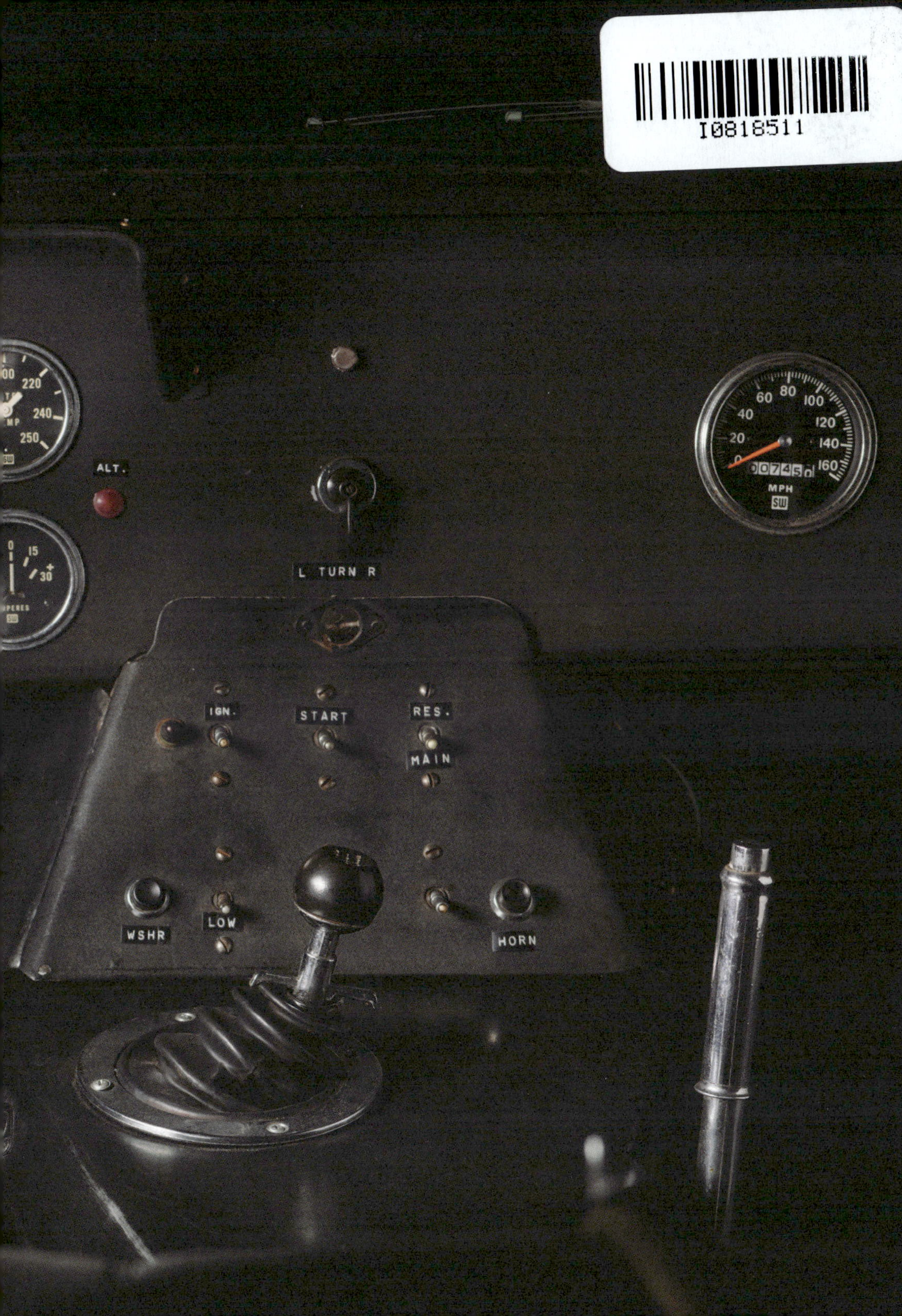
I0818511
ALT.
L TURN R
IGN.
START
RES.
MAIN
WSHR
LOW
HORN
MPH

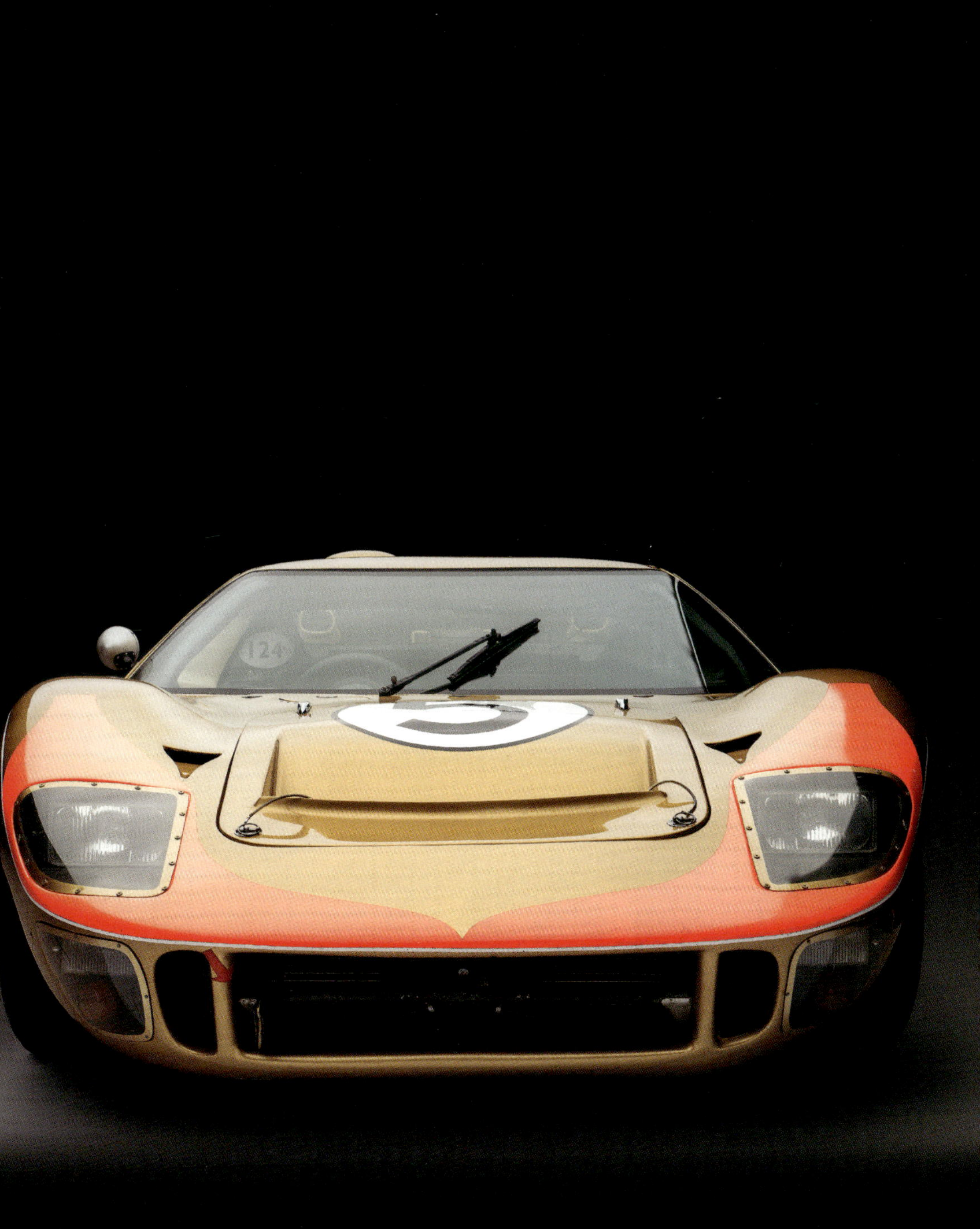
124

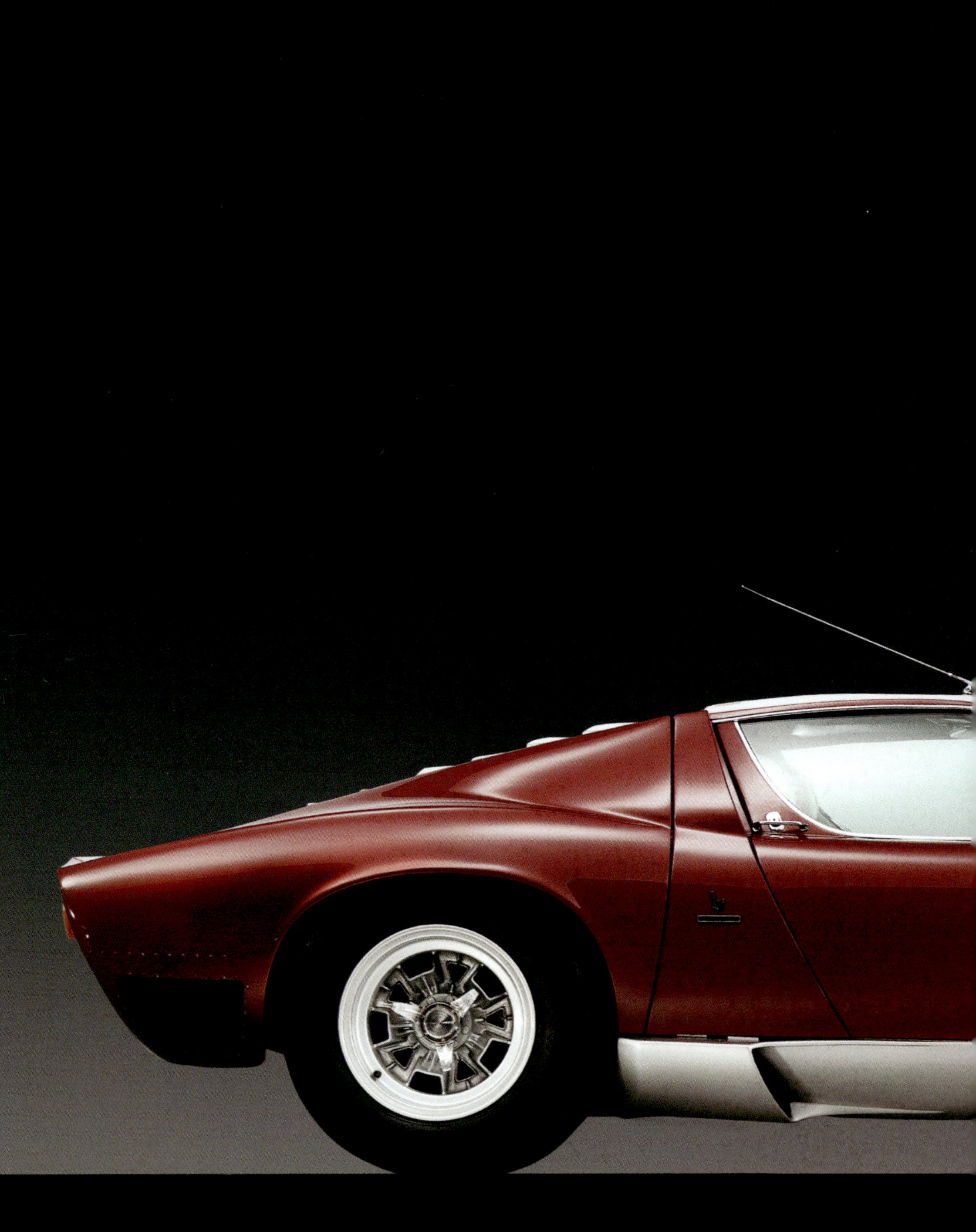

CHARLOTTE & PETER FIELL

Sports Cars

50 Ultimate Collector Cars from the 1910s to the Present

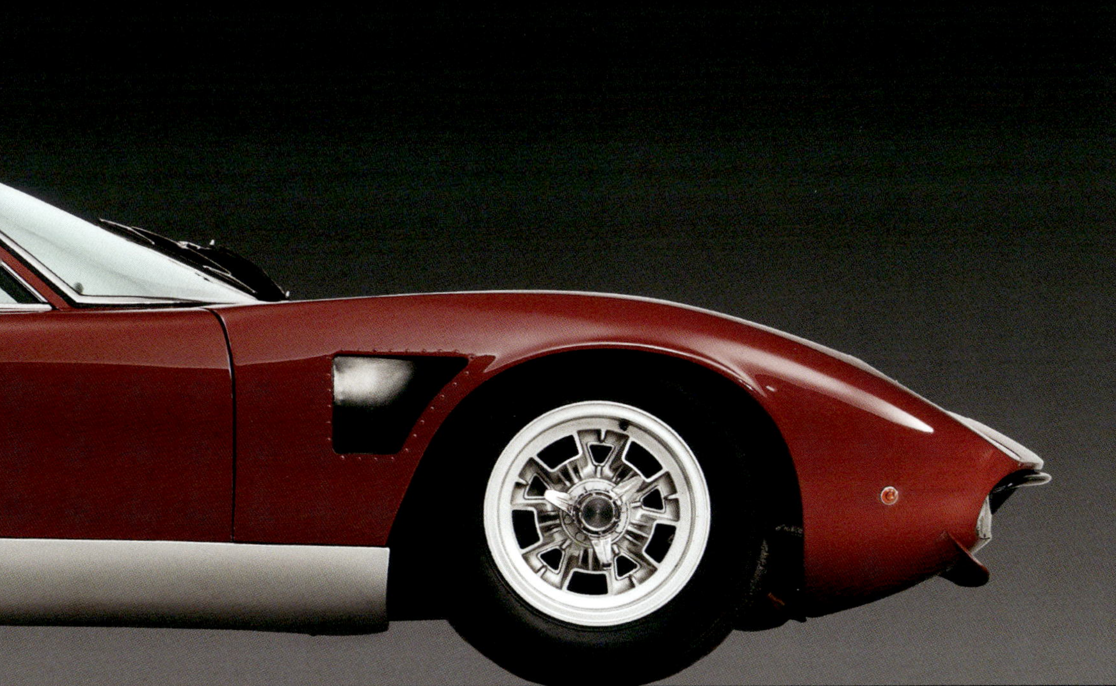

TASCHEN

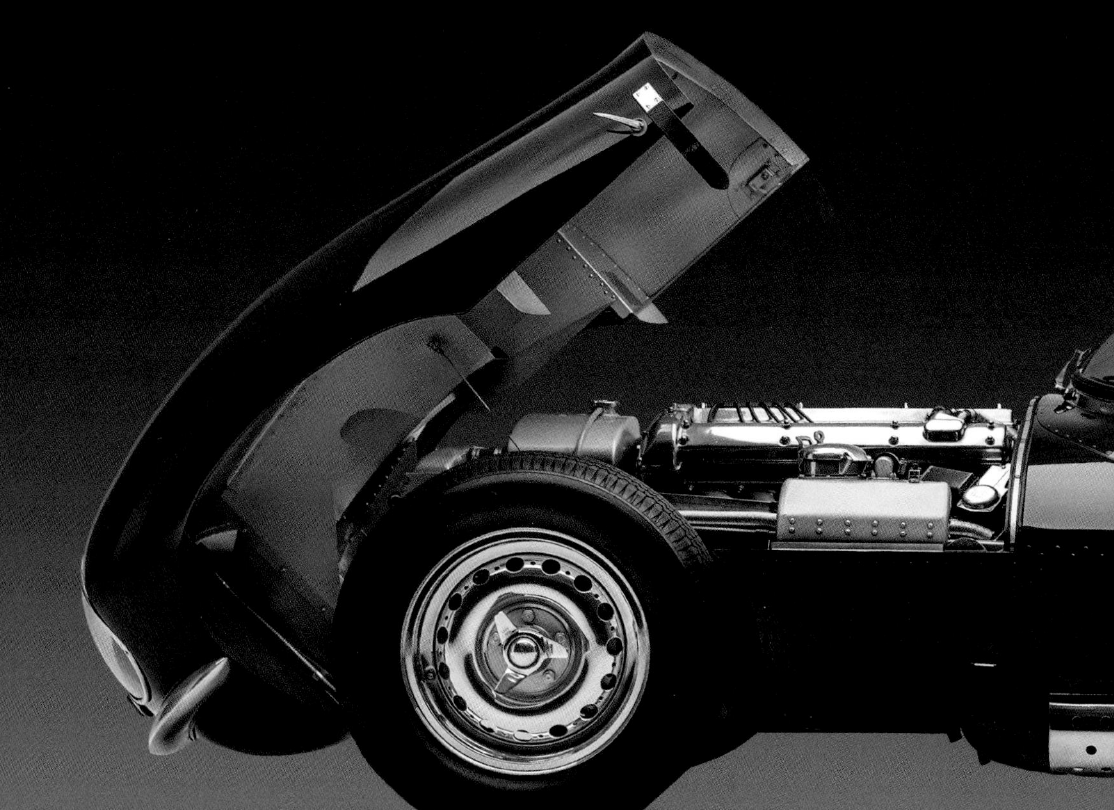

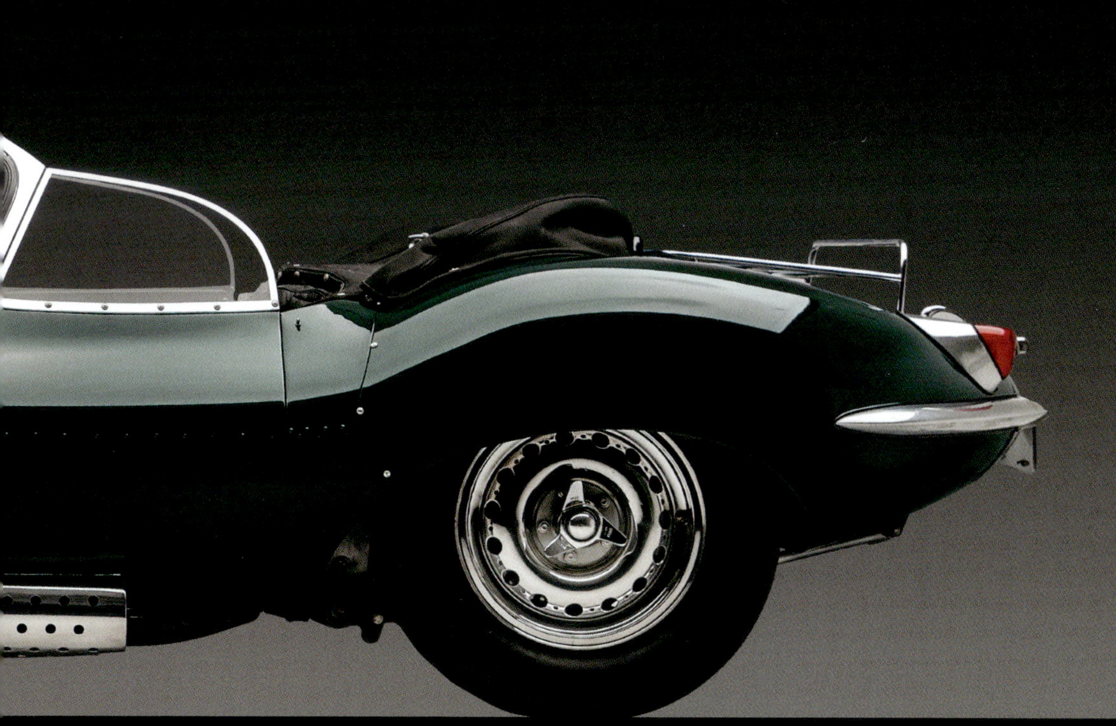

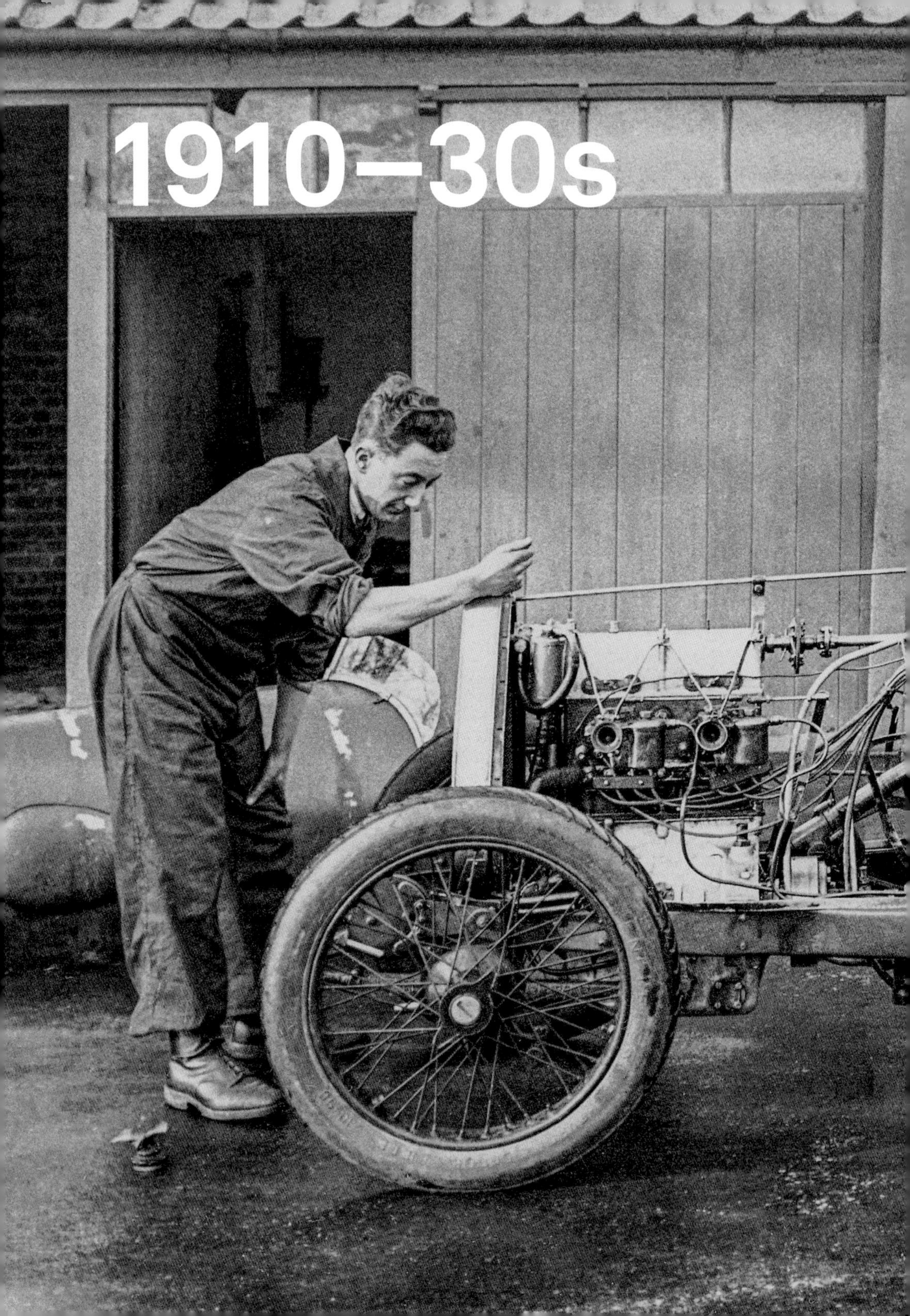
1910–30s

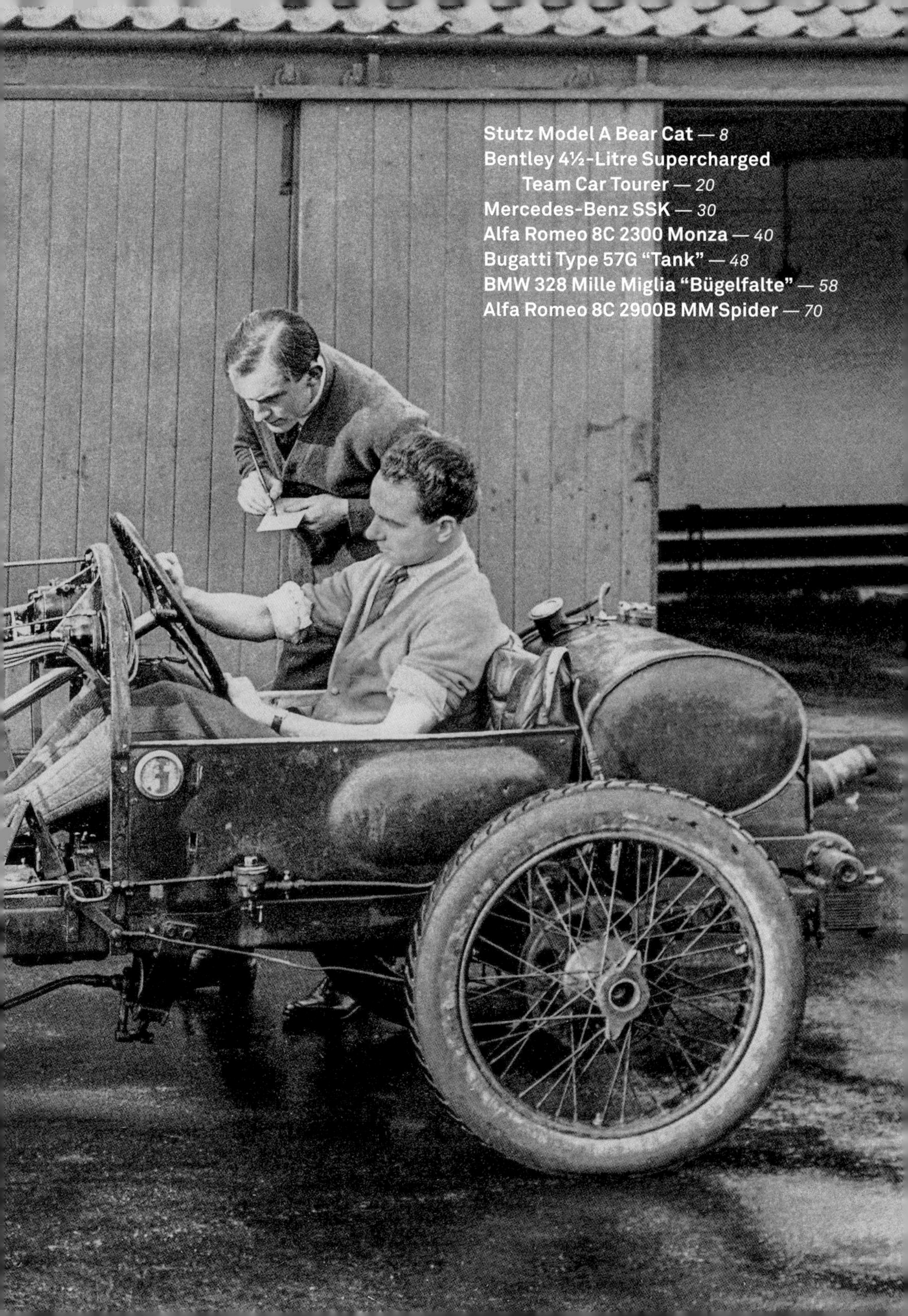

1912

Stutz Model A Bear Cat

MANUFACTURED 1912 | ENGINE 6,391 cc (390 cu. in.), T-head inline 4-cylinder | HORSEPOWER 60 | TOP SPEED 130 km/h (81 mph) TRANSMISSION 3-speed | NUMBER PRODUCED not known (a total of 266 Stutz cars were produced in 1912, which included Model As)

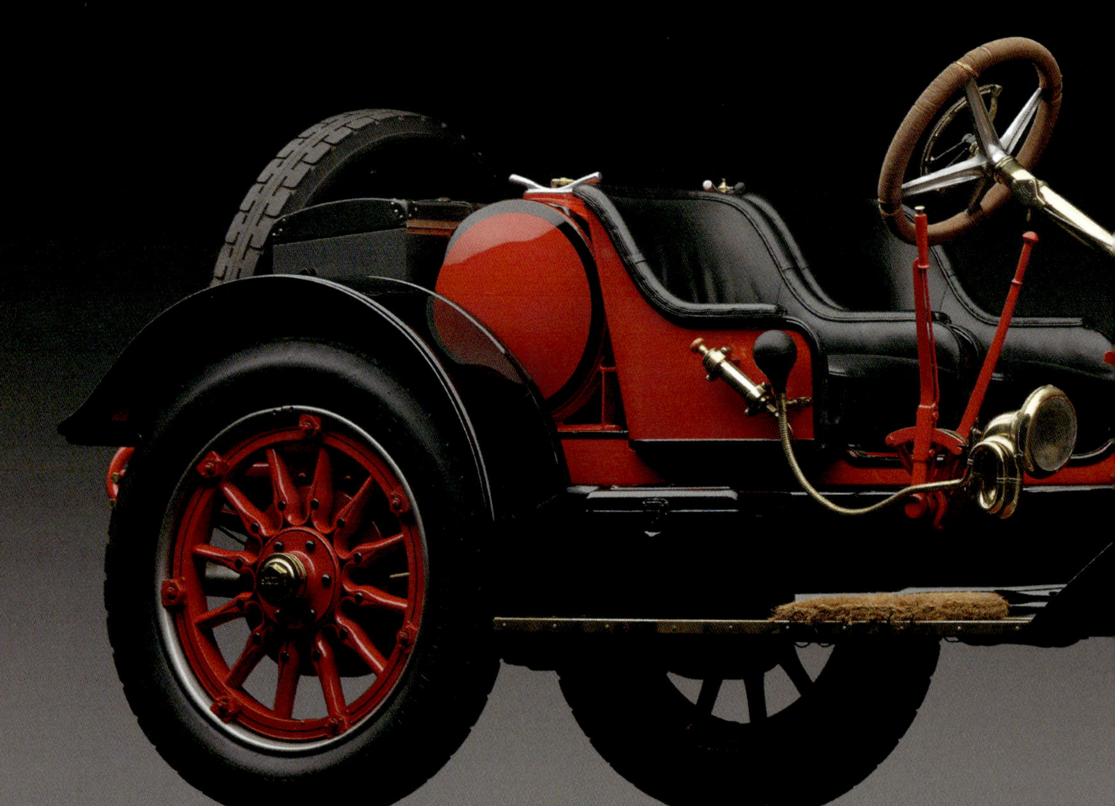

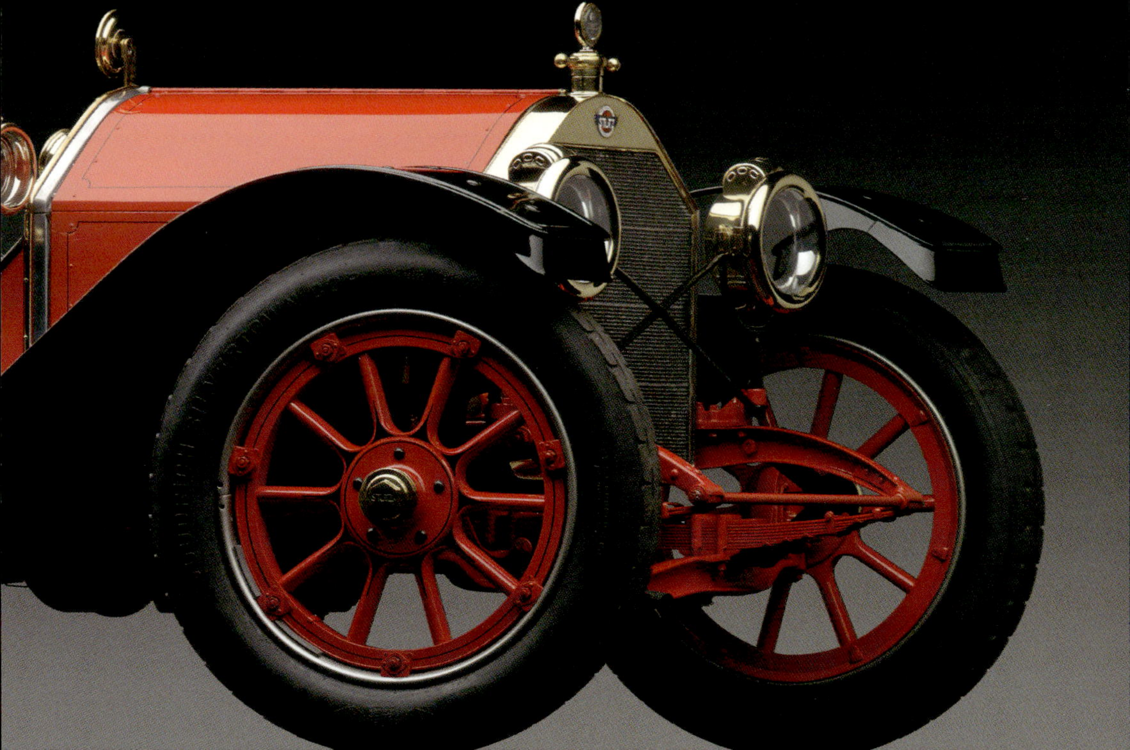

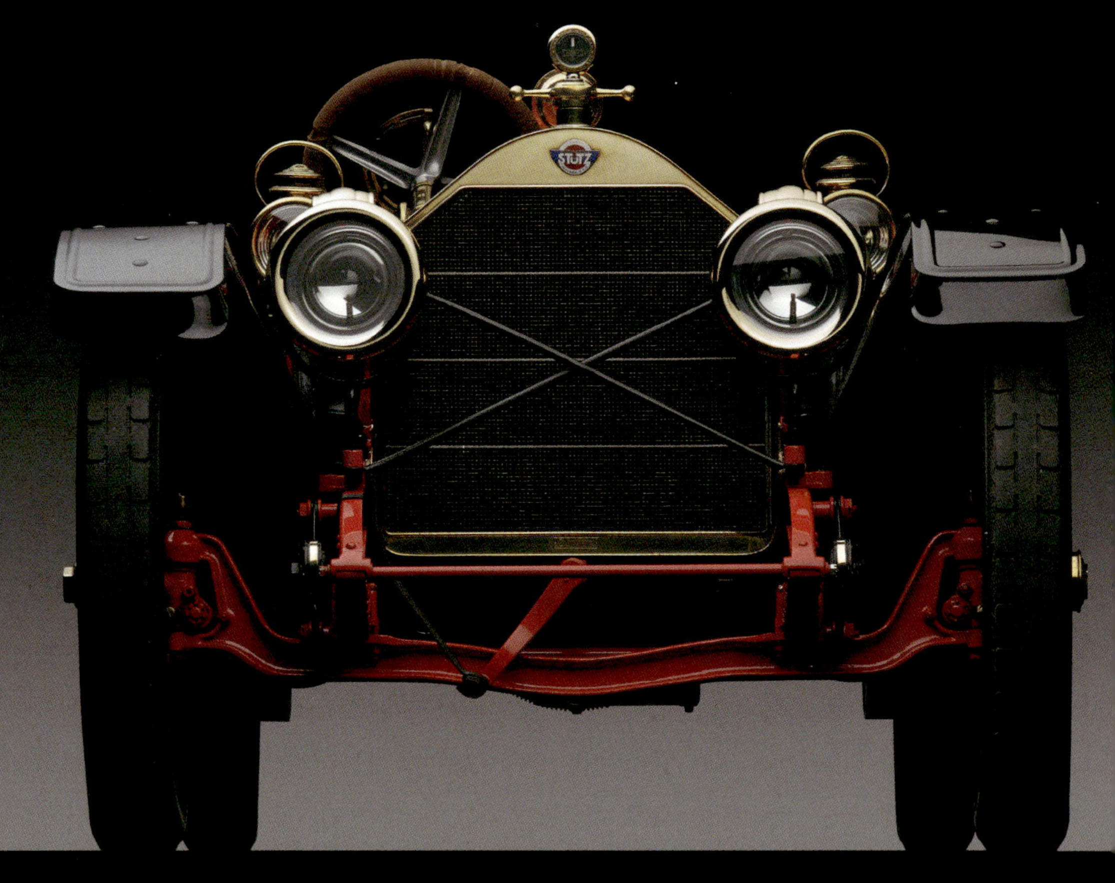
STUTZ

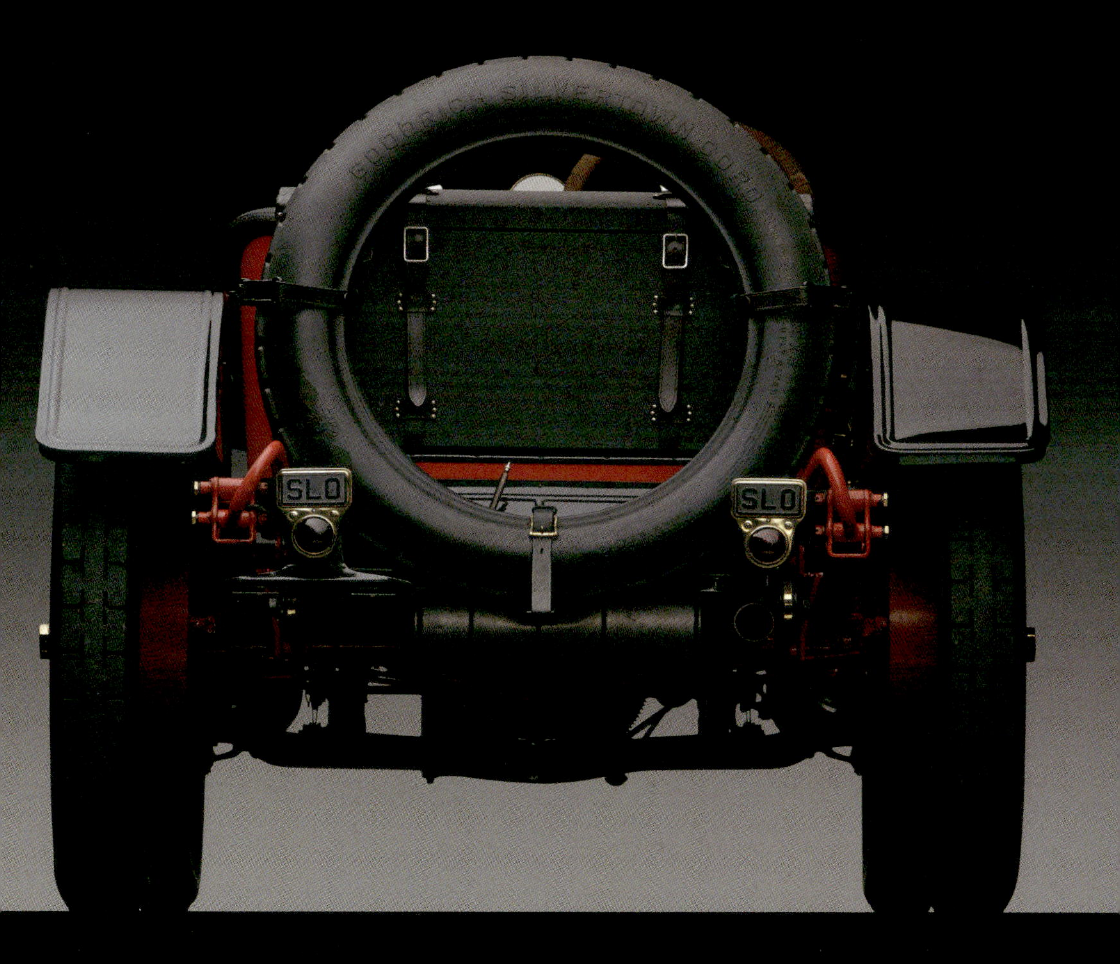
SLO
SLO

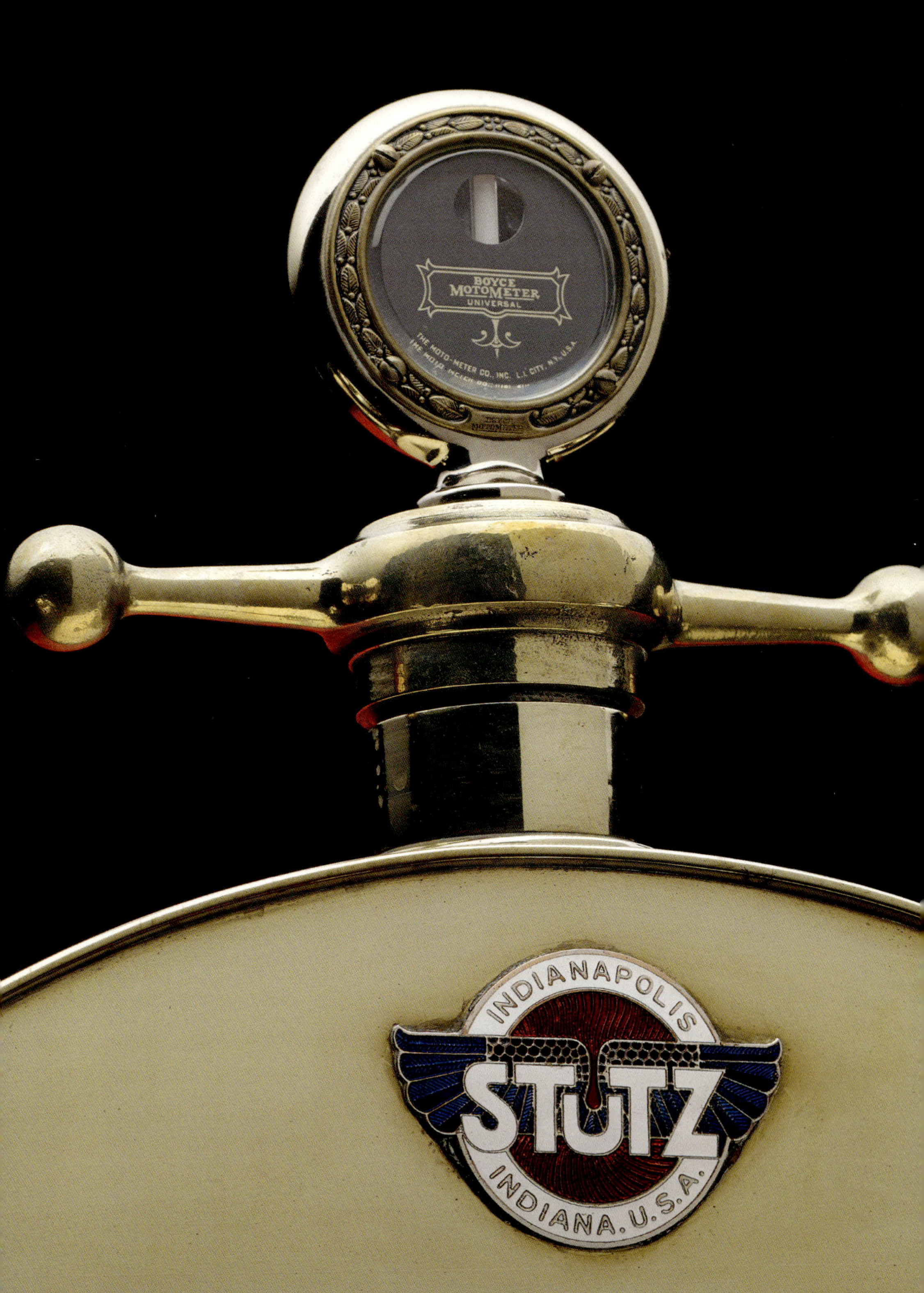
BOYCE
MOTOMETER
UNIVERSAL
THE MOTO-METER CO., INC. L.I. CITY, N.Y. U.S.A.
INDIANAPOLIS
STUTZ
INDIANA. U.S.A.

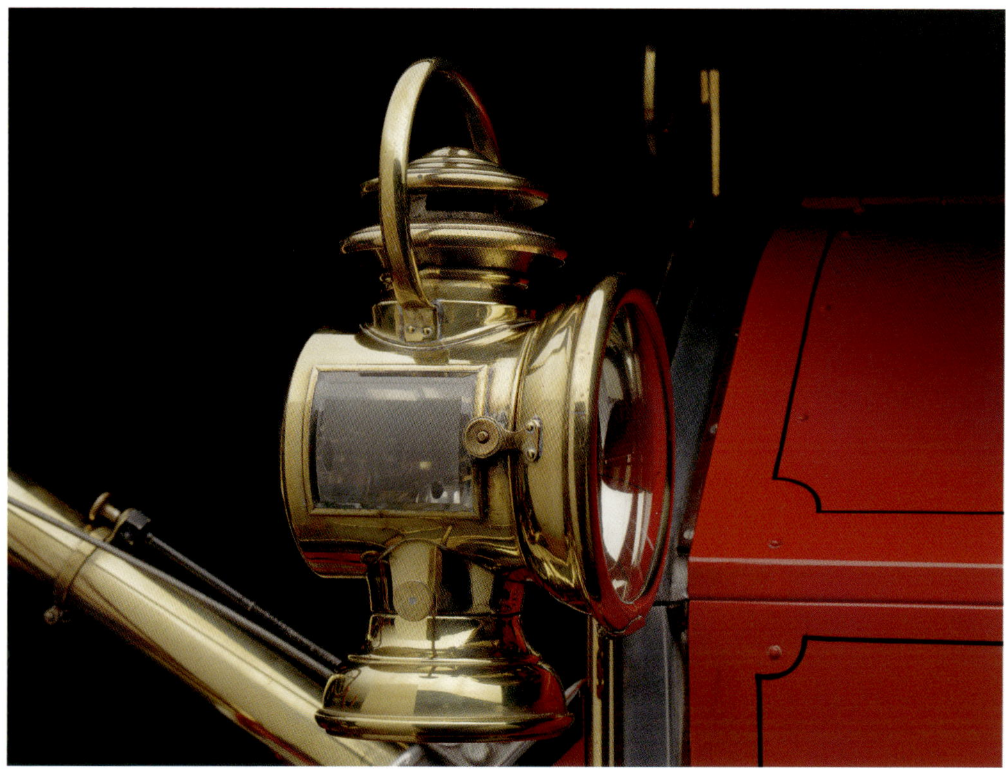

Pages 6–7: Amateur British racing driver Raymond Mays behind the wheel of his 1922 Brescia Bugatti "Cordon Rouge" Type 13 (chassis no. 1318) photographed ca. 1924 with Amherst Villiers (holding note pad) and a mechanic taking the revs of the car. Villiers was a gifted engineer who developed superchargers, particularly remembered for his work on the 4½-litre supercharged "Blower" Bentley.

Opposite: Detail of the Stutz Model A Bear Cat's Boyce MotoMeter positioned on top of the radiator, which also features an enameled Stutz badge. The Boyce MotoMeter was patented in 1912, and was used in automobiles to read the temperature of the radiator. The nonpressurized Thermosiphon cooling systems that were widely used until the 1920s led to a low boiling point. With the MotoMeter drivers now had for the first time information about engine temperature while operating their car.

Above: Detail of brass headlight.

Famed as the car that invented "American performance," the 1912 Stutz Model A Bear Cat was the brainchild of Harry C. Stutz — an Ohio-born self-taught engineer and entrepreneur who was one of the most influential early pioneers of the American automotive industry. In 1911, Stutz built a car under his own name in less than five weeks. He then set up with his friend Henry F. Campbell the Ideal Motor Car Company in Indianapolis in order to produce it. This first Stutz "Bear Cat" was subsequently entered into the Indianapolis 500 that same year, where driven by Gil Andersen it placed 11th. This was a very admirable race performance for a first-time independent-works car and led Stutz to promote

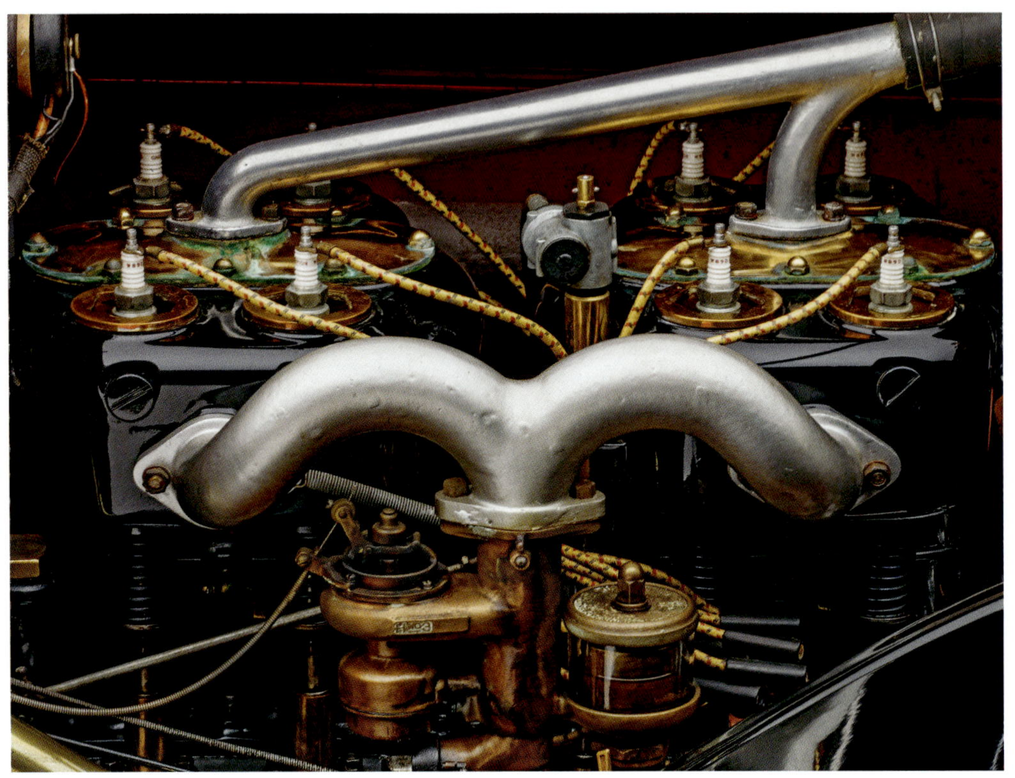

Above: Detail of right side of Stutz Model A Bear Cat's Wisconsin-built 6,391 cc (390 cu. in.) T-head inline four-cylinder engine. Harry Stutz's mechanical brilliance increased the engine's performance to an estimated 60 horsepower, which was fed to the rear wheels through a transaxle — a technological advancement that was some five decades ahead of its time.

Opposite: Detail of one of the Stutz Model A Bear Cat's rear brake lights with illuminated "SLO" warning.

his later production version of the vehicle as "The Car That Made Good In A Day." In fact, Stutz went on to market this model as a faithful duplicate of his racing car, claiming in the company's 1912 catalogue that it was made using "absolutely the same material, workmanship, and design." This production model was the legendary Model A Bear Cat of 1912, a beautiful example of which is shown here.

It was only the 1912 model that bore the two-word name "Bear Cat," which was a tribute to its racing progenitor (later Stutz productions models were known as "Bearcats"). Like its erstwhile competitor, the Mercer Type 35R Raceabout, the Bear Cat was enthusiastically taken up by wealthy amateur racing drivers who put it through its paces on dirt and board tracks across the country, while rival spectators teased each other with such taunts as: "You gotta be nutz to drive a Stutz!" that would then be gleefully countered with "But it's worser to drive a Mercer!"

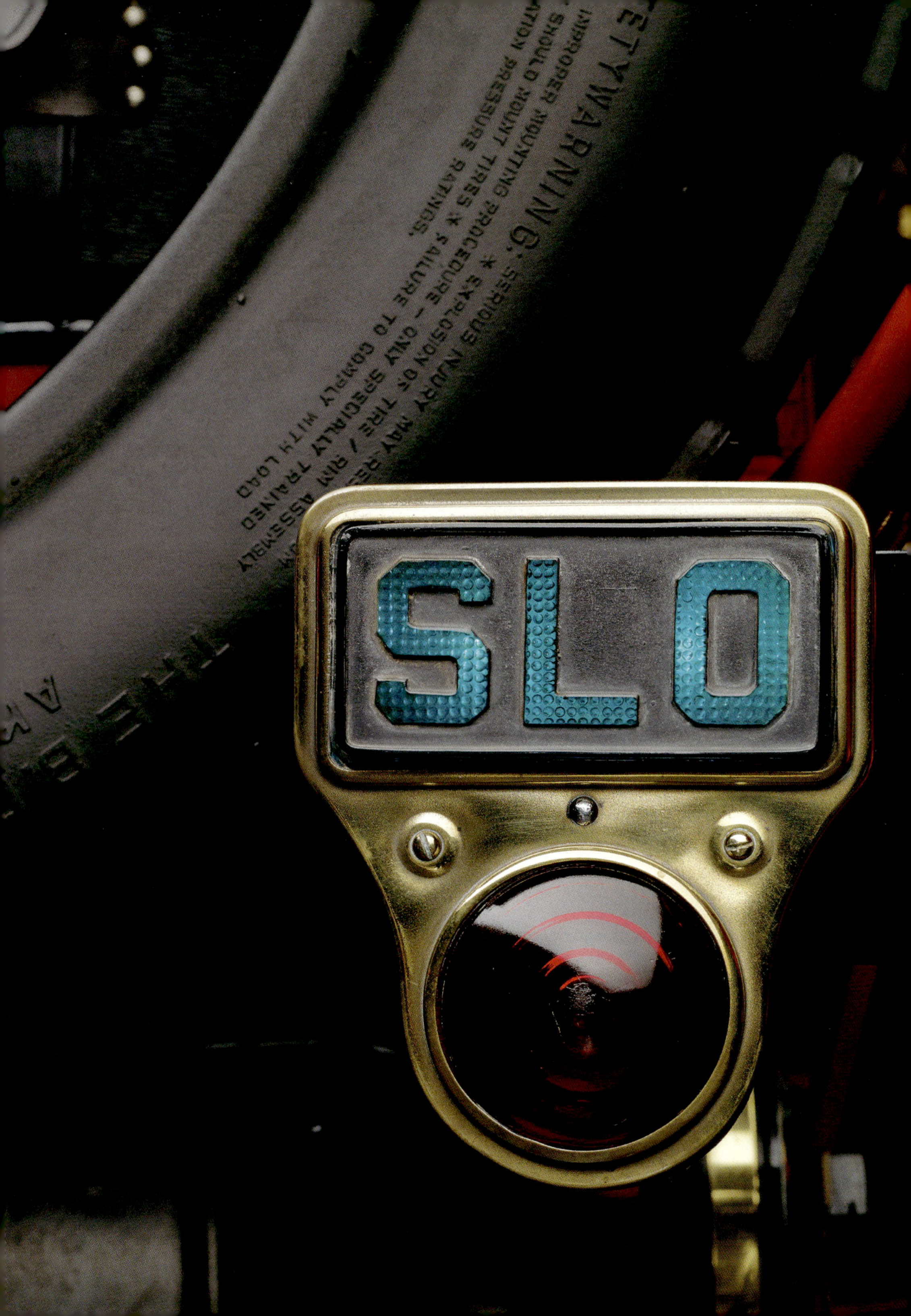
SLO

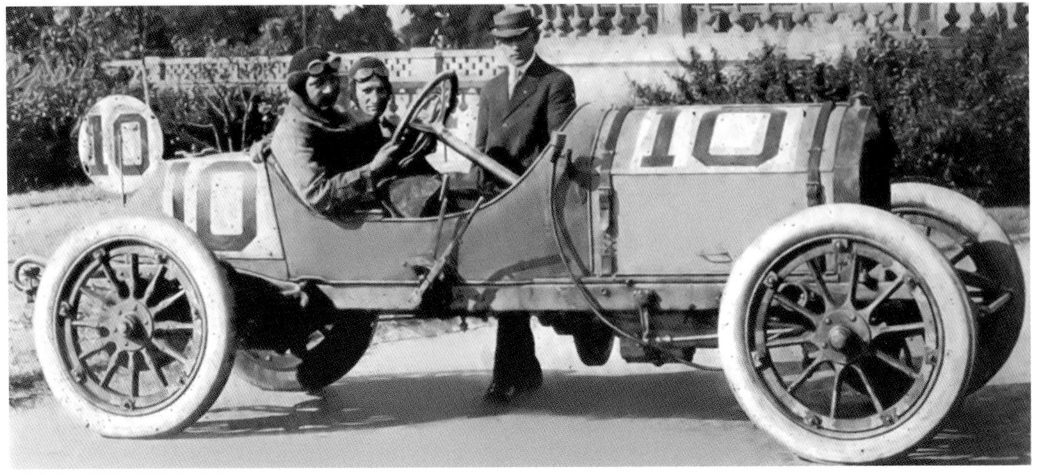

The impressive racing record of the 1912 Stutz Model A Bear Cat was attributable in part to its high performance T-head four-cylinder engine made by the Wisconsin Motor Manufacturing Company, which boasted notable race-enduring stamina. But more than this, Harry Stutz, a genius mechanic, was able to increase the engine's performance to an estimated 60 hp, which was fed through a transaxle to its rear wheels, thereby helping to optimize its driving capabilities at high speed. This type of layout was utterly innovative for its day; in fact, it was some five decades ahead of its time. The Bear Cat's pared down bodywork set on a 120-inch-wheelbase chassis was also a tour de force of essentialist design, and similarly helped to bolster its racing potential by being much lighter in weight than most competing racing models of the time. The manufacturer of its engine later hailed Stutz's Model A as "America's Triumph" and indeed it was, as over the next few years it clocked up a remarkable racing record — including winning the first Astor Cup car race in 1915 — that proved once and for all that brawny and powerful American-made cars could be every bit as thrilling as their European counterparts.

As RM Sotheby's noted in its catalogue in 2013, when it came to sell this glorious example, the 1912 Stutz Model A Bear Cat is "about the engine that starts with a growl and hustles to speed with a steady, ceaseless drumbeat. It is about exhaust that crackles through its open pipe like a roaring autumn campfire. It is about easily experiencing speeds above 70 mph (112 km/h) on an open chassis aimed toward the west wind. It is automotive performance art at its most visceral and soul-stirring." Fitting praise for this groundbreaking, pace-setting all-American automotive legend.

Opposite: 1912 Stutz Bear Cat racer-designer Harry Stutz (standing), Gilbert "Gil" Andersen, driver, and Frank Agan, mechanic.

Below: Gil Andersen aboard the No. 1 Stutz Motor Company Stutz Bear Cat racer holding the inside line alongside Teddy Tetzlaff driving the No. 3 FIAT followed by Len Zengel in the No. 2 Stutz and Ralph DePalma driving the No. 4 Mercedes at the start of the second running of the Indianapolis 500 Mile Race on May 30, 1912, at the Indianapolis Motor Speedway, Indianapolis.

Overleaf: Detail of Bear Cat's steering wheel with central ignition timing control, lights, instrumentation and pedals.

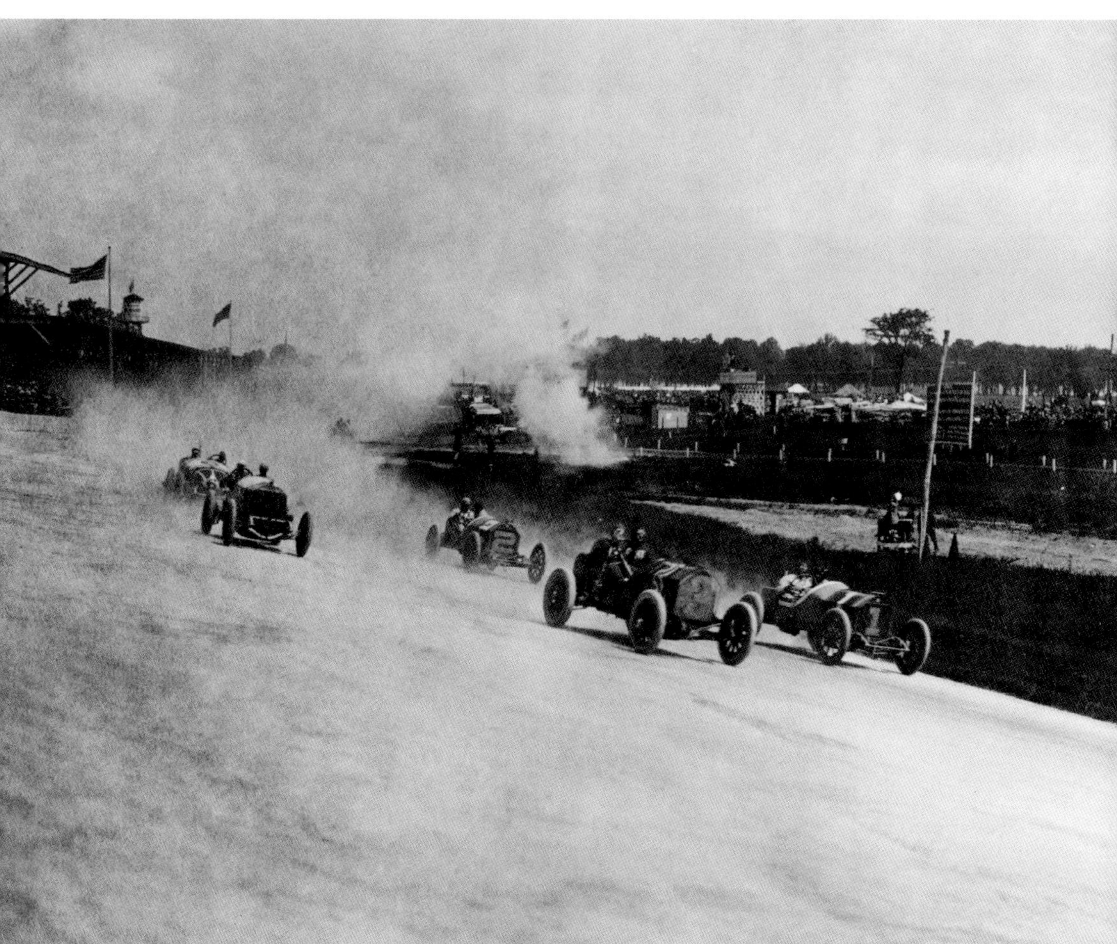

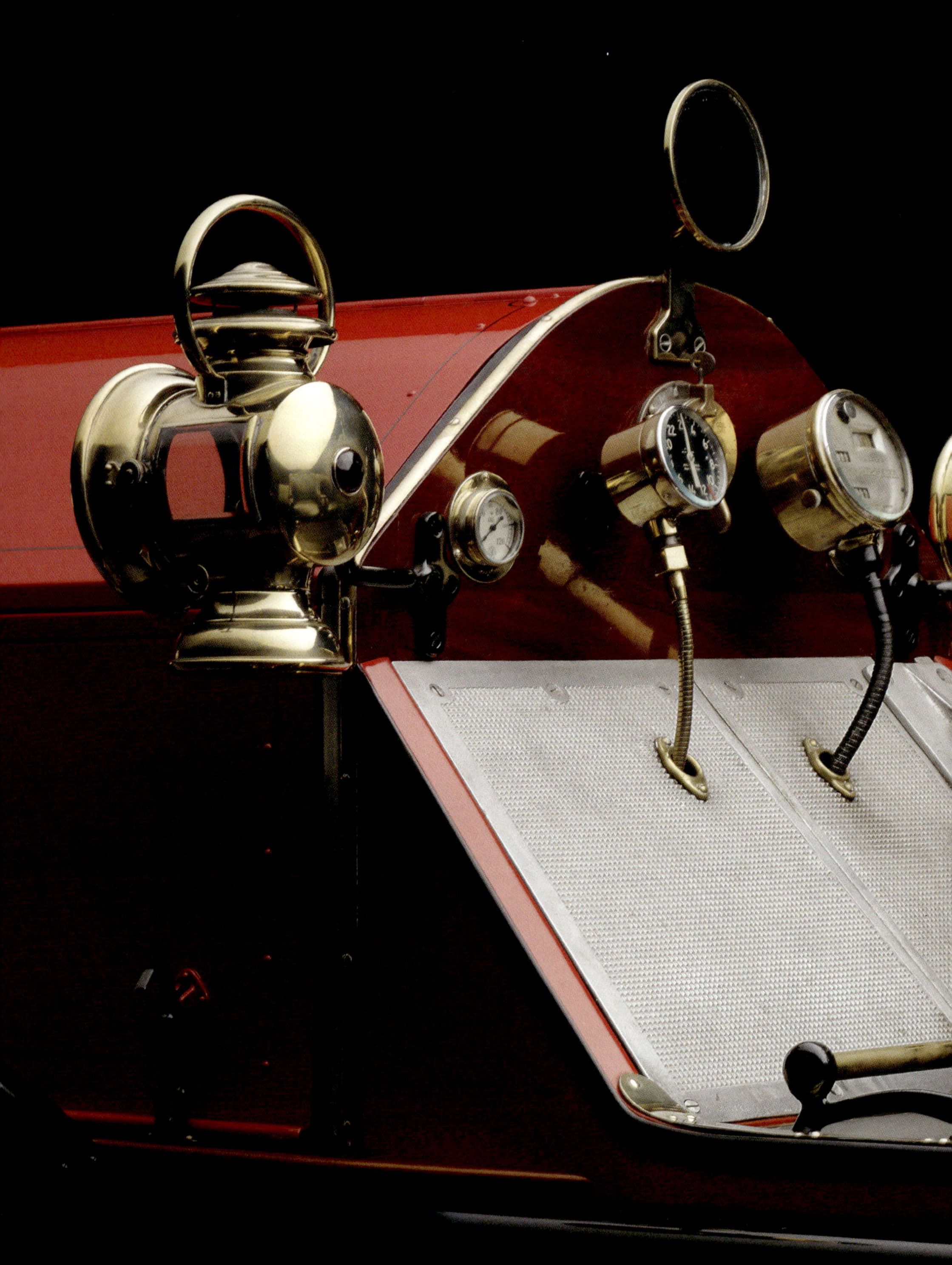

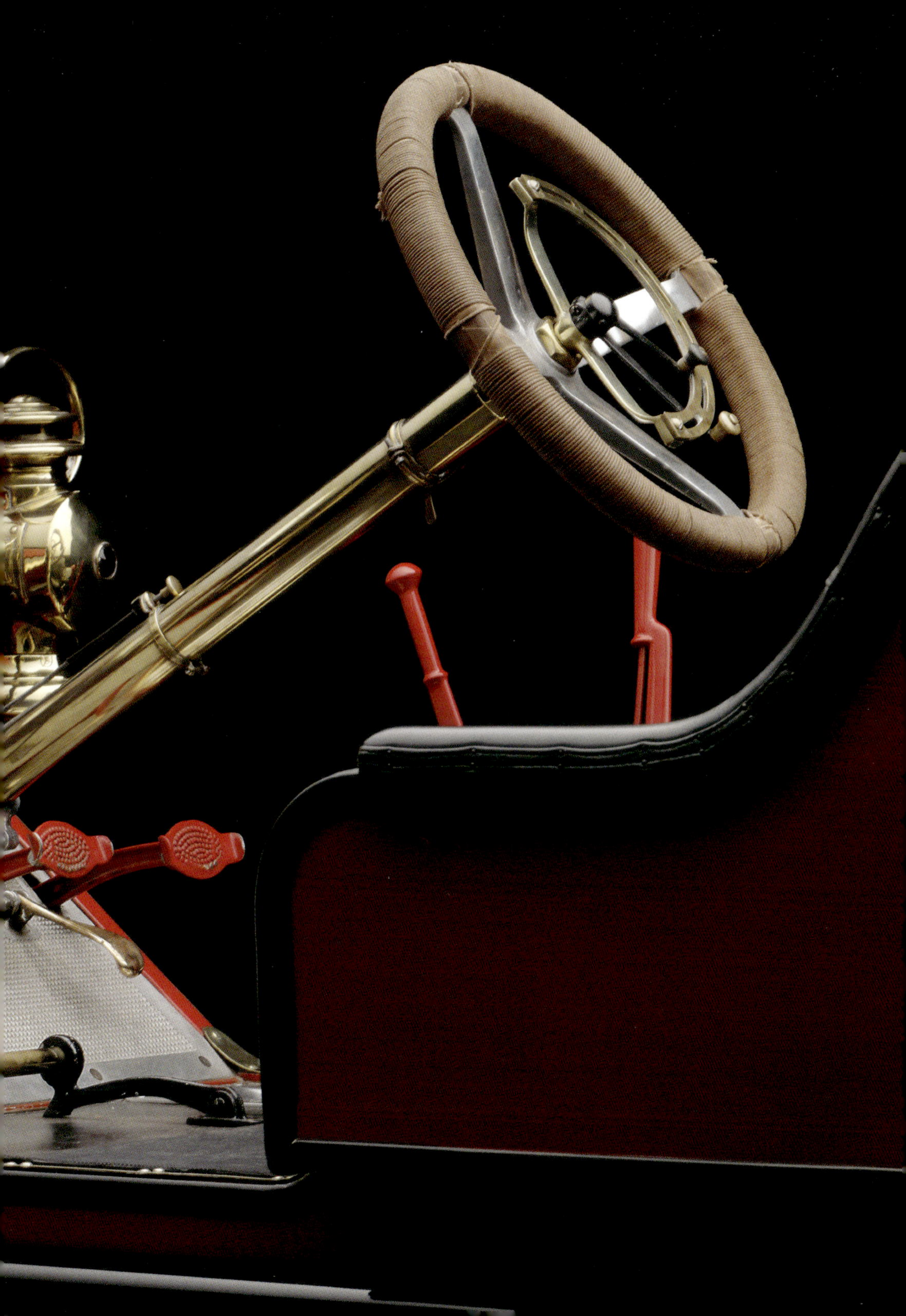

1929

Bentley 4½-Litre Supercharged Team Car Tourer

MANUFACTURED 1929–30 | **ENGINE** 4,398 cc (268 cu. in.), supercharged SOHC inline 4-cylinder | **HORSEPOWER** 240
TOP SPEED 193 km/h (120 mph) | **TRANSMISSION** 4-speed
NUMBER PRODUCED 4 (3 raced & 1 spare)

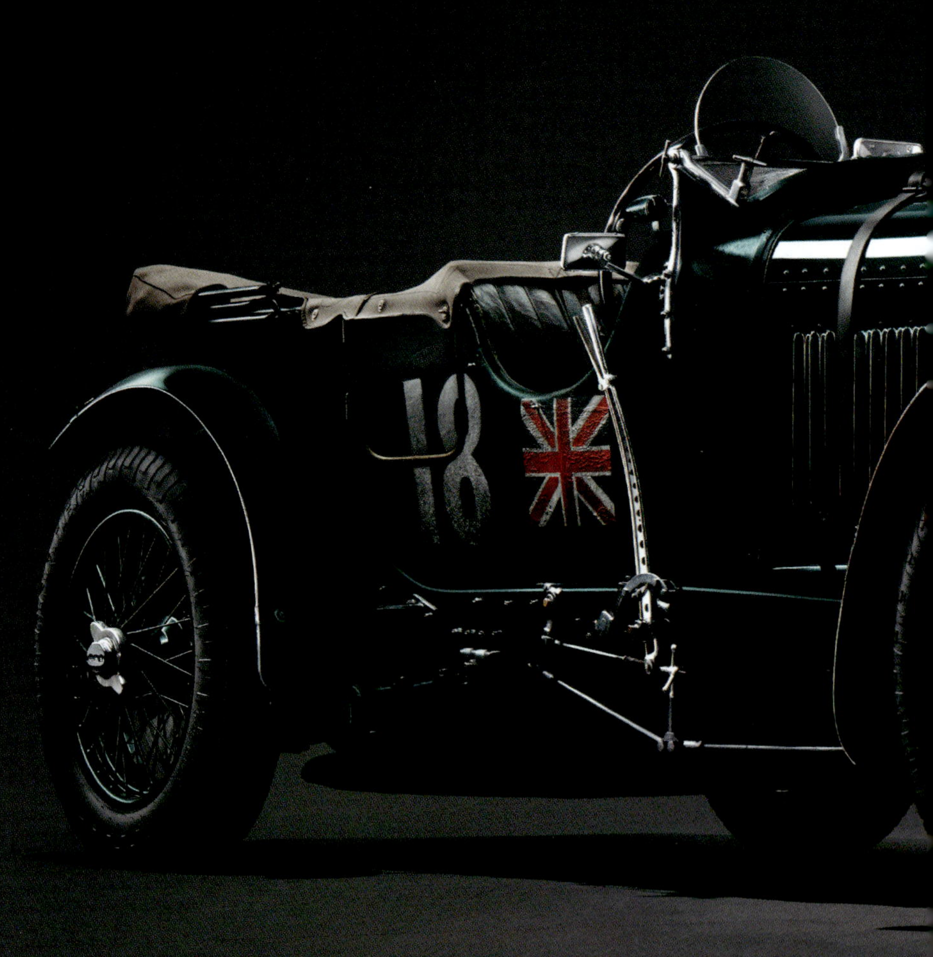

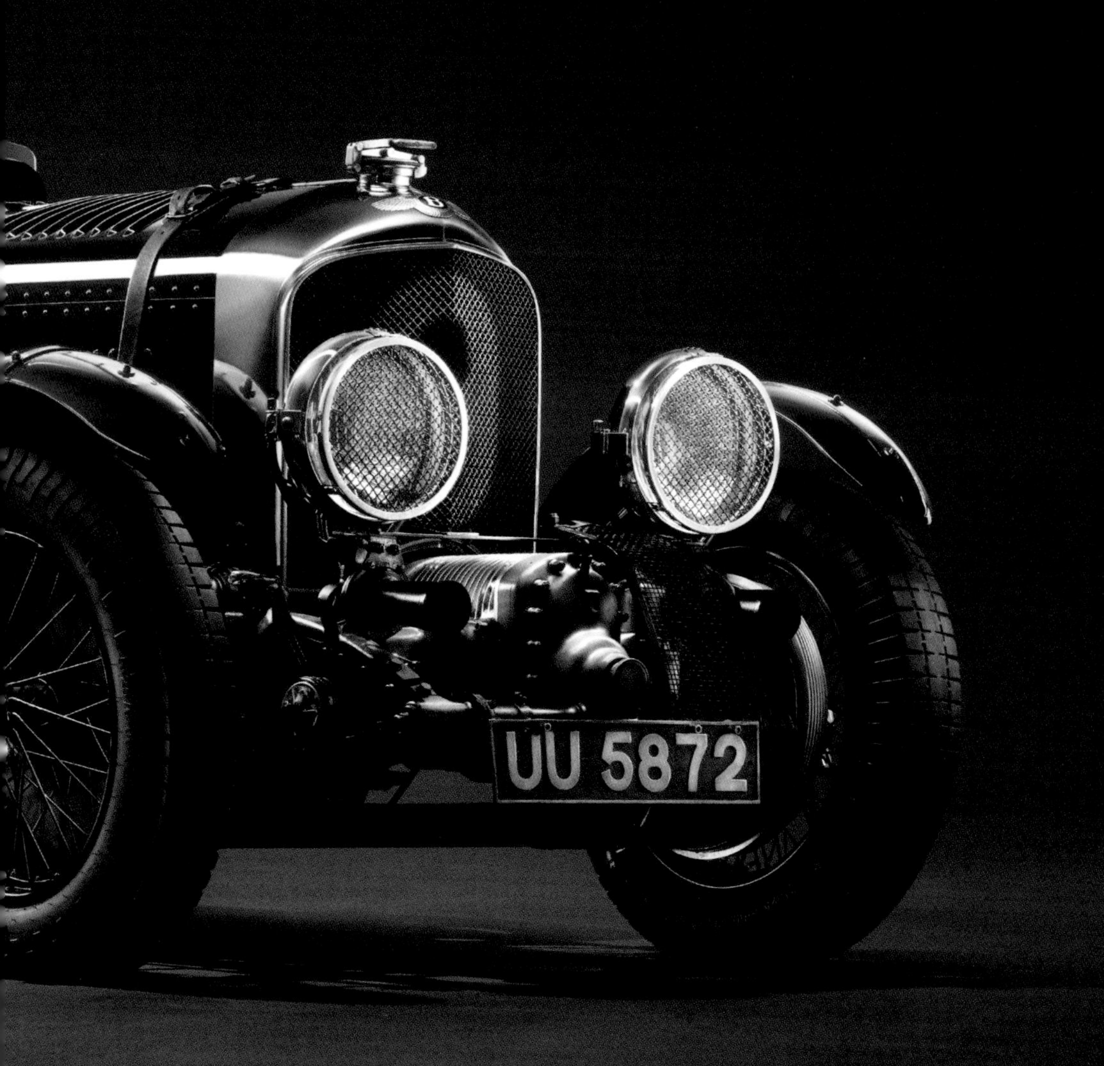
UU 5872

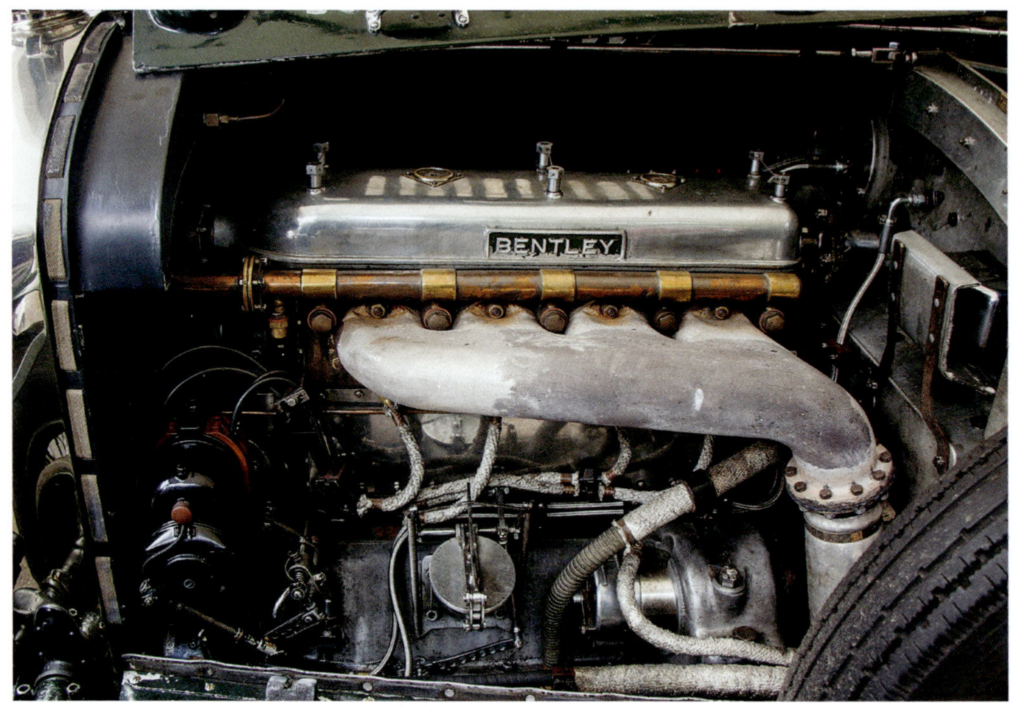

Above: Detail of left side of Bentley 4½-Litre Supercharged Team Car Tourer, with 4,398 cc (268 cu. in.), supercharged SOHC inline four-cylinder engine with two SU HVG5 carburetors.

Originally delivered to Birkin as a naturally aspirated 4½-Litre Bentley, chassis no. HB3403 was the second example to be fitted with a Roots-type supercharger by the engineer Amherst Villiers.

Overleaf: Detail of cockpit, instrumentation and controls.

The "Team Blower" Bentley shown here is one of the original five racing prototypes, and is considered among the most collectible British cars of all time. The Bentley Blower was the brainchild of Tim Birkin, one of the famed Bentley Boys — a group of dashing young men drawn from the upper echelons of society who dominated British motorsports during the 1920s while driving for Bentley's works team. They were responsible for winning not only the 1924 Le Mans race, but a further four consecutive Le Mans victories in 1927, 1928, 1929 and 1930 — thereby sealing the marque's hallowed status within British motorsports history. Birkin's decision to supercharge a 4½-litre Bentley in the quest for more power around the racetrack was not without controversy. His Bentley Blower design was first shown at the 1929 London Motor Show, however, one of the rules for entering the upcoming 24 Hours of Le Mans endurance race the following year was that any competing model had to have a corresponding minimum homologated production run of 50 cars. So apart from the five specially designed supercharged 4½-litre-racing Bentleys constructed by Birkin and his team of engineers, which were funded by the wealthy socialite Dorothy Wyndham

Paget, another 50 production "Blowers" were officially produced by the Bentley factory, then based in Cricklewood.

As for the five racing Blowers, which comprised the single-seater supercharged Blower No. 1 designed specifically for racing at Brooklands, and four additional two-seater 4½-litre competition models — Blowers Nos. 2, 3, 4 and 5 — which were specially developed for the upcoming Le Mans race of 1930 (No. 5 being a spare), they could be said not to have fully lived up to their initially much-hyped promise. At this event — the whole raison d'être of Birkin's supercharging adventure — one of the Blowers failed to start, while the other two did not finish although both clocked up over 20 hours of race time before retiring. Three months later, however, Birkin went on to rack up a very commendable second place at the 1930 French Grand Prix in one of these famous two-seater Blowers, finishing only 14 seconds behind the winning car. Despite this, company founder W. O. Bentley was entirely dismissive of the whole experiment, later observing: "The supercharged 4½ never won a race, suffered a never-ending series of mechanical failures, brought the marque Bentley disrepute and incidentally cost Dorothy Paget a large sum before she decided to withdraw her support in October 1930..." Nevertheless, the Bentley Blowers still retain an almost mythical status among British motorsports aficionados and collectors. Constructed ostensibly for the sole purpose of homologating Birkin's five "Team Blower" racing cars, the production Blowers were formidable road cars in their own right.

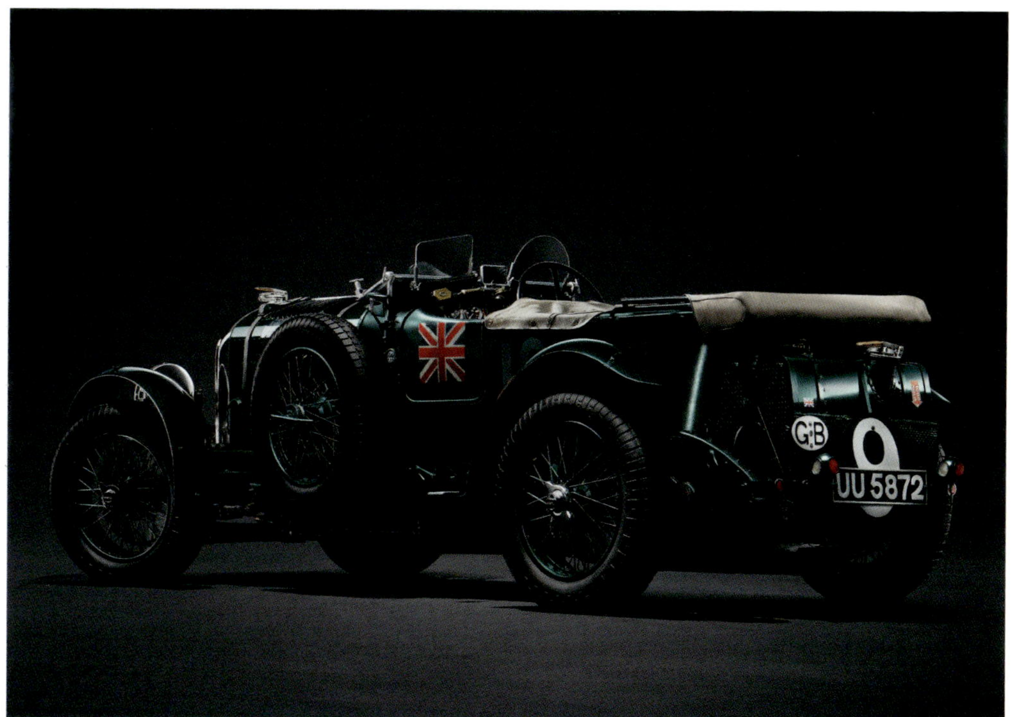

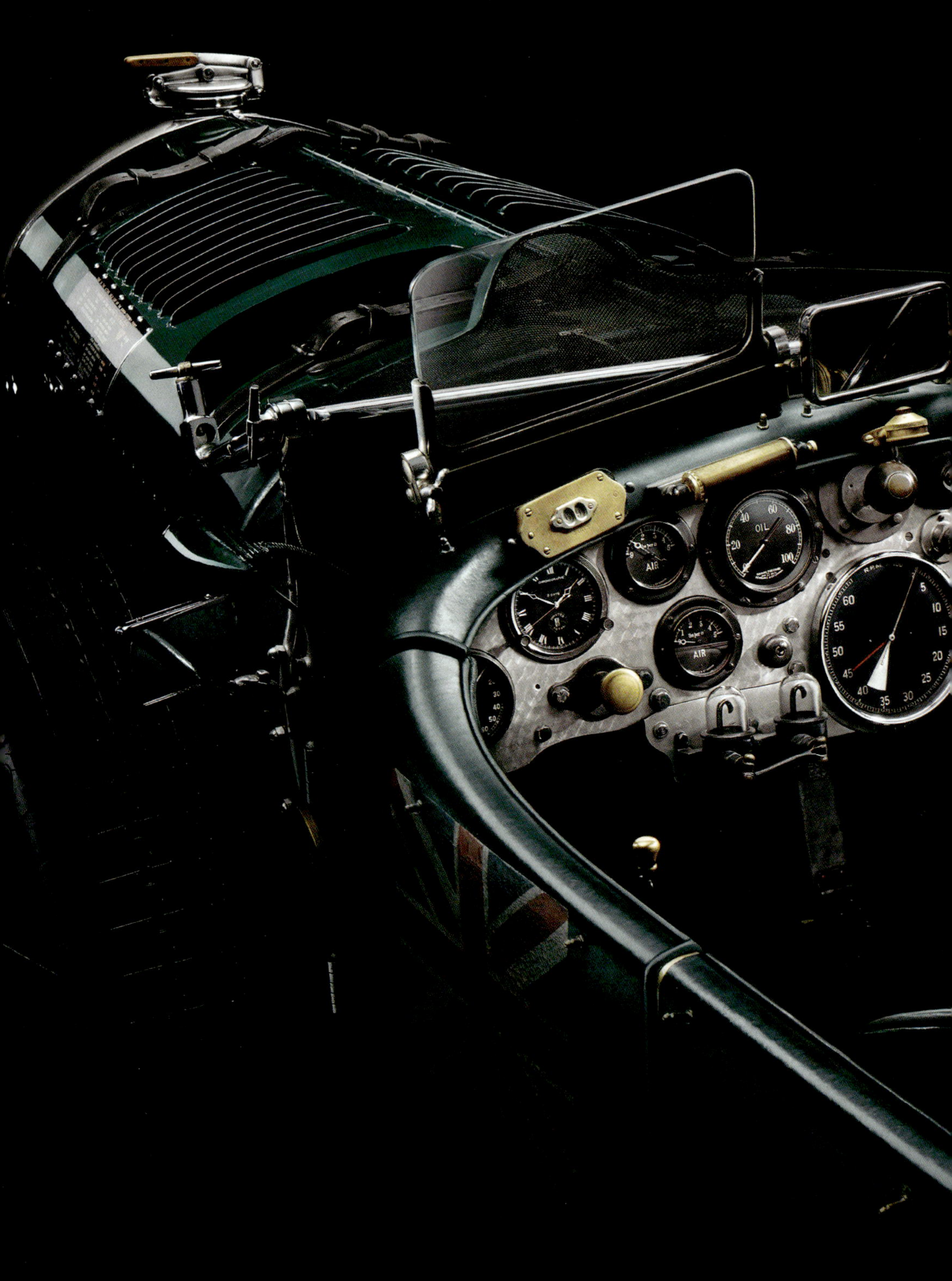
OIL
AIR
AIR

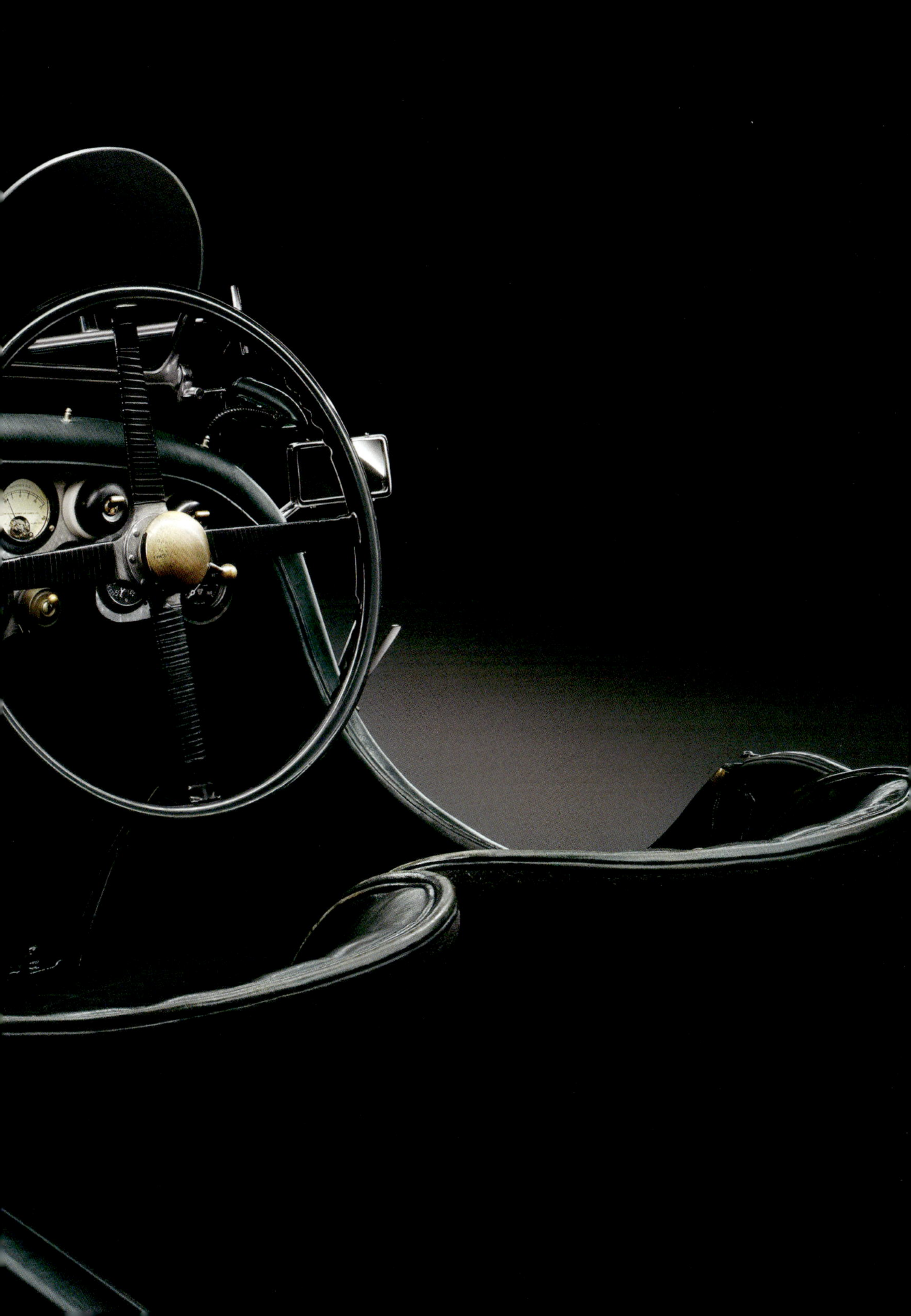

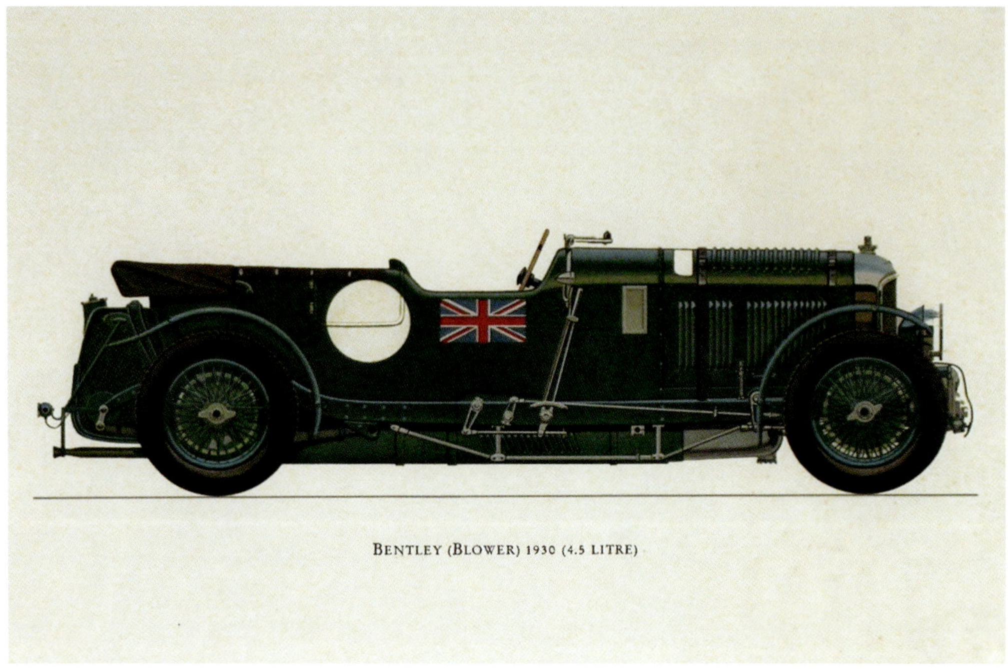

Capable of a top speed of over 100 mph, these supercharged tourers were considered the supercars of their day thanks largely to their intrinsic racing DNA. Indeed, the esteemed *Motor Sport* magazine lauded their "remarkable acceleration" and described them as "a car for the connoisseur of sporting cars." Only five of these production Blowers were originally delivered with saloon bodies — three provided by Freestone & Webb, with the remaining two constructed by Maythorn and Gurney Nutting — one apiece. And as for the ultra-rare No. 2 Team Car Tourer (chassis no. HB3403 / reg. UU5872) shown here, which was Tim Birken's own team racer, it currently resides at Bentley's headquarters in Crewe, where it is lovingly looked after by the marque's heritage team as one of the standout stars of Bentley's collection of rare and historic "B"-mascotted cars.

Above: Drawing of a 1930 Bentley 4½-Litre "Blower" Tourer, ca. 1930s.

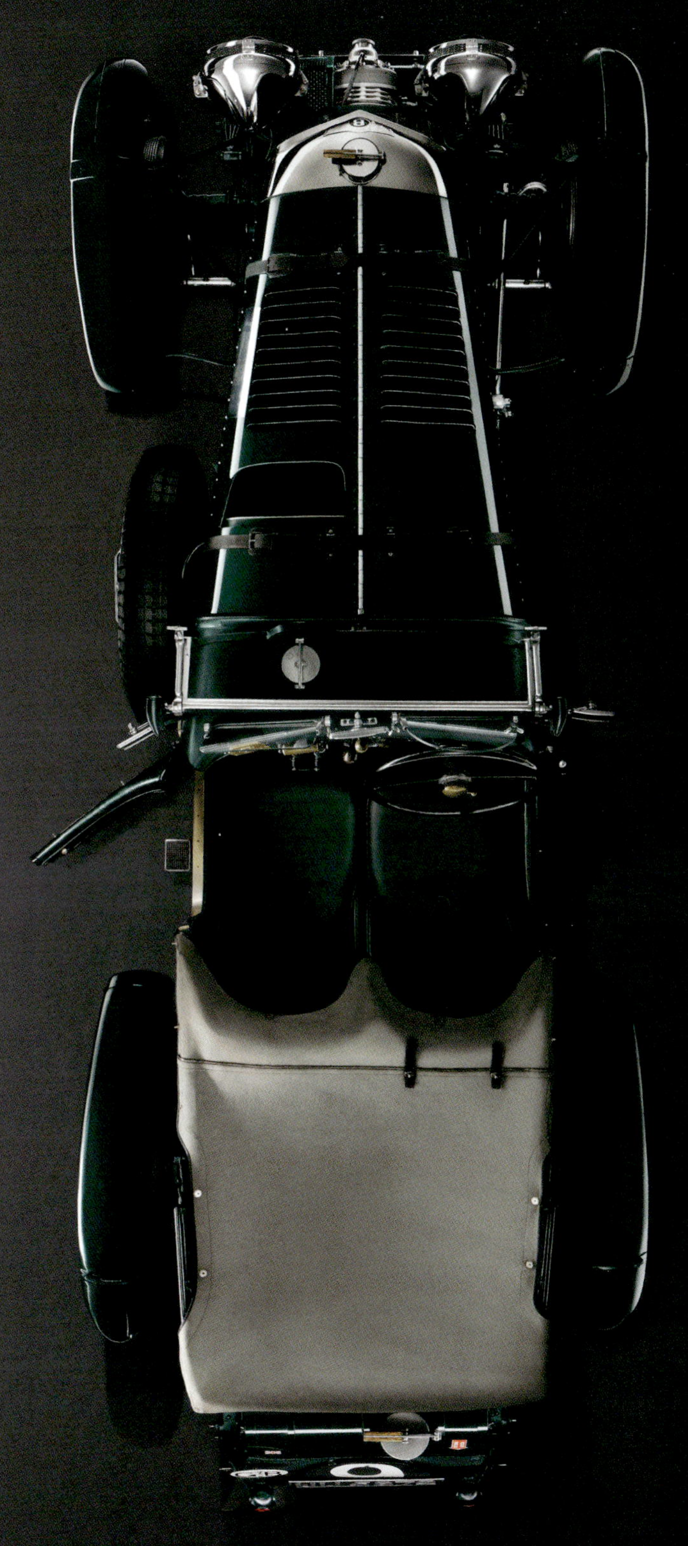

Below: Cutaway drawing by Leslie Cresswell (1896–1979) of the 1929 Bentley 4½-Litre Supercharged Team Car Tourer (chassis no. HB3403) that appeared in the book *The Grand Prix Car 1906–1939*, which was first published 1949.

Opposite (top): Image taken two years before the "Blowers" first ran showing the Bentley Boys at Le Mans, France, June 18–19, 1927: (Front row, left to right) Frank Clement, Leslie Callingham, Baron André d'Erlanger, George Duller, Sammy Davis and John Benjafield; (Second row, left to right) Woolf "Babe" Barnato (directly behind d'Erlanger) and W.O. Bentley (second from the right). The Bentley Boys were a close-knit group of wealthy mainly British playboys, racers and adventurers who drove Bentley sports cars to victory in the 1920s and 30s and kept the marque's reputation for high performance alive. Among the missing from the photo include, Tim Birkin, Glen Kidston and Jean Chassagne.

Opposite (bottom): 1930 24 Hours of Le Mans — Jean Chassagne retires his No. 9 Bentley 4½-Litre Supercharged Team Car Tourer (chassis no. HB3403) in the pits, which was co-driven with Tim Birkin. After 20 hours (138 laps out of a total 152) a connecting rod broke and the the car had to be retired. The massive superchargers fitted to these cars, which boosted their power by 65 hp, put too much stress on their engines for endurance racing.

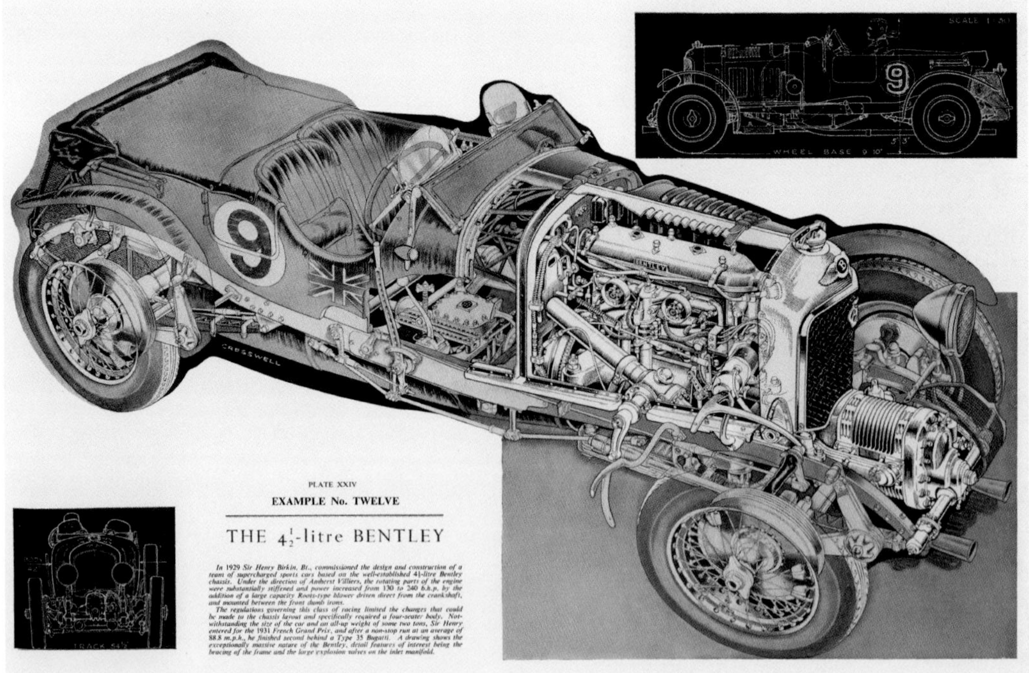

PLATE XXIV

EXAMPLE No. TWELVE

THE 4½-litre BENTLEY

In 1929 Sir Henry Birkin, Bt., commissioned the design and construction of a team of supercharged sports cars based on the well-established 4½-litre Bentley chassis. Under the direction of Amherst Villiers, the rotating parts of the engine were substantially stiffened and power increased from 130 to 240 b.h.p. by the addition of a large capacity Roots-type blower driven direct from the crankshaft, and mounted between the front dumb irons.

The regulations governing this class of racing limited the changes that could be made to the chassis layout and specifically required a four-seater body. Notwithstanding the size of the car and an all-up weight of some two tons, Sir Henry entered for the 1931 French Grand Prix, and after a non-stop run at an average of 88.8 m.p.h., he finished second behind a Type 35 Bugatti. A drawing shows the exceptionally massive nature of the Bentley, detail features of interest being the bracing of the frame and the large explosion valves on the inlet manifold.

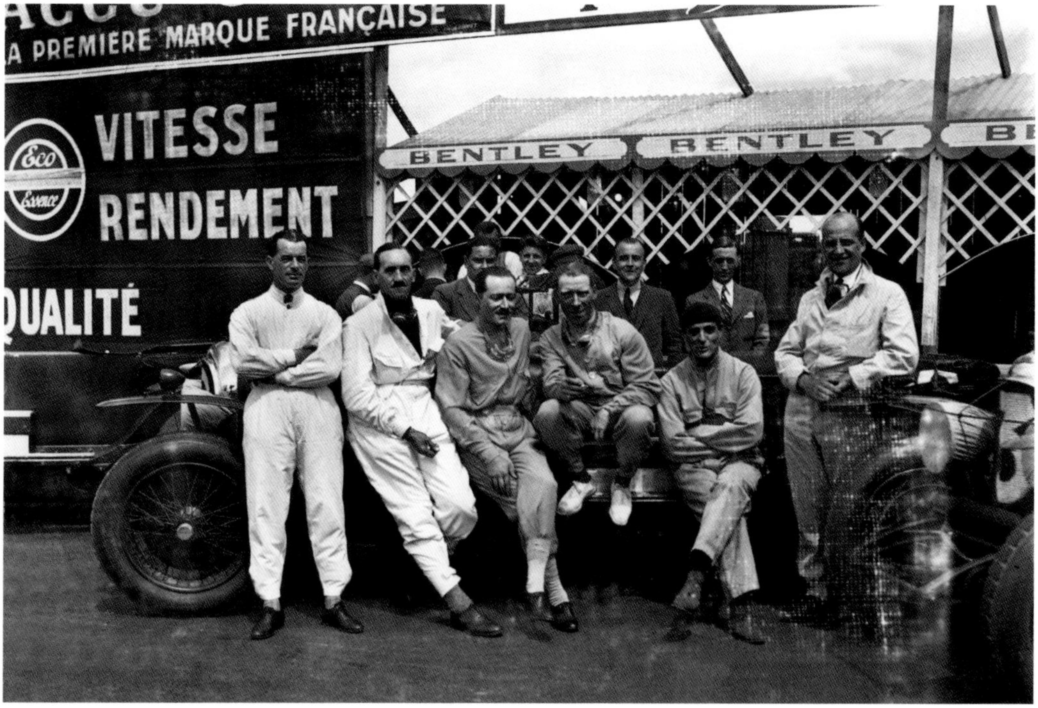
LA PREMIERE MARQUE FRANÇAISE
VITESSE
RENDEMENT
QUALITÉ
BENTLEY
BENTLEY

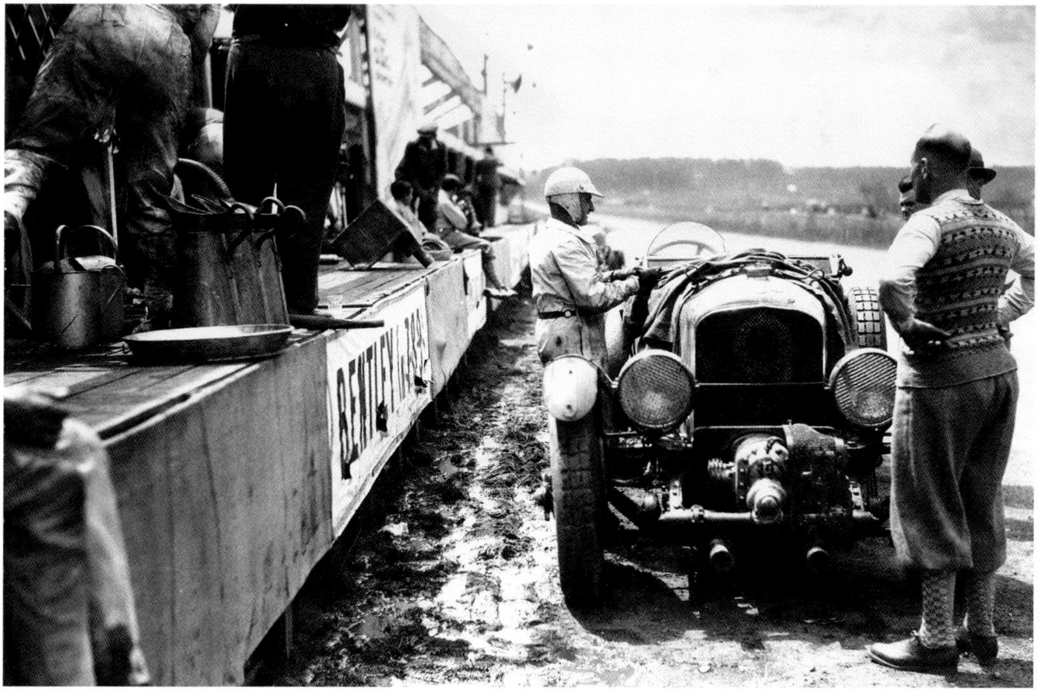

Mercedes-Benz SSK

MANUFACTURED 1928–32 | **ENGINE** 7,069 cc (431 cu. in.), supercharged SOHC inline 6-cylinder | **HORSEPOWER** 225
TOP SPEED 192 km/h (119 mph) | **TRANSMISSION** 4-speed
NUMBER PRODUCED 31

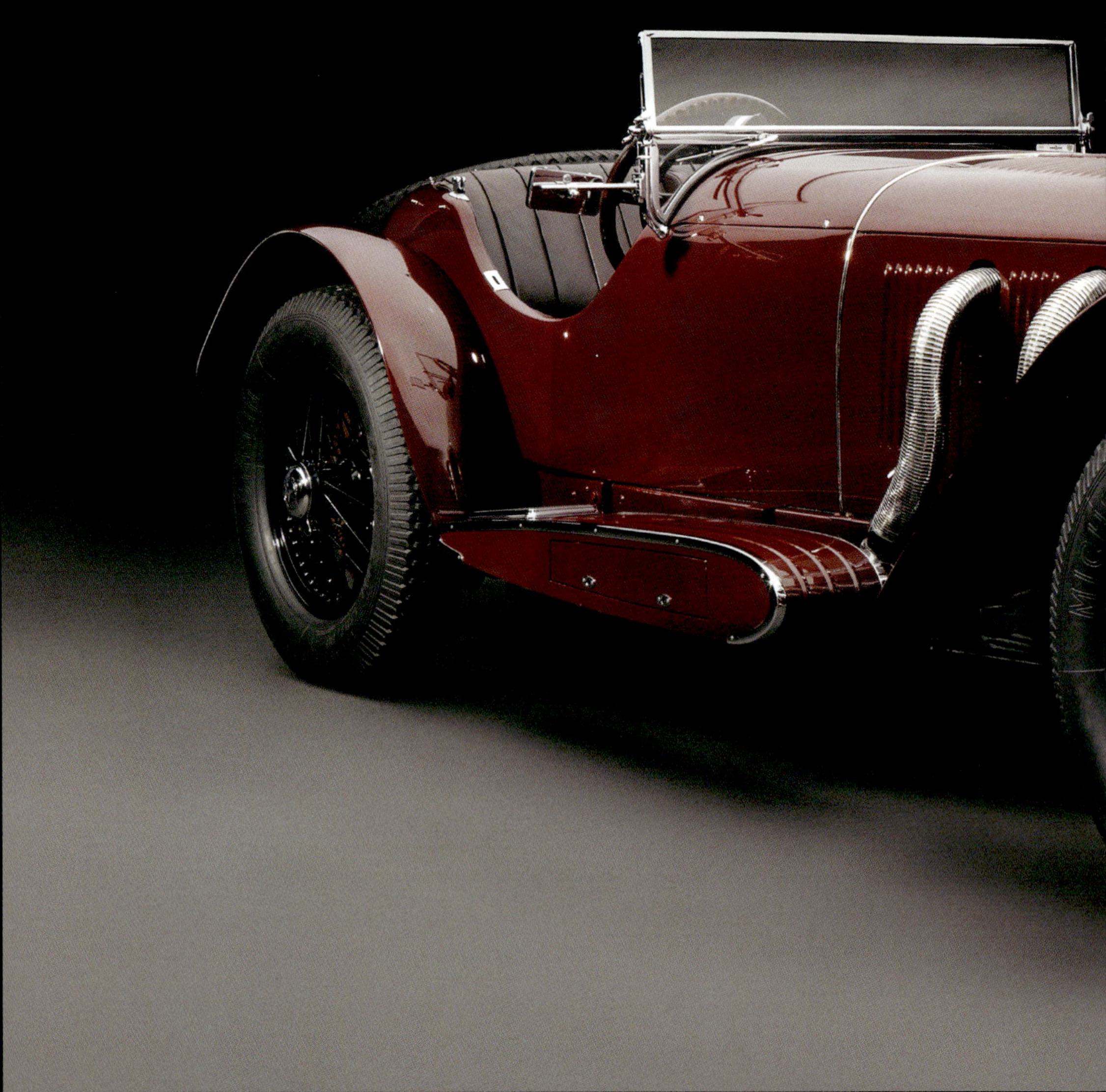

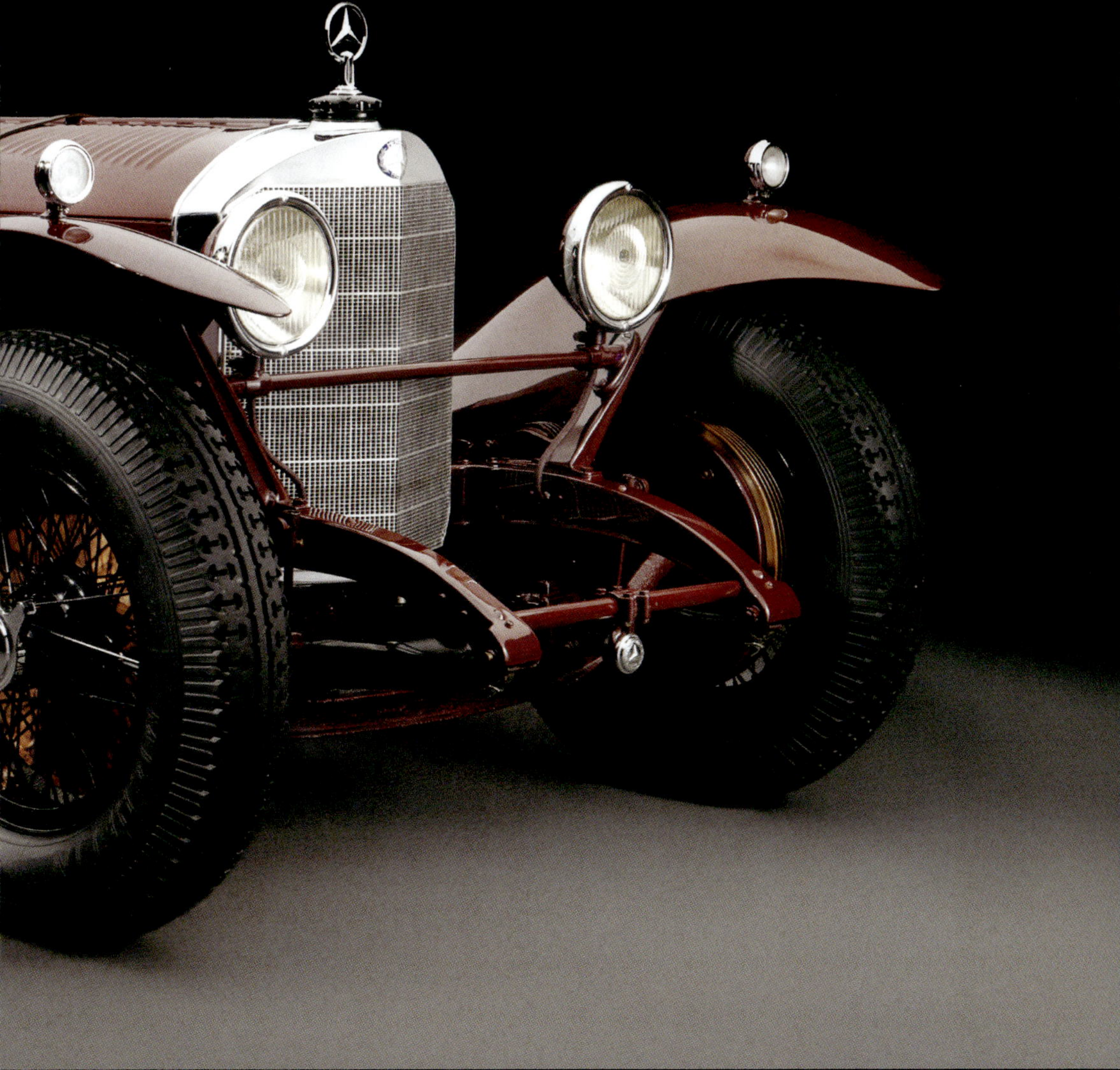

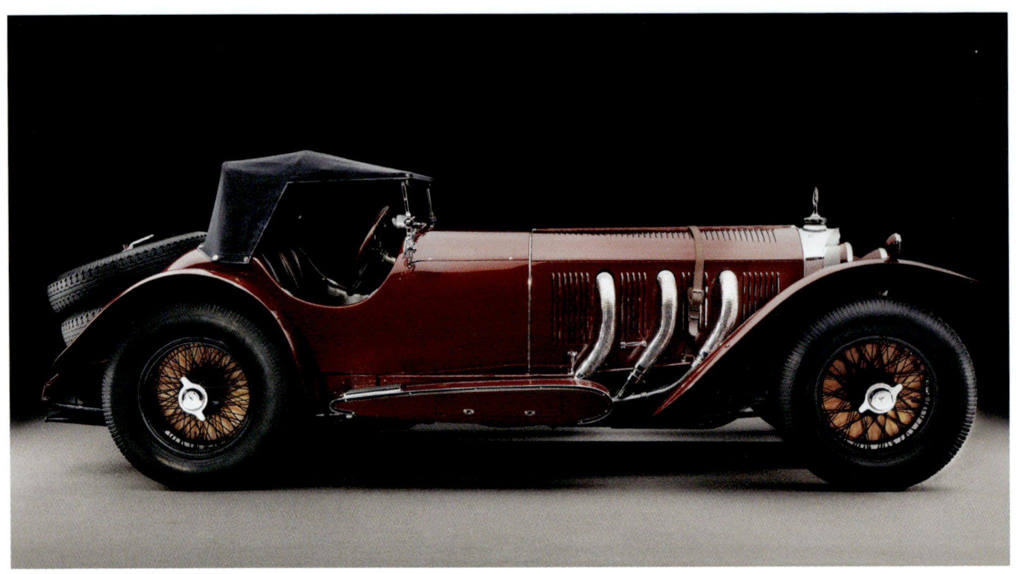

Above: View of car showing external exhaust pipes, which give the SSK a very powerful appearance.

In 1927, Daimler-Motoren-Gesellschaft (DMG) launched its Mercedes-Benz S-Series by debuting the Model S. Designed by the automotive engineering legend Dr. Ferdinand Porsche, this car featured a state-of-the-art yet also very noisy six-cylinder engine, the W 06, that was equipped with an engageable Roots-type supercharger, thereby giving it a considerable amount of power when required both as a race and production car. But more than this, in comparison to earlier Mercedes models, the car's engine was placed an extra 30 centimeters (12 in.) rearward in an attempt to improve weight distribution, while its frame was set lower giving it a deeper center of gravity — all of which helped enhance handling and stability. Right from its outset, the Model S was very sucessful in motorsports, winning its very first competition at the Nürburgring opening race of 1927. In mid-1928, a new variant of the S-series was introduced, the Model SS, which stands for Super Sport, also designed by Porsche. It had an even better-performing engine thanks to increased displacement, which added an extra 40 horsepower and delivered a truly impressive top speed of 192 km/h (119 mph) — which in the late 1920s was around double or triple what most cars could achieve. The problem was, however, that although the Model S and Model SS performed extremely well when racing on straights thanks to their impressive top speeds, they were both pretty unwieldy around bends, which became a major frustration for the works' race manager, Alfred Neubauer. That said, at the SS's debut the factory's ace driver Rudolf Caracciola drove one of its cars to glory at the Bühler Heights Hill Climb and then DMG enjoyed a 1-2-3 finish at the German Grand Prix held at the Nürburgring circuit that same year with its stable of Model SSs. Yet despite these successes in late 1928 Porsche was tasked with developing an improved variant of the Model SS, so that Caracciola would have even more competitive advantage in hill-climb events. The resulting model incorporated the Model S's radiator and the Model SS's supercharged engine, aptly named the "Elephant Blower" because of its fearsome noise. In fact, all the S-Series cars went on to become known collectively as "White Elephants" — a rather unflattering moniker bestowed on them by motorsports fans but, as Daimler explains, "these racing cars in the white color of Germany's racing team, were big, strong and powerful — and the infernal roaring of the supercharger also contributed to their name. But that's about as far as the comparisons with the pachyderms can go."

The new and improved 1929 model, which was marketed as "The Fastest Sportscar in the World," would prove to be a superb race machine. Significantly, it would be Porsche's last design for DMG. Produced until 1932, it was christened the SSK or Super Sport Kurz — with *kurz* being the German word for "short." The name was derived from the fact that the SSK had a significantly shortened wheelbase, measuring 295 cm (116 inches) it equated to around 46 cm (18 inches) less than those of its forebearers. This meant the more compact

Below: Detail of right side of SSK 7,069 cc (431 cu. in.), supercharged SOHC inline six–cylinder engine showing external exhaust pipes. The SSK exhaust note is very loud, but when combined with the scream of the supercharger the car makes an utterly unforgettable sound.

Overleaf: Detail of cockpit, controls and instrumentation.

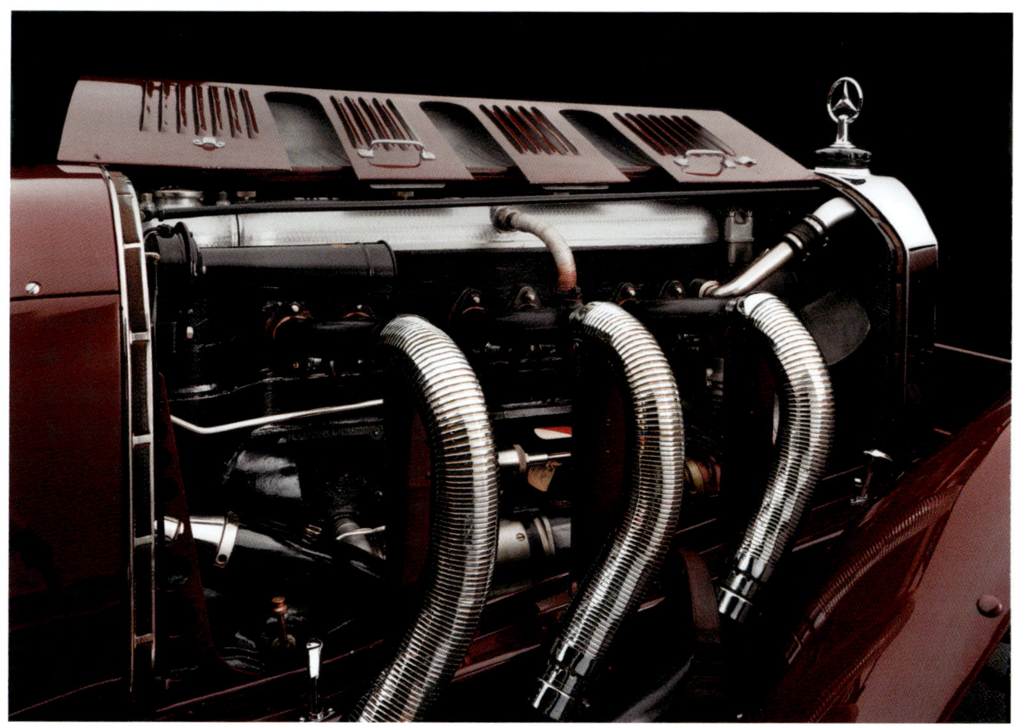

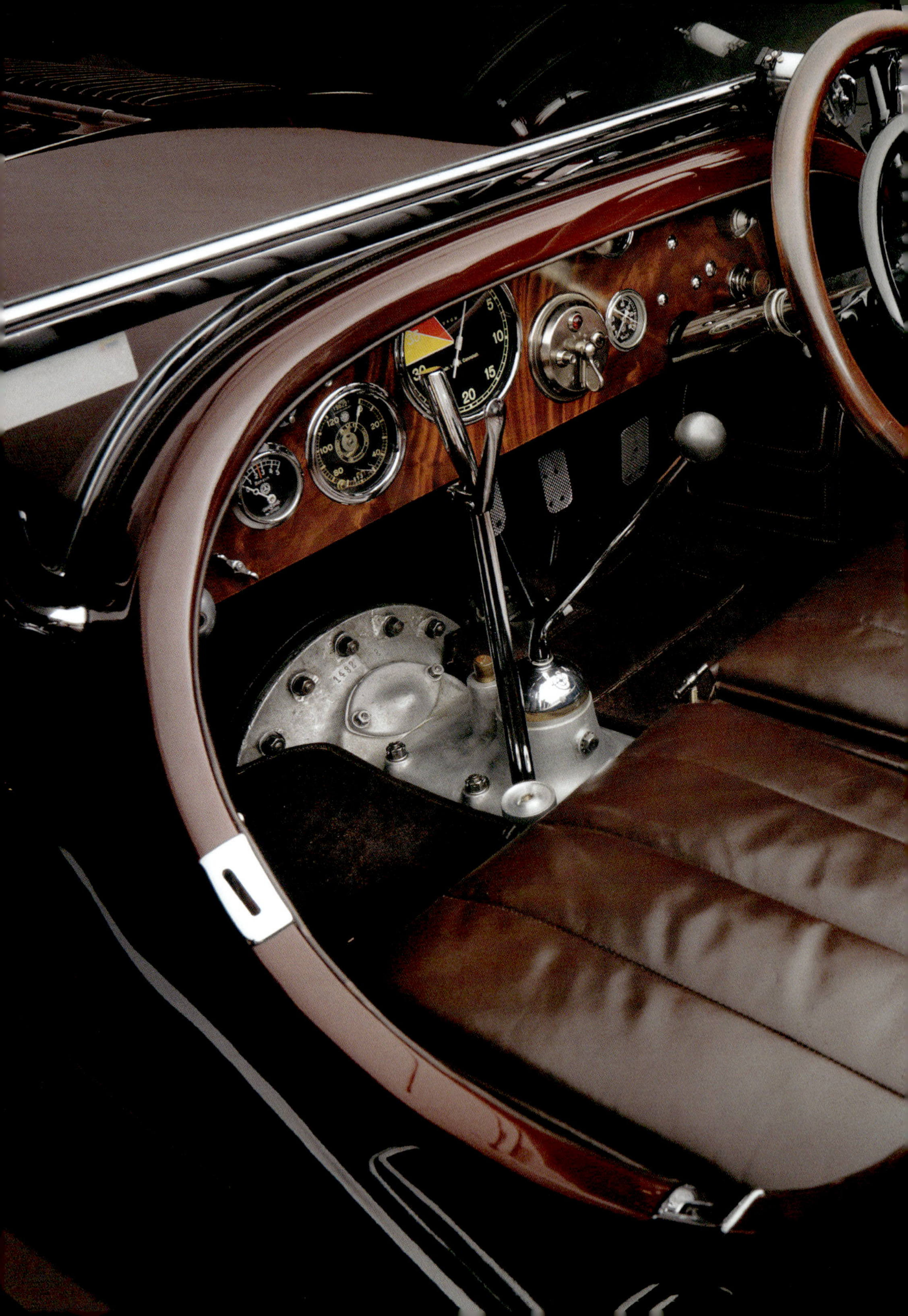

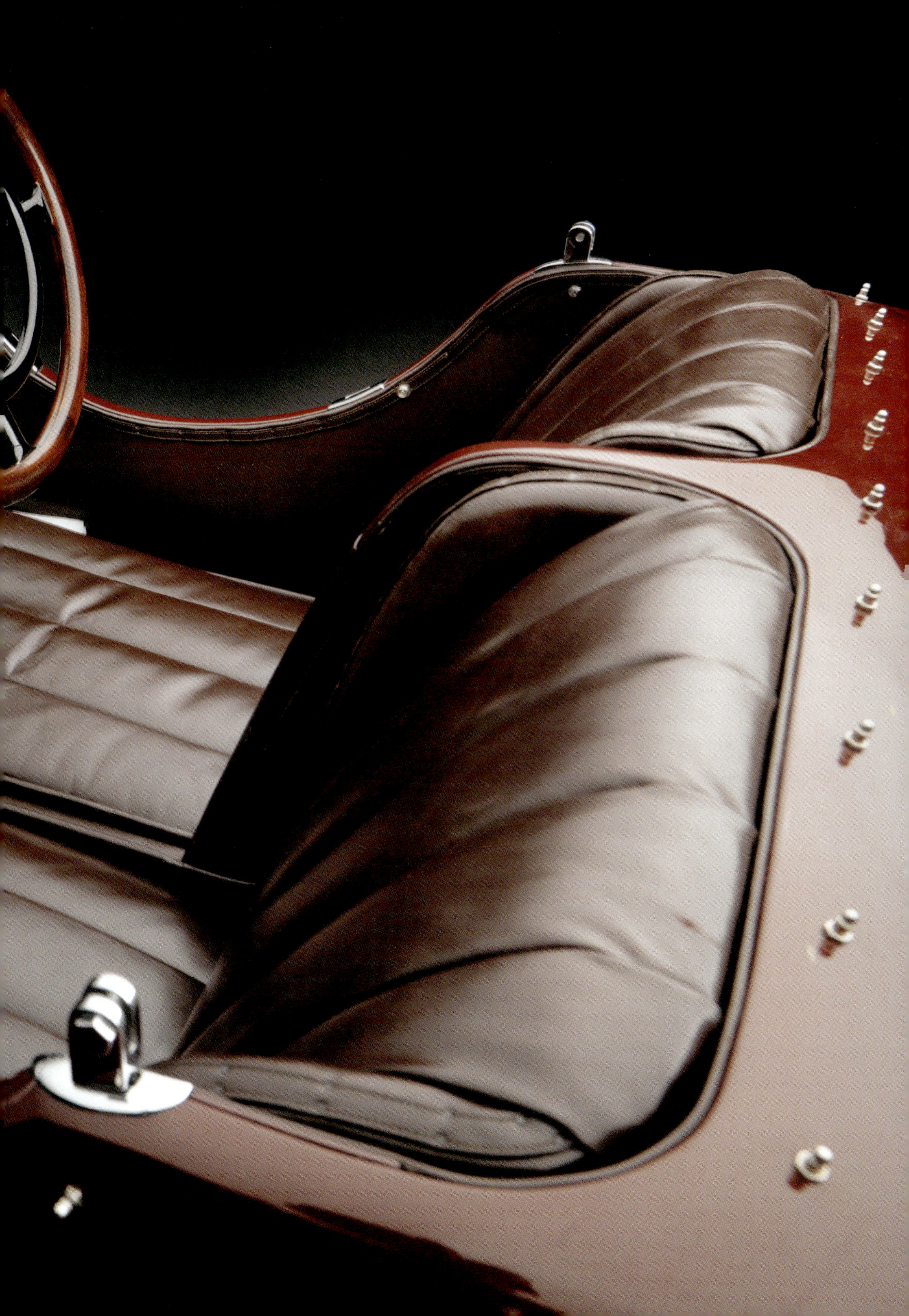

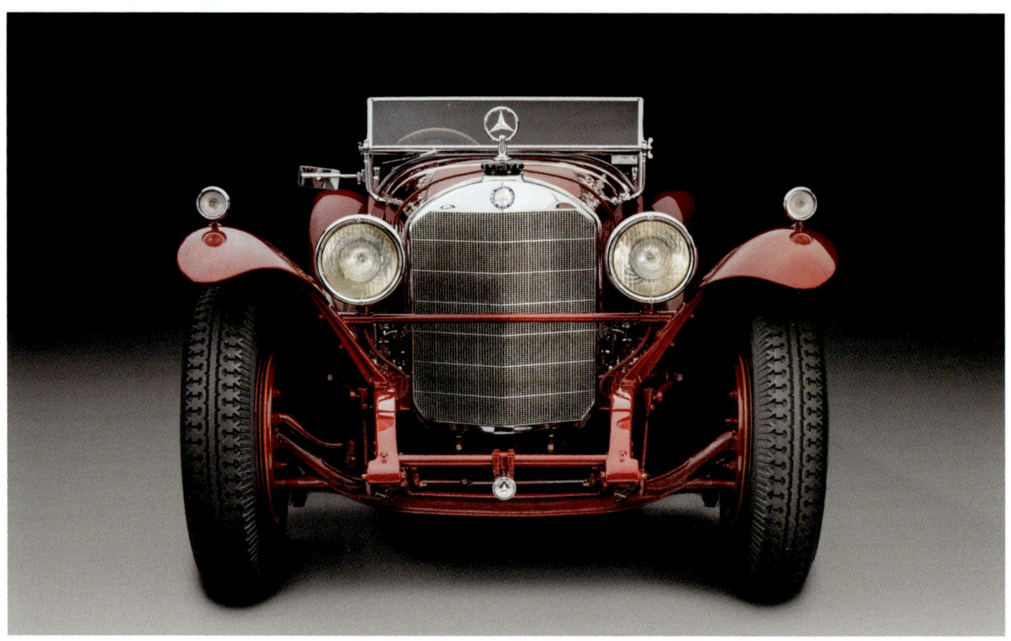

SSK was far nimbler around corners and ultimately quicker in races. It also boasted a slightly improved top speed of 192 km/h (119 mph). Unsurprisingly, this car proved itself spectacularly on hill climbs with Caracciola clocking up 26 wins over the next two years. Indeed, on the racetrack the SSK dominated its class for several years, with Caracciola often in the driving seat. And although only 31 SSK sports cars were built over its four-year production run, it provided Mercedes-Benz with considerable cachet and acres of brand-building publicity. The reason being several were owned by celebrities, including the example shown here, which once belonged to the eccentric British race horse owner, the Hon. Dorothy Wyndham Paget. This "Queen of the Turf" later bankrolled the legendary Bentley Blower race team. In 1931, a new variant of the SSK was launched — the SSKL — with the L standing for *leicht* (light) which, as its name suggested, was lighter in weight thanks to numerous holes being drilled into its chassis to reduce its overall mass by 113 kg (250 lb.). That same year Caracciola became the first non-Italian driver to win the Mille Miglia, while piloting an SSKL. Intended for competition, only a handful of SSKLs were produced and today no genuine examples are thought to have survived — making the handful of extant "Mighty Mercedes" SSKs all the more desirable to collectors.

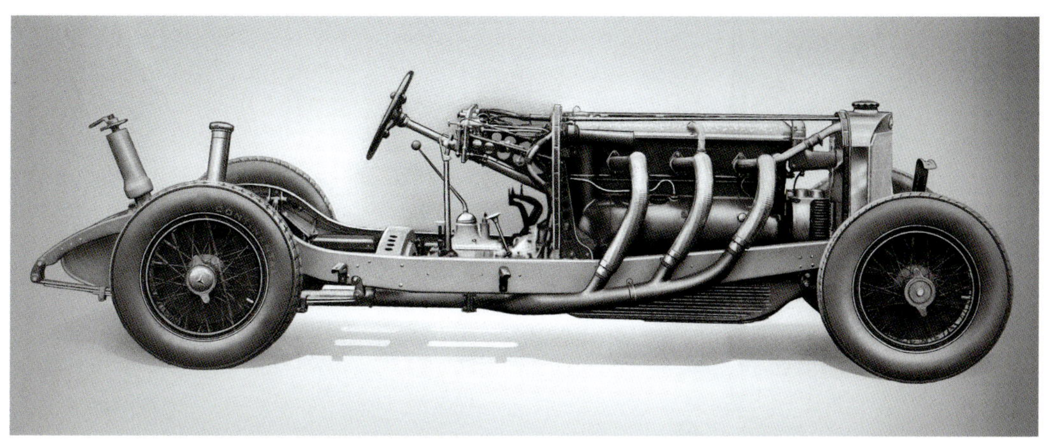

Above: llustration of Mercedes-Benz SSK chassis and powertrain. Built between 1928 and 1932, with its 7-liter supercharged engine the car was very powerful and very dynamic — the fastest car of its day — and dominated many important races throughout the world.

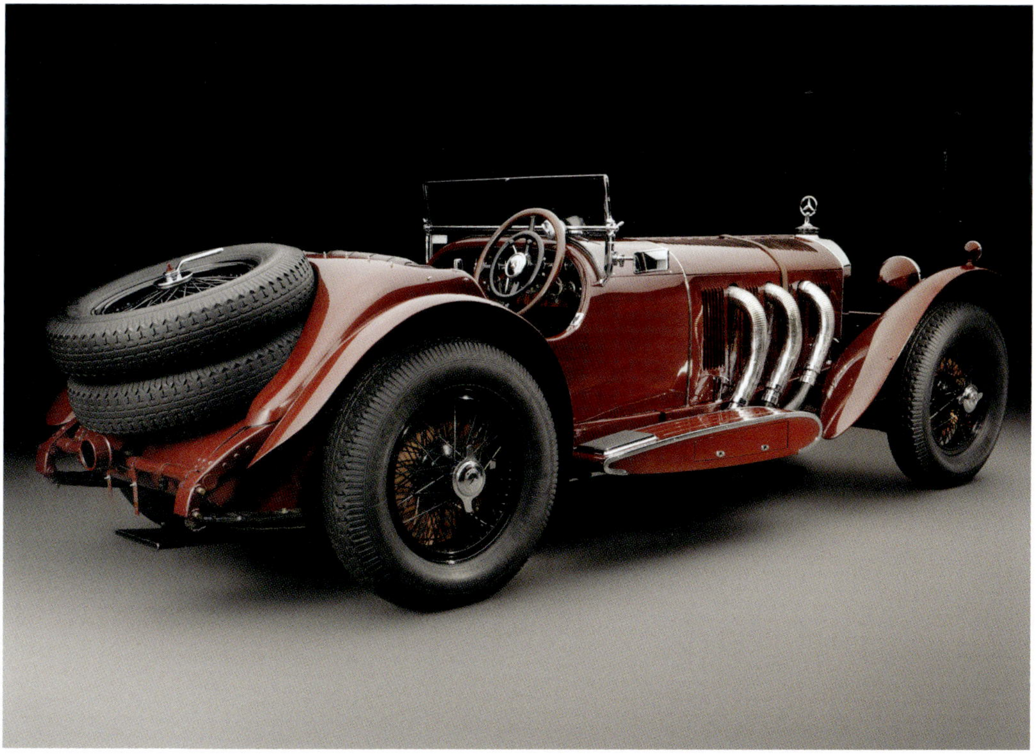

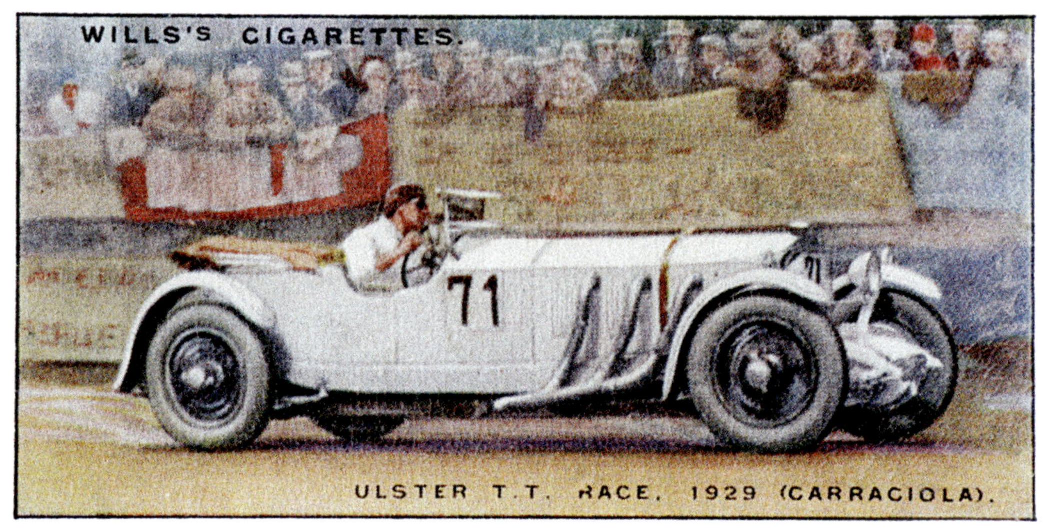
WILLS'S CIGARETTES.
71
ULSTER T.T. RACE. 1929 (CARRACIOLA).

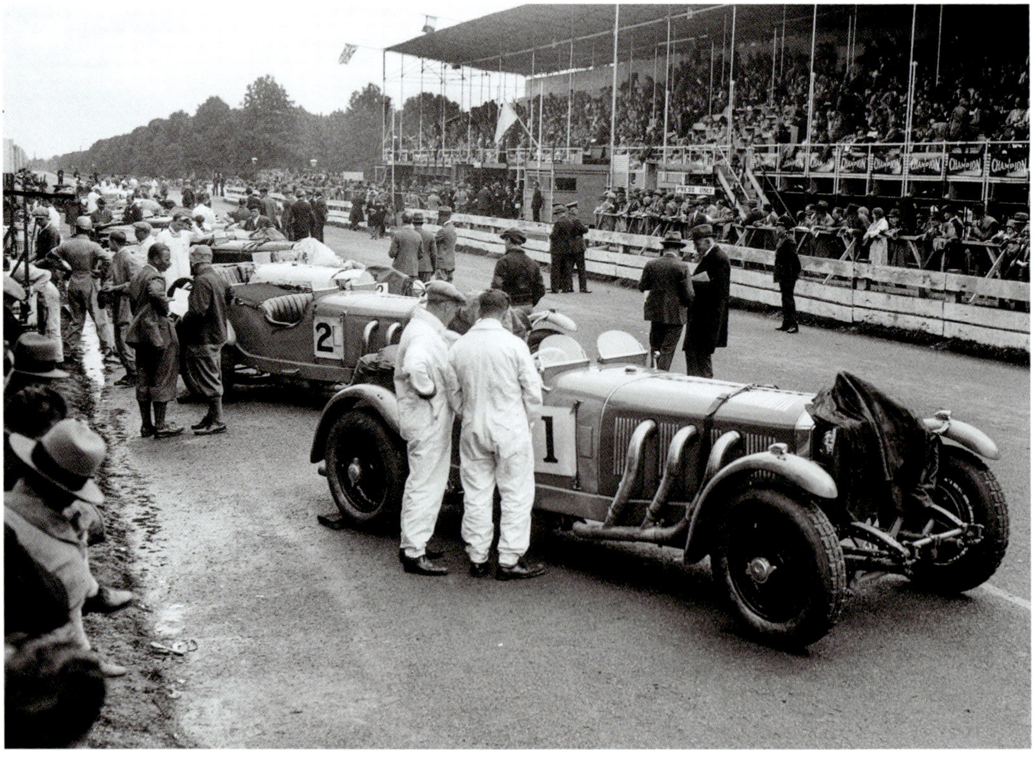

Opposite (top): Wills cigarette card ca.1930 depicting Rudolf Caracciola driving the No. 71 Mercedes-Benz SSK at the 1929 Ulster Tourist Trophy. Having won the race, Caracciola was later described by the press as "A laughing dare-devil in a monstrous Mercedes racer, who staggered the motoring world."

Opposite (bottom): Mercedes-Benz SSKs of Malcolm Campbell (No. 1) and the Earl Howe (No. 2) before the start of the Irish Grand Prix, Phoenix Park, Dublin, 1930. Rudolf Caracciola won the race in another Mercedes-Benz SSK.

Below: International Klausen Hill Climb in Switzerland, August 9–10, 1930. Rudolf Caracciola in the No. 64 Mercedes-Benz SSK won the 8-liter sports car category.

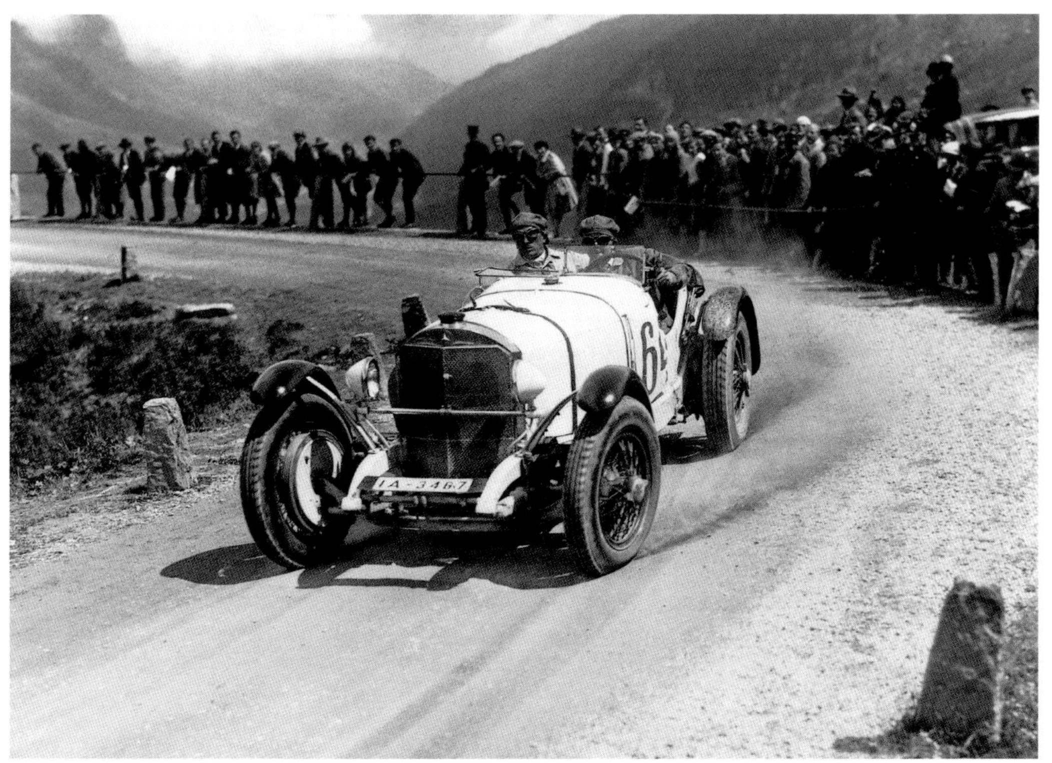

1933

Alfa Romeo 8C 2300 Monza

MANUFACTURED 1931–33 | **ENGINE** 2,327 cc (142 cu. in.), supercharged DOHC inline 8-cylinder | **HORSEPOWER** 165 **TOP SPEED** 225 km/h (140 mph) | **TRANSMISSION** 4-speed **NUMBER PRODUCED** 10

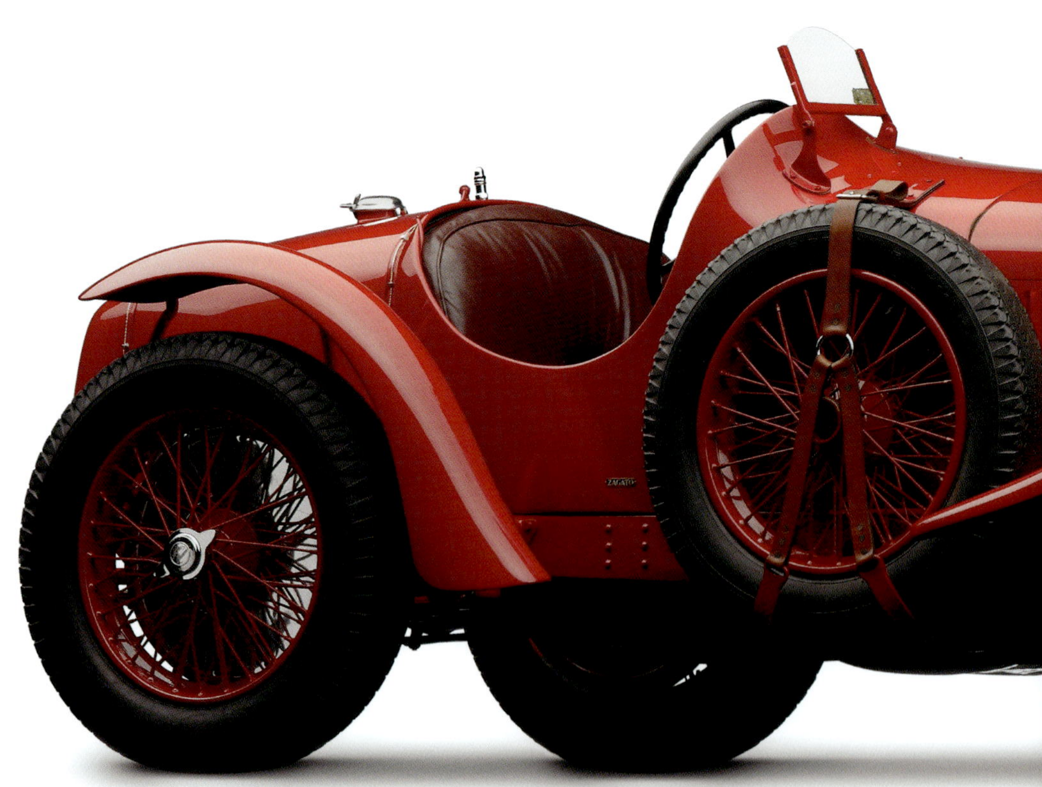

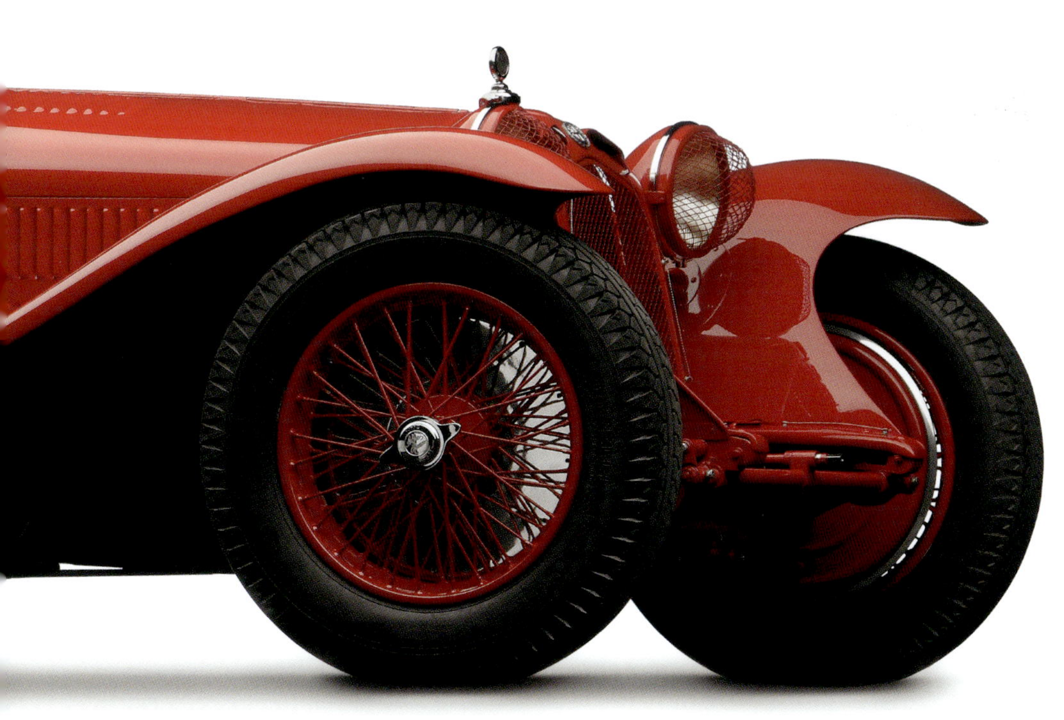

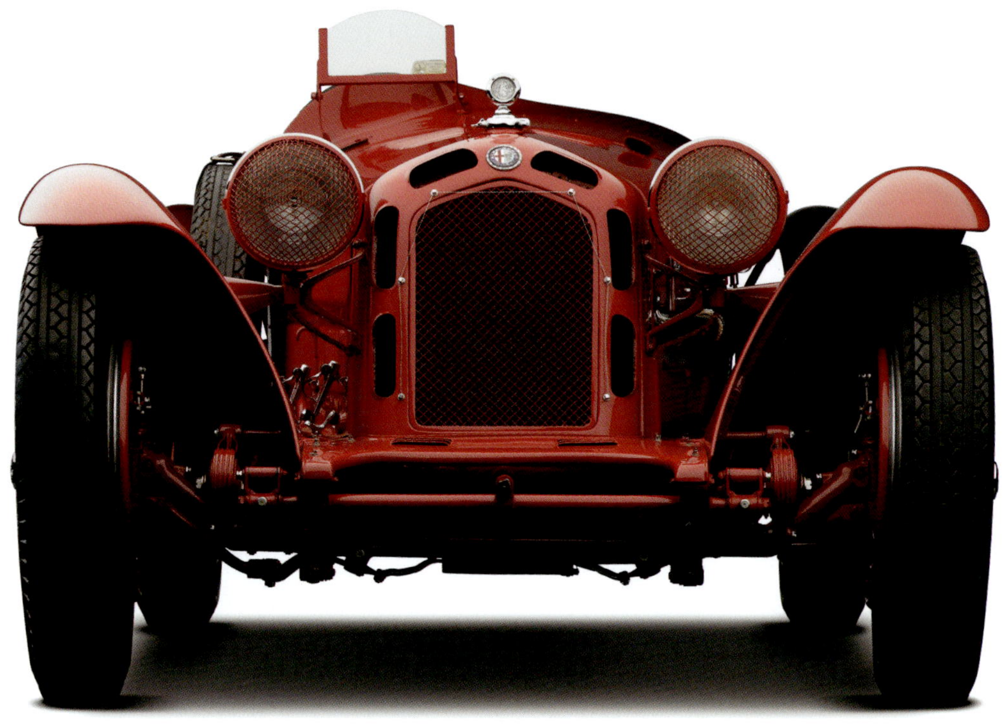

Opposite (top): Alfa Romeo race factory photo prior to the 1931 Mille Miglia showing driver Luigi Arcangeli and mechanic Pietro Bonini in an 8C 2300 Spider Corsa — they had an accident and did not finish the race.

Opposite (bottom): 1933 Alfa Romeo 8C 2600 Monza. In 1933 the supercharged DOHC inline eight-cylinder engine that had been enlarged to 2.6 liters for the Alfa Romeo Tipo B P3 Monoposto was fitted to the Scuderia Ferrari 8C Monzas. By this time Scuderia Ferrari had become the semi-official race department of Alfa Romeo.

The Alfa Romeo 8C 2300 was designed by the talented engineer Vittorio Jano as the marque's second series-production road/sports/race car (after the 6C). It was powered by a formidable 2.3-liter eight-cylinder engine and, shortly after the model's introduction in 1931, was driven to victory by Tazio Nuvolari at the Targa Florio race in Sicily. This success was repeated the following year with Nuvolari again at the wheel. The 8C 2300 also achieved a much celebrated 1-2 finish at the 1931 Italian Grand Prix held at Monza, with the winning car being put through its paces by Nuvolari and his opera-singing co-driver Giuseppe Campari, who had worked for Alfa since he was a teenager. Needless to say, both men went on to become national heroes as a consequence of this historic Italian victory, while the car subsequently earned itself the nickname "Monza." The following year, perhaps even more thrillingly, the 8C 2300 Monza clocked up another landmark triumph at the 1932 Monaco Grand Prix with a repeat 1-2 finish, with Nuvolari again driving the winning car, while Rudolf Caracciola took second place.

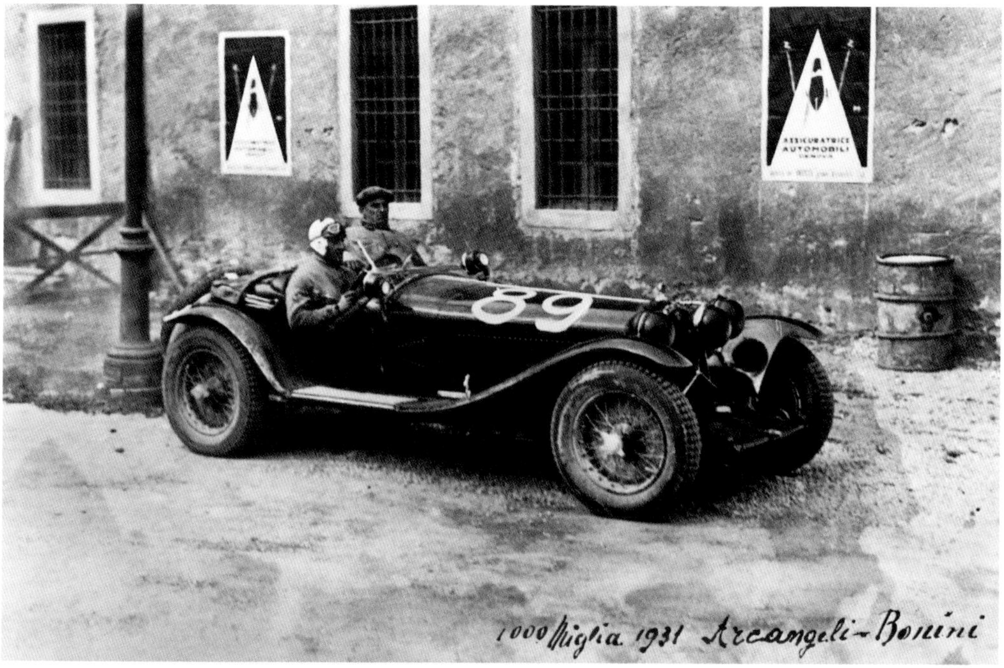

1000 Miglia 1931 Arcangeli-Bonini

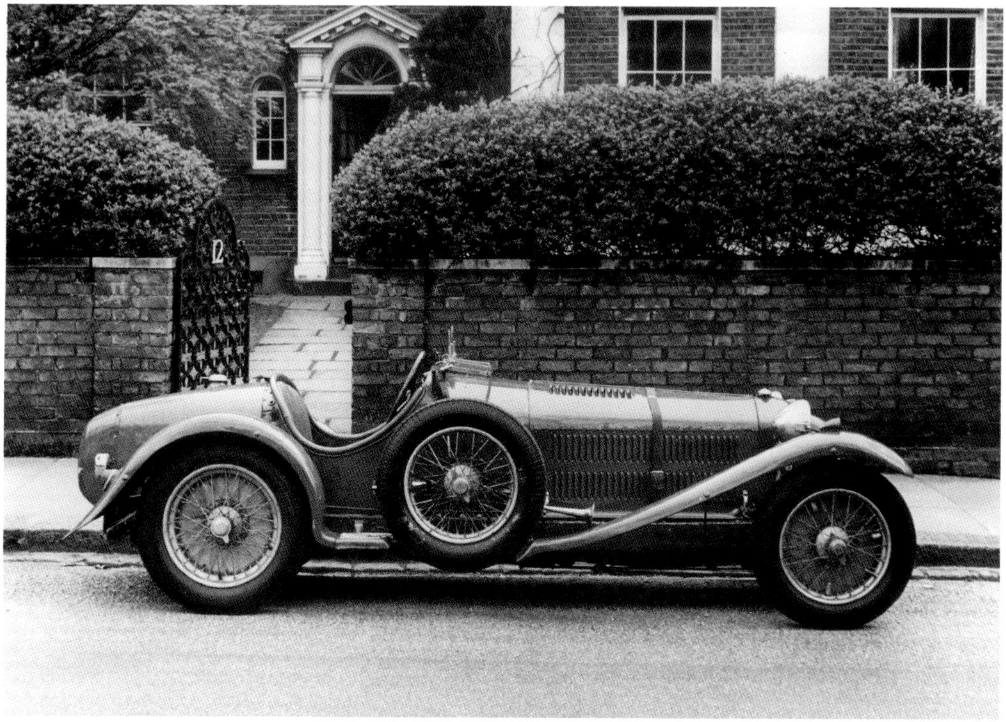

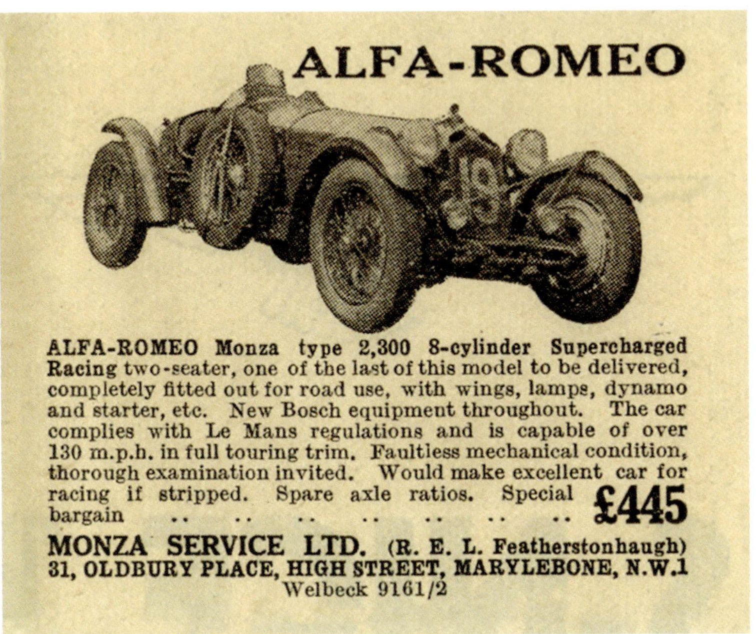

Alfa Romeo produced the 8C 2300 series from 1931 to 1936, which comprised three different models powered by its high performance supercharged double overhead cam engine, which was tailored to suit different types of races. These were: the "Le Mans," which had a longer chassis so that it could accommodate the legendary race's obligatory rear seat rules; the "Mille Miglia" spider, which had a shorter chassis making it better suited to more twisty road racing; and the "Monza" (shown here) which, as mentioned, was a full-out Grand Prix racer that enjoyed great success during the early 1930s. It is known from historic company records that very few factory Monza chassis were actually constructed at Alfa Romeo, and that the majority of the 8C 2300 Grand Prix racers were instead built by Scuderia Ferrari. This enterprise functioned as Alfa Romeo's de facto race team after the firm ran into financial difficulties, which saw it being taken over in 1933 by a state-owned conglomerate that subsequently prohibited it from funding its own works team. Often these Scuderia Ferrari-built Monzas were constructed from converted two-passenger spiders. As the renowned collector Dr. Frederick Simeone explains, "There are specific details which constitute the Monza, mainly chassis changes, special racing wheels and certain mechanical modifications that evolved over its racing career."

The multiple victories — some 50 in total — that the Alfa Romeo 8C 2300 Monza clocked up helped bring valuable publicity to the marque and its production Monzas, which were manufactured from 1931 to 1933 and sold to gentlemen racers as race-ready sports cars. One period British advertisement stated, for example, that the model was "capable of over 130 mph in full touring trim," an astonishing top speed for the early 1930s, and also that it "Would make an excellent car for racing if stripped."

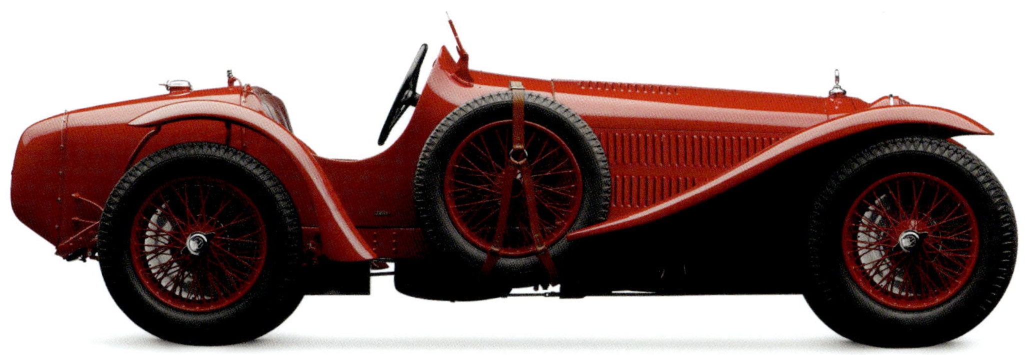

Opposite: 1930s British advertisement for 1933 Alfa Romeo 8C 2300 Monza chassis no. 2211112.

Below: 1933 Alfa Romeo 8C 2300 Monza (chassis no. 2211112) competing in the 1938 24 Hours of Le Mans — driven by Marcel Horvilleur and Yves Matra the car was retired on lap 53.

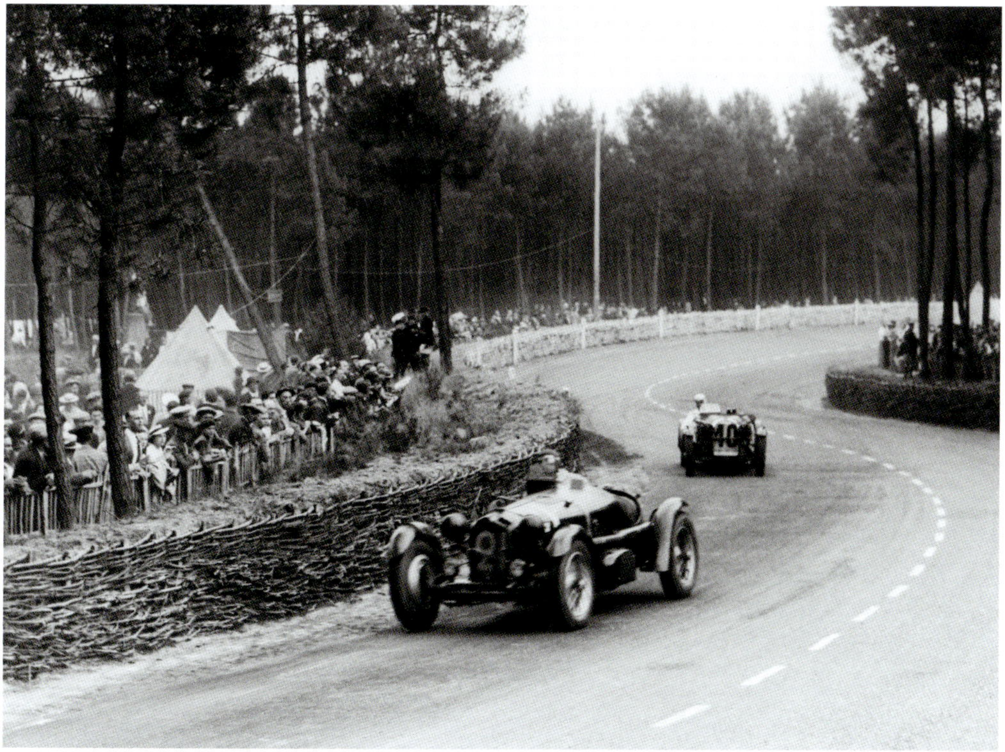

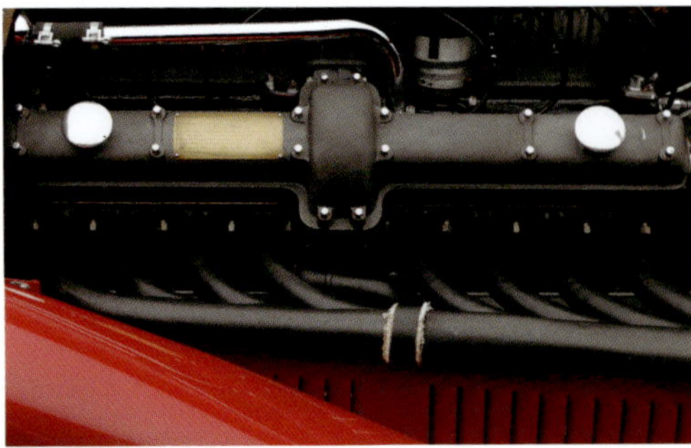

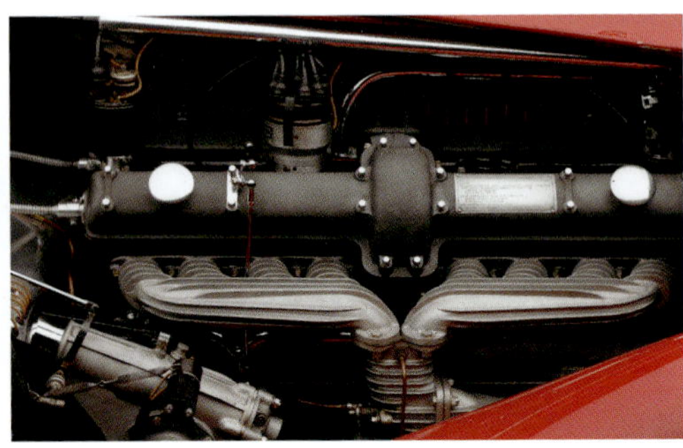

Above: Detail of the left and right side of the Alfa Romeo 8C 2300 Monza 2,327 cc (142 cu. in.), supercharged DOHC inline eight-cylinder engine. This engine was designed by the brilliant Alfa Romeo engineer Vittorio Jano and was built up from two cast aluminum blocks of four cylinders with the gear drive to the overhead camshafts sandwiched in between. This effectively cut in half the length of the camshafts, which are prone to flexing in engines this long. Producing up to 180 hp when fully race tuned, the engine enabled the 8C 2300 to go down into history as one of the finest and most successful sports-racing cars ever constructed.

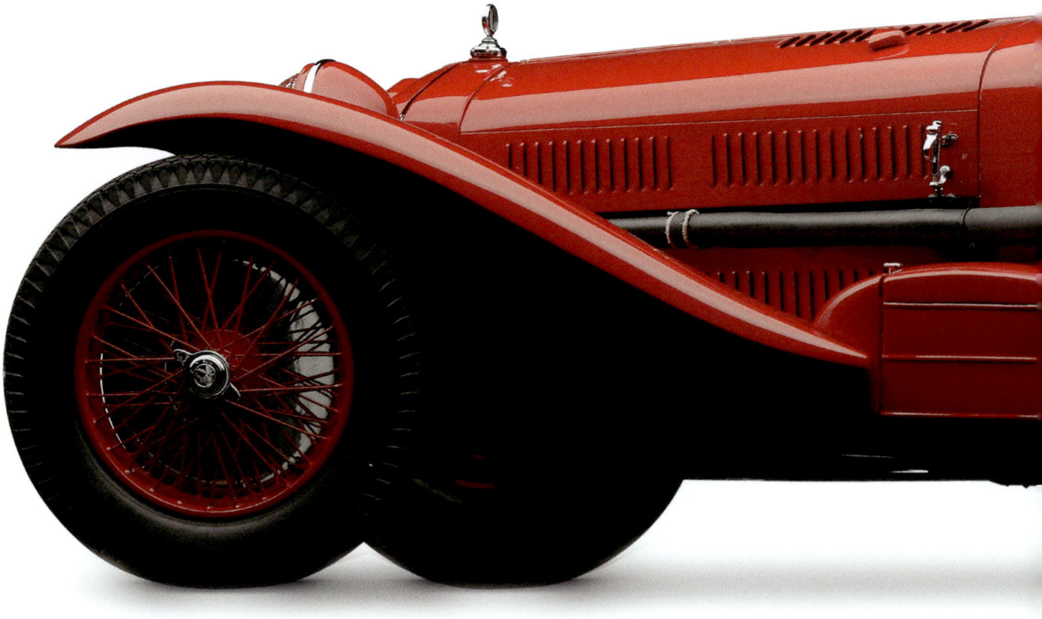

The 1933 Monza shown here (chassis no. 2211112) is from the Simeone Foundation Automotive Museum and is an exquisite example of this beautiful and thrillingly responsive interwar competition car. It was ordered from Alfa Romeo by Count Carlo Castelbarco for him to co-drive/navigate at the 1933 Mille Miglia, along with his driver Franco Cortese. It had a full-on Monza chassis and an aerodynamic body modified by Zagato. The night before the race, however, there was a mishap as a result of a mechanic filling its tank and not realizing an electrician was still working underneath it. A resulting spark ignited the fuel and the car burst into flames. It was subsequently all hands on deck to get the car race ready, and then misfortune struck again an hour before the race when a mechanic mistakenly poured water into its fuel tank, which meant dismounting it, cleaning it and remounting it. Yet despite all these woes, Cortese and Castelbarco managed to get on the grid, and then averaging 200 km/h (124 mph) down the autostrada placed a remarkable second, which was an epic result given the lead up to their race. In fact, at this event various iterations of the Alfa Romeo 8C 2300 took the top eight places, with two other Alfa Romeos (6C 1750 GSs) taking the ninth and tenth spots, testifying to the marque's racing dominance during this era.

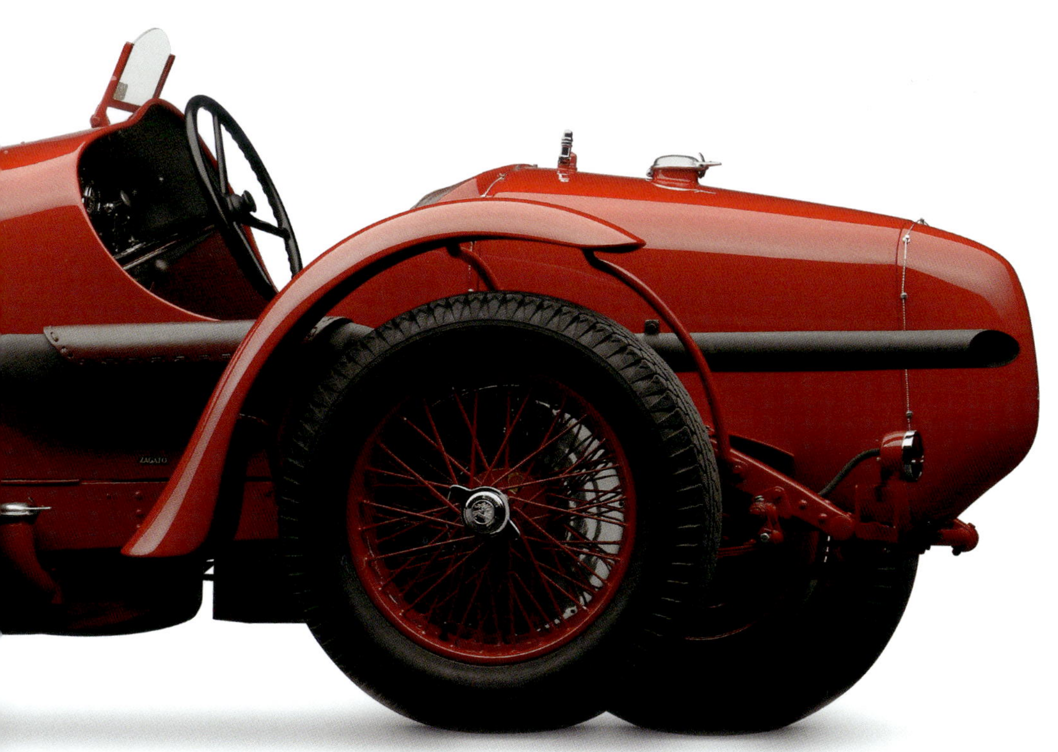

1936

Bugatti Type 57G “Tank”

MANUFACTURED 1936 | ENGINE 3,257 cc (199 cu. in.), DOHC inline 8-cylinder | HORSEPOWER 200
TOP SPEED 220 km/h (137 mph) | TRANSMISSION 4-speed
NUMBER PRODUCED 3

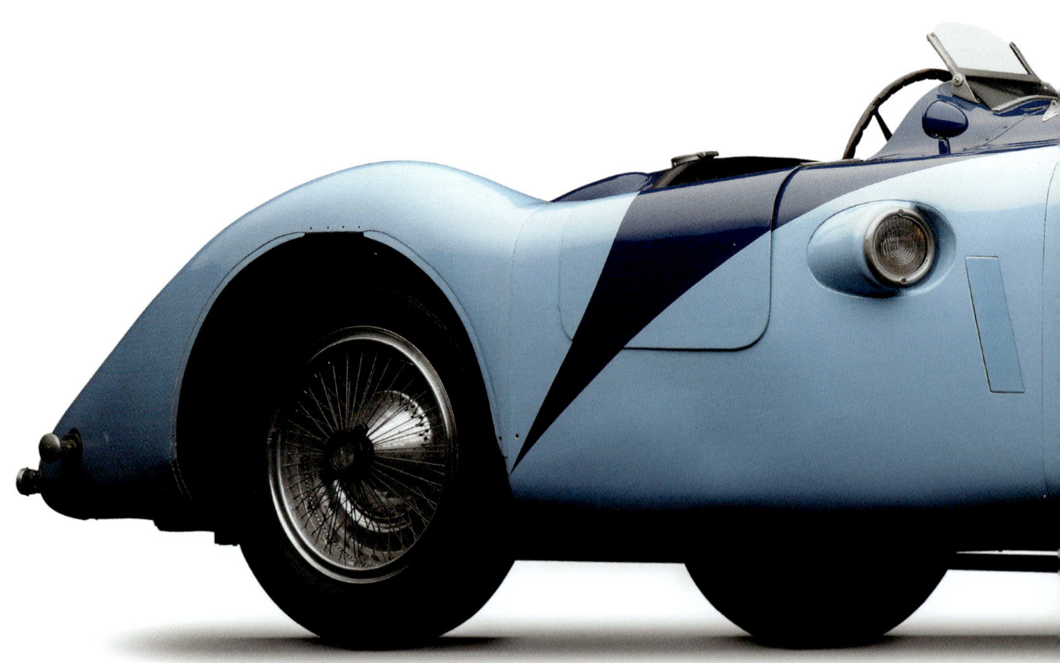

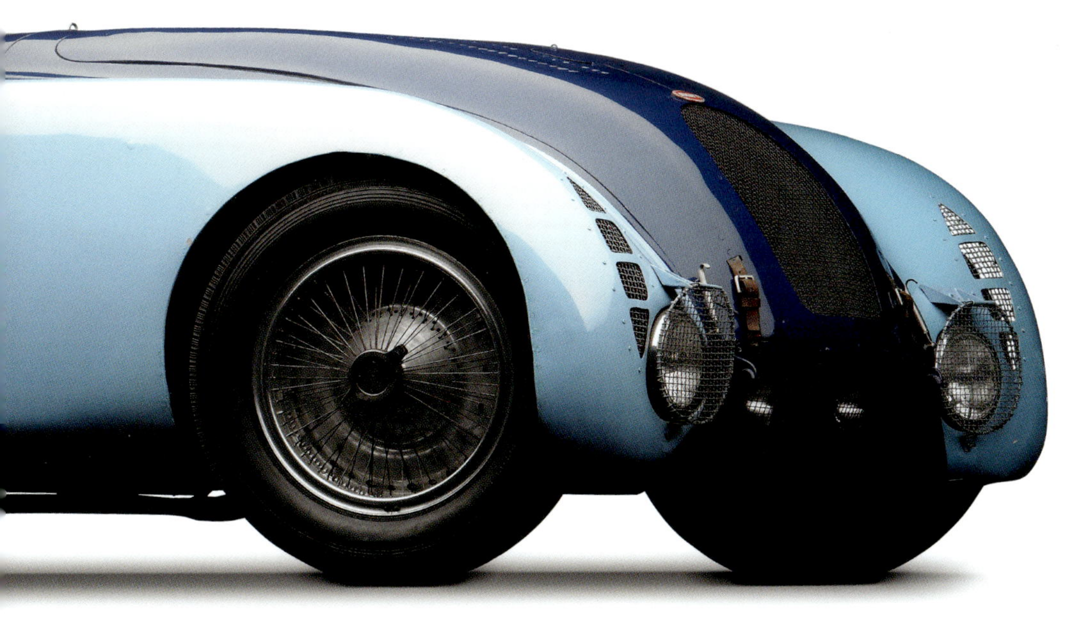

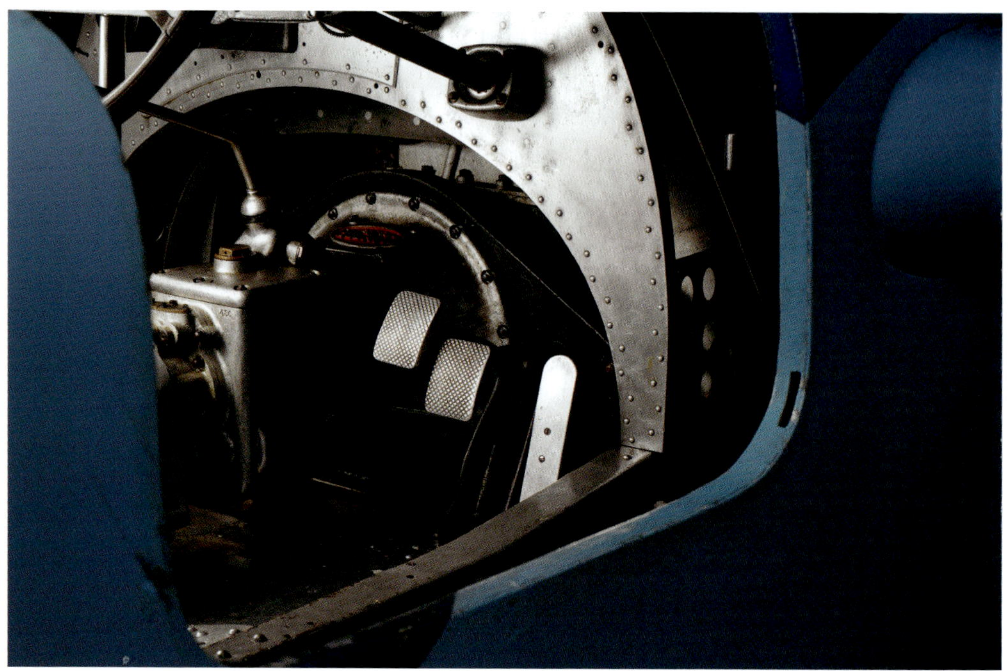

Above: Detail of 1936 Bugatti Type 57G's pedals, inner frame and fire wall. The brake and clutch pedals are notably close together despite the car being wide overall.

Opposite: In June 1936 the Automobile Club de France (ACF) permitted the participation of "Grand Touring Cars" in various race events including the 24 Hours of Le Mans. This category incorporated their definition of sports cars — meaning two-seaters. A few months prior to the rule changes Bugatti had designed a special racing engine, which they called the 57G. This was then married to a car with an unusual streamlined all enveloping body, thereby giving rise to the car shown here — which became known as the prototype Bugatti 57G "Tank."

If rarity, beauty and provenance are the prime drivers of a collecting obsession, then there are very few cars that match the desirability of the 1936 Bugatti Type 57G "Tank." It is a sole survivor, with outstanding good looks and a racing pedigree to match, which gives it "holy grail" status within the car-collecting world. In June 1936, the Automobile Club de France (ACF), which then set the regulations for the French Grand Prix, decided to have a new "Grand Touring Car" category, which meant for the first time the rules allowed all cars to compete with just two seats. Just a few months prior to this announcement, Bugatti had developed a new racing engine, the 57G, which was ostensibly an evolution of the company's high performance eight-cylinder, 3.25-liter 57S engine, in that it had been designed with a lighter crankshaft in order to reduce speed-sapping weight.

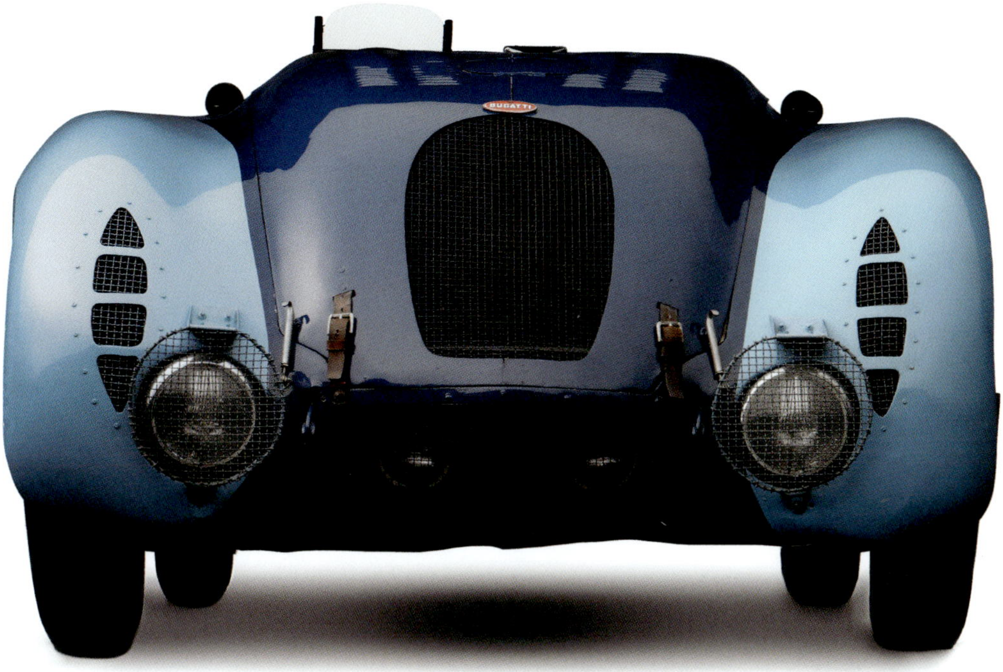

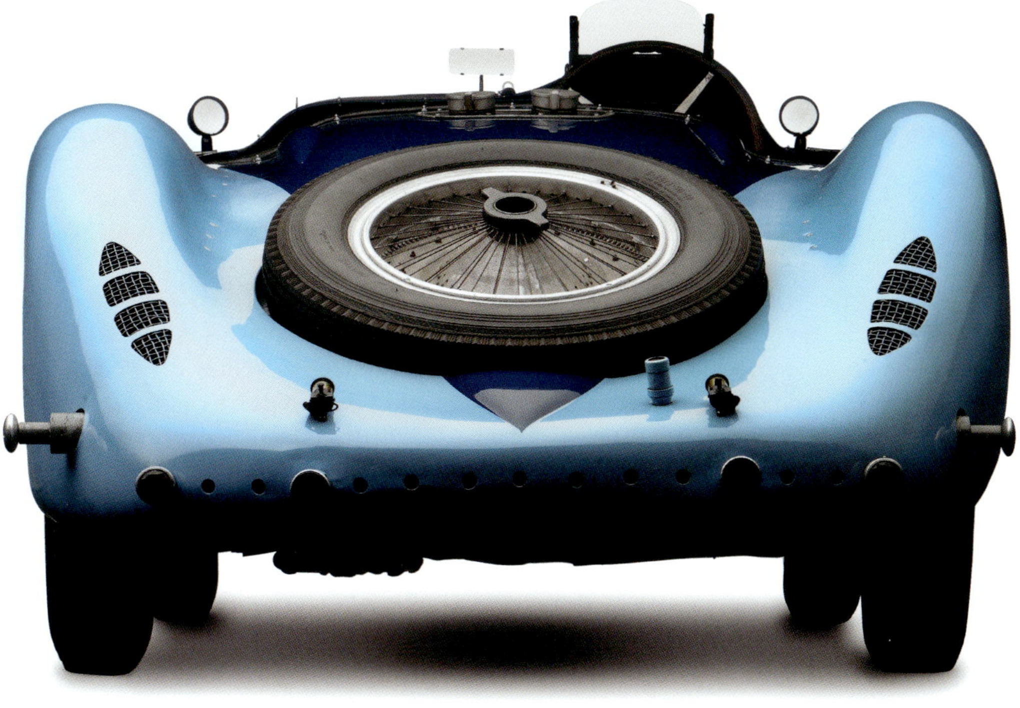

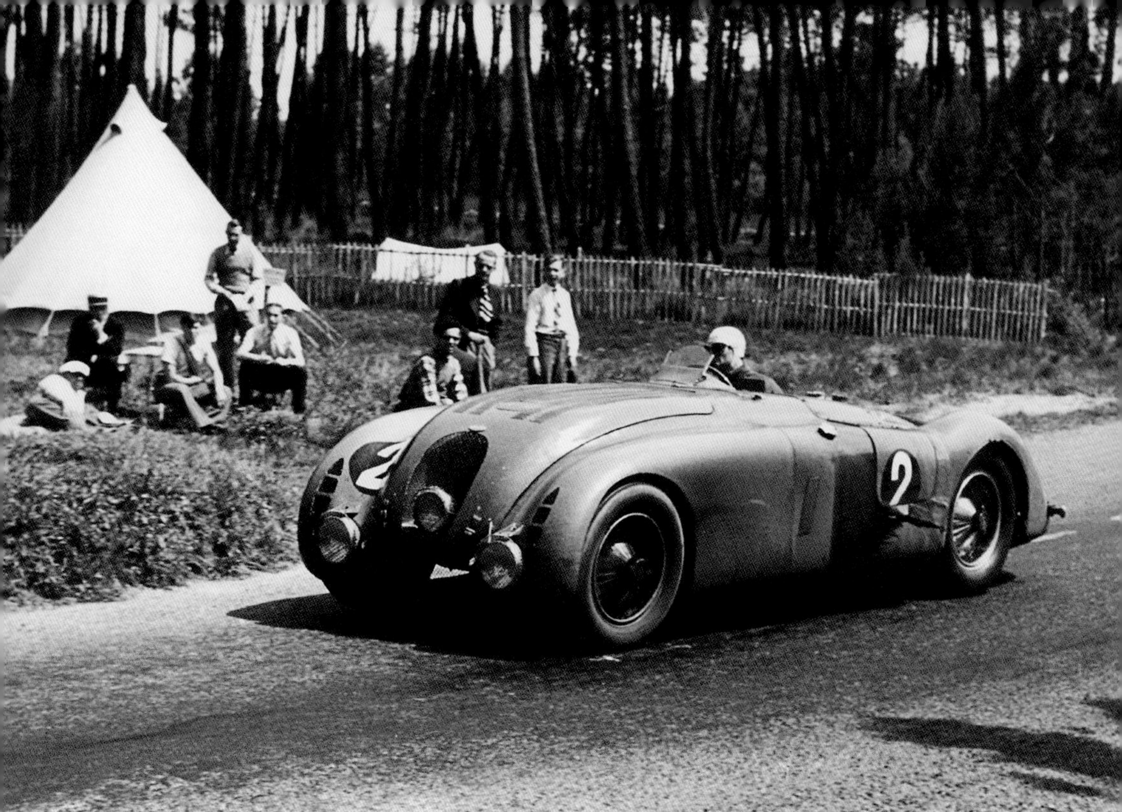

Above: 1936 Bugatti Type 57G (chassis no. 57G 01) at the 1937 24 Hours of Le Mans, which co-driven by Jean-Pierre Wimille and Robert Benoist won the race at an average speed of 137 km/h (85 mph) over a total distance of 3,287.938 km (2,043 miles).

It was this improved engine that lay at the core of a car newly developed by Bugatti with an interesting all-enveloping streamlined body, which was tested on June 7, 1936, at Montlhéry. This experimental model, which earned itself the nickname of "the aerodynamic mule," was the first Type 57G racer and functioned as the blueprint for two subsequent examples that Bugatti hastily constructed just days before the French Grand Prix, held the same year on June 28 at Montlhéry. At this event, the three race-ready Bugatti 57Gs, which were quickly dubbed the "Tanks" because of their enclosed bodies, placed first, sixth and thirteenth. This was a pretty astonishing result given that it was the Tanks' first official outing — with Jean-Pierre Wimille and Raymond Sommer winning the race in the example shown here (chassis no. 57G 01), which now resides in the Simeone Foundation Automotive Museum in Philadelphia. That same year, according to *Actualité Automobile,* the Tanks set various international records, including the 24 hour one. As it noted of this feat, "For the first time on the Montlhéry racetrack, an average speed of 125 km/h (78 mph) was reached over a 24 hour period. It doesn't surprise us that Bugatti was the one to have achieved this accomplishment. The performance was even more remarkable because they accomplished it with a car... without a compressor... To understand the merit of this feat, one would have to see the car speeding through the night at more than 200 km/h (on certain stretches of a track lit only by hurricane lamps. More than once a few spectators shuddered when, at the speed, a fifth of a second could have been fatal. If the car driving on the black line that marked the track's limits moved one meter beyond it, the car would crash. And driving at an average of 125 km/h (78 mph) for an hour at Montlhéry is already an extraordinary feat. To realize the same average for 24 hours is beyond all superfluous commentary."

Not surprisingly, given its outstanding speed the car set record times at this race. Then, a week later this same car, as presented here, put in an even more impressive showing at the XI Grand Prix de la Marne held in Rheims. Driven by Wimille, it again won the race, but with an even more impressive average speed of 140.2 km/h (87 mph). Disappointingly, given the Tanks' competitiveness that year, the 1936 24 Hours of Le Mans was called off because of a general strike.

The following year, however, came the most epic win of all — the French journalist, racing driver and owner, Robert Labric entered all three Bugatti 57Gs into the 1937 Le Mans 24 Hours race. Although two of these 57Gs failed to finish, the other one (the car shown here) driven by Wimille and Robert Benoist drove to glory — constituting a major historic victory for Bugatti. Then two years later, the Type 57 flexed its racing muscles once more, when this time with Wimille and Pierre Veyron at the helm, it seized another Le Mans triumph — and very decisively too, with the Bugatti being way ahead of the second-place car by a remarkable 26 miles. This car with a supercharged engine was a one-off variant of the 57G, known as the Type 57C "Tank," which shortly after this famous race win, on August 11, 1939 was completely destroyed in a tragic accident that killed 30-year-old Jean Bugatti, who was test driving the car not far from the factory on the road near the village of Duppigheim.

Of the three original Type 57Gs constructed — chassis no. 57G 01 is the only example known to still exist. It was reputedly buried underground for the duration of World War II as an act of preservation by the Bugatti family. Its dramatic lines and turquoise color scheme went on to inspire the design of the Bugatti Veyron, introduced in 2005 — testifying to the legendary standing of this celebrated survivor.

Overleaf: Detail of Bugatti Type 57G "Tank" radiator, engine compartment and firewall.

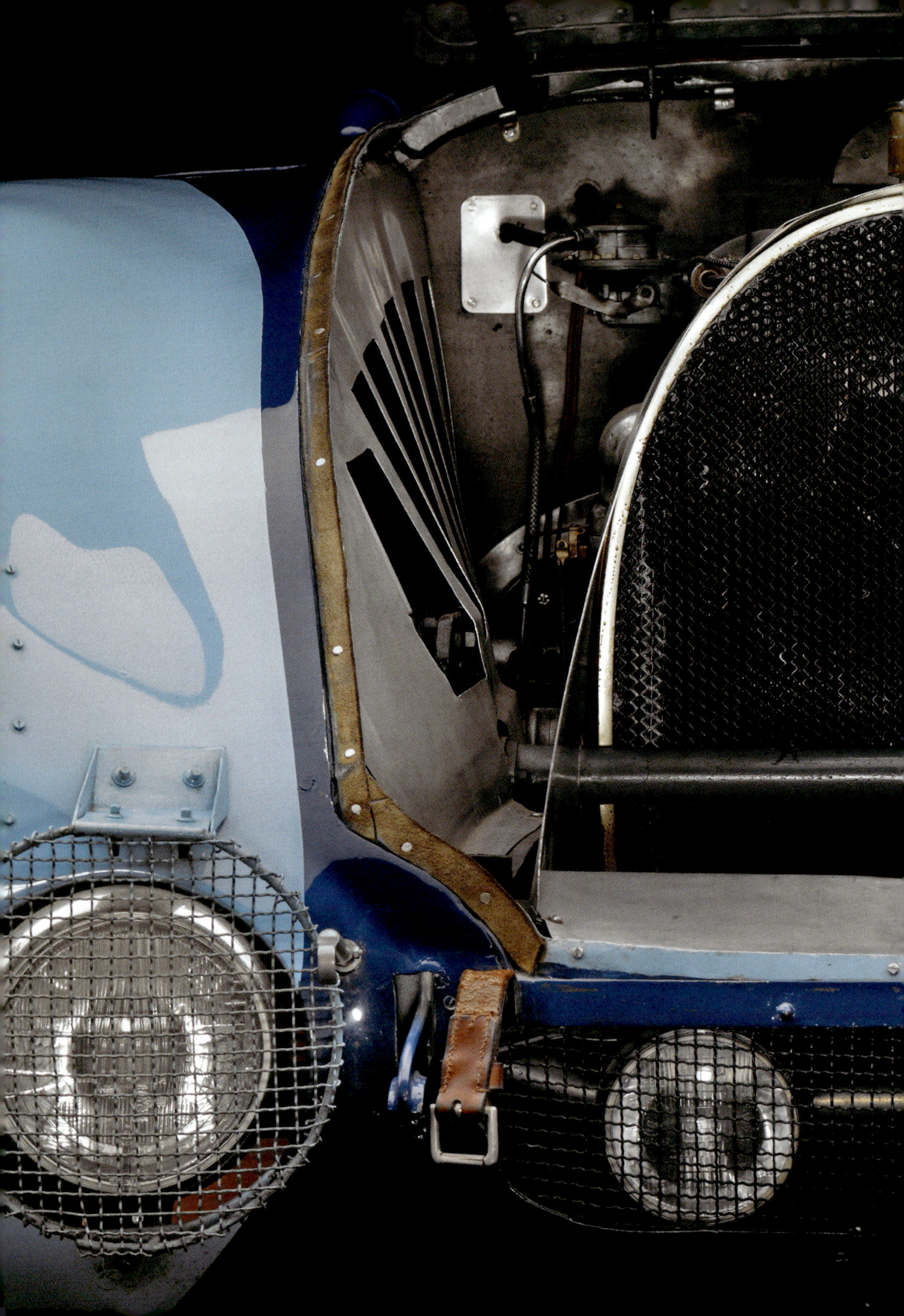

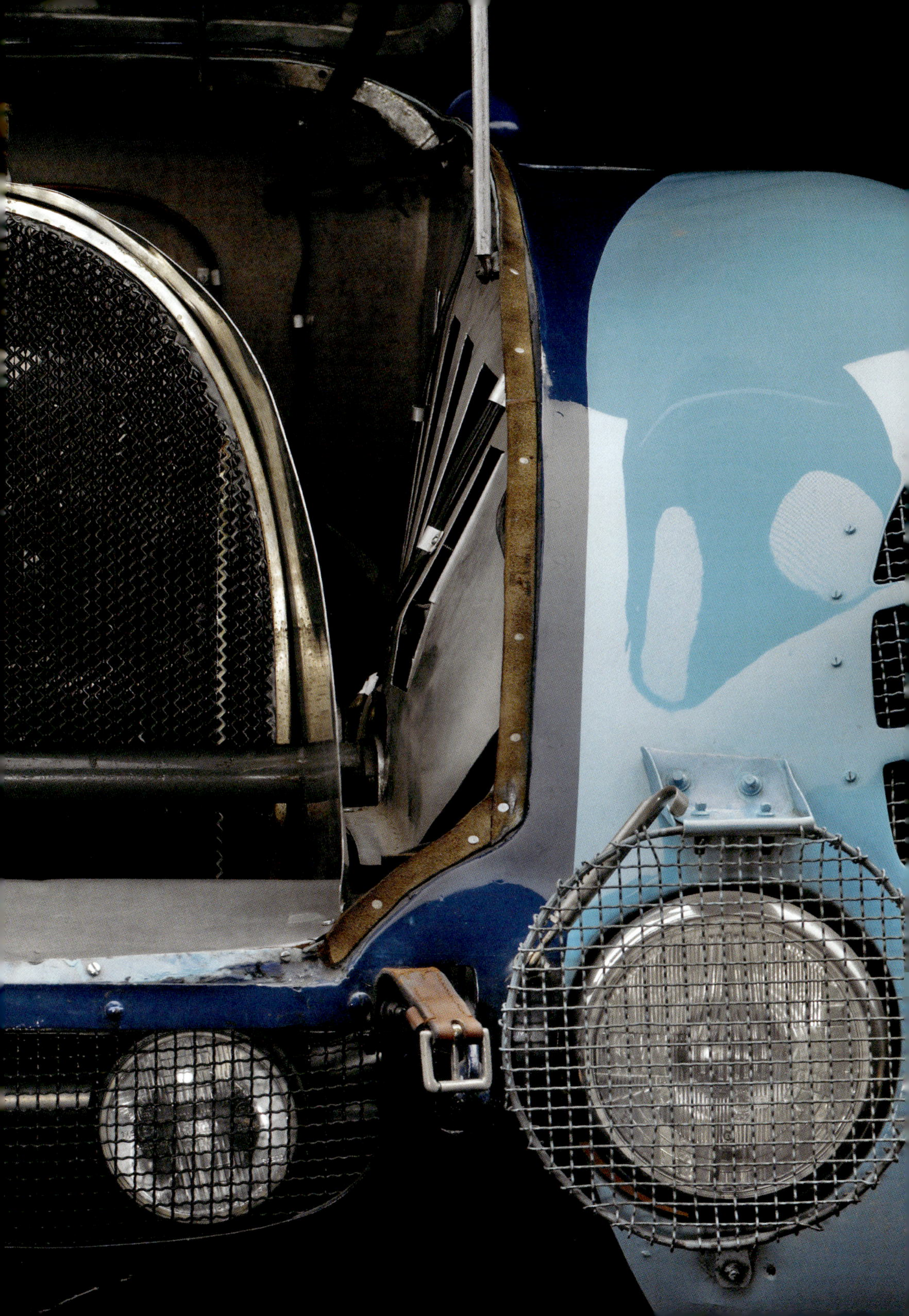

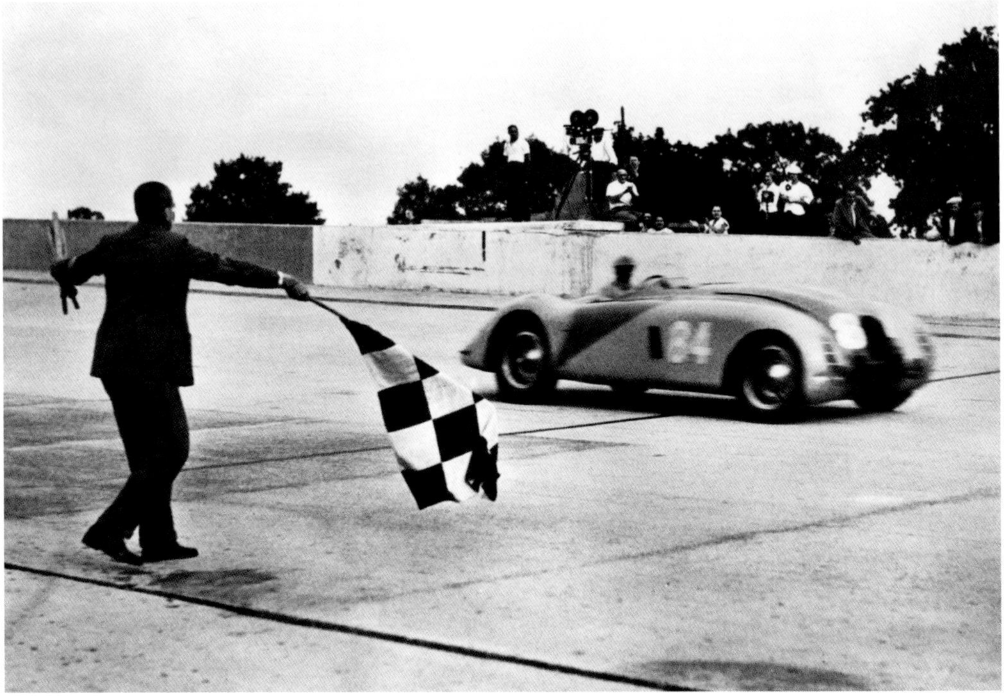

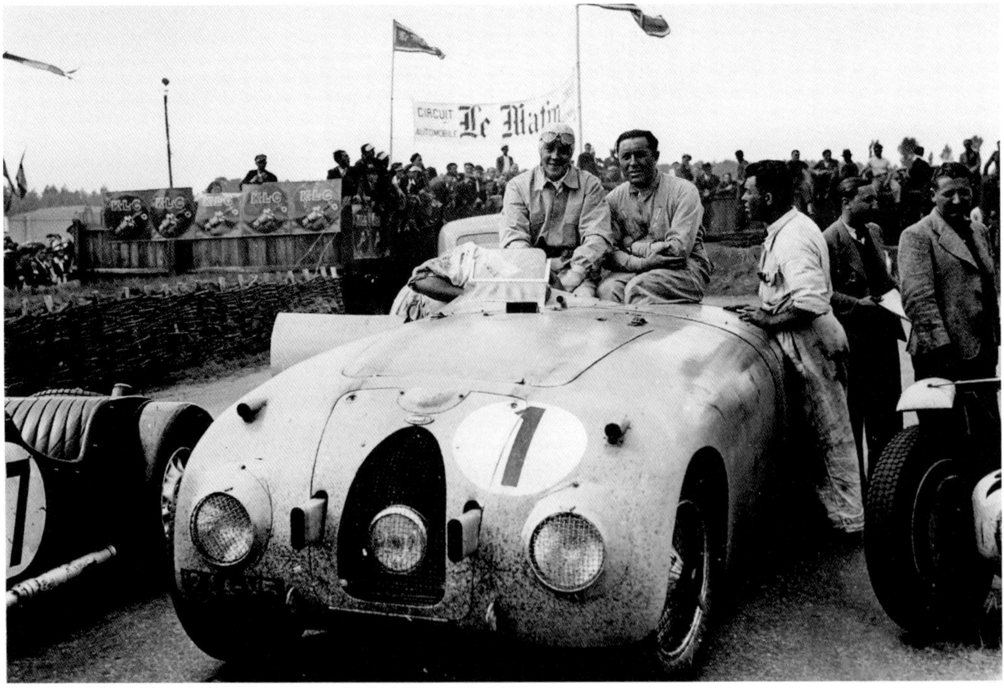
CIRCUIT
AUTOMOBILE
Le Matin
KLG
1

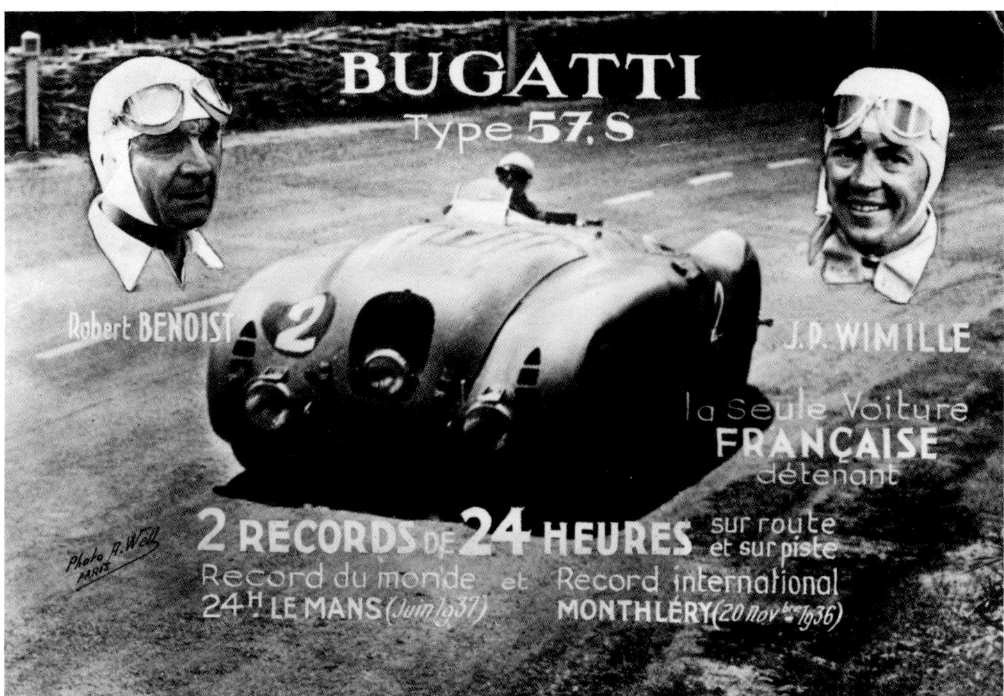

Opposite (top): 1936 Bugatti Type 57G (chassis no. 57G 01) co-driven by Jean-Pierre Wimille and Raymond Sommer wins the 1936 ACF Grand Prix (French Grand Prix) held at Montlhéry going at an average speed of 125 km/h (78 mph) for just under eight hours. One week later, on July 7, Wimille won the Grand Prix de la Marne held at Rheims in the same car at an average speed of 140 km/h (87 mph).

Opposite (bottom): Jean-Pierre Wimille and Pierre Veyron having just won the 1939 24 Hours of Le Mans in a different and one-off variant of the Type 57G "Tank," known as the 57C "Tank." A few weeks later, on August 11, this car was destroyed in a tragic accident that killed 30-year-old Jean Bugatti, who was test driving the car not far from the factory on the road near the village of Duppigheim.

Above: Promotional photograph celebrating Jean-Pierre Wimille and Robert Benoist's win at the 1937 24 Hours of Le Mans in chassis no. 57G 01 — the first time a Bugatti had ever prevailed in that race.

1937

BMW 328 Mille Miglia "Bügelfalte"

MANUFACTURED 1937 | ENGINE 1,971 cc (120 cu. in.), overhead-valve inline 6-cylinder | HORSEPOWER 130
TOP SPEED 200 km/h (124 mph) | TRANSMISSION 4-speed
NUMBER PRODUCED 1

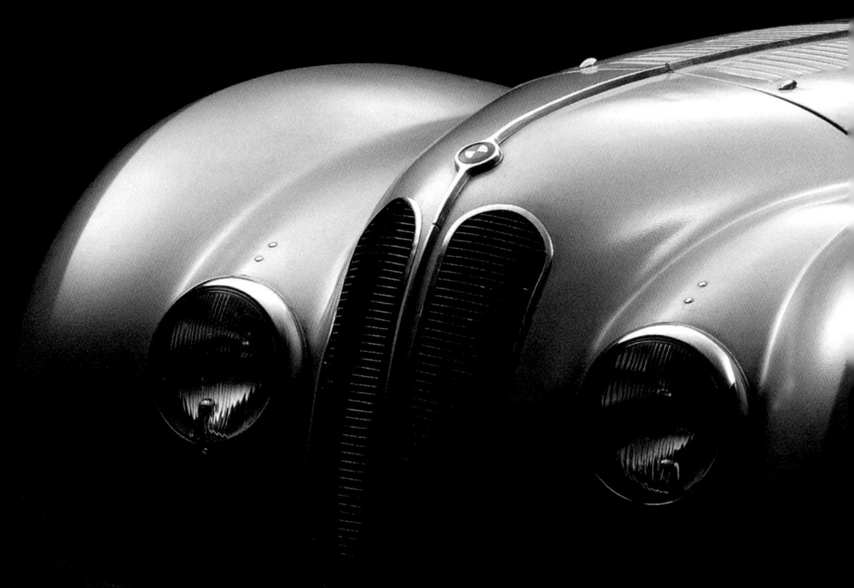

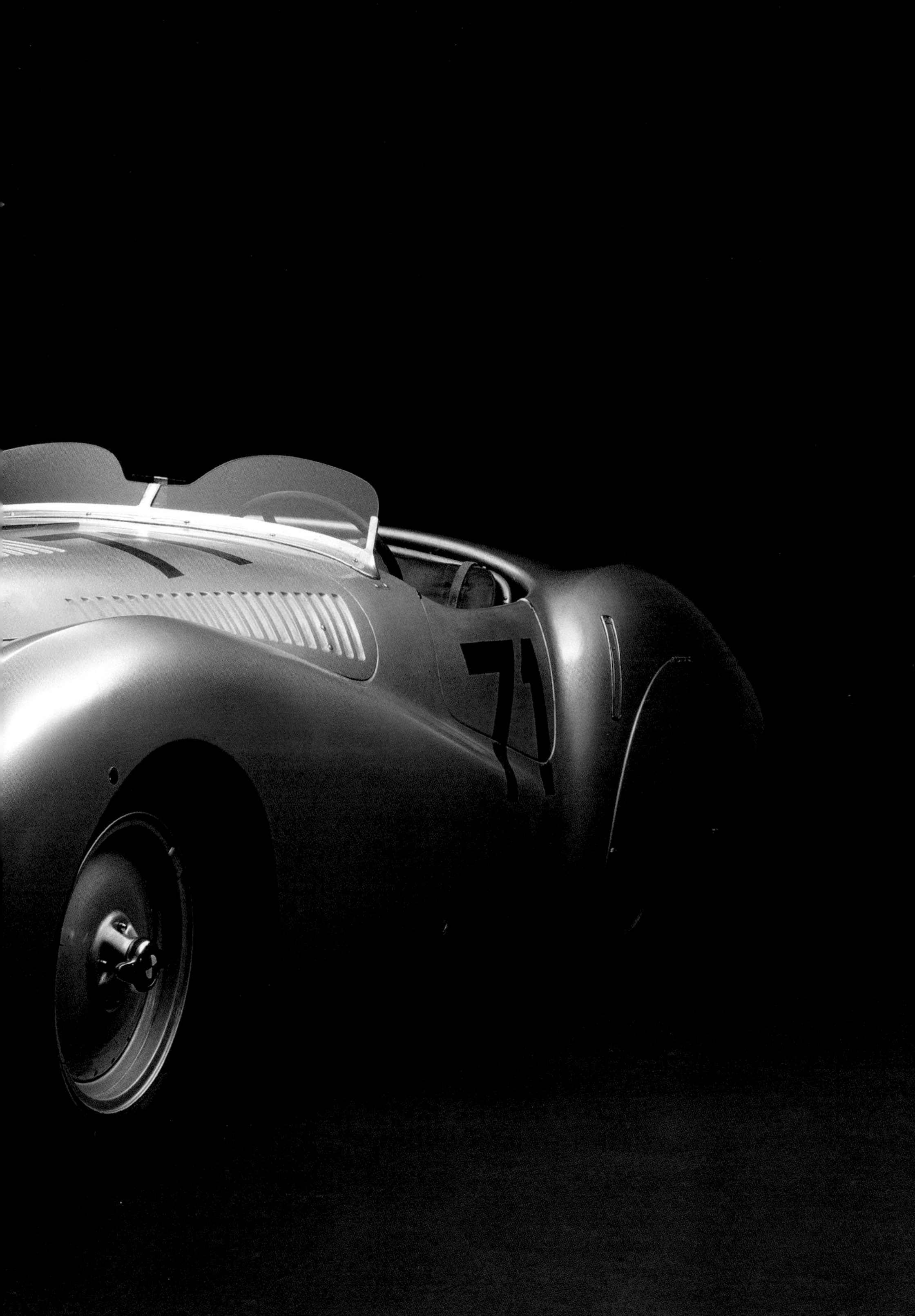

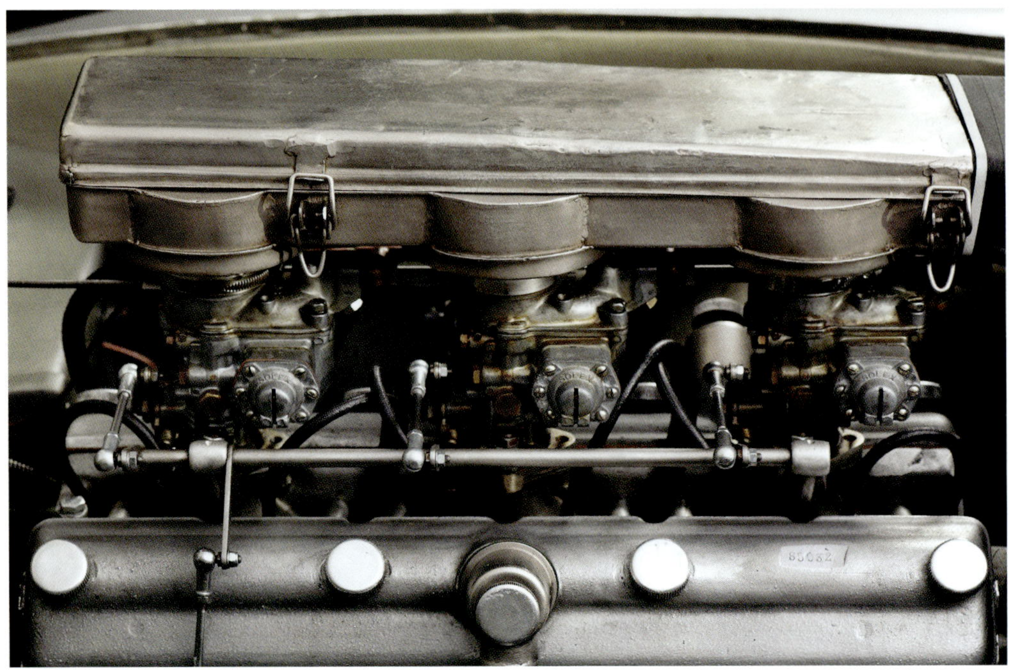

Above: Detail of BMW 328 Mille Miglia "Bügelfalte" Roadster's 1,971 cc (120 cu. in.), overhead-valve inline six-cylinder engine with triple Solex 30 JF carburetors. The car's engine and driveline were sunk deeper into the chassis to reduce the body's frontal area and lower the center of gravity in order to improve handling.

Opposite: Detail of the lightweight tubular space frame of the BMW 328 Mille Miglia Roadster.

Overleaf: Detail of the car's instrumentation panel, including a large centrally positioned tachometer.

This BMW prototypical racer is one of those very rare cars that enjoys such iconic status among classic car aficionados it is frequently referred to just by its moniker "Bügelfalte," which in English translates to "ironing crease." This nickname is derived from the car's remarkable bodywork, which has pleated trouser-like folds running along its fenders. But more than this, its whole body is an exercise in visual and physical integration, with its wheel arches and headlights cleverly absorbed into its main body for enhanced aerodynamic performance. This pursuit of structural unity, spurred on by drag-defying considerations, gave this lightweight open roadster a very modern and forward-looking aesthetic. Around this time — the late 1930s — other marques, most notably Bugatti and Talbot-Lago, were similarly attempting to create more unified bodies, but their resultant models were nowhere near as successful. The innovative Bügelfalte was constructed under the auspices of BMW's new department of Künstlerische Gestaltung (artistic development), previously founded in 1934, which was one of the first in-house design teams of its kind within the automotive industry.

The 1937 Bügelfalte Roadster (chassis no. 85032) is a one-off racing variant of the BMW 328 sports car, which had been developed the previous year. Its overall concept was the brainchild of two renowned BMW specialists: the designer, Wilhelm Kaiser, a very experienced member of the firm's new in-house design team, and its chief stylist, Wilhelm Meyerhuber, who had previously worked for General Motors in the US. The Bügelfalte's structural and visual unity, in fact, chimed very much with wider developments within German design circles. Indeed, from 1923 onward Walter Gropius as director of the influential Staatliches Bauhaus (founded in 1919) had championed the idea of "Art and Technology — A New Unity" and in many ways the Bügelfalte was a three-dimensional realization of this progressive concept. Created specifically to race at the 1940 Mille Miglia, the sleek Bügelfalte Roadster with its innovative streamlined form and distinctive "ironing-crease" fenders represented a masterpiece of unitary design. In fact, when viewed from front on, it is easy to see how its five arching elements so cleverly accommodate its wheels, headlights and hood in an apparently seamless undulation of five rolling waves of hammered-to-perfection metal alloy.

The roadster's body with its bulbous front end and long tapering tail was sculpted according to data gleaned from wind tunnel tests conducted by the pioneering aerodynamicist Wunibald Kamm using a 1:10 scale model. The resultant streamlined bodywork was hand built by "Blasi" Huber in Ernest Loof's racing department utilizing a lightweight state-of-the-art aluminum-magnesium alloy, which had previously been developed for high performance aircraft. This sculptural shell was then mounted on a 328 chassis that was itself

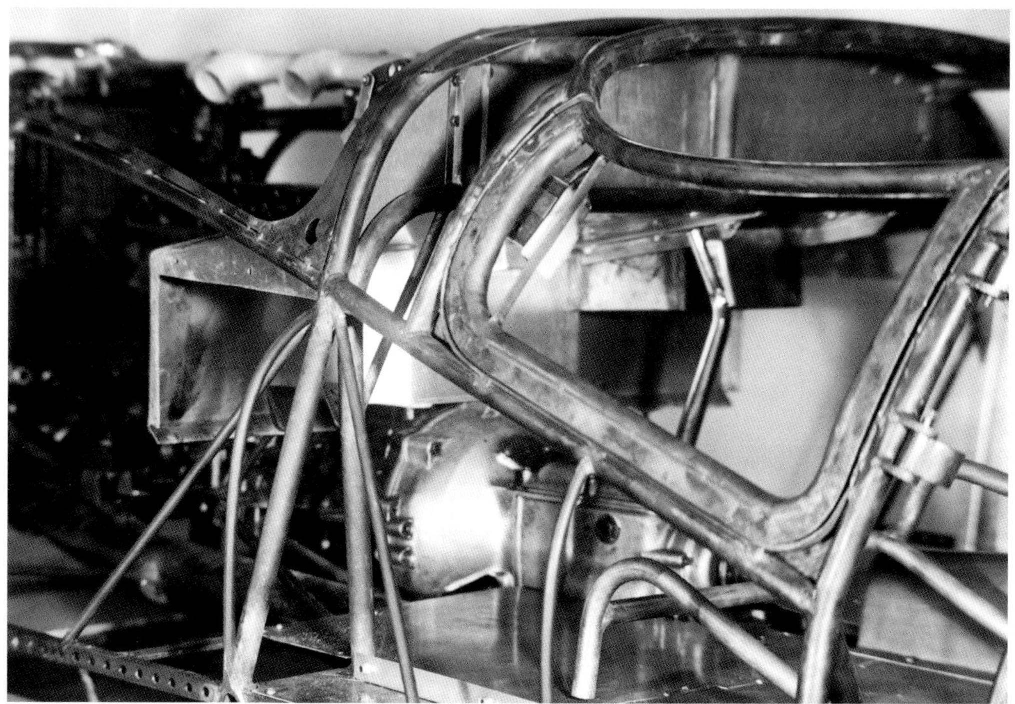

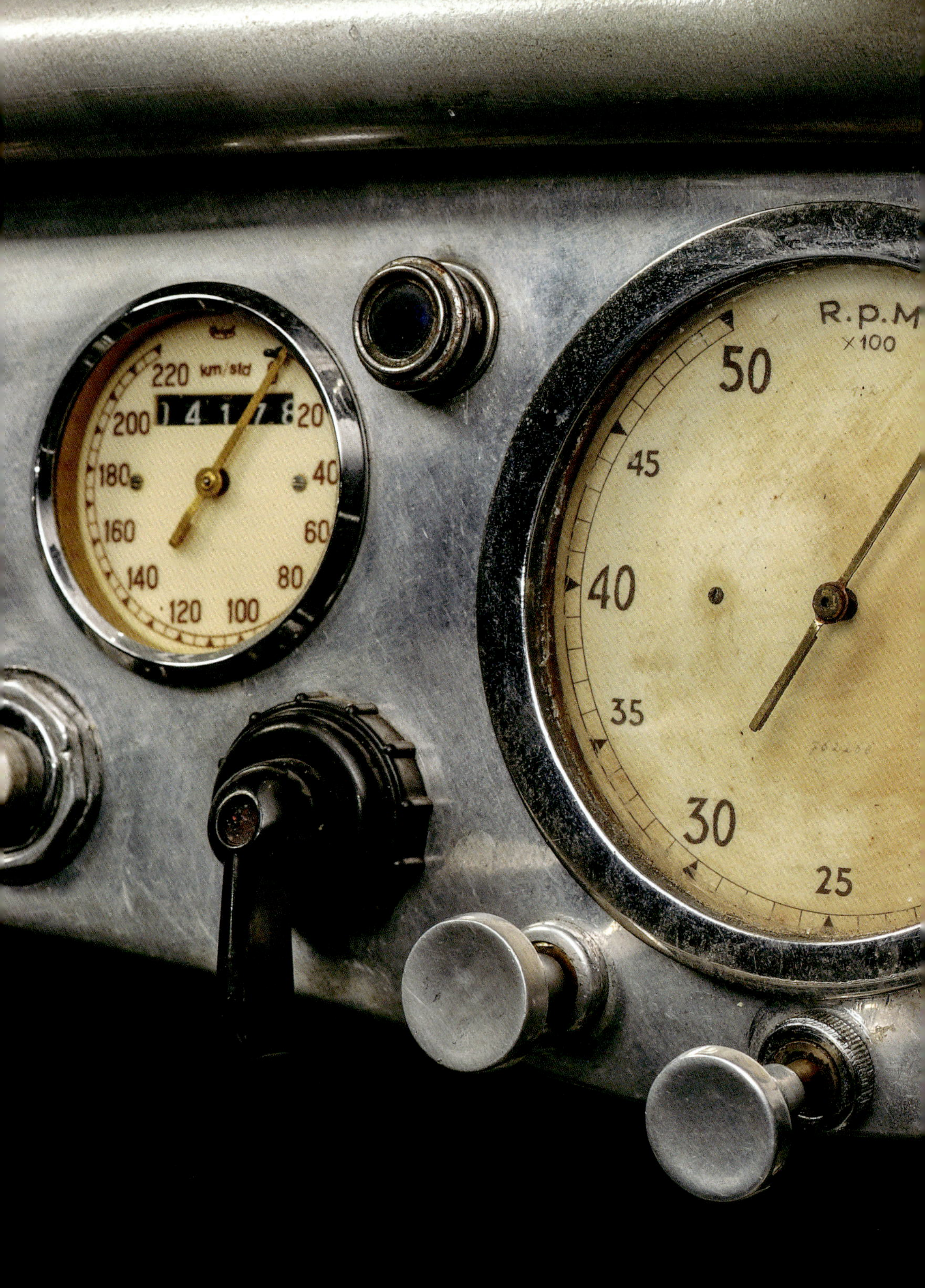
km/std
220
200
180
160
140
120
100
80
60
40
20
R.p.M
×100
50
45
40
35
30
25

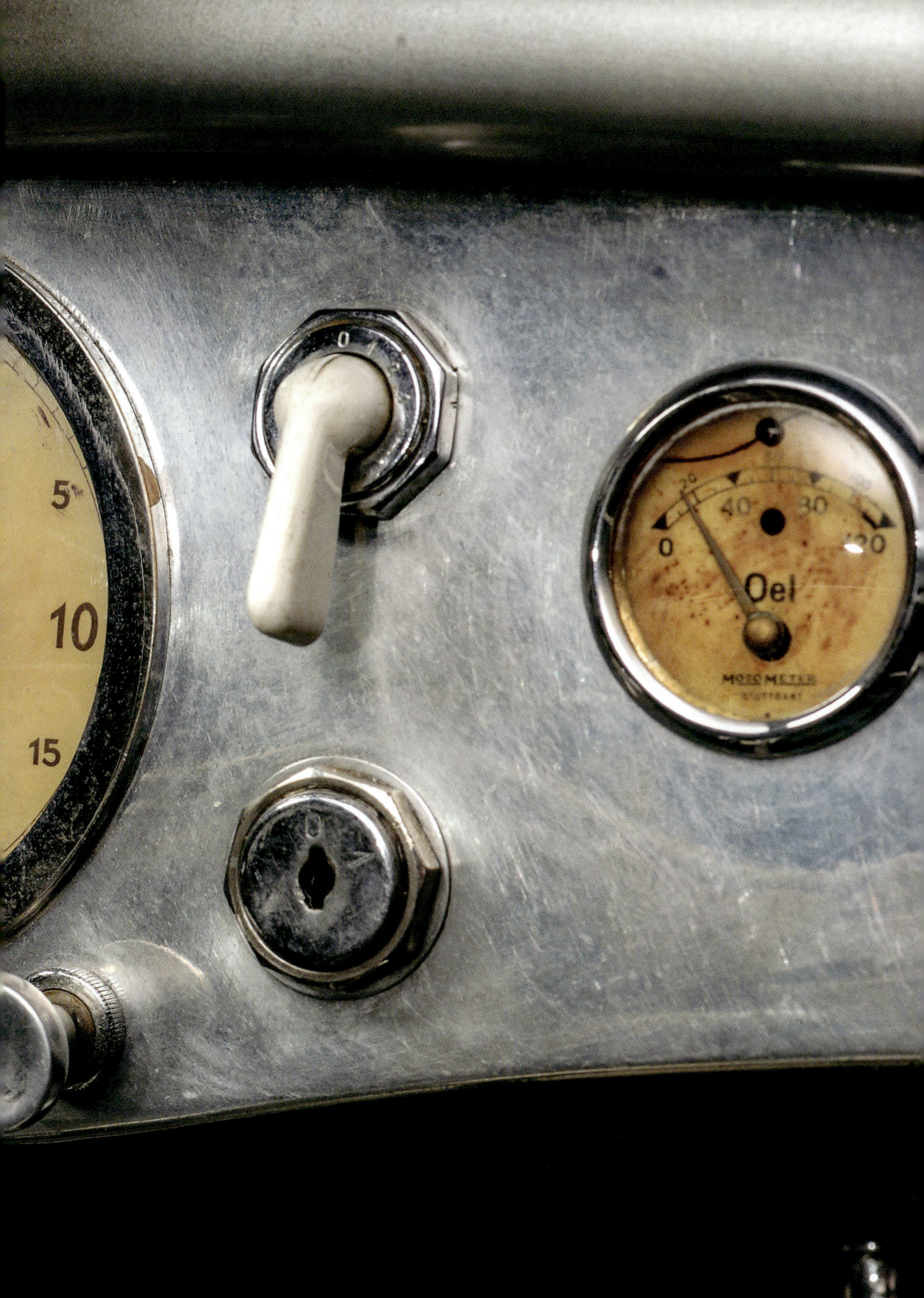

5
10
15
0
40
Oel

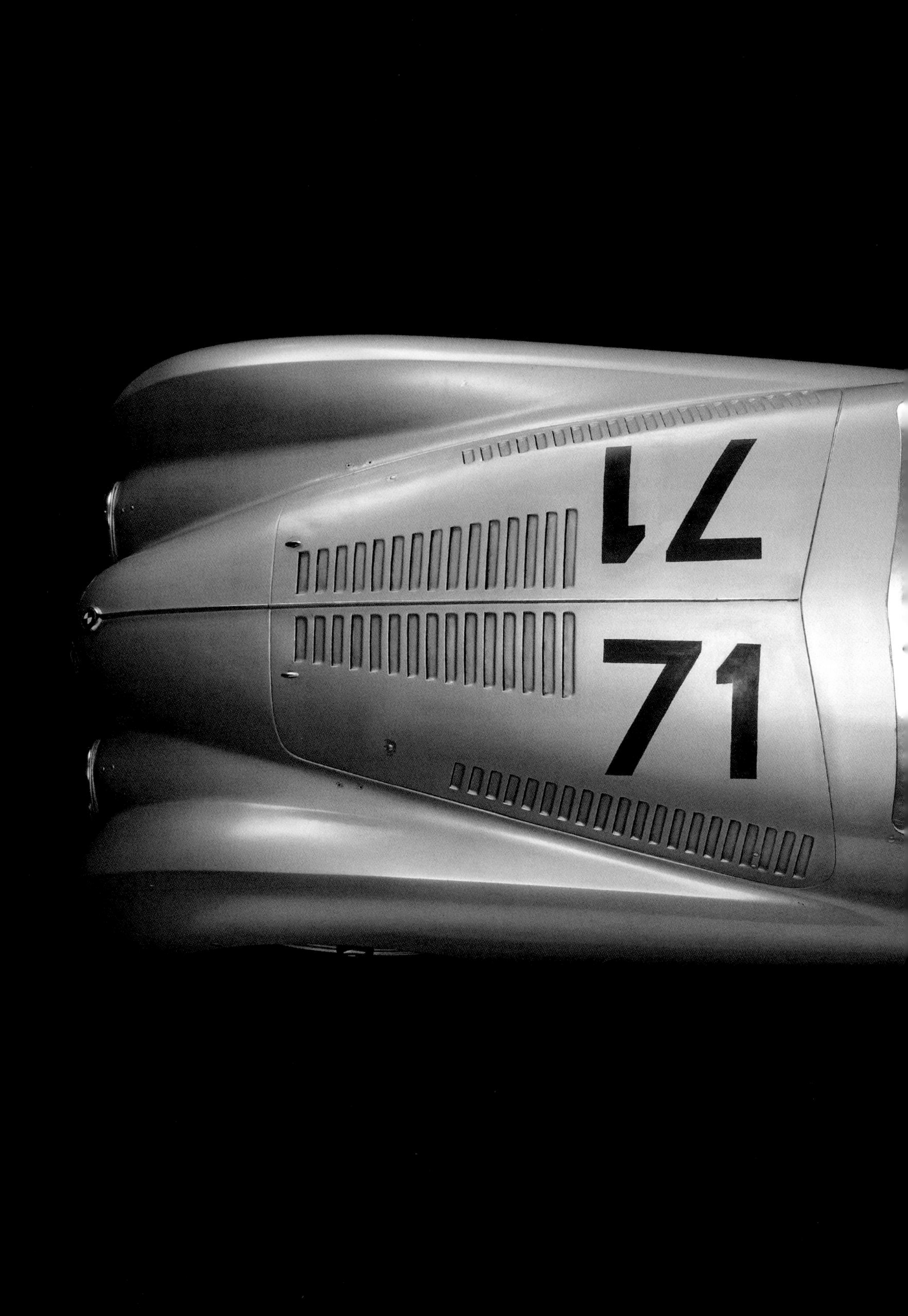

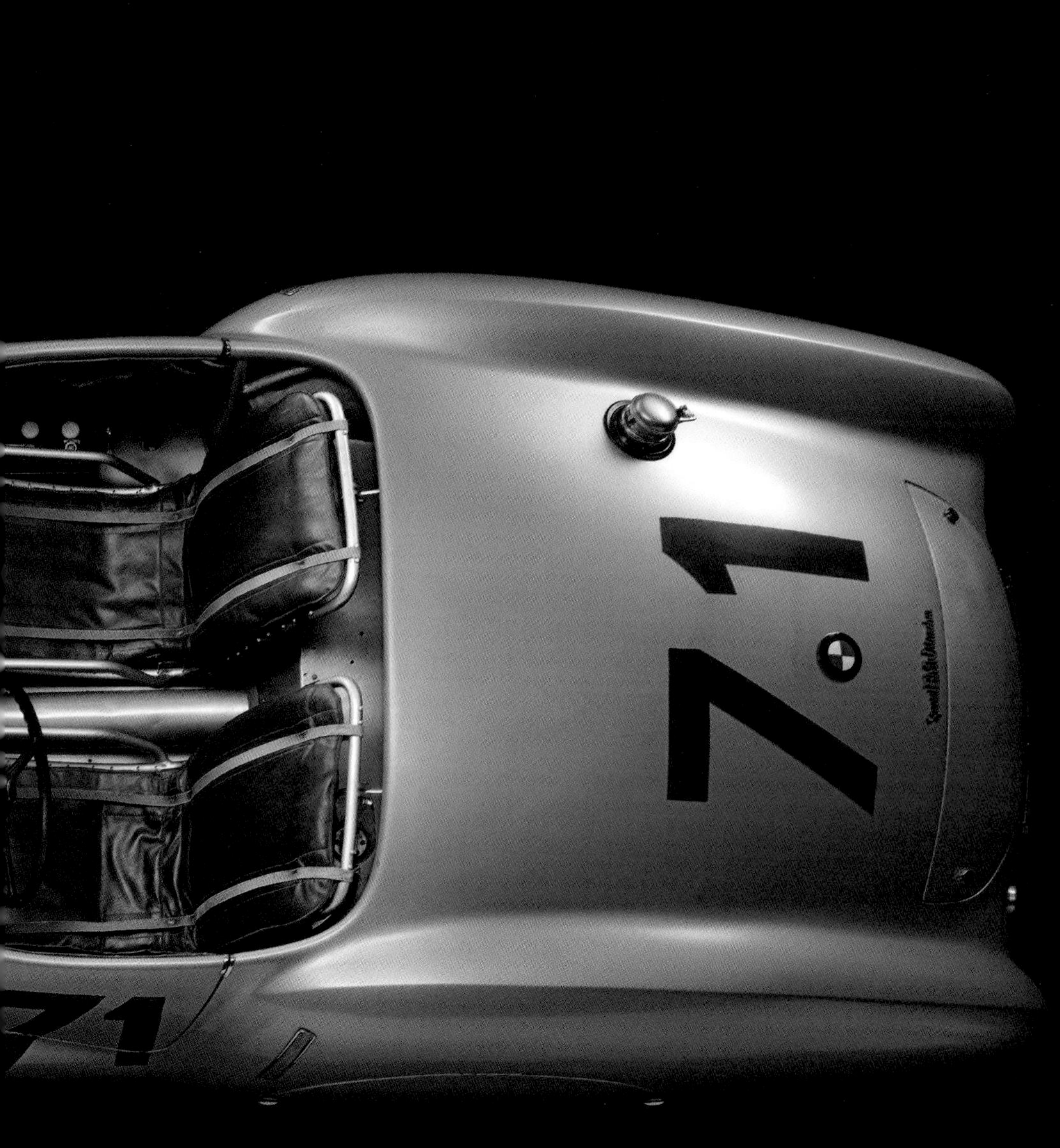

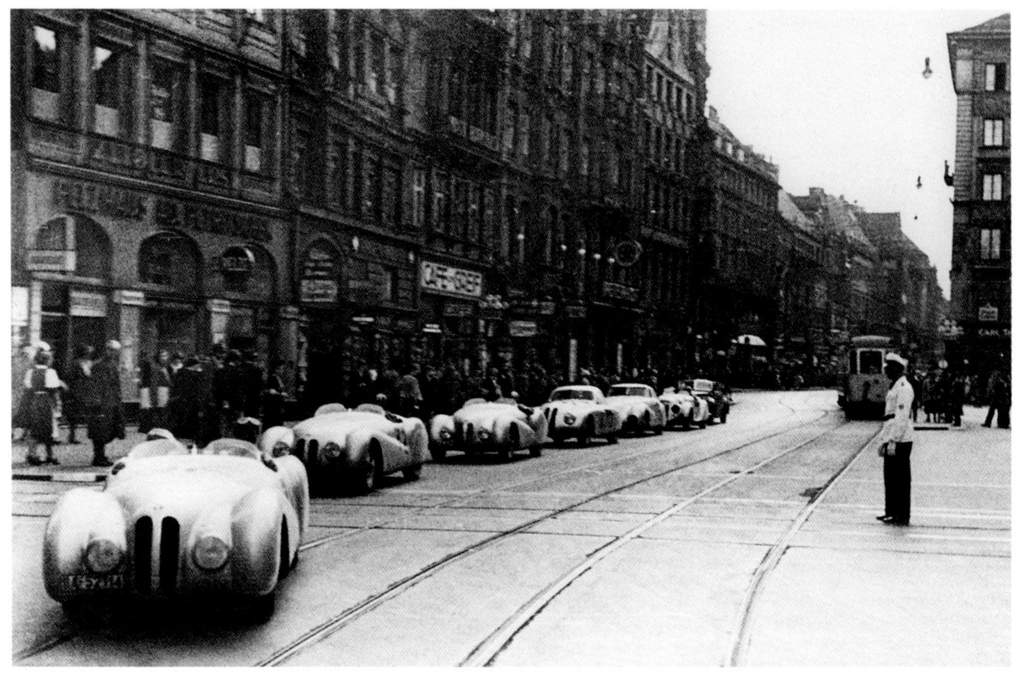

Above: Parade of the BMWs entered in the Brescia Grand Prix, which functioned as a replacement to the 1940 Mille Miglia. To this day many racing enthusiasts dispute whether this 1940 race should be classified as an offical "Mille Miglia" race, due to the reduction of the course by the Mussolini regime. For 1940, racers would still start from Brescia and race to Cremona, then Mantua, before returning to Brescia. This circuit would be lapped nine times, each lap having a distance of 166 km (103 miles) — thereby equating to a total of 1,491 km (927 miles) rather than the usual 1,597 km (992 miles) of a bona fide Mille Miglia race.

a very innovative space-frame design, but which had then been specially modified in order to lower the Bügelfalte's engine and drivetrain within its cat's-cradle-like construction of metal tubing and wire rods. These alterations meant that the car's overall center of gravity was pushed far lower, thereby improving its on-track stability and handling at high speed and around corners. But more than this, the team at BMW went to remarkable lengths to reduce its weight as much as possible; even the seat frames and inside panels were made of a light-but-strong alloy. Eventually, this sublime low-slung racer was put through its racing paces by Hans Wencher and Rudolf Scholz at the 1940 Mille Miglia, where it finished in sixth place. At this race, another BMW 328 — a Touring Coupé — driven by Fritz "Huschke" von Hanstein and Walter Bäumer, however, did achieve victory, which even to this day is regarded as a key milestone in BMW's corporate history. That said, it could be argued that the Bügelfalte Roadster was potentially the more important racer in that its radical aerodynamic design heralded a new forward-looking aesthetic that went on to influence the appearance of an entire generation of postwar sports cars.

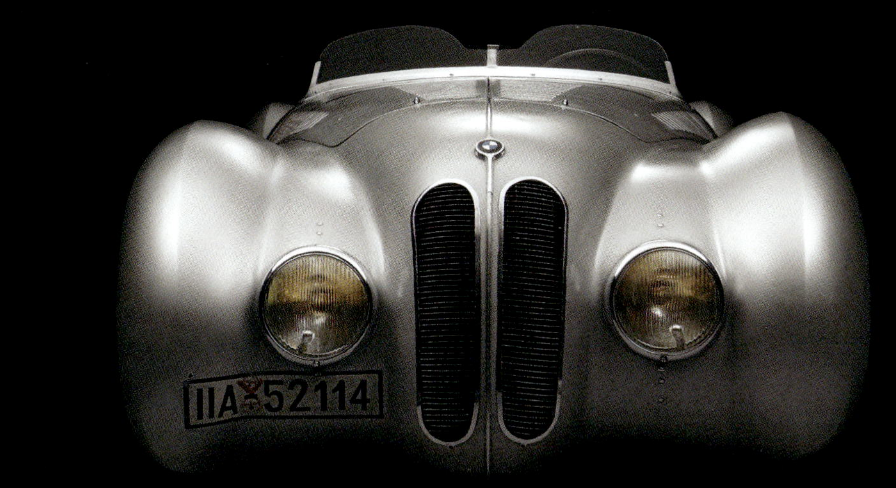
IIA 52114

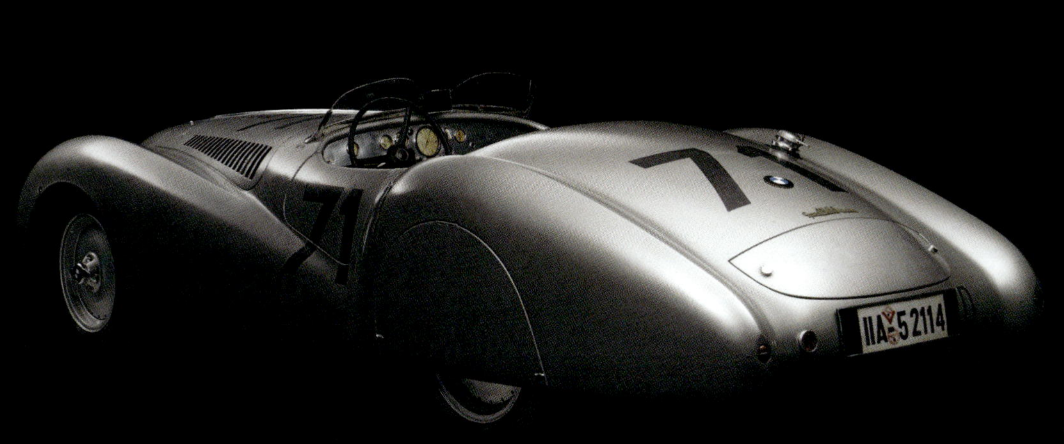
71
71
IIA 52114

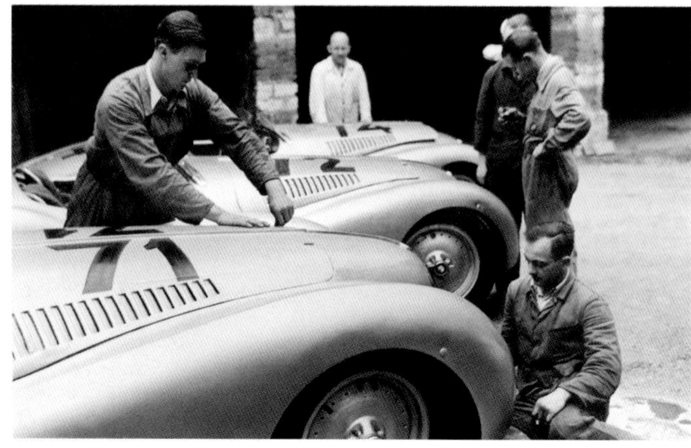

Left: BMW 328 Mille Miglia Roadsters in the BMW paddock in Brescia, April 28, 1940 — the No. 71 "Bügelfalte" (trouser crease) Roadster in foreground, which was driven by Hans Wencher and Rudolf Scholz. Willi Briem and Uli Richter drove car No. 72 and Adolf Brudes and Ralph Roese drove car No. 74.

Below: Hans Wencher and Rudolf Scholz in the BMW 328 Mille Miglia "Bügelfalte" Roadster (chassis no. 85032) during the 1940 Mille Miglia race. They finished in sixth place.

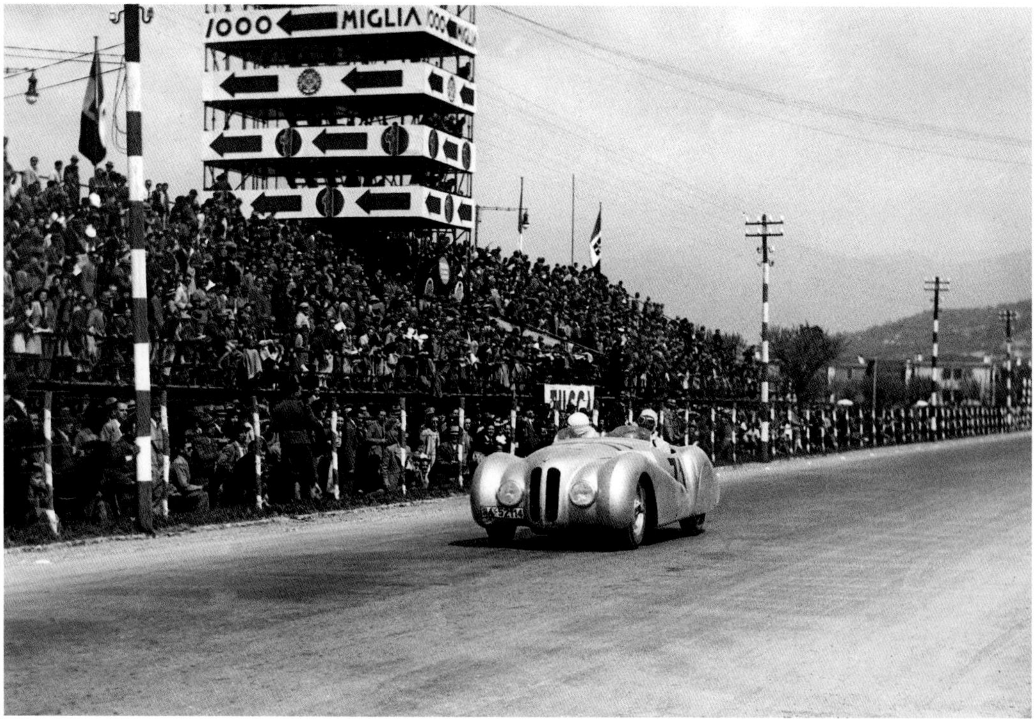

Right: Hans Wencher and Rudolf Scholz in the BMW 328 Mille Miglia “Bügelfalte” Roadster (chassis no. 85032) during the 1940 Mille Miglia race.

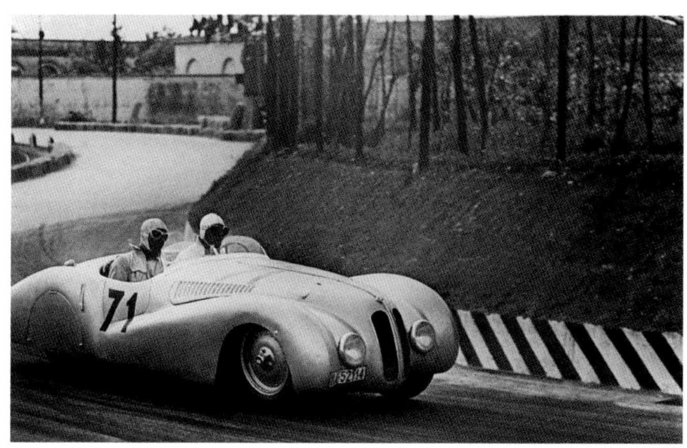

Below: April 28, 1940, Mille Miglia in Brescia, (left to right): BMW 328 “Bügelfalte” Roadster (No. 71); BMW 328 Touring Coupé (No. 70 driven by Fritz Huschke von Hanstein and Walter Bäumer); BMW 328 Mille Miglia Kamm Racing Saloon (No. 73 driven by Giovanni Lurani and Franco Cortese of Italy). Fritz Huschke von Hanstein and Walter Bäumer’s car ultimately won the race at an average speed of 166.7 km/h (103.6 mph).

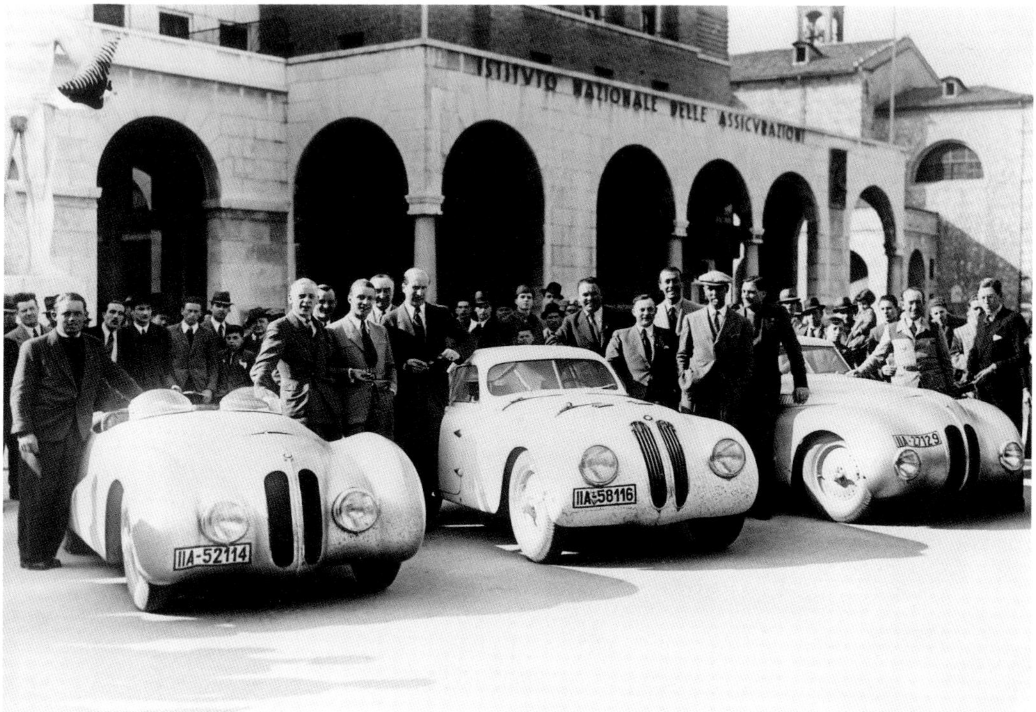

1938

Alfa Romeo 8C 2900B MM Spider

MANUFACTURED 1938 | ENGINE 2,991 cc (183 cu. in.), twin-supercharged DOHC inline 8-cylinder | HORSEPOWER 295
TOP SPEED 220 km/h (137 mph) | TRANSMISSION 4-speed
NUMBER PRODUCED 5

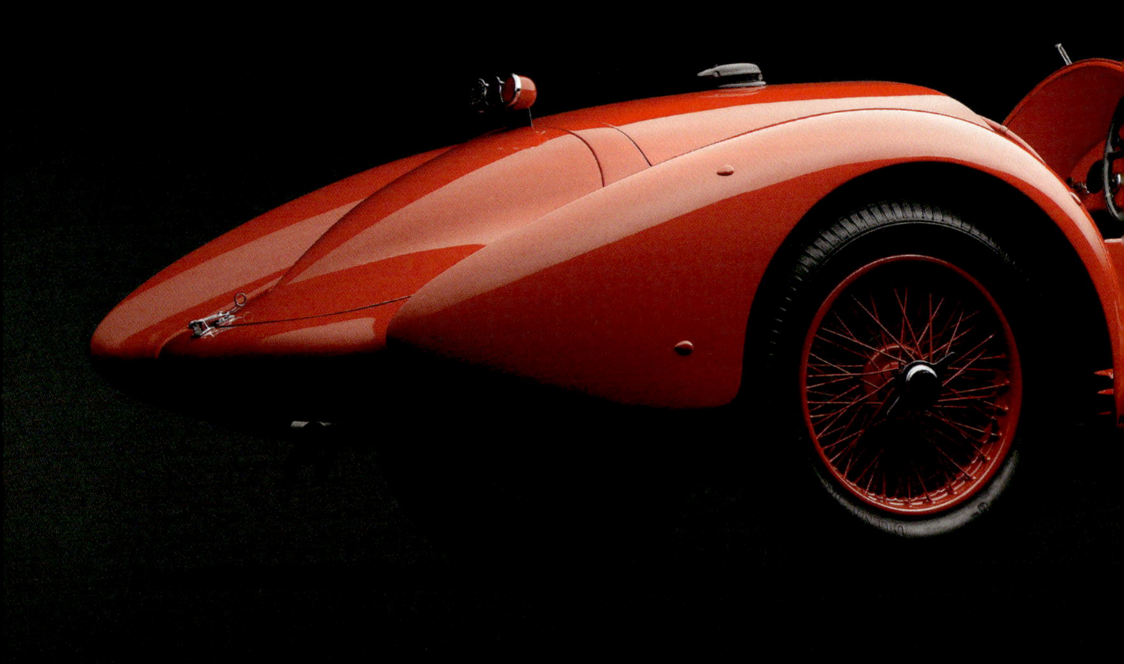

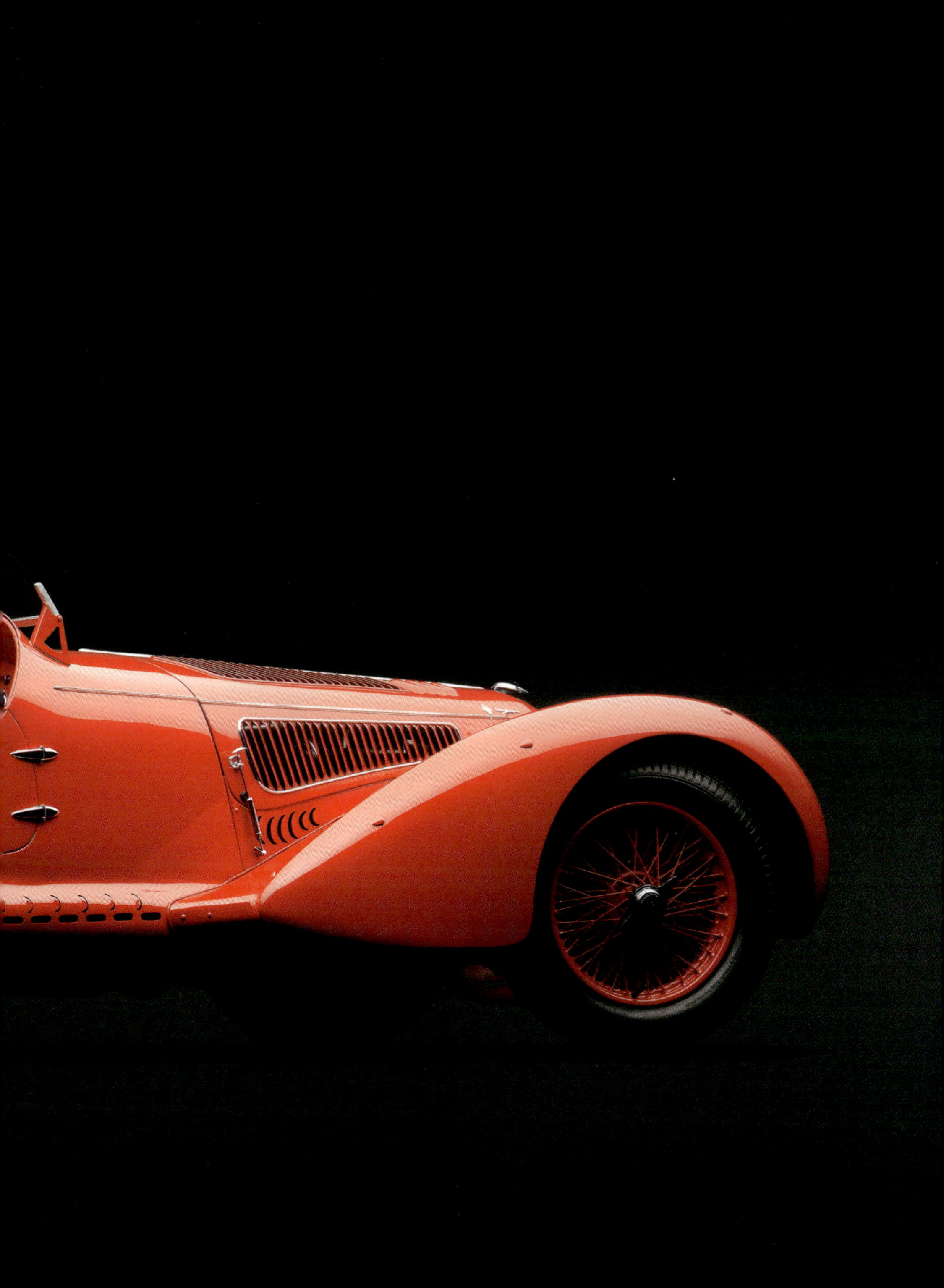

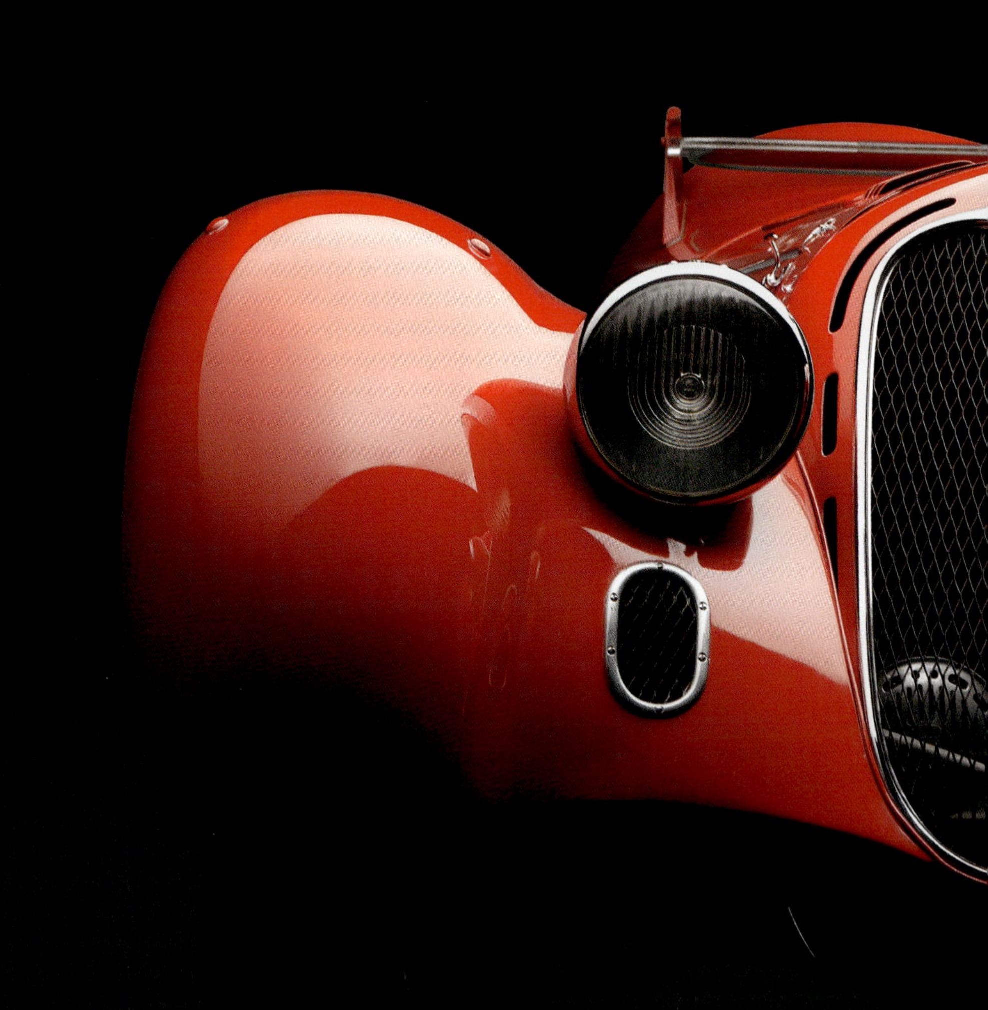

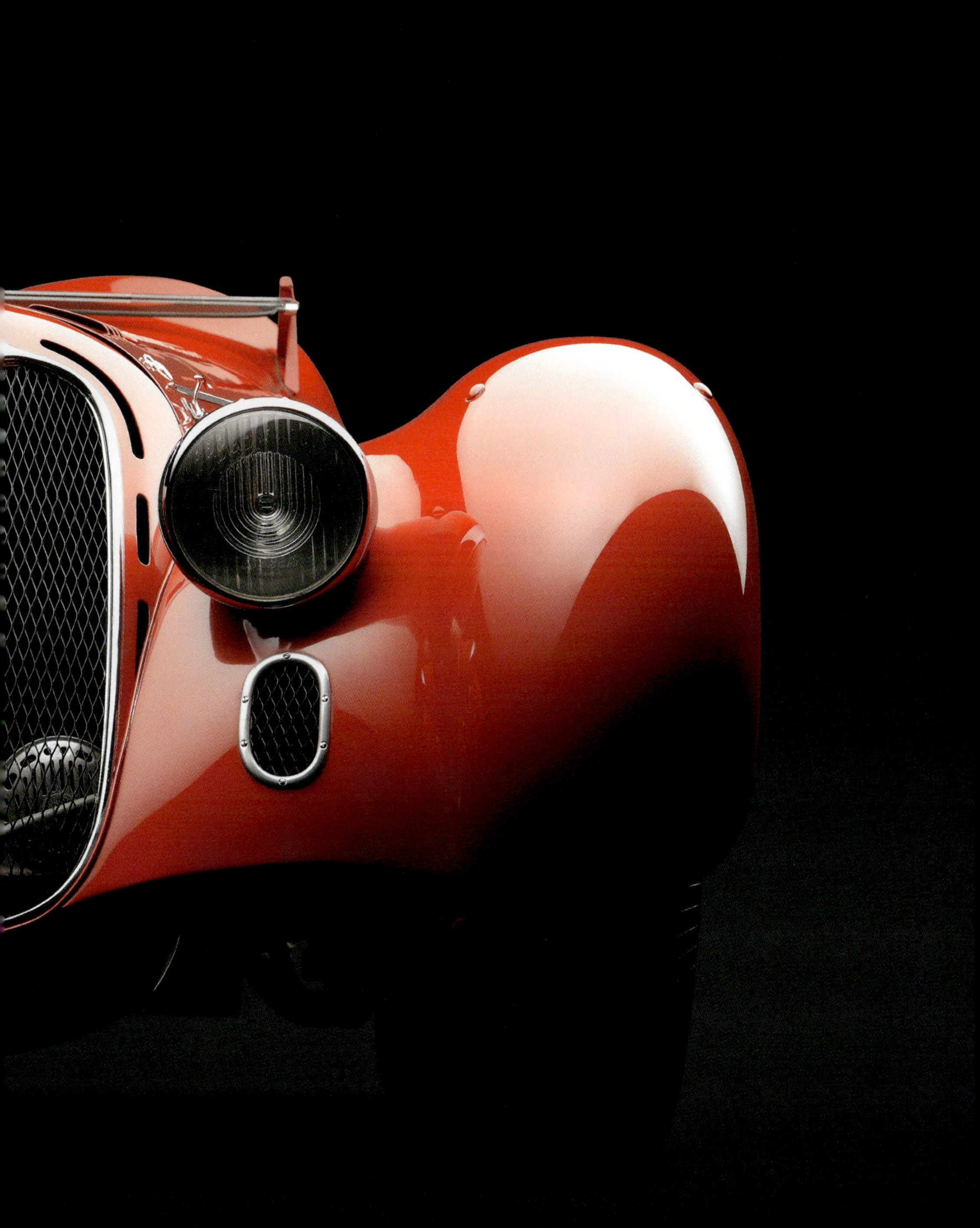

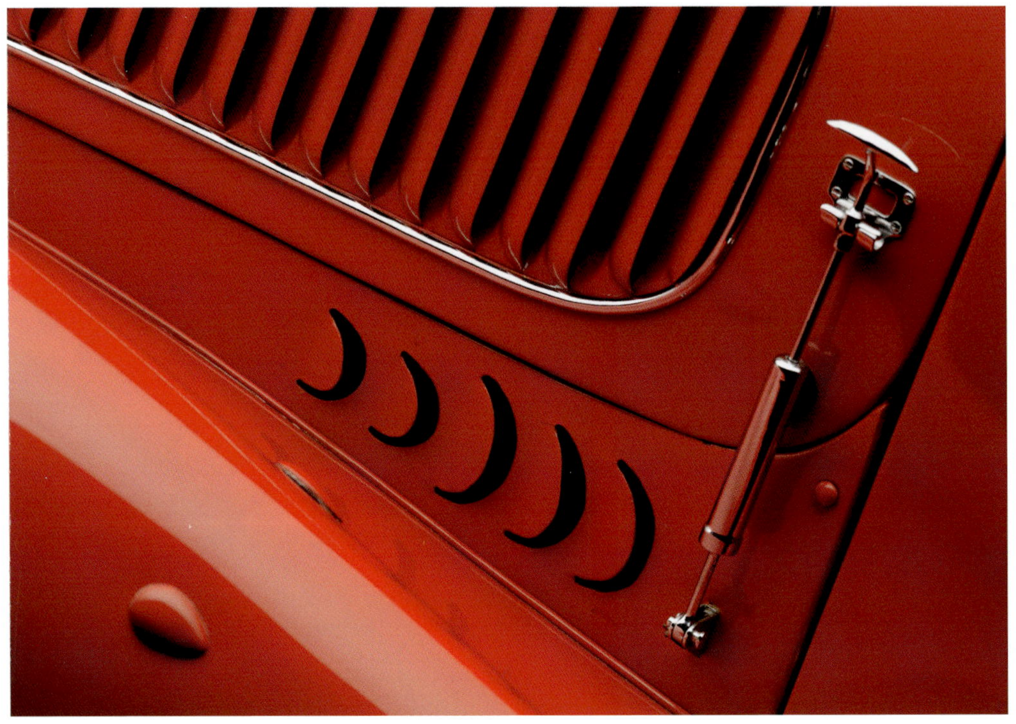

The 1938 Alfa Romeo 8C 2900B MM Spider is considered by many to be the ultimate prewar sports-racing car, thanks to its mix of awesome power and seductive aesthetics. Its sleek curvaceous form, resulting from a synthesis of superlative engineering and exquisite aerodynamic styling, is the very embodiment of the famous *La Linea Italiana* (The Italian Line) for which Italian design has become so renowned throughout the world. Quite simply, this is a car born out of the deeply embedded Italian passion for high-speed performance and beauty. During the 1930s, there was an almost gladiatorial battle raging between the various competing marques with each throwing everything they could come up with on their cars to make them more competitive for the next race, while their drivers were the superstar celebrities of their day. And at the heart of all this thrilling action was Alfa Romeo, then the quintessential high performance Italian marque whose modus operandi since its founding in 1910 was the unrelenting pursuit of racing glory. But Alfa's financial health during the early 1930s did not match its racing ambitions and as a result in 1932 the firm was placed under the control of the state holding company, Istituto per

Opposite: April 1938 advertisement celebrating the victorious 8C 2900B MM Spider in the 1938 Mille Miglia.

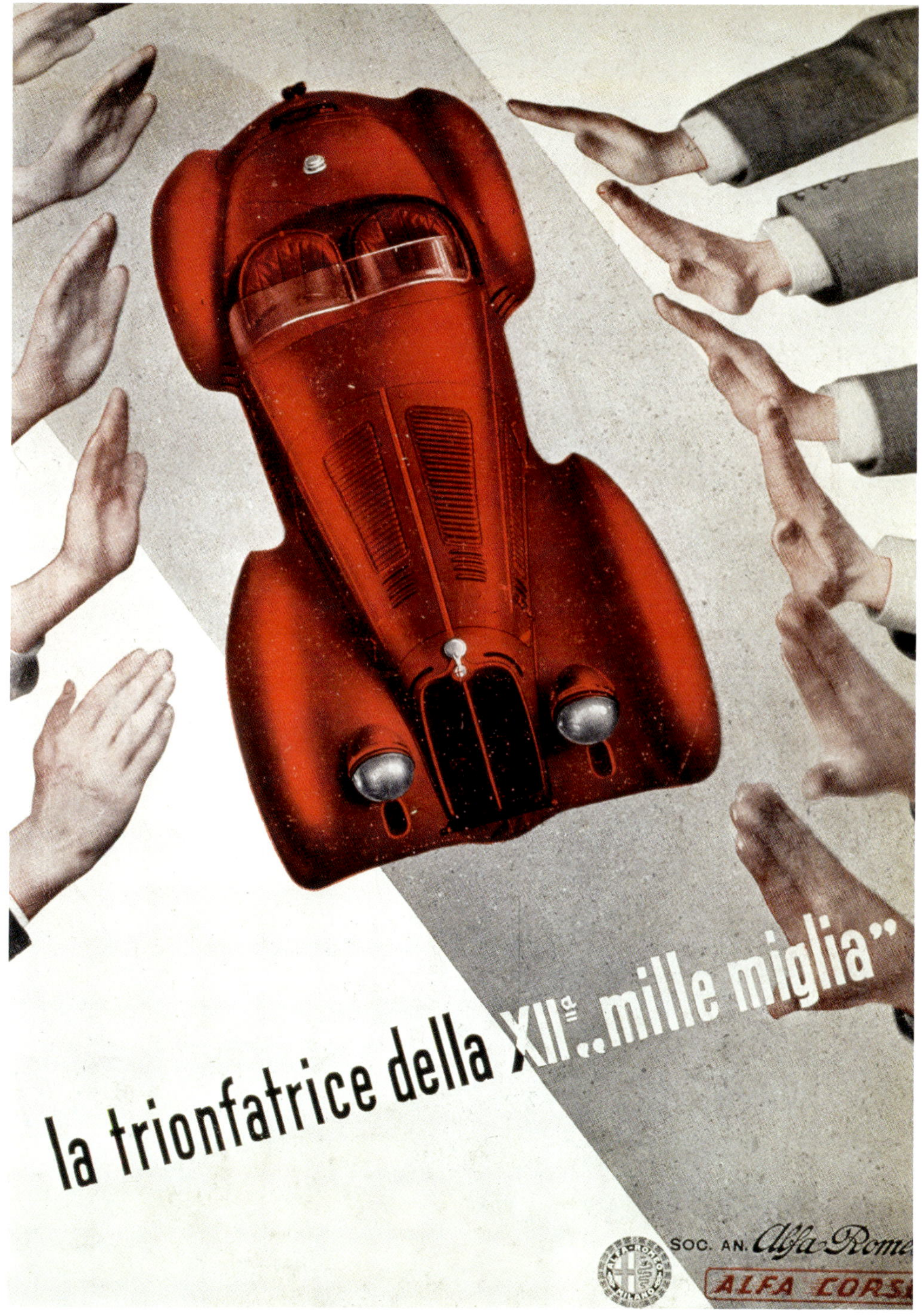
la trionfatrice della XIIa „mille miglia"
SOC. AN. Alfa Rome
ALFA CORS

la Ricostruzione Industriale (IRI). The following year, unable to justify the expense, it was forced to withdraw its in-house racing team from competition. For the next five years, Scuderia Ferrari headed by Enzo Ferrari acted as Alfa's de facto works team, with Alfa eventually acquiring a majority share in the enterprise. However, at the beginning of 1938, it was decided that Alfa Romeo needed to return to racing under its own name, and so launched its official Alfa Corse team. This new entity was basically Scuderia Ferrari, which was disbanded and reformed under the new arrangements, and for the first year of its operation Enzo Ferrari remained at its helm despite being unhappy about this turn of events. Indeed, it caused such a rift that he left the following year. Because part of his severance agreement included a veto on using the Ferrari name for the next four years he established Auto Avio Costruzioni, but this eventually evolved into his own eponymous marque.

This meant that 1938 was a key season for Alfa Romeo because it marked its official return to competition under its own banner. But more than this, it would be the last year that the prodigiously gifted Ferrari headed its in-house works team. Under Ferrari's guidance a new Alfa Romeo racing spider was built for that season. It used as its foundation the firm's existing 8C 2900B chassis, introduced the previous year, onto which was placed an aerodynamic *Superleggera* body specially designed by Carozzeria Touring, which employed an innovative and patented lightweight tubular metal substructure system. As the well-known collector Dr. Frederick Simeone observes, "These cars all had the remarkable combination of features also seen on the 8C 2900A cars, that is double overhead

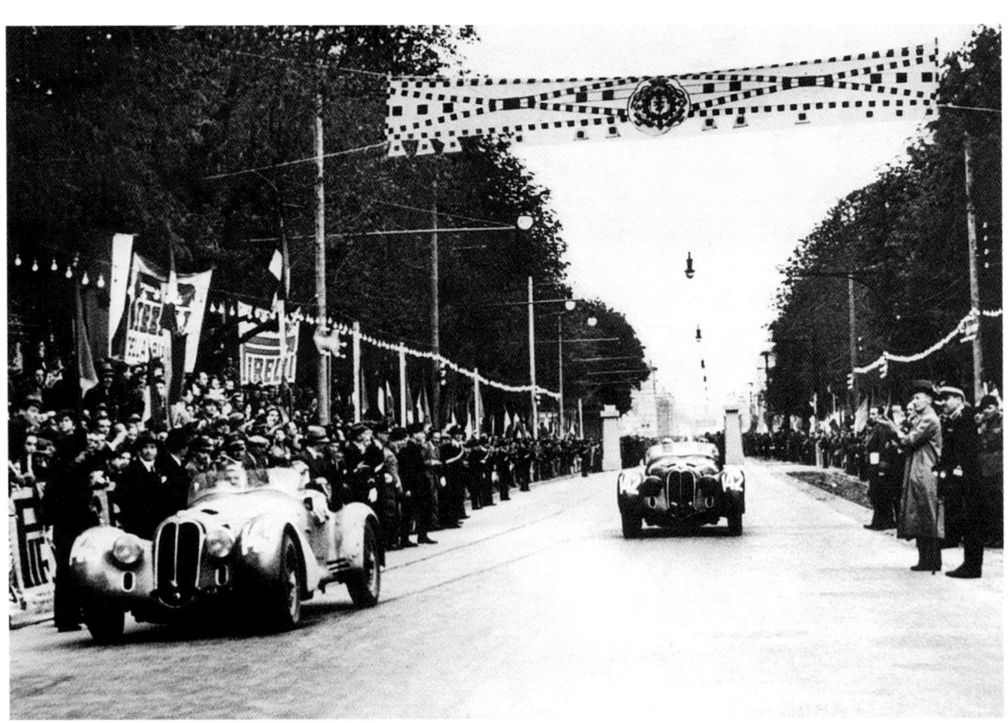

Opposite: Biondetti and Stefani finishing the 1938 Mille Miglia in first place in their Alfa Romeo 8C 2900B MM Spider (chassis no. 412031) followed by Carlo Maria Pintacuda and Paride Mambelli finishing second also in an Alfa Romeo 8C 2900B MM Spider.

Right: Clemente Biondetti and Ado Stefani having just won the 1938 Mille Miglia for Alfa Corse.

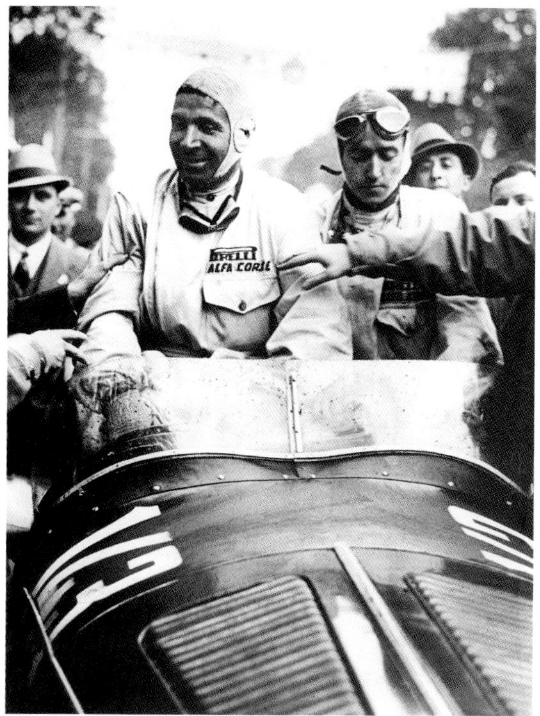

valves [two valves per cylinder], double overhead cams, twin superchargers, independent four-wheel suspension, a transaxle, and suspension dampers — that were adjustable from the seat!"

Five of these gorgeous new Alfa Corse racers were produced for the 1938 Mille Miglia, though when it came to it only four were actually raced at the event. Of these two did not finish, but the other two 8C 2900B MM Spiders more than made up for that disappointment by achieving a glorious 1-2 finish, with Clemente Biondetti driving the victorious car. The example shown here (chassis no. 412031) has been identified as that very same winning car. Significantly, this particular example uniquely featured a bigger Alfa Romeo 308 Grand Prix engine giving it substantially more power, which probably goes quite a way in explaining its triumph over its three siblings. Today, while this car resides in pride of place at the Simeone Foundation Automotive Museum in Philadelphia, the one that came second (chassis no. 412030) is well-known on the Concours d'Elegance circuit having been stunningly restored and now being one of the highlights of Ralph Lauren's world-famous car collection. The other two cars, without their bodywork and having been heavily modified, are to be found at the Cité de l'Automobile-Collection Schlumph in Mulhouse, France.

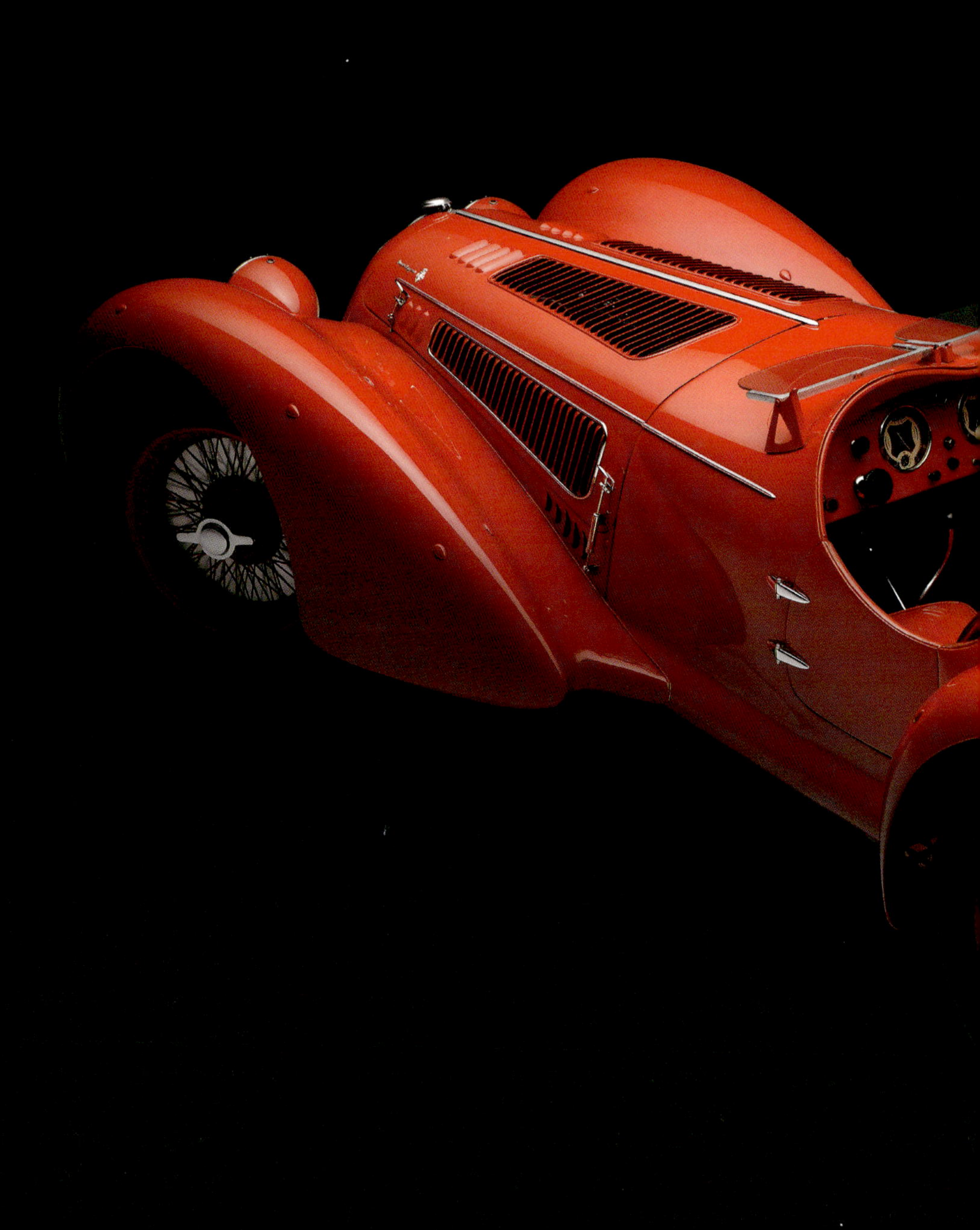

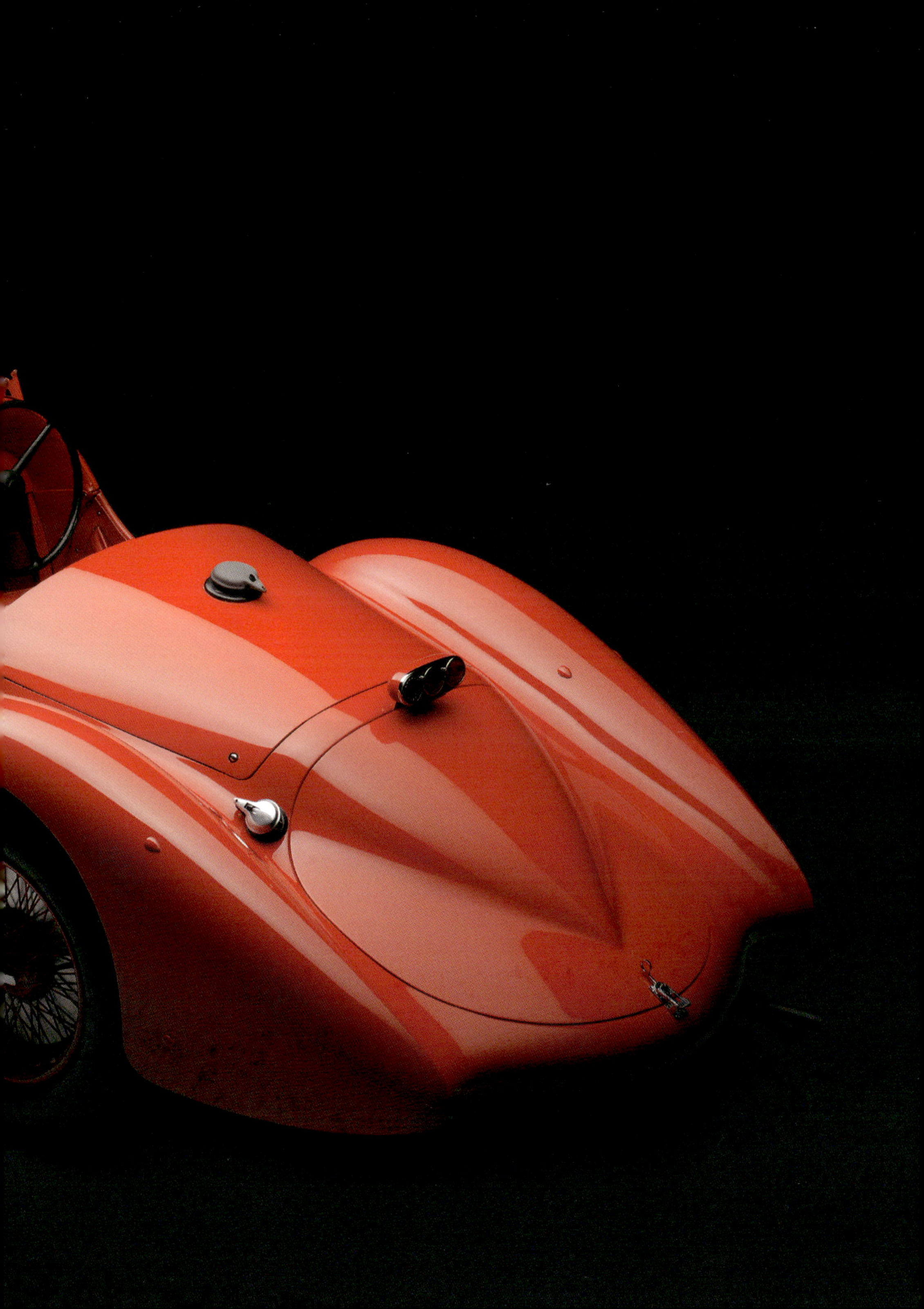

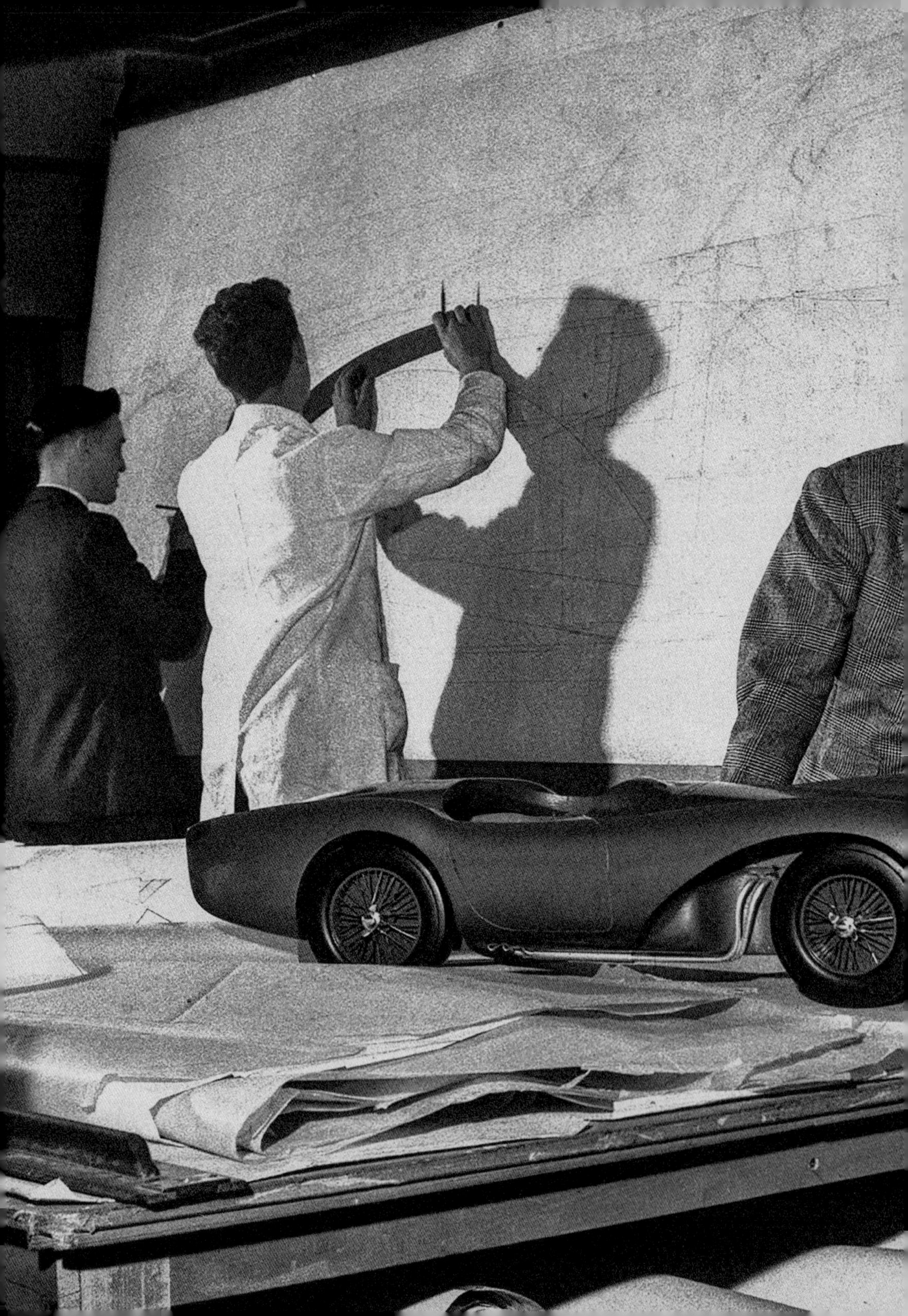

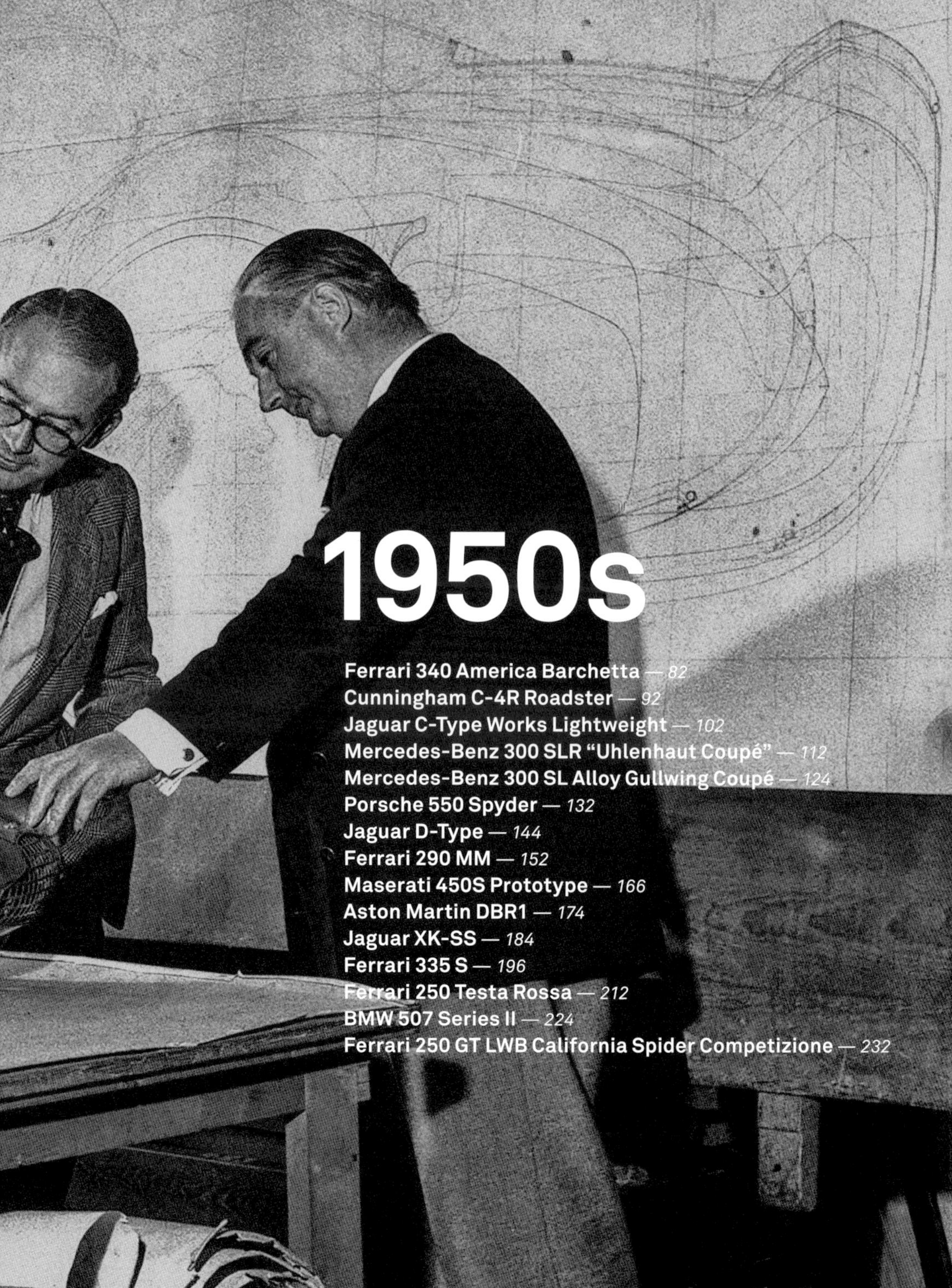

1950s

1951

Ferrari 340 America Barchetta

MANUFACTURED 1951–52 | **ENGINE** 4,101 cc (250 cu. in.), SOHC per bank 60º V12 | **HORSEPOWER** 217
TOP SPEED approx. 241 km/h (150 mph) | **TRANSMISSION** 4-speed
NUMBER PRODUCED 8 by Touring (out of a total 23)

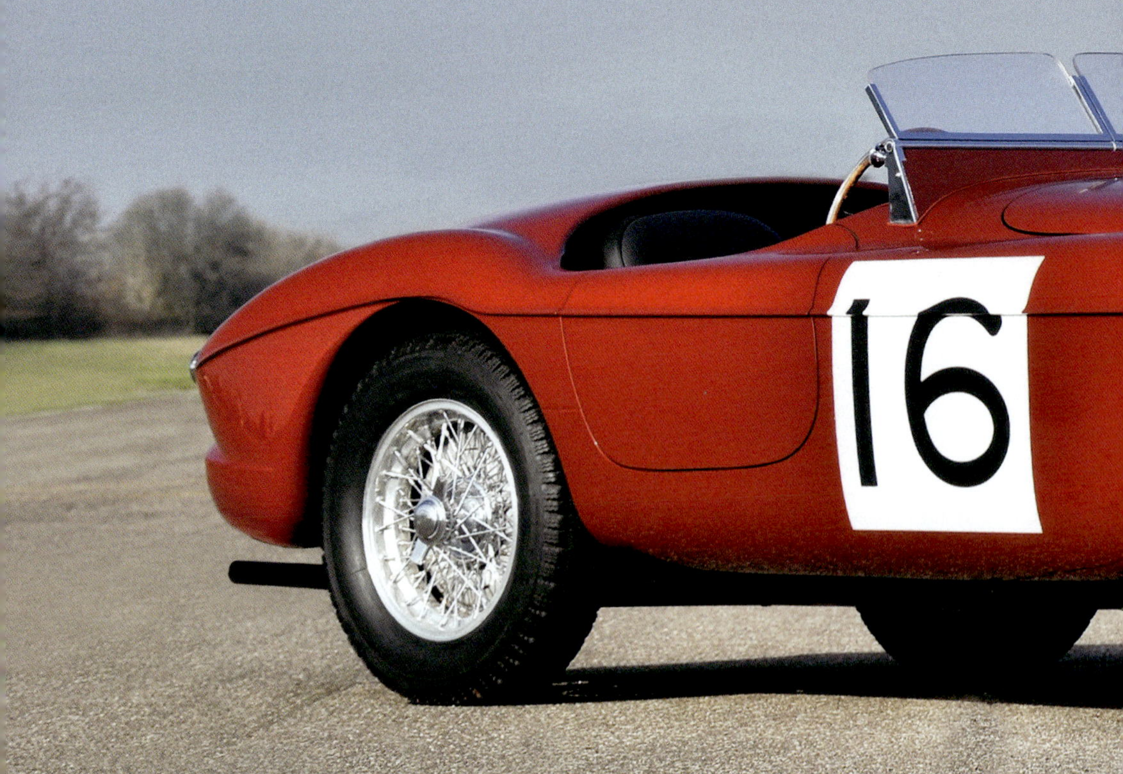

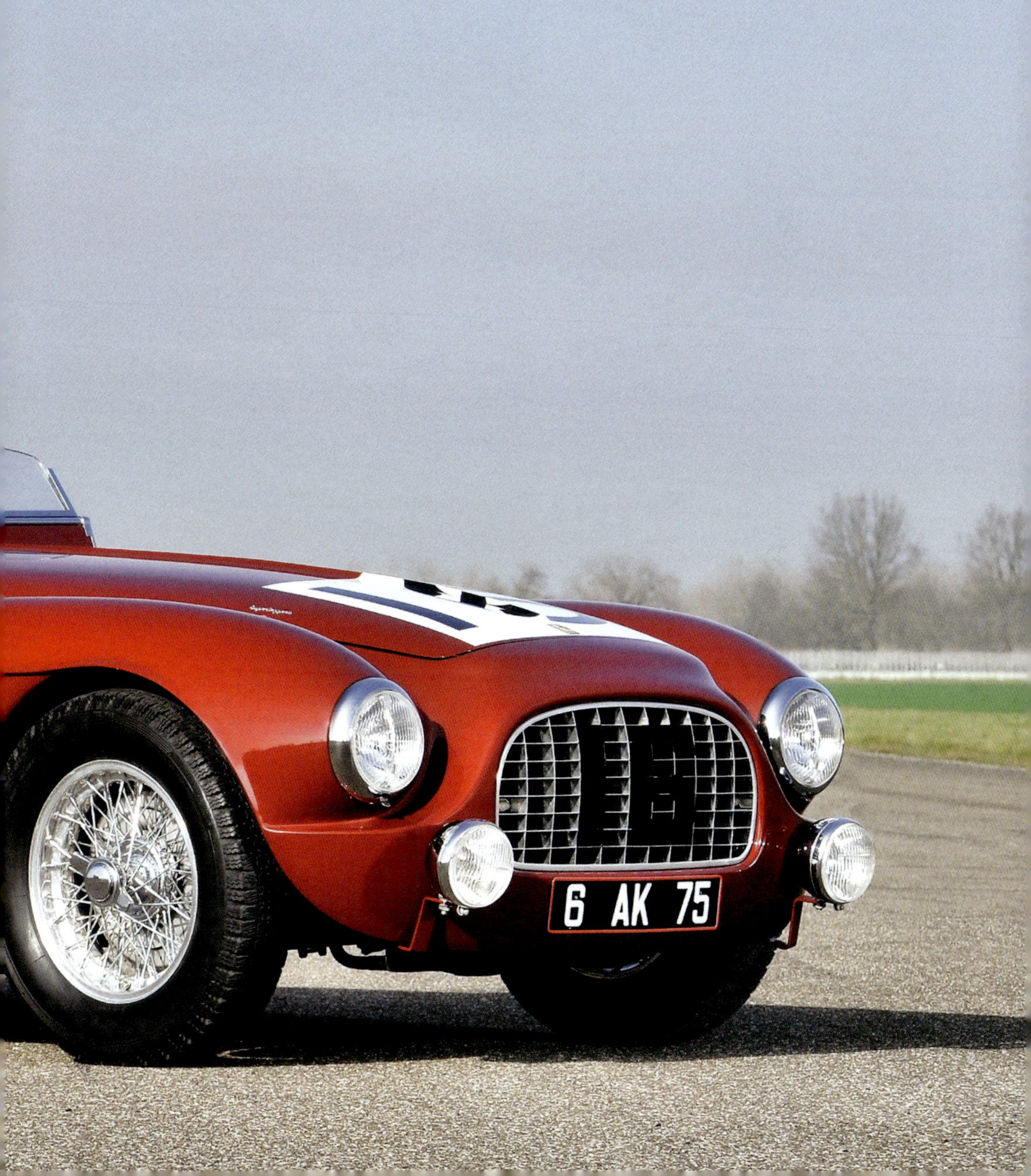
6 AK 75

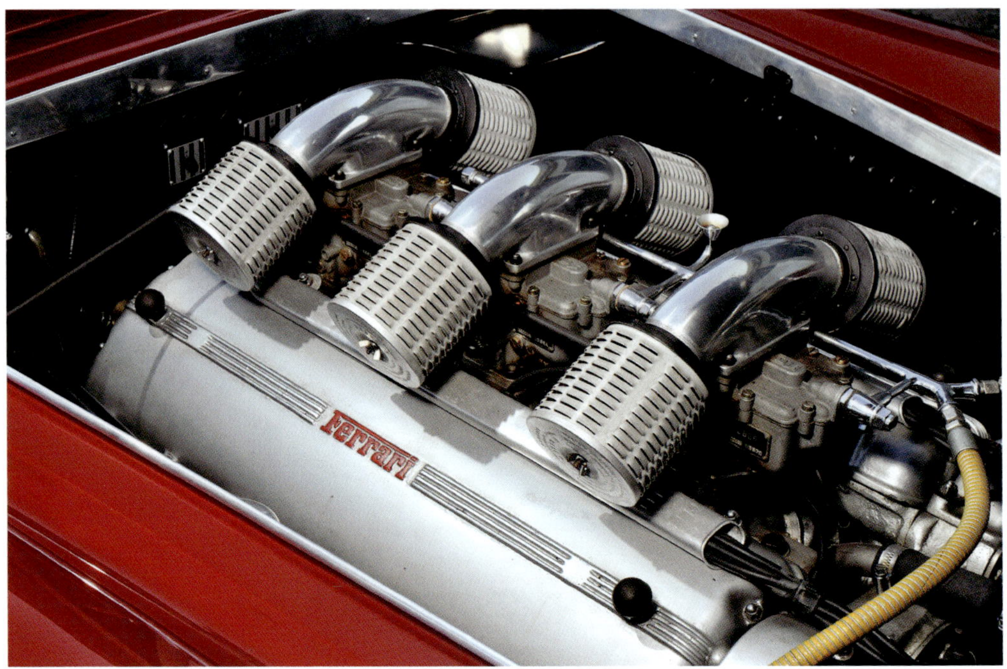

After the devastations of World War II and the ensuing need for rationing in its aftermath, it took a while for European car manufacturers to crank back up and rediscover their creative mojo. Indeed, many of the high-end cars produced in the mid-to-late 1940s, whether produced in the United States or in Europe, were more or less evolutions of earlier prewar models, and as a consequence invariably had a distinctly retro feel. By the early 1950s, however, Italy, which prewar had been one of the greatest nations of automotive innovation thanks to its plethora of highly skilled engineers and mechanics, was getting back on its feet thanks to Marshall Plan aid and the Italian government's implementation of an export-led reconstruction program. As a consequence, Italian carmakers — from Fiat and Alfa Romeo to Maserati and Ferrari — began to look forward optimistically and create cars that embodied the new postwar Italian spirit.

Pages 80–81: David Brown (right), the English industrialist and owner of Aston Martin from 1947–72, inspecting in 1954 a model of a DB3S with Aston Martin body designer, Frank Feeley. Behind them is a design drawing of a DB3S fixed-head coupé.

Above: Detail of right side of Ferrari 340 America Barchetta 4,101 cc (250 cu. in.), SOHC per bank 60° V12 engine with triple Weber 40 DCF carburetors. Designed by Aurelio Lampredi this engine was very similar to Gioacchino Colombo's earlier V12 for Ferrari, though larger in every aspect. The first major sports car win for the Lampredi engine came in 1951 when Luigi Villoresi won the Mille Miglia in a 340 America.

Overleaf: Detail of Ferrari 340 America Barchetta split windscreen, steering wheel, instrumenation and controls.

The gorgeously proportioned, small yet agile 1951 Ferrari 340 America Barchetta styled by Touring was one such vehicle. Only 23 of the 340 chassis were built by Ferrari, and of these only eight were bodied by the legendary Milanese coach builder Carrozzeria Touring. At the heart of the 340 chassis lay a new V12 engine designed by Aurelio Lampredi, which had been specifically developed for Formula 1 competition. The exquisite 340 America shown here (chassis no. 116/A) has an interesting and extensive provenance. According to existing records its engine and chassis were assembled by the renowned Ferrari mechanic Walter Sghedoni between January and April 1951. Then a few weeks later in May it was fitted with its elegant Barchetta coachwork at Carrozzeria Touring, before being returned to Ferrari to undergo its final test-drive. Two days after that it was sold to its first owner, Pierre Louis-Dreyfus, a former French resistance fighter during World War II who later went on to become the CEO of his family's distribution and trading company, Louis Dreyfus et Cie. This highly profitable concern, which had diversified interests ranging from shipping to banking, had made the Louis-Dreyfus family one of the wealthiest dynasties in Europe. In his spare time, Louis-Dreyfus, who was resident in Paris, fed his passion for motorsports by racing cars under the alias "Heldé," derived from an abbreviation of his surname, L-D. From 1931 onward, he had participated regularly in the 24 Hours of Le Mans and it is no coincidence that he took delivery of his new 340 America just a week before the 1951 race. Of the nine Ferraris that were raced that year, four of them were 340 Americas — these

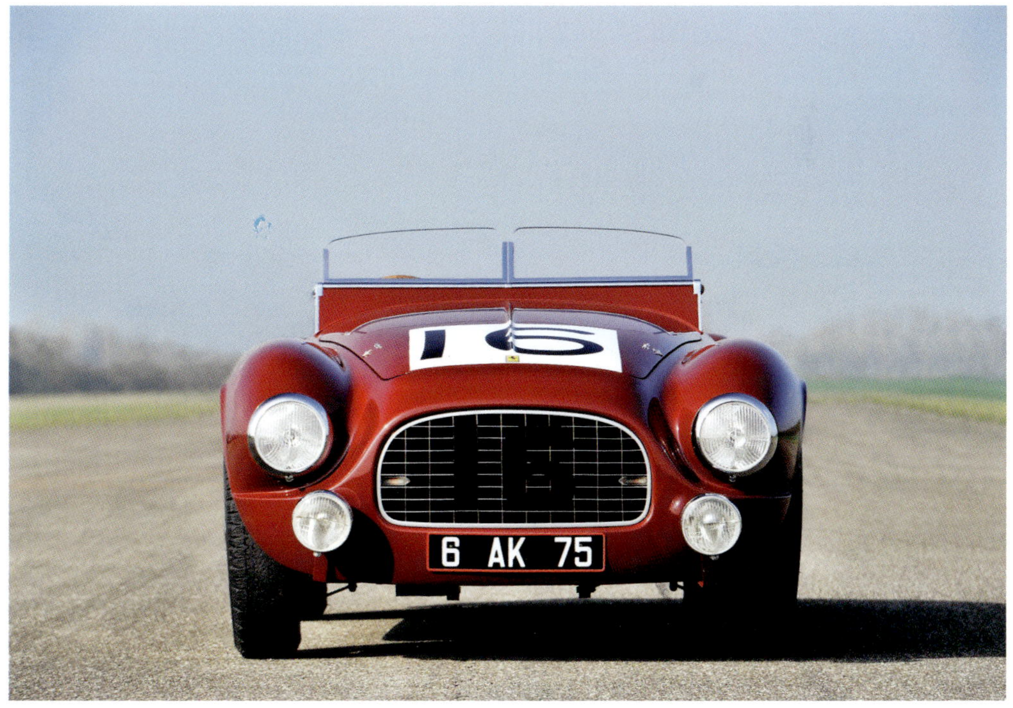

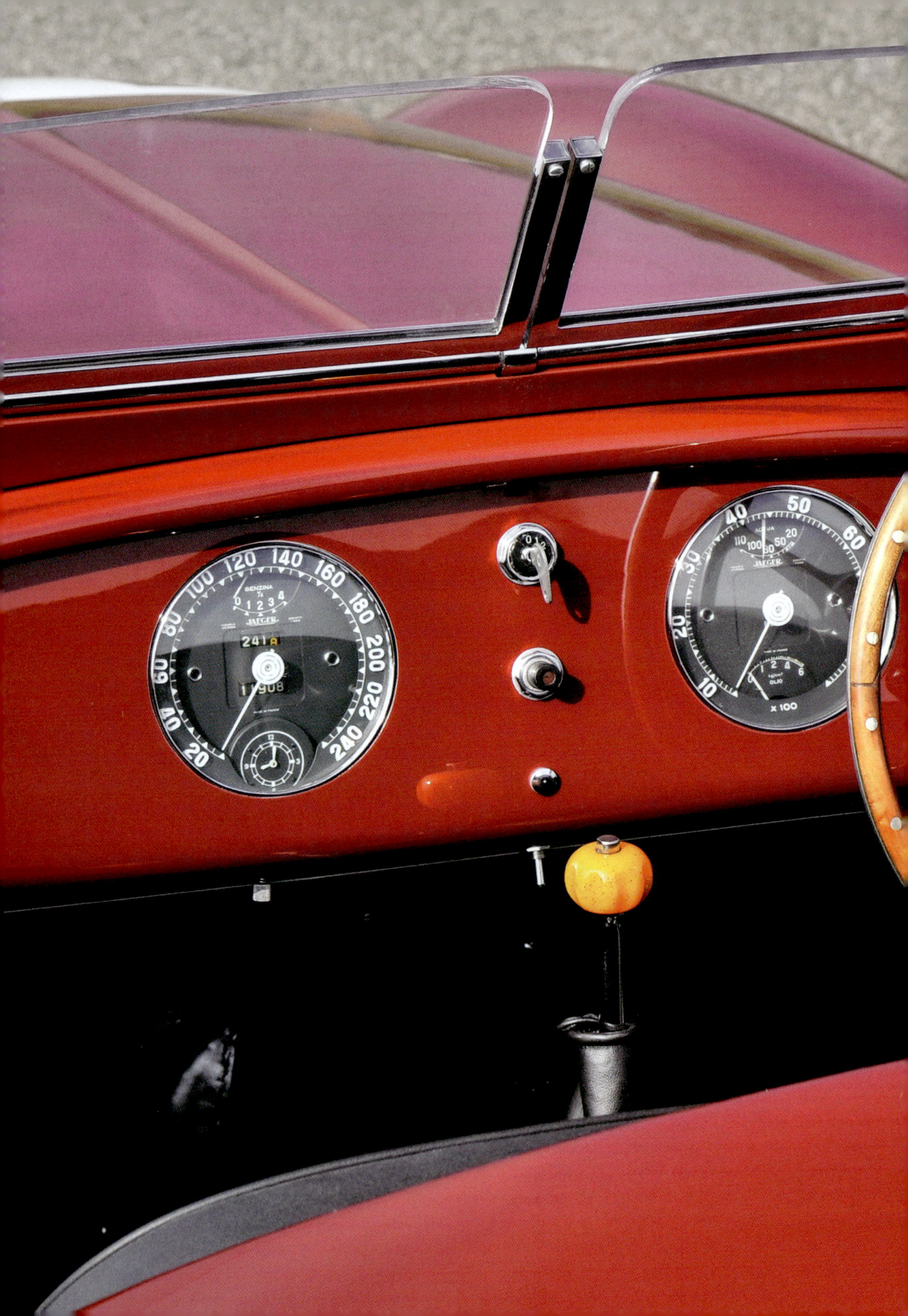
20 40 60 80 100 120 140 160 180 200 220 240
BENZINA
JAEGER
ACQUA
OLIO
x 100

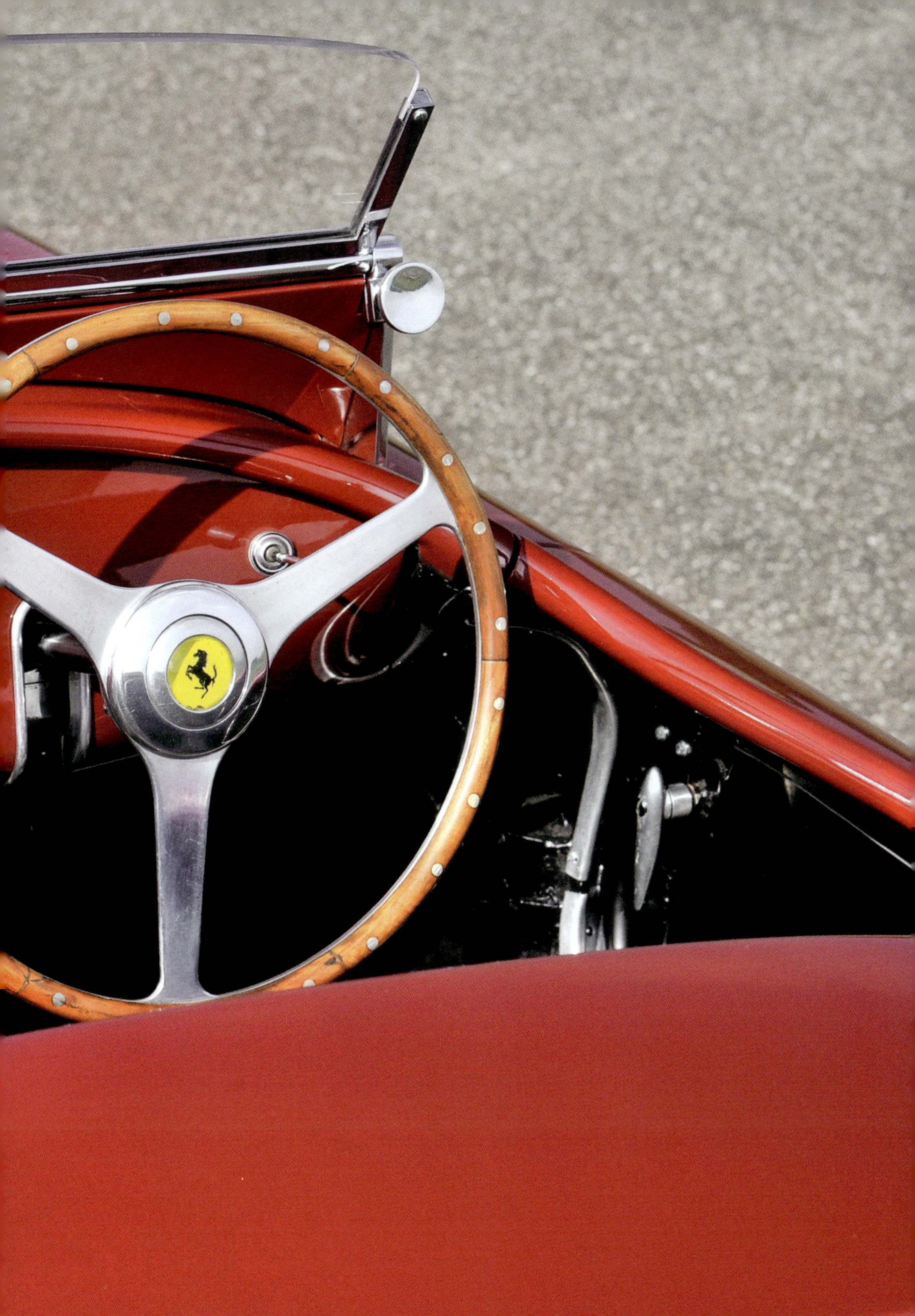

Below: No. 16 Ferrari 340 America Barchetta (chassis no. 0116/A) in the pits during the 1951 24 Hours of Le Mans with its owner, gentleman racer Pierre Louis-Dreyfus at the wheel, who shared driving duties with Louis Chiron. The car was black flagged after only 29 laps because Chiron missed a pit stop and refueled illegally trackside. The car was maintained for the race by Luigi Chinetti.

Opposite: Pierre Louis-Dreyfus driving the No. 16 Ferrari 340 America Barchetta (chassis no. 0116/A) at the 1952 24 Hours of Le Mans. Co-driven by René Dreyfus, the car was again maintained for the race by Luigi Chinetti but this year gained some unique air scoops behind the doors, helping to ventilate the rear drum brakes. Having qualified 15th the car was retired after five hours due to clutch problems.

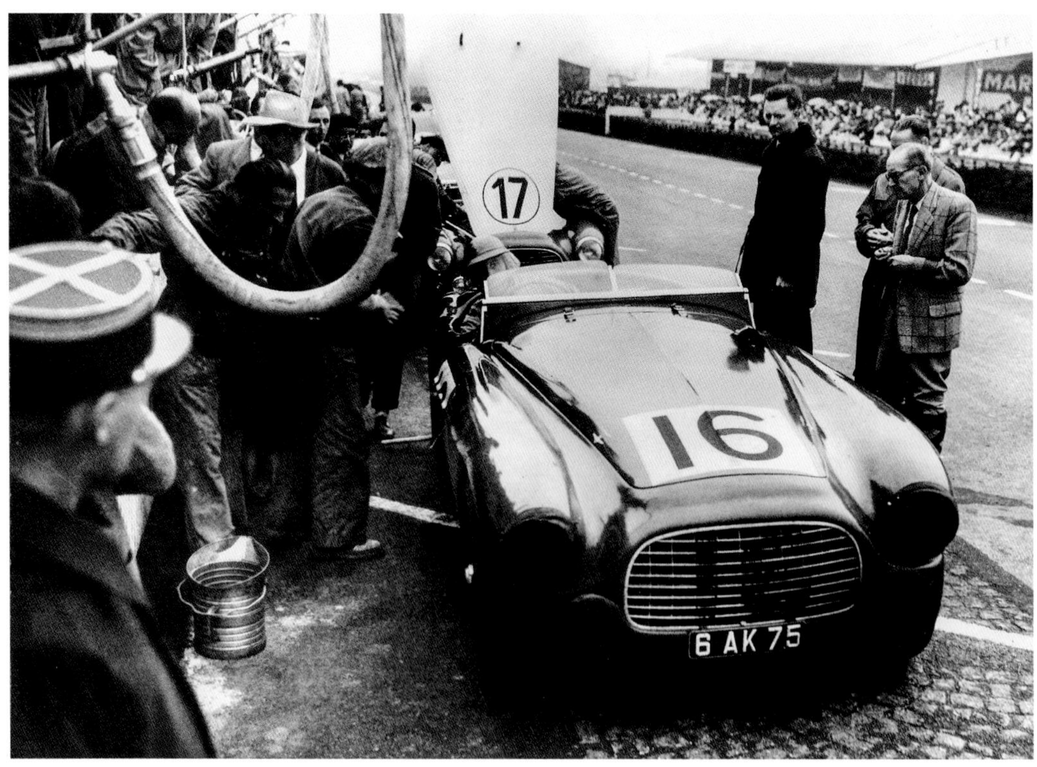

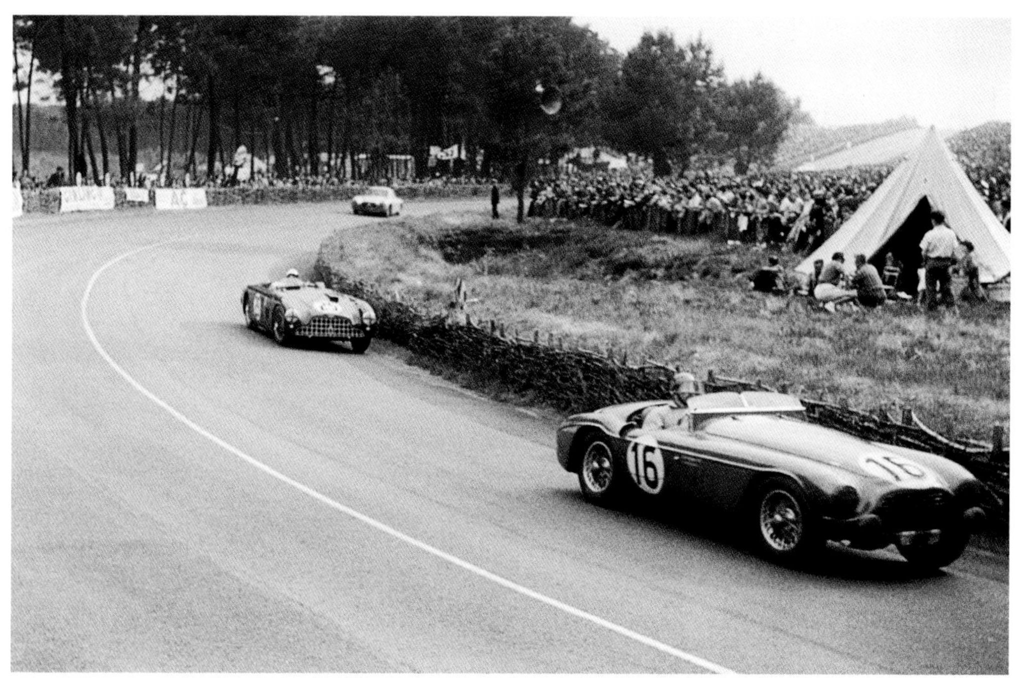

cars were considered the prerace favorites with rumors circulating that they could achieve in excess of 240 km/h (150 mph) on the Mulsanne Straight, which was then considered an astonishing speed. Louis-Dreyfus's newly purchased racer, which was maintained for him by Luigi Chinetti, was among these four entrants and was driven by himself and his good friend, Louis Chiron. Despite the best-laid plans, however, the car (No. 16) was black flagged after only 29 laps, meaning instant disqualification. The reason for this was that Chiron had become so engrossed in a battle with Eddie Hall, also driving a Ferrari 340, that he inadvertently missed his pit stop, which led to his fuel tank running dry and a subsequent illegal trackside refueling. The following year, Louis-Dreyfus reentered the same car (chassis no. 116/A) into Le Mans, with once again Chinetti maintaining it, though this time he shared driving duty with René Dreyfus (no relation) who had previously clocked up a couple of notable Grand Prix victories. But yet again the car did not finish, having had to retire after only five hours due to clutch problems.

The car was later sold on, then changed hands a few times, before being acquired by the noted Ferrari collector, Pierre Bardinon. He had it restored by Ferrari, and since then this beauty has had several owners who have entered it into various competitions, including a least seven "reborn" Mille Miglia events, specifically held for the racing of classic and vintage cars. So, although this remarkable car will soon be entering its seventh decade, it is still very much capable of doing what it was originally designed to do: go around a race circuit fast. And that is the magic of a Ferrari — the stallion might get older, but the thrills it generates never dim.

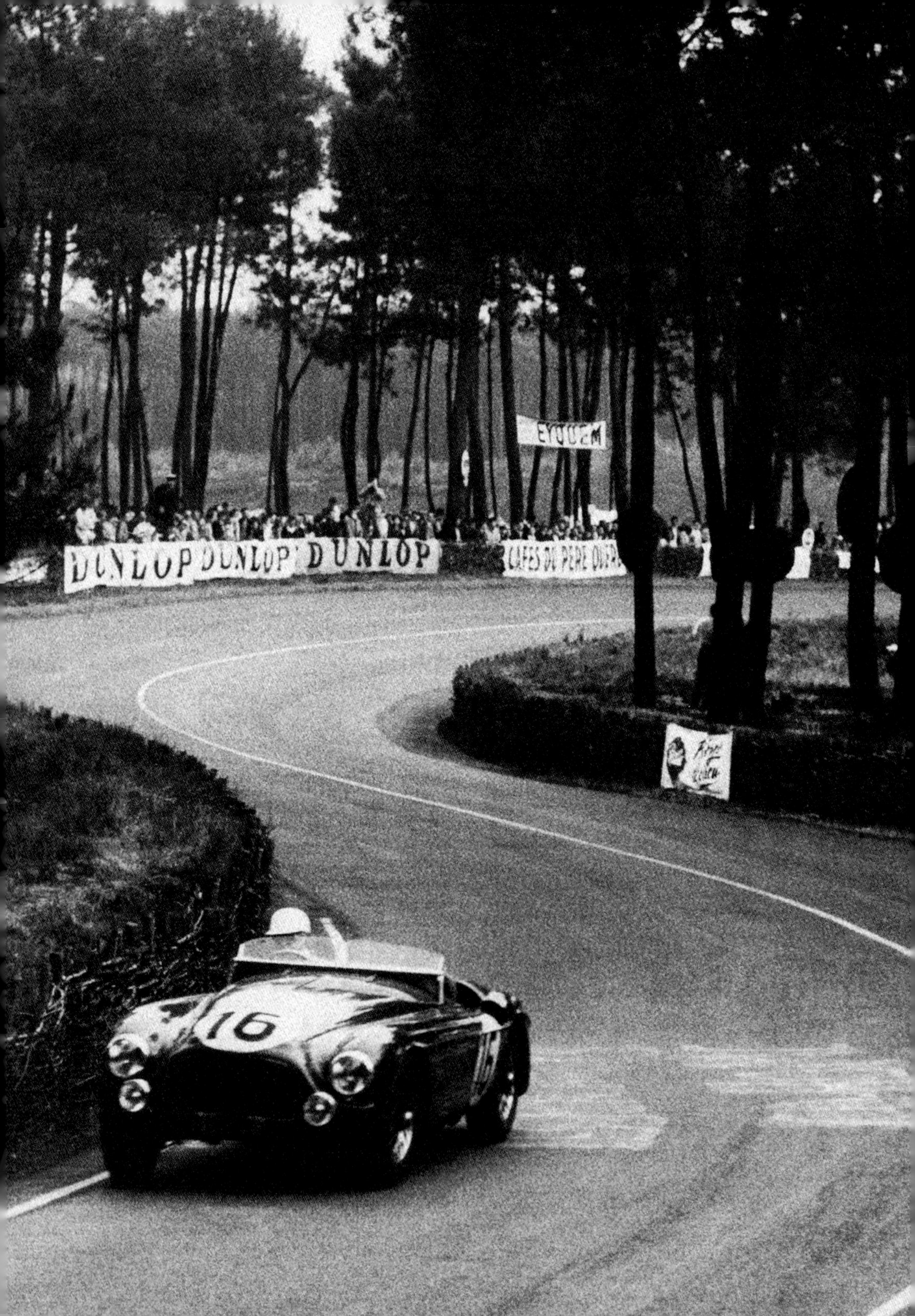
DUNLOP
DUNLOP
DUNLOP
16

Opposite: No. 16 Ferrari 340 America Barchetta (chassis no. 0116/A) being driven by René Dreyfus, the co-driver of car owner Pierre Louis-Dreyfus, at the 1952 24 Hours of Le Mans.

Below: Detail of the Carrozzeria Touring Superleggera badge fixed to the rear end of the car.

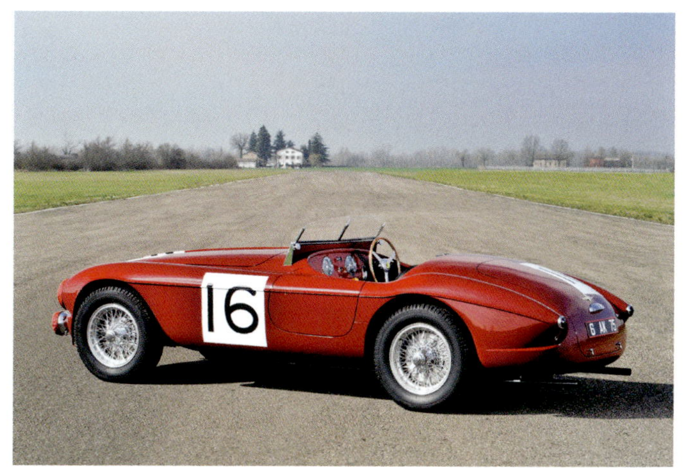

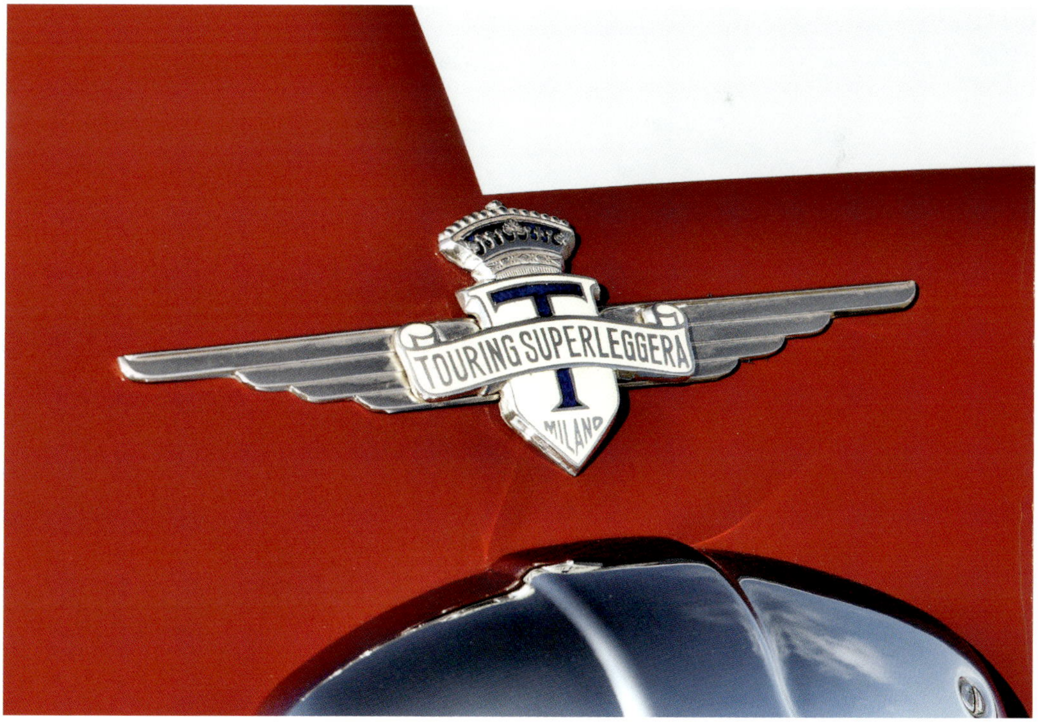

TOURING SUPERLEGGERA
MILANO

1952

Cunningham C-4R Roadster

MANUFACTURED 1952 | ENGINE 5,424 cc (331 cu. in.), overhead-valve Hemi V8 | HORSEPOWER 325
TOP SPEED 250 km/h (155 mph) | TRANSMISSION 4-speed
NUMBER PRODUCED 2 (plus 1 coupe)

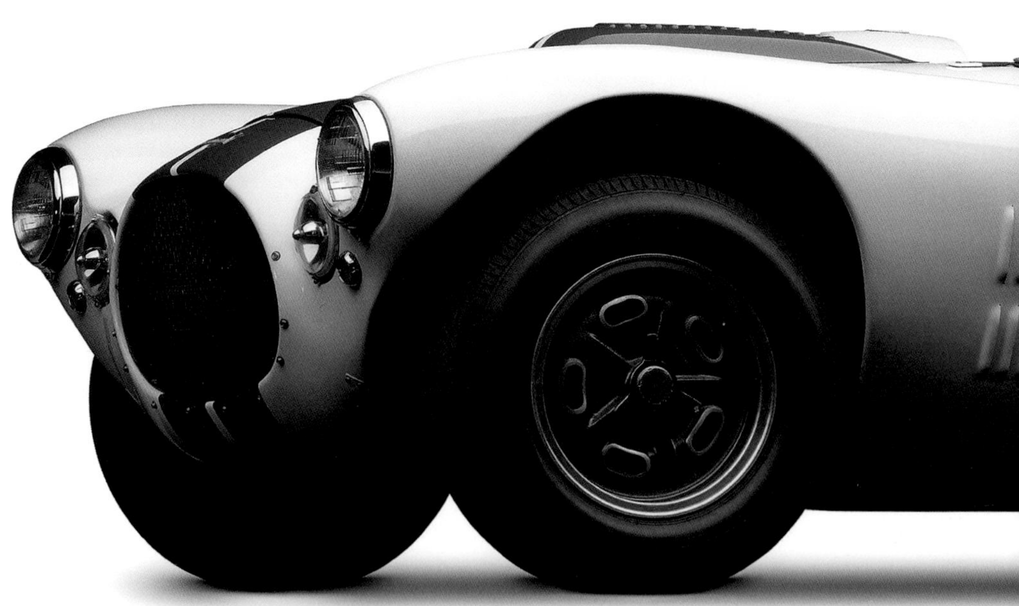

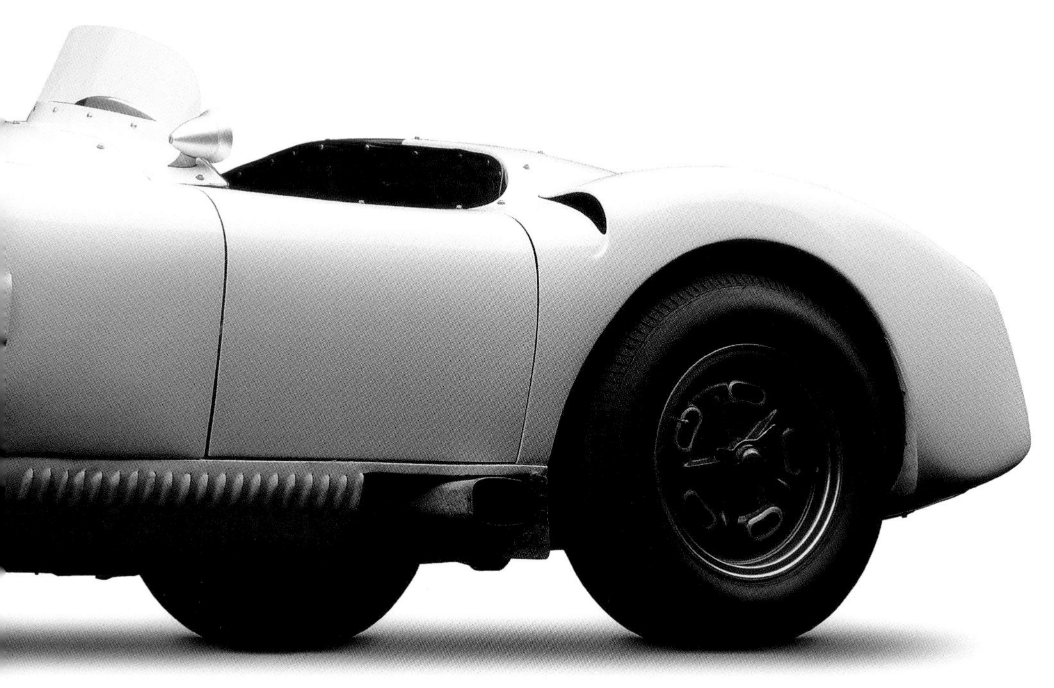

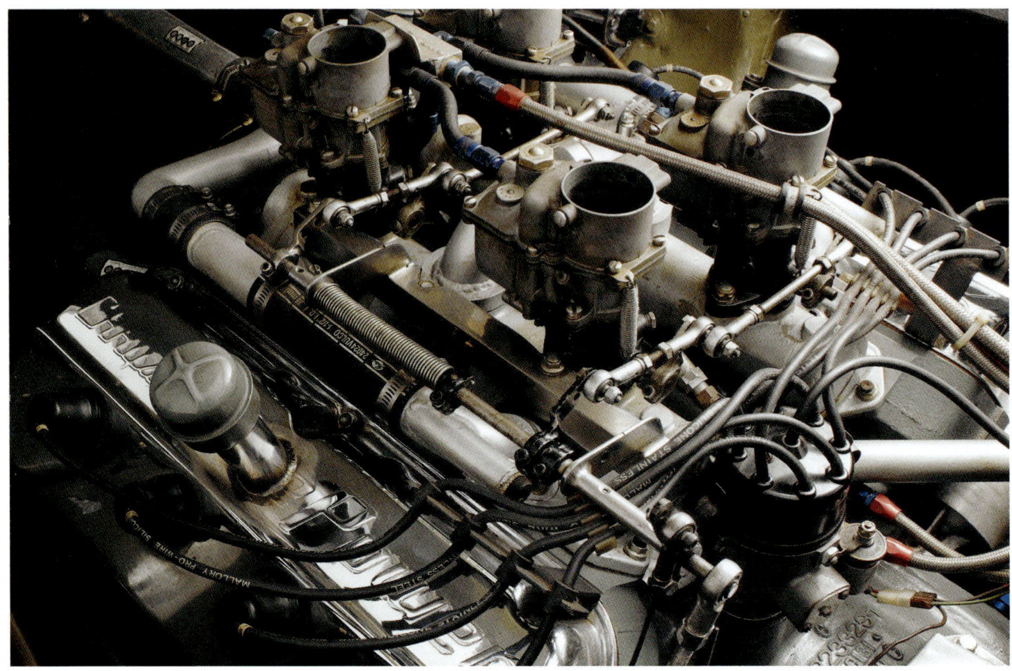

America emerged from World War II stronger and more confident than ever, having reinvigorated its enormous industrial might and shaken off any vestiges of the Great Depression. The factories that had churned out war materiel in truly impressive volumes were now ready to gear up for the production of mainstream consumer goods on an unprecedented scale. But when it came to the development of high performance roadsters during the 1950s, there was only one American marque that made cars to rival those being developed in Europe during this postwar era: Cunningham. Based in West Palm Beach, Florida, B.S. Cunningham Inc. was founded in 1951 by Briggs Swift Cunningham Jr. to produce prototype racers. A millionaire sportsman, Cunningham indulged his passion for motor racing as not only a manufacturer, but also a driver.

Born in Cincinnati, Briggs Cunningham's wealth derived from his family's banking interests there and as a boy his passion for speed and competition was initially sparked by yacht racing. However, when the family acquired a car in 1914, he pestered the family's chauffeur for driving lessons and his passion for cars was further fueled when an uncle built a street racer from a Dodge touring car fitted with a military surplus Hispano-Suiza aircraft engine. The young Briggs reputedly accompanied this uncle to various clandestine street races, although he initially abstained from actually driving himself out of respect for his mother's wishes. When she died, however, he fully immersed himself into motor racing. While studying engineering and technical drawing at Yale University, he became friends with the racing driver Ralph DePalma as well as Miles and Sam Collier, who went on to found the Automobile Racing Club of America. In 1939, Cunningham constructed his first

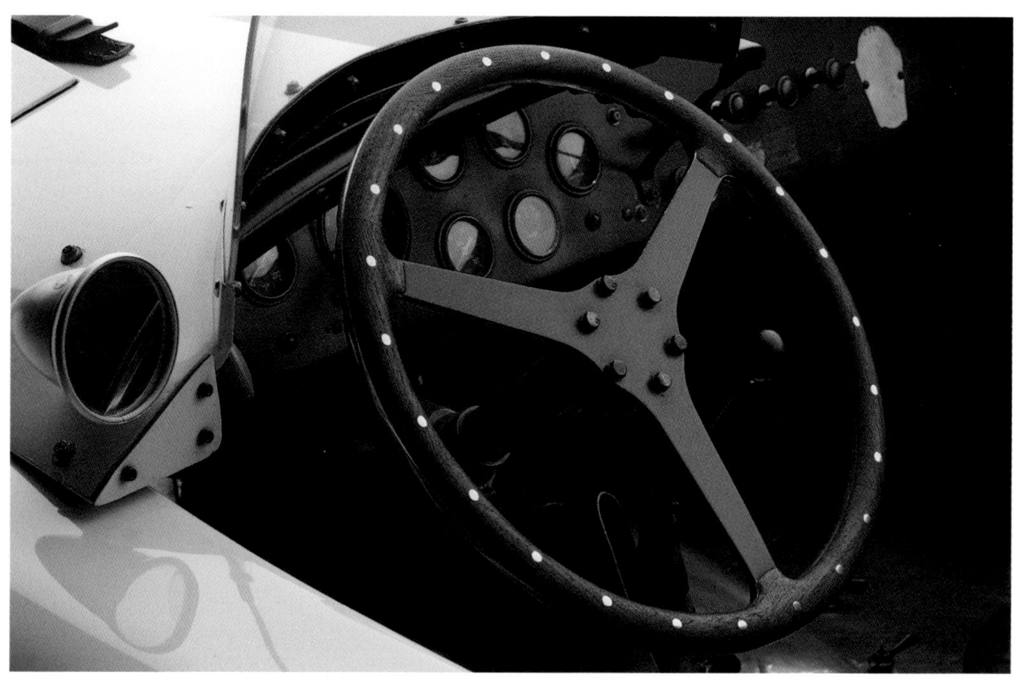

"official" car, the famous Bu-Merc — a Buick chassis mounted with an accident-salvaged Mercedes SSK body created for an impromptu race held at the Colliers's family estate in Westchester County. He later raced this vehicle at the inaugural Watkins Glen Grand Prix in 1948, and as the Revs Institute notes it proved to be "one of the hottest American stock cars on the road at the time."

This early racer was the start of Cunningham's adventure into the construction of superlative high performance road and track cars. B.S. Cunningham Inc.'s first vehicle was the prototype C-1 roadster (chassis no. 5101) built in 1951, which was powered by a V8 Cadillac engine and can be considered the first all-American postwar sports car. Wanting to compete in the 24 Hours of Le Mans race, Cunningham then created three special racing variants, known as the C-2R, that same year, which boasted a bigger 5.5L Chrysler Hemi FirePower V8 engine that provided a top speed of over 150 mph (240 km/h). Importantly, these roaring beasts were the first serious American contenders in this world-renowned endurance race for some 20 years. Prior to the race, anticipation was running high as Phil Walters's Cunningham clocked up the fastest official practice lap.

Opposite: Detail of Cunningham C-4R 5,424 cc (331 cu. in.), overhead-valve V8 engine with four Zenith carburetors. This Chrysler Hemi FirePower engine was substantially modified for competition with a roller tappet camshaft, special carburetion, heavier crankshaft and increased compression ratio so as to produce a very creditable 325 hp at 5,200 rpm.

Above: Detail of steering wheel, instrumentation and controls.

During the race, however, the C-2Rs' weight let them down on a wet and greasy track and their performance was ultimately disappointing, with three DNFs. Undeterred, Cunningham embarked on the construction of three follow-up cars, which became the C-4R model — two roadsters and one coupe. Essentially, the C-4R was a redesign of the earlier Cunningham racers, being 16 inches shorter and an incredible 990 lb. lighter. All three C-4Rs were also equipped with newly designed aerodynamic bodies, conceived by G. Briggs Weaver, that incorporated massive gas tanks capable of holding 50 gallons of fuel. They also featured modified Chrysler Hemi engines that provided 325 horsepower at 5,200 rpm as well as modified suspension systems and four-speed transmissions.

These new features made all the difference in terms of speed and handling at Le Mans the following year, and although two of the C-4Rs were forced to retire, the third, driven by Briggs Cunningham and Bill Spear, clinched a thrilling fourth place — proving that once again American cars were in the running when it came to high performance competition. This was proved again in 1953 when alongside Cunningham's new C-5R which placed third, two of the C-4Rs clocked up very commendable seventh and tenth places. The roadster shown here (chassis no. 5217) went on to win its class at Le Mans in 1954 — the first such victory for a US-based manufacturer, which proved decisively that American automotive muscle was quite literally back on track.

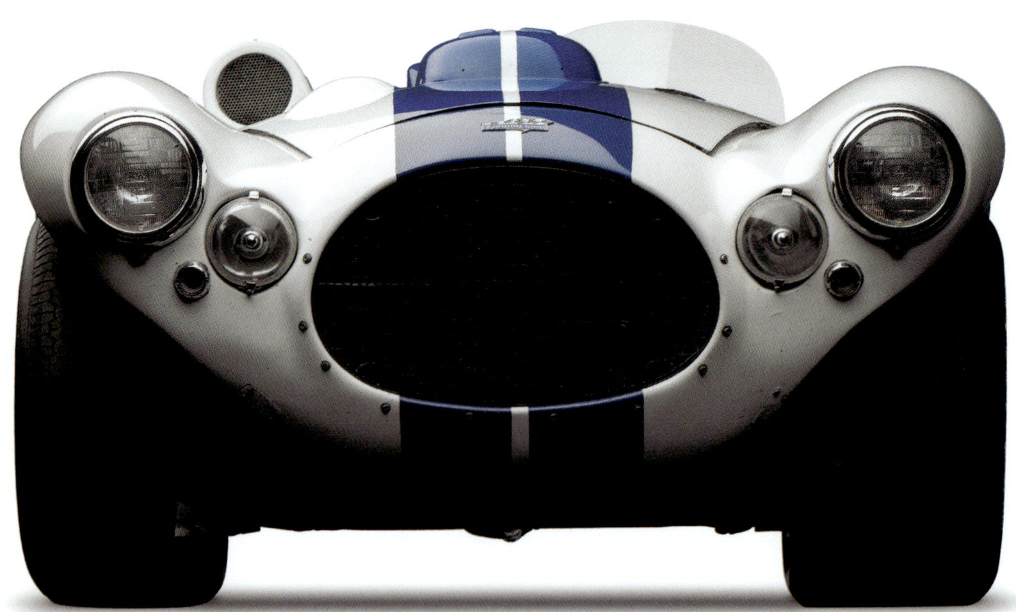

Right: Cunningham Team photographed with two Works C-4R Roadsters outside the West Palm Beach factory, 1952. Briggs Cunningham standing first from right.

Overleaf: Detail of Cunningham C–4R Roadster showing its stripped-down, competition-focused cockpit.

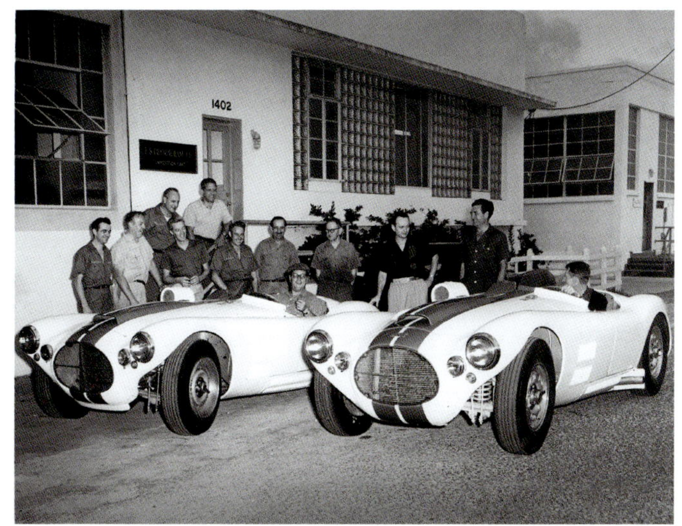

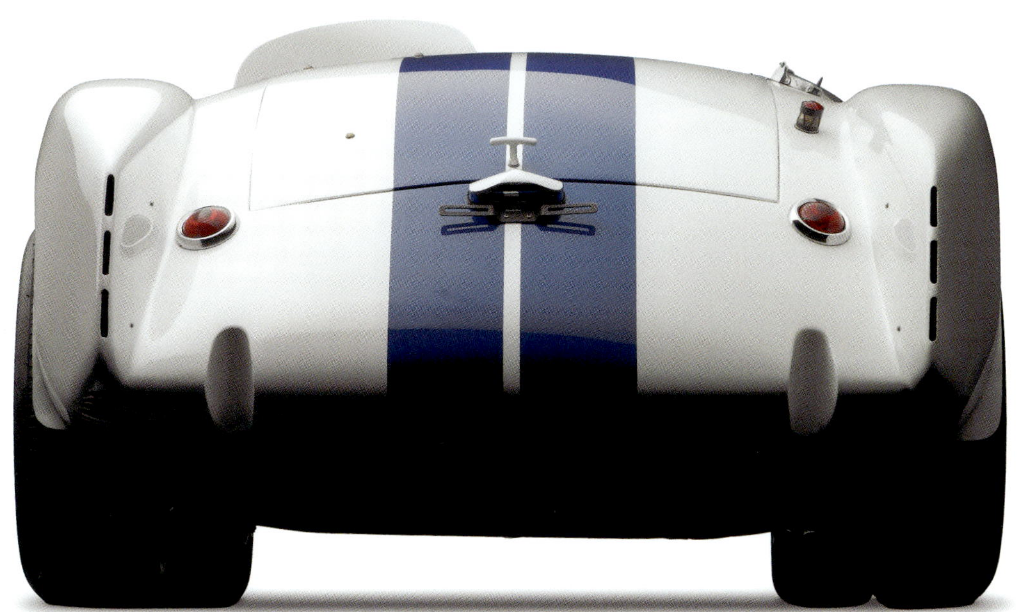

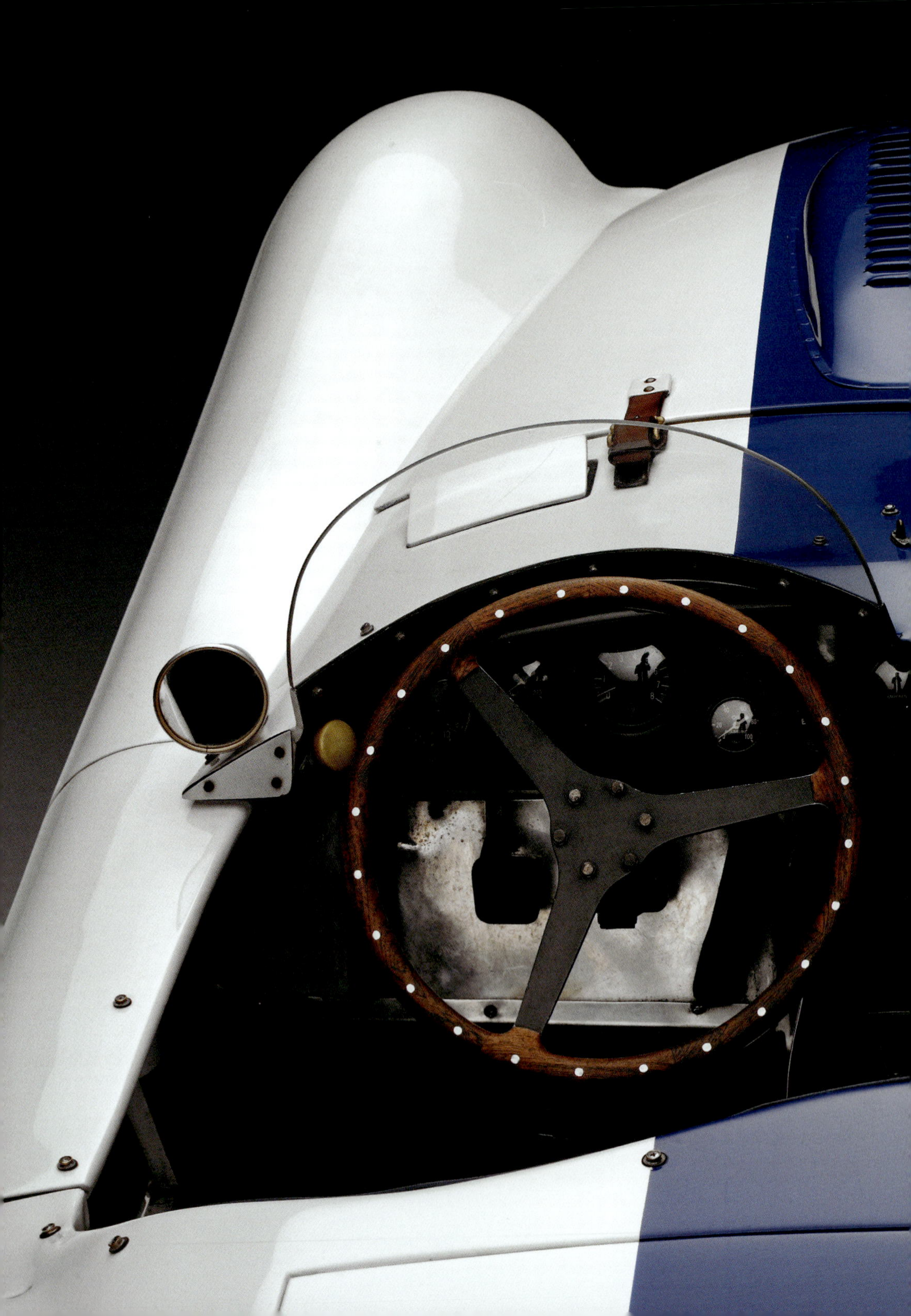

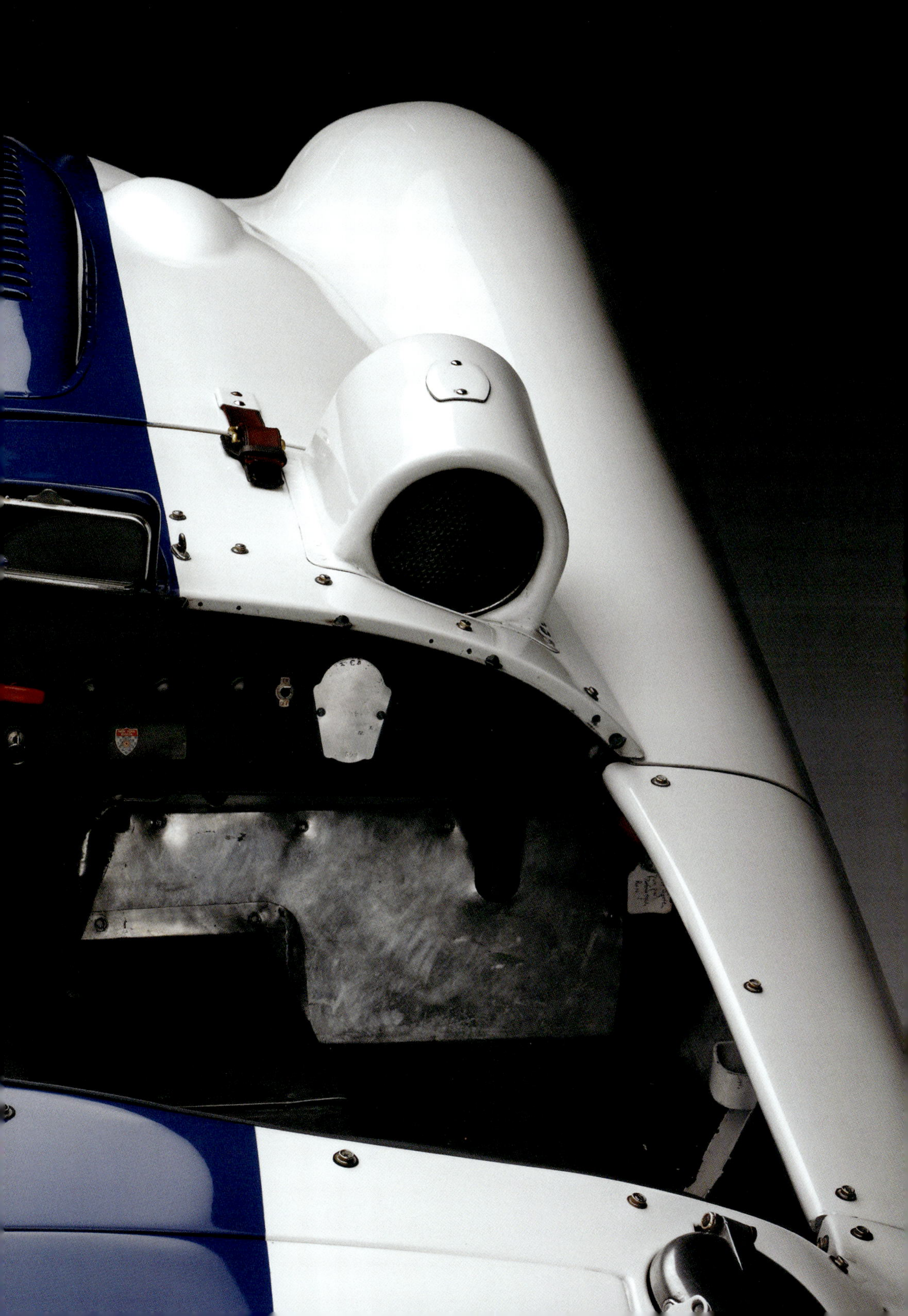

Below: Car No. 2, Works Cunningham C–4R Roadster (chassis no. 5217) at the 1954 24 Hours of Le Mans. Driven by Bill Spear and Sherwood Johnson, this car won its class (over five liter) and placed third overall — the first ever such victory for a US-based manufacturer.

Opposite (top, left): *Time* magazine cover (April 26, 1954), featuring Briggs Cunningham and three C-4R Roadsters. This cover reflected the crucial shift that was taking place within international motorsports during the early 1950s, as American constructors, teams and racers became increasingly competitive.

Opposite (top, right): Color illustration celebrating the Briggs Cunningham team victory of John Fitch and Phil Walters at the 1953 Sebring International 12 Hour Grand Prix of Endurance race in a 1952 Cunningham C-4R (car No. 57). Car No. 30, a Works Aston Martin DB3 driven by Reg Parnell and George Abecassis, placed second.

Opposite (bottom): Start of the 1954 24 Hours of Le Mans. The No. 2 Works Cunningham C-4R Roadster (chassis no. 5217) of Bill Spear and Sherwood Johnston, alongside the Briggs Cunningham team entered No. 6 Ferrari 375 MM of Phil Walters and John Fitch, and the No. 14 Jaguar D-type of Tony Rolt and Duncan Hamilton. The second Works Cunningham C-4R Roadster entered in the race, which was driven by Briggs Cunningham and John Gordon Bennett, finished fifth overall, and second in class (over five liter).

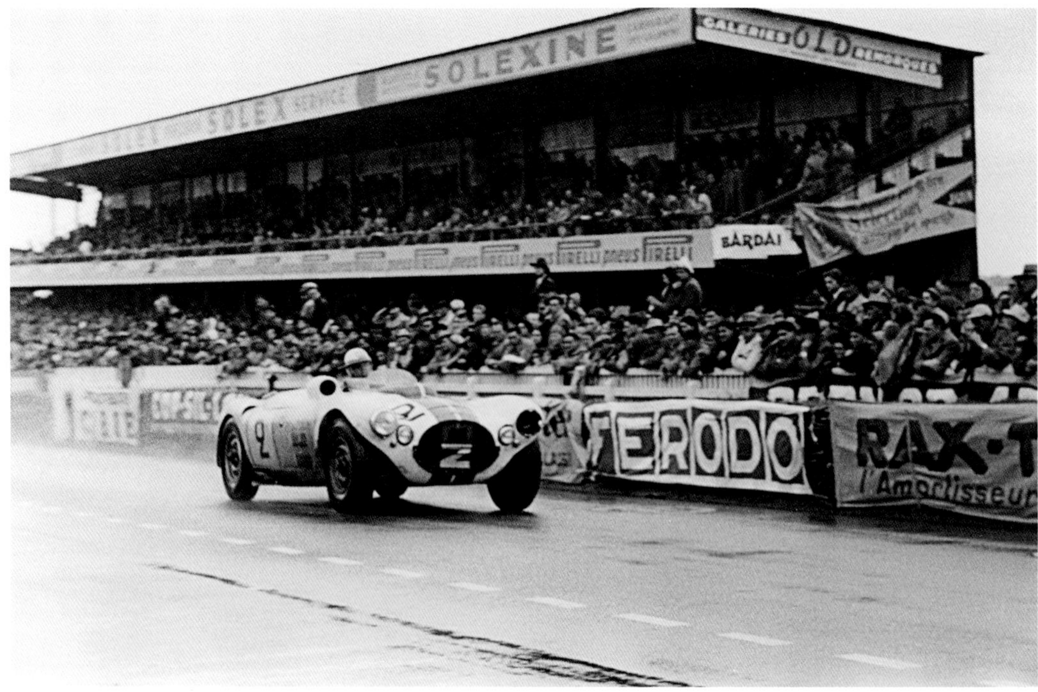

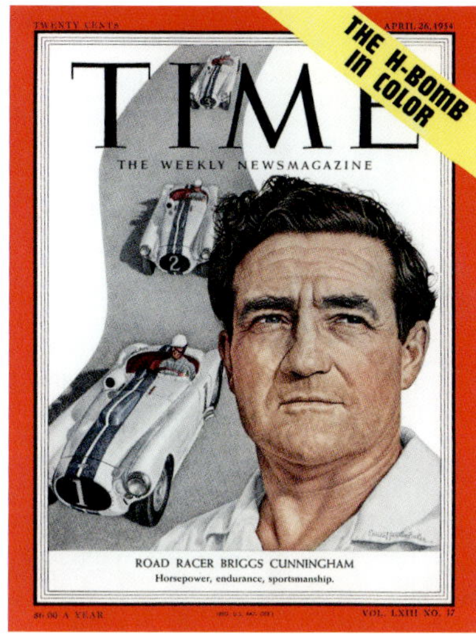
TWENTY CENTS
APRIL 26, 1954
THE H-BOMB in COLOR
TIME
THE WEEKLY NEWSMAGAZINE
ROAD RACER BRIGGS CUNNINGHAM
Horsepower, endurance, sportsmanship.
$6.00 A YEAR
VOL. LXIII NO. 17

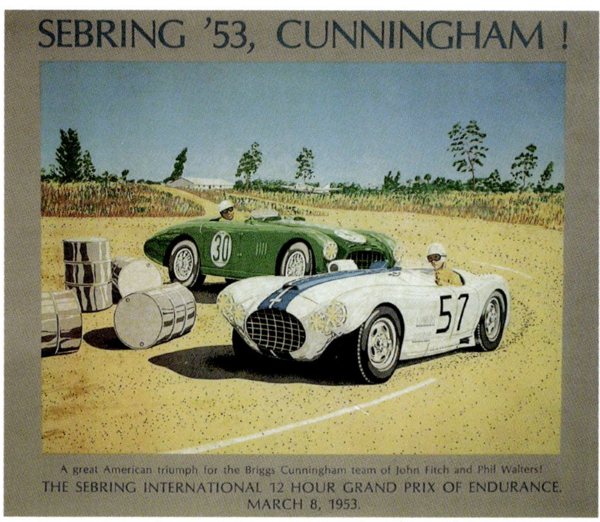
SEBRING '53, CUNNINGHAM !
A great American triumph for the Briggs Cunningham team of John Fitch and Phil Walters!
THE SEBRING INTERNATIONAL 12 HOUR GRAND PRIX OF ENDURANCE.
MARCH 8, 1953.

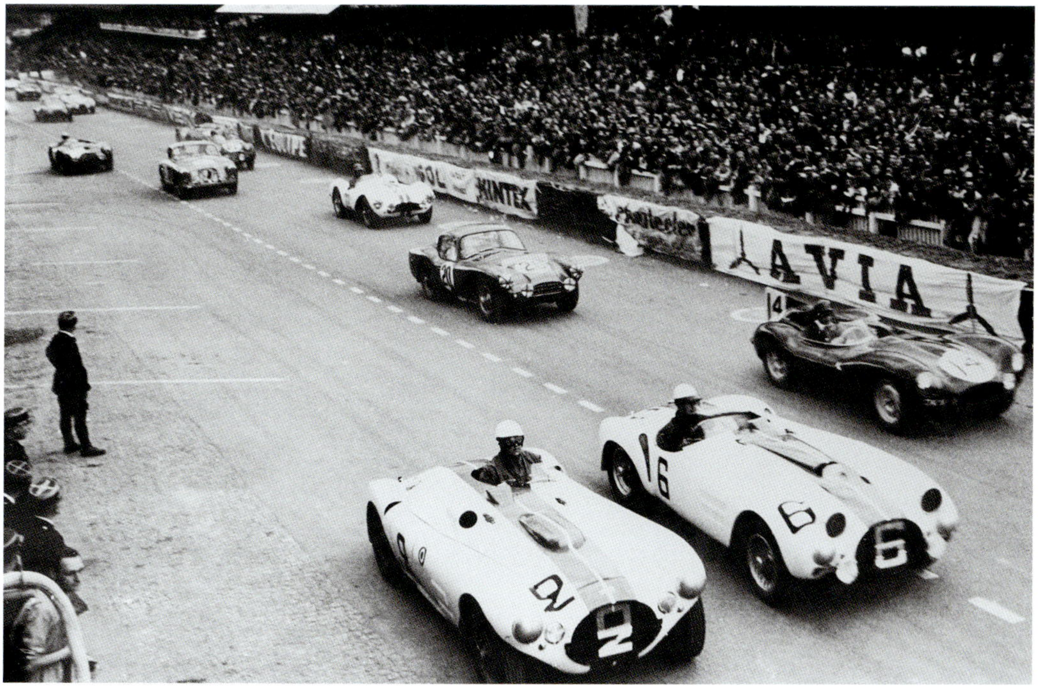

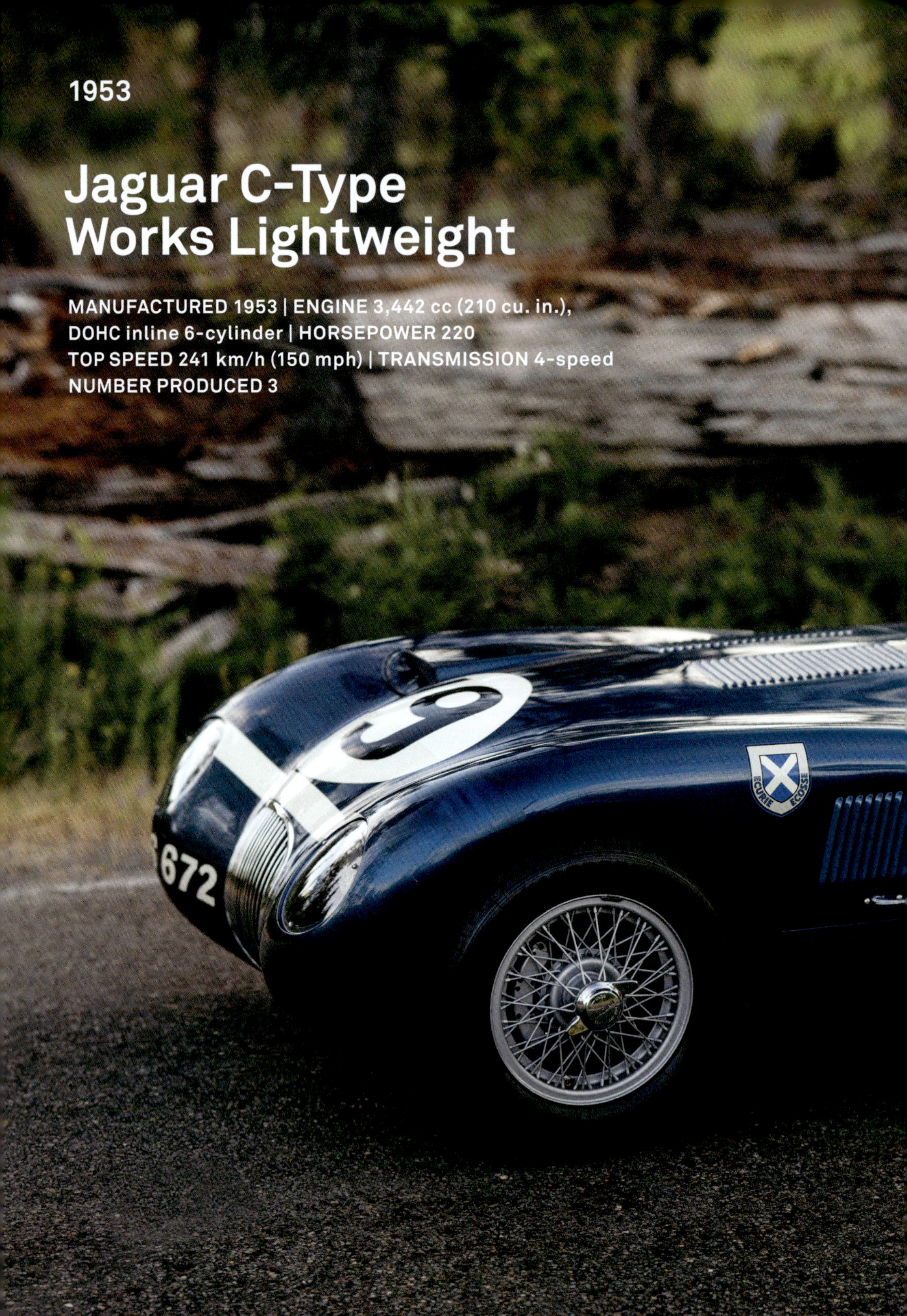

1953

Jaguar C-Type Works Lightweight

MANUFACTURED 1953 | **ENGINE** 3,442 cc (210 cu. in.), DOHC inline 6-cylinder | **HORSEPOWER** 220
TOP SPEED 241 km/h (150 mph) | **TRANSMISSION** 4-speed
NUMBER PRODUCED 3

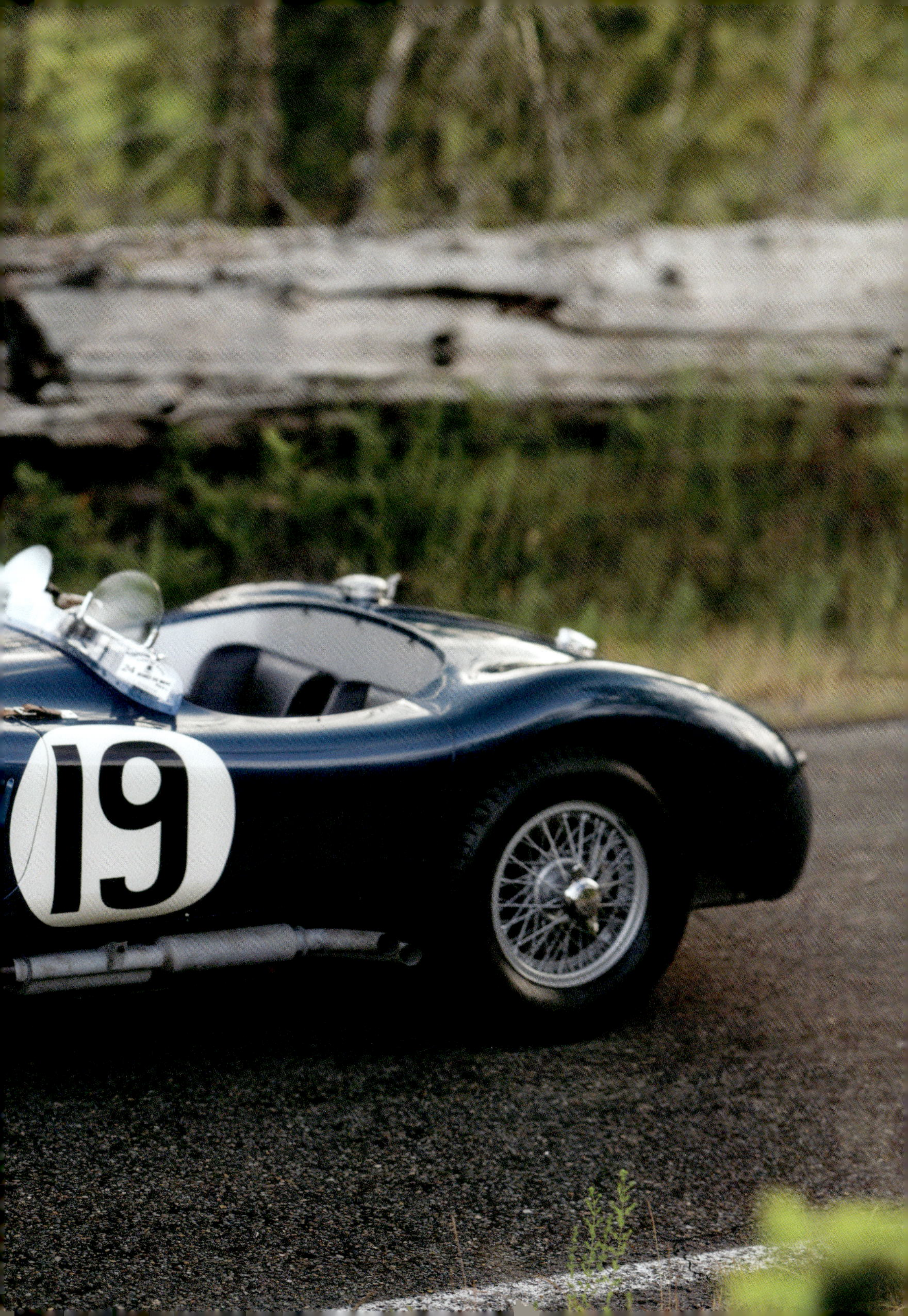
19

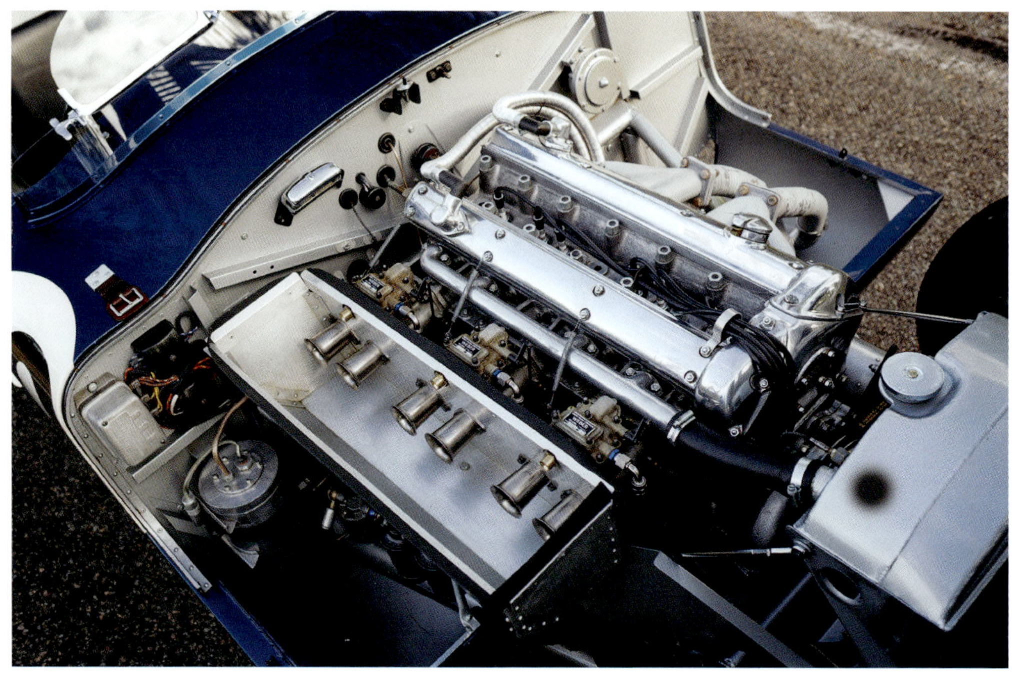

The origins of the Jaguar marque can be traced back to 1922, when the Swallow Sidecar Company was founded by William Walmsley and William Lyons in Blackpool. This venture subsequently diversified into the fabrication of automobile bodies in the mid-1920s. The company was renamed the Swallow Sidecar and Coach Building Company in 1927 and that same year debuted its Austin Seven Swallow — a two-seater open tourer built on an Austin Seven chassis. This car proved popular and the following year a four-seater saloon was launched, which saw more orders pour in. In order to ramp up production to meet demand that same year the firm relocated to Coventry, where there was a large skilled workforce, and soon production had increased fivefold to 50 cars per week. In 1934, Lyons bought out Walmsley and the following year founded S.S. Cars Limited and launched the first car to bear the Jaguar name: the 1935 SS Jaguar 2.5L Saloon. In 1945, the firm was renamed Jaguar Cars and three years later it unleashed its very first sports car, the sensational low-slung XK120 with its distinctive swooping fenders that ran the whole length of its body. Significantly, beneath this exquisite form, which had the poise of a large feline, lurked a new and formidable 3.4-liter twin-cam straight-six engine. This stylish sports car was such a success that its design DNA went on to inform other road-going Jaguars over the next four decades.

Above: Detail of Jaguar C-Type Works Lightweight 3,442 cc (210 cu. in.), DOHC inline six-cylinder engine with triple Weber 40 DC03 carburetors. The performance of this power plant, which was based on the proven 3.4-liter XK engine, was boosted not only by more powerful carburation but also by high-lift camshafts and improvements to the cooling system.

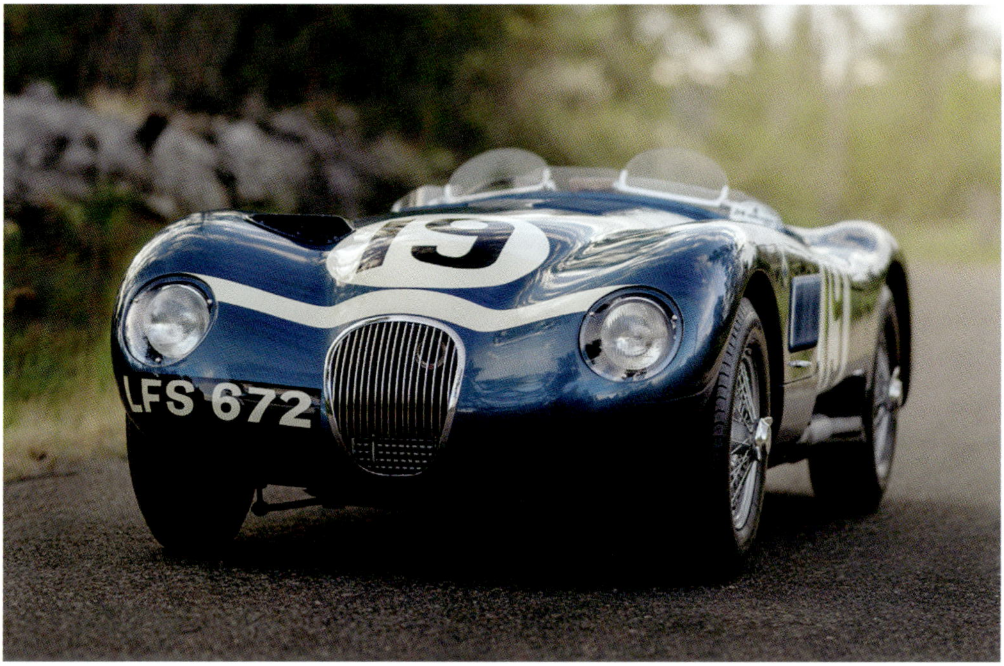

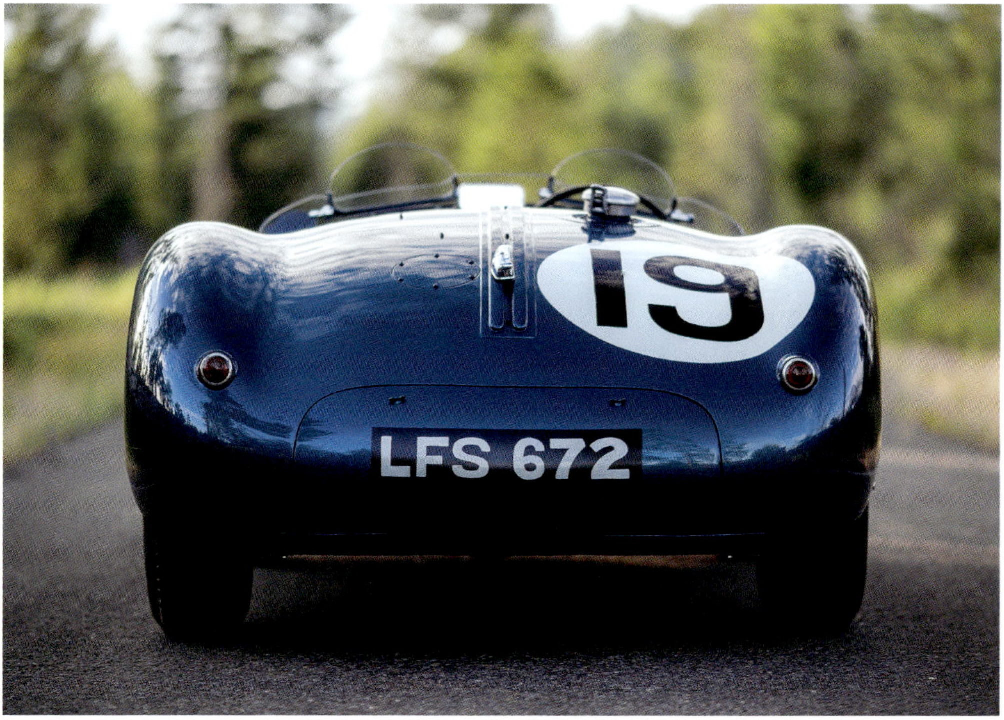

After witnessing the colossal amount of attention generated by the show-stealing XK120, Lyons insightfully grasped the potential publicity value a purebred Jaguar racing car might bring to his company. Based on the XK120 roadster, the resultant XK120C — with the "C" standing for competition — was launched in 1951 and soon thereafter became known as the C-Type. Weighing around 25% less than its progenitor, the C-Type had a lightweight tubular space frame designed by William Heynes (one of the very first uses of the technique in sports car construction) onto which was fixed a stunning aluminum body, the fluid lines of which had been devised by the acclaimed aerodynamicist Malcolm Sayer. The C-Type's XK engine was also modified with the addition of a new cylinder head, high-lift camshafts, racing pistons and an unmuffled dual-exhaust system, all of which helped to increase its output to 200 hp.

Unbelievably, it took only six weeks for the first three C-Types to be hand built in time to participate in the 24 Hours of Le Mans race of 1951. Debuting at this famous endurance race, these powerful-yet-sleek big cats made their mark, for although two retired, the third driven by Peter Walker and Peter Whitehead won the race, finishing a noteworthy 77 miles ahead of the next nearest competitor. As the first British car to win Le Mans for nearly 20 years, it was a legendary victory and as such sparked considerable customer interest. So much so, that the C-Type was put into limited production, with 50 examples subsequently being constructed. At the Le Mans race of 1952, however, all three Works C-Types overheated and were forced to retire. These cooling issues together with that year's dominance of Mercedes-Benz's W 194s (300 SLs), prompted Jaguar's engineers to undertake a number of upgrades in order to get the next three lightweight Works C-Types race-fit for the

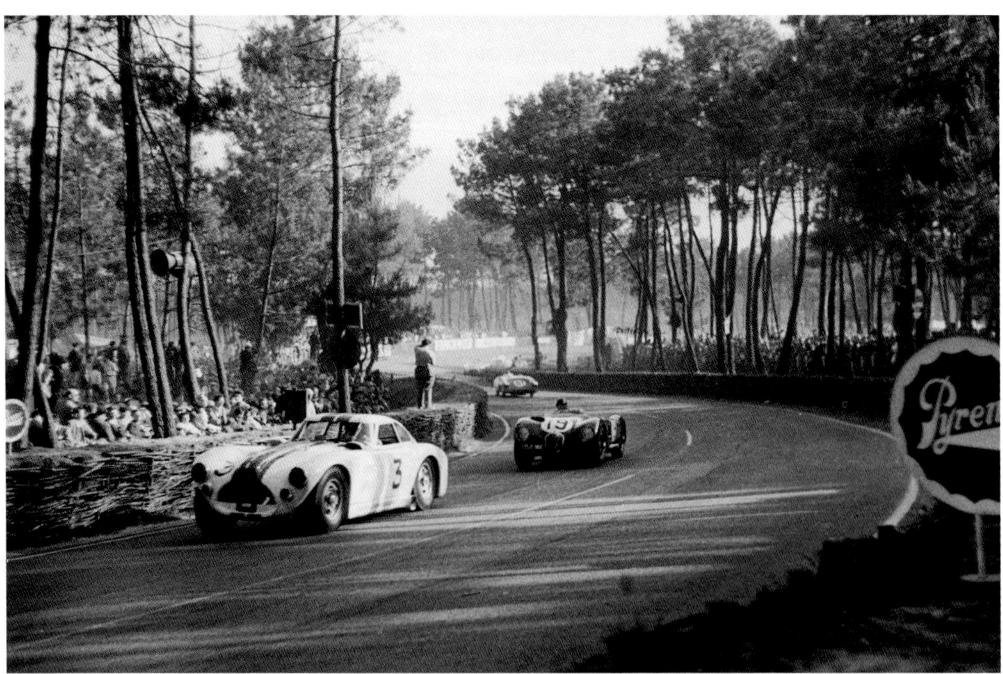

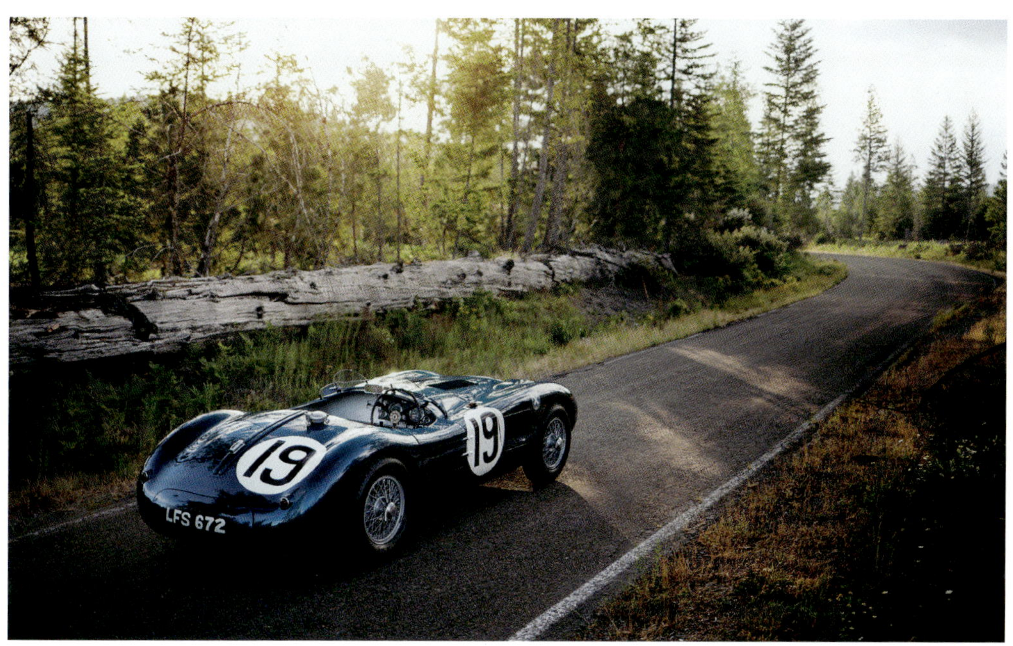

upcoming 1953 Le Mans race. The model shown here is one of these later cars, which were built mid-1953. These new and improved C-Types featured, among other things, bodywork made from thinner-gauge aluminum, more powerful triple twin-choke Weber carburetors, high-lift camshafts, fully synchronized gearboxes, triple-plate clutches, aircraft fuel bladders made of weight-saving rubber, and lastly but by no means least, four-wheel hydraulic disc brakes (the first disc-brake-equipped entrants to ever run Le Mans, and being the only cars so outfitted among the 1953 field) — all of which helped make them lighter, more powerful and more nimble. And so these C-Types achieved in 1953 one of the greatest-ever Jaguar victories at Le Mans, placing as they did first, second and fourth — the fourth-placed car being the example shown here (chassis no. XKC 052). By the end of the 1953 season with Jaguar now developing its next sports-racing model (soon to be known as the D-Type — see p. 144) chassis no. XKC 052 was sold to the famed Edinburgh-based Ecurie Ecosse racing team who successfully fielded it in numerous subsequent races, which included three victories at Goodwood. The car then passed through several collectors' hands, and when eventually in 2015 it came up for sale it became the most expensive Jaguar ever sold at auction. But then its rarity and provenance really make this fabulous C-Type one of the hallowed marque's ultimate big cats.

Opposite: The No. 19 Works Jaguar C-Type Lightweight (chassis no. XKC 052), driven by Peter Whitehead and Ian Stewart (finished fourth), chasing down the No. 3 1952 Works Cunningham C-4RK Kammback coupe (chassis no. 5218R) driven by Charles Moran Jr. and John Gordon Bennett (finished tenth overall) during the 1953 24 Hours of Le Mans.

Overleaf: Detail of steering wheel, instrumentation and controls.

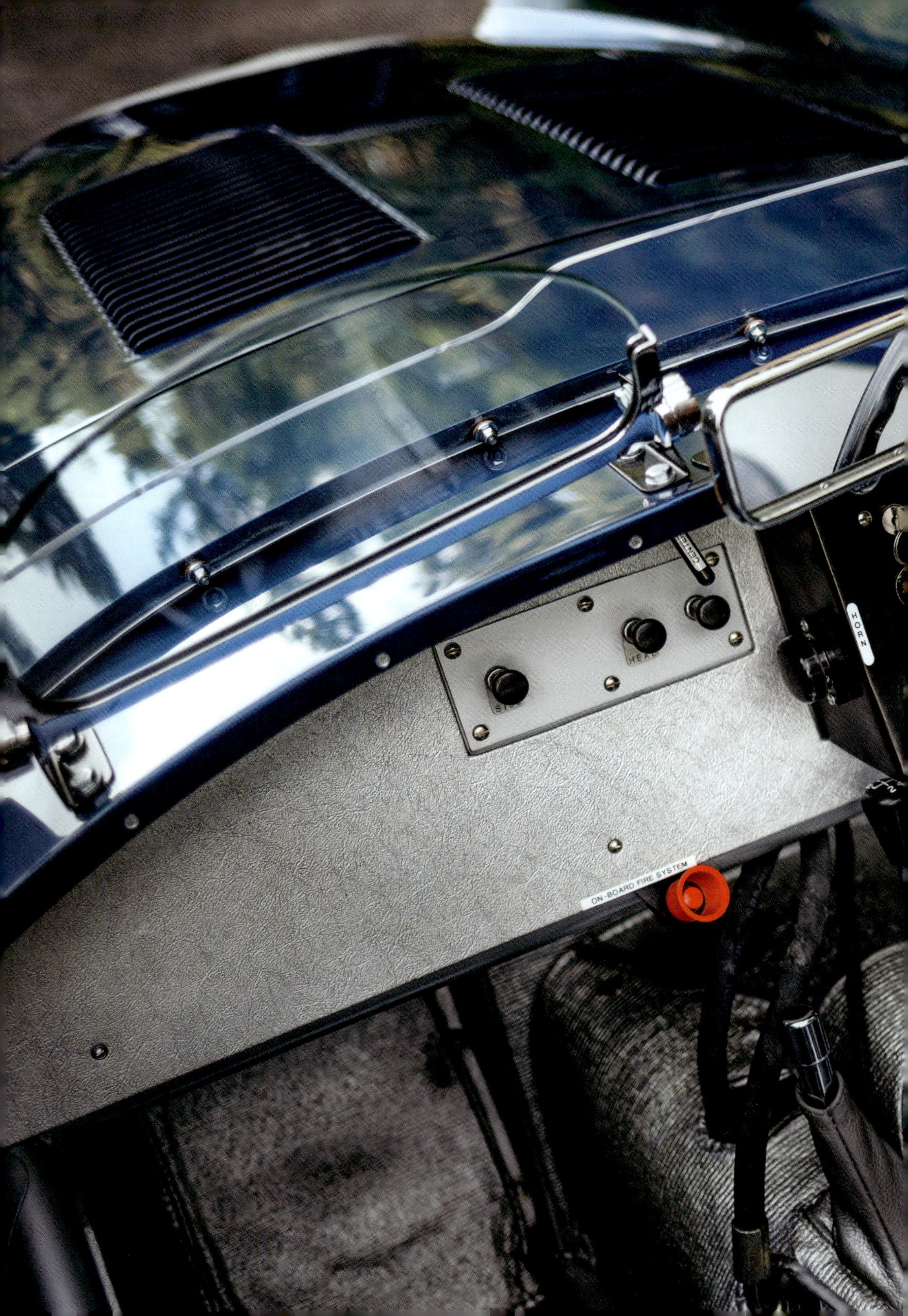
ON-BOARD FIRE SYSTEM
HORN

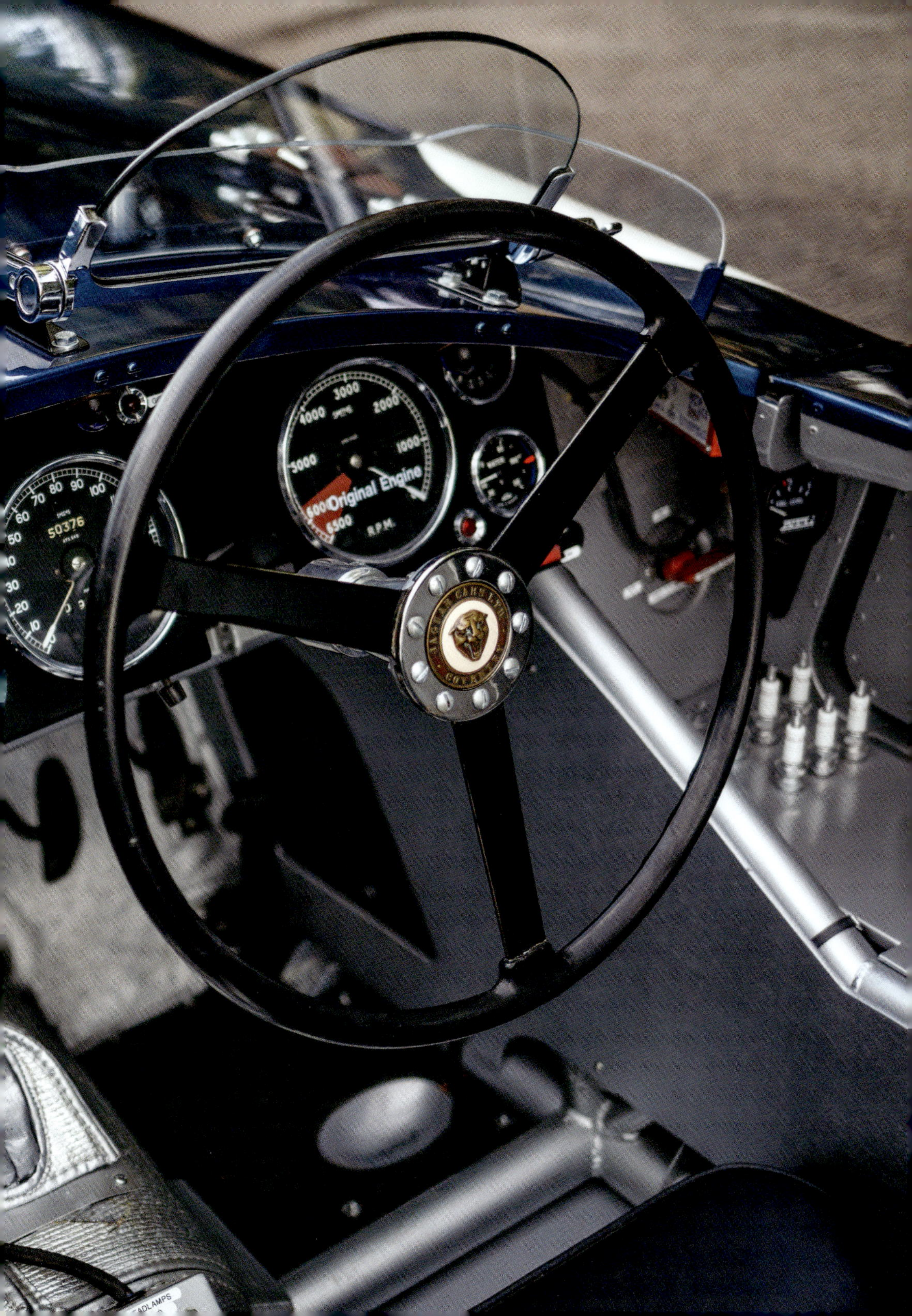
3000
4000
2000
1000
5000
Original Engine
6500
R.P.M.
50376
WATER

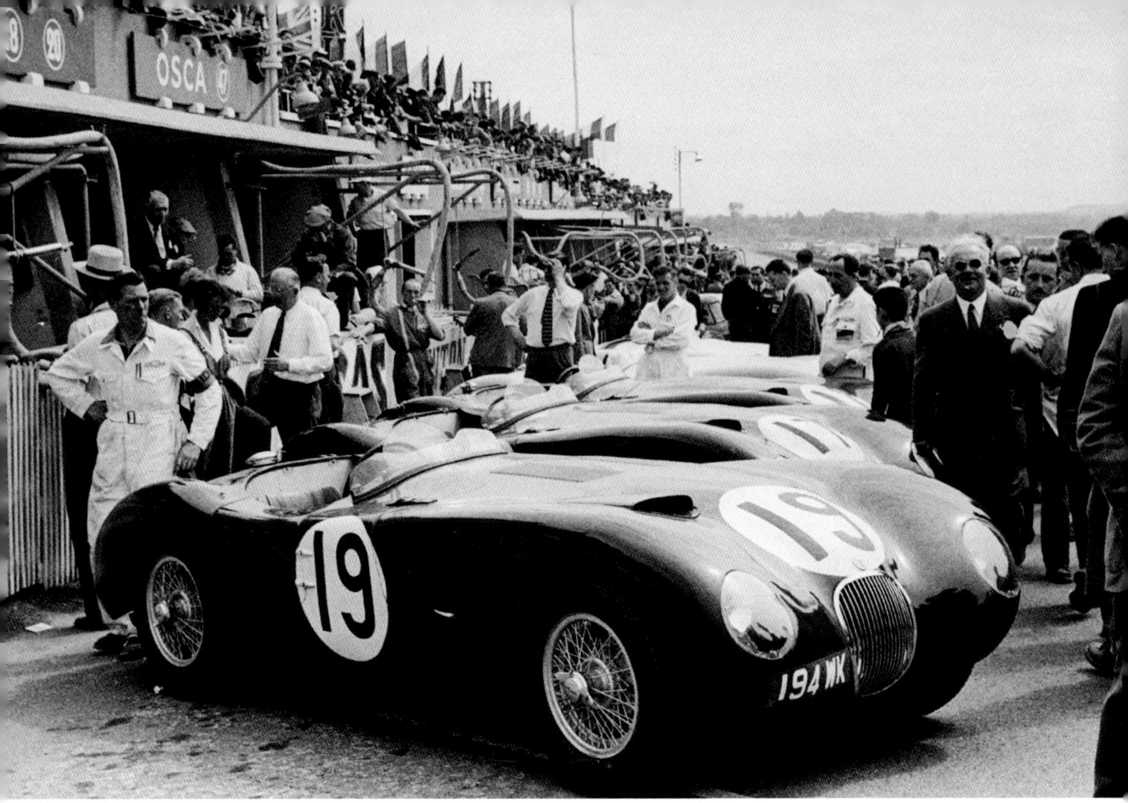

Above: Works Jaguar C-Type Lightweights lined up in pits at the 1953 24 Hours of Le Mans. Car No. 19 (chassis no. XKC 052), driven by Peter Whitehead and Ian Stewart, finished fourth. Car No. 17 (chassis no. XKC 053), driven by Stirling Moss and Peter Walker, finished second. Car No. 18, (chassis no. XKC 051), driven by Tony Rolt and Duncan Hamilton, won the race. Sir William Lyons, the founder of Jaguar Cars Limited, can be seen (in necktie) standing behind the No. 17 C-Type.

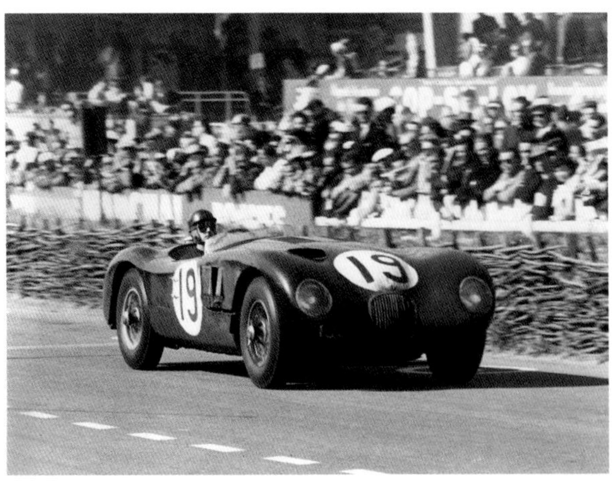

Left: The No. 19 Works Jaguar C-Type Lightweight (chassis no. XKC 052), driven by Peter Whitehead and Ian Stewart, which finished fourth overall, and third in class at the 1953 24 Hours of Le Mans.

Right: Cover of the 1952 24 Hours of Le Mans official program with artwork by Geo Ham (1900–1972) depicting the No. 18 Works Jaguar C-Type of Tony Rolt and Duncan Hamilton ahead of the No. 3 Works Cunningham C-4R Roadster driven by John Fitch and George Viola (aka George Rice) and the No. 26 Works Aston Martin DB3 Spider driven by Dennis Poore and Pat Griffith. None of these cars finished the race.

Below: Car No. 18, the winning Works Jaguar C-Type Light-weight driven by Tony Rolt and Duncan Hamilton, taking the checkered flag to claim victory in the 1953 24 Hours of Le Mans.

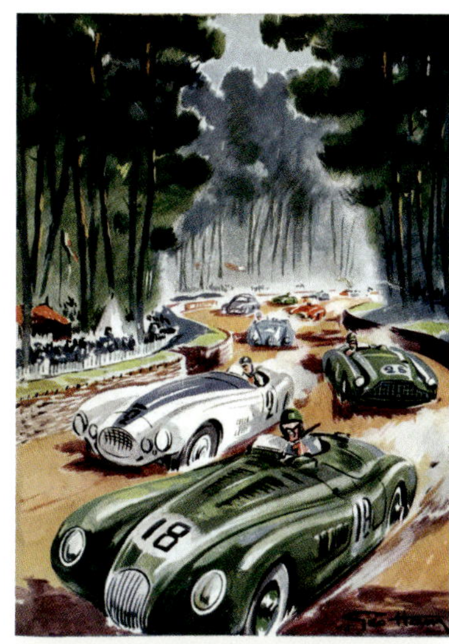

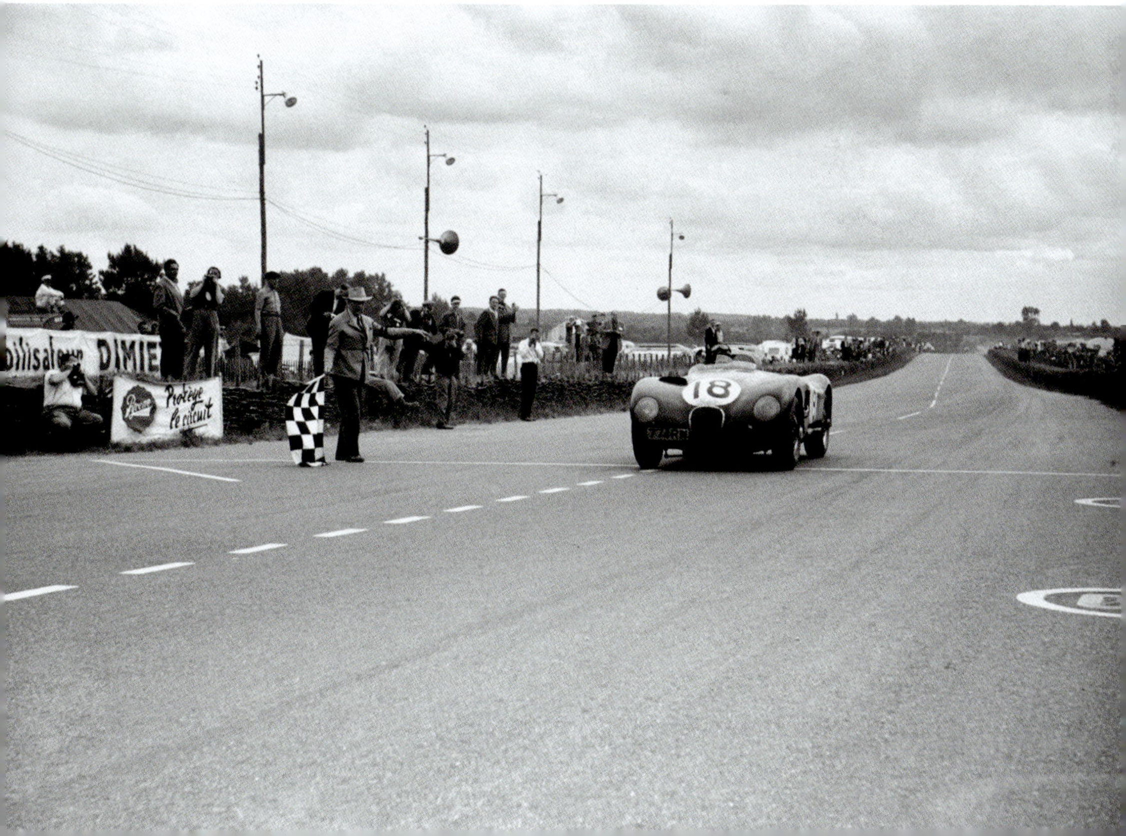

1955

Mercedes-Benz 300 SLR "Uhlenhaut Coupé"

MANUFACTURED 1955 | ENGINE 2,982 cc (182 cu. in.), DOHC inline 8-cylinder | HORSEPOWER 310
TOP SPEED 290 km/h (180 mph) | TRANSMISSION 5-speed
NUMBER PRODUCED 2

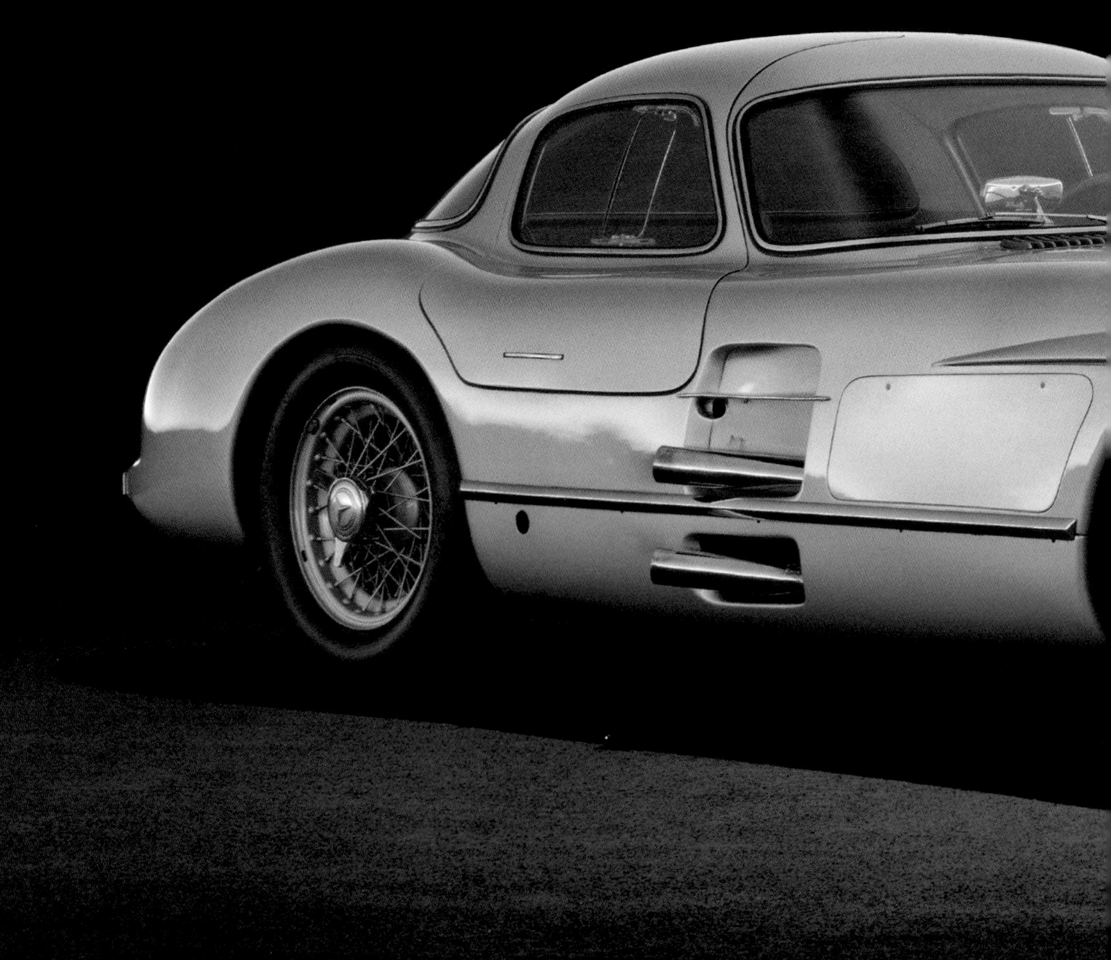

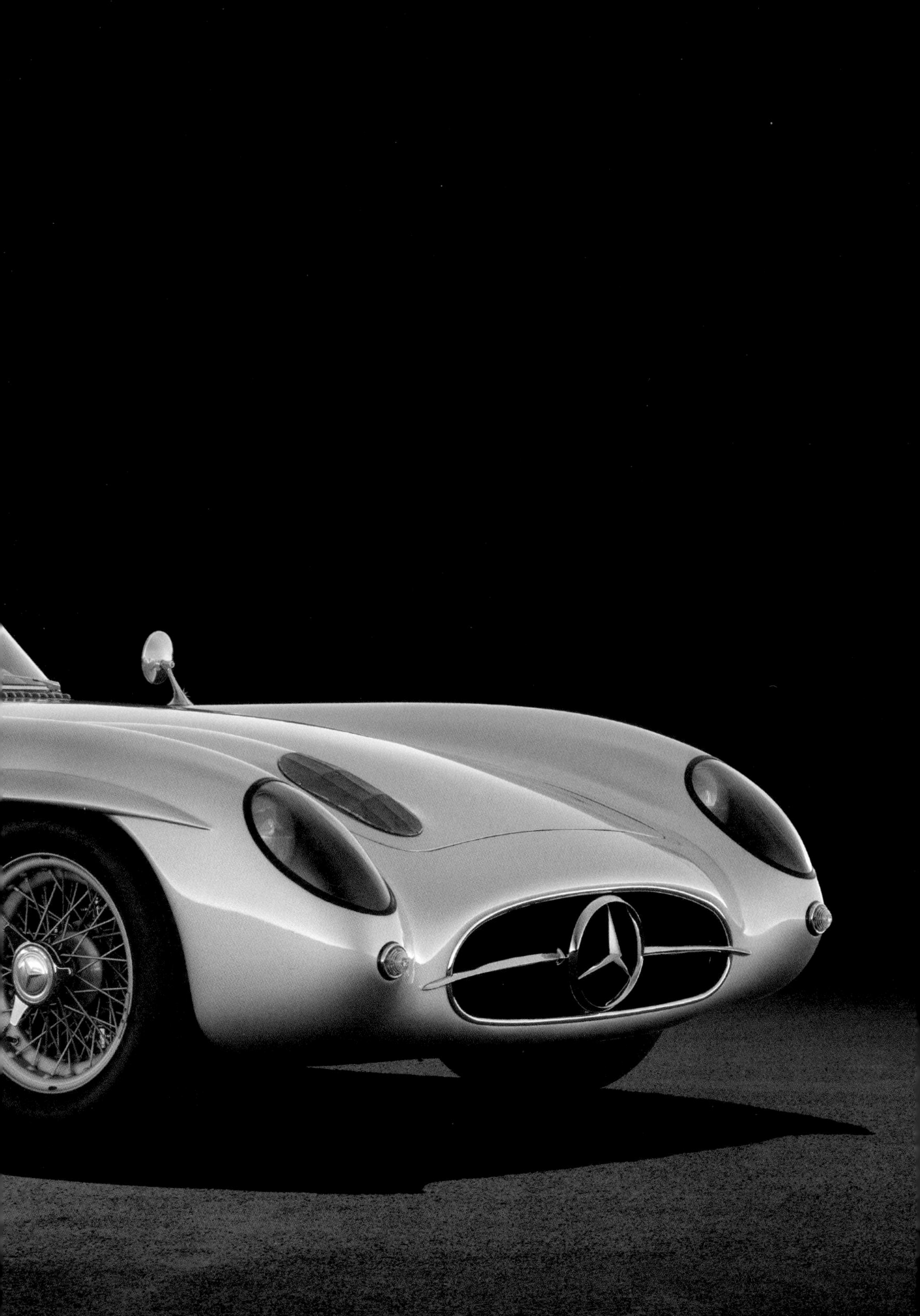

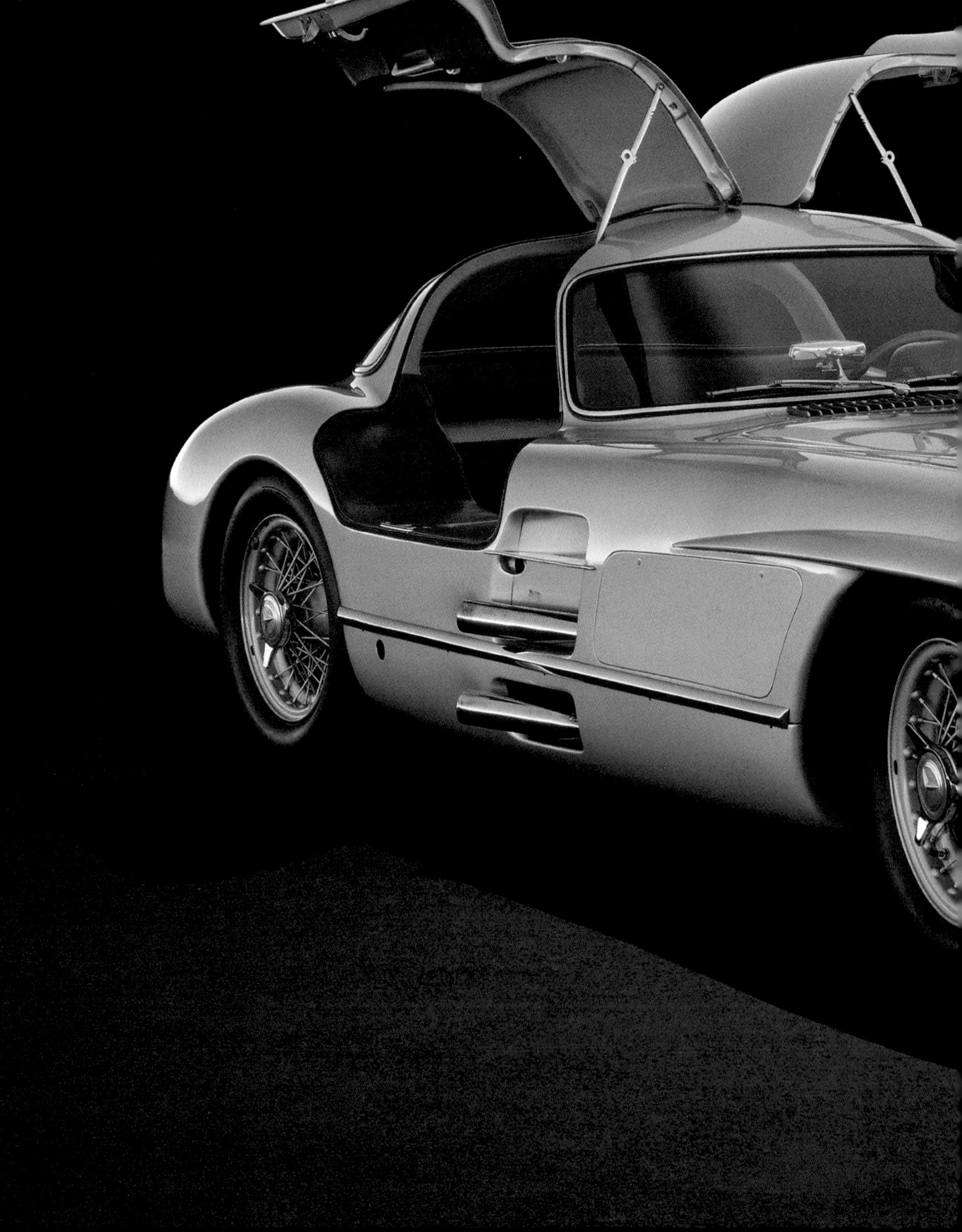

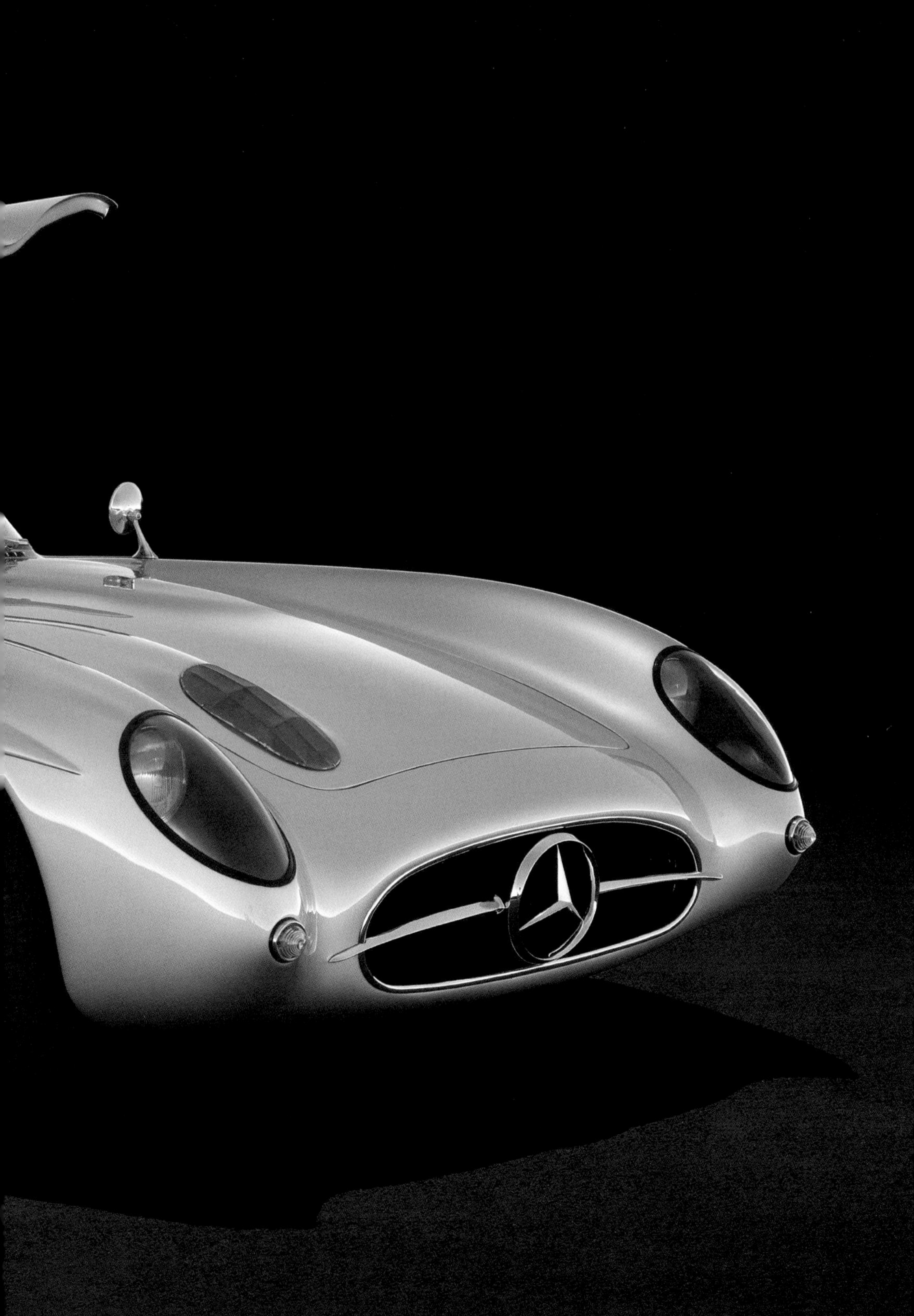

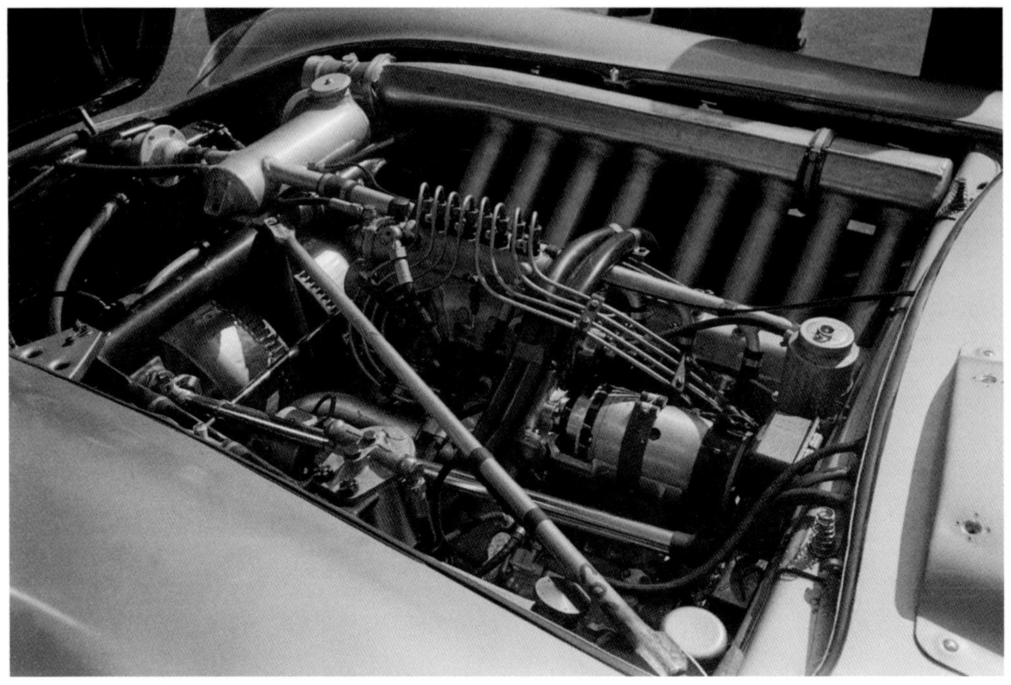

Previous: Side view of the Mercedes-Benz 300 SLR "Uhlenhaut Coupé" showing open exhaust pipes. A suitcase-sized exhaust silencer was retrofitted for a period of time to the car by Rudolf Uhlenhaut to help reduce its deafening engine noise so he could use it as his daily driver.

Above: Detail of the Mercedes-Benz 300 SLR 2,982 cc (182 cu. in.), direct fuel-injected DOHC inline eight-cylinder engine. Derived from the earlier W 196 engine the 300 SLR unit was increased in displacement from 2.5 to 3 liters and was not cast but constructed from sheets of a silicon and aluminum alloy known as silumin. Depending on the engine tune and fuel used, it could produce up to 340 hp. Providing a top speed of 290 km/h (180 mph), this was the power plant of the era's fastest road car.

Sold by RM Sotheby's in 2022 for $143m, by far the highest price ever paid for a car and among the ten highest prices ever achieved for any item at auction, the 1955 Mercedes-Benz 300 SLR "Uhlenhaut Coupé" was originally developed for the 1955 race season. Only two examples were constructed from a run of ten W 196 chassis (nos. 7 & 8). Their open-top 300 SLR siblings famously achieved a remarkable string of victories in their debut 1955 season, including an epic 1-2 finish at the 1955 Mille Miglia with Stirling Moss piloting the winning car. Other notable wins that year included a 1-2 victory at the Targa Florio, a 1-2-3 finish at the RAC Tourist Trophy in Dundrod, Ireland, as well as victories at the German and Swedish Grand Prix — all of which culminated in an overall win of the World Sportscar Championship. But rather than resting on its laurels, Mercedes-Benz's race department was always looking for design improvements in order to retain its competitive edge going into the next race. To this end, Head of the Test Department at Mercedes-Benz, the legendary Rudolf Uhlenhaut, selected the two aforementioned chassis (nos. 7 & 8) for significant modification. These were then widened to create a coupé version of the 300 SLR race car, which thanks to having a "closed" body would help to reduce the inevitable stresses and strains exerted on a driver during a long-distance, endurance race.

The two resulting 300 SLR coupés featured distinctive "gullwing" doors, which opened upward and outward in order to clear their space frames' high sill beams. The intention had been to race these new beautifully bodied beasts at the sixth Carrera Panamericana, however, that race was canceled in August 1955 due to safety concerns following the Le Mans disaster two months prior. This was then followed by Mercedes-Benz's official announcement in October 1955 that it was withdrawing from motorsports competition at the end of that fateful season. This meant that Uhlenhaut's 300 SLR coupés were never put through their paces on the track. As Mercedes-Benz explains, "the fact that the 300 SLR Coupé was not just left to gather dust was down to Rudolf Uhlenhaut, who ultimately had also created this driving machine. An excellent driver himself, Uhlenhaut covered some incredible distances in numerous journeys across Europe in one of the two examples of the car. This proved to be an impressive demonstration of the reliability and high everyday practicality of this top-class 300-hp racing sports car." Nevertheless, Uhlenhaut did make one concession for its road usage — a huge exhaust silencer fitted to one side of the car, which helped reduce the ear-splitting noise of its engine. In fact, its creator used this street-legal racer as his own personal company car, and as a result it went on to become known as the "Uhlenhaut Coupé."

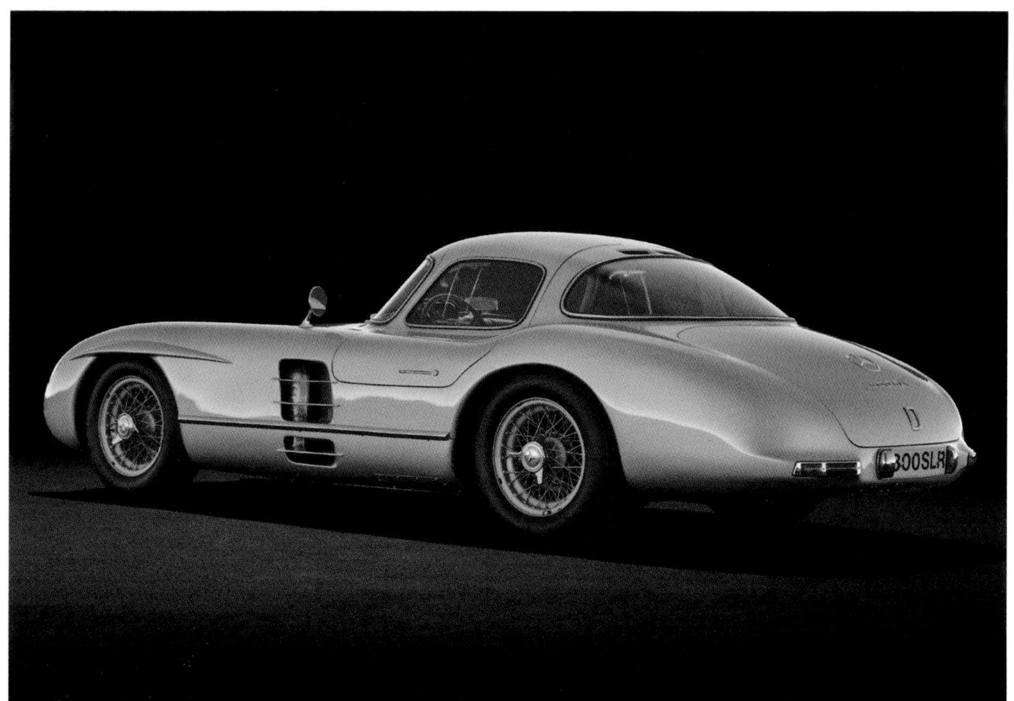

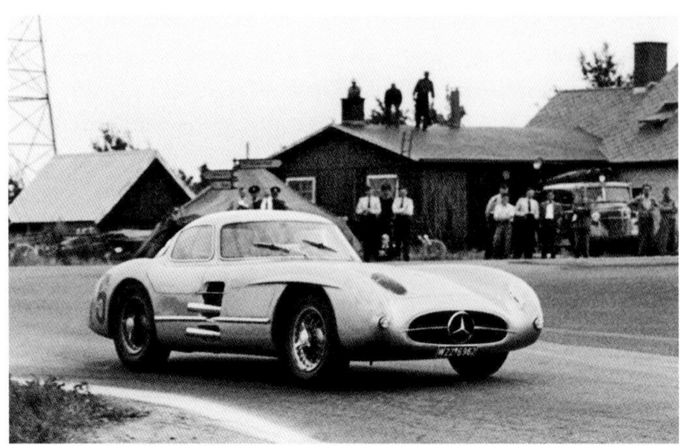

Left: The 300 SLR "Uhlenhaut Coupé" undergoing testing with Rudolf Uhlenhaut at the wheel during the 1955 Swedish Grand Prix in Kristianstad. Uhlenhaut drove the car there himself to undertake some test sessions in order to prove the car's remarkable reliability.

Overleaf: Detail of Mercedes-Benz 300 SLR "Uhlenhaut Coupé" cockpit, steering wheel, instruments and controls.

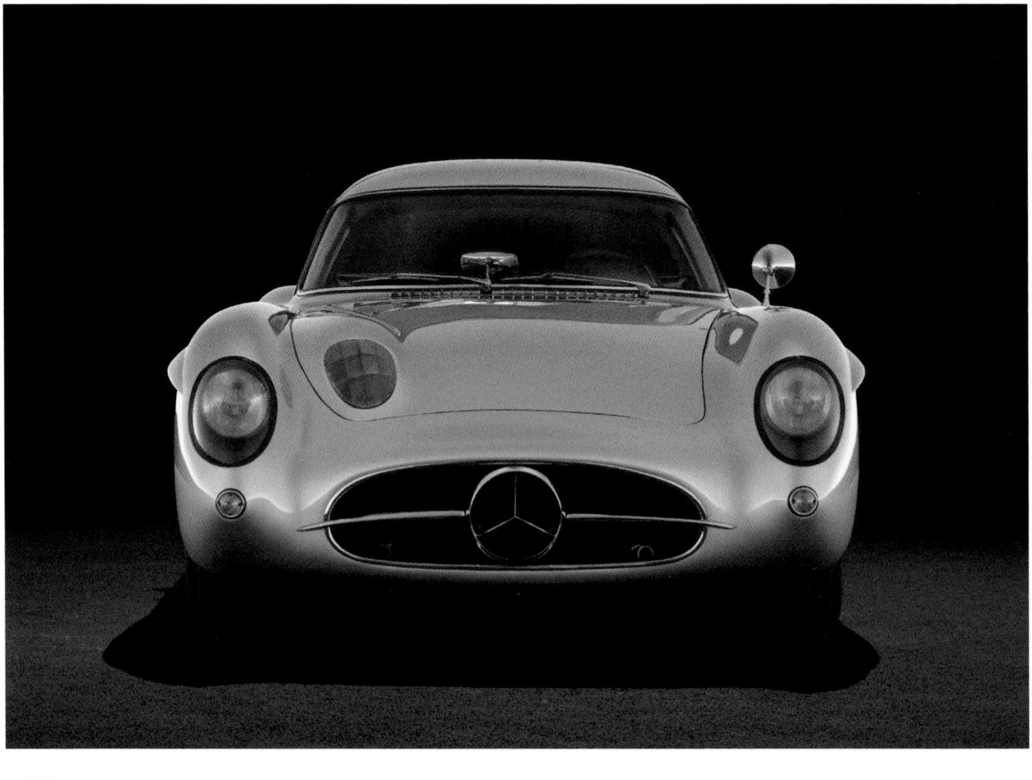

In 1956, this powerful yet beautiful car was subjected to a 3,500 kilometer endurance trial by a test-driver working for the Swiss publication *Automobil Revue*. As he enthusiastically noted, "We are driving in a car which ... overtakes the vehicles of other road users in a matter of seconds, for which 200 km/h on a quiet motorway is a stroll in the park, a car whose cornering safety seems to defy the laws of centrifugal force, a car which uses less petrol at 160 km/h than many a saloon traveling at a more modest speed, but also a car which can never be bought and which no average driver would ever buy either ... Our test car cruised through towns and villages in Switzerland, Germany and Italy, tackled steep mountain roads at full throttle, endured the severest of acceleration and braking trials on the track at Monza, covered long motorway stretches at an average speed approaching 200 km/h, reached a top speed of 284 km/h, once even 290 km/h, and in the meantime served as a pure means of transport without suffering even the slightest breakdown." And if that was not enough, the car had prior to this already clocked up 12,000 kilometers thanks to Uhlenhaut's multiple breakneck-speed trips in it across Europe, proving its high-speed stamina to any would-be doubters. This was, as *Automobil Revue* again jubilantly noted, a car that took "unsensationalism to the extreme ... while observing conventional road etiquette it is still possible to achieve average speeds which seem utopian."

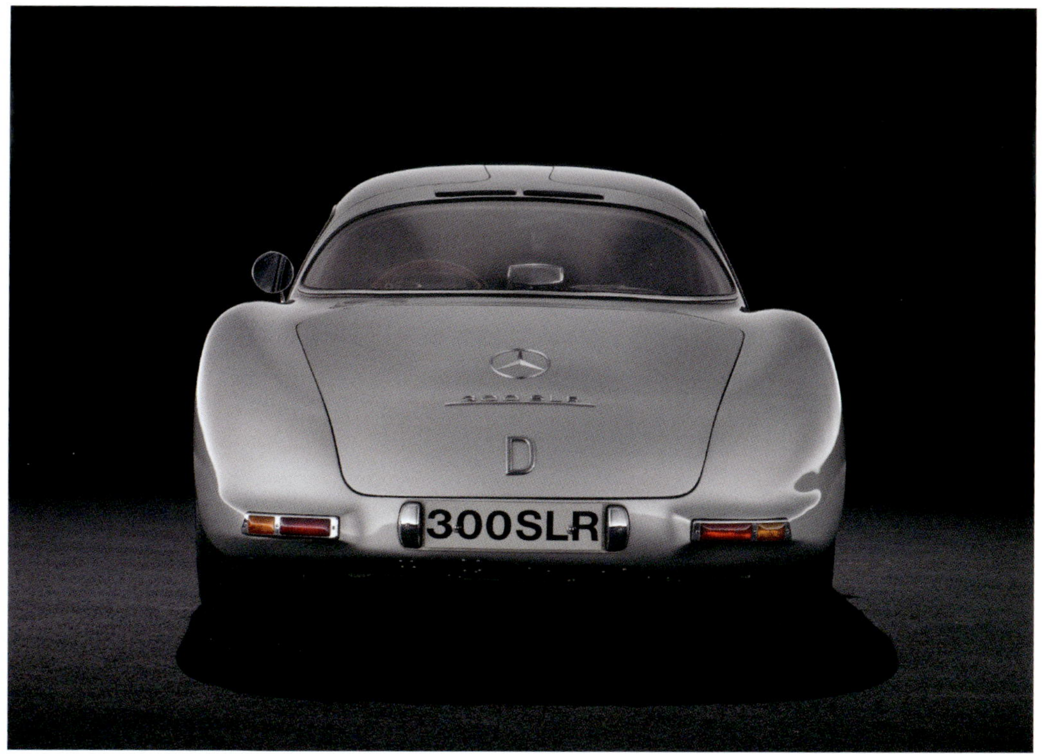

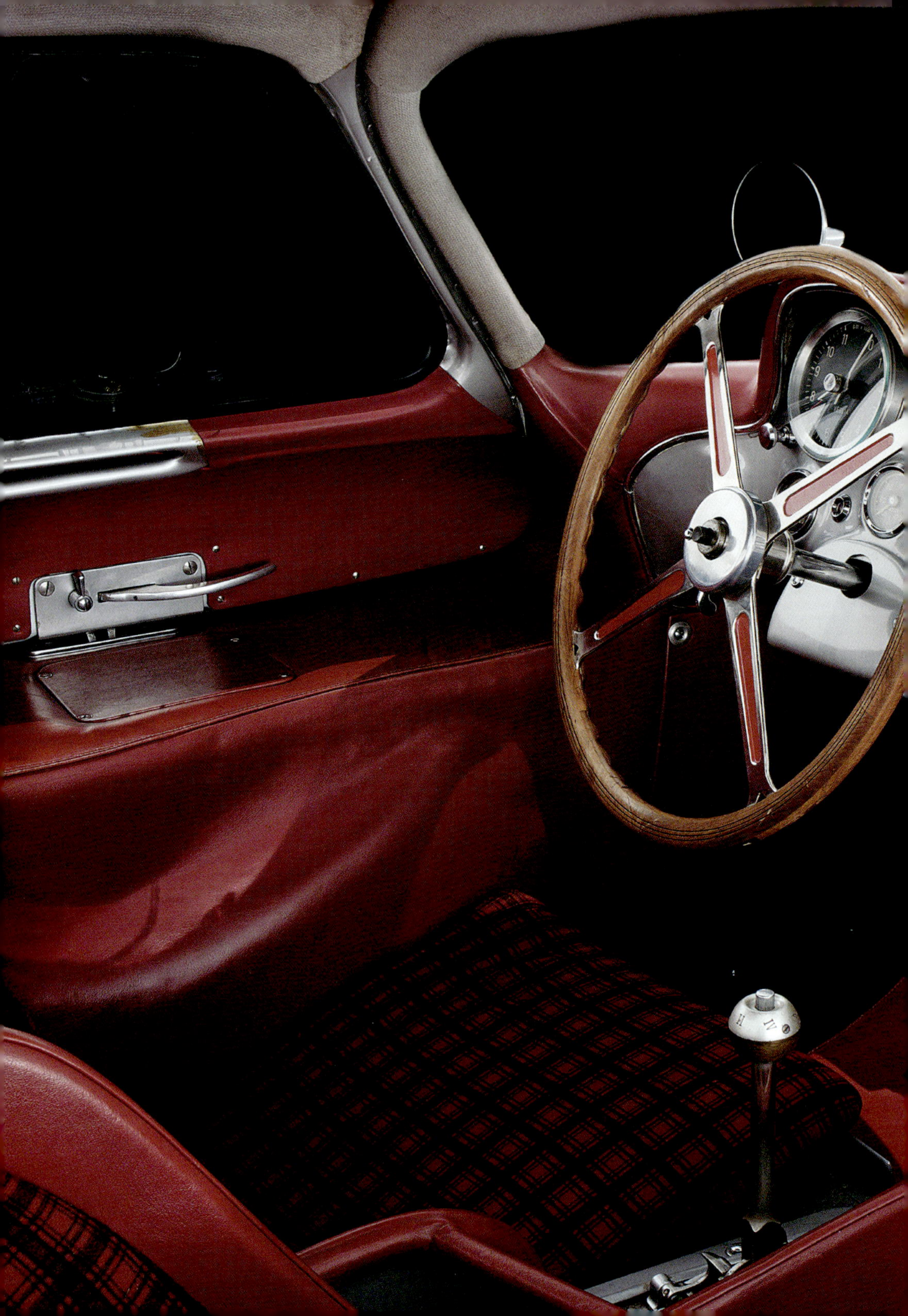

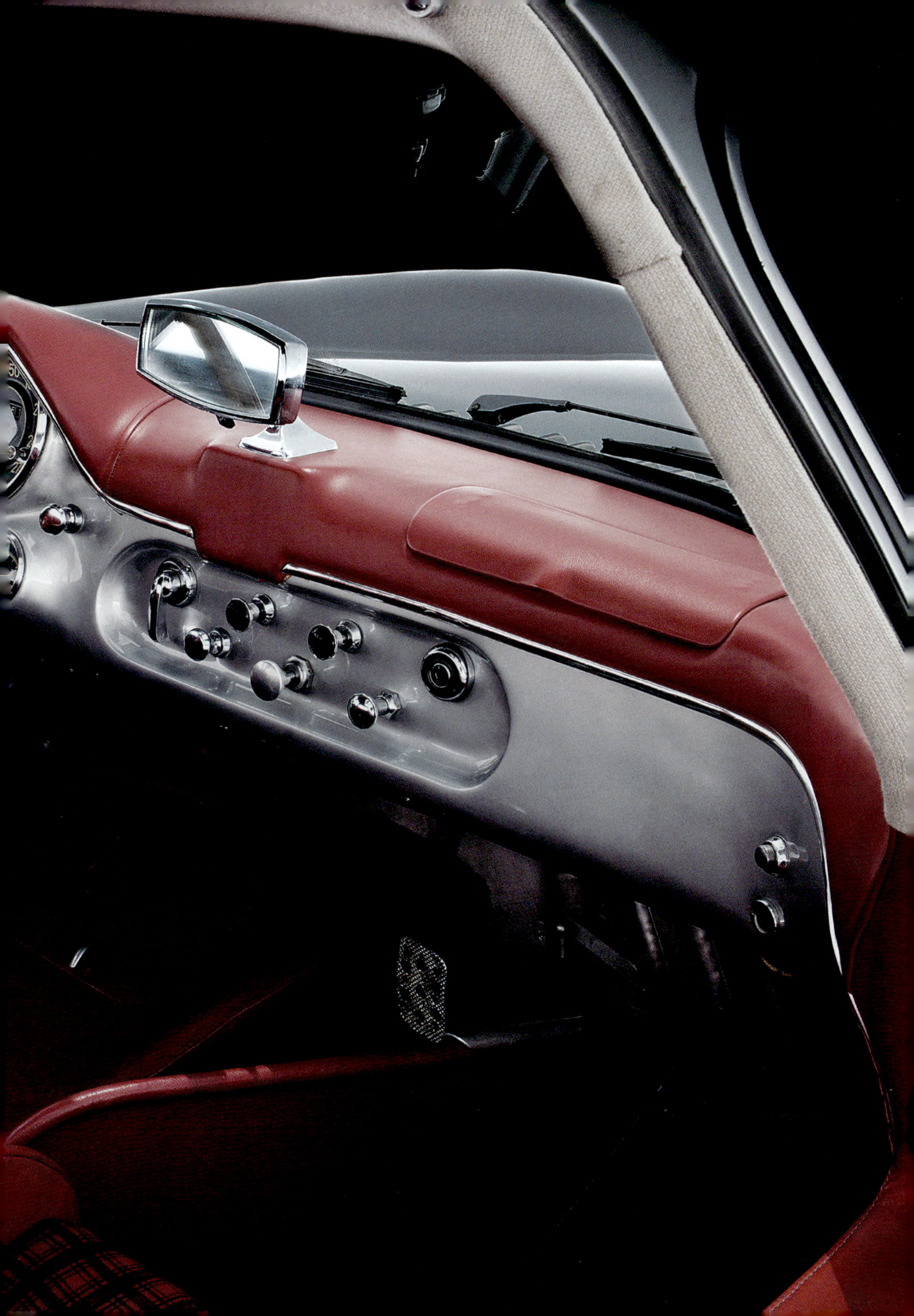

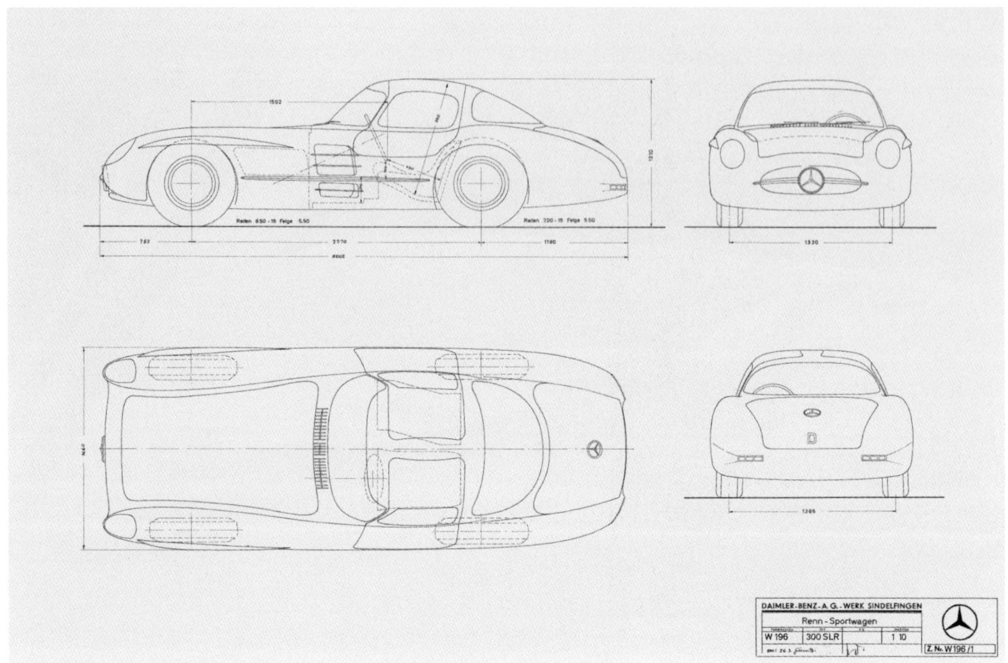

Above: Technical drawing of Mercedes-Benz 300 SLR "Uhlenhaut Coupé," 1955.

Opposite (top:) Mechanic working on the 300 SLR "Uhlenhaut Coupé" between test sessions in Kristianstad during the 1955 Swedish Grand Prix.

Opposite (bottom): Mercedes-Benz engineer and race car designer Rudolf Uhlenhaut with the 300 SLR "Uhlenhaut Coupé," which was a sibiling of the 300 SLR (W 196 S) sports racer that he also designed. Only two coupé variants were constructed and Uhlenhaut used one of them as his daily driver company car.

This type of high praise was for once entirely justified, as the Uhlenhaut Coupé was completely in a class of its own back then. Weighing only 1,117 kilograms (2,462 lb.), this elegant two-seater provided 310 hp, which enabled a top speed of 290 km/h (180 mph)—an astonishing speed for the time that made it the fastest road car of its day. And in many ways, it still remains in a class of its own, at least in terms of collectability. Both Uhlenhaut's iconic gull-winged prototypes formed an important part of Mercedes-Benz's world-class vehicle collection, until 2022 when the present example with a red interior was sold by RM Sotheby's at a world record price. Its stablemate with a blue interior remains in the company's possession. Not surprisingly, they attract a huge amount of attention from the media and public alike, especially when one gets an airing at any concours-type event because, as the renowned motorsports historian Karl Ludvigsen once noted, the Uhlenhaut Coupé is quite simply "one of the most exciting cars that Mercedes-Benz has ever built."

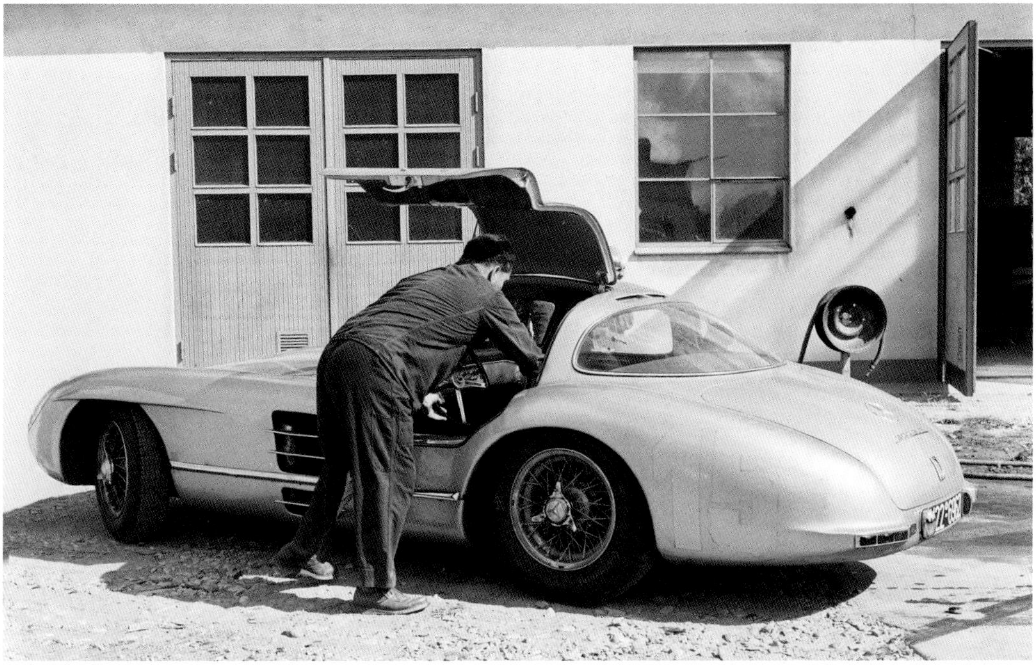

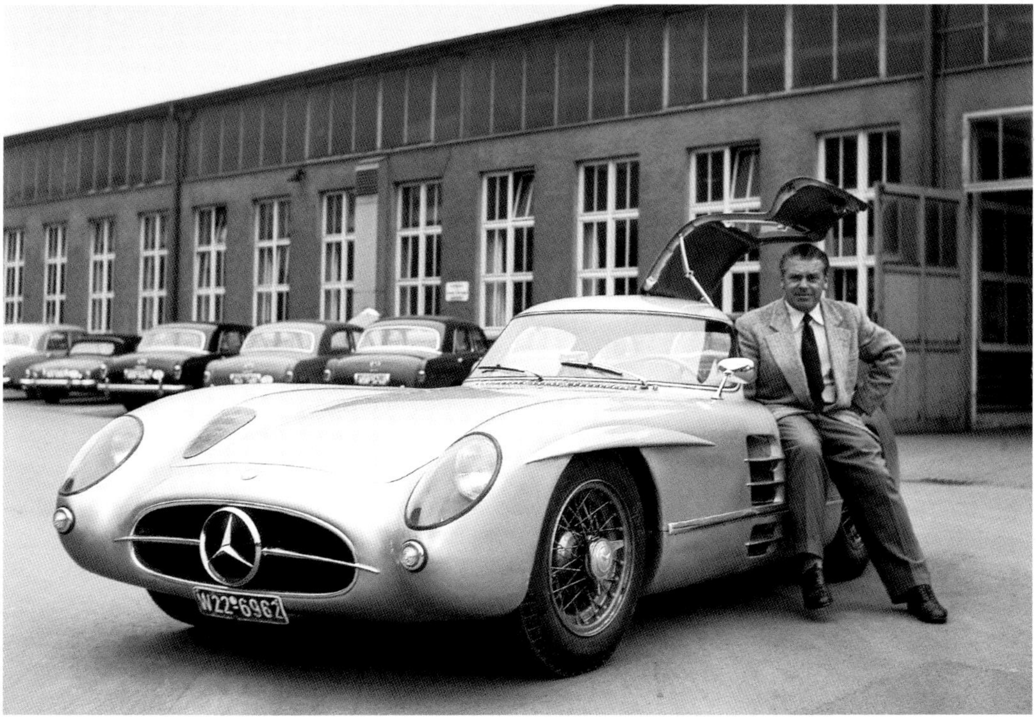

1955

Mercedes-Benz 300 SL Alloy Gullwing Coupé

MANUFACTURED 1955 | ENGINE 2,996 cc (183 cu. in.), SOHC inline 6-cylinder | HORSEPOWER 215
TOP SPEED 250 km/h (155 mph) | TRANSMISSION 4-speed
NUMBER PRODUCED 29

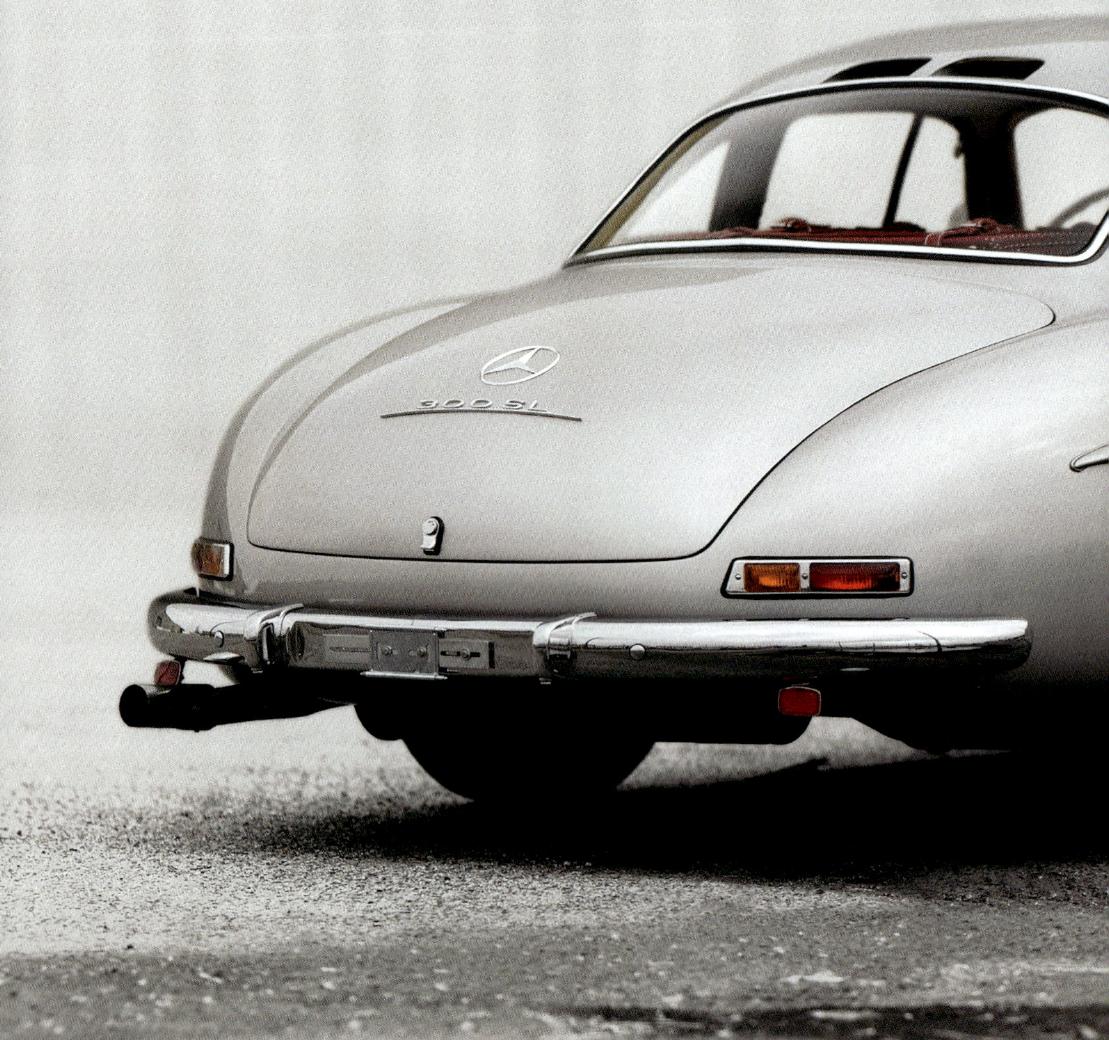

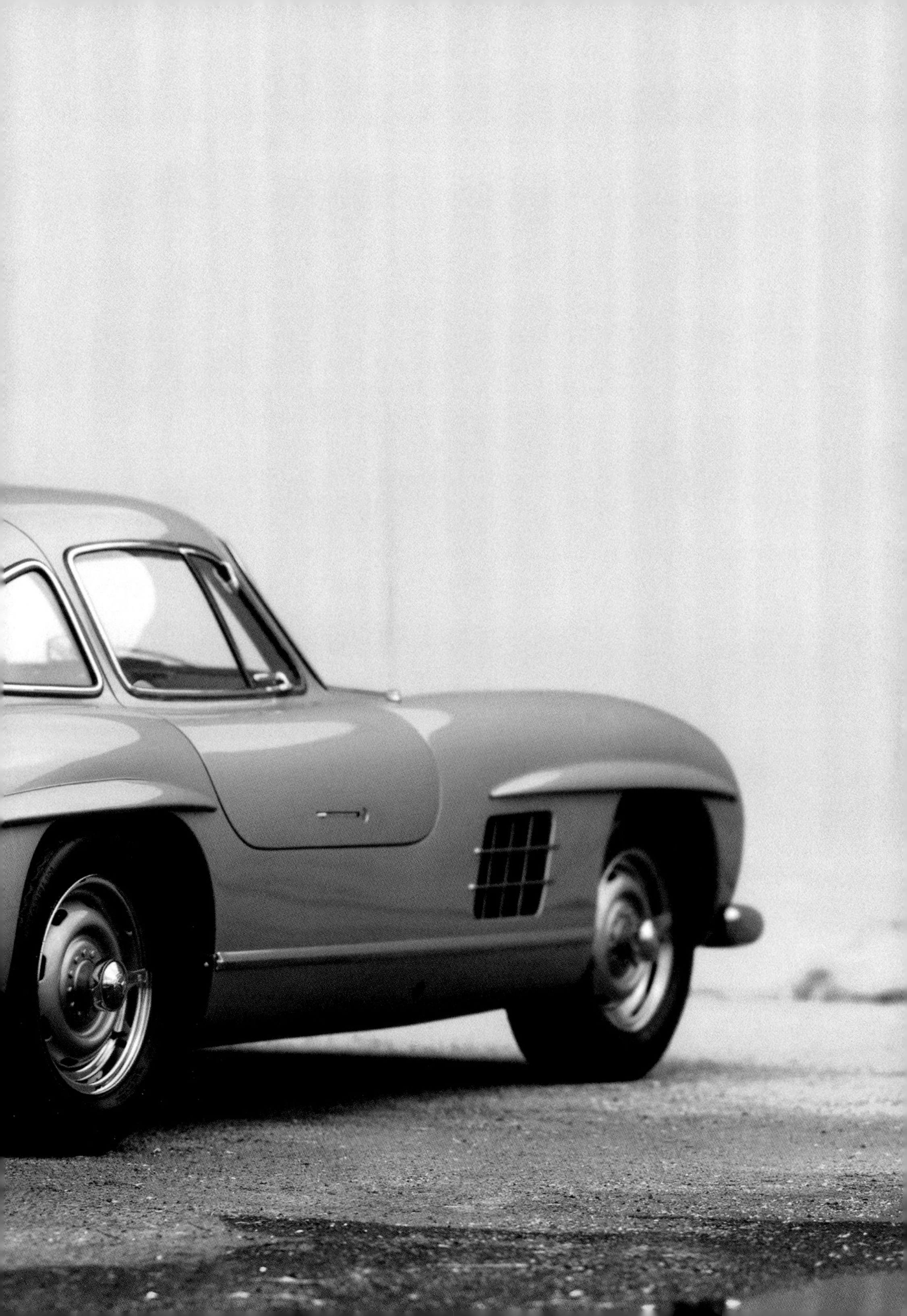

Arguably the best-known Mercedes-Benz of them all, the 300 SL "Gullwing" is simply among the most stunning cars ever produced. Indeed, if a car can be said to have a cool attitude then it has to be this one, with its streamlined purposeful form being a sublime example of Teutonic engineering excellence at its most refined. In fact, the attention to detail lavished on this model by Mercedes-Benz's famed team of ultra-talented designers and engineers was outstanding—from the handy directional pointers on its center caps to its thoughtfully laid out instrument panel to its elegantly profiled side intakes. Yet, this is a car where the whole is so much more than the sum of its exquisitely executed parts.

Not surprisingly, when it was unveiled at the International Motor Sports Show in New York in February 1954, the 300 SL immediately caught the attention of wealthy members of the international jet set as well as the emergent deep-pocketed sports car crowd, because this was a car that had it all: a beautiful body of exquisite proportions that enveloped a race-bred power plant, which provided exceptional performance. It was quickly nicknamed the "Gullwing," thanks to its distinctive roof-hinged doors, which when opened evoke the form of a seabird in flight. Production of the 300 SLs commenced in August 1954, however, the lighter alloy version, as shown here, was introduced the following year. As RM Sotheby's explains, "not all Gullwings were created equal, and if you were a well-heeled sports car enthusiast in 1955, the aluminum-bodied 300 SL was the car to have. Its lighter bodywork made it even more competitive against other British and Italian

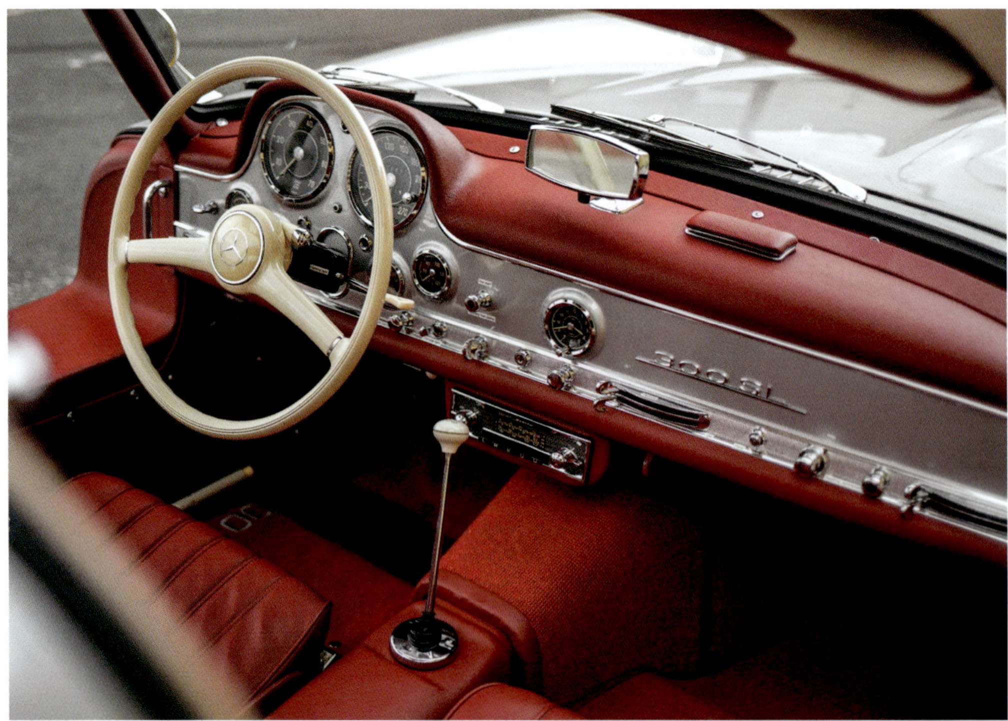

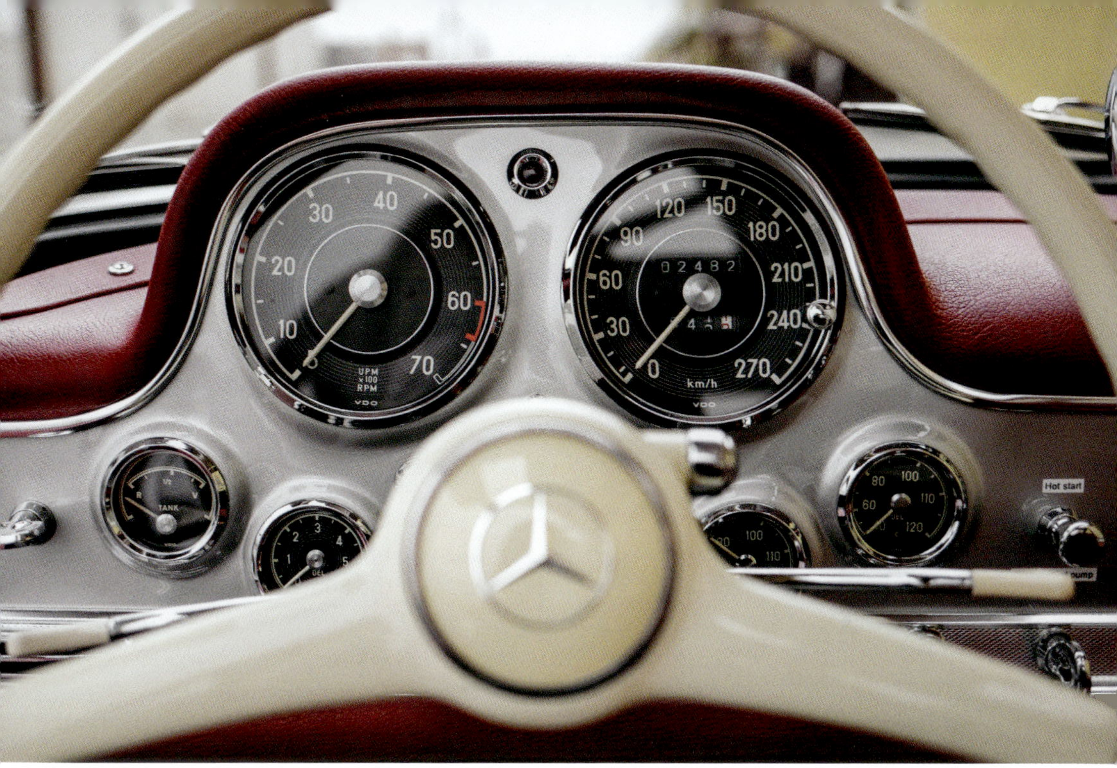

Opposite: Detail of Mercedes-Benz 300 SL Alloy Gullwing Coupé cockpit, steering wheel, instrumentation and controls.

Above: Detail of instrument cluster on 300 SL Coupé dash panel.

3-liter sports cars. Additionally, these cars were also outfitted with the Sonderteile engine, which utilized a competition-spec camshaft, increasing power output by 15 horsepower. With both a slight increase in power and decrease in overall weight, the additional performance in these cars was instantly discernable from behind the wheel." All of this meant that the sleek aluminum-bodied Gullwing was capable of outperforming its competitors, whether as a sports car on a highway or as a racer tearing around a track. As a result, the alloy-bodied Gullwing is rightly considered to be the ultimate variant of this famed model, yet only 29 of these exclusive cars were ever built by Mercedes-Benz, which, of course, makes them especially prized among collectors today. Indeed, the alloy version equated to only two percent of total Gullwing production of 1,400 steel-bodied examples. The matching-numbers 300 SL Alloy Gullwing (chassis no. 5500786) shown here, is an excellent and highly specified example of this rare model, boasting sports suspension, Rudge knock-off wheels and even a special two-piece luggage set. It also possesses an especially nice provenance having been originally ordered by the Swiss industrialist and sports car enthusiast René Wassermann, who picked it up direct from Mercedes-Benz's factory in Stuttgart and then drove it back home to Switzerland himself. Eventually, Wassermann sold the car on and by the early 1960s it had landed up in the United States where it was acquired by

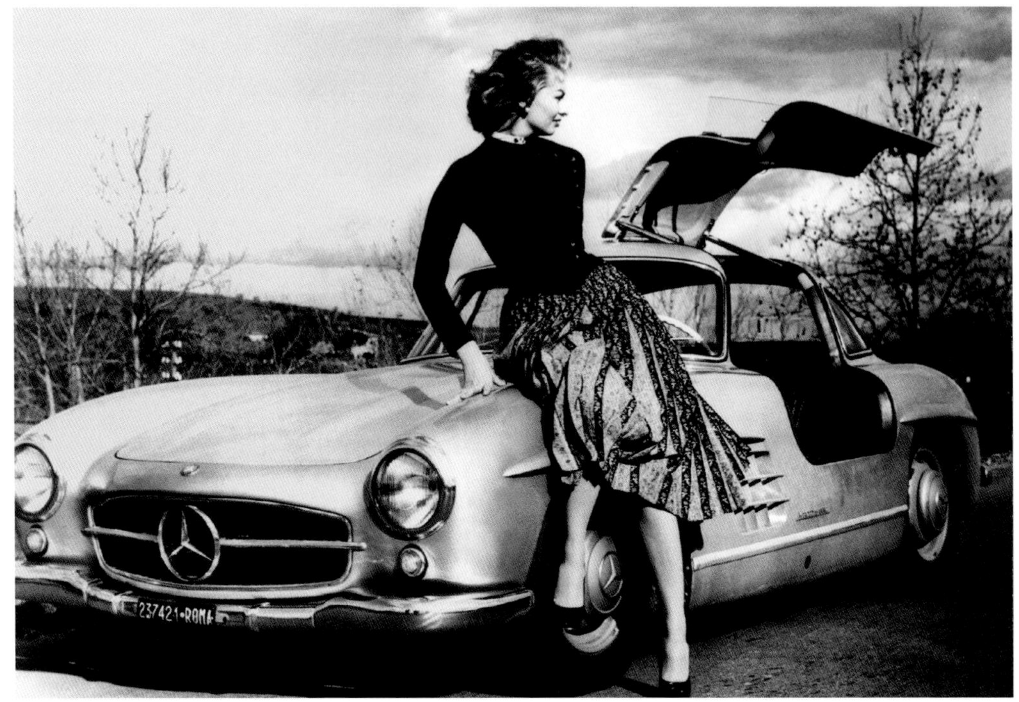

Above: The actress Sophia Loren photographed with her Mercedes-Benz 300 SL Gullwing Coupé, 1955. Perhaps the car she is best known for owning, which she posed with frequently, Sophia Loren received this 1955 steel-bodied Gullwing as a gift from her husband, the prolific Italian film producer Carlo Ponti.

Pennsylvania State Senator Theodore Newell Wood. He was a keen amateur sports car racer who served as president of the Hill Climb Association and also founded the Brynfan Tyddyn Road Races, which were held from 1952 to 1956.

After passing through the hands of several other people over the decades chassis no. 5500786 was subsequently purchased by the Swedish businessman and collector Hans Thulin in around 1989 who then tasked Kienle Automobiltechnik in Stuttgart with its full restoration. Known for being one of the foremost workshops for this specialized kind of work, Kienle prides itself on its meticulous attention to detail and its adherence to absolute factory correctness, and as a result the painstaking restoration of this rare survivor was utterly superb. In fact, this specific example represents many of the key attributes discerning collectors are seeking: a rare variant of an iconic model with matching numbers, a vehicle with a good provenance, and an example that has been sensitively restored by acclaimed marque specialists. Combining beauty and power, such a car will always command top dollar, because there are enough wealthy collectors out there who want only the crème de la crème.

Right: 1954 Mercedes-Benz factory photo showing the lightweight space frame construction of the 300 SL Coupé. It is from this that the "SL" (standing for "Super Leicht" or "Super Light") in the car's name is derived.

Below: Page from the 1955 Mercedes-Benz 300 SL Gullwing Coupé sales brochure.

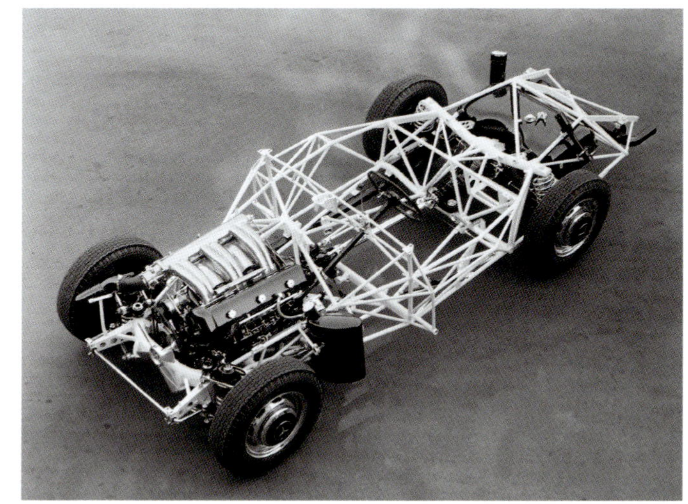

Leistung voraus TYP 300 SL

Den Gewinn aller Siege des Mercedes-Sterns legen die Konstrukteure der Daimler-Benz AG. mit diesem Sportwagen von souveräner Eleganz in die Hände ihrer Kunden.

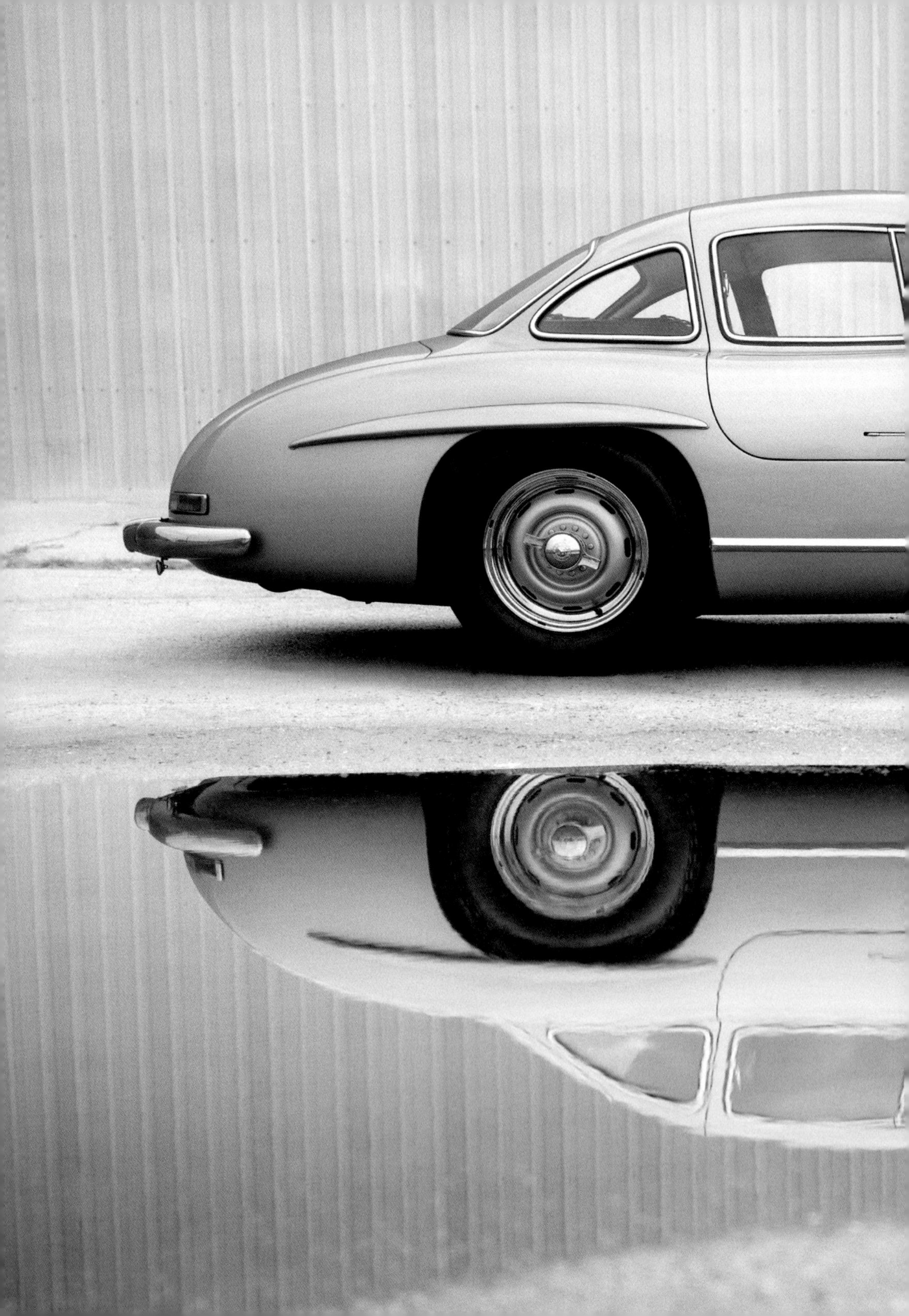

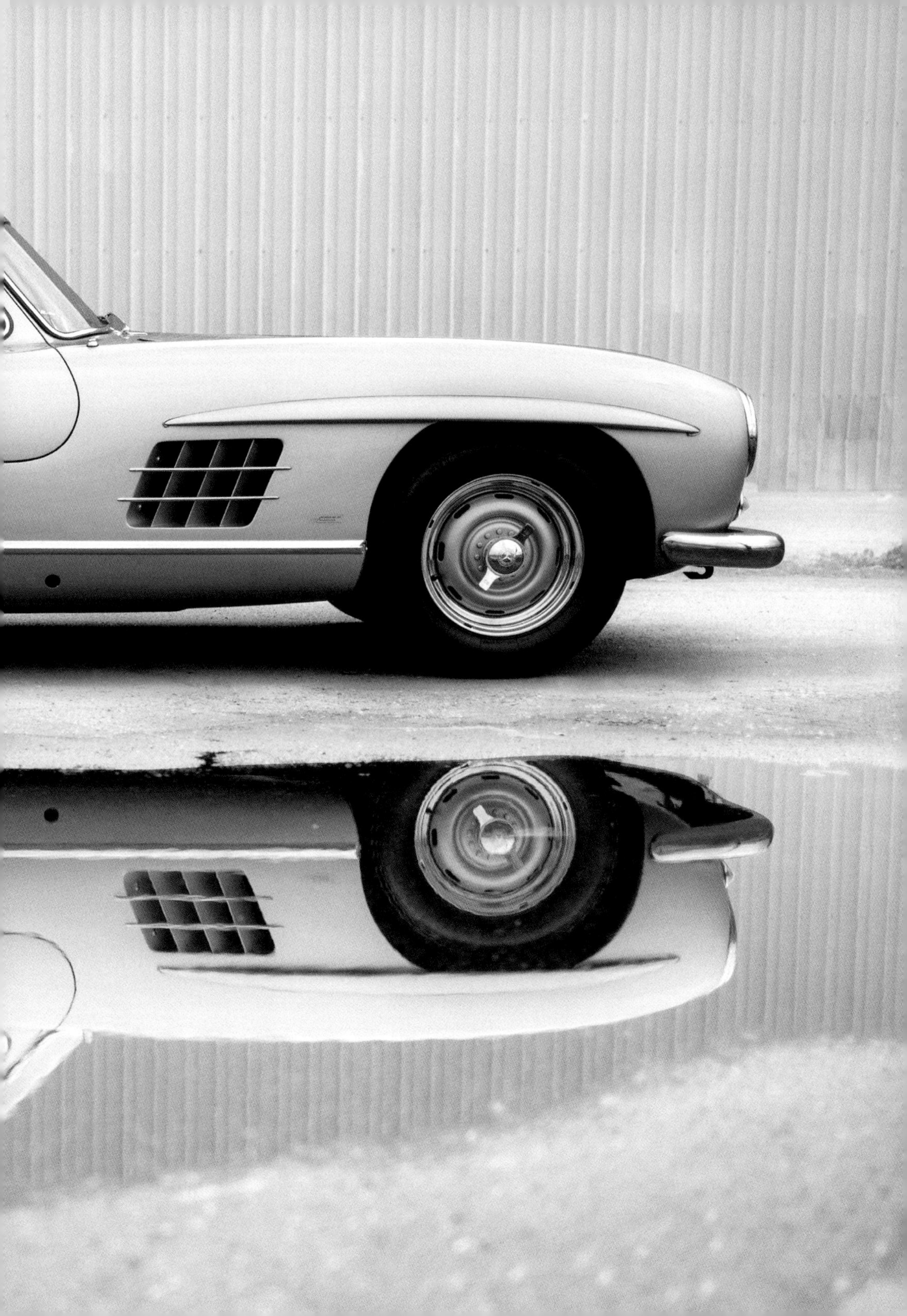

1955

Porsche 550 Spyder

MANUFACTURED 1953–56 | ENGINE 1,498 cc (91.4 cu. in.), DOHC per bank horizontally opposed 4-cylinder | HORSEPOWER 110
TOP SPEED 220 km/h (137 mph) | TRANSMISSION 4-speed
NUMBER PRODUCED 90

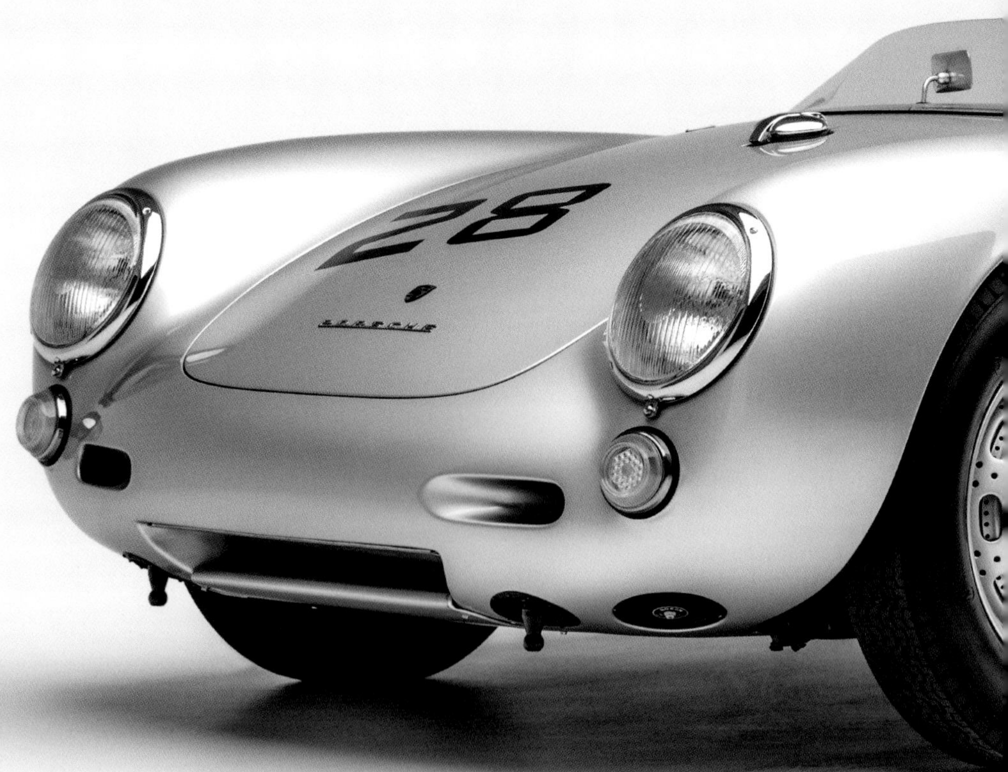

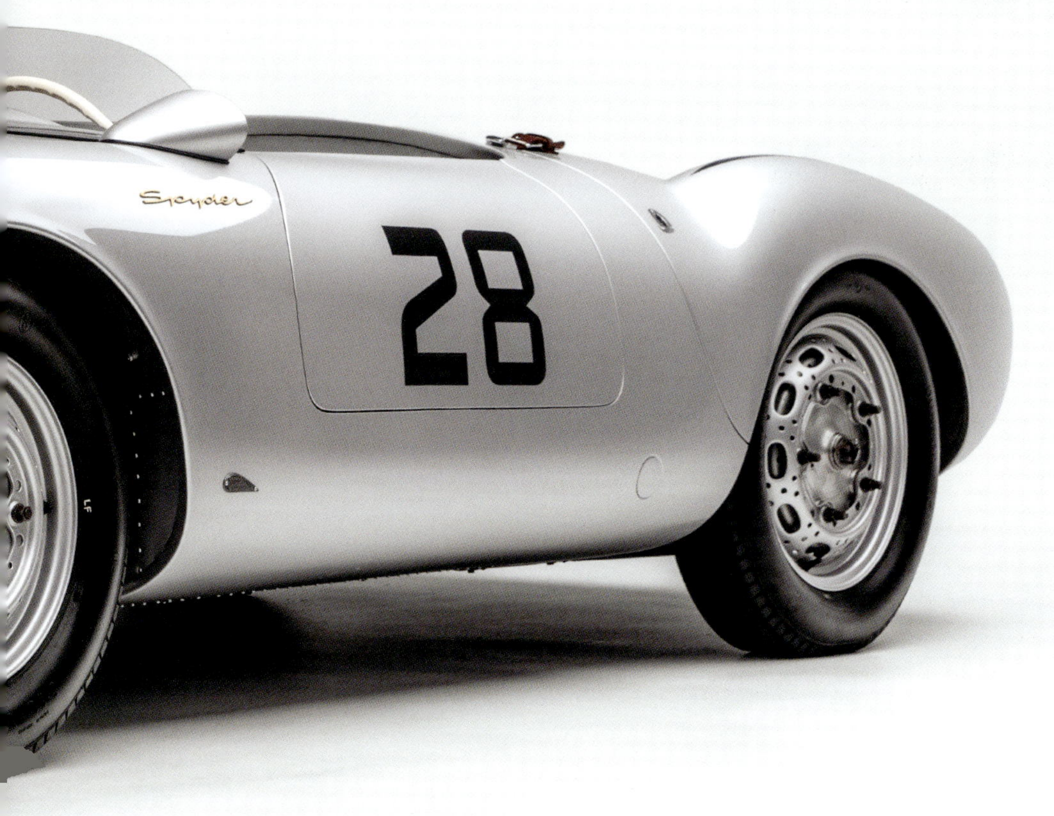
28
LF

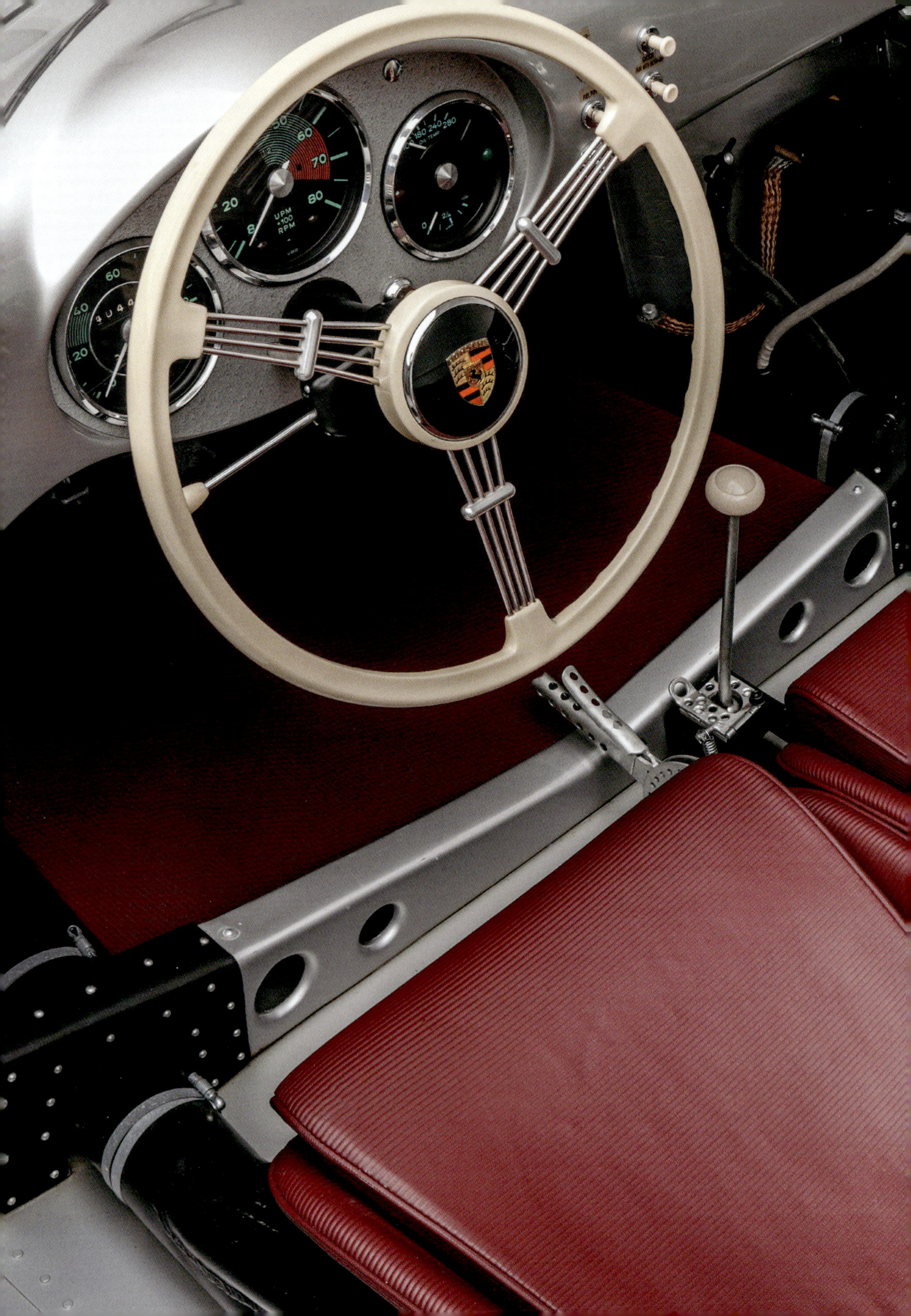

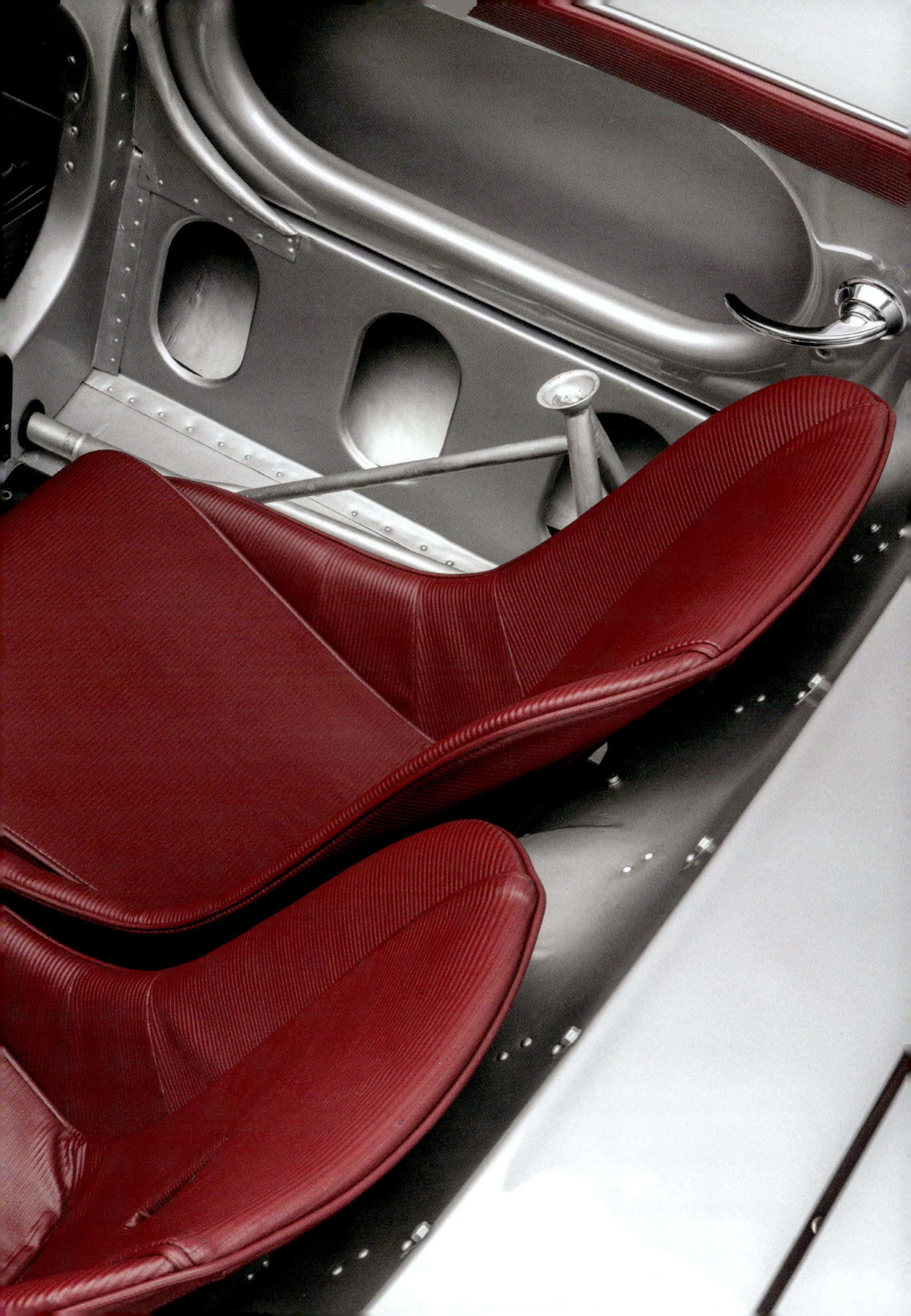

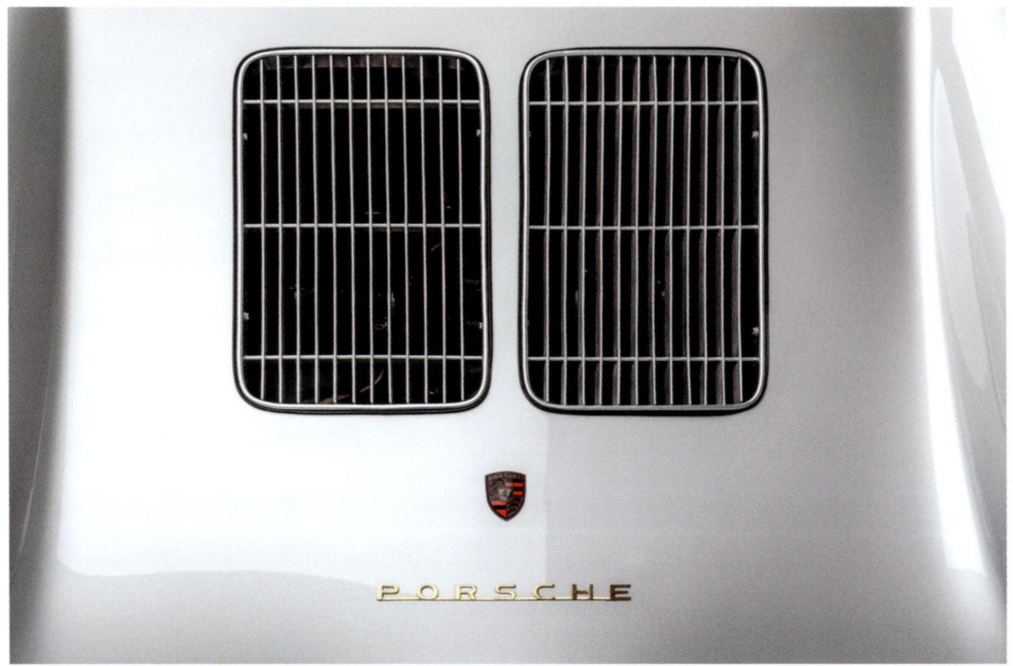

Previous: Detail of Porsche 550 Spyder cockpit, steering wheel, instrumentation and controls. Also showing is the internal structure of the lightweight aluminum body.

Above: Detail of Porsche 550 Spyder air vents on rear engine cover.

The design of the mid-engine Porsche 550 was originally inspired by the Porsche 356, which had been created previously by Ferdinand "Ferry" Porsche in 1948. Unlike this stylish runabout sports car, however, the 550 was a full-on competition-bred sports racer. As such, its design had also been influenced by the spider prototypes that the amateur German racing driver Helm Glöckler had developed and successfully raced in the early 1950s.

Specifically conceived for competition, the Porsche 550 was the first production race car that the Stuttgart-based company developed. By adopting a lightweight aluminum body mounted on a tubular ladder-frame chassis, Porsche's engineers were able to minimize its overall weight for increased high-speed capability. But more than this they also undertook extensive wind tunnel testing to develop and ultimately perfect an aerodynamically refined body form, so as to improve airflow and thereby eliminate as much drag as possible. The 550's bodywork was initially developed with the assistance of Wiedenhausen Karosserie in Frankfurt, which had previously created bodies for the Glöcker racers, and was then later slightly restyled by Erwin Komenda. The 550's distinctive low-to-the-ground

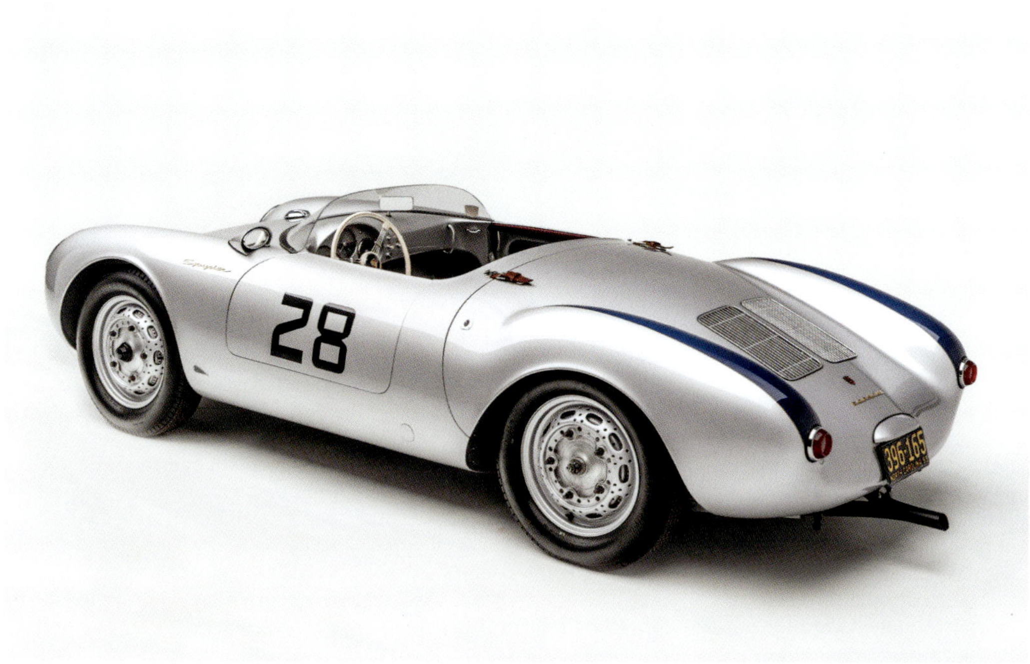

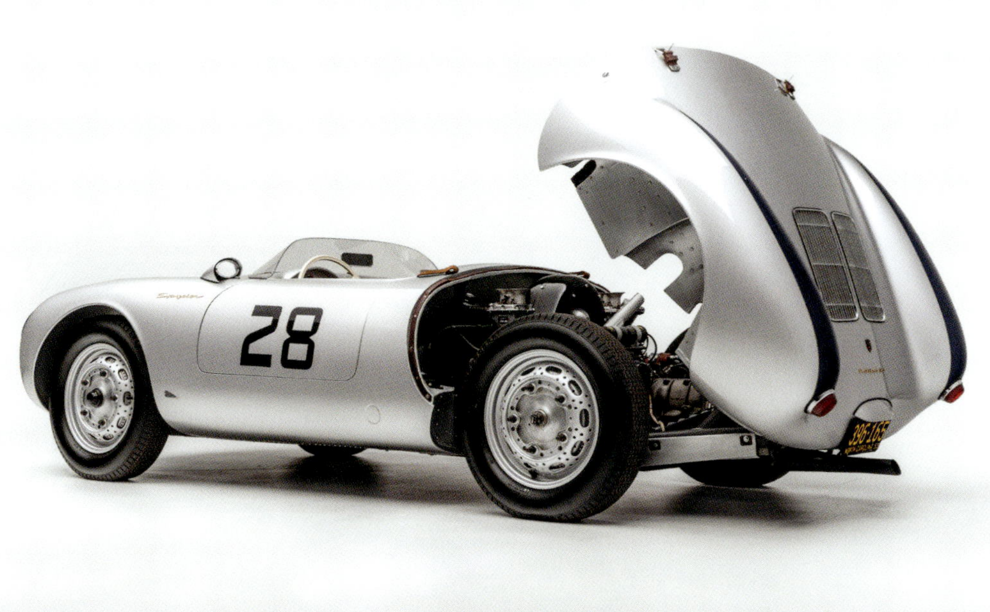
28
396-165

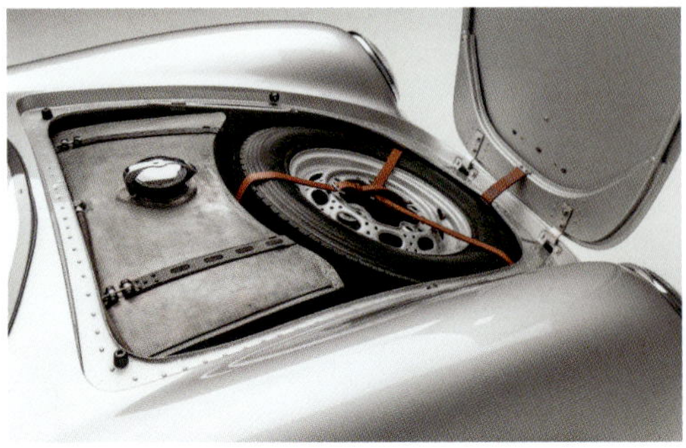

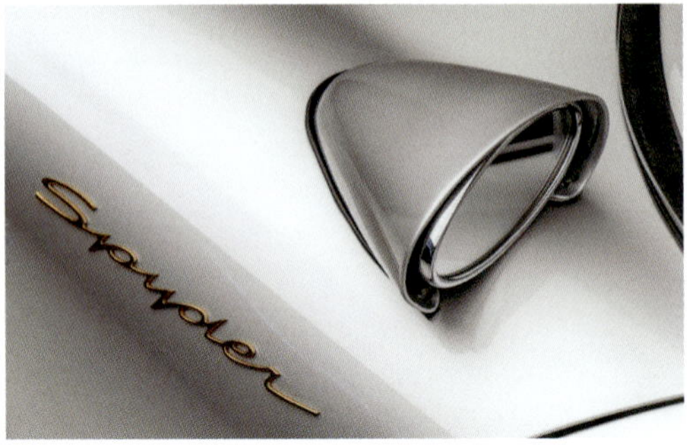

Top, left & right: Details of Porsche 550 Spyder's fuel cell, spare tire and wing mirror.

Below: Detail of Porsche 550 Spyder 1,498 cc (91.4 cu. in.), DOHC per bank horizontally opposed four-cylinder engine with two Solex PJJ carburetors. Known as a "Fuhrmann Engine" (Type 547) named after the engineer, Ernst Fuhrmann, who deveoped it, this all-aluminum air-cooled mid-mounted boxer engine features two overhead camshafts per cylinder bank, which are driven by shafts instead of the more traditional chains or belts, as well as dual ignition with two separate ignition manifolds and two ignition coils.

Opposite: Detail of Porsche 550 Spyder air-cooled mid-mounted Type 547 DOHC boxer engine. With this new power unit, the 550 Spyder was soon established as a consistent winner in small-displacement sports car racing. Production of customer Spyders began in 1955, enjoying a reputation as a very balanced, almost docile racing car with good power and excellent handling characteristics.

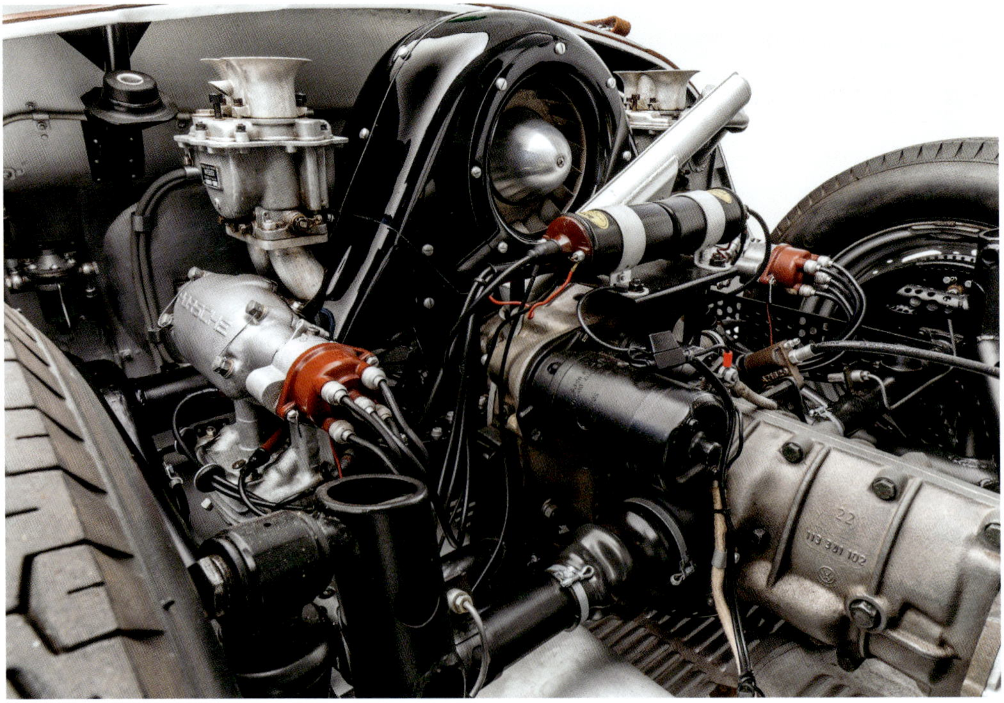

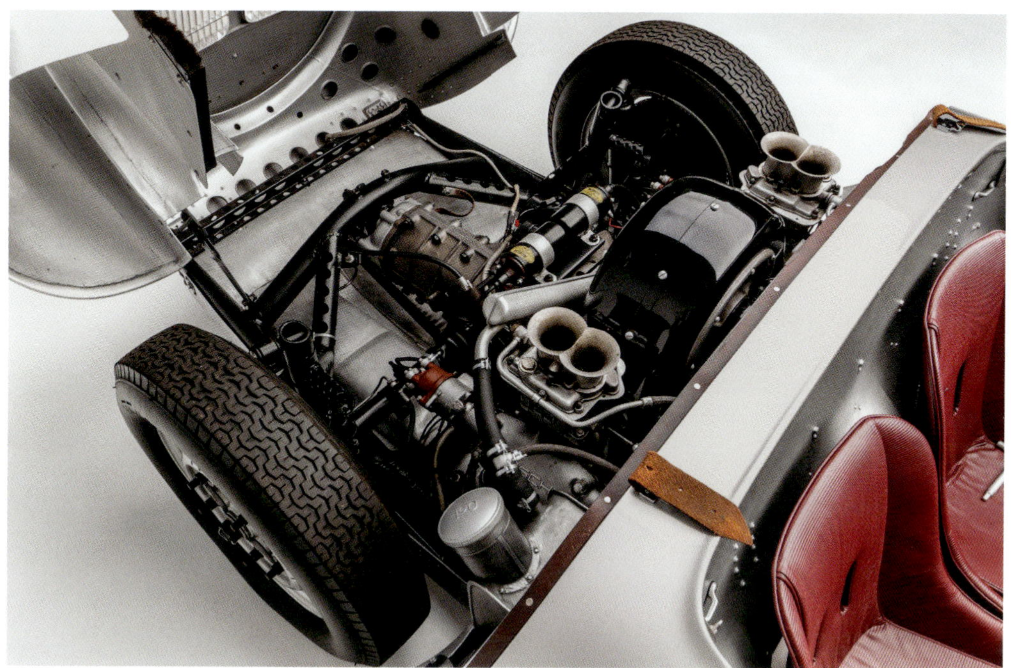

setup was similarly dictated by drag-reducing concerns. In many ways, the 550 was a radical automotive experiment in form following function and testifies to the fact that form derived entirely from functional considerations is often the most beautiful.

Debuting at the Paris Motor Show in 1953, the first three hand-built 550 prototypes had detachable roofs, which could be fitted to improve their aerodynamics for high-speed racing. These cars were not only visually stunning, but from chassis 550-03 onward also impressively powerful thanks to their complex all-aluminum, naturally aspirated 110-horsepower quad-cam (double overhead camshafts on each cylinder bank) four-cylinder boxer engines, which had been developed in-house at Porsche by Dr. Ernst Fuhrmann — who later went on to become the company's chairman. The nimble and responsive "Fuhrmann" Type 547 engine was mounted forward of the rear axle (i.e., mid-engine), which meant the 550s had a well-balanced weight distribution that allowed them to be easily slung around a racetrack fast, although the possibility of over rotation when cornering sharply was a concern.

The 550 Spyder's racing debut was at the Nürburgring Eifel Race in May 1953, and extraordinarily it took first place. Over the next couple of years, the 550 was evolved and refined by the Porsche Works Team and as a consequence clocked up numerous other podium places, including winning its class at the 1955 24 Hours of Le Mans and finishing second in points in its SCCA class for the 1956 season with the car shown here (chassis no. 0073). That same year a new variant of the model was introduced, the 550A, which boasted an even lighter yet more rigid space frame and was famously responsible for

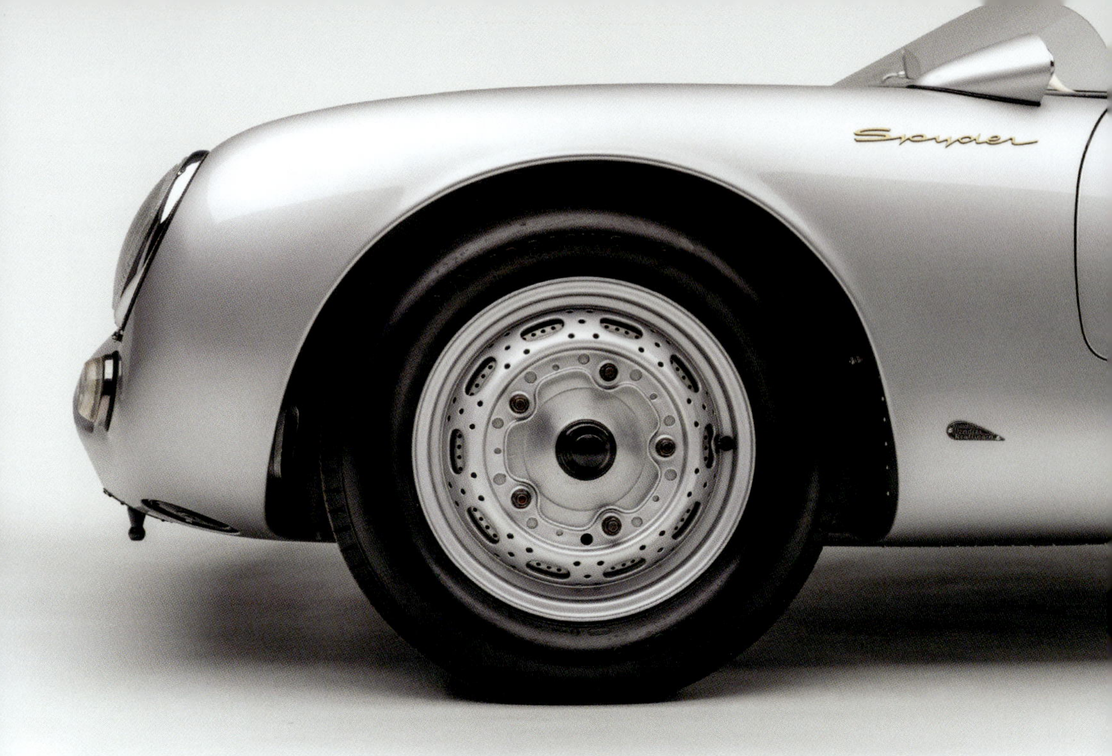

Porsche winning another landmark sporting-calendar event, the Targa Florio — an open-road endurance race held in the Sicilian mountains. In fact, the 550 became known as the "Giant Killer" because despite its diminutive size and soft-edged look, it was able time and again to beat off more powerful and more aggressively styled rivals. The stunning 1955 example shown here, which is part of the Ingram Collection and was included in the Petersen Automotive Museum's "The Porsche Effect" touring exhibition, is probably the finest original 550 Spyder in existence.

With its seductive air-sculpted form, the 550 can be seen as an exquisite embodiment of Ferdinand Alexander Porsche's belief that "Design is not simply art, it is elegant function" — and certainly his later design of the immortal Porsche 911 (1963) can trace its ancestry right back to this earlier landmark race car.

Opposite (top): Publicity photo of the Works Porsche 550 RS Spyder team at the 1955 24 Hours of Le Mans. They took first, second and third for their class (1.5 liter) and placed fourth, fifth and sixth overall.

Opposite (bottom): Porsche 550 RS Spyder main dimensions and traffic requirement No. 550.00.116, technical drawing dated December 6, 1954, scale 1:10.

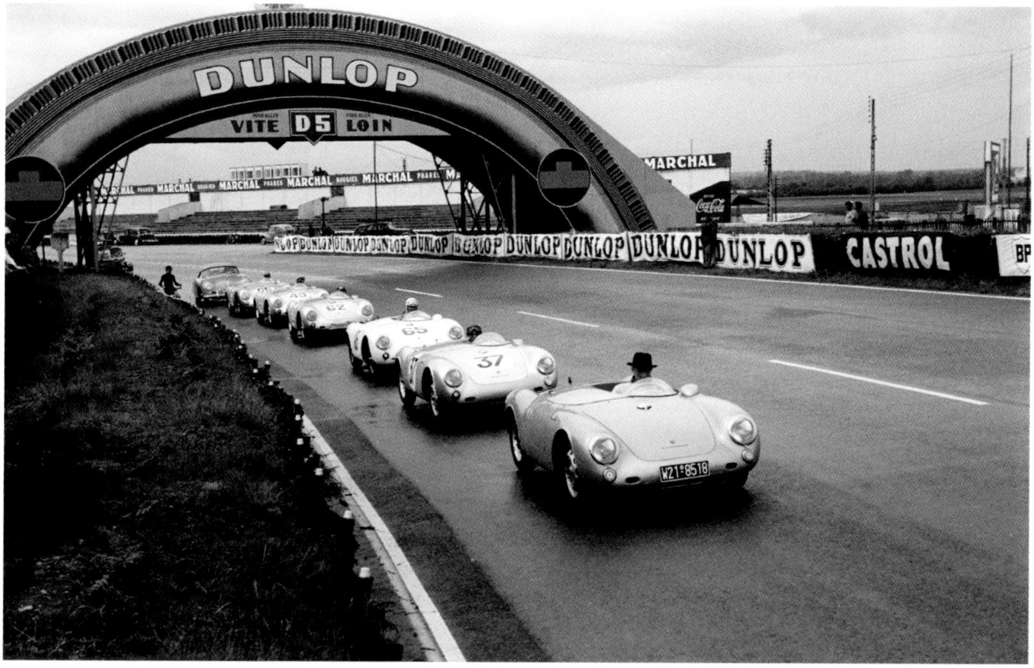
DUNLOP
VITE D5 LOIN
MARCHAL
DUNLOP
CASTROL
W21-8518

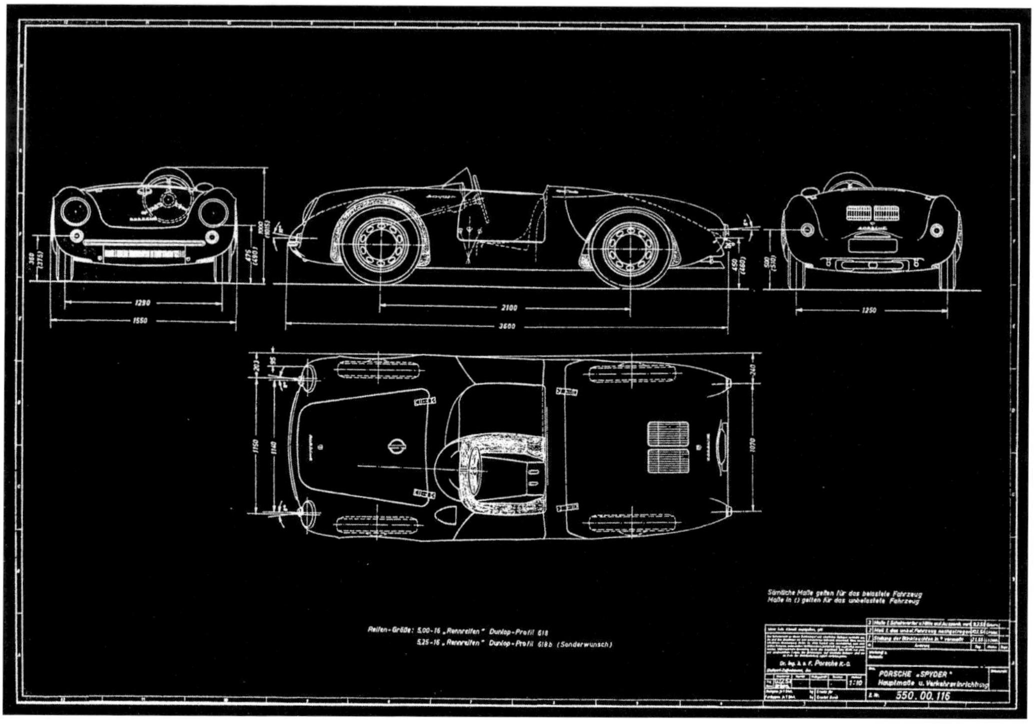
1290
1550
2100
3600
1250
Sämtliche Maße gelten für das belastete Fahrzeug
Maße in () gelten für das unbelastete Fahrzeug
Reifen-Größe: 5,00-16 „Rennreifen" Dunlop-Profil 618
5,25-16 „Rennreifen" Dunlop-Profil 618b (Sonderwunsch)
Dr. Ing. h. c. F. Porsche K.-G.
1:10
PORSCHE „SPYDER"
Hauptmaße u. Verkehrseinrichtung
550.00.116

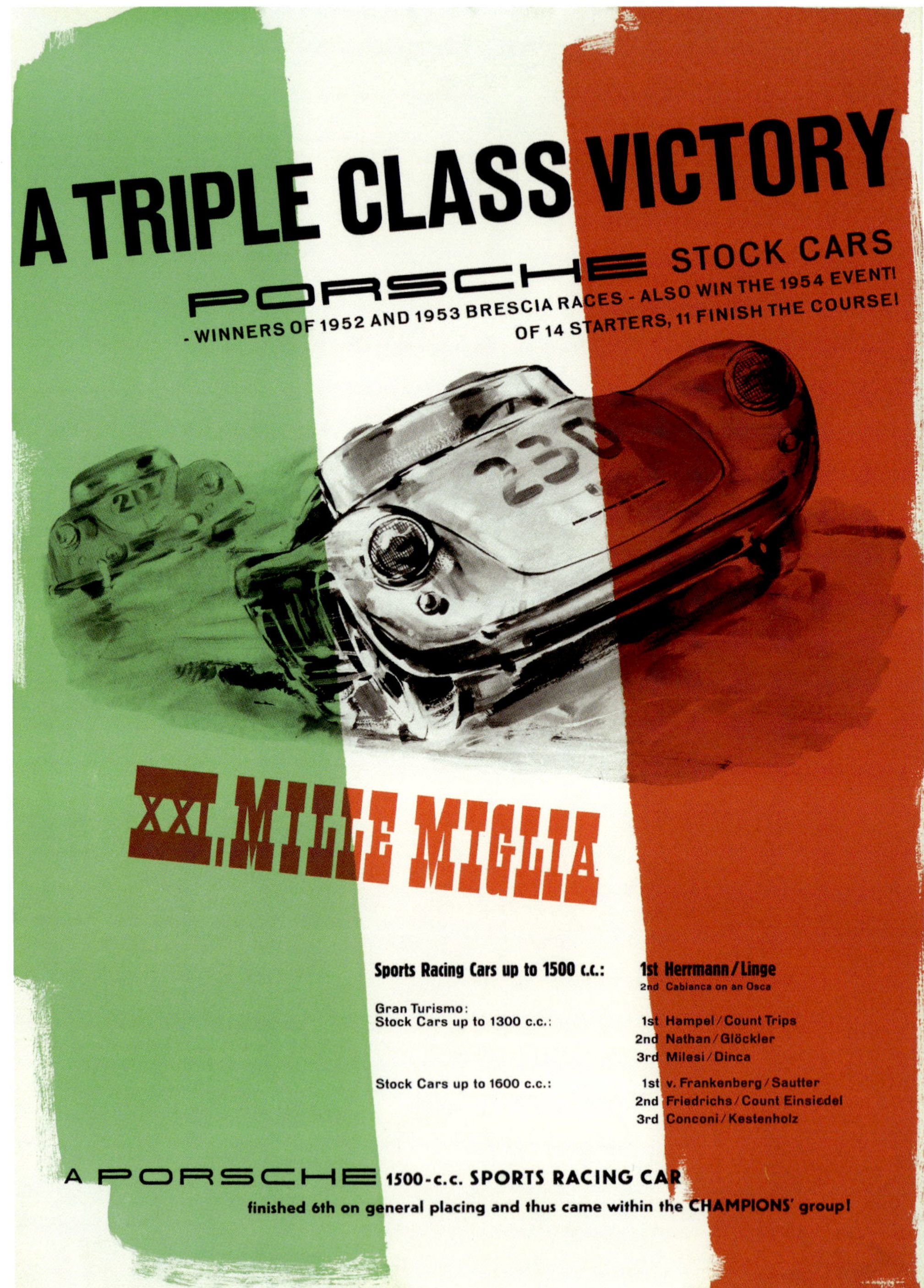
A TRIPLE CLASS VICTORY
PORSCHE STOCK CARS
- WINNERS OF 1952 AND 1953 BRESCIA RACES - ALSO WIN THE 1954 EVENT!
OF 14 STARTERS, 11 FINISH THE COURSE!
XXI. MILLE MIGLIA
Sports Racing Cars up to 1500 c.c.: 1st Herrmann/Linge
2nd Cabianca on an Osca
Gran Turismo:
Stock Cars up to 1300 c.c.: 1st Hampel/Count Trips
2nd Nathan/Glöckler
3rd Milesi/Dinca
Stock Cars up to 1600 c.c.: 1st v. Frankenberg/Sautter
2nd Friedrichs/Count Einsiedel
3rd Conconi/Kestenholz
A PORSCHE 1500-c.c. SPORTS RACING CAR
finished 6th on general placing and thus came within the CHAMPIONS' group!

Opposite: 1954 poster by Erich Strenger (1922–1993) celebrating various Porsche 550 Spyder race results.

Right: Poster by Erich Strenger celebrating Porsche 550 Spyder race results in 1955 at L'autodrome de Linas-Montlhéry, France.

Below: Actor James Dean gives a thumbs-up sign from his brand new Porsche 550 Spyder, which he dubbed the "Little Bastard," while parked on Vine Street in Hollywood. Dean, who had taken up racing the year before, owned the car only nine days when he lost his life in a highway accident while driving the Porsche to a Salinas Road Race event scheduled for October 1 and 2, 1955.

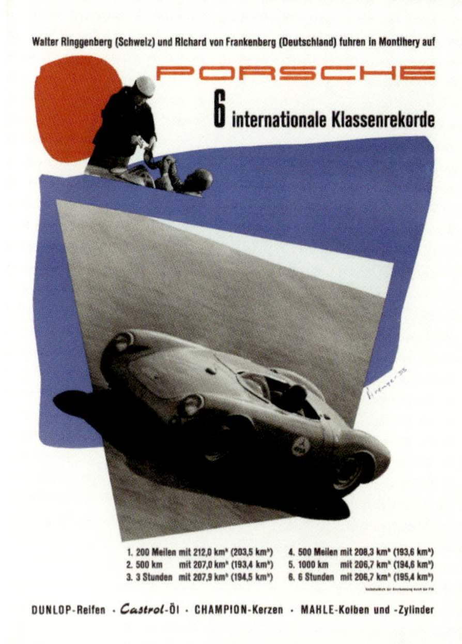

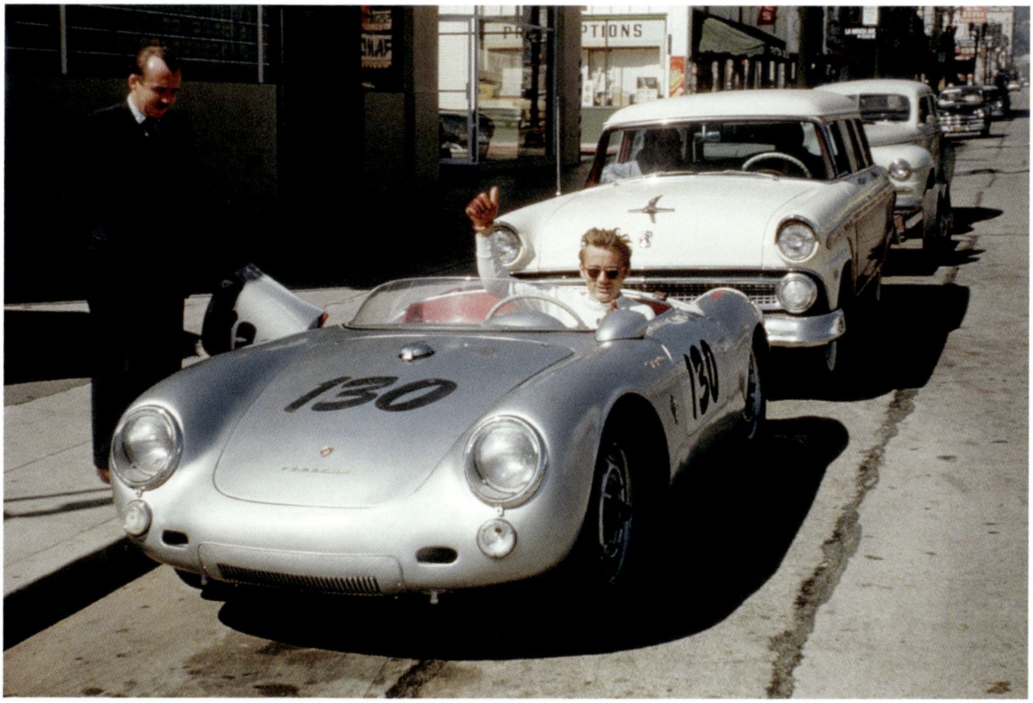

1955

Jaguar D-Type

MANUFACTURED 1954–56 | **ENGINE** 3,442 cc (210 cu. in.), DOHC inline 6-cylinder | **HORSEPOWER** 262
TOP SPEED 272 km/h (169 mph) | **TRANSMISSION** 4-speed
NUMBER PRODUCED 17 factory team cars and 62 customer cars

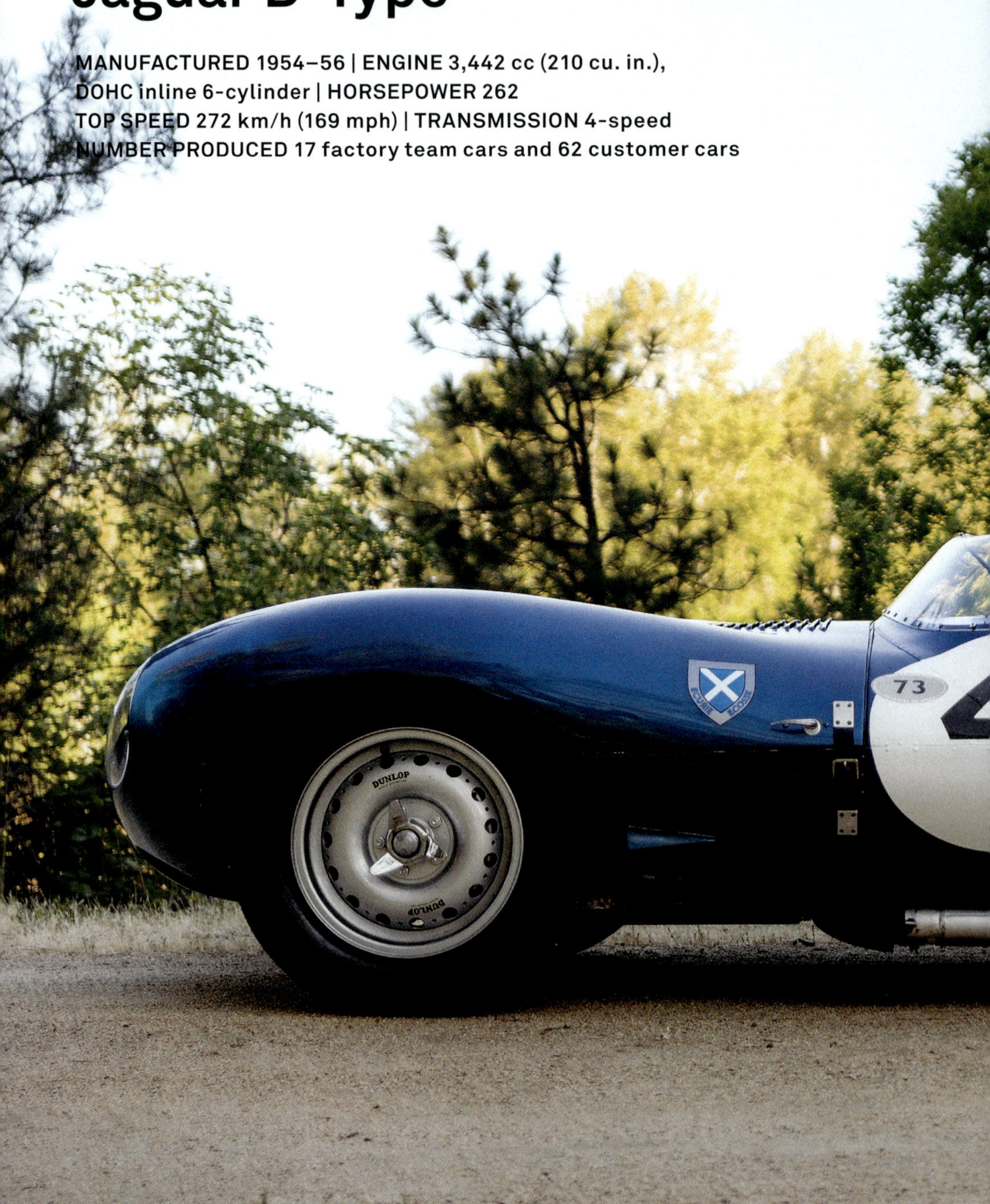

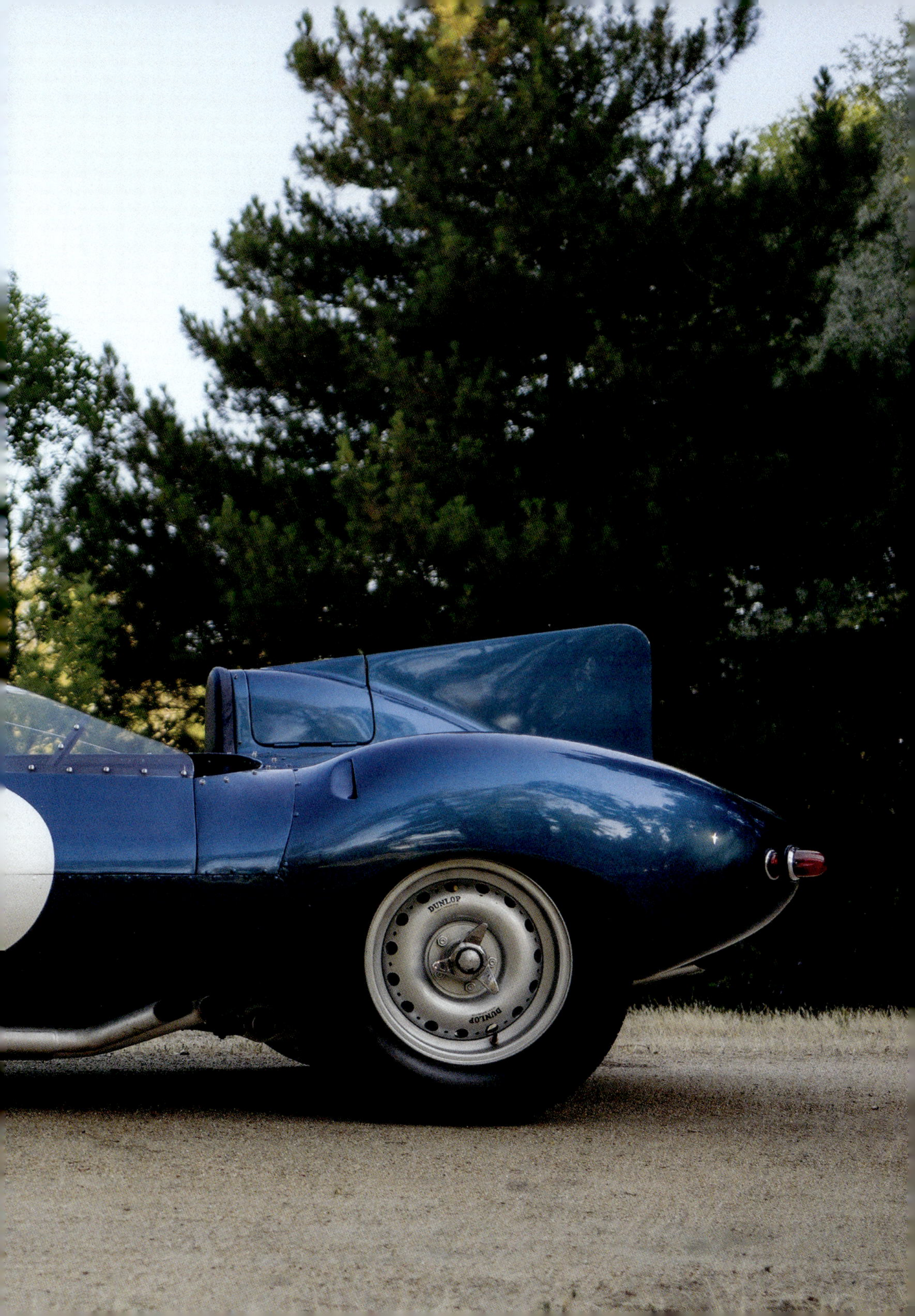
DUNLOP

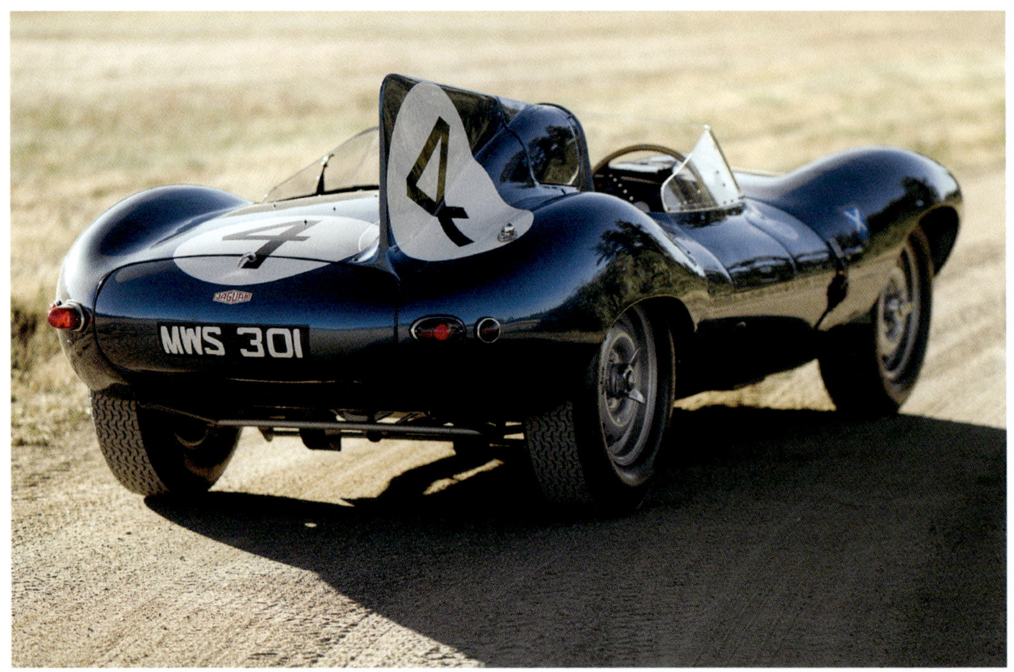

The immortal Jaguar D-Type is one of the sports racers most sought after by collectors, while ownership of one of these rare "big cats" commands instant respect among the automotive cognoscenti. This is hardly surprising because the D-Type represents one of the great high points of Jaguar's illustrious history, and continues to thrill with its distinctive aerodynamic form, not to mention its famed performance. This was the car that ultimately sealed Jaguar's Le Mans legend by clinching a hat trick of thrilling victories between 1955 and 1957. It was the immediate successor of the C-Type (see p. 102), itself a celebrated racer that had famously won Le Mans in 1951 and 1953. But staying competitive on the racetrack was not that easy when you were up against the likes of Mercedes-Benz and Ferrari. Indeed, the threat that such rivals posed, made it perfectly clear to the manager of Jaguar's racing team, Frank "Lofty" England and renowned Jaguar engineer, William Heynes, that a freshly designed and higher-performing model was needed if they were to have any chance of clinching more victories. The resulting D-Type was stronger, lighter and faster than its illustrious progenitor and although at its heart lay the same XK engine, it had been tuned to provide 262 hp versus the C-Type's 220 hp. This power-boosting development helped the XK engine compete with the heavier and more powerful engines used by Mercedes and Ferrari. An additional bonus with reusing this inline six-cylinder dual overhead camshaft engine was that, as the Jaguar Heritage Trust explains, it "meant that private owners could easily buy and maintain these cars, which provided a useful back-up to the works team." The D-Type's lightweight, unitary semi-monocoque construction designed by Heynes — Jaguar's Technical Director and Chief Engineer — was unusual for the time and cleverly combined body and frame for better structural integrity. It, together with the aerodynamic bodywork by the gifted aerodynamicist Malcolm Sayer, significantly boosted the car's performance, as did the fitting of an early fuel-injection system on the later works D-Type racers.

The first prototype of the D-Type (chassis no. XKC401) was completed in May 1954 and was then immediately sent out to France to be put through its paces at a Le Mans testing session, where works driver Tony Rolt broke the lap record by five seconds. It was obvious Jaguar was in the competitive running with this new model, and so the prototype was returned to Coventry where it was used as a platform for more development, while another three D-Types were constructed for the upcoming 24 Hours of Le Mans race of 1954. One of these cars was assigned to Jaguar works team principal drivers Stirling Moss and Peter Walker and was the fastest car during practice, which bolstered Jaguar's hopes of glory. However, all three of these D-Types unfortunately suffered from an engine misfiring issue during the actual race, which was later traced to fuel contamination. This problem meant two failed to finish; although the third, piloted by Tony Rolt and Duncan Hamilton, managed a very commendable second place despite all the frustration. Later that year, a Jaguar works D-Type won the French Grand Prix in Reims and the following year another was victorious at the 12 Hours of Sebring held in Florida. All of this boded well for the upcoming 1955 Le Mans race, which was won by Mike Hawthorn and Ivor Bueb in one of Team Jaguar's D-Types. This victory, however, was entirely marred by one of the most

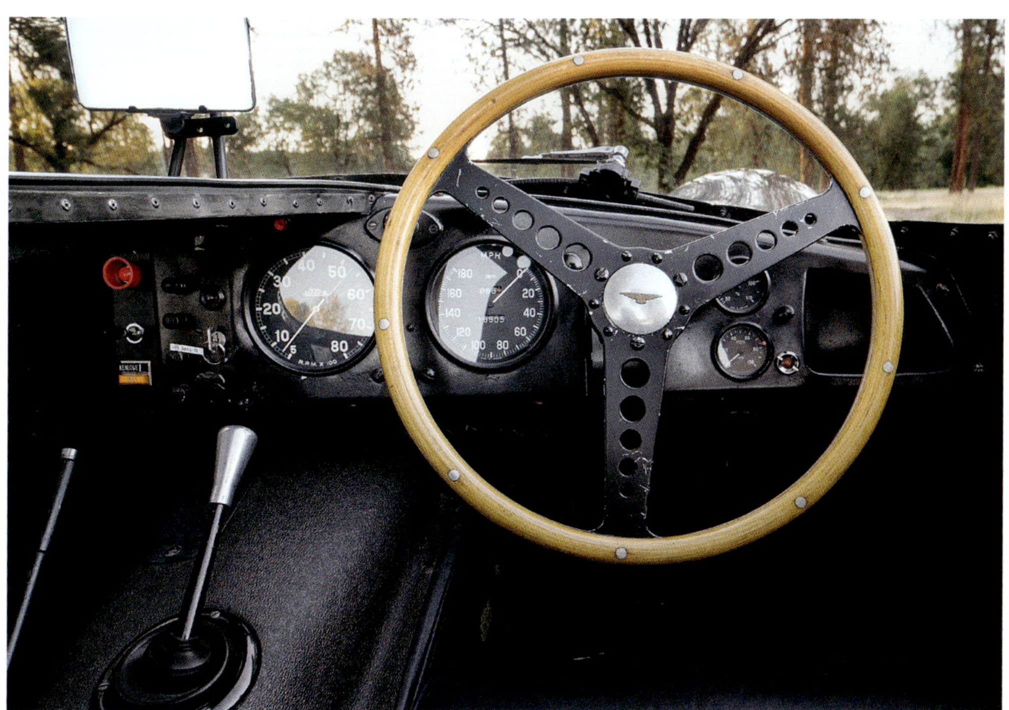

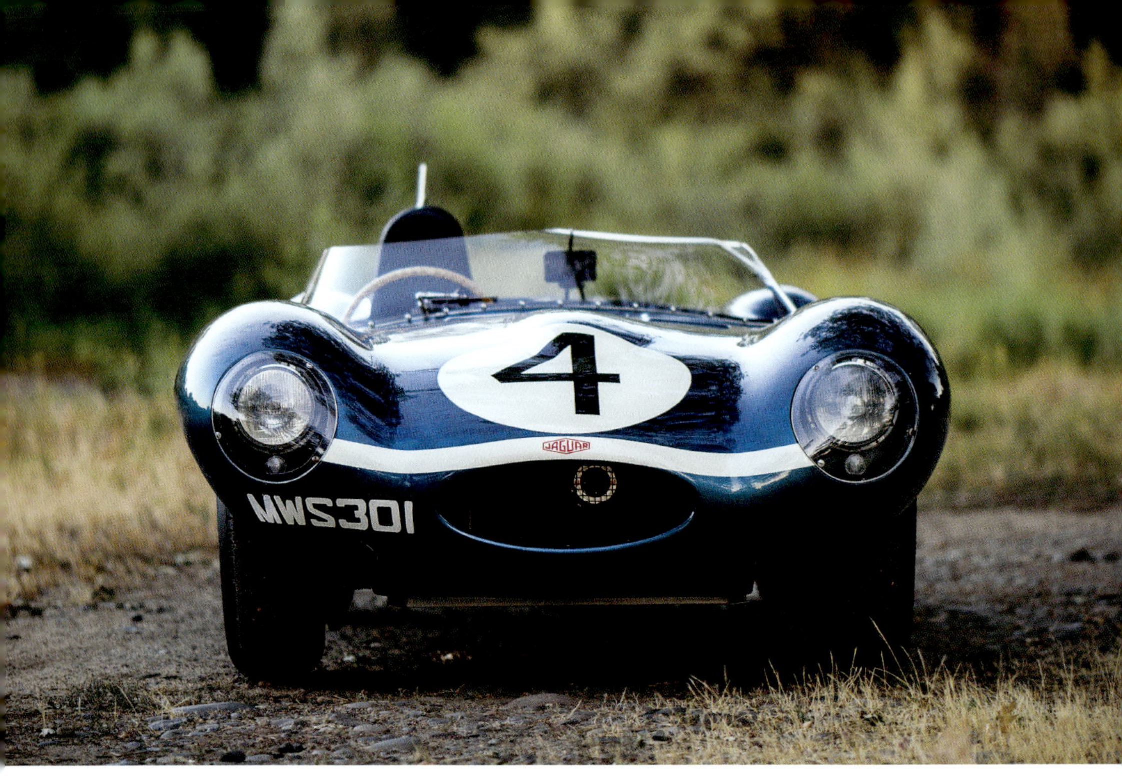

catastrophic crashes in motorsports history, which saw Pierre Levegh's Mercedes-Benz 300 SLR launched into the packed terraces of spectators at 120 mph (200 km/h), killing 83, including Levegh himself, and injuring a further 180. The following year, at the 1956 Le Mans, two of Jaguar's three works D-Types crashed, while the other was retired with engine failure. Nevertheless, the D-Type (chassis no. XKD 501), shown here, which was fielded by the privately owned Scottish racing team Ecurie Ecosse and driven by Ninian Sanderson and Ron Flockhart, ultimately won the race. The reputation of this swift and lithesome Le Mans–winning model was further solidified when Ecurie Ecosse enjoyed a historic 1-2 finish in 1957 with two other Jaguar D-Types, likewise sporting blue and white paintwork that patriotically referenced the flag of Scotland. These epic victories helped to forever immortalize the D-Type in the pantheon of historic motorsports legends.

Opposite (top, left): 1955 D-Type body fabrication at Jaguar's Browns Lane factory in Coventry. The car's lightweight unitary semi-monocoque construction, with the body and frame combining for structural integrity, was highly progressive.

Opposite (top, right): Production of the D-Type at Jaguar's Browns Lane factory, 1955. From 1954 to 1956 17 factory team cars and 62 customer cars were produced there.

Opposite (bottom): The No. 4 Ecurie Ecosse Jaguar D-Type (chassis no. XKD 501) driven by Ron Flockhart and Ninian Sanderson en route to a first-place finish at the 1956 24 Hours of Le Mans.

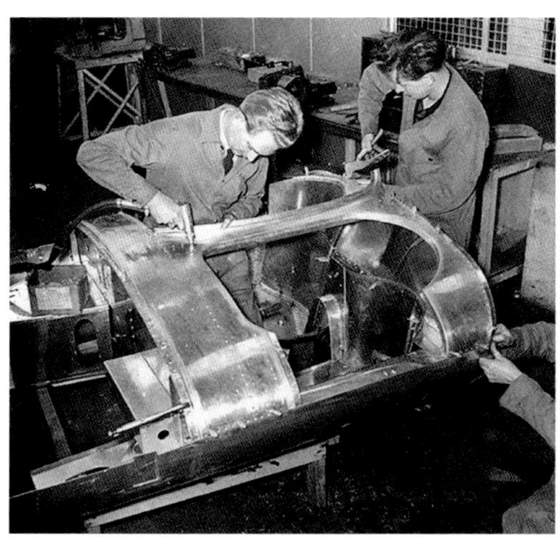

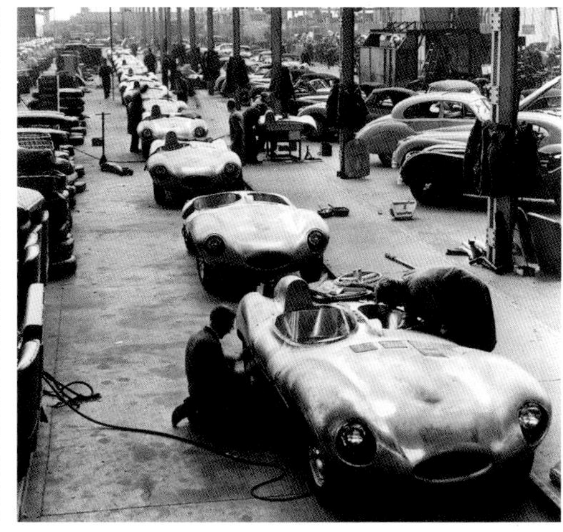

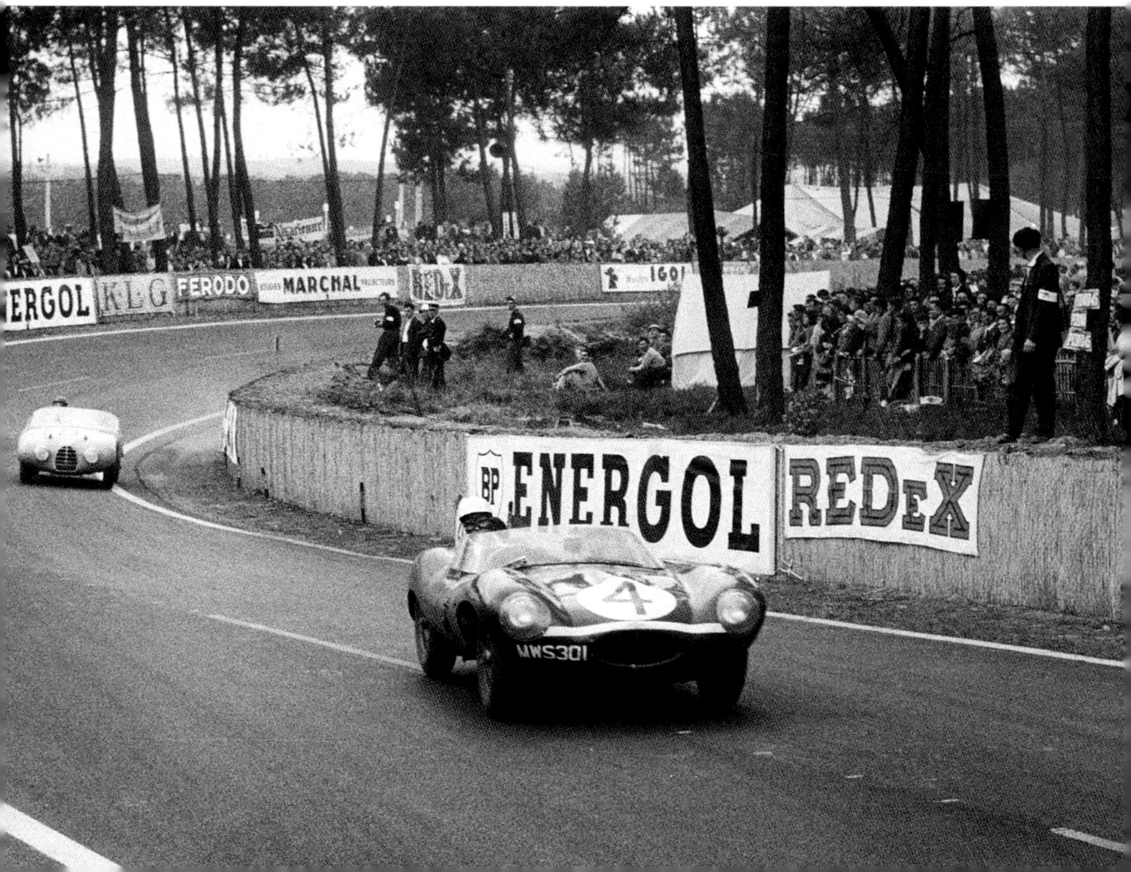

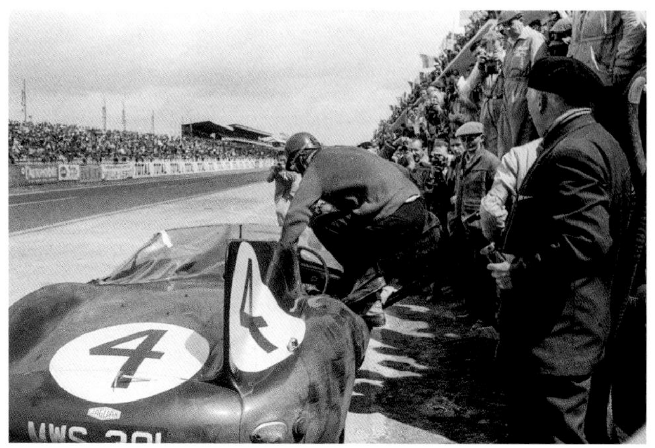

Left: Ron Flockhart / Ninian Sanderson, Ecurie Ecosse, No. 4 Jaguar D-Type, makes a driver change during a pit stop at the 1956 24 Hours of Le Mans.

Below: Ron Flockhart / Ninian Sanderson, Ecurie Ecosse, No. 4 Jaguar D-Type (chassis no. XKD 501) takes the checkered flag to win the 1956 24 Hours of Le Mans.

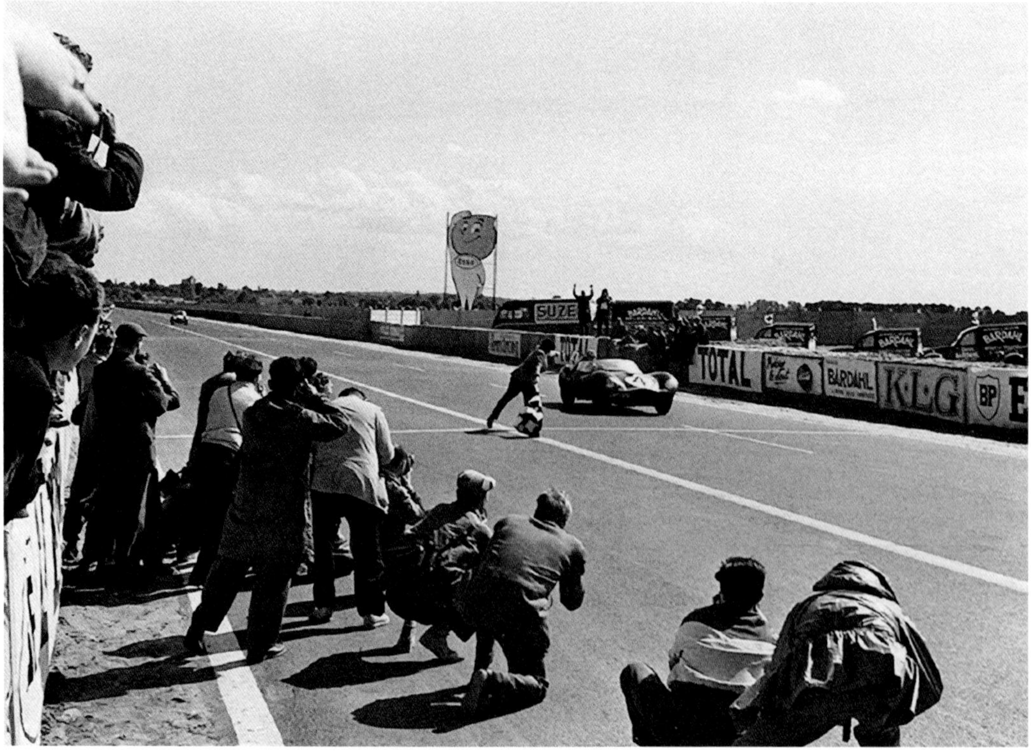

Right: Cover of the 1954 Jaguar D-Type sales brochure, with an illustration by Roy Nockolds (1911–1979).

Below: The overall race-winning Ecurie Ecosse, No. 4 Jaguar D-Type (chassis no. XKD 501) in the finish area of the 1956 24 Hours of Le Mans along with the second-place Aston Martin DB3S of Stirling Moss and Peter Collins.

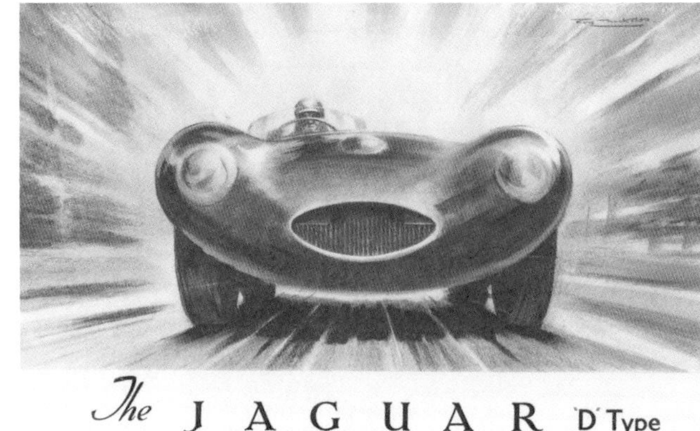

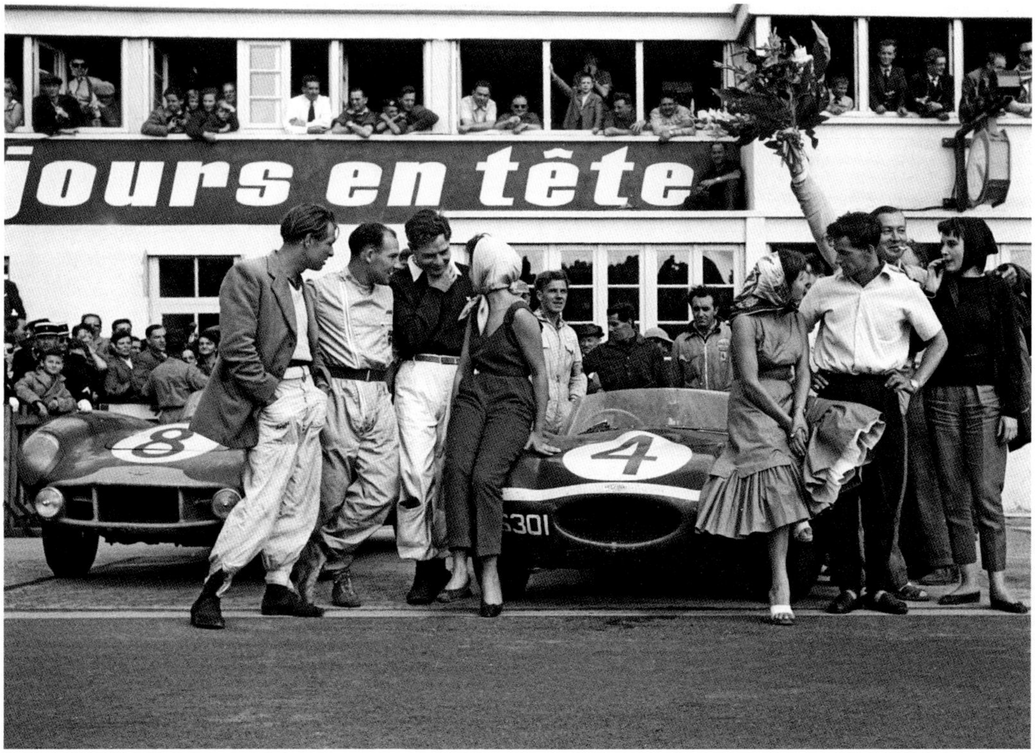

1956

Ferrari 290 MM

MANUFACTURED 1956 | **ENGINE** 3,490 cc (213 cu. in.), SOHC per bank 60º V12 | **HORSEPOWER** 320
TOP SPEED 280 km/h (174 mph) | **TRANSMISSION** 4-speed
NUMBER PRODUCED 4 (one converted from an 860 Monza)

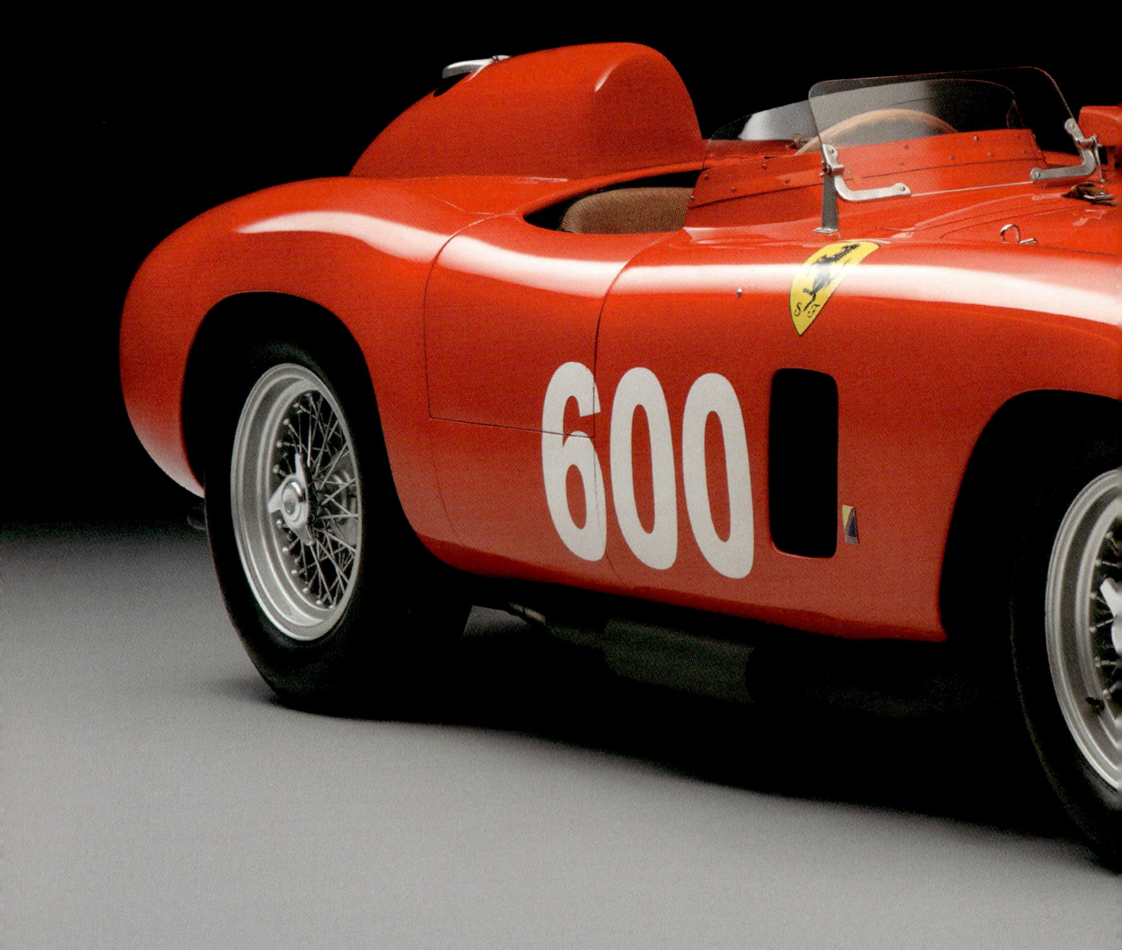

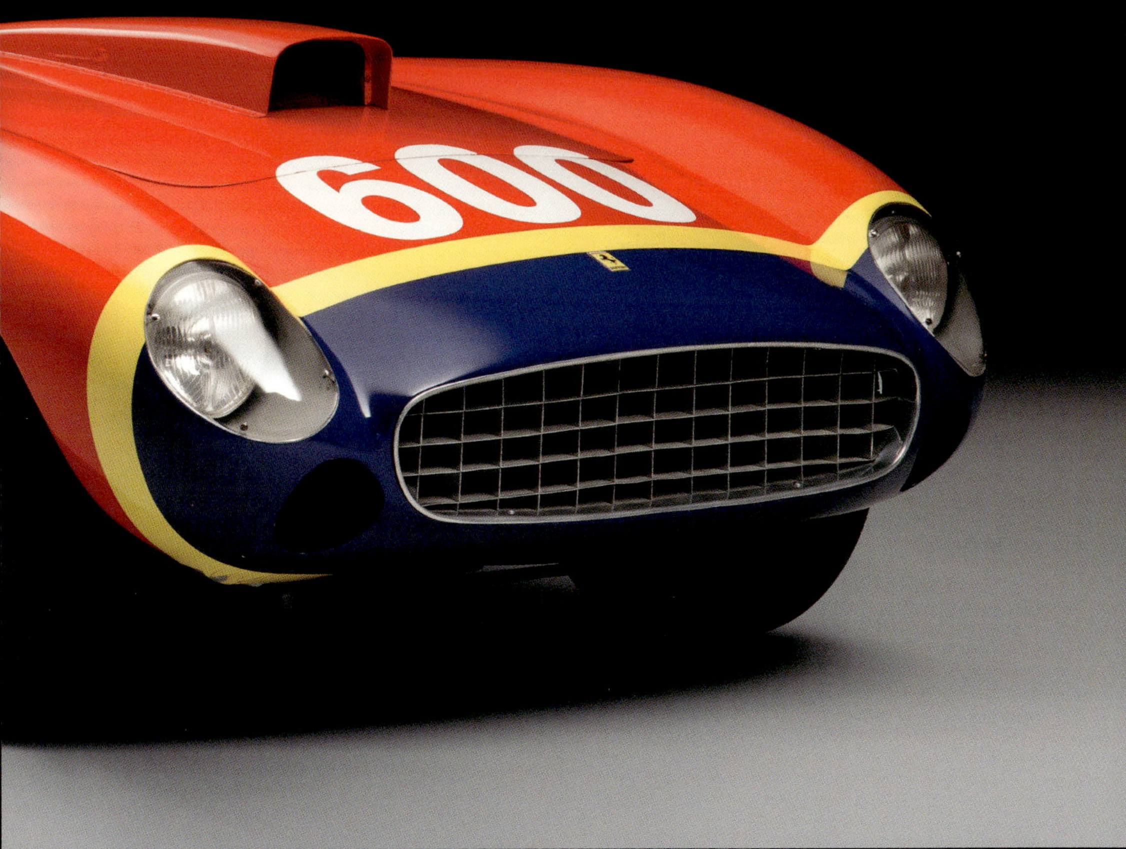
600

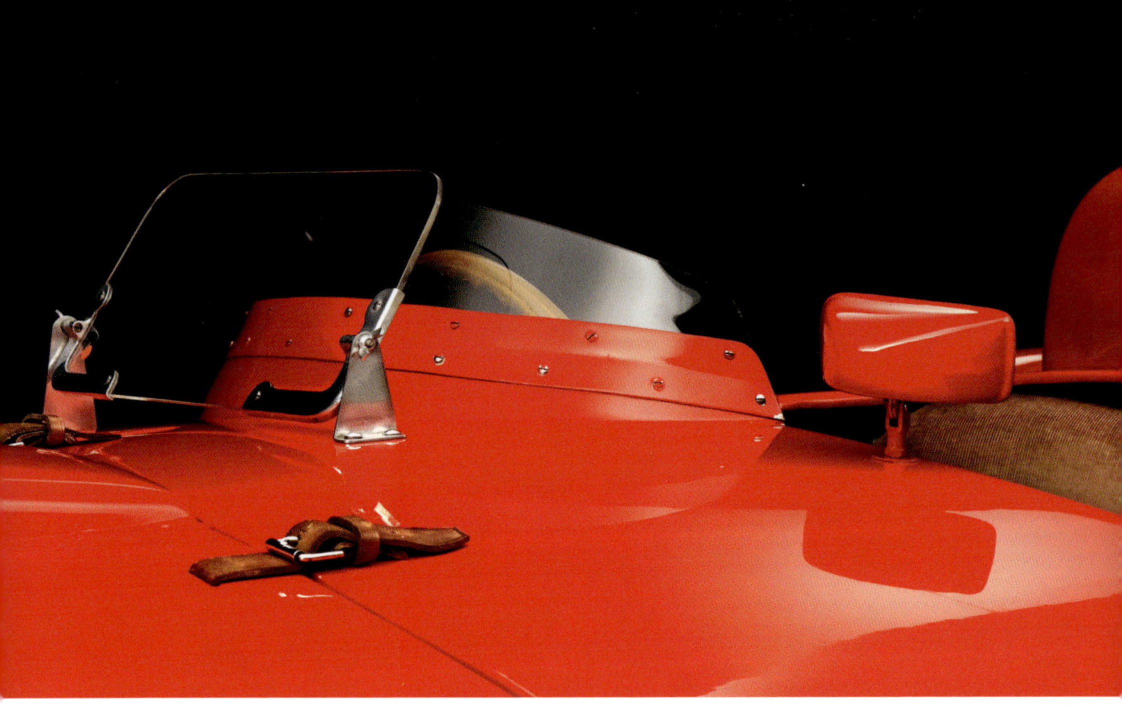

Above: Detail of wind deflector and reduced windshield for improved aerodynamics.

Opposite (bottom): Ferrari 290 MM 3,490 cc (213 cu. in.), SOHC per bank 60° V12 engine with triple Weber 46 DCF3 carburetors. This all-new dry-sump engine featured twin spark-plug ignition with quad Magneti-Marelli distributors and was created by Vittorio Jano and Andrea Fraschetti for the 1956 World Sportscar Championship. Although following principles set by Aurelio Lampredi, with its integral block and cylinder heads with screwed-in wet liners, the new engine was shorter and wider, with considerable effort put into the combustion chamber design to improve inlet and exhaust valve function.

Overleaf: Detail of Ferrari 290 MM cockpit, Nardi wood-rimmed steering wheel, instrumentation, and controls.

Of all the Ferraris ever made the most collectible are the marque's legendary prototype racers and homologated production cars, especially those from the fabled golden era of motorsports racing, which spanned the 1950s and 1960s. Among these, it is those that were Ferrari's own works cars that are, of course, the most highly prized by competition-focused collectors — because, let's face it, a constructor will always keep the best racers for their own team to give itself the best winning advantage. Indeed, it is the direct association with Ferrari's famous stable of drivers that also makes these cars so desirable, because Enzo Ferrari had a knack of attracting the best of the best to drive for him. And of these rare Maranello-stabled thoroughbreds, there are few as special as this astonishing 1956 Ferrari 290 MM by Scaglietti (chassis no. 0626), which was driven by the famous Argentinian racing driver Juan Manuel Fangio at the 1956 Mille Miglia. Although Fangio

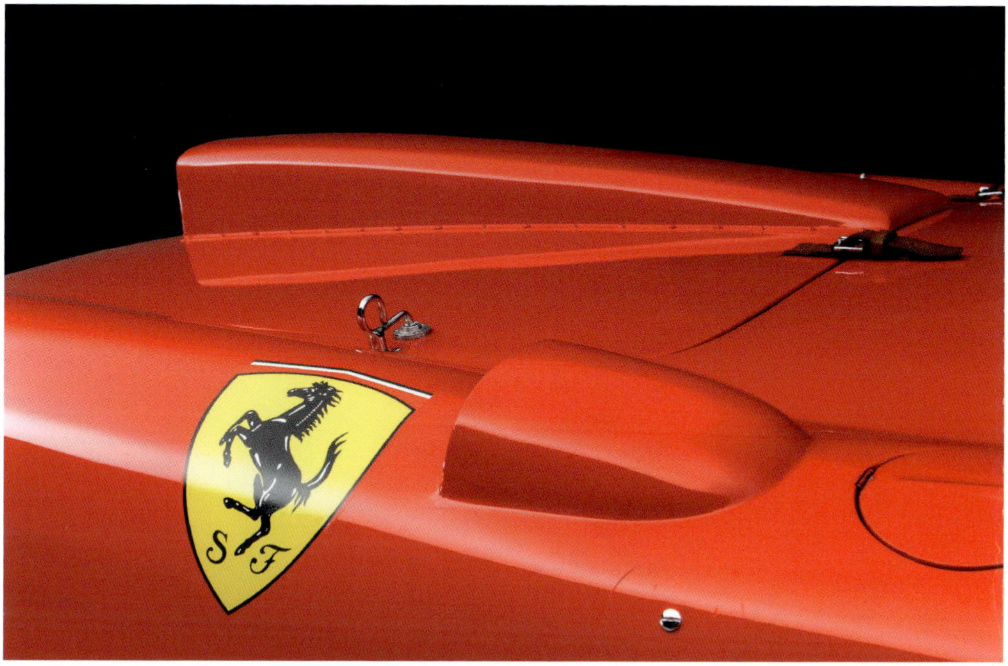

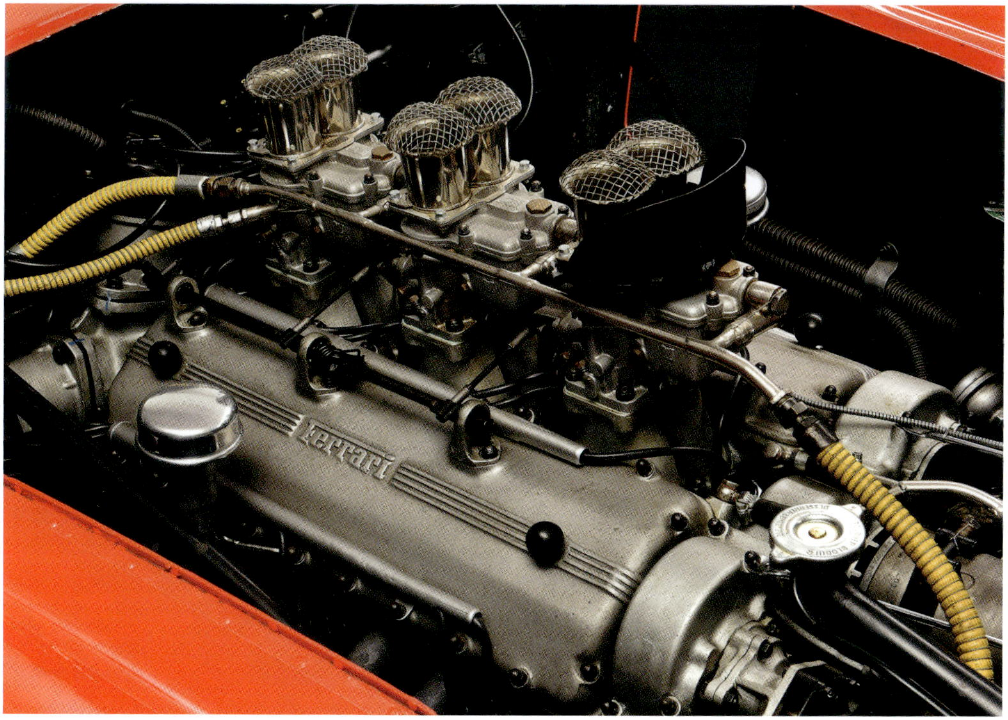

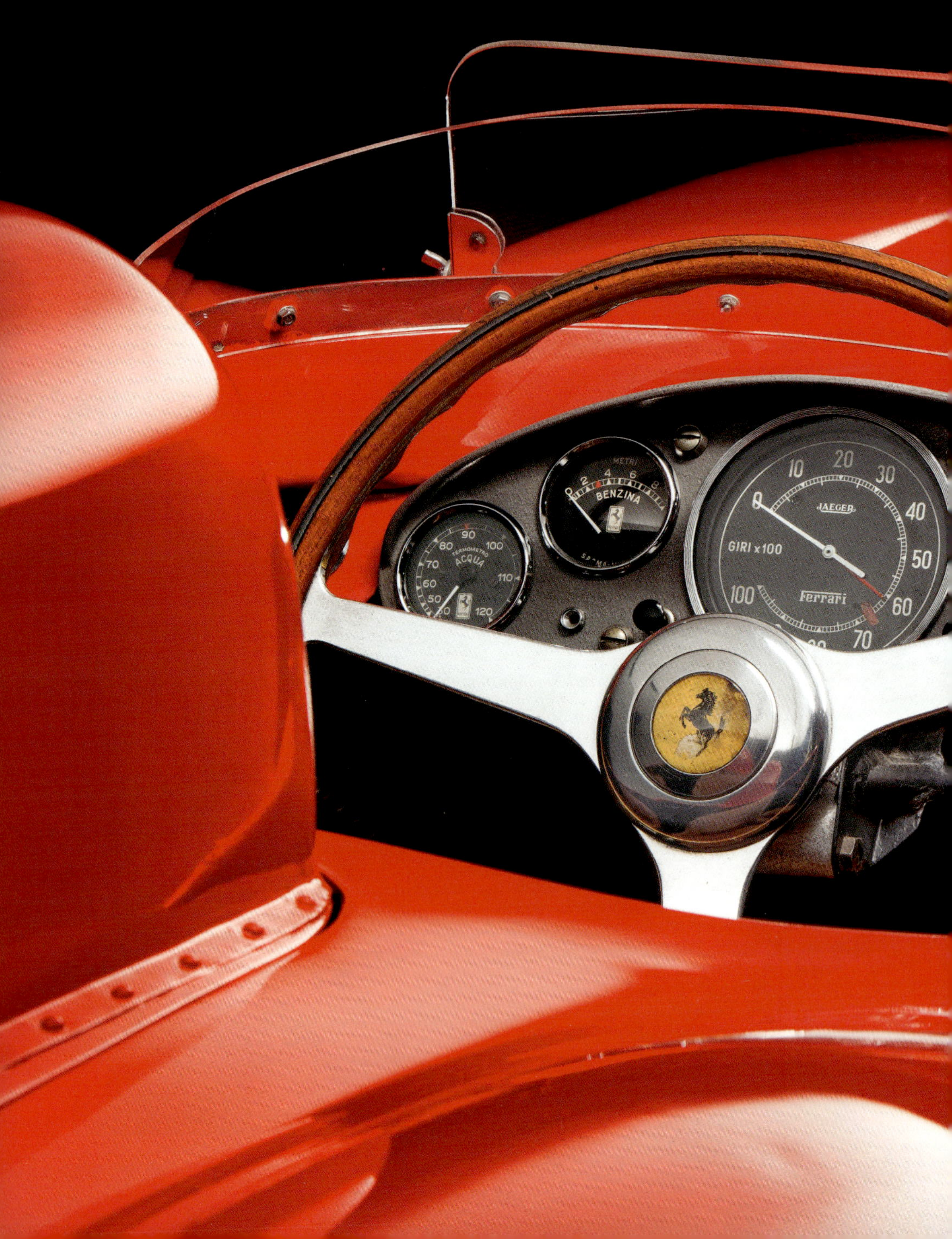
METRI
BENZINA
TERMOMETRO
ACQUA
JAEGER
GIRI x100
Ferrari

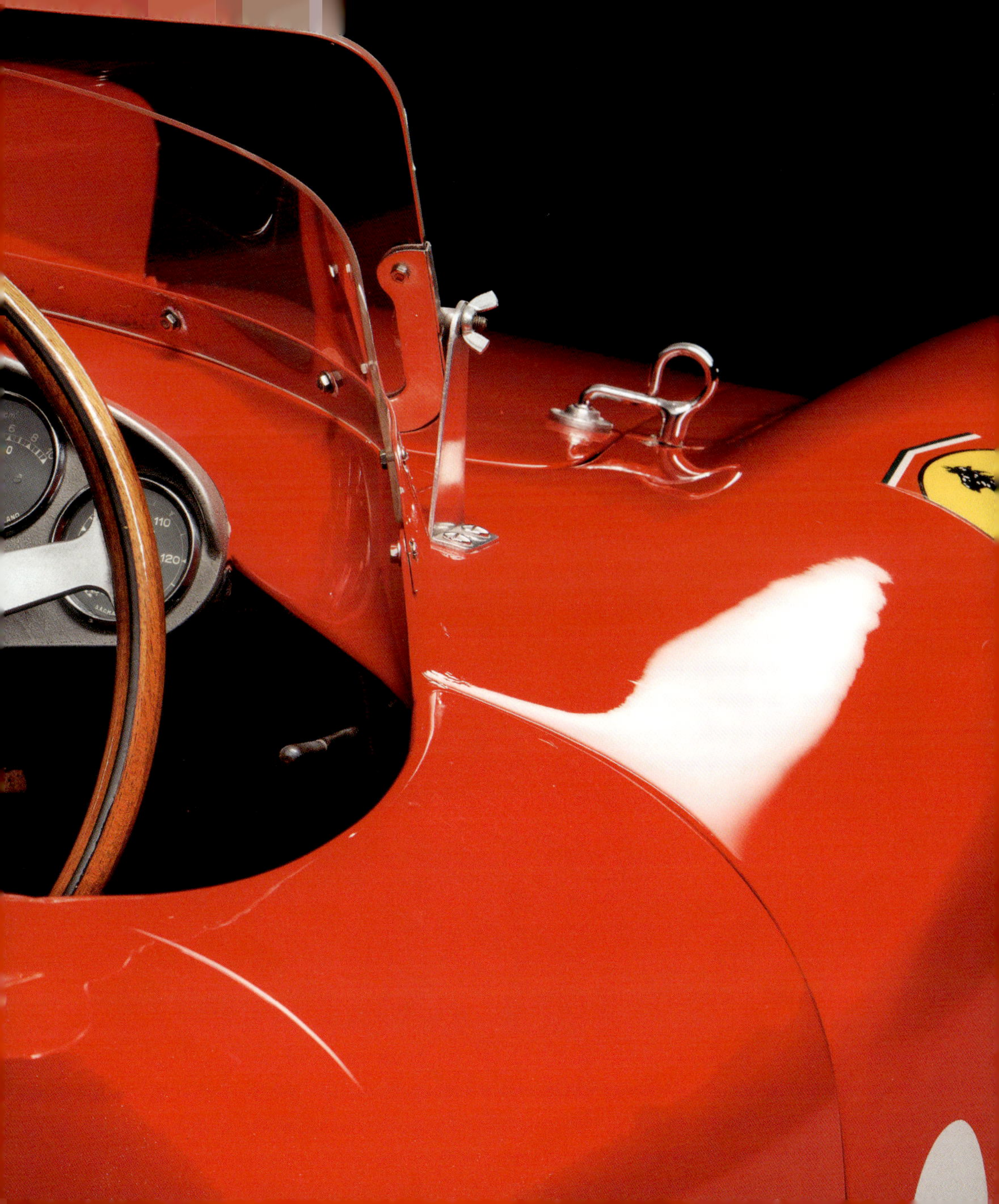
110
120

only came fourth at this race, Scuderia Ferrari did triumph with a memorable 1-2-3-4 finish — the winning car being a sister 290 MM.

This remarkable success testified to Ferrari's extraordinary competitiveness during the mid-1950s, which was born from Enzo's commitment to perpetual innovation as well as his deep-seated work ethic. He once famously quipped, "One must keep working continuously: otherwise, one thinks of death." But more than this, Ferrari's success was also fundamentally an expression of the great man's all-encompassing passion for motor racing, with him once observing, "Racing is a great mania to which one must sacrifice everything, without reticence, without hesitation." It was this uncomprising ethos that made Enzo's "Prancing Horses" such formidable competitors on the racetrack, because it led to inevitable technological advancement. It was Ferrari's dedication to high-tech engineering solutions in the never-ending pursuit of better performance, alongside similar efforts made by other marques during the late 1950s and early 1960s, that helped to gradually professionalize the focus of motor racing and ultimately establish the foundations of today's motorsports competition. By the late 1950s, sports racers that could be driven on the road to a racetrack, often by amateur gentleman owner-racers, were being increasingly sidelined, quite literally, by full-on competition race cars piloted by highly skilled professional drivers.

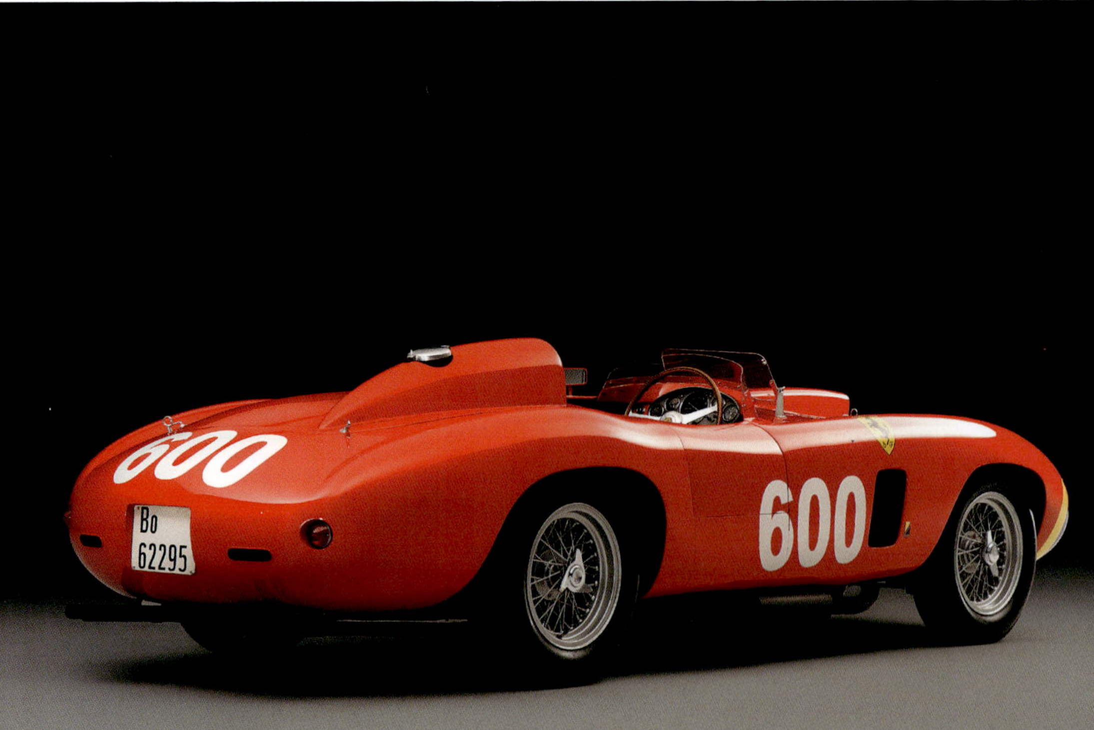

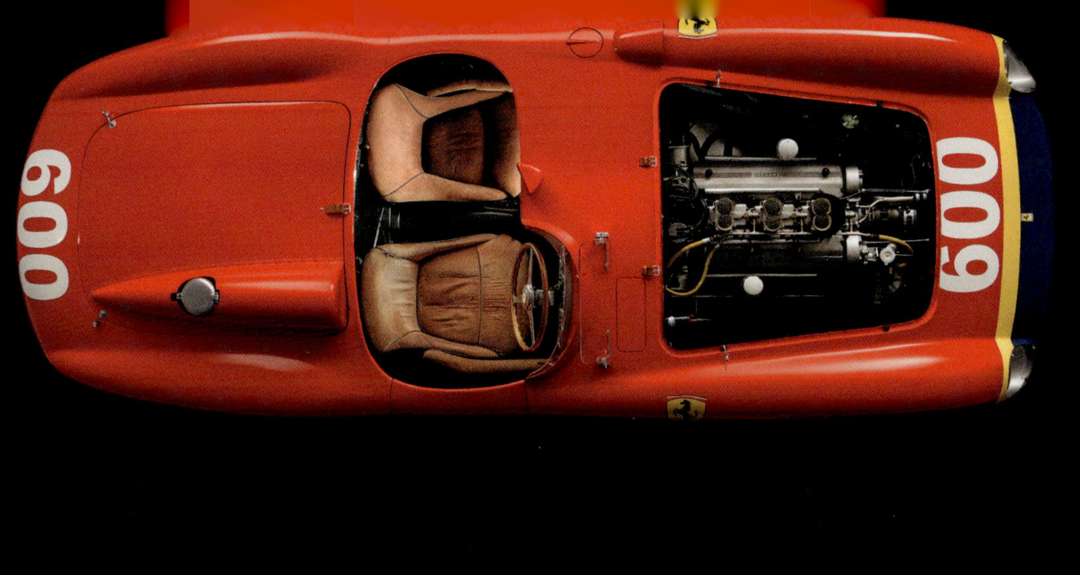

The 290 MM, for instance, was specially built to contest not only the 1956 Mille Miglia, but also that year's World Sportscar Championship (WSC). In fact, Enzo considered it as important to win the WSC as the Formula One World Championship. As a background, Ferrari had won the inaugural 1953 and 1954 WSC championships and won the first race of the 1955 WSC season, only to be spectacularly trounced by Mercedes-Benz's 300 SLRs, which went on to win three of the five remaining events. And if that was not enough, Ferrari's old rival, Maserati, toward the end of the 1955 season unleashed its own formidable new weapon, the 300S. Enzo knew he needed urgently to develop a more competitive car if he was to have any chance of success in the upcoming 1956 season. And so, at the suggestion of the engineering genius, Vittorio Jano, who had only recently returned to Ferrari after a stint at Lancia, a new V12 engine was created, which was notably shorter and wider than previous Ferrari engines. As Ferrari explains, "the 290 MM was mounted with a V12 engine with dual ignition and dry sump derived from the 4.5-liter Grand Prix. Even though this engine could be described as belonging to [the] Lampredi School, its bore and stroke measurements were really more reminiscent of Colombo's V12 than anything else." Much effort was also put into designing its combustion chamber so that inlet and exhaust functions were enhanced. All these developments equated to an increase of 40 bhp over the similar-sized 860 Monza. Unlike today when the specifications of F1 racing cars are heavily regulated — indeed, many would argue completely overregulated — back in the 1950s, racers were not so subject to cylinder capacity restrictions or weight limits, which meant that engineers had the freedom to push existing technical

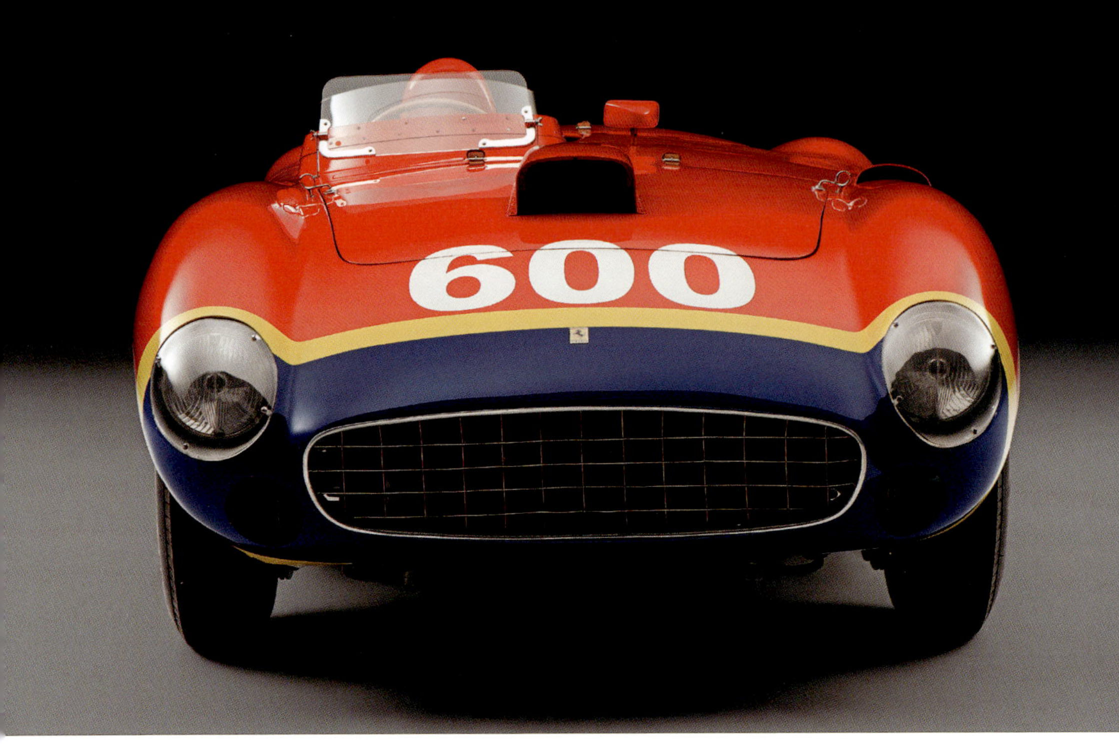

boundaries to the limits of achievability in their pursuit of racing glory. The fruits of their labors were then tested to the absolute maximum on some of the most challenging courses ever to have existed, most notably the aforementioned Mille Miglia. And as for the World Sportscar Championship of 1956, the other main reason behind the present car's development, Ferrari gloriously triumphed over its erstwhile Bolognese nemesis thanks to three wins out of five — two of which were taken by the sublime 290 MM by Scaglietti.

Opposite (top): The No. 600 Ferrari 290 MM (chassis no. 0626) with Juan Manuel Fangio at the wheel during the 1956 Mille Miglia. The car was specifically built for him by Ferrari, but he only managed to finish fourth.

Opposite (bottom): Juan Manuel Fangio in the No. 600 Ferrari 290 MM (chassis no. 0626) at the finish of the 1956 Mille Miglia and looking disappointed having placed fourth behind his teammate Eugenio Castellotti, who won the race in a sister Ferrari 290 MM Scaglietti and two Ferrari 860 Monza Scagliettis that took second and third.

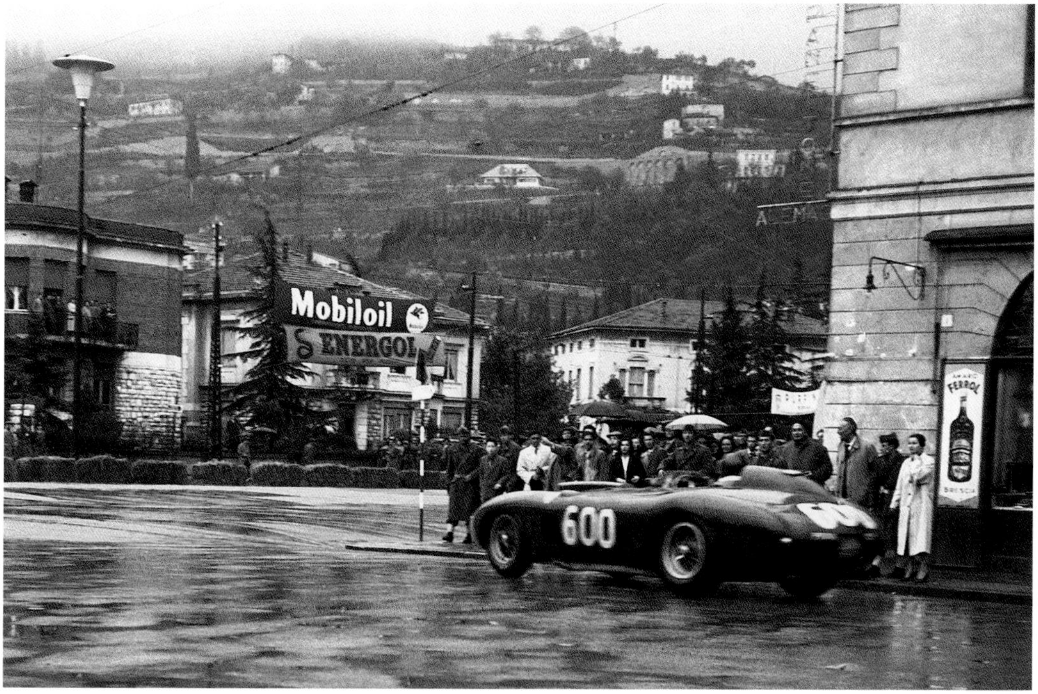
Mobiloil
ENERGOL
600

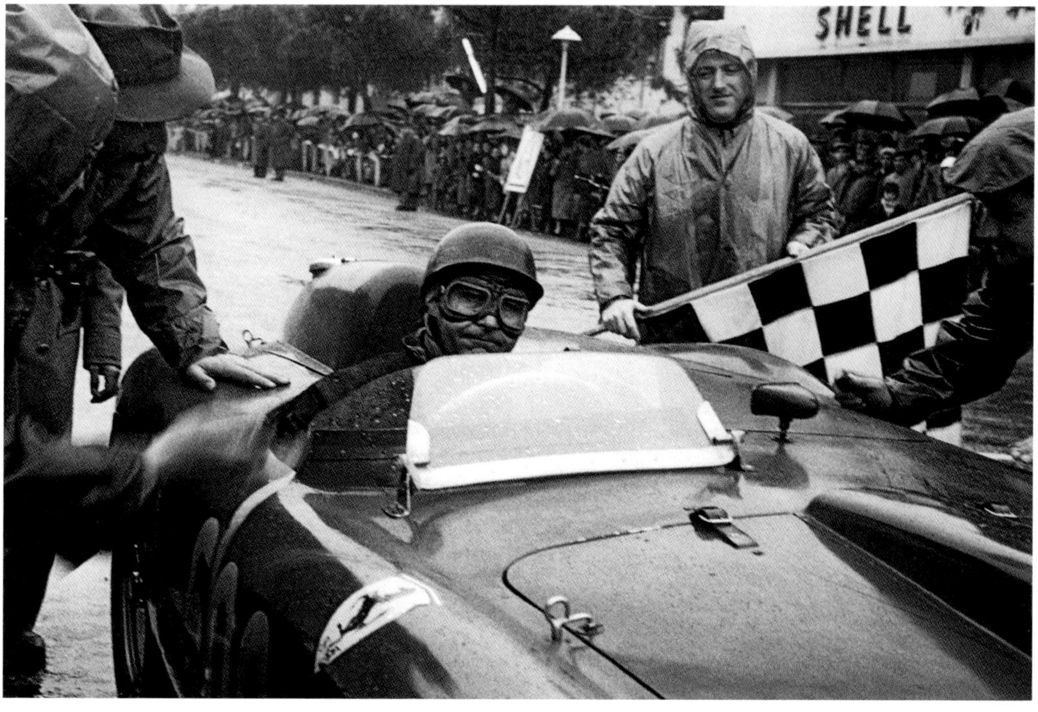
SHELL

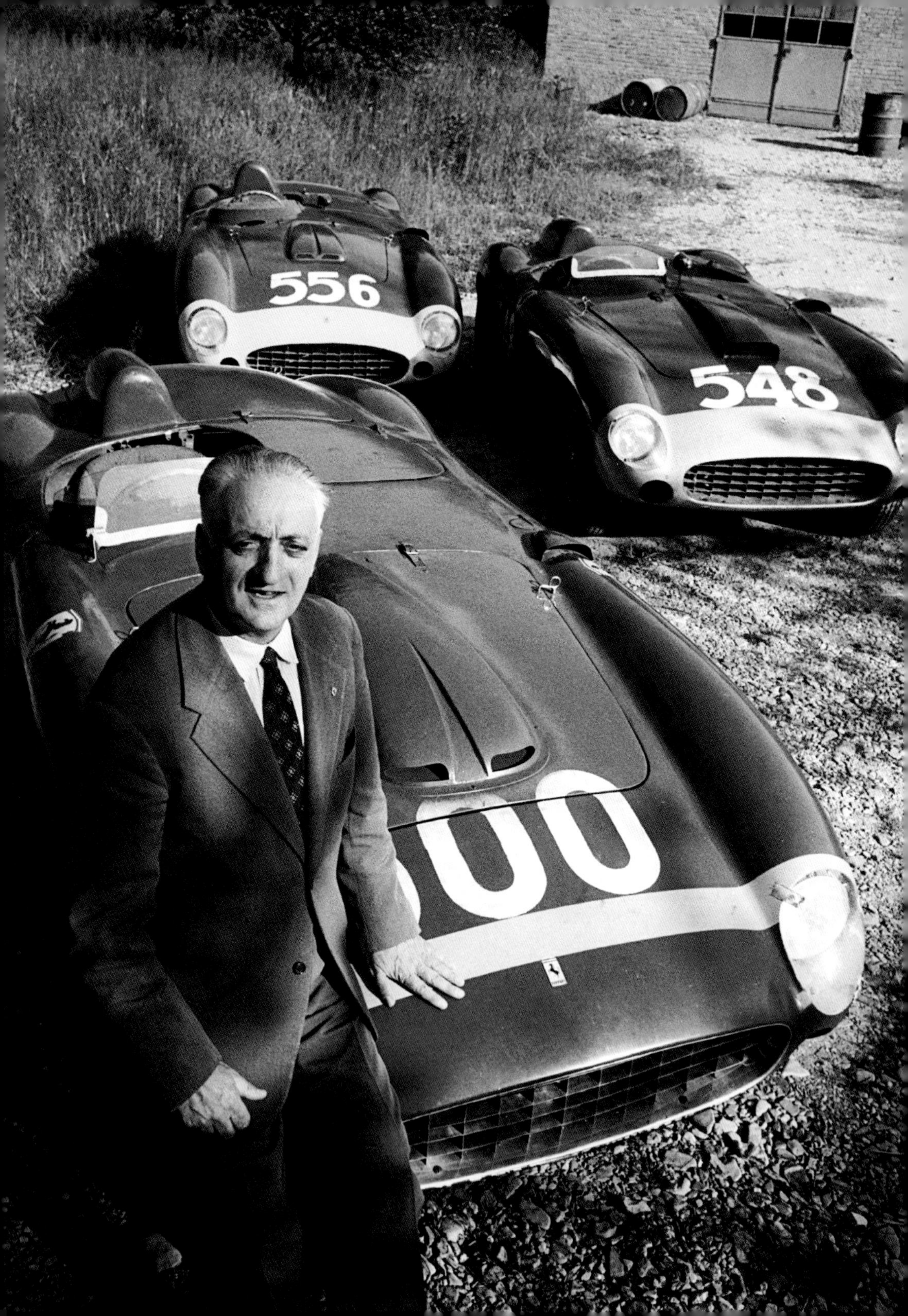
556
548

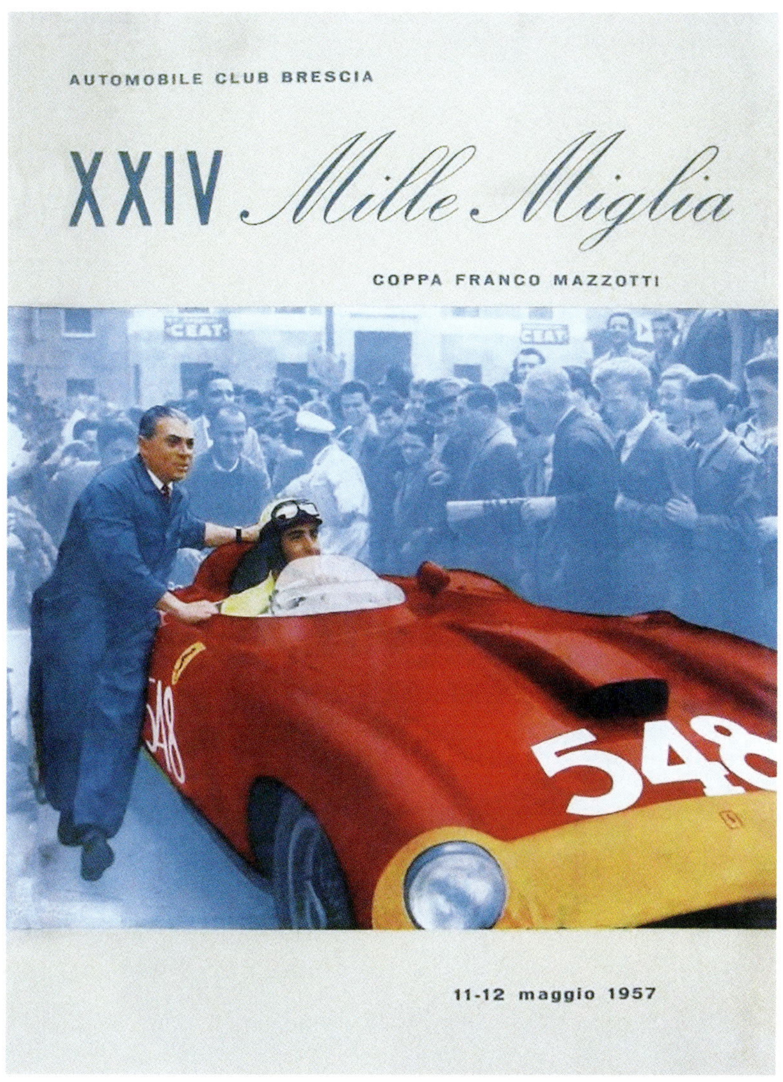

Opposite: Ferrari founder Enzo Ferrari (1898–1988) poses with his Mille Miglia-entered cars, the No. 600 Ferrari 290 MM Scaglietti of Juan Manuel Fangio, the No. 548 Ferrari 290 MM Scaglietti of Eugenio Castellotti and the No. 556 Ferrari 860 Monza Scaglietti of Luigi Musso, at the Ferrari factory, Maranello, Italy, 1956.

Above: 1957 XXIV Mille Miglia official program showing on the cover the 1956 Mille Miglia–winning No. 548 Ferrari 290 MM Scaglietti driven by Eugenio Castellotti.

Overleaf: Juan Manuel Fangio in the No. 600 Ferrari 290 MM by Scaglietti (chassis no. 0626) at the start of the 1956 Mille Miglia.

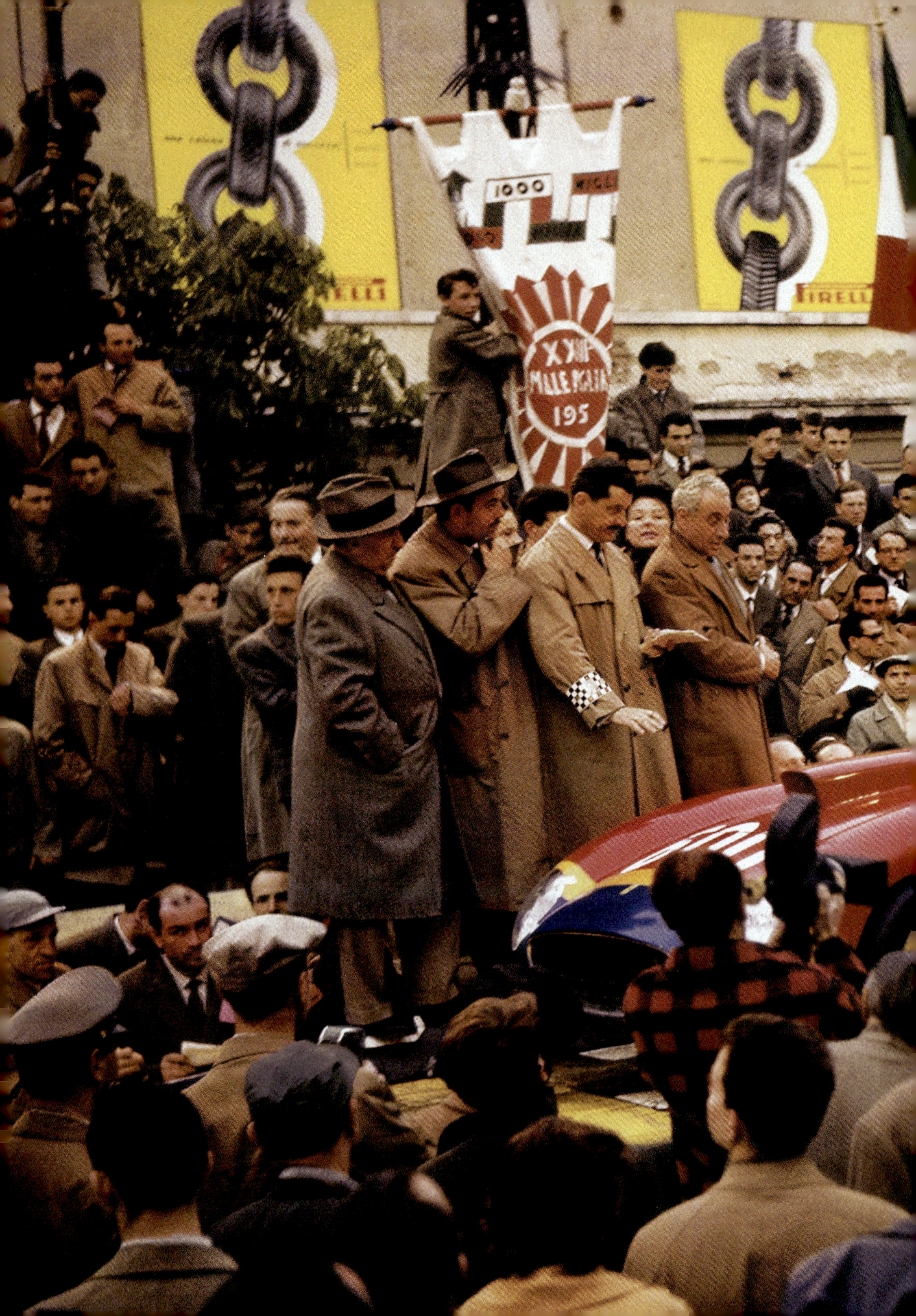
1000
MILLE MIGLIA
195
PIRELLI

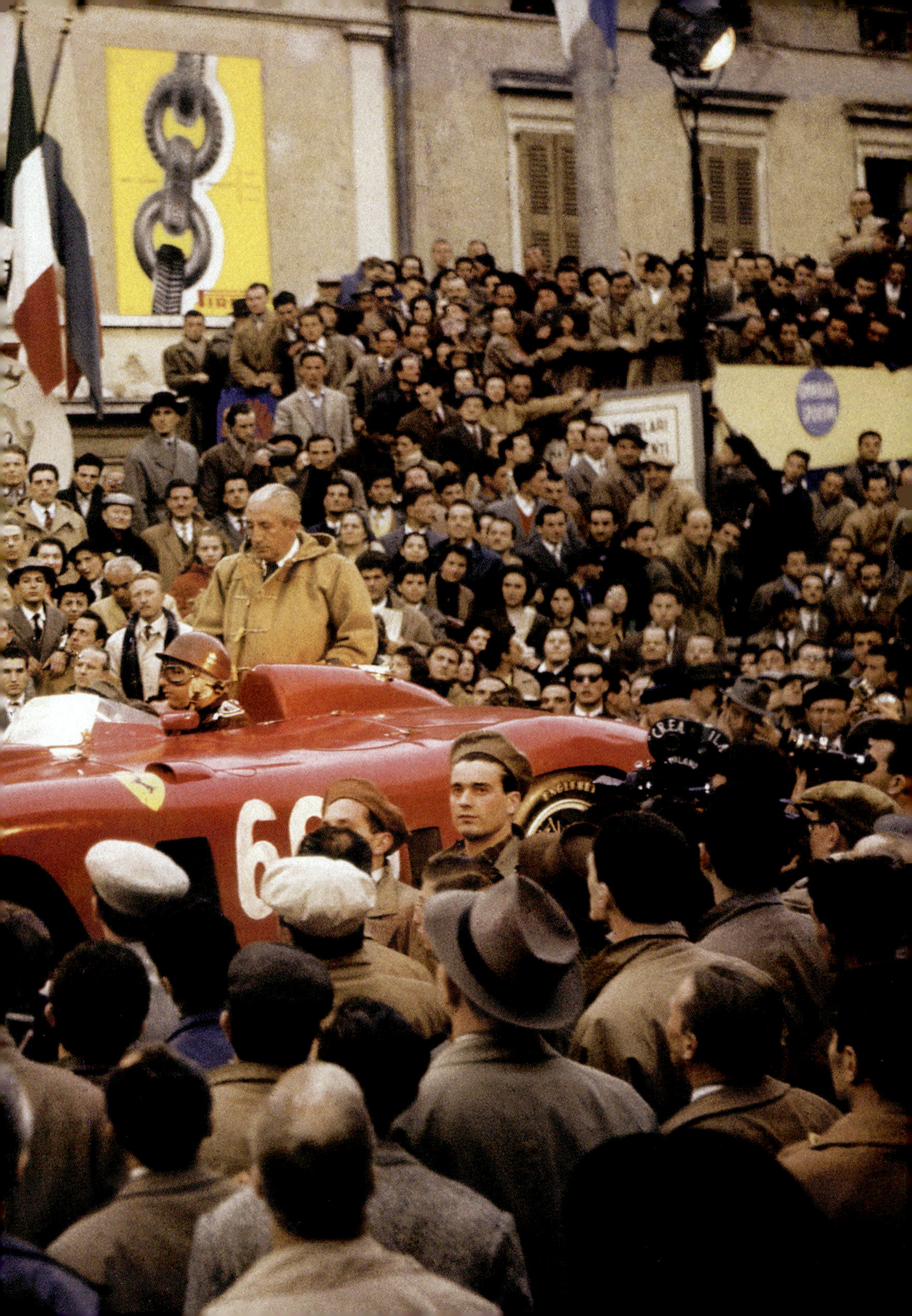

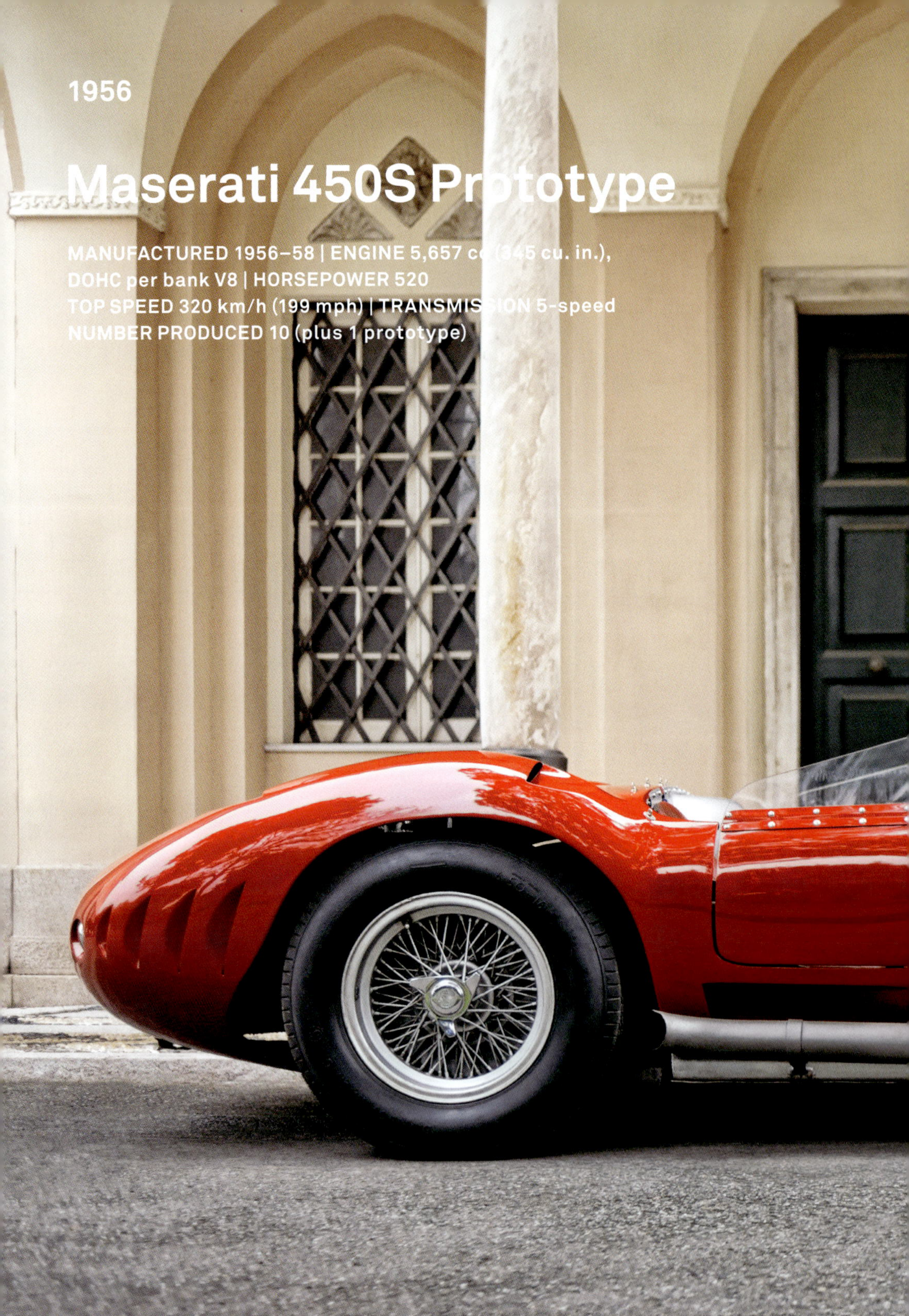

1956

Maserati 450S Prototype

MANUFACTURED 1956–58 | ENGINE 5,657 cc (345 cu. in.), DOHC per bank V8 | HORSEPOWER 520
TOP SPEED 320 km/h (199 mph) | TRANSMISSION 5-speed
NUMBER PRODUCED 10 (plus 1 prototype)

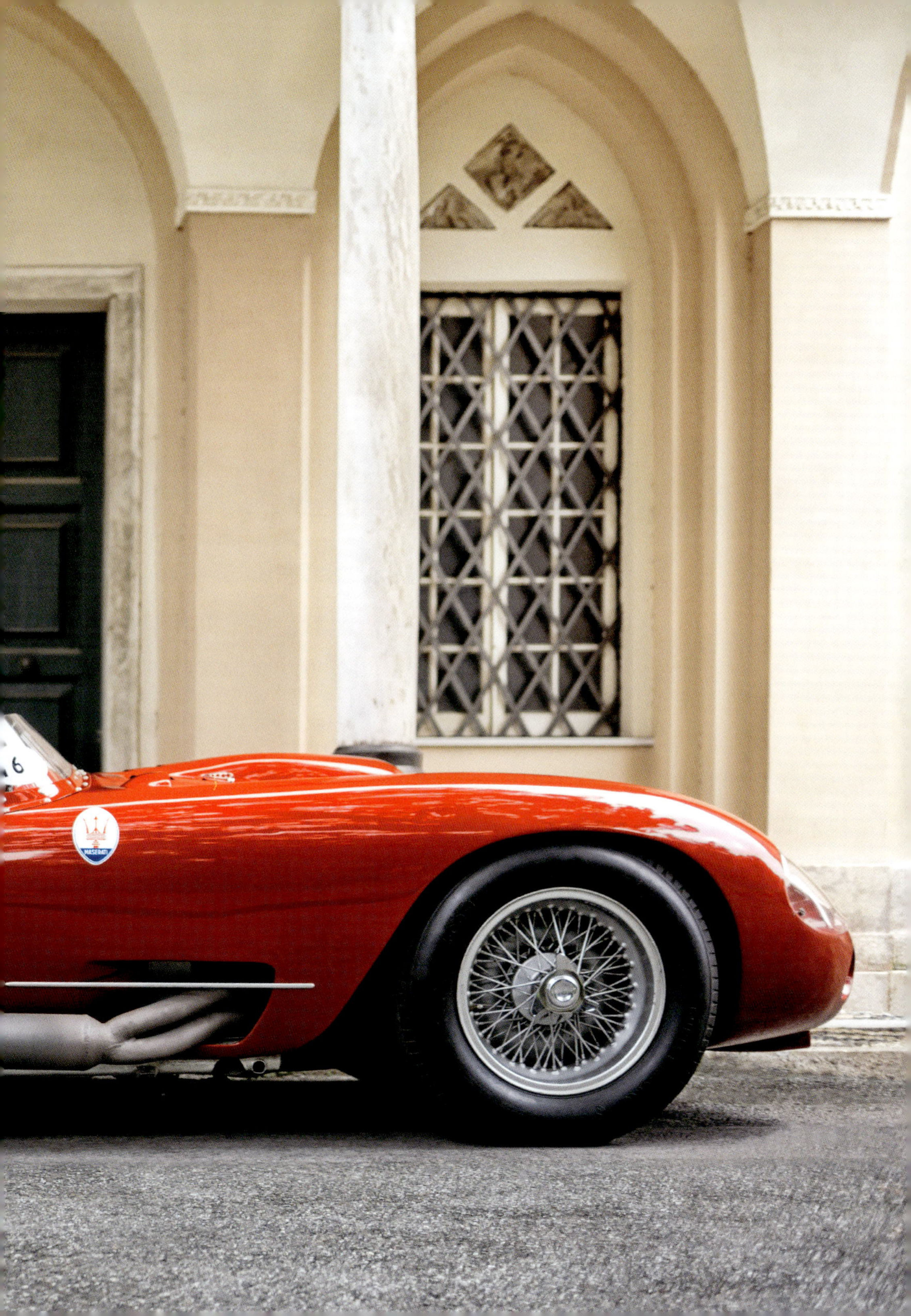
MASERATI

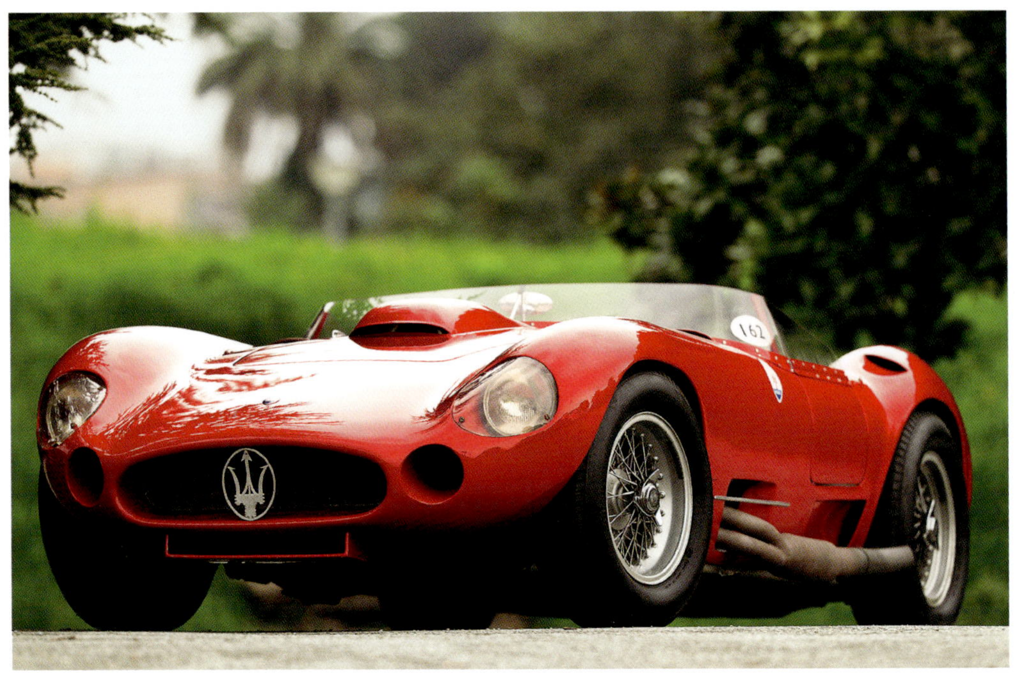

Officine Alfieri Maserati SA was established in Bologna in 1914, marking the nascence of one of Italy's most respected marques. This venture was very much a family affair and Alfieri, the founder, brought his brothers, Ettore, Bindo and Ernesto, into the business. Alfieri, Ettore and Bindo had all previously worked for Isotta Fraschini, a well-known Milanese luxury car manufacturer that was also renowned for producing high performance marine and aeronautical engines. During World War I, the Maserati brothers' technical expertise was focused on designing and manufacturing spark plugs for military aircraft engines. It was over this period that Alfieri developed an innovative and better-performing mica-insulated spark plug, which he patented in 1918 and which improved the reliability and performance of all kinds of engines.

In 1920 three of the Maserati brothers — Alfieri, Ettore and Ernesto — joined forces to create their very first engine. That same year the distinctive Maserati trident logo was devised by another sibling, Mario — it was inspired by Giambologna's bronze Neptune in Bologna's Piazza Maggiore. After redesigning this first Maserati engine, Alfieri and Ernesto were approached by the Turinese manufacturer Diatto to direct its racing team. The brothers also drove for the marque, with Alfieri winning the challenging Susa-Moncenisio mountain race of 1922. In 1926, Diatto decided to withdraw from competition, so the Marquis de Sterlich, who was himself a keen racing driver, provided financing for Alfieri to set up his own Maserati racing venture. Thanks to his dedication to innovation in the late 1920s and throughout the 1930s, Maserati became a serious motorsports contender — so much so that it attracted the great Tazio Nuvolari to its stable of drivers in 1933. Then, six years later,

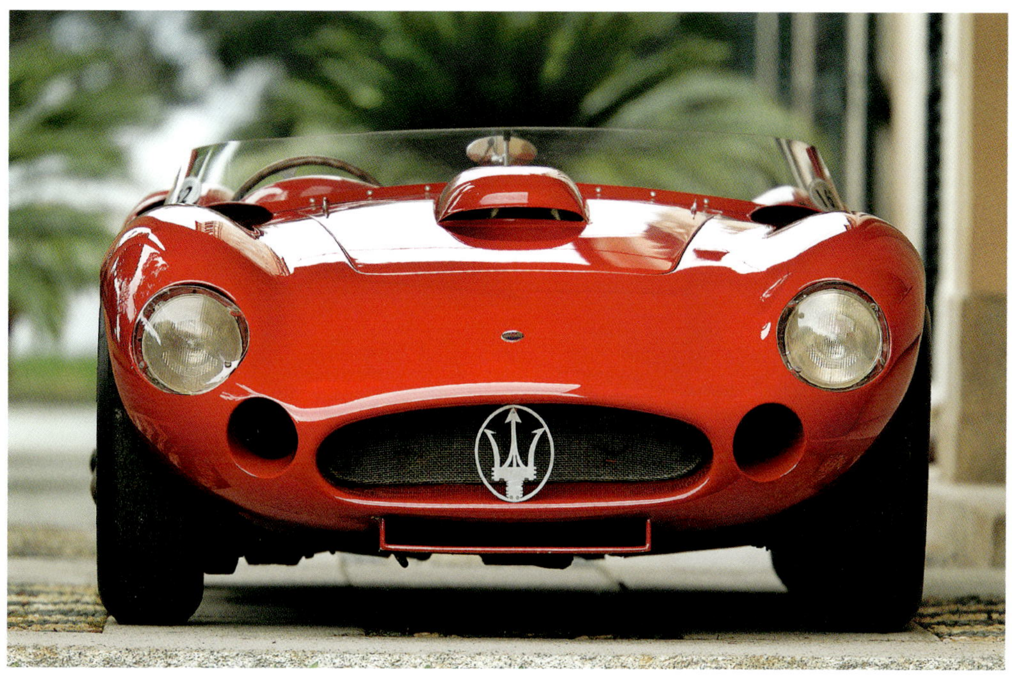

the marque enjoyed its first American victory at the Indianapolis 500 race, which brought it much international acclaim, as did another Indy victory the following year.

During World War II, Maserati's racing efforts were curtailed and the factory moved to Modena, where production was turned over to wartime materiel. Postwar, however, the company quickly resumed car production with the 1946 Maserati A6 grand tourer. In 1954, the marque's works team, racing as Officine Alfieri Maserati, returned to the track. This new dawn for Maserati within the motorsports arena was marked by the victorious debut of the Maserati 250F at the 1954 Argentine Grand Prix, piloted by Juan Manuel Fangio. This was followed up with the development of the legendary Maserati 450S, which was designed for the FIA's World Sportscar Championship — hence the "S" in its designation. The origins of this car go back to the early months of 1956, when the wealthy American property developer Tony Parravano asked the Maserati brothers to develop a new large-bore V8 engine to use with a Kurtis Kraft chassis for the upcoming Indy 500 race. This commission enabled Maserati to complete the development of its Tipo 54 V8 engine, which had been shelved in the wake of the 1955 Le Mans disaster, and to trial the new power plant in its own recently developed sports-racing 350S chassis.

The first example of the resultant Maserati 350S (chassis no. 3501) was raced at the Mille Miglia by Stirling Moss and Denis Jenkinson, although sadly it did not finish. This car's chassis was subsequently elongated to accommodate an all-new V8 engine. Once fitted, the car was transformed into the works 450S prototype, which debuted at the 1956 Swedish Grand Prix, where it showed promise, but also the necessity for a stronger

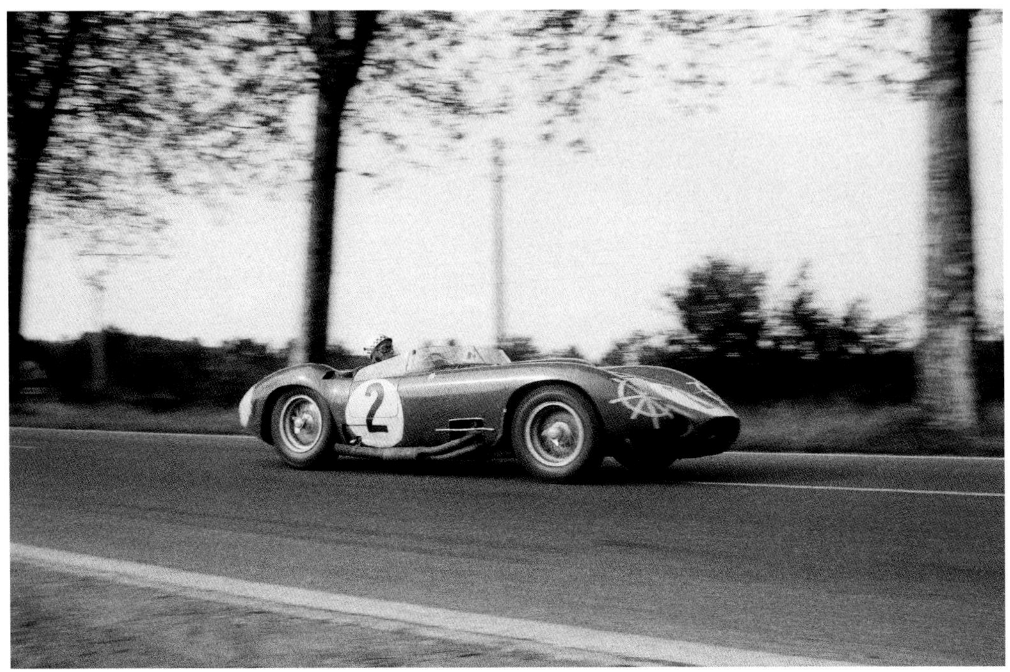

Previous spread: This car, originally built as a six-cylinder 350S and assigned chassis no. 3501, was hastily prepared for the 1956 Mille Miglia and was driven by Stirling Moss, with Denis Jenkinson navigating. They did not complete the race due to an accident. Later in 1956 chassis no. 3501 was elongated to accommodate an all-new 4.5-liter V8 engine and converted to the Works 450S prototype with chassis no. 4501 designation. In the late 1980s the engine was replaced with a 5.7-liter V8.

Above: Jean Behra at the wheel of the No. 2 Works Maserati 450S by Fantuzzi (chassis no. 4503), which he co-drove with André Simon, at the 1957 24 Hours of Le Mans. The car was retired from the race after three hours due to a driveshaft joint breaking, which caused an accident.

purpose-built chassis that could contain the formidable power of its engine. While these new chassis were being built for the follow-on production 450S, other developments were also worked on to get them ready for the 1957 1000 Kilometres of Buenos Aires race, that year's World Sportscar Championship season opener. Fangio, who took pole position, nicknamed the 450S the "bazooka" for good reason, even though he ultimately ended up with a DNF — or in other words a "Did Not Finish." The example, shown here, (chassis No. 3501/4501/350SI-10) is believed to be the 450S prototype, which like its ten production stablemates, has a stunning body that was aerodynamically sculpted by the Modena-based Carrozzeria Fantuzzi. For the following 1957 season, however, the Commission Sportive Internationale (CSI) introduced a new 3.0-liter engine restriction, which meant the 450S was ineligible to race. Nevertheless, the cars did continue to enjoy success on the American SCCA racing circuit. Because of the FIA's new rules only eleven 450S were ever made, including this prototype, making it one of the most collectible Maseratis of all time.

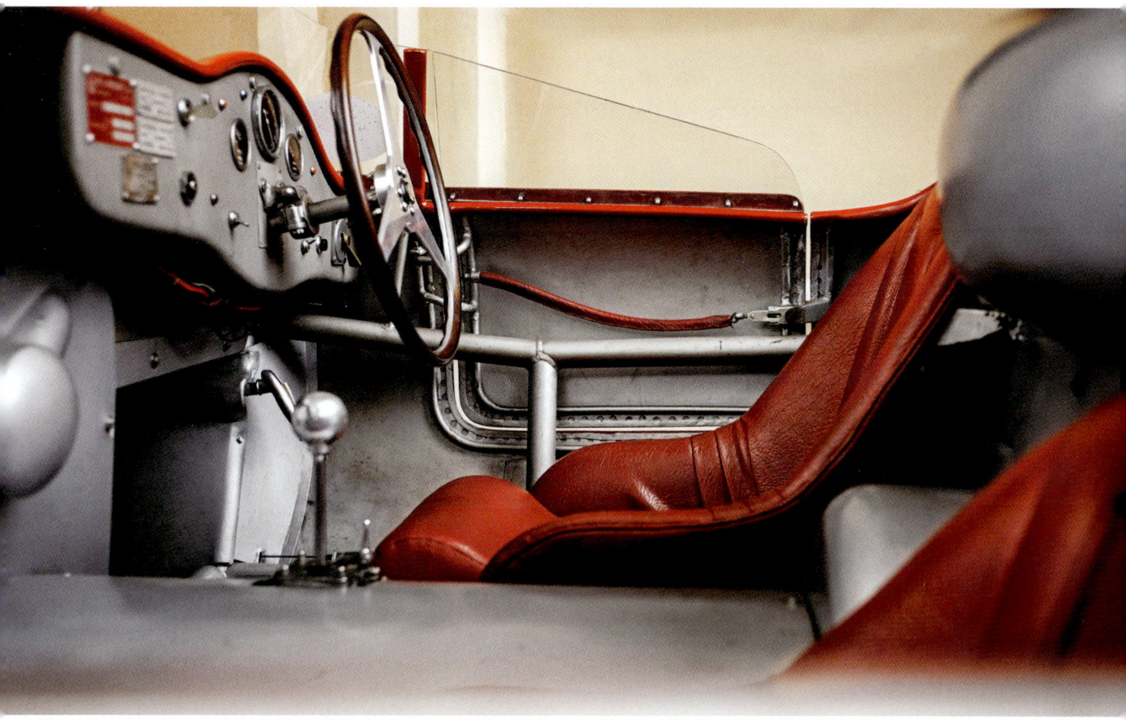

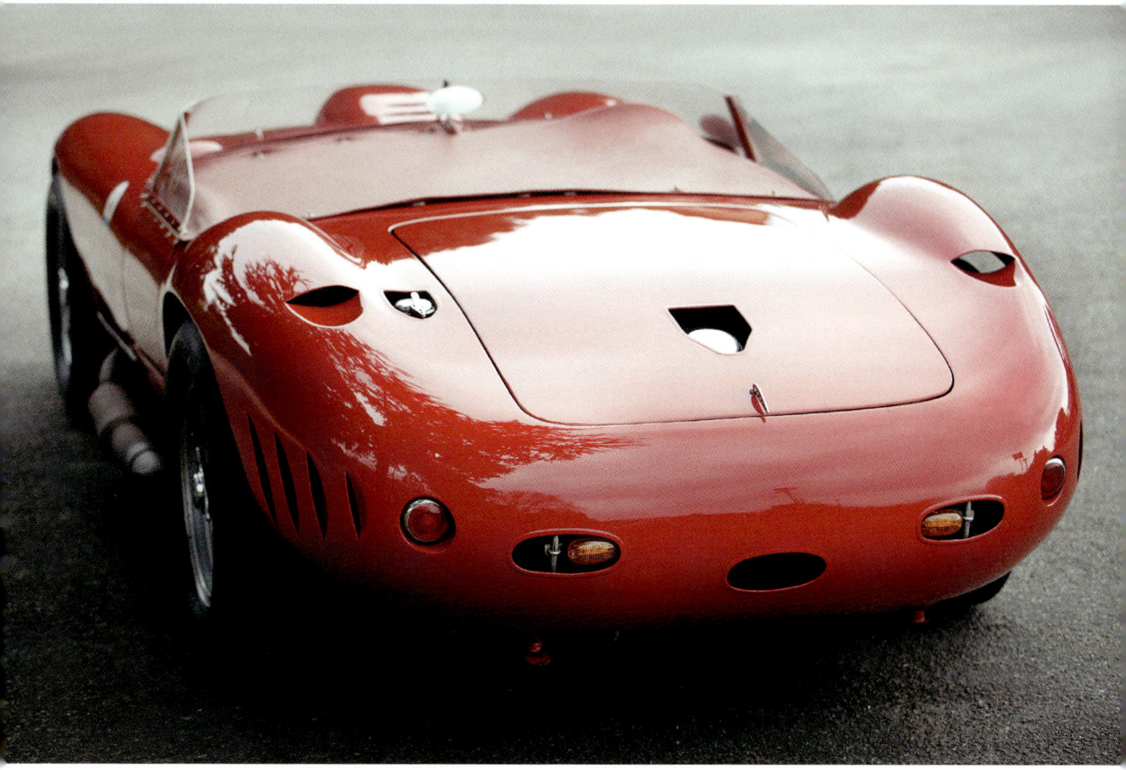

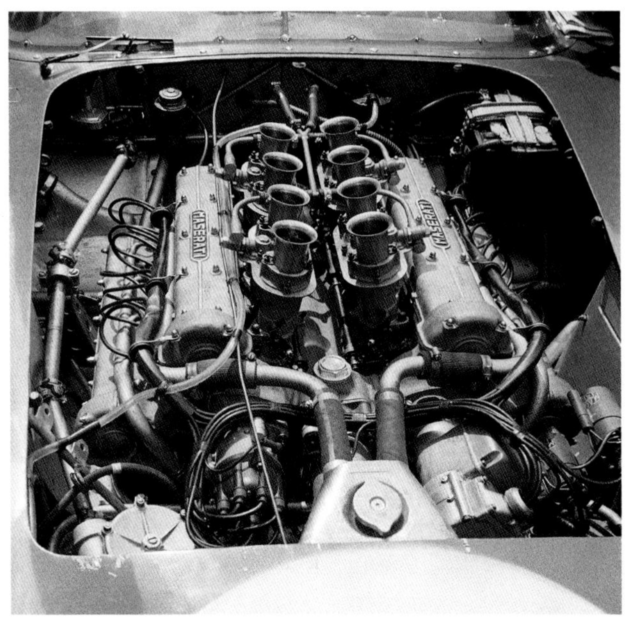

Left: The Maserati 450S 4,478 cc (273 cu. in.), DOHC per bank V8 engine with four Weber 45 IDM carburetors belonging to the car of Stirling Moss and Denis Jenkinson — photographed in Brescia, prior to the start of the 1957 Mille Miglia. With its immense output of 400 hp the quad cam, V8 engined 450S was easily the most powerful sports car of its day.

Below: Technical drawing of the Maserati 450S by Fantuzzi.

Opposite: Stirling Moss and Denis Jenkinson in the No. 537 Works Maserati 450S (chassis no. 4505) at the start of the 1957 Mille Miglia. They retired from the race due to a broken brake pedal.

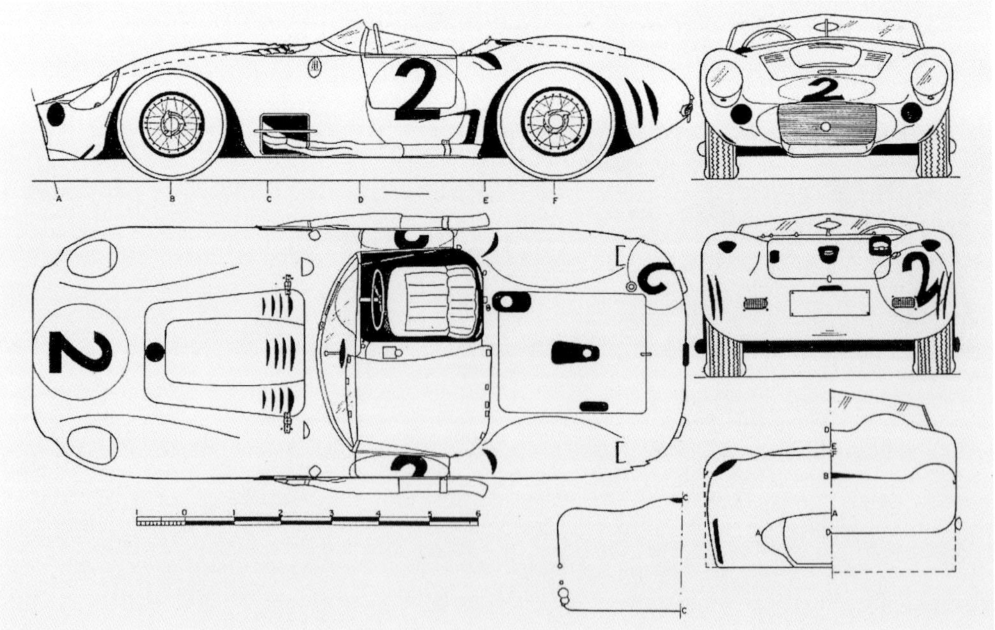

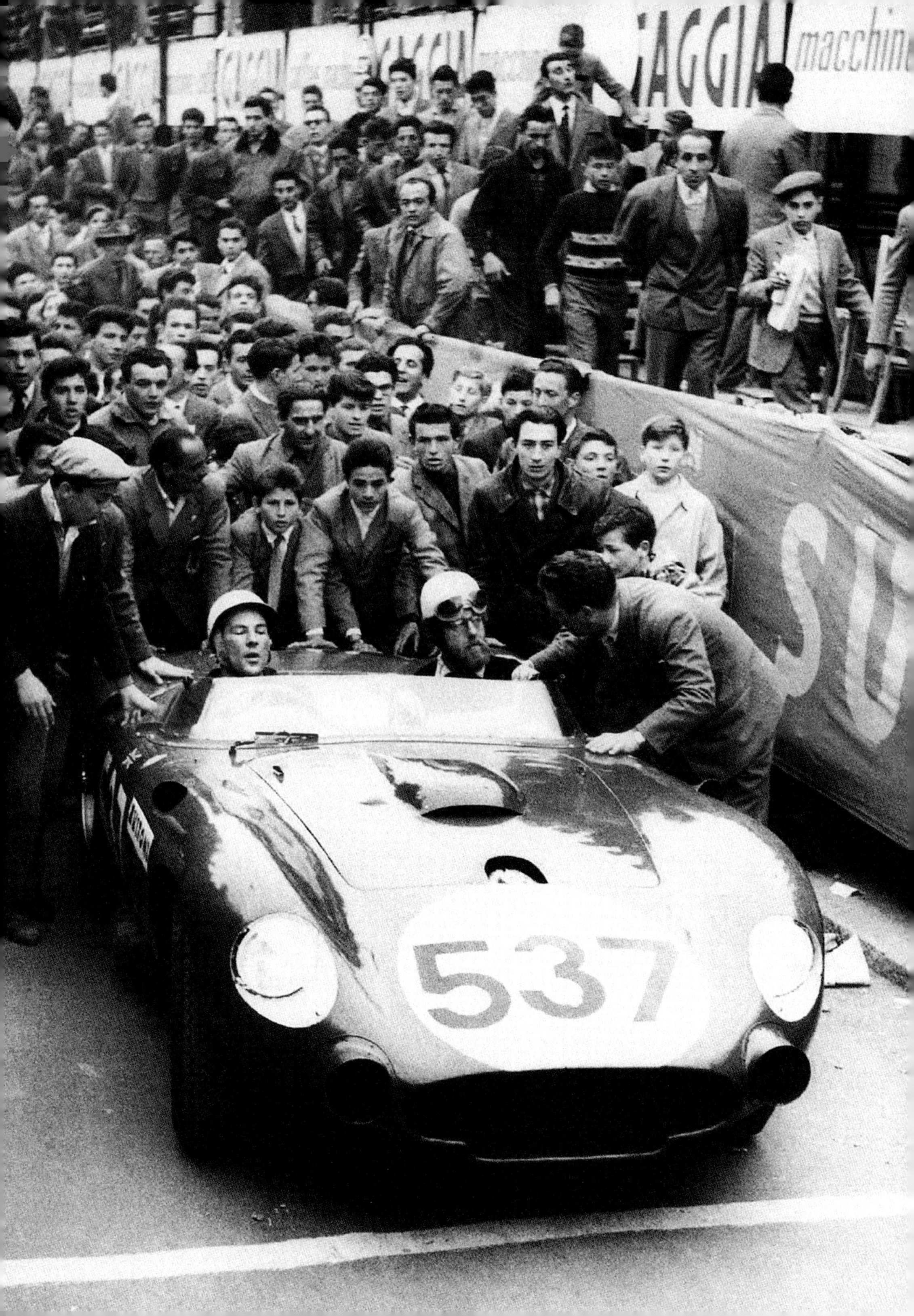
537

1956

Aston Martin DBR1

MANUFACTURED 1956–59 | ENGINE 2,992 cc (183 cu. in.), DOHC inline 6-cylinder | HORSEPOWER 268
TOP SPEED 249+ km/h (155+ mph) | TRANSMISSION 5-speed
NUMBER PRODUCED 5

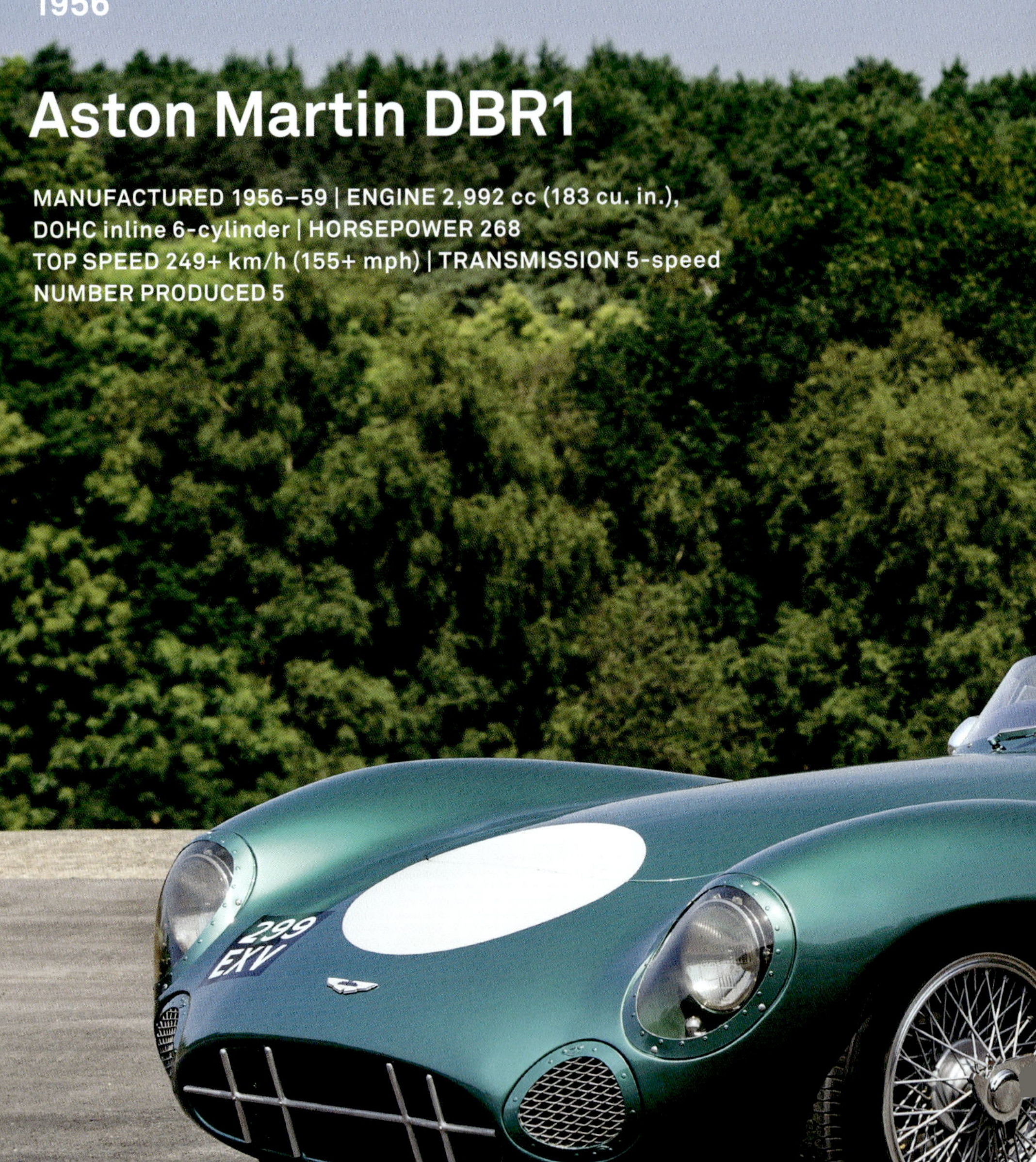

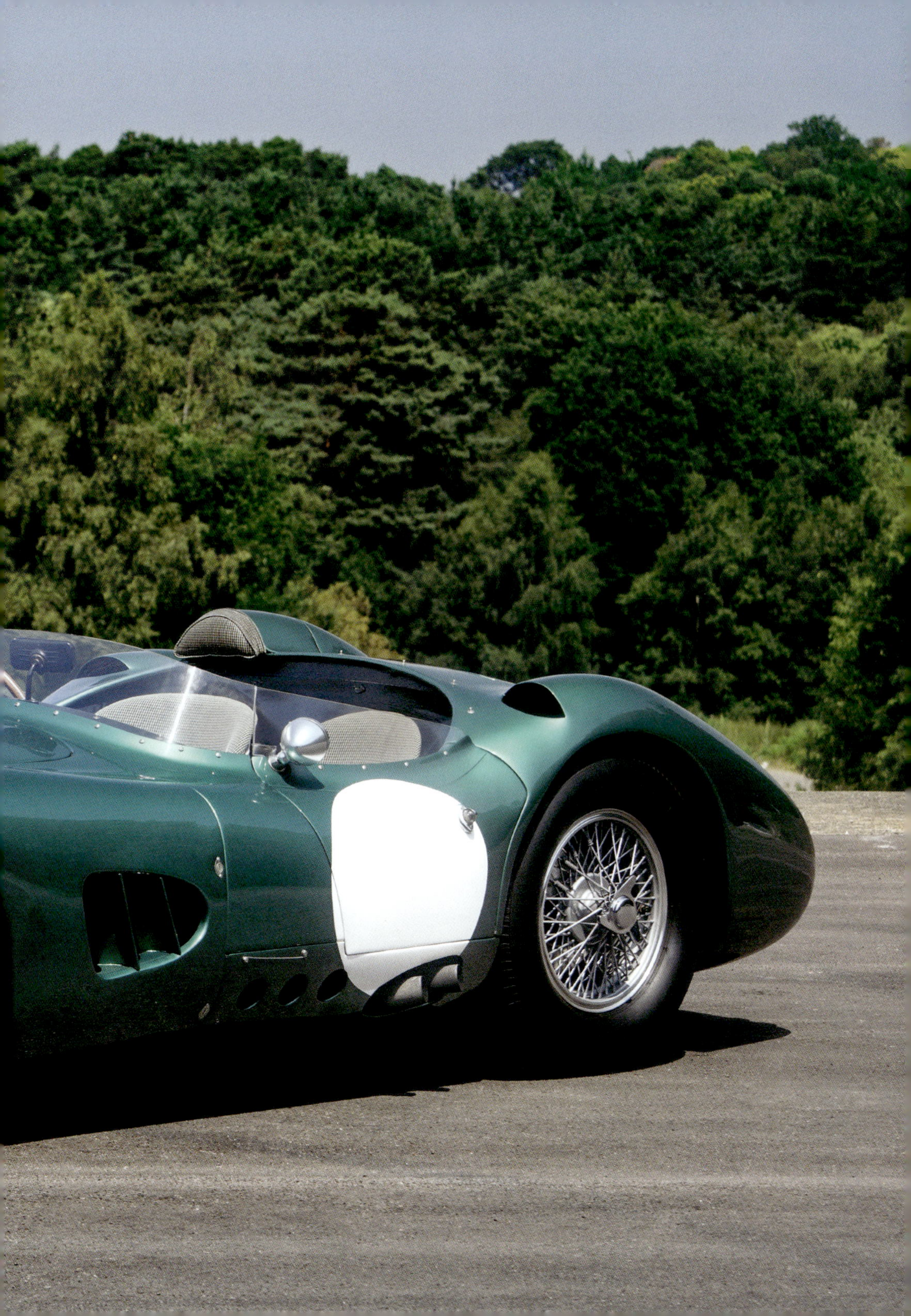

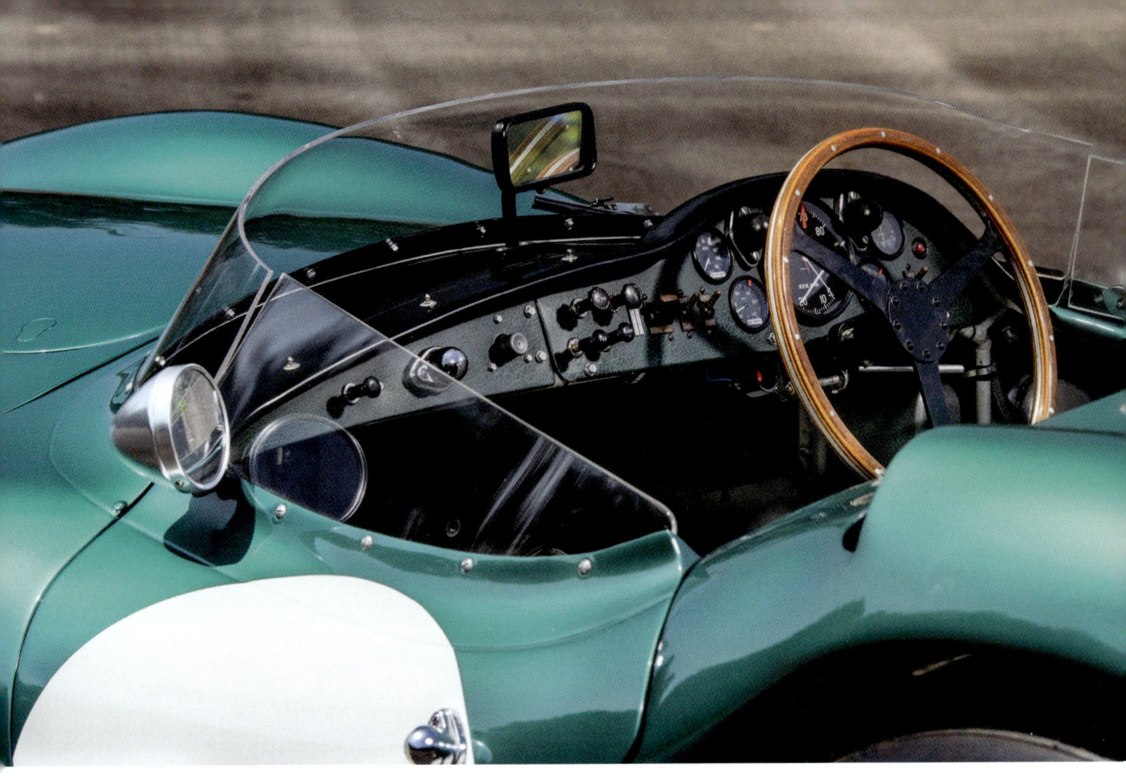

Aston Martin was founded by Lionel Martin and Robert Bamford in 1913 as a small London-based workshop. From these humble beginnings evolved one of Britain's most esteemed and well-loved marques, famed throughout the world for its very beautiful and elegant cars. As the company now explains, "The love of beautiful has always been our guiding principle. And Martin and Bamford's coming together was our earliest expression of it." Indeed, from the venture's outset, its founders were determined to create attractive cars that were based on exceptional engineering and superlative craftsmanship — an ethos that has remained to this day. Its cars from the 1910s right through to the 1930s were all beautifully proportioned and provided exceptional performance, and had a distinctive though subtle look that distinguished them from other luxury cars of the time. Their lines were a little smoother and their overall layout a little more graceful, but that was about it. In 1939, however, the marque created an interesting aerodynamic prototype, known as the Atom, which heralded a new, more sculptural and unified aesthetic that gave Aston Martin cars after the war, when production was resumed, a very definable "signature" appearance. It was the Aston Martin DBR1 sports-racing car that perhaps best exemplifies this forward-looking, purposeful-yet-sensuous new look. Having first appeared in 1956, it was developed to compete in the World Sportscar Championship (WSC), which at that stage included the most epic of endurance competitions of them all: the 24 Hours of Le Mans.

The DBR1's design was prompted by the introduction of a new Le Mans rule, which stipulated that the cars raced on its Circuit de la Sarthe no longer had to be street legal

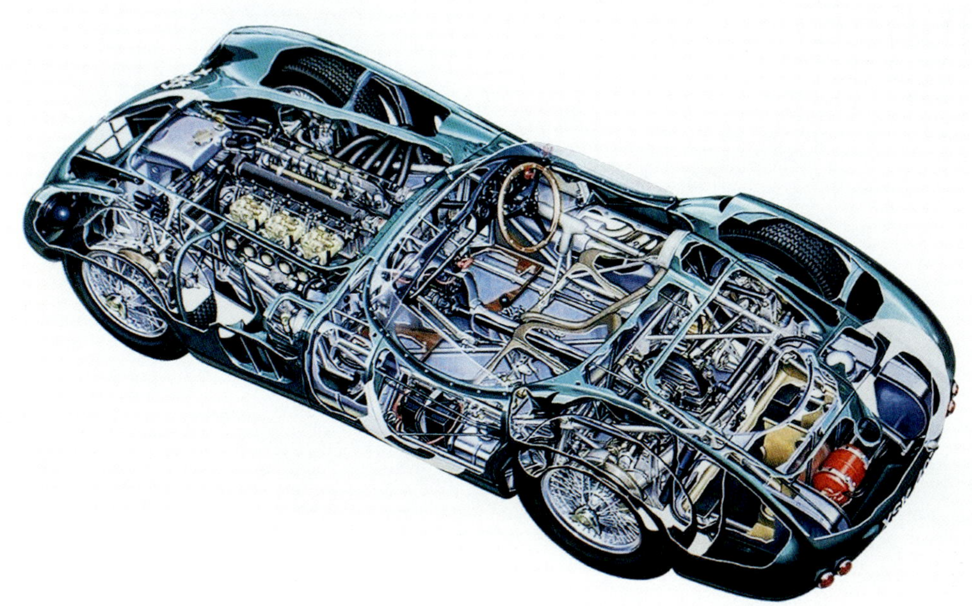

Opposite: Detail of Aston Marin DBR1/1 steering wheel, instrumentation and controls.

Above: Cutaway drawing of the 1957 Works Aston Martin DBR1/2, the single most successful racing car ever built by the company. It scored seven major victories between 1957 and 1959, the most important of which was the win of the 24 Hours of Le Mans in 1959 in the hands of Roy Salvadori and Carroll Shelby.

Below (left): Detail of Aston Martin DBR1/1 2,992 cc (183 cu. in.), DOHC inline six-cylinder engine with triple Weber 45 DCO carburetors. This engine is a correct reproduction unit that was installed in DBR1/1 by a former owner for historic racing purposes. The original RB6/300/3 engine was deemed too precious to risk racing, but came with the car when it was sold by RM Sotheby's in 2017.

Below (right): Details of DBR1/1 cockpit, internal structure of the Ted Cutting–designed ultra-lightweight 20/22 gauge alloy body and perimeter-type, small-tube space-frame chassis.

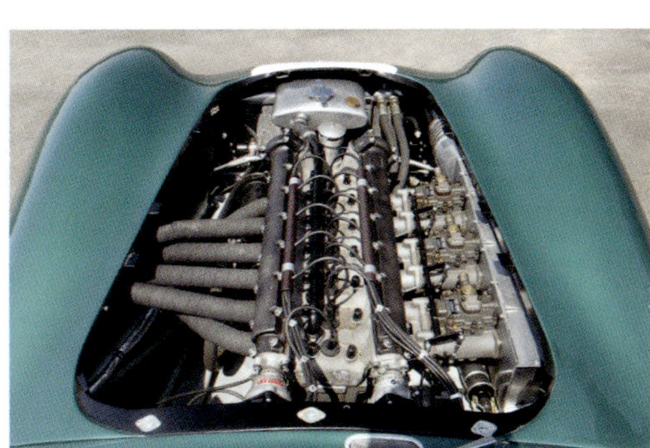

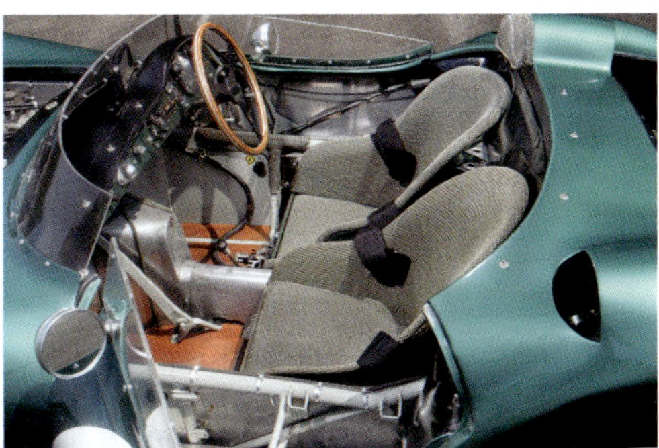

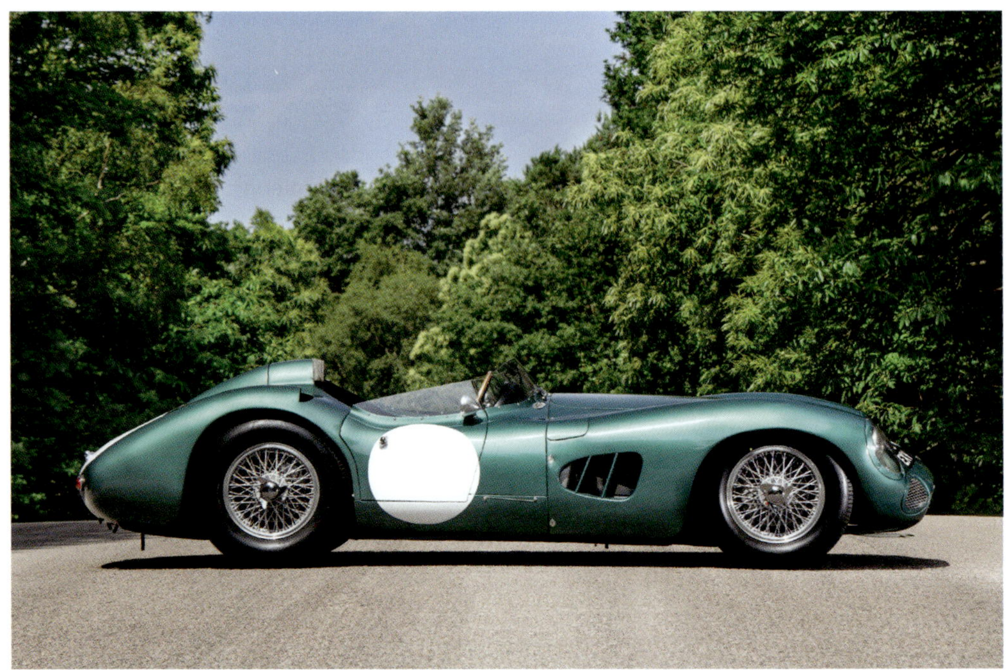

or even based on road-going cars. Prior to this, Aston Martin had been fielding — as per race-entry stipulations — prototypes that were technically road-legal, such as its DB3S, which due its lack of power was just not as competitive as the company would have liked. Its fixed-head coupé variant had also proved to be unstable at high speeds when fielded at Le Mans. The introduction of this new rule effectively offered Aston Martin a clean slate for the design and development of a new works prototype: the immortal DBR1. However, when it was first introduced with a 2.5-liter engine, it was beset with reliability issues. These were all eventually ironed out and by 1959 this stunningly beautiful full-competition racer, with a now upgraded 3-liter engine, was able to flex its well-toned muscles with sensational results. That year it seized a spectacular 1-2 finish at Le Mans, with Carroll Shelby and Roy Salvadori co-piloting the winning car (chassis no. DBR1/2), while Maurice Trintignant and Paul Frère drove its stablemate into second place. With typical Texan grit, Shelby managed to bring his car a lap ahead of Trintignant's in order to orchestrate an unforgettable formation finish. The result of that race made especially interesting reading — the average lap speeds of the two Aston prototypes were 181.16 and 180.75 km/h respectively, while the three road-going Ferrari 250 GT LWB Berlinettas and a 250 GT LWB California Spider Competizione (see p. 232) that followed immediately in their wake had lap times ranging from 164.77 to 166.73 km/h — showing the competiveness of these two British upstarts. Yet, this was only when they were pitted against Ferrari's race-prepped road-going machines, rather than Maranello's full-on racing prototypes, except that is when Stirling Moss was piloting the DBR1.

The DBR1 shown here (chassis no. DBR1/1) was the first of five to be constructed and famously won the 1959 Nürburgring 1,000 km, while being driven by Stirling Moss and Jack Fairman. Over its racing career it was also piloted by Roy Salvadori, Jack Brabham and Carroll Shelby. So buoyed up by the DBR1's success during the 1959 season, Aston Martin's David Brown Racing Department decided to forego sports car racing at the end of that epic season in order to concentrate its efforts on the challenges of Formula 1. With hindsight, this decision to focus on the highest level of open-wheel racing was ill judged, because the DBR4 racers fielded at the Formula One World Championship that same season, 1959, as well as following one were pretty lackluster in comparison to their sports car stablemate. Indeed, so were the follow-up DBR5 F1 cars. The DBR1s' story, however, did not end there as four of them were sold off by the factory and were subsequently raced by privateers in various series for another couple of years, before landing up in museums or private collections. Arguably the most important car ever built by Aston Martin, the DBR1 with its deep-throated engine, its sleek eye-catching body and its formidable performance had an undeniable poise and graceful presence that can be seen to utterly embody the marque's now-guiding motto: "Power, beauty and soul." And it is this last attribute, so difficult to achieve within any man-made object, let alone a car, that has always made Aston's immortal DBR1 so special, so deeply emotionally compelling.

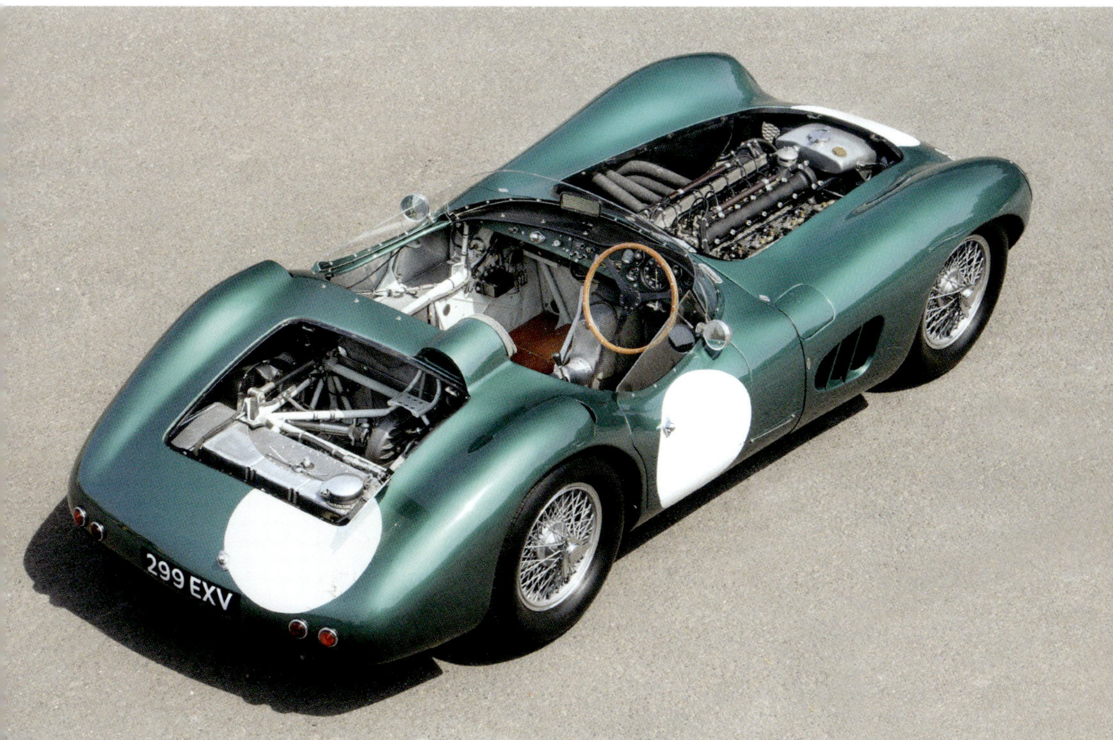

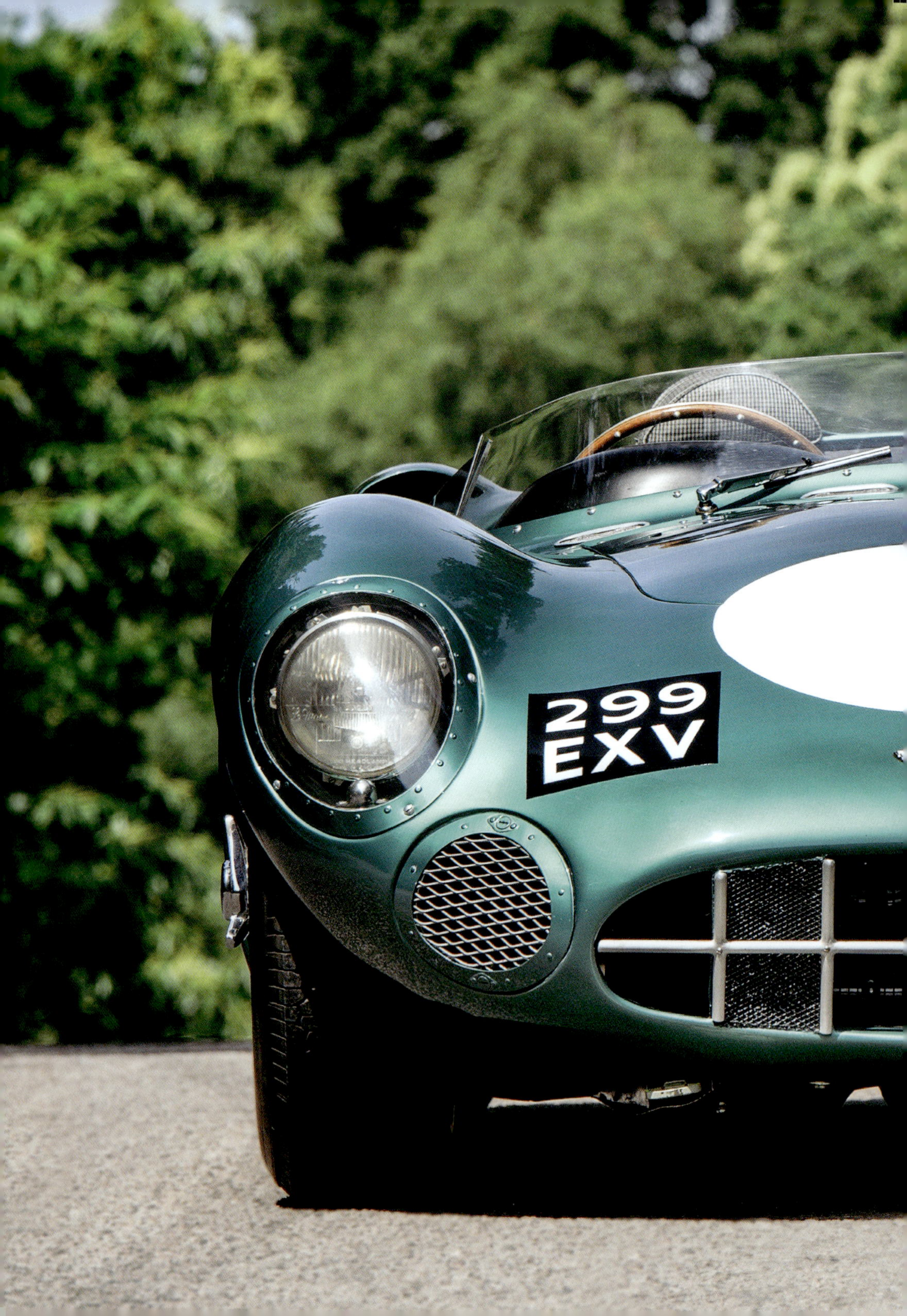
299
EXV

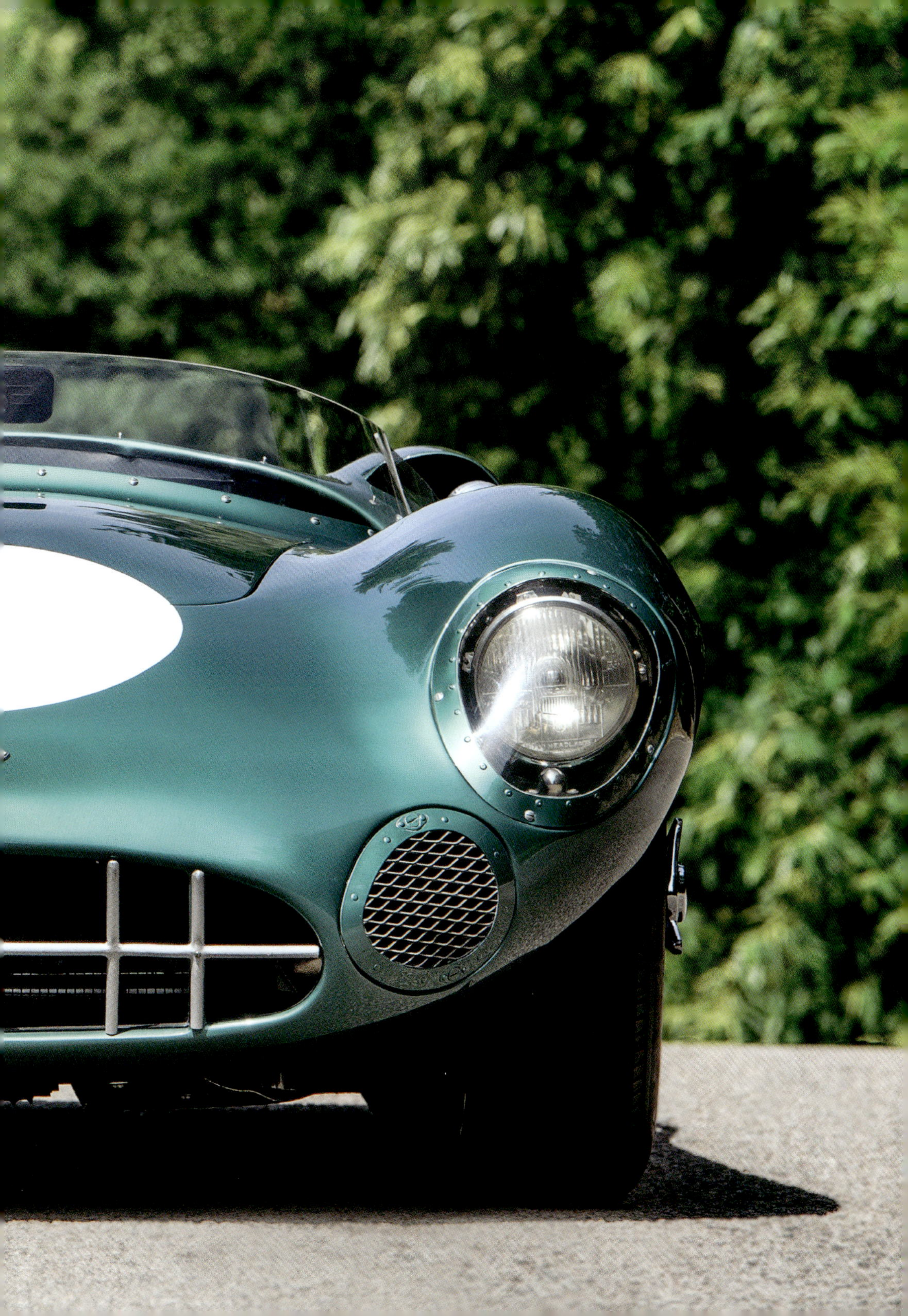

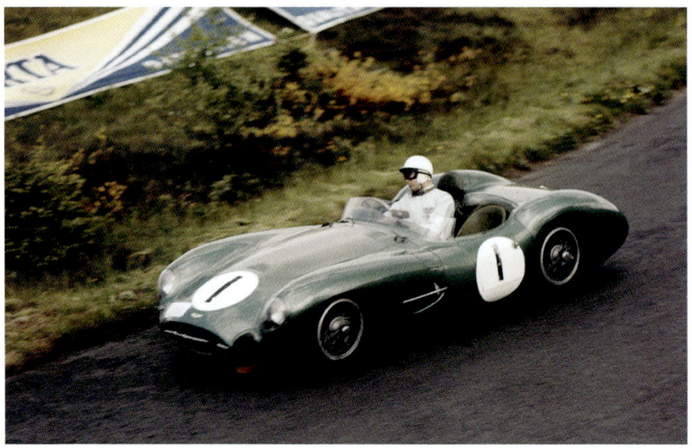

Left: Stirling Moss behind the wheel of the No. 1 Works Aston Martin DBR1/1 at the 1959 1,000 km of the Nürburgring. He won the race spectacularly, breaking the lap record 16 times in one of his greatest-ever drives, with co-driver Jack Fairman having driven only eight laps.

Below: Stirling Moss and Jack Fairman undertake a driver change to their Works Aston Martin DBR1/1 at the 1959 1,000 km of the Nürburgring.

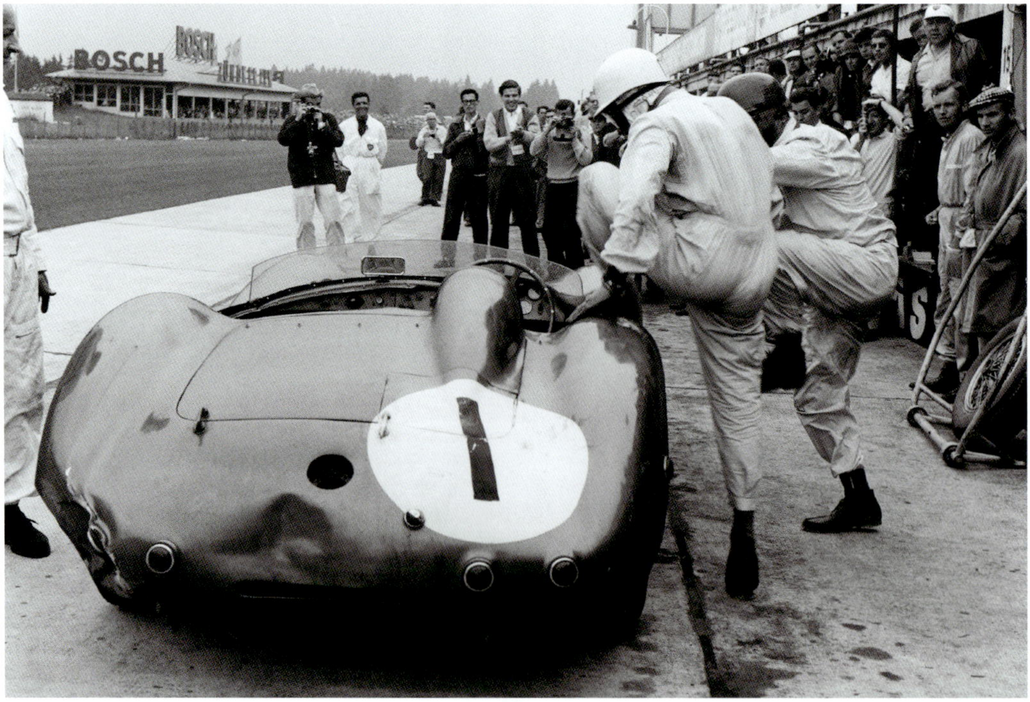

Right: Poster celebrating the first and second place triumph of the Works Aston Martin DBR1s at the 1959 24 Hours of Le Mans.

Below: No. 5 Works Aston Martin DBR1/2, driven by Carroll Shelby and Roy Salvadori, taking victory at the 1959 24 Hours of Le Mans. The No. 6 Works Aston Martin DBR1/4, driven by Maurice Trintignant and Paul Frère, placed second. The next-closest competitor was a distant 25 laps behind the duo. This achievement is considered Aston Martin's finest motorsports triumph.

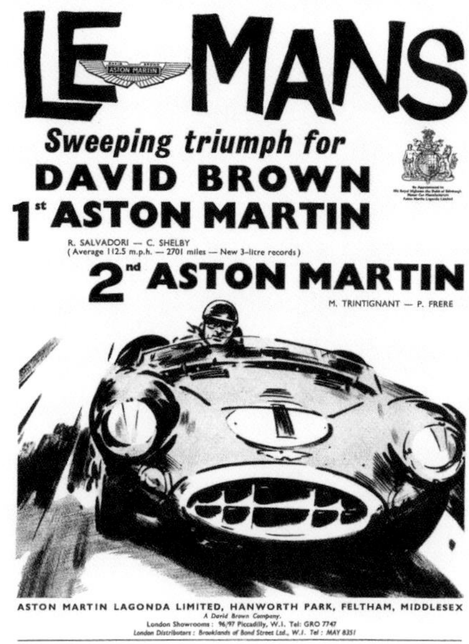

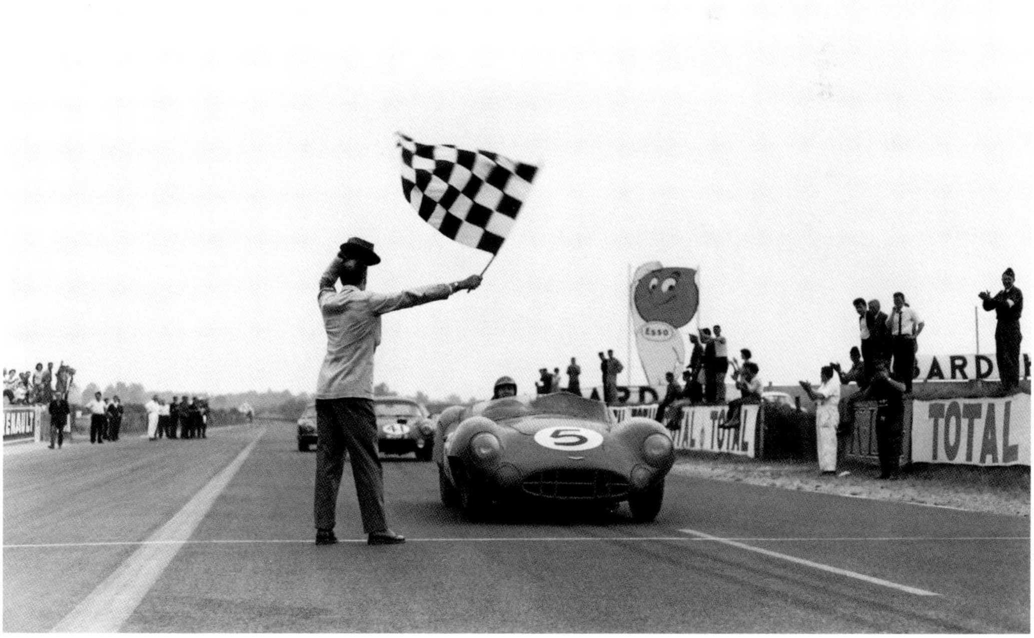

1957

Jaguar XK-SS

MANUFACTURED 1957 | **ENGINE** 3,442 cc (210 cu. in.), DOHC inline 6-cylinder | **HORSEPOWER** 262
TOP SPEED 230 km/h (143 mph) | **TRANSMISSION** 4-speed
NUMBER PRODUCED 16

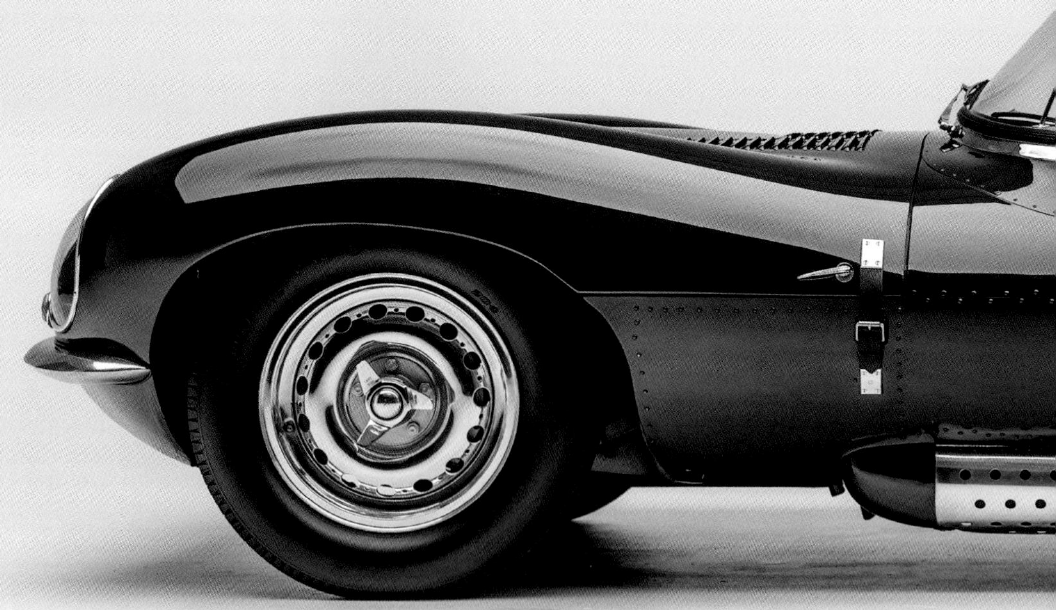

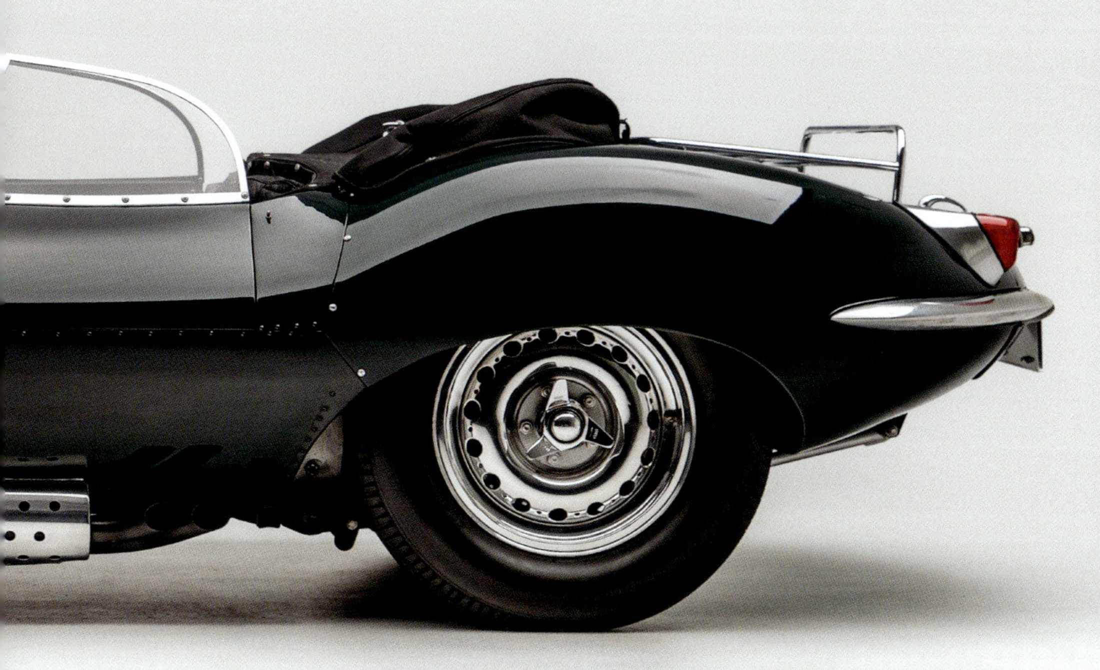

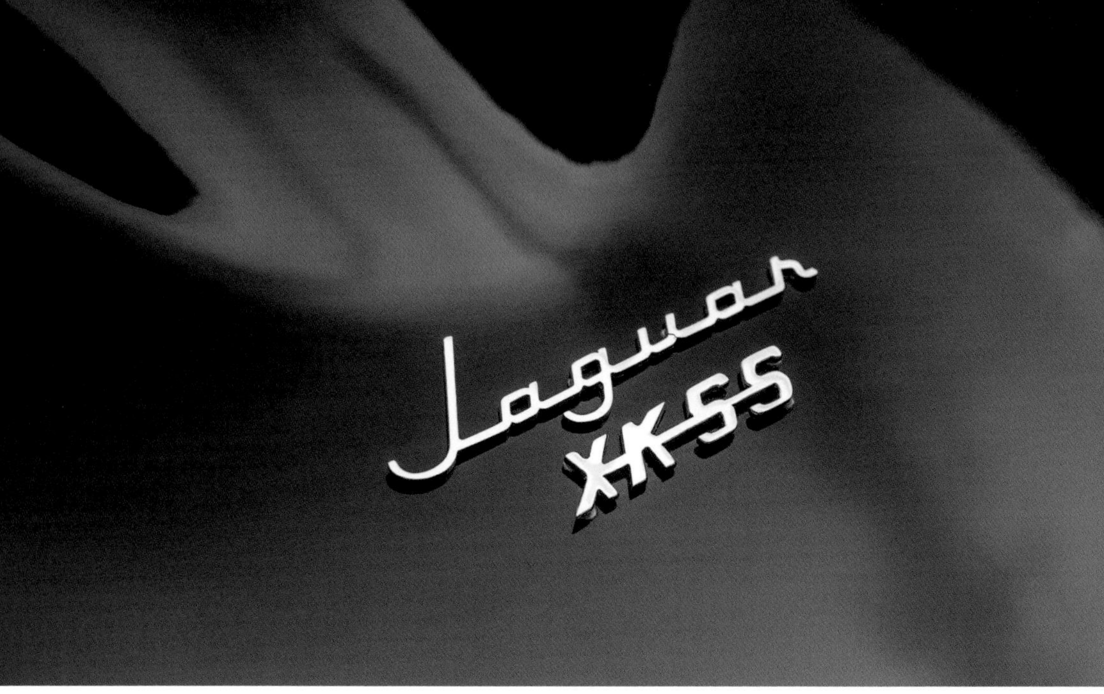

Although it has been irreverently described by *Autoweek* as resembling "part E-Type, part UFO, part frankfurter," the Jaguar XK-SS is a jaw-droppingly beautiful British sports car that famously pulled the heart strings of Steve McQueen, when he first spied one in a studio parking lot on Sunset Boulevard. That particular example was then owned by local radio personality Bill Leyden, who had himself acquired the car from James Peterson, a contractor who had helped develop Riverside International Raceway in California. For McQueen, who was passionate about beautiful fast cars, it was obviously love at first sight because shortly thereafter he managed to cajole his first wife, Neile, into handing over a check for the open-top two-seater to the tune of $5,000 — a princely sum back then. This equates to about $40,000 in today's money, but nothing like what its actual value is today thanks to its rarity and celebrity association. When it first came into McQueen's possession the right-hand-drive XK-SS shown here (chassis no. XK-SS713) was off-white with a red interior. Its bodywork, however, was soon stripped down and repainted in British racing green, while the interior was given an all-black makeover by Tony Nancy, aka "The Loner," a leading Californian hot-rodder.

McQueen later affectionately christened his beloved XK-SS the "Green Rat," and for the next 20 years it was, according to his biographer, Marcelo Abeal, "his favorite weapon in most of his nocturnal raids." Indeed, its distinctive high decibel throaty roar became well known to his neighbors living in the Hollywood Hills as he raced along Mulholland Drive in the early hours. Reputedly, McQueen received so many speeding tickets during the first year of ownership of this car that his license was almost revoked twice.

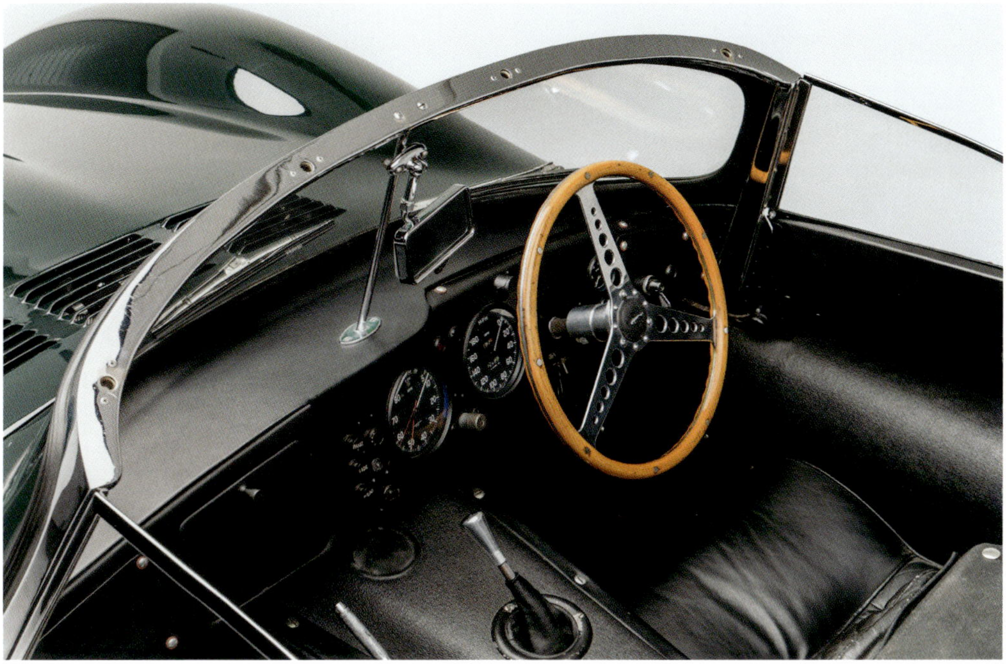

Quickly, this seemingly exotic imported car became inextricably linked to his daredevil persona, and vice versa. Today, this XK-SS is well known within collecting circles as simply the "McQueen Jag." Indeed, the "King of Cool" loved this sporty feline so much that after having regretfully sold it in 1969 he bought it back eight years later and it remained in his possession right up to his untimely death in 1980. This race-bred beauty, with its characterful "smiling" front end, now fittingly resides in the world-renowned Petersen Automotive Museum in Los Angeles.

Above: Detail of Jaguar XK-SS steering wheel, instruments and controls.

Right: Detail of left side of Jaguar XK-SS 3,442 cc (210 cu. in.), DOHC inline six-cylinder engine. This XK engine, which was developed for the D-Type, was the first Jaguar engine to feature an asymmetrical head that was known as the "35/40 head"—the intake valves being mounted at 35 degrees, with the exhaust valves being mounted at 40 degrees.

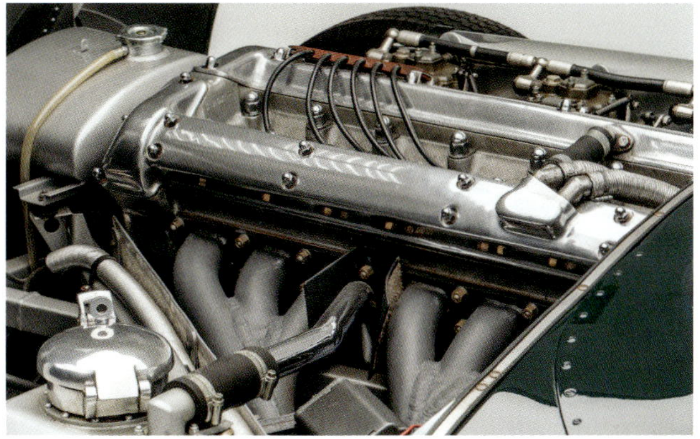

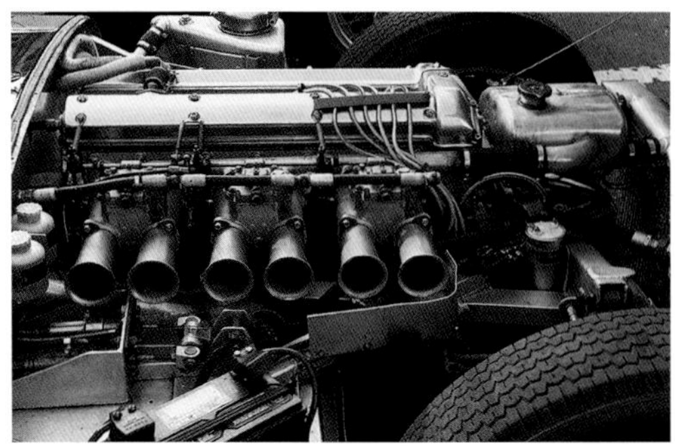

Left: Detail of right side of Jaguar XK-SS engine showing its three Weber 45 DCO3 dual-barrel carburetors.

Opposite (top, right): Detail of Jaguar XK-SS spare tire and open compartment door.

The racing origins of this remarkable sports car with its voluptuous curves can be traced back to Jaguar's D-Type racer (see p. 144) which though having been victorious at Le Mans and Reims, was not nearly so competitive on other tracks. With the D-Type nearing racing retirement, Jaguar decided to withdraw its team at the end of the 1956 season and began casting around for what to do next. As Jaguar explains, "Inspired by a request from the North American market for a class C production racer, the 25 remaining D-Type monocoques were planned for conversion, closely based on the multiple Le Mans winner. XK-SS was a true super car, with all of D-Type's power but it added essentials like a full-width windscreen, bumpers, and a redesigned rear section. The result was stunning."

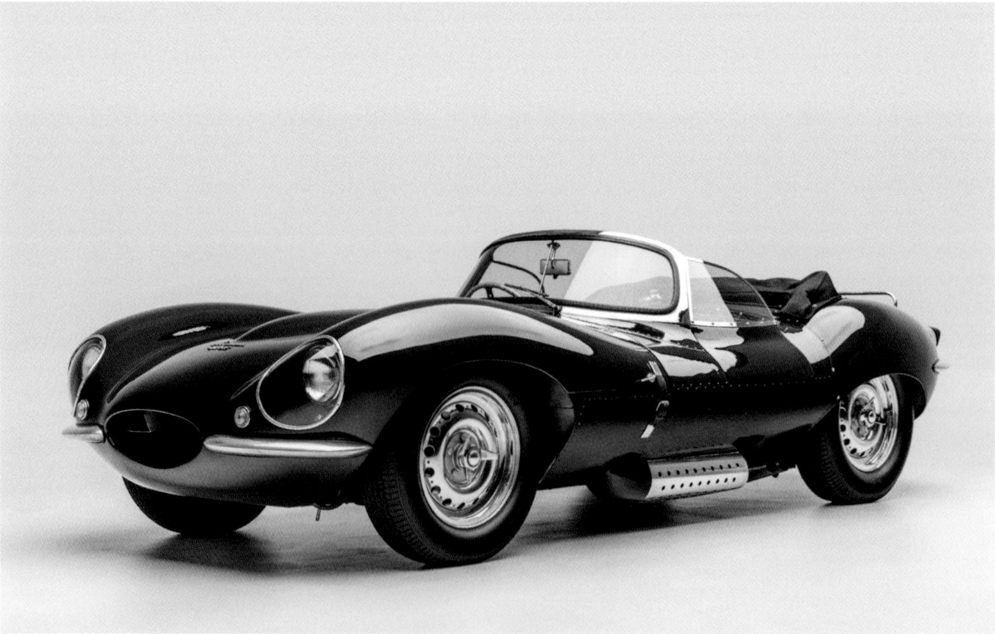

Disaster struck, however, on February 12, 1957, when a raging fire ripped through Jaguar's factory in Browns Lane, Coventry, with devastating consequences. Countless

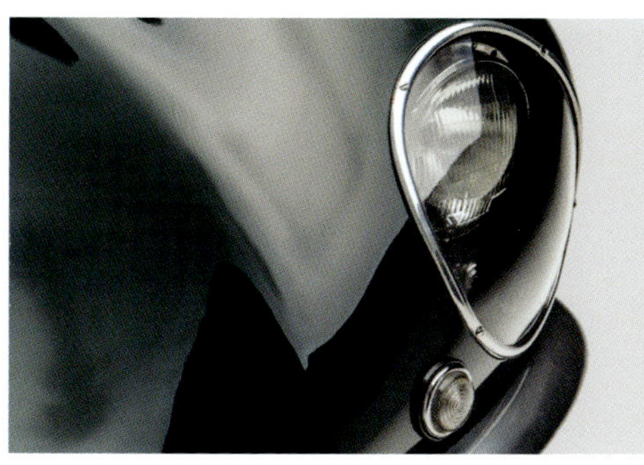

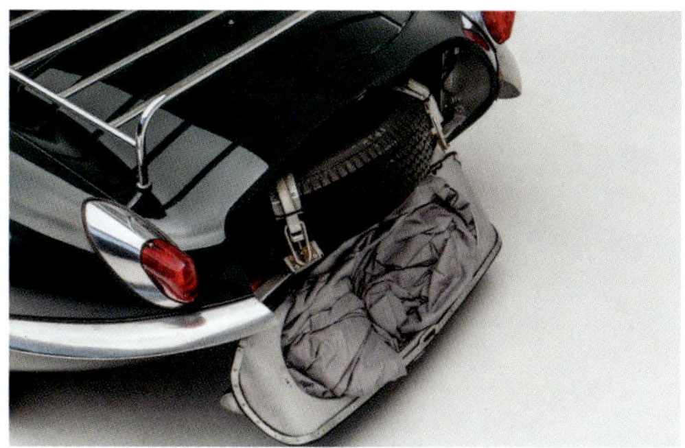

cars were destroyed in the blaze, including five of the 25 D-Types intended for conversion, while four cars were permanently dismantled and never rebuilt to XK-SS specification. This meant that ultimately only 16 XK-SS cars were ever constructed, making it a very rare beast indeed. And while the XK-SS was at its core a highly tuned World Sportscar Championship racer, its windscreen, passenger seat and fabric roof enabled it to be raced in the US as a production sports car, making it thrillingly competitive in its class. And, of course, the ultimate XK-SS for any collector would be McQueen's infamous Green Rat, which achieves the Holy Trinity of collecting — beauty, power and provenance — in one enticingly seductive automotive package. In fact, legendary car collector and enthusiast Jay Leno was left almost speechless when he took this fabulous car for a drive, uttering "I'm stunned, it's unbelievable!"

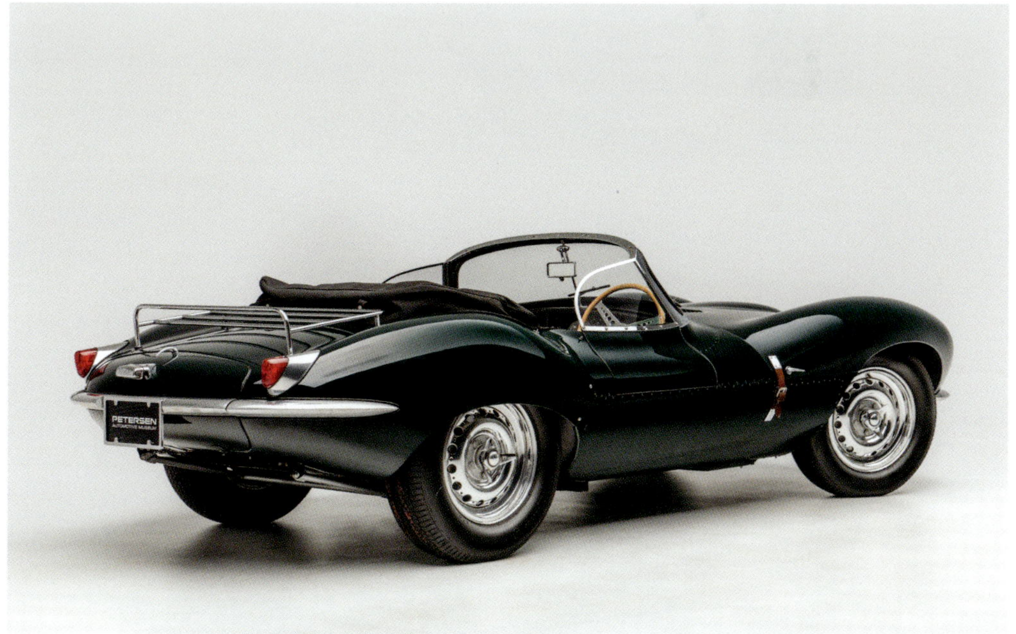

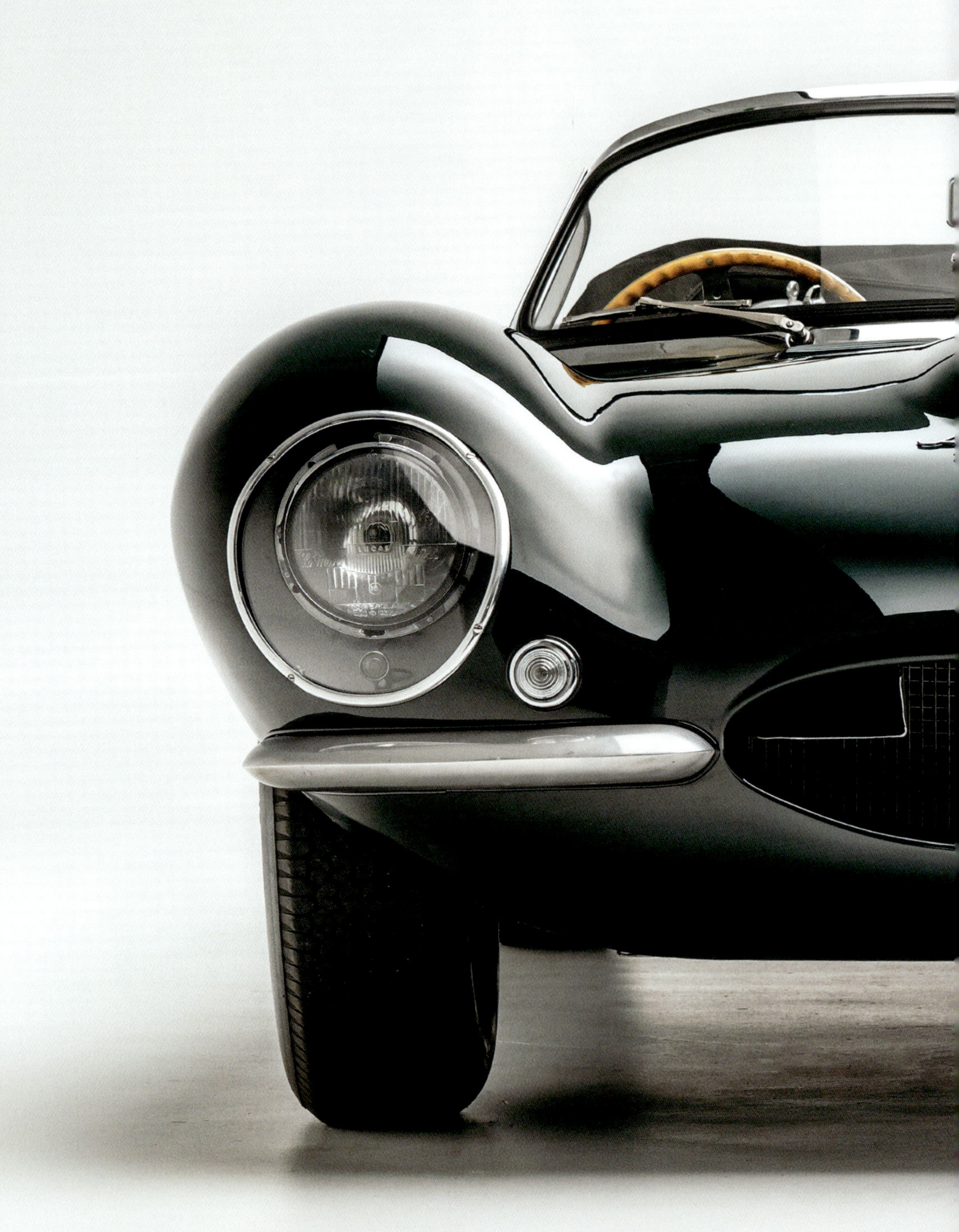

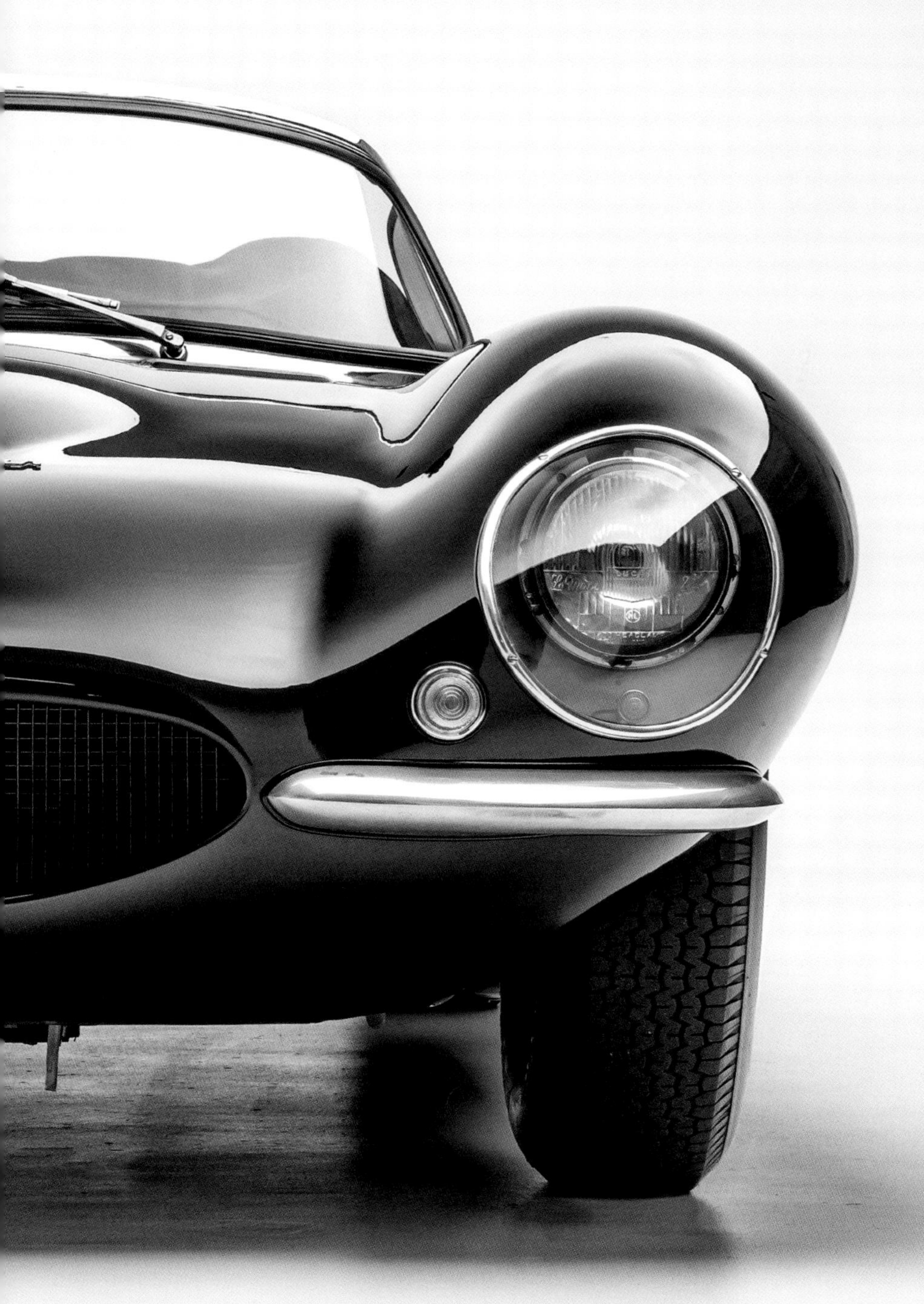

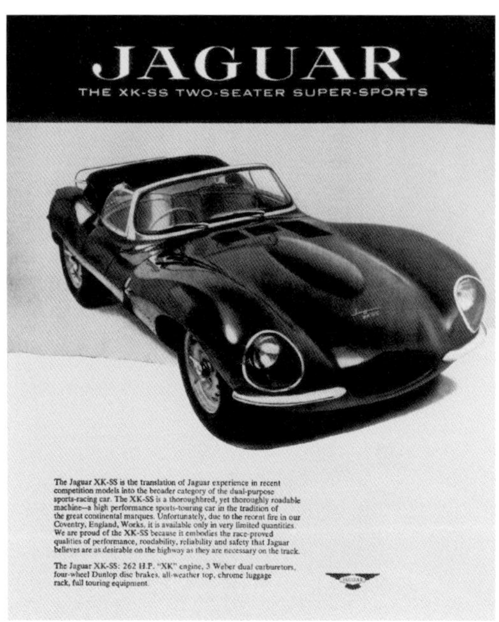

Left: 1957 Jaguar XK-SS US advertisement. Most of the 16 XK-SSs constructed were sold in the United States.

Below: Factory photo of a 1957 Jaguar XK-SS showing its top up and the optional chrome luggage rack on its trunk lid.

Opposite: Steve McQueen discussing his Jaguar XK-SS with a mechanic in Los Angeles, ca. 1963.

Overleaf: Actor Steve McQueen (1930–1980) driving his beloved 1957 Jaguar XK-SS (chassis no. XK-SS713), which he dubbed the "Green Rat," on a Hollywood backlot, June 1963. This car is now in the collection of the Petersen Automotive Museum, Los Angeles, California.

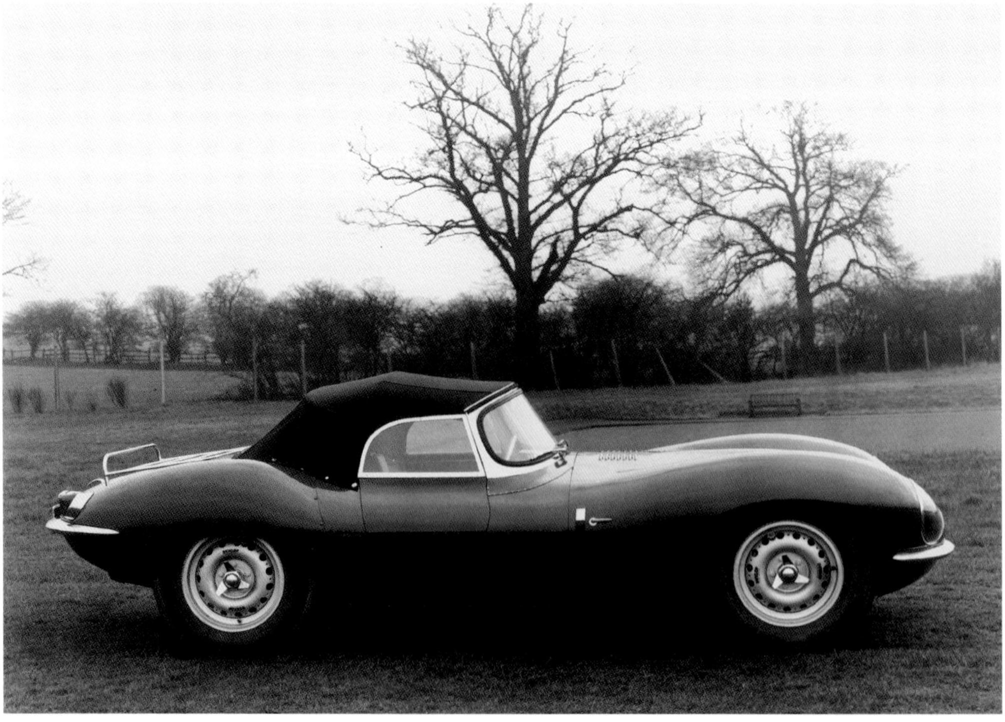

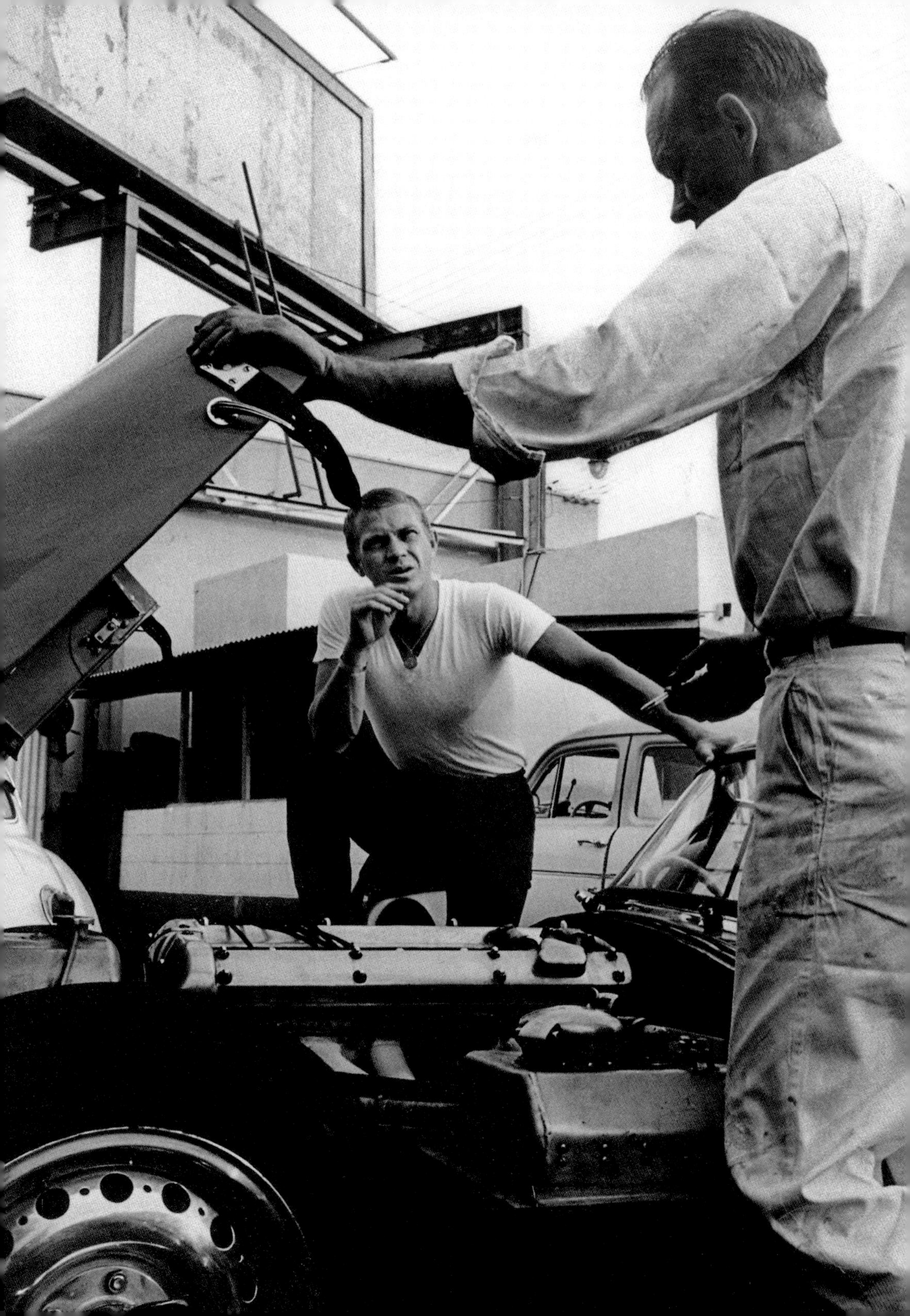

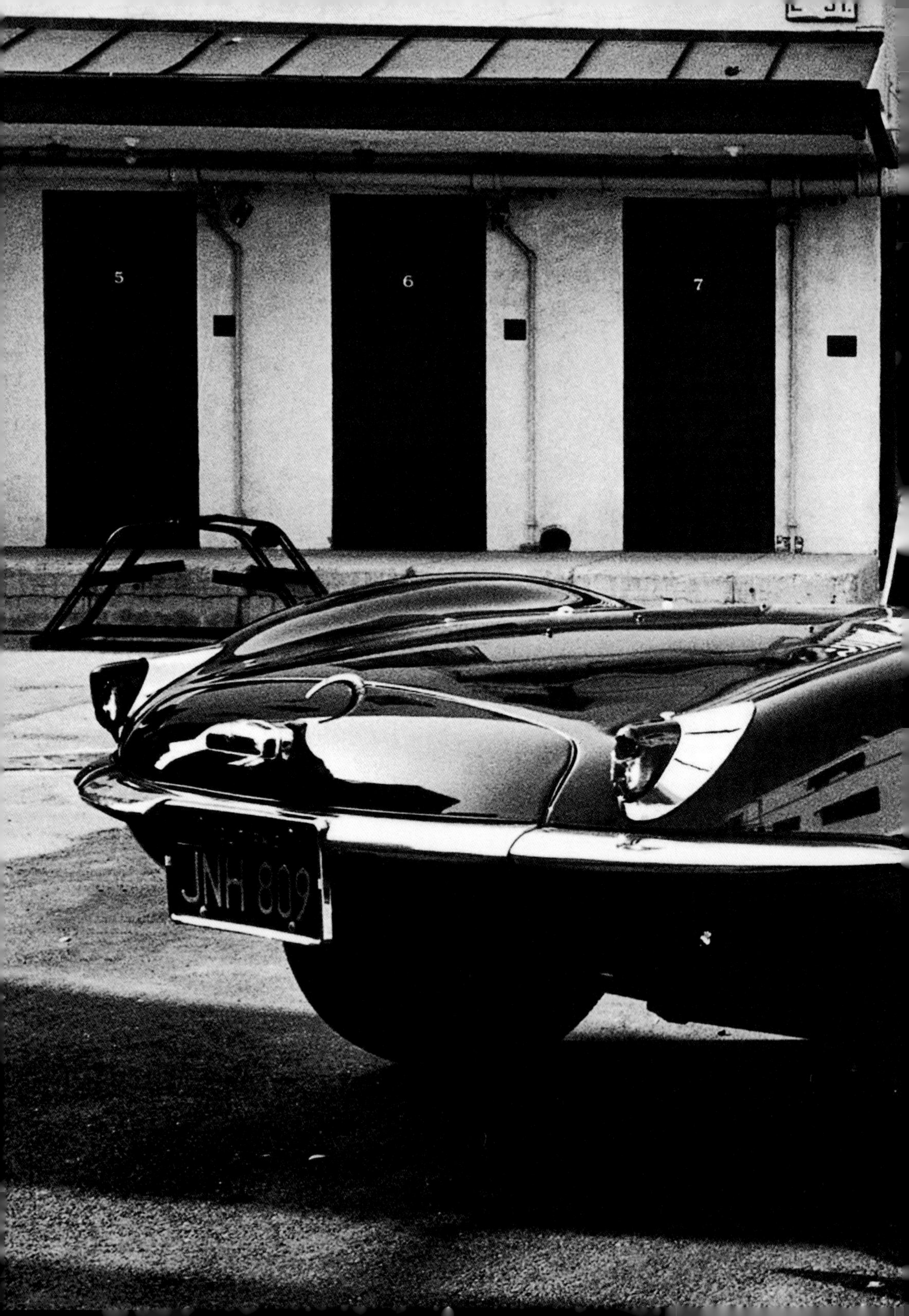
5
6
7
JNH 809

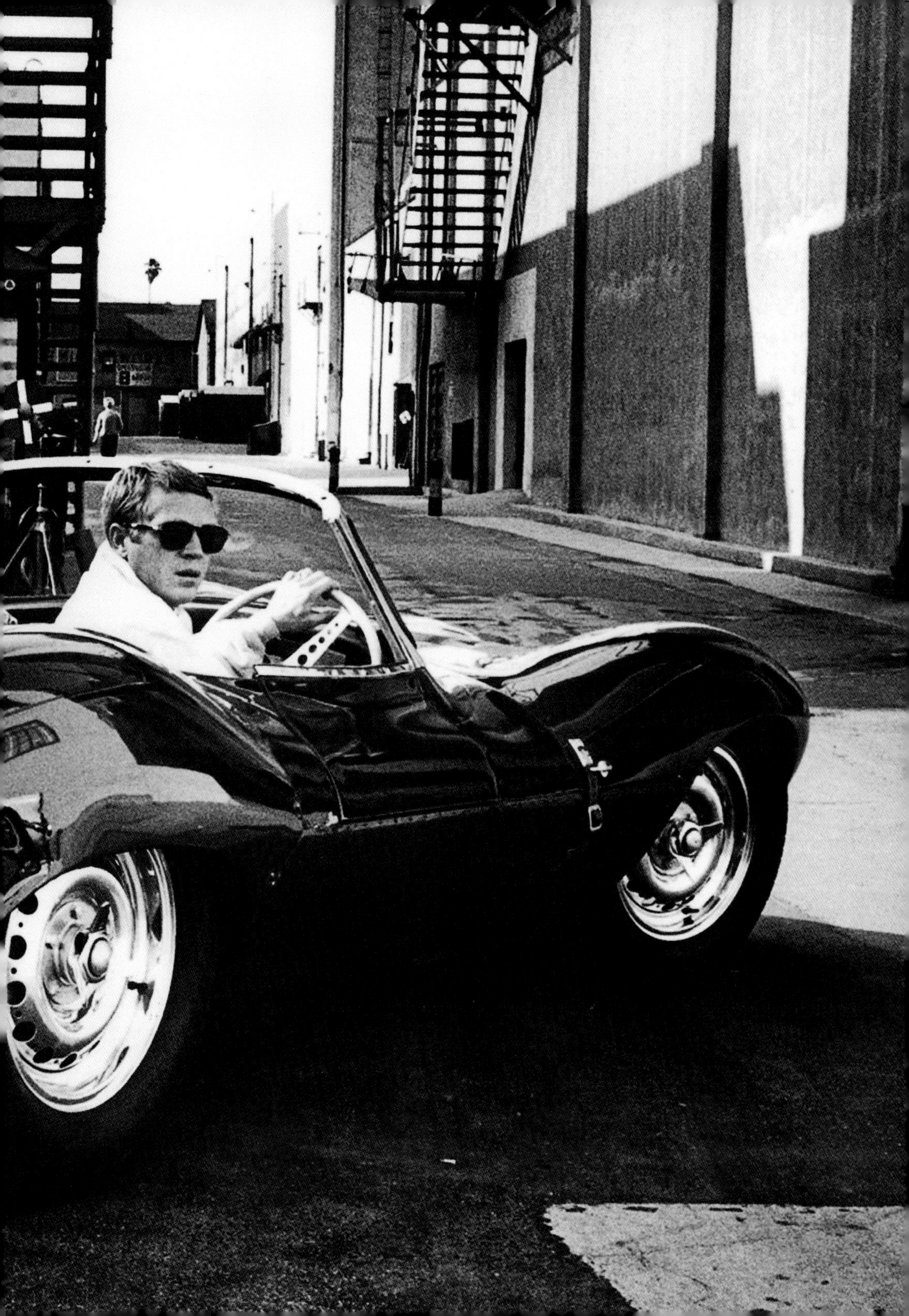

1957

Ferrari 335 S

MANUFACTURED 1957 | ENGINE 4,023 cc (245.5 cu. in.), DOHC per bank 60º V12 | HORSEPOWER 390
TOP SPEED 300 km/h (186 mph) | TRANSMISSION 4-speed
NUMBER PRODUCED 3 (315 S) / 4 (335 S)

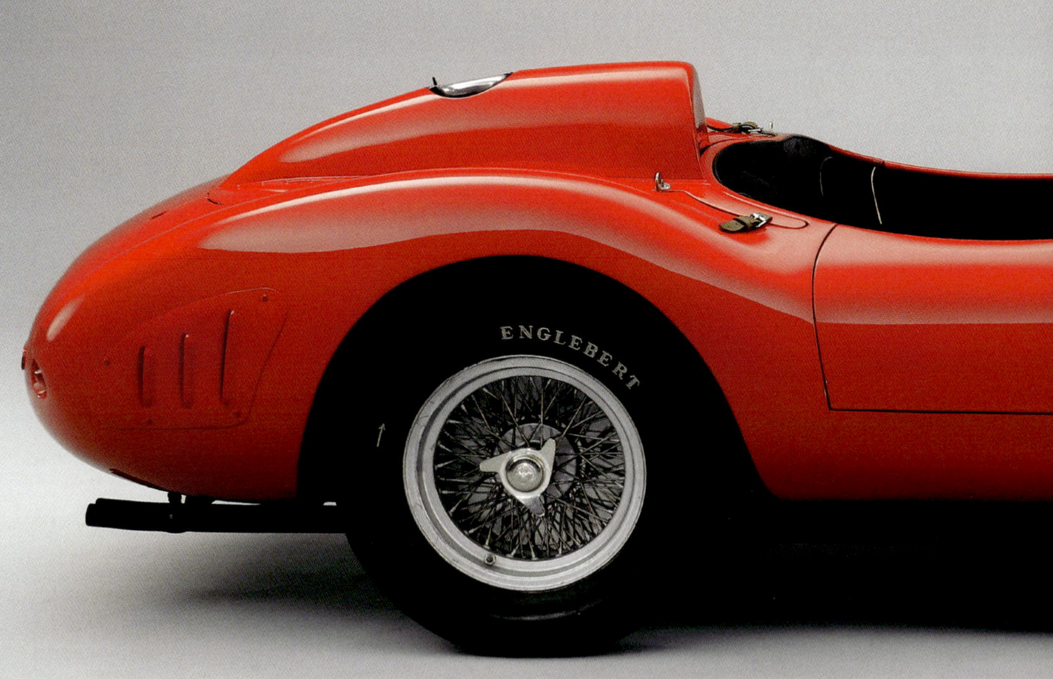

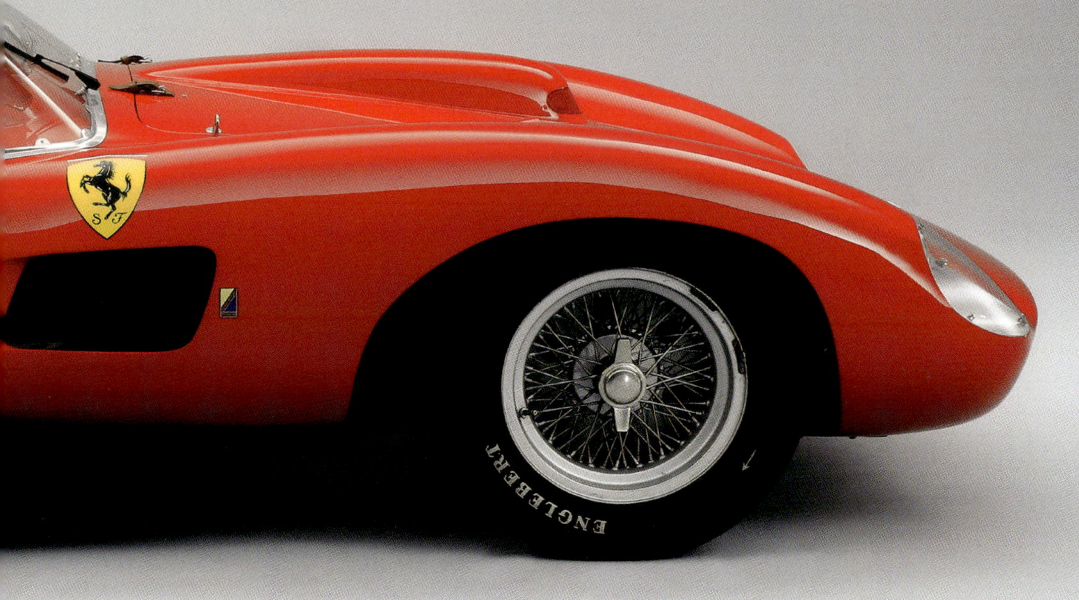
ENGLEBERT

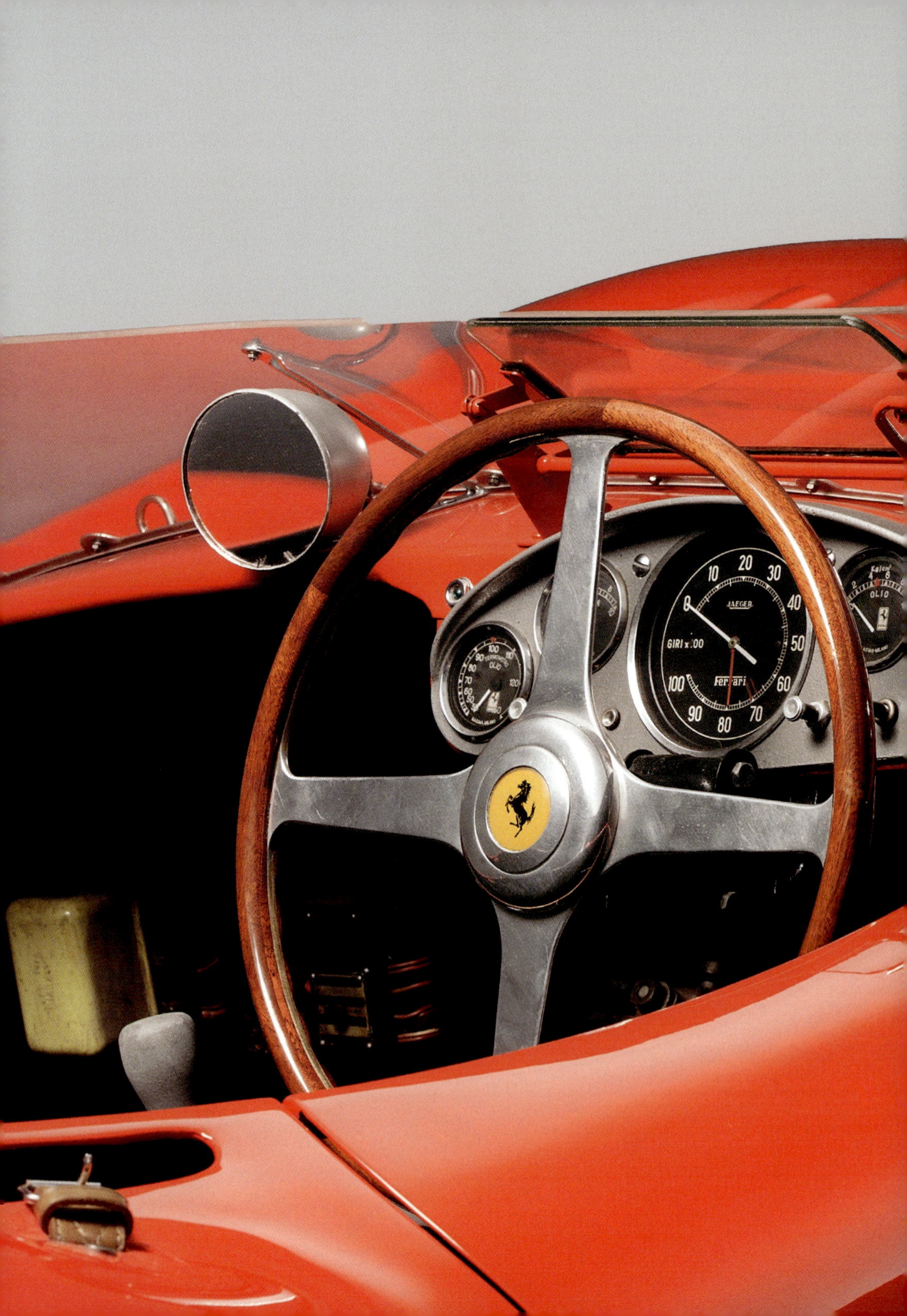
JAEGER
GIRI x 100
Ferrari
OLIO

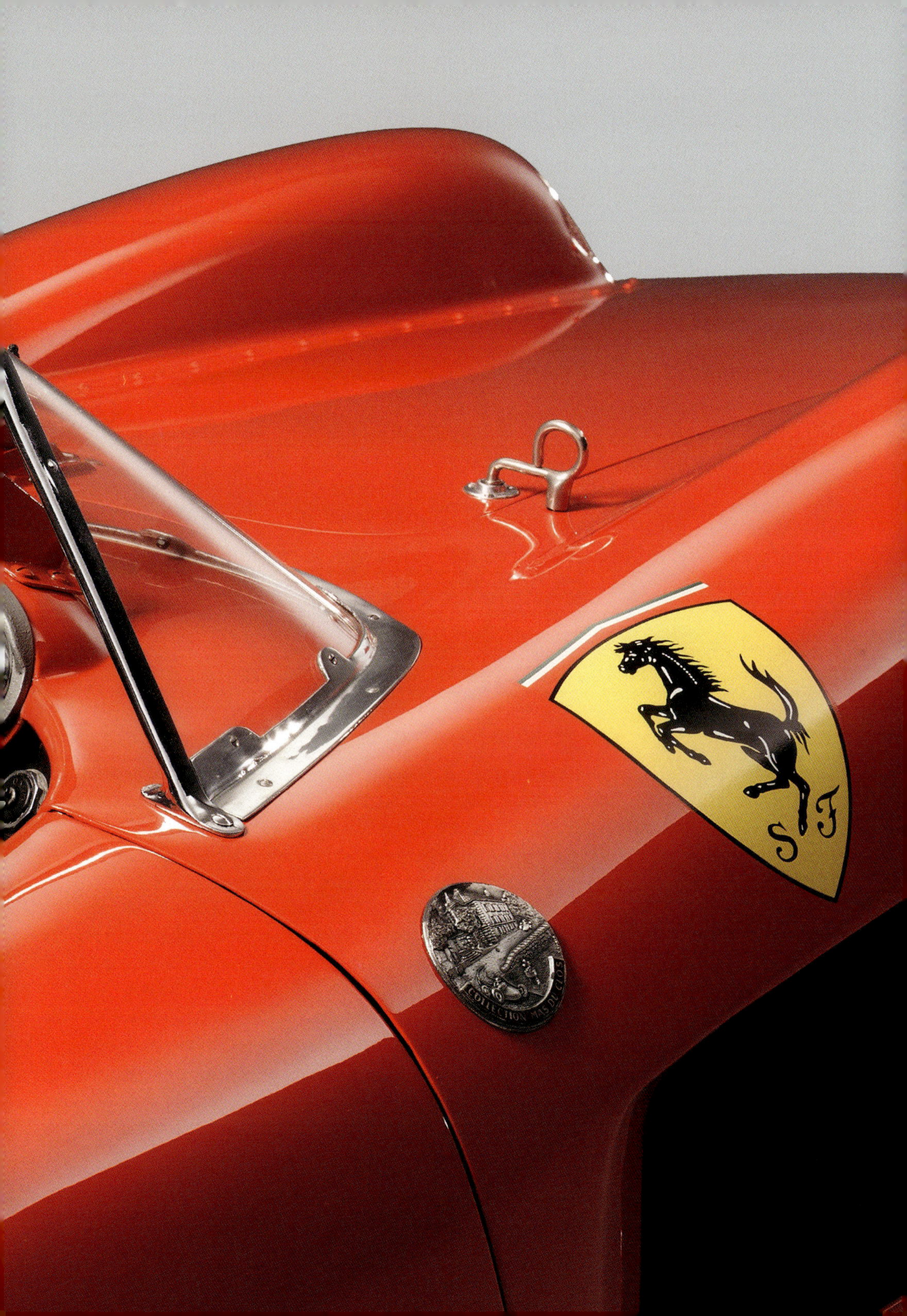
S F
COLLECTION MAS DU CLOS

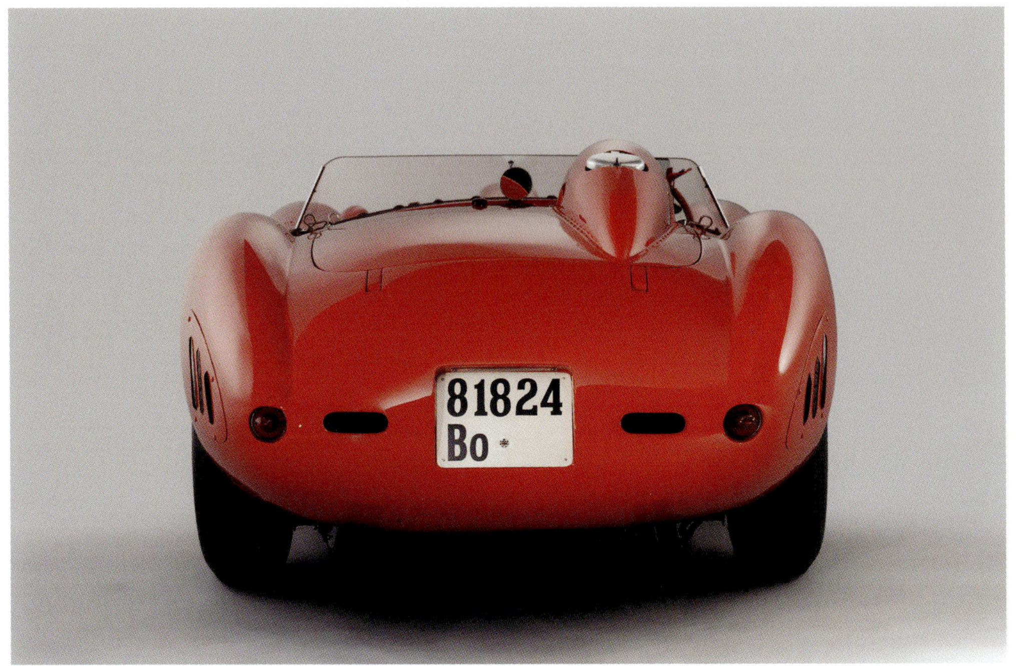

Previous: Detail of Ferrari 335 S steering wheel, instruments and controls. Bodied as a *barchetta* by Scaglietti this car epitomizes the ultimate finesse, purity and lightweight of Italian racing machines from this golden era.

Enzo Ferrari had a genius for attracting some of the very best designers and engineers to his thoroughbred race stable in Maranello. Indeed, the marque's renowned status was built on the extraordinary fruits of their labors. But more than this, Enzo also had a rare gift for getting many of the world's most talented drivers to race his factory cars as part of his celebrated in-house racing division, Scuderia Ferrari. Today, these works Ferraris are some of the most sought-after collector cars on the planet, especially those from the 1950s, which constituted a veritable golden age for the Ferrari racing team. And no wonder they are such objects of desire, given their exceptional rarity, sublime beauty, race histories and remarkable provenances.

This 1957 Ferrari is one of these very rare cars — a purebred factory racer that clocked up various landmark sporting achievements during its racing career. Its design genealogy is confusing, however (as is so common for race cars), for it started life out at the very beginning of 1957 as a Ferrari 315 S (chassis no. 0674). At this stage its aerodynamically sleek *barchetta* body styled by Scaglietti encased a 3.8-liter V12 engine with four (two per bank) chain-driven overhead camshafts. In this guise, the car's racing debut took place at the famed 12 Hours of Sebring endurance race in Florida on March 23, 1957, with the Franco-British duo Maurice Trintignant and Peter Collins co-driving the car.

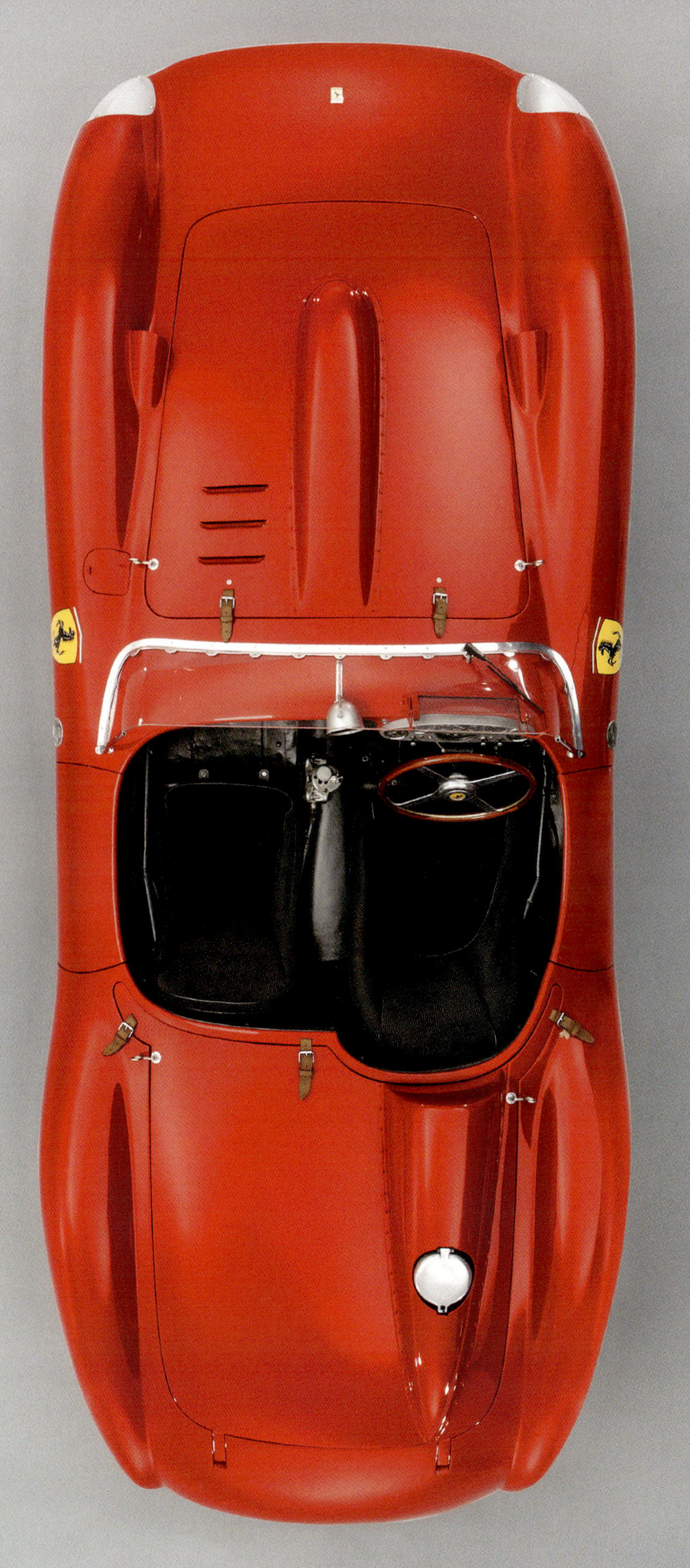

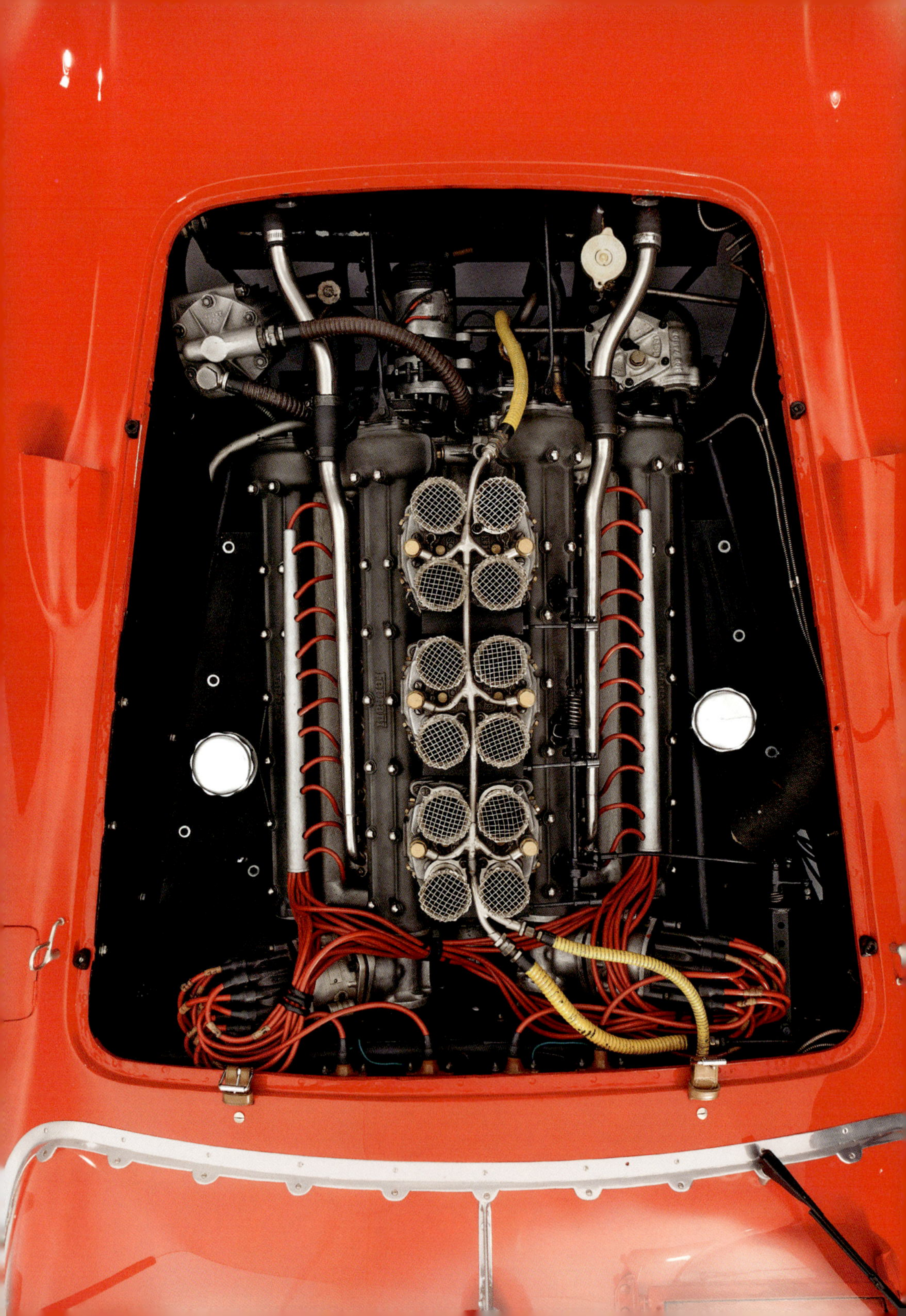

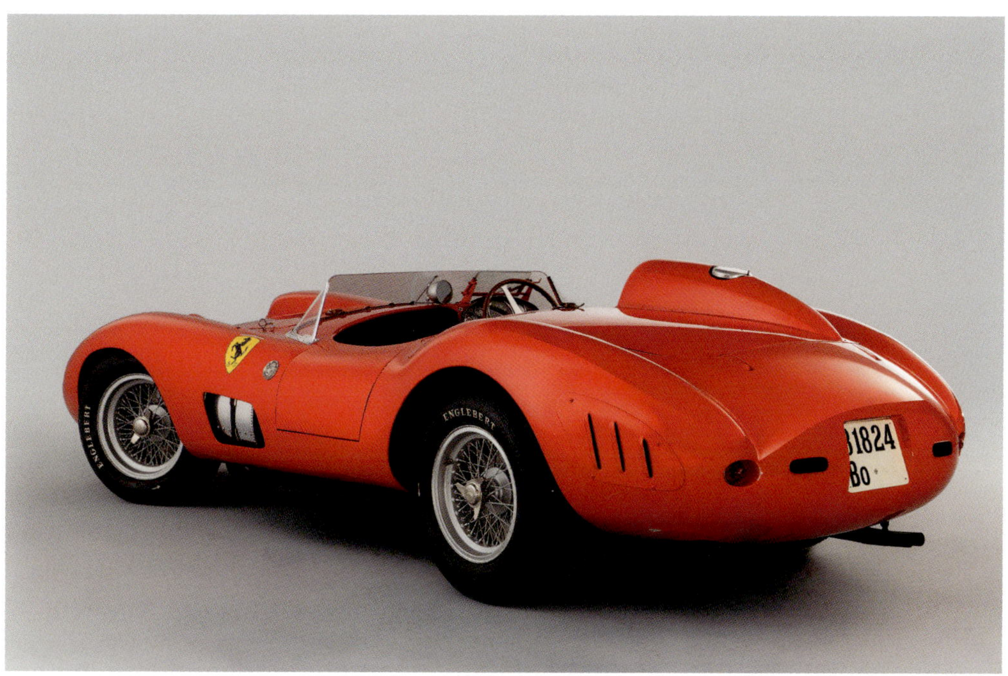

Opposite & overleaf: Detail of Ferrari 335 S 4,023 cc (245.5 cu. in.), DOHC per bank 60° V12 engine with six dual choke Solex 44 mm inverted carburetors. An evolution of the 3.8-liter Tipo 140 V12 engine designed by Vittorio Jano for the 315 S, the awesome all-alloy quad-cam four-liter Tipo 141 of the 335 S with double ignition and four coils represented the most advanced engineering of its day.

For the first 20 laps of this road-course race the car led the pack, but then lost impetus, finally finishing a disappointing sixth. After this trial run the car's next challenge was the 1957 Mille Miglia, then the most famous car race in the world. It was raced by the German driver Wolfgang Graf Berghe von Trips alongside another 315 S driven by his Italian teammate, Piero Taruffi. These two clocked up a 1-2 finish, with Taruffi winning the actual race — a personal triumph given it was his 14th attempt. Ferrari also took third place albeit with a 250 GT TdF Scagletti Berlinetta. Two other Scuderia Ferrari works cars, both 335 S, were also entered into the race, with one failing to finish and the other being involved in a devastating crash. The latter was driven by Alfonso de Portago, who had stepped in at the last minute as a replacement driver for the team. Highly respected and well liked, the Spaniard suffered a catastrophic front tire explosion that saw his 335 S careen off the track near Guidizzolo, killing not only him and his co-driver, but also nine spectators and injuring a further 20 people. This horrific accident prompted the introduction of a ban on all high-speed racing on Italian public roads three days later.

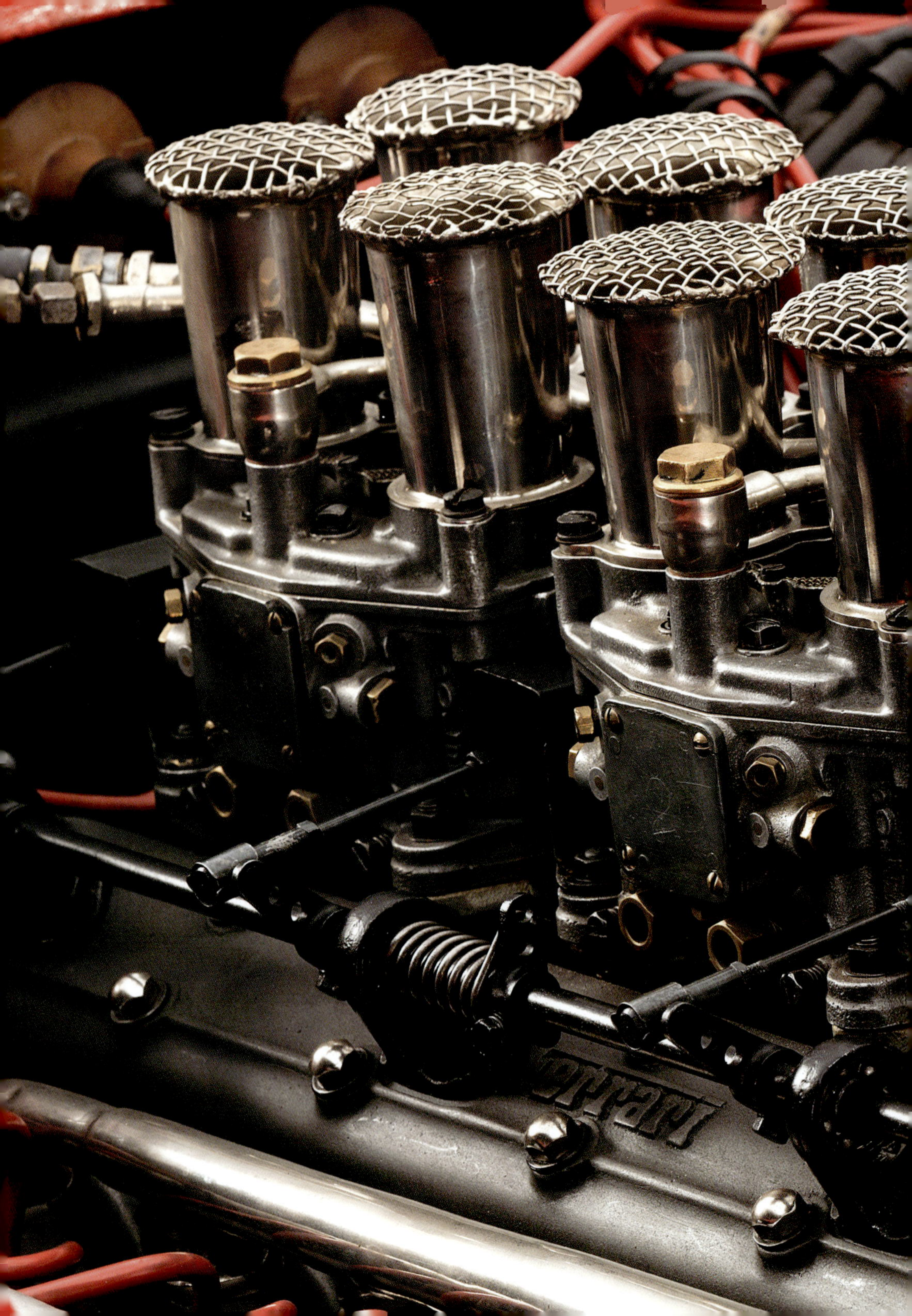

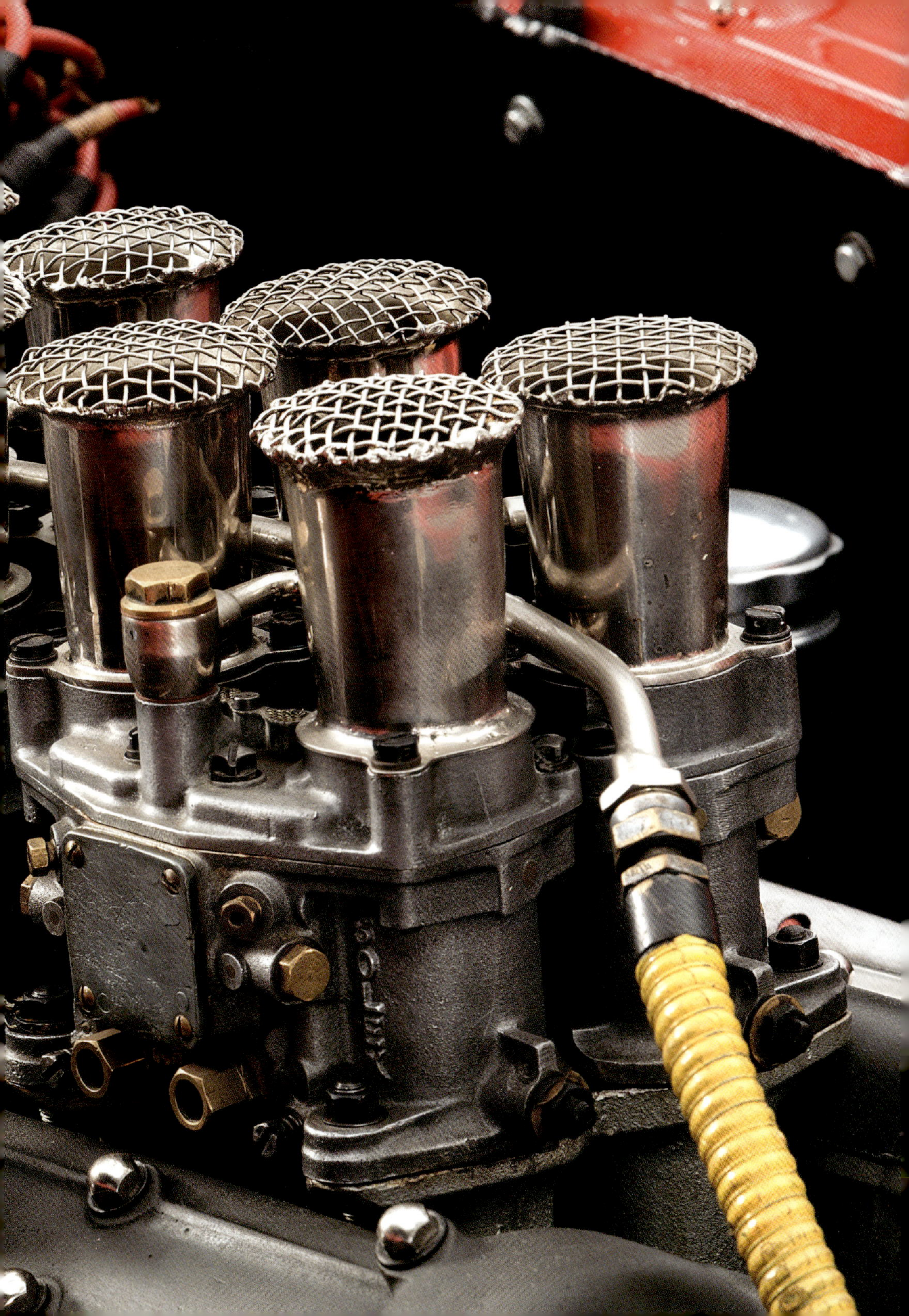

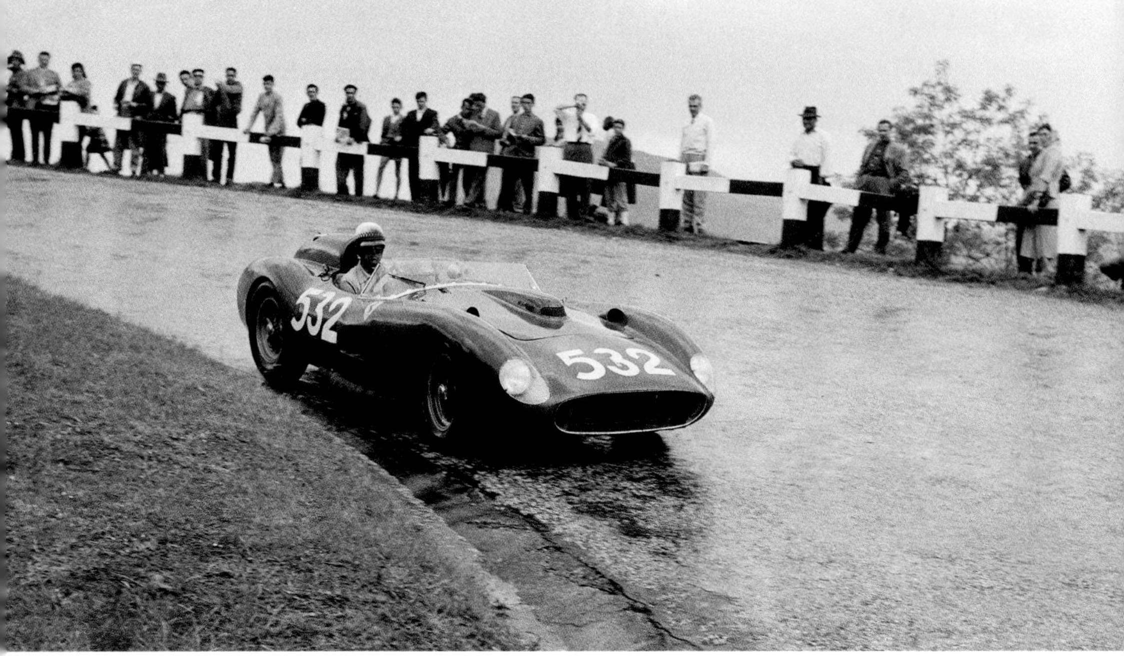

Above: Wolfgang Graf Berghe von Trips in the No. 532 Ferrari 315 S Scaglietti, chassis no. 0674, during the 1957 Mille Miglia, Brescia, May 11, 1957.

The 315 S shown here (chassis no. 0674) was afterward converted into a fully fledged 335 S with the addition of an upgraded V12 engine with an increased displacement of 4,023 cc (versus 3,783 cc) giving it a top speed of 300 km/h (186 mph) versus 290 km/h (180 mph). This modification meant that it became the fourth and last 335 S ever to be constructed. The car was subsequently entered into the 1957 24 Hours of Le Mans race, where co-driven by Mike Hawthorn and Luigi Musso, it managed to break the race record for the average lap speed by exceeding 200 km/h (124 mph). However, it was subsequently forced to retire with engine problems. It then took part in the Swedish Grand Prix, again driven by Hawthorn and Musso, where it placed fourth and sporting a new cooling pontoon fender it later came in second at the Venezuelan Grand Prix as part of an epic Ferrari 1-2-3-4 finish, which helped clinch Ferrari's win of the 1957 Constructors' World Championship Title. This pace-setting car was then given yet another engine upgrade at Ferrari's factory in Maranello and was afterward sold on to Luigi Chinetti, the founder of the Ferrari-affiliated North American Racing Team (NART). Sporting this team's blue and white livery, the car was finally driven to victory by Stirling Moss and Masten Gregory at the 1958 Cuban Grand Prix in Havana — sealing forever its legendary status in automotive history.

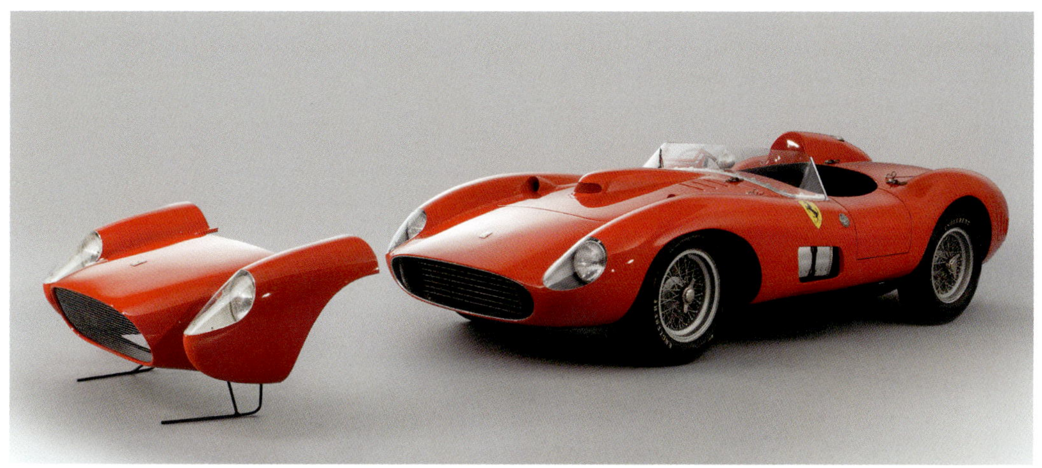

Above: In late 1957 chassis no. 0674 was sent back to the factory where it was modified with a "pontoon fender" front end, to help cool the brakes more effectively in advance of the Venezuelan Grand Prix in November that year. Later in 1981, under the ownership of the great Ferrari collector Pierre Bardinon, the car was restored to its original configuration, with its first front nose. The pontoon fender (as shown here) was retained, however, and sold with the car when it came up for sale in 2016.

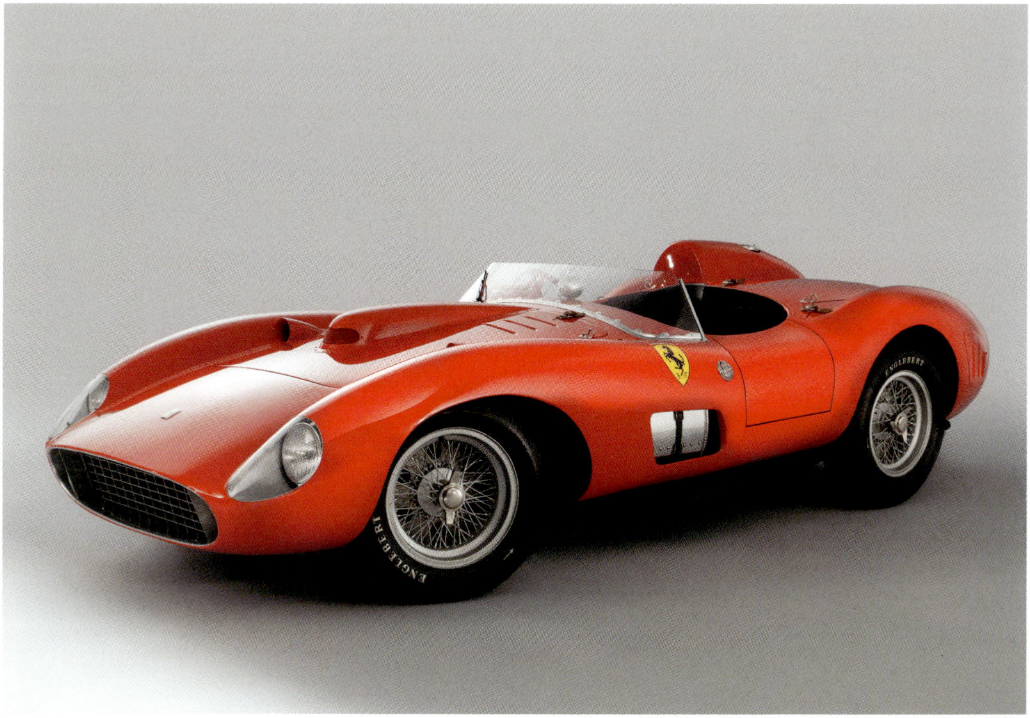

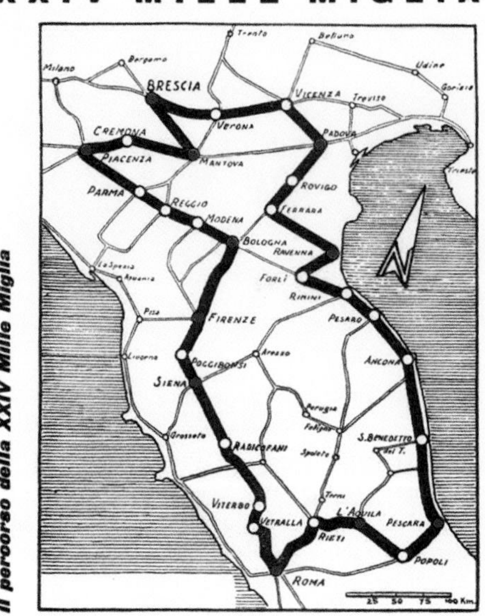

Left: Map of the 24th Mille Miglia, held May 11–12, 1957. The racecourse totaled 992.332 miles (1,597.004 km) and was made up entirely of public roads around Italy. The route was based on a round trip between Brescia and Rome, with the start/finish in Brescia.

Below: Italian driver Piero Taruffi in the No. 535 Ferrari 315 S Scaglietti winning the 1957 Mille Miglia in Brescia, with Germany's Wolfgang Graf Berghe von Trips in the No. 532 Ferrari 315 S Scaglietti, chassis no. 0674, finishing second.

Opposite (top): 1957 24 Hours of Le Mans — Luigi Musso rounds Mulsanne corner in the No. 7 (now upgraded) Ferrari 335 S, chassis no. 0674, which he co-drove with Mike Hawthorn. An engine problem forced the car to retire in the fifth hour.

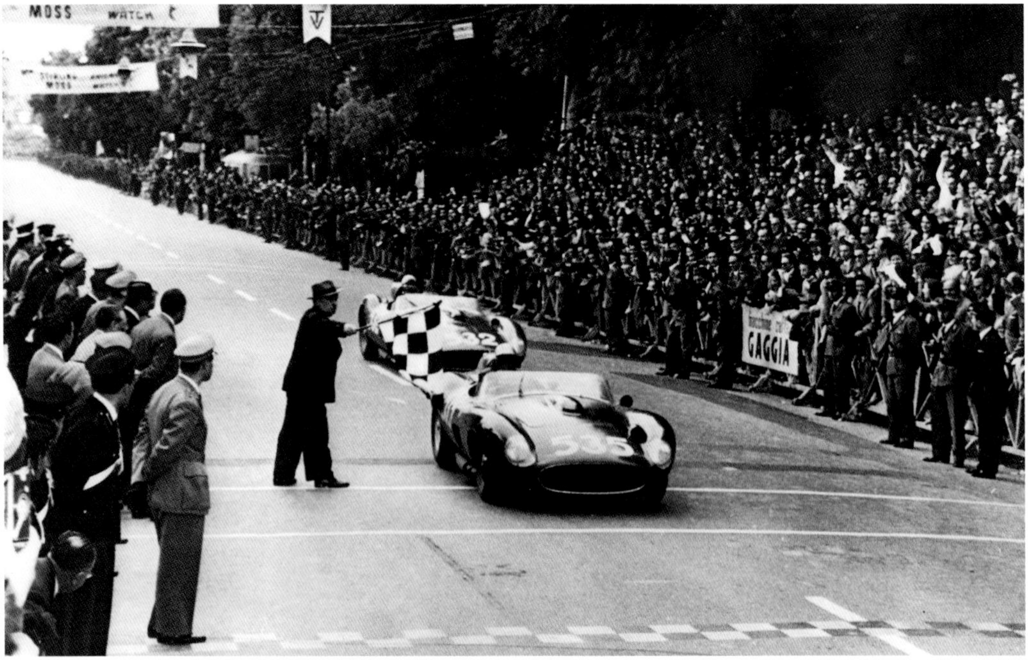

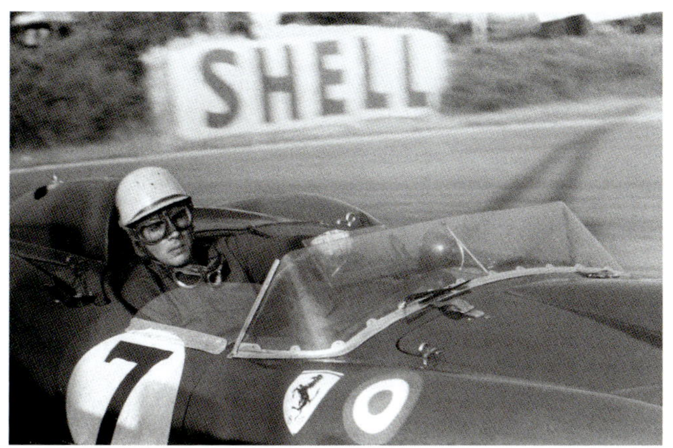

Below: The 24 Hours of Le Mans, June 22–23, 1957. Early in the race the No. 7 Ferrari 335 S (chassis no. 0674) being driven by Mike Hawthorn, who shared driving duties with Luigi Musso, dives into the Esses past the smaller No. 27 Ferrari 500 TRC of Fernand Tavano and Jacques Péron. Neither car would survive the race.

Overleaf: 24 Hours of Le Mans, June 22–23, 1957. The Ferrari team assembles in the pits before the first practice session. The No. 7 Ferrari 335 S (chassis no. 0674), which was co-driven by Mike Hawthorn and Luigi Musso did not finish the race. The No. 8 Ferrari 315 S, which was driven by Stuart Lewis-Evans and Martino Severi, finished in overall fifth place behind four Jaguar D-Types.

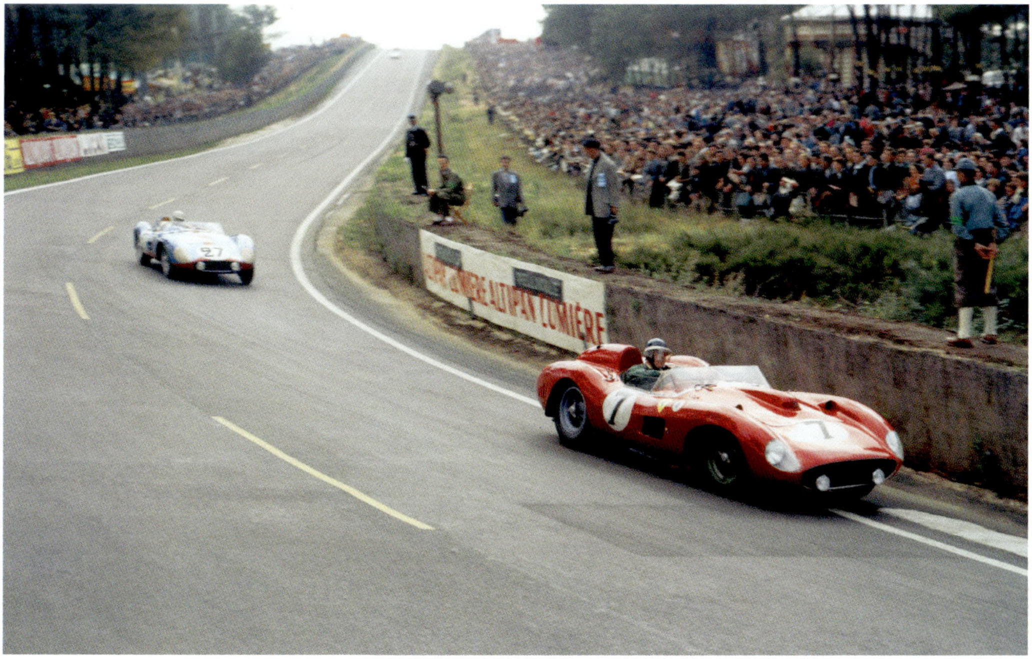

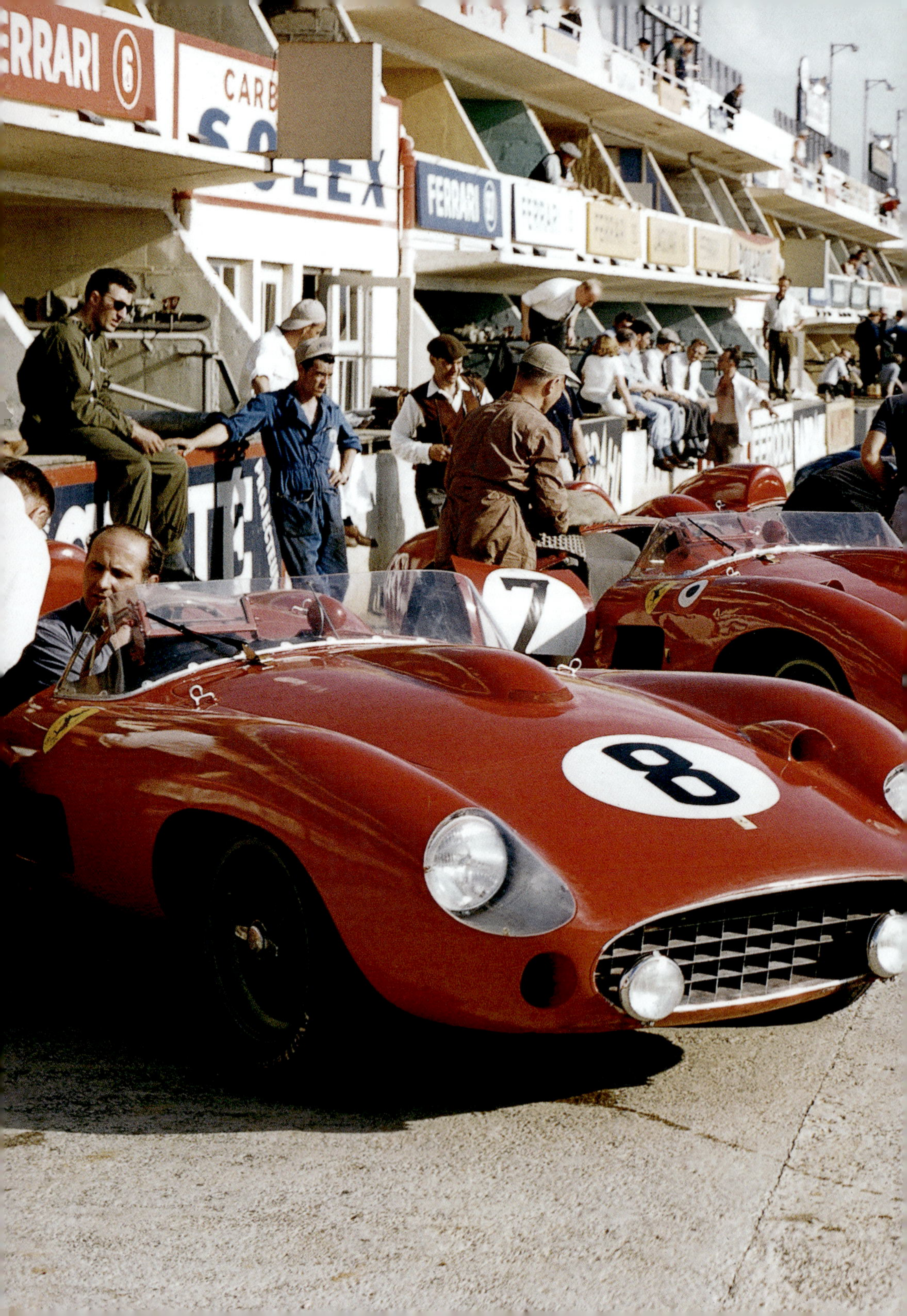
FERRARI
7
8

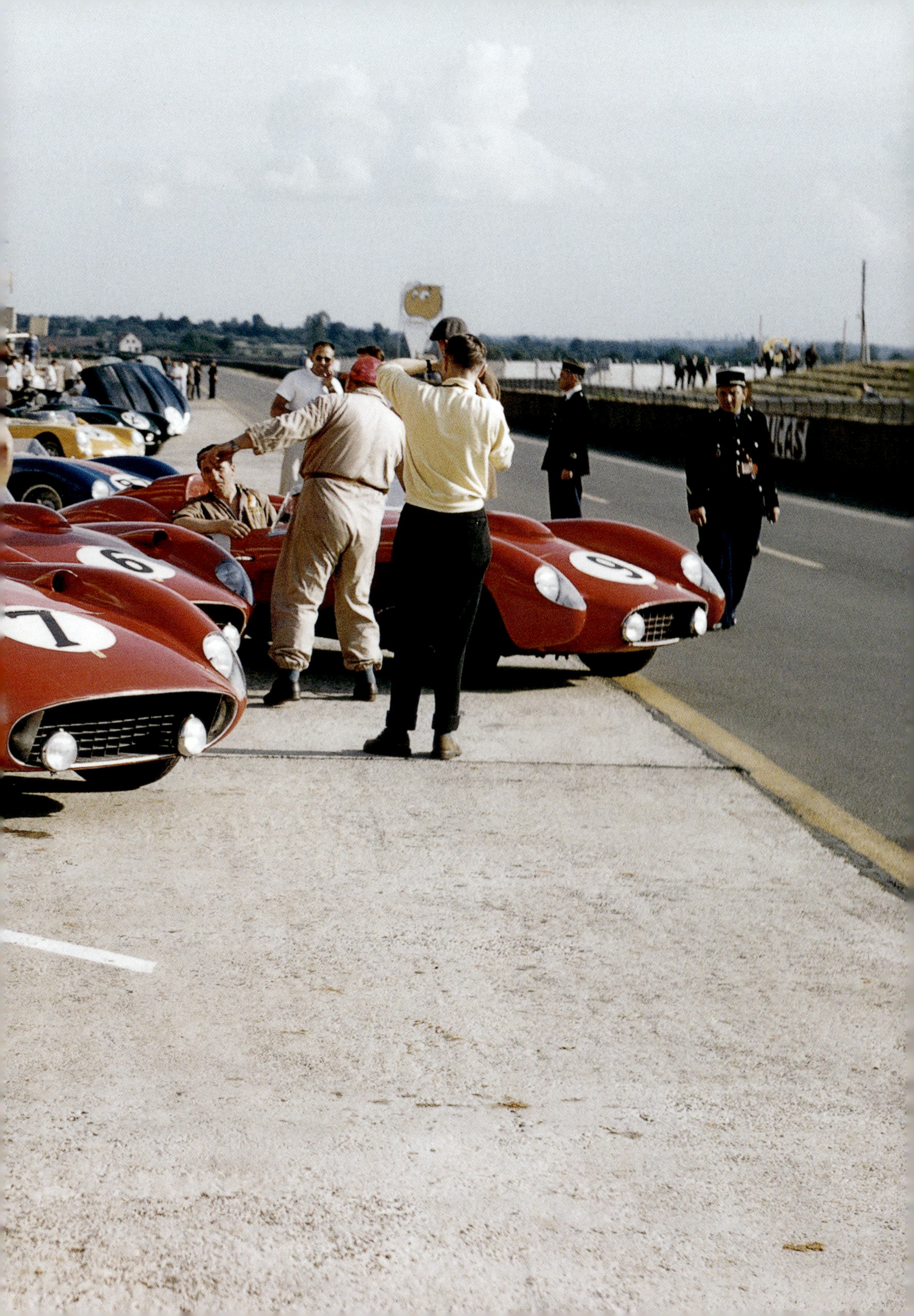
7
6
9

1957

Ferrari 250 Testa Rossa

MANUFACTURED 1957–61 | ENGINE 2,953 cc (180 cu. in.), SOHC per bank 60° V12 | HORSEPOWER 300
TOP SPEED 270 km/h (168 mph) | TRANSMISSION 4-speed
NUMBER PRODUCED 34 (including 2 prototypes and the unique 330 TRI/LM)

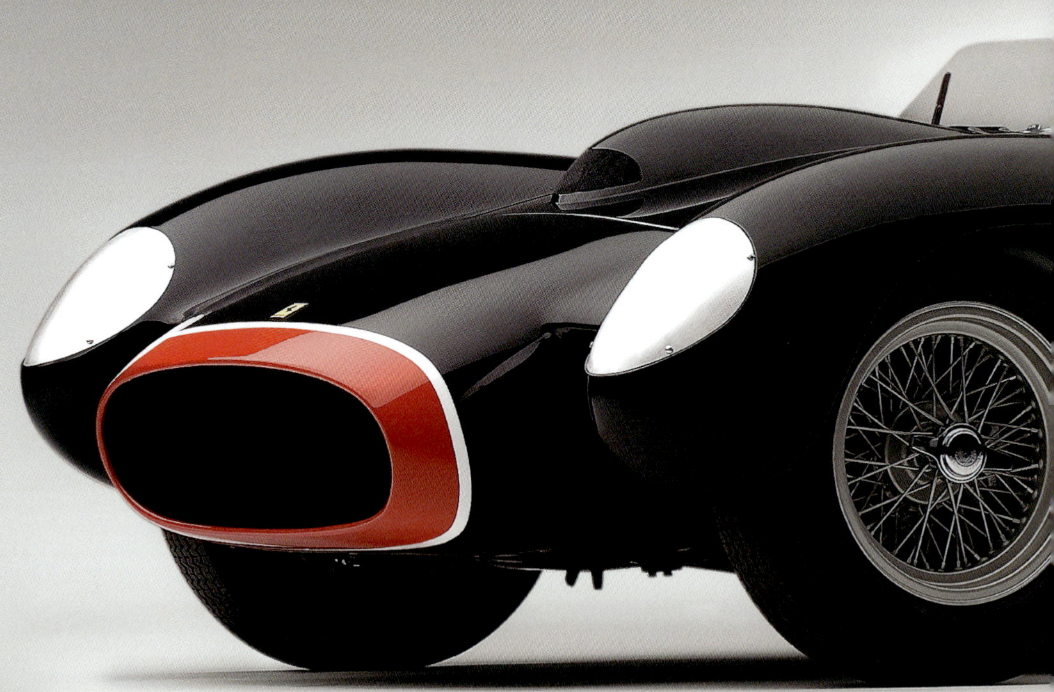

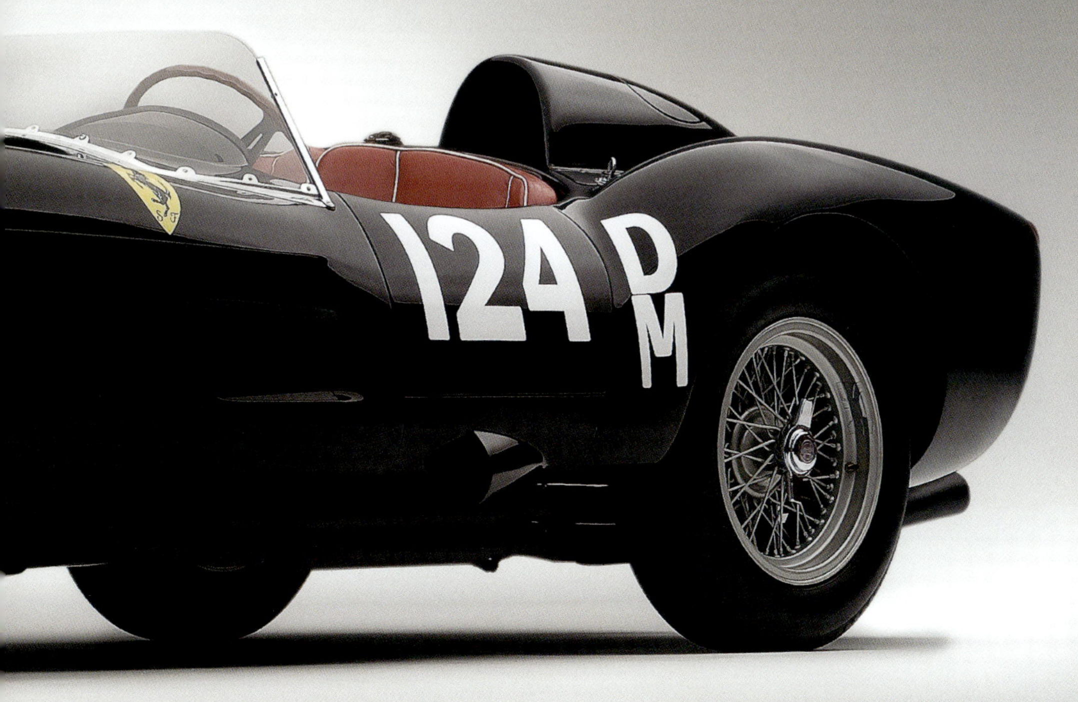
124
DM

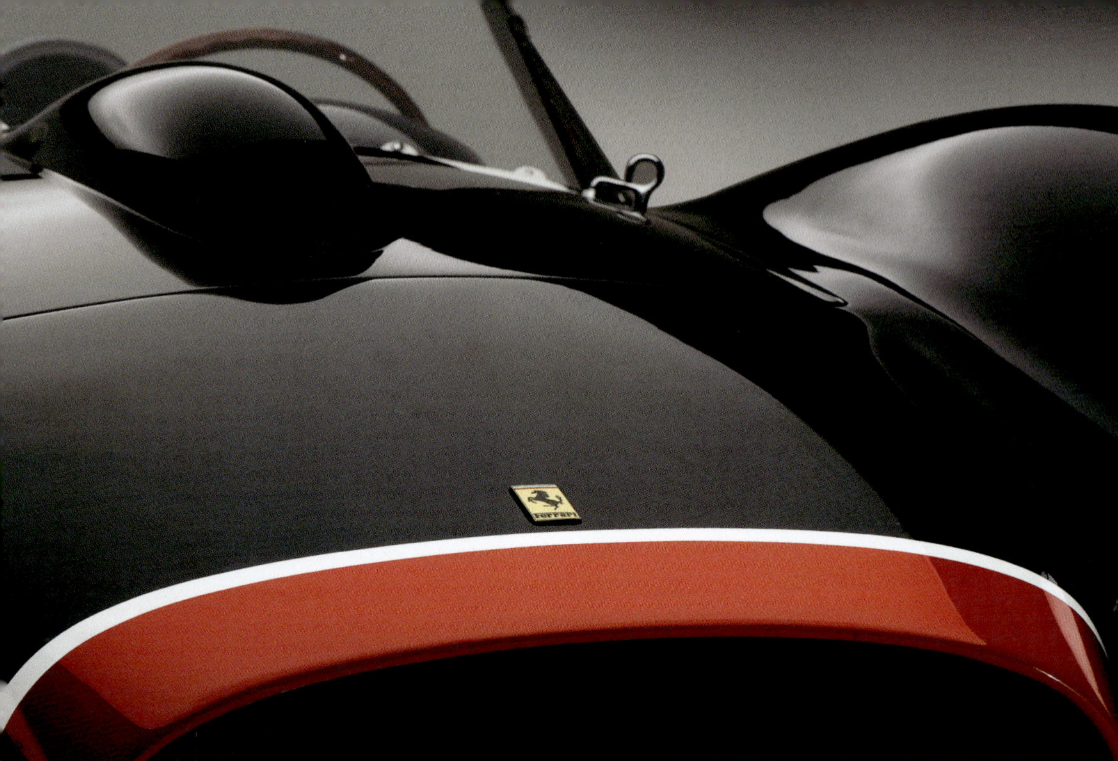

Above: Detail of Ferarri 250 Testa Rossa's distinctive cutaway nose, air intake "power bulge," and the deep channel of its pontoon fender.

Opposite: Detail of Ferrari 250 Testa Rossa 2,953 cc (180 cu. in.), SOHC per bank 60º V12 engine with six Weber 38 DCN carburetors. The sobriquet "Testa Rossa" (red head) was personally coined by Enzo Ferrari and was first used for the 1956 four-cylinder Ferrari 500 TR and then subsequently for the Ferrari 250 Testa Rossa. This famous nickname was derived from the engine's cam covers that were painted a bright crimson. The engine was based on the well-proven Colombo-designed 3.0L V12, which was modified by the engineer Carlo Chiti together with Ferrari engineers to increase performance and reliability. This included cylinder heads that used single overhead cams, two valves per cylinder, helical double-coil valve springs and relocating the spark plugs outside the engine vee between exhaust ports, which allowed for a better spark position and more efficient combustion. Additionally, piston connecting rods were machined from steel billet, rather than forged, which resulted in more stress resistance at higher RPMs. The resulting Tipo 128 LM engine proved remarkably durable and highly competitive.

The Ferrari 250 Testa Rossa is one of the rarest Ferrari racers of all time, making it highly prized among top collectors. When it was first introduced some journalists were pretty dismissive of this *barchetta* (little boat), however, others were more accepting of its low-slung aerodynamic form but, even so, they still had major reservations about its seemingly outmoded single-cam engine setup. Yet the 250 TR and its later modified variations exceeded all expectations and ultimately trashed any criticism with a string of thrilling performances on track.

The car's development started in 1957 when the Commission Sportive Internationale (CSI) began deliberating the introduction of new engine displacement rules in response to the Mercedes disaster at the 1955 24 Hours of Le Mans and then Alfonso de Portago's crash at the 1957 Mille Miglia while at the helm of a Ferrari 335 S (see p. 196). These two tragedies shocked the motorsports world to its core as not only had drivers been killed, but also a large number of spectators. It was realized that such carnage was too high a price to pay and that the sport had to be made safer for both competitors and spectators. Yet despite the latter accident, Ferrari had taken a 1-2-3 finish at that last-ever Mille Miglia, which helped it clinch the 1957 World Sportscar Championship. That said, Enzo Ferrari, perhaps more than anyone given his crash-related manslaughter prosecution (which was ultimately thrown out of court), knew that a reduction in engine capacity was inevitable. Indeed, rumors were circulating that the CSI would be introducing imminently a 3.0-liter engine limit on racing prototypes. So, anticipating this ruling Ferrari began developing a new car for the 1958 season that would meet its predicted requirement. The design ancestry of this car could be traced back to the four-cylinder 500 TR, introduced in 1956, which had been the very first Ferrari to bear the sobriquet "Testa Rossa" (red head). This nickname, coined by Enzo himself, was derived from the engine's cam covers that were painted a vivid scarlet. Developed by Carlo Chiti and his engineering team, the 250 TR retained the excellent handling and impressive reliability of the earlier car by being built on a similar chassis, but was equipped with a much more powerful V12 engine designed by Gioacchino Colombo, which had already proved its mettle in other earlier models from the 250 series. This single cam 2,953 cc V12 power plant was

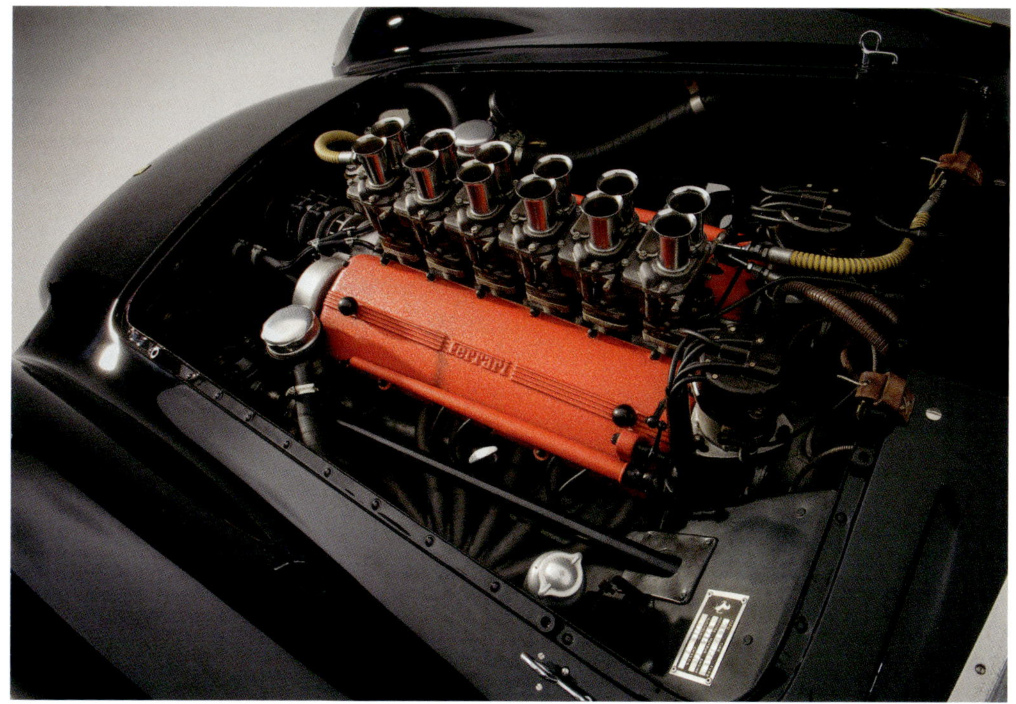

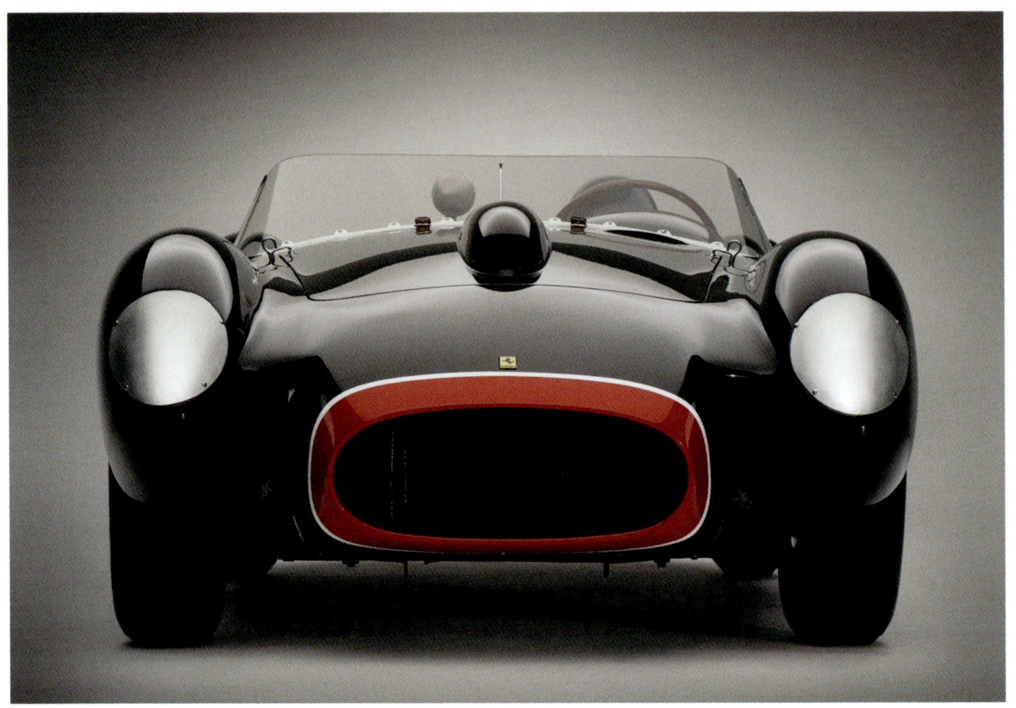

mounted at a 60-degree angle and then fitted with six radically tuned Weber carburetors to provide 300 hp.

The 250 TR's competitiveness was also assisted by its lightweight aerodynamic body, which not only reduced drag, but also directed air to vents that cooled its brakes. Maranello-based Carrozzeria Scaglietti was responsible for the design and execution of the 250 TR's sculptural body with its undulating pontoon fenders that are visually separated from its nacelle body. The irresistibly curvaceous form of the 250 TR epitomized the sculptural elegance of the famed *Linea Italiana* (Italian Line). At the time of its introduction, however, this low-slung body design was pretty controversial, so much so that Enzo Ferrari subsequently commissioned Pininfarina and Carrozzeria Touring to produce other more conventional bodies for the 250 TR's later iterations. It is, though, the original 250 TRs designed by Scaglietti that have the greatest status among collectors.

The Colombo V12 engine combined with the streamlined coachwork was a truly winning formula. Between 1957 and 1961, the 250 TR won ten of the nineteen international championship races it was entered into. It was, however, Ferrari's World Sportscar Championship win in 1958, with its stable of 250 TRs clinching victory in four of that year's six races, that would forever seal this Maranello steed's reputation as a bona fide motor racing legend. Weighing just 800 kilograms, this forward-looking racer with its lithe Scaglietti-designed body was capable of a very impressive for the day 270 km/h (168 mph) top speed.

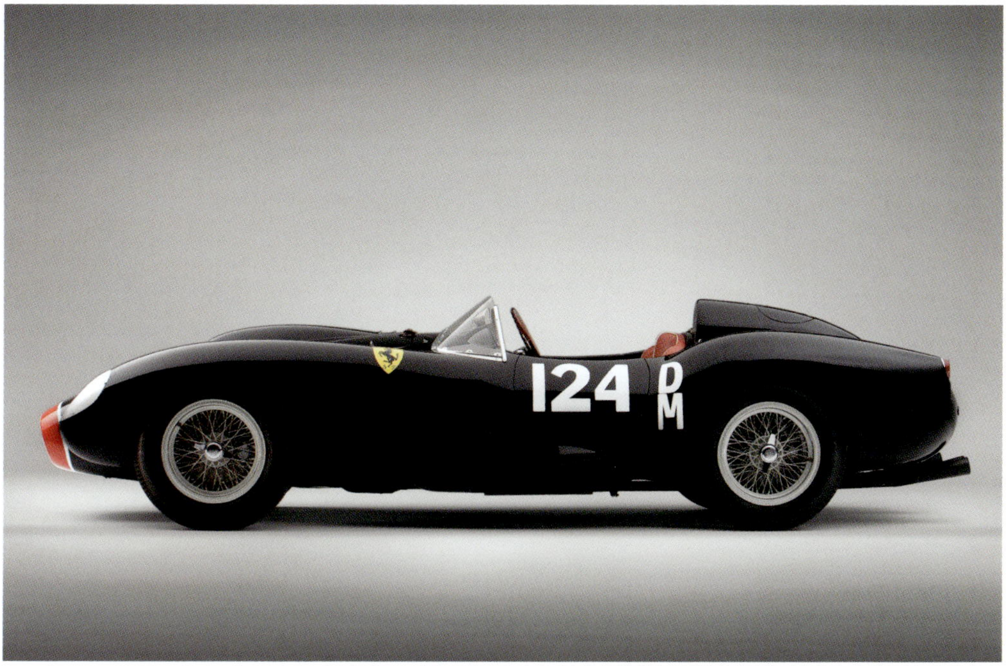

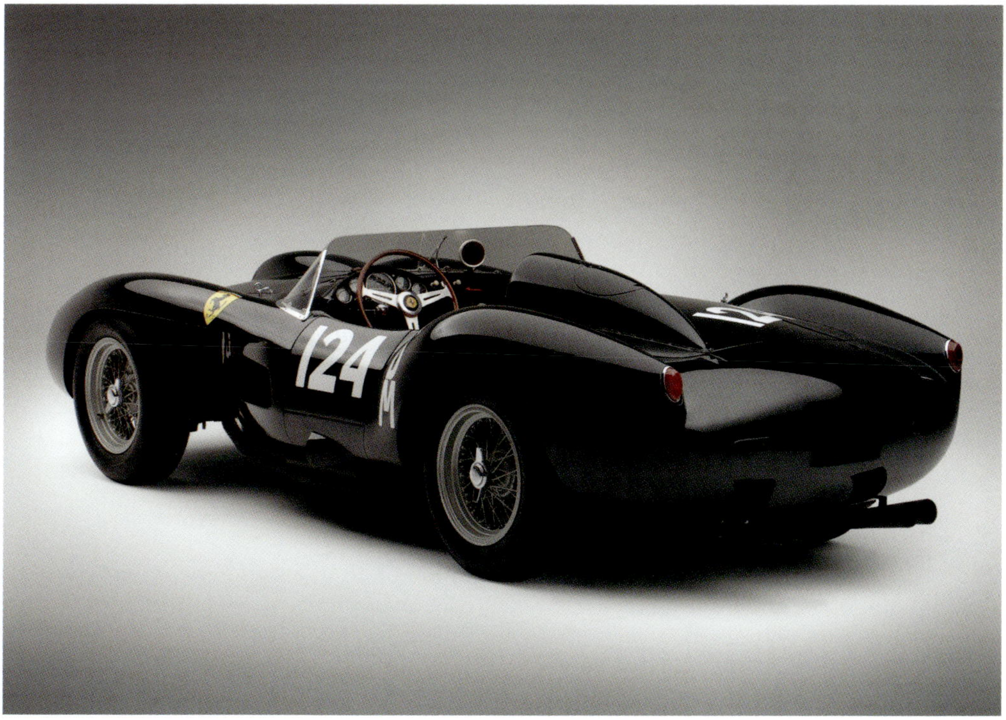

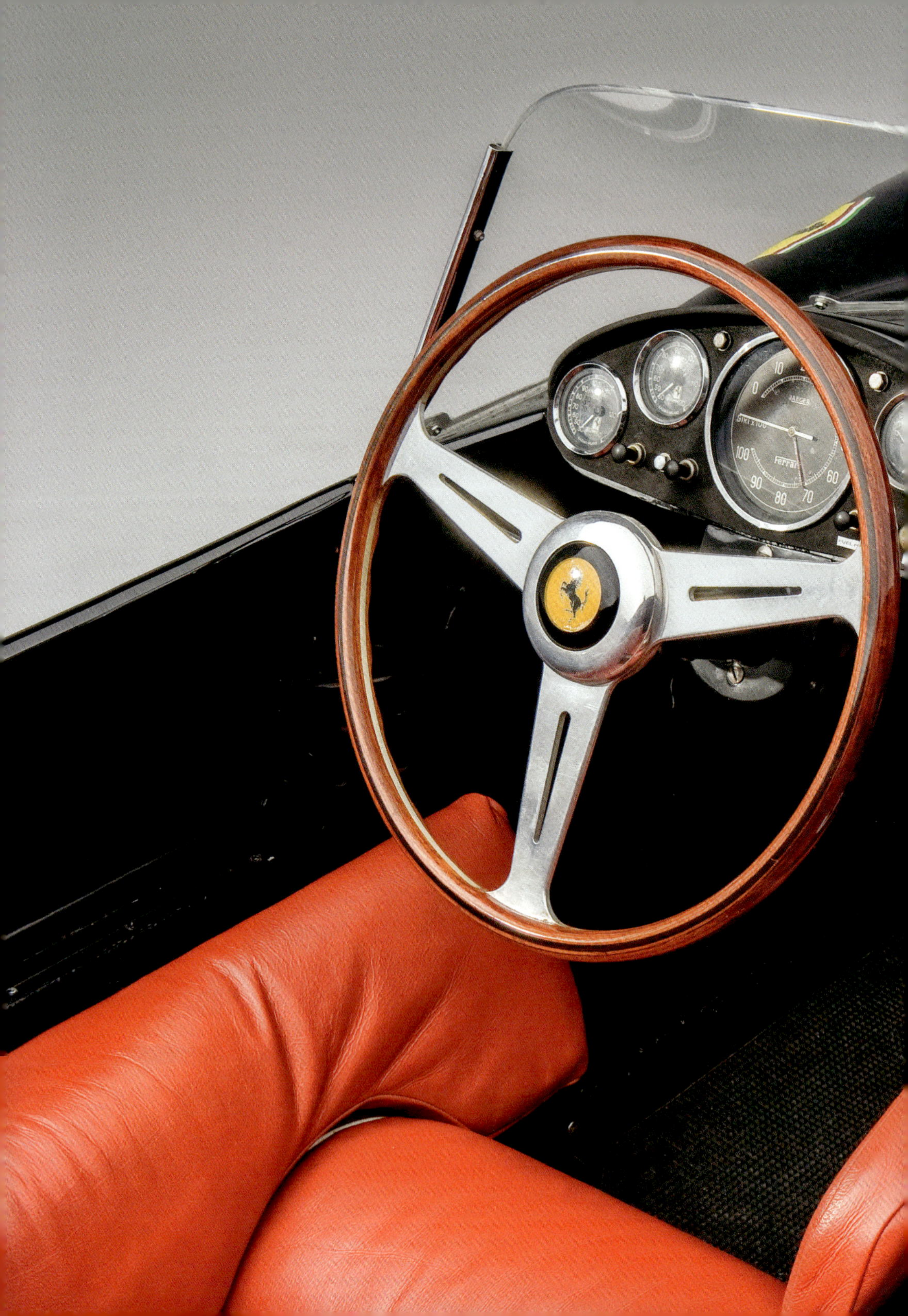

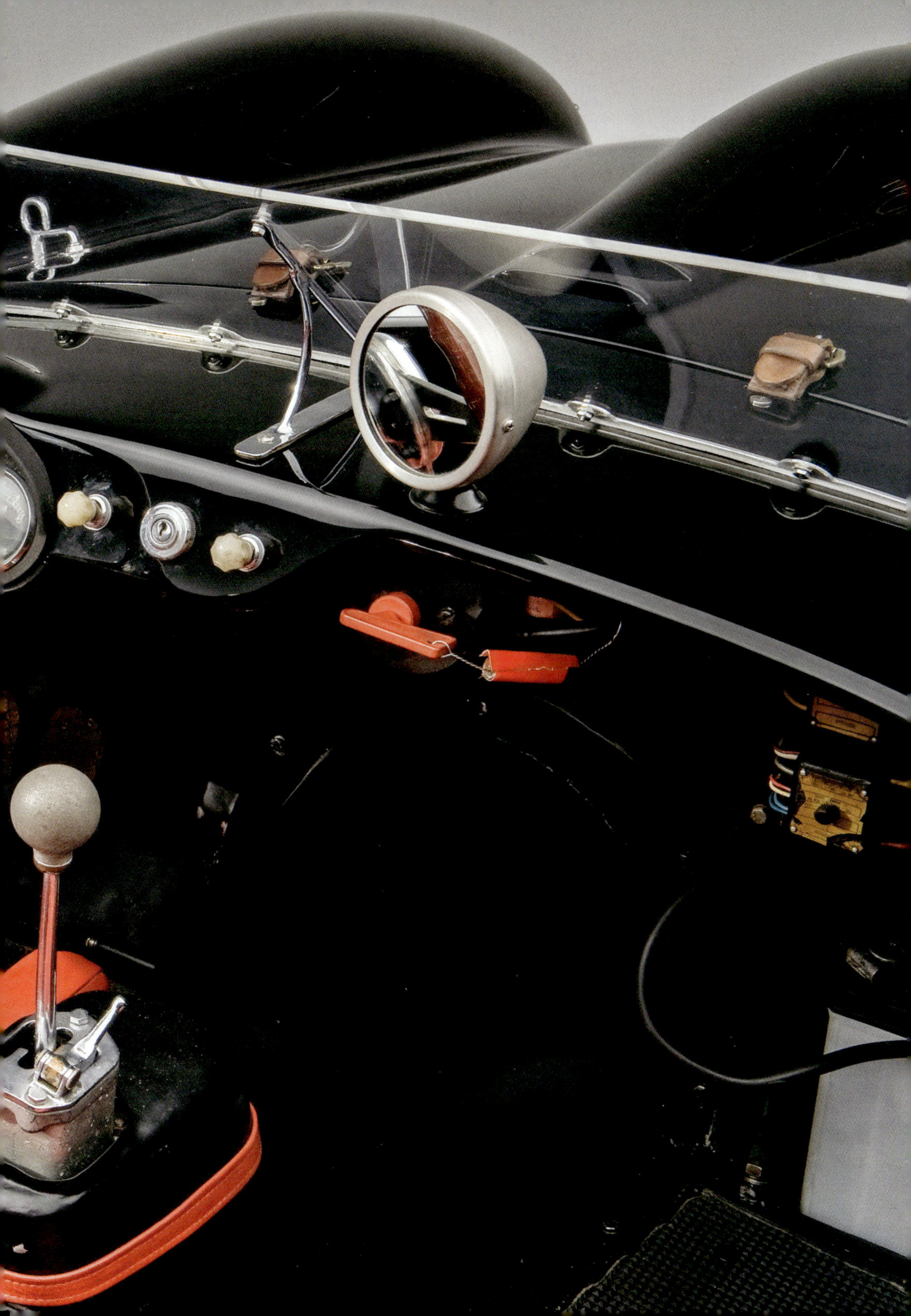

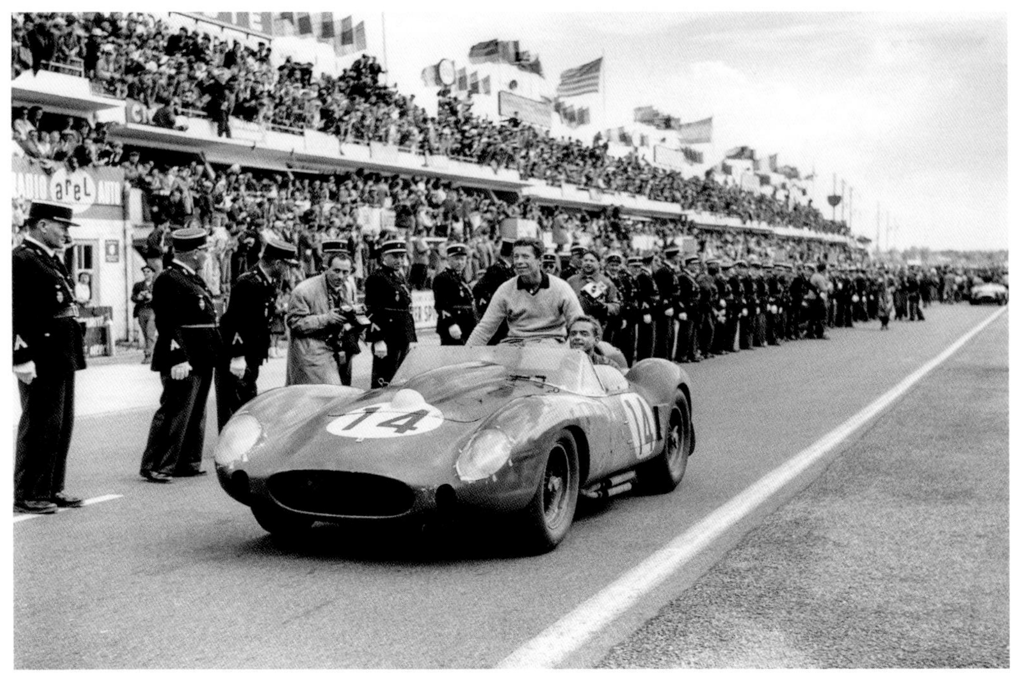

Previous: Designed in collaboration with Scaglietti, the Ferrari 250 Testa Rossa's open interior was appropriately simple and utilitarian, with its instrumentation and controls completely focused around the driver. As with other Ferrari sports cars from the 1950s and 1960s, the 250 Testa Rossa was equipped with an open-gated gear shifter, and a Nardi wooden steering wheel.

Above: Phil Hill (driving) and Olivier Gendebien leading the victory parade in their No. 14 Scuderia Ferrari 250 TR58 (chassis no. 0728TR) having won the 1958 24 Hours of Le Mans.

Overleaf: The No. 14 Scuderia Ferrari 250 TR58 (chassis no. 0728TR) being driven by Olivier Gendebien, which he shared with Phil Hill, in the 1958 24 Hours of Le Mans. Three Works Ferraris were entered into the race and were referred to as "TR58s" in order to distinguish them from the customer TRs (Testa Rossas). Phil Hill and Olivier Gendebien carefully and quickly piloted their TR58 to a well deserved victory with the closest competition a dozen laps (or 100 miles) behind. This was chassis no. 0728TR's only major victory.

And even now its deep, throaty engine roar can send shivers down one's spine. The example shown here (chassis no. 0714TR) is a car that is superlative on so many levels — it is not only beautiful and rare, but also has an impressive race history having begun its competition career with a winning debut at the 1958 1000 Kilometres of Buenos Aires, with Phil Hill at its helm. It was then fielded in various other important race events around the world, clocking up a number of significant finishes. As one of the ultimate and most desirable Ferraris of all time, this stunning beast in its black and red livery set a world record in 2009 as the most expensive car ever sold up till then at auction. This testifies to the enduring allure of this truly iconic Ferrari, which even when standing still looks fast because its design is so infused with pure racing spirit.

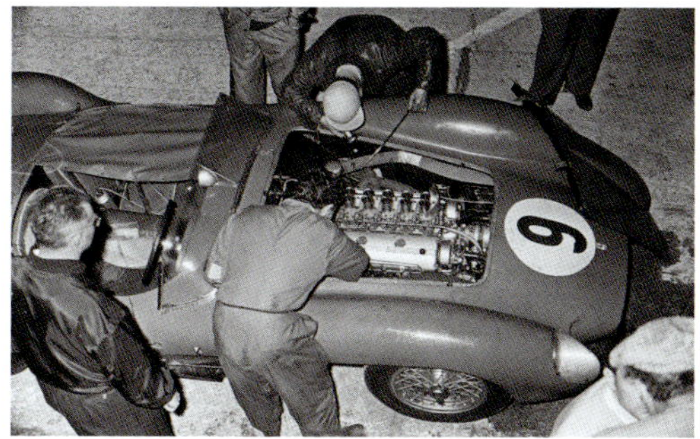

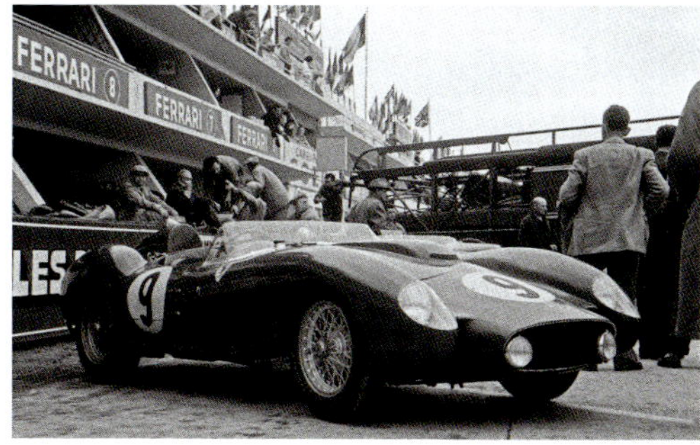

Above (left): Ferrari mechanics working on the engine of Olivier Gendebien and Maurice Trintignant's No. 9 250 Testa Rossa during the 1957 24 Hours of Le Mans. The car failed to finish the race due to a piston problem.

Above (right): The No. 9 Scuderia Ferrari 250 Testa Rossa, driven by Olivier Gendebien and Maurice Trintignant in the pits prior to the start of the 1957 24 Hours of Le Mans. This was the first Ferrari 250 Testa Rossa to appear at Le Mans. It was fitted with a 3.1-liter engine so as not to fall into the competitive three-liter class.

Below: Cutaway drawing of a 1958 Ferrari 250 Testa Rossa (chassis no. 0710 TR) by R. J. Way, which appeared in an article in *The Motor*, 1958.

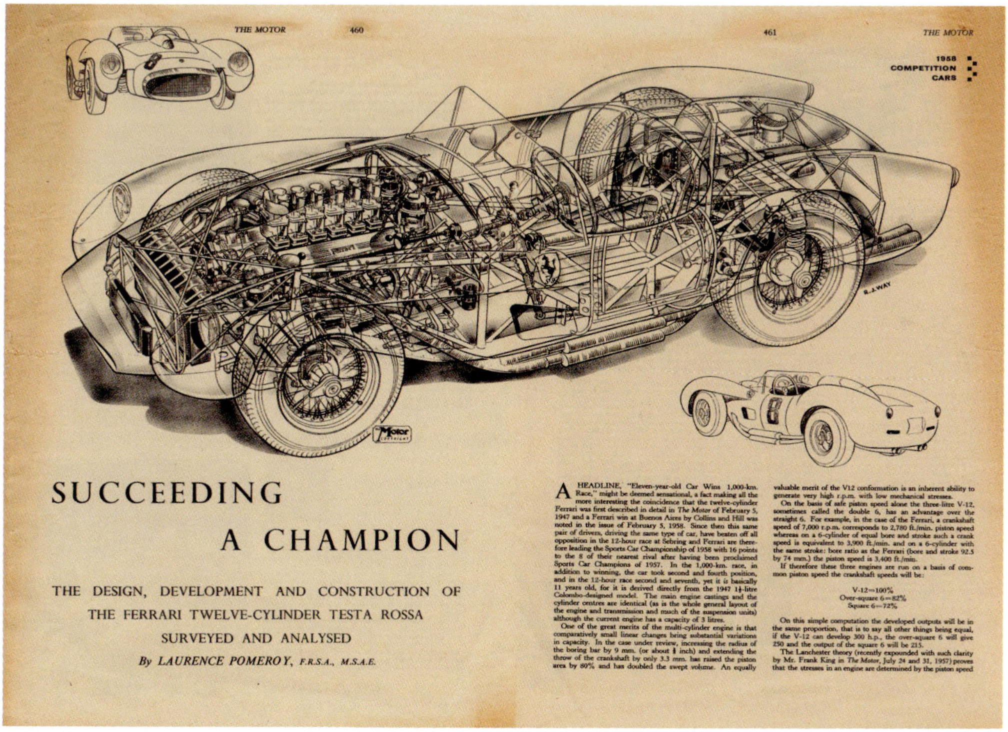

THE MOTOR 460 461 THE MOTOR

1958 COMPETITION CARS

SUCCEEDING A CHAMPION

THE DESIGN, DEVELOPMENT AND CONSTRUCTION OF THE FERRARI TWELVE-CYLINDER TESTA ROSSA SURVEYED AND ANALYSED

By LAURENCE POMEROY, F.R.S.A., M.S.A.E.

A HEADLINE, "Eleven-year-old Car Wins 1,000-km. Race," might be deemed sensational, a fact making all the more interesting the coincidence that the twelve-cylinder Ferrari was first described in detail in *The Motor* of February 5, 1947 and a Ferrari win at Buenos Aires by Collins and Hill was noted in the issue of February 5, 1958. Since then this same pair of drivers, driving the same type of car, have beaten off all opposition in the 12-hour race at Sebring and Ferrari are therefore leading the Sports Car Championship of 1958 with 16 points to the 8 of their nearest rival after having been proclaimed Sports Car Champions of 1957. In the 1,000-km. race, in addition to winning, the car took second and fourth position, and in the 12-hour race second and seventh, yet it is basically 11 years old, for it is derived directly from the 1947 1½-litre Colombo-designed model. The main engine castings and the cylinder centres are identical (as is the whole general layout of the engine and transmission and much of the suspension units) although the current engine has a capacity of 3 litres.

One of the great merits of the multi-cylinder engine is that comparatively small linear changes bring substantial variations in capacity. In the case under review, increasing the radius of the boring bar by 9 mm. (or about ⅜ inch) and extending the throw of the crankshaft by only 3.3 mm. has raised the piston area by 80% and has doubled the swept volume. An equally valuable merit of the V12 conformation is an inherent ability to generate very high r.p.m. with low mechanical stresses.

On the basis of safe piston speed alone the three-litre V-12, sometimes called the double 6, has an advantage over the straight 6. For example, in the case of the Ferrari, a crankshaft speed of 7,000 r.p.m. corresponds to 2,780 ft./min. piston speed whereas on a 6-cylinder of equal bore and stroke such a crank speed is equivalent to 3,900 ft./min. and on a 6-cylinder with the same stroke: bore ratio as the Ferrari (bore and stroke 92.5 by 74 mm.) the piston speed is 3,400 ft./min.

If therefore these three engines are run on a basis of common piston speed the crankshaft speeds will be:

V-12=100%
Over-square 6=82%
Square 6—72%

On this simple computation the developed outputs will be in the same proportion, that is to say all other things being equal, if the V-12 can develop 300 h.p., the over-square 6 will give 250 and the output of the square 6 will be 215.

The Lanchester theory (recently expounded with such clarity by Mr. Frank King in *The Motor*, July 24 and 31, 1957) proves that the stresses in an engine are determined by the piston speed

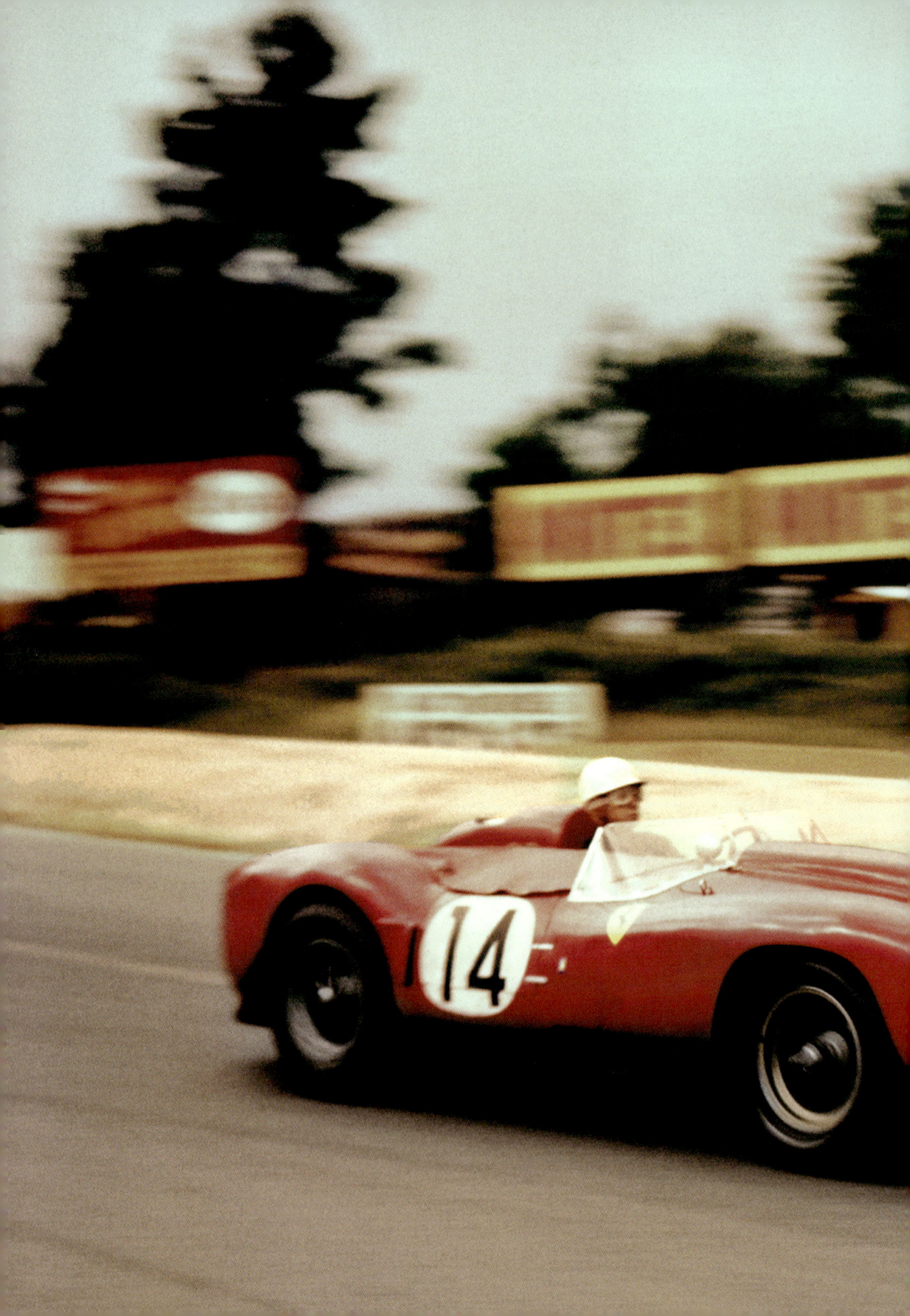
14

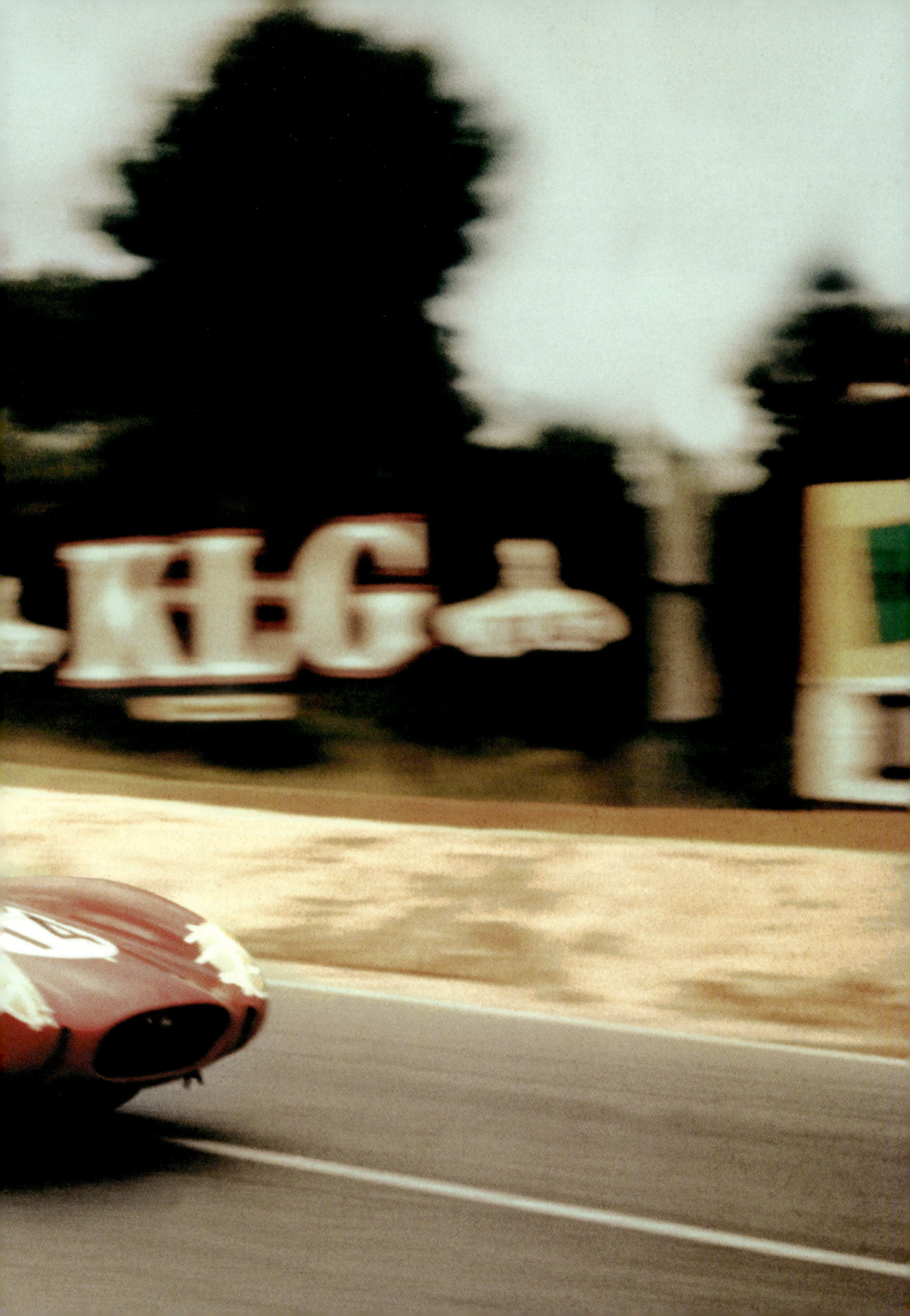

1958

BMW 507 Series II

MANUFACTURED 1956–59 | ENGINE 3,168 cc (193 cu. in.), overhead-valve V8 | HORSEPOWER 155
TOP SPEED 217 km/h (135 mph) | TRANSMISSION 4-speed
NUMBER PRODUCED 217 Series II (out of 252 total 507s)

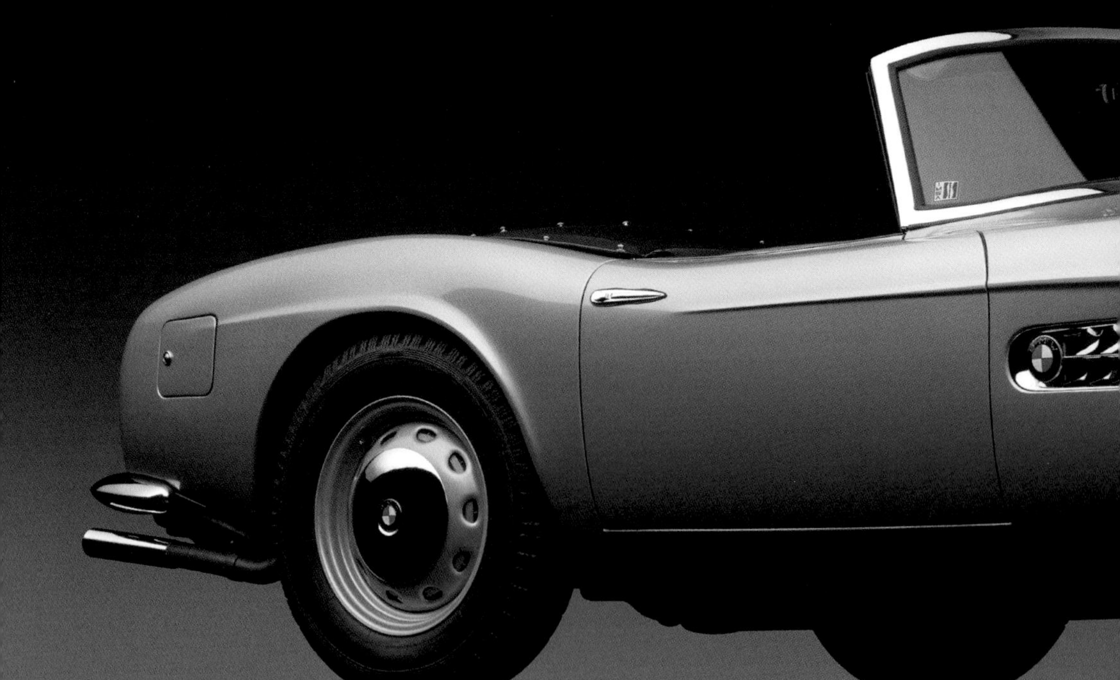

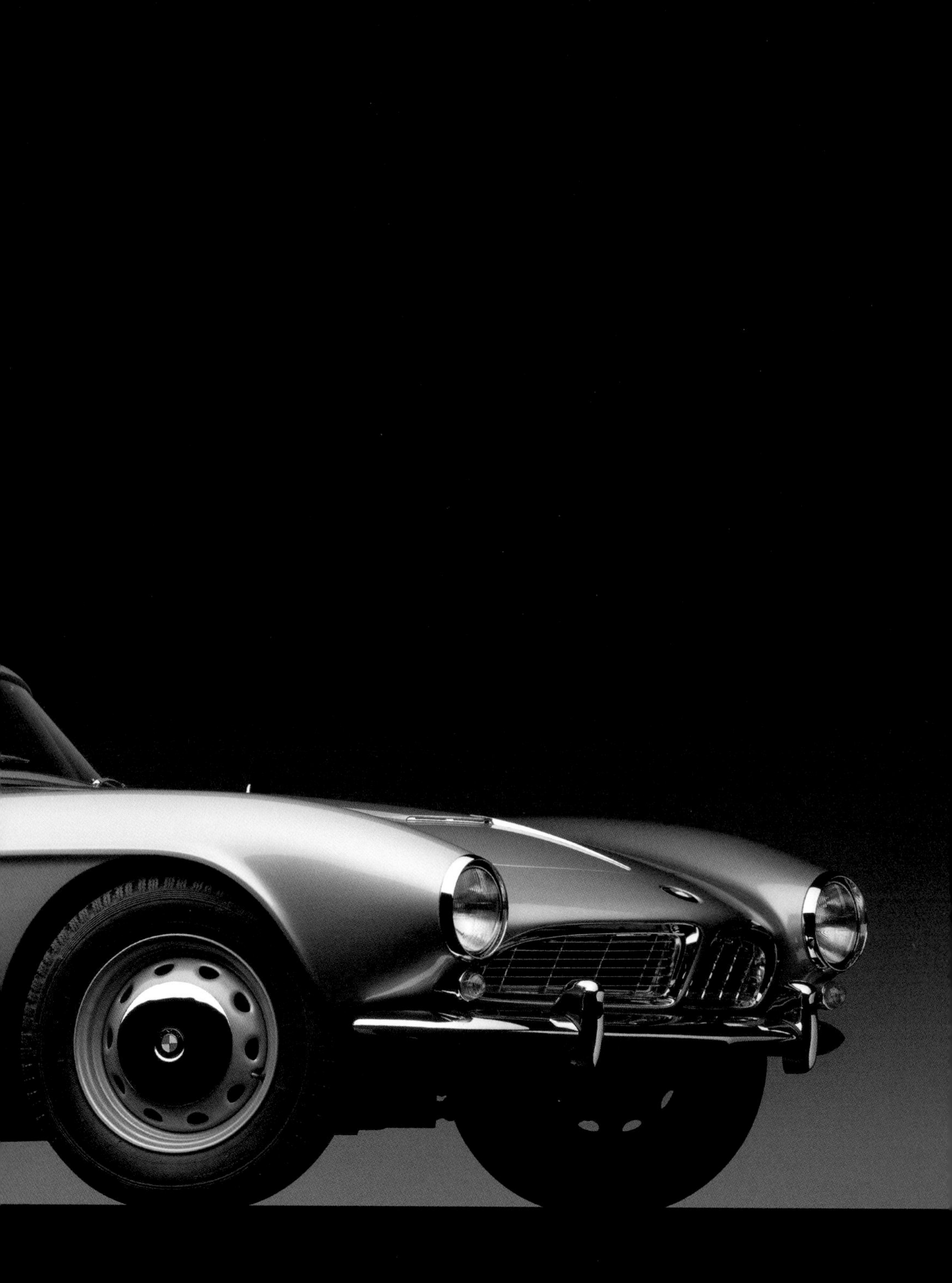

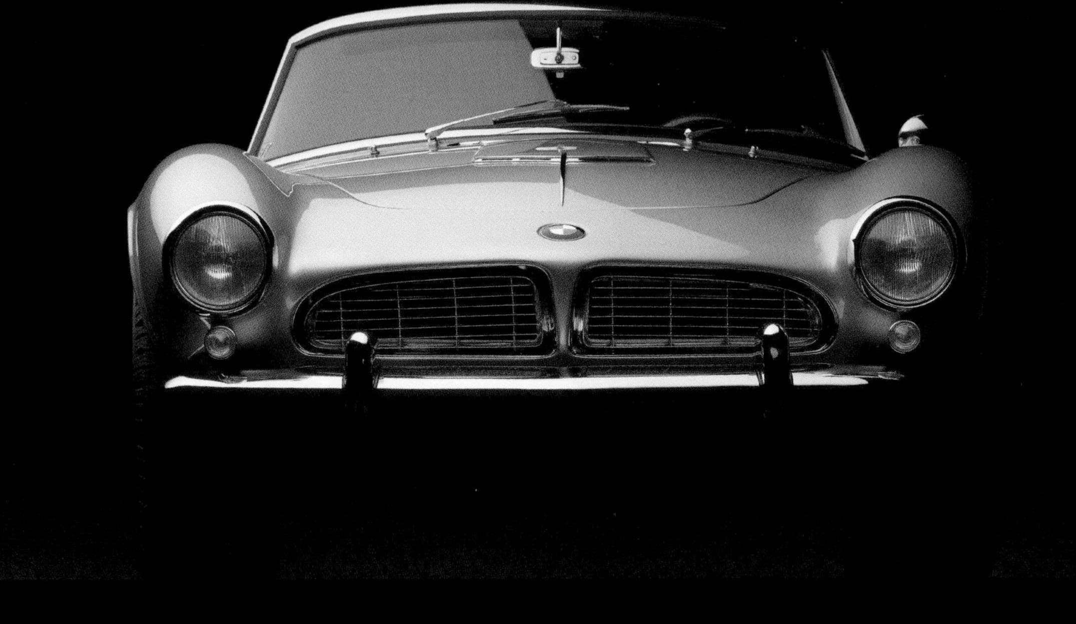

Although not a designer himself, Max Hoffman had a tremendous impact on the design and development of luxury sports cars during the postwar period. Born in Vienna, Hoffmann emigrated to the USA in 1941 with the idea of importing and selling European cars there. But almost as soon as he arrived America entered the war, which put paid to this dream, at least for a while. After the war had ended, however, he opened a Park Avenue showroom in 1947 in New York City with initially just one car on display — a Delahaye. Soon, though, he was importing all sorts of foreign cars to meet the growing demand among wealthy Americans for "exotic" high performance sports cars during the 1950s boom years. Such was Hoffman's remarkable influence in terms of his market-savviness and business acumen, he is quite rightly credited with contributing significantly to the development of several truly iconic sports cars, most notably the Mercedes-Benz 300 SL "Gullwing," the Porsche 356 Speedster and the BMW 507 roadster. Hoffman knew what his clients were looking for and then fed this information back to the manufacturers, who were then able to create models that were tailored to the tastes and needs of the all-important American market. This had a huge impact not only on the cars produced by these luxury high performance marques, but also on the postwar perception of European car brands in general — Hoffman basically helped to make them cool.

And let's face it: What could have been cooler in the late 1950s than the BMW 507 roadster? Employing components sourced from BMW's 502 and 503 series, including a 3.2-liter, overhead-valve aluminum-block V8 engine, which had been upgraded with twin carburetors, this roadster ticked all the power-performance boxes. It was, however, the car's distinctive low-slung body with its seductive curves that really elevated it to its now legendary status, and it was Hoffman who was largely responsible for this. Thanks to his stature as one of the most significant importers of European sports cars into America, he was given final approval of the car's design. As a consequence, Hoffman had requested the design services of Count Albrecht von Goertz, a very talented German-born protégé of the famous industrial design consultant Raymond Loewy. On Loewy's recommendation von Goertz had been given a design job at Studebaker, and it was the futuristic aesthetic of his cars for this marque that drew Hoffman's attention to his skills. As RM Sotheby's observes of the subsequent BMW 507, "Goertz imagined some of the most beautiful lines ever folded into metal." This hand-built imported beauty, however, did not come cheap — a fully optioned example cost over $11,000 back then, roughly equating to about $100,000 in today's money.

It was this high price tag that ultimately led BMW to discontinue the model after only two-and-half years production. As a result, only 252 examples of the 507 were ever built.

Below: The 507 Series II Roadster with optional removable hard-top. Count Albrecht von Goertz "designed in" the 507's hardtop with the result that the car is as striking with this rare optional extra fitted as it is when removed and open to the breeze.

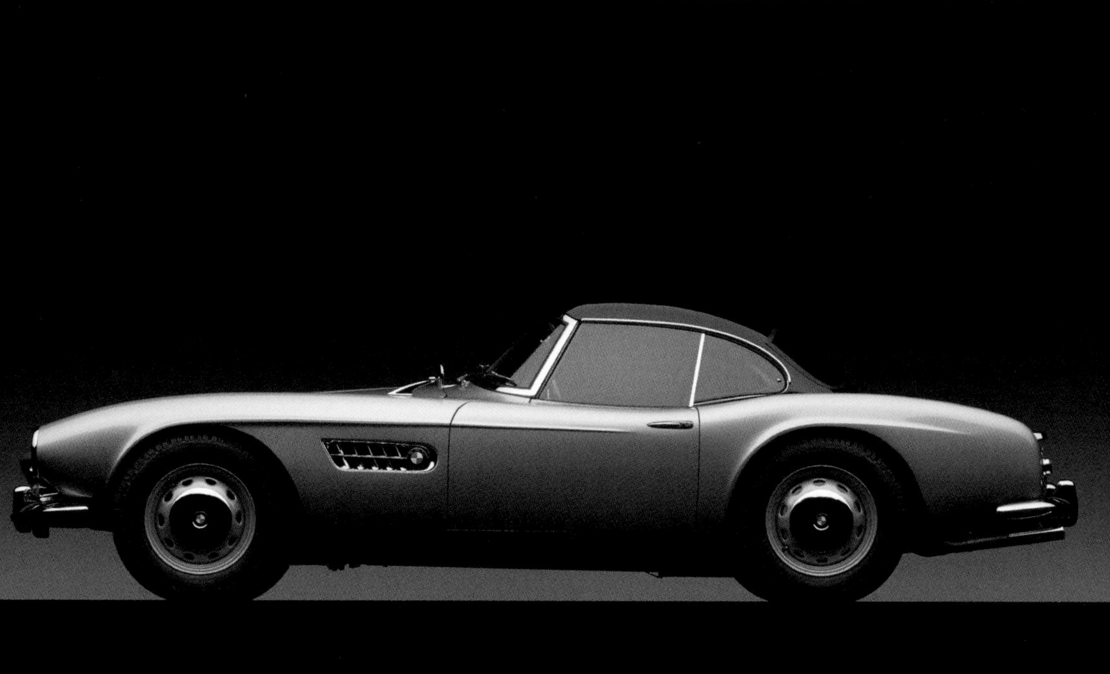

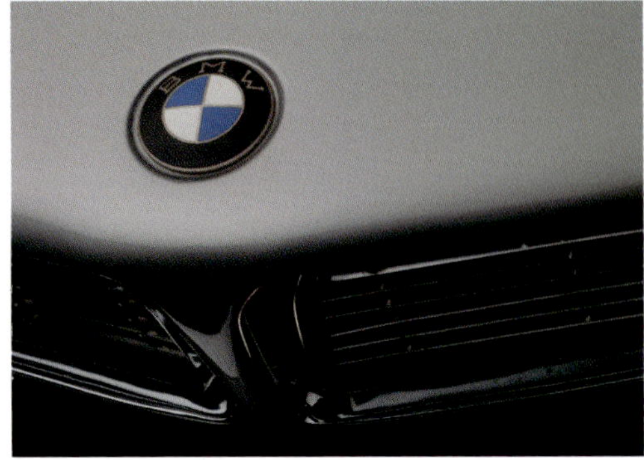

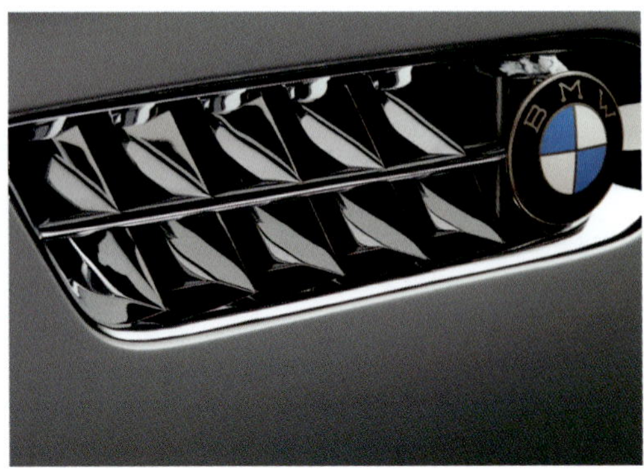

Below: December 21, 1958 — Frankfurt, Germany: Elvis Presley accepts the keys to his newly purchased BMW 507 sports car. Having previously been used by German auto racer Hans Stuck for demonstrations, it came with a racing motor. Presley, however, exchanged it for a tamer touring one, while he was stationed with a US Army unit at nearby Friedberg.

Opposite: Cutaway drawing of BMW 507 by illustrator Serge Bellu. Shown is the 3,168 cc (193 cu. in.), overhead-valve aluminum block V8 engine with dual Zenith twin choke carburetors. The 507 design had a lightness that meant performance was brisk and it provided a comfortable but still sporty ride.

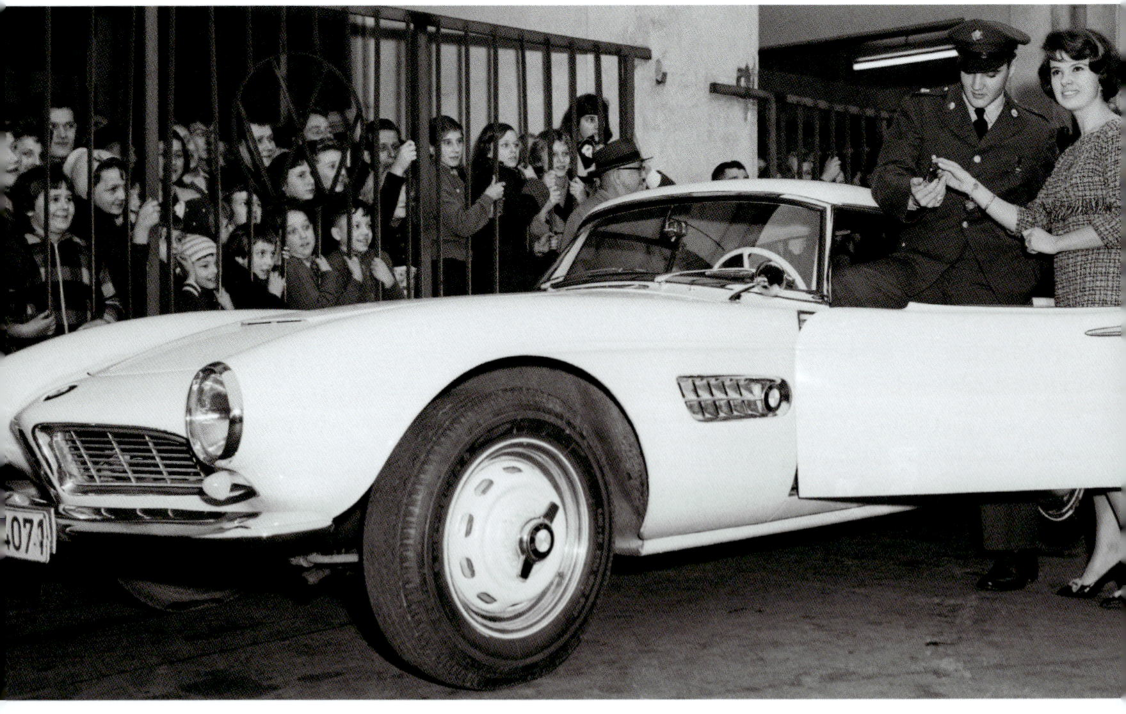

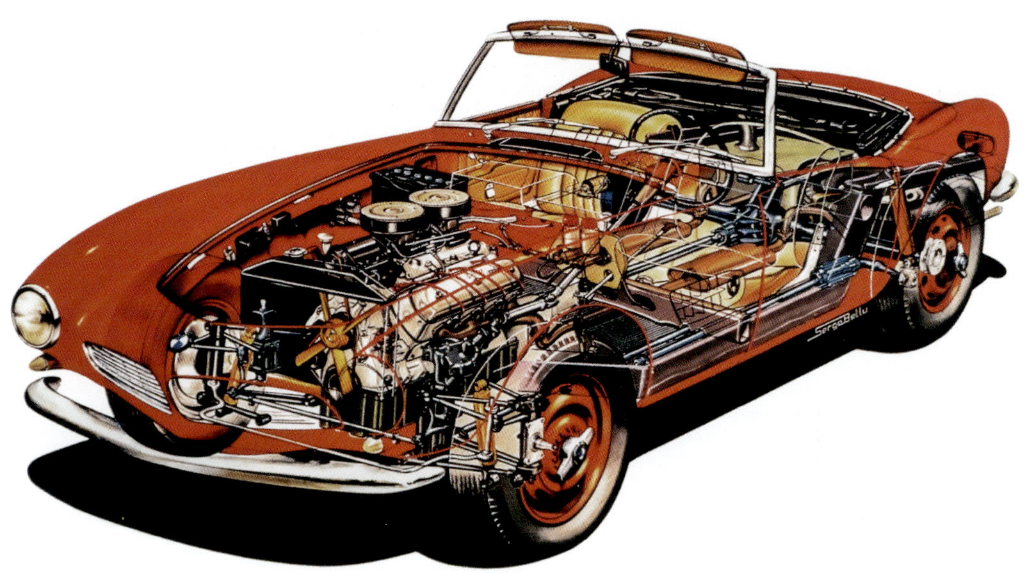

But it is amazing how spellbinding a beautiful car can be, and certainly the 252 original customers who purchased one must have been so taken with its looks that they were able to justify its steep price tag. Reputedly, Elvis Presley gave one to the actress Ursula Andress when she fell for its allure, and presumably he for hers. Another lucky owner was the racing driver John Surtees, who went on to become World Champion. Such was the enduring appeal of von Goertz's forward-looking design that it would later go on to inspire the development of the retro-yet-sporty BMW Z8 roadster in the early 2000s. The 1958 BMW 507, shown here (chassis no. 70180) is a fine example from the later Series II, meaning it had an increased engine output of 155 hp and also boasted a little more space behind its seats in order to provide extra legroom for taller drivers and passengers. The rising appeal of the sports car as an automotive genre during the late 1950s can be seen to have potently embodied the era's rising optimism and prosperity. During this period, high-speed driving in super-stylish roadsters, like this superb BMW 507 Series II, became inextricably linked to a sense of youthful devil-may-care freedom, especially in America where the new interstate highway system offered exciting possibilities for discovery and adventure. And what better vehicle to head out on the highway hurtling toward the horizon with the wind in your hair than this American-tailored, German-engineered automotive masterpiece?

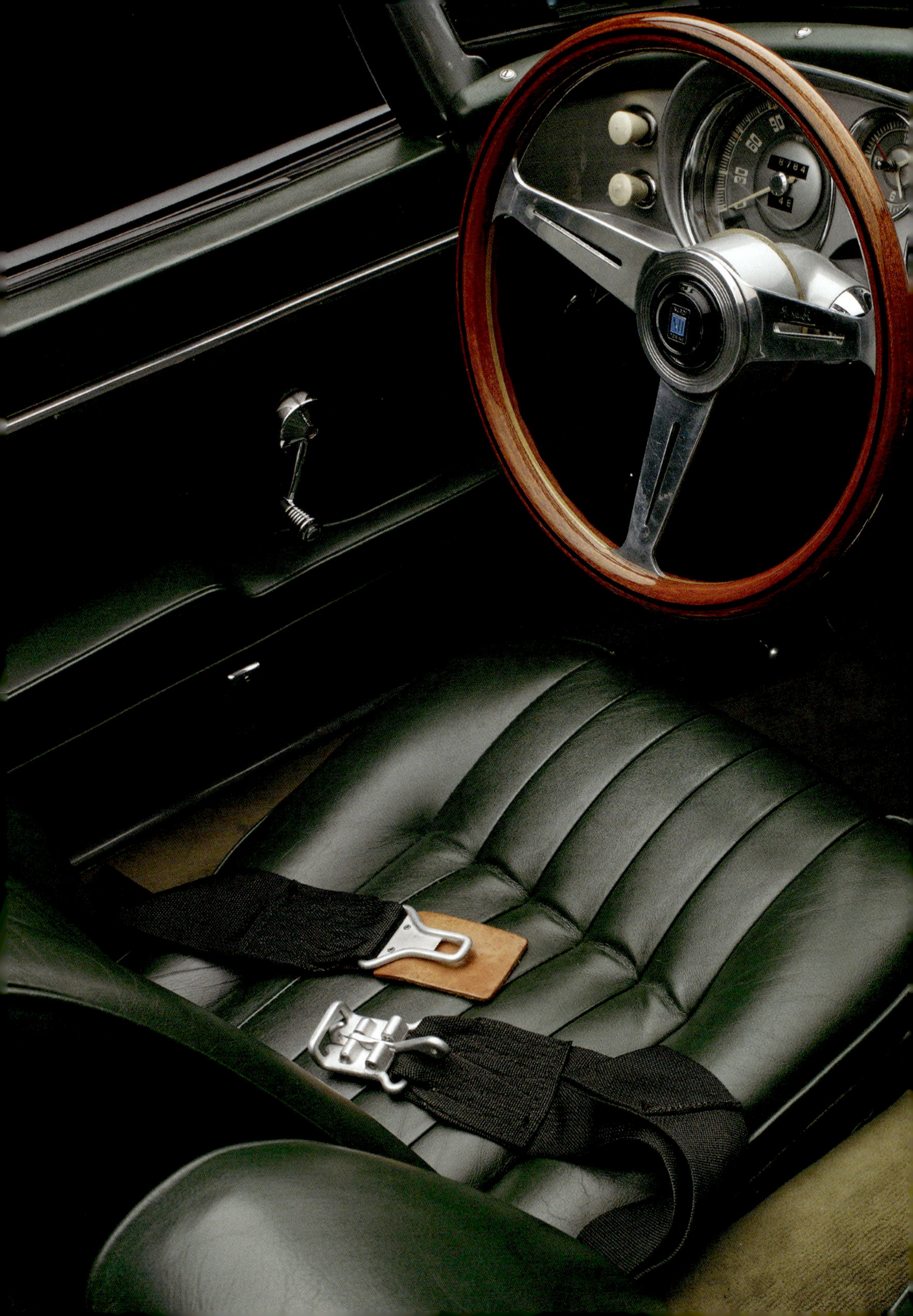

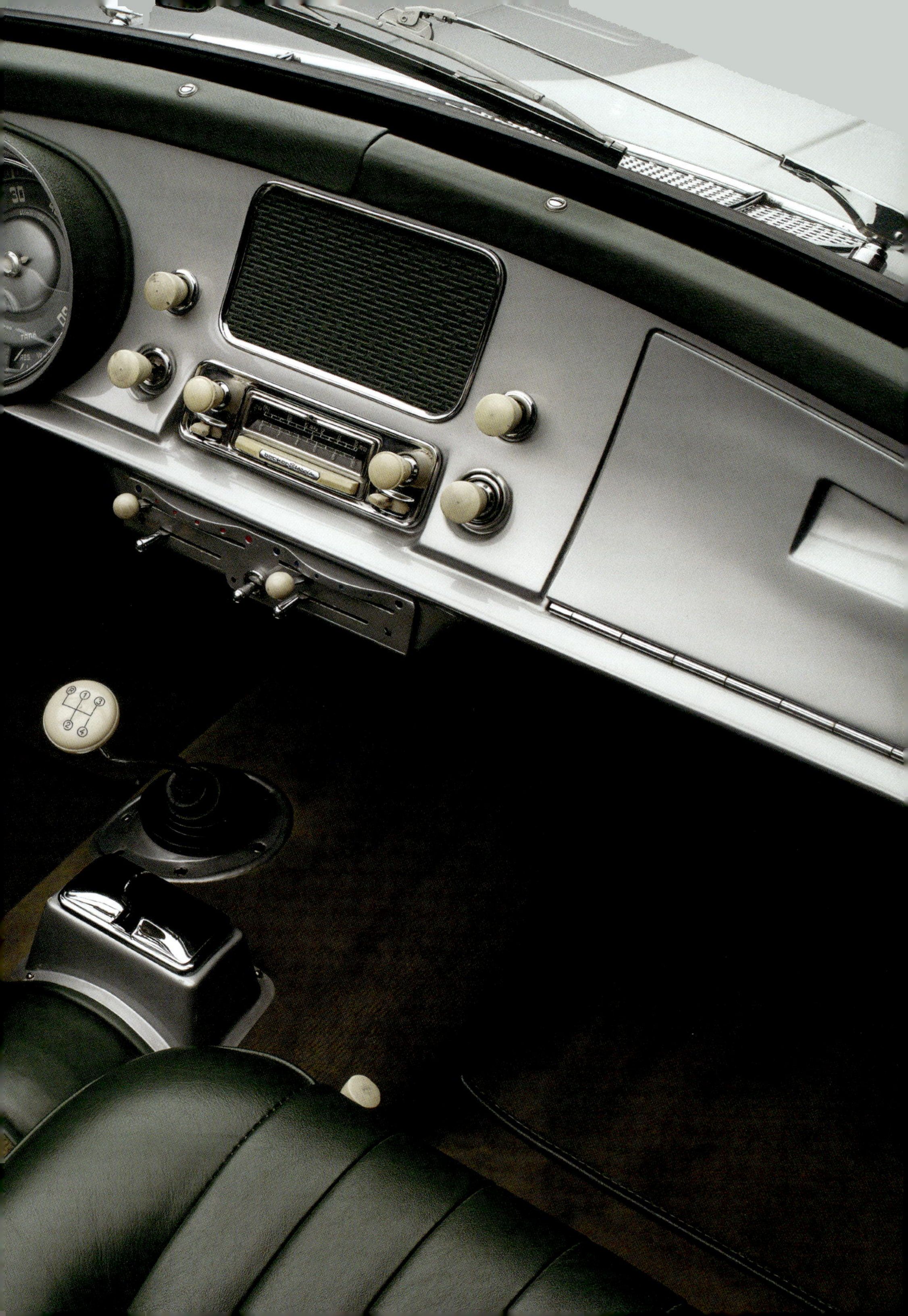

Ferrari 250 GT LWB California Spider Competizione

MANUFACTURED 1958–60 | ENGINE 2,953 cc (180 cu. in.), SOHC per bank 60° V12 | HORSEPOWER 262
TOP SPEED 252 km/h (157 mph) | TRANSMISSION 4-speed
NUMBER PRODUCED 8 alloy-bodied LWB California Spider Competizioni

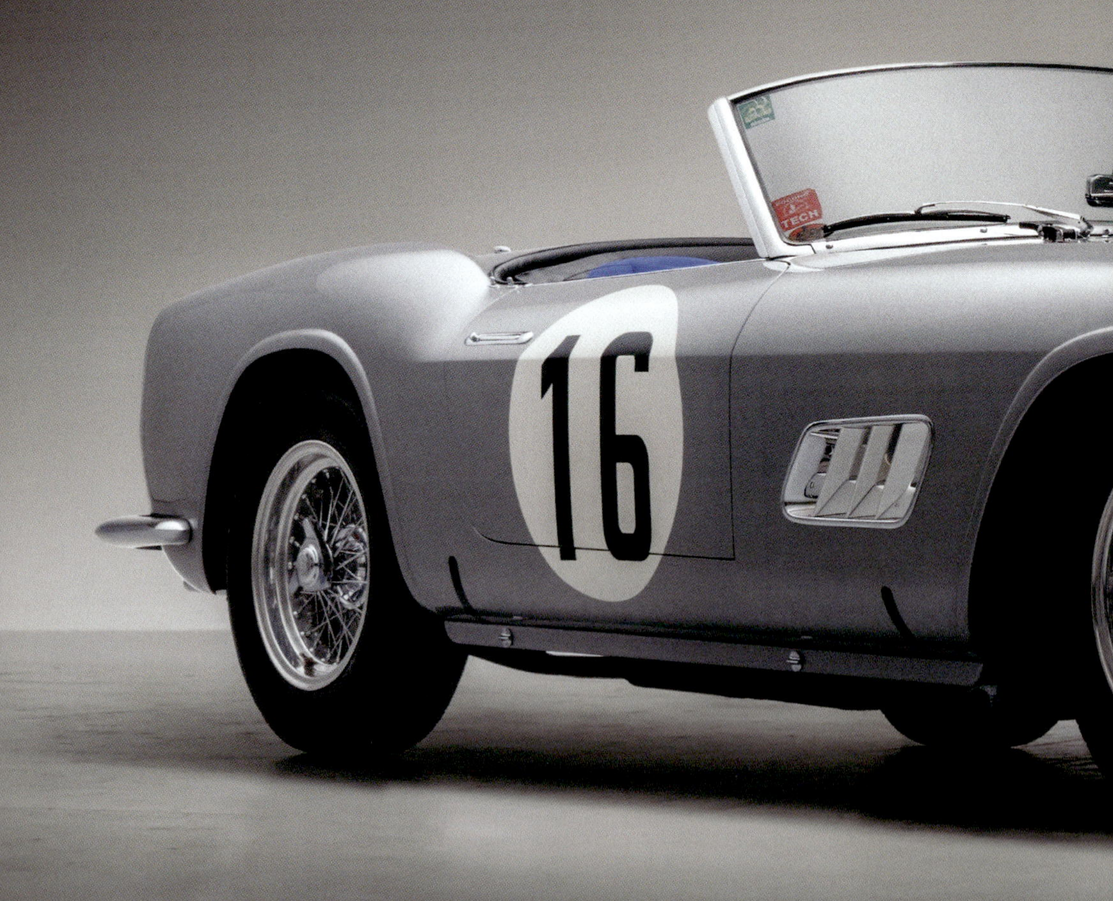

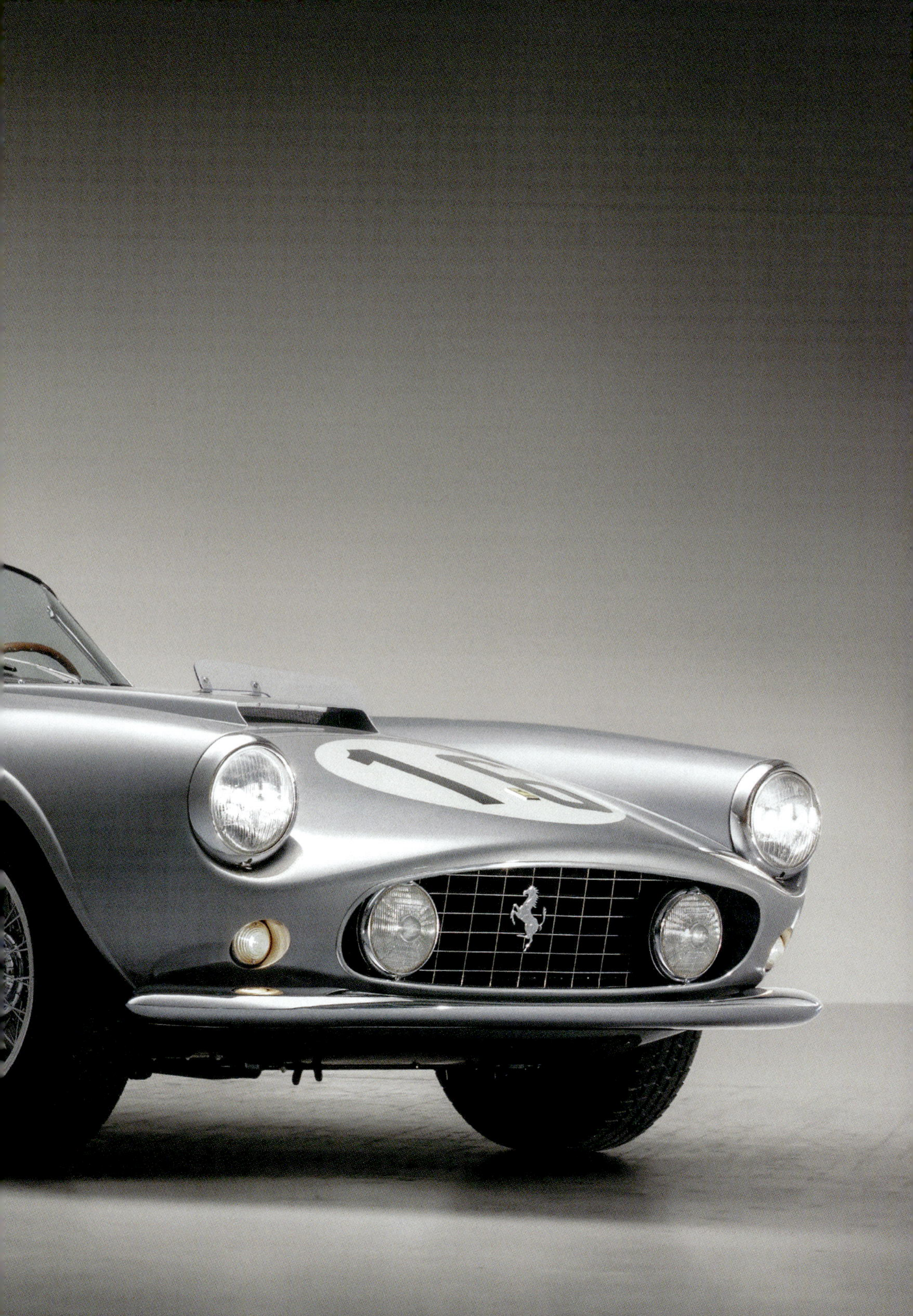

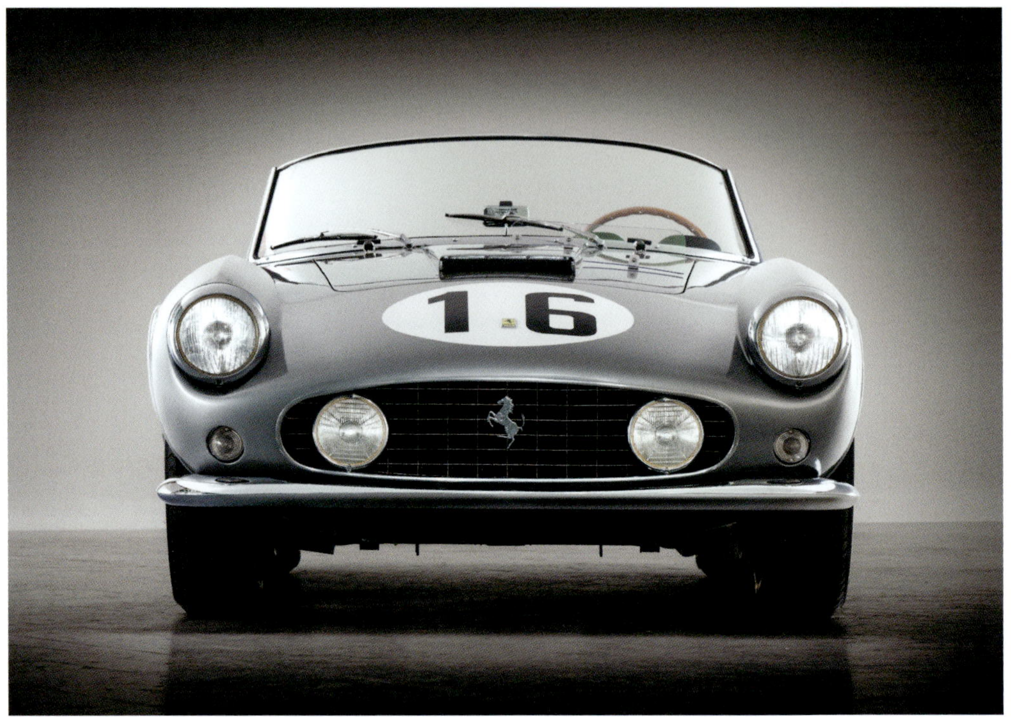

Previous & above: Within the hierarchy of the LWB California Spiders, chassis number 1451 GT sits at the very top of the pyramid. Built to full "competizione" specifications, it was the second of eight California Spiders bodied in aluminum. First owned by the great racing driver Bob Grossman, the car was raced by him under Luigi Chinetti's famous NART banner.

Opposite: Detail of Ferrari 250 GT LWB California Spider Competizione 2,953 cc (180 cu. in.), SOHC per bank 60º V12 engine. This was the first outside-plug, Tipo 128F engine, topped with high-lift camshafts and triple Weber 40 DCL6 carburetors, fitted to a California Spider.

Recalling the sleek profile of a predatory shark, the Ferrari 250 GT LWB California Spider Competizione by Scaglietti has an altogether more angular and muscular demeanor than some of Ferrari's earlier models, which were invariably distinguished by very feminine, curvaceous forms that exemplified the famed *Linea Italiana* (Italian Line). The reason for this is that Enzo Ferrari had always been very aware of the American market, with the vast majority of his firm's car sales having been made there thanks to the enthusiastic efforts of Luigi Chinetti, the marque's main US importer. In the late 1950s John von Neumann, Ferrari's representative on the West Coast, became convinced that there was a potential market for a high performance Ferrari spider that would be suited to open-top driving in the Californian sunshine. He conveyed these thoughts to Chinetti, who was immediately taken with the idea and then managed to persuade Enzo Ferarri to add a sporty convertible such as this to the marque's product line. The resultant model was the

250 GT California Spider, which was first introduced in 1958 and was essentially an open-top version of the 250 GT Berlinetta. Although boasting drop-dead gorgeous European styling and exceptional high-precision engineering, this roadster reflected a definite stateside influence not only through various styling cues but also by the addition of "California" to its name. Although this sports racer might have been built in Ferrari's factory in Maranello and styled by one of Italy's greatest coachworks, Carrozzeria Scaglietti, ultimately Enzo's dreams for this car lay with the sun-kissed Golden State. Certainly, its styling, though utterly exquisite and every inch what you would expect from a Ferrari, gives a distinct nod to more muscular American aesthetics.

To give context to the model's development it is worth remembering that from the late 1950s to the early 1960s was the golden age of sports car racing, when every weekend privateer gentleman racers and manufacturers' works teams would take to racetracks around the world and pit themselves against each other in thrillingly noisy speed battles. As RM Sotheby's explains, "Races varied from fun and seemingly non-competitive to events where the reputations and livelihoods of manufacturers and professional drivers alike would hang in the balance. In many regards, postwar organized motorsport was still in its infancy, allowing for a sort of romanticism to be associated with the events, their participants, the spectators, and the cars themselves." It is nostalgia for this lost motorsports era, when races were perilous life-or-death experiences and drivers were larger-than-life personalities, that drives the prices of the cars that competed in events such as

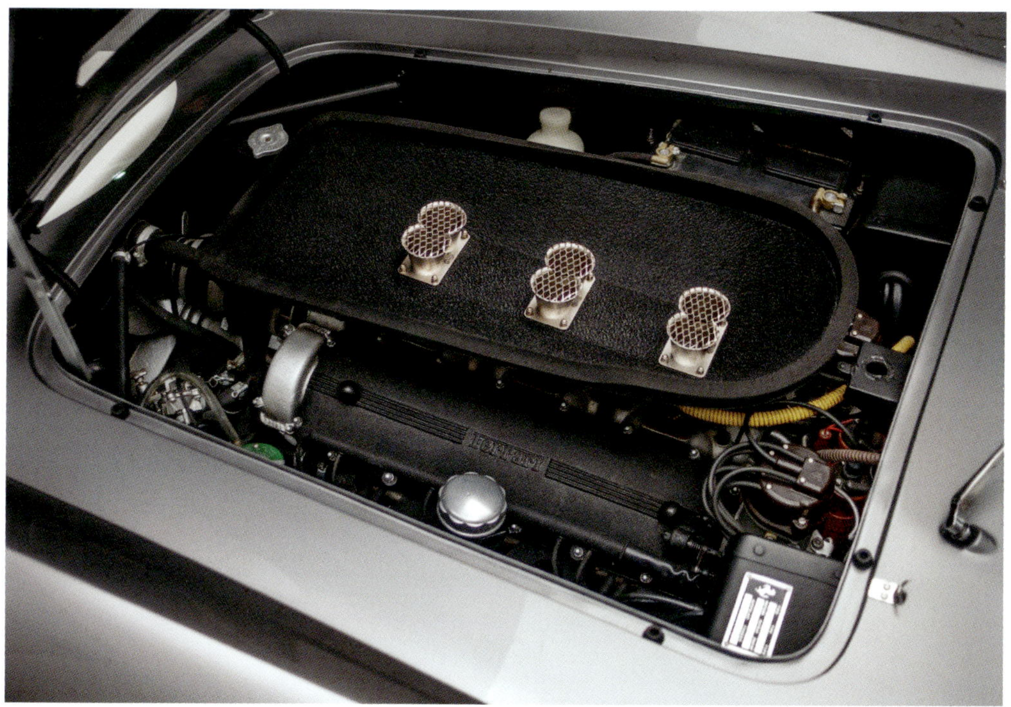

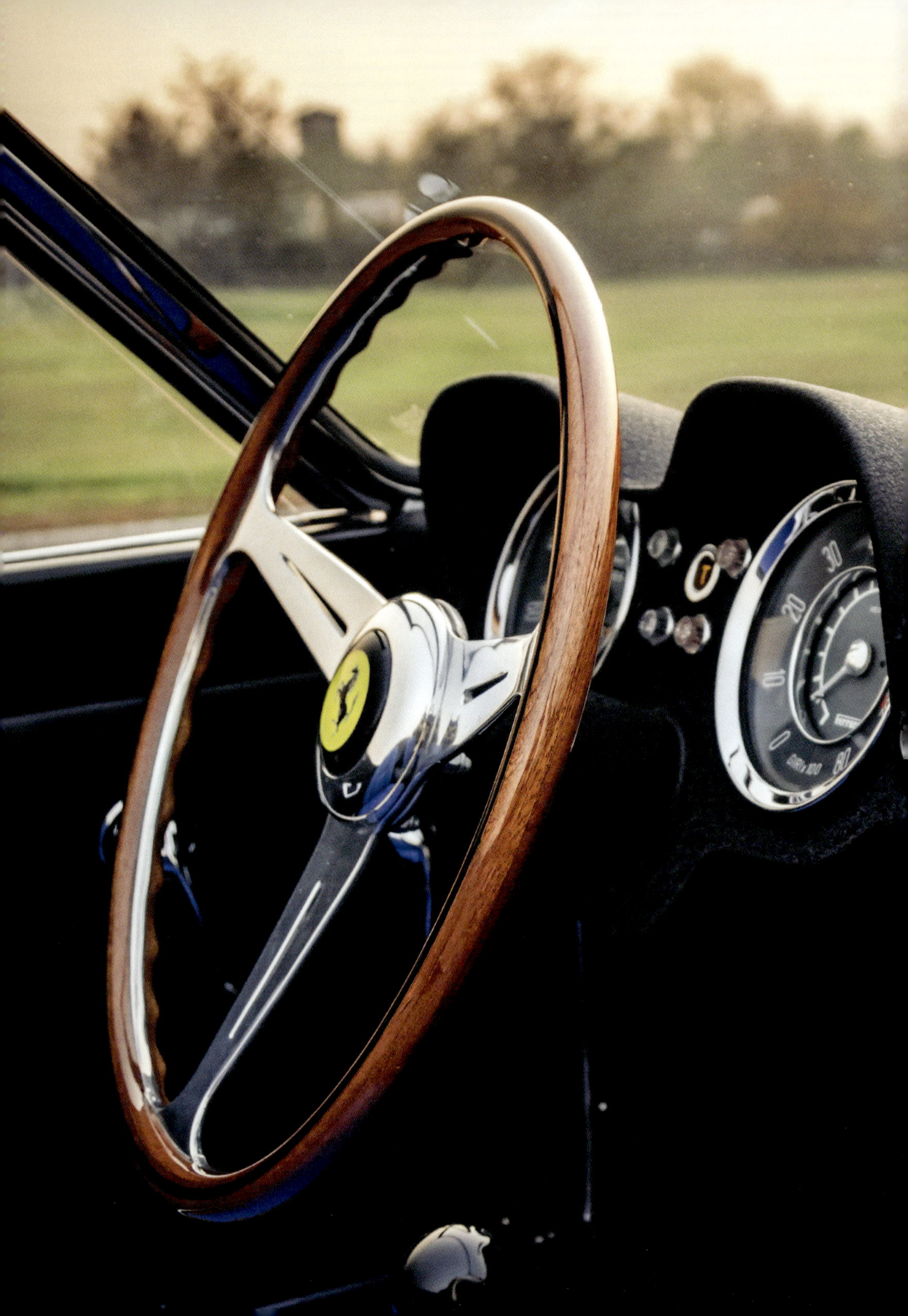
30
20
10
GIRI x 100

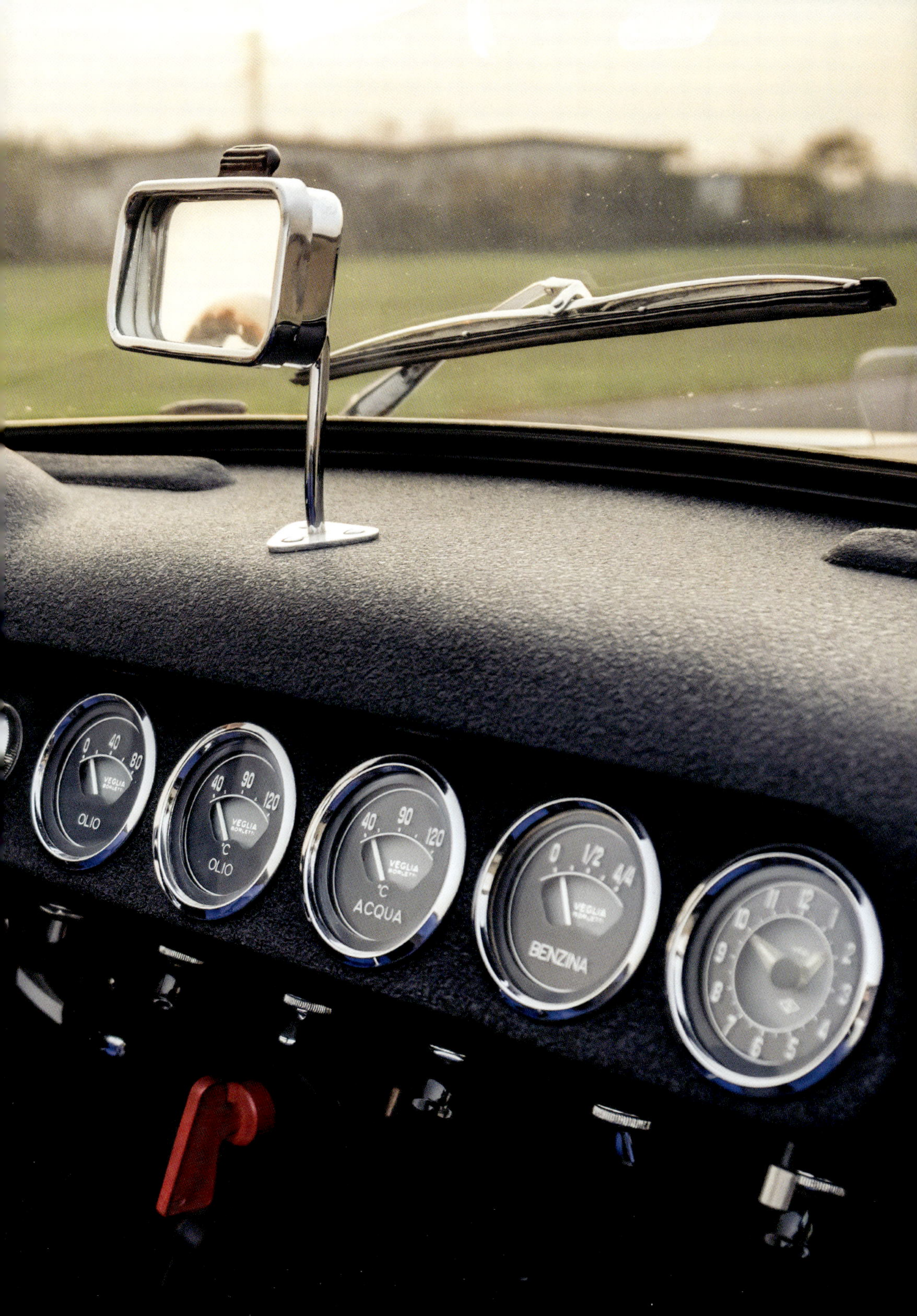
0 40 80
VEGLIA BORLETTI
OLIO
40 90 120
VEGLIA BORLETTI
°C
OLIO
40 90 120
VEGLIA BORLETTI
°C
ACQUA
0 1/2 4/4
VEGLIA BORLETTI
BENZINA
11 12 1
10 2
9 3
8 4
7 6 5

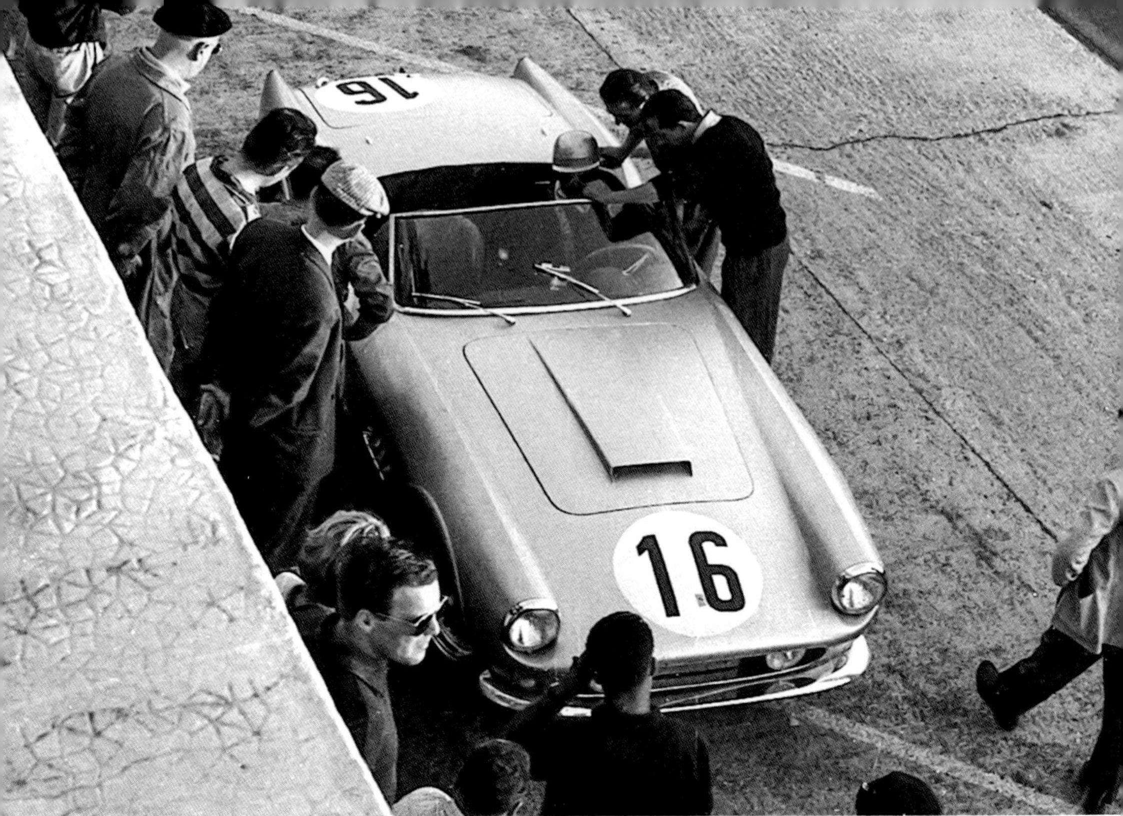

Previous: Detail of 1959 Ferrari 250 GT LWB California Spider Competizione's Nardi steering wheel, instrument cluster and controls.

Above: The No. 16 1959 Ferrari 250 GT LWB California Spider Competizione by Scaglietti (chassis no. 1451 GT) of the North American Racing Team (NART) driven by Bob Grossman and Fernand Tavano making a pit stop during the 1959 24 Hours of Le Mans.

these ever upward. One of the major players in sports car racing during this period was, of course, Chinetti, who was himself a former racing driver whose record was legendary, having won the 24 Hours of Le Mans three times in 1932, 1934 and 1949. This last victory (in a Ferrari 166 MM) was momentous in that it was Ferrari's first race victory. After the war, Chinetti had opened a Ferrari dealership in Paris and then subsequently emigrated to America, where he famously became Ferrari's first and for a while sole US distributor and established the very first and, for quite a time thereafter, only Ferrari-dedicated dealership, Luigi Chinetti Motors Inc. in New York City. Chinetti also later founded the fabled North American Racing Team in 1958 — aka NART — as a means of promoting the Italian marque stateside by participating as an all-American Ferrari team at the world's foremost endurance races — notably Daytona, Sebring and, of course, Le Mans.

The following year, under the auspices of NART, Chinetti entered a trio of Ferrari factory-tuned, race-prepped thoroughbreds into the 24 Hours of Le Mans: a 250 Testa Rossa (see p. 212), a 250 GT SWB Berlinetta and the exquisite competition-specified

250 GT LWB California Spider (chassis no. 1451 GT) shown here. This car was only the second of eight aluminum-bodied LWB California Spiders and its build was completed just five days before the 1959 Le Mans, where it was co-piloted by Bob Grossman (its actual owner, who was a sports car dealer based in Rockland County, New York) and the French racing driver, Fernand Tavano. At the race, this car (No. 16) ultimately placed third in its class and fifth overall, which given the superior speed of Aston Martin's DBR1s (see p. 174) that year, was by anyone's standards highly commendable. After Grossman retired from racing in 1960, this stunning car was sold on several times, before undergoing a full restoration, which was completed in 1983. Afterward, it went on to win first in class at the Pebble Beach Concours d'Elegance. It then underwent another full restoration, which returned it back to its original Le Mans livery. Since then, it has won numerous awards including, somewhat fittingly, the Ferrari Club of America's NART Award of 2016.

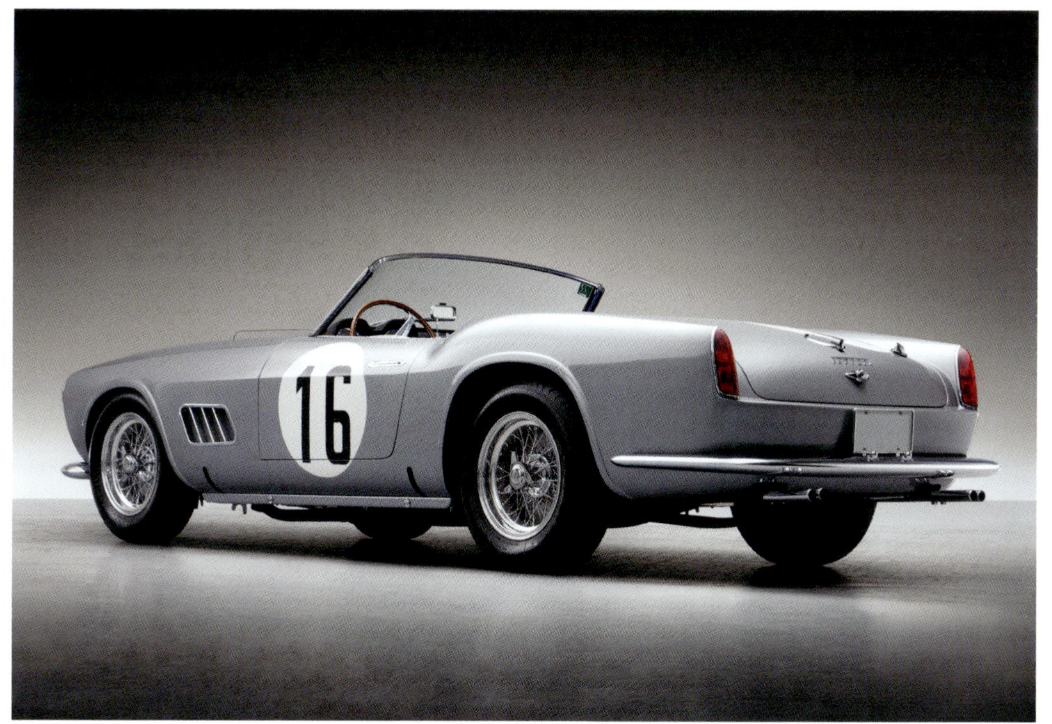

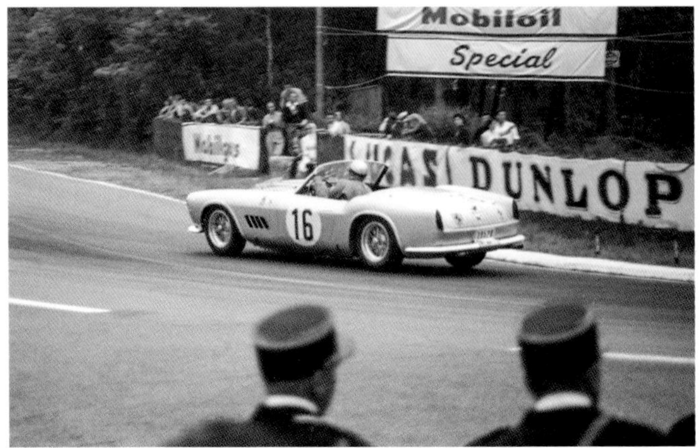

Left, below & opposite (top): The No. 16 NART Ferrari 250 GT LWB California Spider Competizione driven by Bob Grossman and Fernand Tavano in action during the 1959 24 Hours of Le Mans.

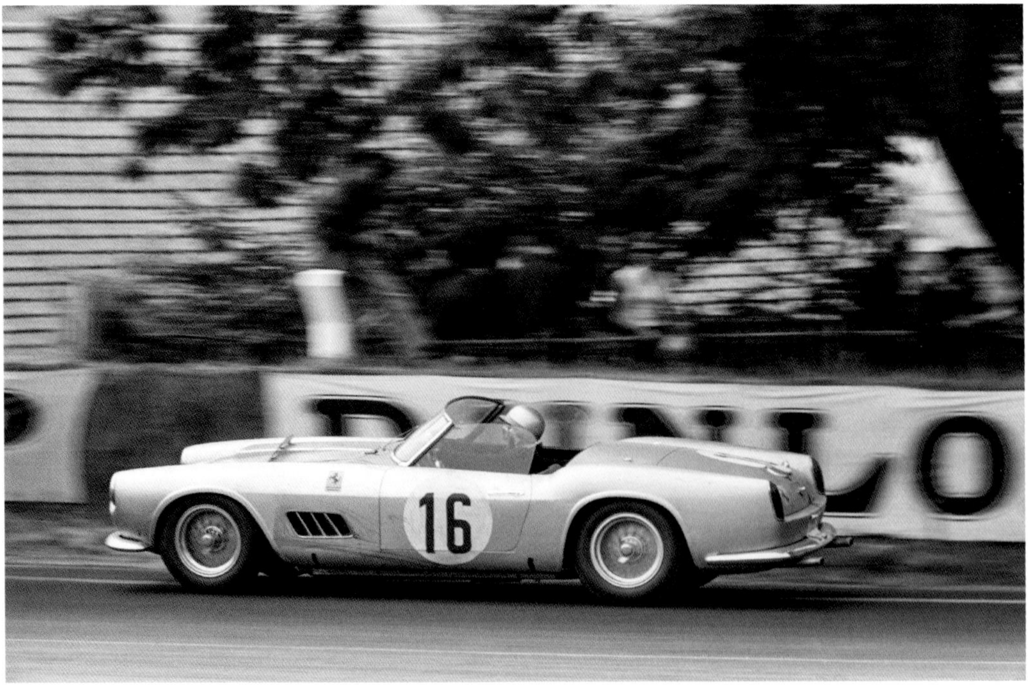

Below: The No. 16 Ferrari 250 GT LWB California Spider Competizione by Scaglietti (chassis no. 1451 GT) driven by Bob Grossman and Fernand Tavano taking the checkered flag and finishing fifth overall and third in their class (GT3.0) at the 1959 24 Hours of Le Mans. The car on the left, the No. 18 Ferrari 250 GT LWB Berlinetta driven by André Pillette and George Arents finished fourth overall and second in their class (GT3.0). Both cars were entered by Luigi Chinetti's North American Racing Team.

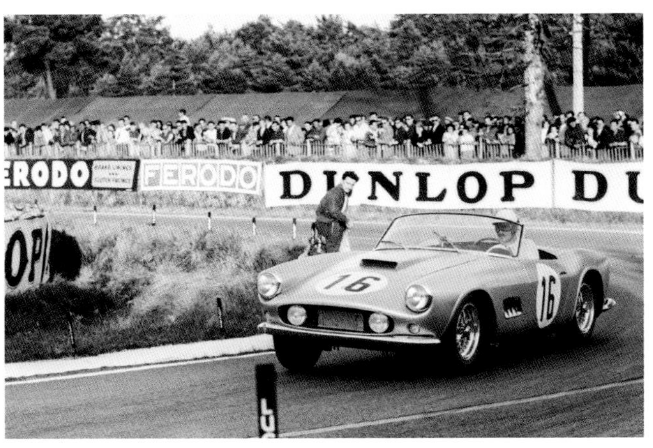

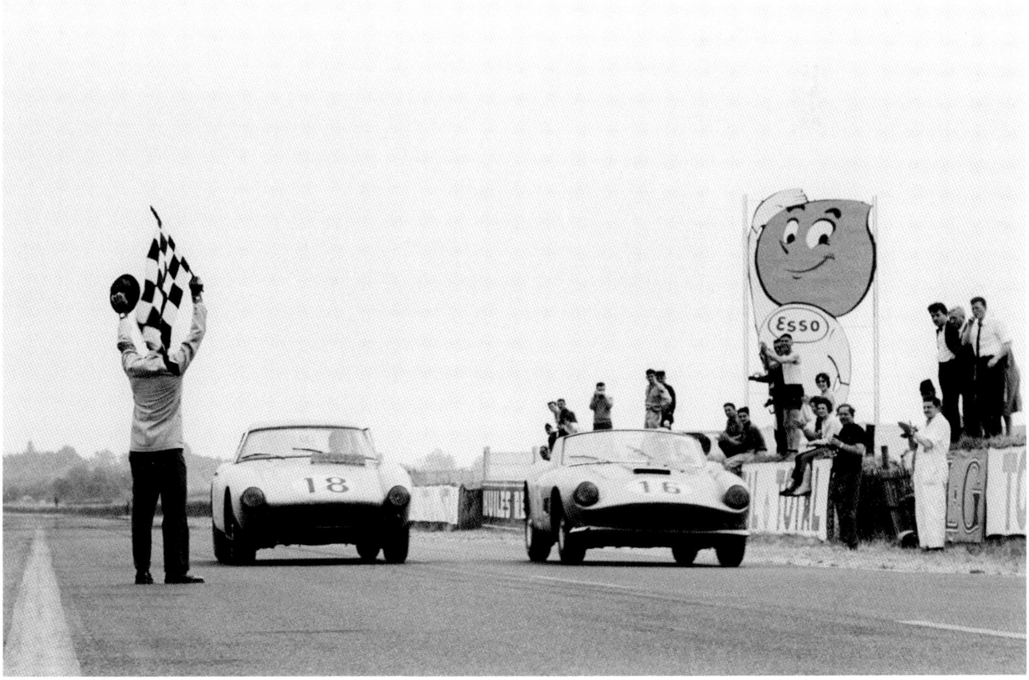

1960s

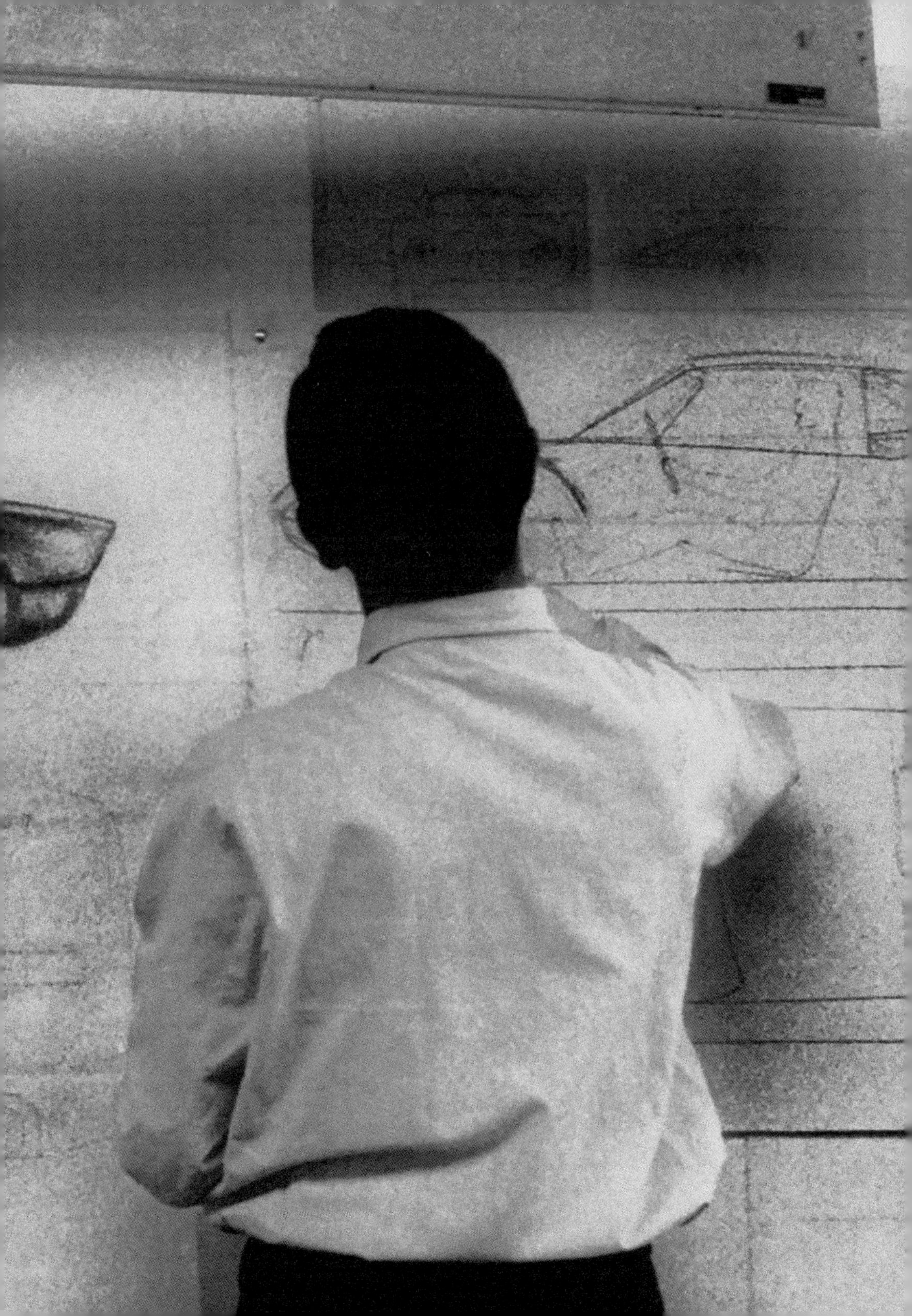

Maserati Tipo 61 “Birdcage”

MANUFACTURED 1959–60 | **ENGINE** 2,890 cc (176 cu. in.), DOHC inline 4-cylinder | **HORSEPOWER** 250
TOP SPEED 285 km/h (177 mph) | **TRANSMISSION** 5-speed
NUMBER PRODUCED 16

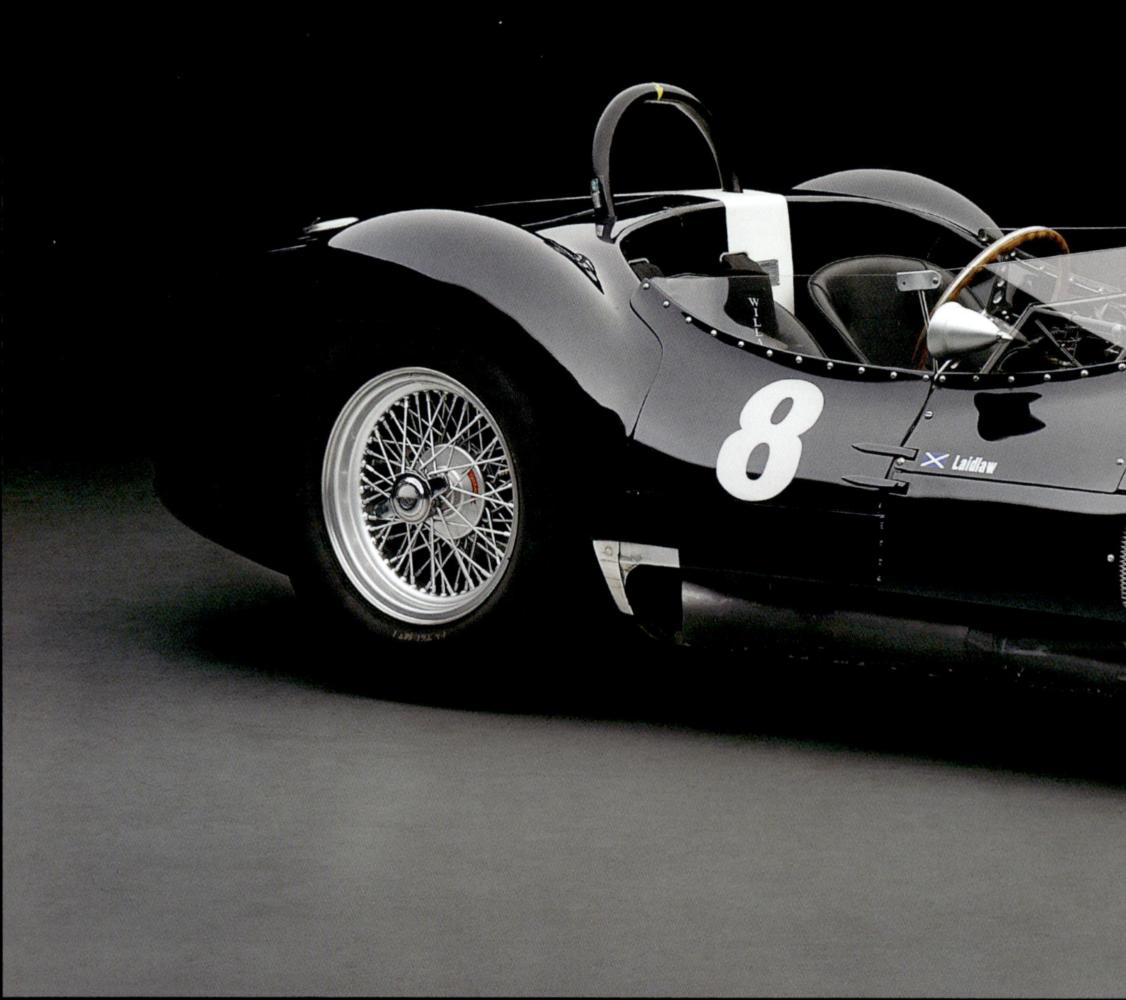

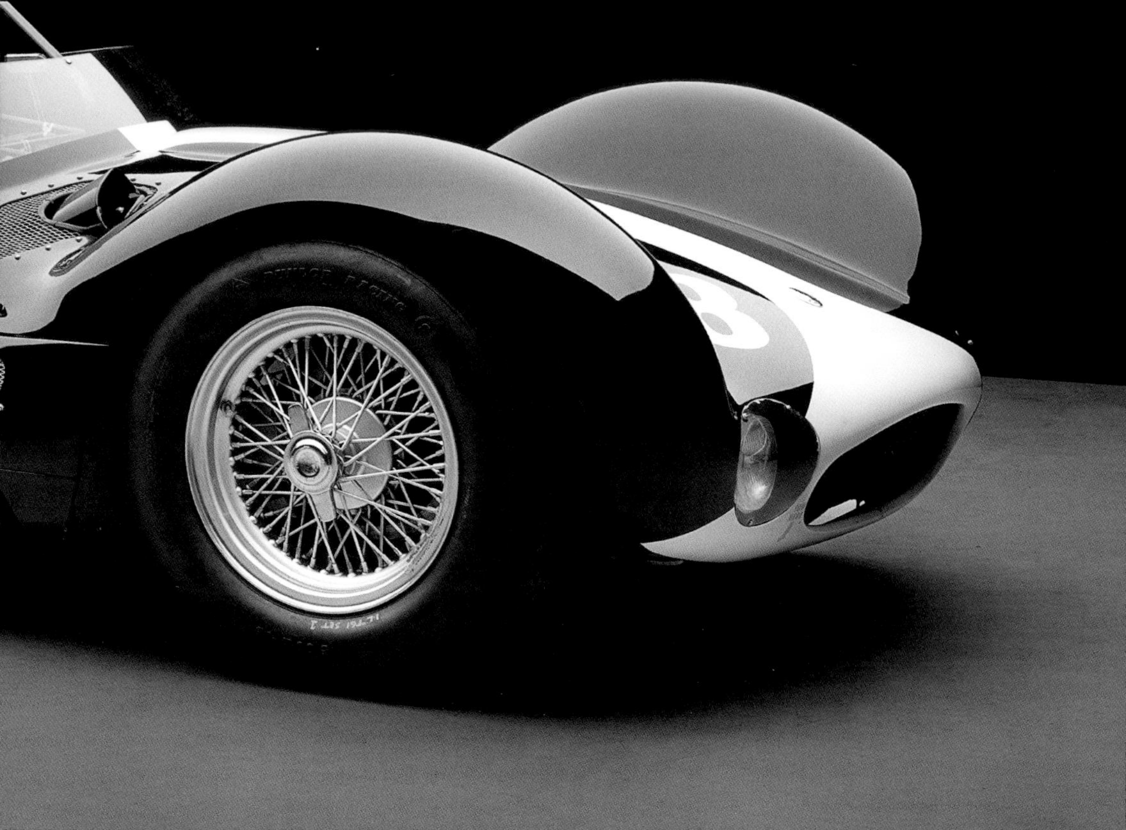

Some cars are just so famous that among auto-aficionados they just go by a nickname. Such is the case for the "Birdcage." One of the most celebrated Maseratis of all time, this sports racer was in its day a stellar example of cutting-edge Italian design, which married progressive styling with state-of-the-art engineering. This absolutely stunning-looking car would go on to become renowned for being excitingly competitive on the racetrack. Its unusual moniker is derived from its lightweight open-work chassis, a trellis-like construction of fine-gauge metal tubes, which was then skinned in one of the most seductively beautiful, aerodynamic body shells ever created. Designed by the engineer Giulio Alfieri and initially powered by a two-liter engine, the first iteration of the Birdcage, the Tipo 60, burst memorably on to the sports racing scene with a victory by Stirling Moss at the Coupe Delamare Deboutteville in July 1959. Six examples of this model were produced before it was upgraded. As RM Sotheby's notes, "In the competitive American racing market, word was already out that Maserati was developing a larger four-cylinder engine, and it wasn't long before an anxious spate of owners lined up for the Tipo 61, a development of the Birdcage with the enlarged 2.9-liter engine."

The immaculate Tipo 61, shown here (chassis no. 2464) was one of five Birdcages that came to be fielded by the independent Camoradi Racing Team (aka CAsner MOtor RAcing DIvision), which was founded in 1960 by Lloyd "Lucky" Casner and Fred Gamble — both of whom would drive for the team. The former was an erstwhile used-Cadillac salesman who dealt cars in order to fund his racing habit, while the latter was a hot-rod enthusiast with

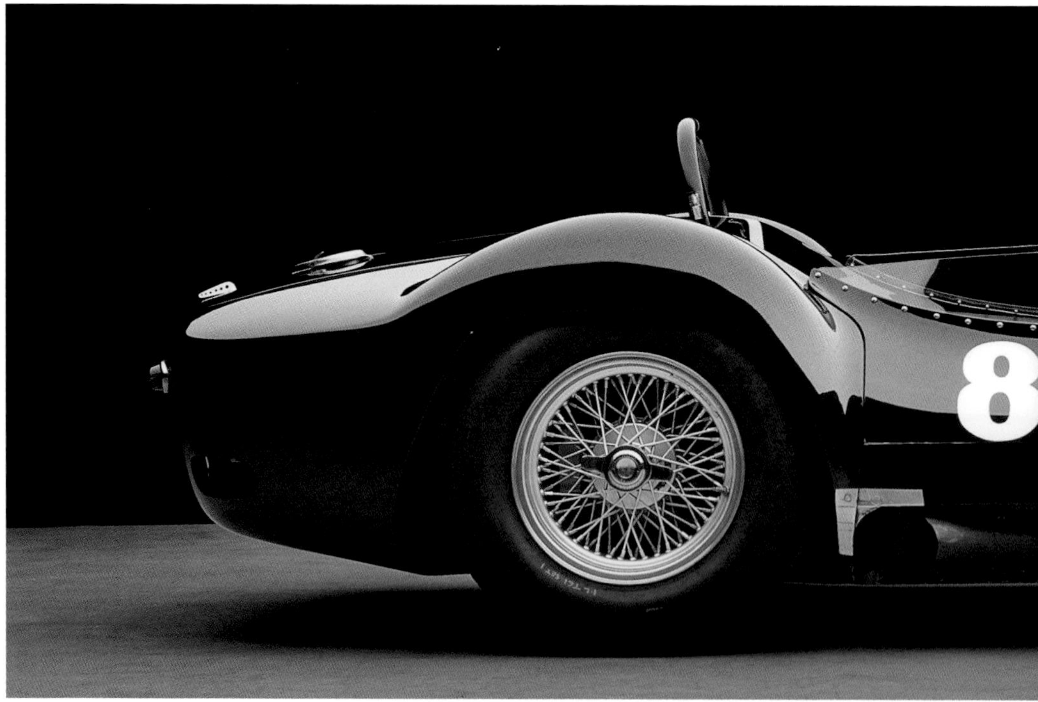

Pages 242–243: Ferdinand Alexander "Butzi" Porsche, the son of "Ferry" and grandson of the great Ferdinand, at the drawing board designing his 904 Carrera GTS, ca.1963. He also designed the equally ground-breaking, immortal Porsche 911.

Right: Stirling Moss and Dan Gurney undertake a driver change to their No. 5 Camoradi Maserati Tipo 61 "Birdcage" (chassis no. 2461) during the 1960 1000 km of the Nürburgring. They won the race. The 11th Tipo 61 produced, chassis no. 2461 went on to claim the most celebrated competition record of any Maserati "Birdcage."

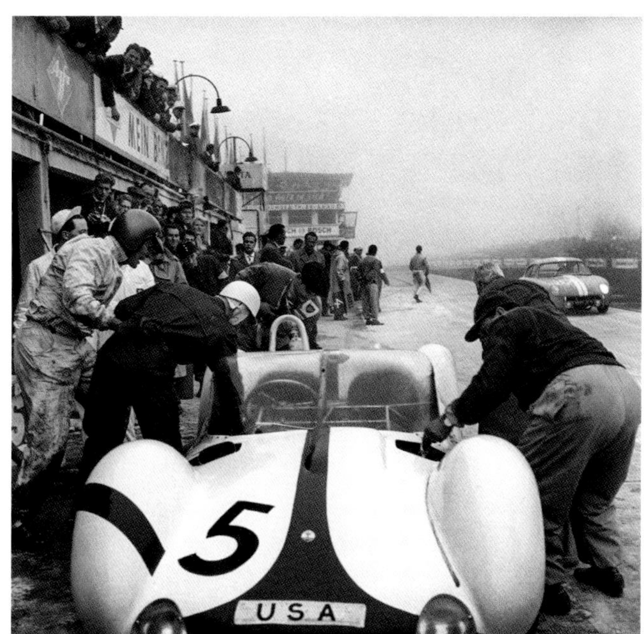

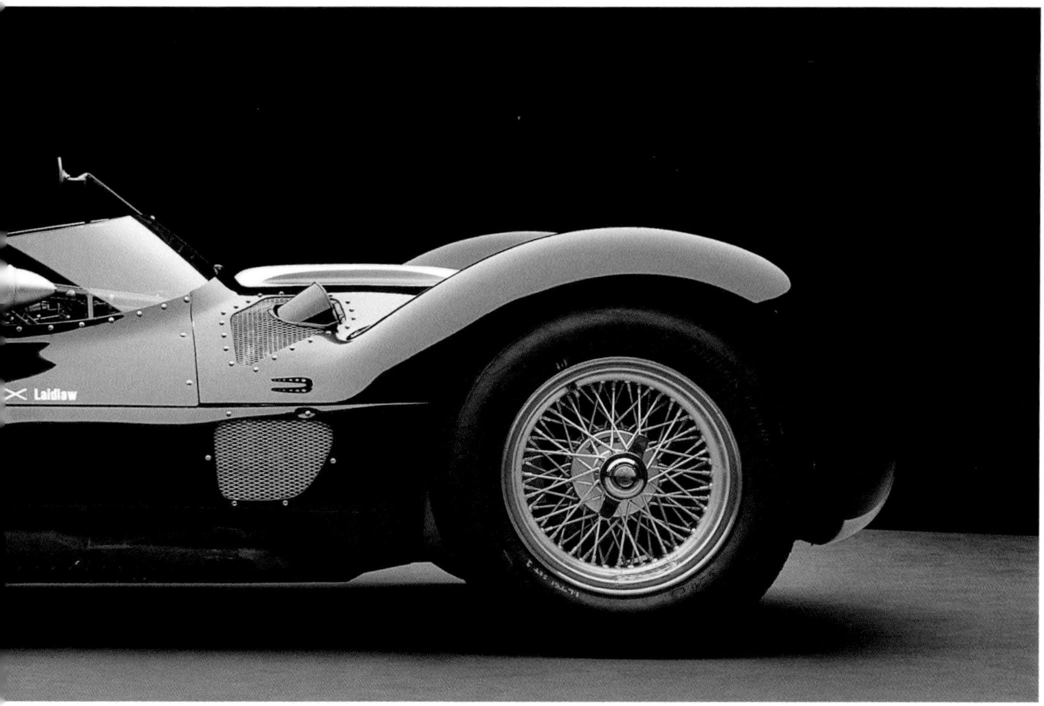

a strong public relations background, who also worked as a motoring journalist. Although a fledgling and undoubtedly maverick team, it somehow managed to secure substantial backing from the Goodyear Tire and Rubber Company via Gamble's contacts at the New York advertising agency Young & Rubicam. Goodyear not only provided tires, but also essential financial and engineering assistance. And with Goodyear onboard, the duo then managed to get further support from a number of other major players in the motorsports world including, Shell, BP and Champion. To get the team going Casner had traveled to Italy to meet with Maserati, which had just developed the new Tipo 61 Birdcage. The company itself had abandoned competition at the end of the 1957 season because it had become overstretched financially in its attempt to win both the Formula 1 and World Sportscar Championship that year. Teetering on the verge on bankruptcy Maserati was, nevertheless, still producing cars for privateers that would be racing ostensibly on the marque's behalf, albeit in their own livery. With his honed sales skills, Casner convinced Maserati to partner with his Camoradi Racing Team for the upcoming 1960 season, and the rest is automotive history. With its stable of five Tipo 61 Birdcages, Camoradi had a spectacularly good rookie season that was kicked off with an epic win by Stirling Moss at the Cuban Grand Prix in February 1960. Two

Below & opposite: The car presented here (chassis no. 2464) is one of the five "Birdcages" that came to be fielded by the independent Camoradi Racing Team. During the 1960 racing season, it garnered a fifth overall at Nürburgring 1,000 km, then got a DNF at the 24 Hours of Le Mans, before finally clinching a first in class and second overall at the Kanonloppet (or Cannon Race) in Sweden. In autumn of 1960, the car was sold to Texan privateer Alan Connell, a well-known SCCA competitor, who repainted it in the present livery and went on to race it very successfully in the US.

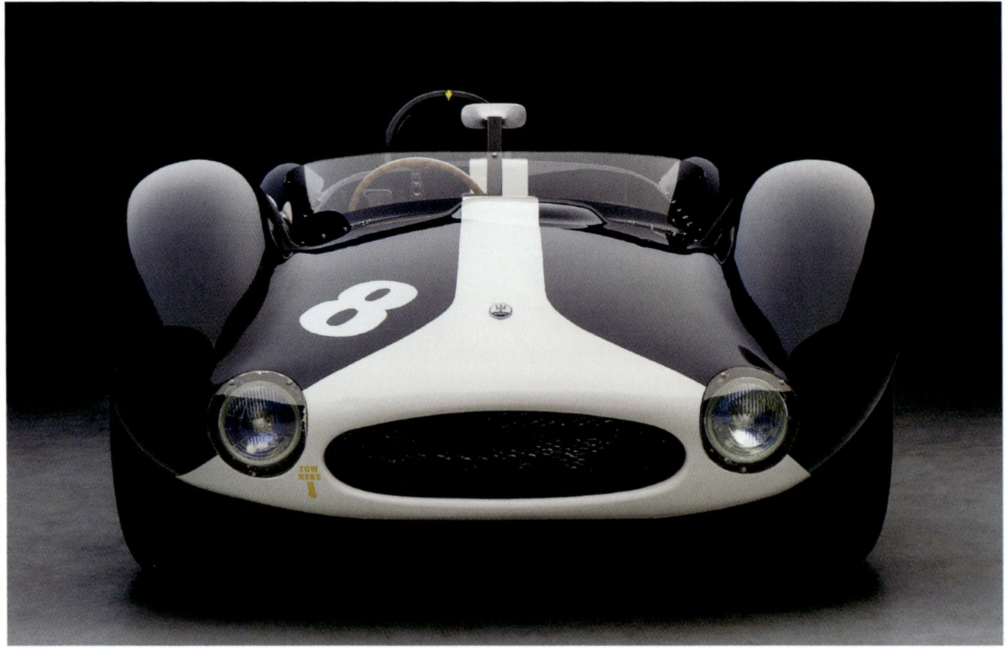

months later, Carroll Shelby enjoyed a victory at the Los Angeles Times Grand Prix held at Riverside International Raceway, and then a month after that came another win at the Nürburgring 1,000 km race with Stirling Moss yet again at the helm together with a fifth place with the car (chassis no. 2464) shown here.

The 1960 24 Hours of Le Mans race — the original raison d'être for the whole Camoradi adventure — was, however, pretty much a blowout for the team due to all three of its Tipo 61s — including the one presented here — retiring with mechanical issues. In terms of these Birdcages, Camoradi's role was primarily financial because the Maserati factory was still responsible for maintaining and race prepping them and when it came to any European races all the logistics were handled by the company as well. The Birdcage, shown here, did however manage to wind up the season with a notable triumph when the Swedish driver Joakim Bonnier piloted it to a class victory and a second-overall finish at the Kanonloppet (Cannon Race) — a forerunner of the Swedish Grand Prix — held at the Karlskoga Motorstadion in August 1960. That autumn, Casner sold this Birdcage along with another (chassis no. 2461) to the Texan privateer Alan Connell, who was a well-known Sports Car Club of America (SCCA) competitor. At this stage both these cars were equipped with "longtail" bodies, specifically suited to straighter racetracks. The alternative shorter "bobtail" body option, which chassis no. 2464 featured originally and is now reequipped with, was meant for courses with shorter straights. It is testament to the Birdcage's remarkable design and performance, that the legendary Carroll Shelby once praised it as the "best cornering fast car" he had ever driven.

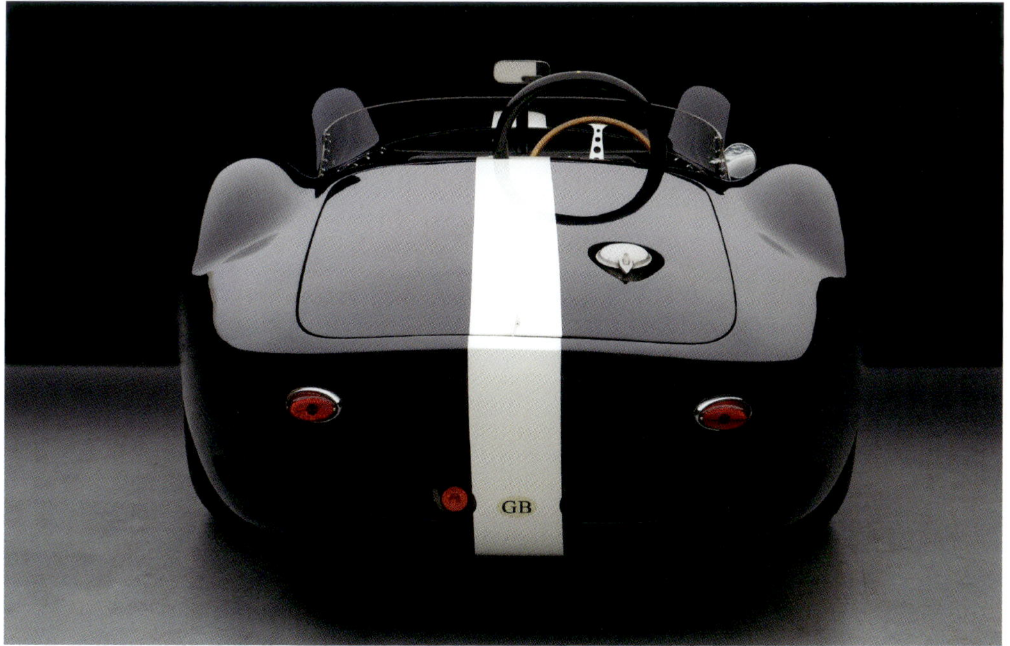

Below: Detail of Maserati Tipo 61 "Birdcage" 2890 cc (176 cu. in.), DOHC inline four–cylinder engine with two Weber 48 DCO3 carburetors sitting within the car's lightweight open-work chassis, an intricate trellis-like construction of fine-gauge chromoly steel tubes, from which the moniker "Birdcage" was derived. Although still ahead of the driver, the engine was mounted well behind the front axle and at a 45° angle to reduce the frontal area and centre of gravity. Derived from Maserati's 200S power unit, the four-cylinder engine featured a redesigned head in which the exhaust and intake ports had swapped sides. An all-new triangular sump was created to allow for the angled installation.

Opposite (top): 1959 Coupe Delamare Deboutteville, Rouen-Les-Essarts — Stirling Moss in obvious disagreement with Maserati chief mechanic, Guarino Bertocchi, while they inspect the prototype Maserati Tipo 60 "Birdcage" (chassis no. 2451). This was a non-championship race that Moss won, which was held the same day as the seventh Grand Prix of Rouen for Formula 2, which Moss also won (in a Cooper-Borgward). Introduced in 1959 the Maserati Tipo 60 "Birdcage" was powered by a 2.0-liter engine, which produced 200 hp, while the Tipo 61 "Birdcage" had a 2.9-liter engine that produced 250 hp.

Opposite (bottom): Designed by the gifted Italian engineer Giulio Alfieri, the Maserati Birdcage's intricate tubular space frame chassis comprised about 200 chromoly steel tubes that were welded together and arranged in a triangular formation in areas of high stress. This extremely innovative multi-tubular construction enabled a lighter weight and more rigid chassis than any other race car at the time, which provided a significant competitive advantage.

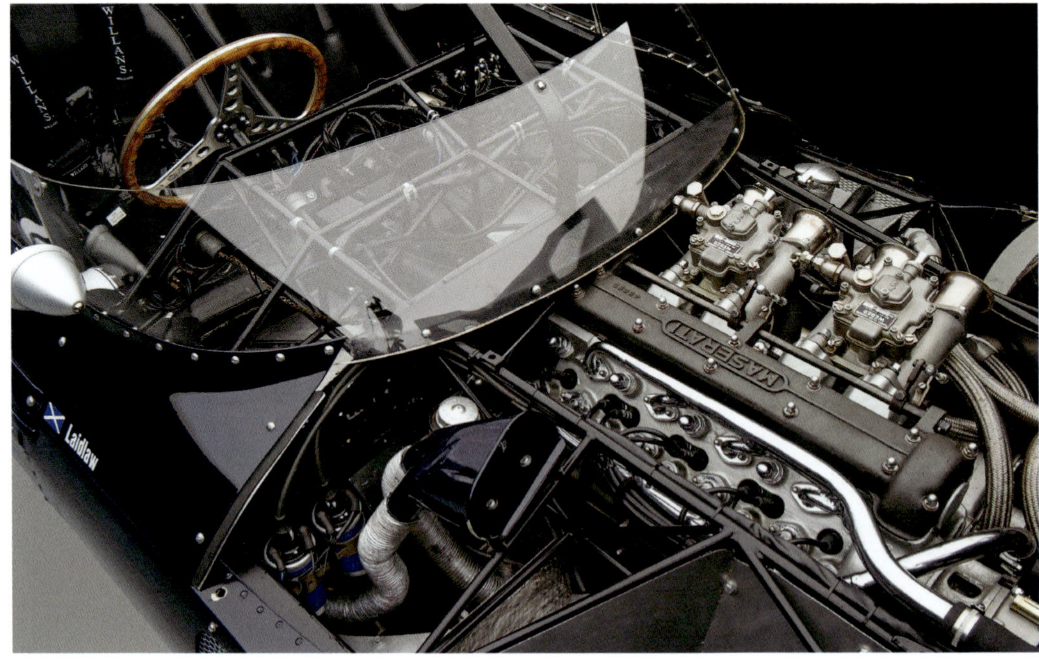

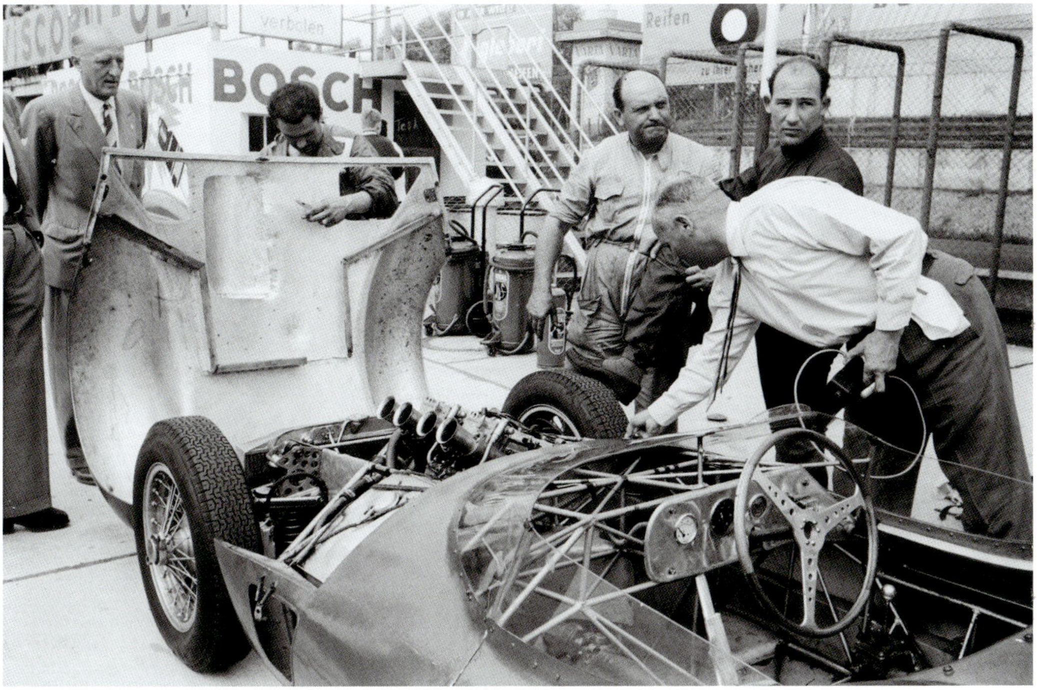
BOSCH
verboten
Reifen

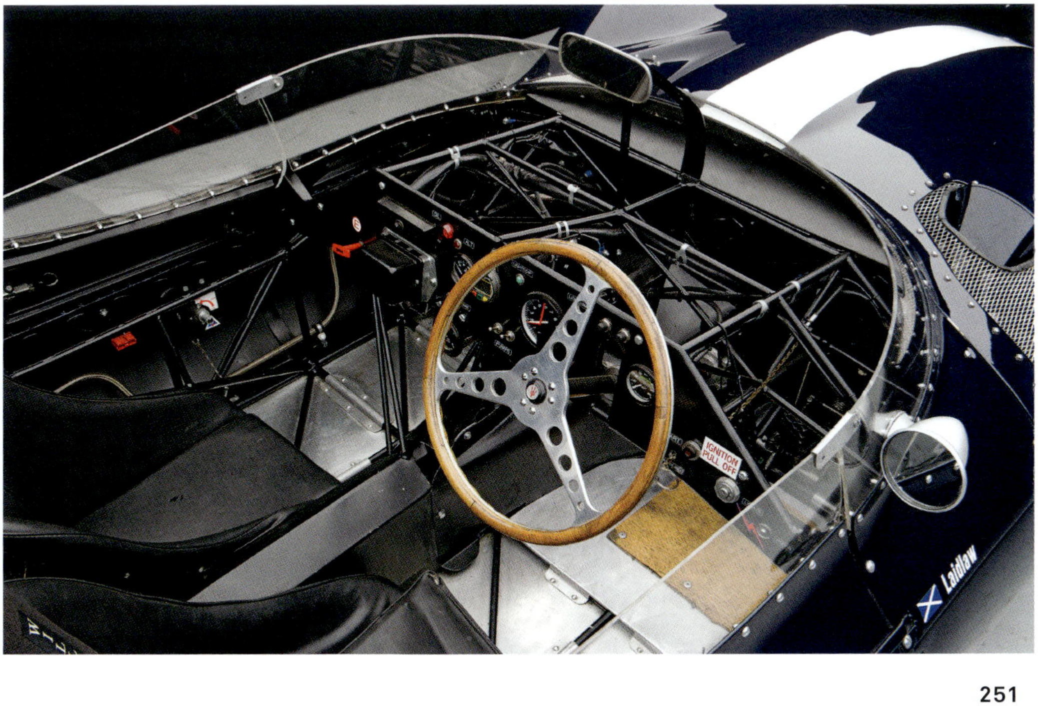
IGNITION PULL OFF
Laidlaw

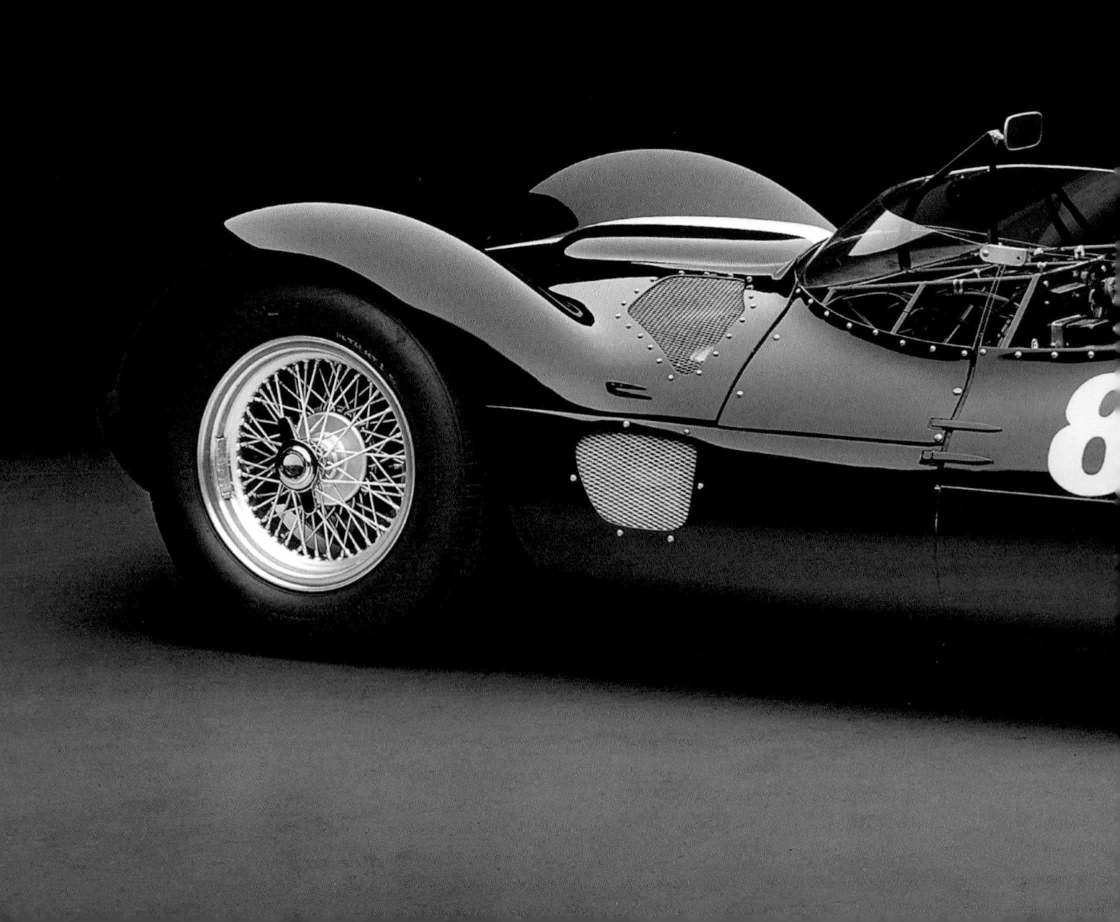

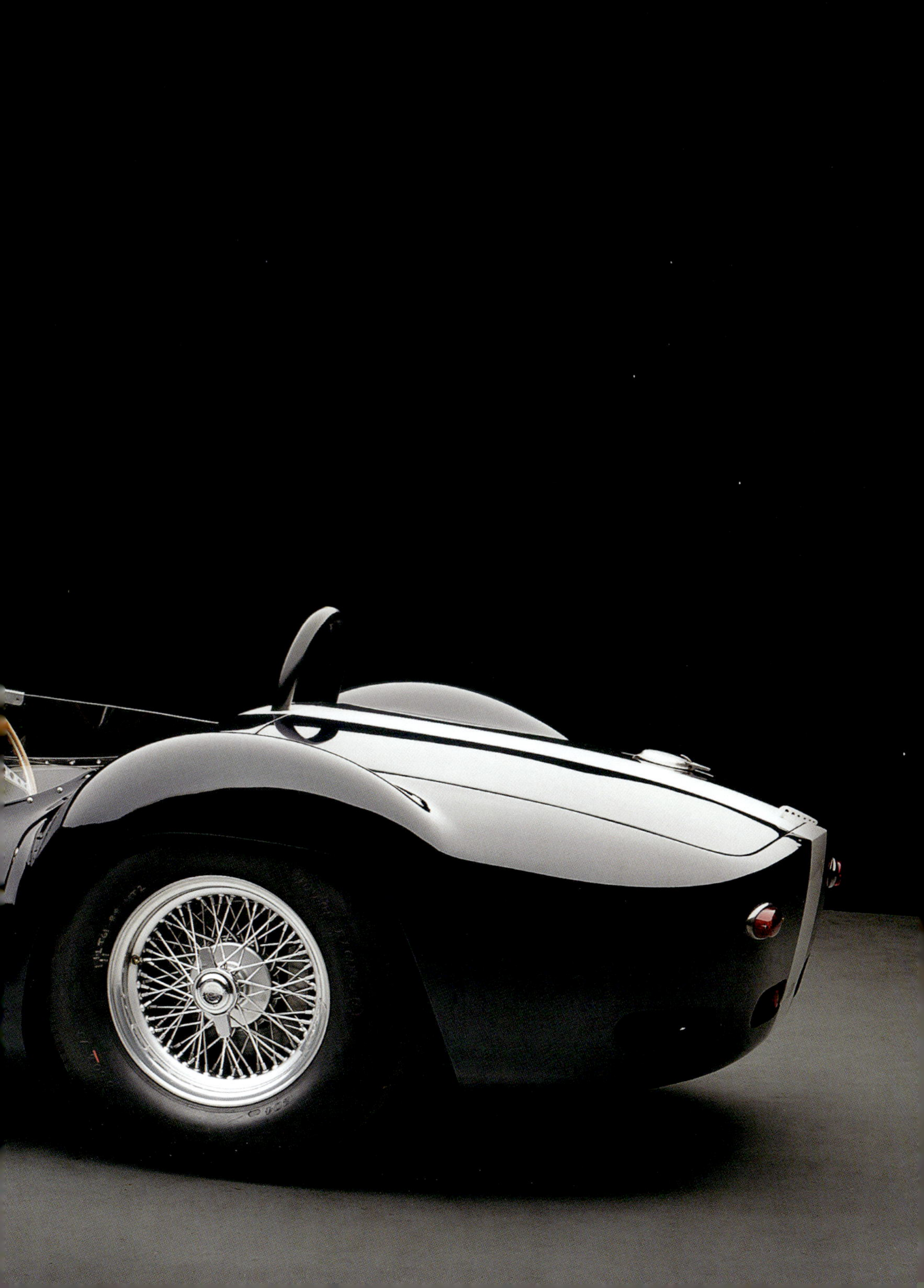

1962

Aston Martin DB4 GT Zagato

MANUFACTURED 1960–62 | ENGINE 3,670 cc (224 cu. in.), DOHC inline 6-cylinder | HORSEPOWER 314
TOP SPEED 245 km/h (152 mph) | TRANSMISSION 4-speed with overdrive
NUMBER PRODUCED 19

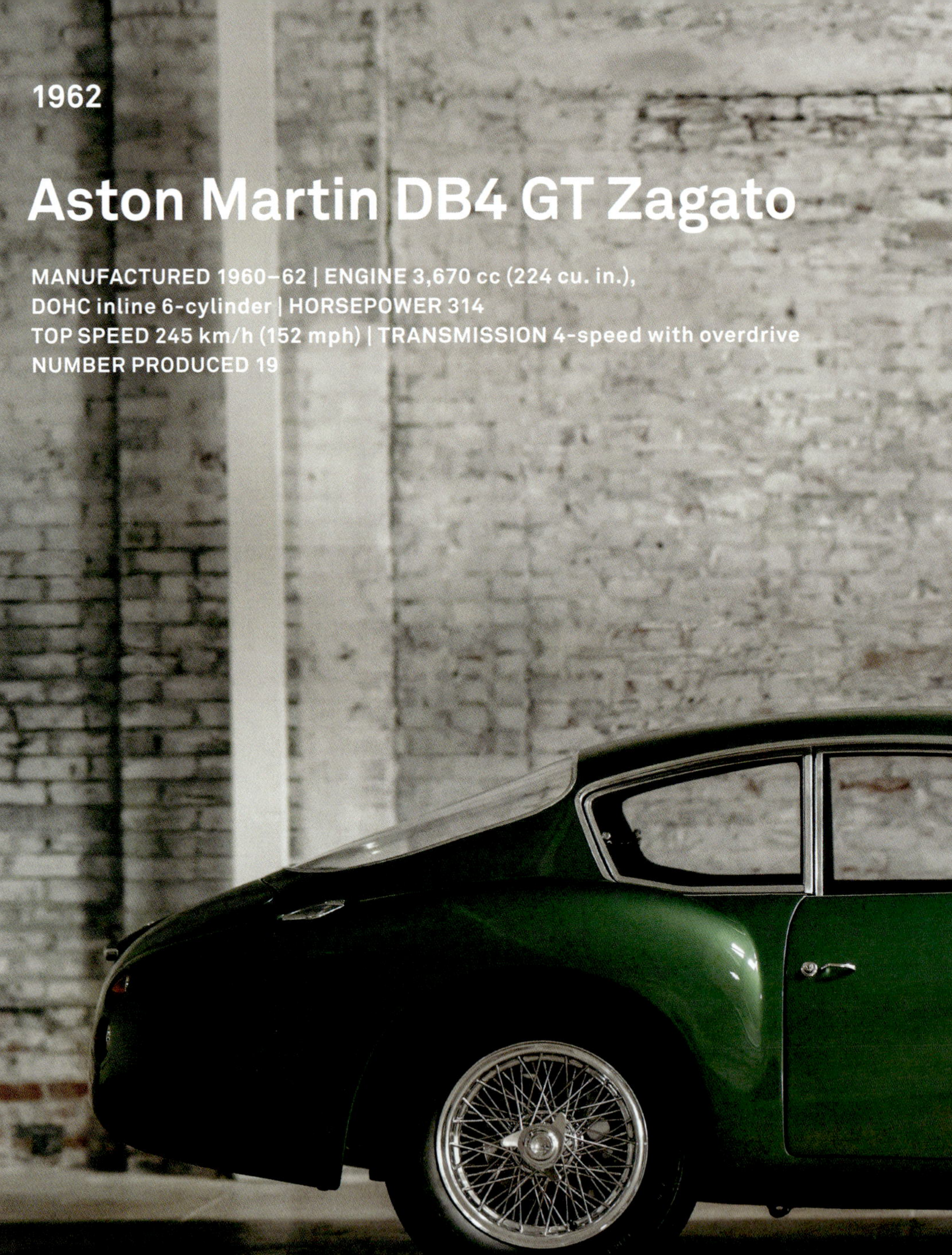

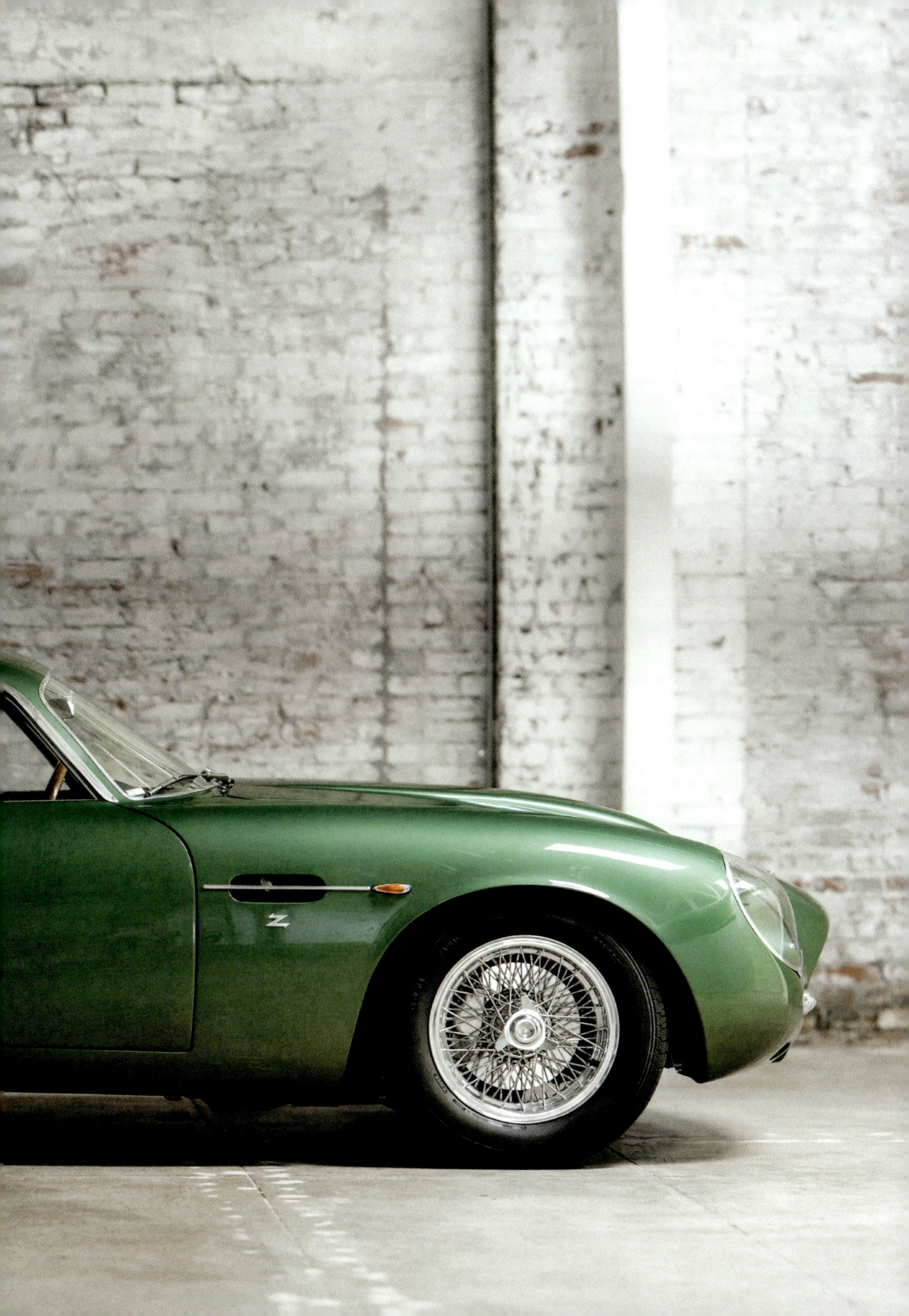

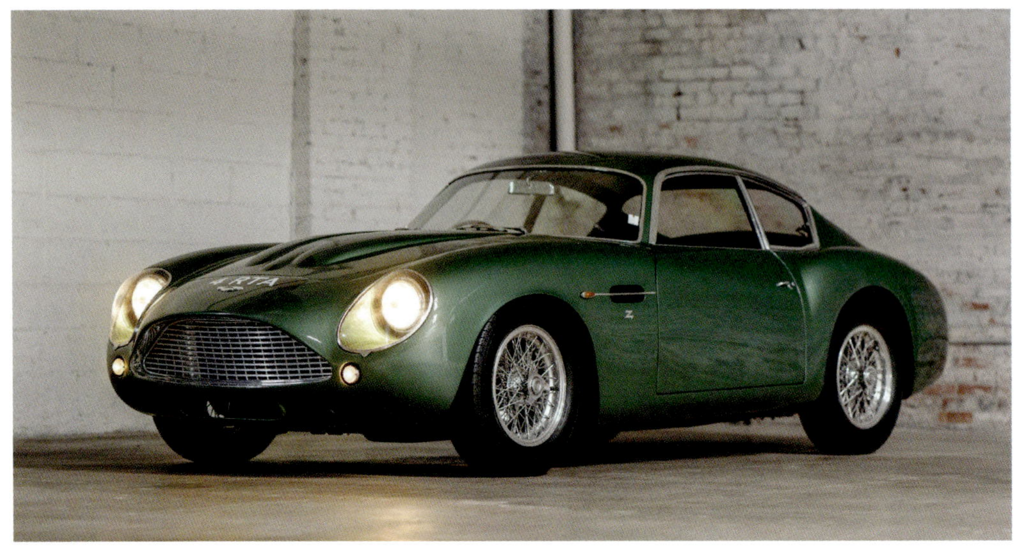

Above & overleaf: Considered by many to be the coachbuilder's finest design, the DB4 GT Zagato is recognizable as both an Aston Martin and a Zagato, thanks to the carrozzeria's ability to blend distinctive design elements from each company into one harmonious work of art.

Opposite: Detail of Aston Martin DB4 GT Zagato 3,670 cc (224 cu. in.), DOHC twin-plug inline six-cylinder alloy engine with triple Weber 45 DCOE carburetors. More powerful than the standard DB4, with the whole vehicle also 110 lb. (50 kg) lighter in weight, Aston Martin produced only 19 examples of this car.

A veritable motorsports legend and one of the most coveted Aston Martins of all time, the DB4 GT Zagato is a very rare and exotic car — only 19 were produced — so on the scarce occasion one does come up at auction it creates an extraordinary buzz of expectation. As a full-bore British sports racer that was exquisitely clad in an elegant Italian suit expertly tailored by Carrozzeria Zagato, it united two of the world's great automotive heritages, British engineering and Italian styling, into a single streamlined entity. Astonishingly attractive yet impressively powerful, it is an exceptional design on so many levels that was highly advanced for its time. But then, ever since its inception, Aston Martin has always pursued impeccable aesthetic form in harmony with superlative performance.

During the early 1960s, Aston Martin was constantly trying to usurp Ferrari's dominance within the GT category of the World Sportscar Championship. After the "upset" of the British marque's 1-2 win at 1959 24 Hours of Le Mans, thanks to the excellent performance of its outstanding DBR1, Ferrari upped its racing stakes with the introduction of its 250 GT SWB Berlinetta Competizione. As a counter move, Aston Martin then launched its DB4 GT in September 1959, but it was just not powerful enough to take on Ferrari's competition-based Berlinettas. So, determined to claw back its competitive edge, the English manufacturer decided the only way to trounce Ferrari would be to build a new model, which would be based on the DB4 GT's existing platform. The idea being that if the existing chassis and engine setup were equipped with a more aerodynamic and lighter-weight body then the marque's chances of victory might be improved. Seeking external specialist help for this, Aston Martin commissioned Zagato, one of Italy's most famous *carrozzerie* to create this new better-performing body. The recently qualified Italian design engineer Ercole Spada — who was only 23 years old and had only just joined this renowned Rho-based coachbuilding workshop — was tasked with coming up with the Aston's new design. In fact, it was Spada's first design for Zagato and although over the years he would go on to create a plethora of other notable cars for the likes of Lancia, Alfa Romeo, Volvo, BMW and Ferrari, none was as fluently beautiful nor as intricately detailed as this youthful early design.

When Spada's resulting lightweight two-seater Aston Martin DB4 GT Zagato was unveiled at the 1960 London Motor Show, it was obvious that this was a design that more than fulfilled its brief. The car's body work had an altogether more dynamic and fluid form, with its elements being better unified into its volumetric body. It also had a more aggressive look, which was no doubt attributable to its more purposeful form following better racing function. Its beauty was, however, not just skin deep. It weighed nearly 110 lbs. (50 kg) less than its progenitor and its 3.7-liter twin-plug engine had been developed to produce a higher compression ratio, providing an extra 12 bhp.

Aston Martin planned a production run of 25 cars with a UK price of £5,157 including tax. When it came to it, however, only 19 were made, presumably because of their high cost, which was no doubt attributable to the complexity of the car's manufacture. Their production involved very complicated logistical handling, with the chassis being built at the Aston

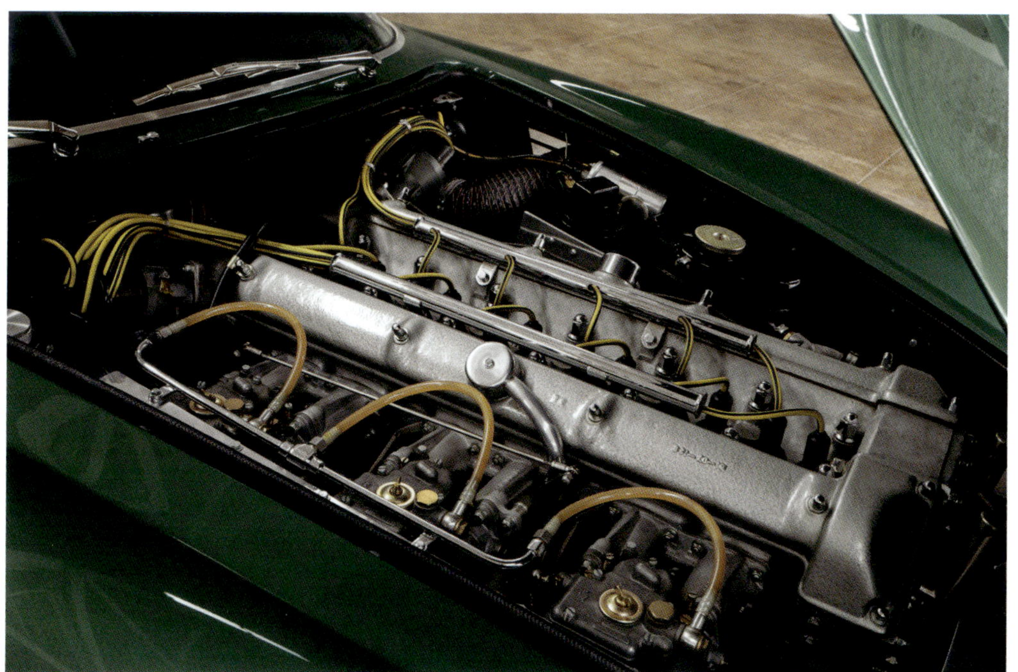

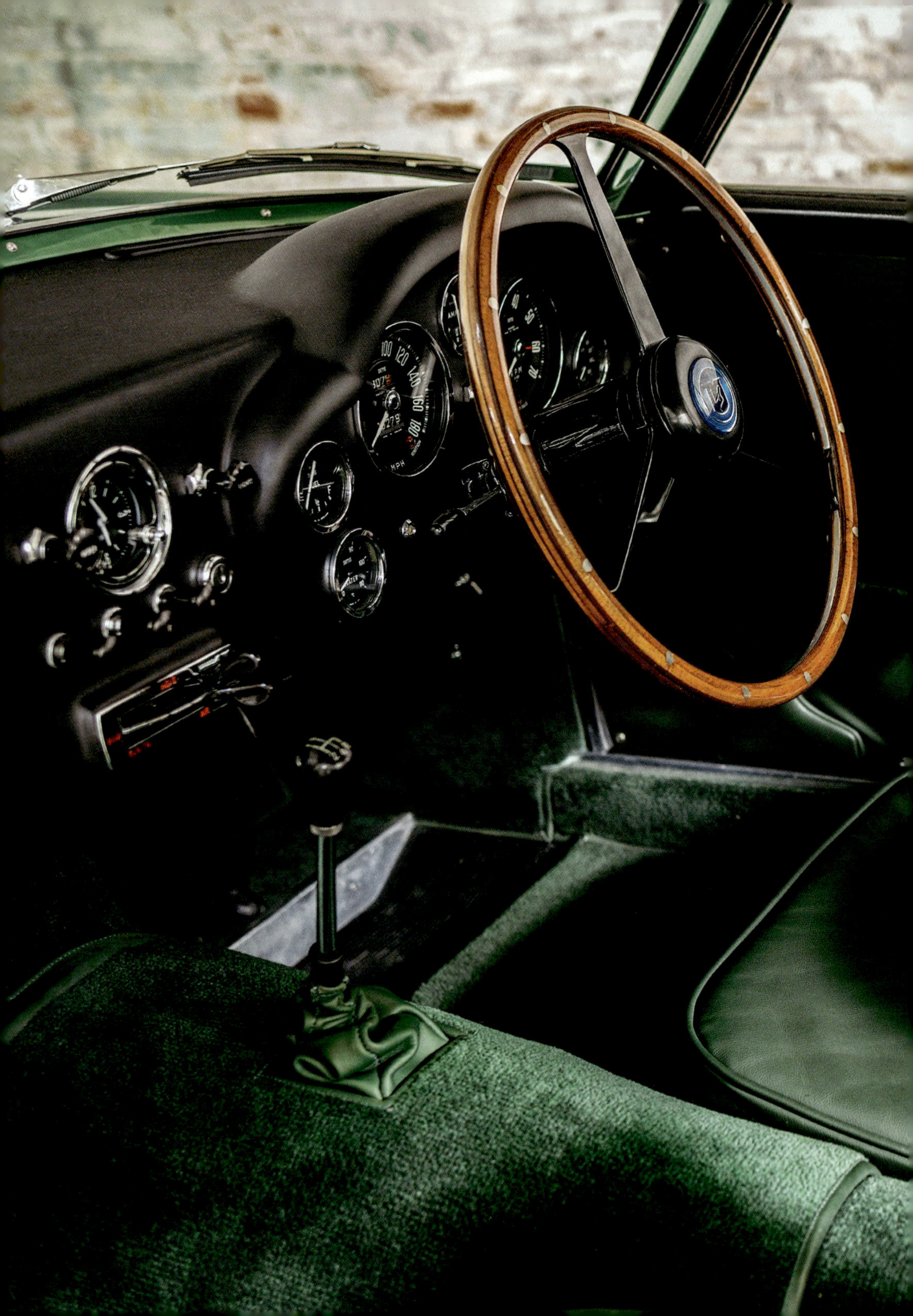
100
120
140
160
180
MPH

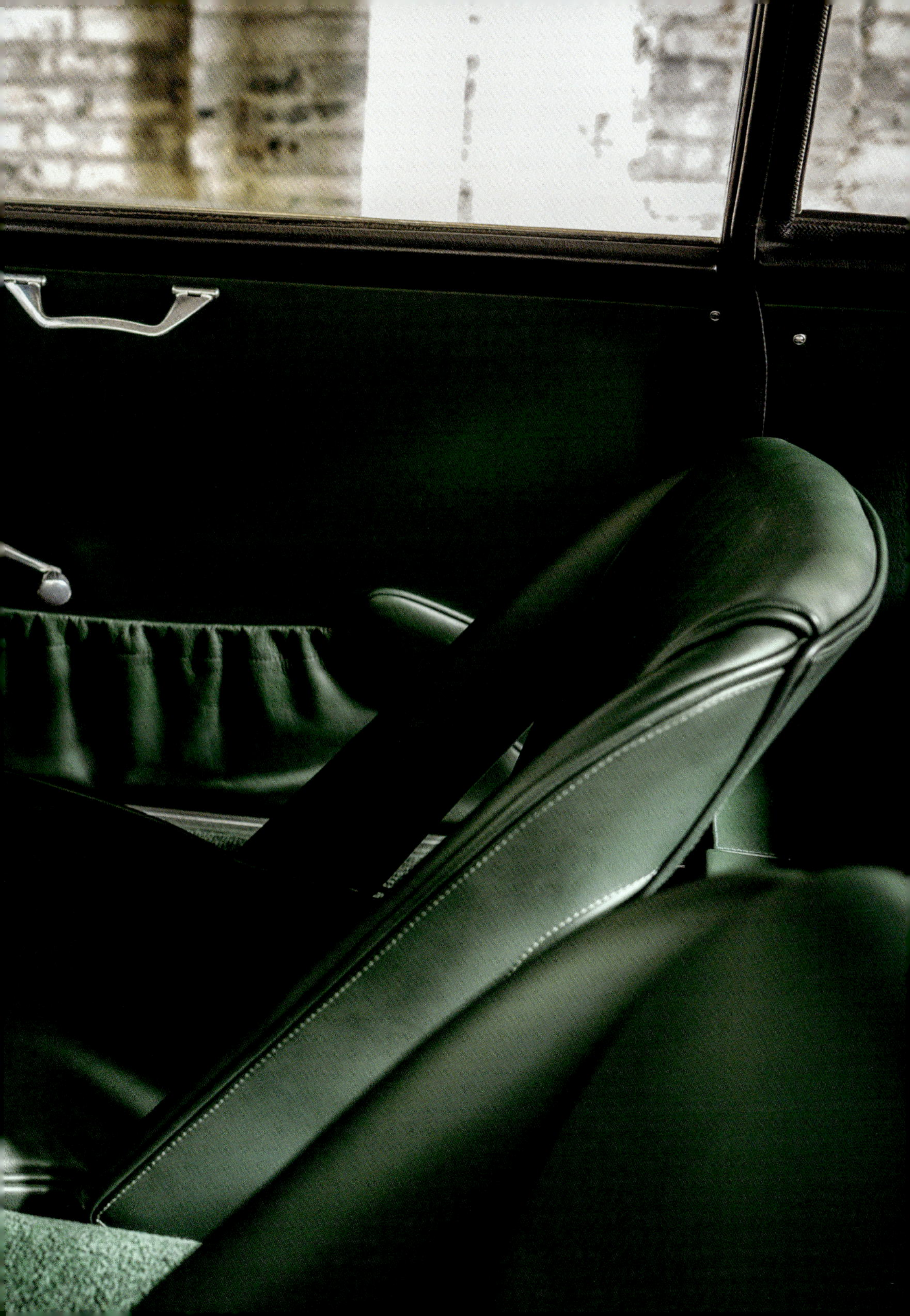

Are you a Racing Driver?

- IF THE ANSWER IS "YES" YOU KNOW ALL ABOUT THIS CAR.
- IF THE ANSWER IS "NO" BUT YOU DRIVE QUICKLY YOU NEED THIS CAR.
- IF THE ANSWER IS "DON'T KNOW" IT DOES NOT MATTER BECAUSE WHATEVER KIND OF DRIVER YOU ARE THIS IS THE SAFEST AND SUREST WAY OF ENJOYING A KIND OF MOTORING THAT LEAVES LITTLE TO BE DESIRED.

FAST . . . . . Yes . . . if need be. 0-100 m.p.h. 14 secs. (approx.)

SAFE . . . . . Always . . . with roadholding to spare

CAPACIOUS . . . . . Luggage for two for a month in the sun

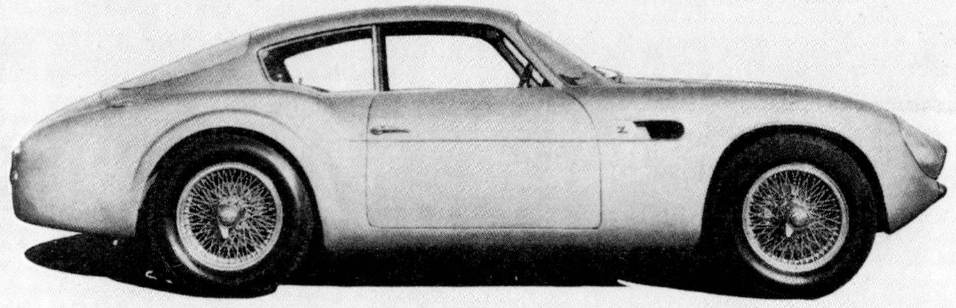

ASTON MARTIN ZAGATO GT

"THE FASTEST ROAD CAR WE HAVE TESTED TO DATE." Autocar

THE ULTIMATE **GRAND TOURING** *CAR FOR TOURING IN THE GRAND MANNER*

- **JOIN THE MOST EXCLUSIVE CLUB IN THE WORLD**

we proudly announce that we have been appointed sole selling agents for the United Kingdom.

H. W. MOTORS (GEORGE ABECASSIS) LTD.

NEW ZEALAND AVENUE. WALTON-ON-THAMES 20404

SPECIALISTS IN THE SALE AND PARTICULARLY SERVICE OF HIGH PERFORMANCE CARS.

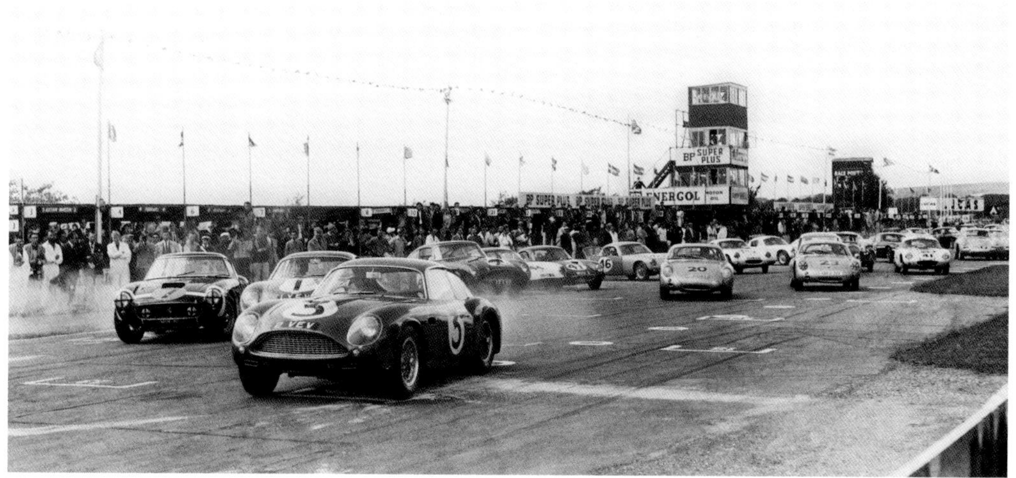

Opposite: Advertisement that appeared in *Autocar*, April 13, 1962.

Above: Jim Clark in the No. 3 Aston Martin DB4 GT Zagato leads at the start of the 1961 RAC Tourist Trophy at Goodwood. He finished in fourth place behind the sister DB4 GT Zagato (chassis no. DB4GT/0182/R) in third place driven by Roy Salvadori and the Ferrari 250 GT SWB Berlinetta Competizioni of Mike Parkes (second) and Stirling Moss (first).

Martin works factory in Newport Pagnell then being shipped to Italy, where they were bodied by Zagato and then being returned to Aston Martin's factory to be trimmed and finished — it is thought that five cars might have had this latter stage undertaken in Italy.

But of course, the ultimate test of any sports racer is on the actual track, and as a result four of Aston Martin's DB4 GT Zagato's chassis were race-prepared by further lightening their chassis by around 150 lbs. (68 kg) — two cars of which were built for the works-backed Essex Racing Stable. Their first outing was at the Fordwater Trophy race at Goodwood in 1961, where the one driven by Stirling Moss enjoyed a promising pole position, but in the race it failed to keep pace and ended up placing third. This finish must have been very frustrating, as the new DB4 GT Zagato's had come in behind an Aston Martin DB4 GT and a winning Ferrari 250 GT SWB Berlinetta Competizione. That year's 24 Hours of Le Mans was also a disappointment with all three participating DB4 GT Zagatos being forced to retire — the Essex Racing Stable's two with engine trouble, while the other one fielded by privateer Jean Kerguen battled with a battery issue. Nevertheless, a DB4 GT Zagato did finally achieve victory at the British Grand Prix Support race held in July 1961, which must have been some consolation given the considerable effort that had gone into creating this eye-pleasing beast of a car. But its racing prowess, or lack thereof, does not really matter when it comes to its collectability today. For as *Classic Driver* journalist Alex Easthope notes "Rarer than a Ferrari 250 GTO, as curvaceous as the most voluptuous of women, and oozing Italian style (yet in a quintessentially British manner), the Aston Martin DB4 GT Zagato is perhaps the most eligible Bond car that never was."

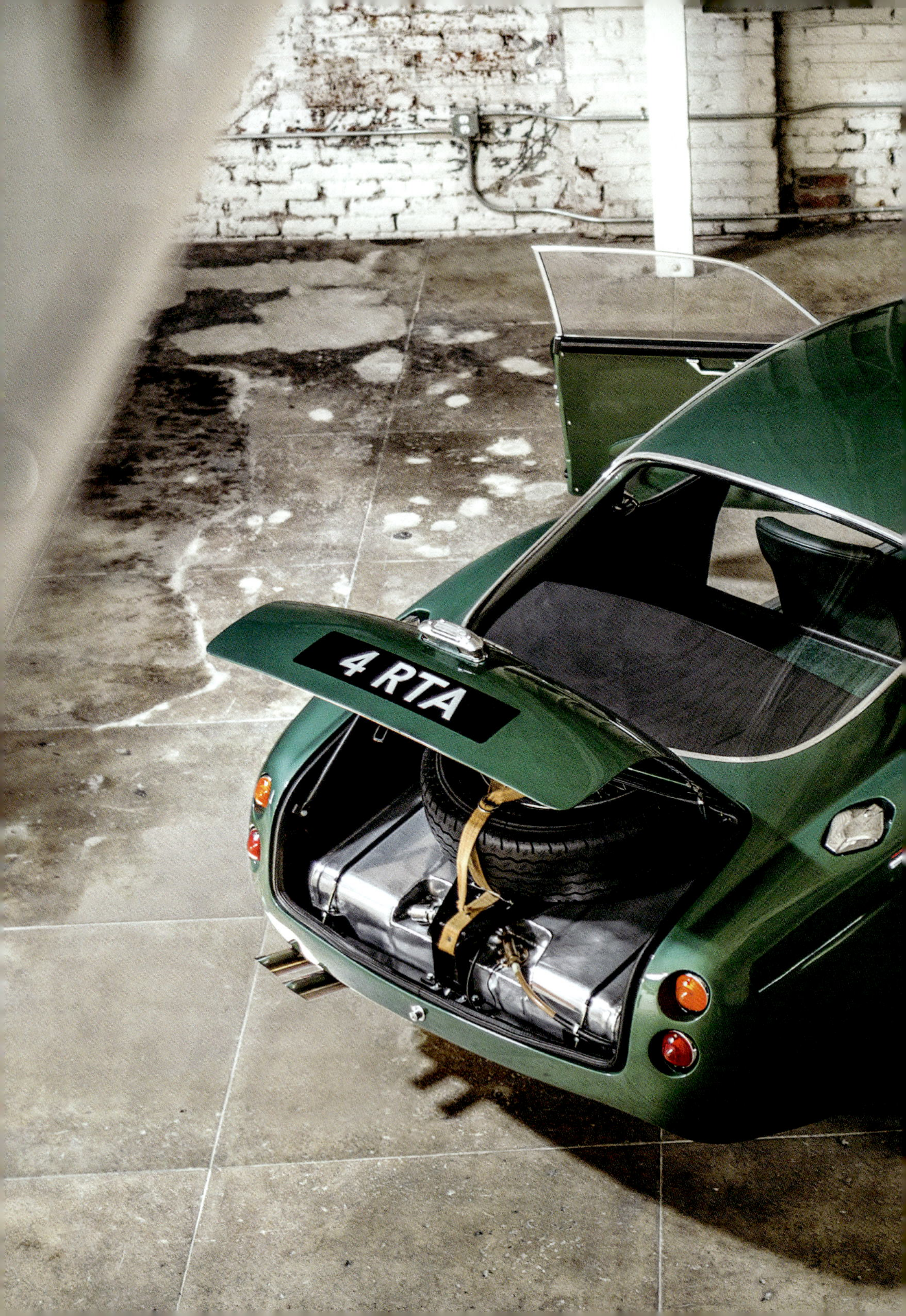
4 RTA

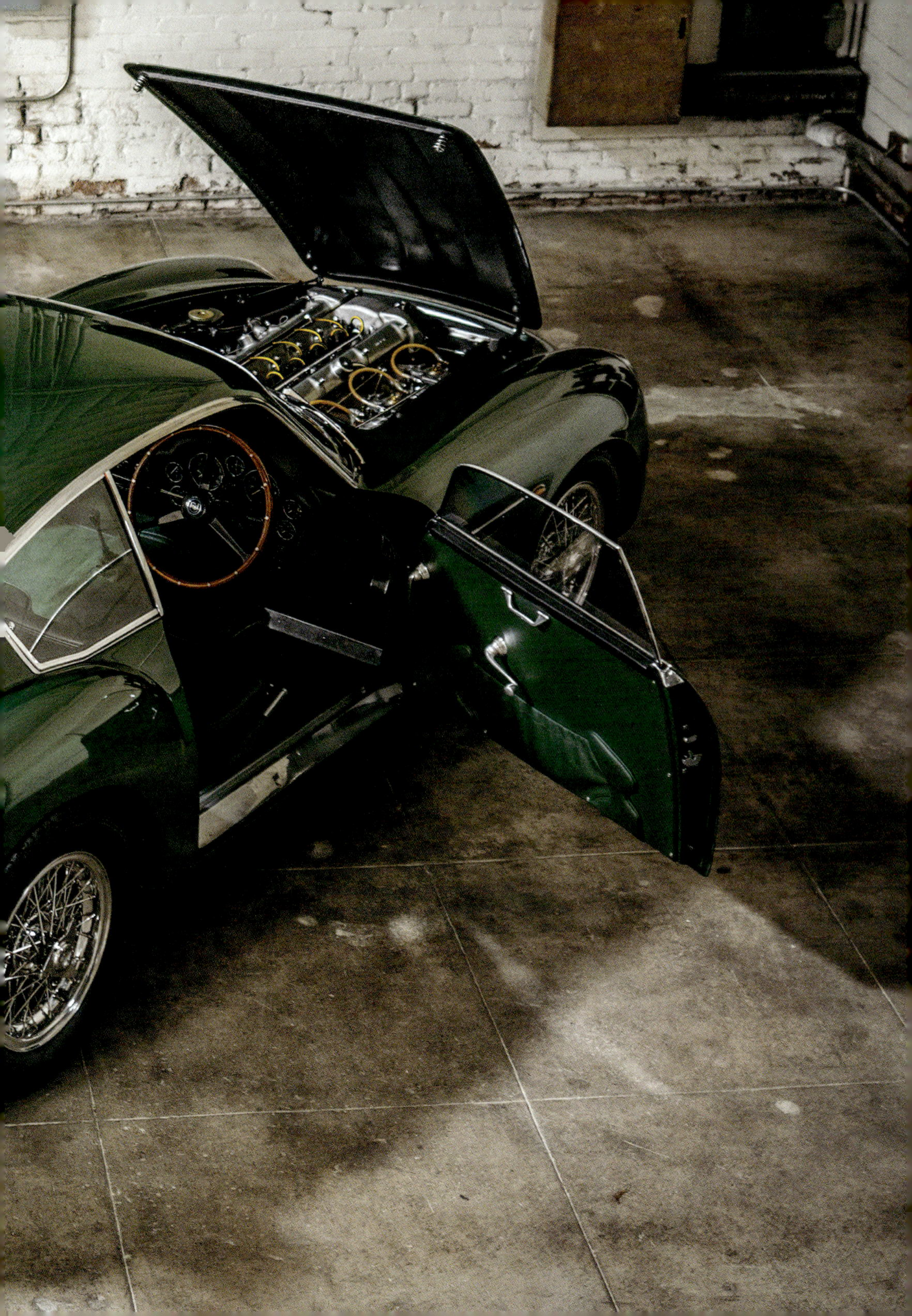

1962/64

Ferrari 250 GTO Series II

MANUFACTURED 1962–64 | **ENGINE** 2,953 cc (180 cu. in.), SOHC per bank 60° V12 | **HORSEPOWER** 300
TOP SPEED 280 km/h (174 mph) | **TRANSMISSION** 5-speed
NUMBER PRODUCED 36 (33 Series I / 3-liter + 3 Series II / 3-liter – this total excludes 3 Series I-bodied / 4-liter cars, 2 prototypes + 1 LMB-body car)

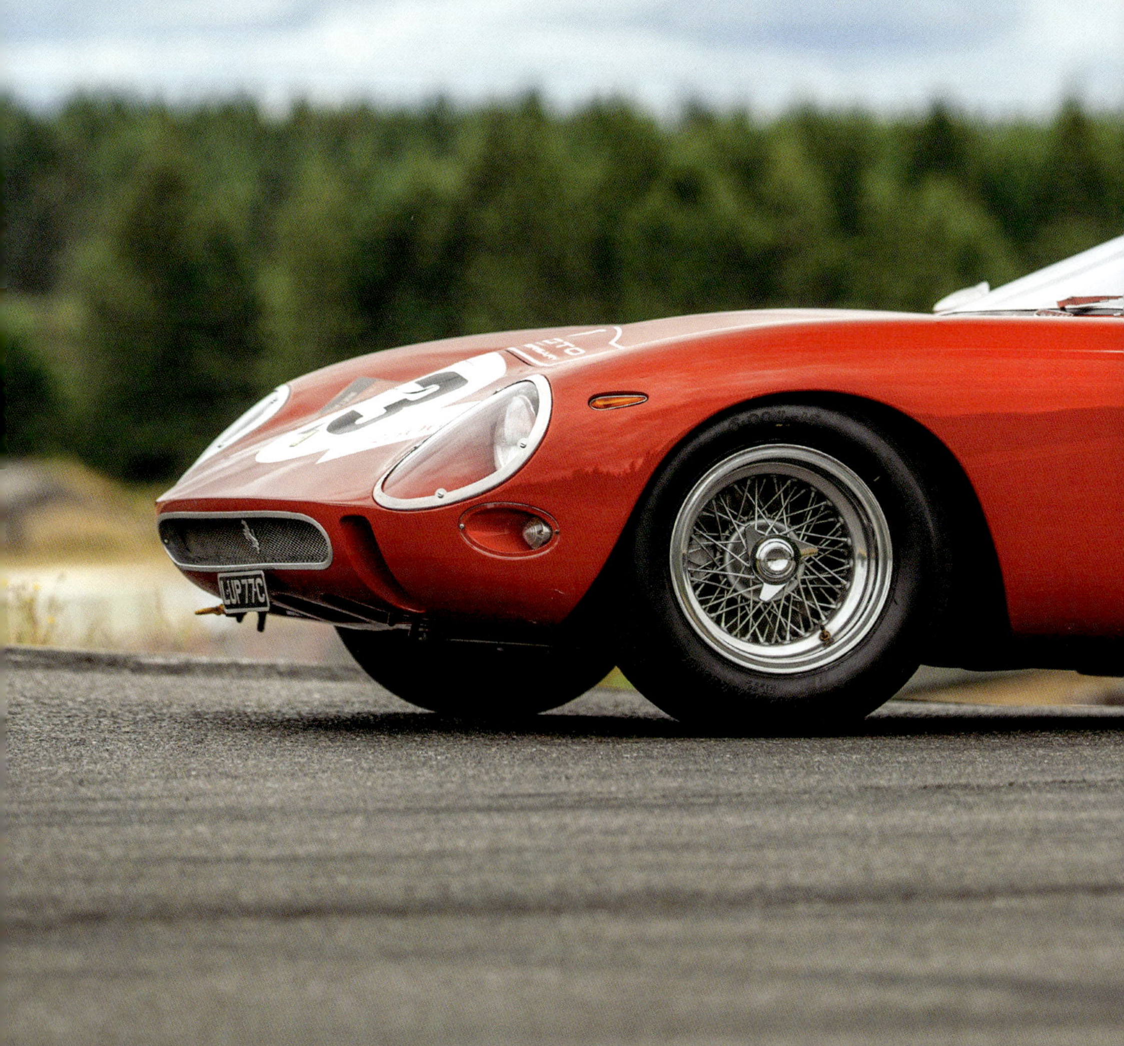

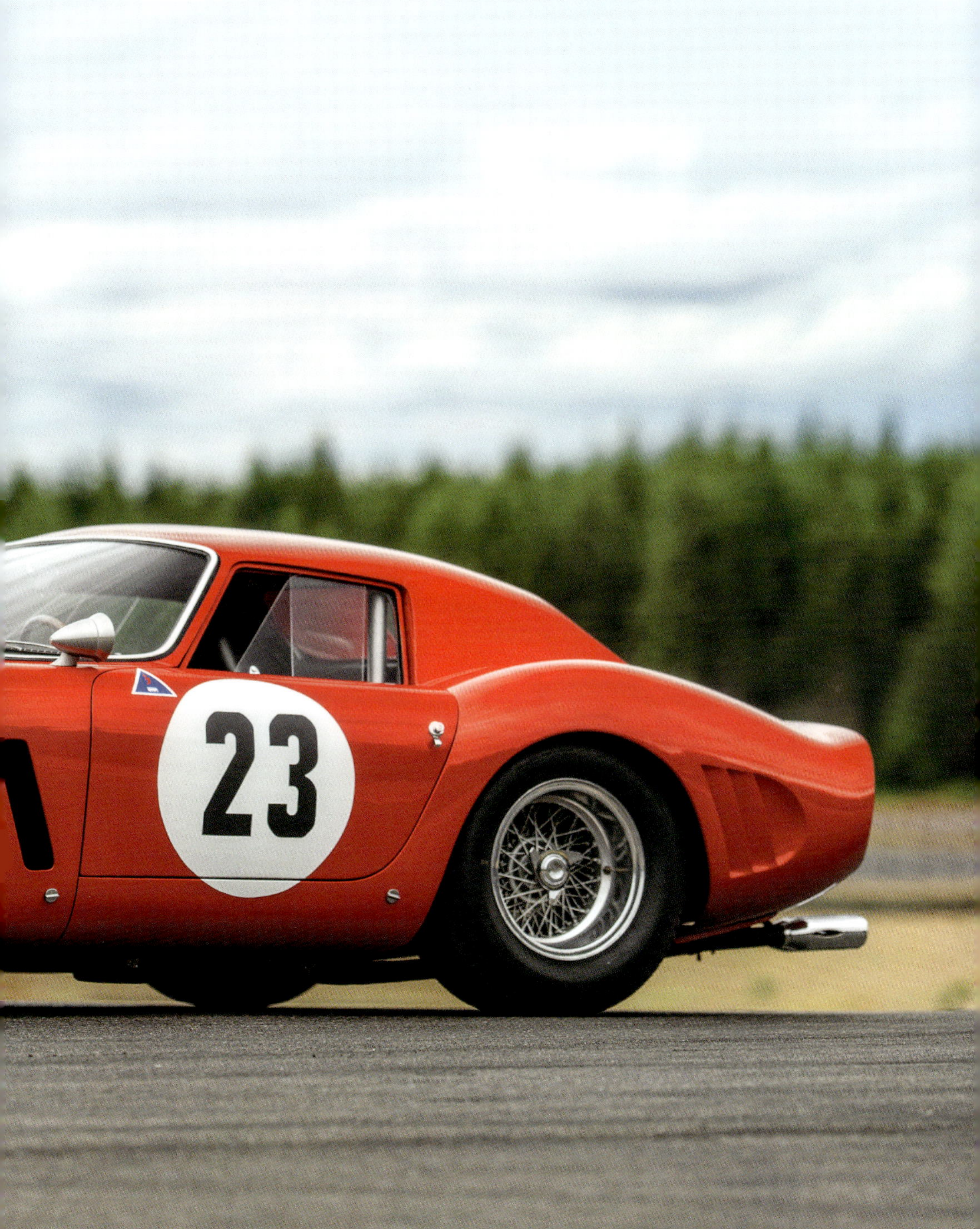
23

The immortal 250 GTO — is there any Ferrari more important, desirable or legendary? Many think not and for good reason: this is the car that perhaps best encapsulates Ferrari's guiding philosophy: "the highest levels of performance and style." But more than this, the 250 GTO will always be remembered for being one of the models to have achieved the highest number of victories within the company's esteemed racing history.

During the 1950s and 1960s, Ferrari became famed as much for its race-winning proficiency on the track as for its production of sublime GT cars. Like Ferrari's racing prototypes, these elegant yet powerful machines have long inspired a passionate following among die-hard Ferrari enthusiasts. Indeed, the fanatical love of these cars, which so perfectly combine raw throaty power with sensual aesthetics, sometimes seems to know no bounds in their country of origin, and certainly elsewhere, too. Of these luxury high performance grand touring models, which were usually two-door coupés, it is the 250 GTO that is commonly acknowledged as the ultimate Ferrari of all time — the "GT" standing for Gran Turismo (grand tourer) and the all-important "O" standing for *omologato* (homologated), meaning that the car was officially certified by the FIA to race within Group 3 GT Class competitions.

Ferrari's chief engineer, Giotto Bizzarrini, initially led the team that worked on the car during its very earliest development phase. At its first test outing at Monza in September 1961, it was mockingly nicknamed *Il Mostro* (the Monster) due to its "rough-hewn and ill-fitting prototype body," but even so, with Stirling Moss as its test-driver it managed to set record times that surpassed those previously achieved by a 250 GT SWB Berlinetta Competizione. The following year there was, as Ferrari puts it, a "Palace Revolution," when Enzo Ferrari decided controversially to sideline Bizzarrini and entrusted Sergio Scaglietti

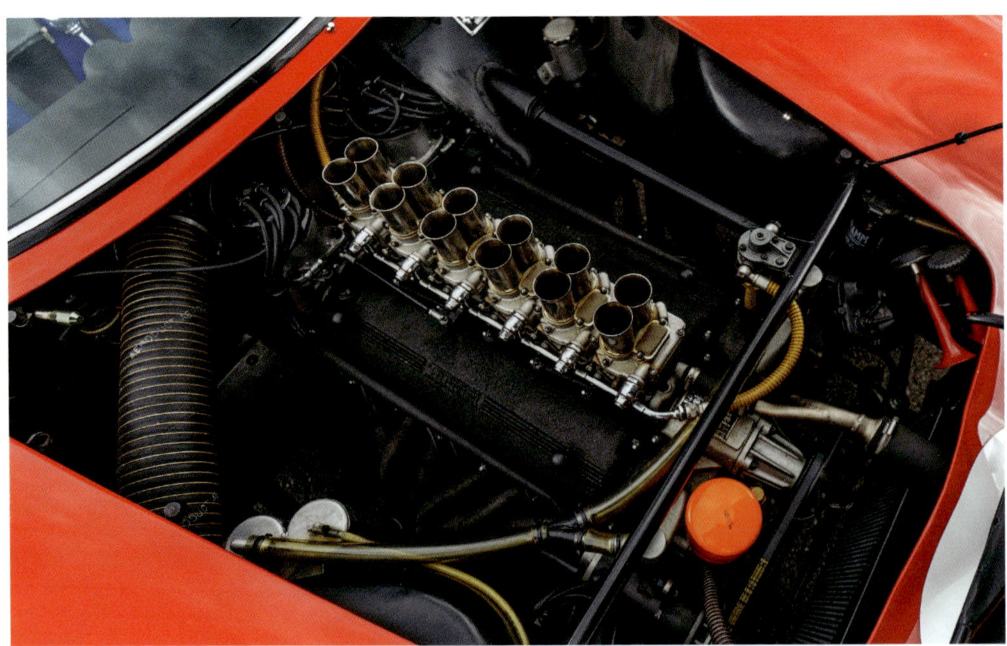

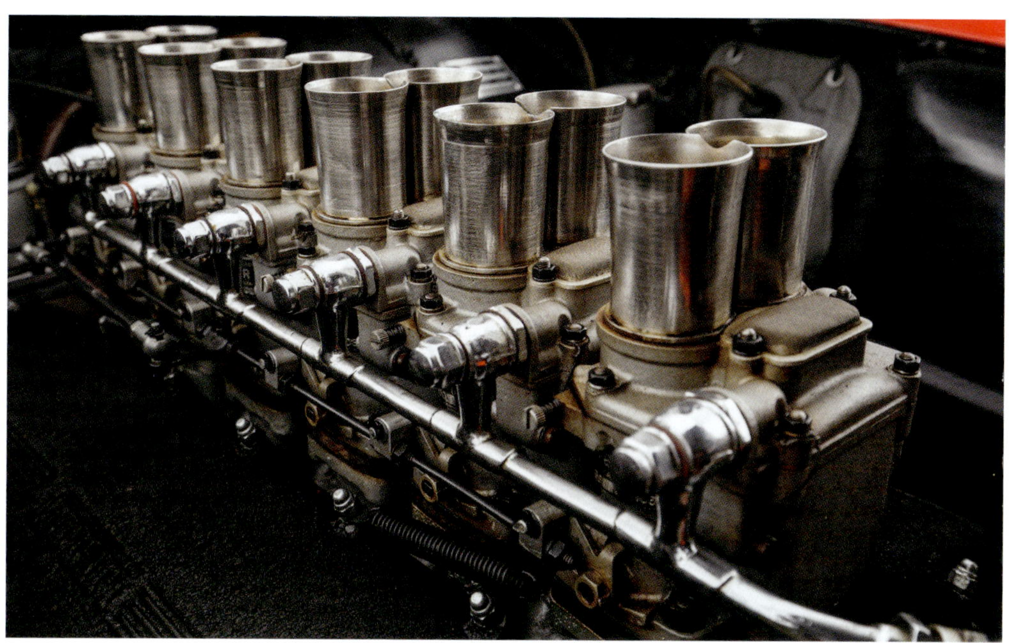

instead with the design and build of the 250 GTO's initial Series I coachwork. Carrozzeria Scaglietti was also tasked with the execution of the later Pininfarina-designed Series II body, introduced in 1963 — as shown on the example here (chassis no. 3413). Using data gleaned from wind tunnel and road track testing, Scaglietti sculpted the Ferrari 250 GTO's aerodynamically efficient aluminum bodywork into something of rare beauty. Under this sculptural skin lay a lightweight tubular steel frame, an A-arm front suspension, a live-axle rear end and four-wheel disc brakes as well as the two-seater Berlinetta's formidable power unit: a 3-liter short-block Colombo V12 that featured six Weber 38 DNC carburetors and produced 300 hp. The car also boasted, as Ferrari explains, "a new 5-speed, all synchromesh gearbox, with an open gate gear-change tower in the cockpit," which enabled quicker gear changing and, thereby, better acceleration.

Ferrari went on to race this low-slung car with its distinctive Borrani wire wheels in Group 3 GT competitions, even though it had only constructed 36 examples when the FIA's homologation regulations clearly stipulated that to compete in such events at least 100 examples of a car had to be produced — Ferrari circumnavigated this troublesome detail by numbering the cars' chassis out of sequence, thereby making it appear that more had been built than actually had been. Constructed between 1962 and 1964, the Ferrari

Opposite & above: Detail of Ferrari 250 GTO 2,953 cc (180 cu. in.), SOHC per bank 60° V12 engine with six Weber 38 DCN carburetors. This engine was the race-proven all-alloy short-block Colombo Tipo 168/62 Competizione three-liter V12 as used in the earlier 250 Testa Rossa Le Mans winner.

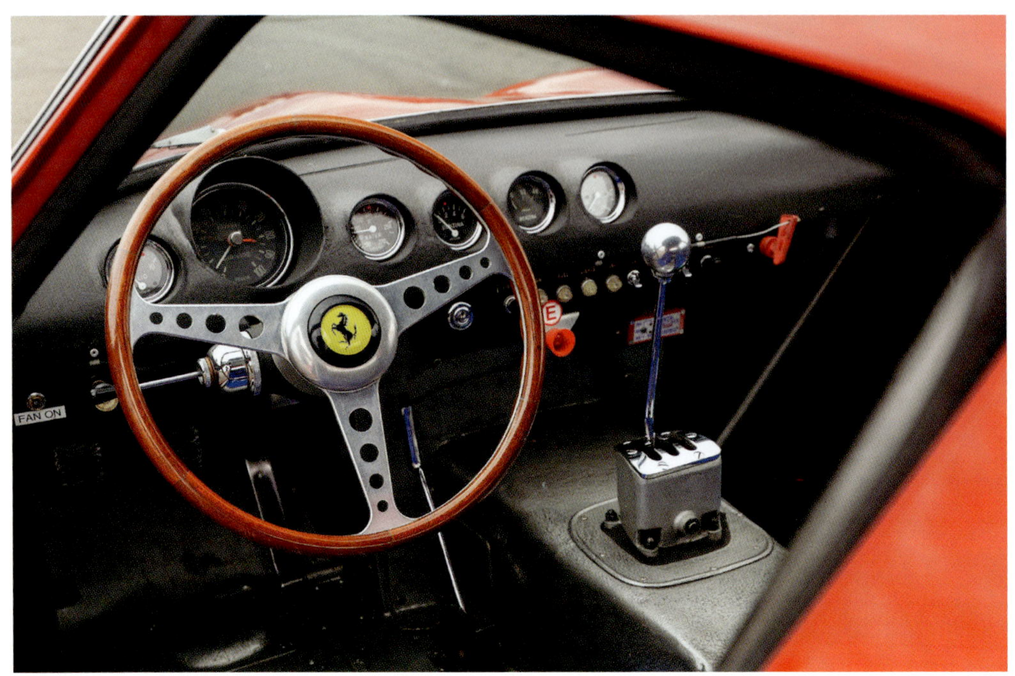

250 GTO enabled the Italian marque to win the GT World Championship over three consecutive years: 1962, 1963 and 1964 — making the 250 GTO a motorsporting legend. Chassis no. 3413, shown here, originally belonged to the wealthy Italian entrepreneur, engineer and privateer Corrado Ferlaino and began its life in 1962 clothed in Series I bodywork. In January 1964, however, it was sent back to the Scaglietti coachworks, where it was fitted with a state-of-the-art Series II body in advance of Ferlaino's first race outing in the car at the Targa Florio held in Sicily. As RM Sotheby's notes, "owner/drivers certainly desired the latest technological offering from Ferrari. Designed by Pininfarina, this improved bodywork was lower, wider, and shorter, with a more aerodynamic, steeply raked windshield, larger tires, wider track, and the engine sitting lower, all with the aim of improving handling and balance — a critical consideration on the curves and shorter straights through the towns and seaside hills along the coasts of Sicily." In fact, this new coachwork was seen as being so desirable a further two 250 GTOs were given similar body upgrades (four older 1962–63 Series I 250 GTOs were subsequently updated with 1964 Series II bodies).

Believed by many to be the Ferrari model that best exemplifies the attributes of the marque, chassis no. 3413 became the world's most expensive car ever sold at auction ($48,405,000 inc. premium) when it appeared at RM Sotheby's 2018 Monterey sale (surpassed in 2022 by the "Uhlenhaut Coupé" — see p. 112). But then, when it comes to this specific model collectors have always been prepared to dig deep knowing that their future investment is likely to appreciate because, let's face it, there will only ever be 36 Series I- and Series II-bodied 250 GTOs in total out there.

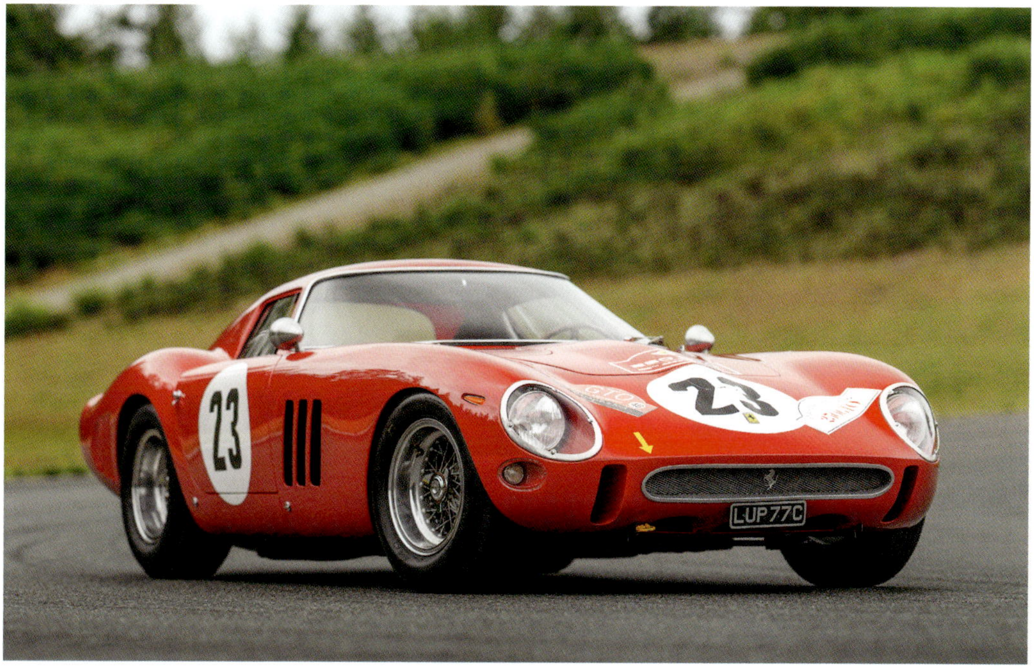

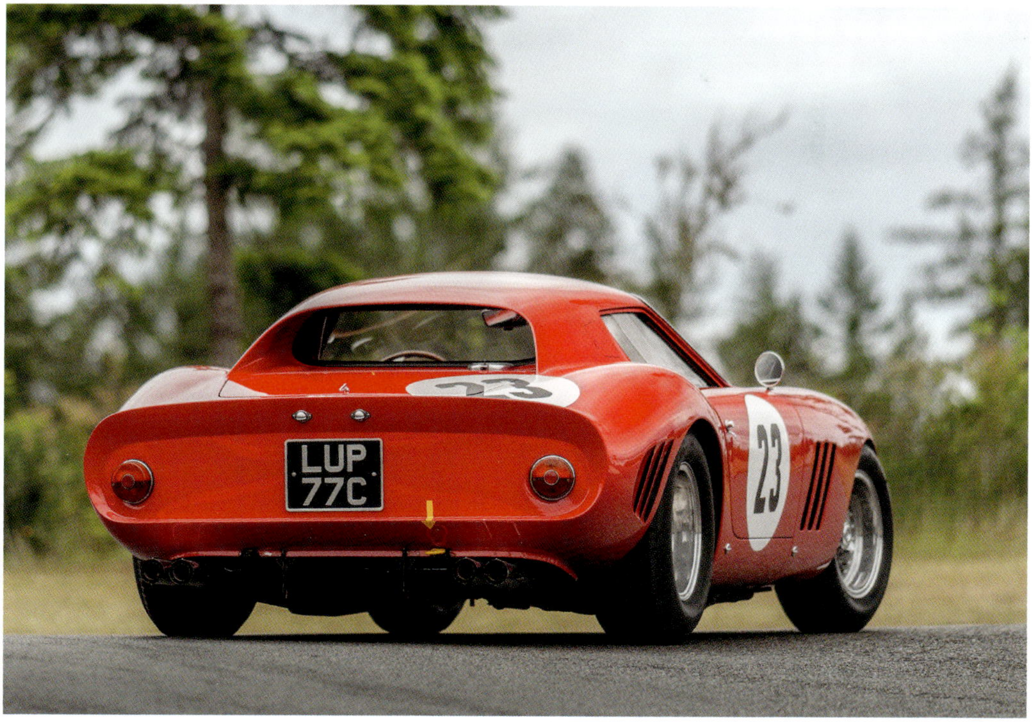

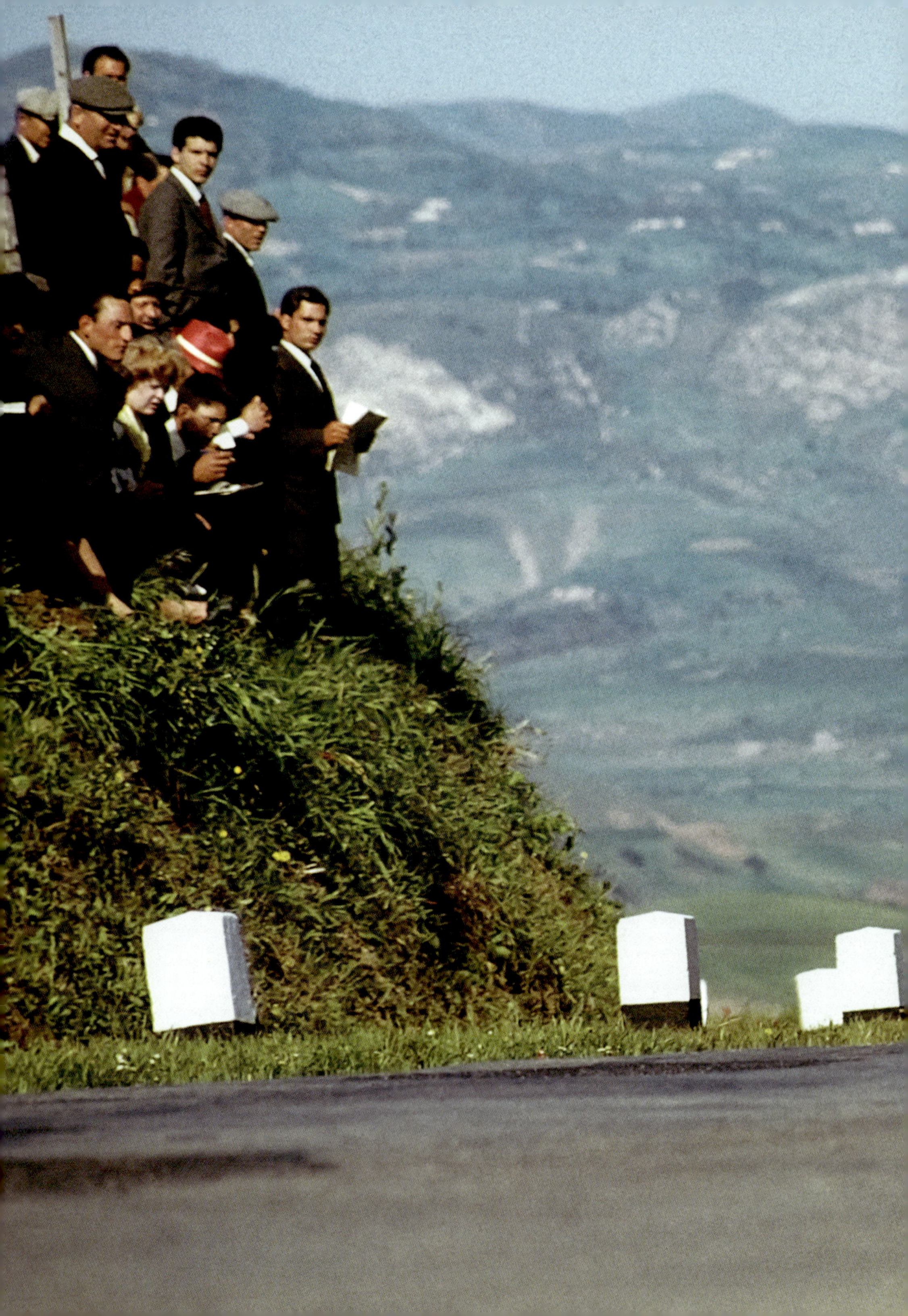

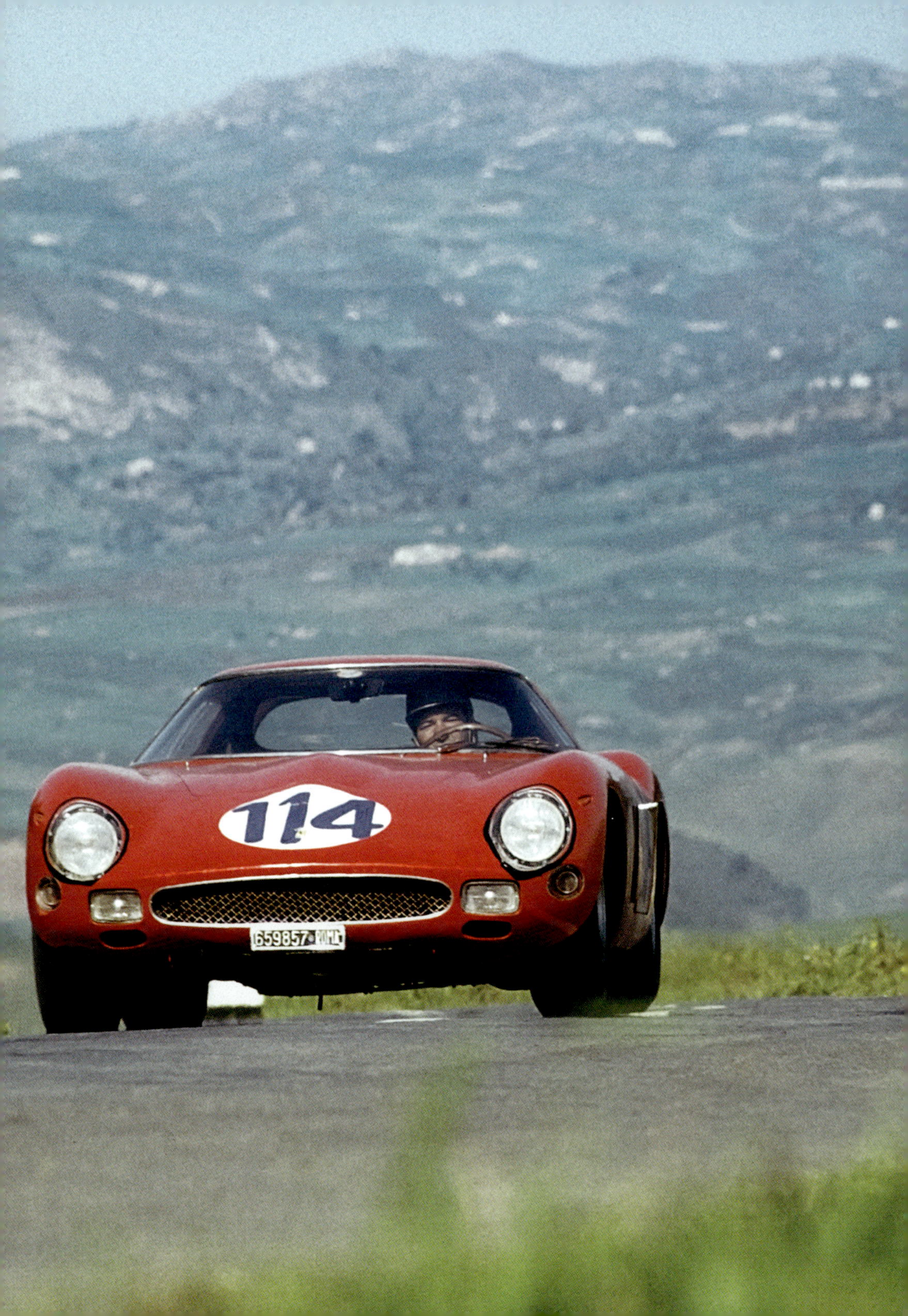
114
659857

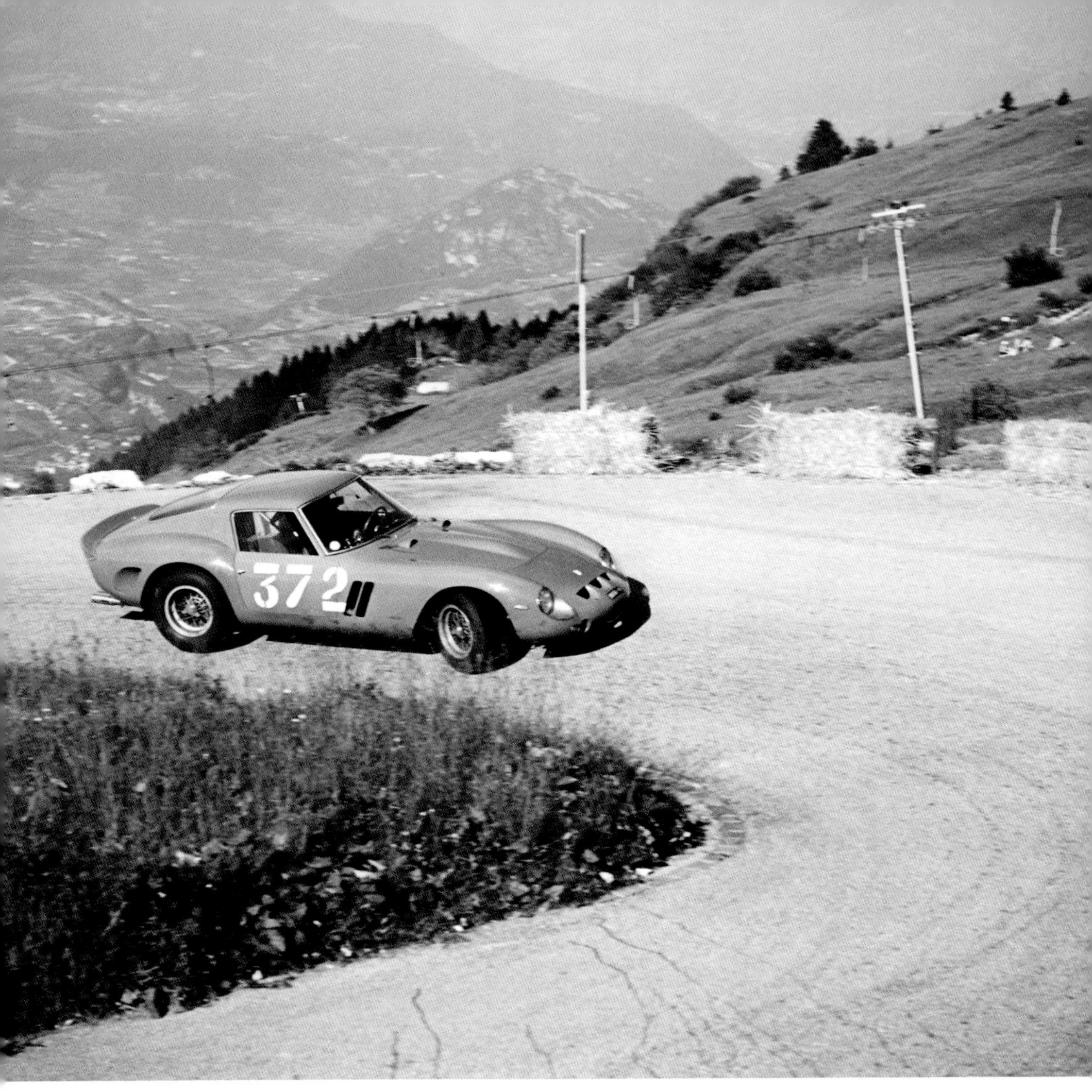

Previous: The No. 114 1962 Ferrari 250 GTO by Scaglietti (chassis no. 3413) at the 1964 Targa Florio, Sicily. Driven by privateers Corrado Ferlaino and Luigi Taramazzo, the car finished first in class (GT3.0) and fifth overall. In December 1963, before the start of the World Sportscar Championship season, owner/driver Ferlaino purchased chassis no. 3413 — a 1962 Ferrari 250 GTO in Series I bodywork. He subsequently had the factory send the car to its official coach builder at Scaglietti in Modena, where the GTOs were all bodied from the outset, and upgraded to Series II coachwork.

Above: The No. 372 Ferrari 250 GTO (chassis no. 3413) of Edoardo Lualdi-Gabardi in Series I bodywork at the 1962 Trento-Bondone Hill Climb, where he took a GT3.0 class win. It was the third production Ferrari 250 GTO built and was acquired by Lualdi-Gabardi in 1962. He campaigned with great success, winning the GT3.0 class at the 1962 Italian GT Championship.

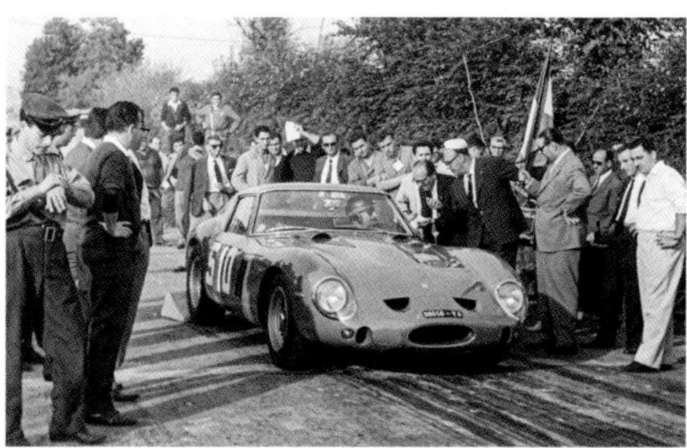

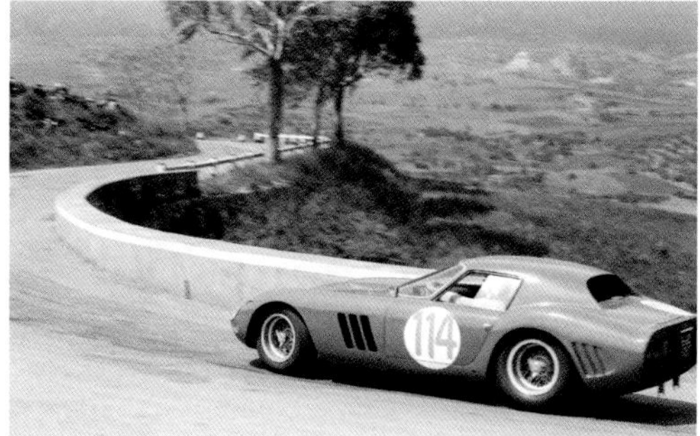

Above (left): Edoardo Lualdi-Gabardi in the No. 510 Ferrari 250 GTO (chassis no. 3413) at the Coppa Fagioli, Ancona hill climb in September 1962 in which he won overall first place.

Above (right) & below: The No. 114 1962 Ferrari 250 GTO with Series II bodywork by Scaglietti (chassis no. 3413) of Corrado Ferlaino and Luigi Taramazzo in action and in the pits at the 1964 Targa Florio, Sicily, where they won first in class (GT3.0) and fifth overall.

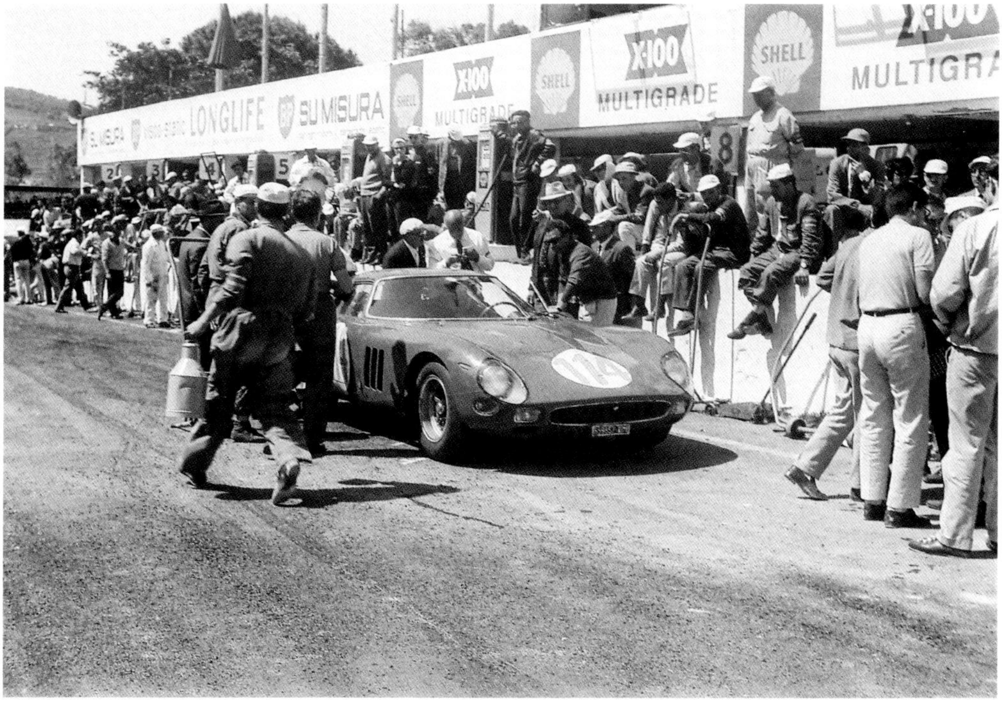

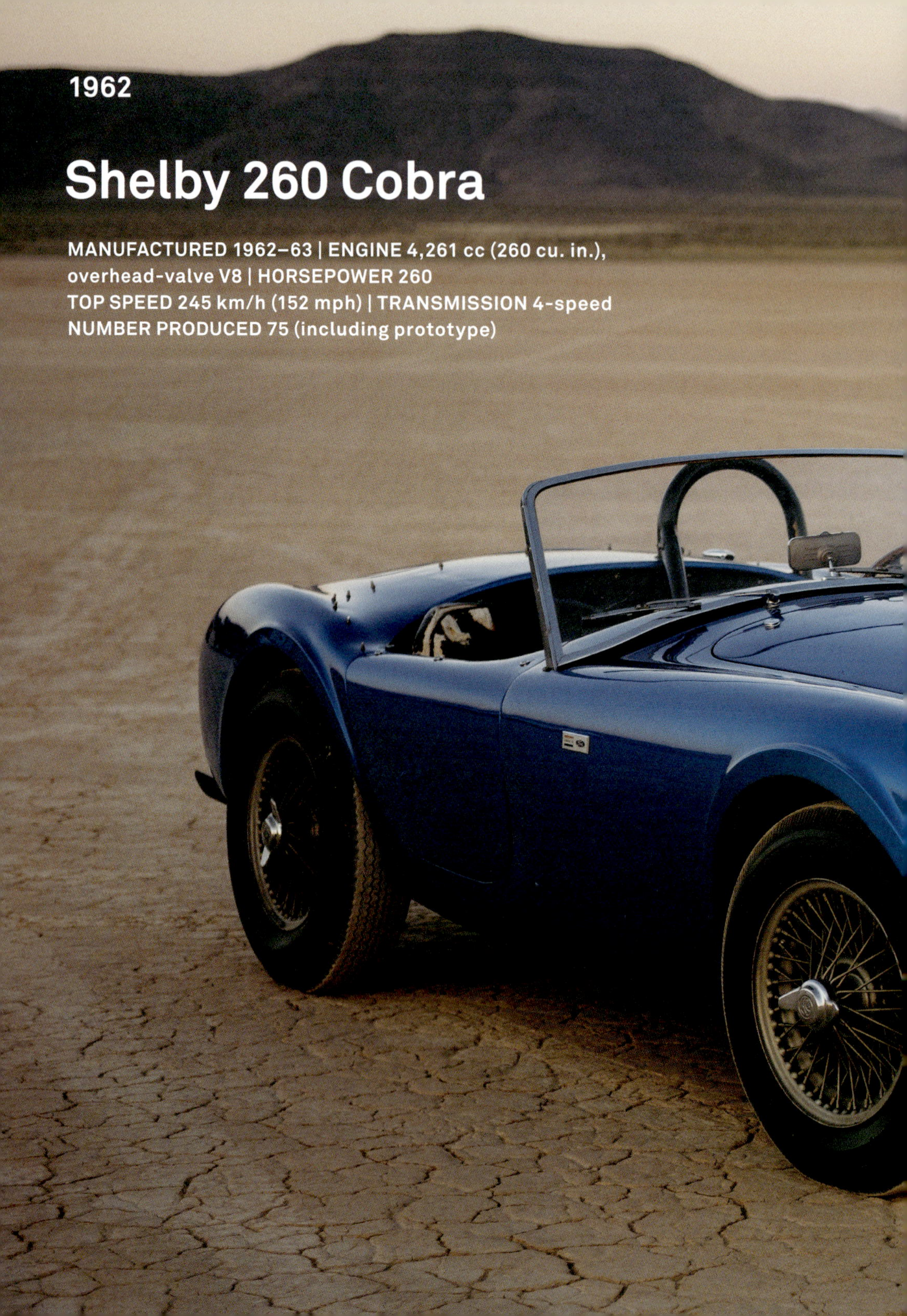

1962

Shelby 260 Cobra

MANUFACTURED 1962–63 | **ENGINE** 4,261 cc (260 cu. in.), overhead-valve V8 | **HORSEPOWER** 260
TOP SPEED 245 km/h (152 mph) | **TRANSMISSION** 4-speed
NUMBER PRODUCED 75 (including prototype)

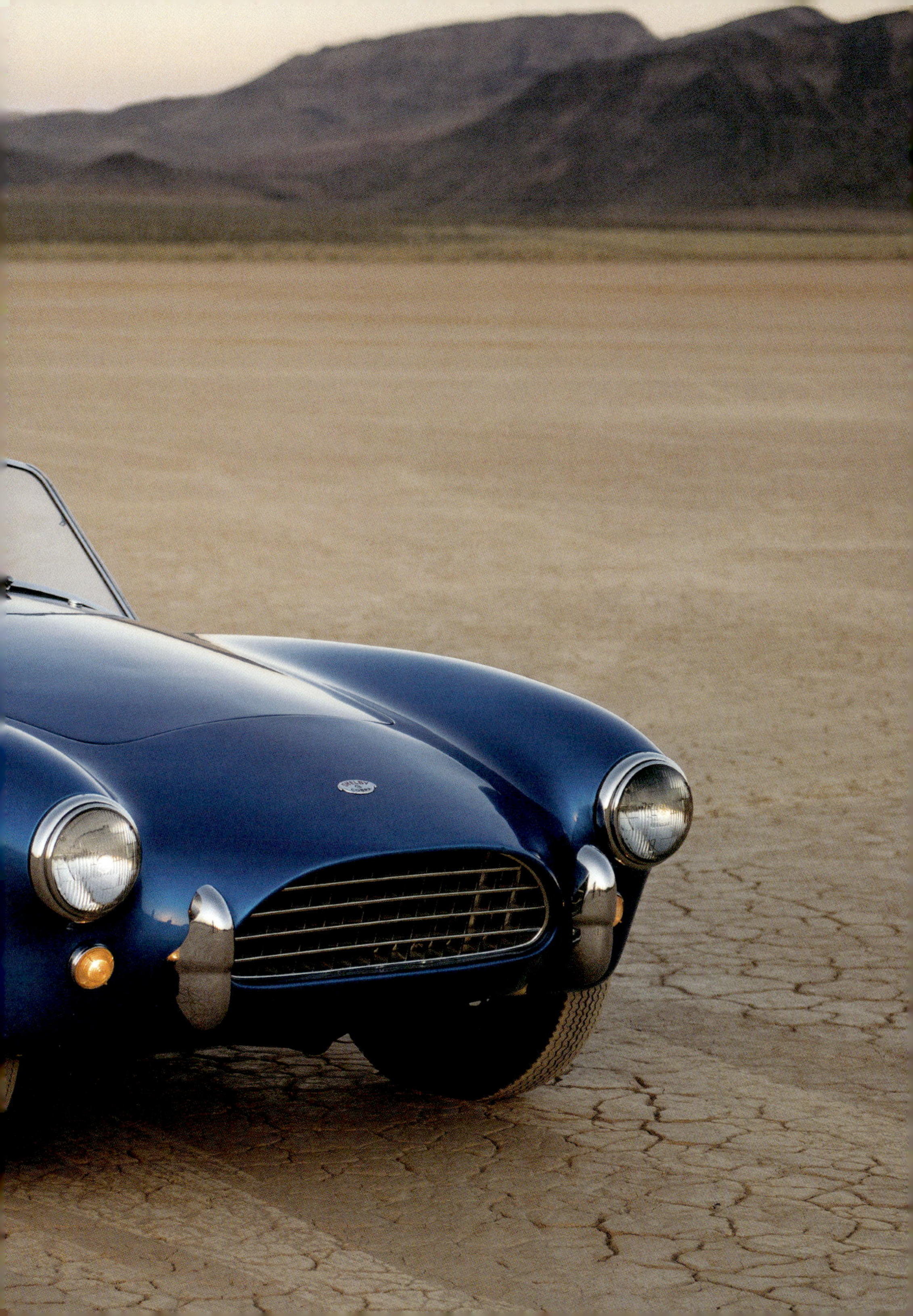

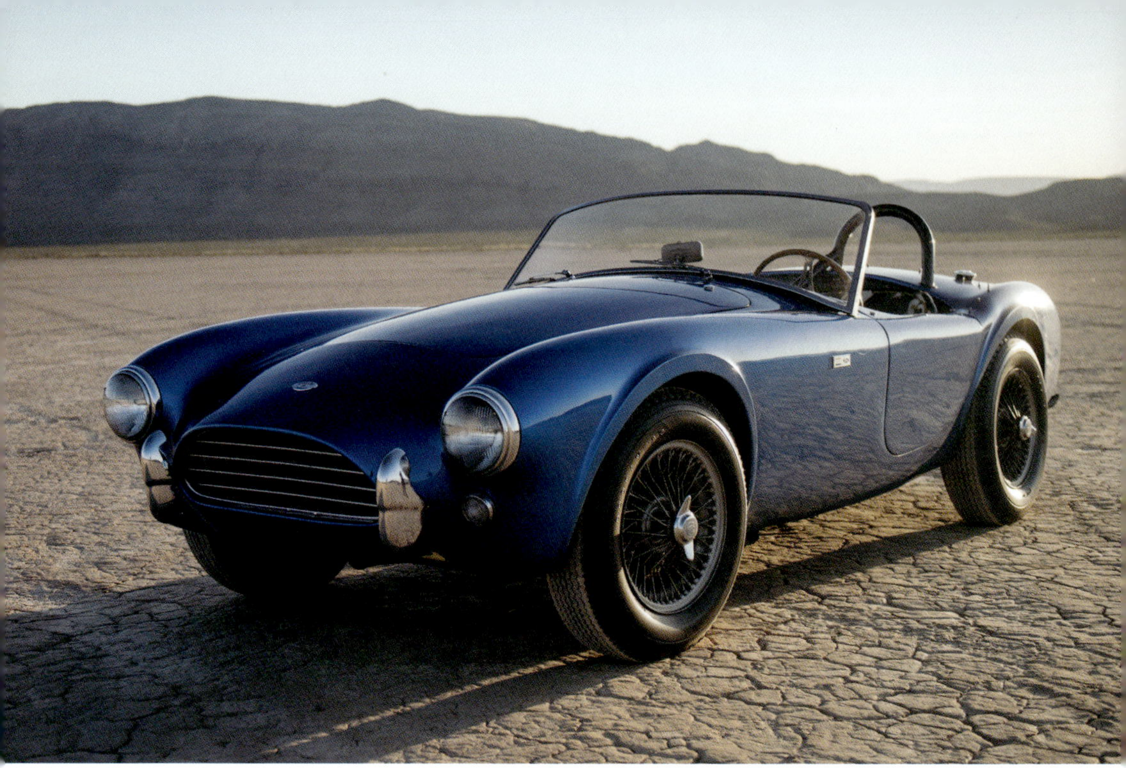

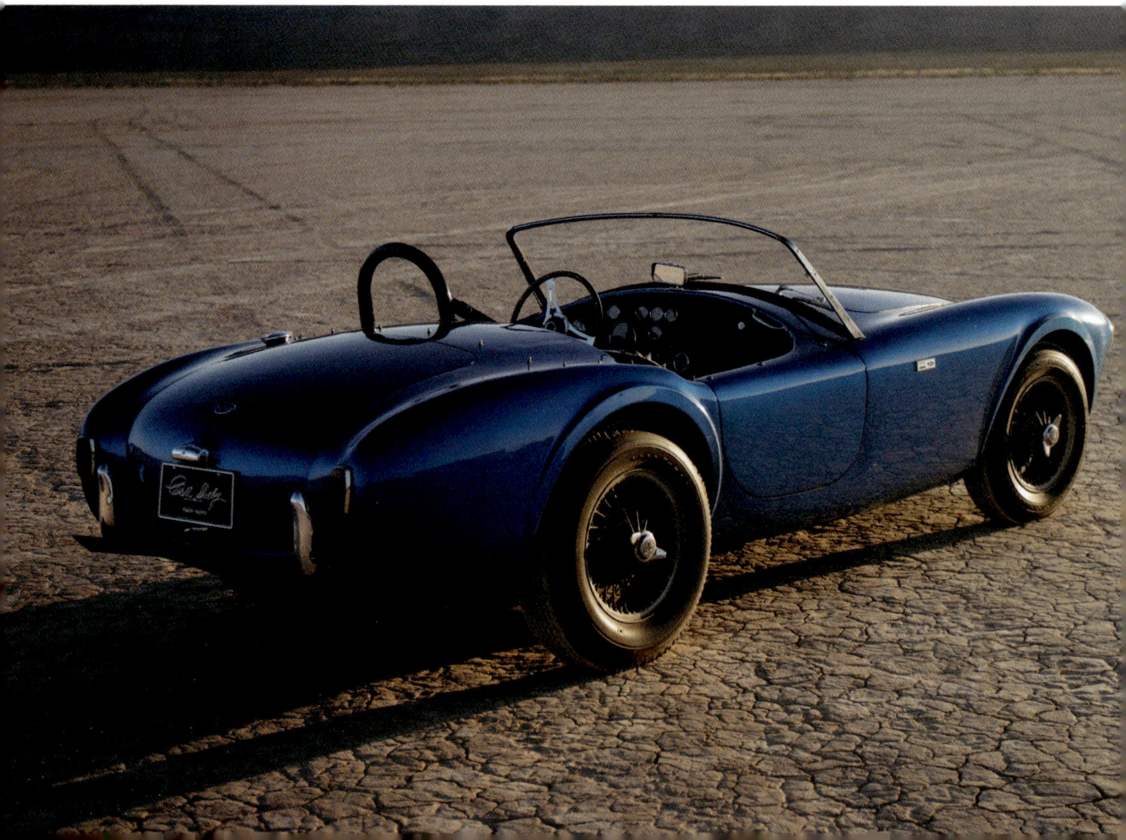

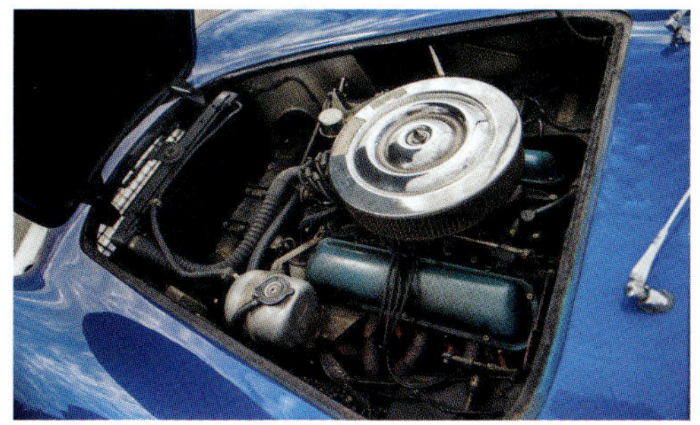

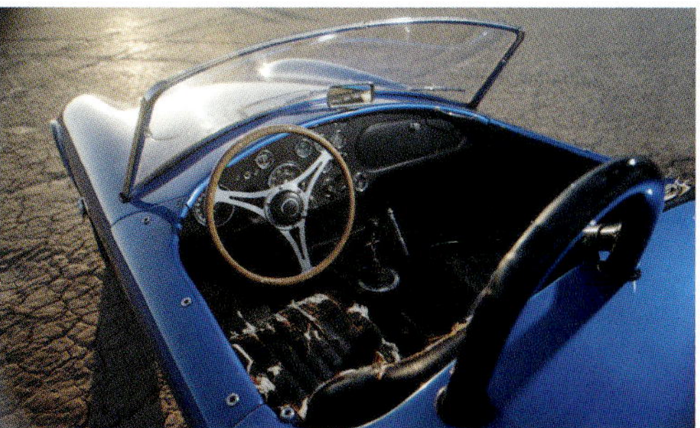

Above (left): Detail of Shelby 260 Cobra 4,261 cc (260 cu. in.), overhead-valve V8 engine with a single Holley four-barrel carburetor. A variety of options were available to increase performance, with the top-spec combination producing over 335 hp. The engine bay here shows the car's astonishing originality.

Above (right): Detail of highly original cockpit including flat AC Ace dashboard.

The immortal Shelby Cobra was the outcome of an extraordinary synthesis of Anglo-American engineering, which ultimately led to a new and exciting chapter in sports car design. Its creator was the legendary Carroll Shelby, who over his career as a racing driver drove for Aston Martin, Austin-Healey, Maserati and, very briefly, Ferrari. In 1959, he famously co-piloted an Aston Martin DBR1 (see p. 174) with Roy Salvadori to a glorious victory at the 24 Hours of Le Mans. Mid-season the following year, however, he was forced to retire from racing due to a heart problem. Not prepared to abandon motorsports altogether, the 37-year-old Shelby decided that more than anything he wanted to build an American sports car that would rival those produced by Enzo Ferrari, whom he personally blamed for the death of his good friend Luigi Musso at the 1958 French Grand Prix while driving a Ferrari.

With this aim, in September 1961, Shelby contacted AC Cars of Thames Ditton in England, after learning that it had lost its source of straight-six engines for the company's small but feisty AC Ace two-seater sports car due to Bristol Cars discontinuing their manufacture. Shelby proposed that the firm carry on building its lightweight chassis, but modify it so that it could accommodate an American V8. AC's owner, Charles Hurlock, agreed to this plan and so Shelby began casting around for a suitable power plant. Fortuitously, Ford was developing just such an engine, a lightweight 221 cu. in. small-block V8, which enabled Shelby to construct a preliminary test vehicle using a borrowed AC Ace.

The car shown here, which became the prototype Shelby Cobra (chassis no. CSX 2000), was air freighted from the UK in February 1962 minus an engine and transmission to Los Angeles airport, where it was picked up by Shelby and his friend and colleague, Dean Moon, a well-known hot-rodder, and taken back to Moon's workshop. They immediately set to work and within less than eight hours had installed a newer, larger-displacement high performance Ford 260 cu. in. engine and a Borg-Warner four-speed transmission. They then tested it and, as Moon recalled, "We got drunk and drove it around an impromptu road course we had set up between the oil derricks. When it didn't break, even after all that rough treatment, well, then we knew we had a good car."

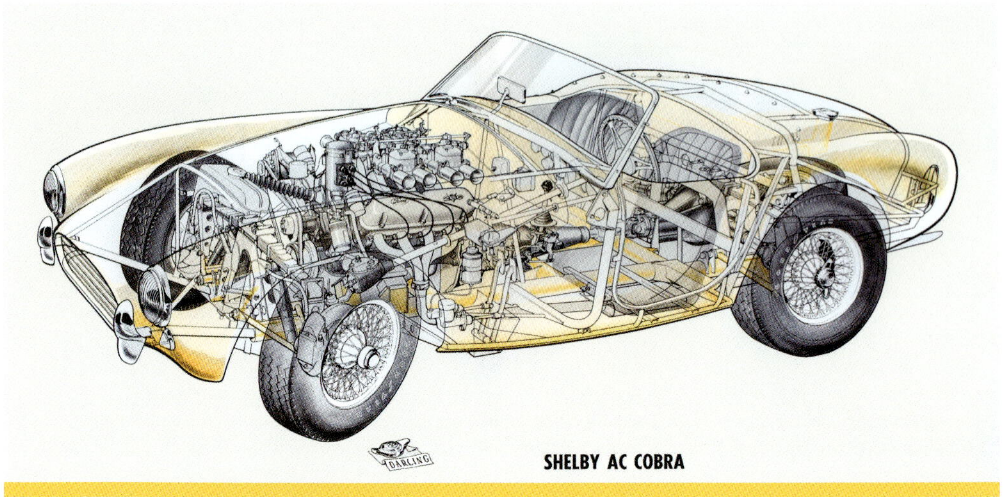

Above: Cutaway drawing by Darling of Shelby 260 Cobra (chassis no. CSX 2000), which appeared in *Sports Car Graphic*, August 1962. The drawing shows the engine with the optional top-spec induction system of a quadruple twin-choke Weber carburetor combination on a ram-tuned manifold. This set up alone produced an increase of 42 hp, taking the total to over 300 hp.

The following month, Shelby American opened up a workshop in Venice, California, and brought in Ray Geddes to help coordinate Ford and AC's involvement in the production project. Worried about the possibility of liability, Ford had opted to keep a low profile, but still helped to facilitate the car's development with funding and expertise. The eventually completed CSX 2000 roadster was astonishingly quick, boasting a 0–60 mph (96 km/h) acceleration of 4.2 seconds when it was tested by both *Car Life* and *Road & Track* magazines. This first-ever Shelby Cobra was repainted in different colors for PR purposes, so it appeared to the press that more examples existed than actually did. This stunning and very fast sports car was debuted on Ford's stand at the 1962 New York Auto Show, and immediately dealers began placing orders for it. In fact, so many were received that Shelby American was able to commit to putting the Cobra into serial manufacture — with CSX 2001 becoming the first production car and CSX 2002 going on to be the first competition Shelby Cobra. Shelby subsequently constructed a new higher-powered Cobra with a Ford 289 cu. in. (4.7-liter) V8 engine. This upgraded variation was known as the 289 Cobra, 51 examples of which were produced 1962–63 together with 75 examples of the 260 Cobra. The cars manufactured by Shelby American during this period are known as Mk I Cobras. The Mk II Shelby 289 Cobra was produced 1963–65 and was adapted to accommodate rack and pinion steering. Its competition variants were first fielded at the 24 Hours of Le Mans in 1963, and their platform was then modified into the iconic Shelby Cobra Daytona Coupe, which won the GT category of the 1965 World Sportscar Championship. This landmark victory can be traced to CSX 2000 — the first Cobra — which potentially makes it, according to RM Sotheby's, "The most important American sports car in history."

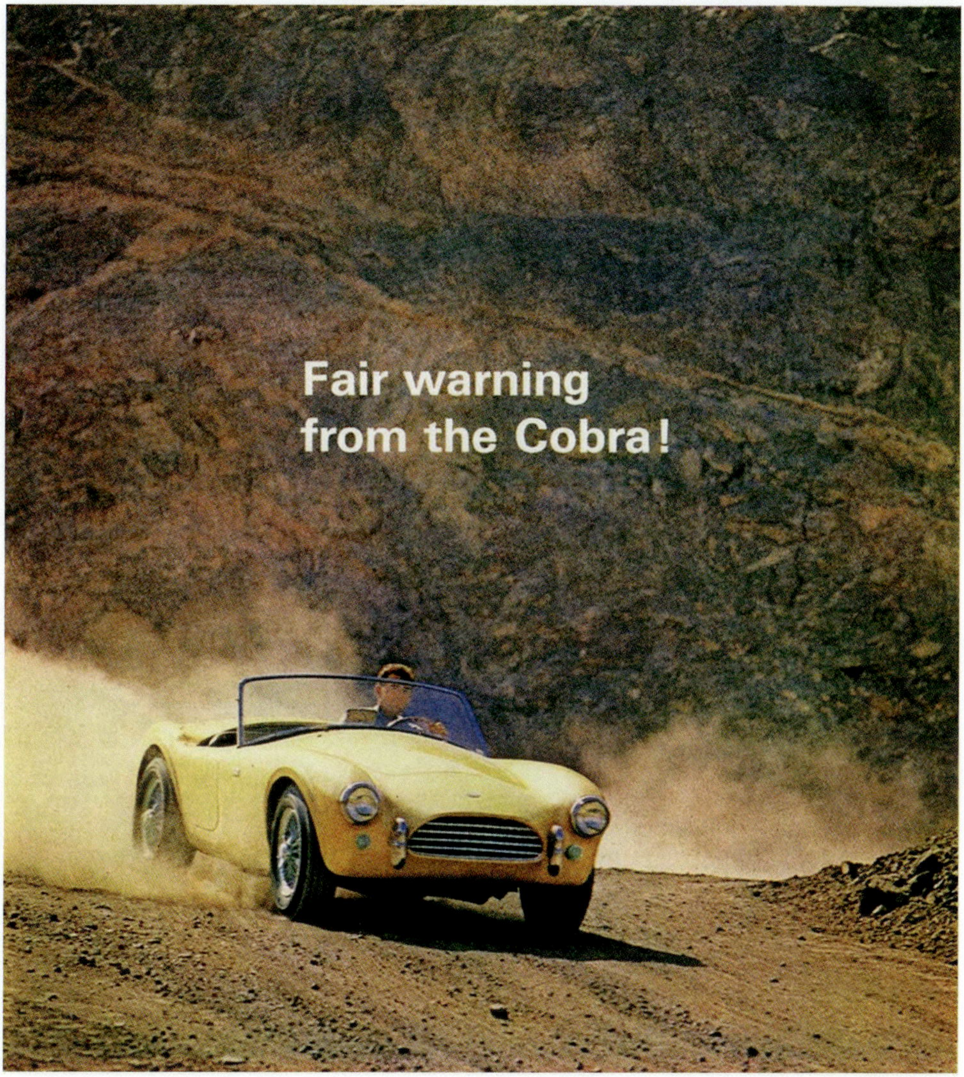

From this day on, drivers of the world's proudest sports cars are advised to stick to the right-hand side of the road. For at any moment an AC/Cobra can come storming past, belly low to the road with twin pipes ripping out a curt "good-by!"

There's not much point trying to argue with this potent new combination of super-hot Ford Fairlane V-8 and super-light AC chassis—260 solid American horsepower on tap all day long in a car that weighs 2,020 pounds curbside. The AC/Cobra roadtests zero to 100 in a breath-stopping 10.8 seconds . . . and comes smoking down to zero again in the grip of disc brakes big enough for a Diesel truck. The seats are deep glove-soft leather, the suspension is supple four-wheel independent, and the way it claws around corners rewrites all the laws of centrifugal force. The V-8 is a real piece of magic. Product of Ford's research in precision-molded "thin wall" cast iron, it is short, narrow, light—and ready to look at the other side of 150 mph (and 7,200 rpm) any time your foot slips. But even whispering around town it doesn't know what "temperament" means and that, coupled with the generous cockpit room, the civilized ride, the reasonable luggage space and the sleek Italianate lines of the hand-formed aluminum body, make the AC/Cobra a *touring* sports car of the very first rank.

Unhappily, the production is severely limited and, since the price is only $5,995 p.o.e., only those who drop a line right now to Carroll Shelby Enterprises, 1042 Princeton Drive, Venice, California, will be able to know what it feels like to drive the most explosively exciting car you can own.

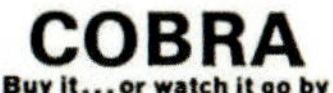

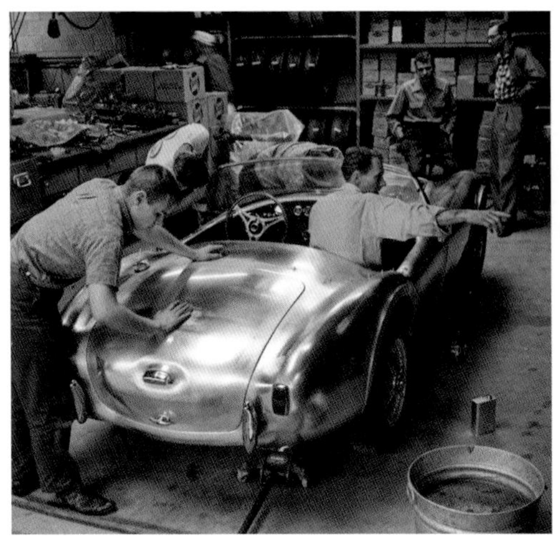

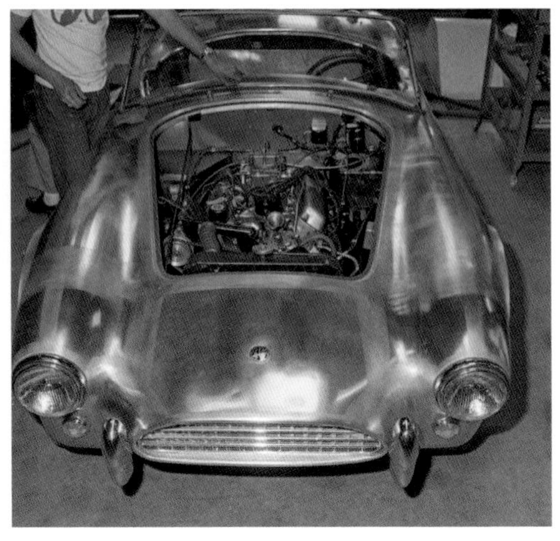

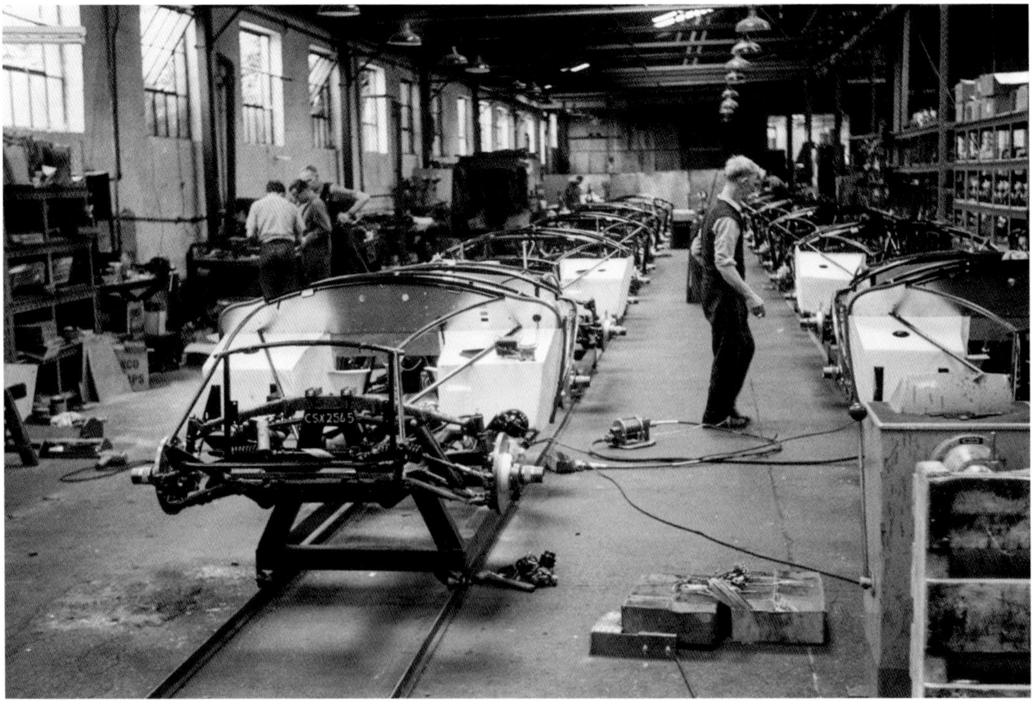

Page 279: 1962 magazine advertisement for the Shelby 260 Cobra featuring the prototype, chassis no. CSX 2000, painted yellow. This car was repainted several times in 1962 in different colors for PR purposes, so it appeared to the press that more examples of the model existed than actually did.

Opposite (top, left & right): The first prototype Shelby Cobra (chassis no. CSX 2000) being built in Dean Moon's Hot Rod Shop in Santa Fe Springs, California, February, 1962. Carroll Shelby took the auto enthusiast world by storm when he pulled the straight-six engine from a lightweight British AC Ace roadster, replaced it with a Ford V8, and created the Shelby Cobra. Between the 1962 and 1967 model years, Shelby American produced just under 1,000 Cobras variously equipped with 260-, 289- or 427-cubic-inch Ford V8 engines.

Opposite (below): Shelby Cobra construction at AC Cars Ltd., Thames Ditton, England, 1964. Starting in 1962 AC exported completed, painted, and trimmed cars (less engine and gearbox) to Carroll Shelby who then finished the cars in his Shelby American International workshop in Los Angeles by installing the engine and gearbox and correcting any bodywork flaws caused by the car's passage by sea. A small number of cars were also completed on the east coast of the US by Ed Hugus in Pennsylvania.

Below: 1962 Shelby American promotional photograph showing a very early production Shelby Cobra.

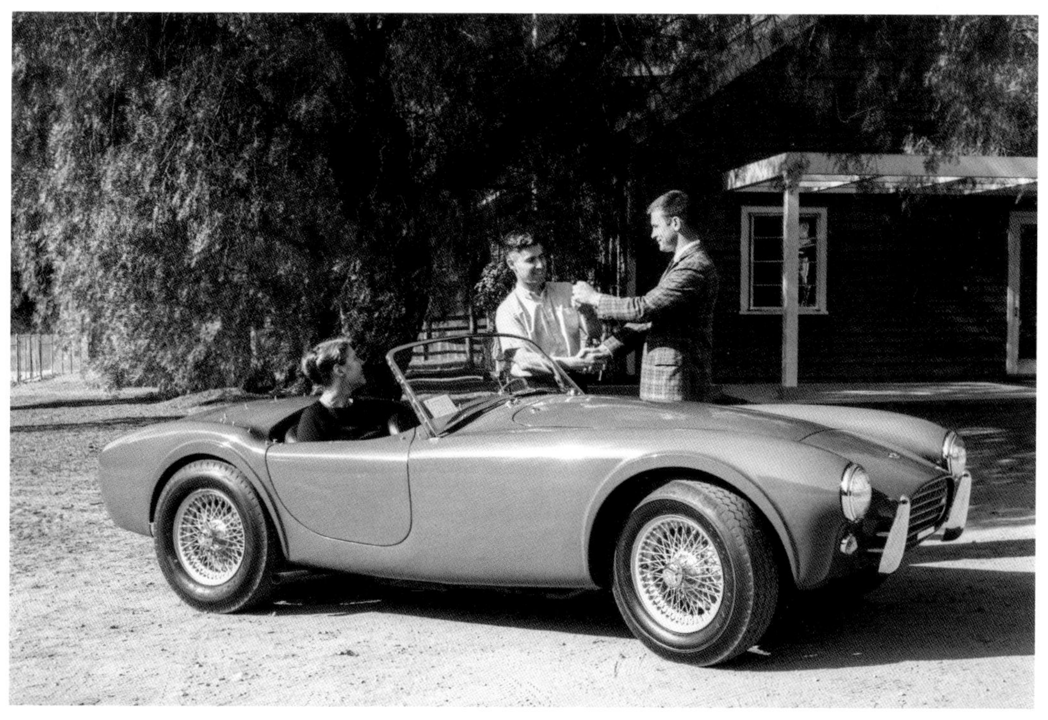

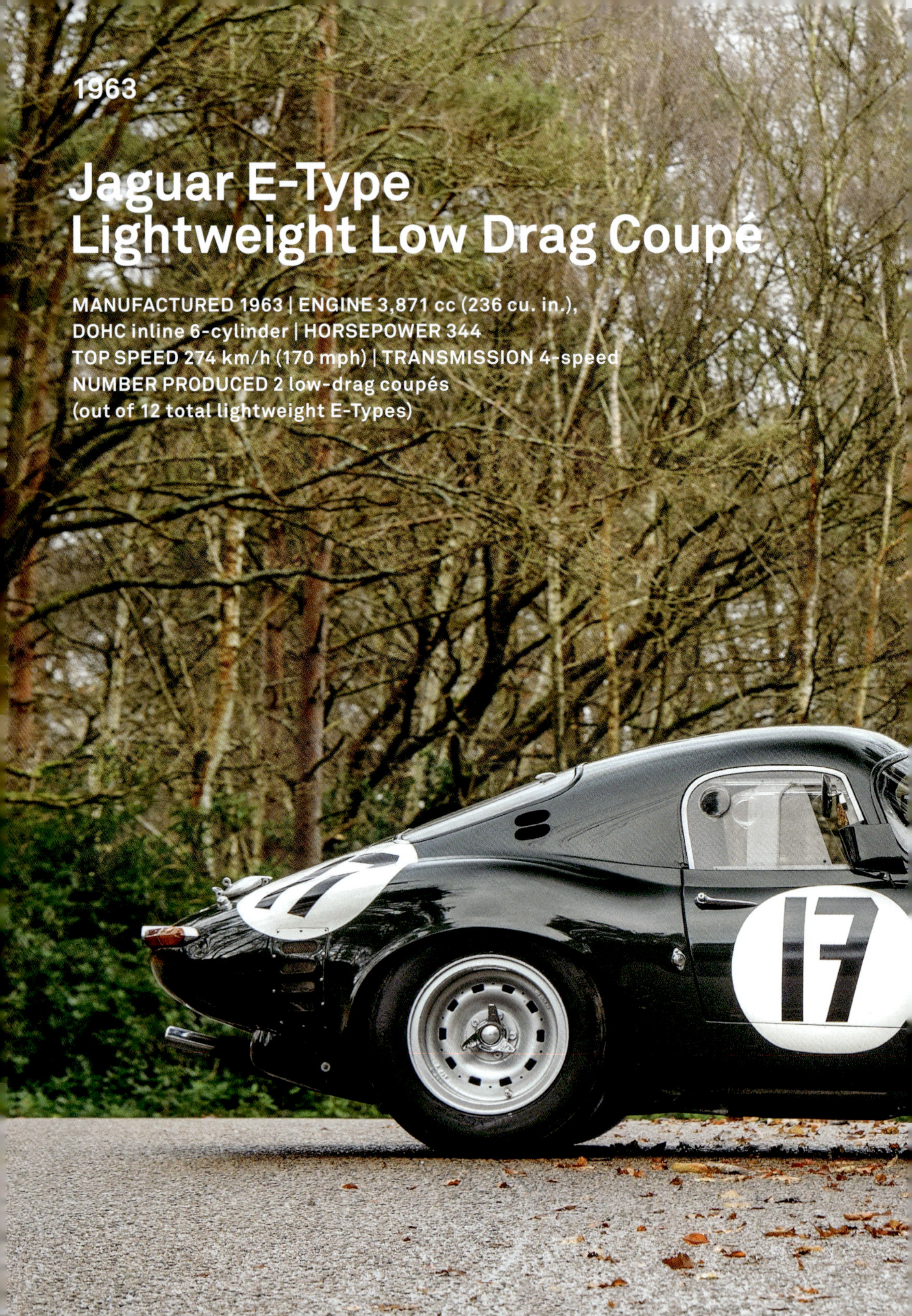

1963

Jaguar E-Type Lightweight Low Drag Coupé

MANUFACTURED 1963 | ENGINE 3,871 cc (236 cu. in.), DOHC inline 6-cylinder | HORSEPOWER 344
TOP SPEED 274 km/h (170 mph) | TRANSMISSION 4-speed
NUMBER PRODUCED 2 low-drag coupés (out of 12 total lightweight E-Types)

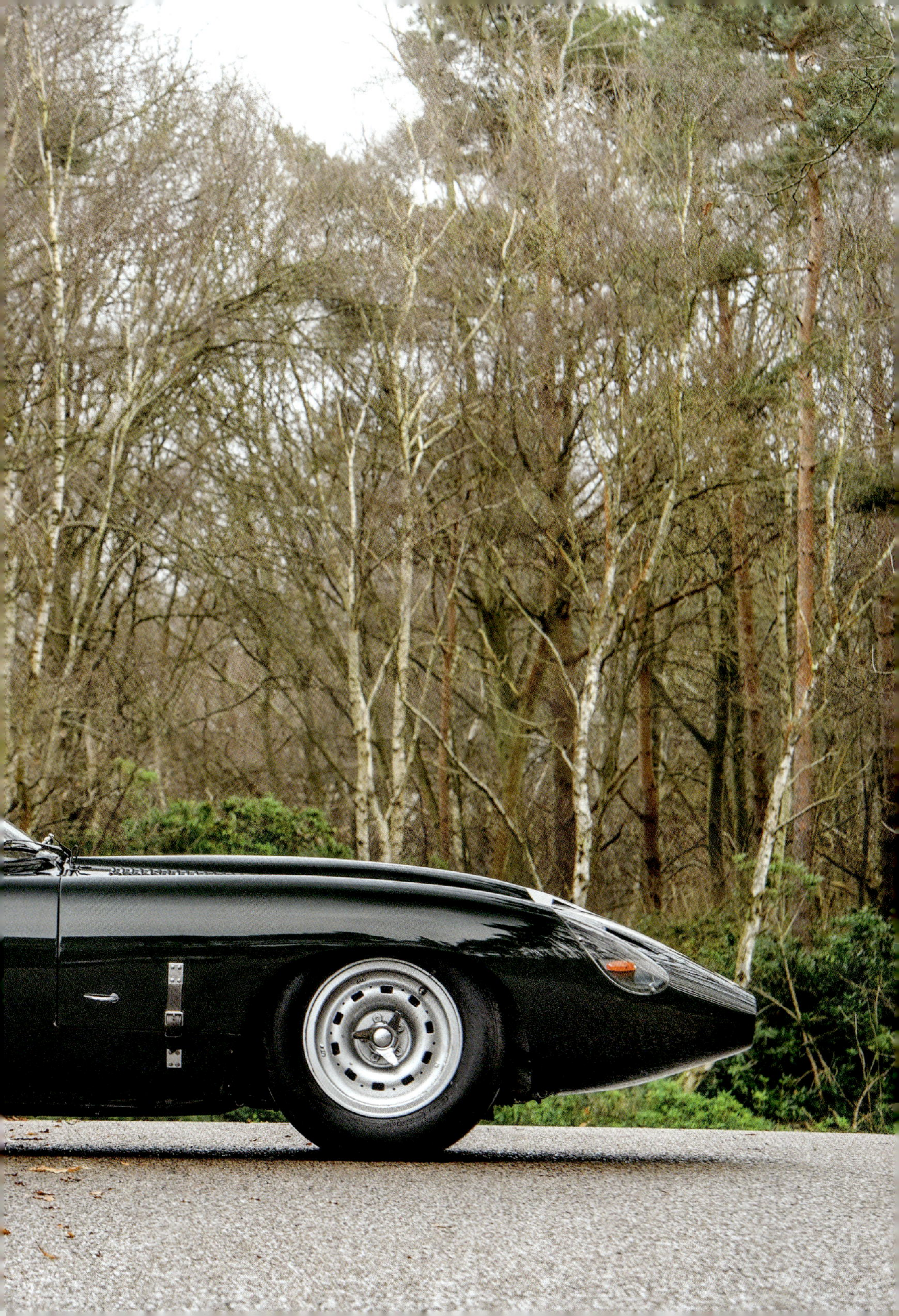

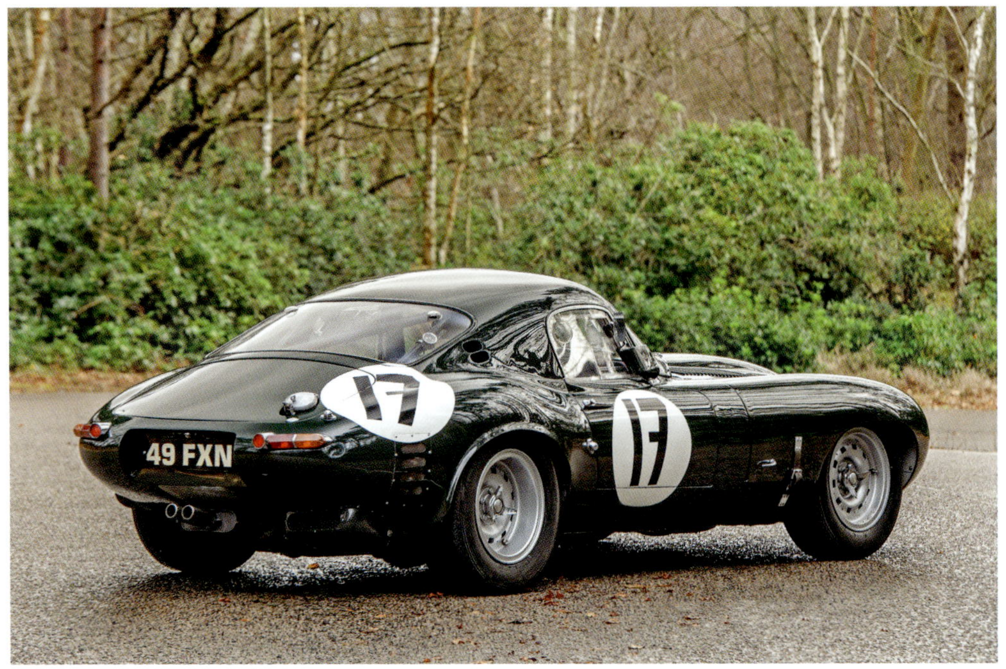

One of the most beautiful sports cars ever produced, the Jaguar E-Type encapsulates in its sensuous curves and flowing lines a quintessentially British approach to engineering and design that is shaped by function, rather than governed by it. Tempering a sense of modern purposefulness with a craft sensibility, this model had an engaging emotive quality that set it apart from its contemporaries. The iconic E-Type was famously designed by Malcolm Sayer who studied at the Department of Aeronautical and Automotive Engineering at Loughborough University, before working for the Bristol Aeroplane Company during World War II. While there, Sayer honed his knowledge of aerodynamics, which he then put to good use designing beautiful, fast cars when he joined Jaguar in 1951. His tenure at the company would become legendary and resulted in a series of exceptional cars. Shortly after his arrival, he developed the first postwar British racing car capable of challenging the likes of Ferrari and Mercedes. This model was the groundbreaking C-Type (see p. 102), which went on to win the 24 Hours of Le Mans in 1951 and 1953.

Sayer's follow up car was the equally competitive D-Type (see p. 144), which thanks to its innovative lightweight monocoque body was victorious at Le Mans in 1955, 1956 and 1957. Sayer then went on to create an evolution of the D-Type: the Jaguar E2A prototype racer,

Above & opposite: Only 12 aluminum-bodied lightweight competition E-Types were constructed by Jaguar. Of these, just two were equipped with modified bodywork to reduce drag. The car shown here, (chassis no. S850663), which is known by its registration, 49 FXN, is one of these rare feline beasts, which was uniquely modified with a roof section created by Dr. Samir Klat that featured a broader, flatter and higher rear in order to further reduce drag as well as lift.

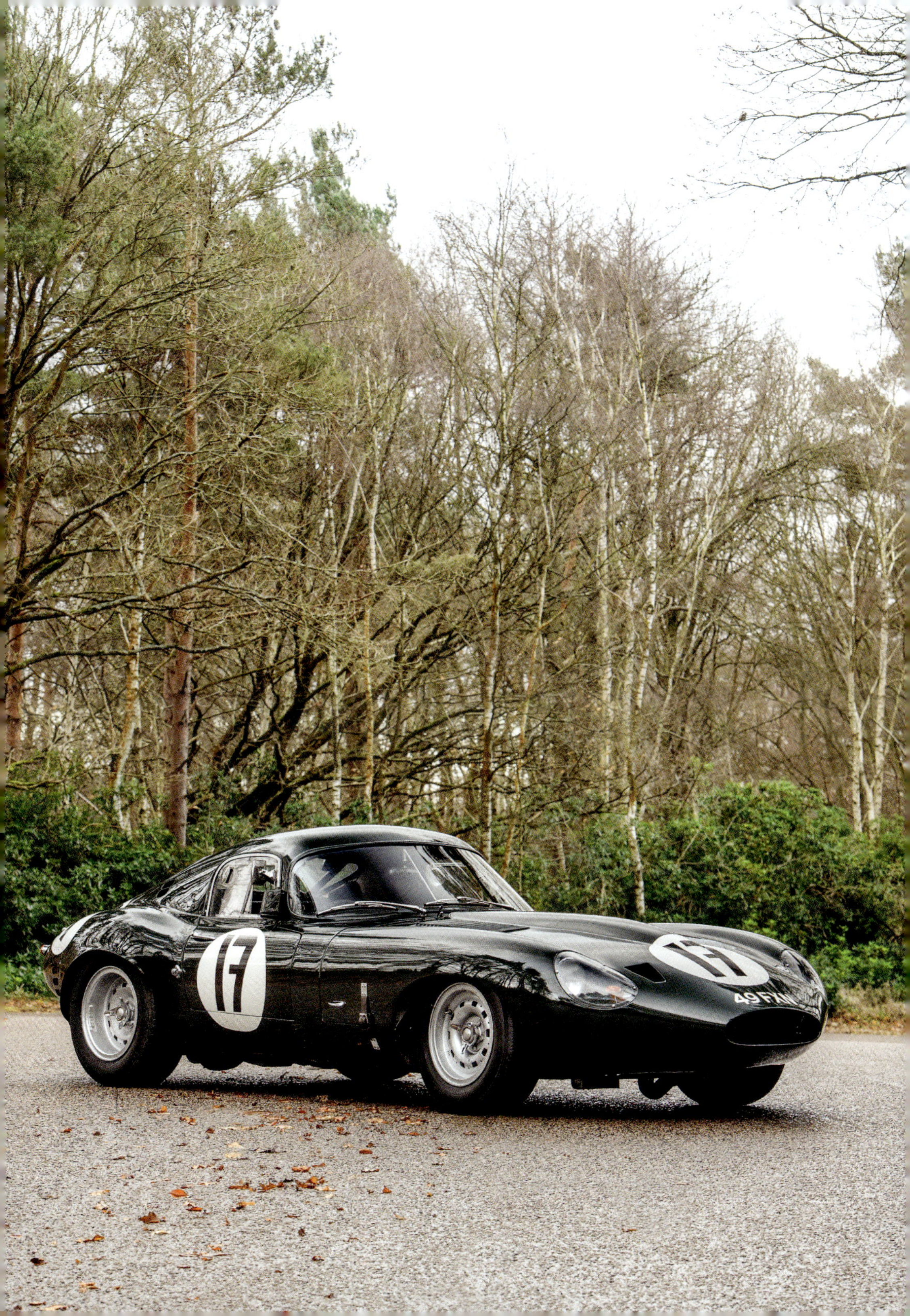
17

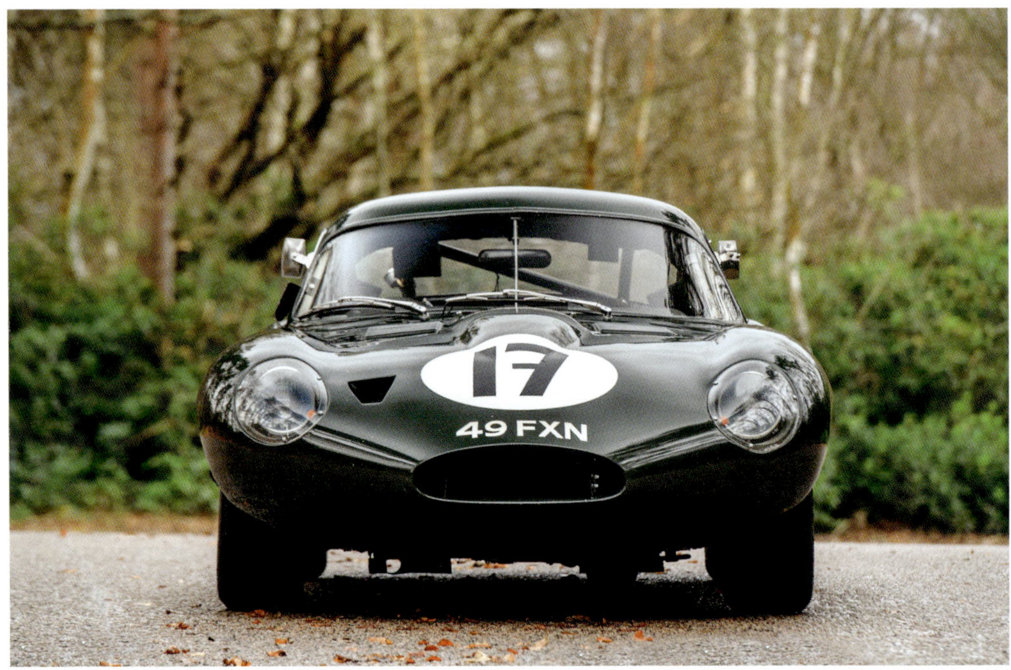

which was designed to meet the new 1960 sports car regulations that set minimum heights for both cars and their windscreens. This last stipulation meant the use of a larger windscreen than the one used on its predecessor, which changed the aerodynamics of the car completely. In order to maximize aerodynamic efficiency, Sayer elongated the car's nose by six inches, which gave it that distinctive E-Type look. The E2A prototype, which was ordered by privateer Briggs Cunningham to compete at the 1960 24 Hours of Le Mans, was the evolutionary bridge between the earlier D-Type racer and the later production E-Type. Driven by Dan Gurney and Walt Hansgen, it unfortunately retired on lap 89 with a blown head gasket.

A year later in 1961, the E-Type, which like its predecessors had a mathematically precise aerodynamic form, caused a sensation when it was unveiled at the Geneva Motor Show. It employed a similar monocoque construction to the D-Type, utilizing 20-gauge sheet steel in conjunction with a tubular steel subframe in order to support its powerful 3.8-liter straight-six engine, as well as its gearbox and suspension system. Its final drive assembly unit, by contrast, was bolted onto the rear of its bodyshell using rubber blocks. This model's racing potential was not lost on a number of privateers and as a result 12 aluminum-bodied lightweight competition E-Types were specially created. Of these, only two were equipped with modified bodywork to reduce drag. The car shown here (chassis no. S850663) which is known by its registration, 49 FXN, is one of these rare feline beasts. In advance of the 1963 season this E-Type Lightweight, which was jointly owned by Peter Lumsden and Peter Sargent, was race-prepped by Jaguar. Already heavily modified, it was now given another slew of upgrades devised by the gifted young engineer, Dr. Samir Klat.

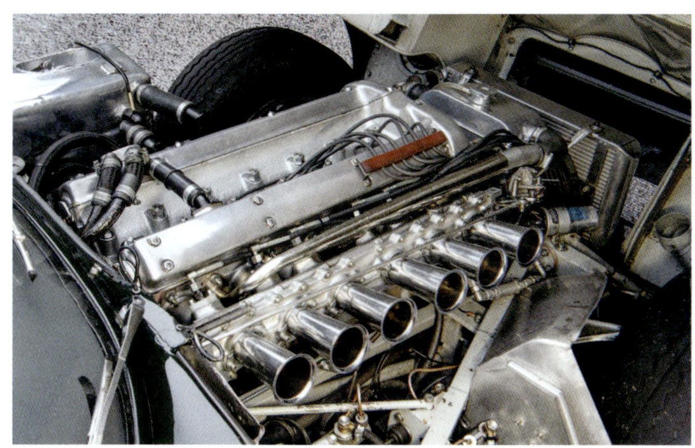

Left & below: Details of Jaguar E-Type Lightweight Low Drag Coupé 3,871 cc (236 cu. in.), direct fuel-injected DOHC inline six-cylinder engine. This was an all-alloy tuned version of the XK engine developed for the D-Type with an asymmetrical 35/40 cylinder head and dry-sump.

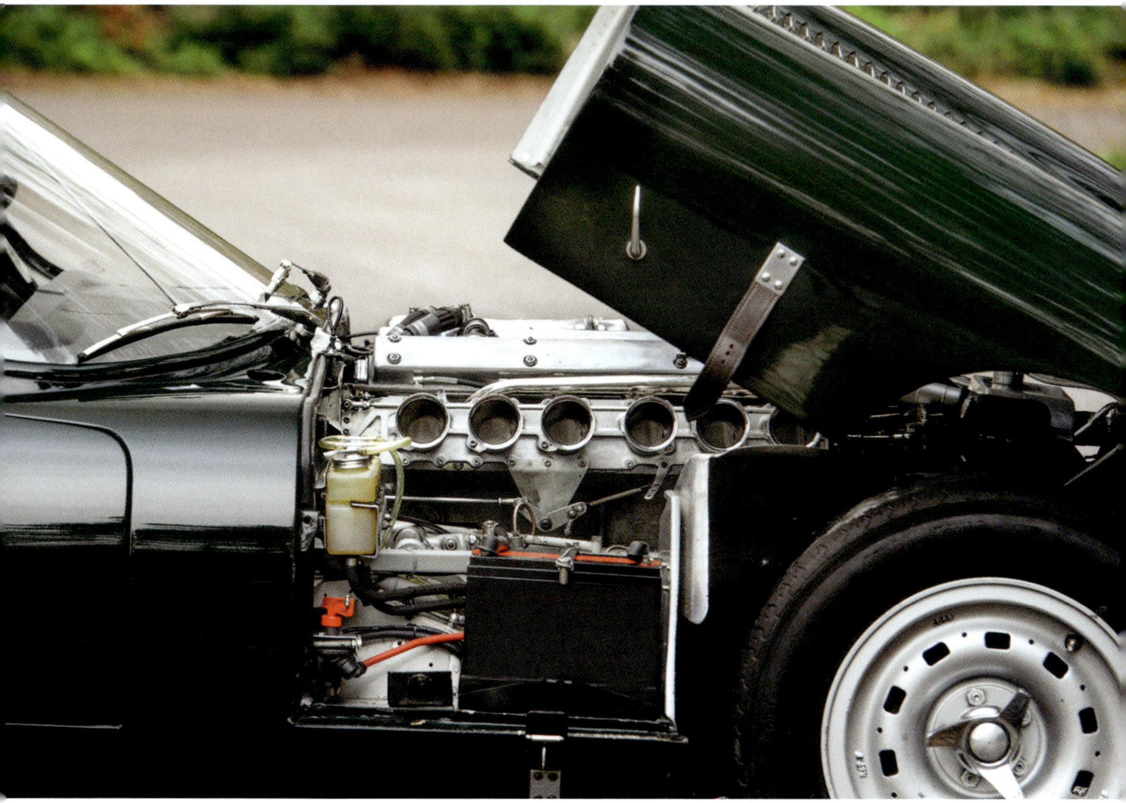

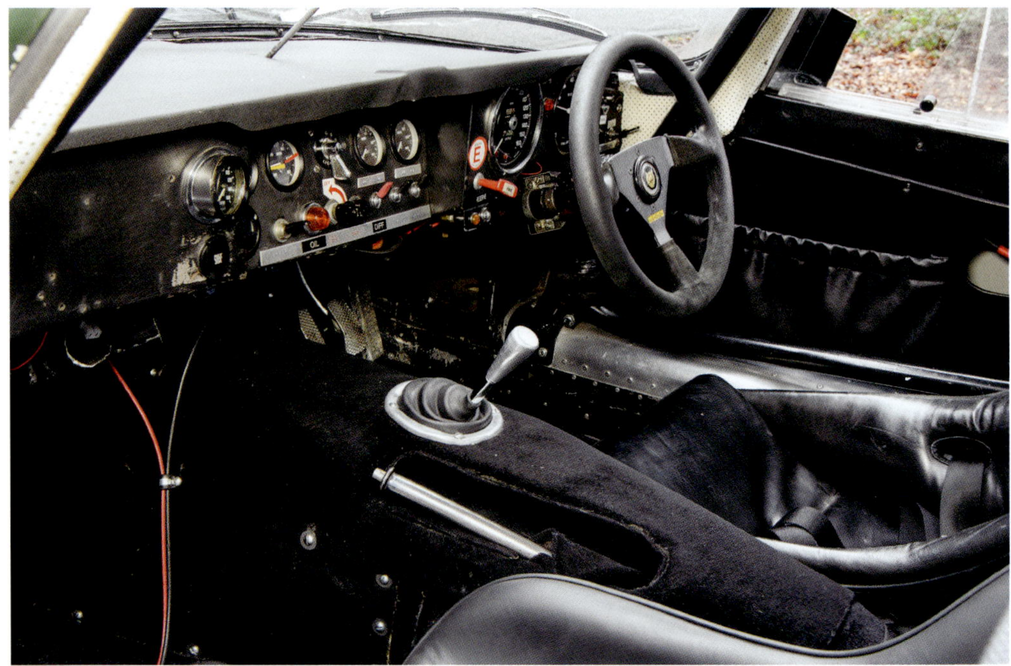

The resultant 49 FXN had its first outing in 1963 at the 1,000 km of Nürburgring, piloted by its owner-drivers. While battling it out in fourth place, Lumsden lost control on the wet circuit and unceremoniously left the track. He was OK, but 49 FXN less so.

The car was immediately sent back to Jaguar and rebuilt so it could compete for the rest the season. As a result even more modifications were implemented, including a new roof section created by Klat that featured a broader, flatter and higher rear that reduced drag as well as lift. As a way of refining its form during testing, little pieces of yarn were tied to this new element, so when the car was driven it could be seen where it needed to be resculpted — if the strings were blown flat, the aerodynamics were working. To reduce blanking in its air intake, Klat also lengthened the car's nose and reduced the size of the inlet aperture, which again resulted in less drag and lift. The suspension was also overhauled by being rigidly mounted using Rose joints, while its engine was upgraded with, among other things, new camshafts. By 1964, the car had been completely souped up and in its new guise reappeared for the Sussex Trophy at Goodwood in 1964, where it placed seventh. It then competed in the 1,000 km of Nürburgring, where due to clutch issues it placed at the very back of the pack. At Le Mans, however, the car showed its mettle early in the race — at the four-hour mark it was placed 16th overall. It also clocked up 174 mph (280 km/h) on the Mulsanne straight, before a faulty gearbox forced it to retire. And although a victory remained elusive during the rest of the season, just competing in this golden period of GT racing is enough to make the utterly gorgeous 49 FXN perhaps the most covetable Jaguar E-Type Lightweight of all time.

Opposite: Detail of 49 FXN's competition focused cockpit. With the exception of the windshield, all cockpit "glass" was Perspex.

Right: Motorway testing the new Klat roof section of the Jaguar E-Type Lightweight Low Drag Coupé (chassis no. S850663) on the M1 Motorway, 1963–64.

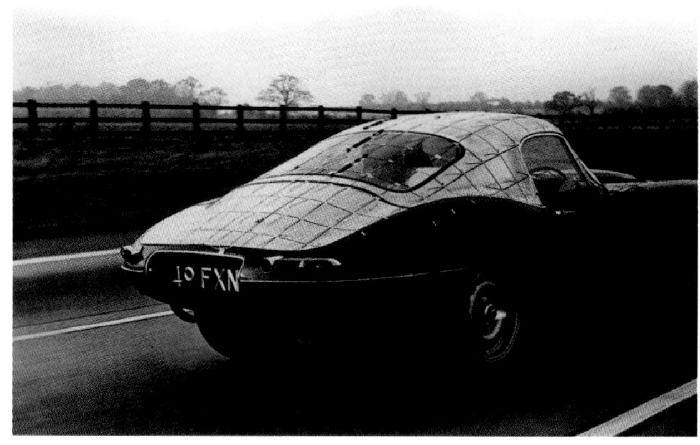

Below: The privately entered No. 17 Jaguar E-Type Lightweight Low Drag Coupé (chassis no. S850663) of Peter Lumsden and Peter Sargent leads the No. 31 Porsche System Engineering, Porsche 904/4 GTS of Gerhard Koch and Heinz Schiller and the rest of the field during the 1964 24 Hours of Le Mans. The Jaguar failed to finish the race due to a broken gearbox after eight hours.

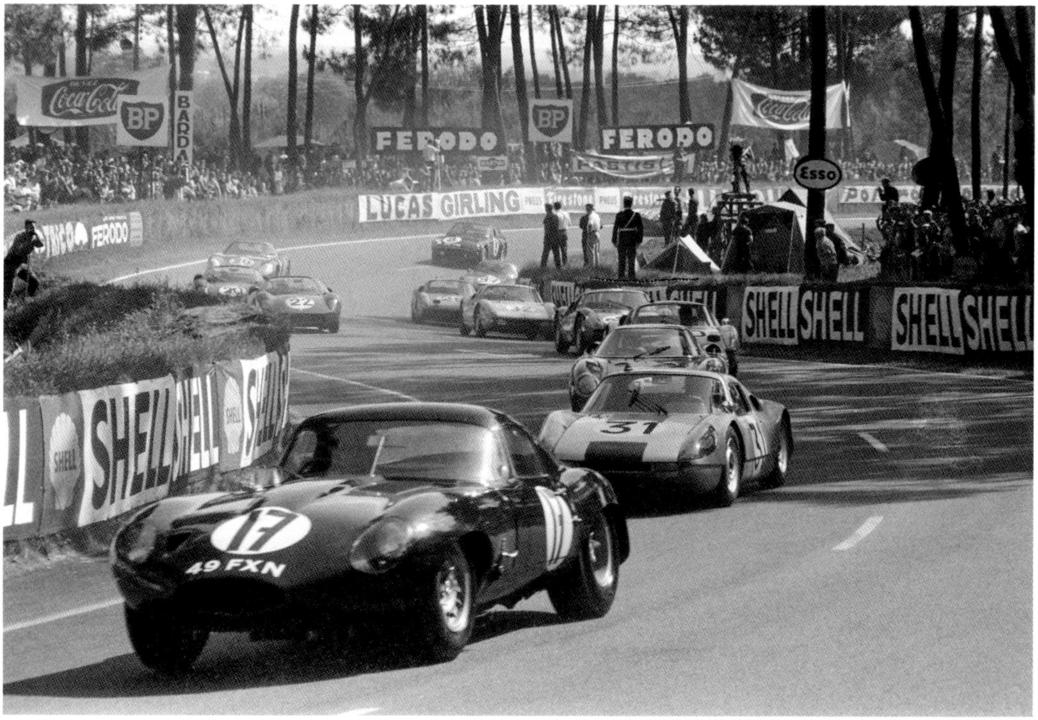

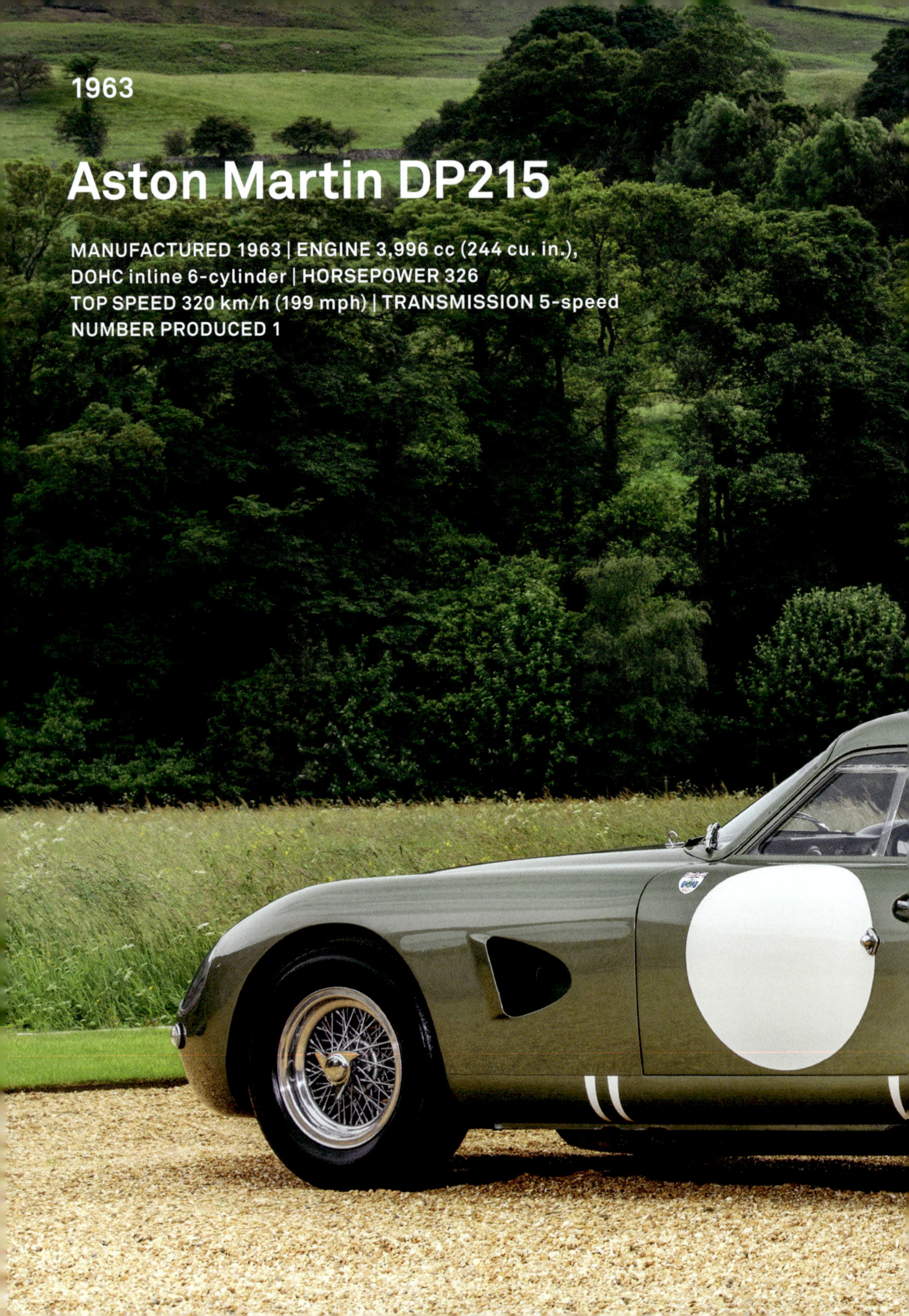

1963

Aston Martin DP215

MANUFACTURED 1963 | ENGINE 3,996 cc (244 cu. in.), DOHC inline 6-cylinder | HORSEPOWER 326
TOP SPEED 320 km/h (199 mph) | TRANSMISSION 5-speed
NUMBER PRODUCED 1

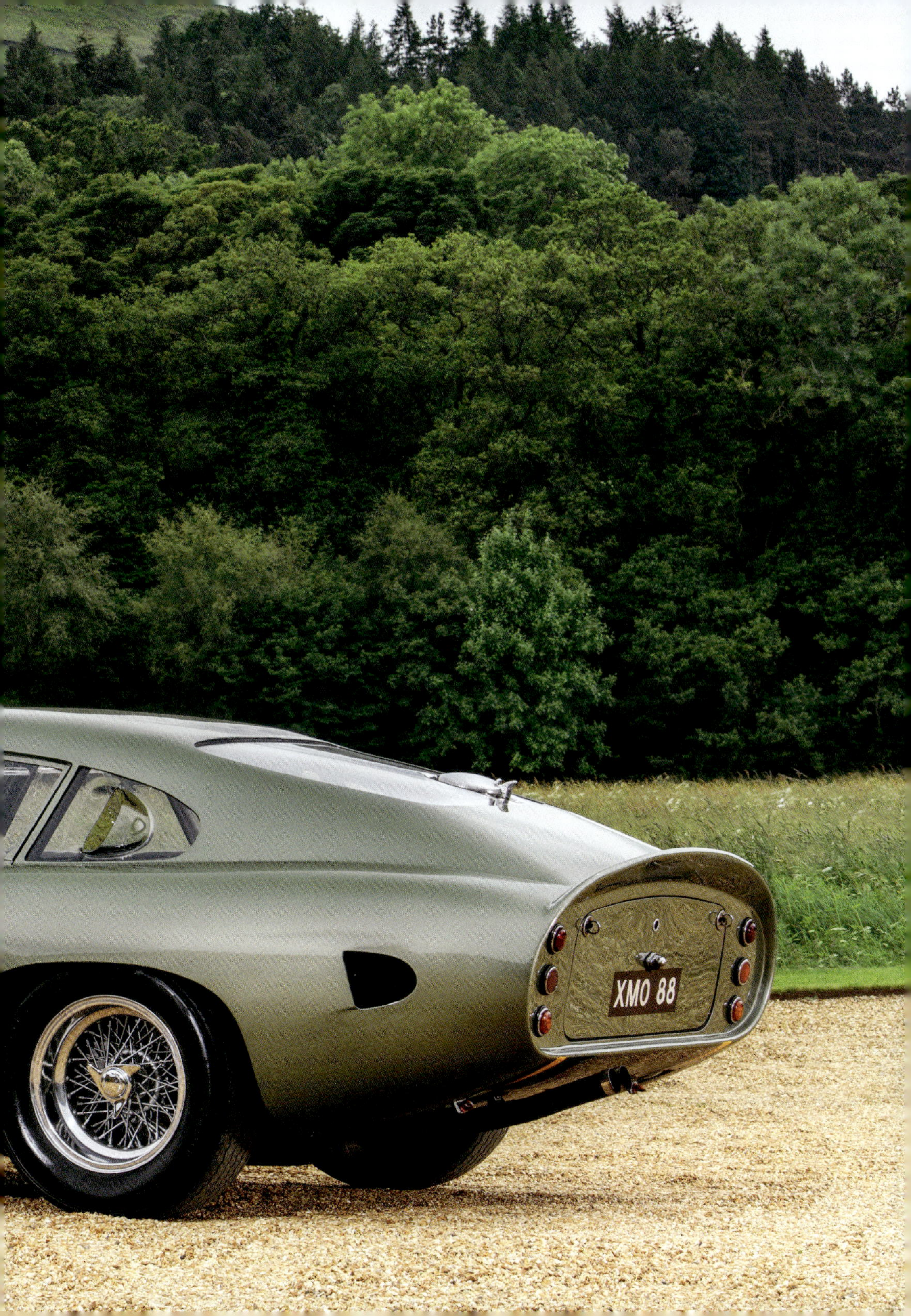
XMO 88

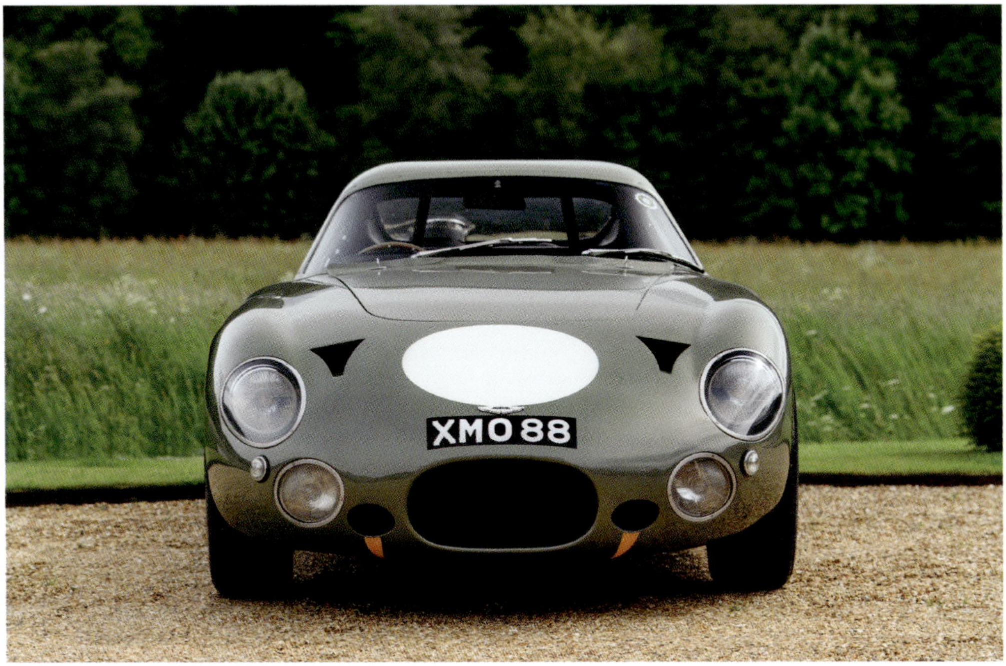

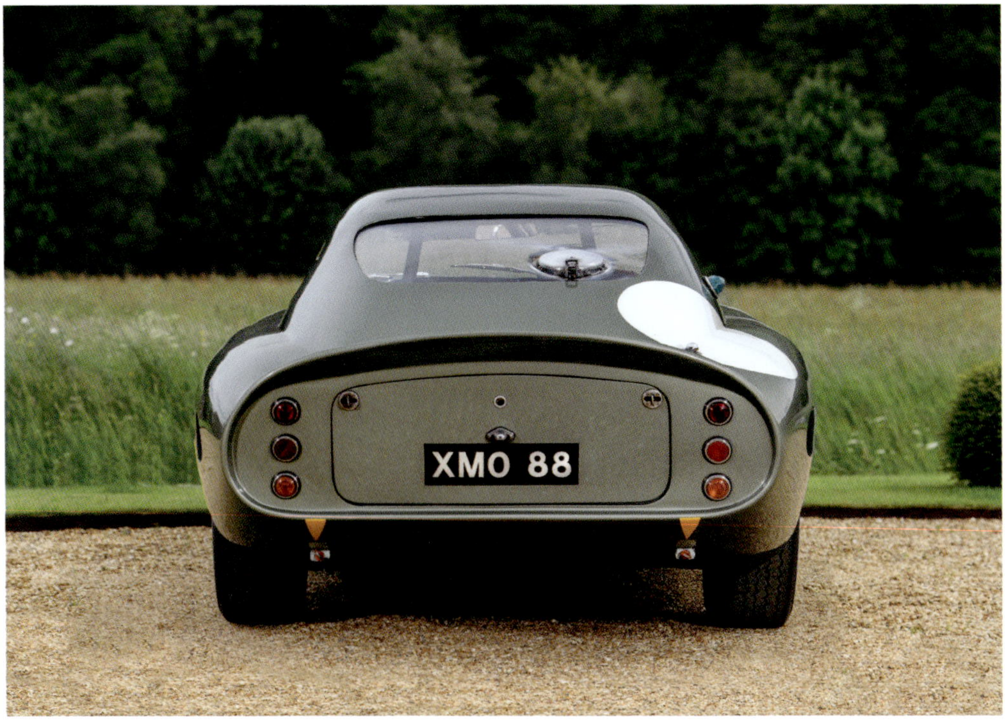

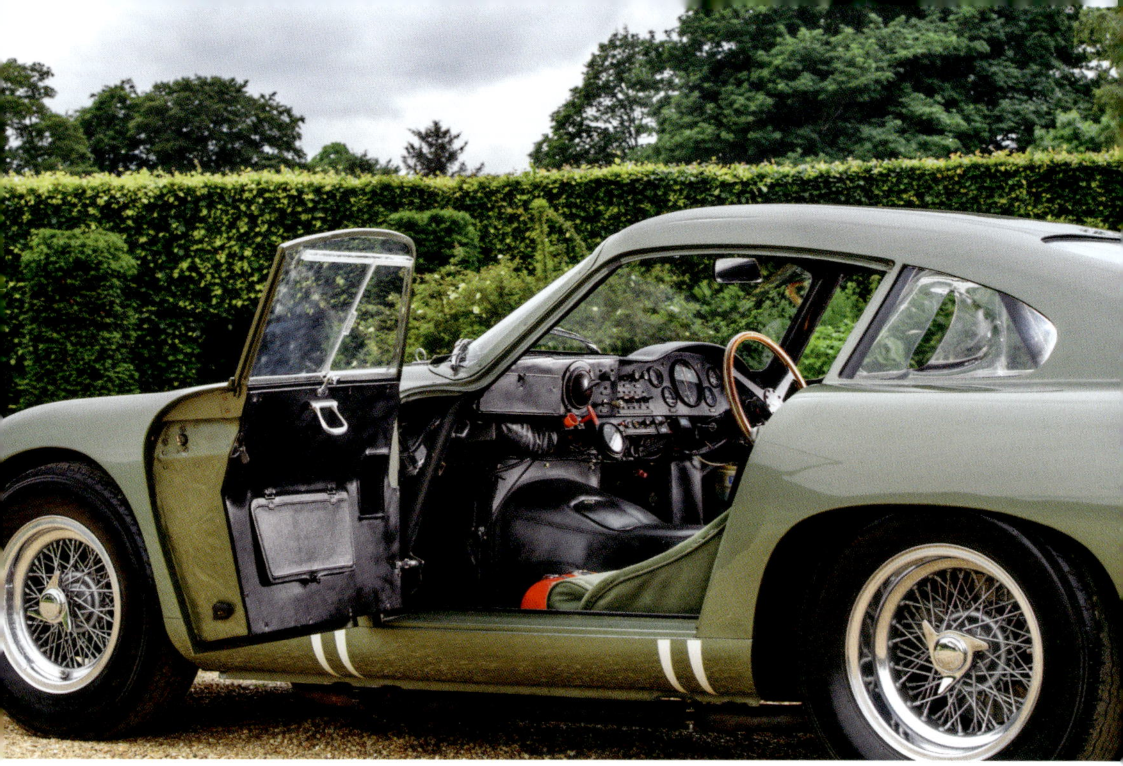

The Aston Martin DP215 Grand Touring Competition prototype is a one-of-a-kind car, and although there were plans to construct more, they never materialized — thus, making this example exceptionally desirable. As any Aston Martin devotee will be able to tell you, after winning the World Sportscar Championship in 1959, following victories with the DBR1 (see p. 174) at Le Mans, the RAC Tourist Trophy, and the Nürburgring 1,000 km, the then-owner of Aston Martin, David Brown, decided to withdraw the company from sports car racing. The reason being Brown, buoyant from his GT successes, wanted Aston's race department to concentrate its efforts on the continuing development of cars for Formula 1 competition. The resultant DBR4 and DBR5, however, were not up to the challenges of this highly competitive race category and after a disappointing single season Aston's works racing department was closed. This did not mean that the marque stopped producing racing cars, but constructed them for privateers instead of its own team.

Not having to oversee a works team, now meant David Brown could focus on the production of road cars, which is exactly what he did with the DB4 GT (see p. 254). As RM Sotheby's explains, "It was not long, however, before the Aston Martin dealers on the continent were begging for a return to Works [GT] racing. Their thinking being, rightly so, that factory competition helps sell cars — and so David Brown approved what would become the first of what would eventually come to be four "Project cars" — sports car racing vehicles all developed from the DB4 GT chassis." The first Design Project prototype was the DP212. Completed within five months, it featured a stunning streamlined body made of a lightweight magnesium/aluminum alloy, which had been aerodynamically sculpted

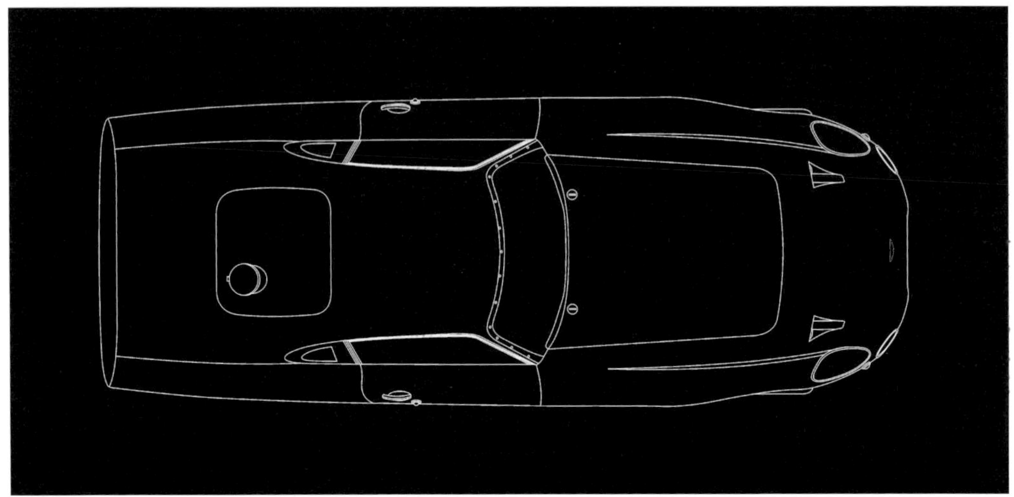

Above: Drawing of plan view of the Aston Martin DP215 Grand Touring Competition Prototype.

to handle the high-speed challenges of Le Mans. When Graham Hill and Richie Ginther drove the car in 1962 at Le Mans, however, it experienced serious stability issues due to a rear-lift problem, before an oil pump pipe fracture forced it to retire. To mitigate its rear lift problem, the car was subsequently fitted with a new Kamm tail spoiler, and its nose was extended and lowered. Crucially, these tweaks informed the development of Aston's later Design Project cars that were unveiled in 1963. These included two DP214s, which had drilled chassis to lighten their weight and engines shunted eight inches (20 cm) rearward in an attempt to solve the rear-lift problem.

These experimental cars were then followed by the unique DP215, shown here, which was likewise unveiled in 1963. This full-out competition car was Aston's works entry for that year's 24 Hours of Le Mans race. It fully showcased the extraordinary skill and dedication of the marque's engineering team, led by its chief engineer, Ted Cutting, who was responsible for its design. The car's development time, like that of its predecessors, was extremely short. Aston Martin's team manager John Wyer sent a detailed design brief to the company's engineering department in March 1963, giving them only three months before the car needed to be ready for Le Mans. As RM Sotheby's notes, "Though very similar in looks to the two prior DP214s, DP215 is a very different car under the skin. Originally created as a vehicle for Tadek Marek's yet-to-be-developed V8, for the 1963 season, DP215 was equipped with a 4-liter version of the DP212 six-cylinder twin plug engine... Modifications to the steel box-frame chassis included allowing for the engine to be fitted a full 10 inches further back than in DP212, as well as independent rear suspension."

Unbelievably, given how many adaptations were made, DP215 was finished in time to compete in the 1963 Le Mans race, where it was co-piloted by Phil Hill and Lucien Bianchi.

During practice, while being driven by Hill, DP215 became the first car ever to break the 186 mph (300 km/h) barrier down the Mulsanne Straight, which Cutting later claimed to be the proudest moment of his career. But that was not the car's top speed — during practice it clocked up an astonishing 198.6 mph (319.6 km/h). This remarkable quickness appeared to put it on a competitive footing with Ferrari's mid-engine prototypes. Indeed, it was lapping 12 seconds faster than the Ferrari 250 GTOs (see p. 264) in the GT class. Yet, this early promise was not realized in the actual race. Just two hours in, the car was forced to retire with gearbox trouble. Two weeks later, the now-repaired DP215 was entered into the GP at Reims, but again it did not manage to finish because of an over-revved engine. Shortly after this, Wyer handed in his notice, and with its engineering genius gone David Brown decided to shut down Aston's works racing team again — this time for good. All of which means that DP215 holds a very significant place in Aston Martin's history, being the last-ever factory racer from that illustrious David Brown era.

Page 293: During an 11-year restoration, which was completed in 1991, the DP215's interior was restored in similarity to the original, but with a few differences: the transmission tunnel was insulated and covered in leather, pockets were built into the doors, and a speedometer and electric fan were added.

Below: Detail of Aston Martin DP215 3,996 cc (244 cu. in.), DOHC inline six-cylinder engine with triple Weber 50 DCO carburetors. Designed by the great engineer Tadek Marek this twin spark, dry-sump engine with aluminum block and head powered what was to become the last racing car built by the factory, and the ultimate evolution of the Aston Martin GT racers.

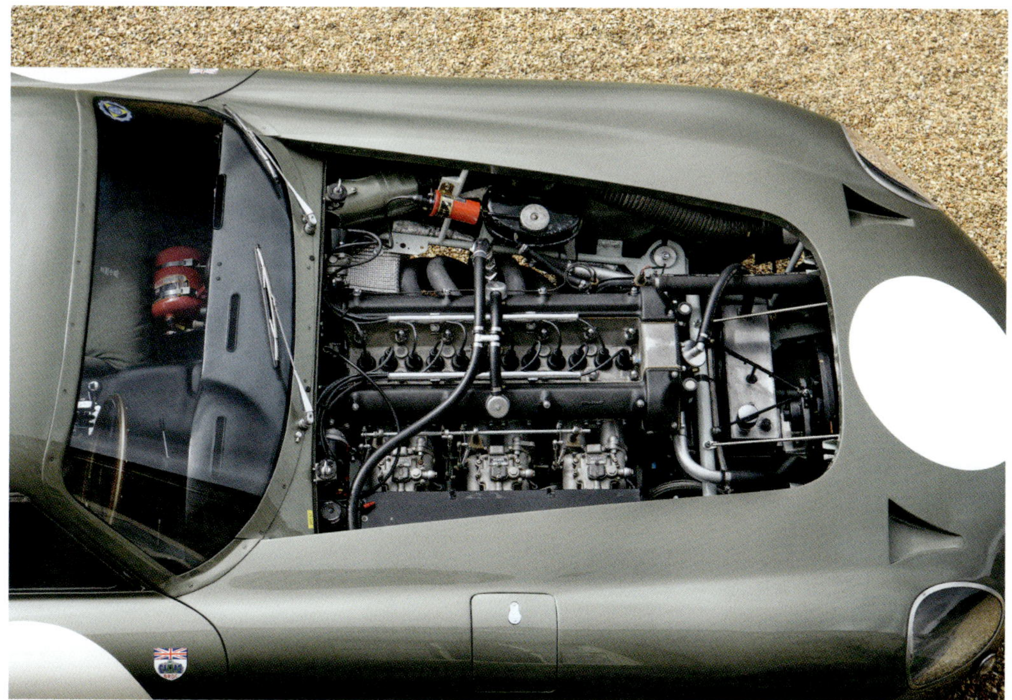

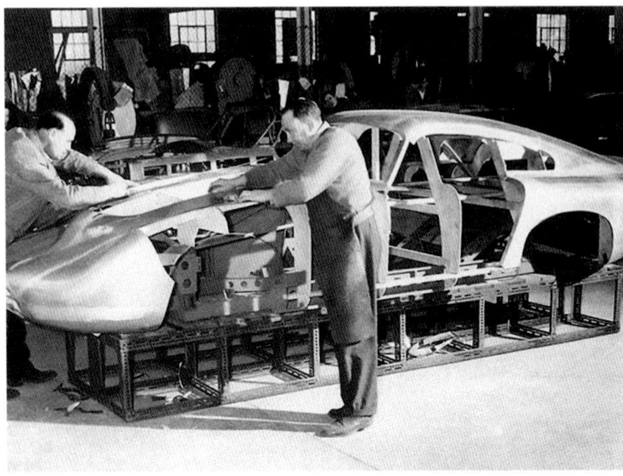

Left: Master sheet metal worker Bert Brookes, in apron, affixes the magnesium/aluminum alloy (Hiduminium) panels to DP215 in the Aston Martin factory, Newport Pagnell. This unique Works design project was specially developed to compete at Le Mans. It was the last racing car built by the factory and the ultimate evolution of the Aston Martin GT racers.

Opposite: The Phil Hill and Lucien Bianchi No. 18 Aston Martin Works DP215 leading the No. 10 Ferrari 330 TRI/LM driven by Pedro Rodriguez and Roger Penske and the rest of the field shortly after the start of the 1963 24 Hours of Le Mans. The Aston Martin failed to finish the race due to a gearbox problem after four hours.

Below: The No. 18 Aston Martin Works DP215 driven by Phil Hill and Lucien Bianchi leads the No. 10 Ferrari 330 TRI/LM driven by Pedro Rodriguez and Roger Penske and the rest of the field at the start of the 1963 24 Hours of Le Mans.

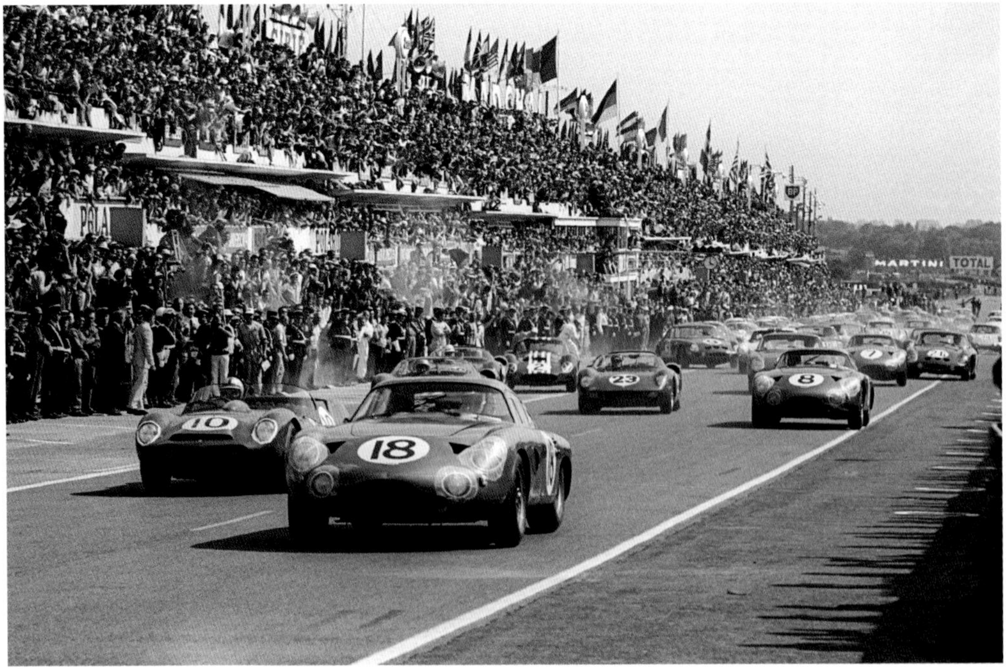

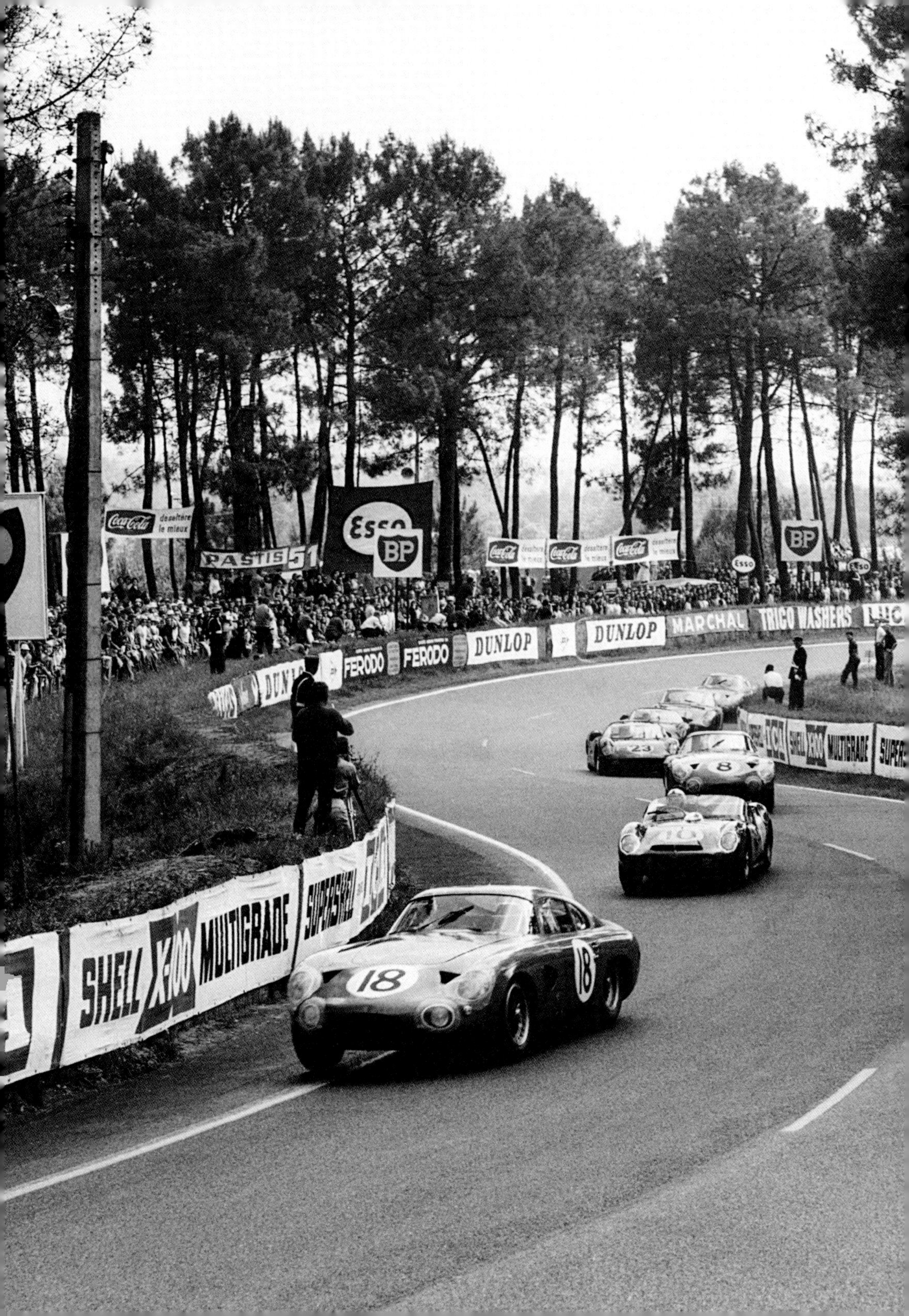
Coca-Cola
désaltère le mieux
PASTIS 51
Esso
BP
DUNLOP
MARCHAL
TRICO WASHERS
FERODO
SHELL X-100 MULTIGRADE
SUPERSHELL

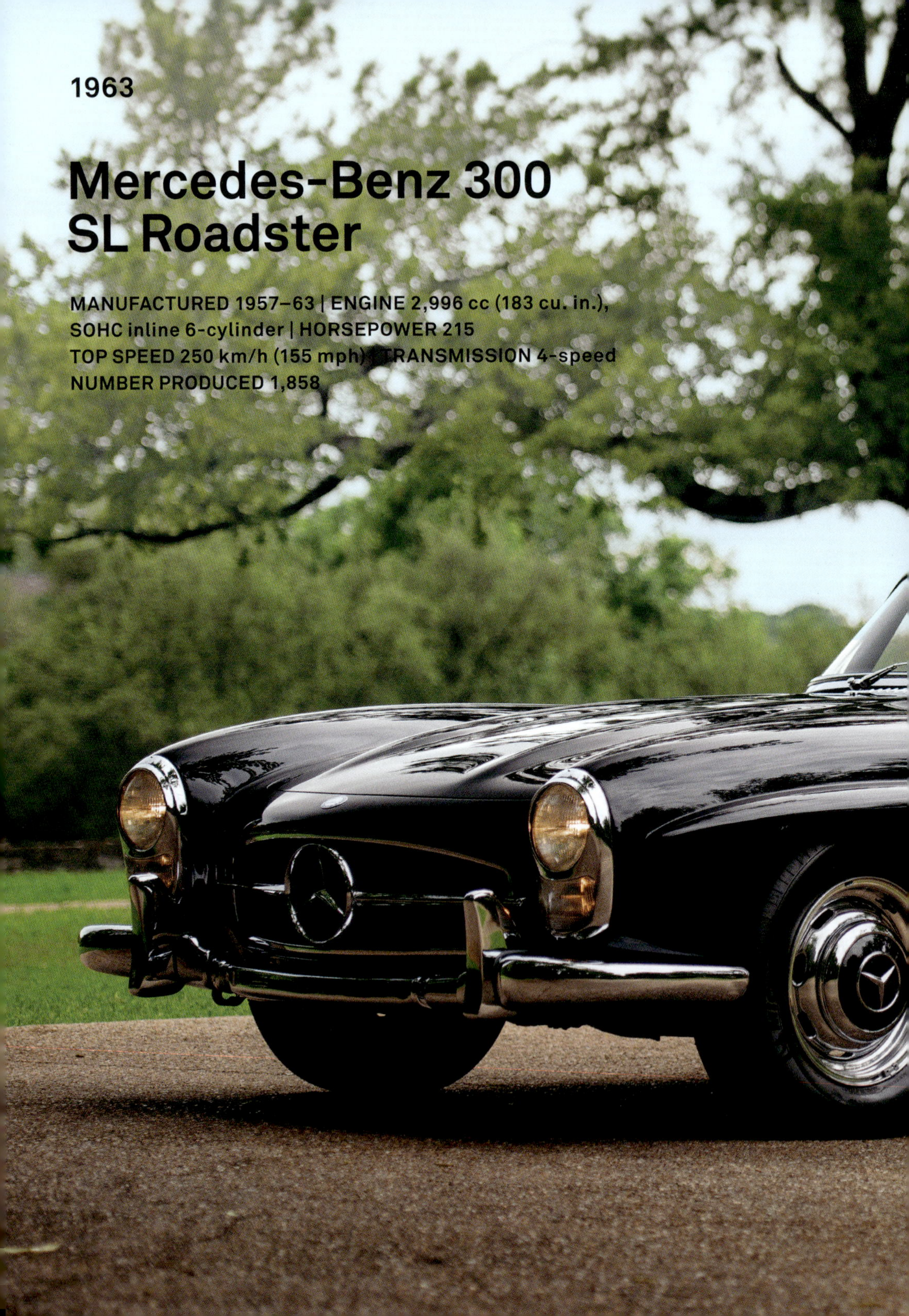

1963

Mercedes-Benz 300 SL Roadster

MANUFACTURED 1957–63 | **ENGINE** 2,996 cc (183 cu. in.), SOHC inline 6-cylinder | **HORSEPOWER** 215
TOP SPEED 250 km/h (155 mph) | **TRANSMISSION** 4-speed
NUMBER PRODUCED 1,858

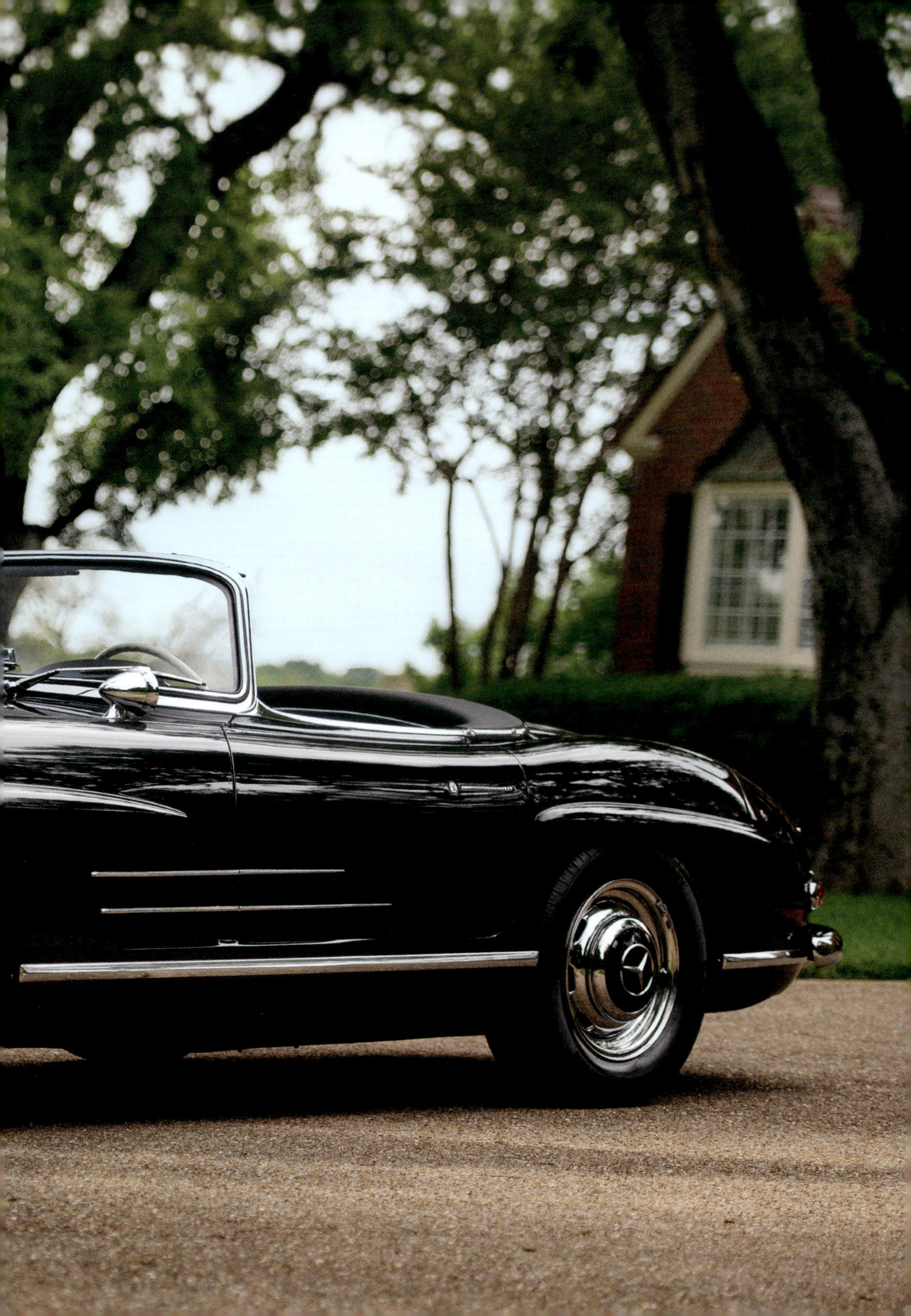

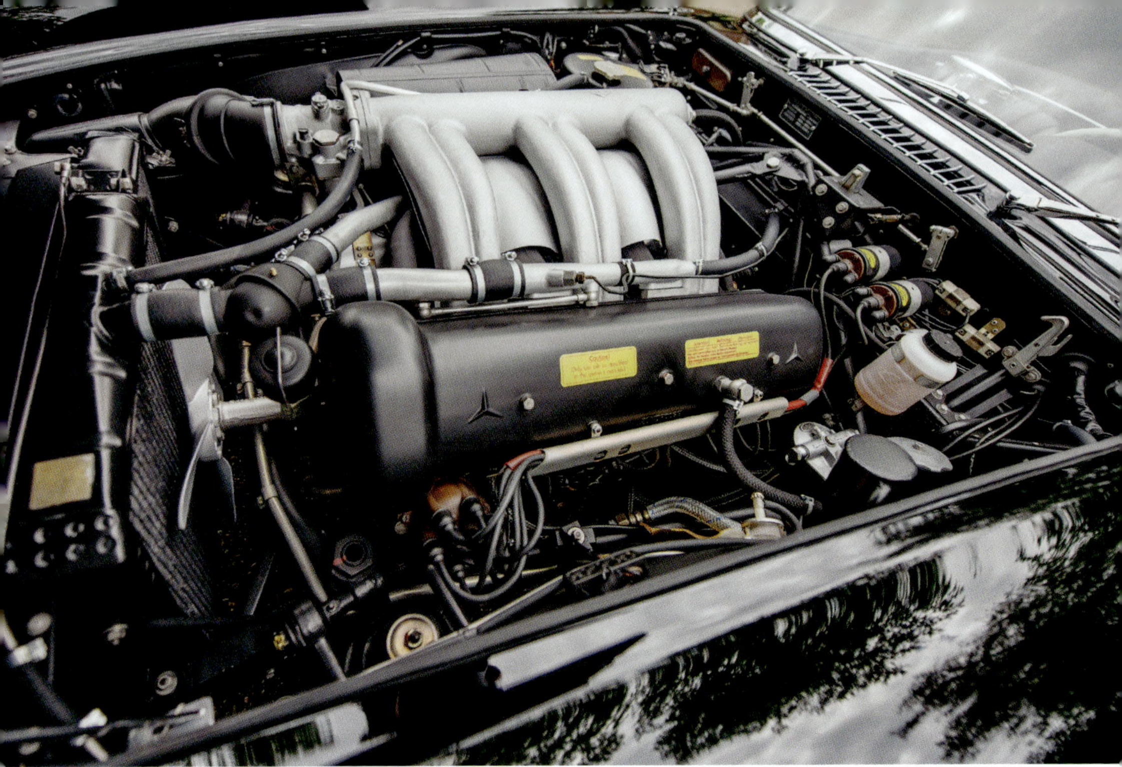

Above: Detail of Mercedes-Benz 300 SL Roadster 2,996 cc (183 cu. in.), direct fuel-injected SOHC inline six-cylinder engine.

Overleaf: Detail of the Mercedes-Benz 300 SL Roadster's luxuriously appointed interior. The very rare factory black exterior with black interior is considered the most desirable combination for this model.

In 1954, Mercedes-Benz launched its attention-grabbing 300 SL coupé — the legendary "Gullwing" with its innovative roof-hinged doors (see p. 124). Then, just three years later at the Geneva Motor Show a convertible version of the Gullwing was unveiled, testifying to Mercedes-Benz's desire to conquer the American luxury market. Indeed, it had been Max Hoffman, the marque's influential US distributor, who convinced the Mercedes-Benz management to create this roadster in the belief that demand for the 300 SL on the West Coast of America would be much greater if it could provide the thrill of top-down motoring.

Although the Gullwing was renowned for its exquisite proportions and exceptional power, it was also well-known for being quite difficult to handle. The roadster, which had the official Mercedes-Benz's designation of W 198, was an evolutionary refinement on the original 300 SL and was much easier to control. Crucially, among various upgrades, the roadster featured a new rear axle design, which with its lower pivot-point helped to reduce the Gullwing's proclivity to oversteer. Produced from 1957 to 1963, the 300 SL Roadster amply shared the high performance capabilities of its precursor, both on and off the track, but in a more driver-friendly way.

As Mercedes-Benz notes, "Concealed beneath the stylish bodywork, the spaceframe remained the roadster's load-bearing structure, although it featured a number of modifications. Lower at the sides, the new frame design now made conventional front-hinged doors possible. This not only made getting into and out of the car easier, it was also a key design prerequisite for any open top vehicle." But more than this, the frame's flatter rear end, as well as a rethought fuel reservoir, allowed the spare wheel to be stowed under the floor, thereby freeing up space for a small though functional trunk.

As one would expect from any Mercedes-Benz, the roadster featured an exceptional level of detailing and boasted numerous thoughtfully considered design elements, such as its special hatch behind the seats, which neatly concealed its easy-to-access soft top when it was not in use. In 1958, the company offered its customers the additional option of an easy-to-fit hardtop for use in colder weather, and in 1961 the 300 SL roadster became the marque's first production car to boast disc brakes on all four wheels, thereby helping to make it safer. It would also be the last Mercedes-Benz passenger car to have an independent frame, marking the end of an era in terms of how its cars were put together.

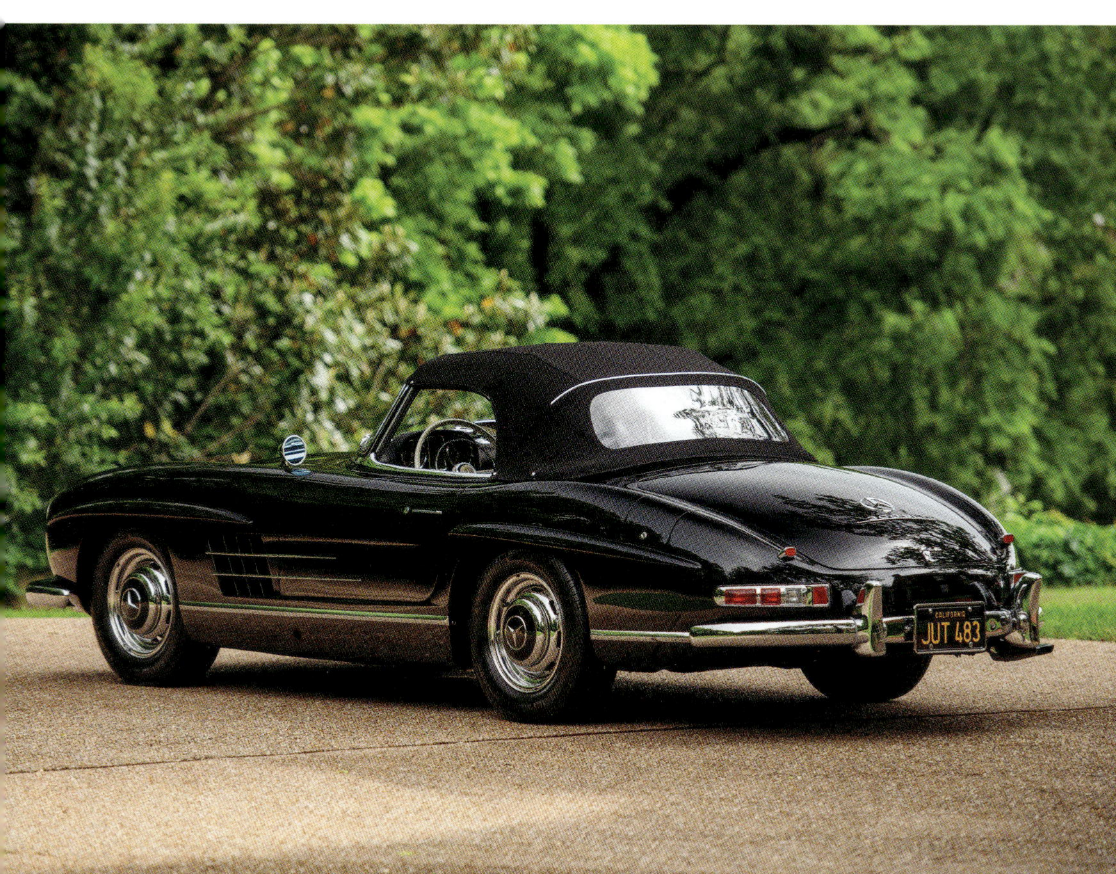

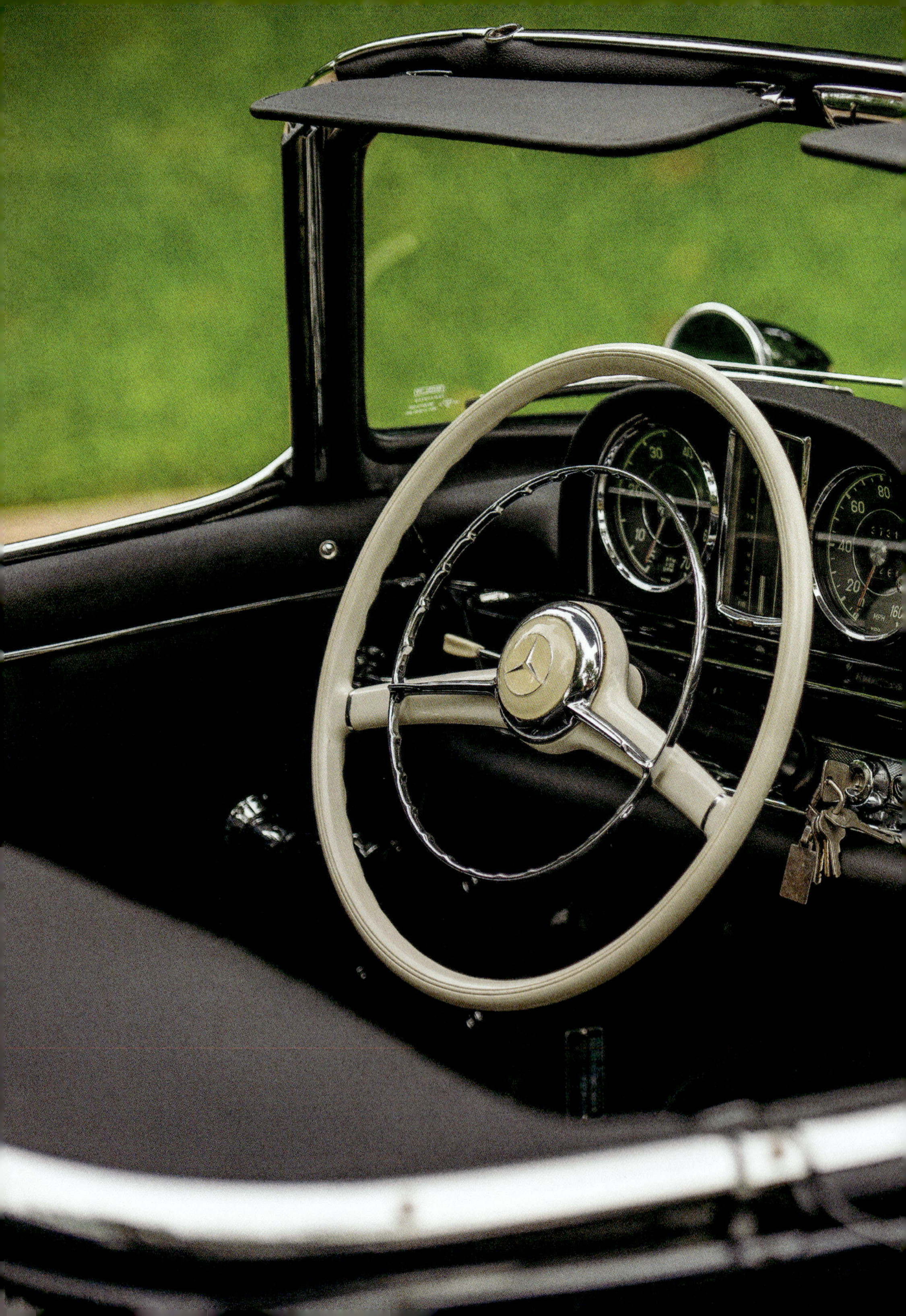

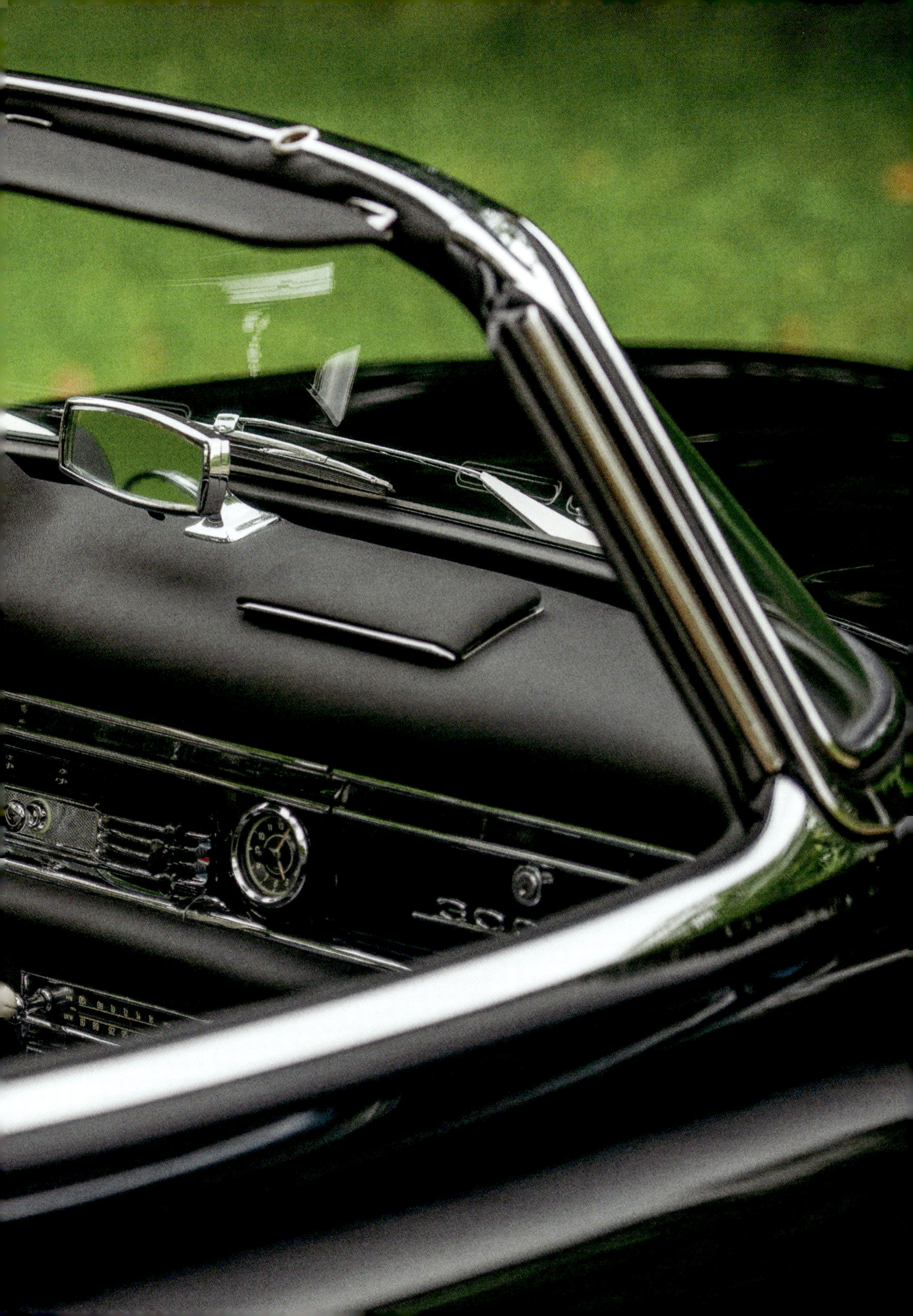

A slimmed down and lighter weight competition-bred version of this stunning roadster was also developed, the 300 SLS — standing for Super Leicht Sports (Super Light Sports). This variant was famously used by the American racing driver Paul O'Shea to win Class D of the Sports Car Club of America (SCCA) Championship by an impressive margin in 1957, after he had already won the championship in 1955 and 1956 with a 300 SL Gullwing. As for the 300 SL roadster shown here, (chassis no. 198.042.10.003116), it is a very desirable late-production example that came equipped with both disc brakes and a lightweight alloy late-model engine block. Restored to its original triple black finish, which so beautifully shows off the sensational lines of its form-follows-function design, this Teutonic stunner has spent most of its life in California — which was exactly the American Dream that Max Hoffman had envisioned for the model all those years ago.

Below: Factory photo of the Mercedes-Benz 300 SL Roadster showing the easy removal of the optional hardtop, 1958.

Opposite: 1957 Mercedes-Benz advertisement for the 300 SL Roadster with the catch phrase "Elegantly controlled power."

Overleaf: Mercedes-Benz promotional photo of the 300 SL Roadster, ca.1960.

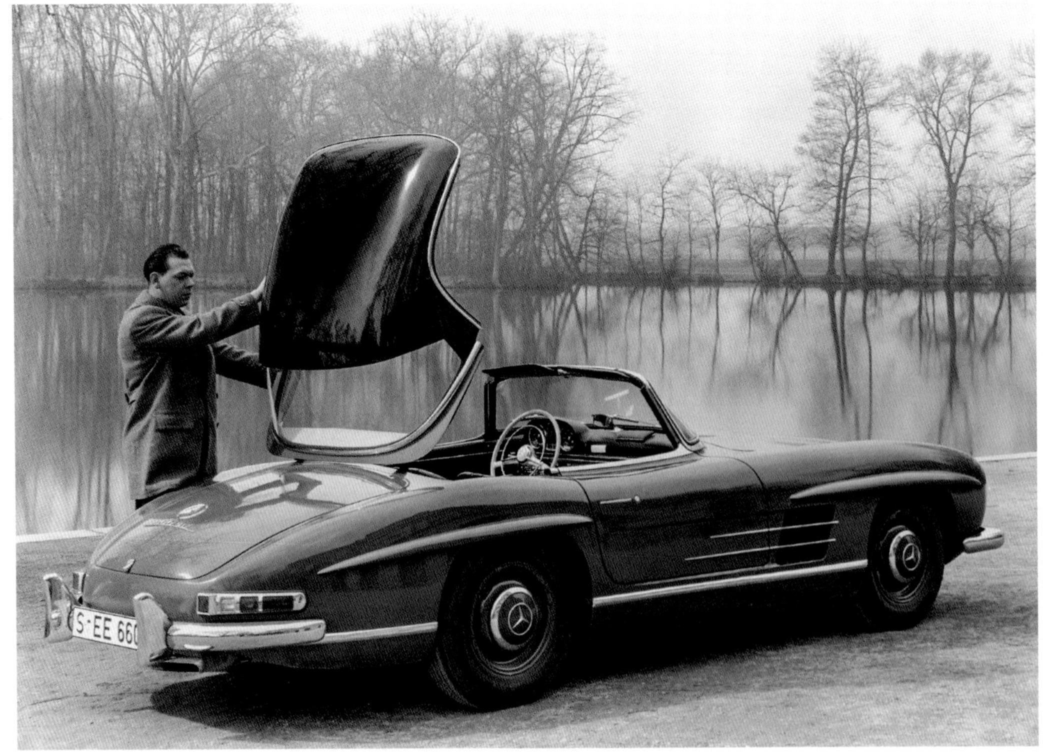

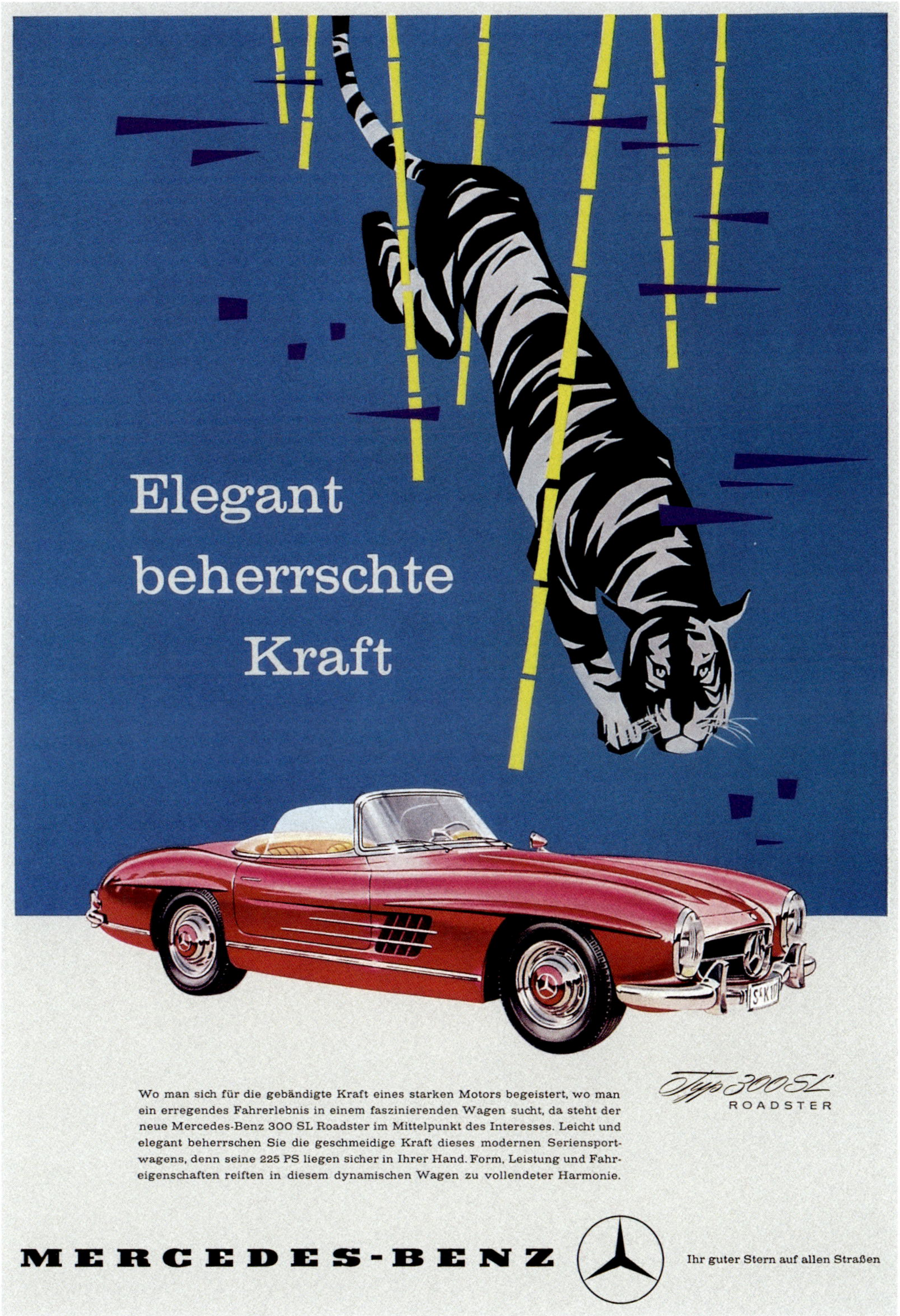

Elegant beherrschte Kraft

Typ 300 SL
ROADSTER

Wo man sich für die gebändigte Kraft eines starken Motors begeistert, wo man ein erregendes Fahrerlebnis in einem faszinierenden Wagen sucht, da steht der neue Mercedes-Benz 300 SL Roadster im Mittelpunkt des Interesses. Leicht und elegant beherrschen Sie die geschmeidige Kraft dieses modernen Seriensportwagens, denn seine 225 PS liegen sicher in Ihrer Hand. Form, Leistung und Fahreigenschaften reiften in diesem dynamischen Wagen zu vollendeter Harmonie.

MERCEDES-BENZ

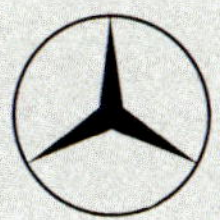

Ihr guter Stern auf allen Straßen

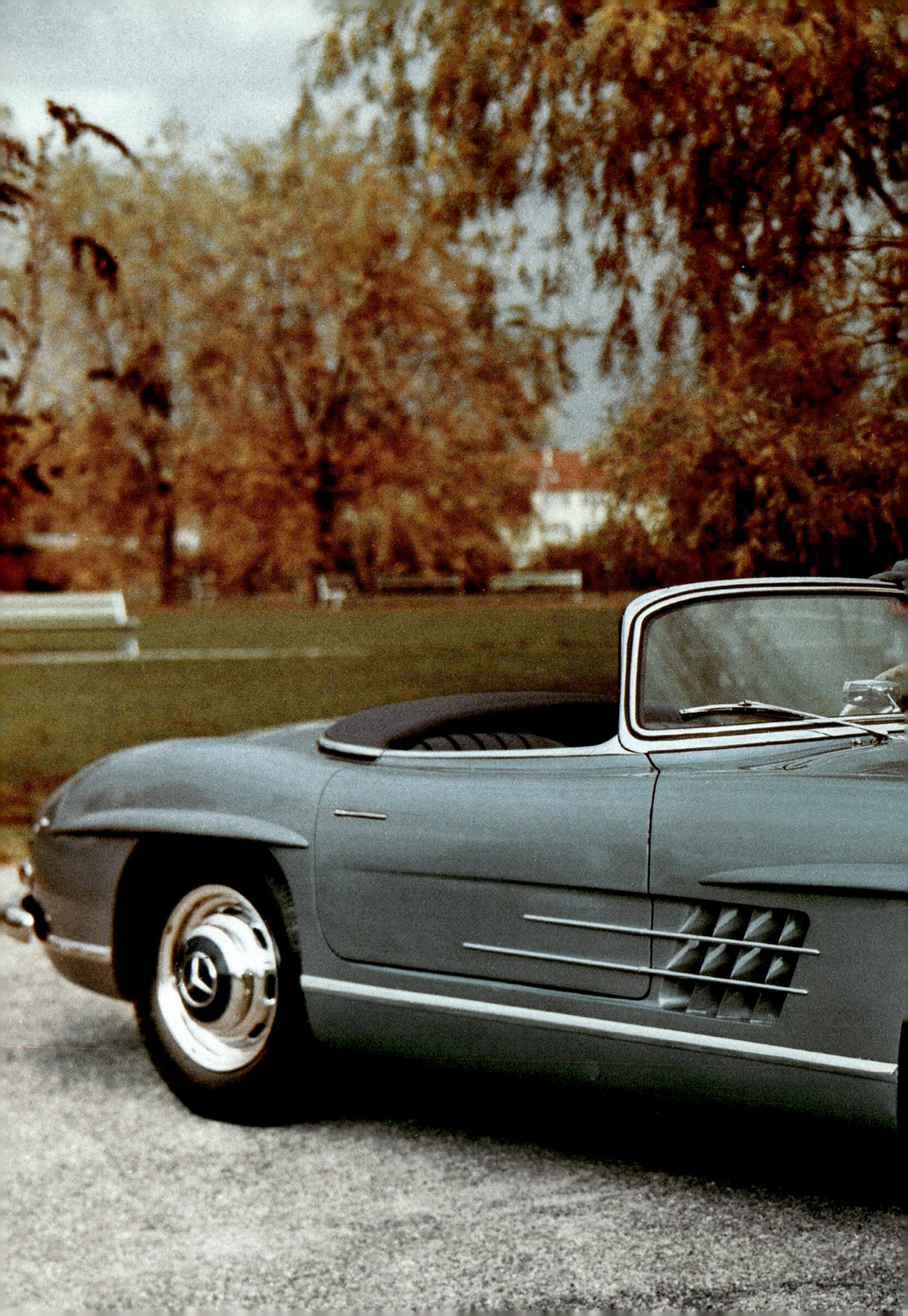

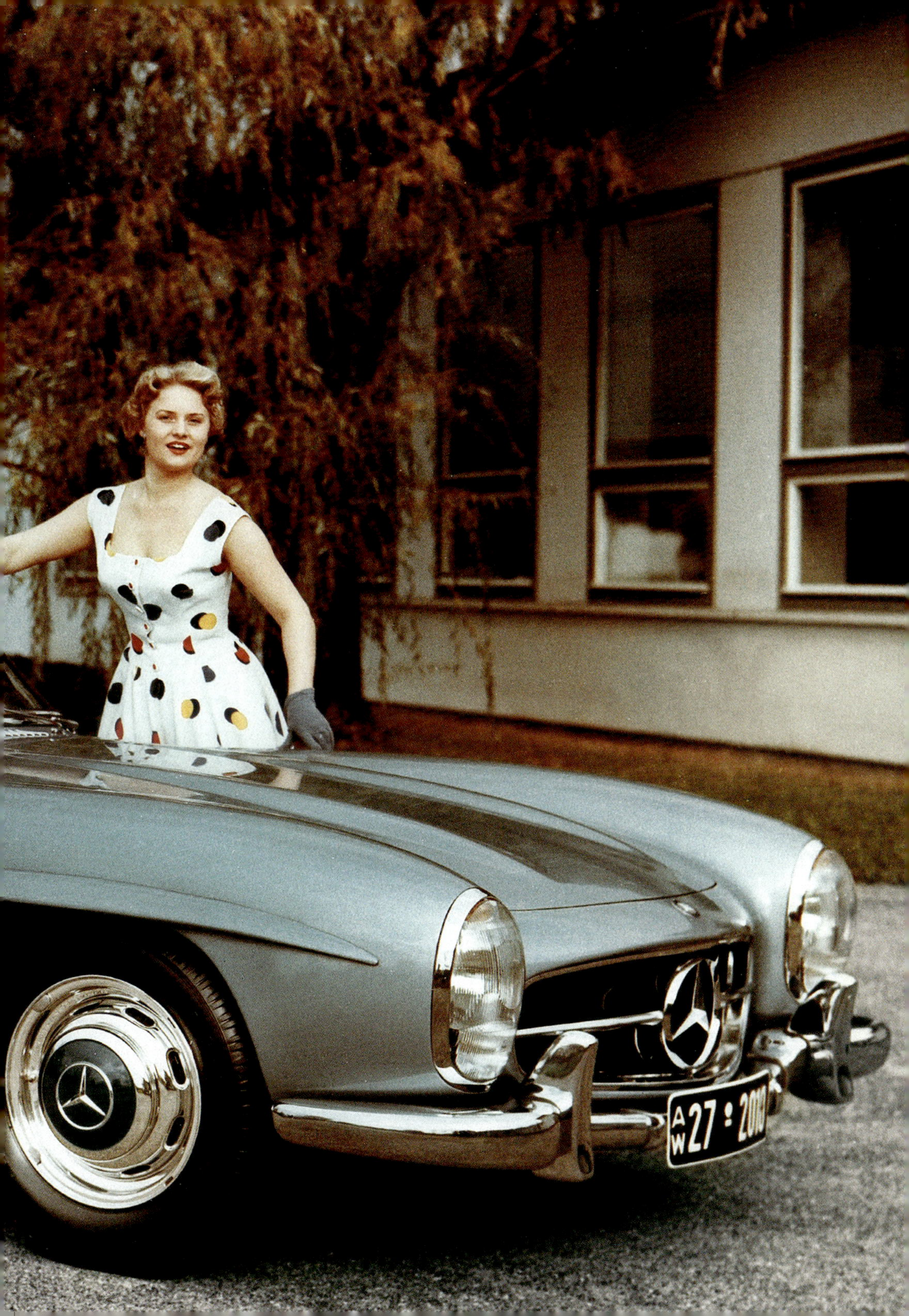
AW 27

1964

Ferrari 250 LM

MANUFACTURED 1963–66 | ENGINE 3,286 cc (200 cu. in.), SOHC per bank 60º V12 | HORSEPOWER 320
TOP SPEED 295 km/h (183 mph) | TRANSMISSION 5-speed
NUMBER PRODUCED 32

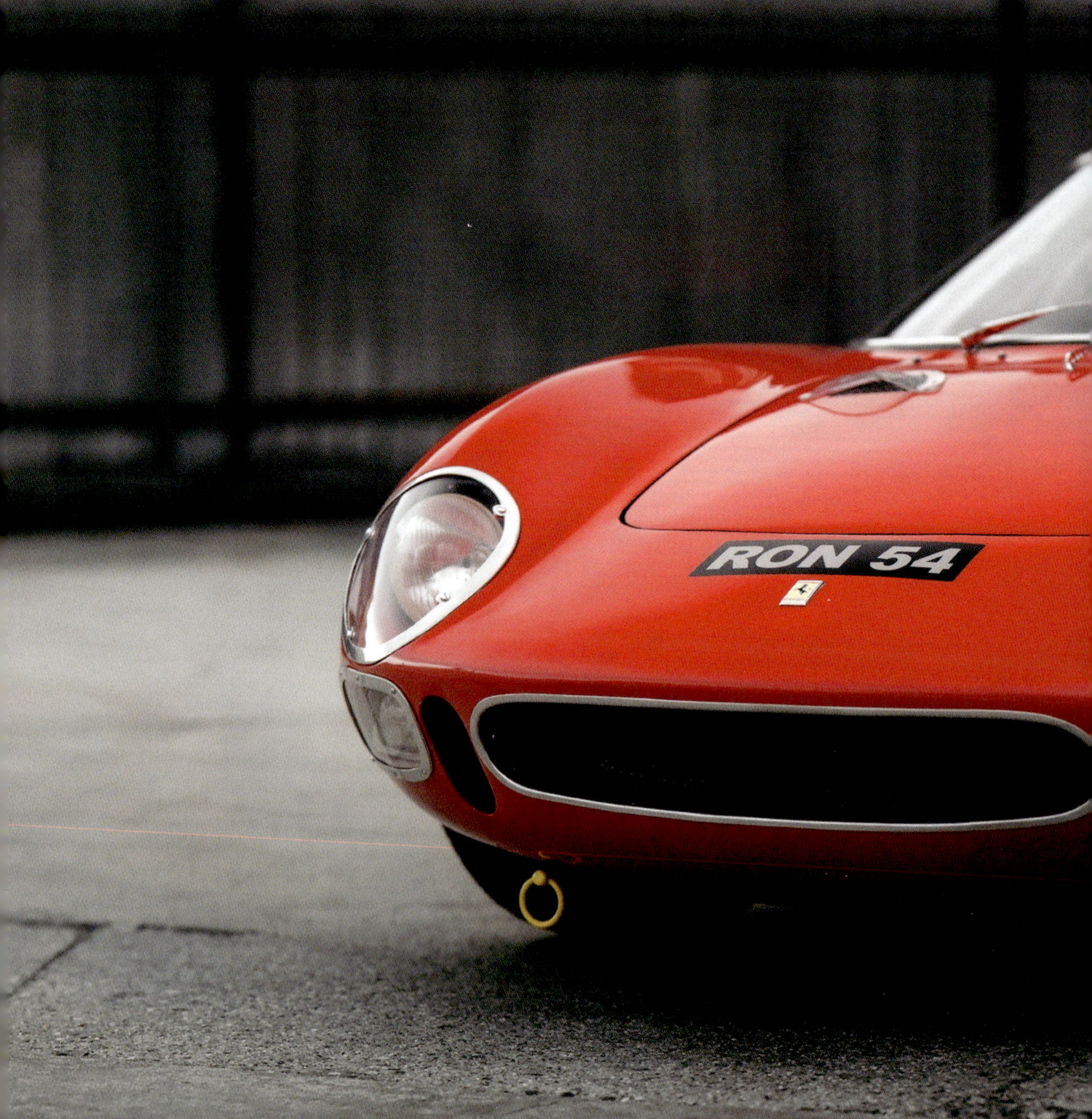

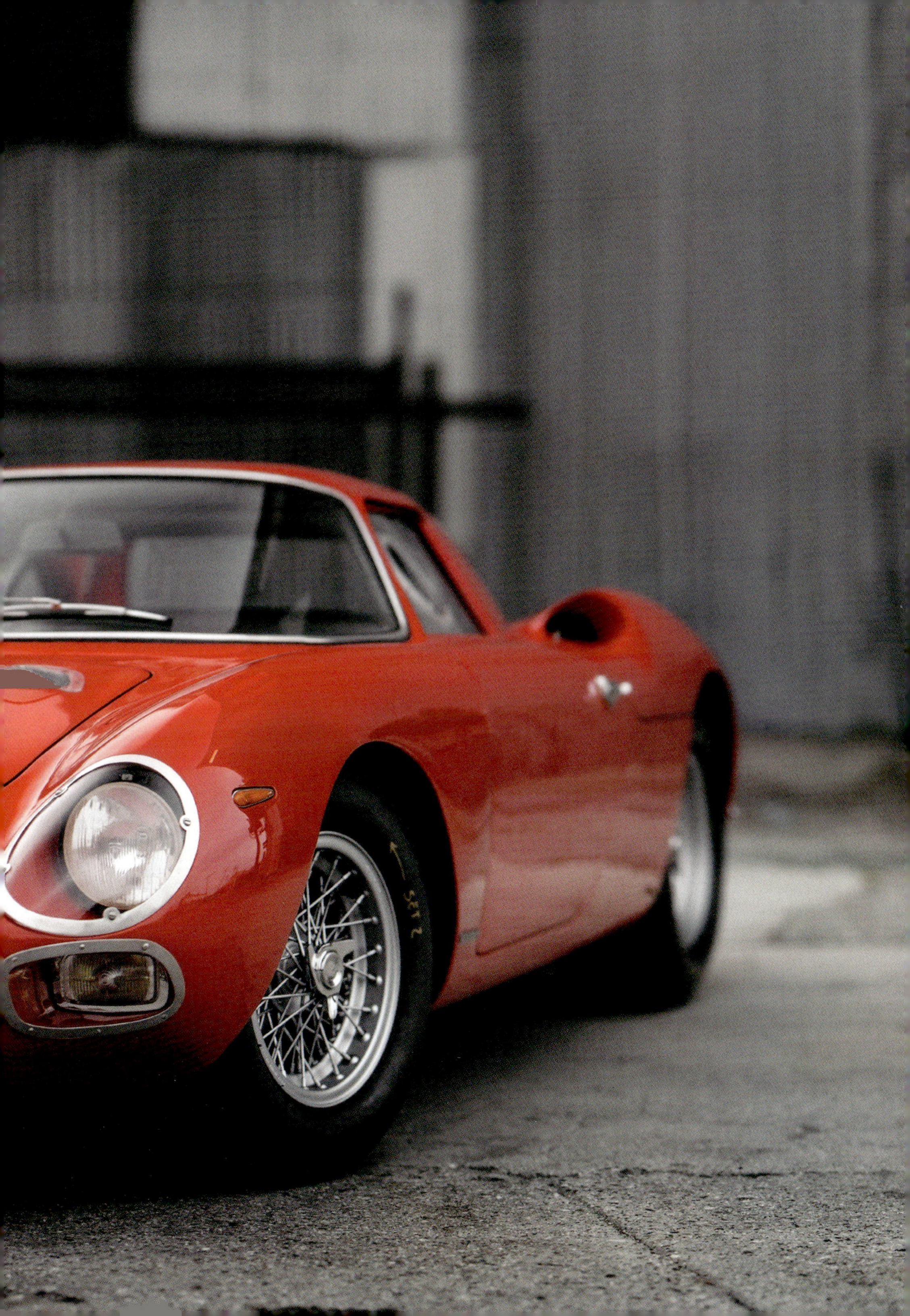

A red-blooded Italian beauty, the Ferrari 250 LM was unveiled at the 1963 Paris Motor Show. It was essentially a two-seater coupé variant of Ferrari's 250 P sports prototype racer, which had been produced in response to the FIA's introduction of a prototype class for the upcoming 1963 World Sportscar Championship season. The mid-engined 250 P designed by Mauro Forghieri at Scuderia Ferrari utilized a tubular steel space-frame chassis that held a longitudinally mounted 60° V12 engine. This was the first instance of a V12 engine being mid-mounted in a Ferrari race car, and drew much controversy because Enzo Ferrari had been notoriously resistant in going over to this configuration despite the trend having been set by Jack Brabham's 1959 World Championship of Drivers victory in the mid-engined Cooper T51. Positioning an engine behind the driver, though, had a decisive design advantage because it freed up the space ahead of a driver, which meant that the front end of the car could be sculpted into a lower, more aerodynamic shape. But more than this, having an engine centered in a car also helped even out weight distribution and thereby improved handling, which in turn enabled the car to be designed lower to the ground. All of which improved performance, especially when competing at high speeds.

As a direct follow-up GT racer the Ferrari 250 LM — with "LM" standing for Le Mans — used the same tubular chassis and running gear as the 250 P, albeit with a few minor modifications. Its bodywork by Scaglietti also shared the same, as Ferrari puts it, "wonderful clean, sharp line" that had been originally created by Pininfarina for the

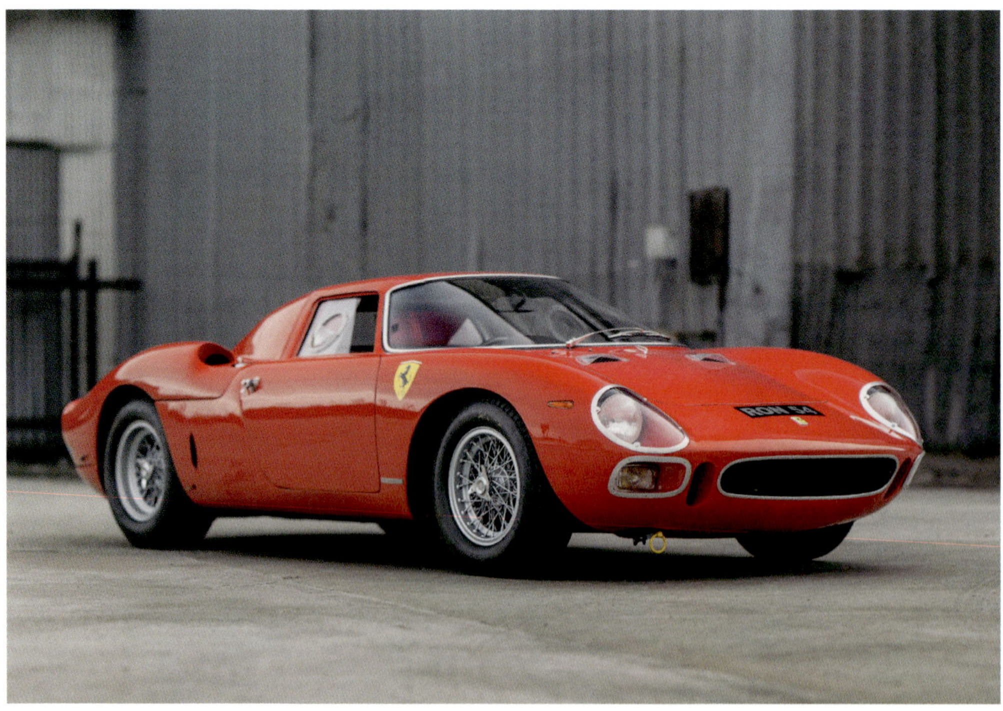

250 P. Indeed, it is a tribute to Scaglietti's formidable design skills just how eloquently the design DNA of the 250 P open-top race car, with its steeply raked windscreen, highly distinctive volumetric rear fenders and slightly up-swooping tail, was adapted into a closed-top sports coupé. The dramatic sloping lines of its fixed roof give the 250 LM a much more edgy and dynamic appearance than its open-topped predecessor. Indeed, there are all sorts of minor design modifications which taken as a whole bestow the 250 LM with its very own distinctive identity.

Originally, it had been intended for the 250 LM to be a street-legal Grand Touring racer, however, as Ferrari explains, "The FIA's refusal to homologate it as a GT car damaged its sales potential and the decision forced the car to compete with true prototypes, thus decreasing its chances of victory." In many ways, this was indicative of the era in which it was created, for during this period there was an increasing demarcation between road and race cars and, ultimately, an ever-growing professionalism within motorsports racing in terms of teams, drivers and their cars. In fact, when it came to it, only 32 examples of the 250 LM were ever constructed, with all of them being destined for the racetrack.

The fine example shown here (chassis no. 6105) was initially acquired by the noted British privateer Ronald Fry, heir to a confectionery fortune. Although a very different beast to the heavier front-engine 250-series Ferraris that had preceded it, the 3.3-liter V12 250 LM was a very fast and nimble machine, which boasted good handling and horsepower, and as a result notched up a number of noteworthy successes on the track. This design's

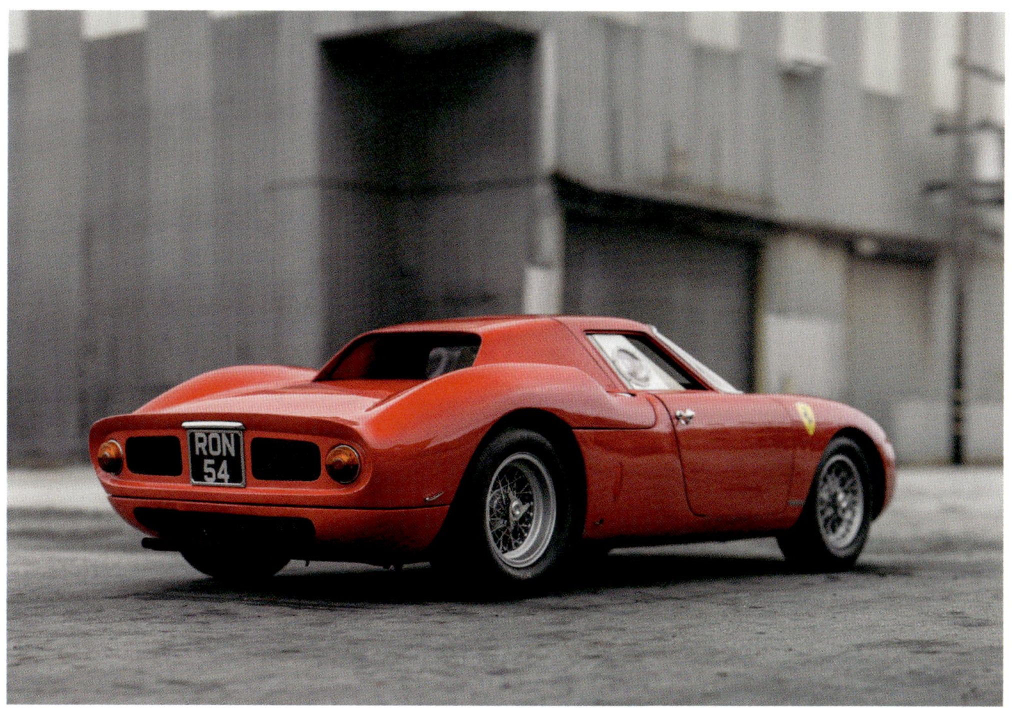

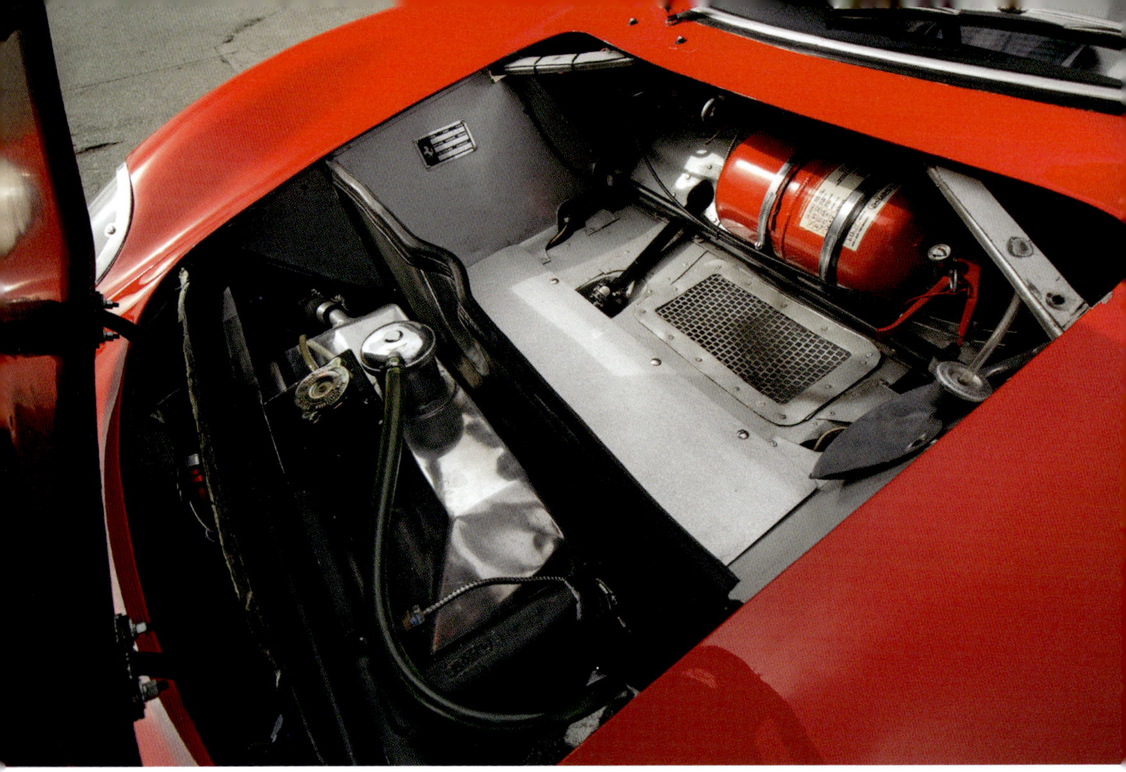

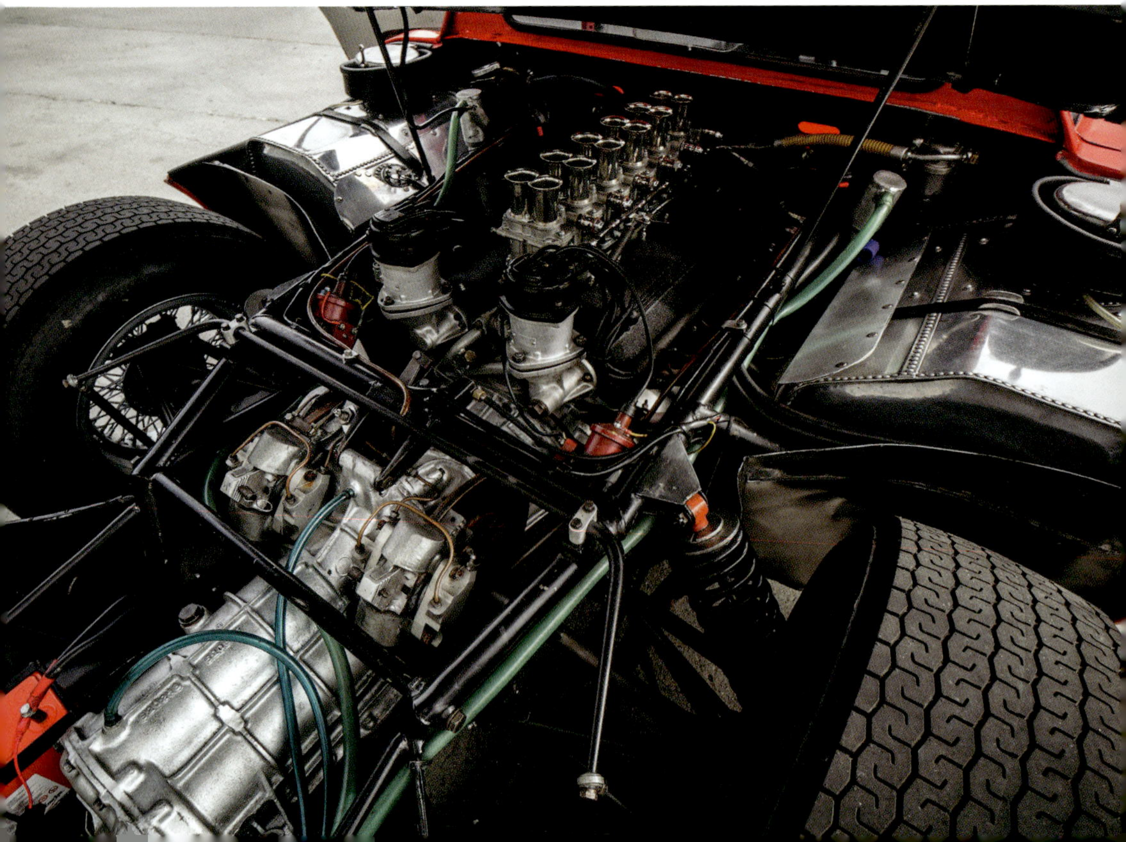

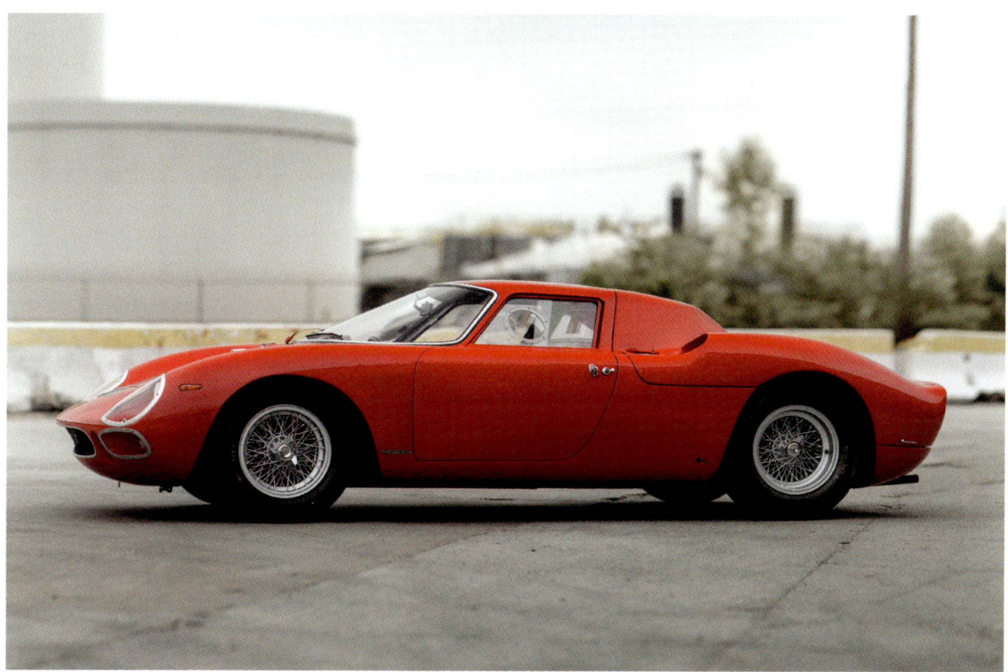

Opposite (top): Detail of radiator and fire extinguisher in the front end of the Ferrari 250 LM. Because the engine of this car was mid-mounted it freed up space ahead of the driver, which meant the front end could be lower, more aerodynamic and enable better forward visability.

Opposite (bottom): Detail of Ferrari 250 LM 3286 cc (200 cu. in.), SOHC per bank 60º V12 engine with six Weber 38 DCN carburetors. The car was developed with this new mid-mounted engine for the GT class but forced to compete as a sports prototype due to the FIA's refusal to homologate it. Nevertheless, it proved to be highly successful on the track, powering the 250 LM chassis no. 5893 to its greatest ever victory — overall first place at the 1965 24 Hours of Le Mans.

racing apotheosis, however, came in 1965 when a 250 LM fielded by Luigi Chinetti's North American Racing Team (NART) and driven by Masten Gregory and Jochen Rindt won the 24 Hours of Mans. In the same race another 250 LM entered by privateer Pierre Dumay and driven by him and Gustave Gosselin placed second. This historic 1-2 victory at the Circuit de la Sarthe cemented the 250 LM's legendary status in automotive history, being as it was Ferrari's last ever overall win at Le Mans.

As one of the most sought after of all Ferraris the 250 LM has long been prized by collectors. And no small wonder, for the 250 LM is not only one of the most historically important Ferraris ever made, but one of the most beautiful, too.

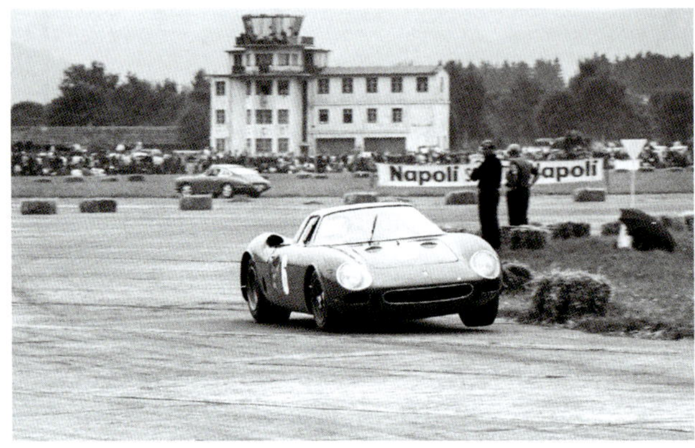

Left: The No. 6 David Piper Autoracing Ferrari 250 LM (chassis no. 6105) at the Zeltweg 500 Kilometers support race during the 1967 Austrian Grand Prix where, driven by Piper and David Skailes, it placed fourth overall and third in its class (S2.0).

Below: No. 21 NART Ferrari 250 LM of Masten Gregory and Jochen Rindt at the 1965 24 Hours of Le Mans. Ed Hugus, the reserve driver, later claimed he drove this car for one stint during the race when Gregory pitted unexpectedly exhausted and with his glasses' vision impaired by the predawn mist, and co-driver, Rindt was sleeping and could not be found. If this had happened, it would have been controversial because, according to the rules, Gregory should not have been allowed to drive again once Hugus replaced him and so the car should have been disqualified. But this incident was never officially recorded, and since then, the story has been dismissed by Doug Nye, one of the world's most renowned authorities on Ferrari's racing history, as "utter garbage."

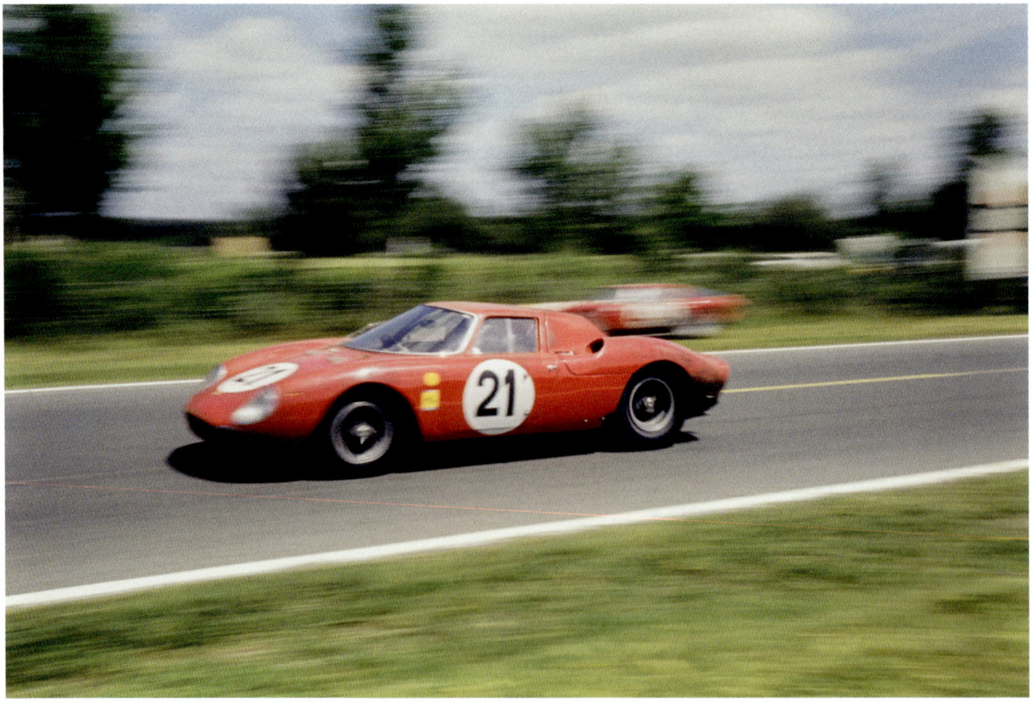

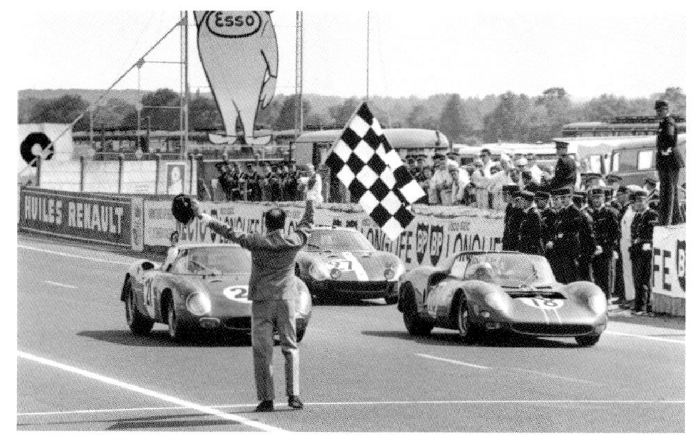

Left: The No. 21 NART Ferrari 250 LM (chassis no. 5893) of Masten Gregory and Jochen Rindt taking the checkered flag and winning the 1965 24 Hours of Le Mans, with the No. 18 NART Ferrari 365 P2 Spider of Nino Vaccarella and Pedro Rodriguez finishing seventh, and the No. 27 Ferrari 250 LM of privateers Armand Boller and Dieter Spoerry finishing sixth. This sensational win for the North American Racing Team would turn out to be the last outright victory for Ferrari at Le Mans.

Below: Masten Gregory and Jochen Rindt in their No. 21 NART Ferrari 250 LM (chassis no. 5893) driving along the pits having just won the overall 1965 24 Hours of Le Mans, surrounded by jubliant colleagues.

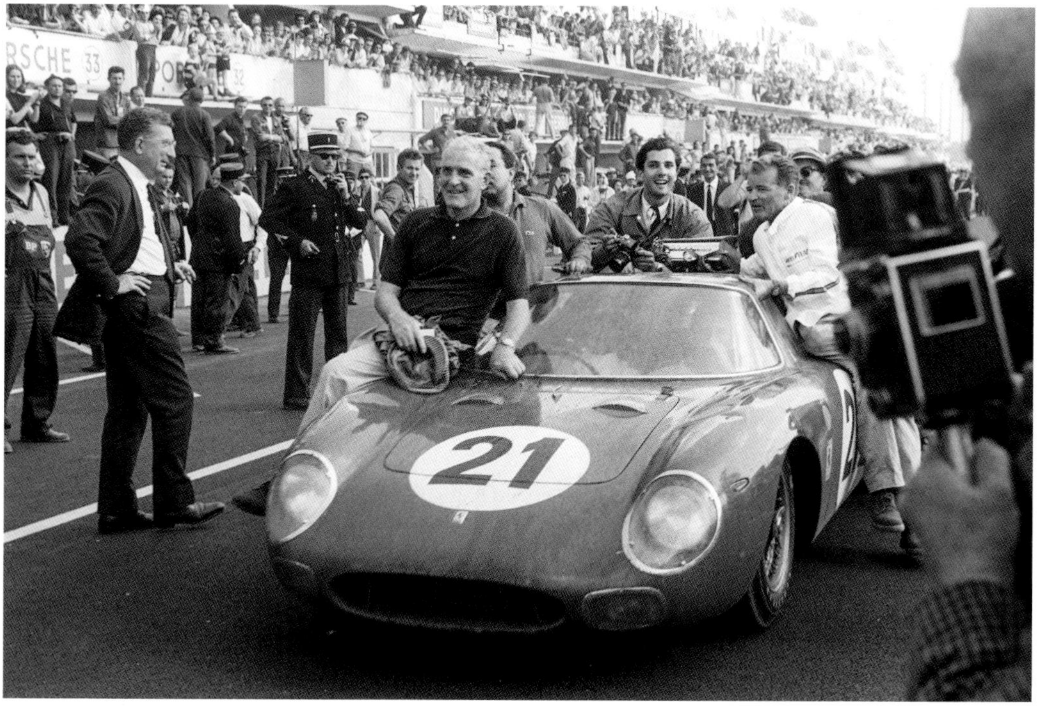

1964

Shelby Cobra Daytona Coupe

MANUFACTURED 1964–65 | ENGINE 4,736 cc (289 cu. in.), overhead-valve V8 | HORSEPOWER 390
TOP SPEED 307 km/h (191 mph) | TRANSMISSION 4-speed
NUMBER PRODUCED 6

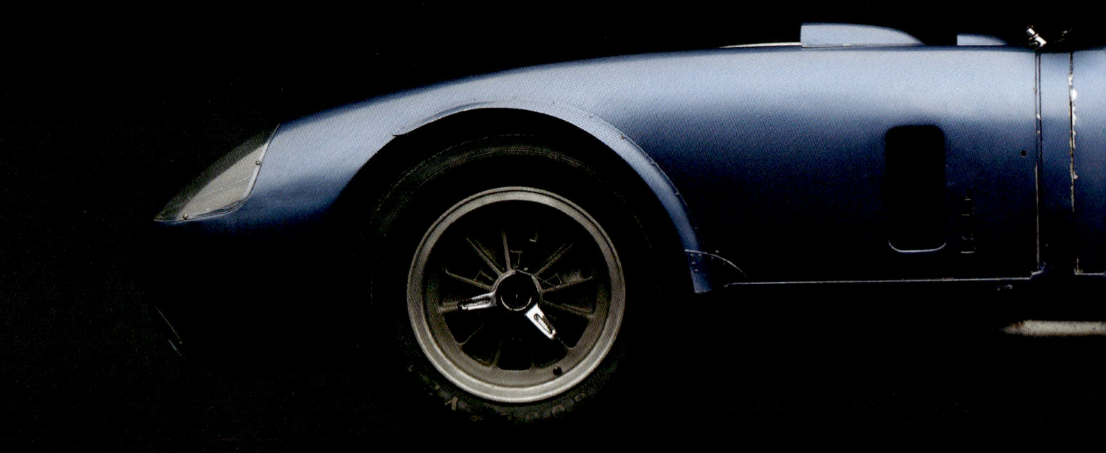

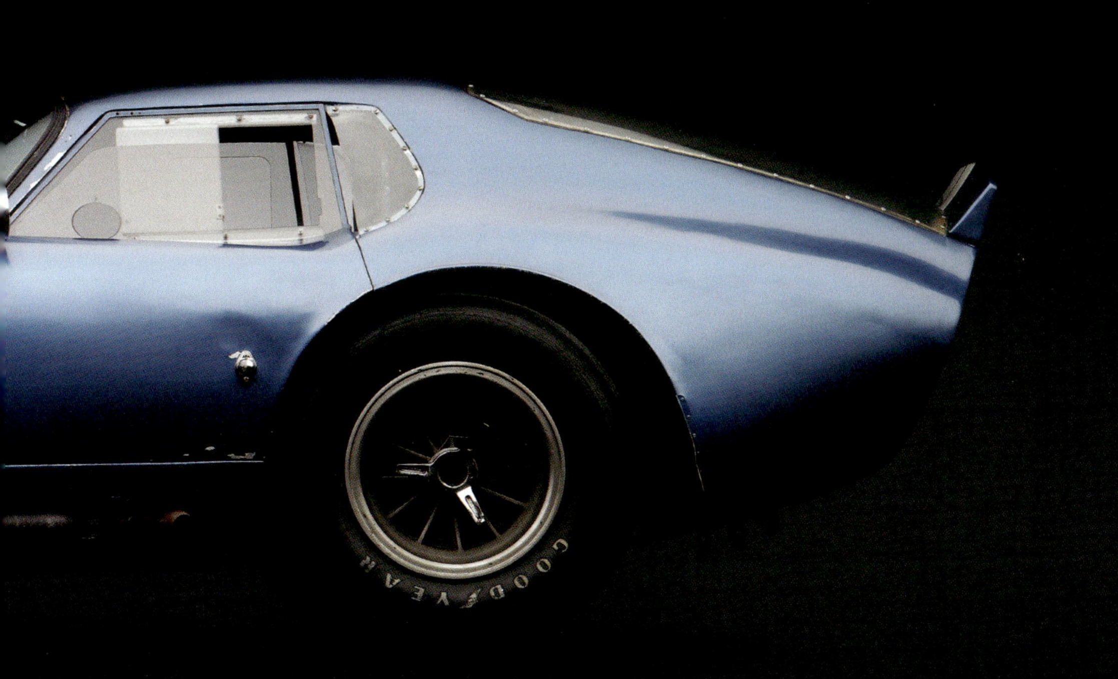
GOODYEAR

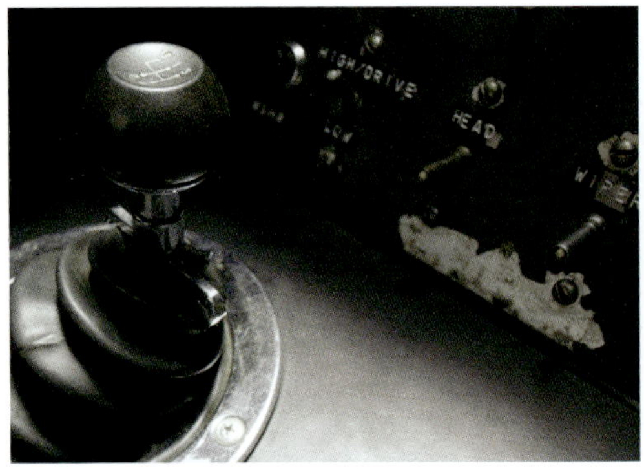

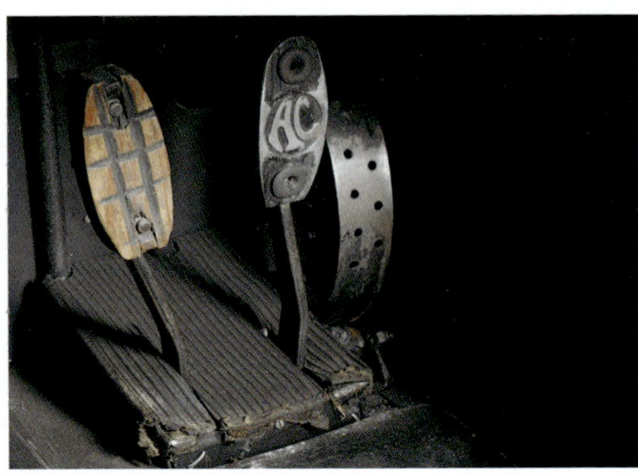

Above (left & right): Detail of Shelby Cobra Daytona gearshift, switches and pedals, which attest to this car's astonishing originality.

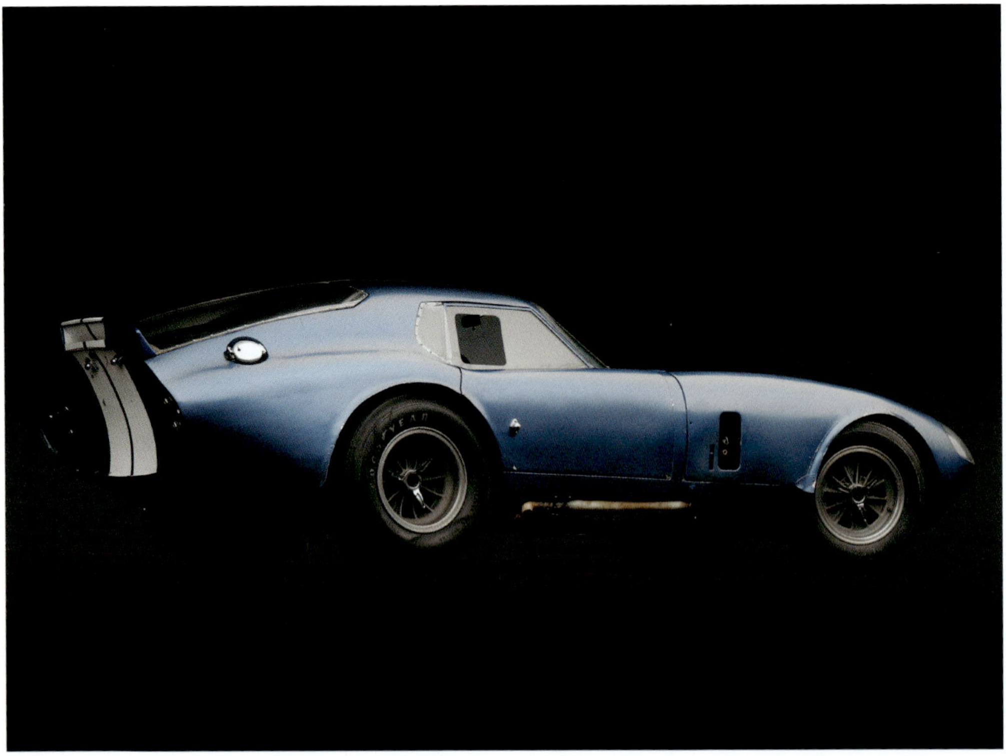

The Shelby Cobra Daytona Coupe was a world-beating car that enabled its creator, Carroll Shelby, to finally dent the dominance of Ferrari's 250 GTOs (see p. 264) during the mid-1960s with a spectacular overall win of the Group 3 category (over 2000 cc) of the World Sportscar Championship in 1965. This was something that Shelby had long dreamt of accomplishing because, having once driven for Enzo Ferrari, though briefly, he hated the way "Il Commendatore" psychologically pitted his drivers against one another in the belief that it would make them more competitive, and firmly believed that this tactic had led to several of their deaths. After battling it out race after race with the Ferraris during the 1963 season in his 289 Cobras, Shelby realized that what he needed was a more aerodynamic version of this car if he was to stand any chance of beating the Scuderia in the upcoming 1964 season.

With this goal fixed in his mind, Shelby tasked his chief designer, Pete Brock, with creating a new aerodynamically honed body. Prior to this, Brock had worked in General Motors' famed Styling Section, where he had worked on the design of the 1959 Corvette XP-87 Stingray racer-concept car. When the youthful Brock came to design the Daytona Coupe, he put all the lessons he had learnt from the development of the Stingray into the creation of this groundbreaking racer. Brock determined that the only way to get better performance out of the 289 Cobra was to either reduce drag or increase horsepower. As he explained to

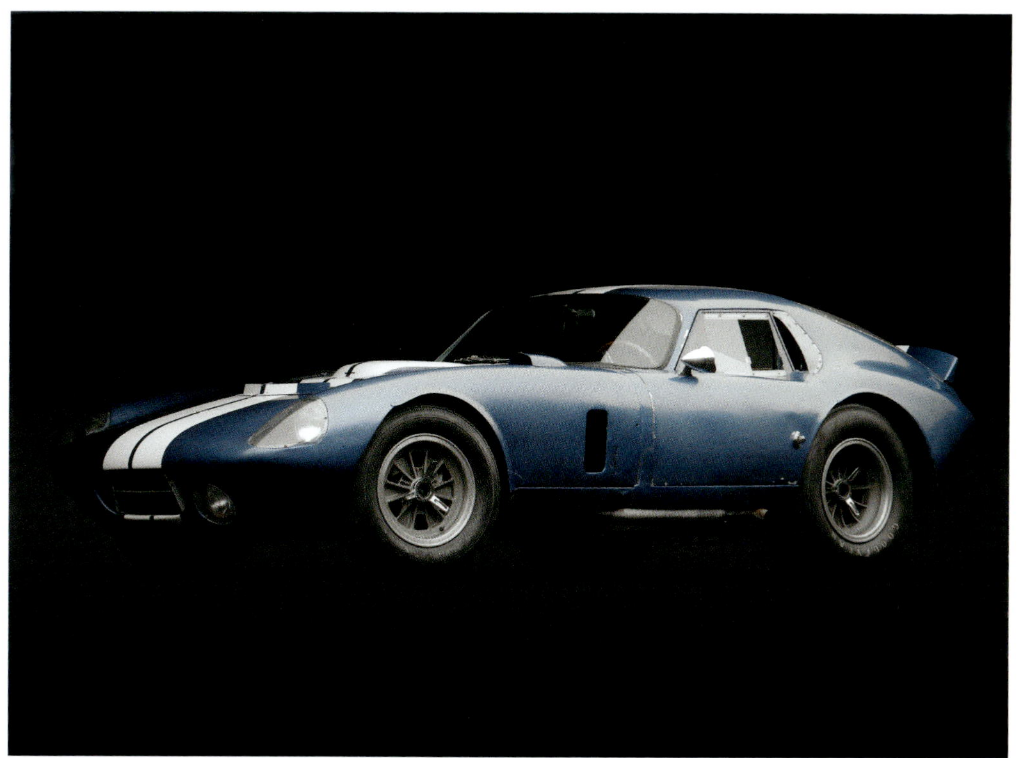

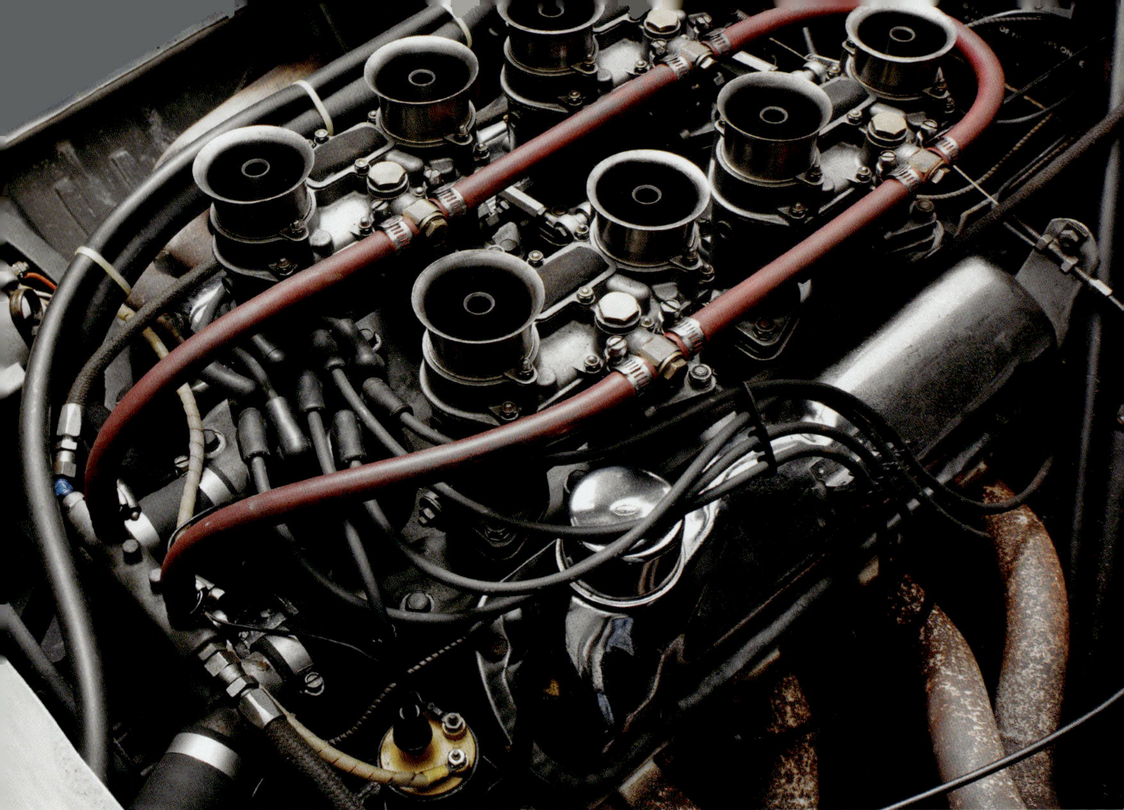

Above: Shelby Cobra Daytona engine with four Weber 48 IDM carburetors. Shelby's original plan was to use an all-aluminum Ford 427 engine, in order to challenge Ferrari at the 1964 24 Hours of Le Mans. But Ford would not make it, claiming the block's bore spacing and thin walls would cause overheating.

Shelby, "If you double the speed, the drag goes up by the square... so unless we change the body there's no hope." Brock then sketched what the car would look like and explained that it was going to have to look very different from its progenitor. Shelby, however, did not seem concerned about what it would look like as long as it went fast. Brock then meticulously studied advanced aerodynamic data that had been produced in Germany prior to World War II by the likes of Erwin Komenda, Wunibald Kamm and Reinhard von Koenig-Fachsenfeld. While most of their work had been destroyed during the war, Brock had managed to find a series of mimeographed sheets of technical data, which the allies had seized after the war, that had landed up in the library of GM. By poring over these "secrets of German aerodynamic design," as Brock referred to them, he was able to gain a much better understanding of the aerodynamics needed to engineer a really fast car.

The resulting design with its dramatic Kamm-tailed rear end was a completely radical design departure, which the engineers working for Shelby American Inc. were not particularly keen on developing. The general consensus being that it was a pretty ugly car. However, a new recruit to the engineering team, a New Zealander by the name of John Ohlsen, took an interest in it, as did the driver-engineer Ken Miles. After getting Shelby's blessing to go ahead with the concept, Brock worked with these two on the car's realization, which took only 90 days from first sketch to first race. The streamlined and very dynamic looking Shelby Daytona marked a paradigm shift within the design of American race cars. In comparison to its Cobra predecessors, for instance, it looked as though it belonged to a completely different generation. And when it underwent its first test outing at Riverside International Speedway in February 1964, Ken Miles, its driver, was seriously impressed with its performance. With its new tubular chassis reinforced with an "unauthorized" triangulated subframe and its sculptural air-slipping body, this racer clocked up a top speed of 185 mph (297 km/h), which was 20 mph (32 km/h) faster than the 289 Cobra roadsters, although it shared the same Ford 289 cu. in. HiPo engine, chassis and drivetrain. Crucially, it meant that Shelby was now in the running to outclass and outpace the Ferraris.

Ultimately, only six Shelby Cobra Daytona Coupes were constructed between 1964 and 1965 for Ford, which bankrolled their development and provided technical assistance. The example shown here (chassis no. CSX 2287) is known as "The Original" because it was the first prototype that was built entirely at Shelby American's race workshop in Venice, California. Importantly, this particular car won the GT class at the 12 Hours of Sebring race in 1964, piloted by Dave MacDonald and Bob Holbert. It also during its racing career

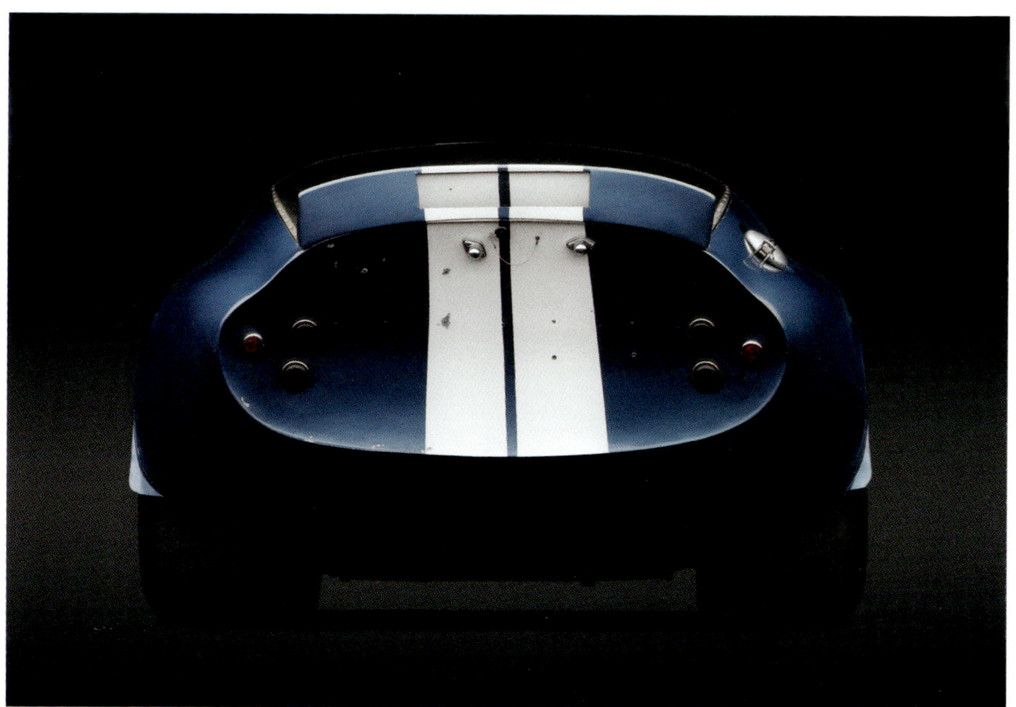

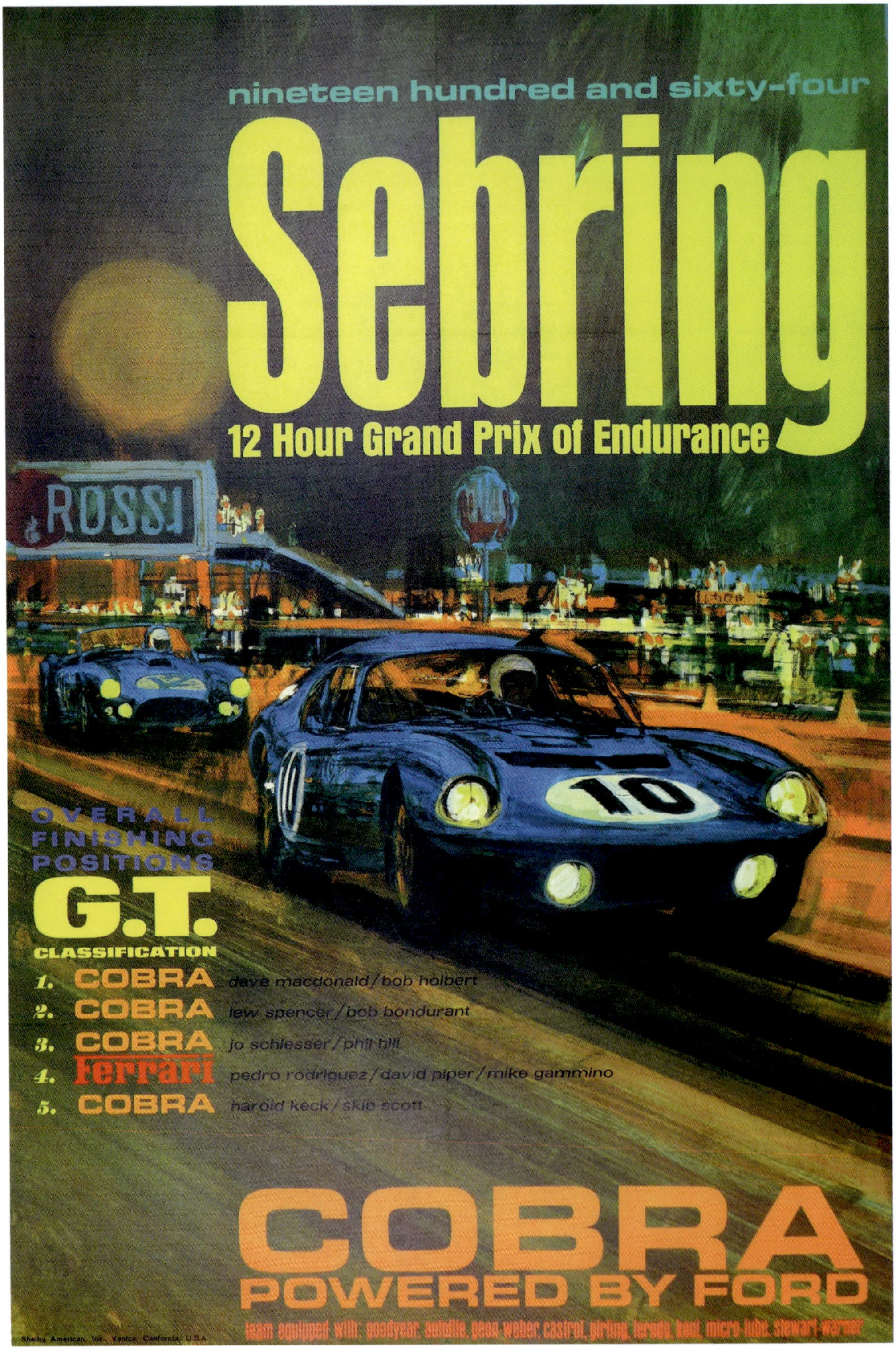

nineteen hundred and sixty-four

Sebring

12 Hour Grand Prix of Endurance

ROSSI

OVERALL FINISHING POSITIONS

G.T.

CLASSIFICATION

1. COBRA dave macdonald / bob holbert
2. COBRA lew spencer / bob bondurant
3. COBRA jo schlesser / phil hill
4. Ferrari pedro rodriguez / david piper / mike gammino
5. COBRA harold keck / skip scott

COBRA

POWERED BY FORD

team equipped with: goodyear, autolite, geon-weber, castrol, girling, ferodo, koni, micro-lube, stewart-warner

Shelby American, Inc., Venice, California, U.S.A.

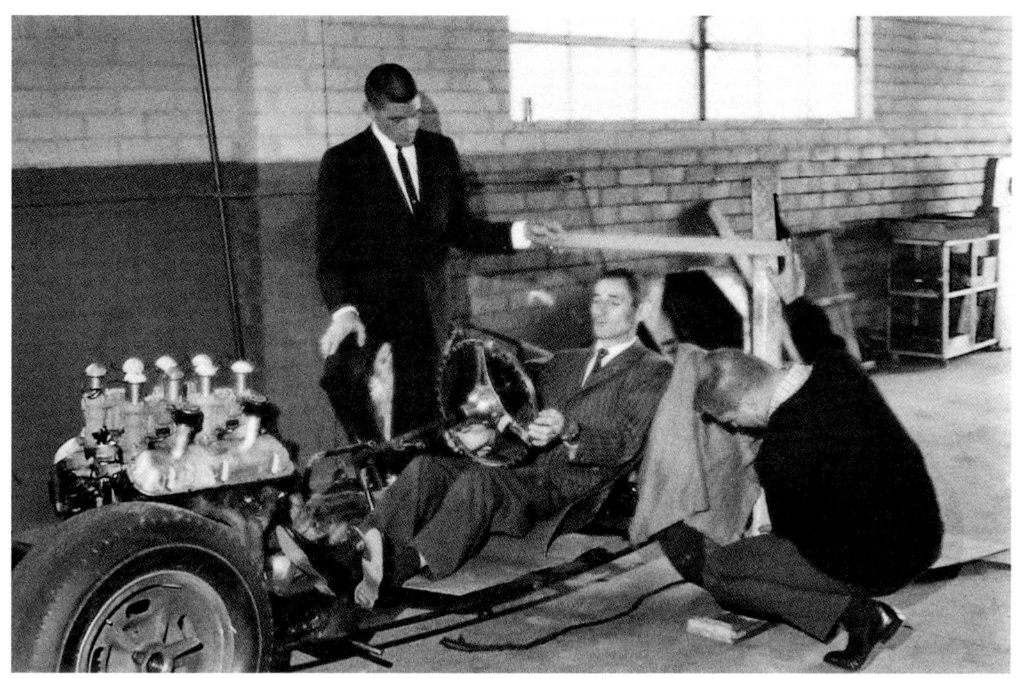

clocked up 25 USAC/FIA speed world records at the Bonneville Salt Flats in Utah in 1965. The car was then sold by Shelby American to a private owner in 1966 and was never again raced. Now owned by the Simeone Foundation Automotive Museum, it is the only Shelby Cobra Daytona Coupe in original, unrestored condition. In 2014, CSX 2287 had the honor of being the very first car to be listed on the National Historic Vehicle Registry of the Historic Vehicle Association (HVA), testifying to both its extraordinary cultural and historic importance.

Opposite: 1964 Sebring 12 Hour Grand Prix of Endurance poster by George Bartell (1933–2013) showing the No. 10 Shelby Cobra Daytona Coupe (chassis no. CSX 2287) driven by Bob Holbert and Dave MacDonald leading the No. 12 Shelby 289 Cobra (CSX 2301) driven by Bob Bondurant and Lew Spencer. The poster was published in 1965 to celebrate Ford's four finishes in the top five at this event.

Above: Testing, design and construction of the Shelby Cobra Daytona Coupe chassis at the Shelby American factory, Venice, California, 1962–63. Chief designer Pete Brock, kneeling; race/test-driver-engineer Ken Miles, sitting; and race driver Dave MacDonald, standing.

SHELBY COBRA DAYTONA COUPE

Below: Shelby Cobra Daytona Coupe, chassis no. CSX 2287, at the Bonneville Salt Flats, Utah, November 6, 1965, having just set a new 12-hour endurance record with drivers Craig Breedlove and Bobby Tatroe clocking up more than 1,931 miles at an average speed of 150 mph. The pair went on to set a further 23 national and international speed records in this car. The first Shelby Cobra Daytona Coupe, CSX 2287, is the only one of the six examples to feature an American-built body — the five others were built in Italy by Carrozzeria Grandsport in Modena.

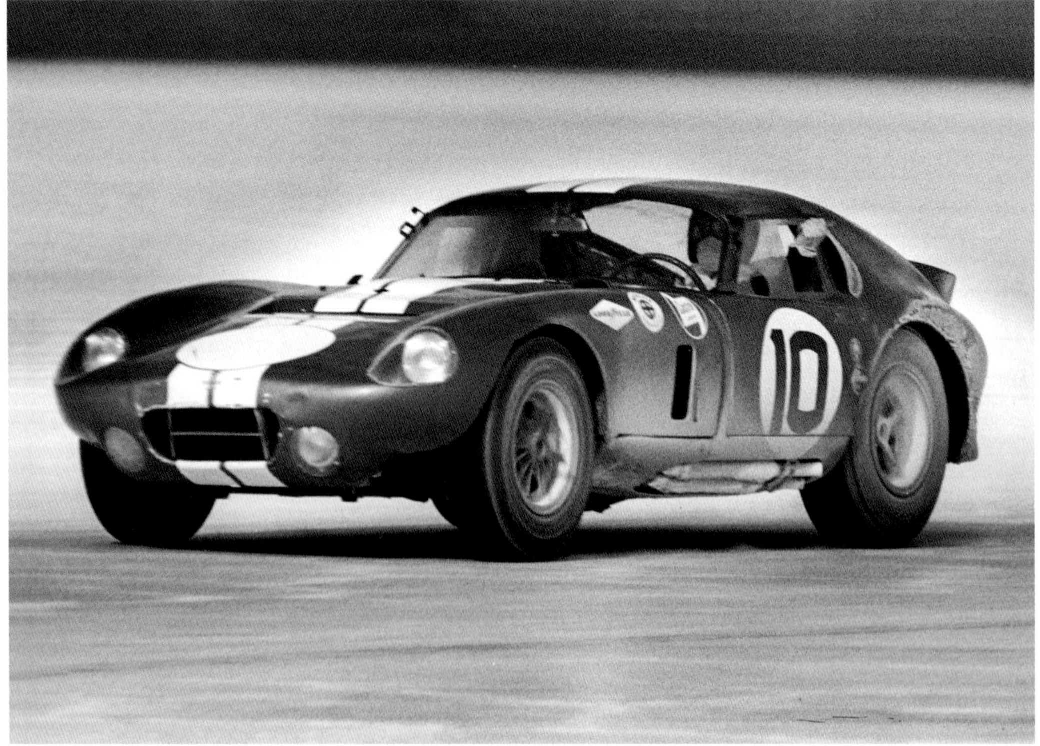

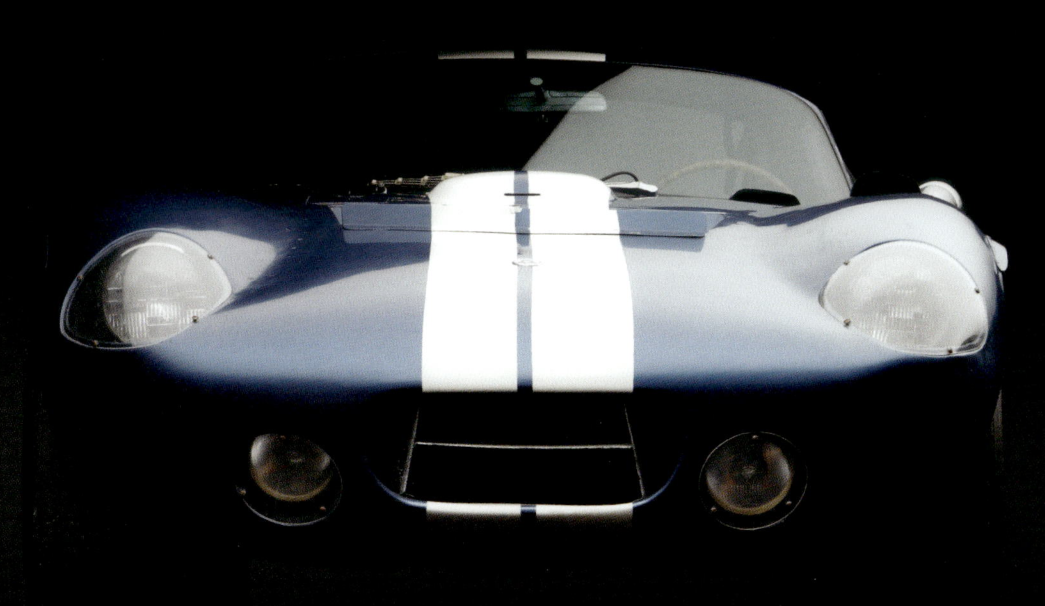

1964

Ferrari 275 GTB/C Speciale

MANUFACTURED 1964–66 | ENGINE 3,286 cc (200 cu. in.), SOHC per bank 60° V12 | HORSEPOWER 320
TOP SPEED 282 km/h (175 mph) | TRANSMISSION 5-speed
NUMBER PRODUCED 4 (3 constructed 1964–65, 1 constructed 1966)

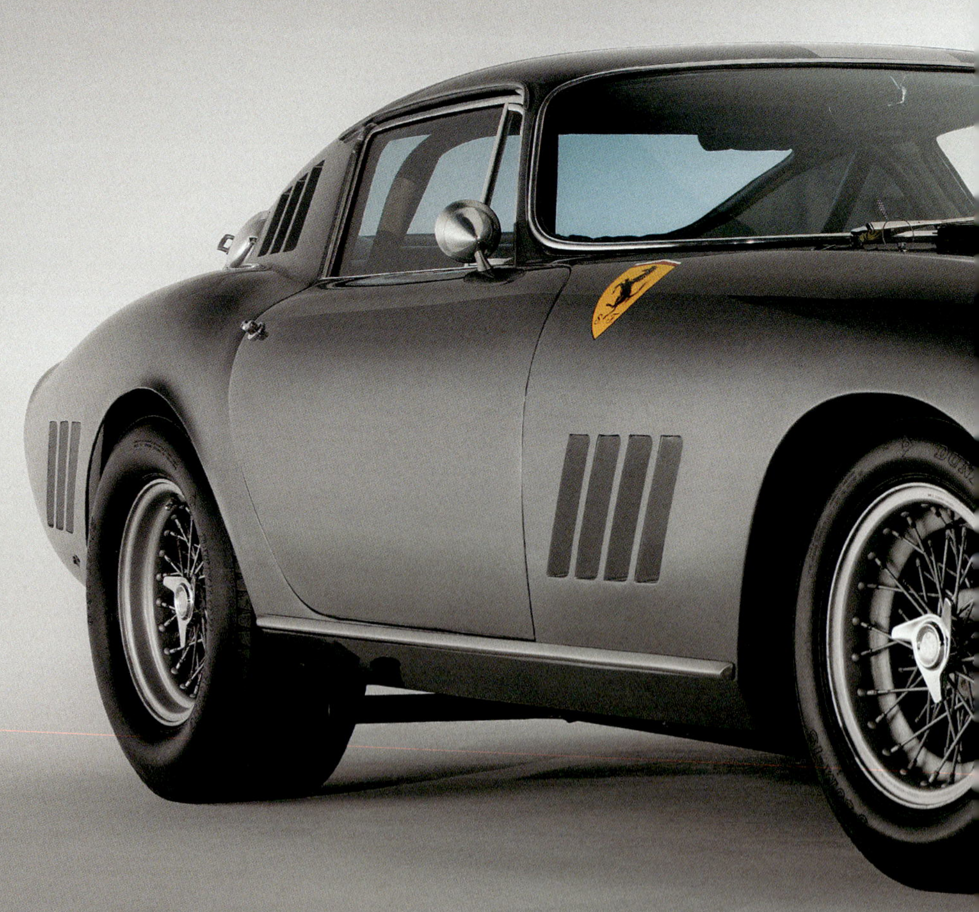

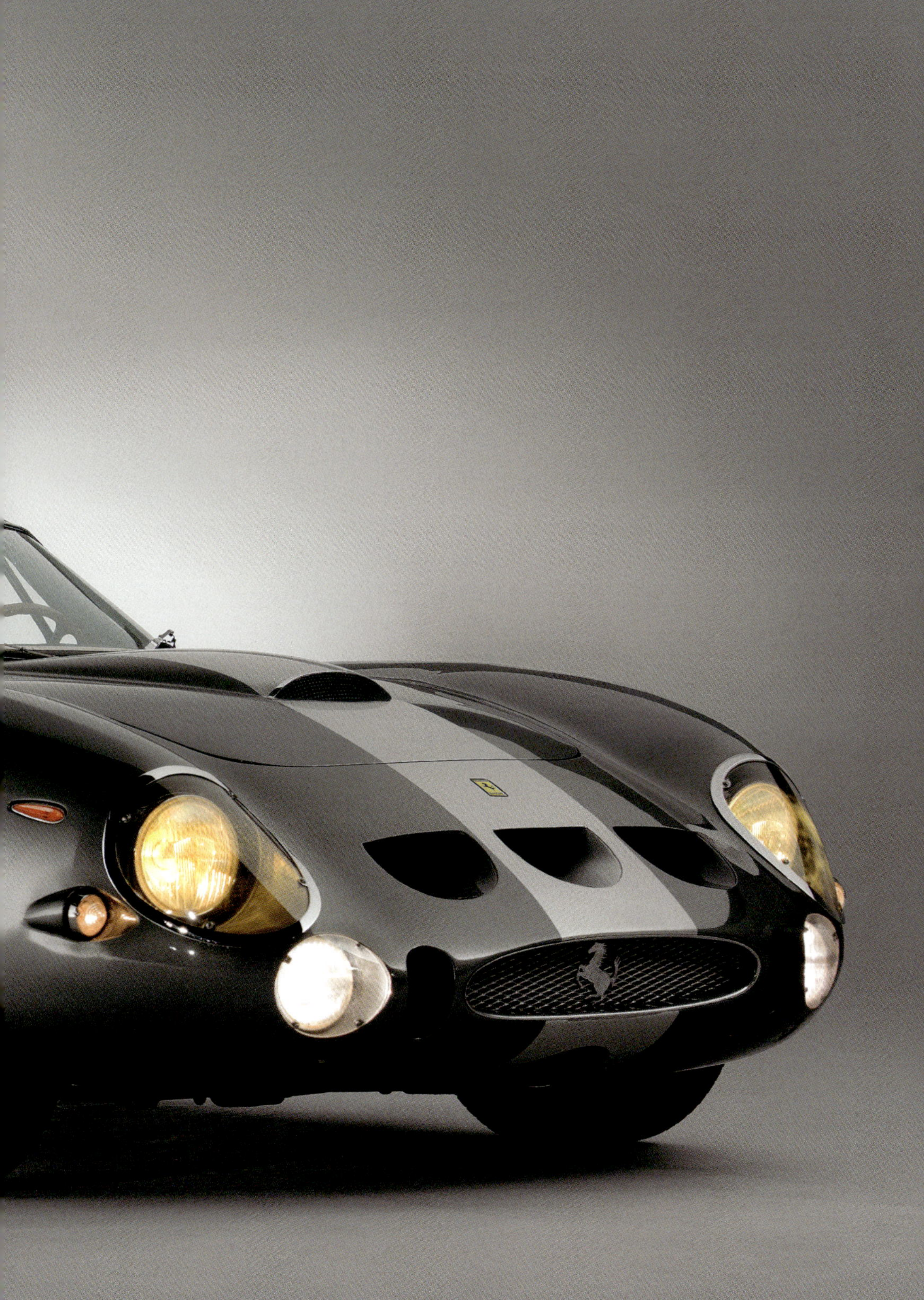

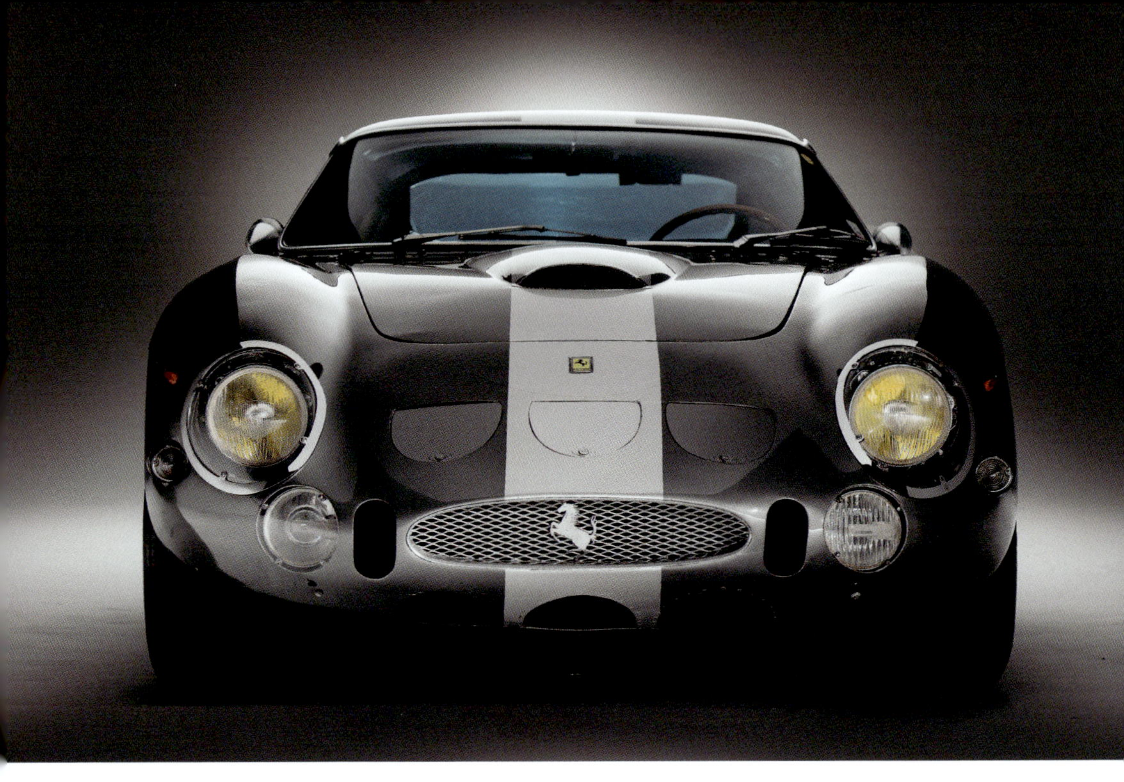

Ferrari famously introduced its 250 series of competition cars in 1953, which ultimately culminated in the fabled 250 GTO (see p. 264), produced from 1962 to 1964. However, when the FIA declined to homologate the GTO's successor, the 250 LM (see p. 308), for the 1965 season — because a sufficient number had not been made for it to qualify as a production GT racer — Ferrari built between 1964 and 1965 three 275 GTB/C Speciales, which combined 250 LM-specification engines with super-lightweight bodies designed by Scaglietti, and then one additional example of the car in 1966. At first glance the front and rear ends of the 275 GTB/C Speciale and the 250 GTO fitted with Scaglietti-created Series I bodywork seem pretty similar. On closer inspection, however, the 275's additional brake-cooling vents and egg-crate-patterned aluminum grille give the car a slightly more aggressive appearance. As Ferrari explains, "The body featured powerful curves with overall lines that had echoes of the 250 GTO, with a long forward section and a set-back cabin falling sharply into the short Kamm tail, carrying circular combination tail/turn light units on a lightly recessed panel similar to that of its predecessor... The cabin was a three window design with a large deeply curved windscreen and an almost flat rear screen bounded by sail panels that featured triple cabin exhaust air slots that matched the quadruple arrangement on the front wings." The 275 GTB's body was designed by Pininfarina and built by Scaglietti, with the production road-going version constructed of steel, but with aluminum doors, hood and trunk lid. By contrast, the works competition Speciale version, as shown here, had an ultra-lightweight all-aluminum body for enhanced racing performance. As a full-on factory racer,

Right: Poster advertising the 1967 24 Hours of Le Mans. The scene depicted shows the prestart lineup from the 1966 race — the No. 29 Maranello Concessionaires Ltd. Ferrari 275 GTB/C of Piers Courage and Roy Pike (finished eighth and won its class), the No. 36 Maranello Concessionaires Ltd. Dino 206 S of Mike Salmon and David Hobbs (DNF), the No. 57 Ecurie Francorchamps Ferrari 275 GTB/C of Pierre Noblet and Claude Dubois (finished tenth).

Below: Detail of Ferrari 275 GTB/C Speciale 3,286 cc (200 cu. in.), SOHC per bank 60° V12 dry-sump engine with six Weber 38 DCN carburetors. This is the same Tipo 213 specification engine that powered the 250 LM, which featured a special crank-shaft, pistons, connecting rods and sodium-filled Nimonic valves. Additionally, many engine cast-ings were made from the light-weight magnesium alloy, Elektron.

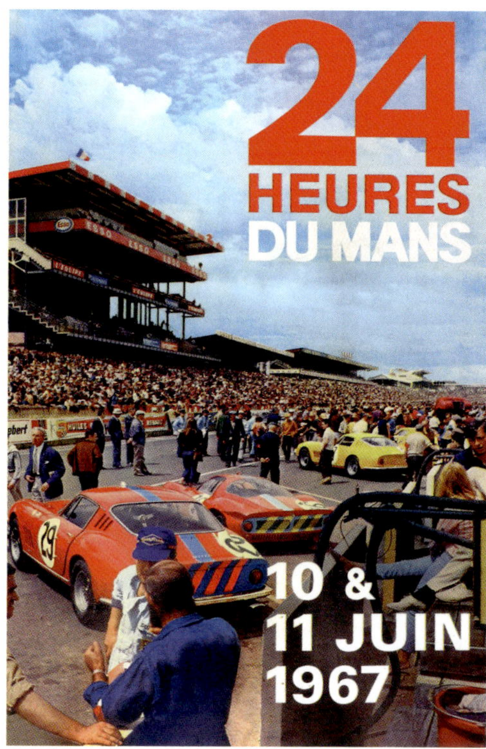

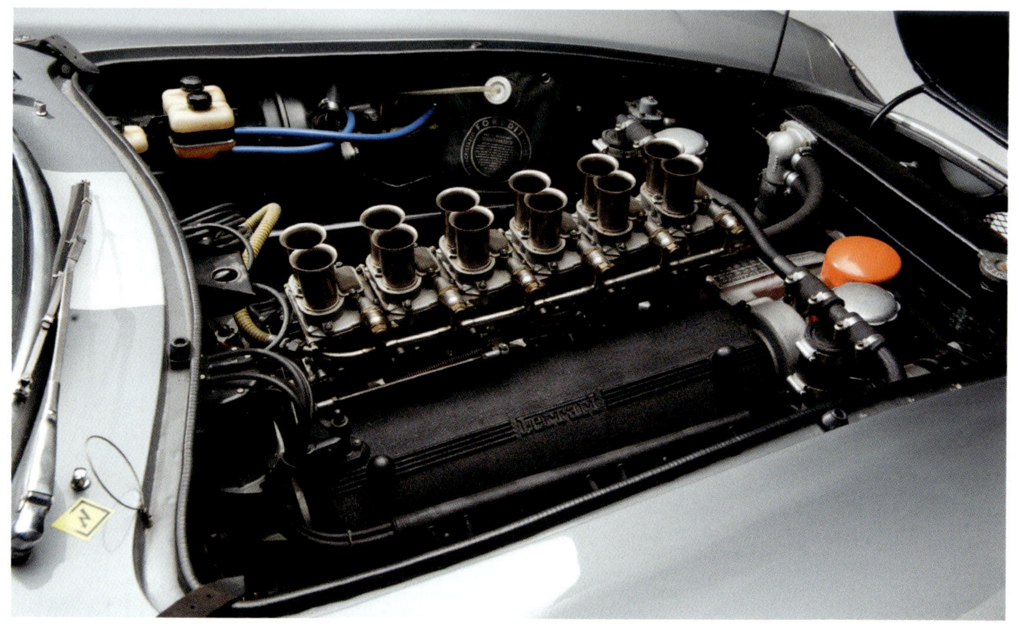

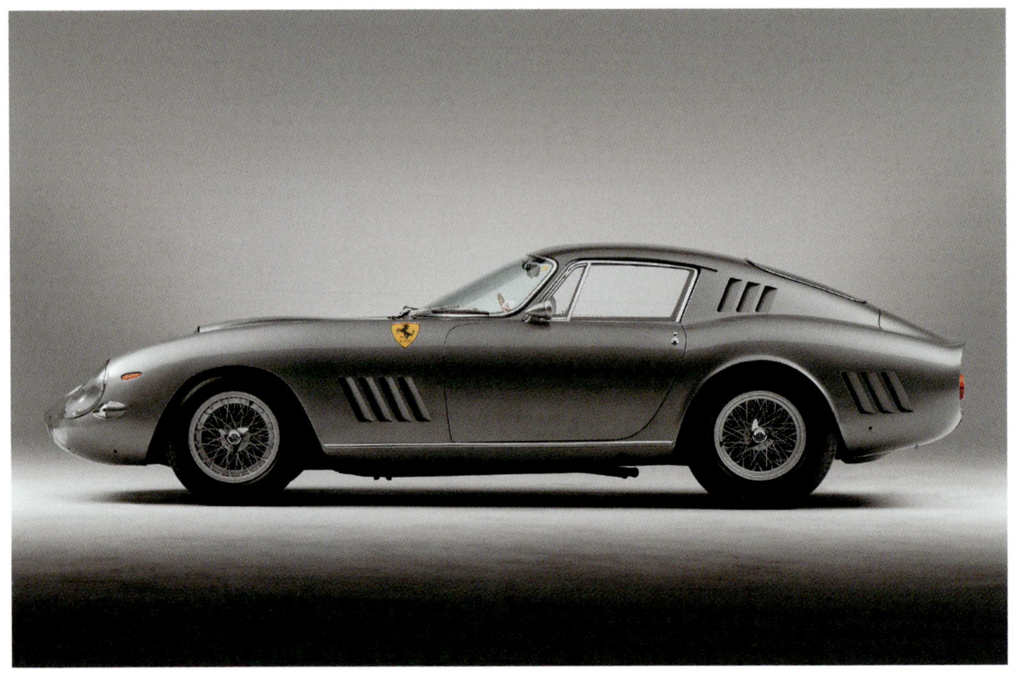

it was also given a “C” designation standing for *competizione* (with “GTB” standing for *Gran Turismo Berlinetta*).

The design of the race-ready 275 GTB/C Speciale was supervised by Mauro Forghieri and boasted a number of other key differences from the production models. These included a drilled chassis, drilled interior panels, a revamped nose, rear-wheel vents, a hood scoop and Plexiglass windows. But perhaps the most notable thing about it was its reduced weight, which in full race trim could be as little as 1,070 kg (2,350 lbs.) — around 150 kg (331 lbs.) less than the alloy-bodied road model.

Having been unveiled at the 1964 Paris Motor Show, the 275 went into serial production the following year with two on-road models — the 275 GTB coupé and 275 GTS convertible (with the “S” standing for spider). Mechanically the two cars were exactly the same, however, while Pinifarina designed both, the GTB definitely had a meaner, edgier look and was quite different to the spider. Once the Speciale berlinetta competition variant was completed in early 1965, however, the FIA initially refused to homologate the model into the GT Class, but eventually settled on a compromise when Enzo Ferrari threatened to withdraw from competing in that class altogether unless it was. This argument caused such a delay that only one 275 GTB/C Speciale was raced during that first 1965 season. It, nevertheless, took a very credible third place at the 24 Hours of Le Mans, and then went on to win the Nassau Tourist Trophy, thereby demonstrating the model's racing potential.

The stunning matching-numbers 275 GTB/C Speciale shown here (chassis no. 06701) was the first of the four works racers. Each of these hand-built cars was slightly different from one another as Ferrari's engineers worked out progressively how to optimize their aerodynamics. As a consequence, chassis no. 06701 has a marginally more aggressive look than its stablemates. Ferrari also, as a follow up, built ten *competizione clienti* cars with alloy bodywork, which were sold to privateers. In addition, for the upcoming 1966 season, a dozen redesigned, lightweight 275 GTB/C racers were constructed, which unlike the earlier Speciales and the client competition cars did not have rear wheel vents. In 1967, ten examples of a four-cam convertible variant, known as the 275 GTS/4 NART Spider were also produced at the behest of Luigi Chinetti.

The 275 GTB/C Speciale works racer, however, is undoubtedly the supreme variant of this most elegant of Ferrari models and is also one of the most desirable Ferraris of all time. The outstanding example shown here, chassis no. 06701, was originally painted Rosso Cina (China Red), but its paintwork was later changed by the factory to two-tone metallic silver-gray before being sold to its first private owner, an Italian paper-manufacturing magnate. It subsequently changed hands a number of times, at some point during which it was repainted red and had three cooling vents cut into its elegant front end, much like a Series I-bodied 250 GTO. Eventually, it landed up in the collection of Brandon Wang, who had the sense to restore it to its stunning Grigio Scurro Metalizatto livery, which so perfectly sets off its dynamic lines. When it came up for sale in 2014 this super-rare thoroughbred, not surprisingly, entered the rankings as one of the most expensive cars ever to sell at auction.

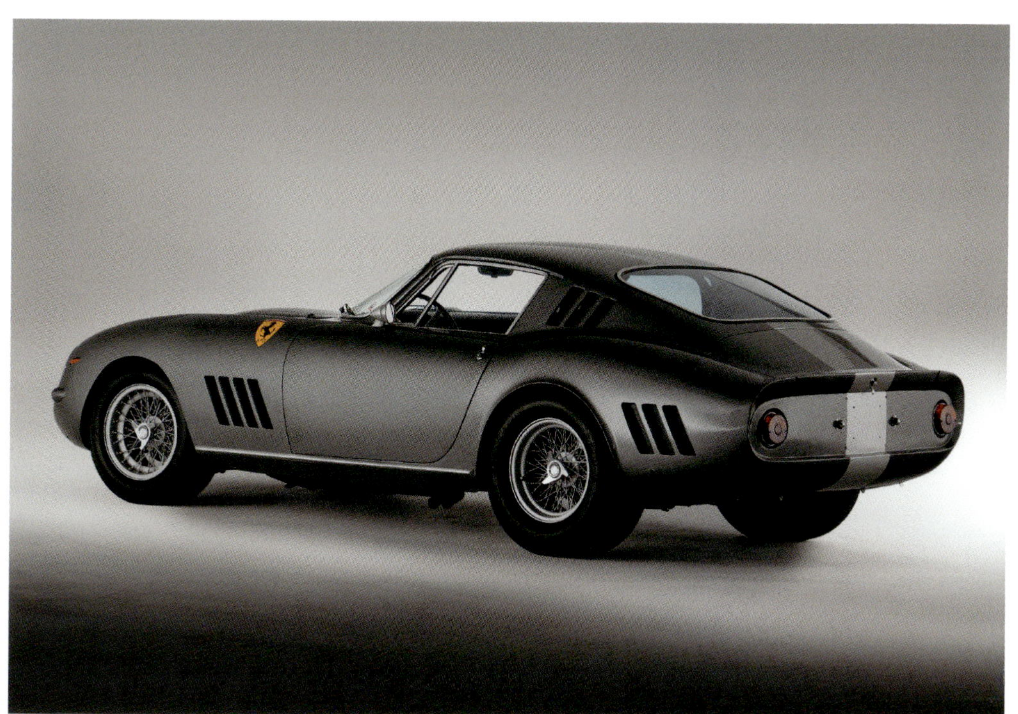

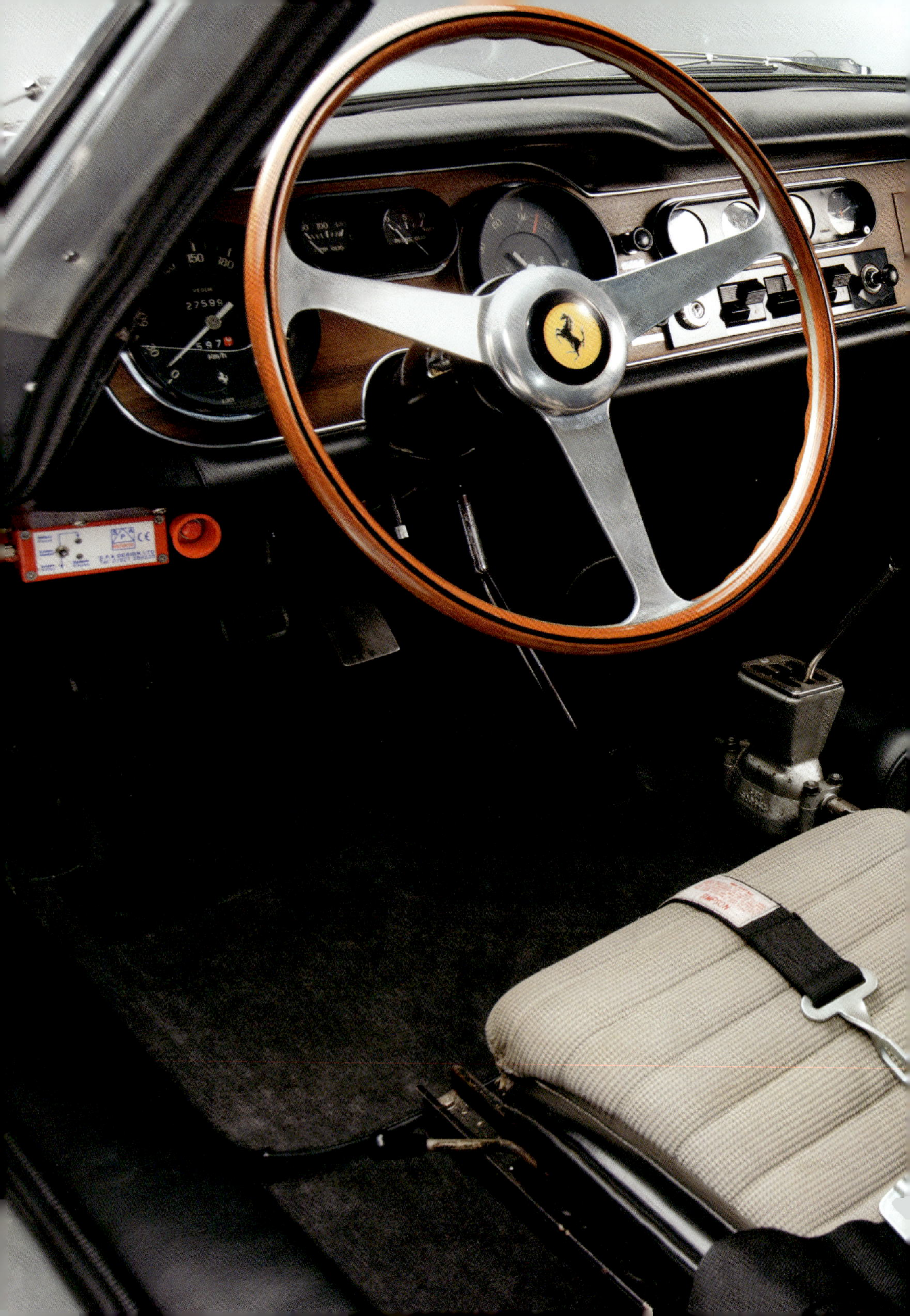
150
180
27599
S.P.A DESIGN LTD

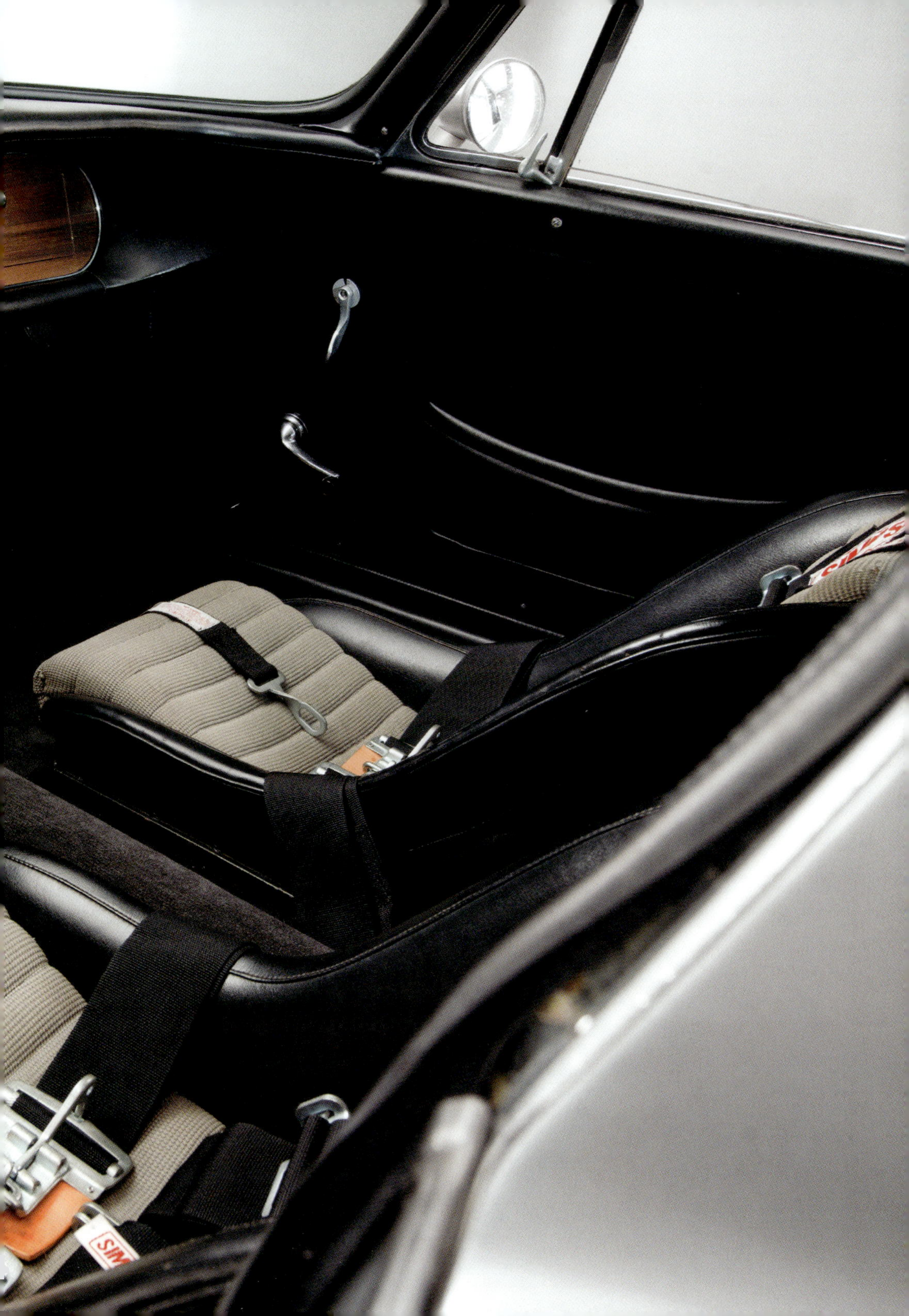

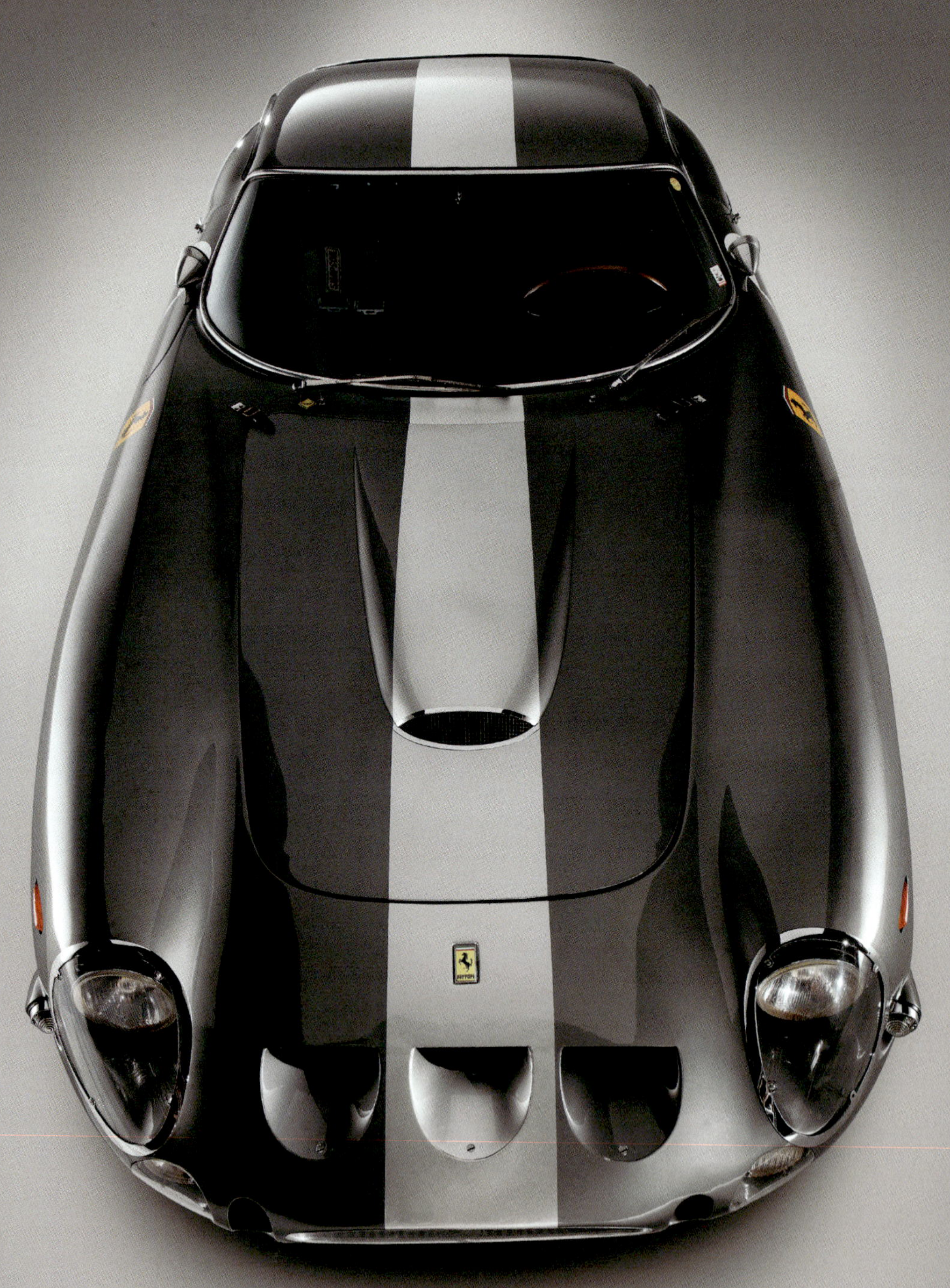

Right: The No. 24 Ecurie Francorchamps Ferrari 275 GTB/C Speciale of Willy Mairesse and Jean Blaton making a pit stop during the 1965 24 Hours of Le Mans.

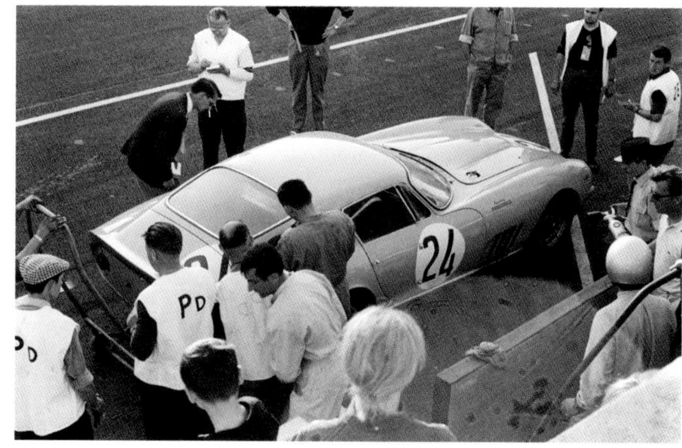

Below: The No. 24 Ecurie Francorchamps Ferrari 275 GTB/C Speciale by Scaglietti (chassis no. 6885) at the 1965 24 Hours of Le Mans. Driven by Willy Mairesse and Jean Blaton the car placed third overall and won its class (GT4.0). Due to the imbroglio between the FIA and Enzo Ferrari over the model's homologation this was the only 275 GTB/C Speciale that competed during the 1965 season.

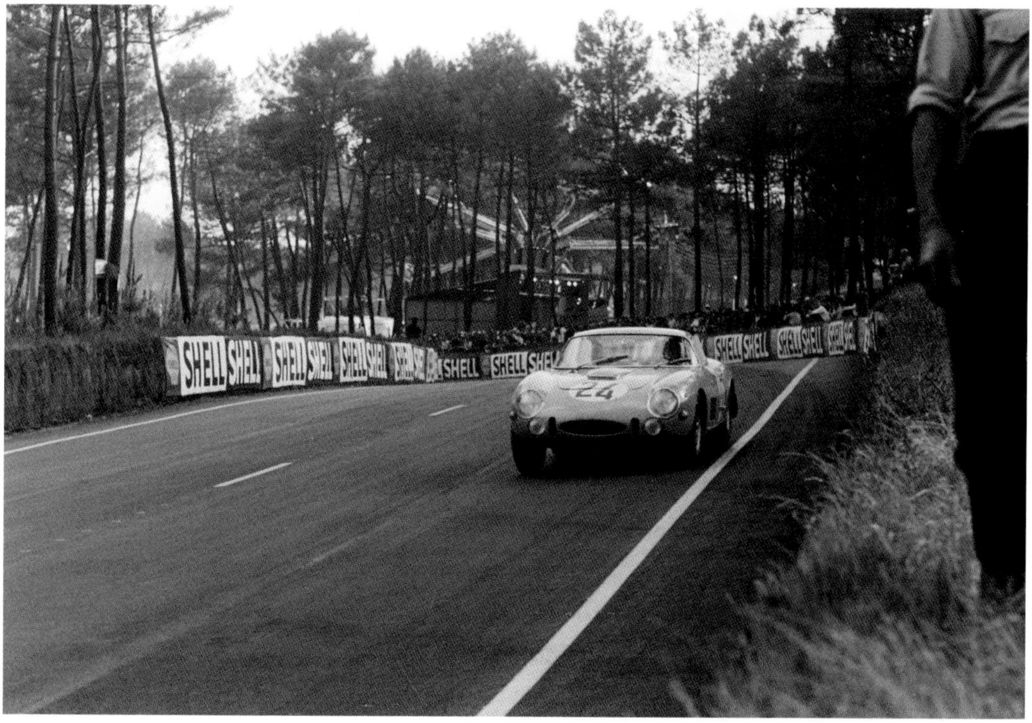

1965

Porsche 904/6 Carrera GTS

MANUFACTURED 1963–65 | ENGINE 1,991 cc (121 cu. in.), SOHC per bank horizontally opposed 6-cylinder HORSEPOWER 200 | TOP SPEED 257 km/h (160 mph) TRANSMISSION 5-speed | NUMBER PRODUCED 6 with Type 901 6-cylinder engine (out of 118 total 904s)

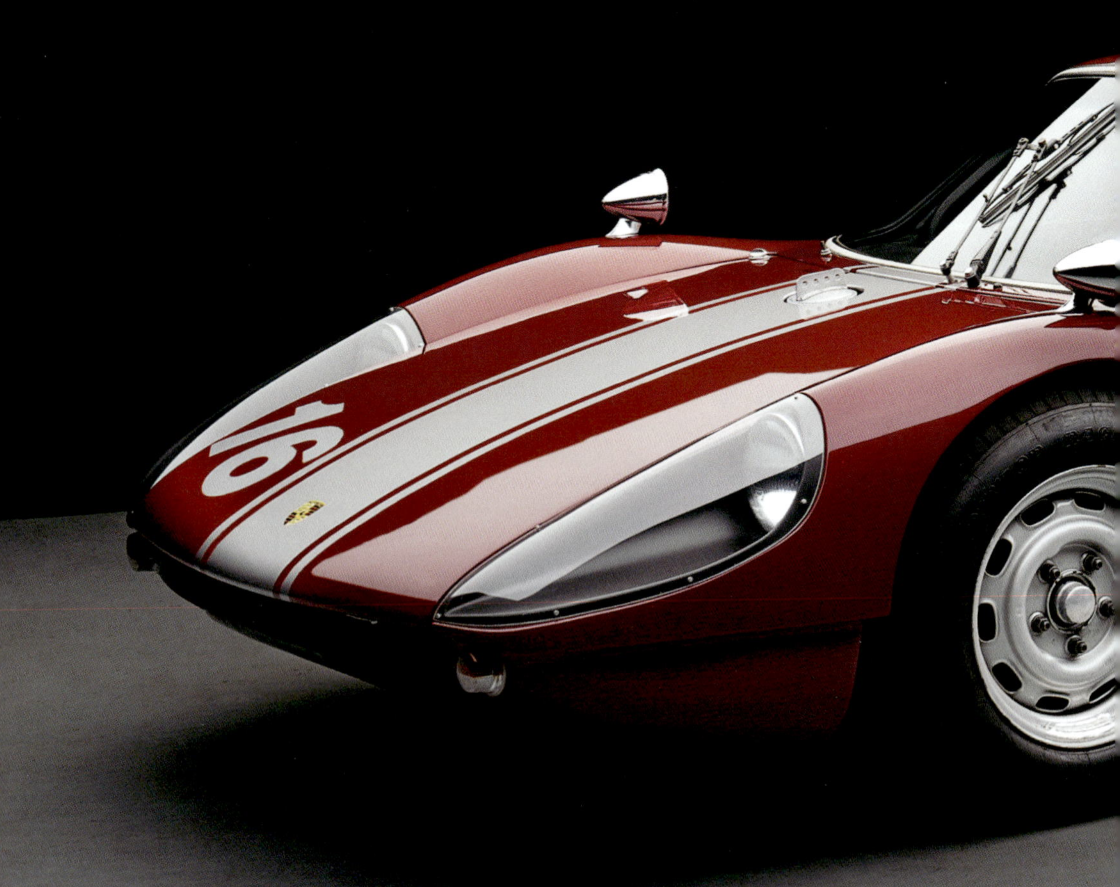

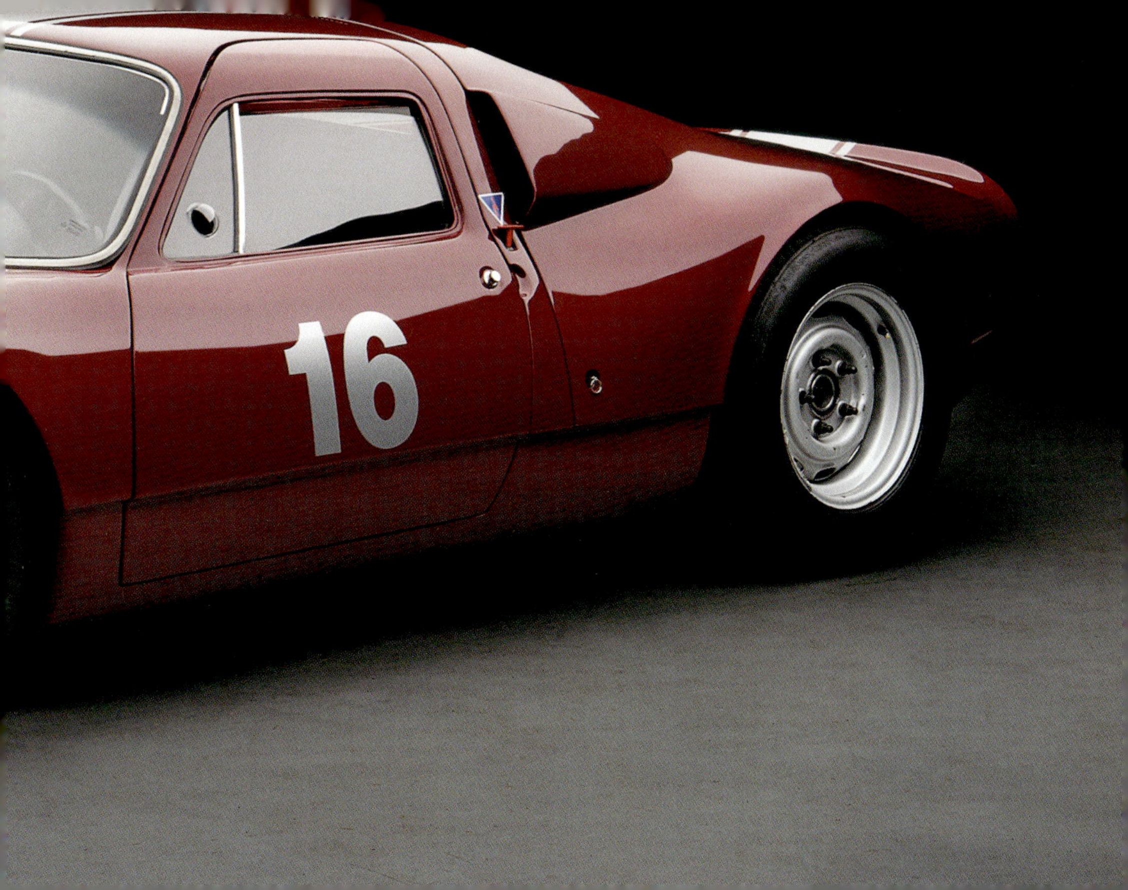
16

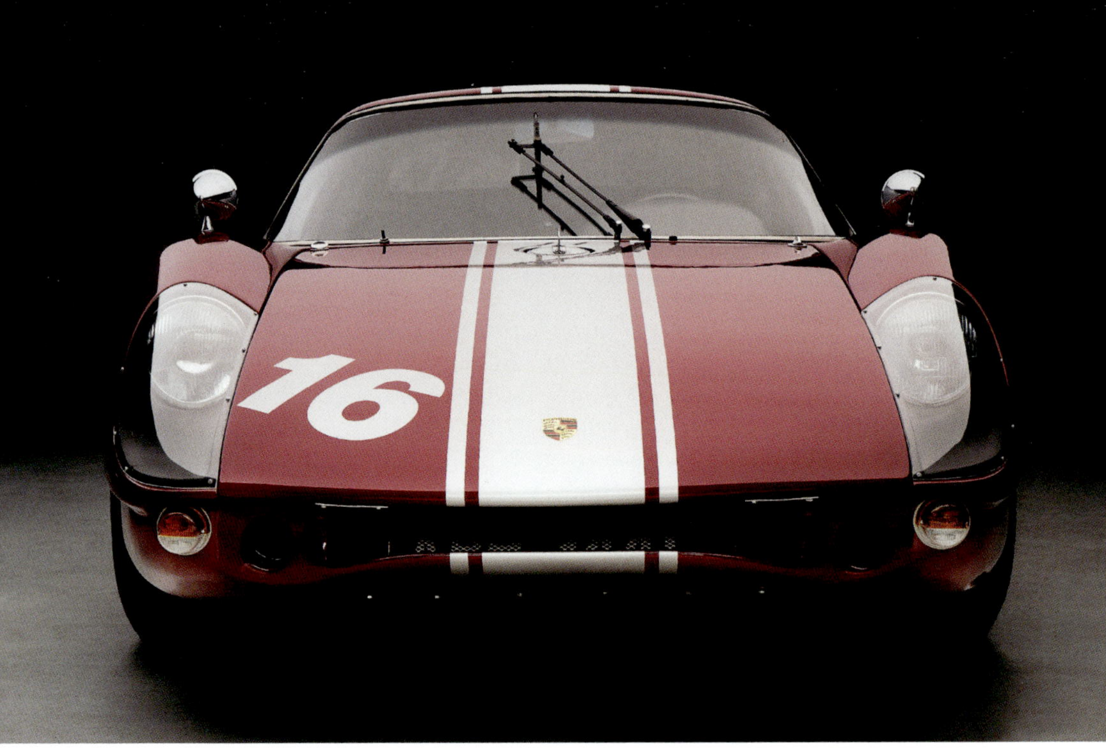

The FIA's homologation rules meant that for any model to be eligible to race in the two-liter GT class of the World Sportscar Championship a minimum of 100 units had to be produced within a 12-month period. The problem with this for manufacturers, however, was that very often there were not enough customers who wanted to purchase out-and-out race cars. The solution, therefore, was to produce very fast street-legal cars that could also be raced competitively on tracks. Porsche had already been successful in this regard with the manufacture of its earlier 550 Spyder (see p. 132).

Ferdinand Alexander "Butzi" Porsche, the son of "Ferry" and grandson of the great Ferdinand, joined the Porsche Design Studio in 1958 and became its head four years later. At the 1963 Frankfurt Motor Show his radically modern 911 was unveiled for the first time as a state-of-the-art successor to the Porsche 356. Alongside it, however, was another design created by Butzi that was equally groundbreaking: the Porsche 904 Carrera GTS.

Unlike the 911, which was intended as a fun and sporty 2+2, the Porsche 904 came to be regarded by many as one of the best Porsche race car designs ever. Having withdrawn from Formula 1 racing the previous season, Porsche was now consolidating its efforts on creating a car that would be guaranteed to bring it sports car racing victory and this stunning model was its solution. As *Porsche Road & Race* notes, "The Porsche Carrera GTS represented a watershed in the company's march toward motorsports fulfillment. Gone was the space frame and aluminum construction of the 550s, the Type 904 ushered in a completely new way of thinking... it is not just the new car's design and overall shape that set it apart, it was the overall construction of the car that was revolutionary." For the first

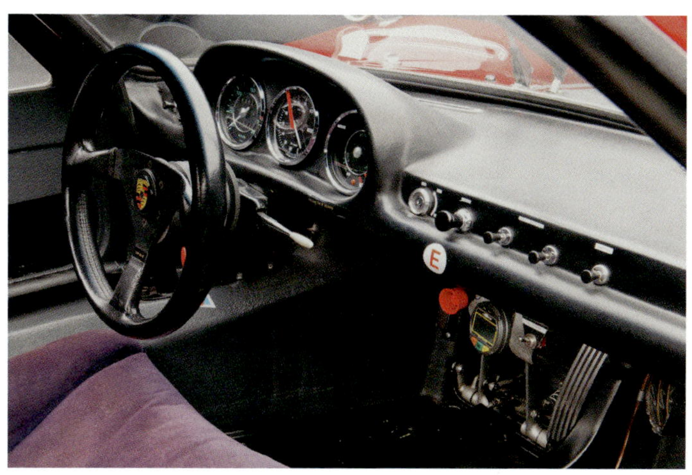

Right: Detail of steering wheel, central instrument cluster and controls. The Porsche 904/6 Carrera GTS's competition-focused cockpit was tight and spartan.

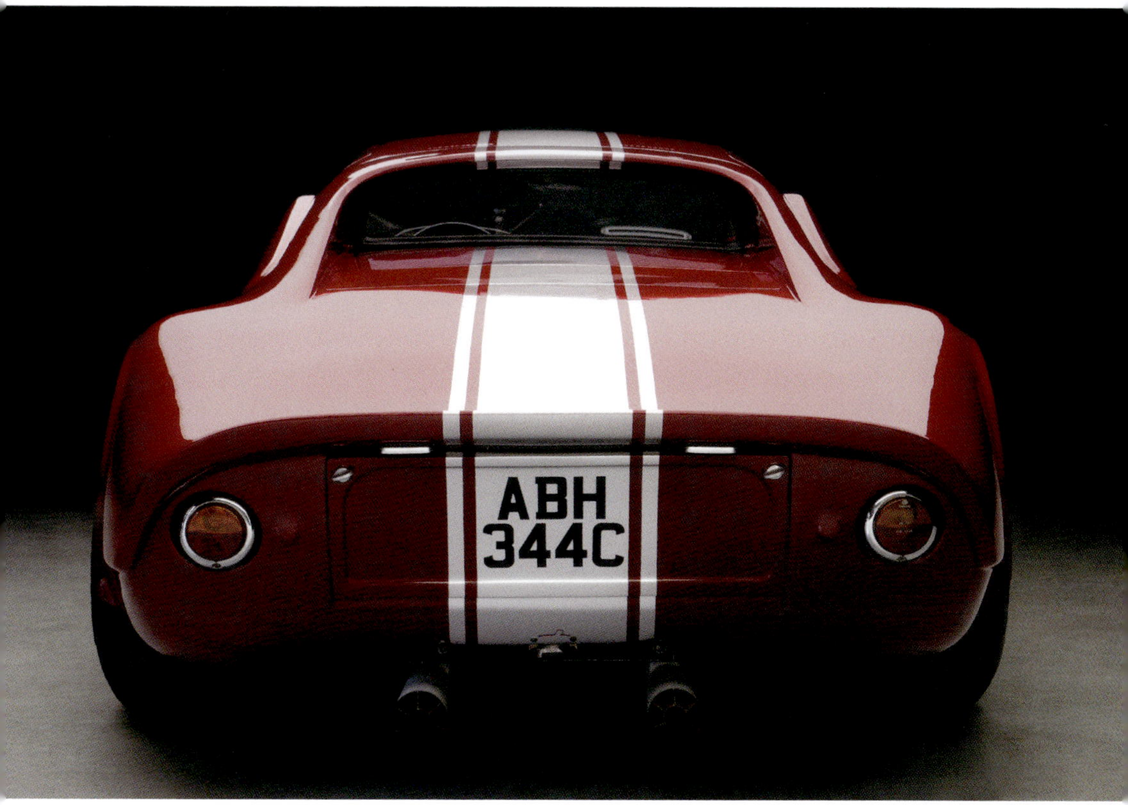

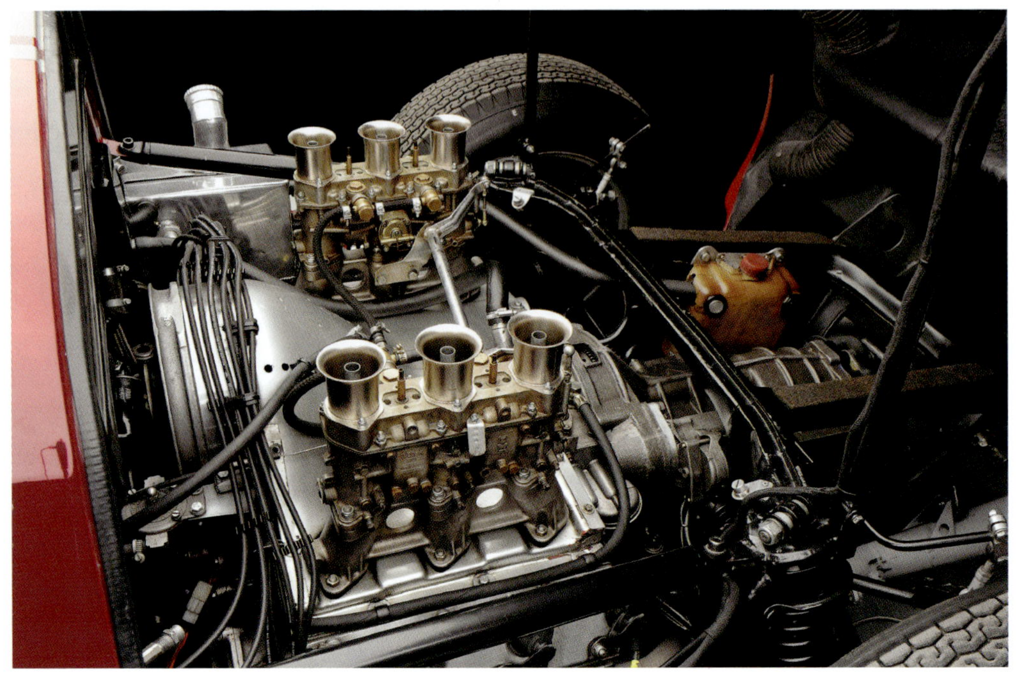

Above: Detail of Porsche 904/6 Carrera GTS 1,991 cc (121 cu. in.), twin-plug, SOHC per bank, air-cooled horizontally opposed six–cylinder mid-mounted engine, with dual Weber 46IDA3C carburetors. Because so few 904s were built with this engine the car could not be homologated, so it was restricted to racing in the prototype class.

time, the Stuttgart-based company used a box-section steel frame construction, which was then skinned with a fiberglass body. The problem for Porsche was although it needed to create 100 examples to satisfy the FIA's homogolation rules in order to race the car, it was not sure there were a hundred customers to buy them. So the company decided to price them very competitively at DM29,700 (equating to $7,481). As a consequence, the first hundred cars were preordered quickly, and then another 18 were made to fulfill unexpected demand for the model. At this time, however, Porsche had no experience of serially producing fiberglass bodies, so it had to turn to the expertise of the aircraft maker Heinkel, to which it subcontracted their construction. Each body had 50 separate parts, which meant Heinkel could only produce two a day, but even then the Porsche factory struggled to build the required chassis for them to go onto. Once Porsche had built a chassis it was dispatched to Heinkel, where the sculptural body was then directly bonded onto the steel frame to help strengthen the car and enhance its rigidity.

The great thing about using fiberglass, apart from it being lighter and cheaper than hand-beaten aluminum, was that it was easier to create complex forms out of. Indeed, the stunning body shape of the 904 attests to this. But as the Revs Institute notes, "its beauty cloaked the fact that it wasn't as aerodynamically perfect as it might have been, and it was

Right: The No. 32 Porsche System Engineering team 904/6 Carrera GTS of Herbert Linge and Peter Nöcker at the 1965 24 Hours of Le Mans. The car performed extremely well having placed forth overall and winning its class (P2.0). Linge and Nöcker's trouble-free run also netted them the Index of Performance prize ahead of the winning Ferrari 250 LM. This Works Porsche 904/6 Carrera GTS (chassis no. 906-001) was the very first six-cylinder engine Porsche sports racer. Previously in May of that year Porsche factory test-driver Herbert Linge and Umberto Maglioli had achieved a fifth place overall in the Nürburgring 1,000 km in the same car.

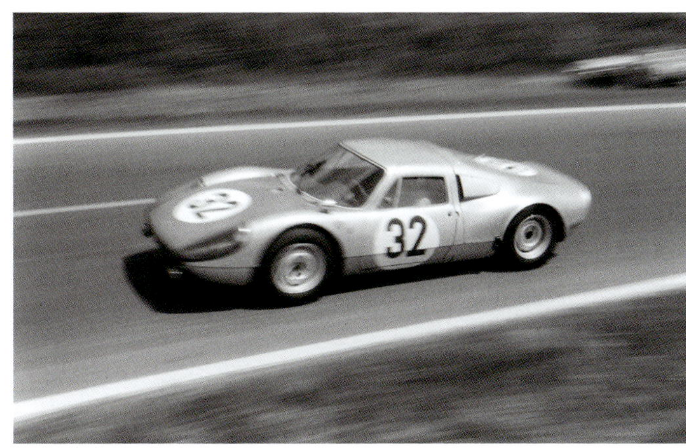

Below: The 904 Carrera GTS was Porsche's first closed mid-engine car; four-, six- and eight-cylinder versions were offered. This example is one of only six built with the Type 901 6-cylinder engine.

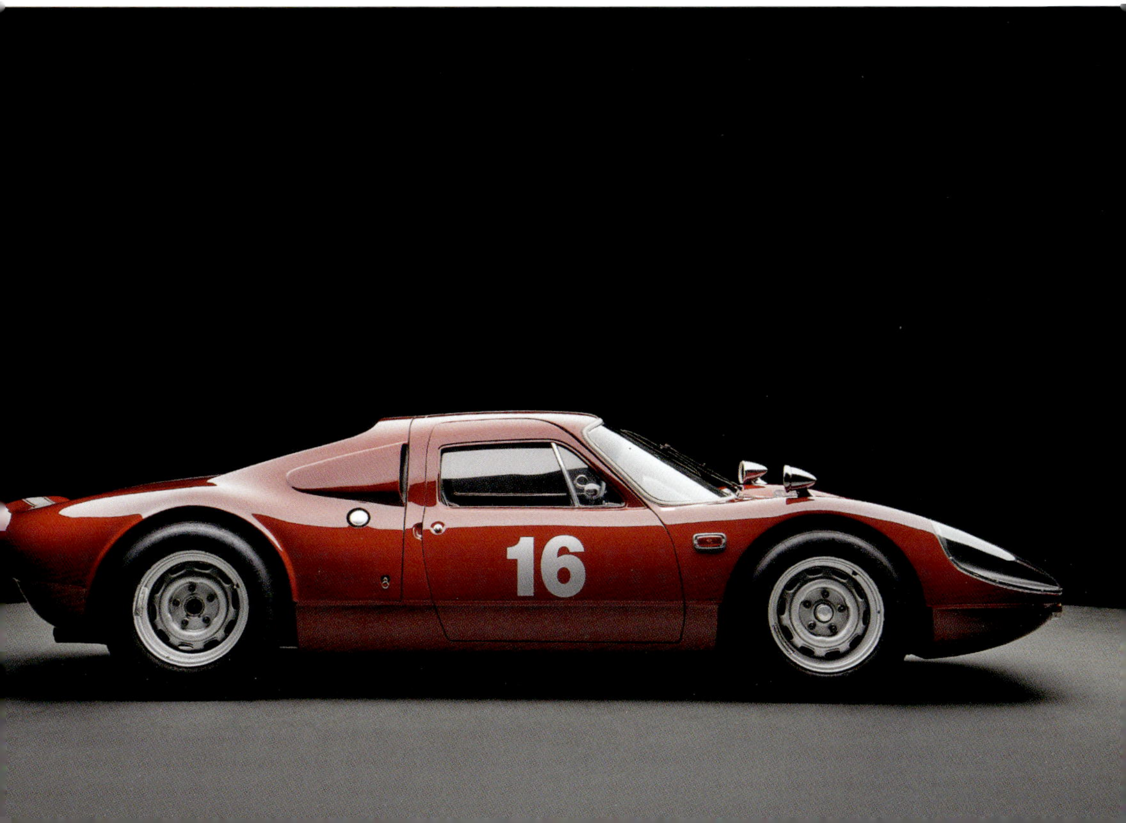

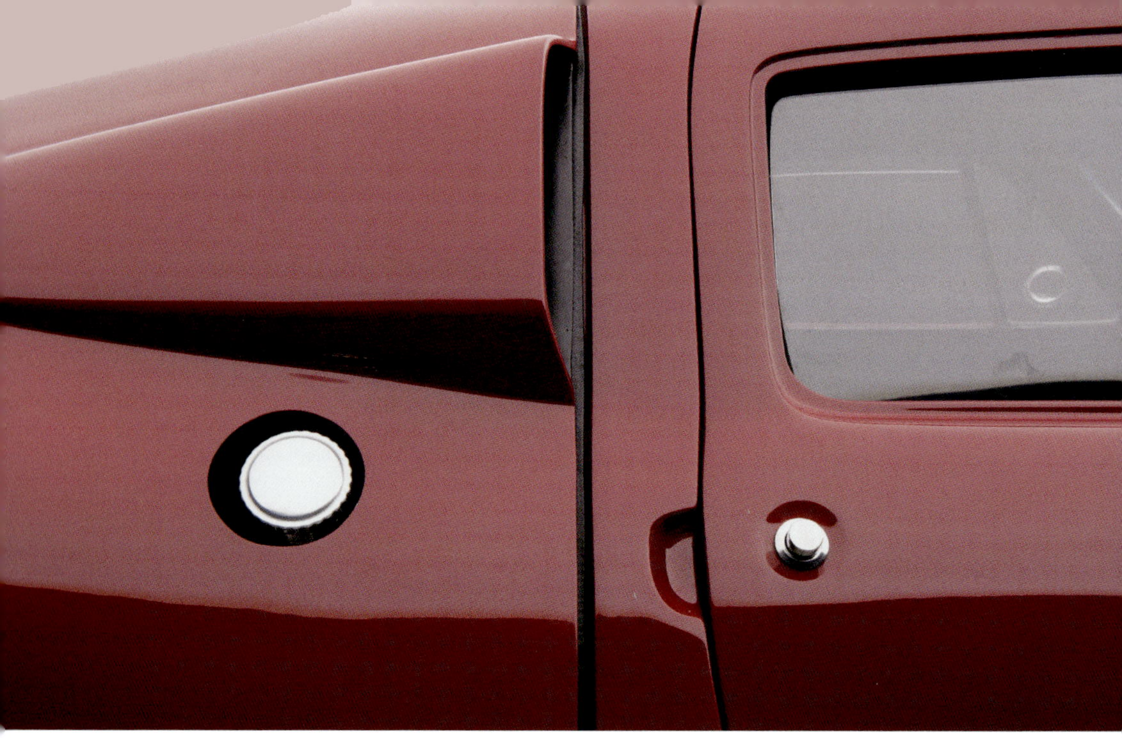

Above: The six-cylinder 904s were easily differentiated from the four-cylinder variants by the broader side air scoops for brake cooling, vertical lift windows and central fuel filler caps, while some differences in brake ducts, fog lights and other details varied from car to car, as development was a continual and rapid process.

Opposite: Detail of fuel cell with centrally located filler cap, a feature unique to the 904/6's.

Overleaf: The styling of the 904 was typical of competition coupés at the time in that the door shut line reached up onto the horizontal roof section, thereby creating easy access to the cockpit. This was possible because the complex curves required in the construction were far easier to achieve in fiberglass than hand-beaten aluminum.

overweight, too. Moreover, as caution dictated that the intended but untried 911-based engine be scratched, it used the aging but reliable 180 horsepower Carrera four-cam unit." Of the 118 examples produced of the 904 Carrera GTS, 109 were fitted with this Type 587/3 two-liter, four-cylinder boxer engine. Just six cars were fitted with the more powerful Type 901 two-liter, six-cylinder boxer engine, which was the engine originally intended for the 904. Even fewer were fitted with the Type 771 two-liter, flat-eight engine. According to its original Le Mans entry paperwork, the example shown here (chassis no. 906-012) was an official works racer and was initially fitted with an eight-cylinder engine, but this was then swapped out for the two-liter flat-six ahead of the 1965 racing season — making it one of the six to be equipped this way.

This model's racing debut had, however, occured the previous year, when five Porsche 904 Carrera GTSs had been fielded at the Sebring 12-Hour race in 1964. Two did not finish, while the other three went on to clock up ninth, 31st and 37th positions, which was a pretty inauspicious start for this brand new sports racer. Nevertheless, the next month it finally proved itself spectacularly, with a 1-2-6 finish at the Targa Florio, which with its twisting mountain roads was better suited to the 904's nimble handling. In fact, this model was never intended to be a dominant race winner, being as it was, up against the likes of Ferrari's legendary 250 GTOs (see p. 264). Yet, over the course of 1964 and 1965, the 904s continued to prove themselves race after race, especially on tight courses. In fact, Porsche's entire competiton strategy until the late 1960s was, as auto-journalist Andrew Frankel explains, "to mop up class honors." This approach ultimately enabled Porsche to take Division II (2,000 cc) of the International Championship for GT Manufacturers in 1964. As a road-going car, the 904 would be overshadowed by the ascent of the 911, but then this model had always been intended as a bona fide series production car, unlike its race-born sibling. Yet, in terms of its fluid aerodynamic styling the 904 set an important benchmark for successive generations of racing Porsches, not least the 906s.

The stunning Stuttgart-born racer (chassis 906-012) shown here, initally bore the Works' silver-gray livery and was entered by the factory team twice during the 1965 season — obtaining, on its debut, a sixth place at the Nürburgring 1000 km, but then sadly retiring with valve problems at that year's 24 Hours of Le Mans. The following year, its was sold on, without its motor, to American racing driver/privateer, George Drolsom, who reinstalled a correct six-cylinder engine and then fielded it at various races, which ultimtately led to a 1st in class at the 1967 12 Hours of Sebring. It subsequently passed through various hands, before ending up in Lord Laidlaw's renowned collection in 2003, where it was given a full competition overhaul and refinished in the distinctive Laidlaw colors. Since then, this sublime ex-Works racer has participated in many historic meetings, from the Le Mans Classic to the Goodwood Revival.

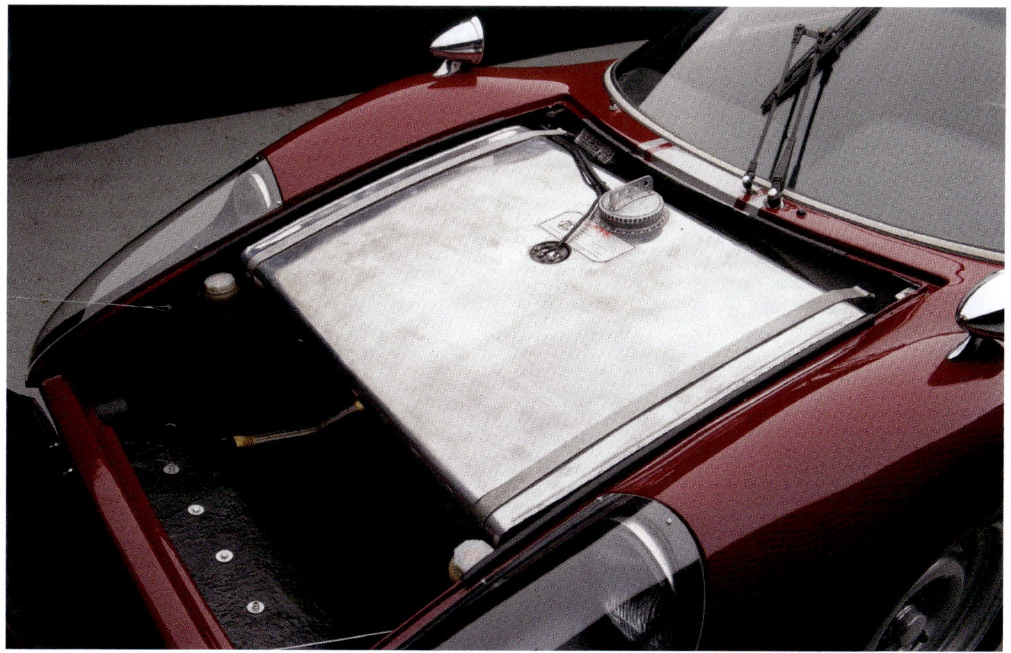

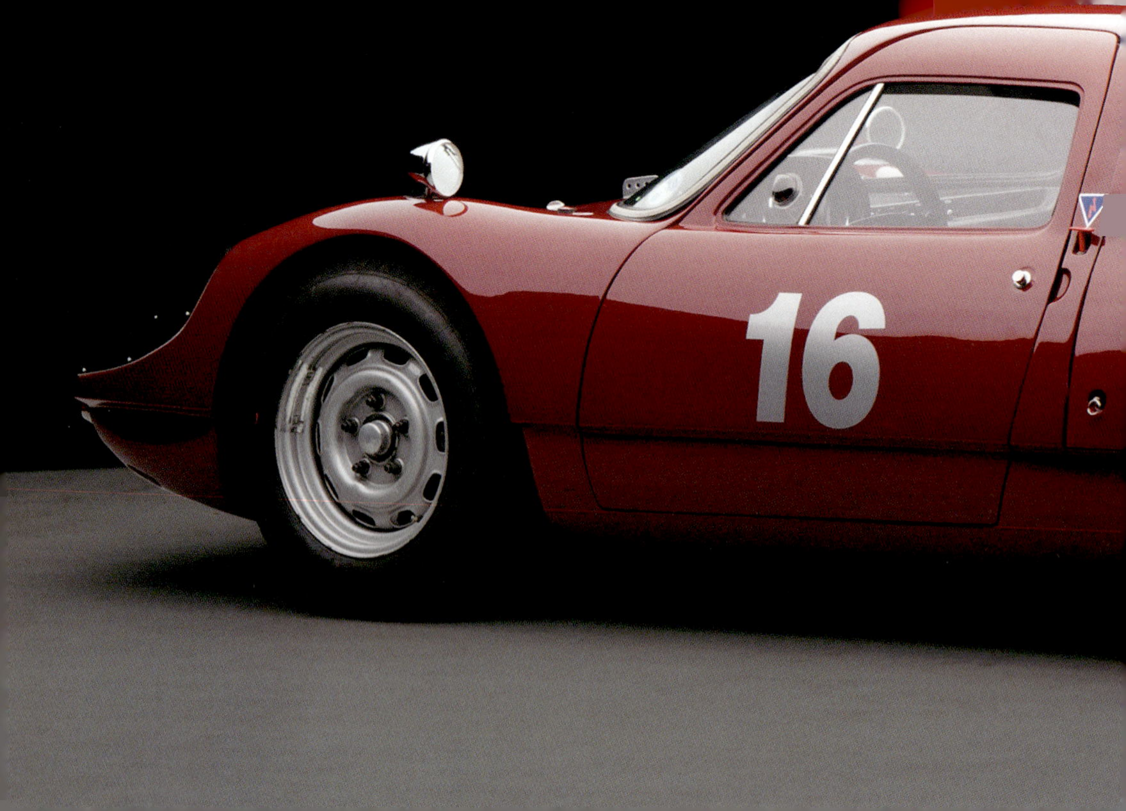
16

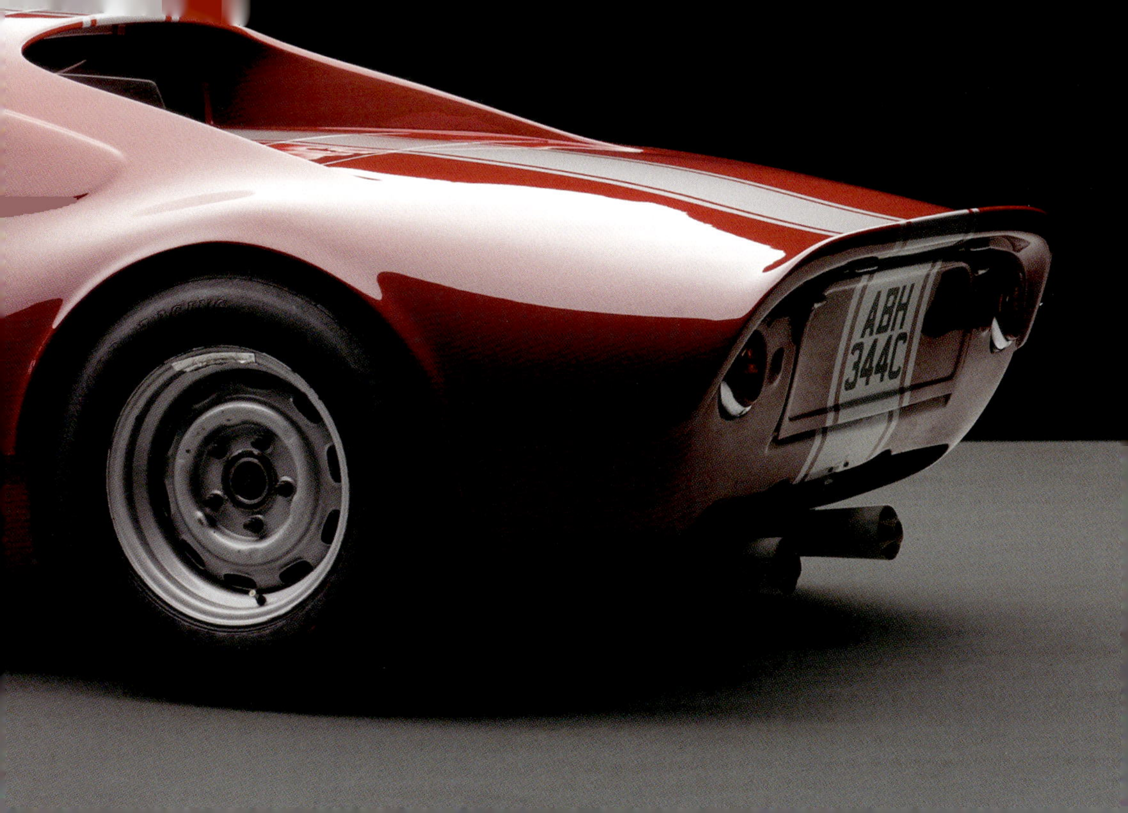
ABH
344C

1966

Shelby 427 Cobra S/C

MANUFACTURED 1965–66 | ENGINE 6,997 cc (427 cu. in.), overhead-valve V8 | HORSEPOWER 485
TOP SPEED 298 km/h (185 mph) | TRANSMISSION 4-speed
NUMBER PRODUCED 29

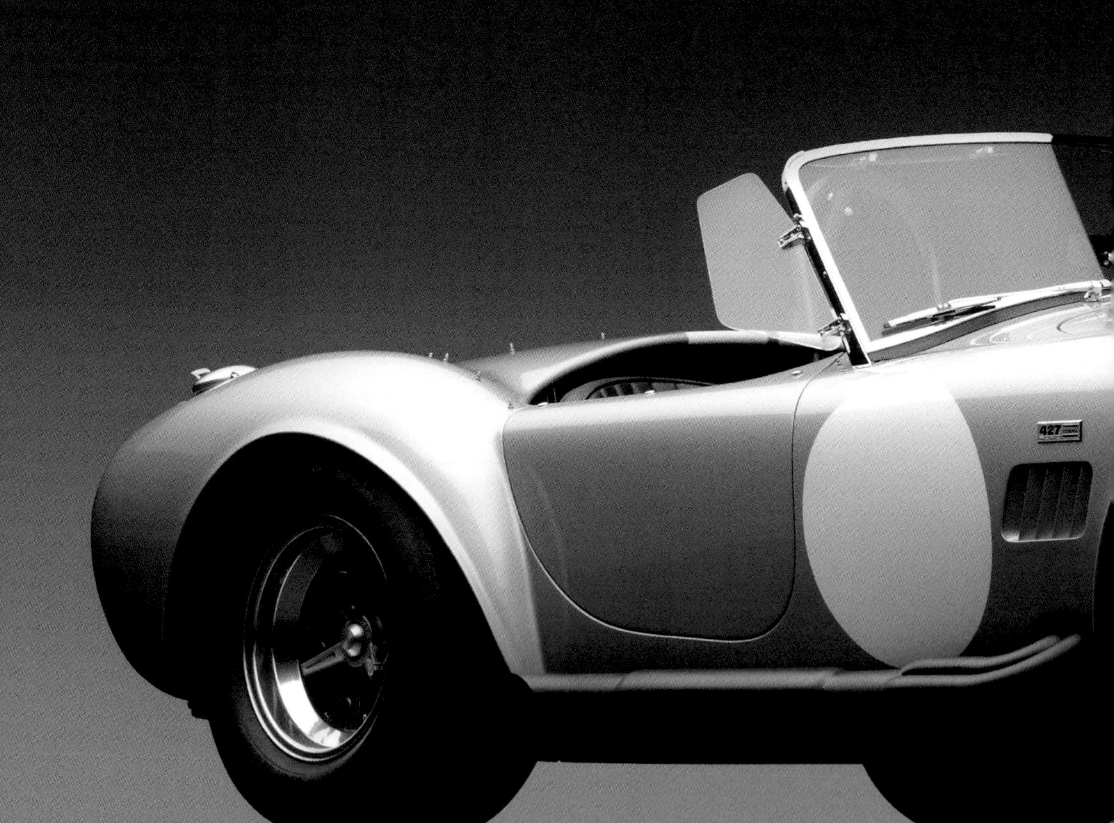

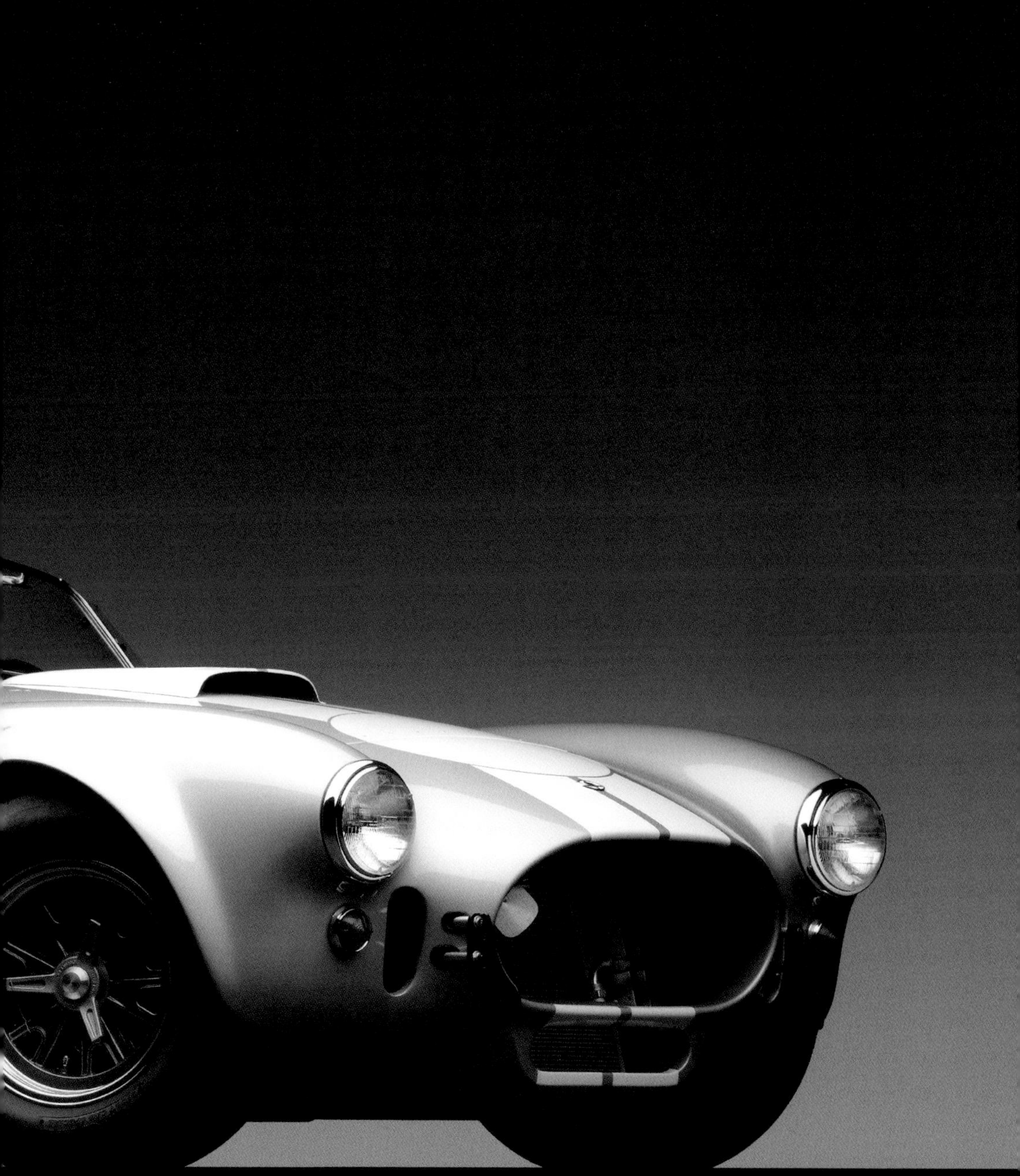

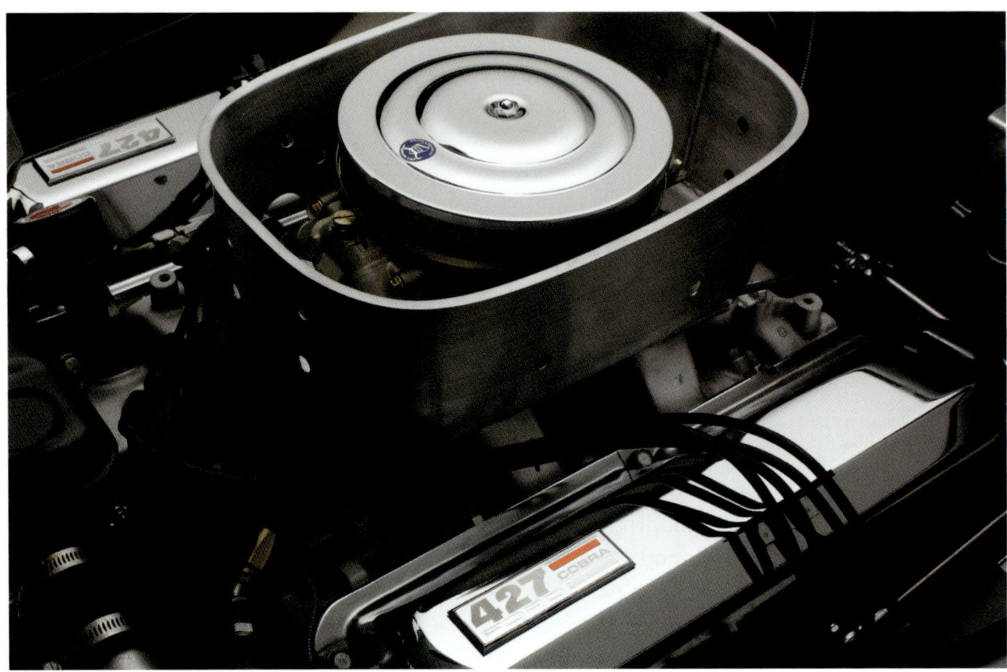

Some cars are all about graceful aesthetics, others opulent luxury, and then there are those that are all about sheer visceral power. The Shelby 427 Cobra S/C falls unequivocally into this latter category. As RM Sotheby's noted when it came to selling the outstanding present example, "It was classic Carroll Shelby, a delightfully mad idea made even madder: take the already ferocious 289 Cobra ... and 'upgrade' it with a 427." The resultant 427 Cobra S/C certainly had all the prerequisite credentials of a testosterone-fueled American sports racer: awesome power under the hood provided by a mighty 427 cu. in. V8; a strong, resilient chassis that could tolerate the intense forces exerted on the car when driven hard and fast; and a well-toned yet lightweight body with bulges in all the right places.

Shelby had always intended to race the 427 Cobra (aka the Cobra MK III), and so the original plan was to build 100 units in full competition trim so as to meet the FIA's strict homologation "GT Class" rules for the upcoming 1965 season. Unfortunately, however, progress was slow in this regard and when FIA inspectors showed up at Shelby's facility in early 1965 only 51 examples had thus far been constructed, which meant he was denied racing approval. As a result of this, he halted production of the full-out competition 427 racers because their whole raison d'être had evaporated. By this stage, however, 16 had already been sold on to privateer-run teams. Then in June 1965, the FIA introduced a new "Competition GT" class, which had a reduced homologation threshold of 50 units, which might have seemed fortuitous. The problem was this was the same class that the Ford GT40 (see p. 362) would be racing in. Shelby had famously helped Ford develop this car, so to avoid any conflict of interest he promised Ford that he would not competitively field his 427 Cobras.

Opposite: Shelby 427 Cobra "Semi Competition" engine with single four-barrel 780 CFM Holley carburetor. Weighing only 2,282 lb. (1,035 kg), the power-to-weight of this car (0.40 hp/kg) was thrilling.

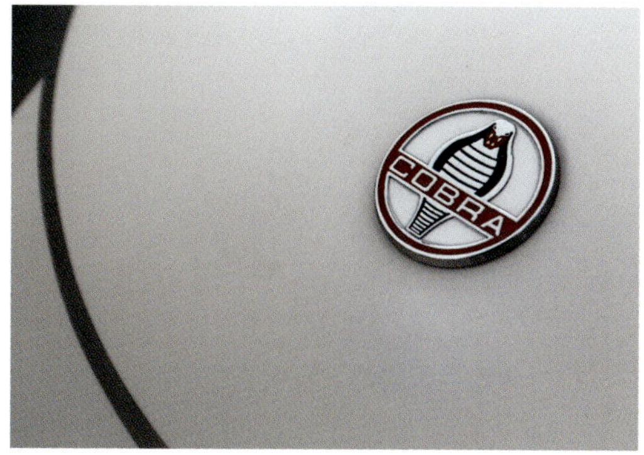

In addition to the 51 competition 427 Cobra chassis that were built there were two prototypes and one that was sent to Ford Engineering. Of the remaining unsold competition chassis, 29 were subsequently repurposed into factory-built 427 S/C or "Semi-Competition" street racers that had been adapted with road-use windscreens, slightly altered engines and quasi-stripped semi-competition trim. When first unveiled in 1965, the 427 S/C was the world's fastest street-legal car. Its Ford 427 cast-iron block V8 provided 485 hp and a top speed of 185 mph (298 km/h). In large part, the 427 S/C was able to achieve this remarkable flat-out speed thanks to its lightweight and highly compact design. Incredibly, it only

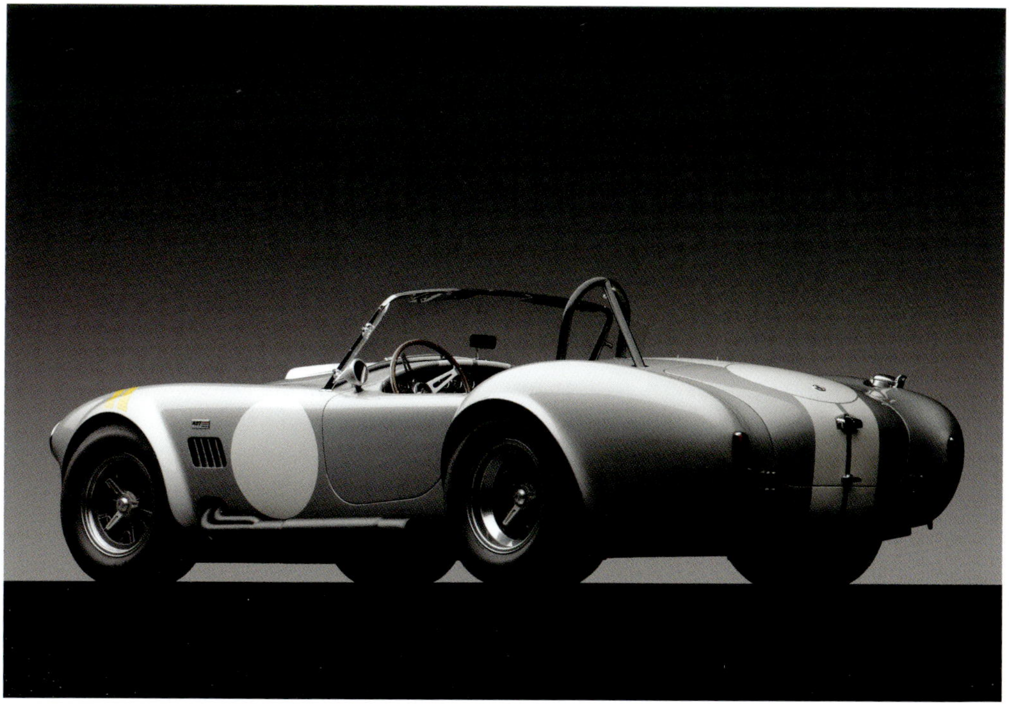

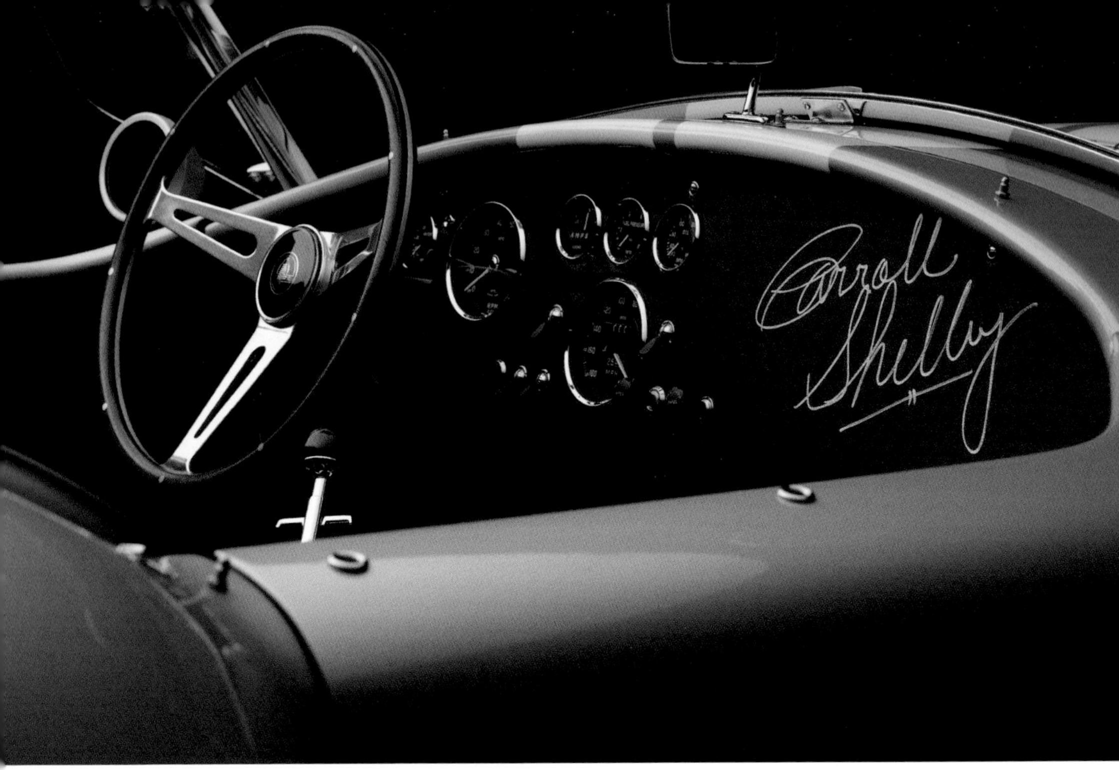

Above: Detail of cockpit (chassis no. CSX 3040) with Carroll Shelby's signature on the dash panel.

weighed 2,282 lb. (1,035 kg), while its internal layout was a truly masterful exercise of space-saving engineering.

Not surprisingly, these race-bred road beasts retained many of the features found on the full-on competition model, including its riveted hood scoop, oil cooler, roll bar, distinctive flared fenders, side exhausts, dual lightweight batteries, a 42-gallon fuel tank and an external quick-fueling access point. Outrageously quick, these street-legal semi-competition roadsters were actually faster than many full-bore racers of the period. Unlike many other 427 Cobra S/Cs, which were very often hammered into the ground by their owners, the stunning example shown here (chassis no. CSX 3040) is unusually well preserved and documented, with only four long-term caretakers since new. As an authentic matching-numbers 427 S/C, which has undergone a sympathetic restoration by Cobra expert Mike McCluskey, CSX 3040 can rightfully be regarded as one of the ultimate "street" Cobras out there.

Right: 1965 Shelby American, Inc. magazine advertisement for the 427 Cobra, with two 427 Cobra S/Cs in the background.

Below: Phil Hill driving the No. 7 Shelby 427 Cobra S/C at the 1965 SCCA National Candlestick in San Francisco, California. He did not finish the race. Because Carroll Shelby was helping Ford develop the GT40 program, he promised not to competitively field the 427 Cobras, and so the Competition and S/C variants of the Shelby 427 Cobra were only ever raced by privateers.

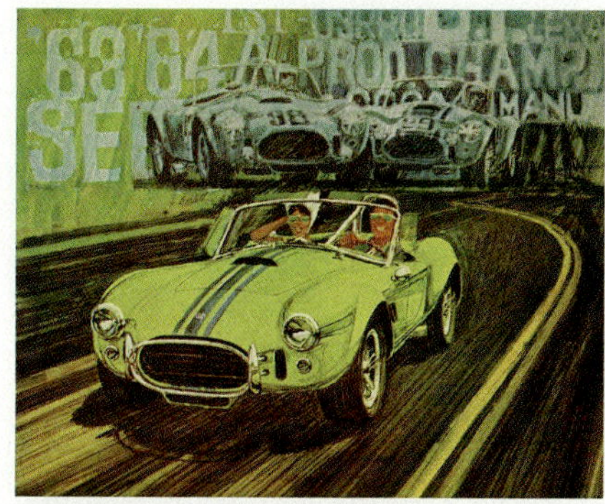

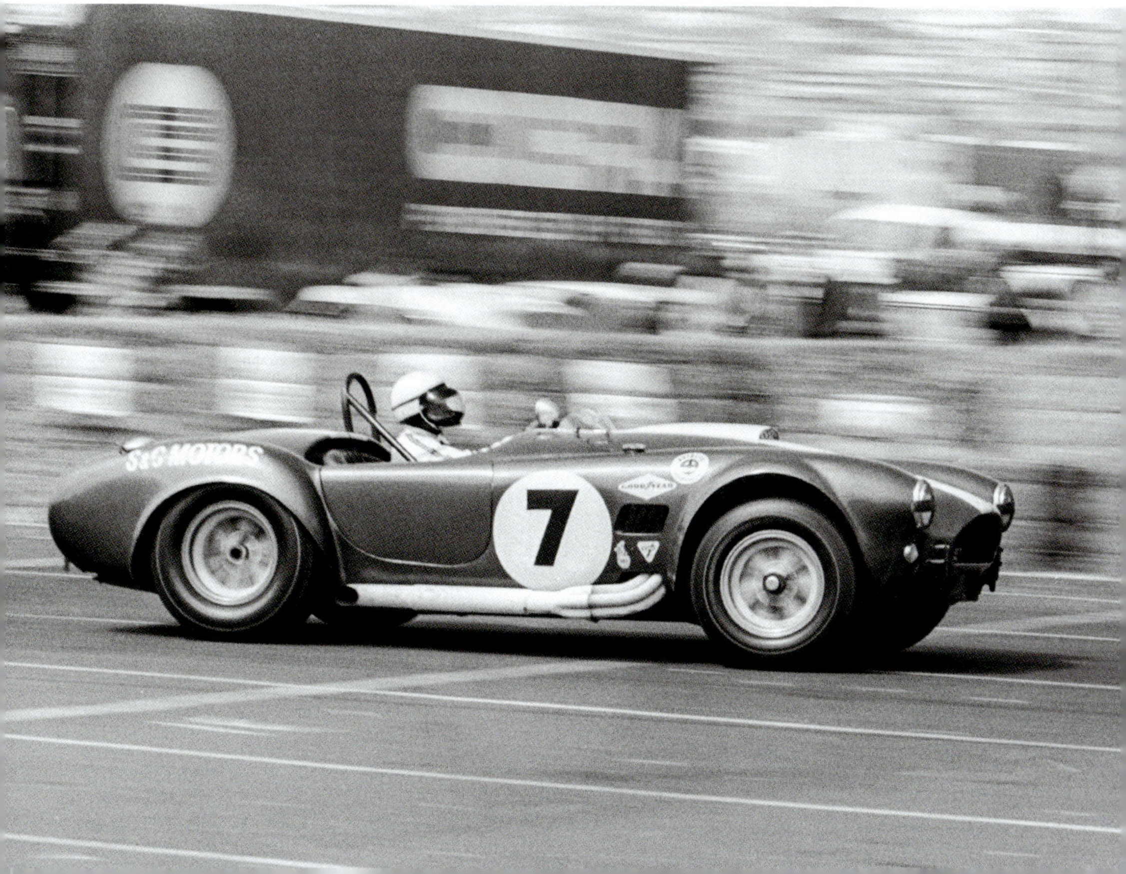

1966

Jaguar XJ13

MANUFACTURED 1966 | ENGINE 4,991 cc (305 cu. in.), DOHC per bank V12 | HORSEPOWER 502
TOP SPEED 287 km/h (178 mph) | TRANSMISSION 5-speed
NUMBER PRODUCED 1

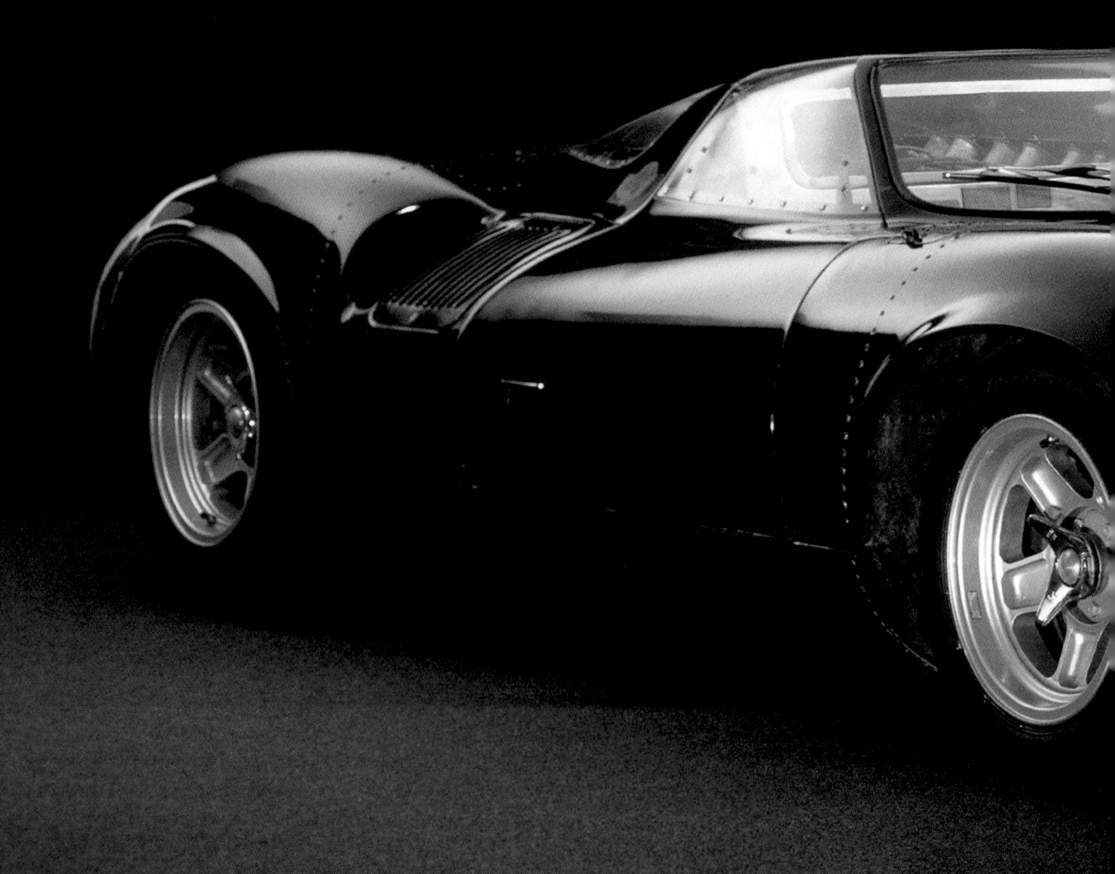

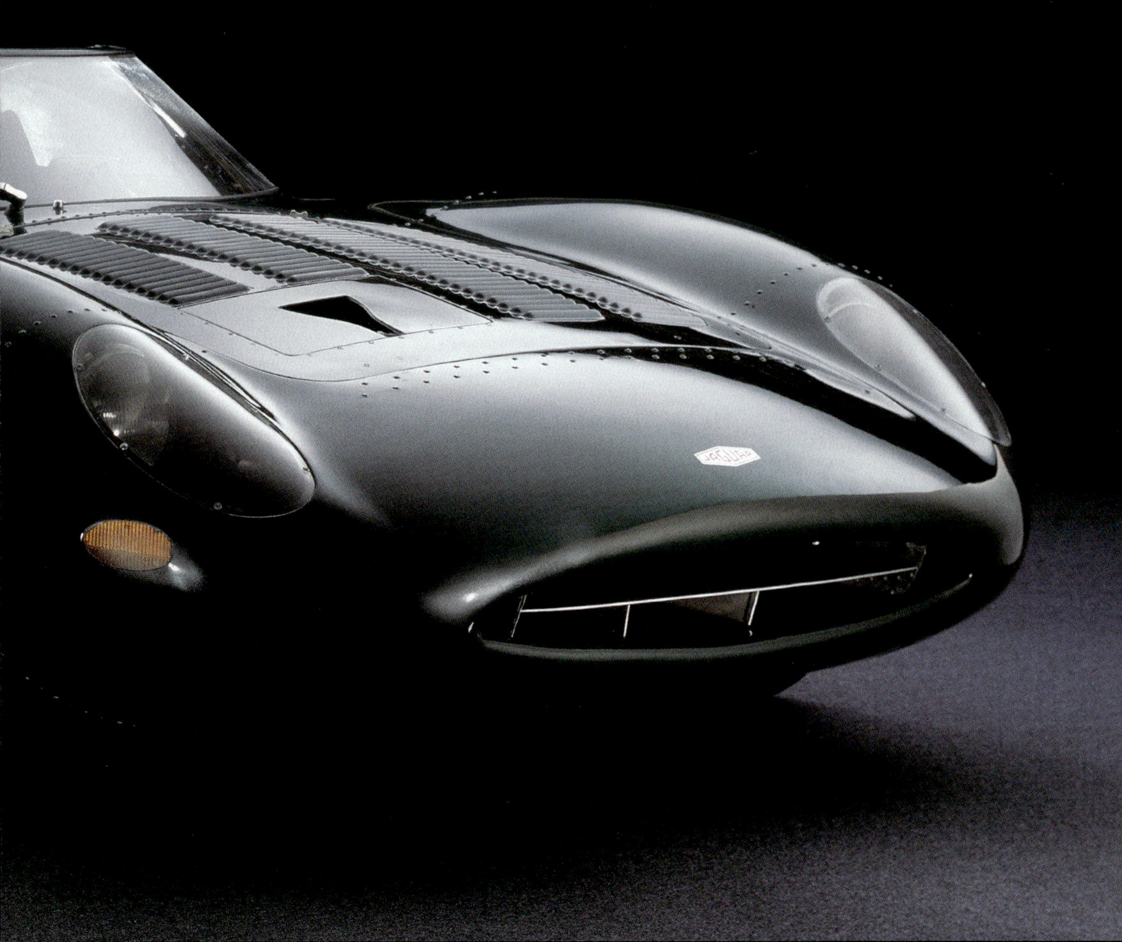
JAGUAR

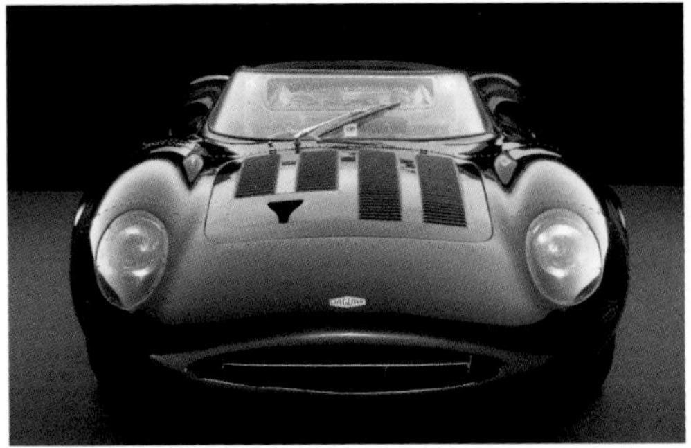

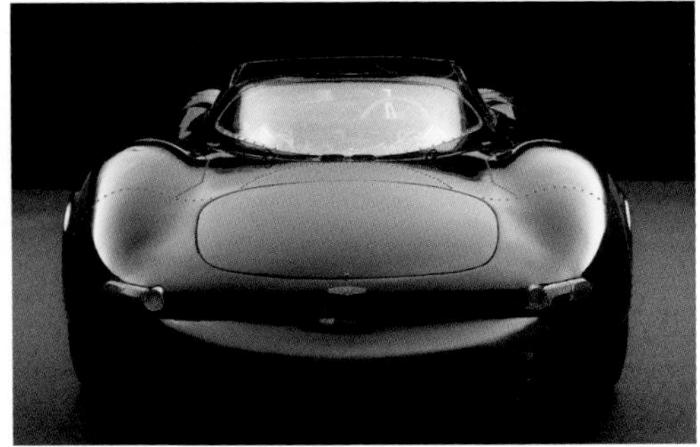

Overleaf: Detail of Jaguar XJ13 cockpit, steering wheel, instrumentation and controls. The car's mighty V12 engine, which was mounted longitudinally behind the driver, was used as a stressed chassis member together with the five-speed manual ZF Transaxle gearbox.

Described by the well-known motoring journalist Andrew Frankel as "The finest Jaguar that never was," the XJ13 is a bit of an enigma for although it was built for the 24 Hours of Le Mans, its racing prowess was never properly tested in competition. Today, this one-off racing prototype resides at the British Motor Museum in Gaydon, Warwickshire. Like the Jaguar C-Type, D-Type and E-Type (see pp. 102, 144, & 282) before it, the XJ13 was designed by the legendary aerodynamicist Malcolm Sayer. Jaguar Cars' director William Heynes initially approached the experienced racing driver Jack Brabham to help with its development vis-à-vis high-speed testing, but in the end this role was taken up by David Hobbs along with Norman Dewis and Richard "Dickie" Attwood.

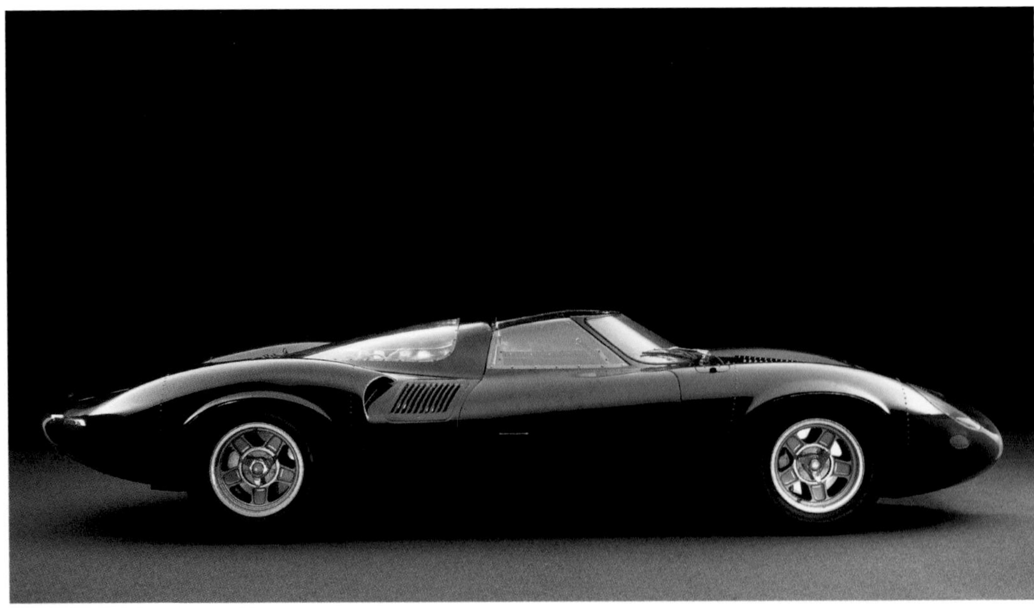

Prior to the XJ13, all of Jaguar's racing cars and practically all of its road cars had been powered by the marque's highly regarded XK6 six-cylinder twin-overhead-cam engine, which had been famously developed by the firm's chief engineer, William Heynes, in around 1943. In contrast, the XJ13 had at its heart a new five-liter quad-cam V12 engine, known as the XK12. This awesome power plant designed by Heynes in collaboration with Claude Baily was made of lightweight aluminum alloy rather than iron. It comprised a pair of twin-engines joined at a 60-degree angle that utilized a common crankcase and crankshaft. It was the glorious culmination of Jaguar's long-held desire to build a racing V12 engine, designs for which had first been sketched by Heynes as far back as 1954.

This powerful, responsive V12 was placed mid-engine and functioned as a stressed chassis component alongside the XJ13's five-speed manual ZF transaxle. Initially, the XJ13 was intended to be raced at Le Mans during the mid-1960s, but its development got sidetracked by Jaguar's merger with BMC in 1966 and the parallel development of an important new road car for the company, the XJ6 saloon, which was launched in 1968. This critical delay meant that by the time the XJ13 was nearing completion in late 1966, its design was pretty much obsolete at least when compared to its potential competitors, namely the Ferrari 330 P4 (see p. 374) and the Ford GT40 (see p. 362). So much so, Jaguar's co-founder and still managing director, Sir William Lyons, became uneasy about racing it, believing the potential for negative publicity if it was seen as a failure far outweighed its slim chance of victory. Plus, he did not want it to detract attention away from the success of the E-Type road car. He decided, therefore, to shelve the project and instructed his team not to test the XJ13 any further. Yet despite this, the car would still go on to become a legend. Ultimately, it was just too much of a temptation for its engineering team not to find out what

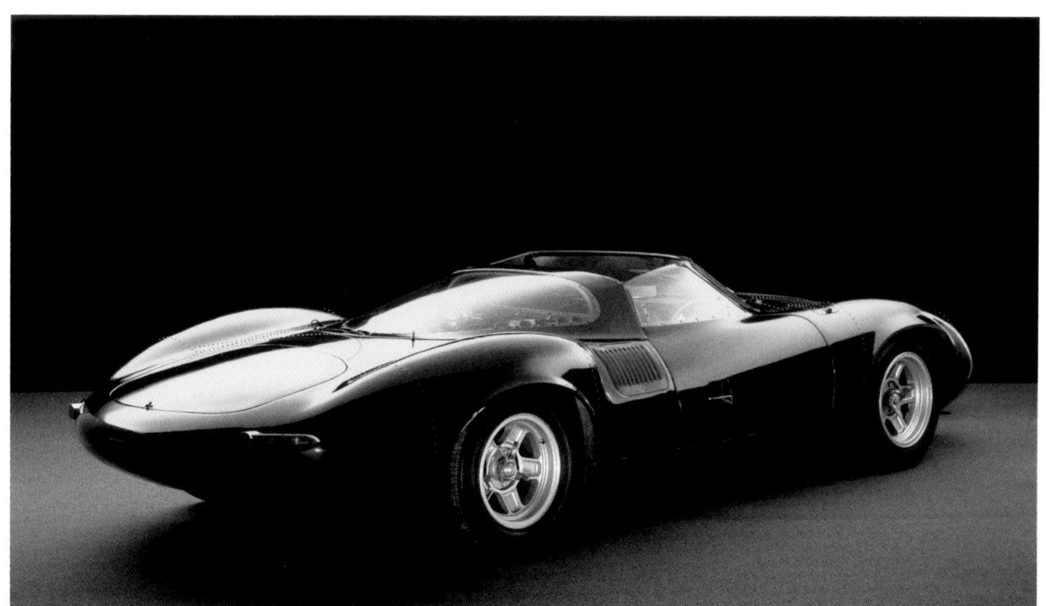

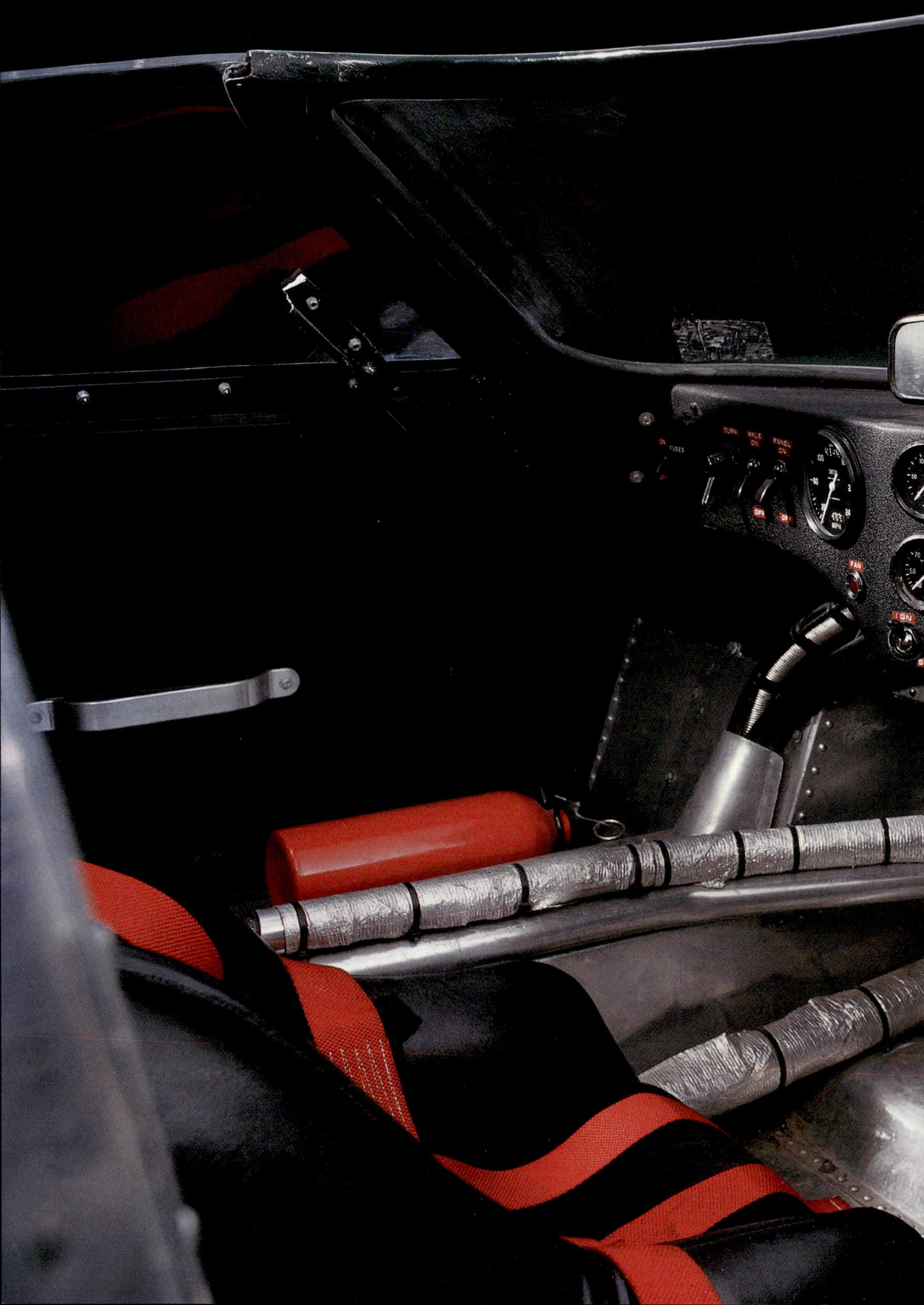
FUSES
TURN
AXLE ON
PANEL ON
MPH
FAN
IGN

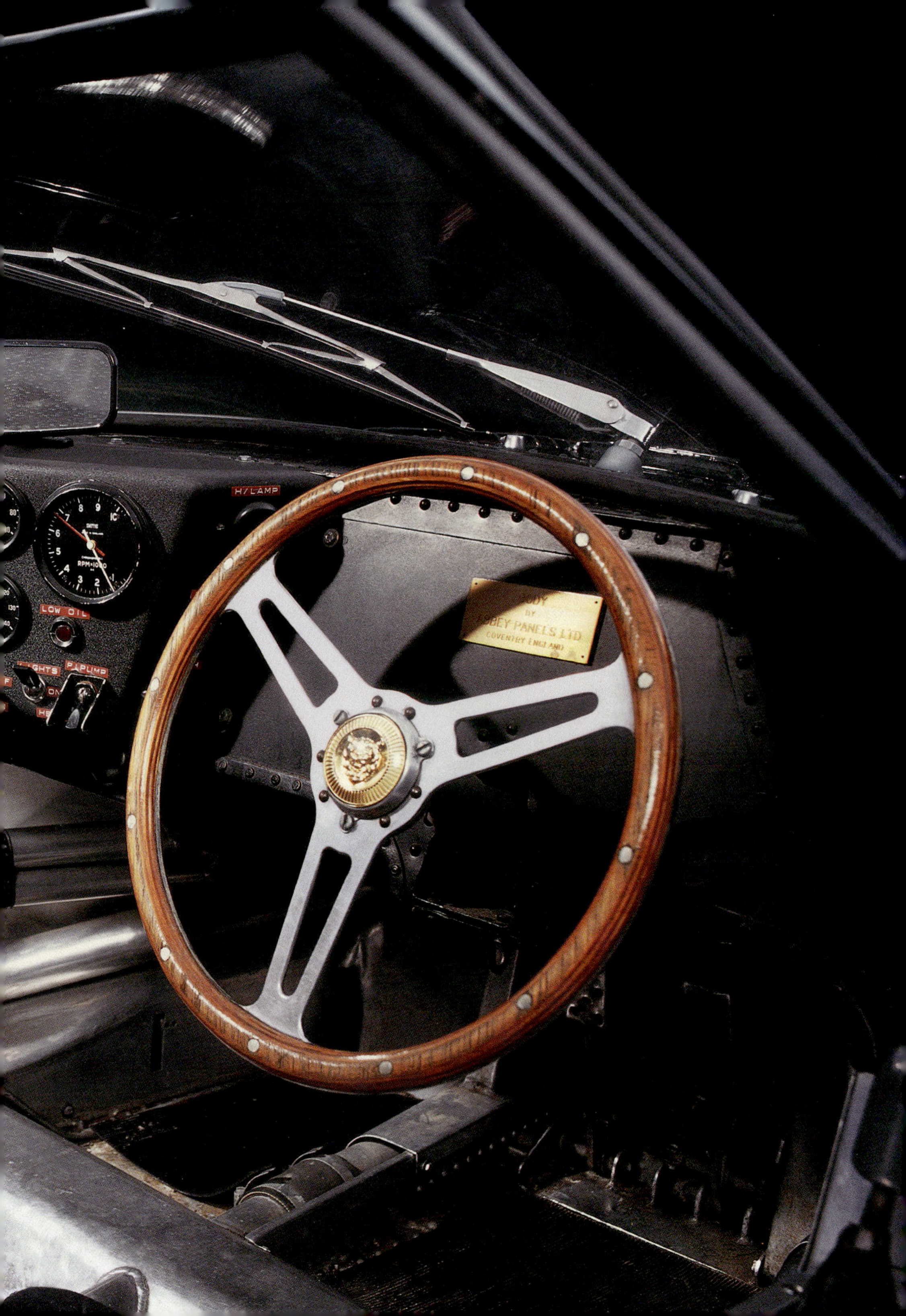
H/LAMP
LOW OIL
BY
COVENTRY ENGLAND

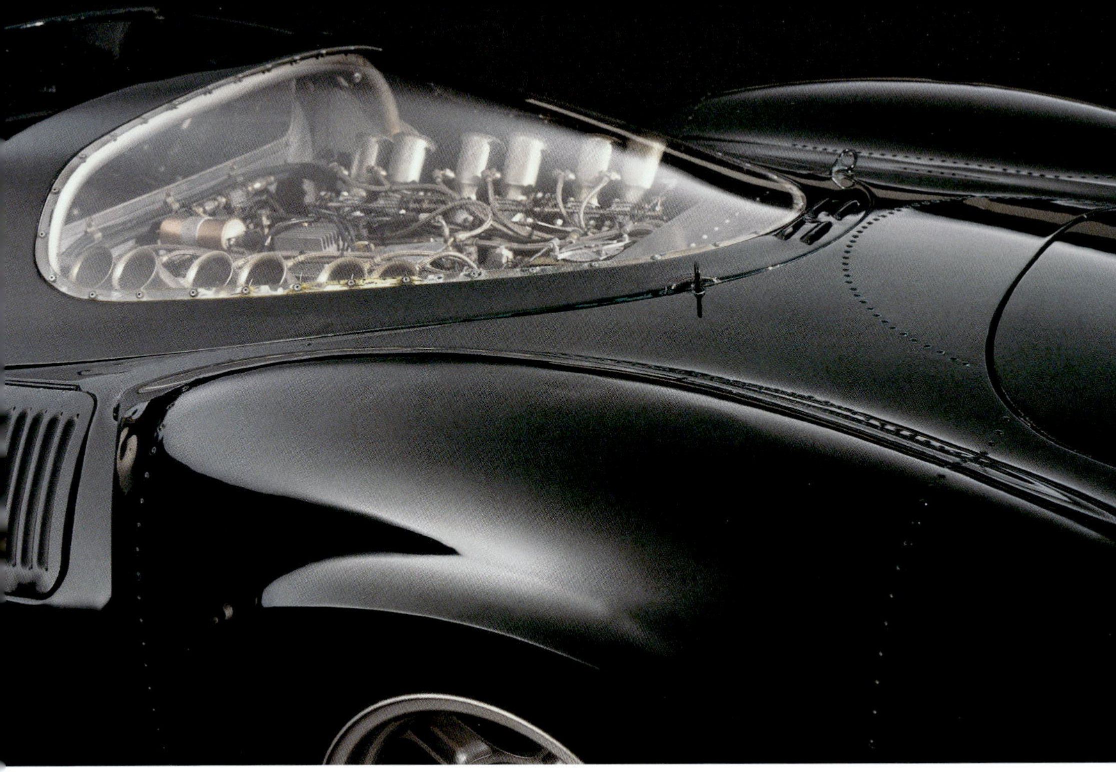

this experimental uni-bodied car's top speed might be. So secretly, Norman Dewis put it through its paces at the British Motor Industry Research Association (MIRA) proving ground in March 1966, where he managed to get it up to in excess of 175 mph (280 km/h). On learning about this unsanctioned speed test, Lyons was utterly furious and hauled Dewis into his office to tear a strip off him, but as he was leaving the "Old Man," feigning nonchalance, famously asked, "So, how fast did it go then?"

Lyons eventually relented somewhat and allowed the XJ13's development to be continued by Jaguar's enthusiastic engineering team, but only on weekends. Once the car was finally completed, it enabled David Hobbs to lap at over 161 mph (259 km/h) during an early testing session held at MIRA's test track in 1967. As Dewis later recalled, "The idea emerged that the new Jaguar V12 engine in the Series 3 E-Type should be launched to the press at Geneva in March 1971 amid the sight and sound of a previously unrevealed, mid-engined V12 Le Mans car emerging into sight from behind the trees." A film crew was

Above & opposite: Detail of Jaguar XJ13 4,991 cc (305 cu. in.), direct fuel-injected DOHC per bank 60º V12 mid-mounted engine. This awesome all-aluminum quad-cam power unit, which comprised a pair of XK6 engines joined at a 60-degree angle and utilizing a common crankcase and crankshaft, was designed by William Heynes in collaboration with Claude Baily. It was the glorious culmination of Jaguar's long-held desire to build a racing V12 engine with Le Mans specifically in mind.

assembled at MIRA's test track and Dewis took to the helm of the XJ13, despite some misgivings about its new tires. The first two laps went well, but then the car suffered a catastrophic wheel failure, which saw it careen into the safety fence and spectacularly barrel roll off the track into a field. Unbelievably, Dewis walked away from this 135 mph (217 km/h) crash, but the XK13 was left severely damaged. A year later, phoenix-like, however, the car reappeared after an extensive rebuild. Thankfully, most of its mechanical parts — engine, suspension, steering — as well as its monocoque had survived the crash, but its bodywork was a total write off and so was recreated by Abbey Panels, with a few modifications including wider arches to accommodate its new fatter wheels and tires. There will always be a big "if" hanging over the XJ13 as to how competitive it might have been, especially in relation to Ford's GT40. As Dewis always maintained, "We were way ahead of the GT40 in many respects, in the performance values alone... Had we gone to Le Mans I'm sure we would have put up a damn good show."

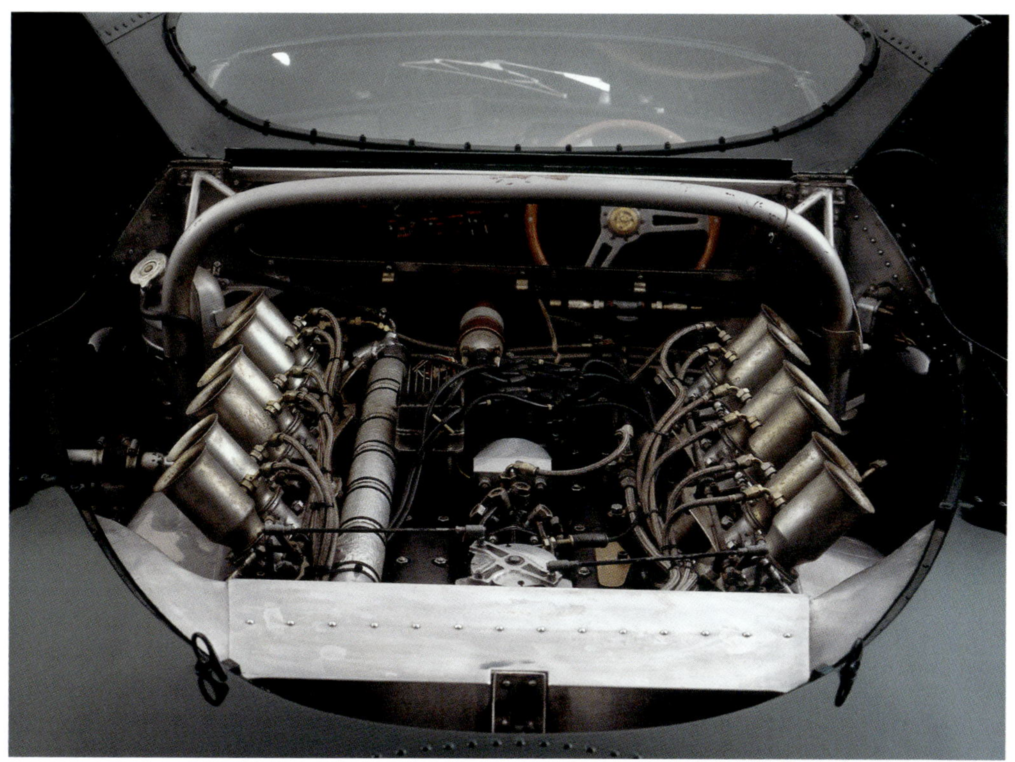

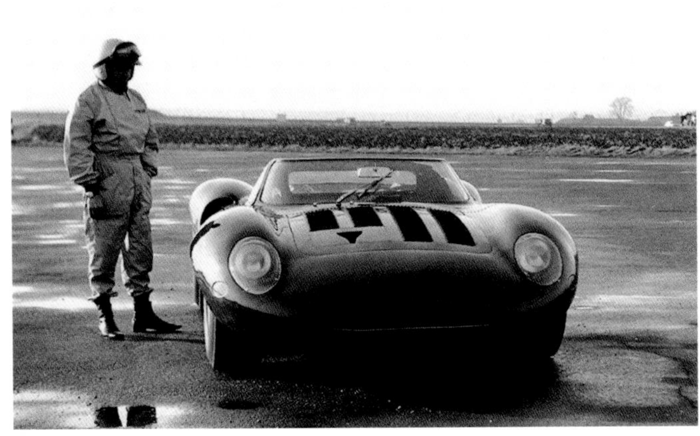

Left: By the time the XJ13 was completed, its design had become obsolete against new cars from the likes of Ferrari, Ford and Porsche. In 1971, having spent four years sitting under a cover in the Jaguar factory, it was taken out of mothballs and returned to the MIRA test track to be filmed for the E-type V12 launch. Here, Jaguar test-driver Norman Dewis is preparing for the run.

Below: The film crew setting up to record the XJ13 with Jaguar test-driver Norman Dewis at the wheel, about to set off.

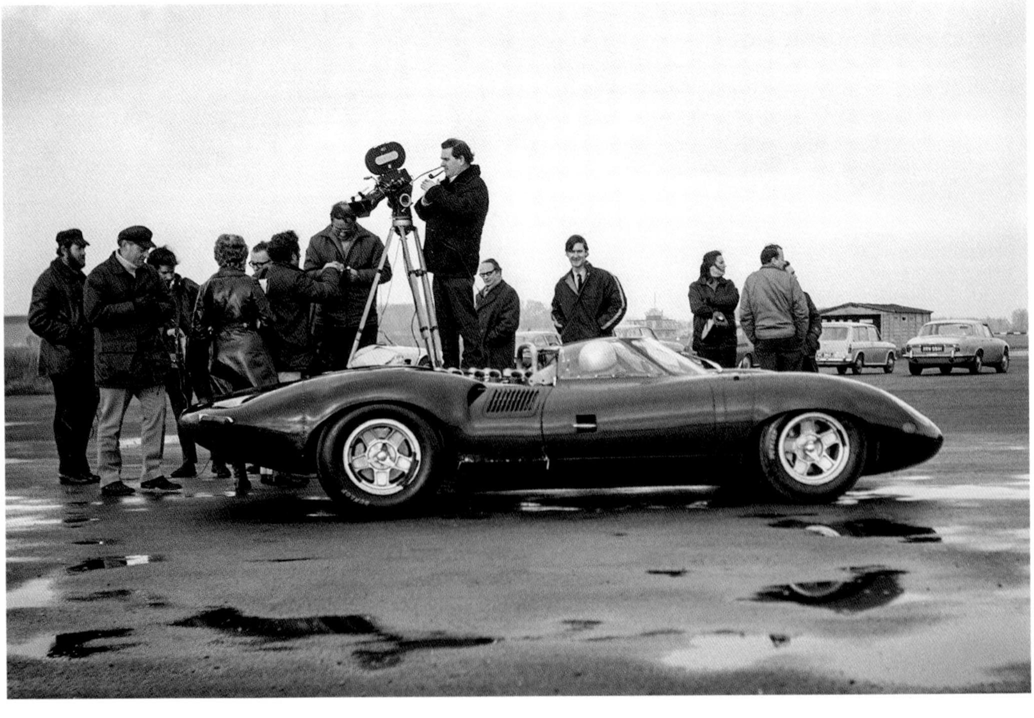

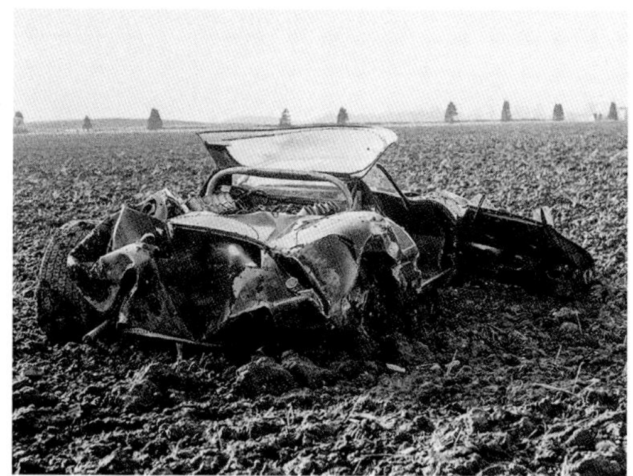

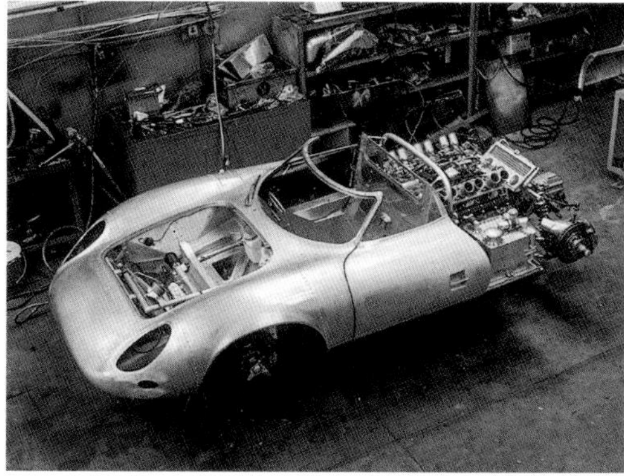

Above (left): Aftermath of the accident. Miraculously, Dewis walked away unhurt.

Above (right): While most of the XJ13's mechanical parts — engine, suspension, steering — survived the crash, its bodywork was a complete write off, but was beautifully recreated by Abbey Panels, with a few modifications including wider arches to accommodate new fatter wheels and tires, and the car was subsequently rebuilt at the Browns Lane factory (shown here).

Below: Factory photo taken one year after the crash — phoenix-like, the XJ13 reappeared after its extensive rebuild. Today, this astonishing one-off racing prototype resides at the British Motor Museum in Gaydon, Warwickshire.

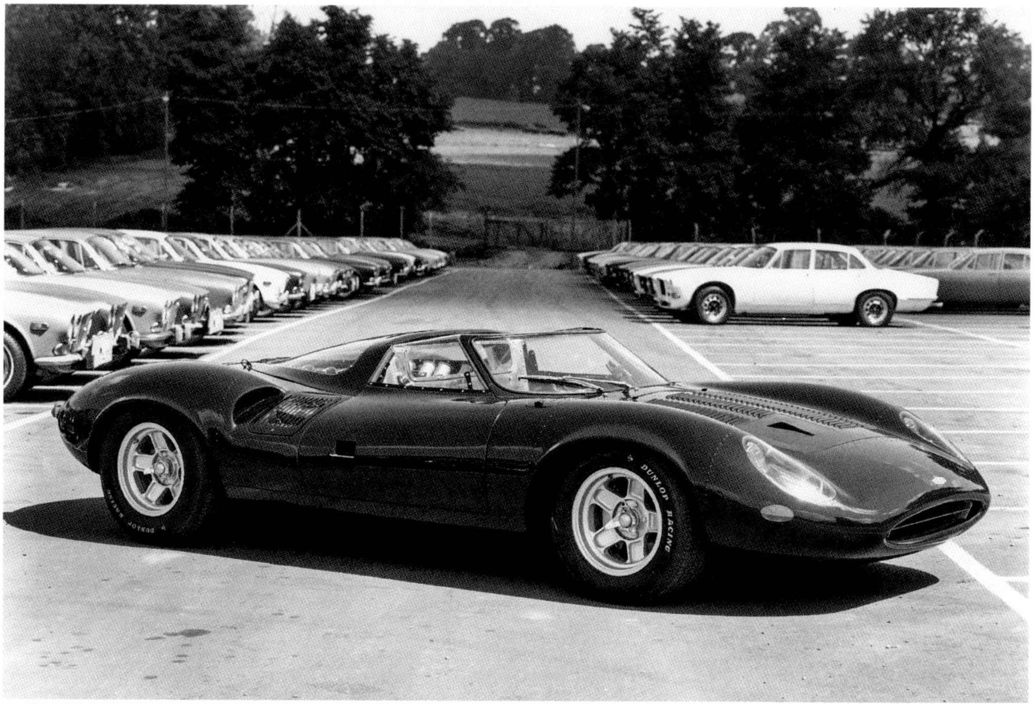

1966

Ford GT40 Mark II

MANUFACTURED 1966 | **ENGINE** 6,982 cc (426.1 cu. in.), overhead-valve V8 | **HORSEPOWER** 485
TOP SPEED 346 km/h (215 mph) | **TRANSMISSION** 4-speed
NUMBER PRODUCED 8

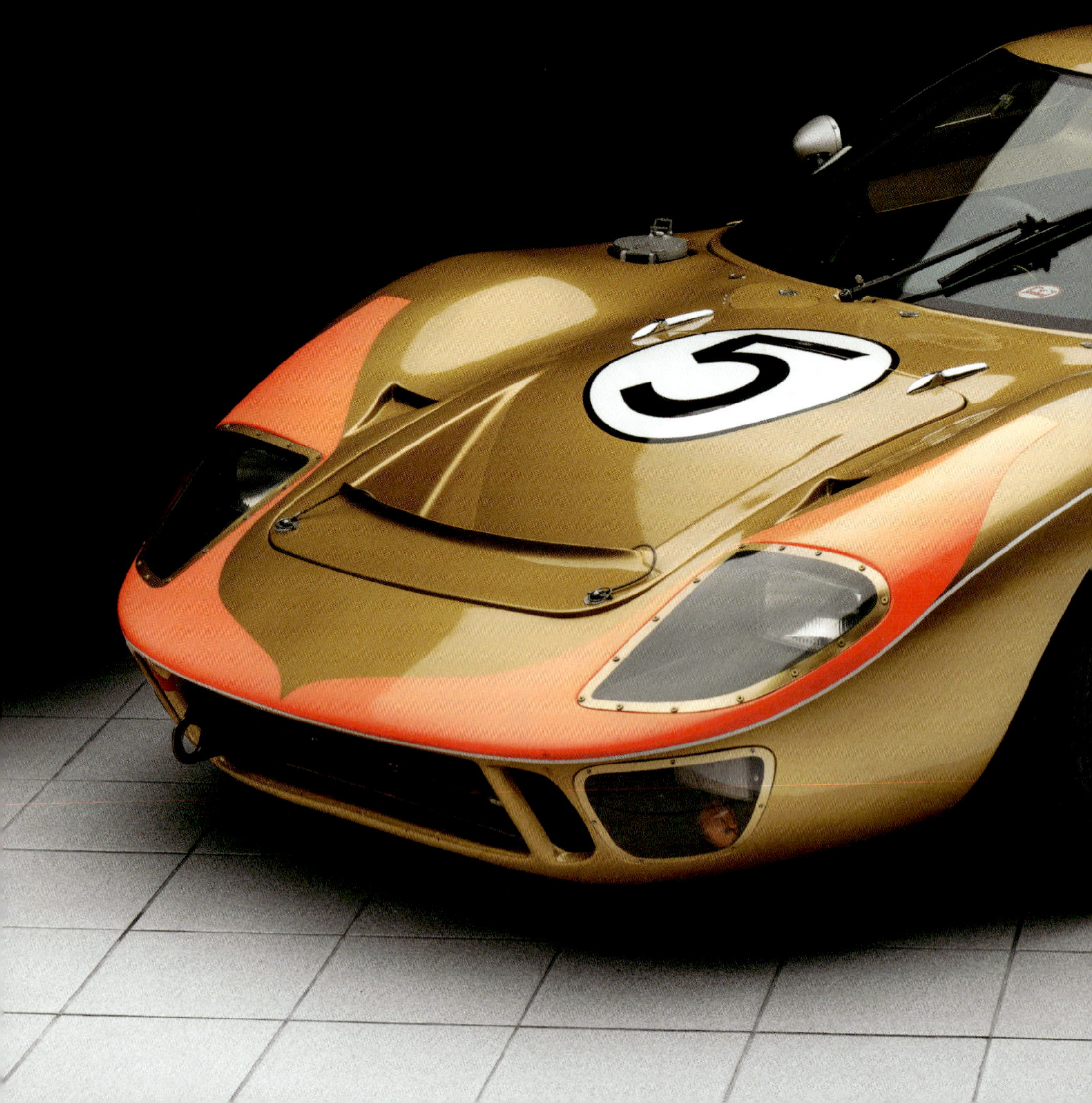

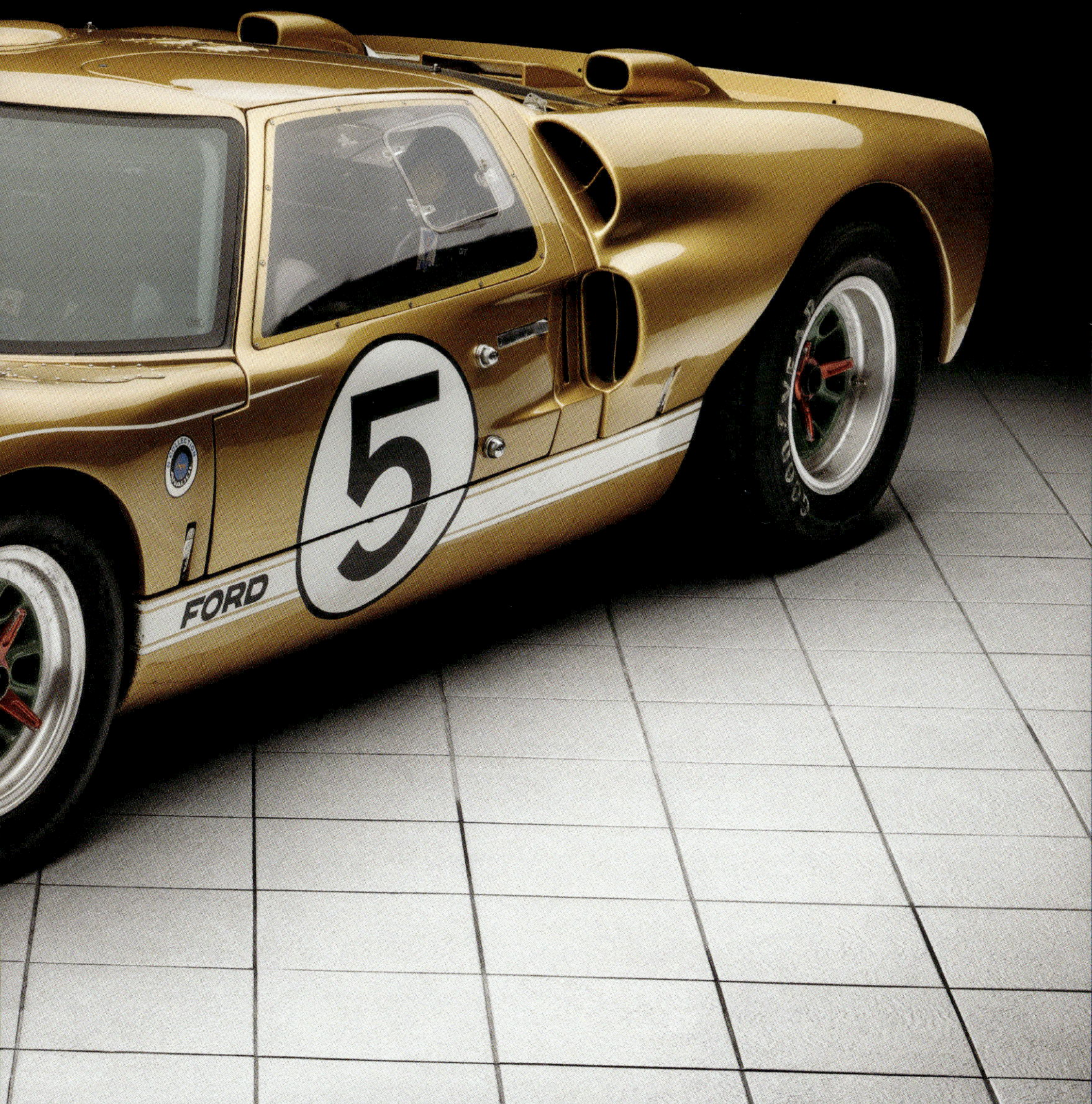
5
FORD

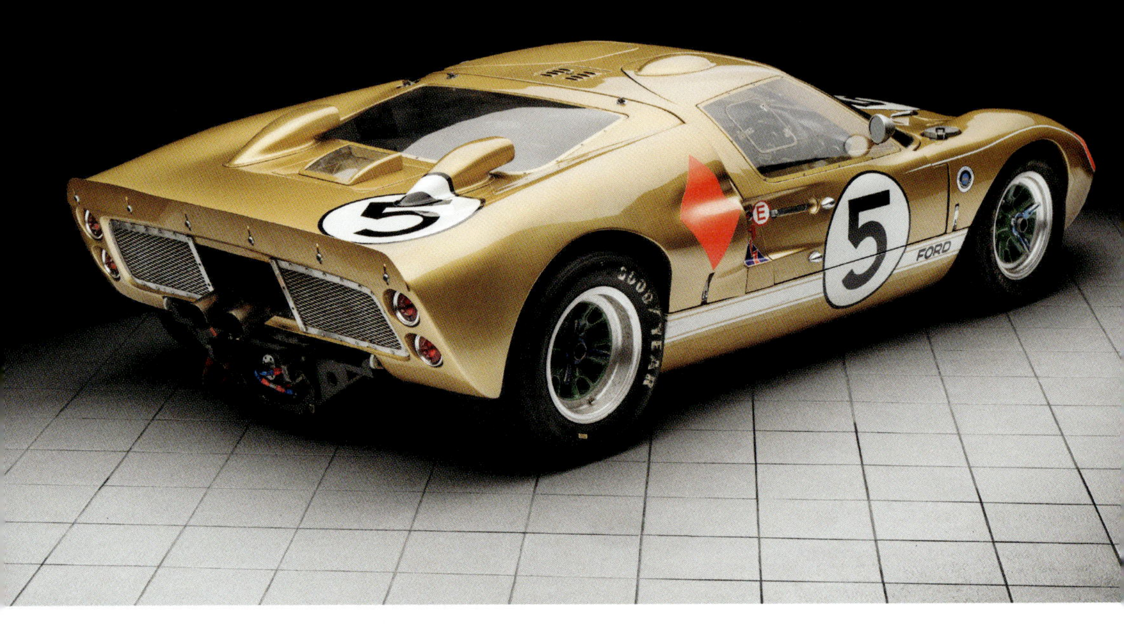

The Ford GT40 was born from a grudge. Like many powerful men, Enzo Ferrari had managed to annoy a number of important people, most notably Henry Ford II, then-president of the Ford Motor Company. The acrimony between the two stemmed from Ford's attempt to acquire the Italian marque in 1963. For some time, Henry Ford II had wanted to expand Ford's motor-racing presence, especially at the 24 Hours of Le Mans. To this end he had entered into negotiations with Enzo to buy the Maranello-based carmaker, which had won every Le Mans from 1960 to 1965. A $16 million deal was agreed, only for Enzo to then pull out at the last minute over a disagreement about the operational control of Scuderia Ferrari. This was pretty astounding given that it was Ferrari's racing division that was the whole reason behind Ford's interest in the company's purchase in the first place. Needless to say Ford and his envoys, who had gone over to Italy to ink the deal, were completely exasperated by this turn of events, and were left fuming. When the negotiating team returned to Dearborn, Henry Ford II called an emergency meeting of his top executives and ordered them to "Build me a car that will crush Ferrari at Le Mans." This desire to exact revenge would be the catalyst for the GT40's development.

Opposite (bottom): GT40 Mark II tail section showing adjustable rear spoiler and twin brake-cooling "snorkel" air intakes.

Overleaf: Detail of GT40 Mark II Plexiglass windows and side-mounted engine air scoops.

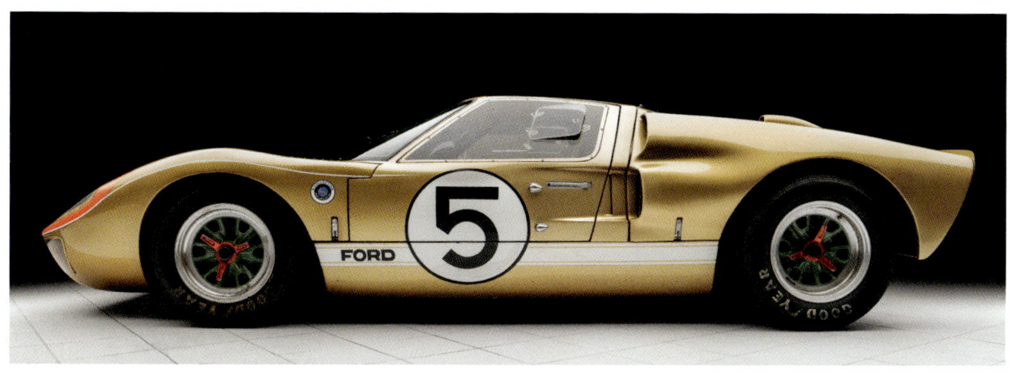

To this end, it was decided to develop the new racer in England, where there was a synergetic cluster of skilled motorsports engineers. Assembled in 1963, the Ford Advanced Vehicles (FAV) team comprised Eric Broadley (founder of Lola Cars) as lead designer, Roy Lunn (previously at AC Cars and Aston Martin) as lead engineer and John Wyer (formerly at Aston Martin) as project manager. This team immediately began development of a high performance racer based on Broadley's experimental Lola Mk6 GT. The outcome of their labors was the GT40 MK I — so named because it was only 40 inches high. A trio of GT40 MK

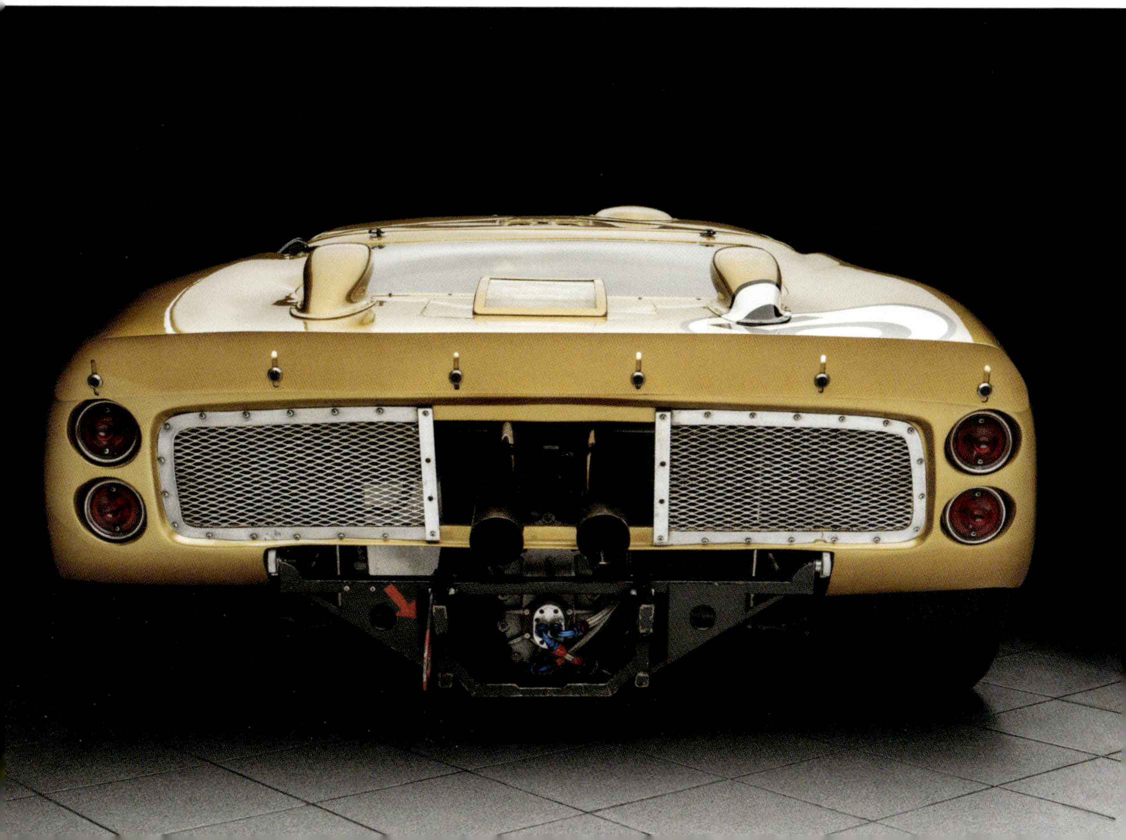

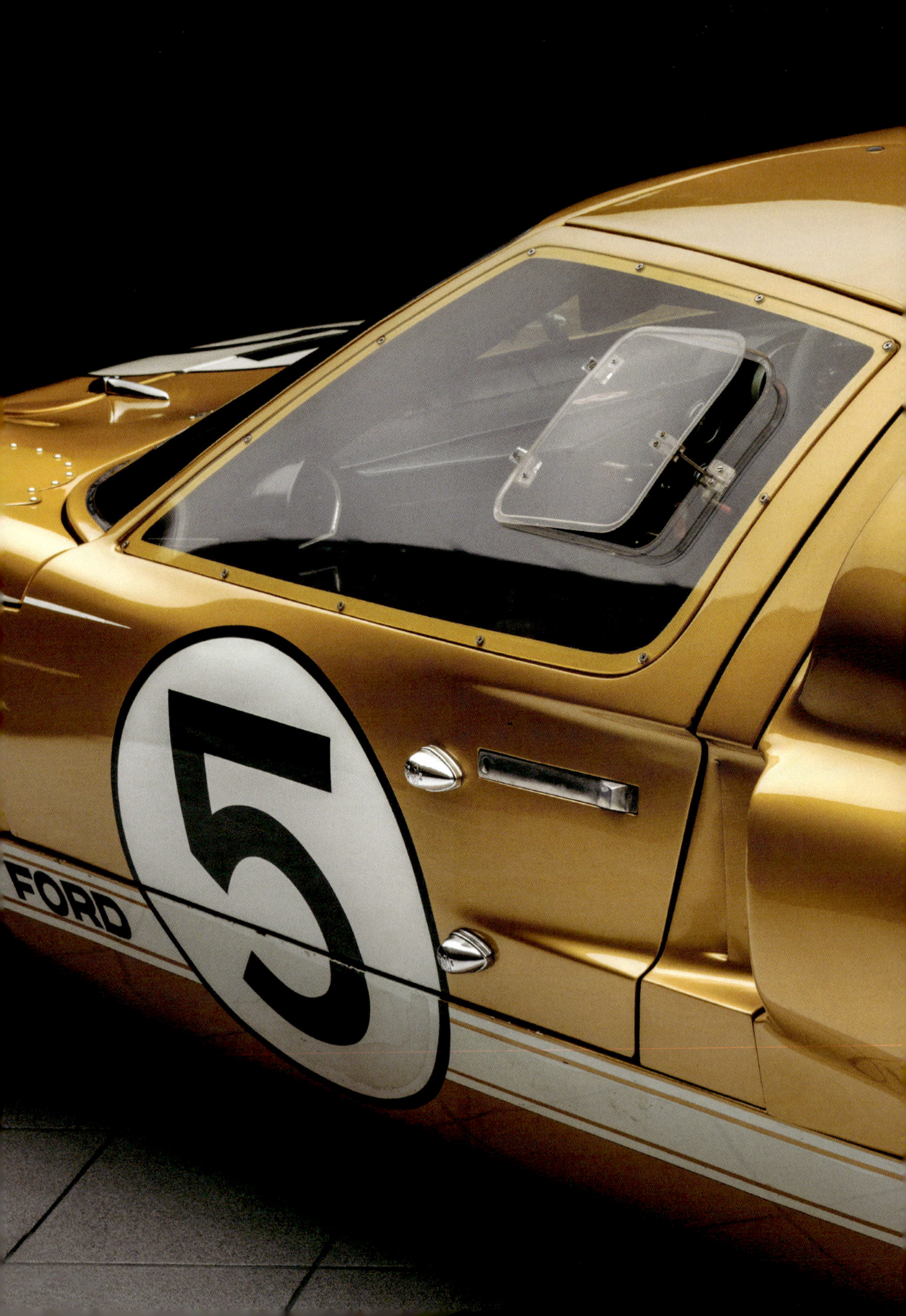
5
FORD

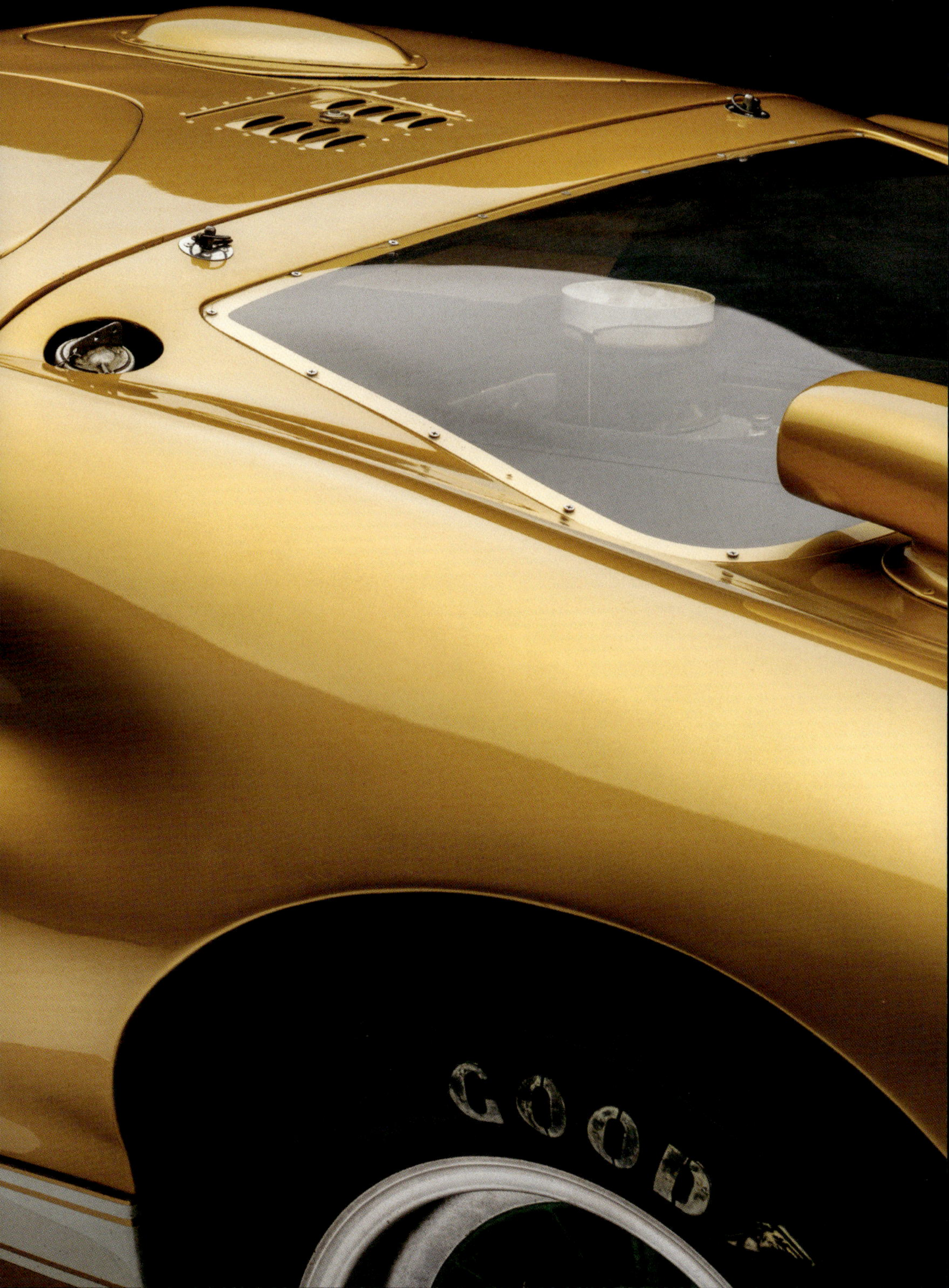
GOOD

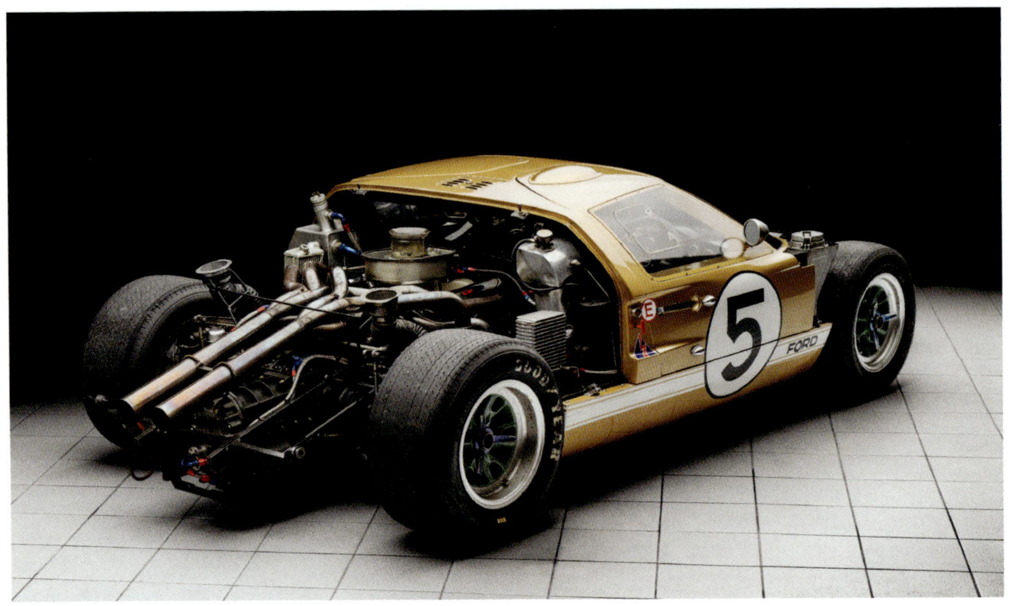

Is debuted at the 1964 24 Hours of Le Mans race sporting 4.2-liter aluminum-block Ford Fairlane V8 engines, tuned to provide a top speed of 210 mph (340 km/h). Their Colotti five-speed gearboxes, however, struggled to cope under endurance conditions, forcing two to retire, while the third failed to finish due to a fire. Two GT40 MK Is were then entered into the Nassau Tourist Trophy, where their performance was equally lackluster. As a result of this, the GT40 program was handed over to Carroll Shelby's Shelby American team, which had more racing experience. With only eight weeks to go until the next race, Shelby got Bob Bondurant to test a FAV-developed car. His verdict was that it was "bloody awful" thanks to its tendency to slide. To overcome its instability issue various modifications were undertaken, including the fitting of new Halibrand wheels and fatter Goodyear tires, as well as the aerodynamic reprofiling of its front end. These revisions enabled the Ford GT40 to achieve its first victory at Daytona in 1965, which saw Ken Miles and Lloyd Ruby win by an epic five-lap margin. The 1965 24 Hours of Le Mans, however, was another washout — all six GT40s retired, two of which were GT40Xs fitted with more powerful 427 cu. in. engines.

Desperate for a redemptive Le Mans victory Henry Ford II gave Ford's VP, Don Frey, free rein to implement whatever changes were needed. Frey's first move was to remove Shelby as program manager and allocate three GT40 chassis built to improved MK II specifications to Holman-Moody, a Charlotte-based racing operation that already had proven itself with the running of Ford's NASCAR program. Wanting to enhance durability, Kar Kraft — Ford's R&D specialist facility — stiffened these chassis by using thicker-gauge steel. More robust engine mountings and a heavier driveshaft were also added, as was an advanced suspension system and ventilated Kelsey-Hayes disc brakes. Likewise the GT40Xs existing 427 cu. in. engine was further developed to provide 485 hp. The bodywork

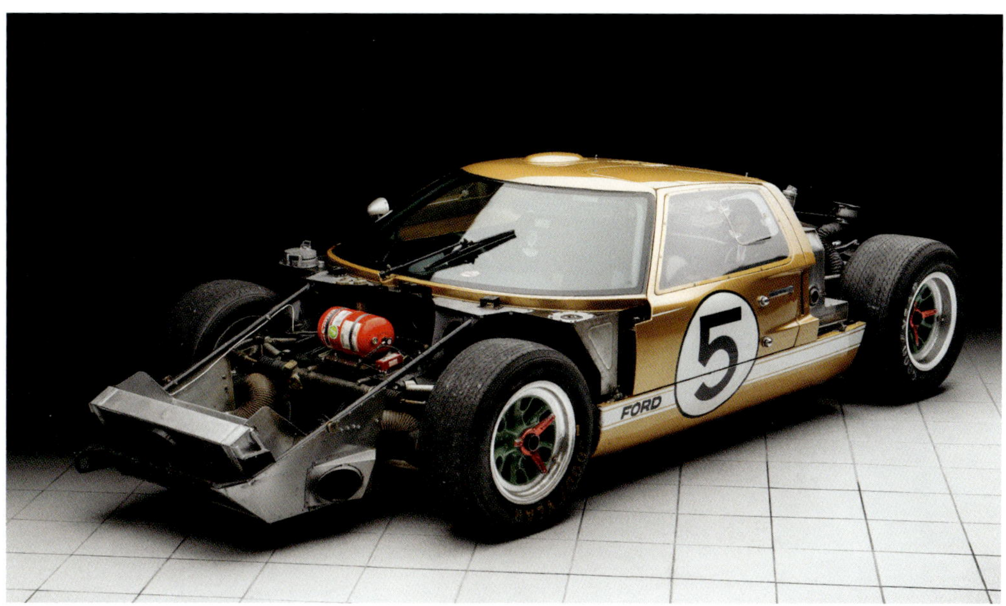

also got a makeover in order to accommodate the MK II's fatter wheels. To optimize performance, the new GT40 featured additional engine scoops as well as an adjustable spoiler. The car shown here, chassis no. P/1016, is the fourth of eight GT40 MK IIs built. For the 1966 Daytona 24 Hours race five GT40 MK IIs were fielded — three by Shelby American and two by Holman-Moody. At this race, a podium clean sweep was achieved as well as a fifth placing — although the example featured here, chassis no. P/1016, failed to finish. It was subsequently given a new Kandy Gold paint job and then was raced in the 12 Hours of Sebring, where it achieved a 12th-place finish. It also participated in the 1966 24 Hours of Le Mans race, where Ford's GT40 MK IIs enjoyed a 1-2-3 clean sweep, with chassis no. P/1016 being the third-placer. By contrast, only two Ferrari 275 GTB Competizioni, fielded by the British Maranello Concessionaires team and Belgian Ecurie Francorchamps, managed to finish in eighth and tenth position respectively, while the three Ferrari works 330 P3 racers either did not finish or did not start. This constituted an absolute flop, given how dominant the Scuderia had been in the preceeding Le Mans races. What more can be said, but that revenge had been gloriously exacted with hard-hitting American brawn.

Opposite: Detail of Ford GT40 MKII mid-mounted 6,982 cc (427 cu. in.), overhead-valve V8 engine. This power plant featured a dry-sump lubrication system, which allowed the V8 to sit lower in the chassis. Breathing through a single Holley four-barrel 780 CFM carburetor, the big block produced so much power and torque that no available gearbox could take it. This was addressed by hastily constructing a brand new four-speed gearbox in-house in time for the 1966 race season.

Above: Detail of GT40 Mark II front end structure including enormous radiator and fire extinguishing system.

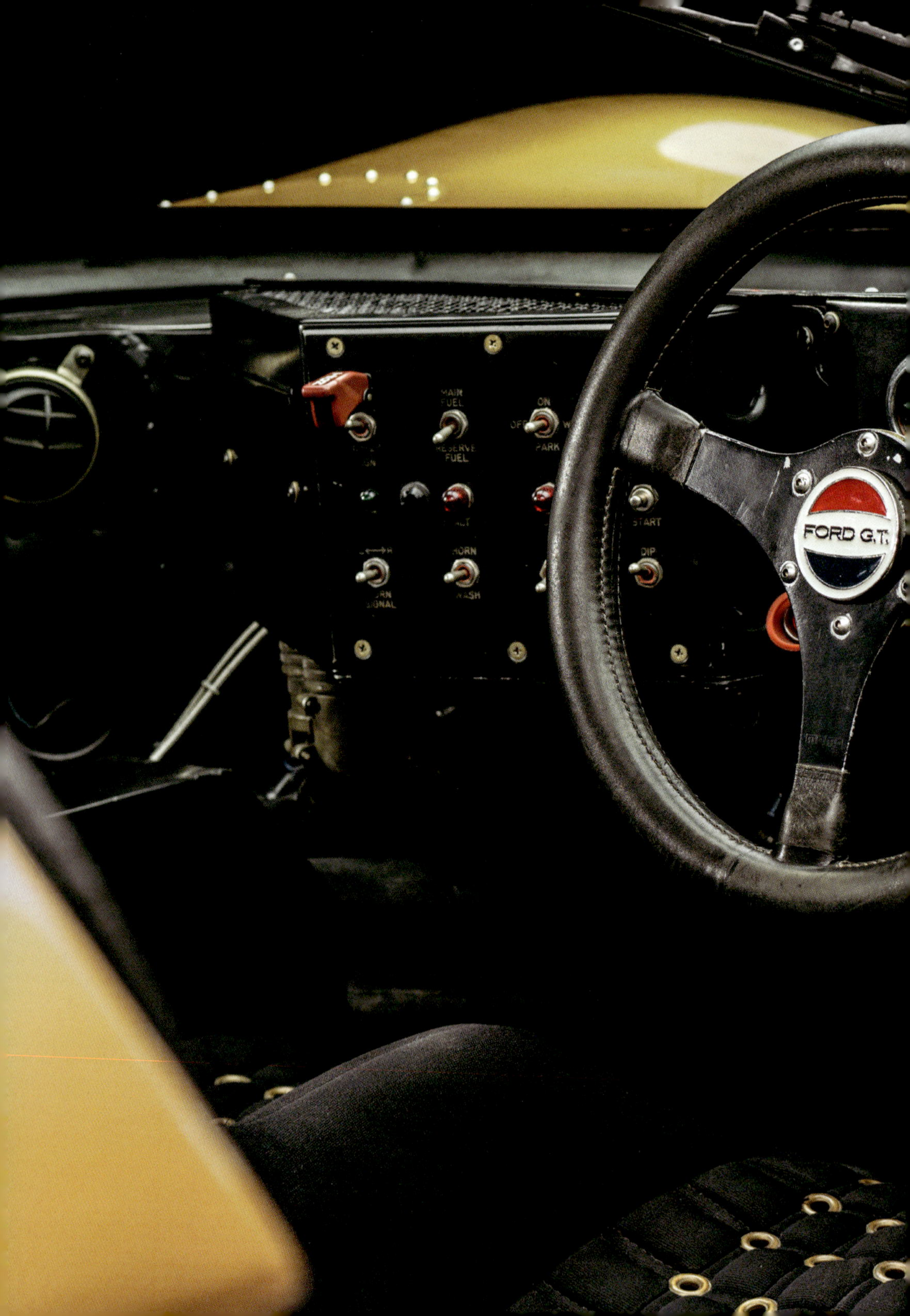
MAIN FUEL
RESERVE FUEL
ON
PARK
START
HORN
WASH
DIP
FORD G.T.

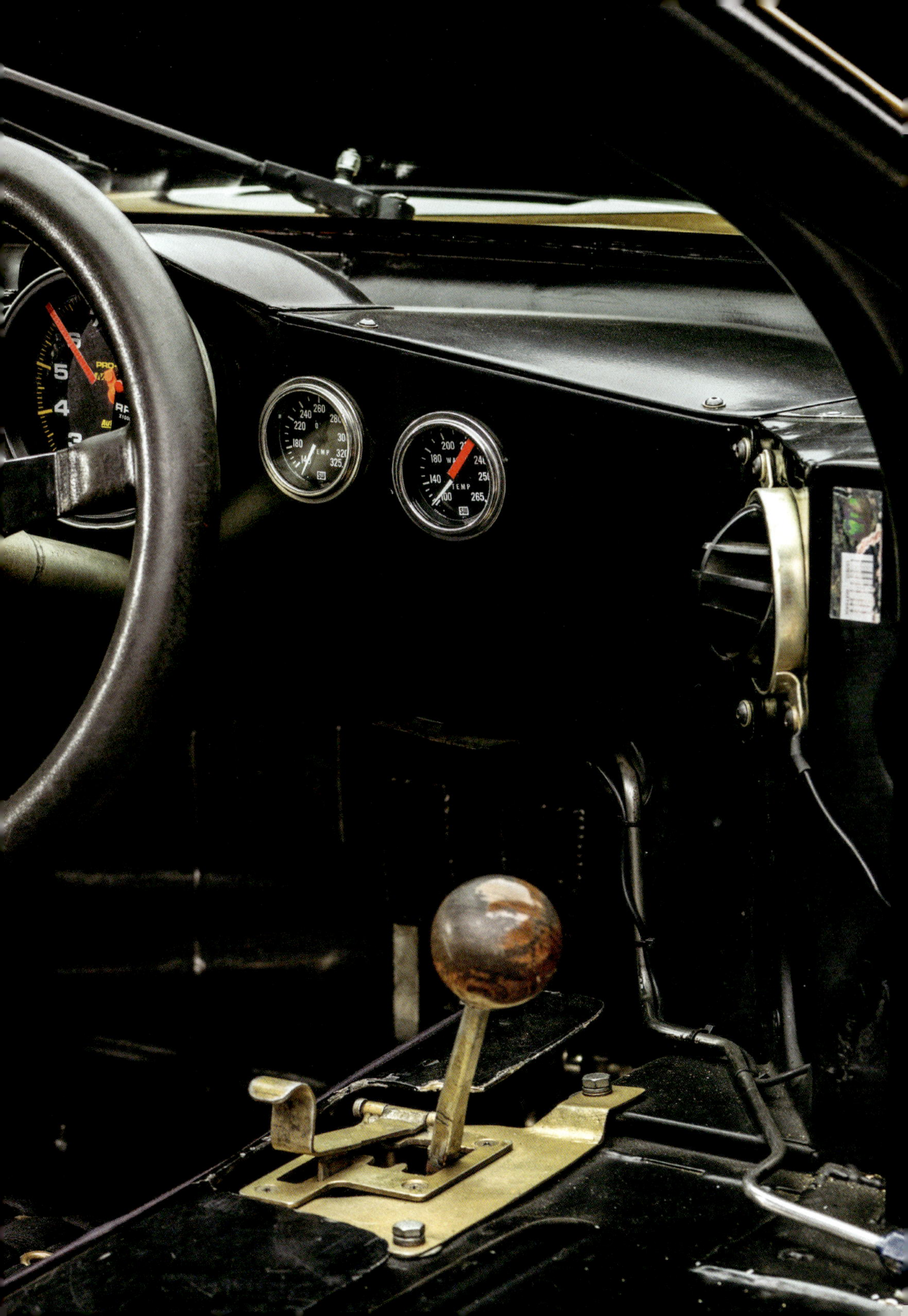
6
5
4
3
260
240
220
180
280
TEMP
320
325
200
180
240
140
TEMP
100
265

Right: The No. 5 Holman-Moody Ford GT40 MK II at the 1966 24 Hours of Le Mans. The fourth of eight MK II examples built, this car was raced in the three major long distance races in 1966: Daytona, Sebring and Le Mans. Its best result was a third place at the historic 1966 24 Hours of Le Mans, where it was driven by Americans Ronnie Buckman and Dick Hutcherson.

Below: The No. 5 Holman-Moody Ford GT40 MK II of Ronnie Buckman and Dick Hutcherson undertaking a driver change during the 1966 24 Hours of Le Mans.

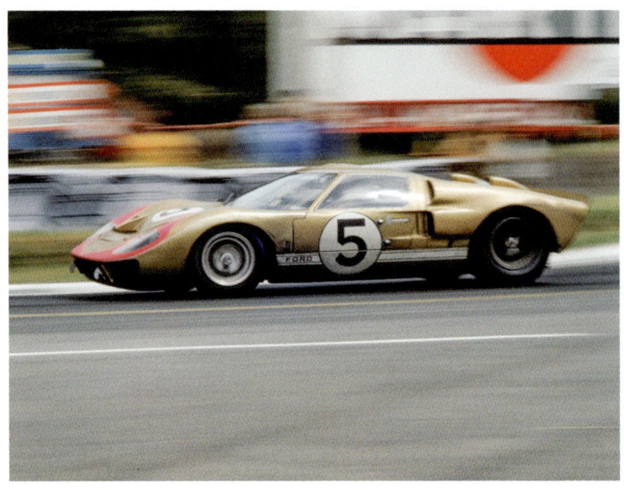

Opposite: Formation finish of the 1966 24 Hours of Le Mans, where Ford's GT40 MK IIs produced a legendary 1-2-3 hat trick. Car No. 2 (chassis no. P/1046) driven by Bruce McLaren and Chris Amon in first place; car No. 1 (chassis no. P/1015) driven by Ken Miles and Denny Hulme in second place; and car No. 5 (chassis no. P/1016) driven by Ronnie Buckman and Dick Hutcherson in third place.

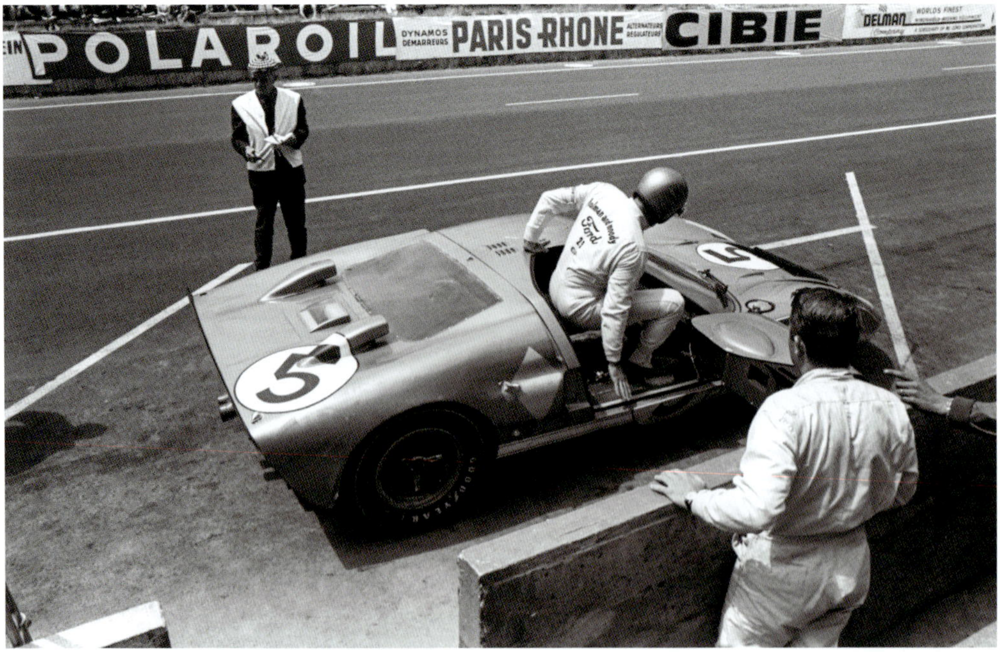

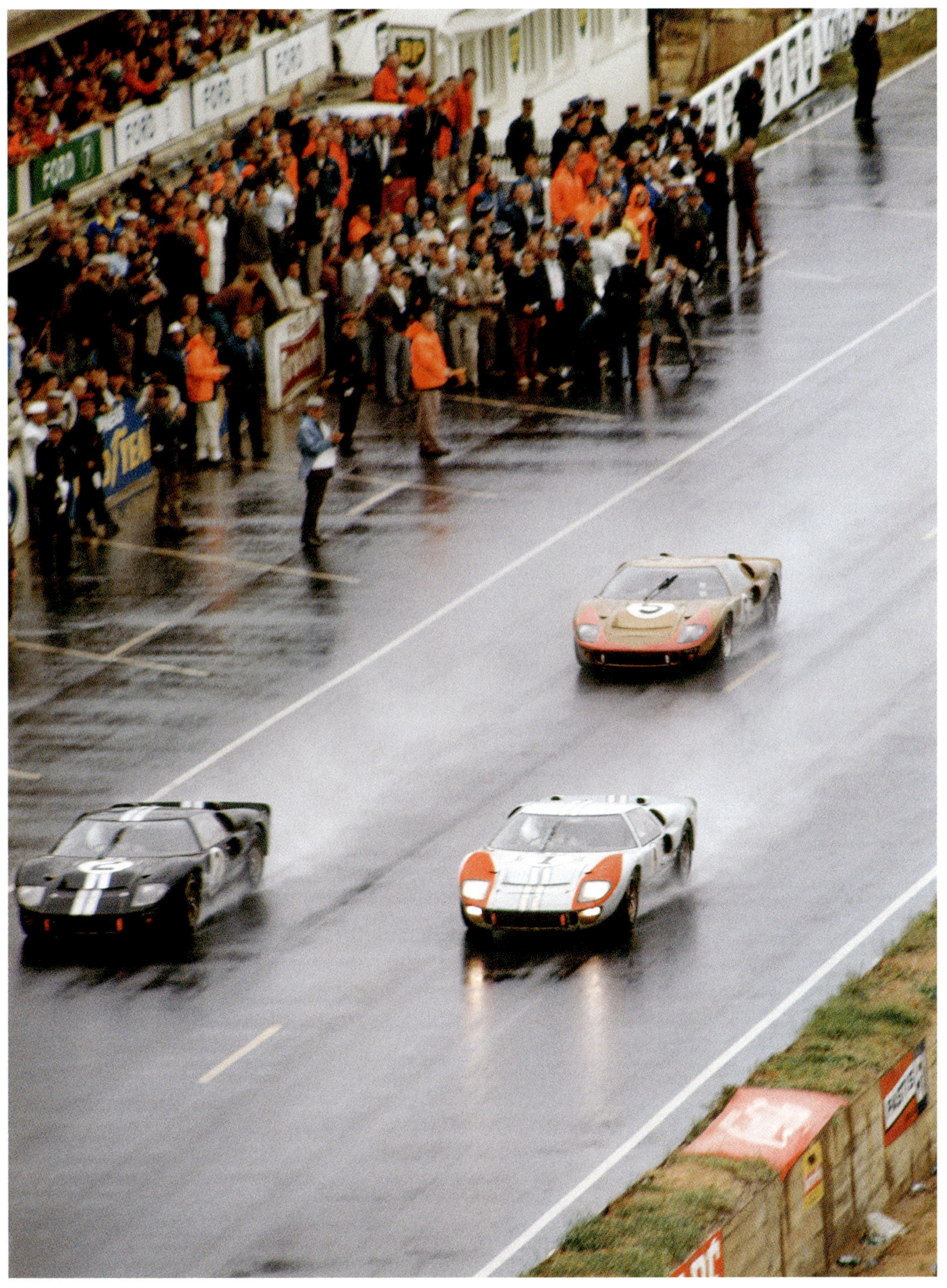
FORD

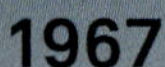

1967

Ferrari 330 P4

MANUFACTURED 1967 | ENGINE 3,967 cc (242 cu. in.), DOHC per bank 60° V12 | HORSEPOWER 450
TOP SPEED 338 km/h (210 mph)
TRANSMISSION 5-speed | NUMBER PRODUCED 3

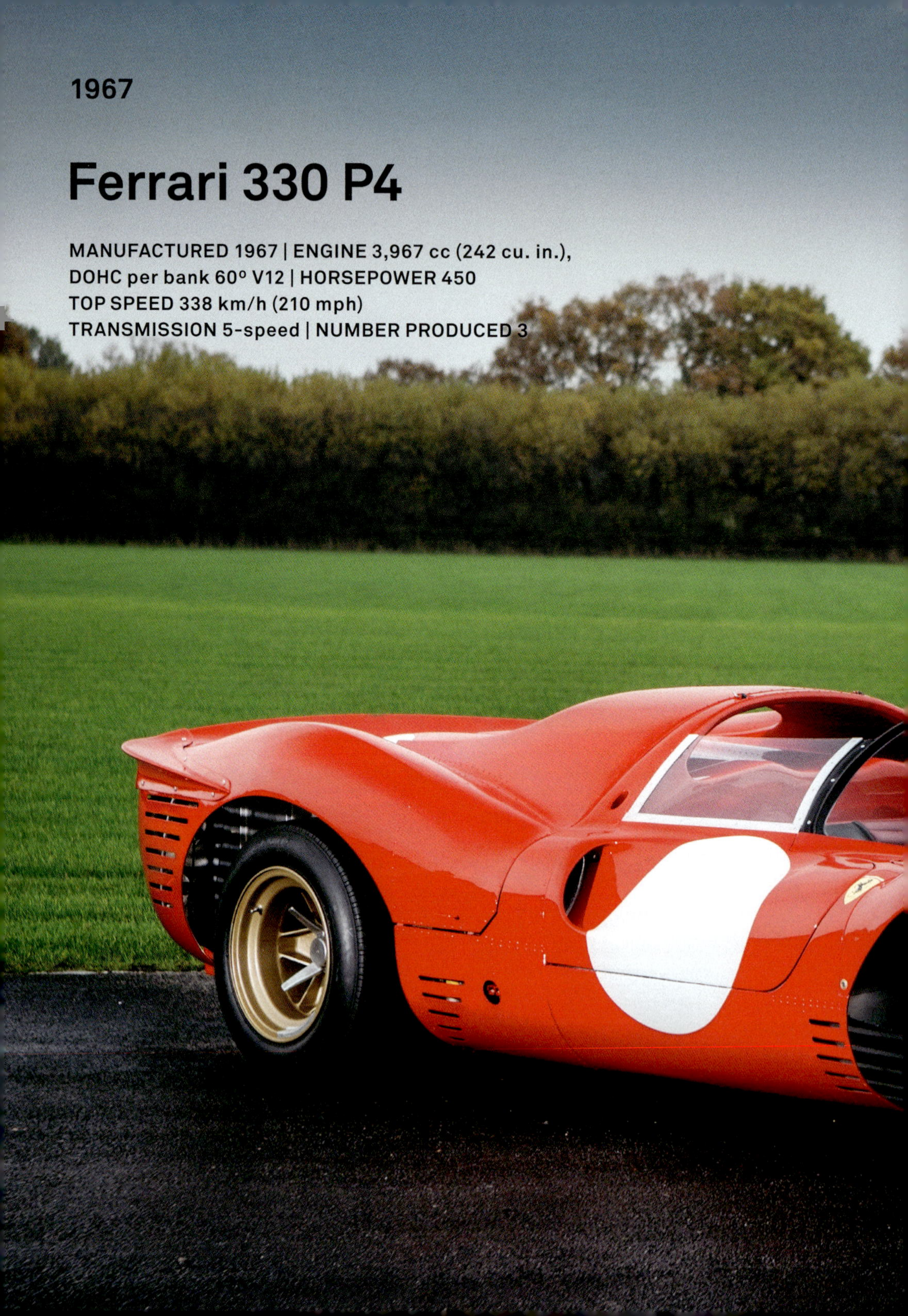

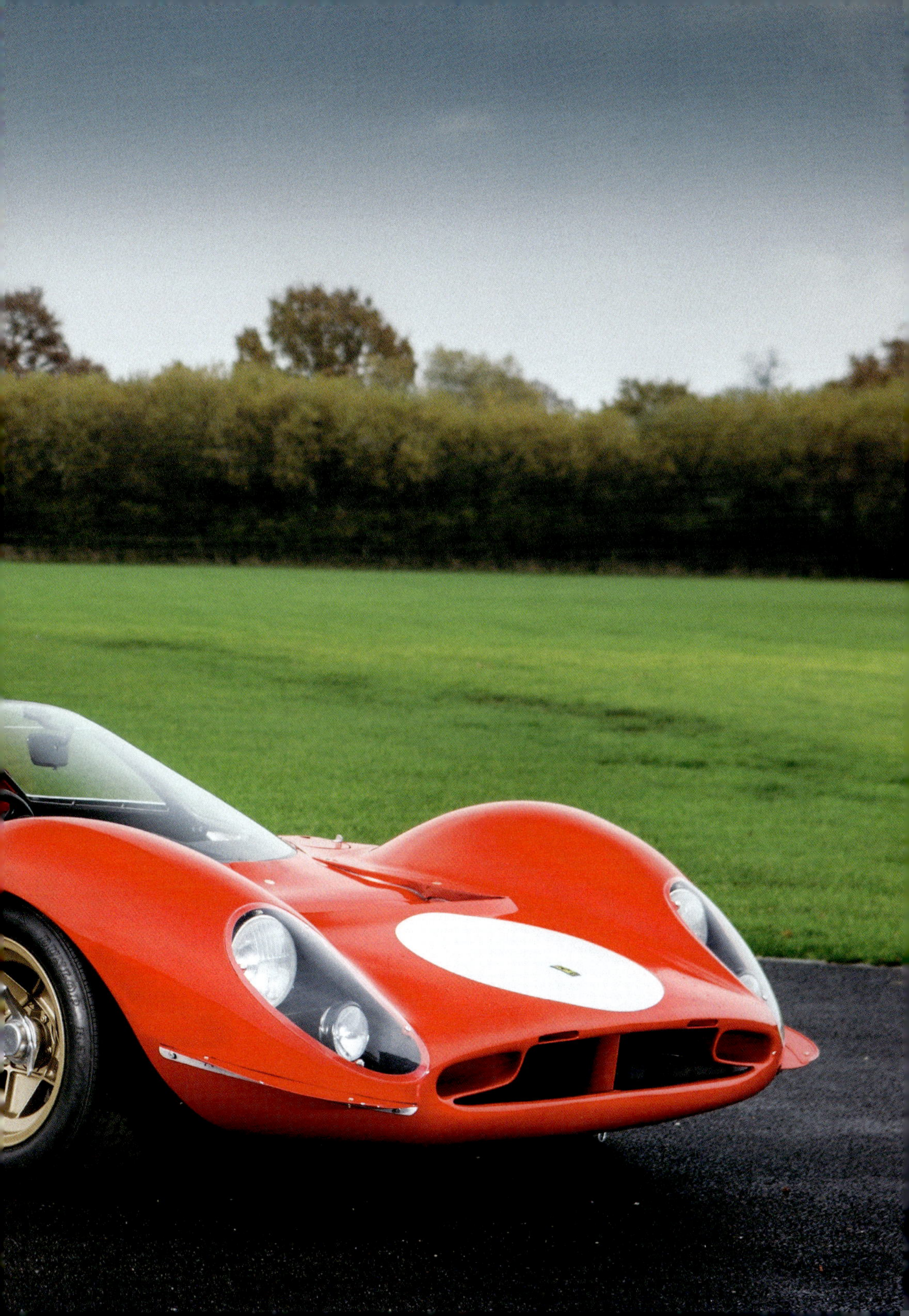

If rarity, beauty, high performance and race history are the Holy Grails of race car collecting, then the 1967 Ferrari 330 P4 is up there among the most desirable cars of all time. In fact, only three examples were ever built, making it one of the rarest and most revered Ferrari models in existence. Piero Drogo of Carrozzeria Sports Cars in Modena designed the visually seductive, aerodynamically curvaceous body of this low-slung racer. Thanks to his previous experience as a Formula 1 driver, Drogo knew exactly how to create a body with formidable high-speed racing capability, which is presumably why Enzo Ferrari entrusted him with designing the model in the first place.

The 1967 330 P4 belongs to the famed P-series of prototype racers produced by Ferrari during the 1960s and early 1970s. The initial development of the P-series was prompted by Jack Brabham and the Cooper works team famously winning the Formula One World Championship in 1959 with a mid-engine car, the Cooper T51, which was a world first for this type of layout. This historic win not only disrupted Ferrari's long-running dominance of top-level motor racing during the 1950s, but also marked a new chapter in F1, as soon other teams began adopting mid-engine designs. Although Enzo Ferrari was initially reluctant about implementing this configuration, he soon came round to the idea and as a result Ferrari produced its first mid-engined prototype racer, the 246 P F1, which debuted at the 1960 Monaco Grand Prix.

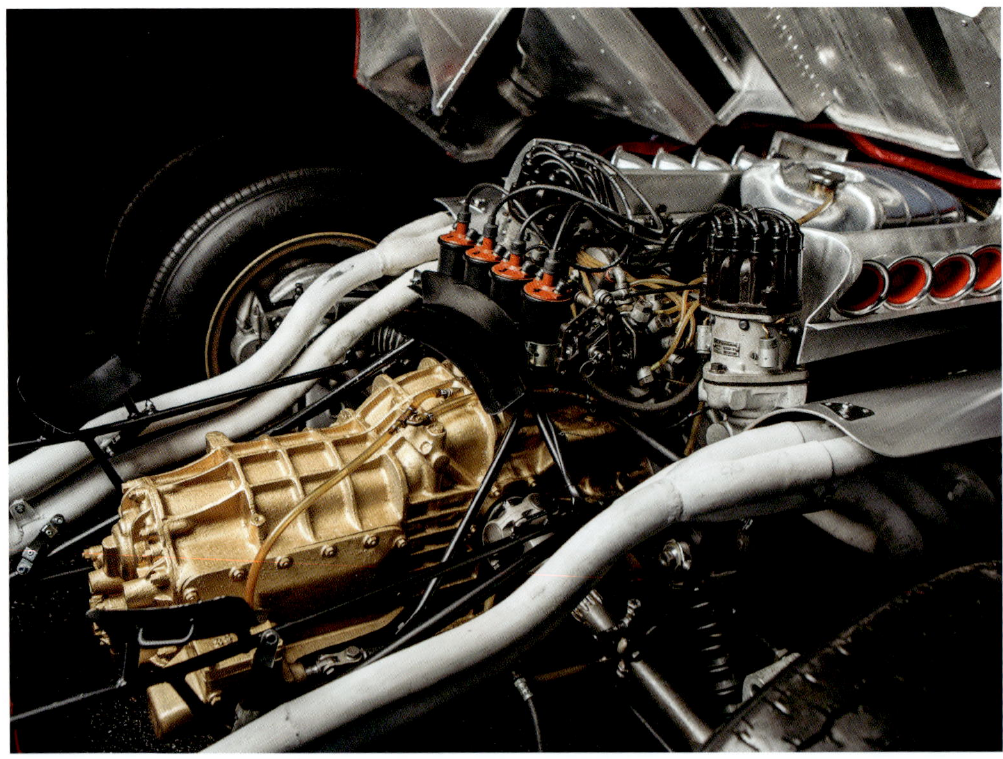

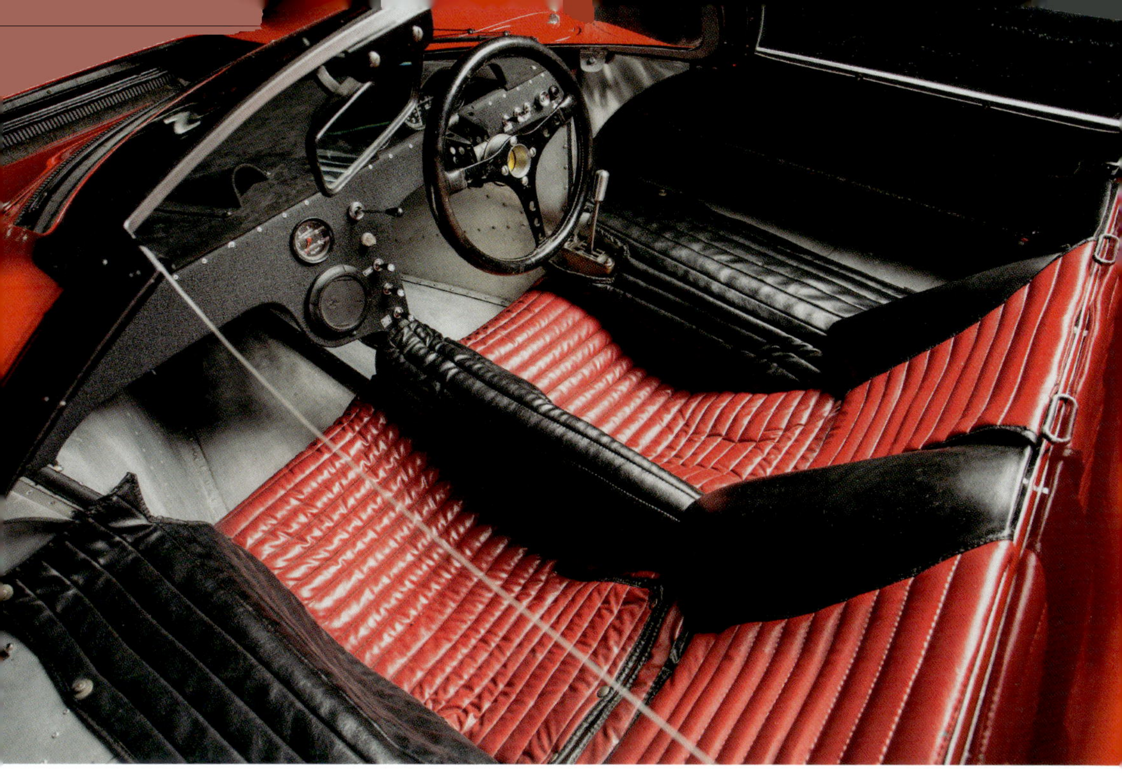

Over the following years other P-series racers were developed by Ferrari, notably the 12-cylinder mid-engined 1963 250 P styled by Pininfarina that was victorious at Sebring, Le Mans and Nürburgring; the more aerodynamically styled 1965 275 P2; the 1965 330 P2 that had a lower and lighter chassis; and the transmission-failure-prone 1966 330 P3, which was a very early fuel-injected Ferrari. Yet of all the P-series racers it was Drogo's aggressively styled replacement for the problematic 330 P3, the 1967 330 P4, shown here, that was without question the standout model in the Scuderia, both in terms of performance and looks. This remarkable showstopper of a car was powered by a mighty four-cam V12 engine that had been radically redesigned by the former aircraft engineer Franco Rocchi, who was one of Ferrari's most trusted colleagues since joining the company in 1949. The main modification to the engine was the incorporation of a three-valve cylinder head (two inlets and one exhaust per cylinder), which provided significantly more power than that produced by the two-valve cylinder head of the earlier 330 P3's V12.

The Ferrari 330 P4 also boasted a much-improved Lucas fuel-injection system that helped give it an output of up to 450 hp at 8,200 rpm. This stunningly beautiful race car also had fiberglass doors, which was the first time Ferrari had used this lightweight composite

Opposite: Detail of Ferrari 330 P4 3,967 cc (242 cu. in.), direct fuel-injected DOHC per bank 60° V12 engine. This mighty four-cam power plant, which was designed by key Ferrari engineer Franco Rocchi, featured a three-valve cylinder head (two inlets and one exhaust per cylinder), which provided significantly more power than that produced by previous Ferrari V12s.

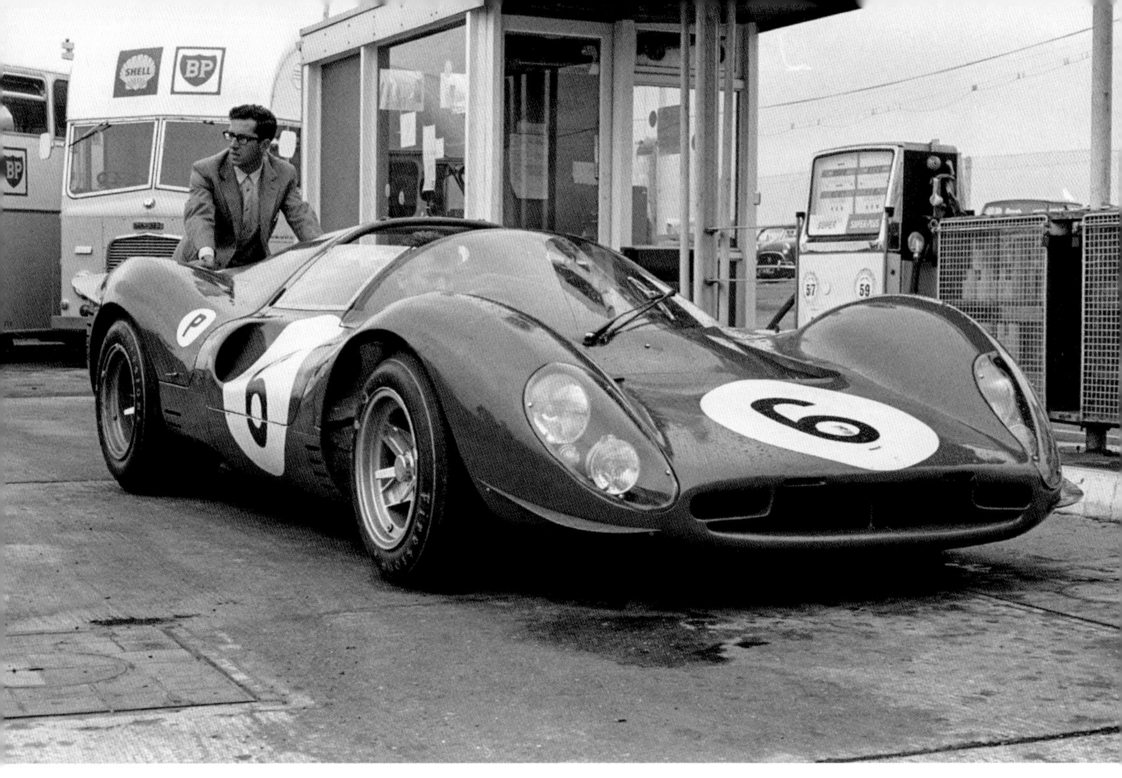

material instead of alumimum in its racer prototypes, and an open-air frame, both of which helped to reduce speed-sapping weight. In addition, the P4's chassis was slightly shorter than its predecessor's, while a new suspension system also improved its road-holding, which meant it was safer to drive at high speed, which ultimately meant it could be driven faster round a circuit. As a result of their thoughtful better-by-design developments, these remarkable racing cars clocked up numerous impressive wins. One of these victories was a truly momentous 1-2-3 finish at the 24-hour race at Daytona in 1967 — which saw two 330 P4s place first and second, alongside a third-placing Ferrari 412 P. This legendary Italian victory on American soil was so sweet for Enzo Ferrari that right up until his death he kept in pride of place a photograph of this winning trio on their final lap of triumph. All three 330 P4s built for the 1967 season were originally constructed and raced as coupés, but by the season's finale at Brands Hatch they had all been modified into spiders, or in other words they had their roofs removed in order to reduce weight.

The 330 P4 featured here, chassis no. 0858, competed under coupé, spider and later Can-Am configurations. Its distinguished racing career includes a second overall at the 24 Hours of Le Mans in 1967 and a second place the same year in the 1,000 km race at Monza. Eventually, it was beautifully and expertly restored back to its earlier spider configuration over two years by the renowned Ferrari specialist David Piper.

Since then, the car has been restored by Franco Meinert back to its initial Le Mans berlinetta configuration using several original panels found in Italy. This work was completed in 2020 and the car was shown in this renewed guise for the first time at Rétromobile.

Opposite: The No. 6 Ferrari 330 P4 of Jackie Stewart and Chris Amon being pushed to the fuel pumps by Ferrari designer and racing technical director Mauro Forghieri prior to the start of the 1967 BOAC International 500 at Brands Hatch.

Right: Poster by Dexter Brown (b.1942) celebrating the 1-2-3 triumph of the Works Ferraris at the 1967 24 Hours of Daytona — No. 23 330 P4 of Lorenzo Bandini and Chris Amon (first), No. 24 330 P4 of Mike Parkes and Ludovico Scarfiotti (second) and No. 26 330 P3/412P of Pedro Rodriguez and Jean Guichet (third).

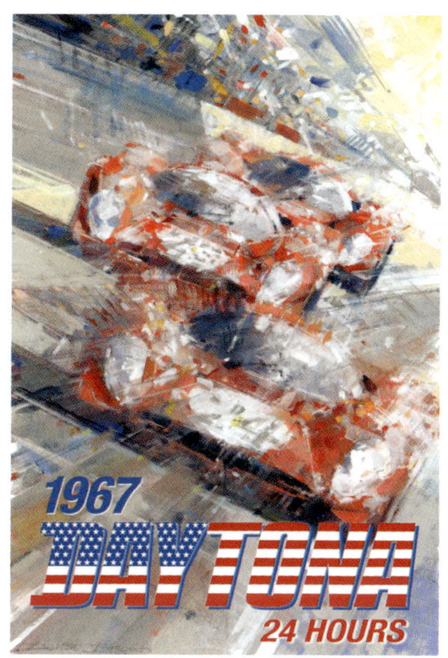

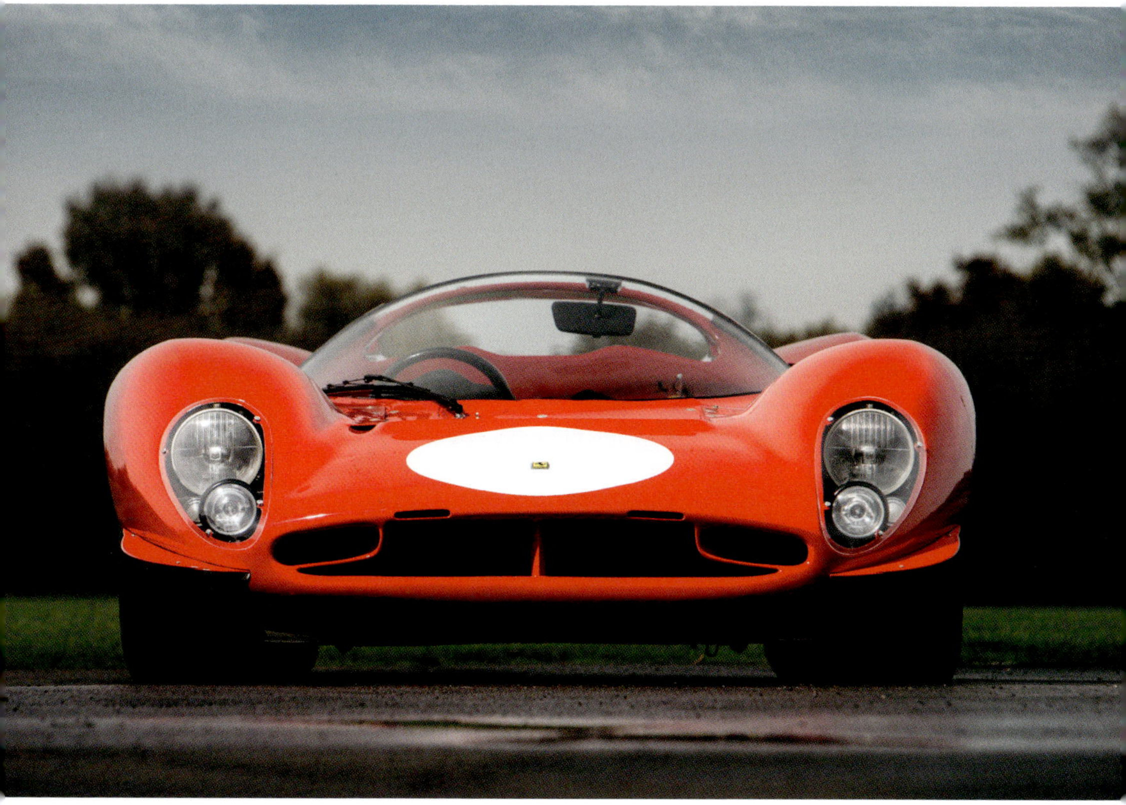

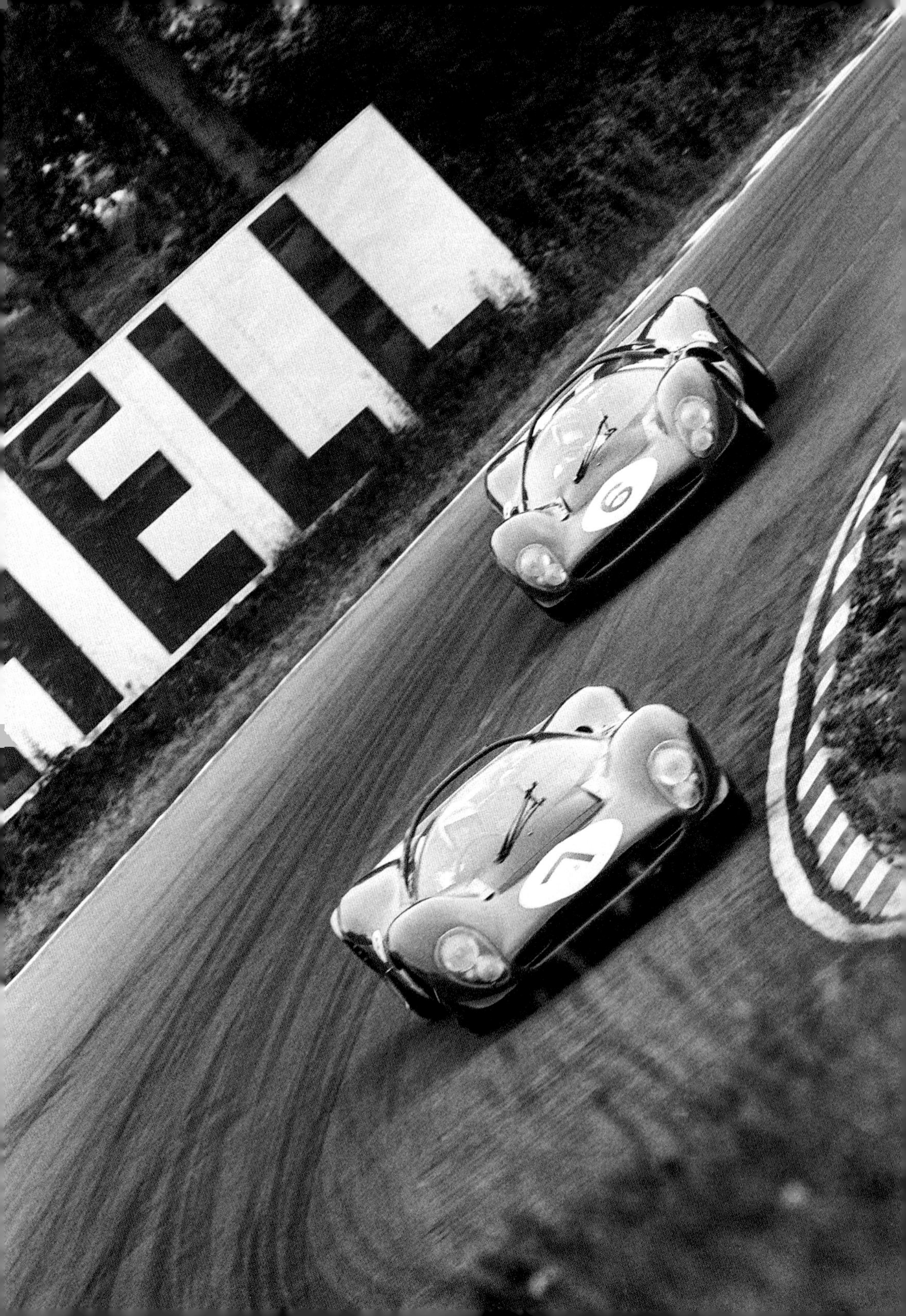

Opposite: The 1967 BOAC International 500, Brands Hatch — the No. 6 Ferrari 330 P4 (chassis no. 0860) driven by Jackie Stewart and Chris Amon finished in second place and the No. 7 Ferrari 330 P4 (chassis no. 0856) driven by Ludovico Scarfiotti and Peter Sutcliffe finished in fifth place.

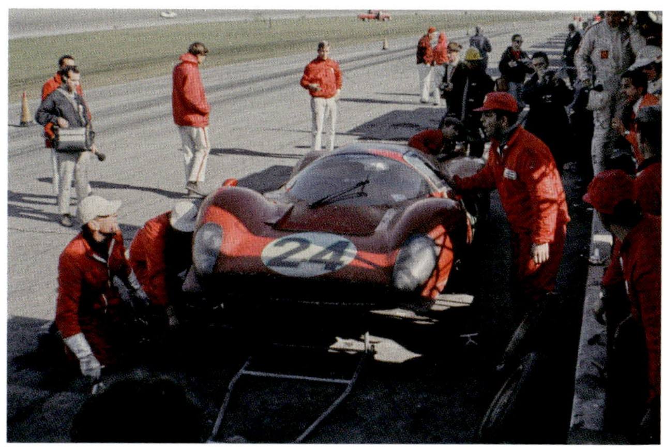

Right: No. 24 Ferrari 330 P4 (chassis no. 0856) of Mike Parkes and Ludovico Scarfiotti making a pit stop at the 1967 24 Hours of Daytona. They finished in second place. After this race the car's roof was cut off, thereby reducing its weight considerably.

Below: Ferrari designer and racing technical director Mauro Forghieri (second from left) screams instructions as second placed Chris Amon brings a smoking Ferrari 330 P4 (chassis no. 0860) — also now without roof — into the pits to allow Jackie Stewart to take over at the 1967 BOAC International 500, Brands Hatch.

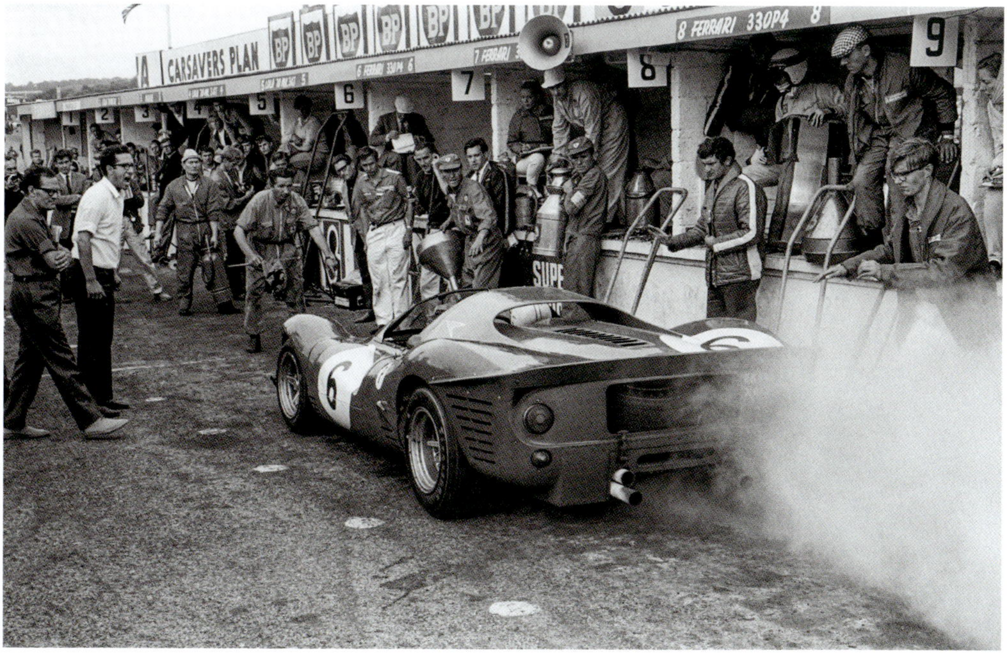

1967

Alfa Romeo 33 Stradale

MANUFACTURED 1967–69 | **ENGINE** 1,995 cc (122 cu. in.), DOHC per bank 90° V8 | **HORSEPOWER** 230
TOP SPEED 260 km/h (162 mph) | **TRANSMISSION** 6-speed
NUMBER PRODUCED 18

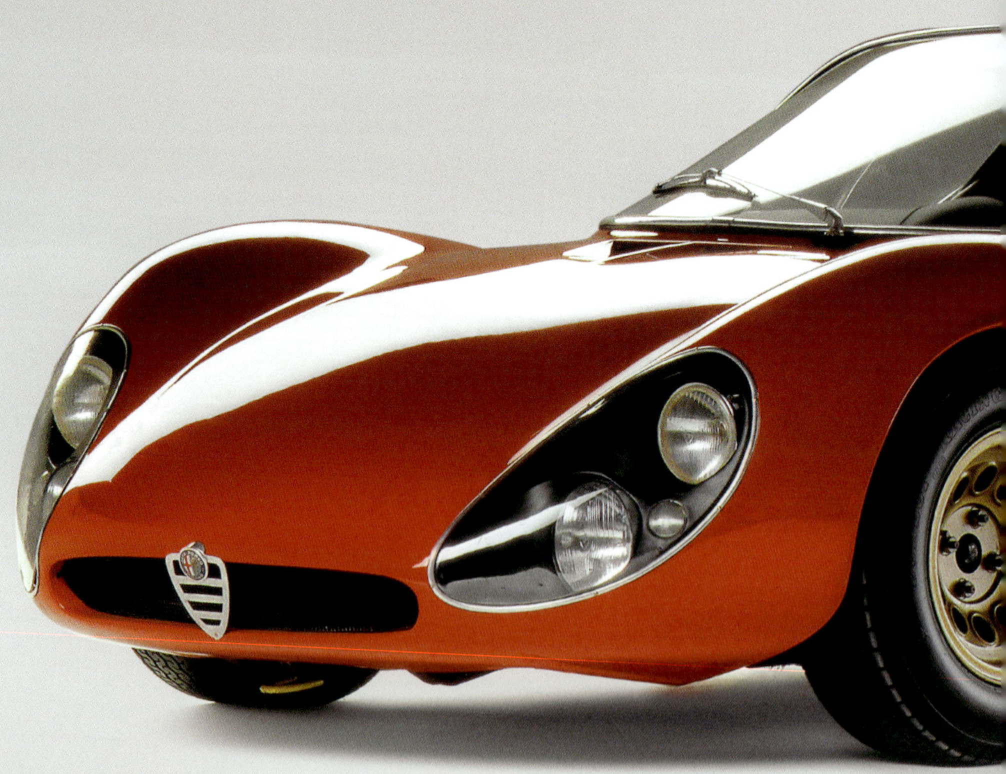

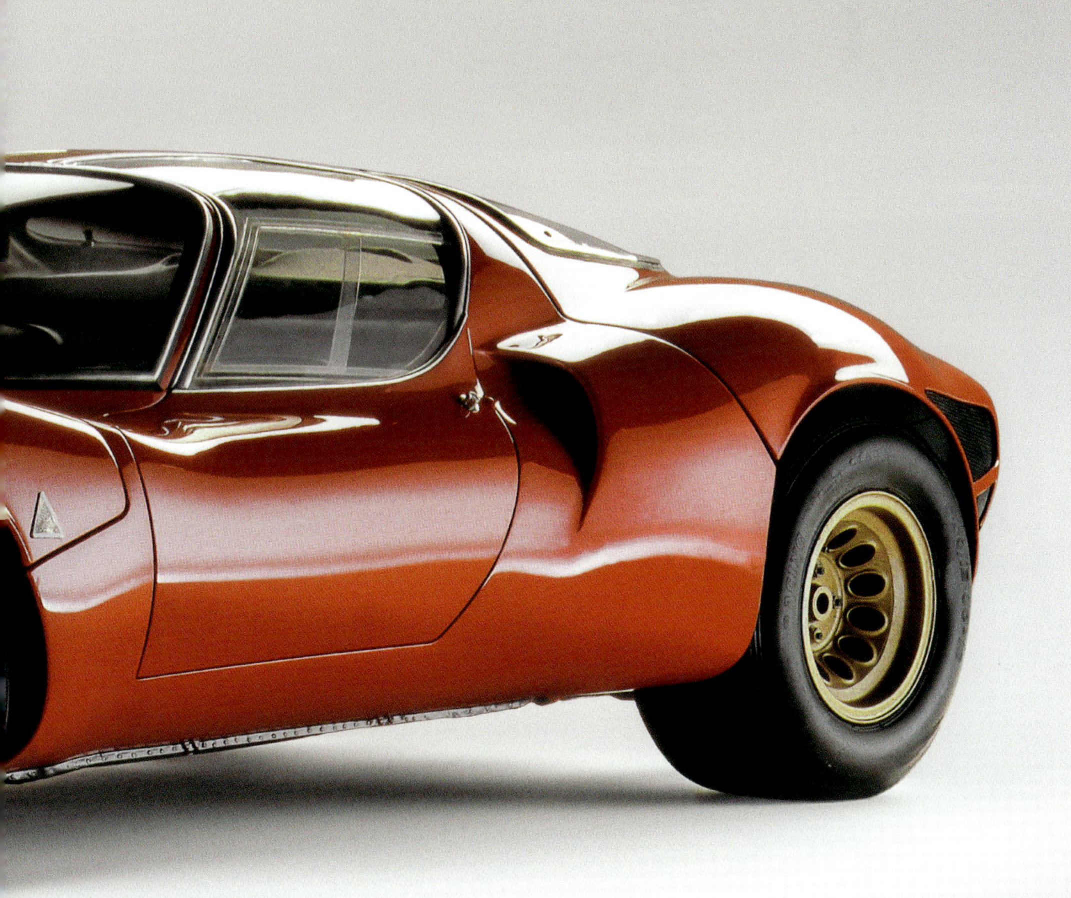

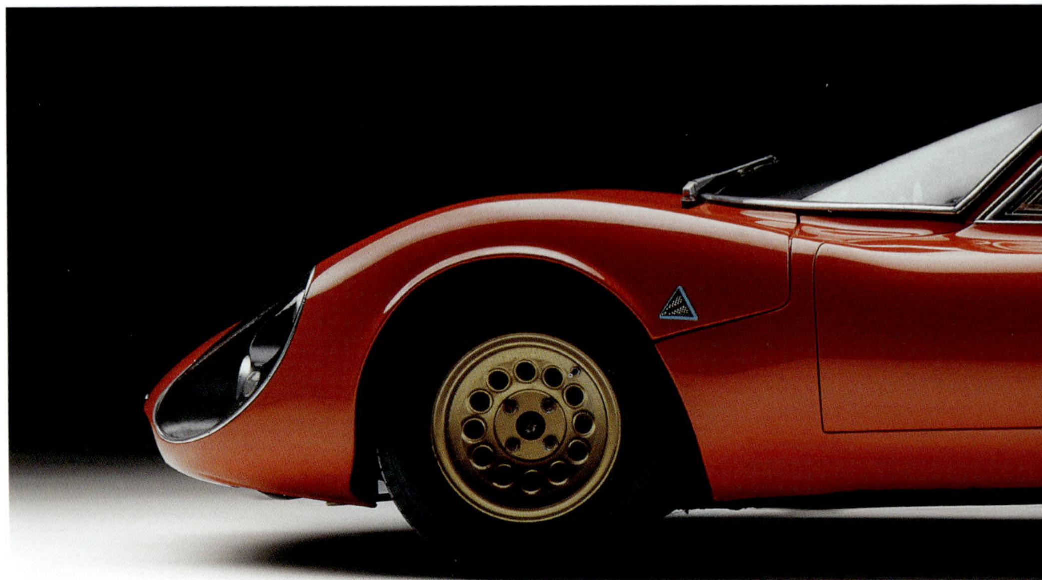

Many consider the Alfa Romeo 33 Stradale one of the most beautiful cars ever made thanks to its exquisite proportions and elegant gestural lines, which are so stunningly exemplified by the way its butterfly doors sweep vertically skyward when opened. This is a luxuriously appointed sports car that reflects in its seductively voluptuous form a deep-seated Italian passion for cutting-edge design blended with innovative high performance engineering. But more than this, in Italy there is the well-known concept of *La Bella Figura* (the beautiful figure), which is all about making a good first impression and emphasizes the importance of surface appeal. The Alfa Romeo 33 Stradale utterly embodies this idea with its dazzlingly attractive body, which was sculpted by one of the undisputed maestros of Italian coach-building, Franco Scaglione. But the 33's beauty is a lot more than just skin deep for at its heart sits a mid-mounted longitudinal 1,995 cc (122 cu. in.) quad-cam V8 capable of 230 hp at 8,800 rpm — in other words, a ridiculously high-revving engine for a car intended for road use.

The origins of this legendary sports car can be traced back to 1967, when the Alfa Romeo Tipo 33 racing prototype made an impressive debut at the Côte de Fléron Hill Climb in Belgium, which it won to everyone's astonishment. Bolstered by this maiden victory, which came on top of the other wins that Alfa Romeo's racing cars had been notching up on tracks around the world, the company's then-president, Giuseppe Luraghi, decided that the next step should be for the marque to build its own European-style "dream car" based on the chassis of the successful Tipo 33. The model was intended as an exclusive, low-volume, high performance sports coupé, which would rival anything then built by the likes of Ferrari or Maserati. Interestingly, the resultant 33 Stradale — with *stradale* meaning "road-going" (a term often used by Italian car manufacturers to indicate a street-legal version of a racing

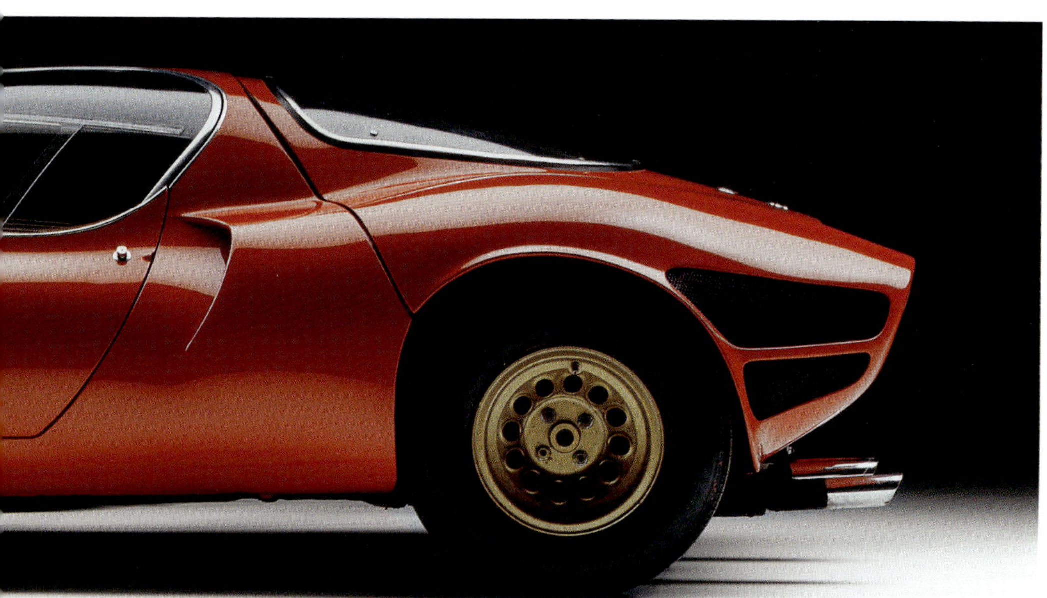

car) — possessed a very distinctive Alfa look about it, with its beautiful profile and visually seductive lines. Indeed, Scaglione's refined body was a complete tour de force of the coach builder's art, with the car's concave air vents being perfectly offset by its large raked windscreen, rear and side windows. Even without its famous badge, one would instantly recognize it to be from the Alfa stable because of its inherent and easily identifiable design DNA. And thanks to its powerful engine and aeronautically inspired lightweight chassis made entirely from a combination of tubular steel and cast magnesium alloy elements, it also offered exceptional performance for its time. Weighing in at just over 700 kilos, this 3.97-meter-long and one-meter-high road-rocket boasted impressive acceleration of 0–60 mph in 5.5 seconds and a top speed of 260 km/h (162 mph).

Carrozzeria Marazzi constructed only 18 examples of the model between 1967 and 1969, which of course makes it nowadays a very rare and highly sought after automotive icon. The example shown here (chassis no. 10533.12) was the second Alfa Romeo 33 Stradale to have been built. It features an experimental magnesium body and is easily distinguished from later versions by the twin headlights and the lack of vents behind the front wheels. This particular 33 Stradale was never sold and remains in the Alfa Romeo collection. It can be seen in the Museo Storico Alfa Romeo, just outside of Milan, where it is one of the most prized exhibits.

In its day, the 33 Stradale was always intended to be highly exclusive. When it was introduced at the Monza Sports Car Show in 1967 it cost nearly 10 million Italian lire, making it the highest-priced sports car on the market at the time, costing roughly twice as much as any Jaguar or Ferrari. But then this is a car that transcends form and function by embodying pure driving emotion, or to put it another way, it is quite simply the most alpha of all Alfas.

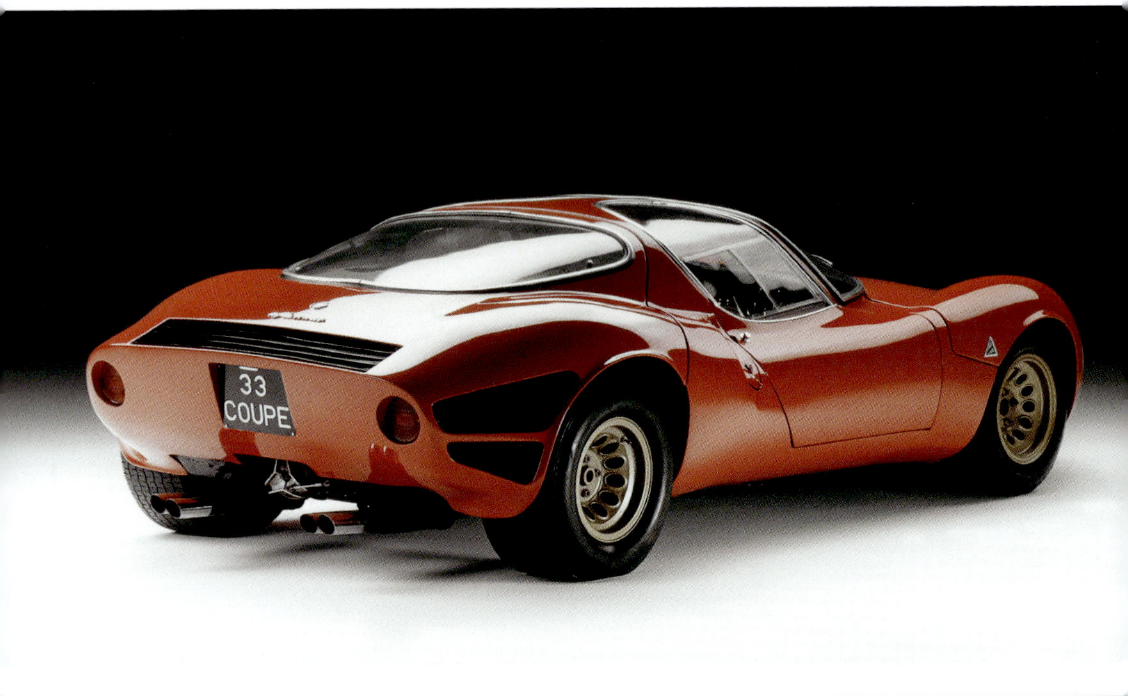

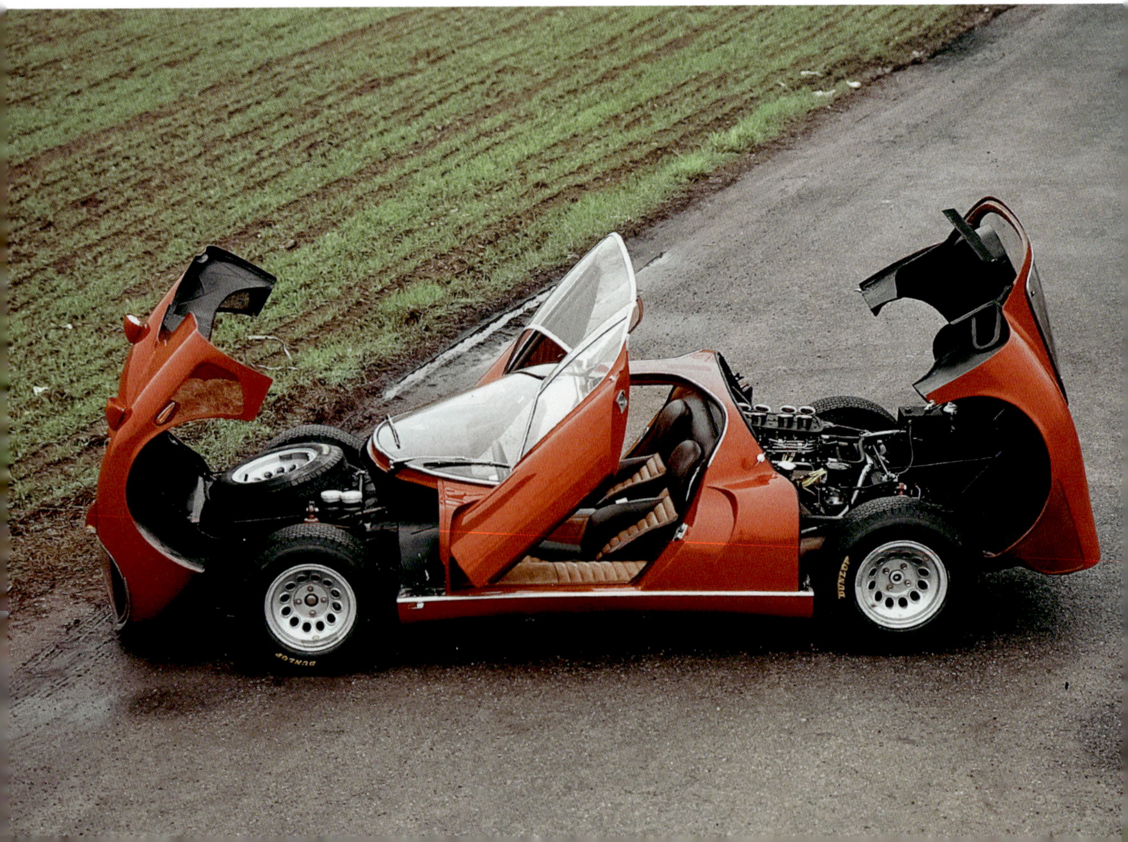

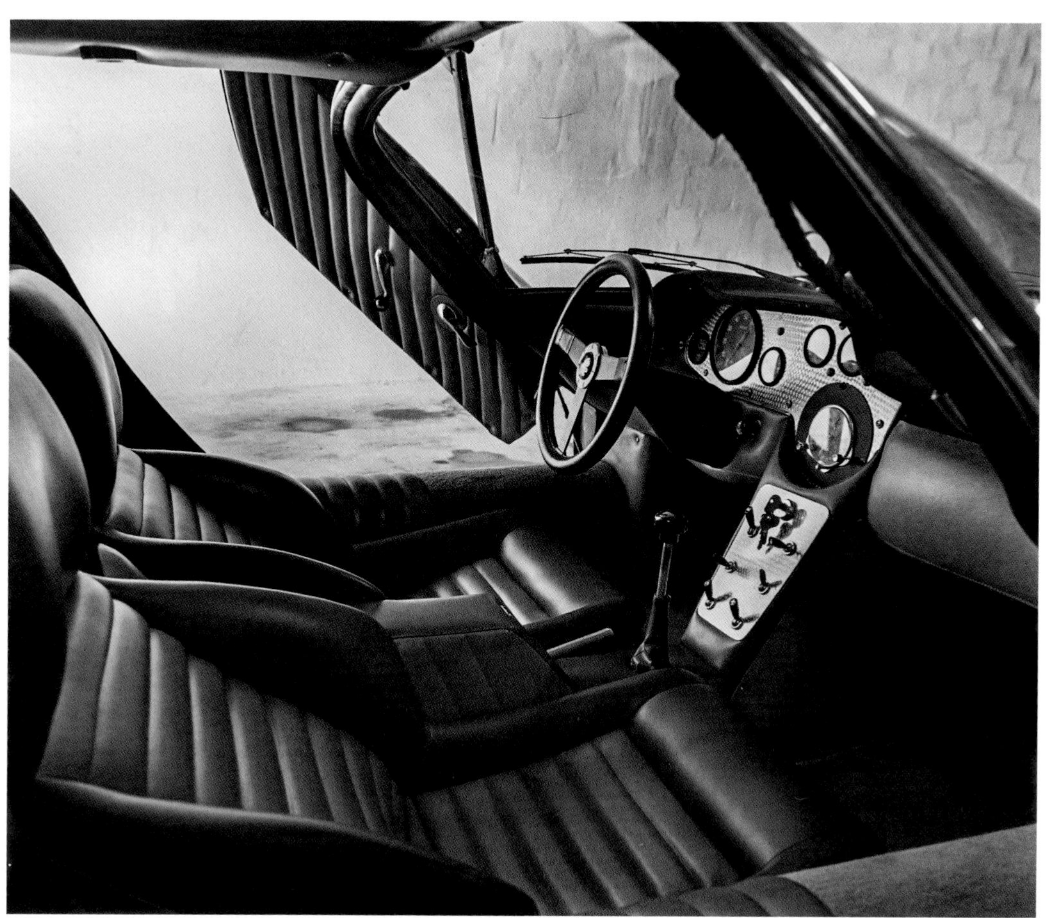

Opposite (bottom): Factory photo showing detail of the Alfa Romeo 33 Stradale's mid-mounted, direct fuel-injected 1,995 cc (122 cu. in.), DOHC per bank 90° V8 engine. This high-revving power unit was capable of producing as much as 270 hp, but for reliability reasons was restricted to 230 hp for road use. This was Alfa Romeo's first V8 engine and was constructed entirely of aluminum. The Alfa Romeo 33 Stradale was the first production vehicle to feature dihedral doors, also known as butterfly doors. The car shown here is a later model with vents added behind both the front and rear wheels to allow hot air from the brakes to escape.

Above: Detail of the Alfa Romeo 33 Stradale cockpit. This was a luxuriously appointed interior for what was in effect a road-going race car. The dashboard and center console feature beautifully engine-turned aluminum details.

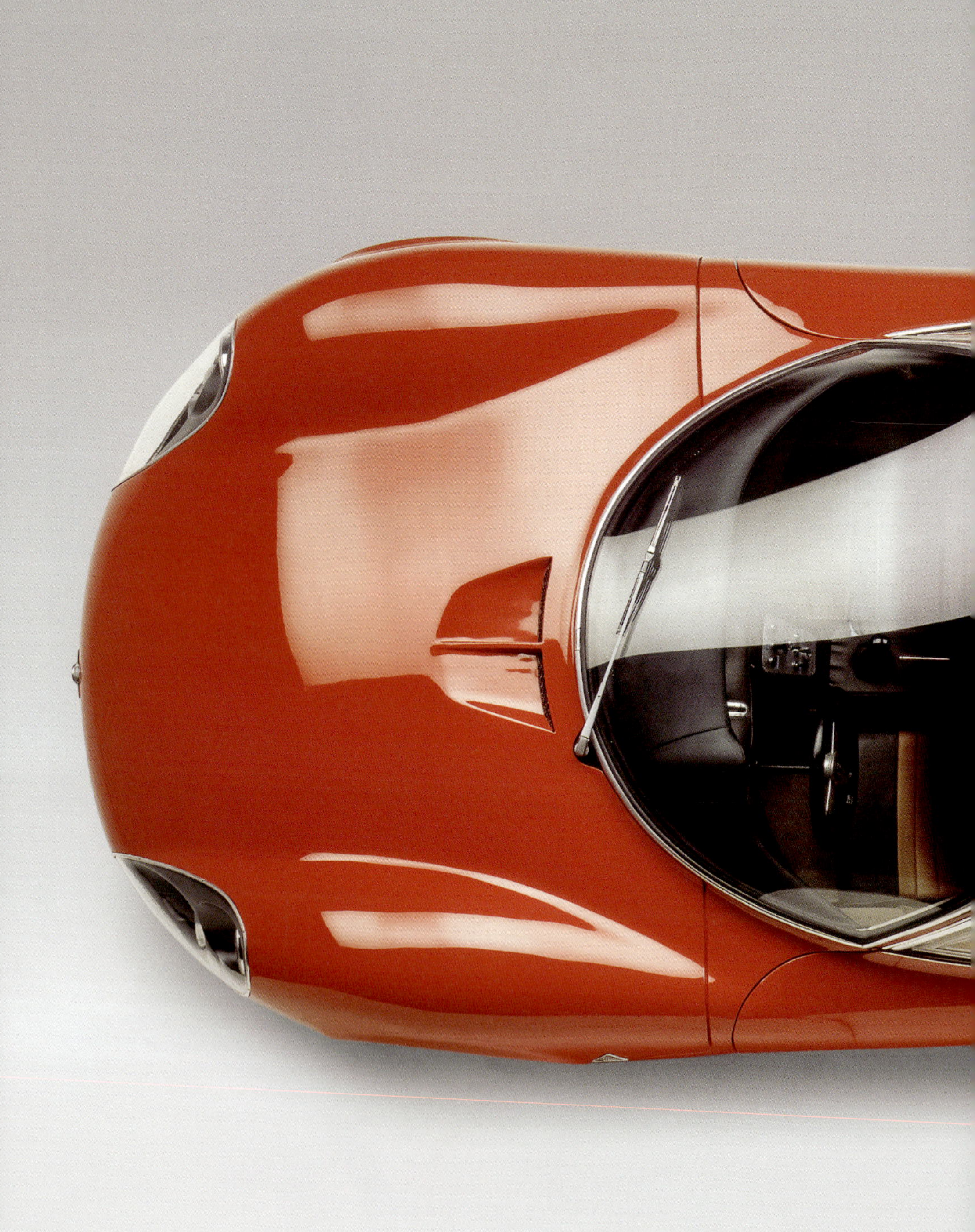

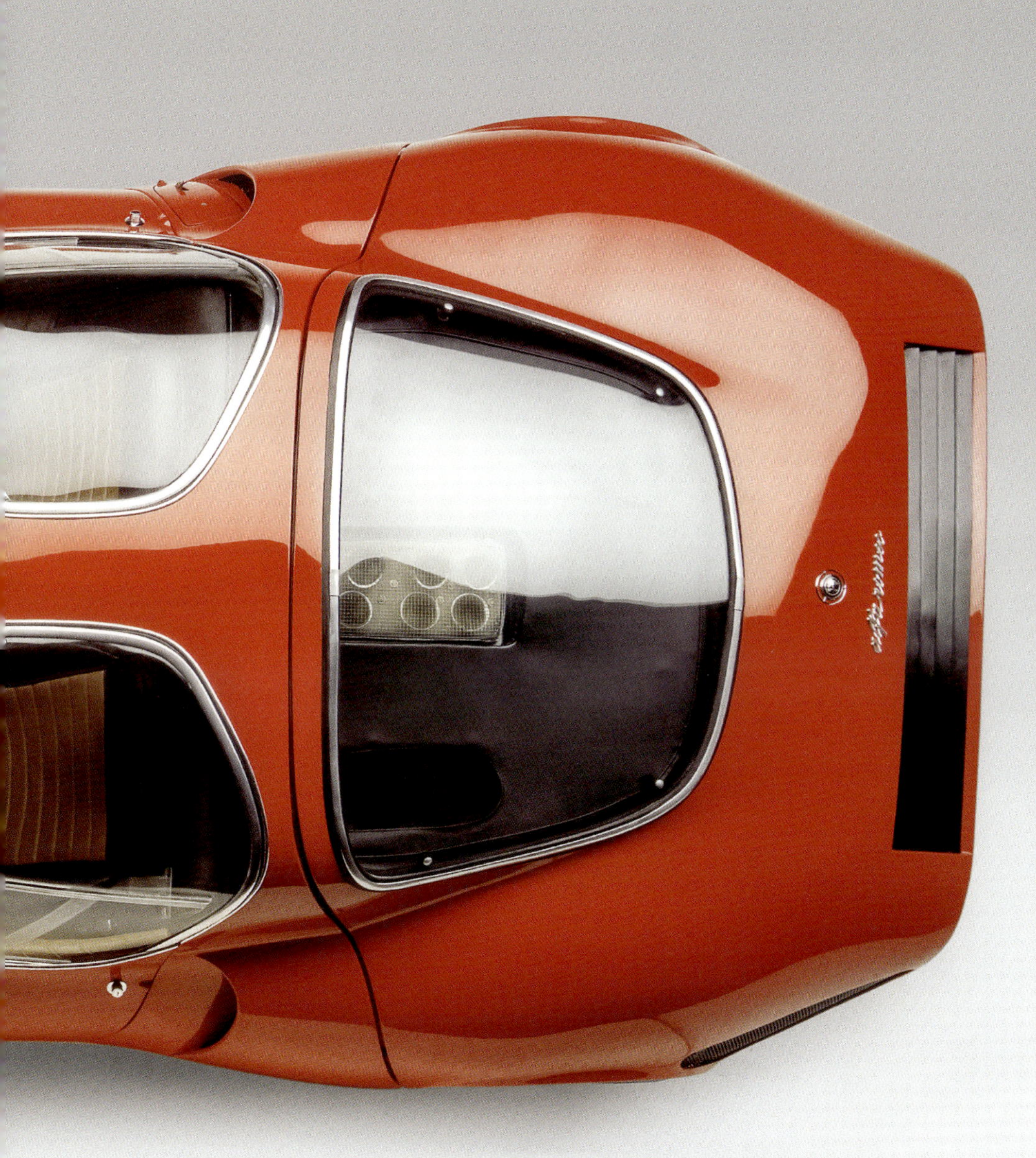

1967

Chevrolet Corvette Sting Ray L88 Coupe

MANUFACTURED 1967 | ENGINE 6,997 cc (427 cu. in.), overhead-valve V8 | HORSEPOWER 430 (claimed) / approx. 540 (actual)
TOP SPEED approx. 274 km/h (170 mph) | TRANSMISSION 4-speed
NUMBER PRODUCED 20

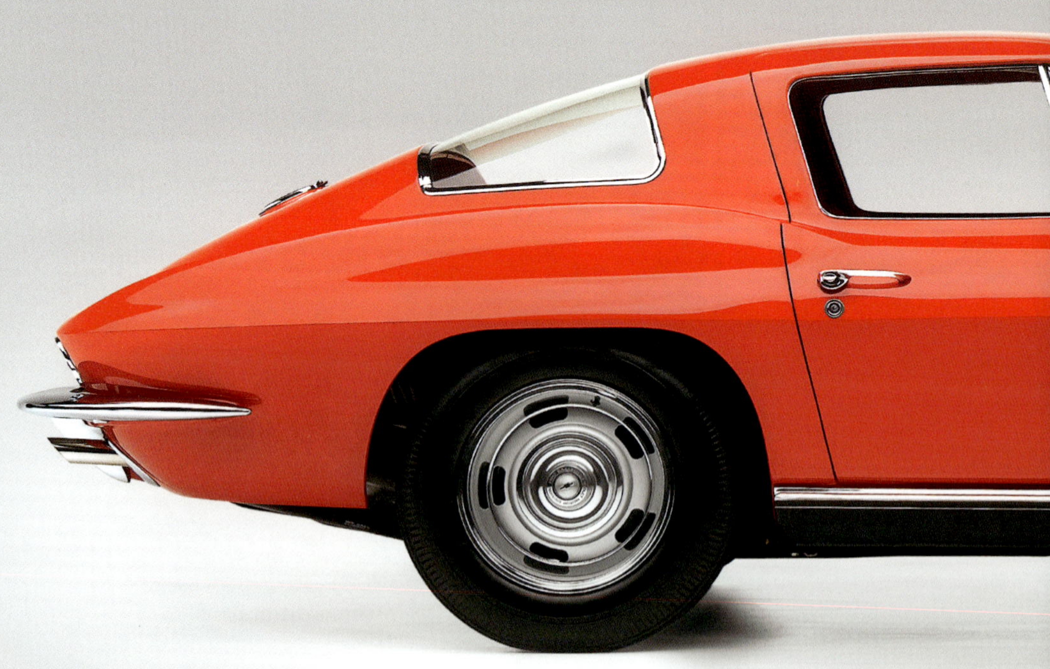

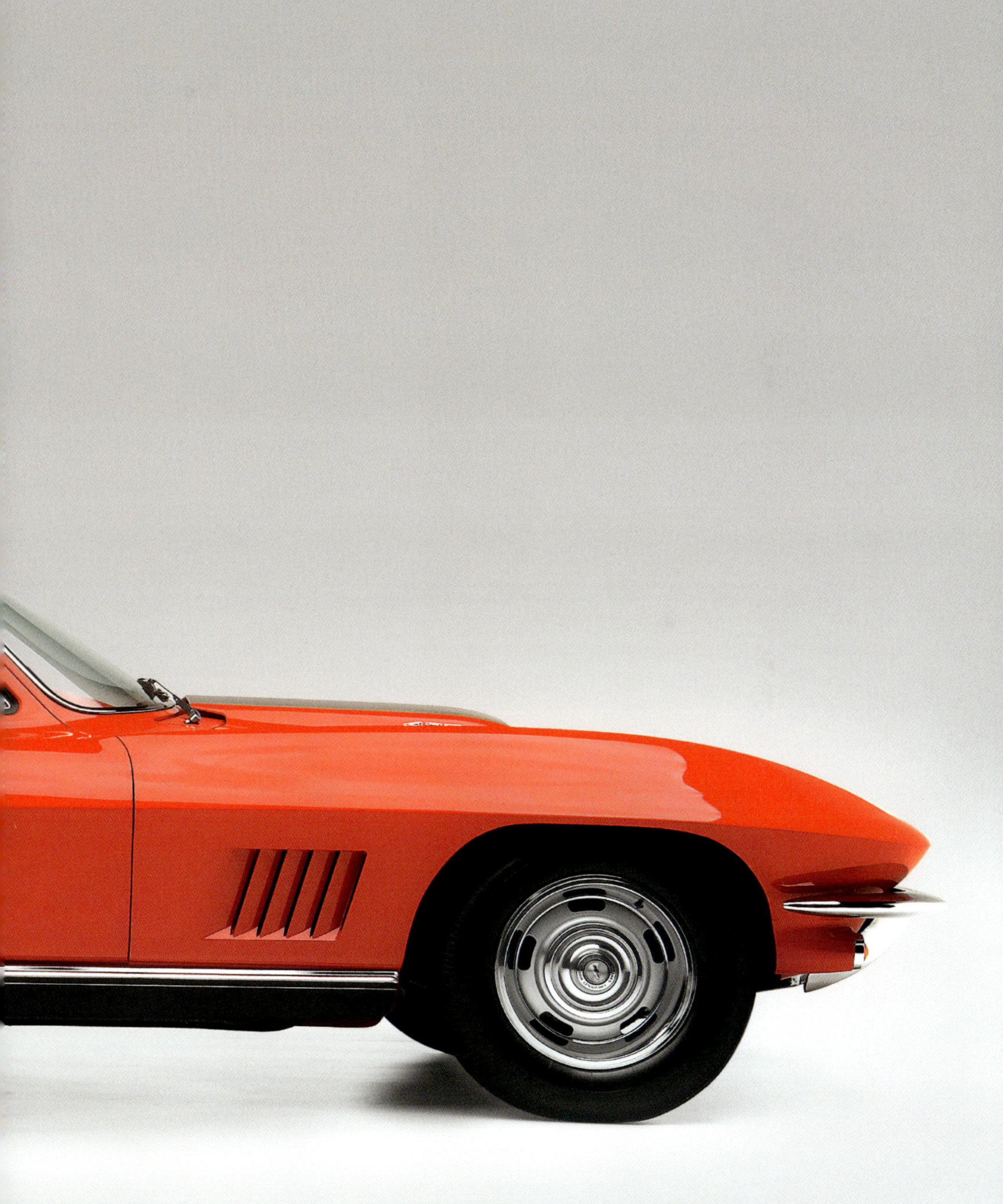

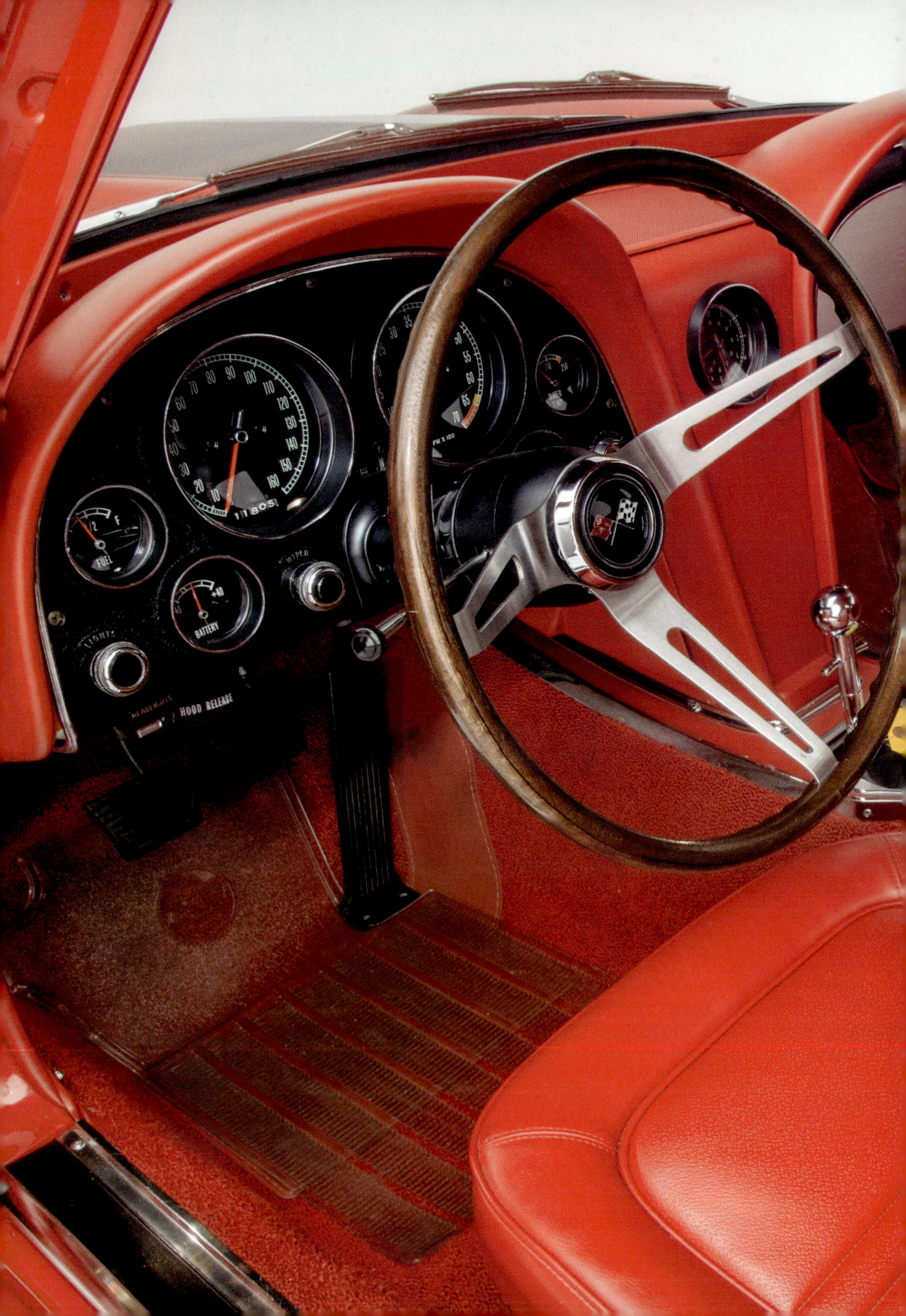
FUEL
BATTERY
WIPER
LIGHTS
HOOD RELEASE

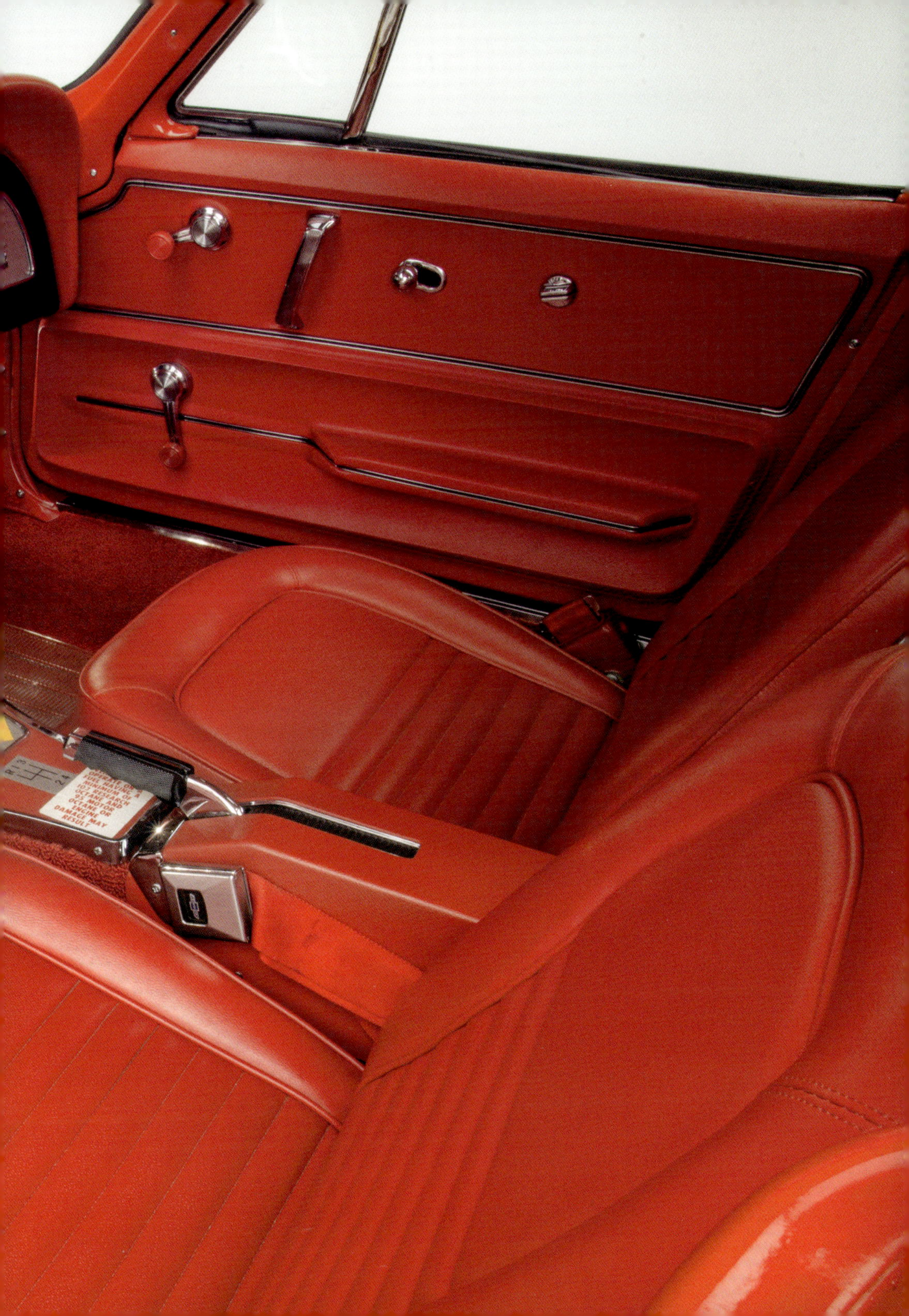
OPERATE ON A
FUEL HAVING A
MINIMUM OF
103 RESEARCH
OCTANE AND
95 MOTOR
OCTANE OR
ENGINE
DAMAGE MAY
RESULT

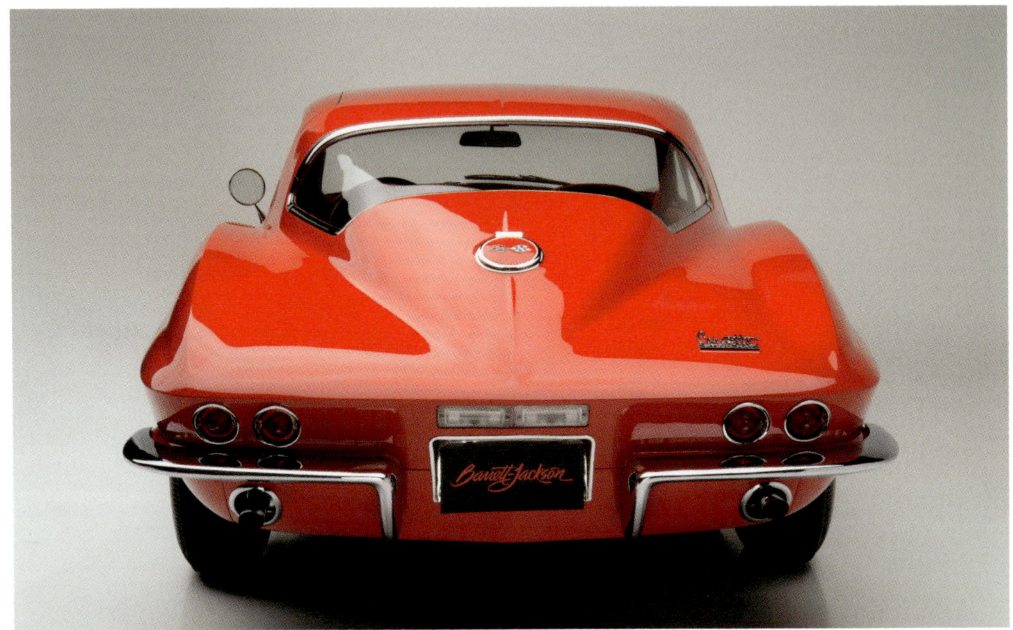

Previous: Detail of Chevrolet Corvette Sting Ray L88 Coupe cockpit, steering wheel, instruments and controls. This vehicle (VIN no. 194377S10015791) — the sixth L88 built — is the only known 1967 red/red L88 produced. For the Sting Ray L88 the normal radio and heater were deleted to reduce weight and discourage the car's use on the street.

Above: Detail of Chevrolet Corvette Sting Ray L88 Coupe's fastback. 1967 was the last year of the second generation (C2) Corvette, but the first year that the mighty L88 was available in a regular production Corvette, thus making this variant one of the rarest and most desirable Corvettes of all time — only 20 were built.

Opposite: 1967 General Motors magazine advertisement for the Chevrolet Corvette Sting Ray L89. This was a mighty V8 engine that was also introduced in 1967. It featured three dual-barrel carburetors and produced 435 hp. The L89 was a beast, but not nearly as ferocious as the L88, which was never advertised publicly.

The first-generation Chevrolet Corvette (C1) was launched in 1953, which thanks to its popularity went on to become known as "America's Sports Car." It was a design that perfectly catered to a new and affluent home grown demographic that desired more speed and better all round performance. Beautifully styled, this early lightweight fiberglass bodied, front-engine, rear-wheel-driven, two-seater reflected a stylistic shift within sports car design. A decade later, it was followed up by its visually impactful second-generation successor, the Corvette Sting Ray (C2), which was produced from 1963 to 1967. In the final year of the Sting Ray's production the awesome 427 L88 engine option was introduced. Only 20 cars were built with this engine in 1967, which makes this particular model the most covetable of all Corvettes.

From the late 1950s and throughout the 1960s there was a lot of design inspiration going back and forth between America and Europe, especially when it came to the creation of high performance automobiles. American manufacturers were becoming increasingly

Wolf in wolf's clothing.

Some cars tell you all about themselves at first glance. A big soft family sedan. (Ho-hum) An utterly practical station wagon. (Ehhh) A plodding sort of economy car. (Wheee) Or a Corvette. A tough, wide-tired, bulge-hooded "let's go driving" Corvette. A Sting Ray with the 427-cubic-inch 435-horsepower three-deuces V8 you can specify.
It *is* what it looks like.

'67 Corvette

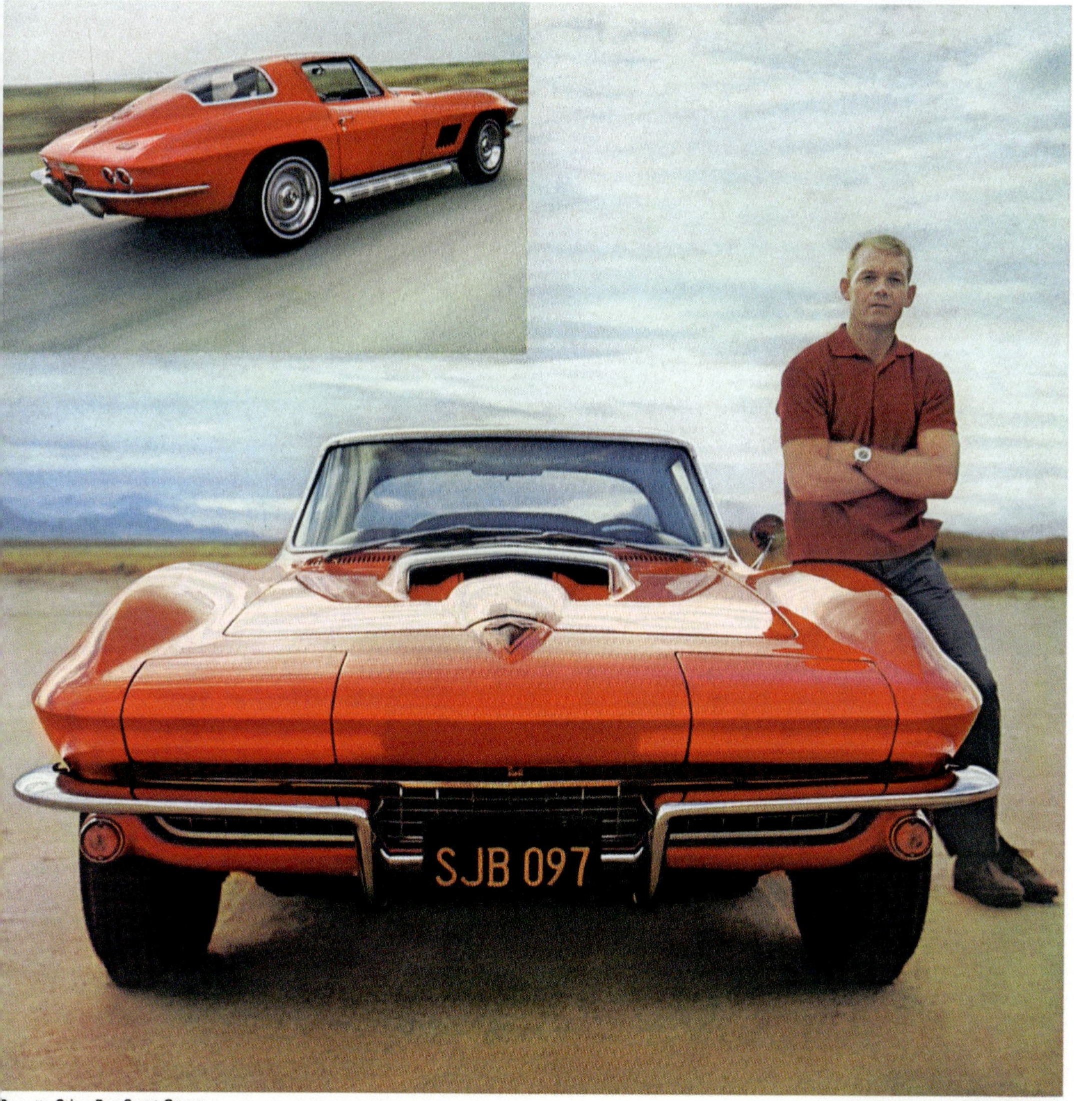

Corvette Sting Ray Sport Coupe with features like four-way hazard warning flasher standard for your added safety.

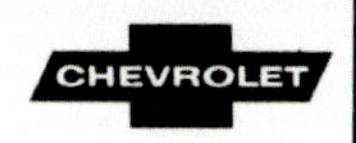

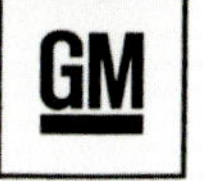

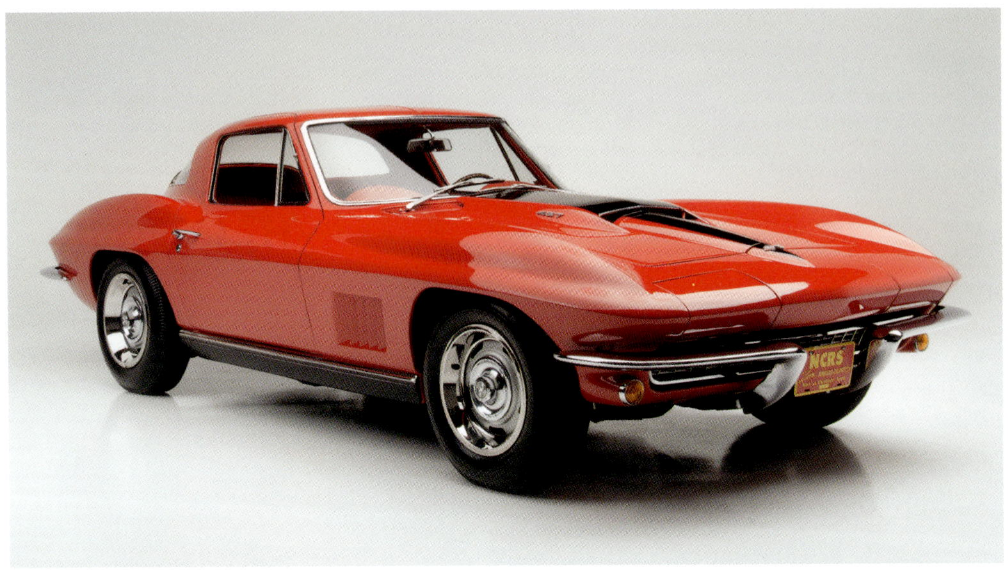

influenced by the elegant, high-end yet super-fast racers and sports cars being produced by the likes of Ferrari, Jaguar and Maserati, while conversely European manufacturers with an eye on the all-important US export market were beginning to create race-derived roadsters better attuned to open-top West Coast driving. The popularity of motorsports during this period also had a lot to do with this transatlantic creative exchange, which saw manufacturers battle it out week in, week out during the racing season in the knowledge that a win at Le Mans, Daytona or Sebring would translate into acreages of free publicity and enhanced brand prestige, which would in turn help boost sales of new cars. But more than this the racing circuits were, as they remain to this day, important incubators and testbeds for new design and engineering innovations.

In fact, the Corvette Sting Ray L88 can trace its ancestry directly back to two GM experimental projects: The first was the "still-born" mid-engine Q-Corvette fast-back concept proposal of 1957, which had been instigated by Chevrolet's director of high performance vehicle design and development, Zora Arkus-Duntov. It featured, among other things a rear transaxle, independent rear suspension and in-board drum brakes. The second project was a concept car designed in 1959 by the General Motors designers, Pete Brock, Bill Mitchell and Larry Shinoda. Known as the Corvette XP-87 Stingray Racer, it borrowed a number of design elements and styling cues from the earlier Q-Corvette. Like the trio's concept racer, the follow-up production Corvette Sting Ray married a lightweight chassis with a powerful V8, with one of the engine options being the monstrous 427 L88. This legendary developed-for-racing power plant, the creation of which was personally instigated by Duntov, boasted phenomenal 12.5:1 compression, a hi-lift cam, an 850 cubic feet per minute (cfm) four-barrel carburetor and aluminum heads. Introduced in 1967, it was quite simply one of the most powerful US-built engines you could lay your hands on. Its racing debut was at Sebring in 1967, when it was sunk into a Chevrolet Corvette L88 Sunray DX race car. Later that same year, the 427 L88's mettle was further tested during the 24 Hours of Le Mans in a red, white and blue Corvette racer piloted by Dick Guldstrand, Bob Bondurant and Don Yenko. This was the Corvette's first participation at Le Mans, and although the car was forced to retire in the 13th hour with trouble emanating from its near-stock big-block engine, Guldstrand nevertheless managed to get this Sting Ray up to an impressive 171.5 mph (276 km/h) along the infamous Mulsanne Straight.

Today, only 17 of the street-legal 1967 L88 Corvettes can be accounted for, with the other three presumably lost to the mists of time. As Barrett-Jackson, who sold this magnificent example in 2014, notes, "The true intent of the L88 was all-out performance on the race-track. L88s were delivered without fan shrouds, they did not have chokes and were a bear to keep running until they came up to operating temperature, there was no radio and no heat-er." Moreover, General Motors intentionally underrated the engine at 430 hp, because if the truth of its awesome power had been revealed in all likelihood it would have been banned from street use — stock, as delivered L88s have reputedly been dyno-tested at up to 560 hp. Indeed, you had to be pretty well connected to even be able to get one of these big block engines fitted into a Corvette Sting Ray, which meant these cars were always the preserve of serious, deep-pocketed petrol-heads — much like they still are today. Although the L88 engine was only offered in production cars between 1967 and 1969, its design was hugely influential, so much so its legacy continues to reverberate in Chevrolet's latest-generation big-block engine, the ZZ427. The well-documented Corvette Sting Ray L88, shown here, VIN no. 194377S10015791 (the sixth L88 built) probably represents the finest example in existence — it is the only known red-on-red version to have been produced in 1967 and it received the National Corvette Restorers Society Duntov Mark of Excellence Award in 2001 for its stunning restoration.

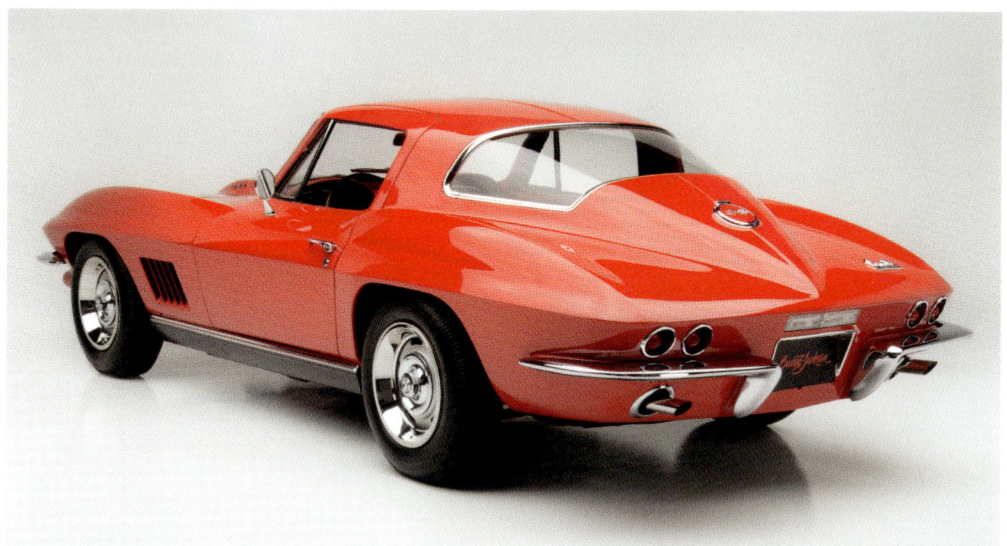

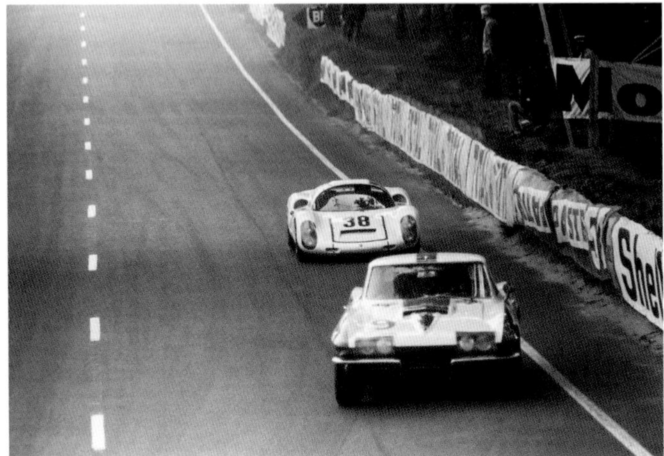

Left: The No. 9 Dana Chevrolet Inc. Corvette Sting Ray L88 of Bob Bondurant, Dick Guldstrand, and Don Yenko leads the No. 38 Works Porsche 910 Kurzheck of Rolf Stommelen and Jochen Neerpasch (finished sixth overall) in the 1967 24 Hours of Le Mans.

Below: Several hours into the 1967 24 Hours of Le Mans the No. 9 Dana Chevrolet Inc. Corvette Sting Ray L88 leads the No. 19 Scuderia Ferrari 330 P4 of Günter Klass and Peter Sutcliffe (DNF). This was the Corvette's first participation in the 24 Hours of Le Mans, and although the car was forced to retire in the 13th hour due to trouble with its near-stock big-block engine, Guldstrand nevertheless managed to get this Sting Ray up to an impressive 171.5 mph (276 km/h) along the infamous Mulsanne Straight.

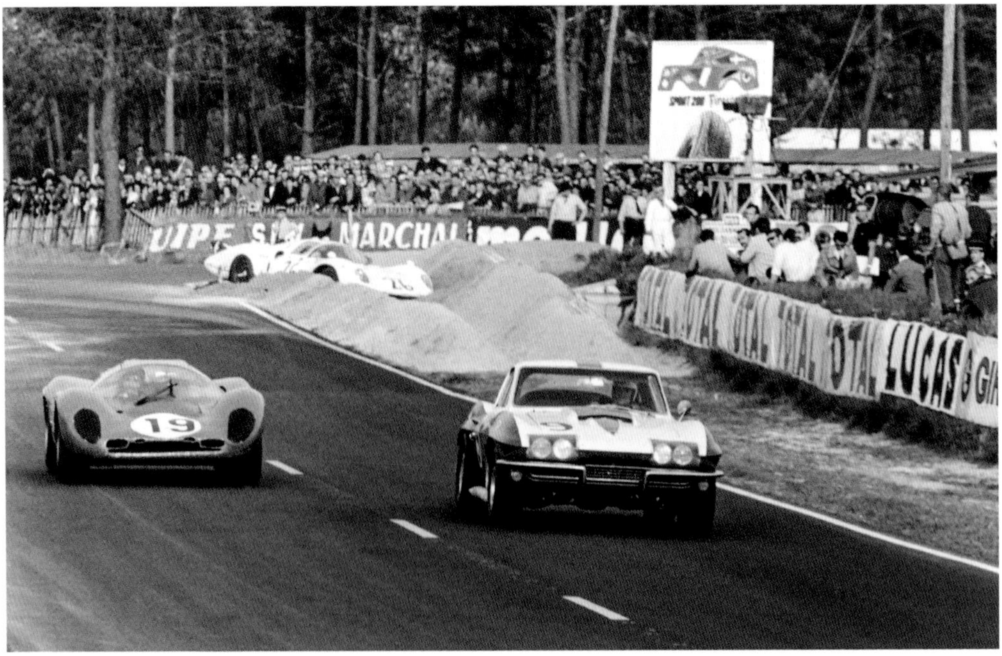

Right: Zora Arkus-Duntov (1909–1996), the Belgian-born American engineer, photographed in 1974, whose work on the Chevrolet Corvette earned him the nickname "Father of the Corvette." Duntov was also a professional racing driver, appearing at the 24 Hours of Le Mans four times and taking a class win in 1954. He was made chief engineer for Corvette in 1967, a position he held until his retirement from GM in 1975.

Below: Detail of 1967 Chevrolet Corvette Sting Ray L88 6,997 cc (427 cu. in.), overhead-valve V8 engine. Boasting phenomenal 12.5:1 compression, a hi-lift cam, a single Holley 850 cfm four-barrel carburetor and aluminum heads, the L88 was in its day one of the most powerful engines available for a road car, producing an outstanding 540+ hp. Its development was instigated by the legendary GM engineer Zora Arkus-Duntov.

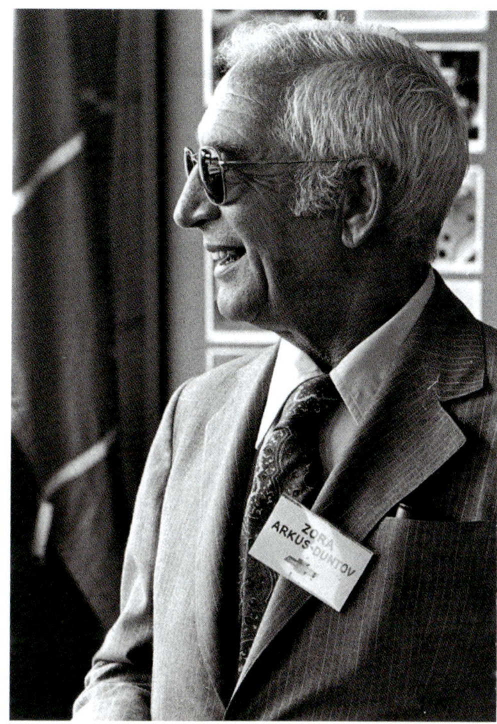

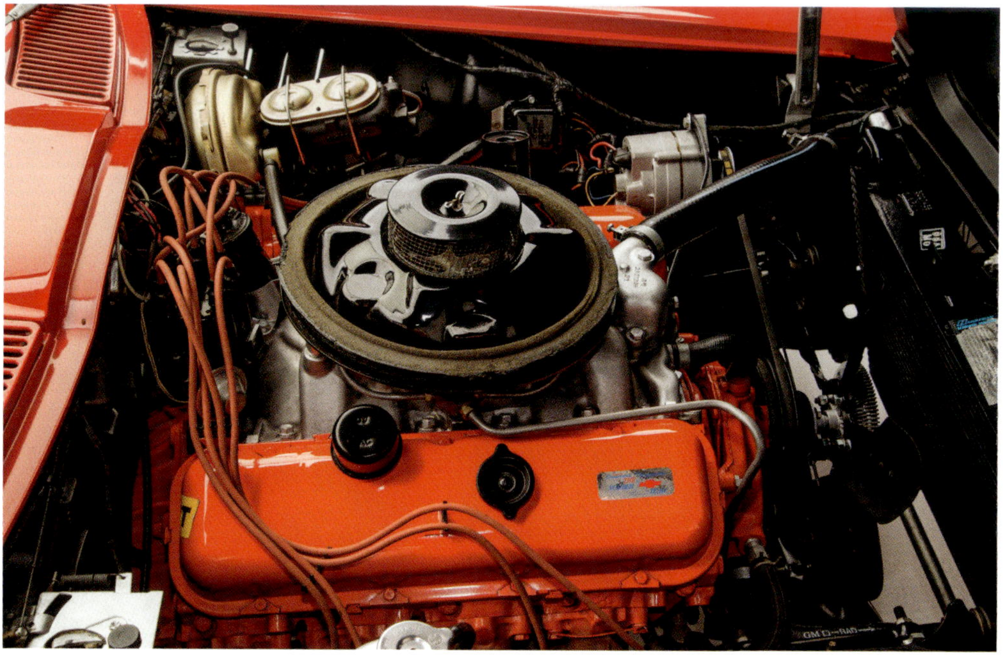

1970–90s

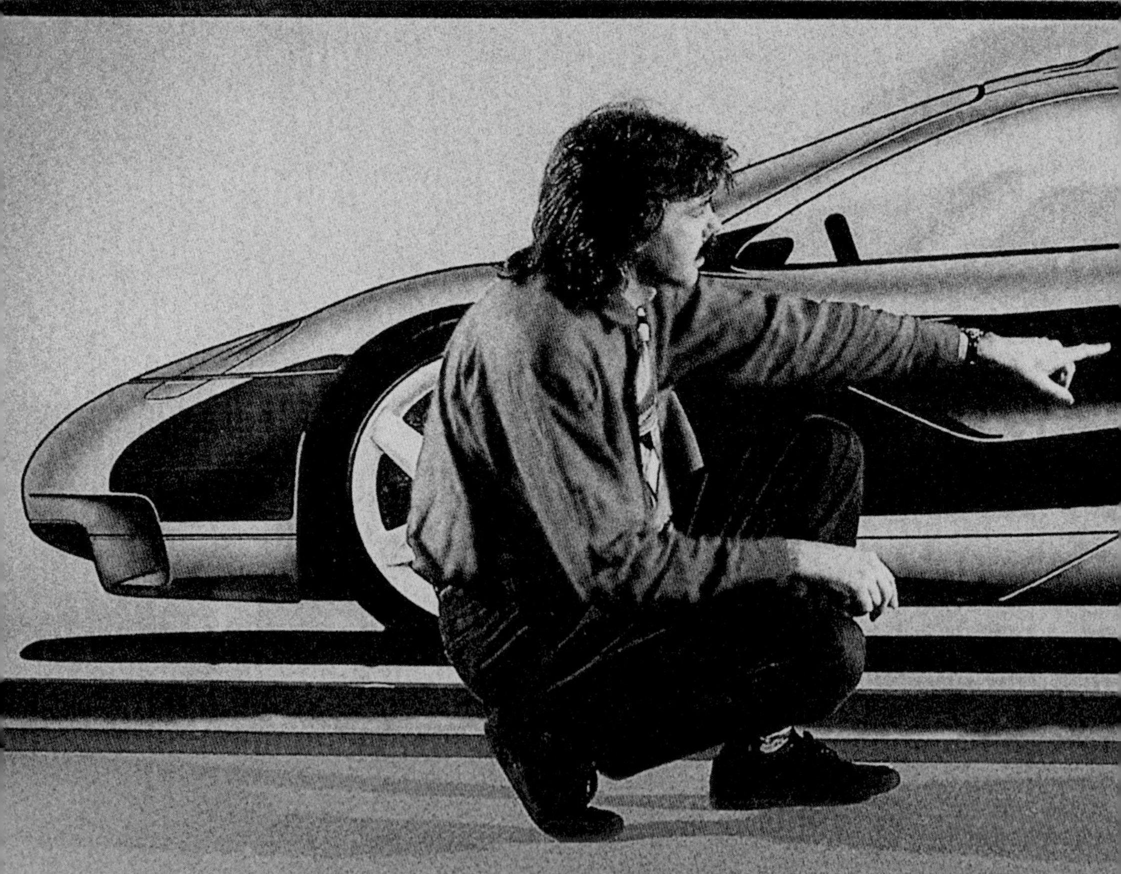

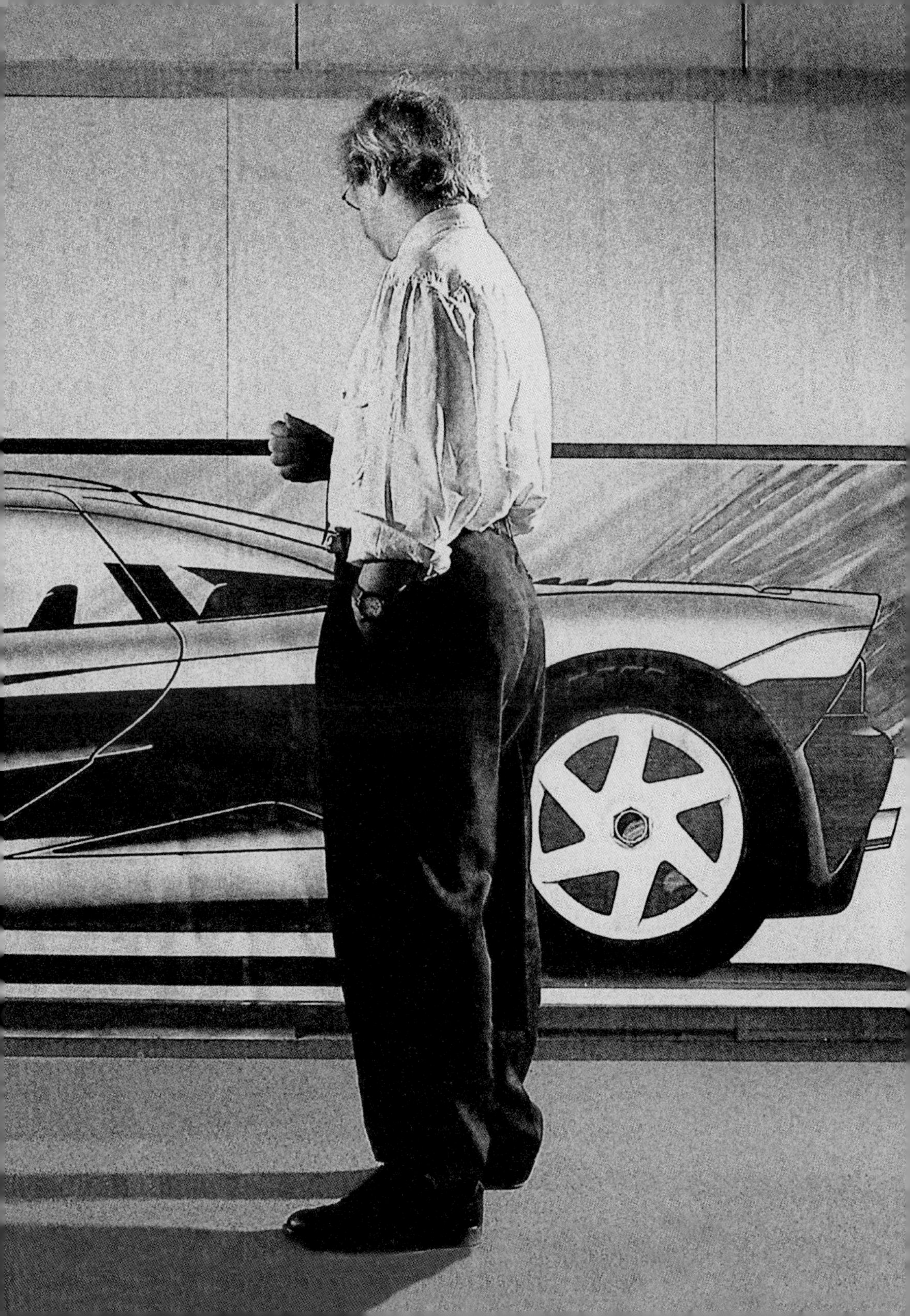

1971

Lamborghini Miura P400 SVJ

MANUFACTURED 1971–73 | ENGINE 3,929 cc (240 cu. in.), DOHC per bank transverse 60° V12 | HORSEPOWER 385
TOP SPEED 290 km/h (180 mph) | TRANSMISSION 5-speed
NUMBER PRODUCED 4 (original factory built)

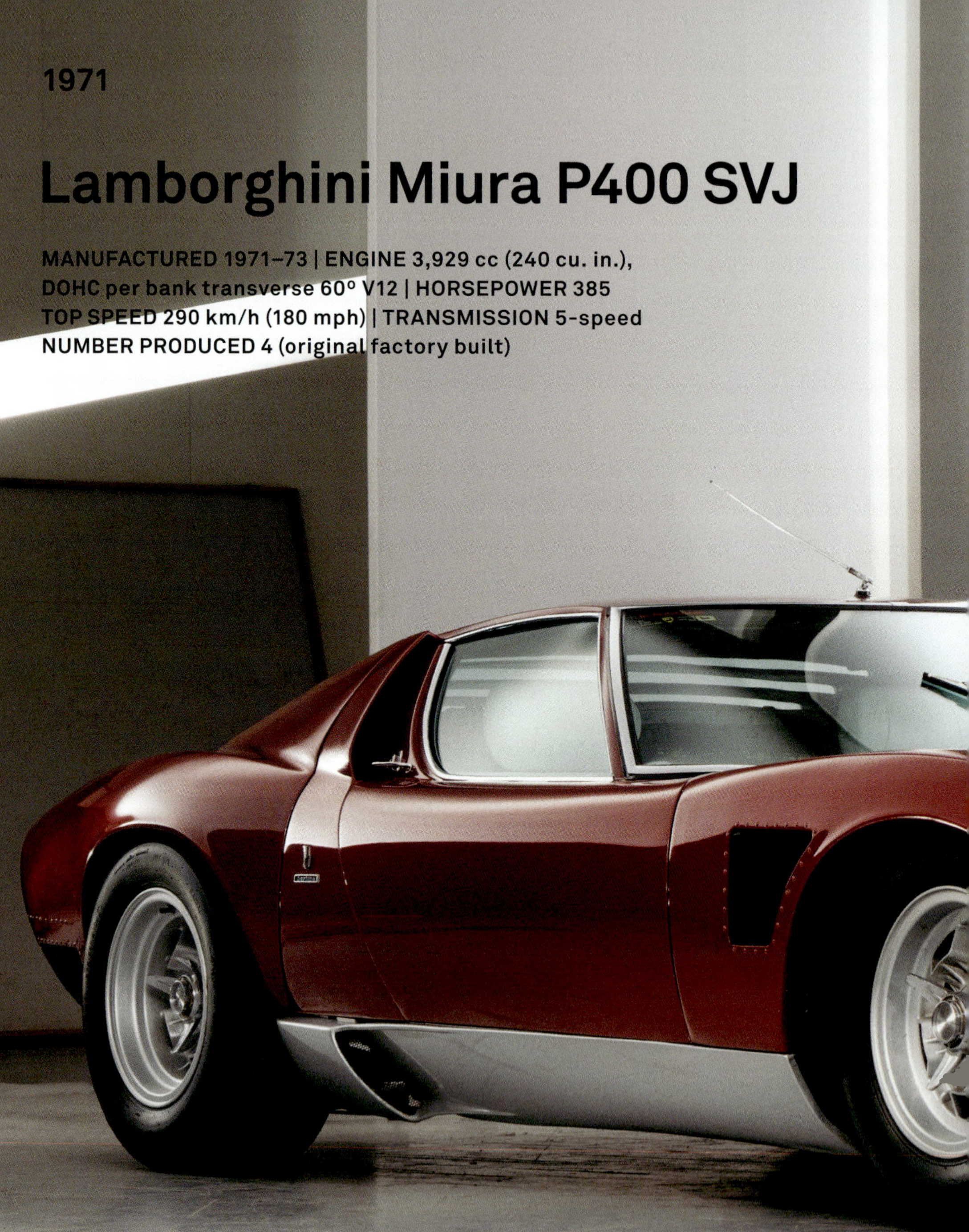

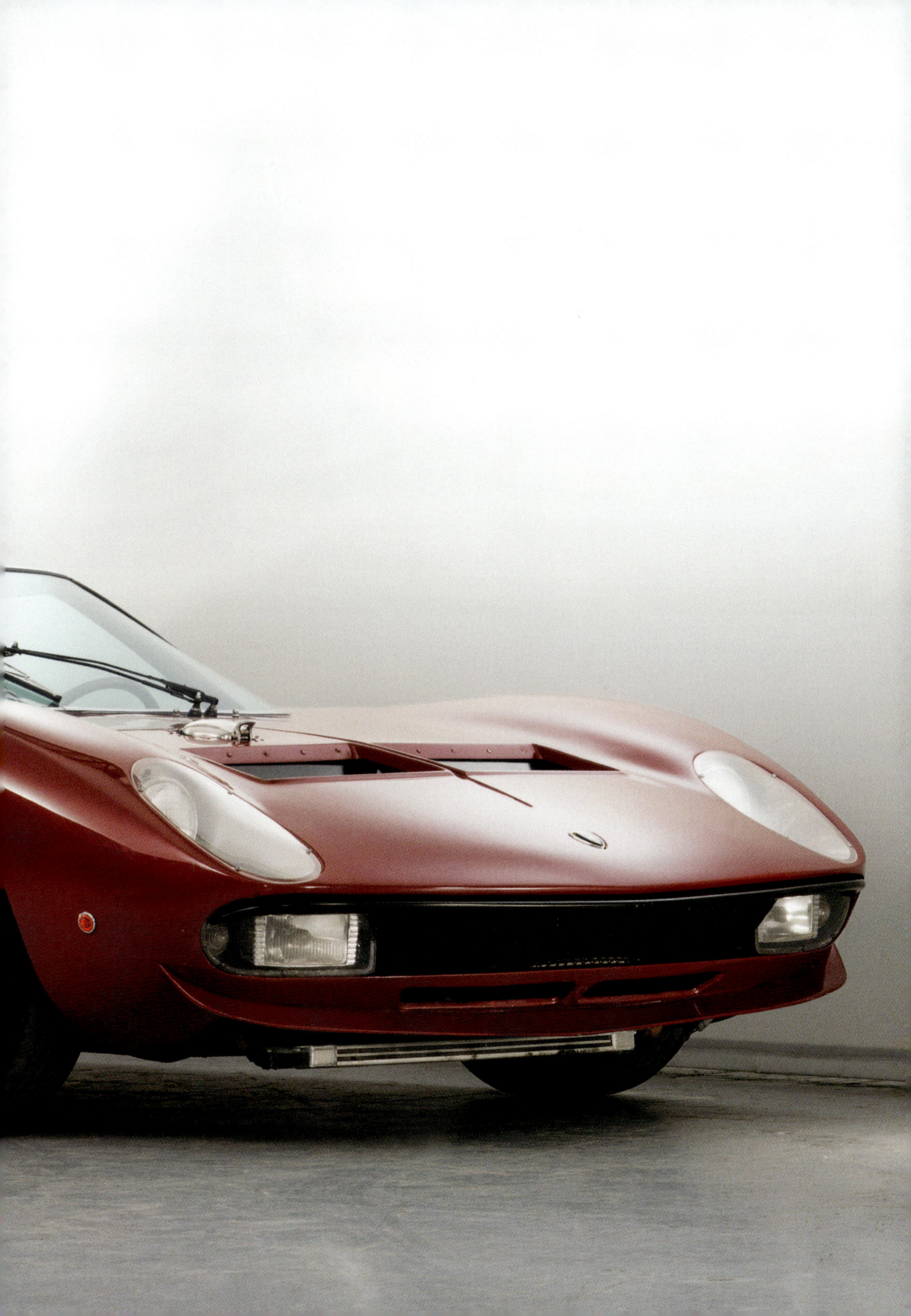

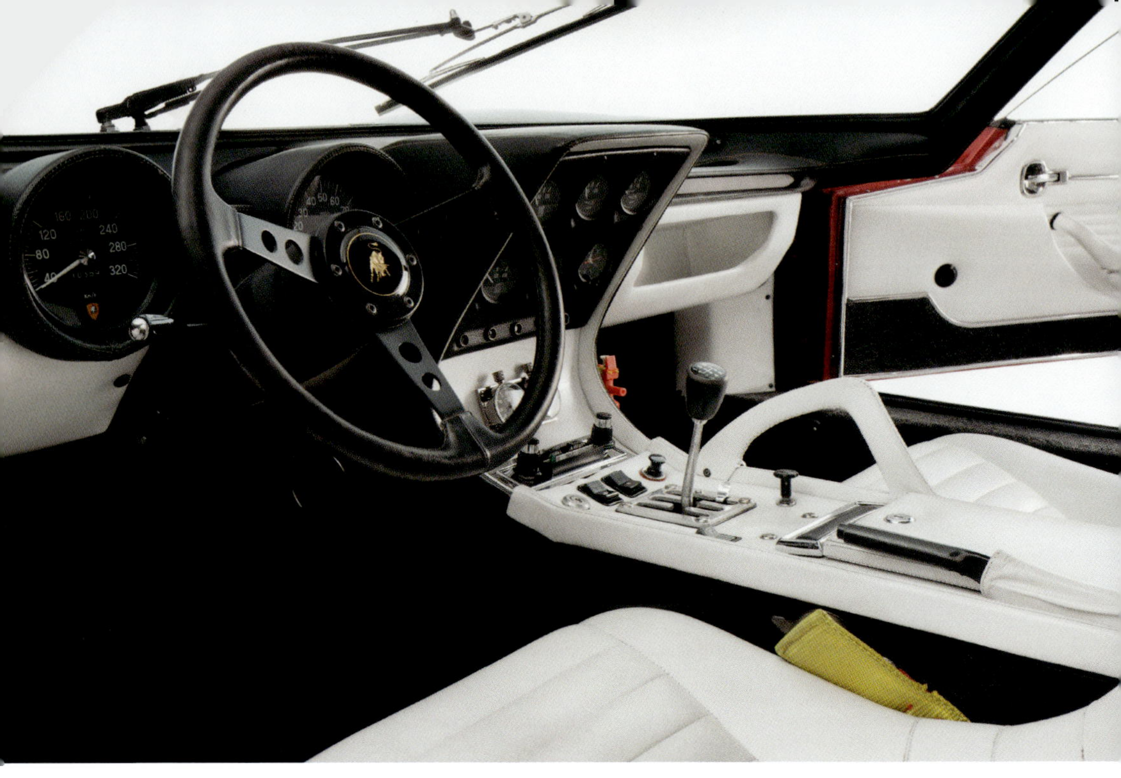

Above: Detail of Lamborghini Miura P400 SVJ's beautifully designed and appointed cockpit including five-speed gated gear shift.

Regarded by many as the finest Lamborghini ever made, the Miura P400 is also generally considered the world's first supercar — the term reputedly having been coined by the British journalist L. J. K. Setright to describe the vehicle in an expanded article in *Car* magazine in 1967/68. The Miura was famously named after a well-known Spanish cattle ranch renowned for the breeding of fighting bulls — like the one emblazoned on the marque's badge.

The genesis of this legendary car can be traced to a Lamborghini-developed 3.5-liter four-cam V12 prototype engine created in 1963. This engine was then installed into a barebones rolling chassis created by the marque's chief designer, Gianpaolo Dallara and his team of talented engineers. When this setup was subsequently unveiled at the Turin Motor Show in 1965, it created a complete stir because of its radical layout, which had the 60° V12 engine transversely mid-mounted, thereby upending all preexisting notions of how a production sports car should be built. This controversial chassis was then later adorned with a seductively attractive body created by Carrozzeria Bertone, which spectacularly reimagined what a high performance street-legal coupé could look like. Although the Miura's dynamic lines referenced slightly earlier all-out racers like Ford's GT40 MK II (see p. 362) and Ferrari's 250 LM (see p. 308), their gestural fluidity was so perfect the model seriously upped the ante in the stylishly good-looking stakes. While Marcello

Gandini is generally credited with the design of the Miura's s voluptuous bodywork its initial concept was conceived by Giorgetto Giugiaro, as extant early sketches attest. But the beauty of the Miura was a lot more than surface deep, for under its sculptural coachwork lay a formidable high performance package. First shown at the 1966 Geneva Motor Show, the Miura was a showstopper that perfectly reflected Lamborghini's utter commitment to technological innovation in the pursuit of superlative performance.

That said, the marque's founder, Ferruccio Lamborghini, was only interested in producing road-going sports cars and was reticent about getting involved in the creation of competition racers. He had, though, working for him a young, gifted New Zealand–born engineer, Bob Wallace, who had previously worked at Maserati on the development of the groundbreaking Tipo 61 "Birdcage" (see p. 244). During the Miura's development, Wallace undertook extensive testing of Miura prototypes and the later production cars, which had then informed the creation of the model's updated S and SV variants. Working so closely on the car's development convinced him that it had real racing potential and so he persuaded Ferruccio to let him develop a special one-off "test mule" Miura prototype that would meet the FIA's Appendix J sporting regulations in 1970 — with the "J" inspiring its eventual naming: the P400 Jota. Wallace took a standard Miura chassis and engine and then modified it extensively. To reduce the car's overall weight, steel chassis components and panels were replaced with lighter elements made of Avionel, the side and rear windows were made of Perspex, and lighter-weight cast-magnesium Campagnolo wheels

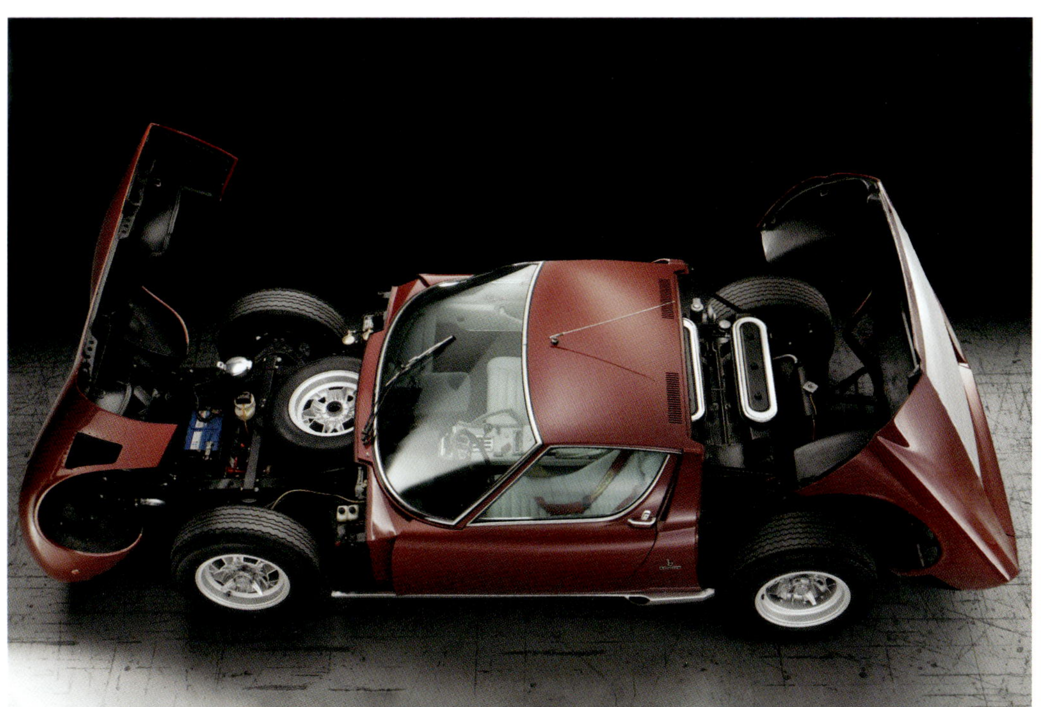

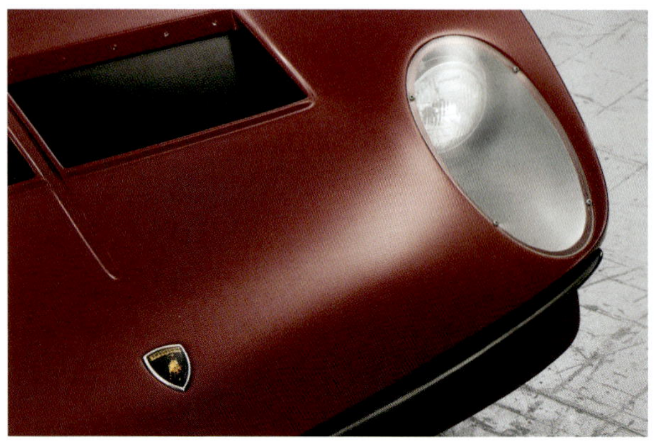

Left & opposite: The idea behind the SVJ was to modify an existing Miura P400 SV so that it not only provided better performance, but looked racier too, like the original Jota prototype. It featured a host of modifications including the adding of brake-cooling vents behind the front and rear wheel arches, Perspex headlight covers, and a competition-style rapid fuel filler.

were fitted. Then, to enhance its handling and stability, a front spoiler was added, while the suspension system was completely overhauled and widened. And then came the ramping up it is engine, with its compression ratio upped from 10.7:1 to 11.5:1 thanks to new hot camshafts being added, while a competition exhaust with four megaphone outlets was installed to enhance gas flow. All of this helped to produce an impressive 440 horsepower at 8,000 rpm. A host of other tweaks were also made by Wallace, so that when the Jota was finally completed it weighed just 880 kilograms (1,940 lb.), boasted a claimed top speed of 317 km/h (197 mph) as well as an acceleration of 0–60 mph in under four seconds. The racing mettle of this one-off supercar, however, was never proved. It was subsequently sold to Dr. Alfredo Belponer, the owner of the Scuderia Brescia Corse racing team, via InterAuto, a Lamborghini dealership in Brescia, founded by one of Belponer's erstwhile drivers, Enrico Pasolini. Fancying himself a bit of a racer despite the fact that his only prior claim to racing fame appears to have been failure to qualify for Le Mans, Pasolini decided to take the Jota on an unauthorized, high-speed test along the autostrada. The resulting crash was so bad that only the Jota's engine was salvageable, and it was deemed a miracle that Pasolini and his passenger were not killed in the mangled wreckage.

But Wallace's dream of a super Miura lived on and as a result another model was constructed, the P400 SVJ, of which only four factory-built examples were made (excluding a handful of conversions) during the Miura's original production run. The first of these is the car shown here (chassis no. 4934), which was built for Mohammad Reza Pahlavi, the Shah of Iran, a well-known car collector. The idea behind this model was to modify an existing Miura SV so that it not only provided better performance, but looked racier too, like the original Jota. As Wallace later recalled, "The Shah wanted something special and he was willing to pay for it." In fact, this special SVJ — with the "J" standing for Jota — cost over 60 percent more than a regular Miura P400 SV. The modifications undertaken included adding brake vents behind the front and rear wheel arches, Perspex headlight covers, a competition-style fuel filler, a downforce-enhancing chin spoiler, single pantograph windscreen wiper and a straight-through exhaust system, plus a safety harness for the driver — all of which helped to make this Miura very special indeed.

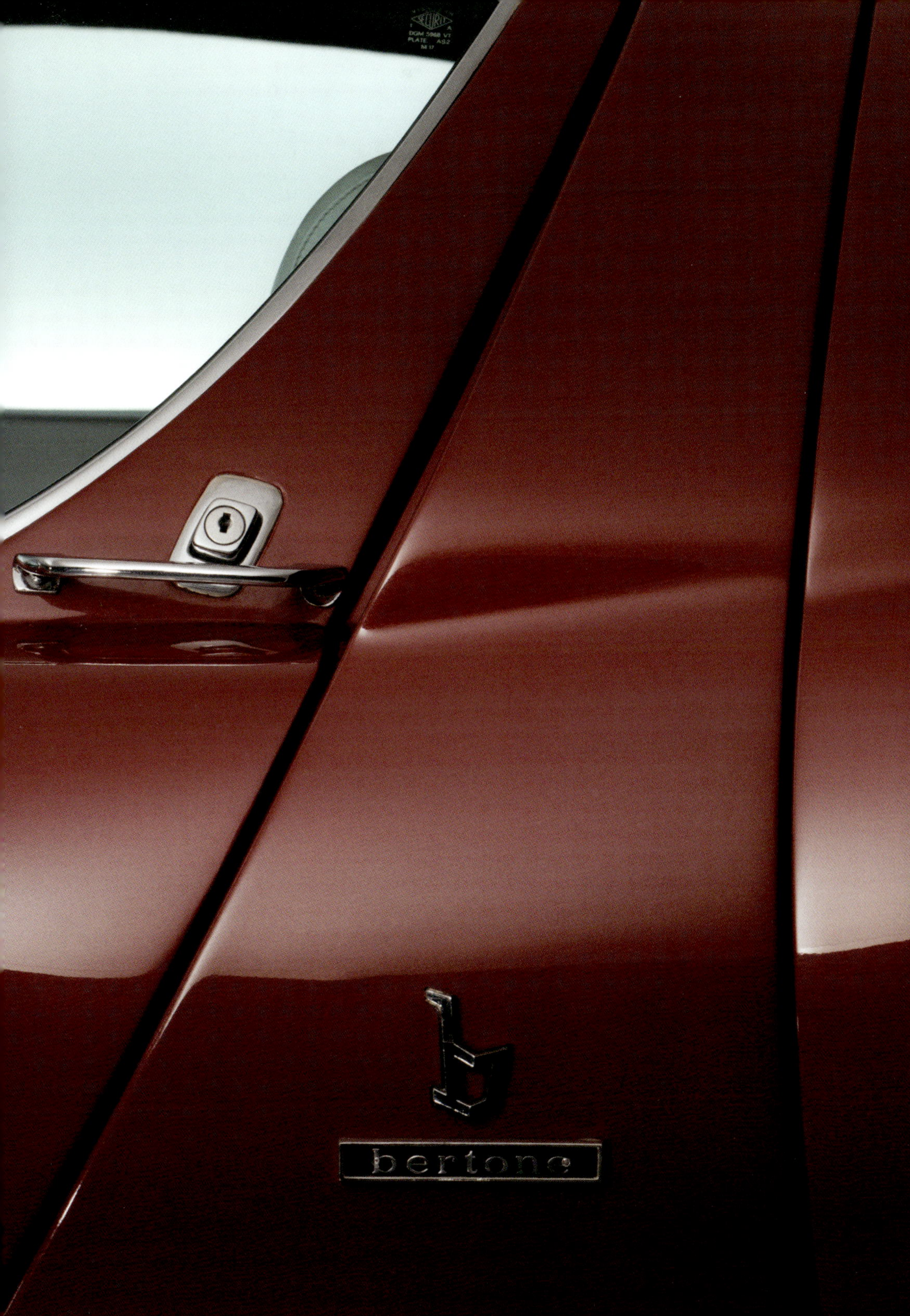
bertone

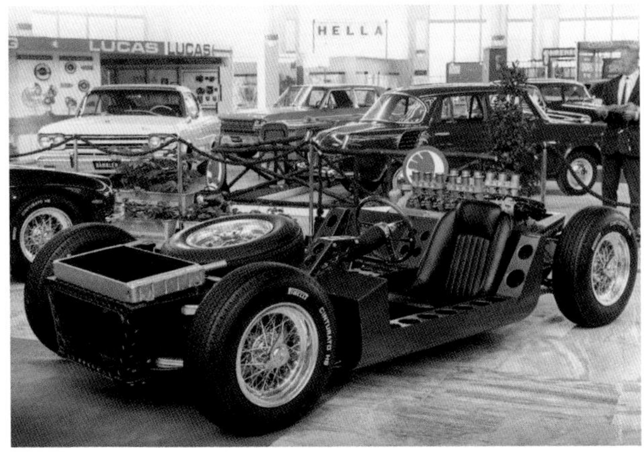

Left: Genesis of the Miura — the rolling chassis created by chief designer Gianpaolo Dallara with the transversely mid-mounted Lamborghini-developed 3.5-liter quad-cam 60° V12 engine with four Weber 40 IDL triple-barrel carburetors, which was unveiled at the Turin Motor Show in 1965. This radical layout caused a sensation.

Below: The unveiling of the Lamborghini P400 Miura at the 1966 Geneva Motor Show. The marque's founder, Ferruccio Lamborghini, is standing behind the car (second from left).

Opposite (bottom): Bob Wallace's vision of super Miura was realized by the P400 SVJ, of which only four original factory-built examples were made during the original production run. This factory photo shows the first SVJ (chassis no. 4934) built for the Shah of Iran.

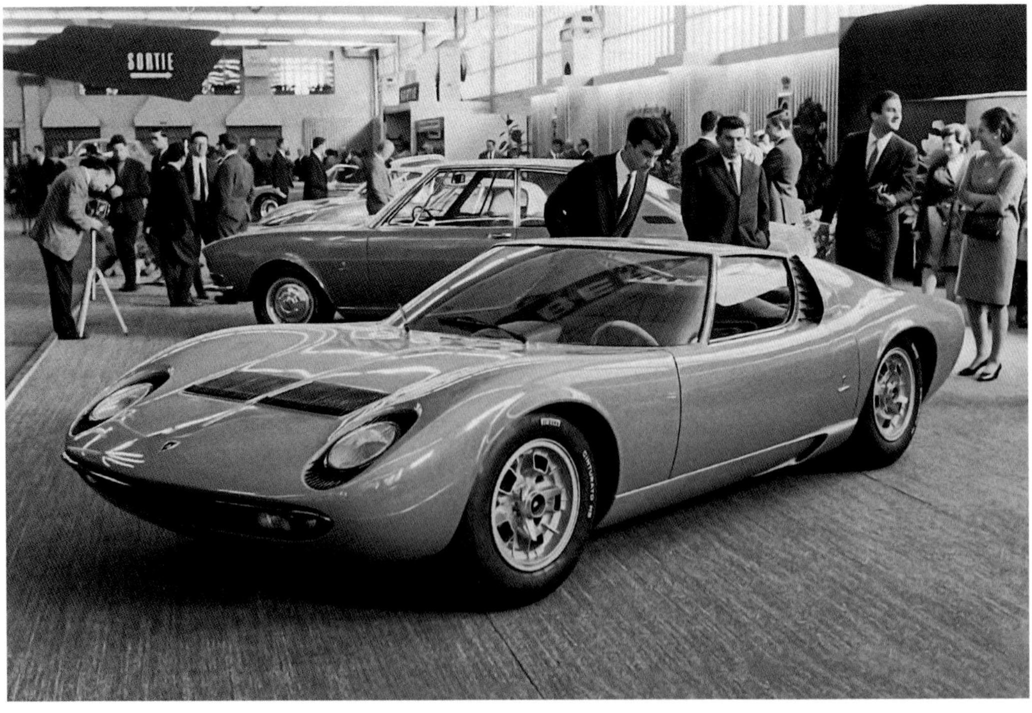

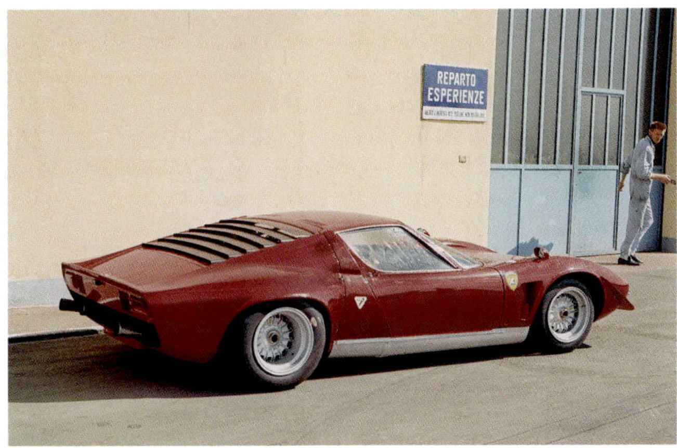

Right: The original Jota prototype ca.1970 with the engineer Bob Wallace who was instrumental in the Miura's development. He convinced Ferruccio Lamborghini to let him create a special one-off "test mule" that met the FIA's Appendix J sporting regulations for a competition Miura P400 SV. The Jota featured a host of performance upgrades, with engine output increased to 440 hp and a claimed top speed of 317 km/h (197 mph). All this came to nothing; the Jota was destroyed in an accident in 1971.

Pages 400–401: Gordon Murray (kneeling) and Peter Stevens, designers of the McLaren F1, discussing the car's dihedral door access to its cockpit with one-plus-two seating, 1992. For this revolutionary design Murray (who conceived the car's original concept) articulated McLaren's goal thus: "Our main objective has been to create the purest driver's car, a new beginning, a design which simply rewrites all existing standards."

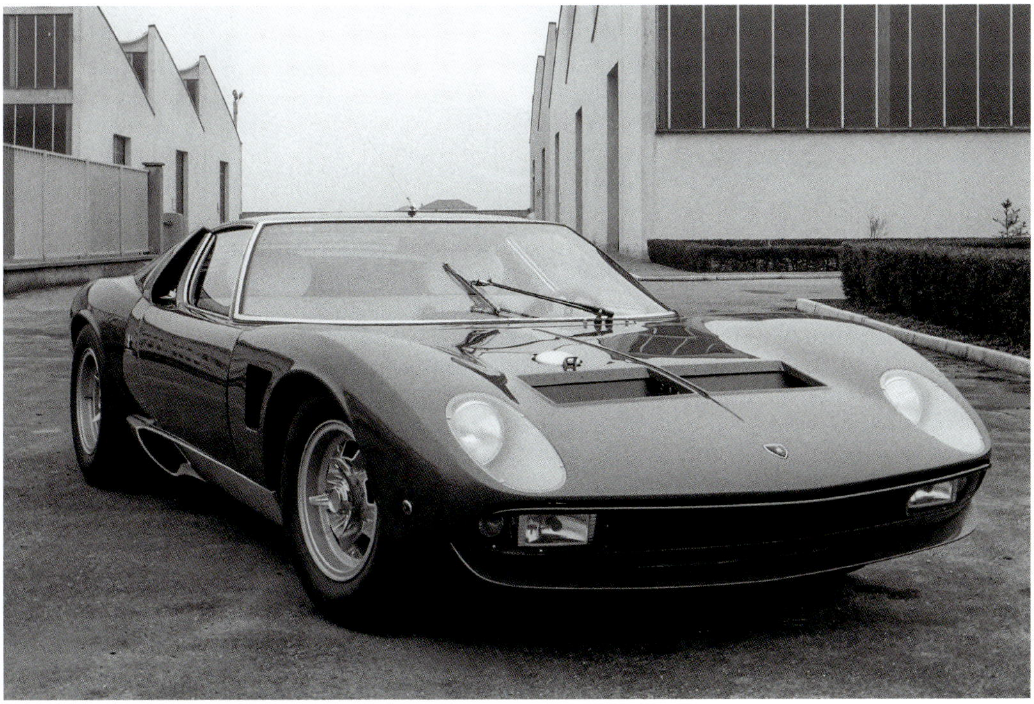

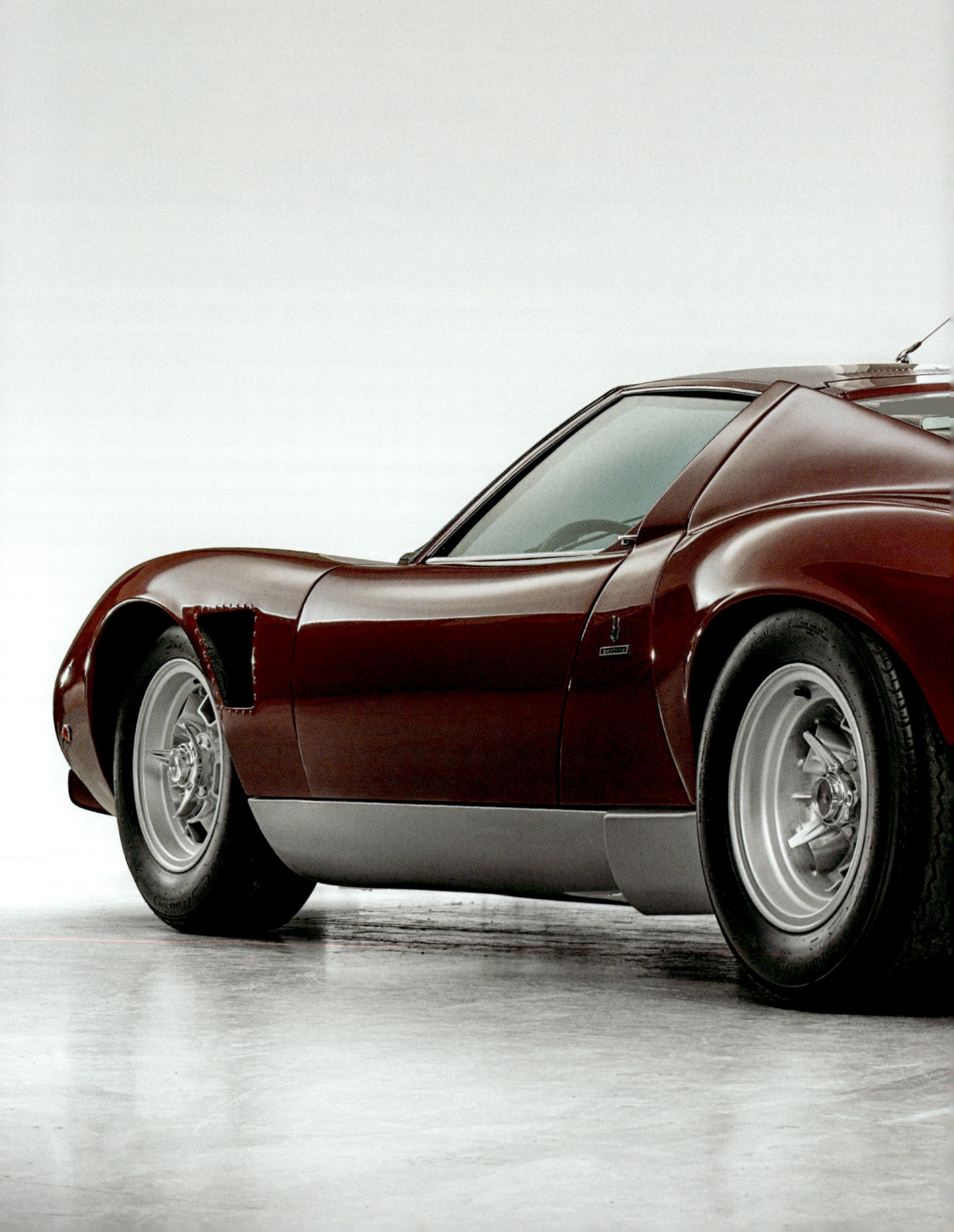

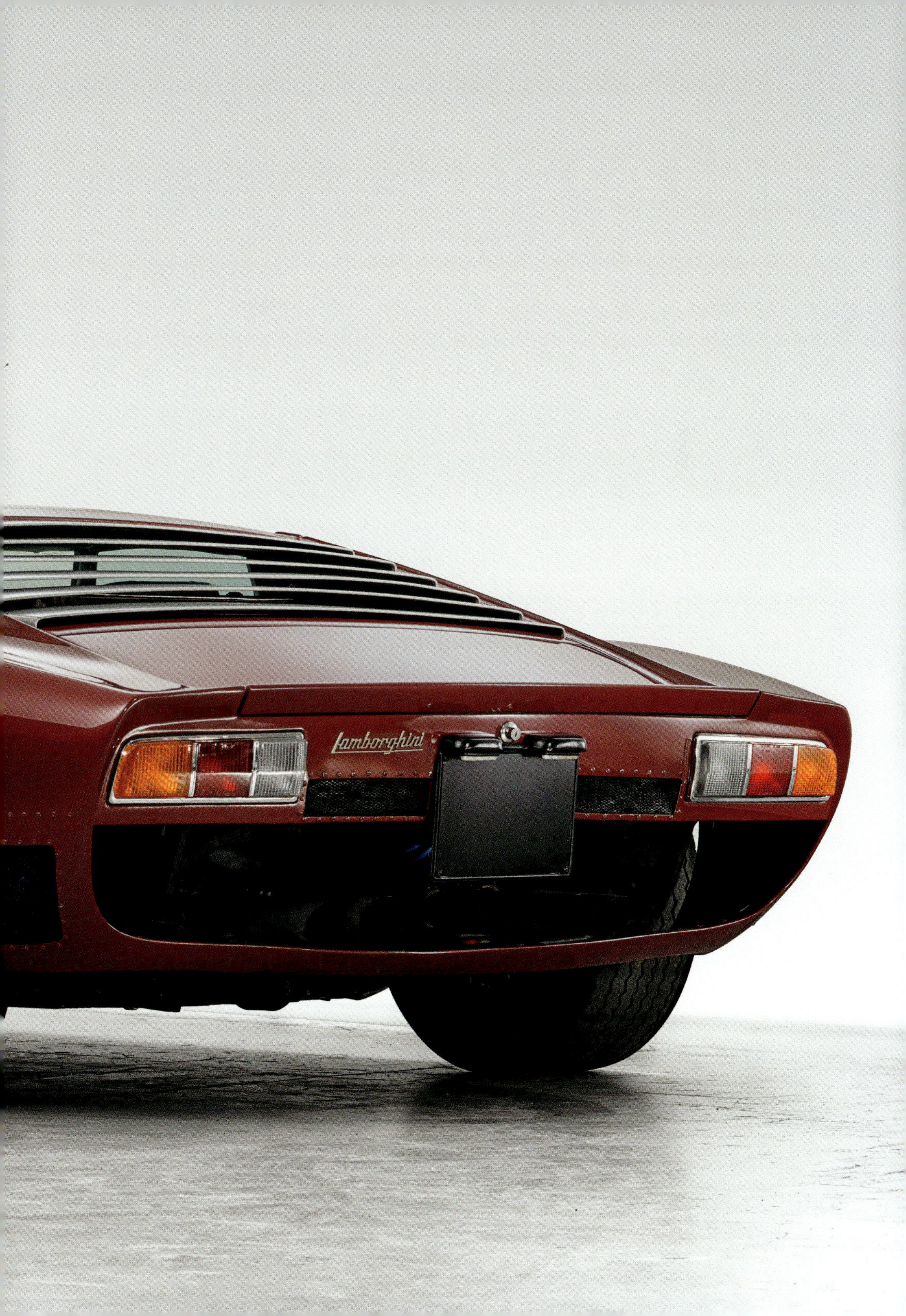
Lamborghini

1985

Ferrari 288 GTO

MANUFACTURED 1984–86 | ENGINE 2,855 cc (174 cu. in.), twin-turbocharged DOHC per bank V8 | HORSEPOWER 400 TOP SPEED 305 km/h (189 mph) | TRANSMISSION 5-speed NUMBER PRODUCED 272

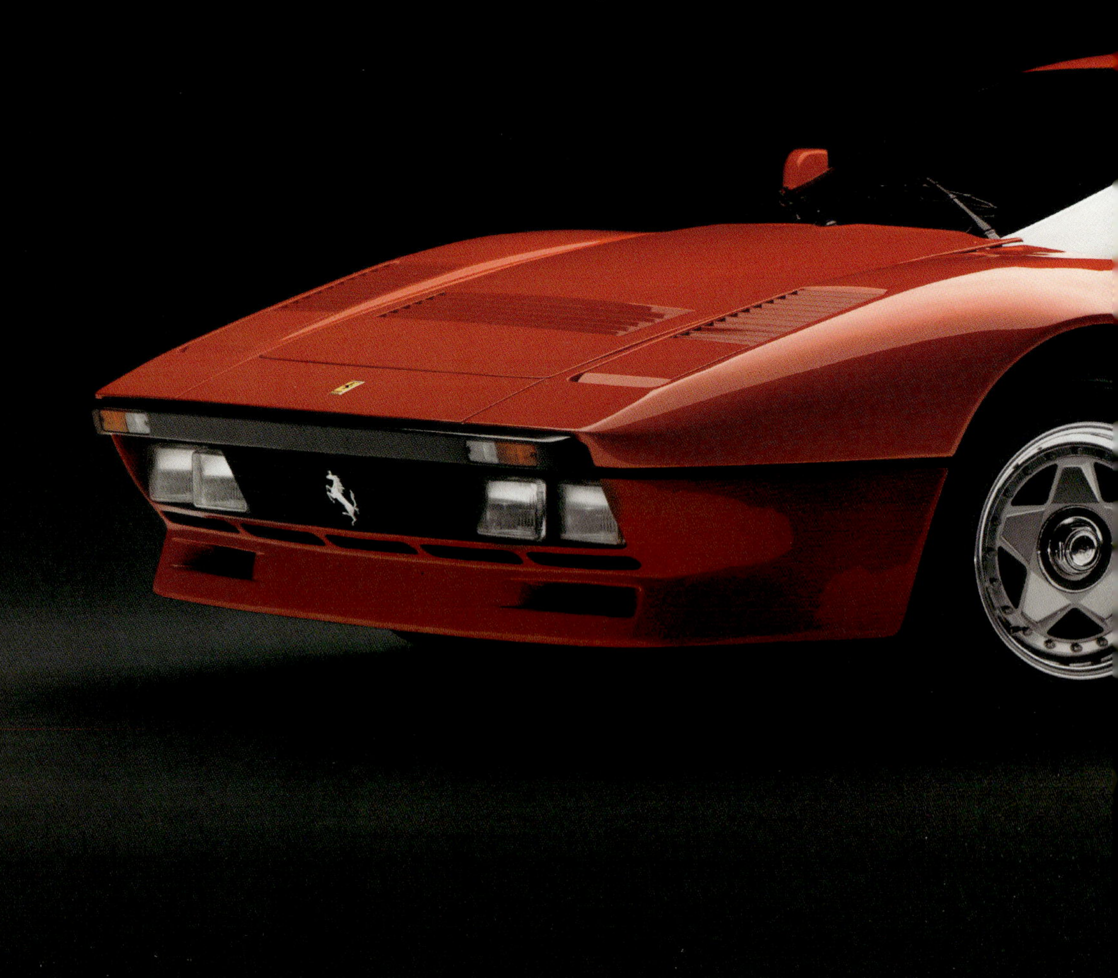

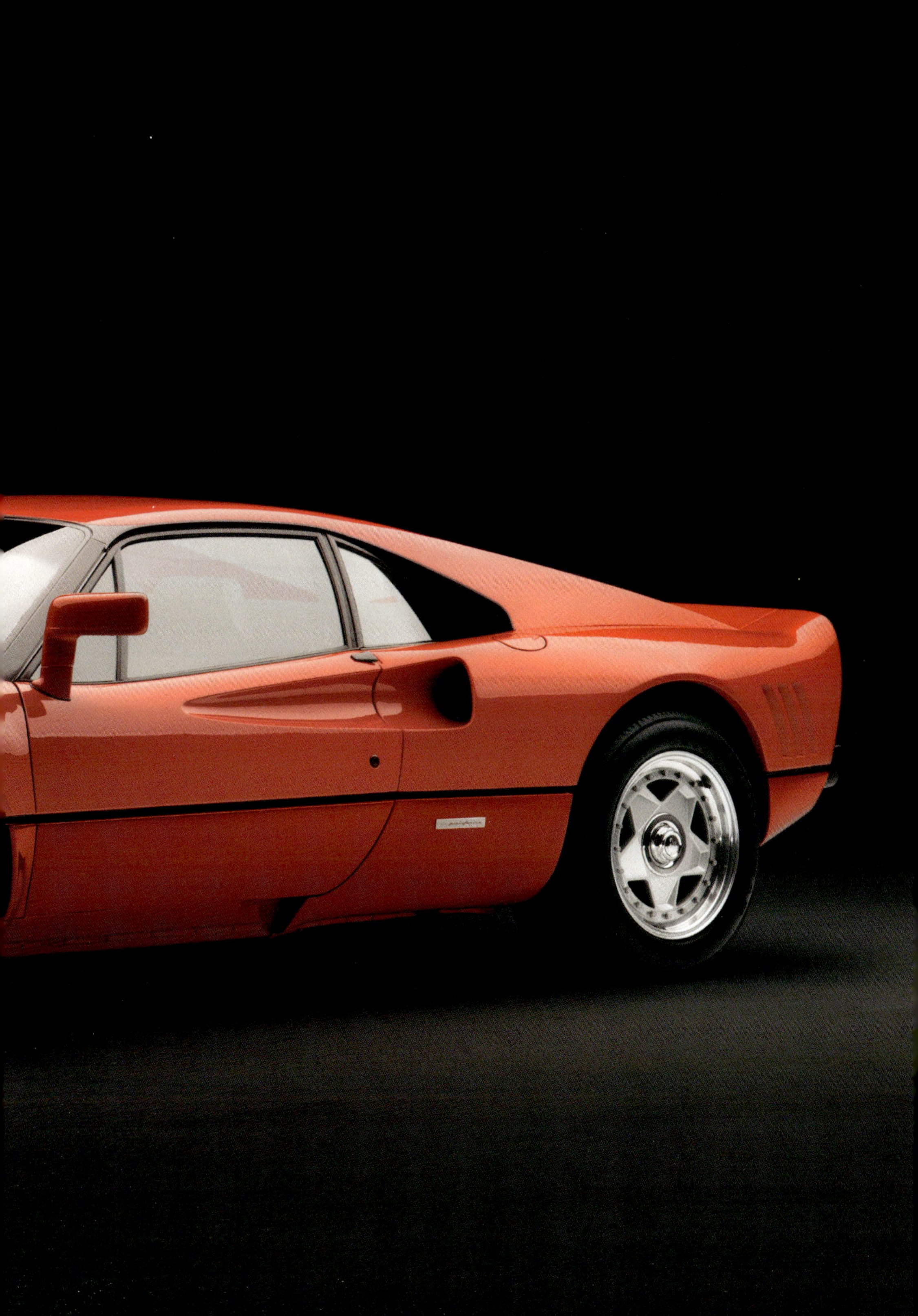

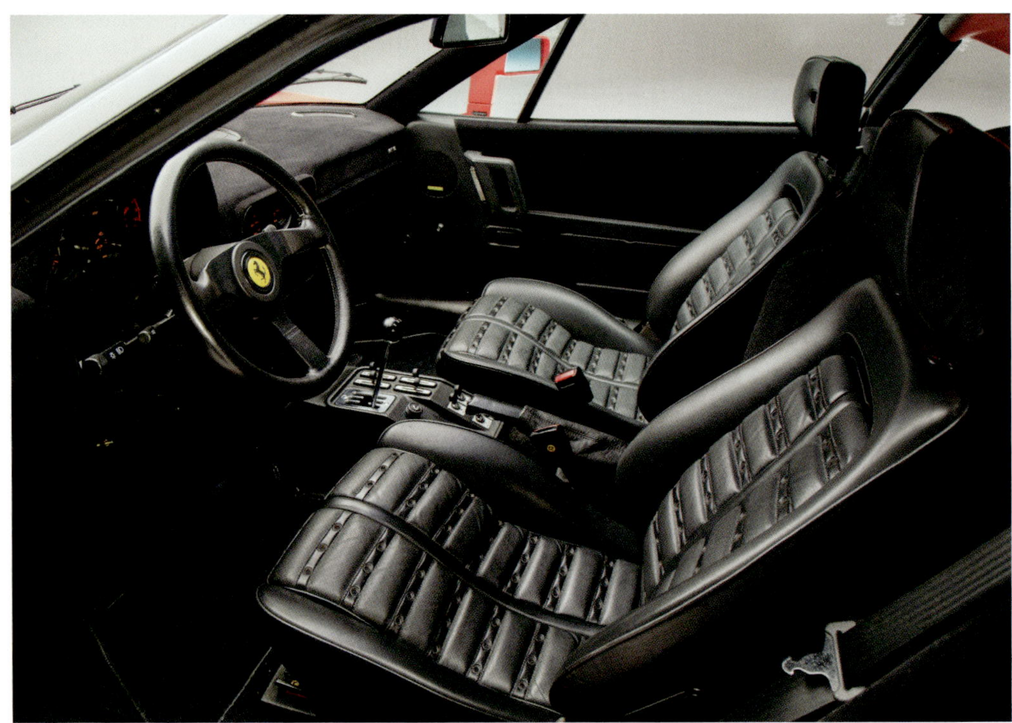

During its early years, Ferrari constructed most of its road-going cars in very limited series. However, from the late 1950s onward, as demand increased for its coupés and roadsters especially in the United States, its models were produced increasingly in higher volumes. In fact, the firm completely abandoned limited-production road models after the 365 California, which was manufactured between 1966 and 1967. There were a number of reasons for this. One was that by the end of the 1960s Ferrari was struggling financially, while another was that the later 1973 oil crisis and prolonged period of global stagflation that ensued saw the bottom drop out of the high-end car market. By the mid-1980s, however, the world's economy began to boom once more, and as a consequence the market for rare and expensive cars began heating up. Perfectly timed, Ferrari returned to its low-volume roots with the launch of the Ferrari GTO at the 1984 Geneva Motor Show. Yet while this simple three-letter designation has always been the car's official title, today it is more commonly referred to as the Ferrari 288 GTO in order to better distinguish it from its spectacular forefather, the Ferrari 250 GTO (see p. 264).

This beautiful angular-yet-lithe supercar, styled by Pininfarina's Leonardo Fioravanti, was created while Enzo Ferrari was still very much at the helm of the company and he officially sanctioned its development as a GT racer. Its numerical nomenclature was derived from its mid-mounted 2.8-liter eight-cylinder engine, while its racing origins meant it would become only the second car in the marque's illustrious history to be given

Opposite: Detail of Ferrari 288 GTO cockpit. The 255th example built, chassis no. ZFFPA16B000057709 is perhaps the finest and most original example in existence. Finished in Rosso Corsa over Nero leather with matching black inserts, the car was ordered without power windows or a radio for weight-saving performance purposes and is believed to be one of 19 examples ordered as such.

Below: Detail of Ferrari 288 GTO 2,855 cc (174 cu. in.), twin-turbocharged and electronic fuel-injected DOHC per bank 32-valve V8 engine. The model's nomenclature was derived from this mid-mounted 2.8-liter power plant, which produced an impressive 400 hp. Only the second vehicle in Ferrari's history to bear the fabled GTO (Gran Turismo Omologato) moniker, the model was conceived to compete in Group B rallying but the series was disbanded before the 288 GTO ever turned a wheel in anger. Nevertheless, the 200 cars built to homologate it sold out so quickly that an additional 72 were constructed. The 288 GTO is rightly considered to be the very first Ferrari supercar.

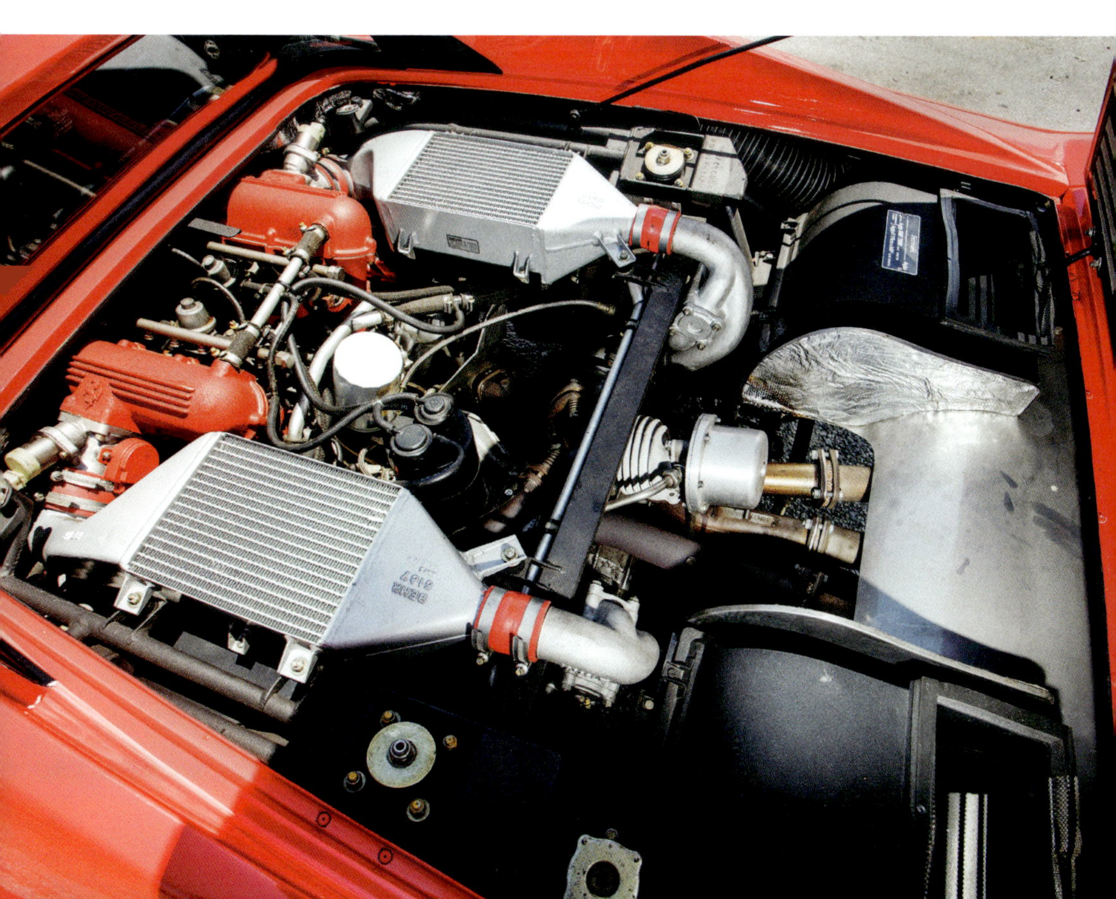

the famed GTO (Gran Turismo Omologato) designation. For this model, Ferrari embraced various new technologies in the pursuit of racing glory, including the extensive use of advanced techno-materials for the building of both its Kevlar/Nomex body and its tubular steel chassis, which was strengthened with a layered composite made of Kevlar, fiberglass and aluminum. As Ferrari explains, "Initially the reason was not to provide a select few clients with an exclusive form of transportation, but to satisfy the two-hundred-unit build number for homologation purposes as a Group "B" competition car. However, the regulations changed, so here was a competition orientated car with nowhere to compete." Nevertheless, the car had caused such a sensation when it was unveiled in Geneva that very soon afterward the planned production run of 200 cars had completely sold out. In fact, to cope with additional demand the total production was increased to 272 units — all of them painted red, except for a single black example. The success of this low-volume, high-cost car marked the real starting point of what became known as "Supercar Syndrome," which involves a car being sold on for a sizable profit, even before it has been delivered to its initial purchaser. A knock-on consequence of this phenomenon was that the classic and sports car markets got caught up in a whirlwind of investment speculation, and values soared unsustainably upward through the mid-to-late 1980s. But as ever, what goes spectacularly up often comes down with a very heavy

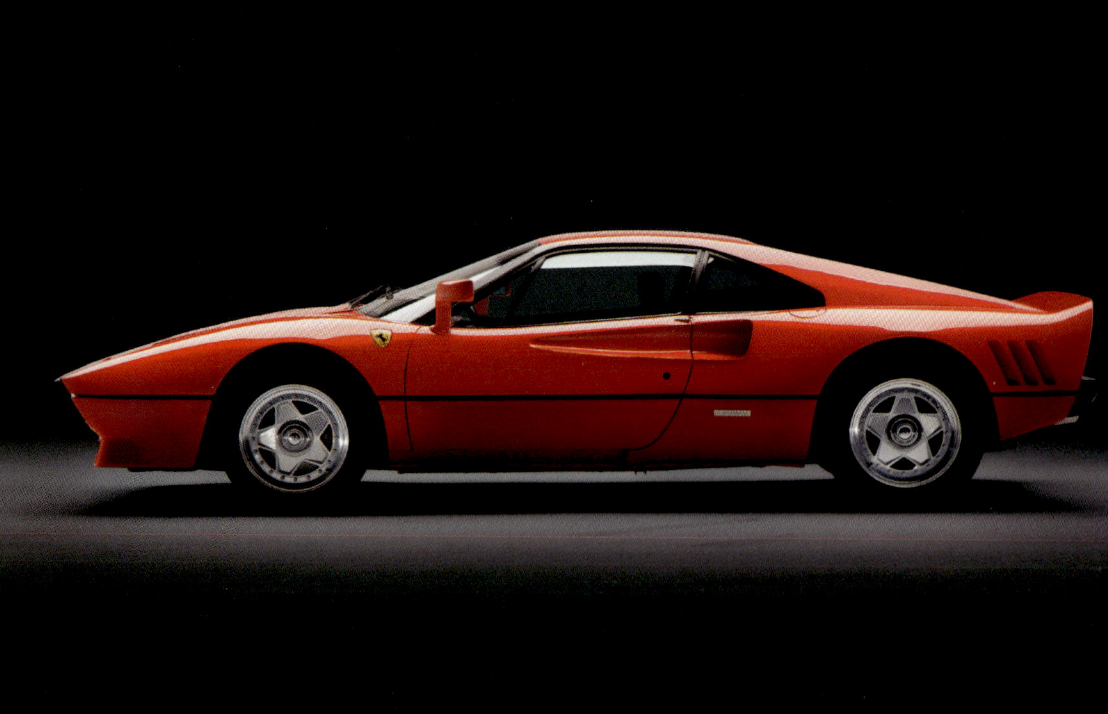

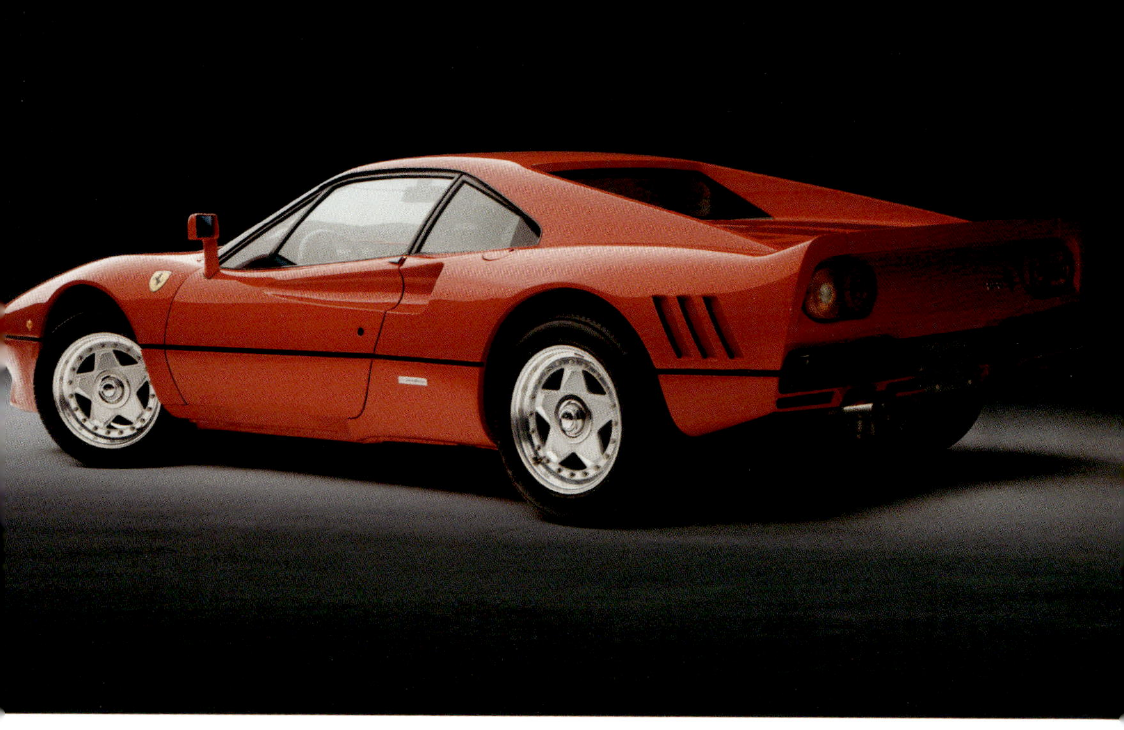

bump, which is exactly what happened to the collector car market in the early 1990s. However, if you had been lucky enough to have purchased a Ferrari 288 GTO when it was first launched at its suggested list price of $83,000 then you would have seen a sizable appreciation of that investment in recent years. For instance, the exquisite 288 GTO shown here (chassis no. ZFFPA16B000057709), which was one of only 19 light-weight examples that came without a radio or electric windows, sold at auction in 2017 for over $3.2 million, equating to nearly 40 times its original cost. The reason for this high price is that the 288 GTO has a rare significance: it was arguably Ferrari's very first supercar, and as such was the progenitor of the epic F40, Enzo Ferrari and LaFerrari (see p. 470).

1995

McLaren F1 LM

MANUFACTURED 1995 | ENGINE 6,064 cc (370 cu. in.), DOHC per bank 60° V12 | HORSEPOWER 680
TOP SPEED 362 km/h (225 mph) | TRANSMISSION 6-speed
NUMBER PRODUCED 5 plus 1 prototype

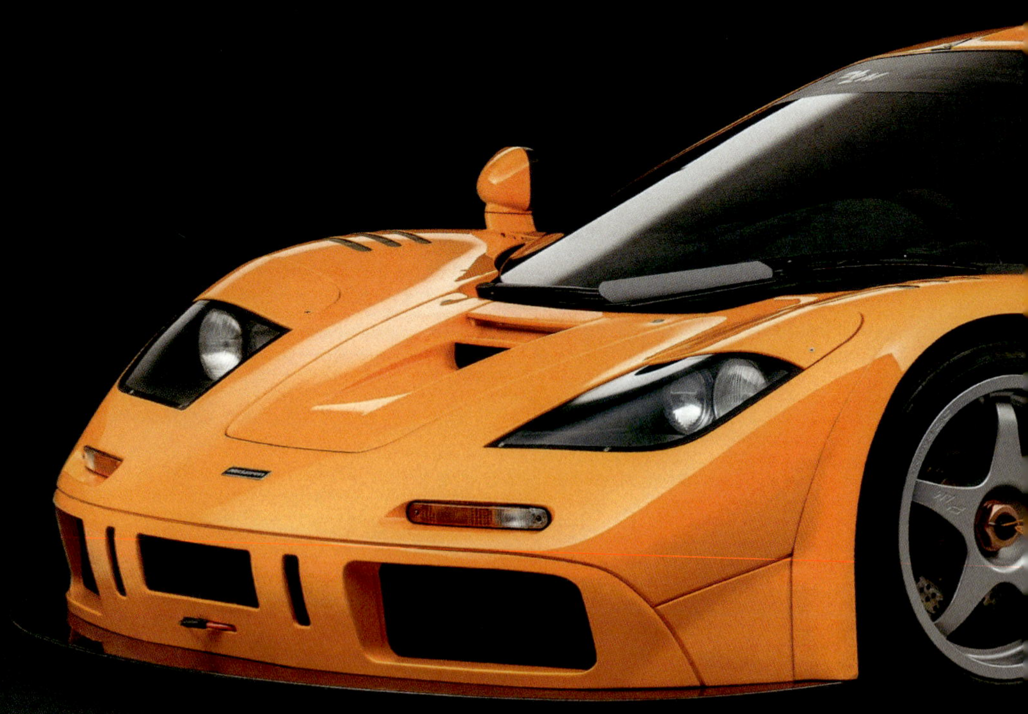

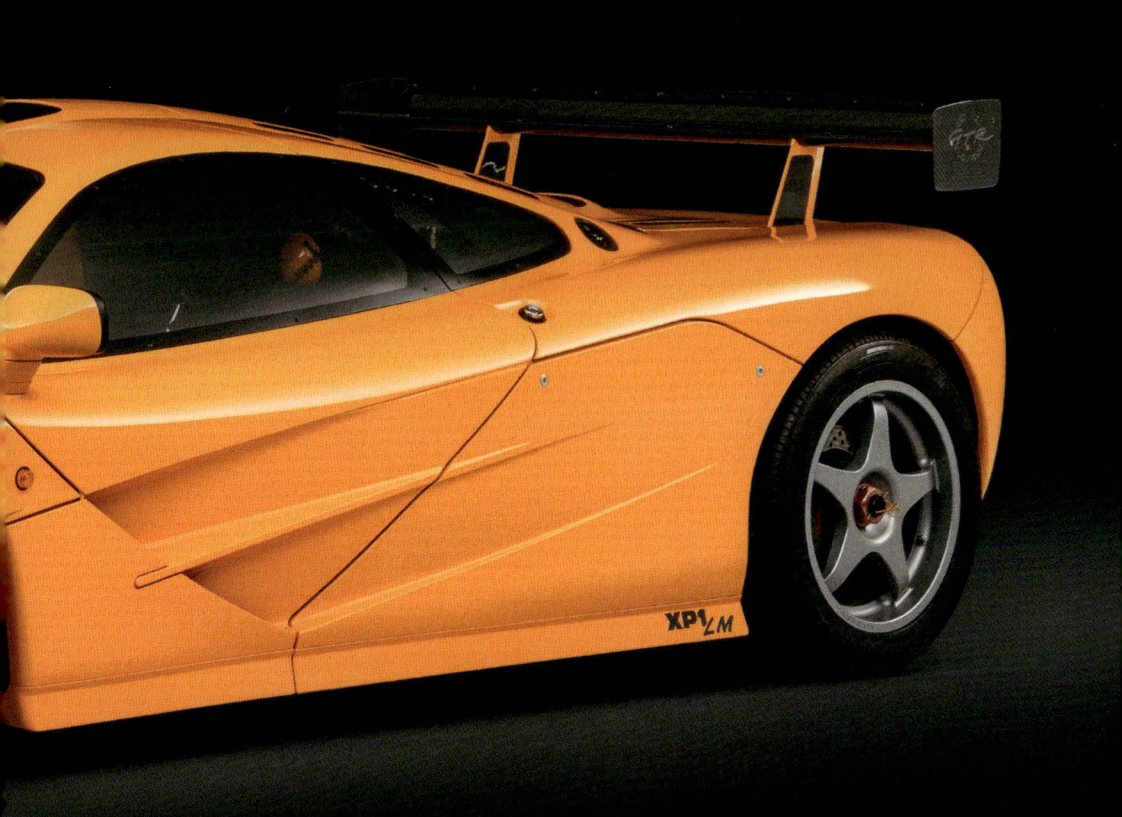
XP1 LM

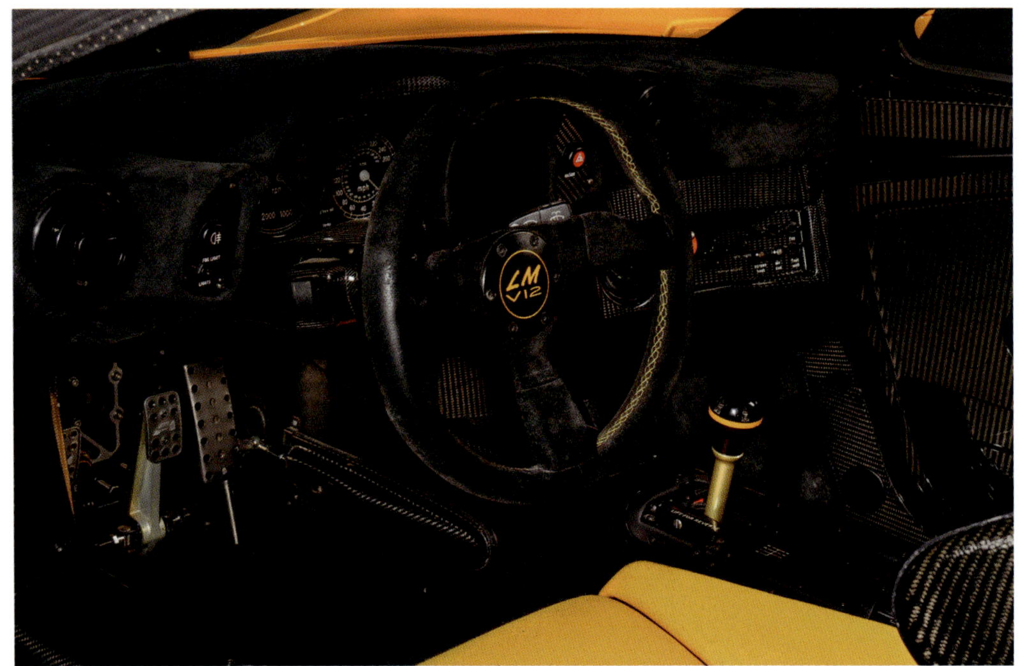

Above & opposite: Detail of McLaren F1 XP1 LM prototype cockpit showing the slightly forward, central driving position of its three-seat layout.

Since the end of World War II, Britain has been at the epicenter of Formula 1 research and development, and today McLaren is the nation's highest profile constructor as well as being one of the most famous teams on the F1 circuit. Its origins go back to 1963, when the New Zealander F1 driver Bruce McLaren founded the company with the sole purpose of building advanced race-winning cars. To this end, it was one of the very first teams to build an F1 racer around a carbon fiber monocoque. In 1981, the McLaren Formula 1 team was acquired by Ron Dennis and it was subsequently named the TAG McLaren Group, in recognition of its partnership with Mansour Ojjeh's TAG Group.

After 25 years of continuous development of superlative racing cars, many championship winning, it was decided in 1988 that McLaren would expand its portfolio by designing and building, "the finest sports car the world had ever seen." The idea for this project came from the company's head of design, Gordon Murray, who wanted to create a "disruptive" supercar. He then famously managed to convince Dennis of its viability during an unscheduled delay at Milan's Linate Airport, following the 1988 Italian Grand Prix. A development team was assembled in 1990 that included designer, Peter Stevens, who was put in charge of exterior styling. For this new model, Murray was determined to use a naturally aspirated engine, which would not only sound far better, but also have more revving ability and superior throttle response than those with superchargers or turbochargers, and so approached various manufacturers. Eventually, he concluded that BMW was the right partner and its motorsport division head, Paul Rosche, subsequently designed and constructed a special six-liter V12 engine, known as the BMW S70/2. This mighty power plant exceeded Murray's original brief by being 14% more powerful, but also 16 kilograms (35 lb.) heavier. With its aluminum block and heads and its dry-sump lubrication, this quad-cam engine also boasted variable valve timing, which afforded better control over its four valves per cylinder, while a chain drive was used to action the camshafts in order to maximize reliability. The engine was then held within a monocoque structure made of carbon-fiber-reinforced polymer (CFRP), making the McLaren F1 the world's first production car ever to feature this state-of-the-art setup. Indeed, the DNA of Formula 1 ran through every atom of this highly seductive, aerodynamically styled car, from its use of high-tech and expensive materials, such as carbon fiber, Kevlar, titanium, magnesium and gold, right through to its central driving position ahead of the engine and the fuel tank, as well as its flanking passengers seats. Another distinctive feature was its butterfly doors that with a scissor-like action open upward and outward. In 1994, after famously road testing the F1, Andrew Frankel wrote in *Autocar* that it was "the finest driving machine yet built for the public road ... We are convinced that the F1 will be remembered as one of the great events in the history of the car." Unquestionably, its introduction marked a watershed moment for

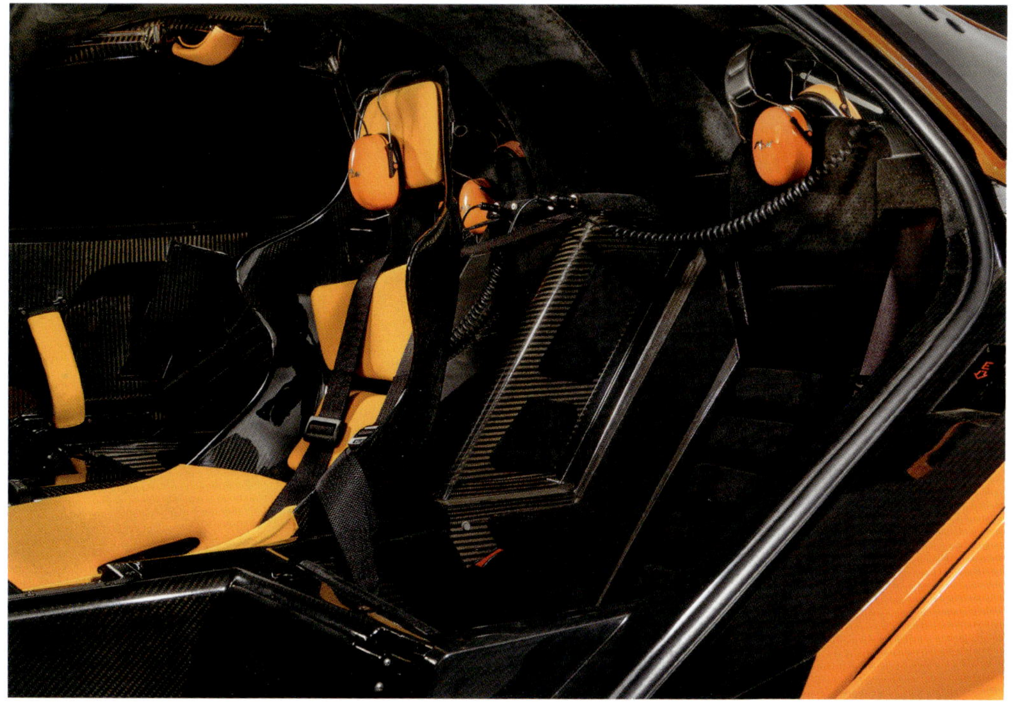

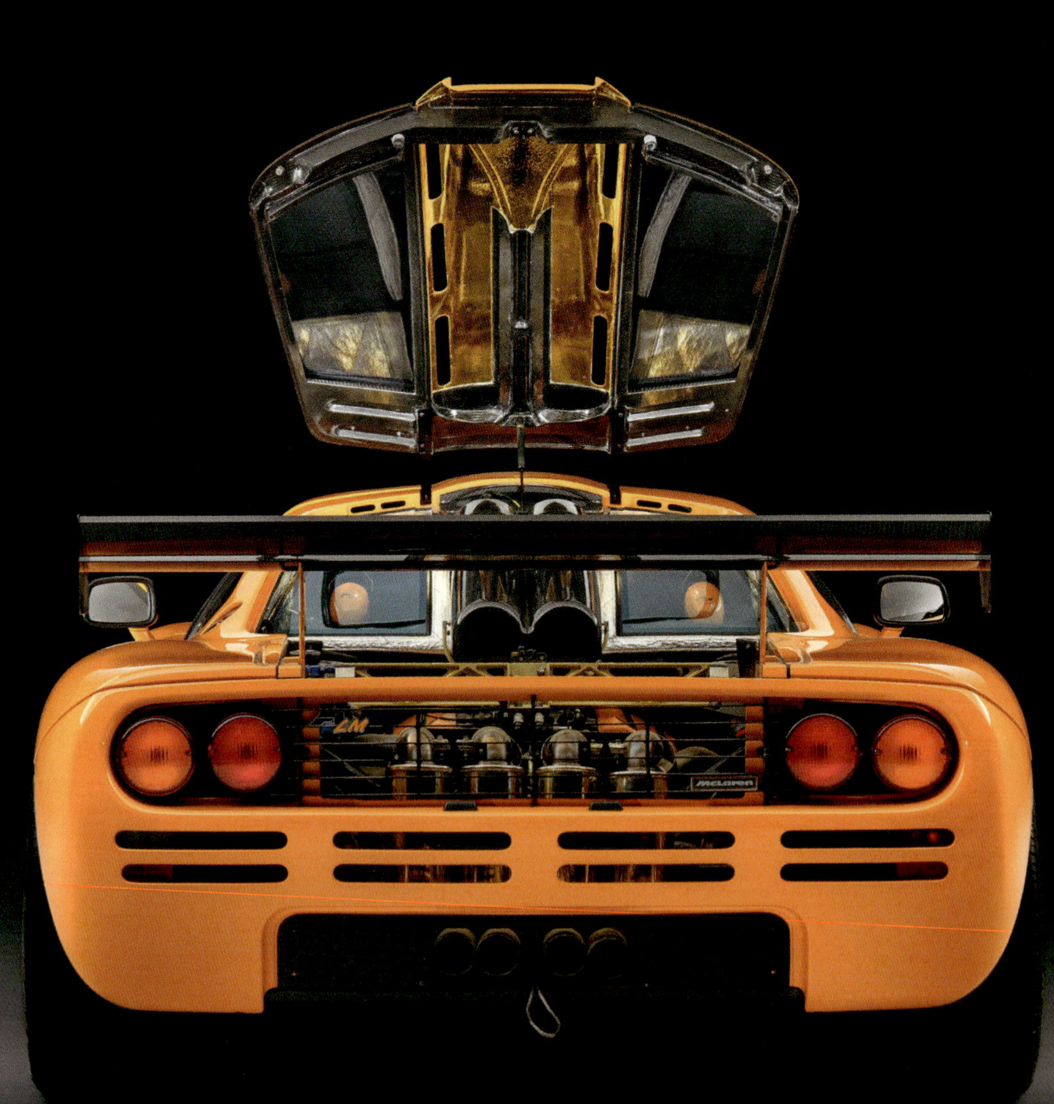
LM
McLaren

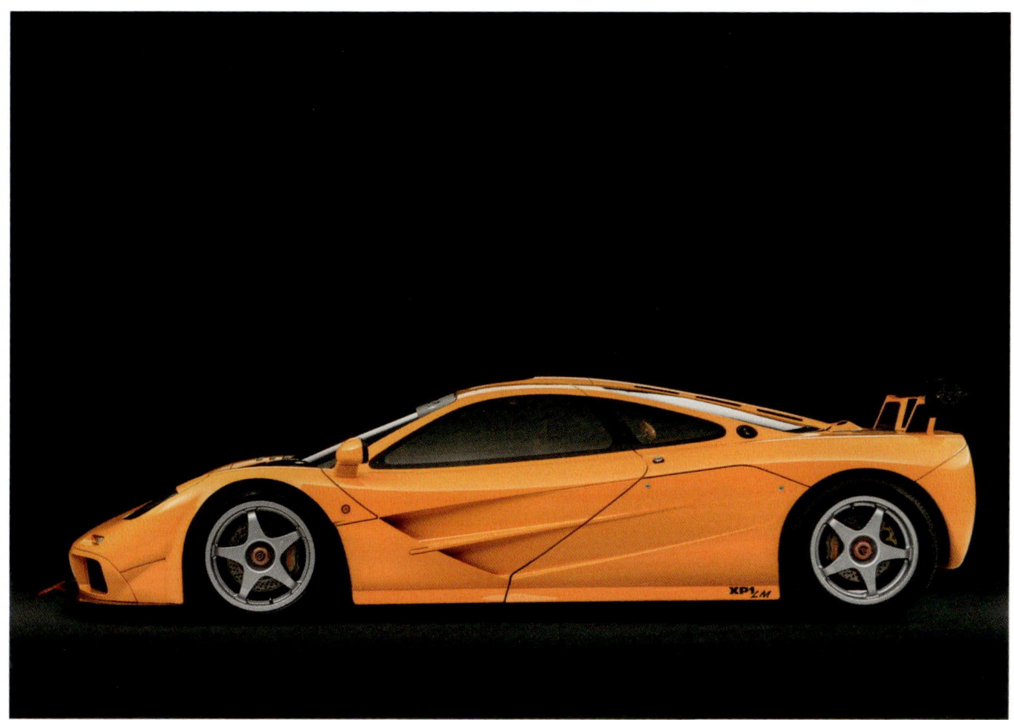

here was a race-bred hypercar that is still widely regarded as one of the greatest achievements of automotive design and engineering and remains one of the fastest naturally aspirated cars on the road.

But however awesome the original 1992 F1 was, there were increasing calls from owners wanting a racing variant. This led to the competition-specced F1 GTR being introduced in 1994. Despite having been developed in just three short months, an F1 GTR co-piloted by J. J. Lehto, Yannick Dalmas and Masanori Sekiya went on to win the 24 Hours of Le Mans the following year — enabling McLaren to become the only constructor ever to win the Formula 1 World Championship, the Indianapolis 500 and the 24 Hours of Le Mans. As Dennis notes, "The F1 is a technological tour de force... Whether endurance racing or on road, it is supremely fast, agile and yet comfortable. Its styling is enduring and will never fade. I enjoy driving mine more today than ever before because I find its technical purity highly satisfying; the F1 remains one of McLaren's proudest achievements."

Opposite: Detail of the McLaren F1 XP1 LM engine cover. To better insulate the heat from the tight engine bay the inside of the engine cover was lined with gold foil, which is highly heat reflective. 16 grams (0.8 ounce) of gold was used on each F1 and variants of the model.

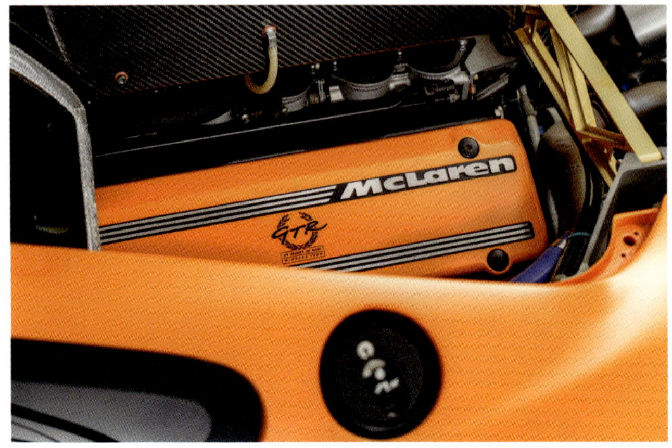

Below: The "Boulevard" at the McLaren Technology Centre in Woking, Surrey. On display (right to left) are the F1 LM XP1 prototype, the 1995 Le Mans–winning No. 59 Kokusai Kaihatsu Racing and Lanzante managed F1 GTR prototype (chassis no. 01R) and the No. 41 Gulf Team Davidoff McLaren F1 GTR Long-tail (chassis no. 20R) which finished second overall and first in the GT class at the 1997 24 Hours of Le Mans.

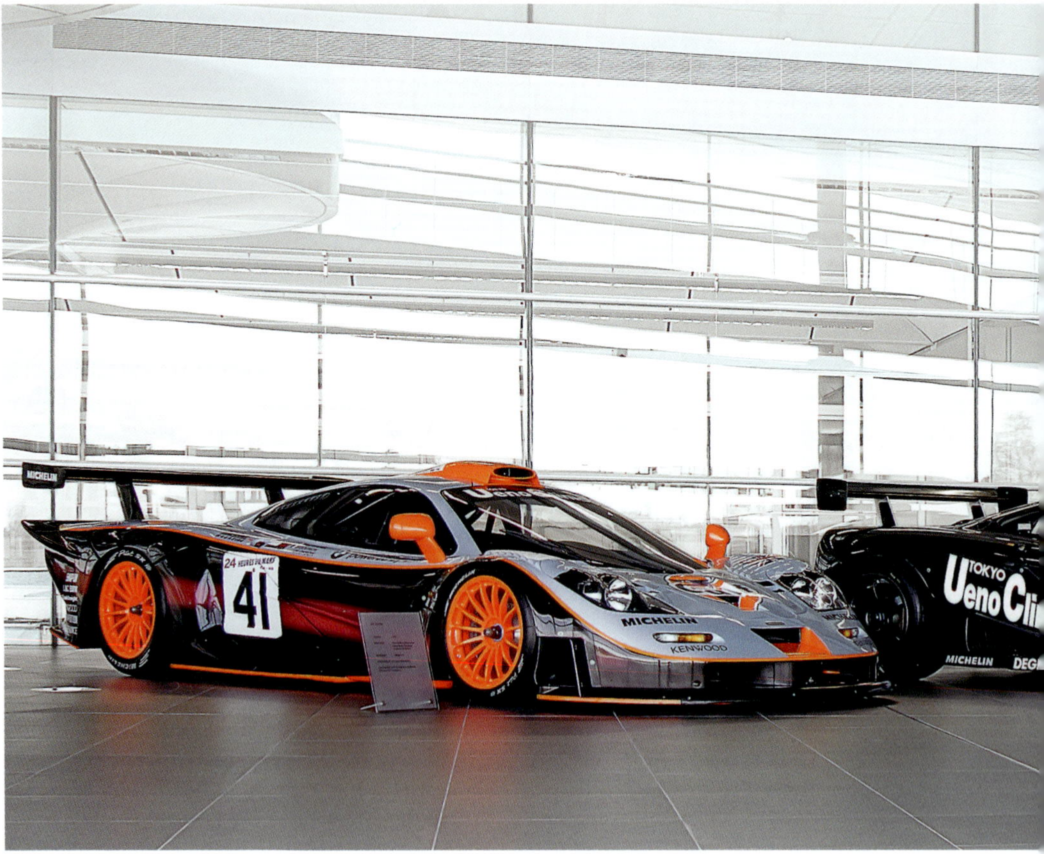

At that famous Le Mans race of 1995, a total of five McLaren F1 GTRs were fielded, where they took four of the five top places, including the aforementioned win. In tribute to this achievement, five LM variants were created, in addition to a single prototype known as the XP1 LM, as shown here, which remains in McLaren's own prized collection of cars. These five additional LM examples were the ultimate road-going version of the F1 complete with race engines and weight-reduced interiors. The original concept was that they would all be offered in "Papaya Orange" paintwork, like the prototype, in tribute to Bruce McLaren's original racing colors. However, the Sultan of Brunei who bought three of the five had other ideas, ordering two in gray. Another of these original LMs is in Ralph Lauren's renowned car collection, while the fifth is reputedly owned by an American collector. It is, however, the famed XP1 LM prototype that is the all-out star of this rarefied F1 LM lineup.

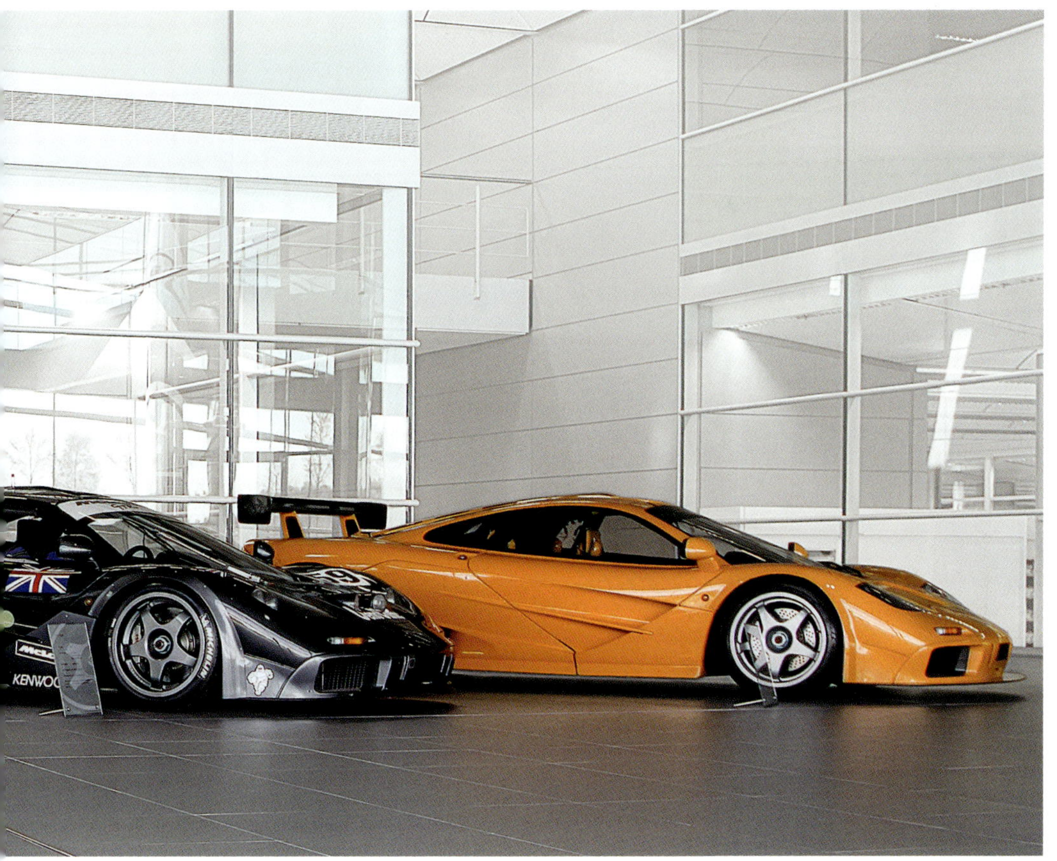

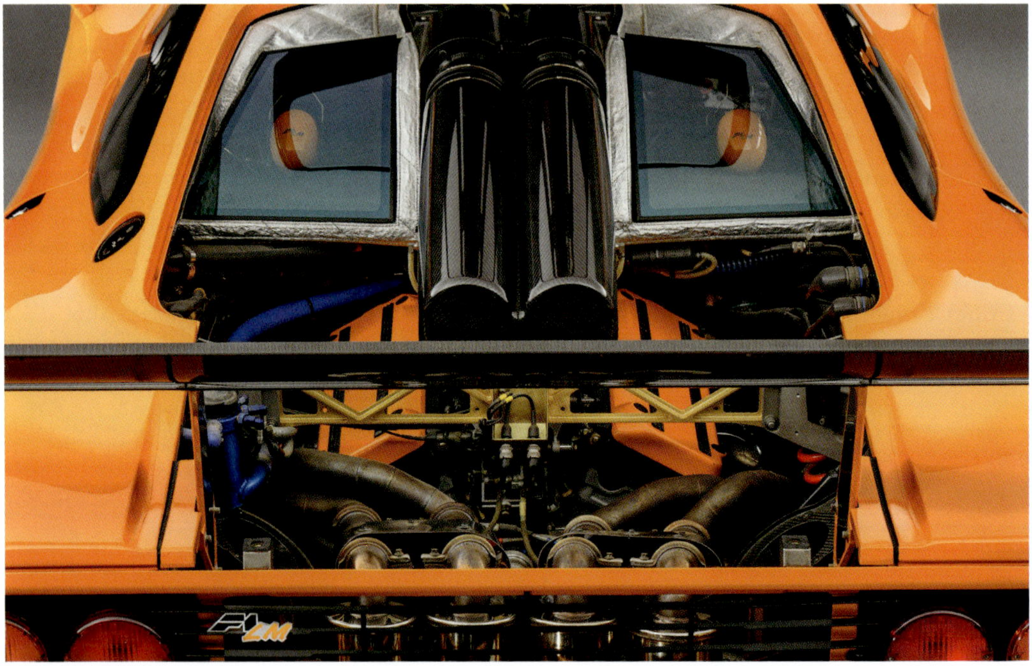

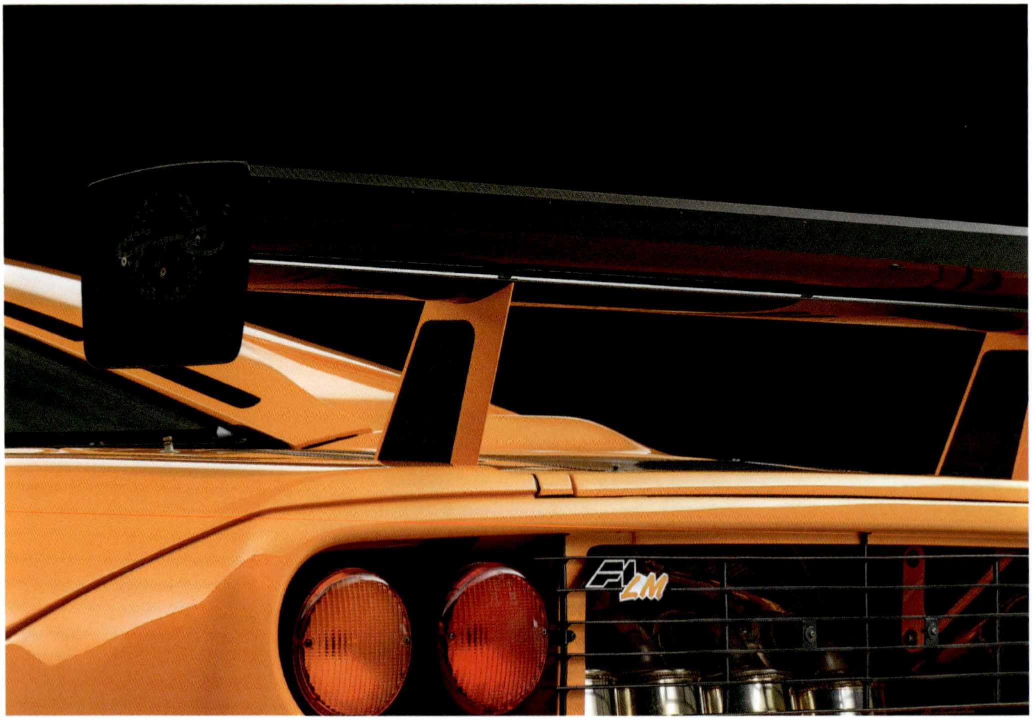

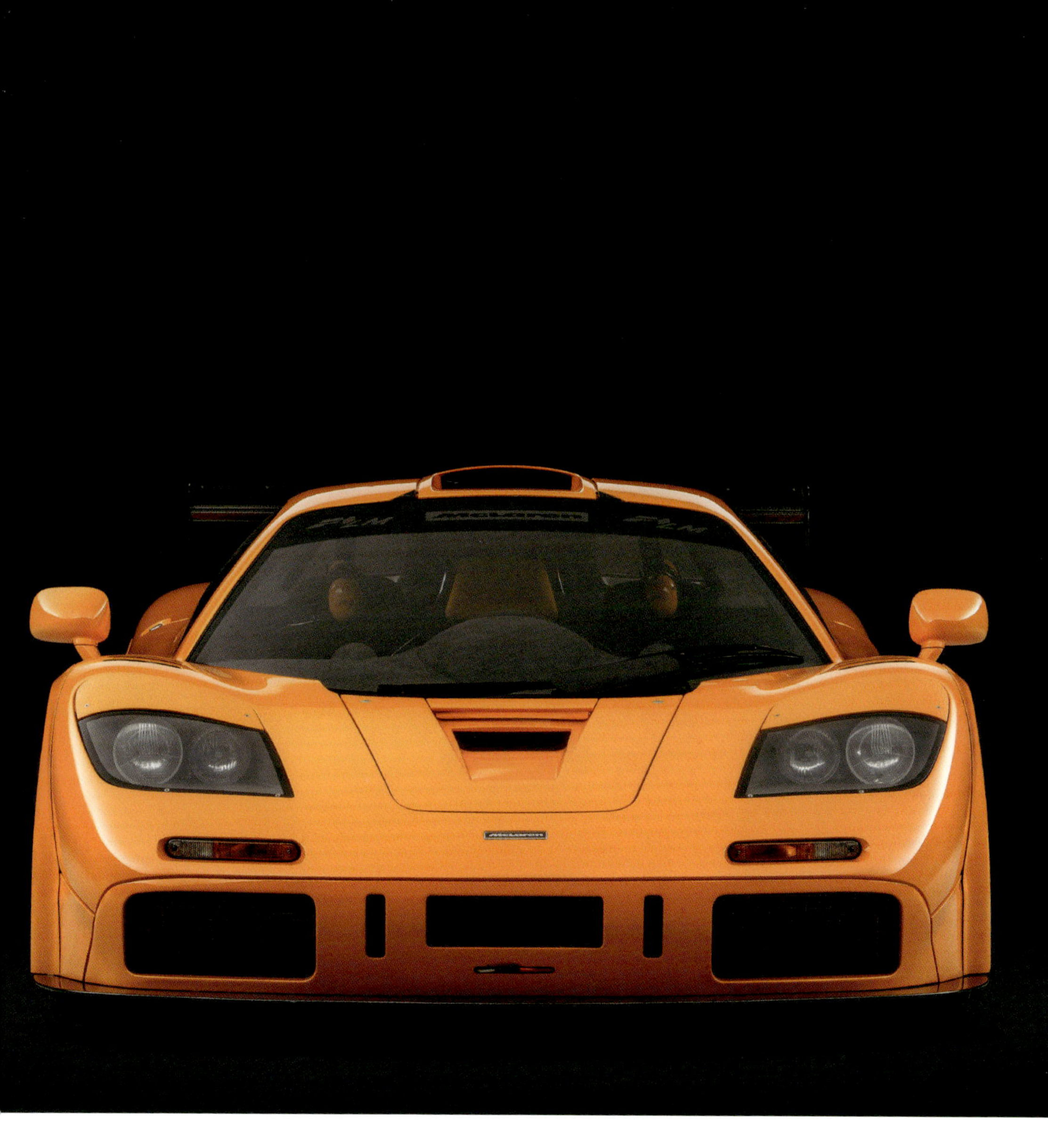

Opposite (top): Detail of McLaren F1 XP1 LM prototype 6,064 cc (370 cu. in.), all-alloy, fuel-injected DOHC per bank 48-valve 60° V12 engine. This was the full-specification, unrestricted BMW S70/2 GTR racing engine that produced 680 hp and a top speed of 225 mph (362 km/h). All F1 LMs were equipped with it.

Opposite (bottom): Detail of rear wing end plate commemorating the historic McLaren F1 GTR victory at the 1995 24 Hours of Le Mans.

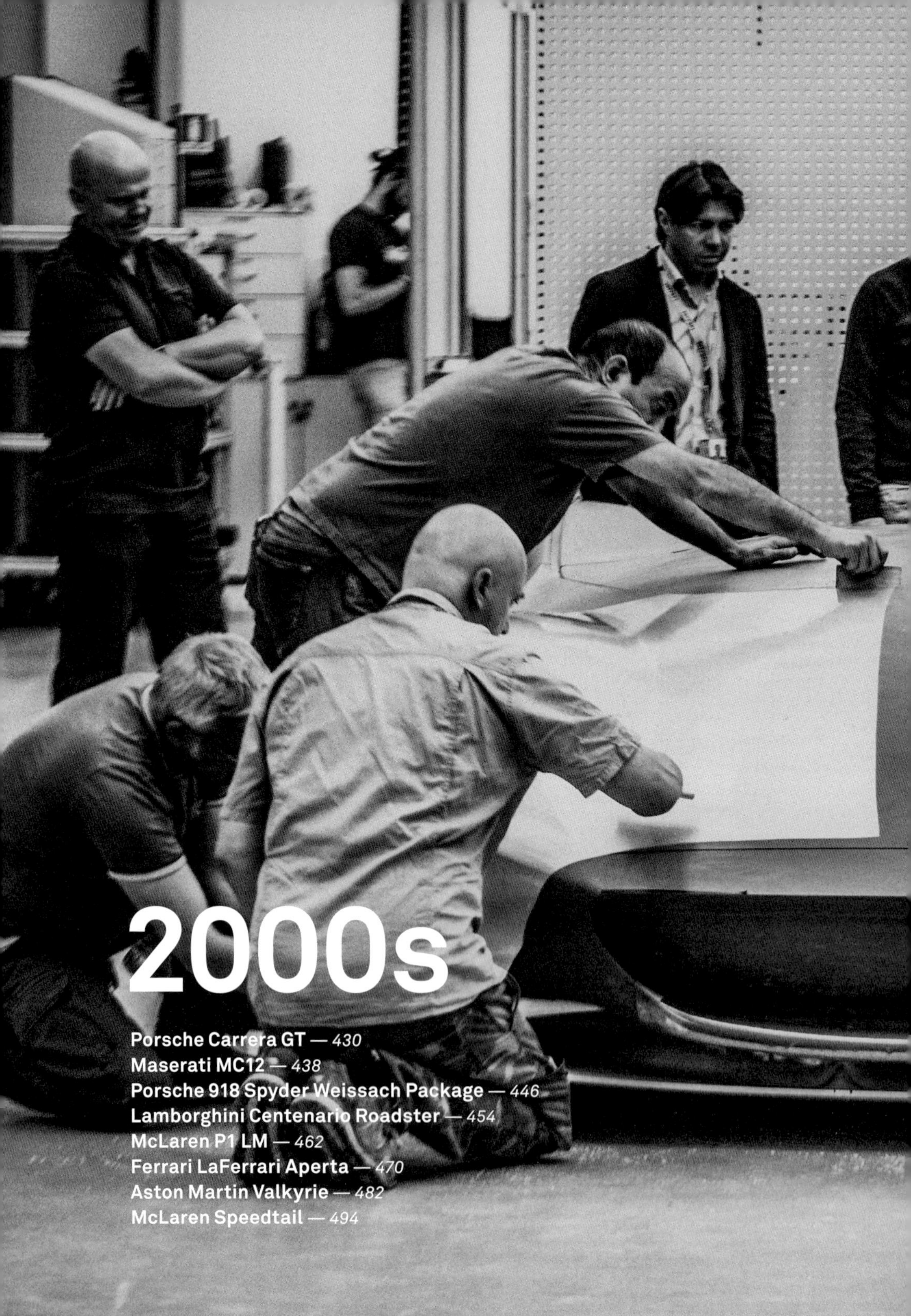

2000s

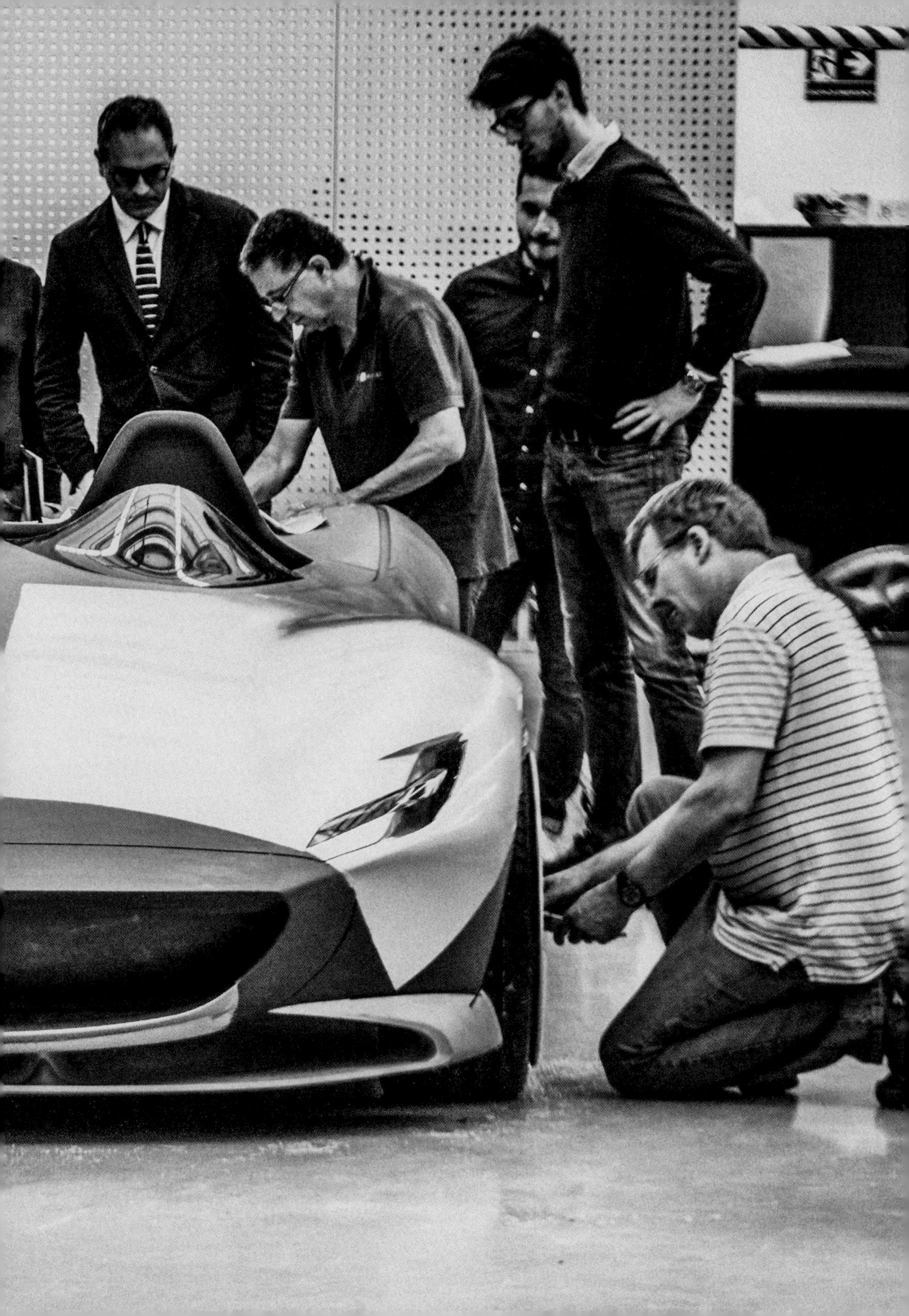

2004

Porsche Carrera GT

MANUFACTURED 2003–07 | ENGINE 5,733 cc (350 cu. in.), DOHC per bank 68° V10 | HORSEPOWER 612
TOP SPEED 330 km/h (205 mph) | TRANSMISSION 6-speed
NUMBER PRODUCED 1,270

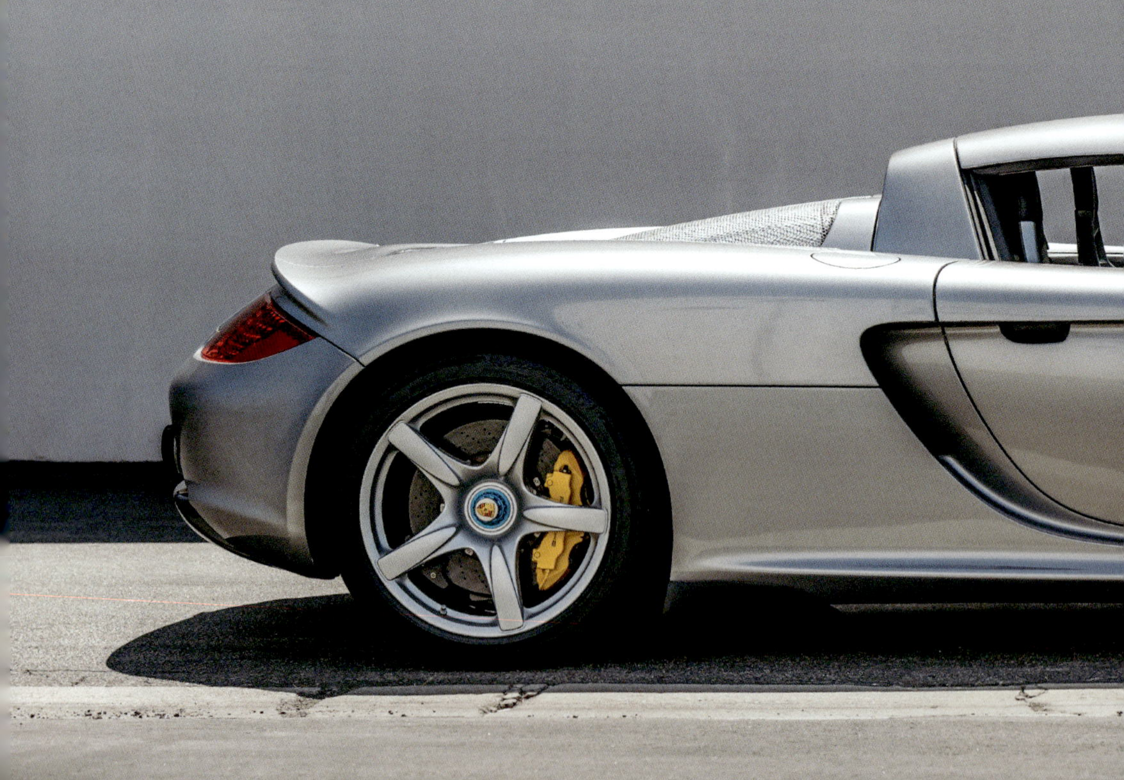

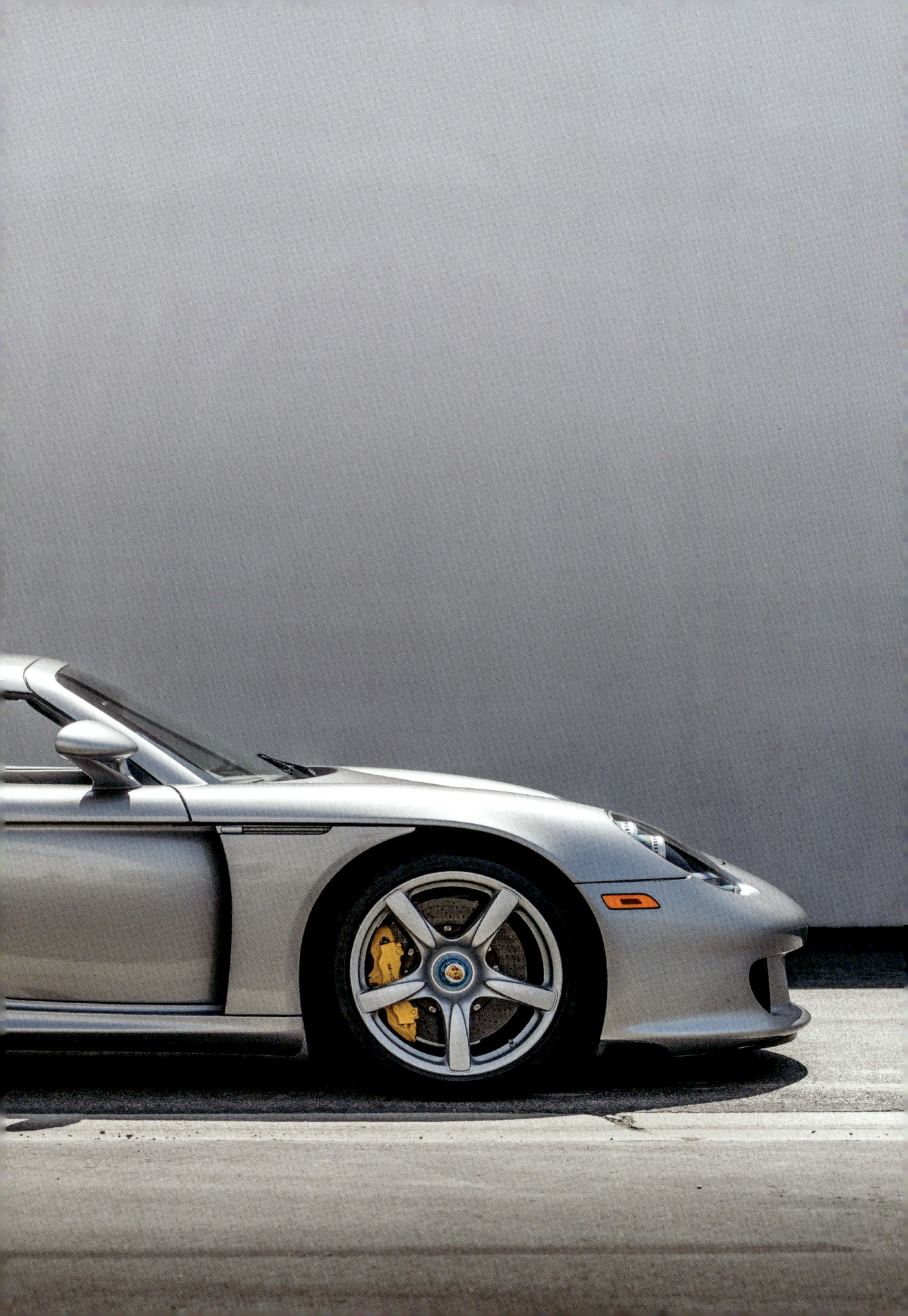

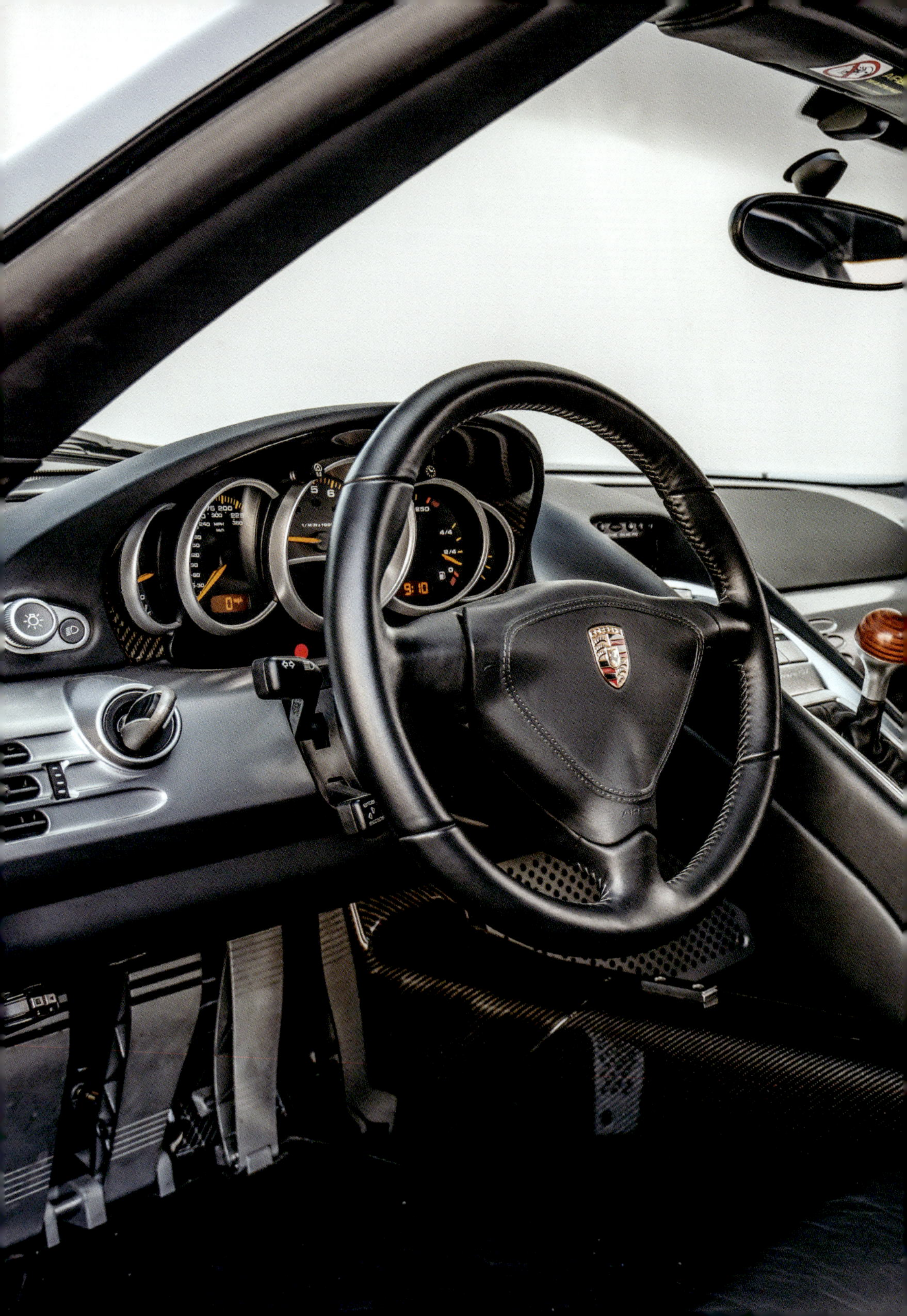

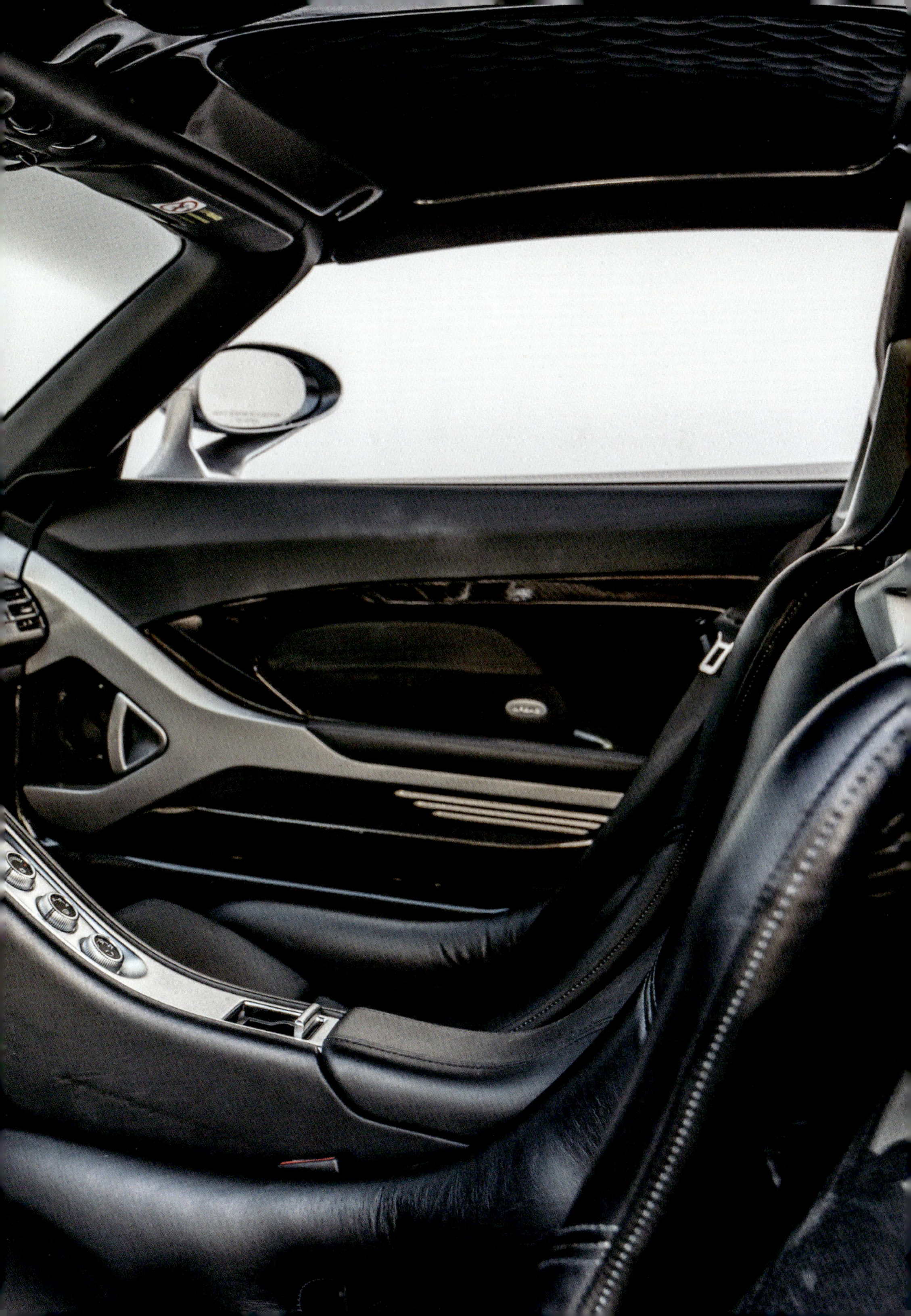

As any fan will know who closely follows car racing, from F1 to the World Rally Championship, the FIA — the all-powerful governing body of motorsport — is constantly changing its rules and regulations in response to health and safety concerns or as a way of making competition more exciting or relevant to an ever-evolving audience. The upshot of this is that constructors have to continuously respond to the FIA's shifting directives, which can be anything from a reduction in engine capacity to a maximum overall height restriction. Sometimes quite a lot of costly research, design and engineering can go into the development of an upcoming race car, only for the FIA rules to change, meaning that everyone has to go back to their drawing boards. But rather than throwing in the proverbial towel on all the work already undertaken, constructors will often reimagine their competition car concepts into exclusive limited-run high performance, street-legal sports cars as a way of recouping some of their R&D outlay. As a road-going variant of Porsche's GT racing cars, the Porsche Carrera GT represents one such transference of competition-bred design and technology.

With its dynamic sweeping lines, the Carrera GT recalls the sporty curves of a much-earlier Porsche racer: the iconic Type 550 (see p. 132) from the 1950s. With its carbon fiber monocoque, the Carrera GT's design lineage can also be traced to two more recent Porsche racing cars: the 911 GT1 (1996) and the LMP1-98 (1998). The former was specifically created to compete in the GT1 class of sports car racing, while the latter was a sort of mutant Le Mans prototype that had originally been designed as a collaborative project between Tom Walkinshaw Racing (TWR) and Jaguar. Originally, two examples were built using TWR

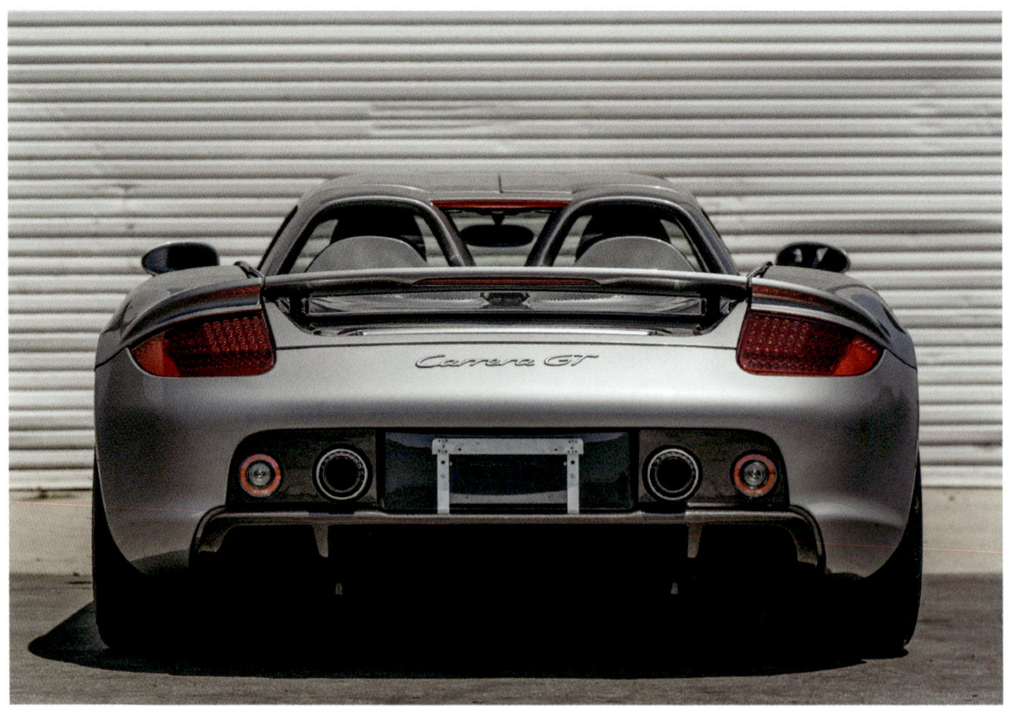

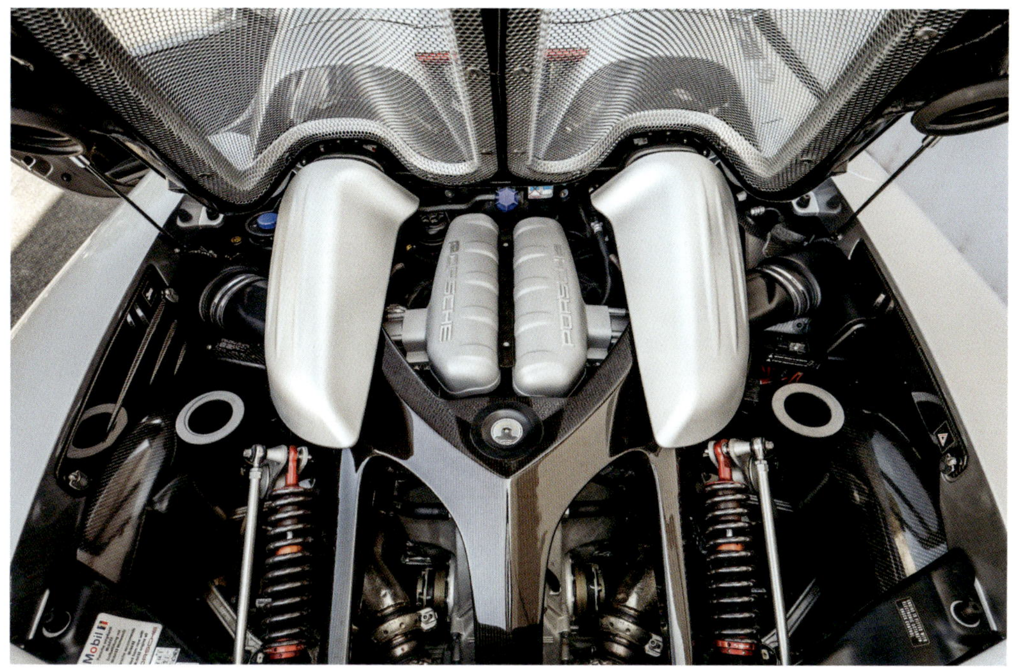

Previous: Detail of Porsche Carrera GT cockpit with magnesium and carbon-fiber elements throughout. The elegant, sporting style seats were the first-ever in a production car made of composite carbon and aramide fibers and weighed only 10.7 kg each — half the amount of conventional bucket seats.

Above: Detail of Porsche Carrera GT 5,733 cc (350 cu. in.), all-alloy, Bosch Motronic ME 7.1.1 fuel-injected DOHC per bank 40-valve 68° V10 engine. This was the first V10 engine used in a Porsche and it proved to be the defining feature of the model, providing the car with incredible performance.

chassis fitted with Jaguar engines. Porsche then modified these racers for TWR with new bodywork and three-liter Porsche flat-six turbo engines. Eventually, these two racers were upgraded with 3.2-liter power plants and it was at this stage that they were officially adopted by the Porsche factory team as works cars and renamed the LMP1-98s. In 1998 the FIA and ACO (Automobile Club de l'Ouest — the creator and organizer of the 24 Hours of Le Mans) introduced rule changes that meant that neither the 911 GT1 nor the LMP1-98 was eligible to compete in the forthcoming 1999 season. In the meantime, Porsche's motorsports division had also been developing a new Le Mans prototype with a newly developed 5.5-liter quad-cam V10 for the upcoming 1999 season. With the introduction of new FIA rules, which it did not meet, the development of this car was pushed to one side. Another reason for this sidelining was that Porsche was in the midst of developing its Cayenne SUV and as a result needed to redeploy its motorsports division's engineering expertise toward this more commercially driven project. However, the Le Mans prototype project slowly crept along in the background and eventually morphed into a brand-new

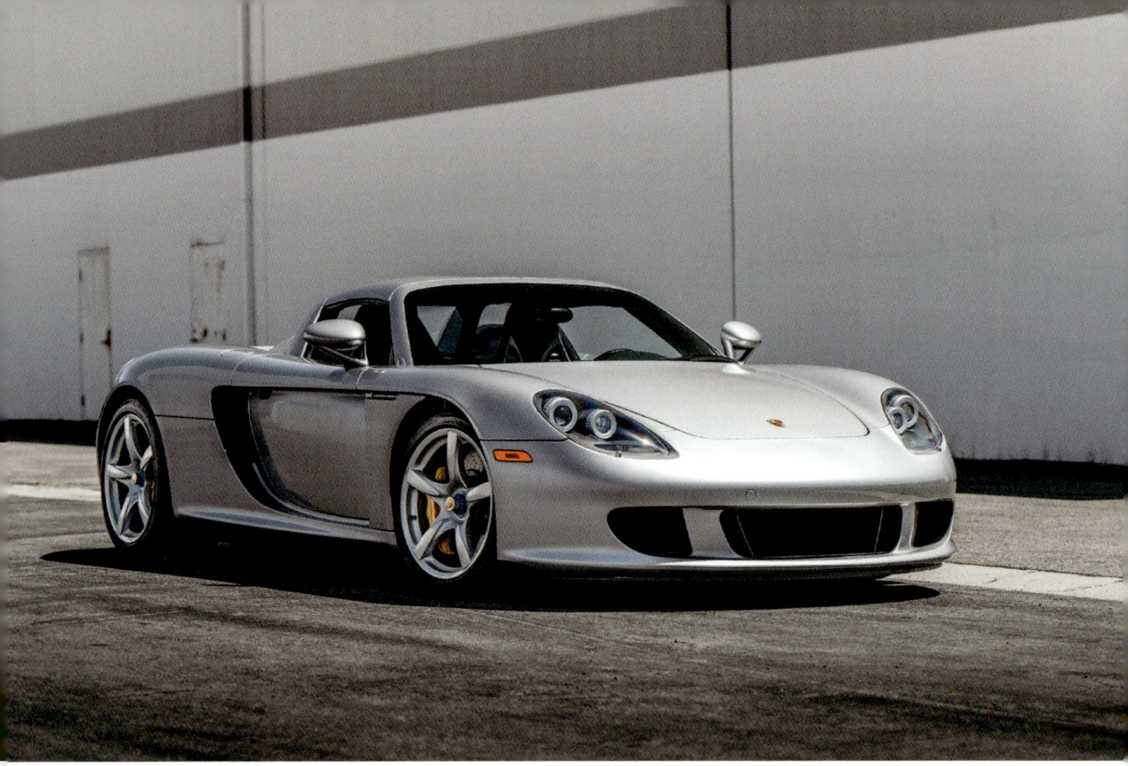

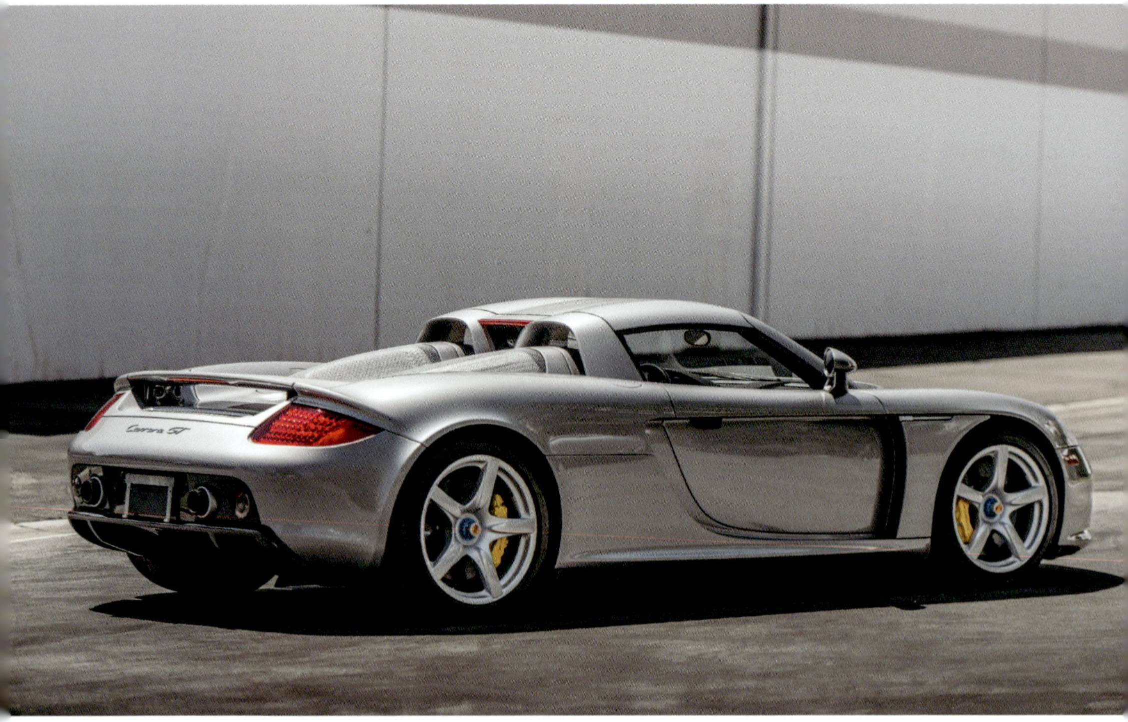

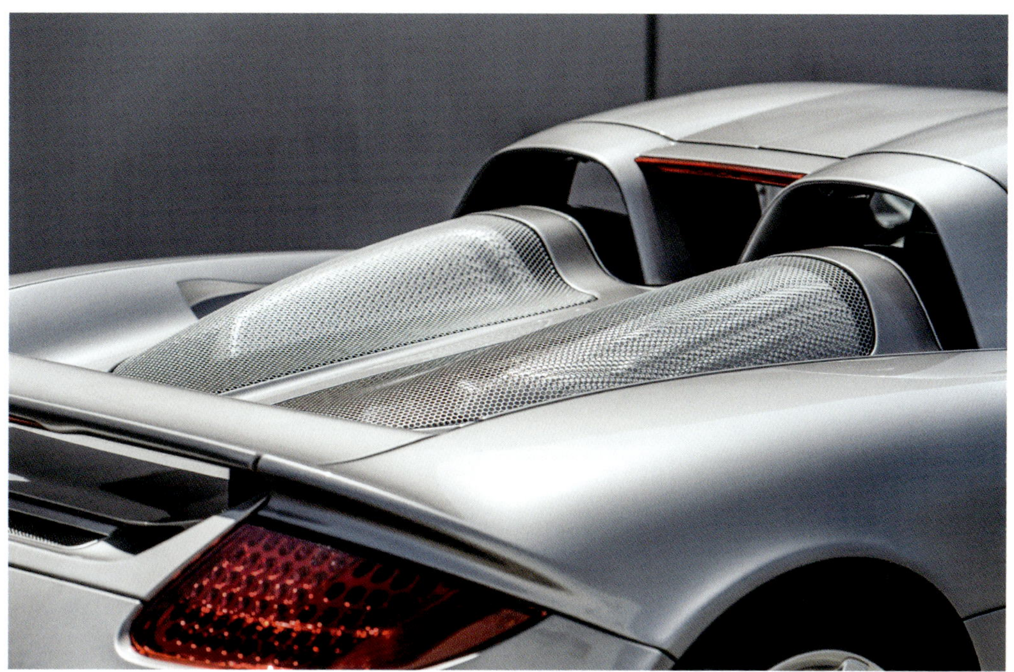

concept car showcased at the 2000 Paris Motor Show, which had the quad-cam V10 racing engine sunk into it.

This mid-engine supercar — known as the Carrera GT — with its radically styled bodywork made of carbon fiber was intended to be a showstopper that would draw attention toward Porsche's stand and was never actually meant to go into production. It caused much more of a sensation than expected, however, and so Porsche, a few years later, decided — on the back of the sales success of the Cayenne — to produce a limited number of street-legal Carrera GTs at its newly opened factory in Leipzig. Despite its $448,000 price tag, it proved popular with a total of 1,270 units being built between 2003 and 2007. The engine used for the production Carrera GT model was actually bigger than the one used for the prototype, being a 5.7-liter quad-cam V10 engine that produced an impressive 612 hp. As the Porsche Museum notes of this masterpiece of Teutonic engineering, "This car delivers a driving experience that is as pure as it is memorable" and goes on to explain, "Its very [distinctive] looks single out the Carrera GT as an uncompromising high performance athlete. It incorporates all the values of a modern racing car — exceptional performance, extreme lightweight construction and high safety." As a consequence, this standout design has over the years generated adulation from various august quarters, with it receiving *Popular Science*'s "Best of What's New" award in 2003 before topping *Sports Car International*'s list of "Top Sports Cars of the 2000s." Such accolades not only testify to its benchmark-setting status within Porsche's canon of great cars, but also help to explain why the Porsche Carrera GT enjoys such an enduring level of desirability among collectors.

2005

Maserati MC12

MANUFACTURED 2004–05 | ENGINE 5,998 cc (366 cu. in.),
DOHC per bank 65° V12 | HORSEPOWER 630 | TOP SPEED 330 km/h (205 mph)
TRANSMISSION 6-speed semi-automatic | NUMBER PRODUCED 50

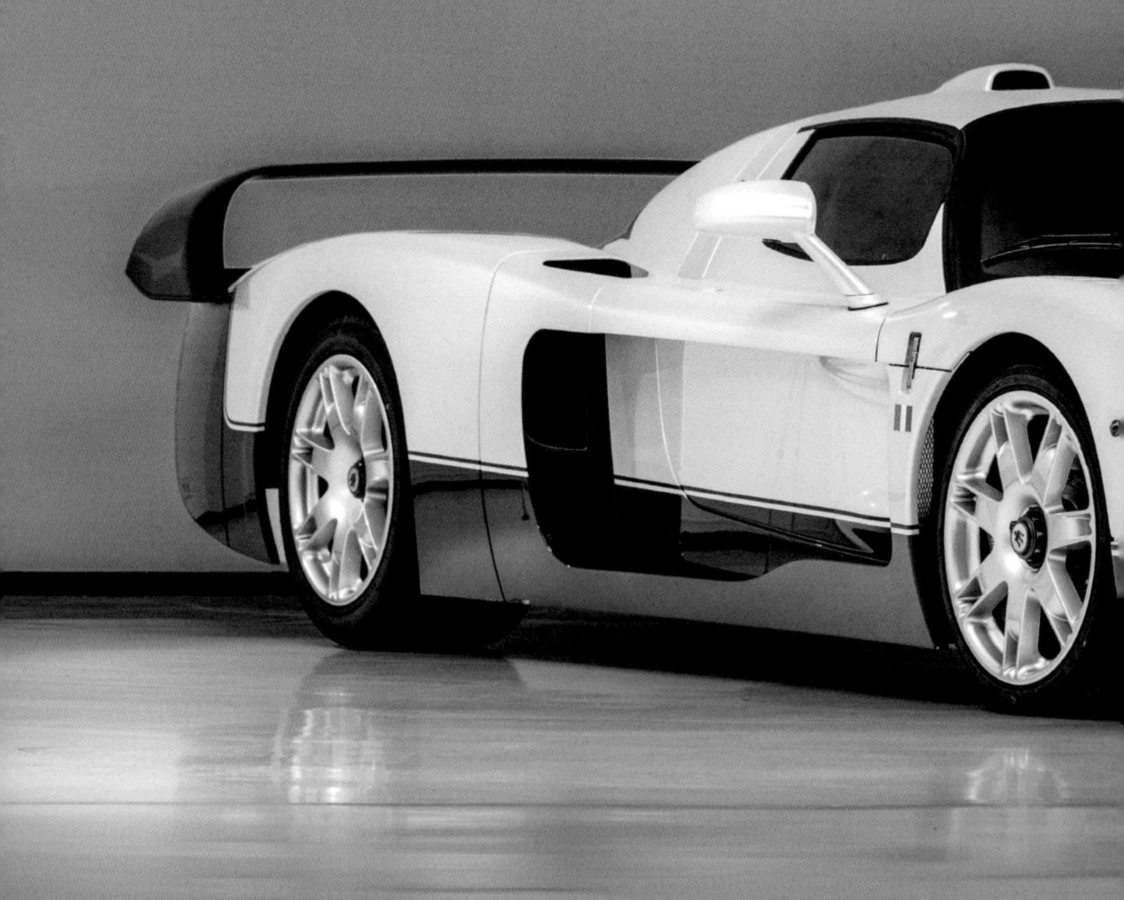

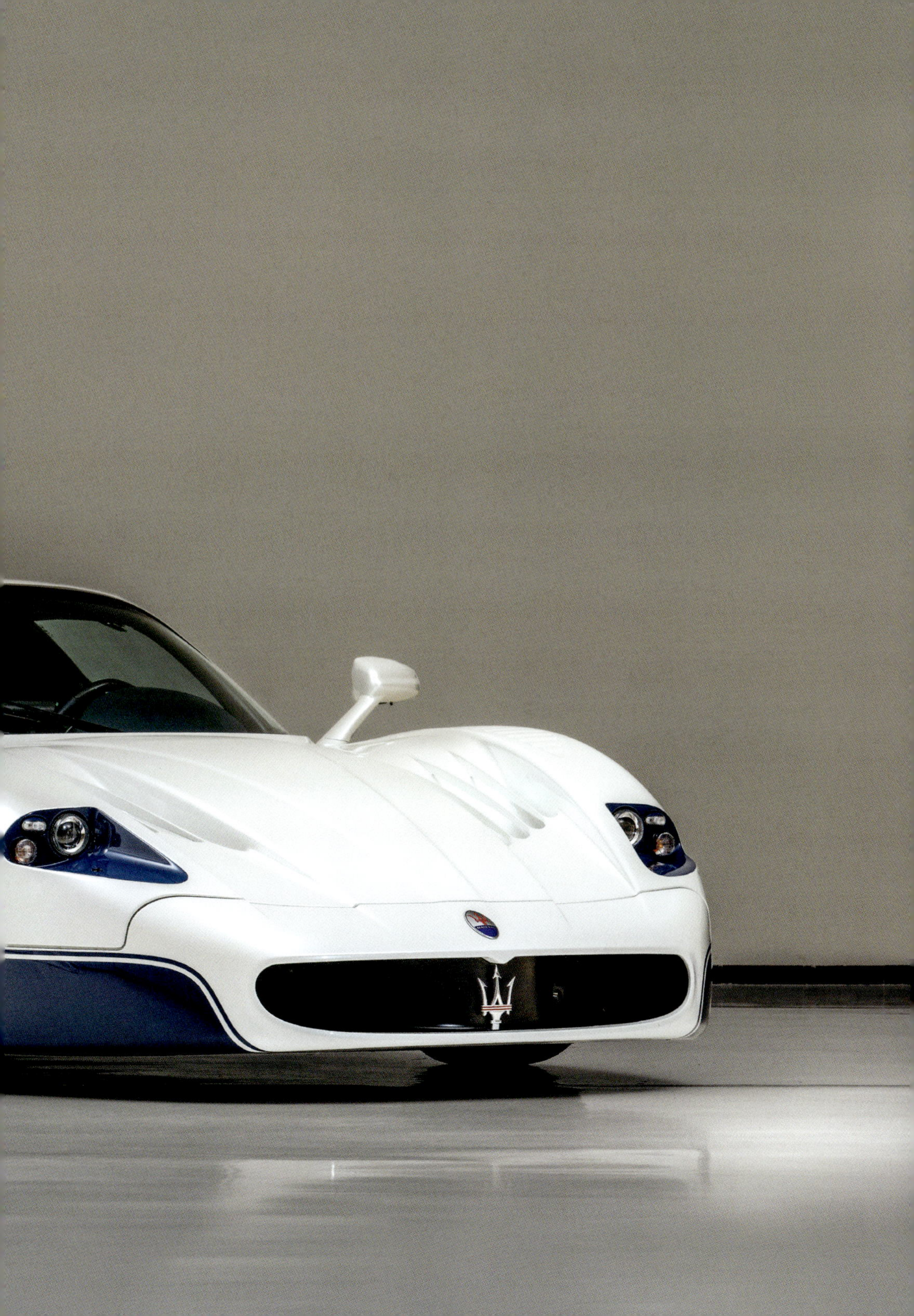

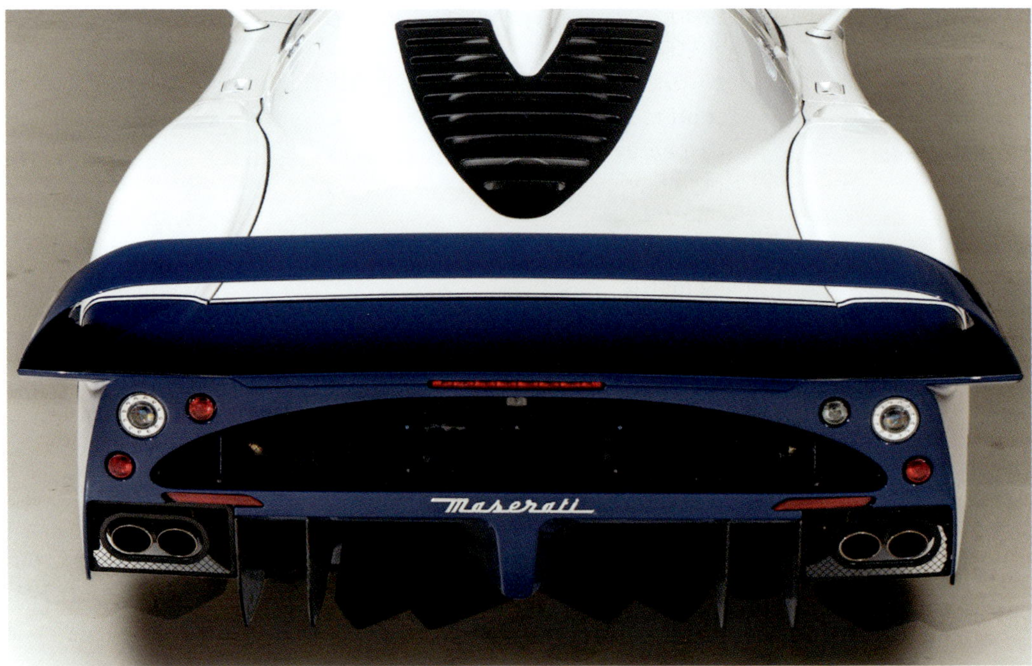

After years of financial instability and having been taken into the ownership of FIAT S.p.A., thanks to the sales successes of its Spyder, Coupé and Quattroporte models, by the mid-2000s Maserati was back on top form and looking to develop a new "halo" car. The resulting Maserari MC12 was a head-turningly beautiful road-going supercar that was initially produced as a short run of 25 units in order to homologate the MC12 GT1 racing variant so that it could compete in the 2004 FIA GT Championship season. With its stunning low-slung, air-cleaving bodywork designed by the legendary Giorgetto Giugiaro and Maserati's chief designer, Frank Stephenson, the MC12 had a very distinctive Maserati look, which somewhat belied the fact that it was built on a Ferrari Enzo Ferrari platform and utilized the same awesome V12 engine. The reason for this slightly surprising marriage was that since 1969, FIAT also had a controlling stake in Ferrari. The Maserati MC12 was, however, not just about visual appeal and viscercal power. Thanks to its massive rear spoiler (which provided significant downforce), its lightweight carbon fiber and Nomex monocoque strengthened with aluminum sub-structures (that shaved off around 45 kilograms, or 100 pounds, in weight compared to the Enzo) and an all-independent wishbone suspension with pushrod coil springs and dampers, it provided superbly sporty handling. Unlike the Enzo, it also had a removable hardtop, which allowed a thrilling wind-in-your-hair driving experience. As RM Sotheby's explains, "The differences between the two were more than just skin deep. The MC12 boasts slightly different engine mapping and traditional dampers instead of the electric dampers of the Enzo, as well as gear-driven cams rather than the Enzo's chain-driven cams."

This supercar's high performance, however, was not confined to the streets, as its competition sibling, the MC12 GT1, which was first fielded in the FIA's GT Class 1 World Championship Series of 2004, proved to be a formidable contender. This first season for the GT1, however, did not get off to the best of starts because production of the 25 homologated cars took longer than expected, and as a consequence the three MC12 GT1s fielded by the factory-backed AF Corse team were not allowed to take points until the season's final race: the LG Super Racing Weekend Zhuhai, held in November. That race, though, saw an MC12 GT1 take overall victory. But even before this, these competition cars had already more than shown their racing mettle, though unofficially — for their debut at Imola, the eighth race of the season, they placed second and third, and then at Oschersleben, the ninth race on the calendar, they took the victory. It was, however, thanks to that first official win in Zhuhai that AF Corse managed to finish seventh in the Teams Championship, which boded extremely well for the following season. In fact, the 2005 season was completely dominated by the MC12 GT1s, which were raced by two teams, Vitapoint Racing and JMB

Below: Detail of Maserati MC12 5,998 cc (366 cu. in.), all-alloy, Bosch Motronic ME7 fuel-injected DOHC per bank 48-valve 65° V12 engine. This was the same Ferrari engine that powered the Enzo. There were differences, however, between the two — the MC12 boasted slightly different engine mapping and had gear-driven cams rather than the Enzo's chain-driven cams. Not surprisingly, the Ferrari had a higher top speed.

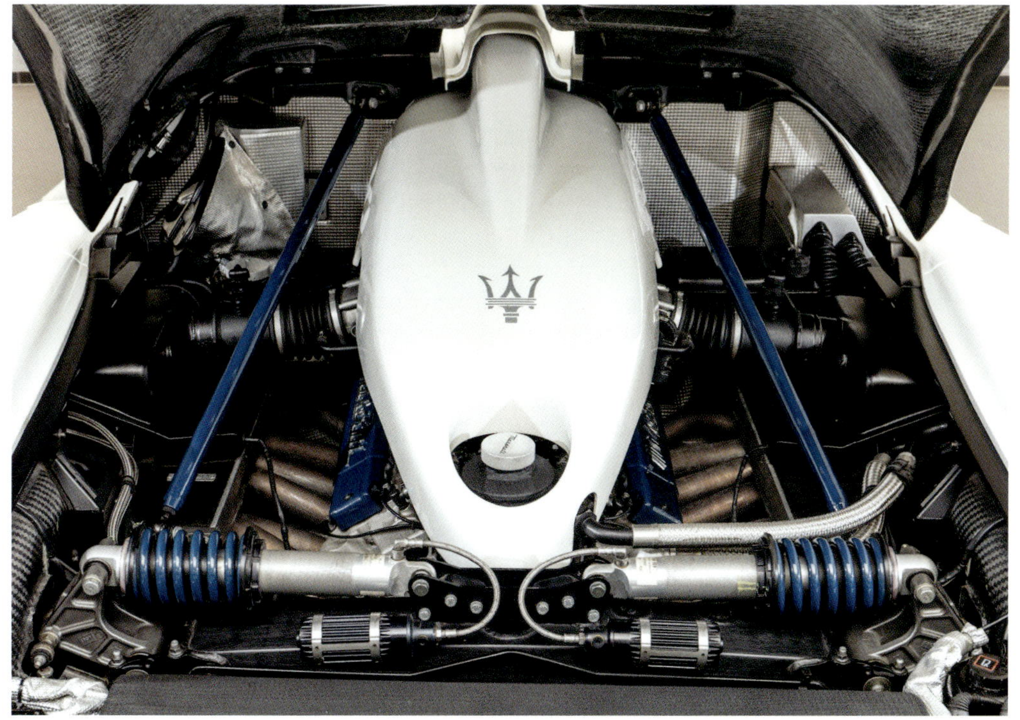

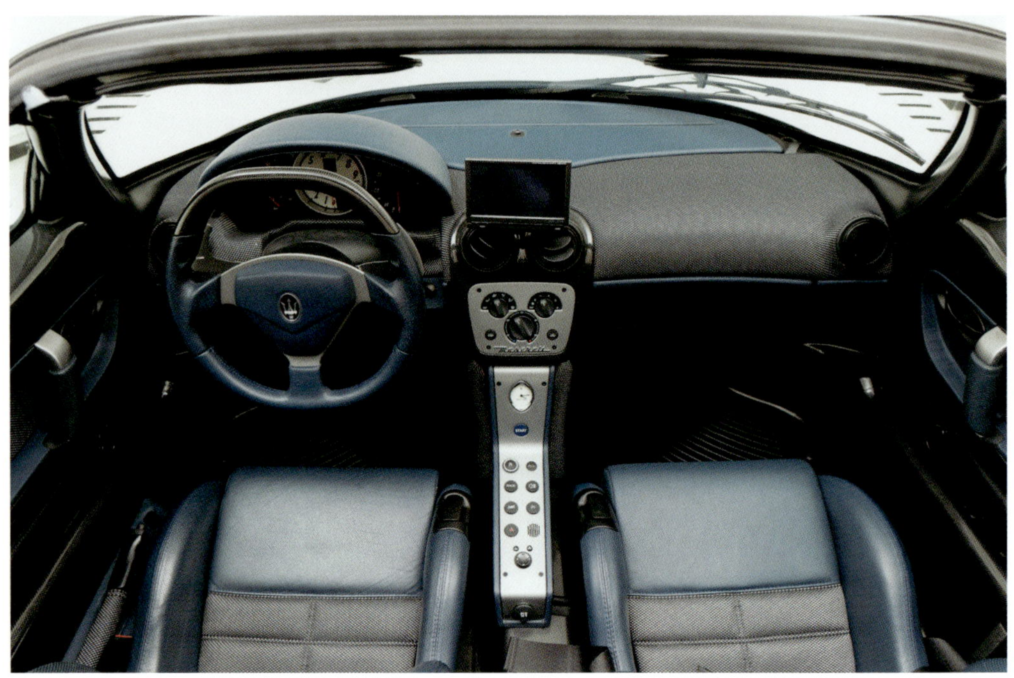

Racing, and took first and second place respectively in the Teams Cup. That same year, Maserati clinched the FIA GT Manufacturers Cup with 239 points, almost double the score of Ferrari, which came second. Importantly, this was the start of a Maserati winning streak, with Vitapoint Racing going on to secure a further four consecutive team championships and Maserati winning a follow-up Manufacturer's Cup in 2007. Remarkably, of the 94 races that the MC12s officially competed in from 2004 to 2009 they won 40. And, unsurprisingly, these victories made the homologated MC12s all the more desirable. These cars offered their lucky owners two driving modes, either "sport" or "race," which were actuated by the press of a button, with the latter providing faster gear changes and a stiffer suspension. A later racing variant of the MC12, introduced in 2006, was known as the Corsa and was specifically developed for European racing and rallying. The MC12 "stradale" shown here — chassis no. ZAMDF44B000012085 — was one of the first to be constructed, out of an eventual total production run of 50, and with only 12,500 kilometers on its odometer it is one of the finest examples of this truly iconic 21st-century Italian supercar.

Above, opposite & overleaf: The outcome of intensive wind tunnel testing and advanced mathematical computations the MC12's air intakes, vents, rear spoiler and other aerodynamic components, including the the sinuous lines formed by two large tapering apertures on the hood, optimized very efficiently air flow and downforce. While the MC12 was designed and built on the chassis of the Enzo Ferrari it is much larger, but has a lower drag coefficient.

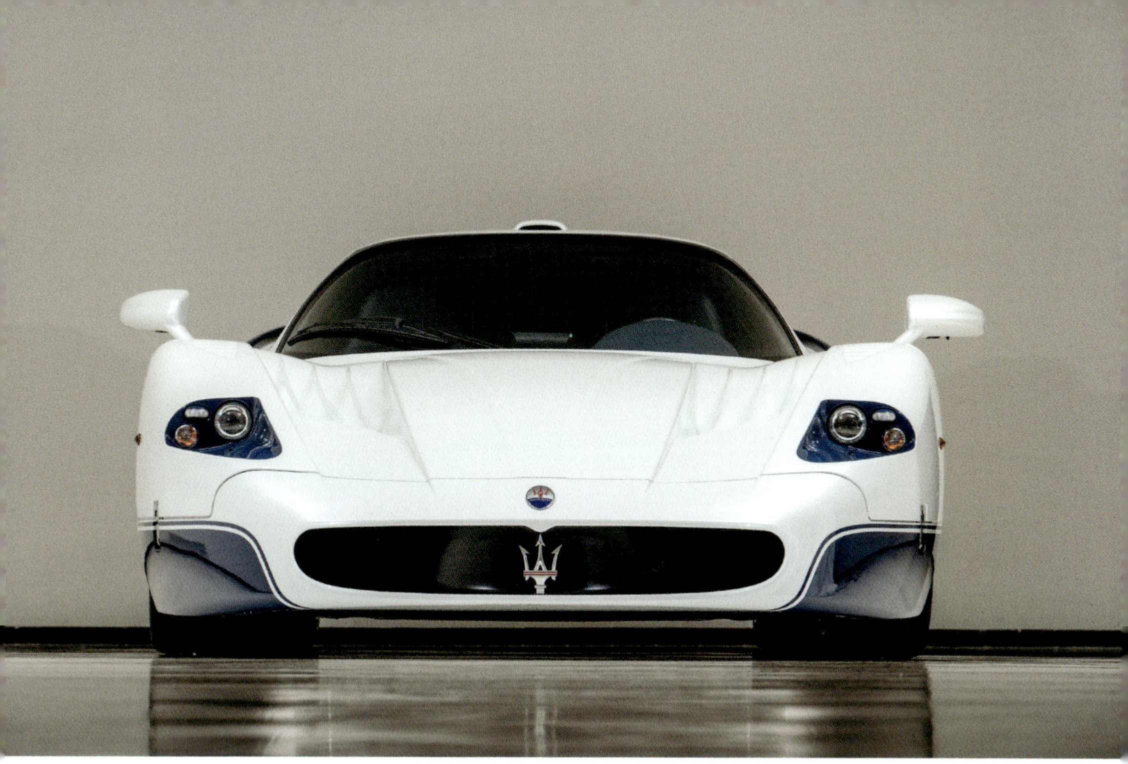

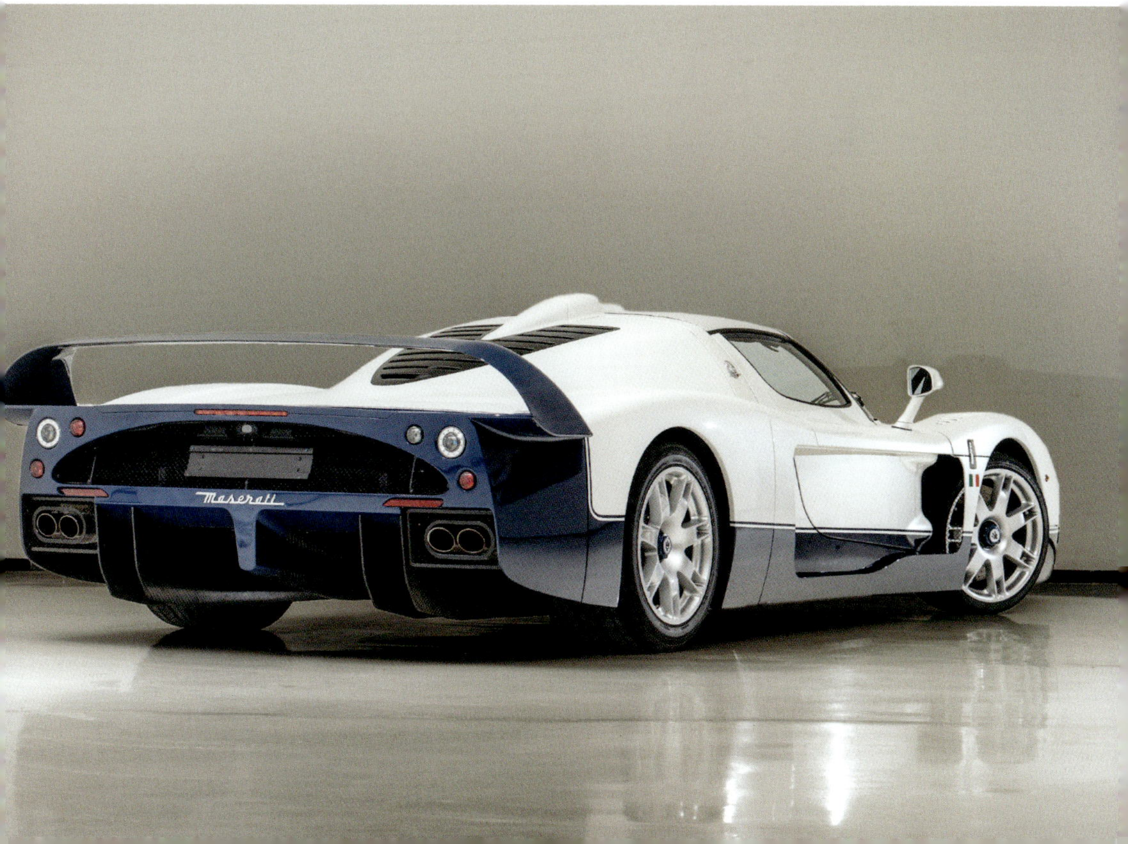

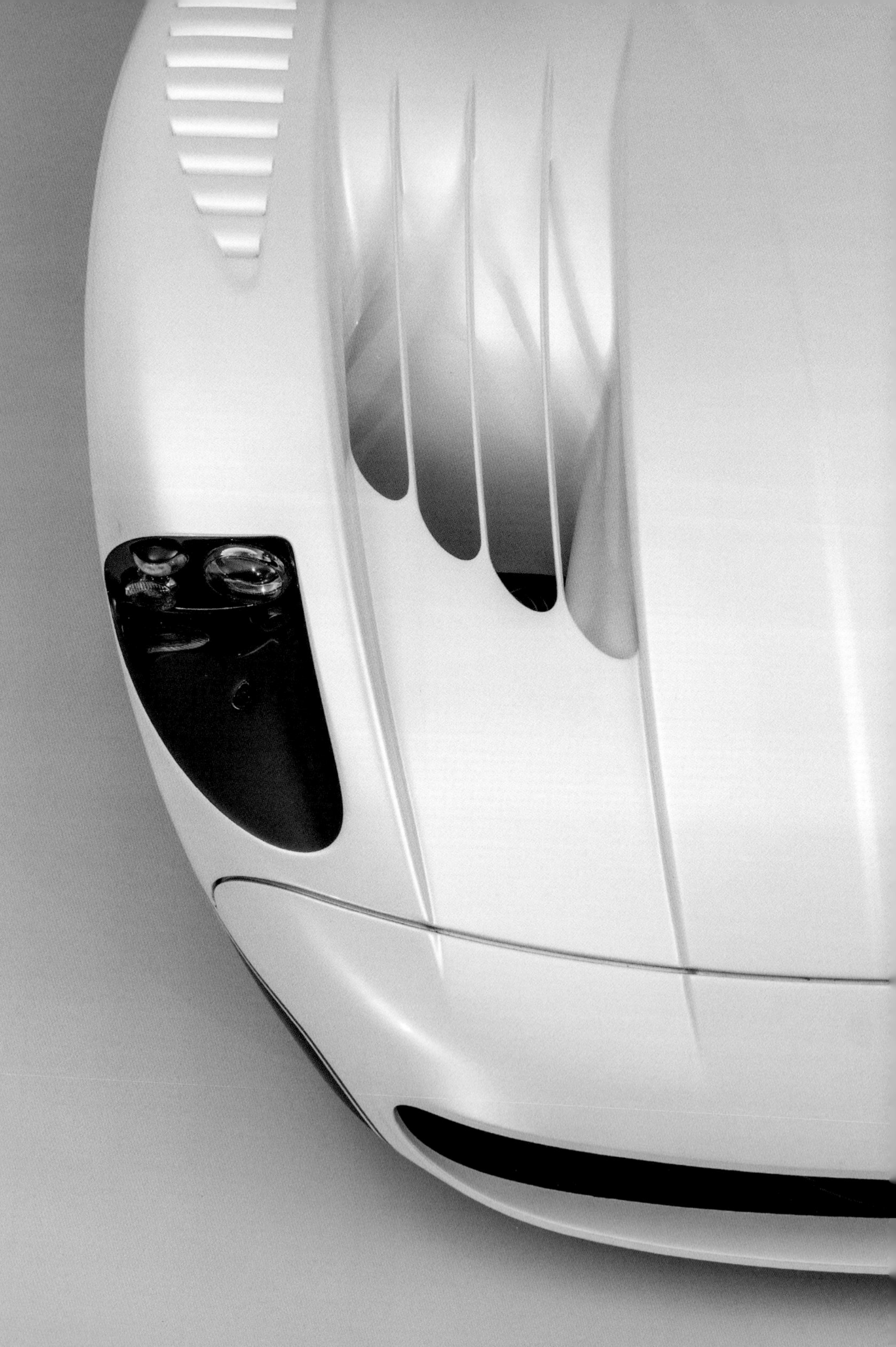

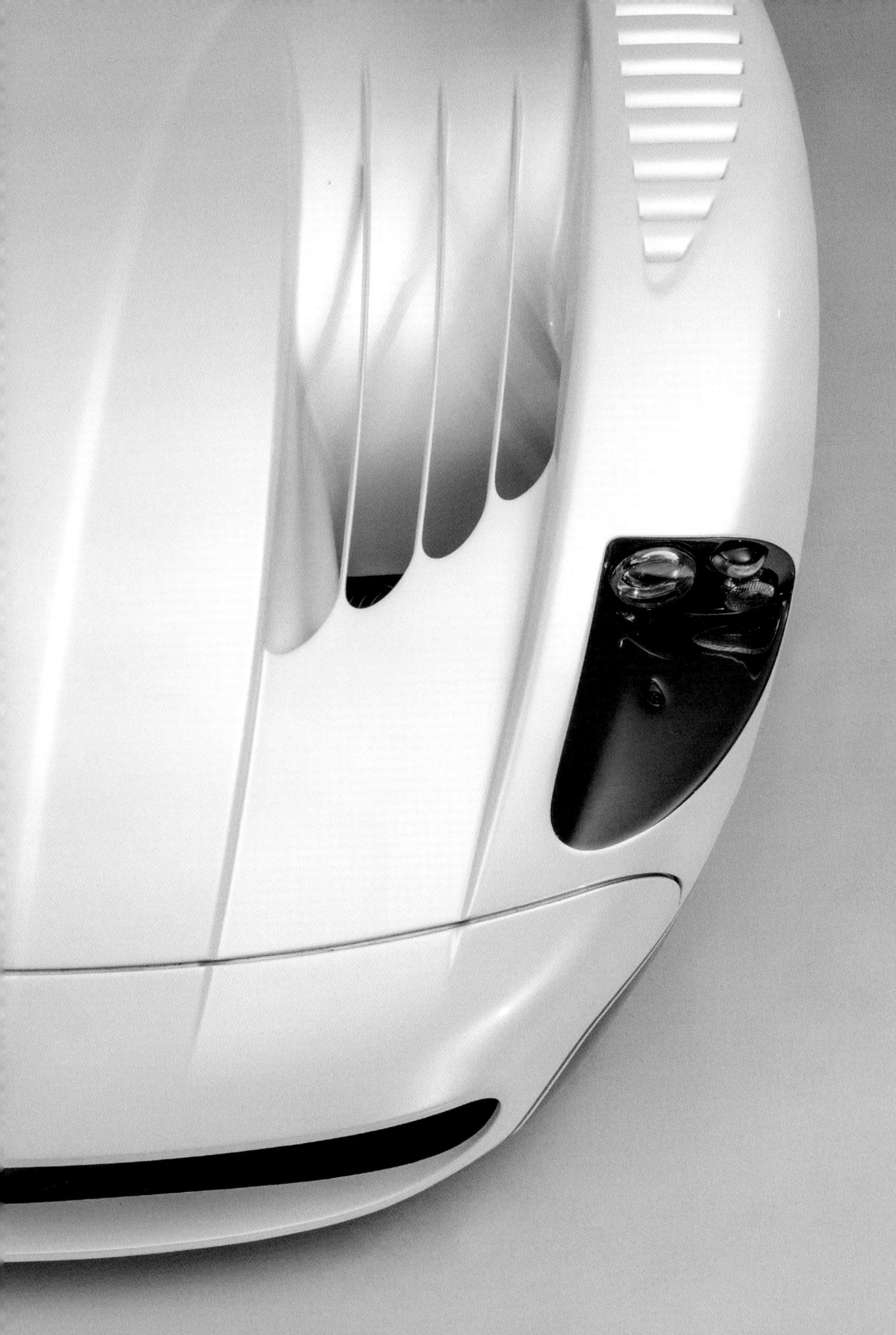

2015

Porsche 918 Spyder Weissach Package

MANUFACTURED 2013–15 | ENGINE 4,593 cc (280 cu. in.), DOHC per bank V8 & dual electric motors | HORSEPOWER 893 peak combined (608 hp & 156 hp & 129 hp) | TOP SPEED 345 km/h (214 mph) TRANSMISSION 7-speed PDK dual-clutch | NUMBER PRODUCED 918

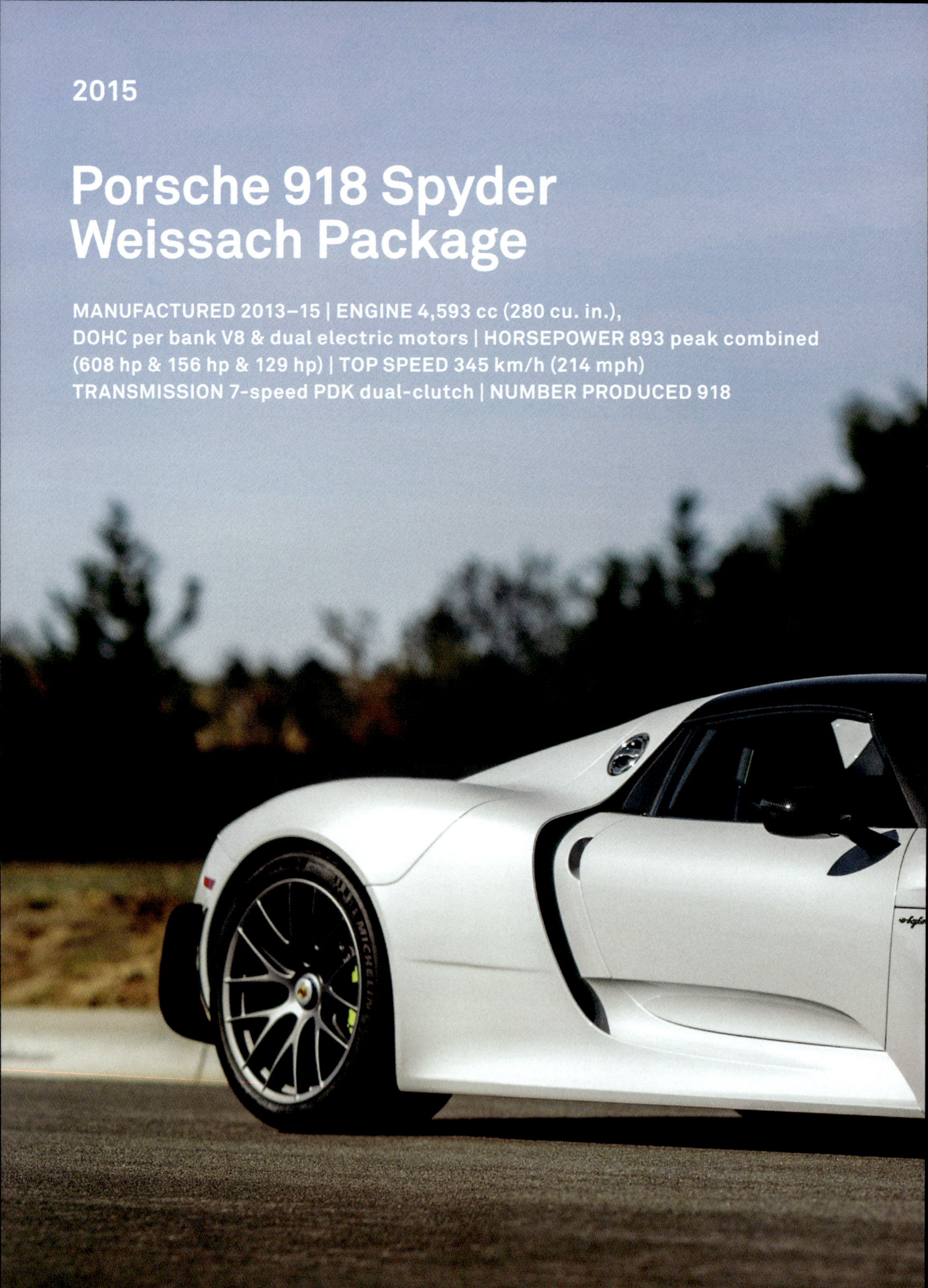

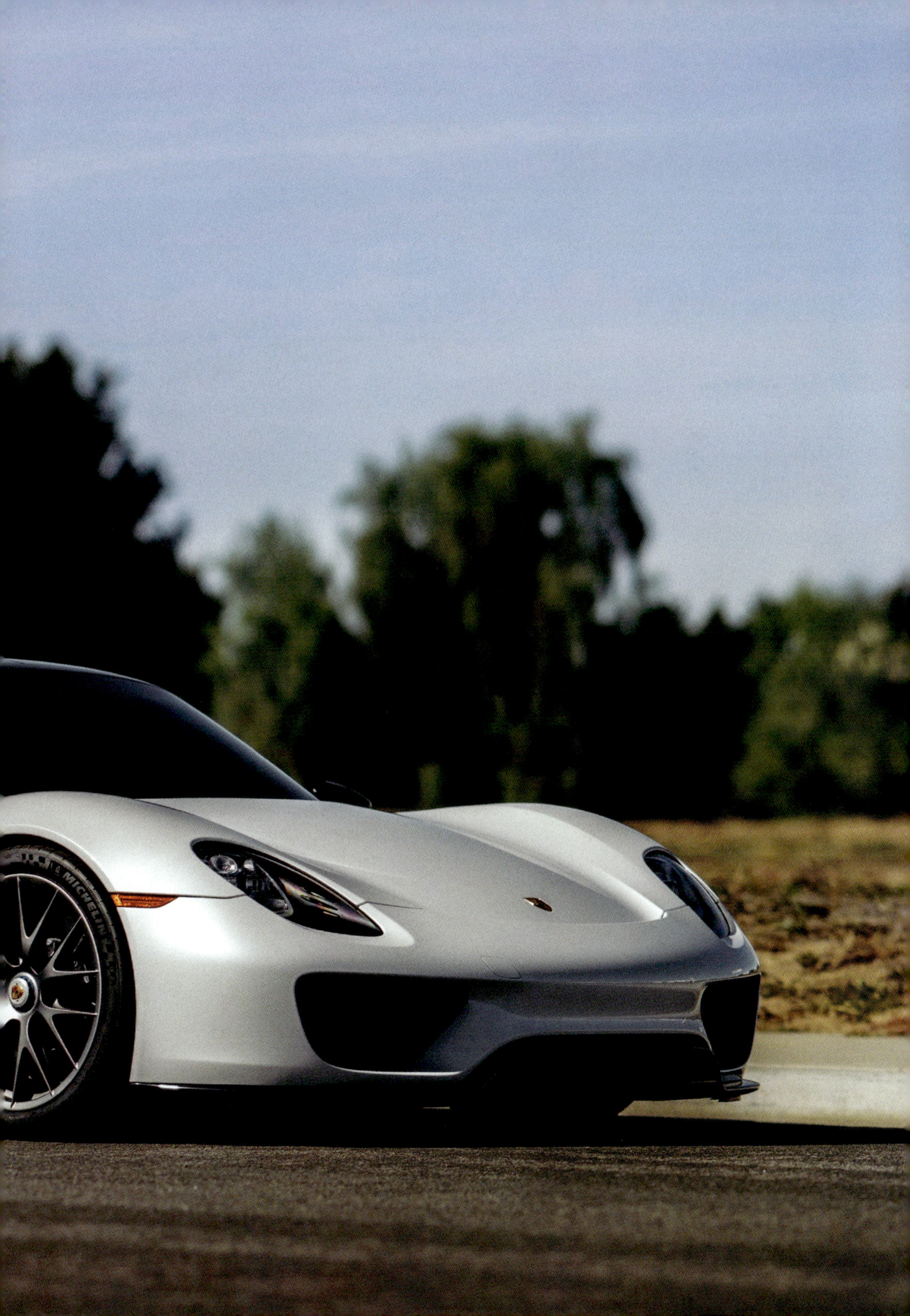
MICHELIN

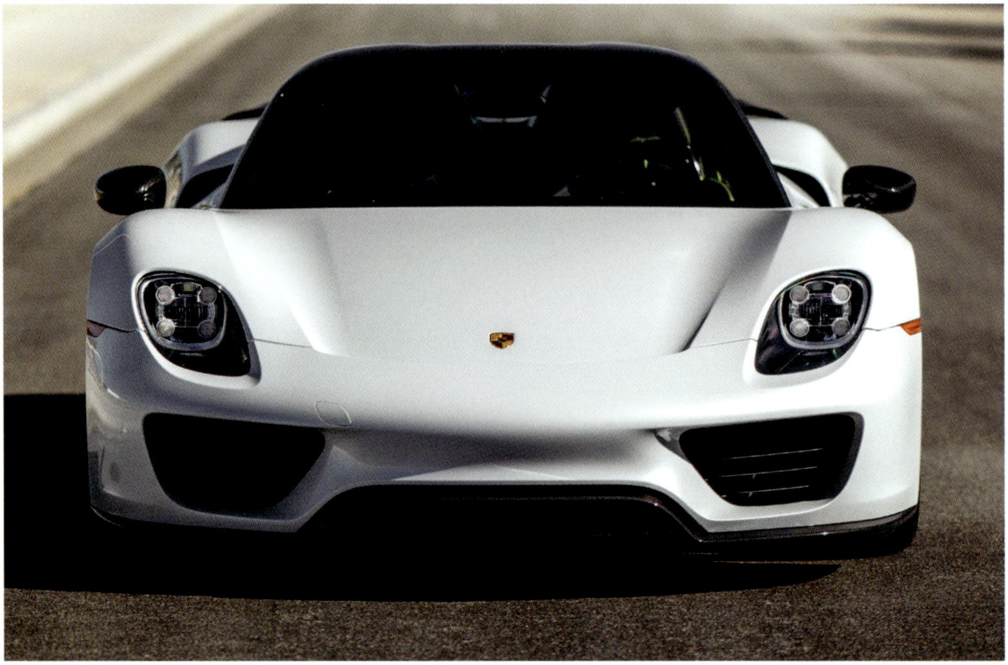

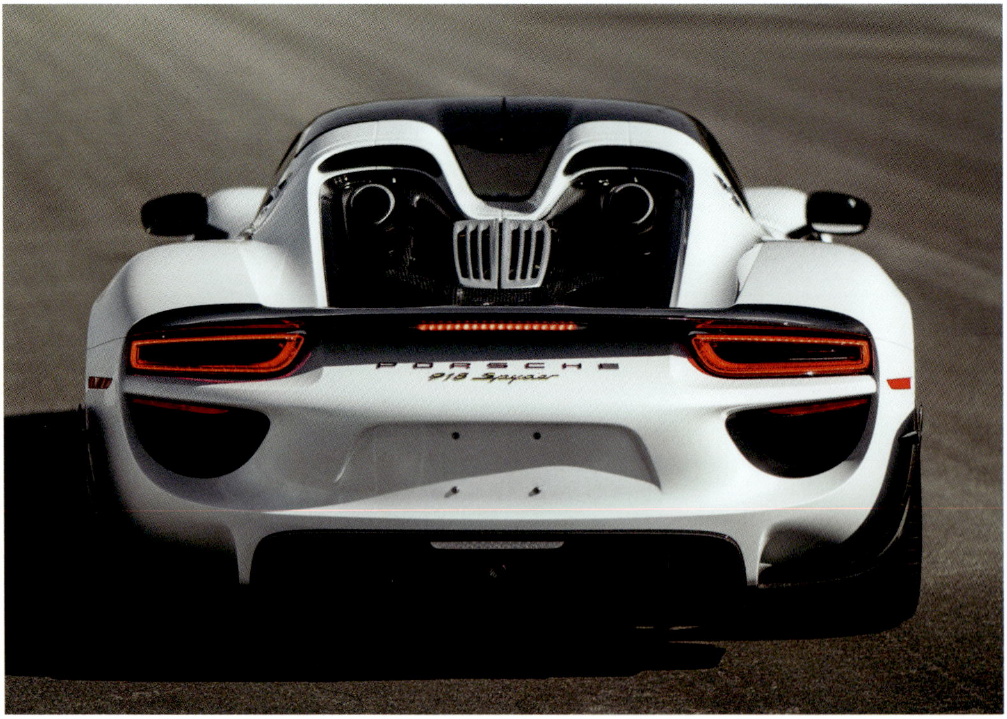

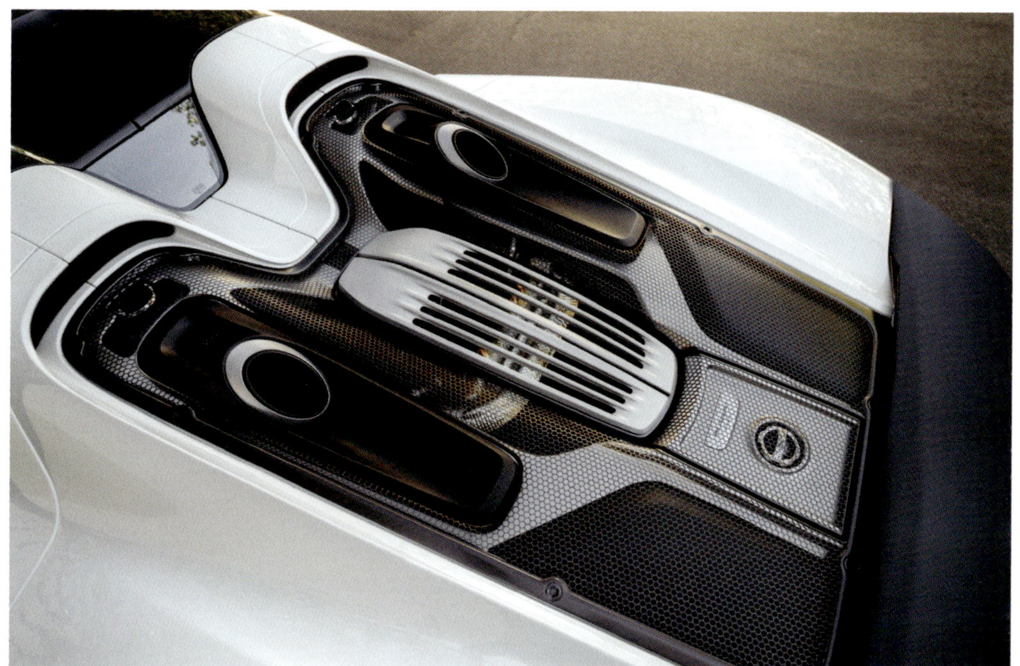

Above: Detail of the Porsche 918 Spyder's engine cover. The mid-mounted all-alloy 4,593 cc (280 cu. in.), direct fuel-injected DOHC per bank 32-valve 90° V8 engine underneath is this hybrid-drive hypercar's principle source of propulsion, which on its own produces an impressive 608 hp. A striking feature of the engine is that it does not support any auxiliary systems — there are no external belt drives and so the engine is particularly compact. It achieves a power output of 132 hp/liter — an outstanding figure for a naturally aspirated engine.

Porsche unveiled its 918 Spyder concept at the 80th Geneva Motor Show in March 2010 and within just four months this supercar, which boasted advanced hybrid technology, had clocked up 2,000 declarations of interest. This led Porsche AG's board to sanction its development as a bona fide production model, which was subsequently unveiled at the Geneva Motor Show in 2013. Two years later, the 918 Spyder was finally made available for purchase with a starting price of $845,000 and a production run limited to 918 units. As one of the first super-hybrids, the 918 Spyder was very much of its time because while the noughties had seen the creation of supercars with huge naturally aspirated engines, the following decade witnessed a complete sea change as hybrid technology became evermore efficient. Moreover, as RM Sotheby's explains, "Manufacturers quickly realized that hybrid powertrains could not only be used to reduce emissions and create highly fuel-efficient vehicles but could also be used to increase performance in ultra-high performance sports cars. By using the electric powertrain to support the conventional powertrain at its weakest, performance could be pushed to boundaries never thought possible, all while decreasing emissions in an industry becoming ever more scrutinized for carbon pollution."

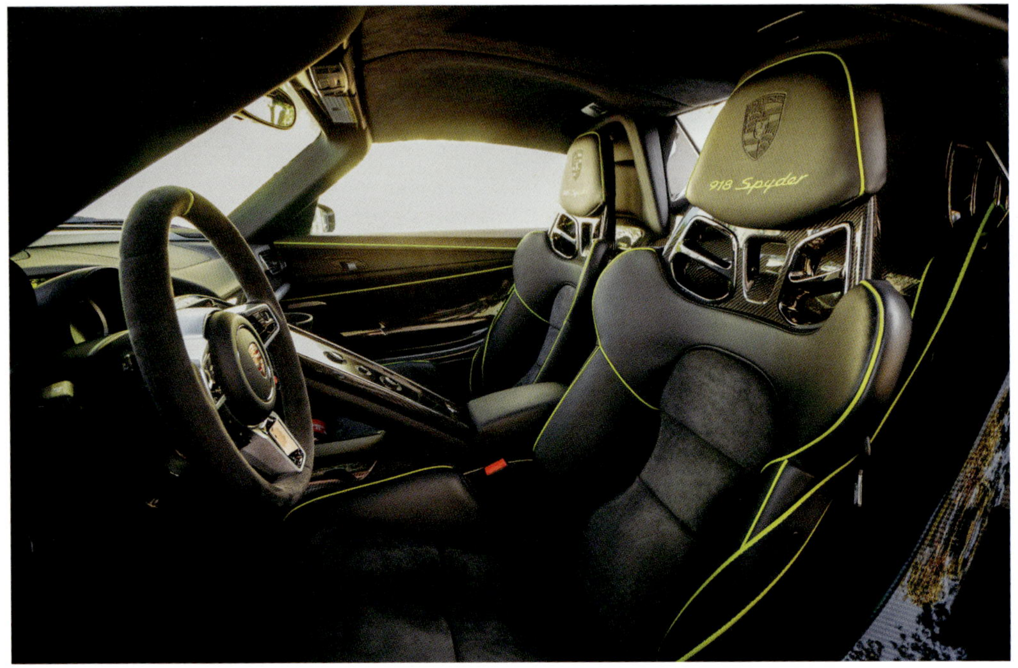

Above: This Porsche 918's interior features black Alcantara offset with acid green highlights with matching accent stripes on the seat belts — providing a very distinct and striking look.

And while this upside "boost" was used by Ferrari and McLaren to create ultra-performance hybrid hypercars, Porsche instead saw it was an opportunity to create a model that was more practical. The resultant 918 was a super-hybrid that unlike its competitors could be used as an everyday driver, though no less impressive for that. While its predecessor the Carrera GT (see p. 430) had been more of a race car for the road, the 918 in contrast blended advanced technology with a thoughtful design that afforded a much greater degree of comfort. It also boasted a four-wheel drive system as well as a rear-axle steering system that provided better stability and handling, with this latter feature enabling it to turn on a dime.

The 918's race-derived, normally aspirated, 4.6-liter quad-cam V8 engine (608 hp) and two electric motors (285 hp combined), one for each axle, produces a combined peak output of 893 hp. This awesome power is delivered via Porsche's famed Doppelkupplung (PDK) — a seven-speed dual-clutch gearbox originally developed by Porsche for sports racing in the 1980s, which enables rapid gear changing with no interruption to the flow of power and allows the 918 to achieve breathtaking performance. It is this perfect engine-gearbox combination that transfigures German precision engineering into automotive poetry in motion. The 918 is also seriously quick from a standing start, with *Car and Driver* magazine verifying an acceleration rate of 0–60 mph in just 2.2 seconds.

For customers wanting the optimum 918 driving experience Porsche created its "Weissach" package, named after the town where Porsche's research center is located. This option featured various weight-saving modifications: lighter Alcantara (synthetic suede) replaced leather, aluminum components were swapped for those made of carbon fiber, and super-light magnesium wheels were fitted. Because of this option's high price of $84,000 only around 25 percent of all 918s were specified with it.

The Weissach package represented a painstaking exercise in weight reduction that lessened the 918's overall weight by 45 kilograms (99 lb.), thereby maximizing performance while also helping to minimize fuel consumption. The 918 Spyder (chassis no. WP0CA2A13FS800804), shown here, is not only outfitted with this highly covetable option, but also boasts a nonstandard "paint to sample" metallic white exterior as well as a bespoke black Alcantra interior featuring acid green accents. The seatbelts continue this distinctive colorway, while the car also features a host of other high-spec options, including a front-axle lift system. All of which makes this example one of the most desirable Weissachs in existence. Given its rarity and high performance credentials, the Weissach variant is the most prized of all 918s and no doubt will come to be regarded as one of Porsche's defining auto-stars of the early 21st century.

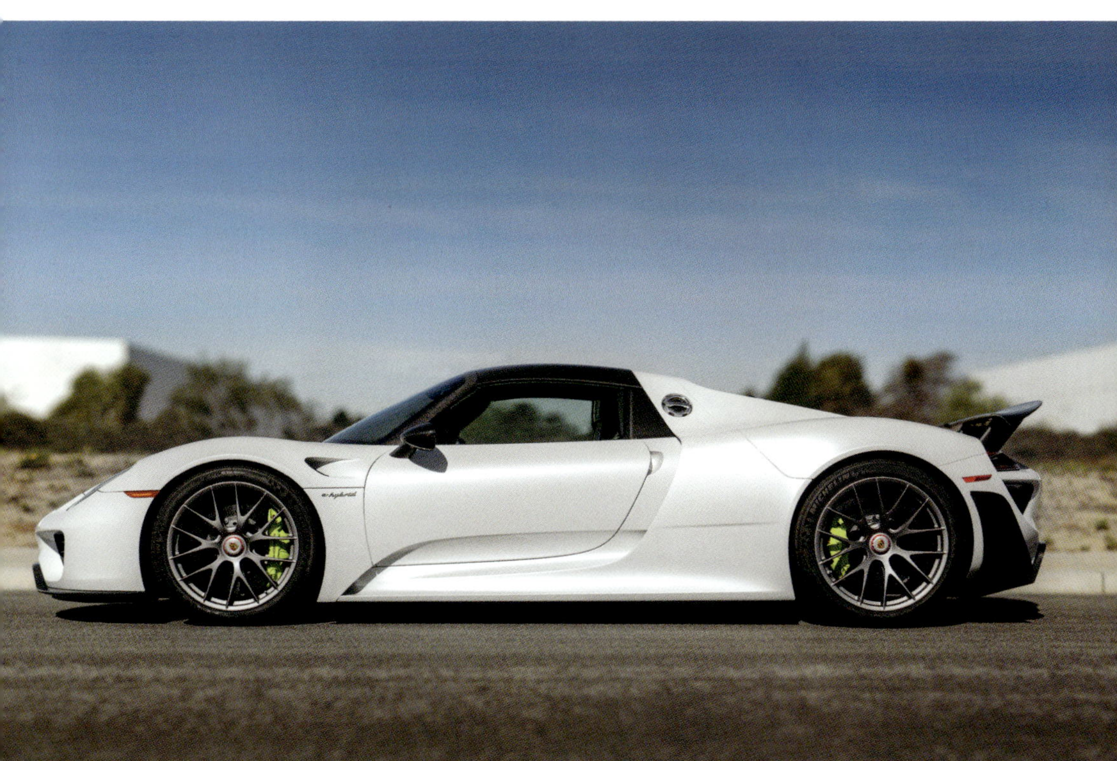

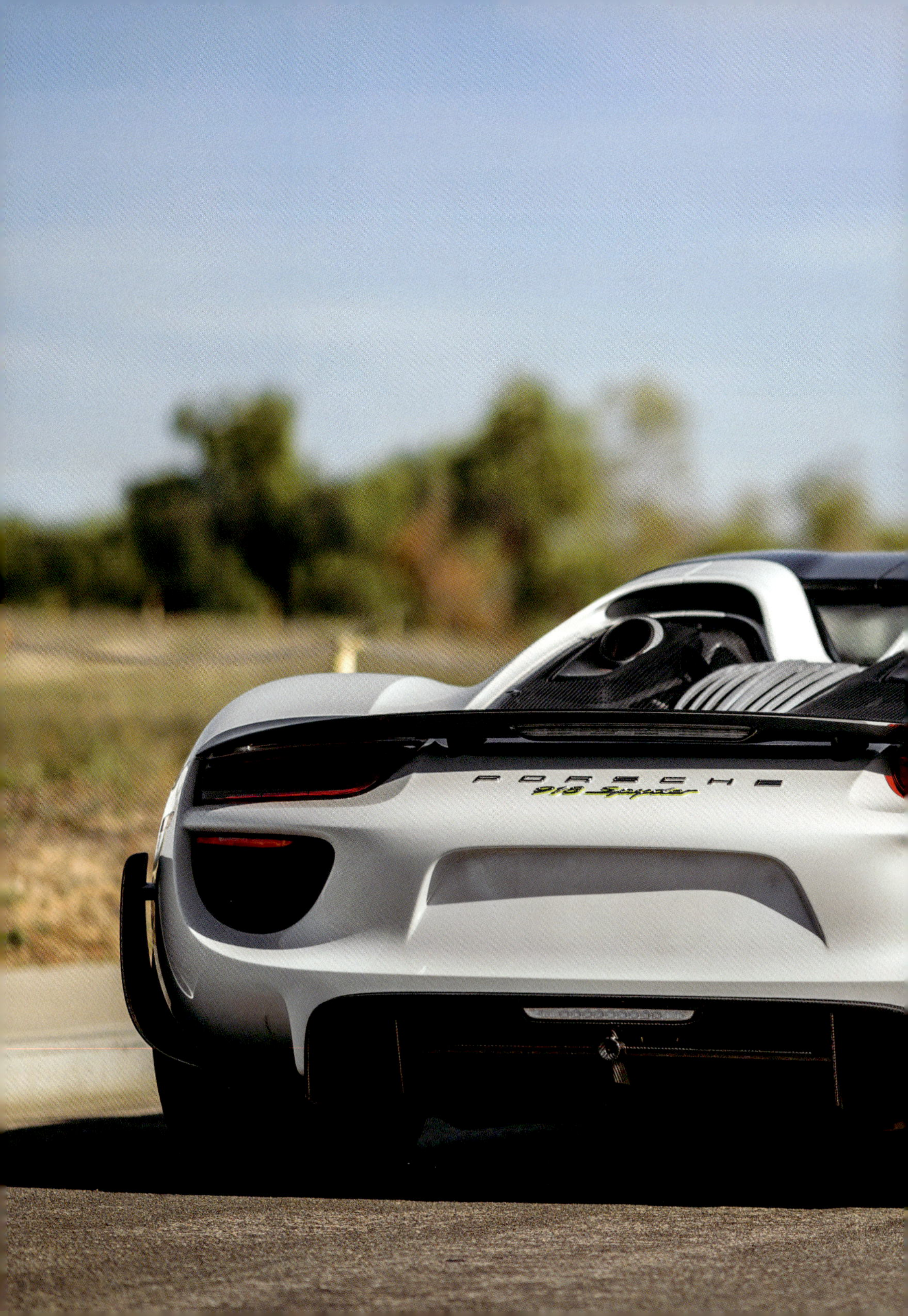
PORSCHE
918 Spyder

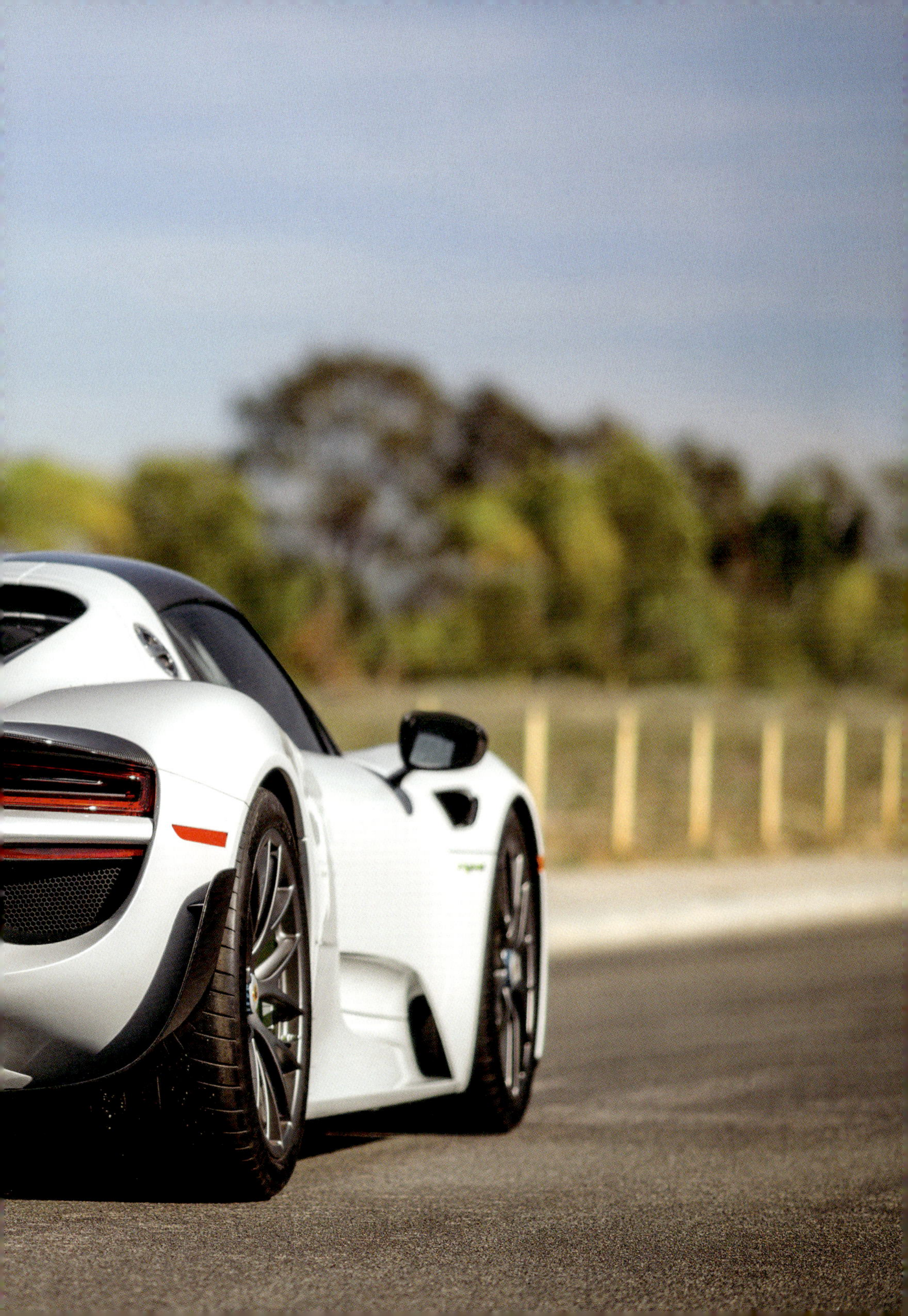

2016

Lamborghini Centenario Roadster

MANUFACTURED 2016–17 | ENGINE 6,498 cc (396.5 cu. in.),
DOHC per bank 60° V12 | HORSEPOWER 770
TOP SPEED 350 km/h (217 mph) | TRANSMISSION 7-speed ISR semi-automatic
NUMBER PRODUCED 20 roadsters & 20 coupés

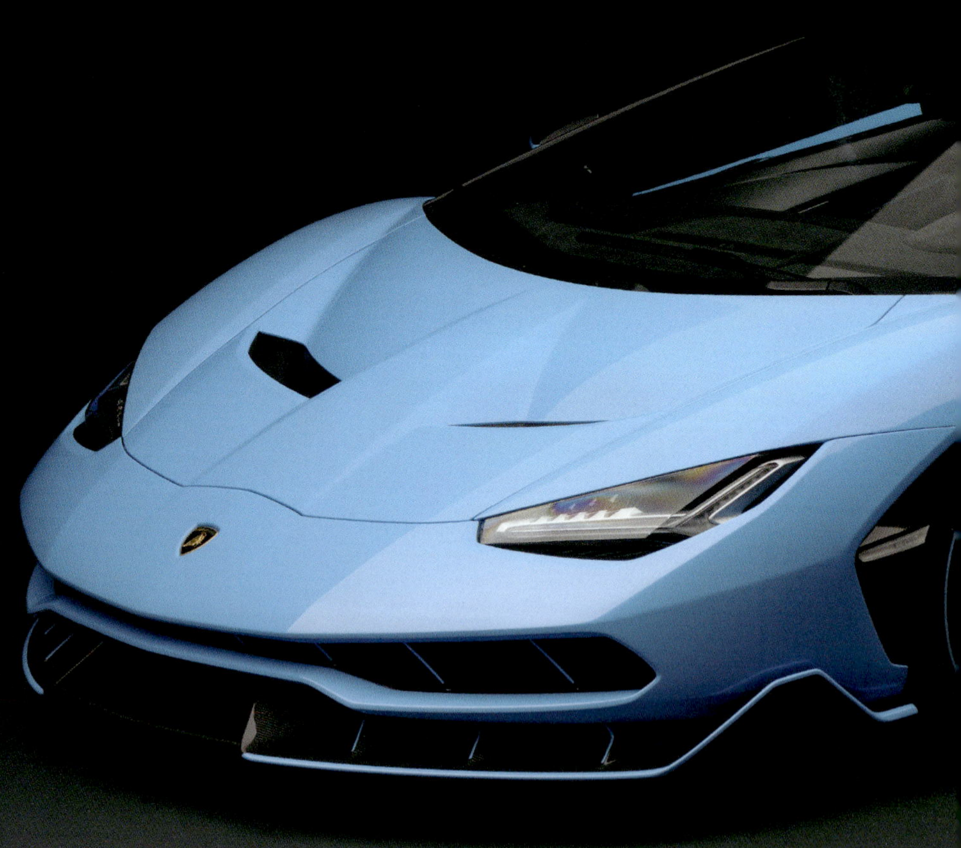

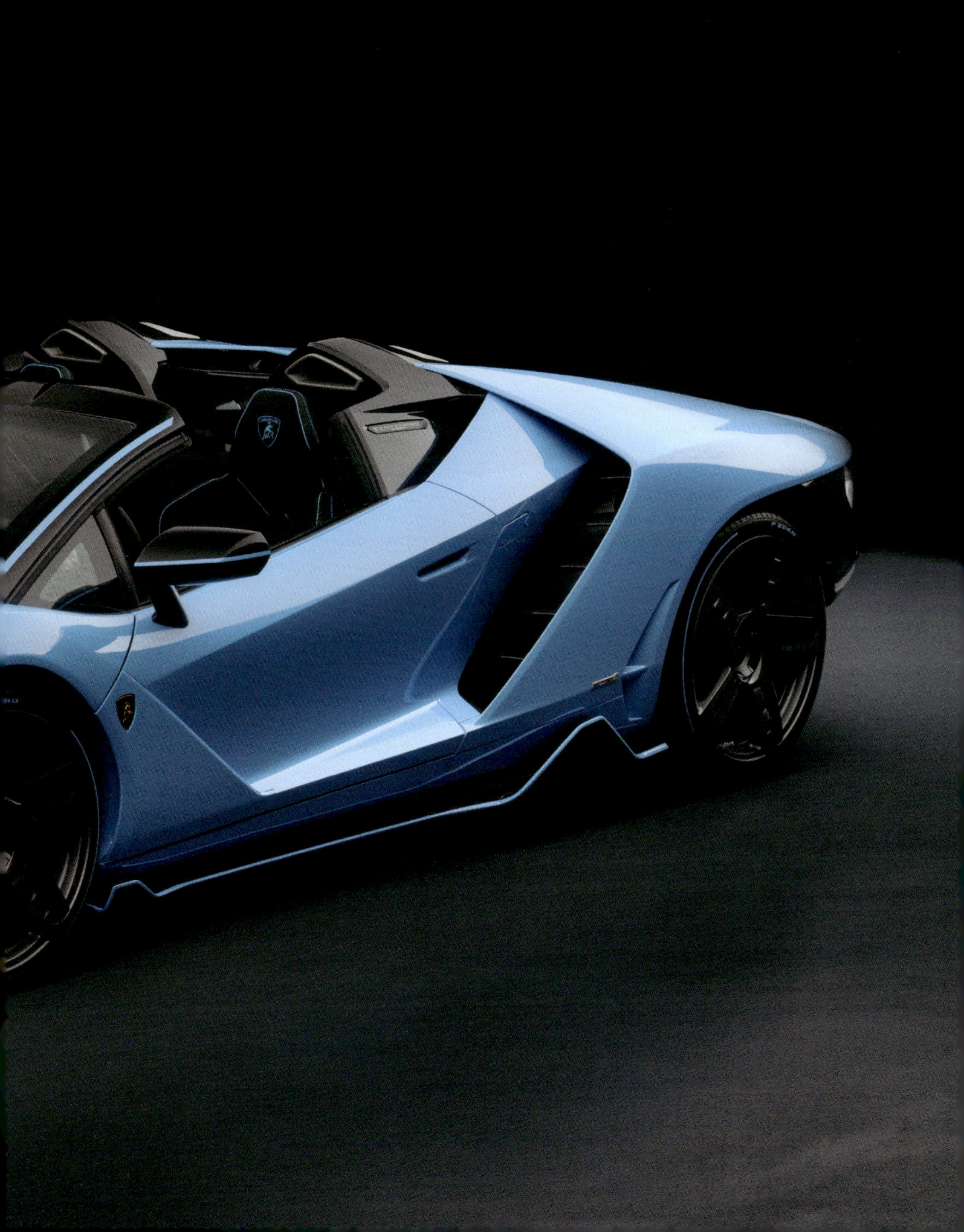

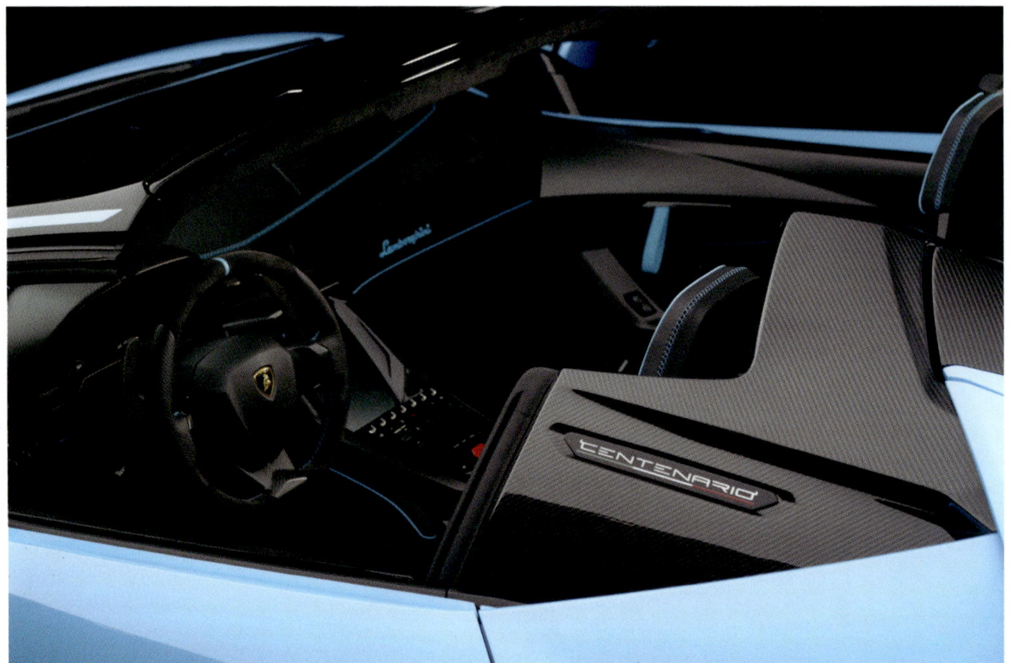

Launched at the Geneva Motor Show in 2016 to commemorate the 100th anniversary of company founder Ferruccio Lamborghini's birth, the aptly named Centenario Coupé was, as Lamborghini explains, "an homage to this visionary man and to the future he believed so much in." But even more than this it represented another bold technological leap forward within the marque's lineage of outstanding supercars, which can be traced right back to the legendary Miura (see p. 402). Over the five and half intervening decades the bull-branded manufacturer — its logo referring to its founder's Taurian zodiac sign — has experimented obsessively with progressive technical solutions for as it notes "time changes form, but not substance." This steadfast performance-driven mission has been unwaveringly and passionately adhered to, but then the marque was itself founded on Ferruccio's overwhelming desire to build the world's most perfect sports car. This is an important distinction for while Enzo Ferrari like so many of the other constructors featured in this volume was always obsessively focused on racing and the next track win, Ferruccio by contrast was far more interested in the creation of high-design, ultra-performance road cars with eye-catching "wow" factor. And to this extent, the Centenario does not disappoint with its dramatic and futuristic angular form.

The design of the Centenario Coupé was based on Lamborghini's production Aventador SV, and as such utilizes a carbon fiber monocoque as well as a competition-derived in-board suspension system. At the heart of this all-out hypercar lies a highly tuned version of the Aventador's 6.5-liter quad-cam V12 engine, which provides a top speed of 350 km/h (217 mph). The most visually striking differentiators between these two models

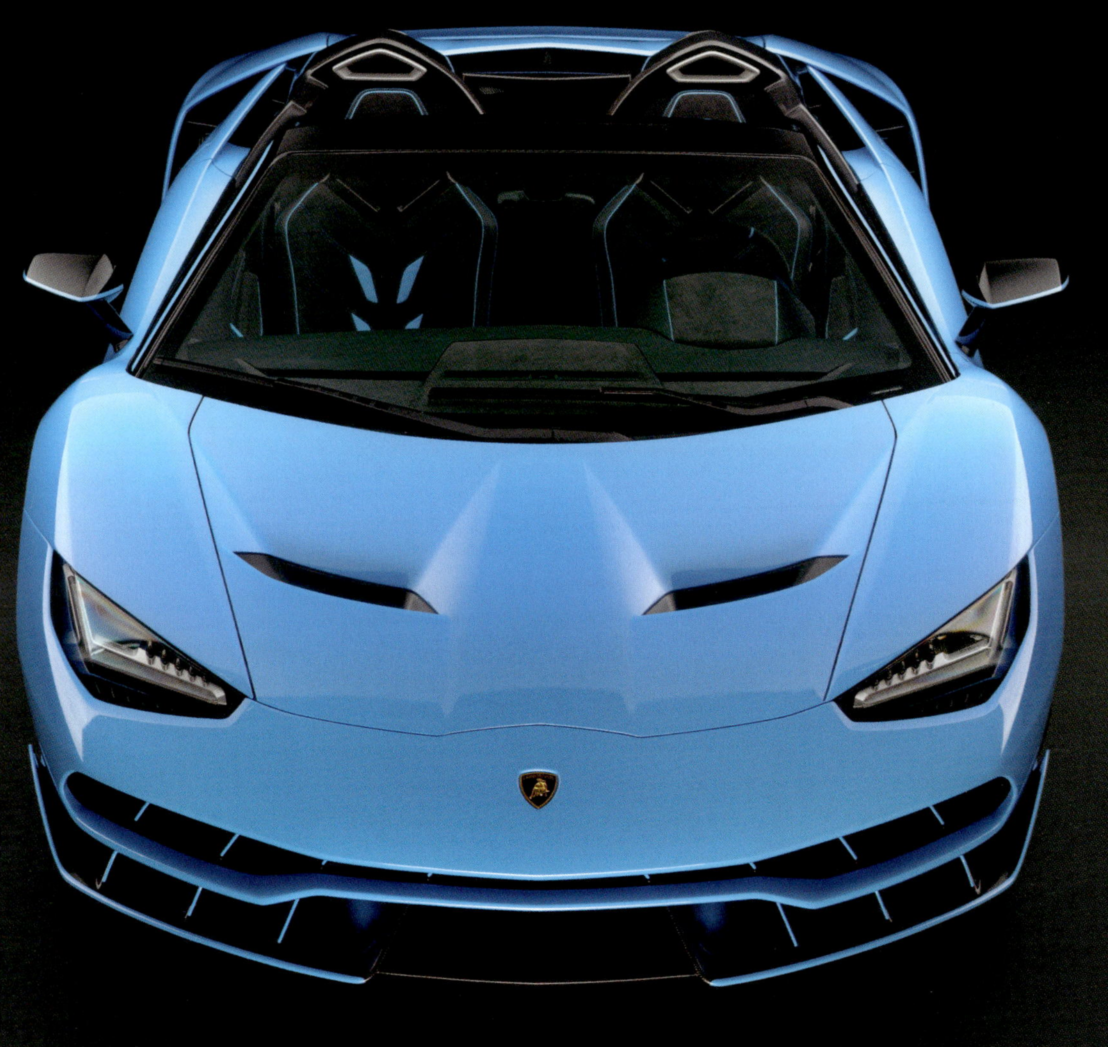

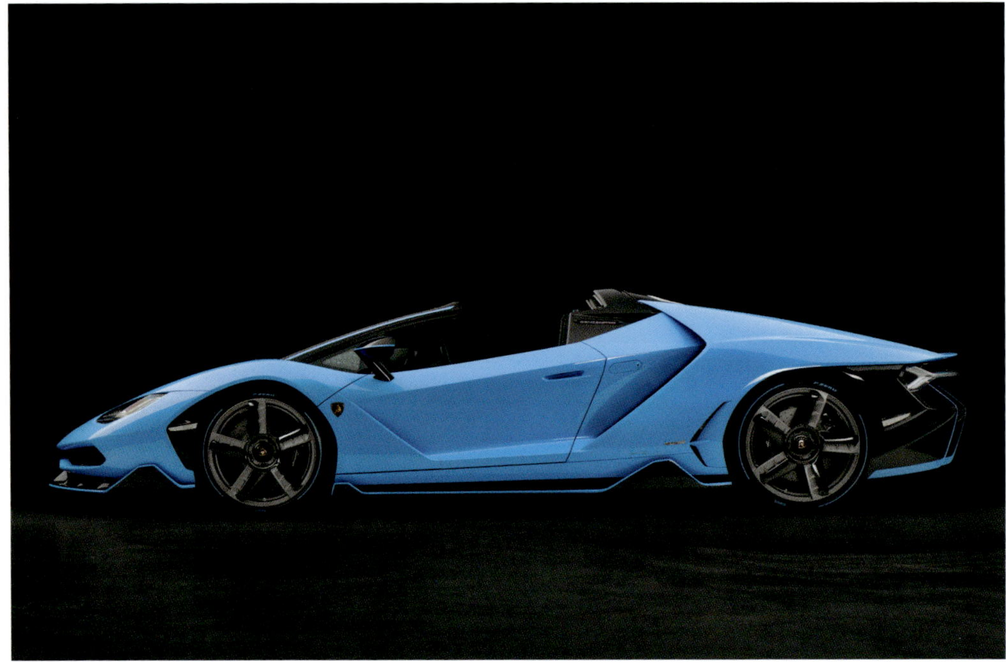

Above & opposite: A hyper performance-led car, the Lamborghini Centenario Roadster is built on a carbon fiber monocoque and the body parts are made of carbon fiber.

are the Centenario's enormous jutting diffuser set on top of its two-tiered front splitter as well as its electronically activated dual-plane rear wings, which considerably increase downforce in order to maximize agility and performance. But more than this, the limited-edition Coupé — restricted to a production run of just 20 examples — had a list price that reflected its exotic rarity. At $1.9 million, this stunning hypercar cost three times more than an Aventador, but that did not put off wealthy collectors as all 20 were snapped up immediately. Like other cars produced by the marque, the Centenario Coupé could also be fully personalized by its purchasers thanks to Lamborghini's Ad Personam service, which seemingly allows an infinite variety of interior choices and exterior finishes.

Later in 2016, the follow-up Centenario Roadster was premiered at The Quail, A Motorsports Gathering, during Monterey Car Week. This sensational open-top version of the Centenario — again produced in an exclusive limited edition of 20 examples — like its sibling Coupé was a masterful synthesis of automotive art and engineering; its fine detailing is utterly exemplary with each dynamic line flowing into the next and capturing that distinct edgy formal vocabulary so redolent of Lamborghini's supercar design DNA. Unsubtle and loud, this high-revving roadster brazenly announces its presence, yet for all its pent-up macho energy it boasts a remarkable sense of poise that is born of absolute design and engineering precision. In fact, this hypercar created by Centro Stile Lamborghini

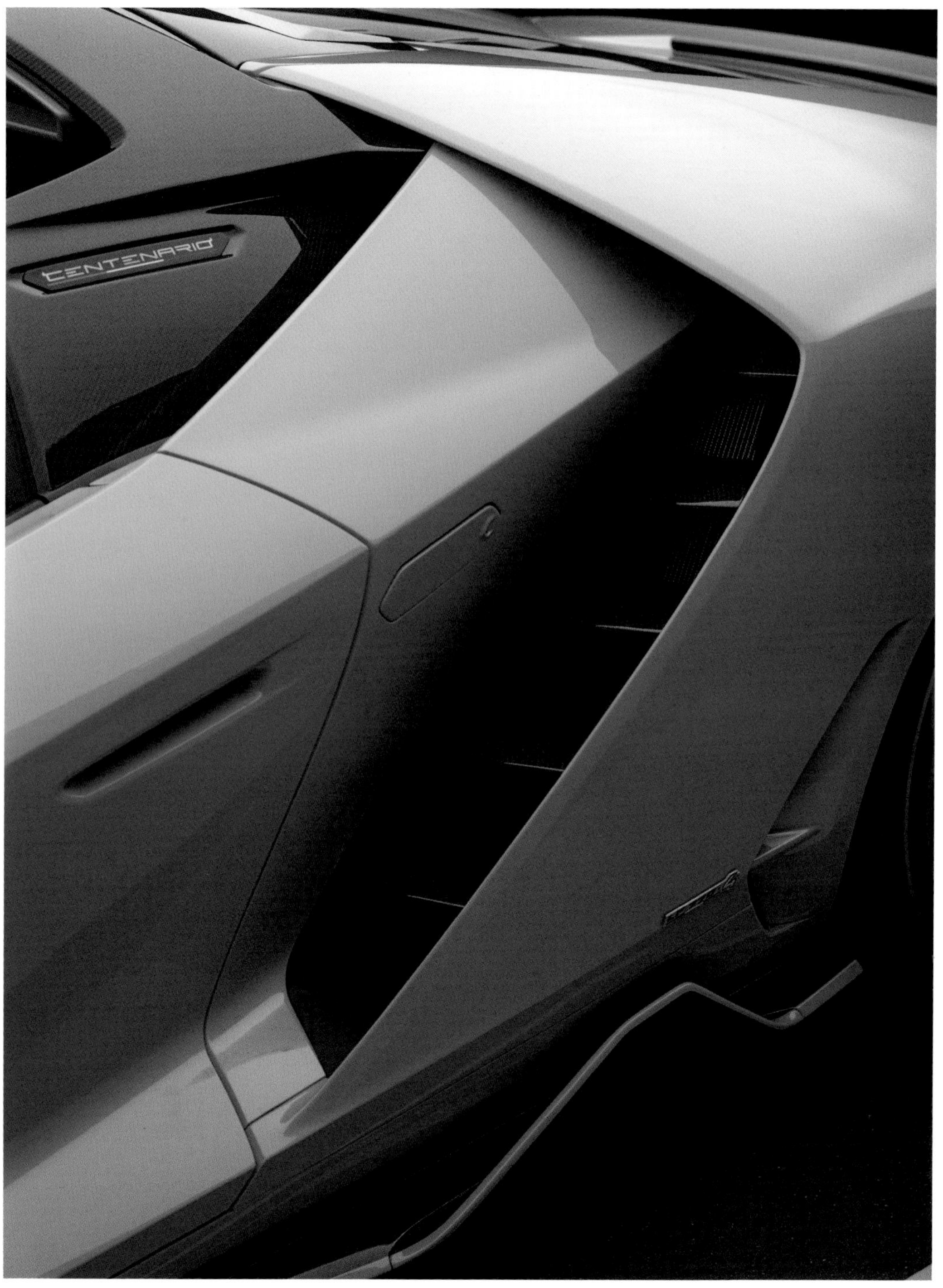
CENTENARIO

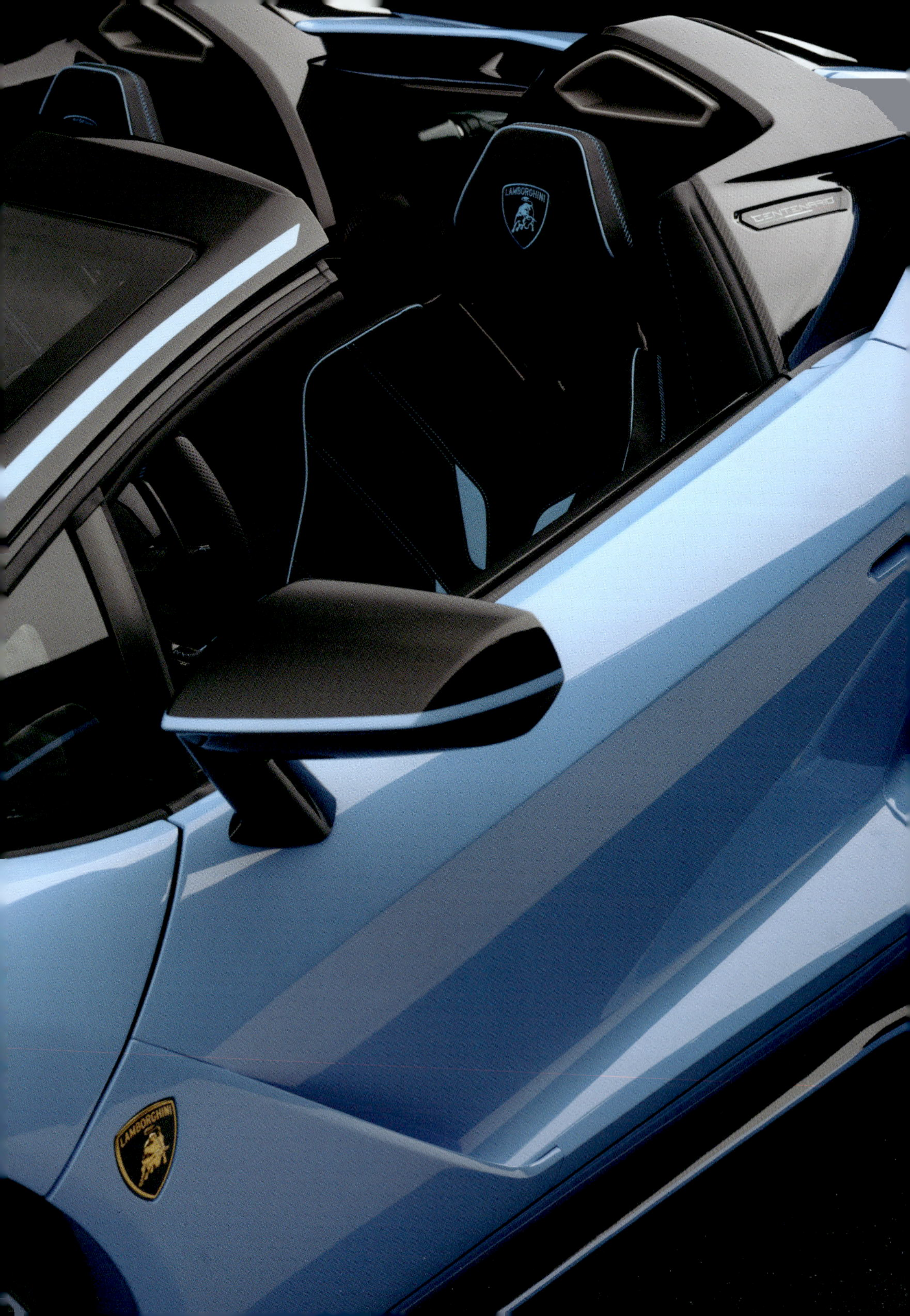
LAMBORGHINI
CENTENARIO
LAMBORGHINI

perfectly reflects the bold sculptural swagger of Italian design at its most stylishly ebullient. Known for experimenting with new cutting edge colors, Lamborghini designers developed special exterior colors, devised exclusively for the Centenario Roadster, to accentuate its dramatic profile. With its futuristic carapace-like body shell, the Centenario in both its guises is an undoubted tour de force of advanced aerodynamic design. As the marque's former CEO, Stefano Domenicali, observed of the roadster at its launch, "Lamborghini prides itself on the relentless pursuit of experimentation. We are proud to unleash Centenario's further potential in the form of a classic roadster; the perfect harmony between innovation and timeless design. This unique engineering achievement... embraces the freedom of a true open-top super sports car for a pure drive experience." Indeed, the Centenario Roadster is perhaps the most visceral Italian distillation of the hypercar genre created to date, and as such must be seen as a highly laudable next-level inheritor of Lamborghini's "ultimate car" mantle.

Below: The integrated rear diffuser dominates the back of the car, its large size optimizing air flow distribution, maximizing the car's downforce and aesthetically emphasizing the importance of aerodynamics in the Centenario. An extendable rear wing is also neatly integrated into the tail section.

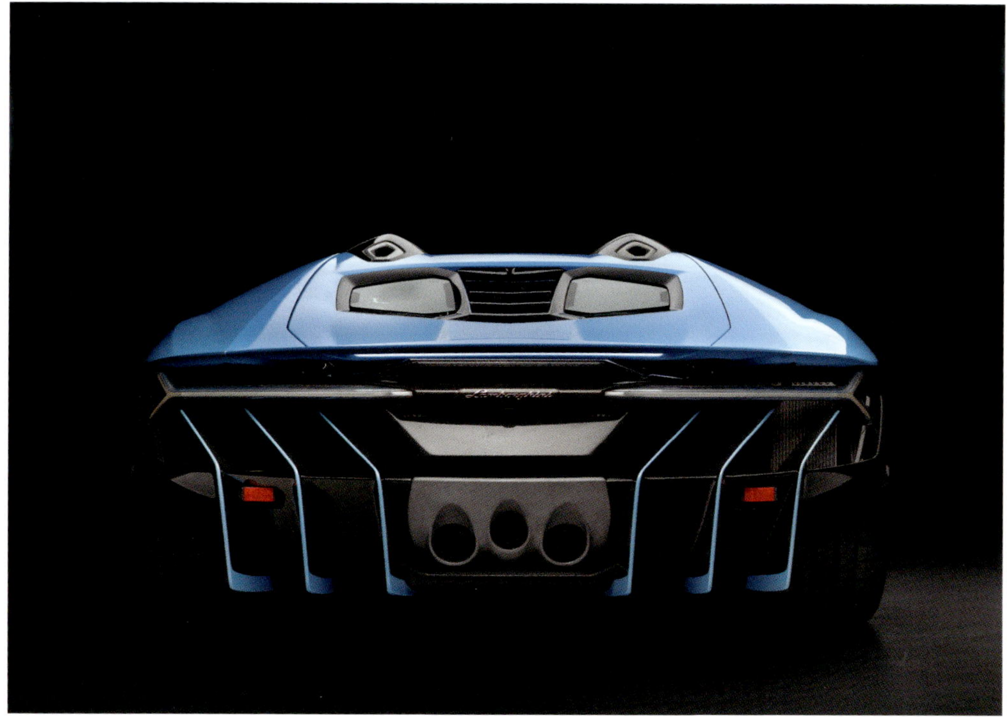

2016

McLaren P1 LM

MANUFACTURED 2016 | ENGINE 3,994 cc (244 cu. in.), DOHC per bank V8 & electric motor | HORSEPOWER 1,000 combined (803 hp & 197 hp) TOP SPEED 345 km/h (214 mph) | TRANSMISSION 7-speed dual-clutch automatic NUMBER PRODUCED 5 & 1 prototype

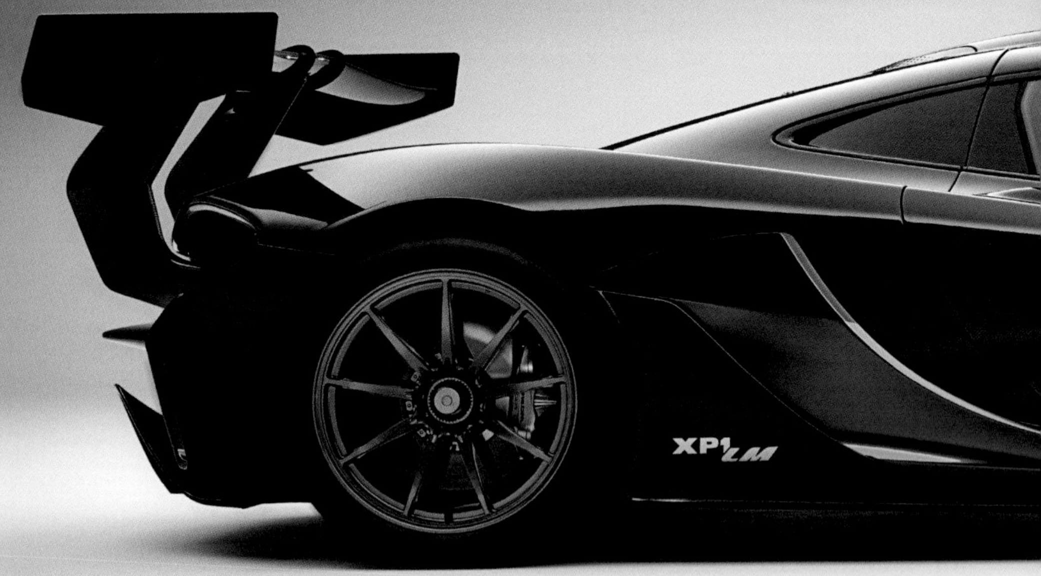

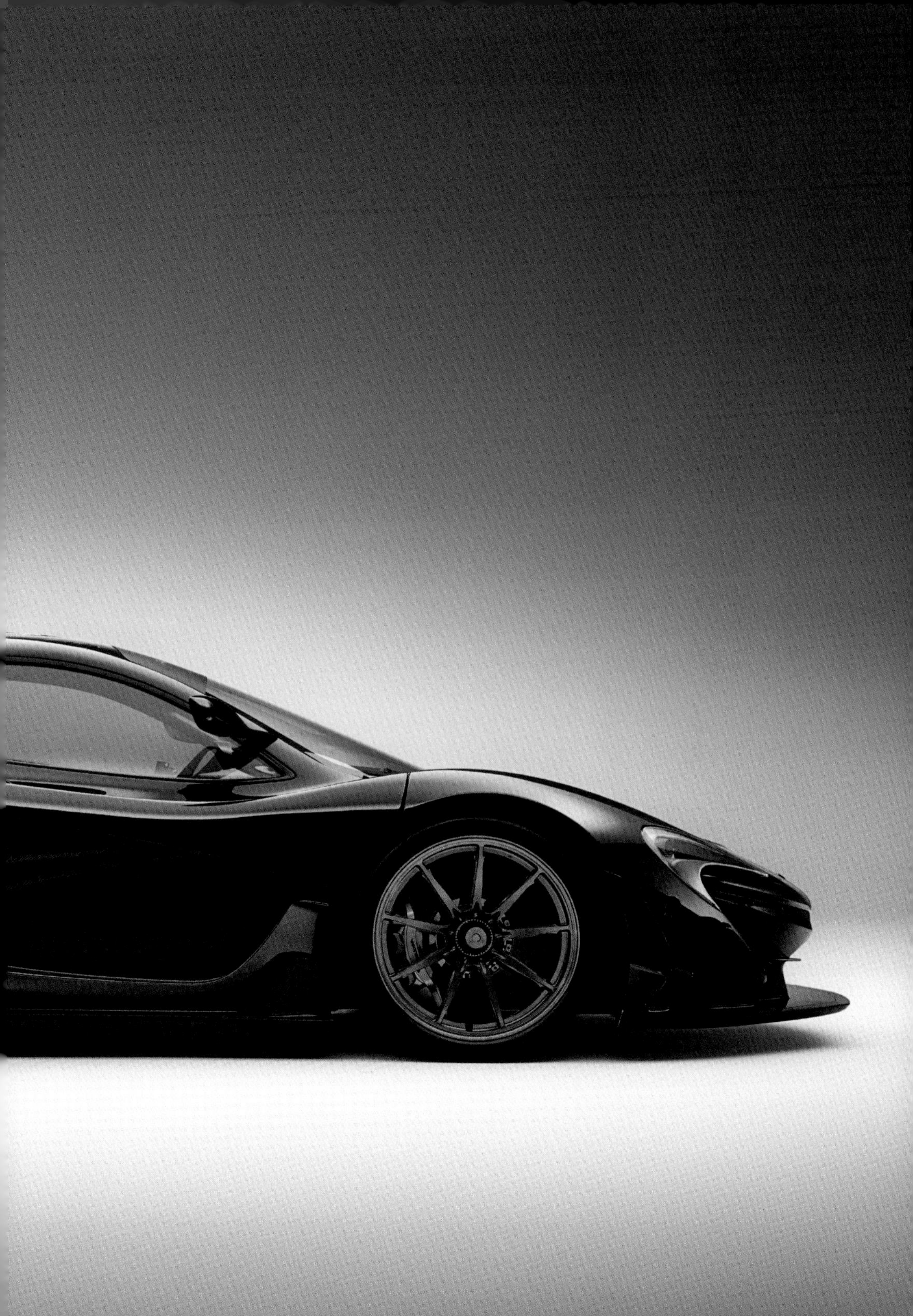

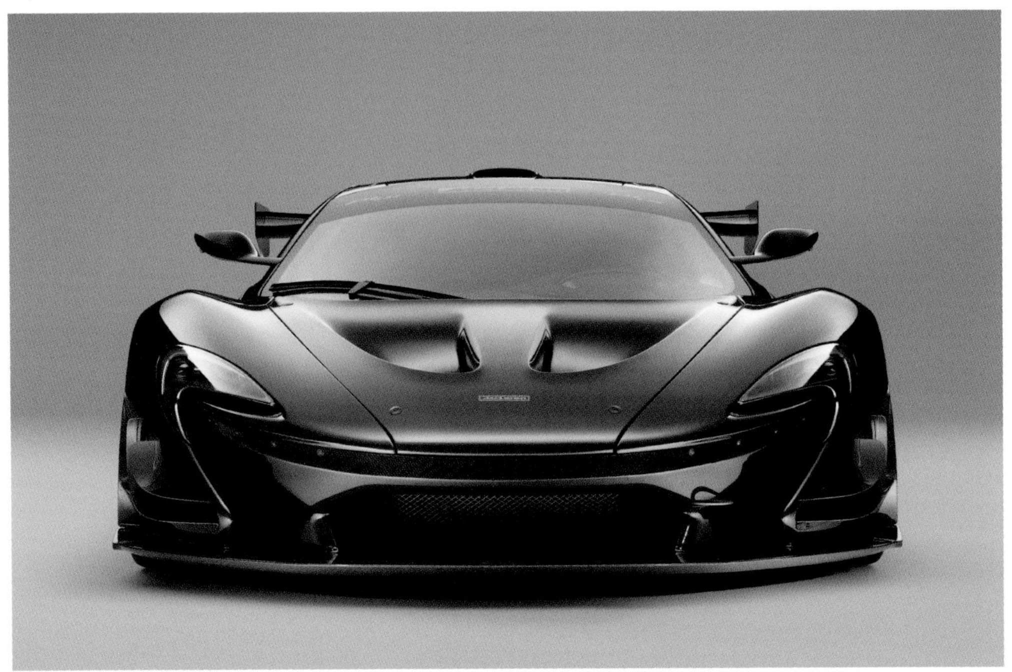

When the McLaren P1 debuted at the 2012 Paris Motor Show there was a lot of speculation as to whether it would be a creditable successor to the legendary F1, which though introduced 20 years earlier was still seen as one of the greatest auto-engineering achievements ever. Following in the F1's tracks was never going to be easy, yet McLaren's design and engineering team were determined to do just this with the creation of a 21st century hybrid hypercar. During the intervening two decades between the launches of these two vehicles a lot had happened in the world of automotive design with the tools of the trade having been utterly transformed by the digital revolution that heralded a new transformative age of highly sophisticated CAD/CAM technology. These new tools enabled the creation of much more complex "fat-free" forms. As with the construction of cars for Formula 1 competition, the earlier F1 had been an obsessive exercise in weight reduction in order to enhance speed, acceleration, handling and fuel economy. This same approach was carried through to the design and development of the P1, so that it possessed not a single extraneous detail and its data-fed undulating surfaces were as aerodynamically efficient as possible, all for the sake of maximizing performace.

As McLaren explains, "The bodywork is 'shrink-wrapped' as tightly as possible over the mechanical hard points of the car and the cockpit sits right at the centre. This approach helps to reduce frontal surface area, but also makes it easier to manage airflow over the surface of the bodywork and into the engine's roof snorkel intake and to the active aero components." This tight-skinning approach twinned with ensuring that all the mechanical elements lurking underneath are fitted together as closely as possible provides functional

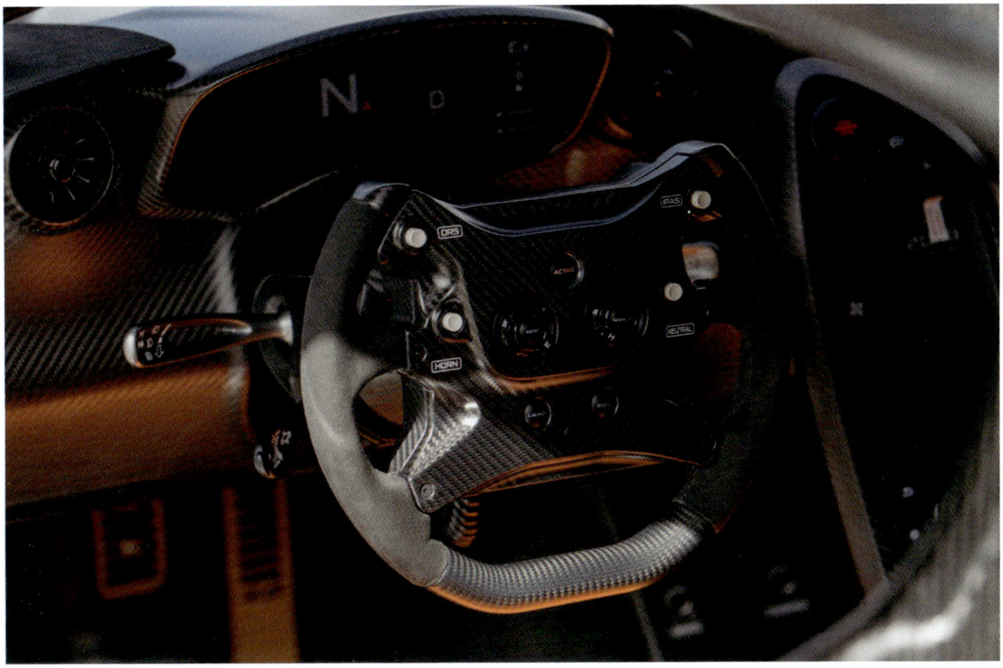
N
IPAS
DRS
ACTIVE
NEUTRAL
HORN

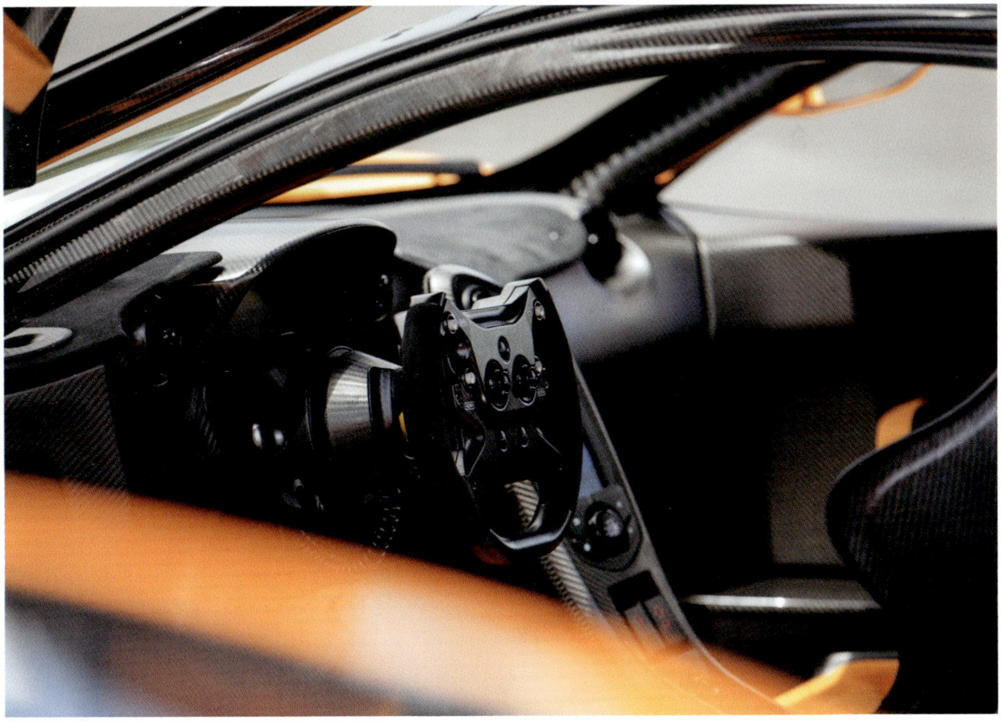

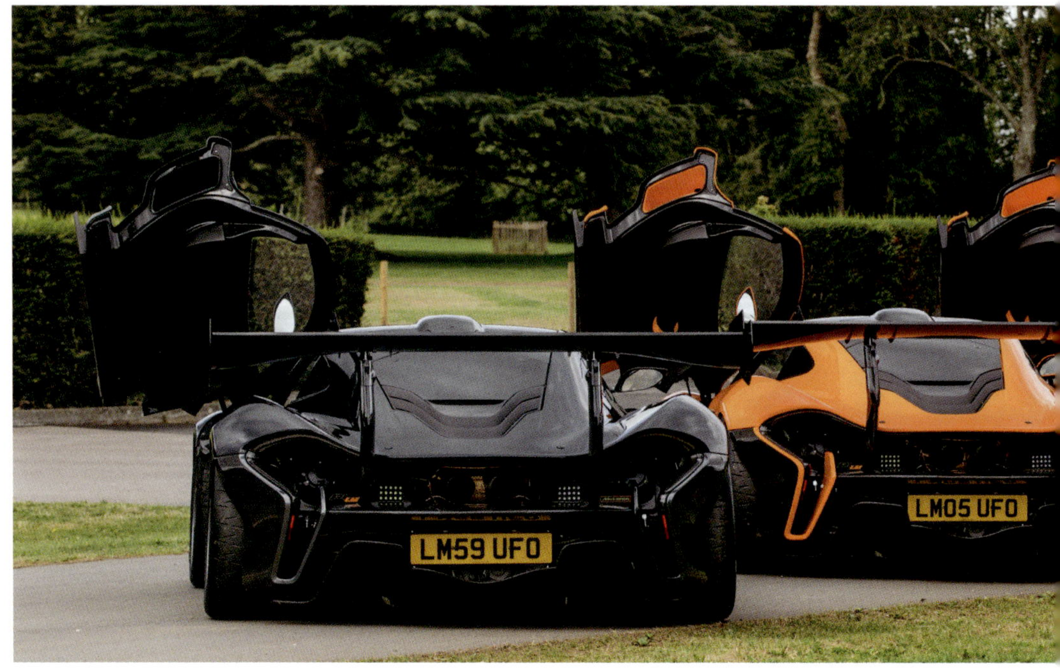

Above: A line up of the six McLaren P1 LMs photographed at Goodwood in 2016. The XP1 prototype is on the left.

efficiency and a gorgeous form-follows-function aesthetic. The oft-used saying in the aviation industry, "If it looks right, it flies right," could equally pertain to the P1 — for its dramatic visual "rightness" is fundamentally an outcome of its purposeful design-engineering. As McLaren's Design Director, Frank Stephenson, further explains, "It's as though we stuck a tube inside and sucked all the air out — a dramatic, honest shape but also a very beautiful one. It was all part of the engineering and design approach to fanatically take out weight." In fact, the complexity of the technology found onboard the P1 is more akin to an aircraft than a conventional car, but then it was always intended as a showpiece of McLaren's superlative engineering know-how. The car's mid-mounted V8 was derived from the earlier McLaren 12C's engine, however, it was fitted with larger high-pressure dual-turbochargers and twinned with a potent hybrid powertrain developed to cope with the challenges of endurance track use. Meanwhile the P1's active aerodynamics maximize downforce, while its RCC (Race Active Chassis Control) system provides the chassis with unparalleled adjustability.

Just as McLaren created a race-going variant of the immortal F1, so the marque also created a track-only GTR version of the P1 after all of the 375 "standard" units had been sold out in celebration of the 20th anniversary of the company's F1 GTR 's

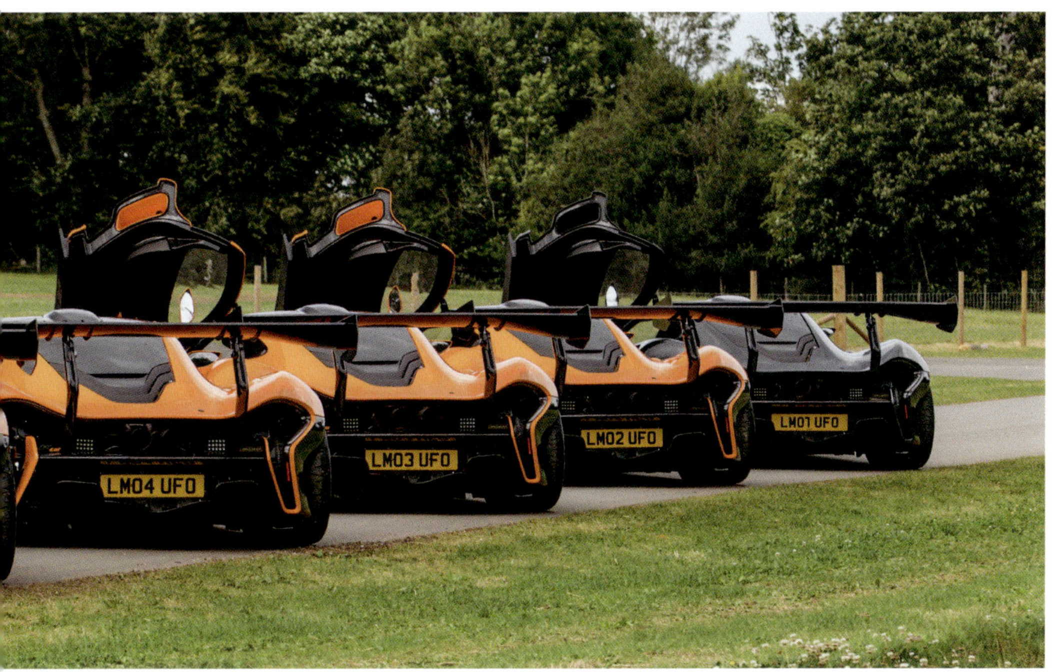

victory at Le Mans in 1995. This stripped-down racer was debuted as a concept at the 2014 Pebble Beach Concours d'Elegance. A total of 58 P1 GTRs were subsequently constructed between 2015 and 2016. By late 2015, however, the Hampshire-based automotive specialist Lanzante — the race team that had so memorably driven the on-loan McLaren F1 GTR prototype to glorious victory at the 1995 24 Hours of Le Mans — was undertaking street-legal conversions of P1 GTRs for clients who wanted to use their race-ready machines on the road. In 2016, with the production of the P1 GTRs complete, Lanzante commissioned McLaren's special ops division to create a further six P1 GTRs so that it could develop them into a special edition (five plus one prototype) of road legal LM variants. These super-rare Lanzante McLarens underwent various performance-enhancing modifications, including uprated drivetrain hardware, a gold-plated engine bay for better heat shielding, redesigned lightweight intercoolers able to operate more efficiently at higher temperatures, a restyled rear wing and larger front splitter and dive planes to improve aerodynamic performance, in addition to a host of weight-lightening material modifications to the car's windows, seats and exhausts among other components. All these better-by-design tweaks helped increase output to a combined 1,000 hp and achieve a weight reduction of 60 kilograms (132 lb.) as compared to the P1 GTR as well as a 40% increase in downforce.

The example, shown here, is the XP1 LM prototype, in which Kenny Bräck set the fastest time (47.07 seconds) for a road car up the Goodwood hill climb at the 2016 Goodwood Festival of Speed. He then set the fastest lap for a road car at the Nürburgring in 2017, but because the XP1 LM ran without a front number plate, it was not deemed official.

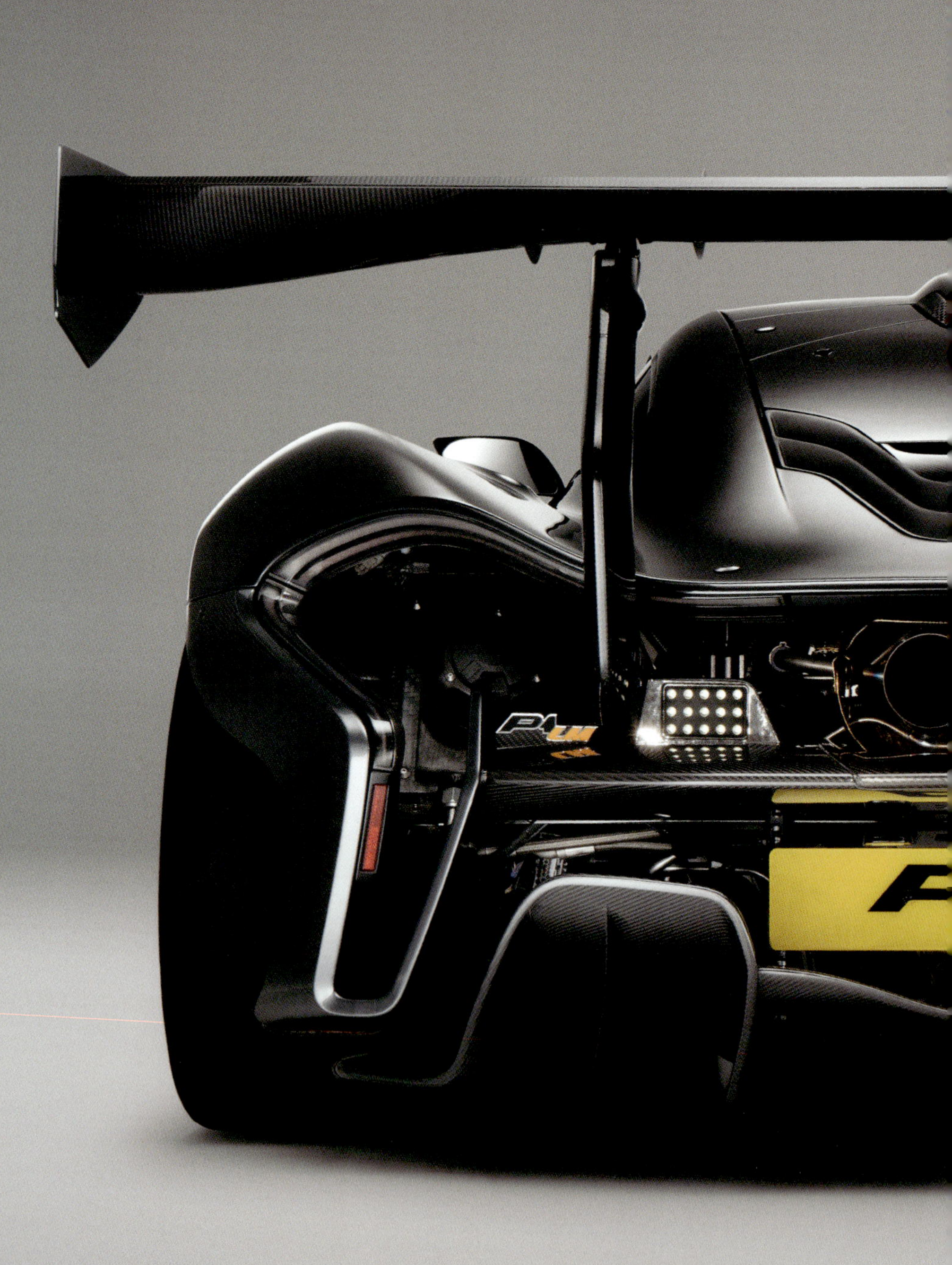

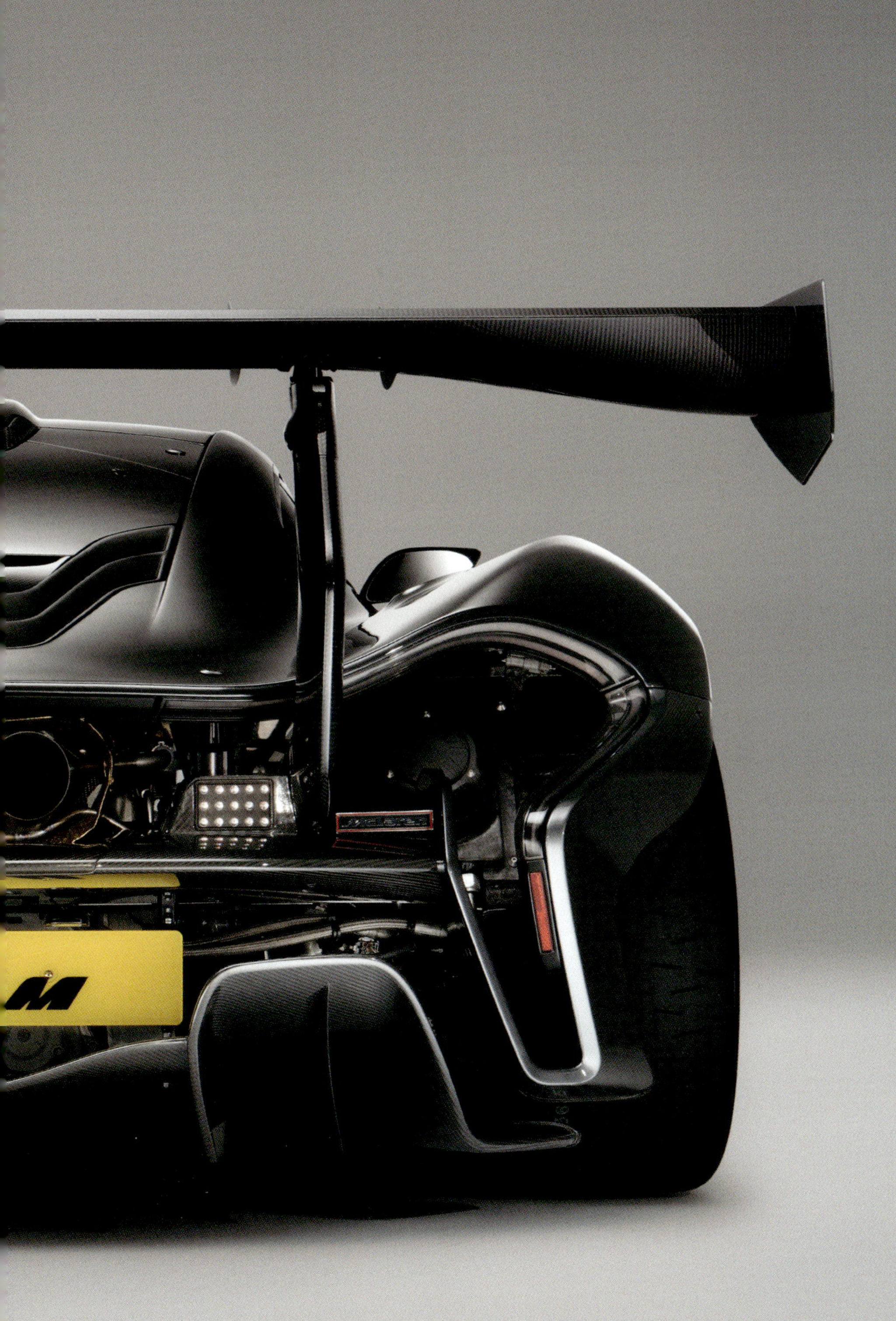

2017

Ferrari LaFerrari Aperta

MANUFACTURED 2016–18 | **ENGINE** 6,262 cc (382 cu. in.), DOHC per bank V12 & electric motor | **HORSEPOWER** 950 combined (789 hp & 161 hp) | **TOP SPEED** 350+ km/h (217+ mph)
TRANSMISSION 7-speed dual-clutch automated manual
NUMBER PRODUCED 210

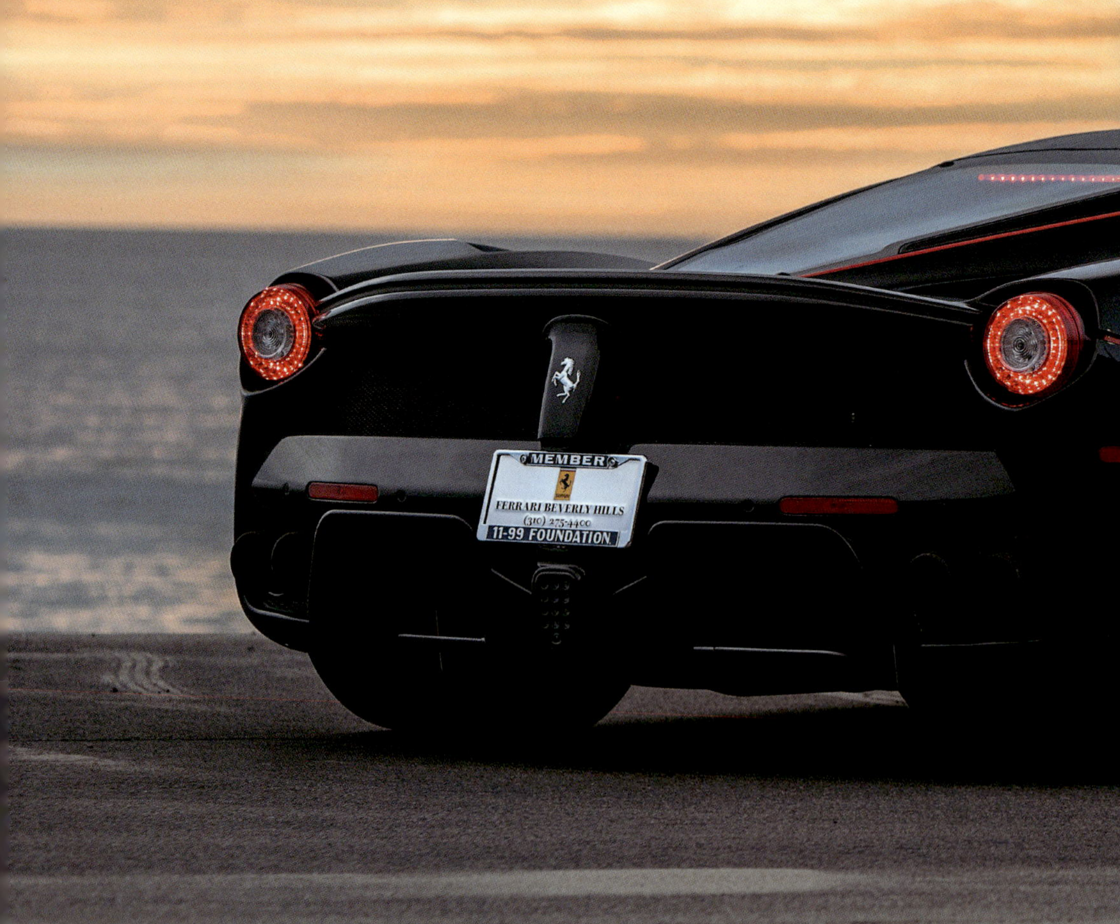

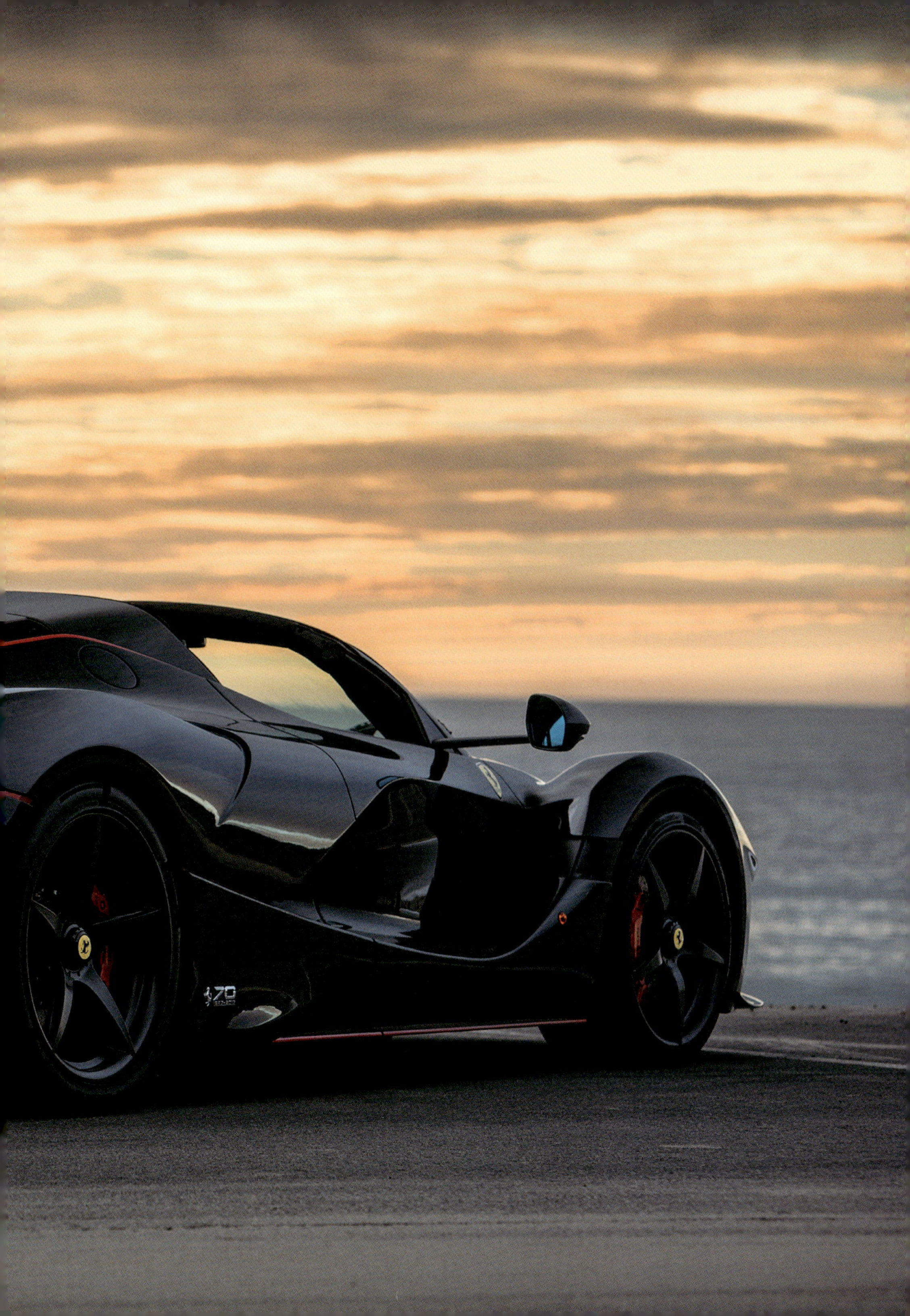

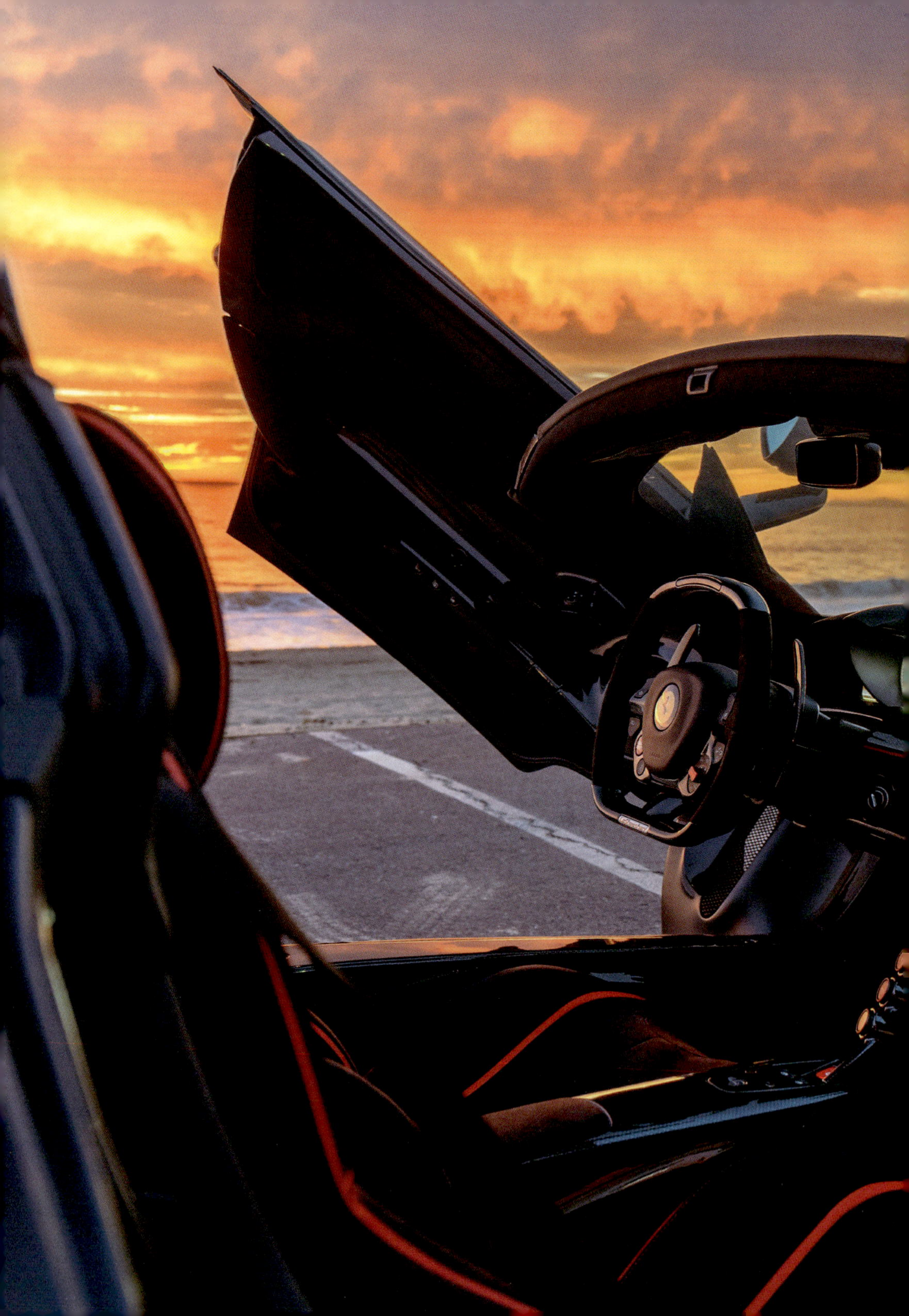

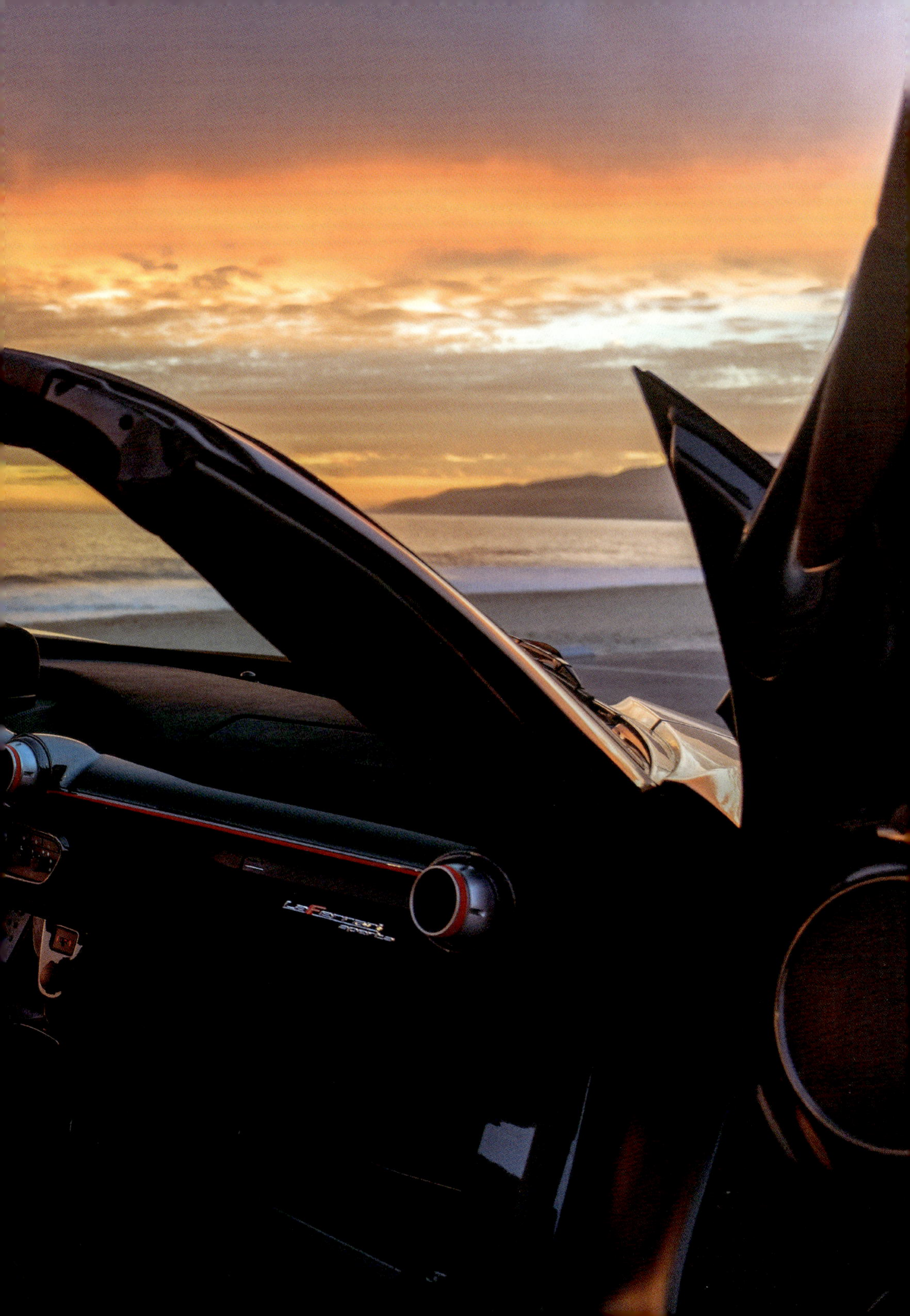

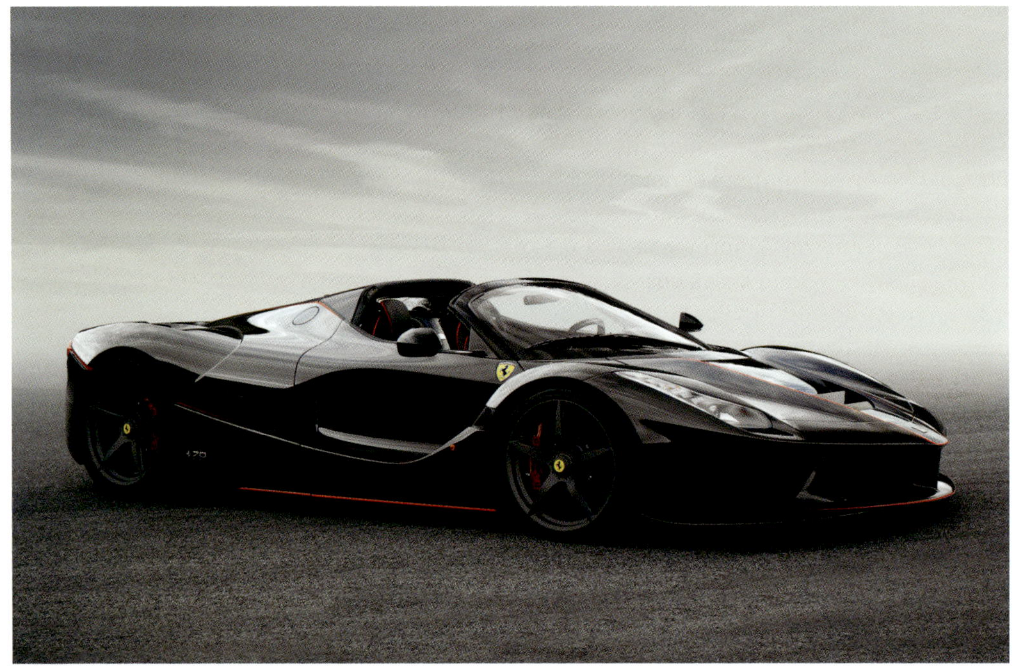

Described by Ferrari as a "futuristic and absolutely extreme car" the LaFerrari Aperta is an open-top version of the fabled LaFerrari hybrid hypercar (2013) and was introduced in 2016. With a top speed of over 350 km/h (217 mph) maxing out this vehicle without a roof in place, on the rare occassion when this might be possible, must be an astonishing and utterly thrilling experience. With its 6.2-liter quad-cam V12 and 120 kilowatt electric motor producing a combined 950 hp, this is a model that is by anyone's standard a complete beast. Nestled under its aerodynamic bodywork, the car's hybrid powertrain utilizes Formula 1 KERS (kinetic energy recovery system) technology that has been specially engineered for road use. When the engine is let loose by depressing the car's bright red ignition button, it emits a bloodcurdling howl, which is a suitable foretelling of the Aperta's heart-stopping acceleration of 0–200 km/h (124 mph) in less than seven seconds. This impressive performance is also aided and abeted by the roadster's fluid aerodynamic lines.

When developing the Aperta, Ferrari's engineering team was determined to achieve the same drag coefficient as its hard-topped brother and so skillfully manipulated the airflow by repositioning its radiators among other things. As the company explains, "In terms of open-top aerodynamic comfort, an innovative integrated system was developed. The high-speed airflow that would otherwise enter the cabin from top of the windscreen is captured by an angled wind-stop fixed to the parcel shelf. The wind-stop is angled to channel the flow through spaces in the car's interior structure before exiting at a slower speed behind the passenger seats." The upshot of all this is that the Aperta enjoys similar levels of driving comfort to other less-extreme convertibles in Ferrari's stable thanks to this drag-reducing setup. Various modifications were also made to the LaFerrari's existing chassis, with its carbon tub reengineered, so that this follow-up model would boast the same torsional rigidity and beam stiffness despite its open-top layout.

As with the LaFerrari coupé the Aperta's active aerodynamics and hybrid system are not only integrated, but are constantly interacting with its other dynamic control systems thanks to the employment of Ferrari's clever proprietary algorithms. This provides the car with exhilarating performance that is lightning-quick in its responsiveness. And with all this power urging to break out, the Aperta has been equipped with a Brembo braking system that has been specially developed to incorporate discs made of an advanced carbon ceramic in order to aid rapid heat dissipation. Although this is very much a 21st-century hypercar Ferrari has managed to imbue the Aperta with a number of classic Ferrari styling cues, which gives it a lot of character and emotional pull.

First unveiled at the Paris Motor Show in 2016, the Aperta was aimed, as Ferrari noted at the time, specifically at "clients and collectors that refuse to compromise on the joy of drop-top driving even when at the wheel of a supercar." Originally priced at $2.2 million, only 200 examples of the Aperta were initially made available for sale, all of which were presold following a special preview for "listed" clients, all of whom already owned a LaFerrari coupé. Then a further ten examples were constructed, nine of which were subsequently used by Ferrari during its 70th anniversary celebrations in 2017. As

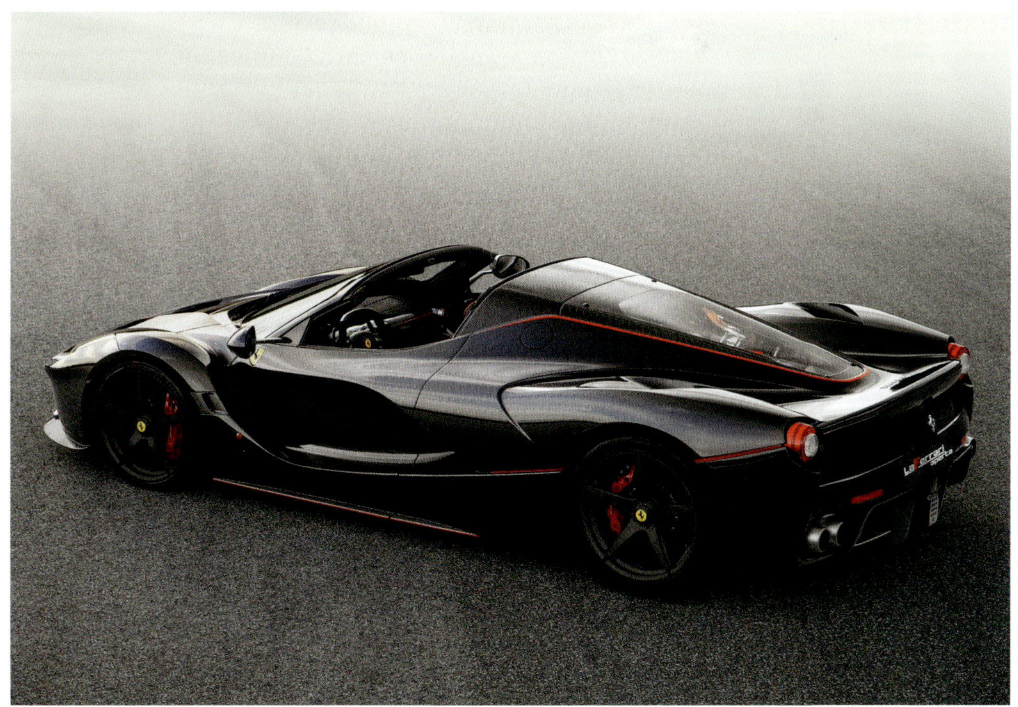

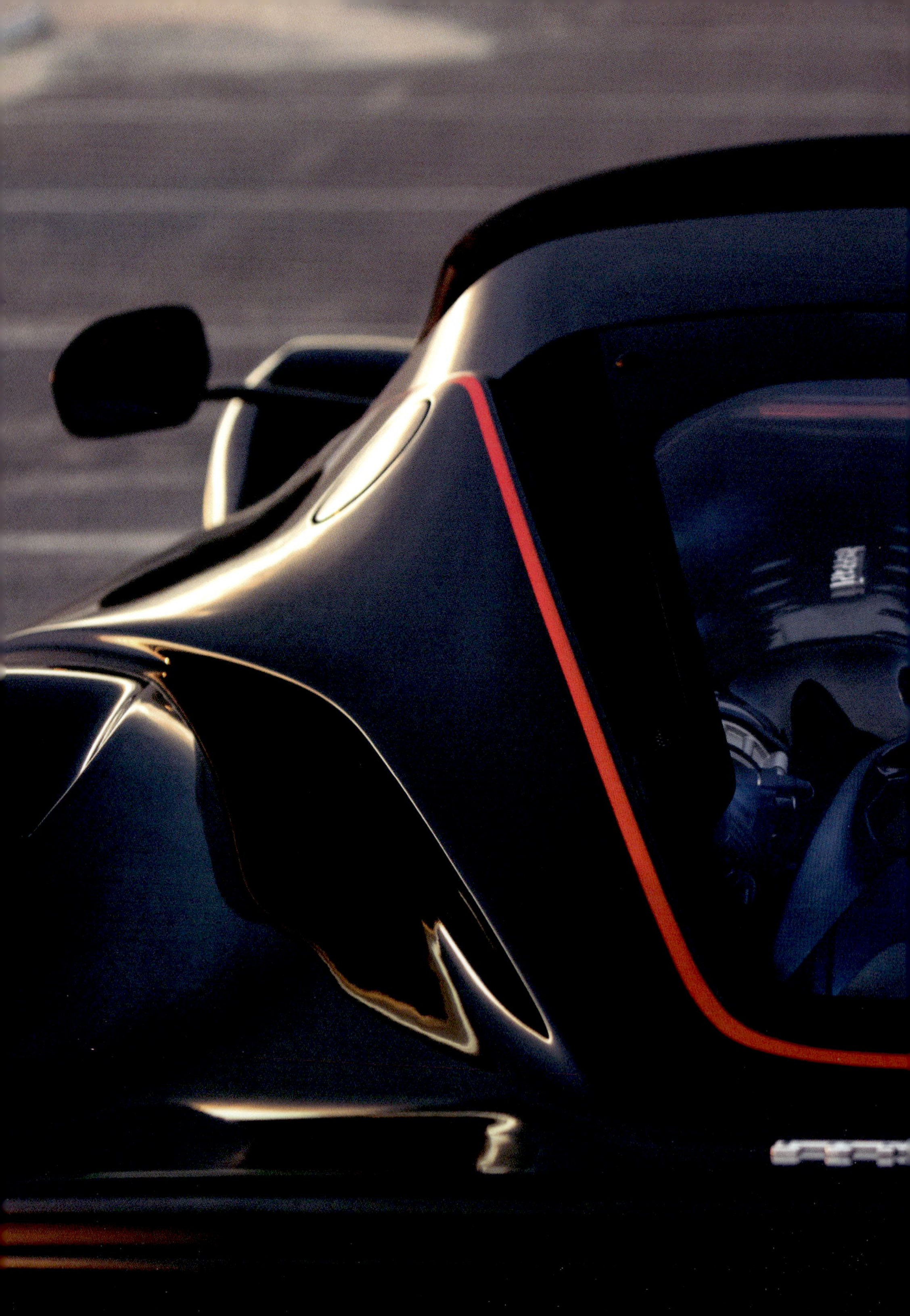

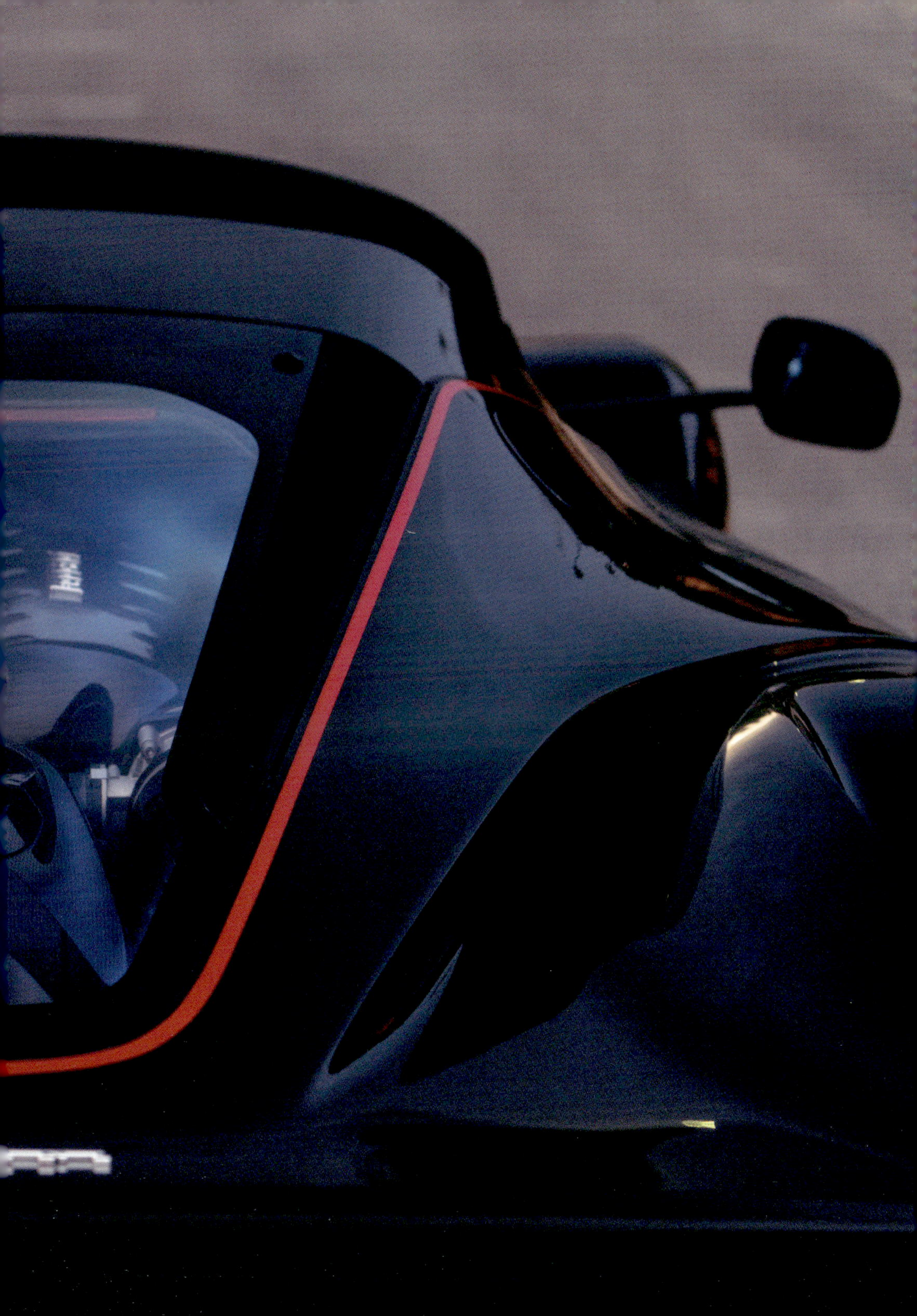

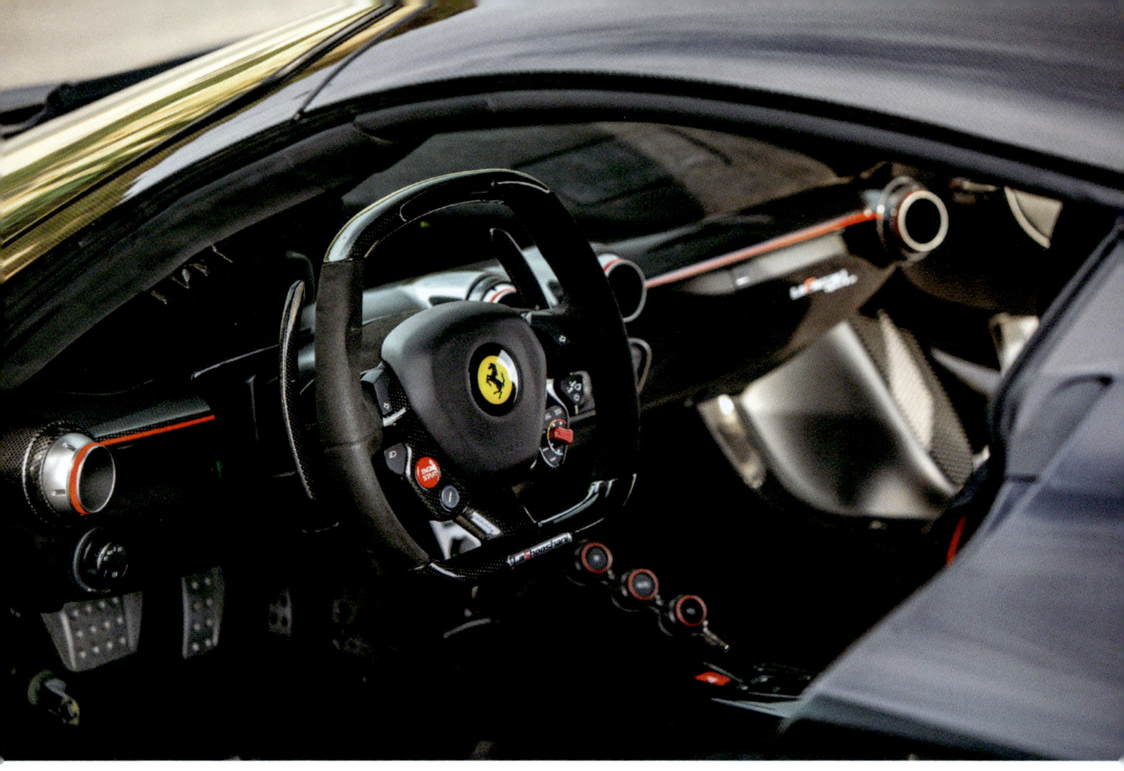

a limited-edition special series of one of Ferrari's most stunning cars to date, the Aperta is everything a Ferrari collector could possibly wish for — rare, beautiful and providing a thrilling level of high performance. As Ben Miller of *CAR* magazine noted after a test drive on a winding Italian road, the Aperta's responsiveness was akin to "a kind of physical poetry." There is no doubt that the car is a complete masterpiece of Italian design and engineering at its very best. And, what is more, the Aperta perfectly embodies the 21st-century spirit of Ferrari, which has been honed and passionately evolved over its 70-year history with a succession of remarkable models that have consistently raised the bar both technically and aesthetically.

The fine Aperta, shown here (chassis no. ZFF86ZHA2H0224581), features a striking color scheme of Nero Daytona with bright red accents both for its exterior and interior, an option that was only ever made available for this specific model. As an all-options specced example, it also boasts "the full carbon package," which includes a detachable roof panel made of exposed carbon fiber. When it came up for sale at RM Sotheby's in 2019, this Maranello-bred black beauty had only around 1,500 miles (ca. 2,400 Km) on its odometer, making it a serious contender for any world-class collection of Ferraris.

Previous: Detail of LaFerrari Aperta engine cover.

Opposite & overleaf: The striking red accents throughout the Nero Daytona exterior and interior is a feature that was done only for the Aperta.

Below: Cutaway drawing of the Ferrari LaFerrari showing the mid-mounted all-alloy 6,262 cc (382 cu. in.), direct fuel-injected DOHC per bank 48-valve 65° V12 engine, which is this hybrid hypercar's principal source of propulsion producing on its own 789 hp, and the 120-kilowatt electric motor that provides an additional 161 hp. The electric motor was developed in conjunction with Magneti Marelli and offers the same torque density and efficiency as the KERS motor used in Ferrari's F1 race cars.

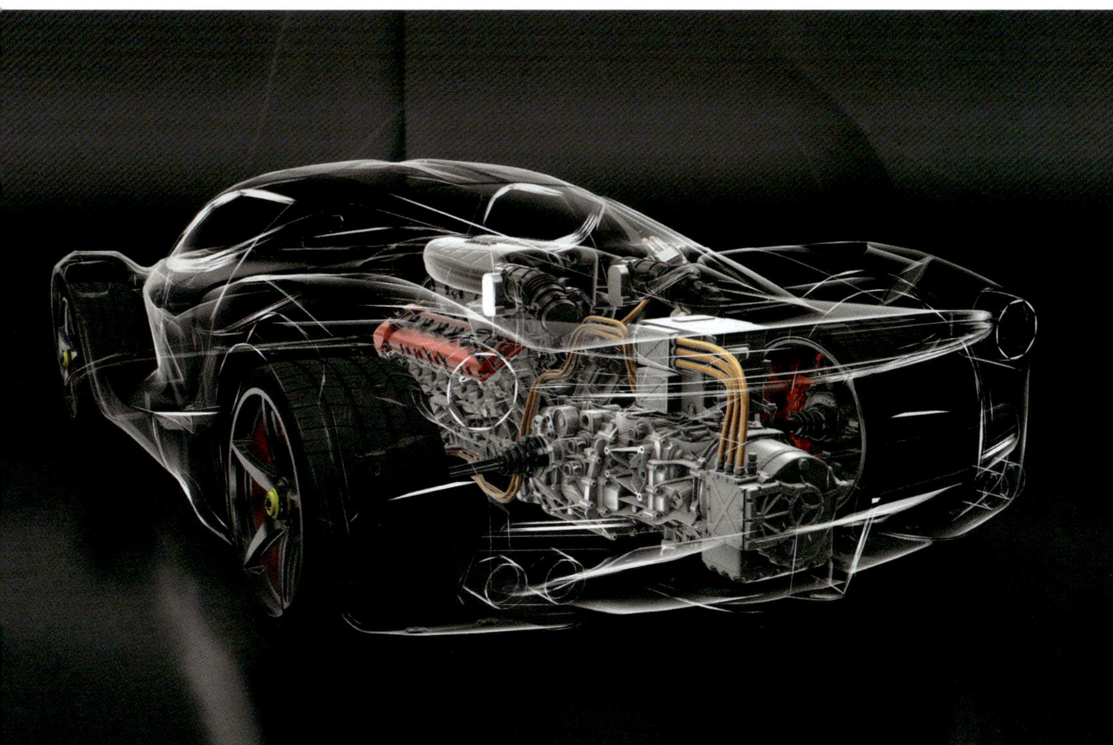

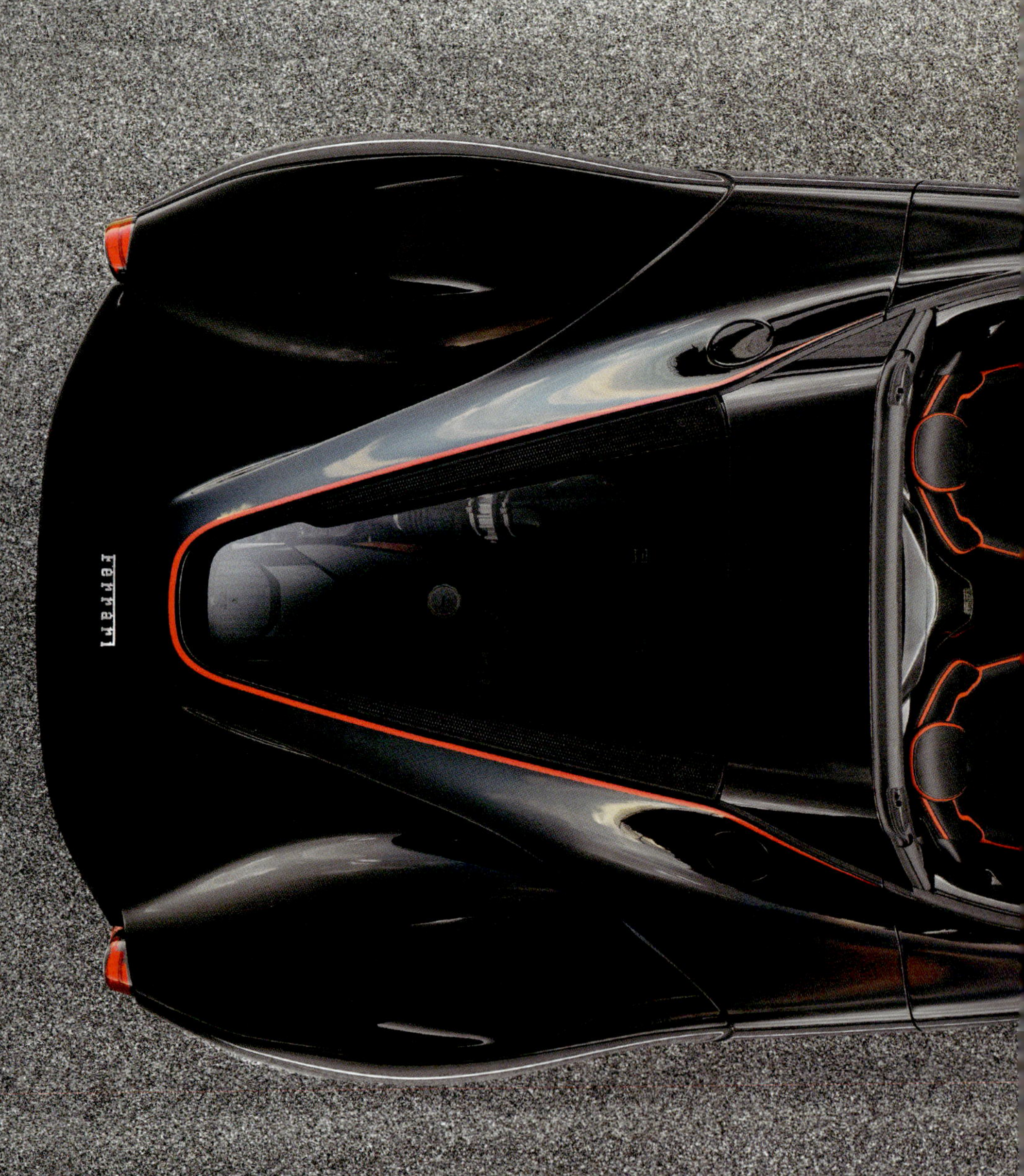

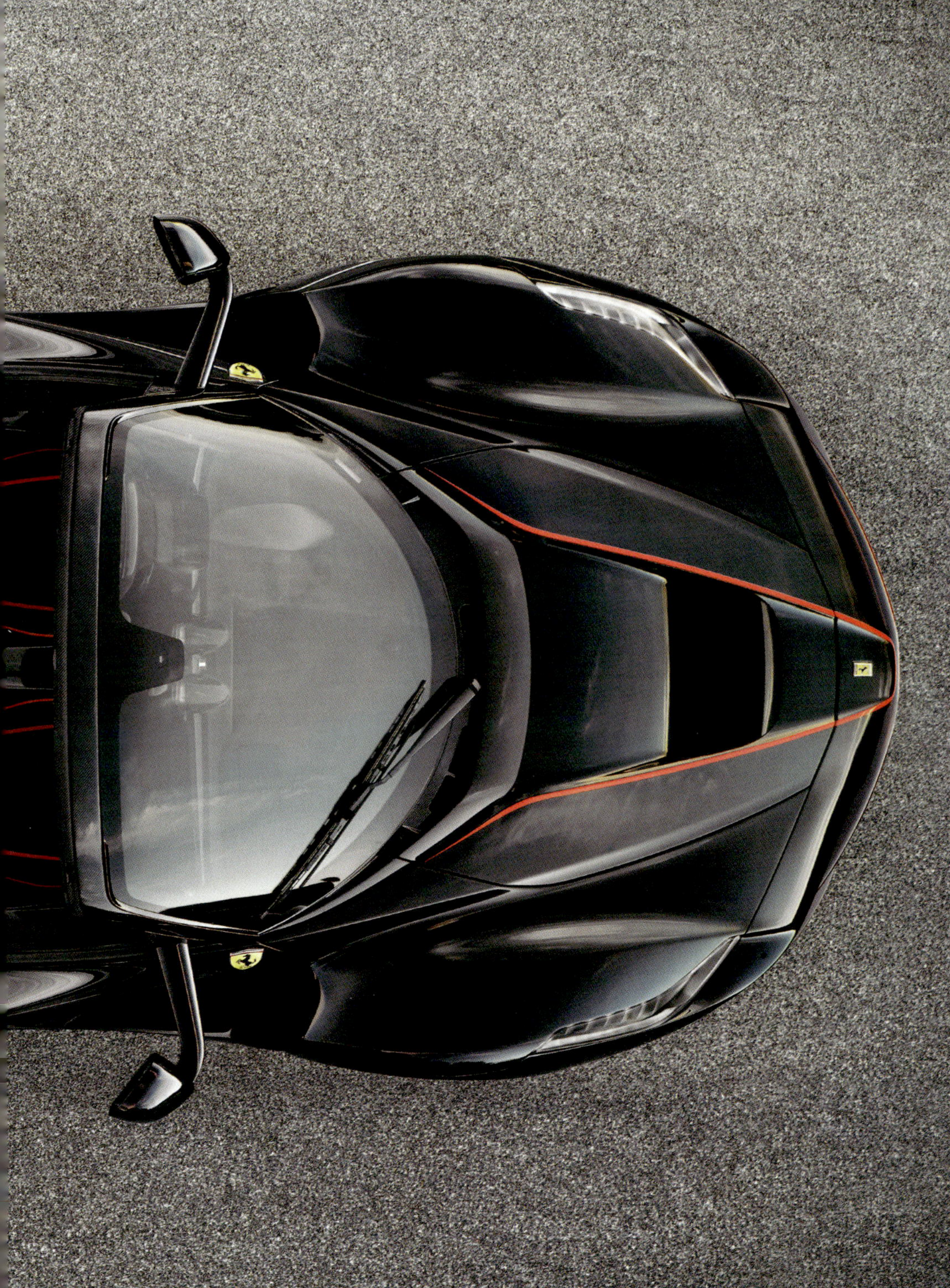

2020

Aston Martin Valkyrie

MANUFACTURED 2020–21 | ENGINE 6,500 cc (397 cu. in.), DOHC per bank 65° V12 & electric motor
HORSEPOWER 1,160 combined (1,000 hp & 160 hp)
TOP SPEED 402 km/h (250 mph) | TRANSMISSION 7-speed automatic
NUMBER PRODUCED 150 & 25 competition variants

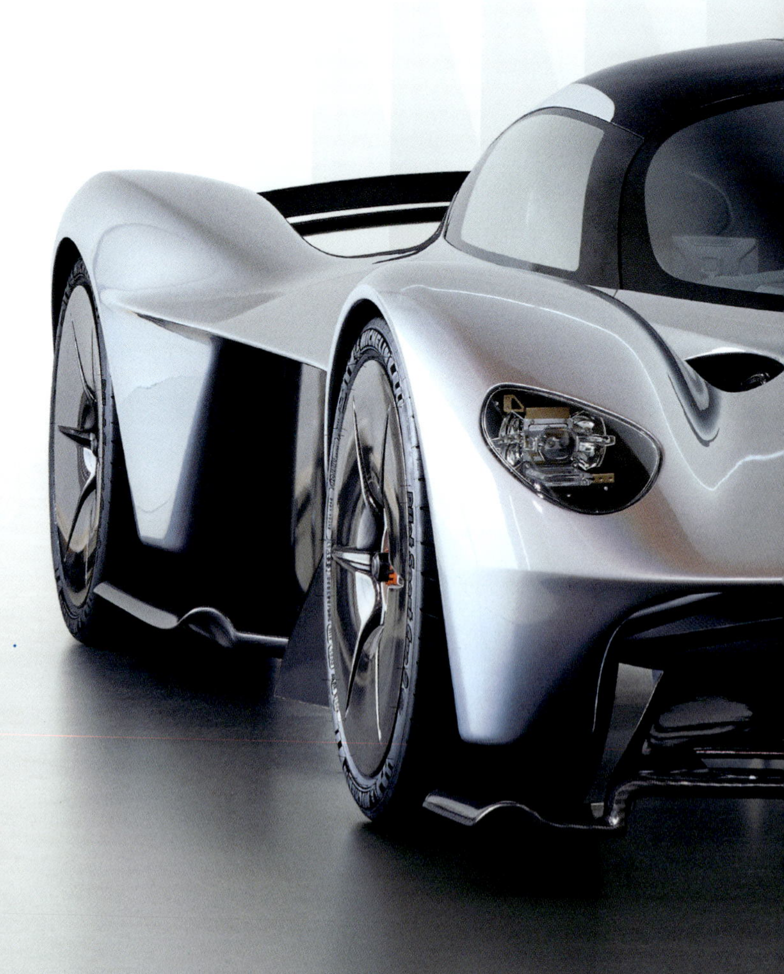

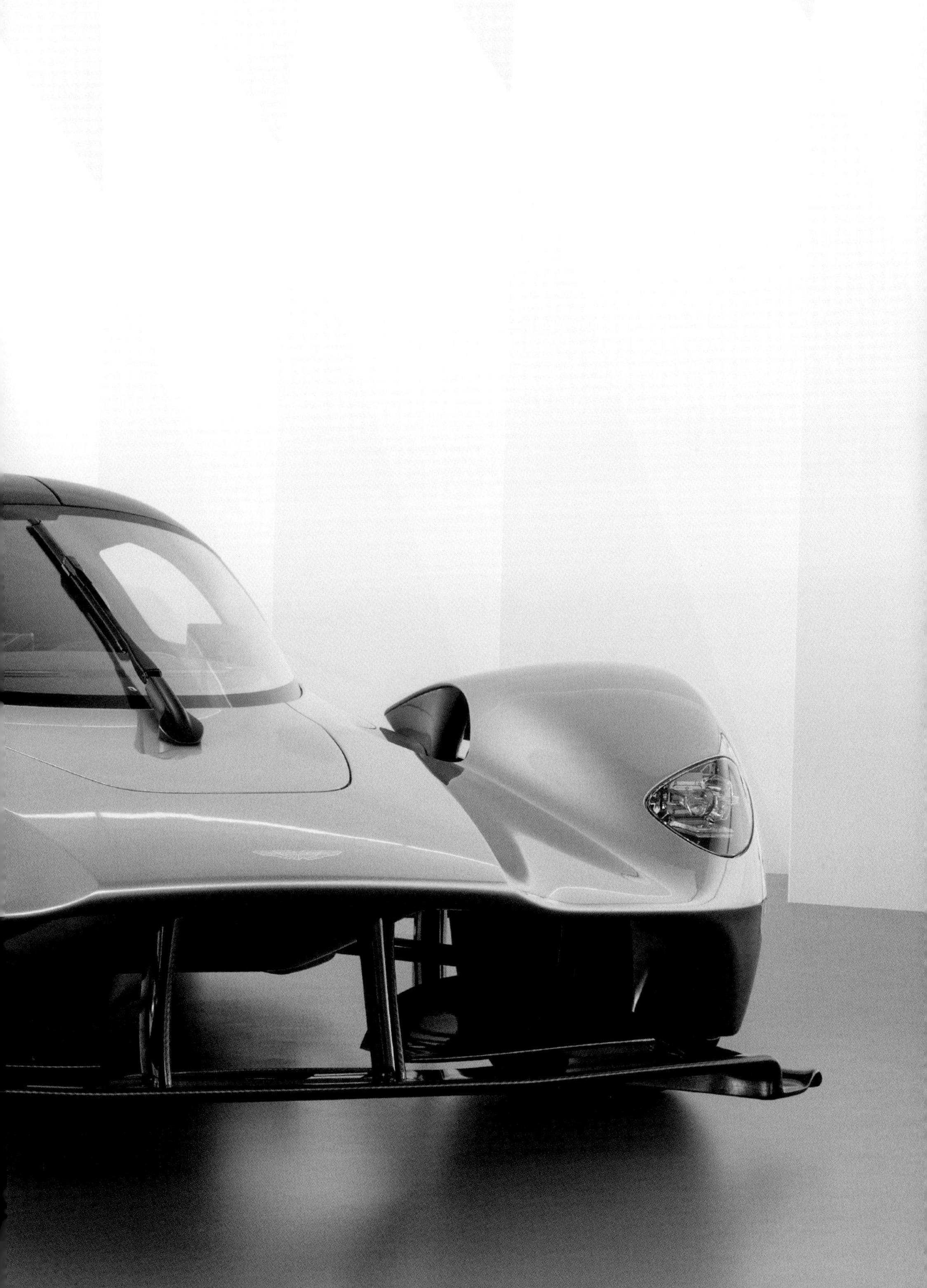

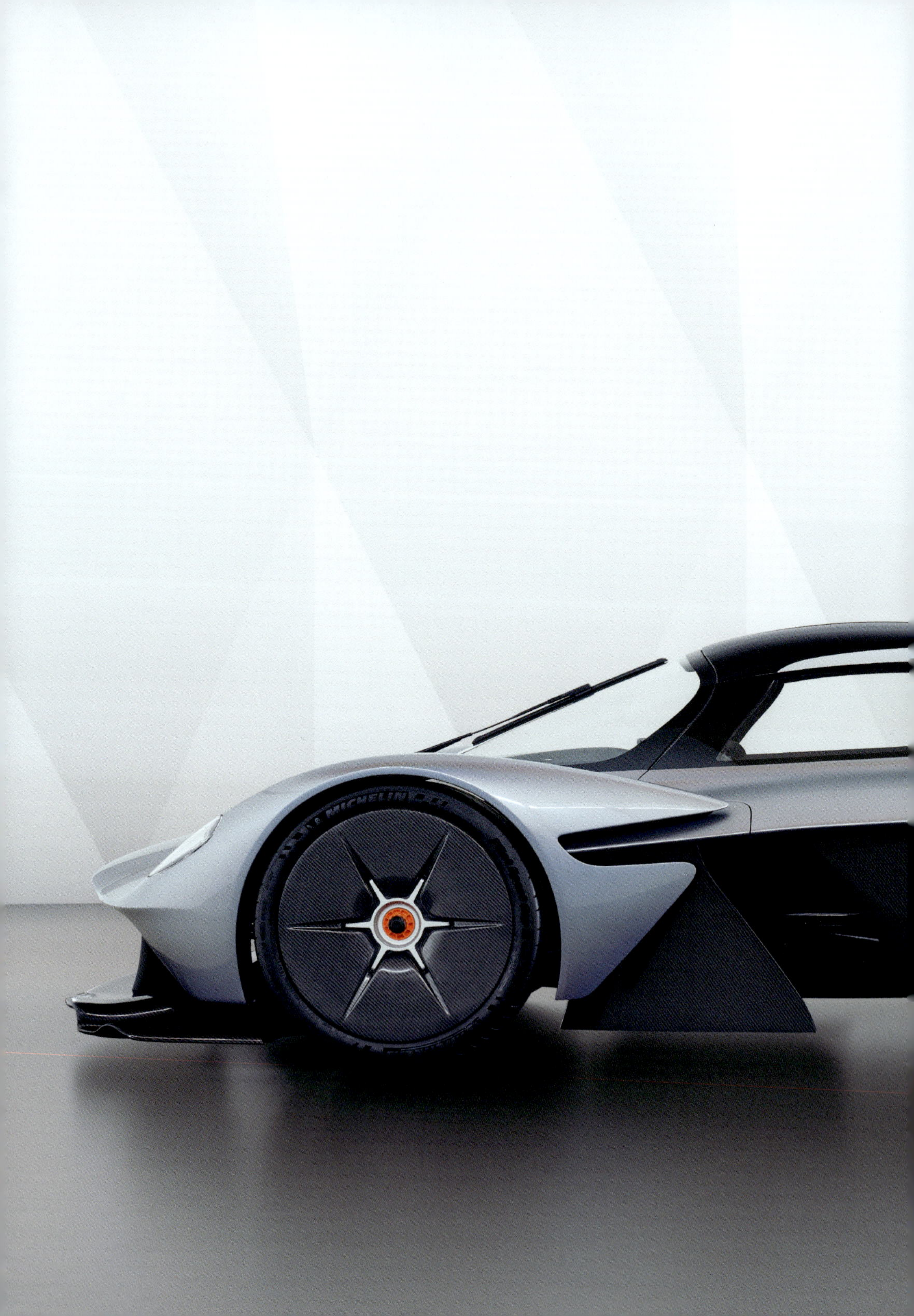
MICHELIN

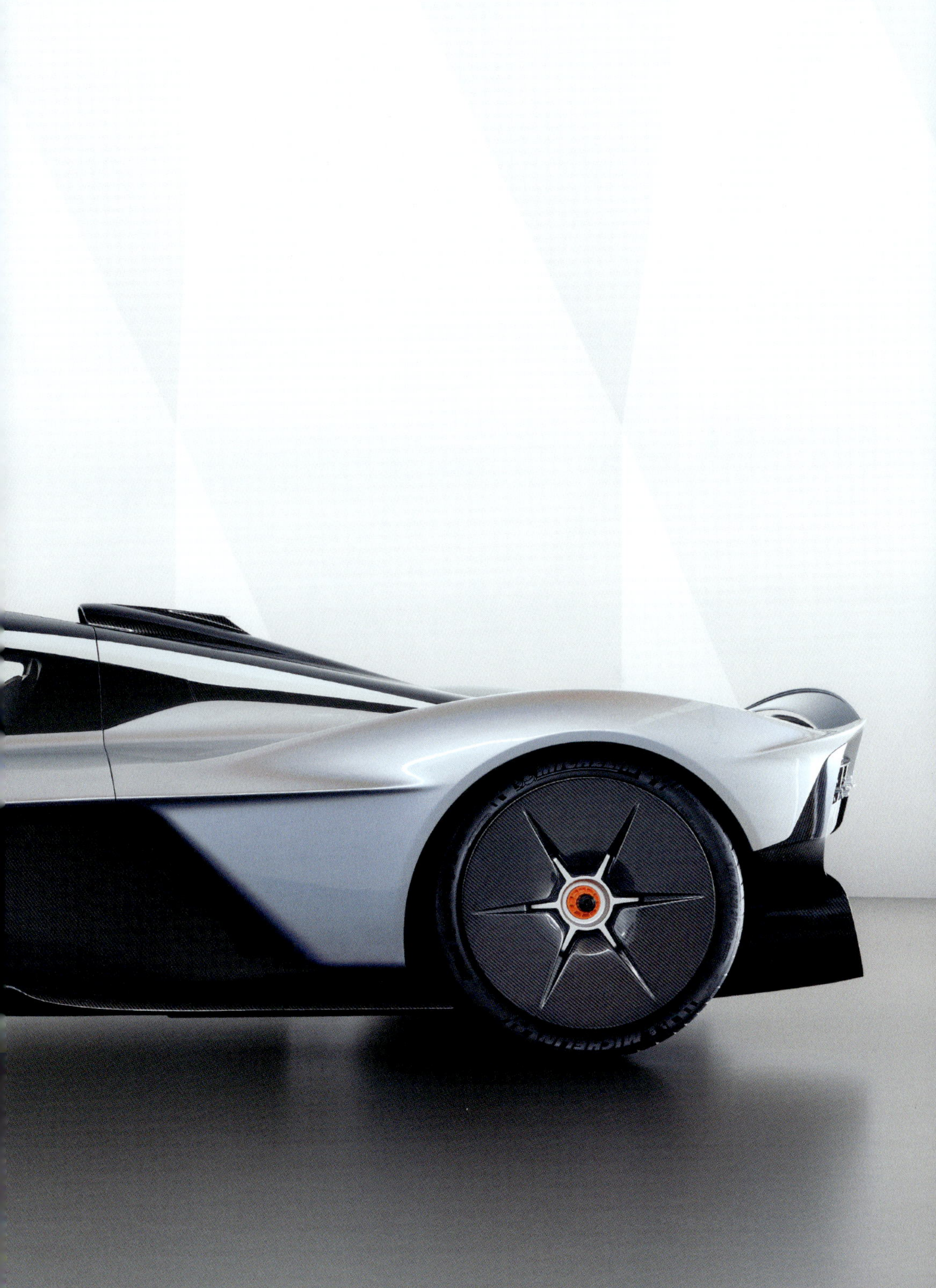
MICHELIN
MICHELIN

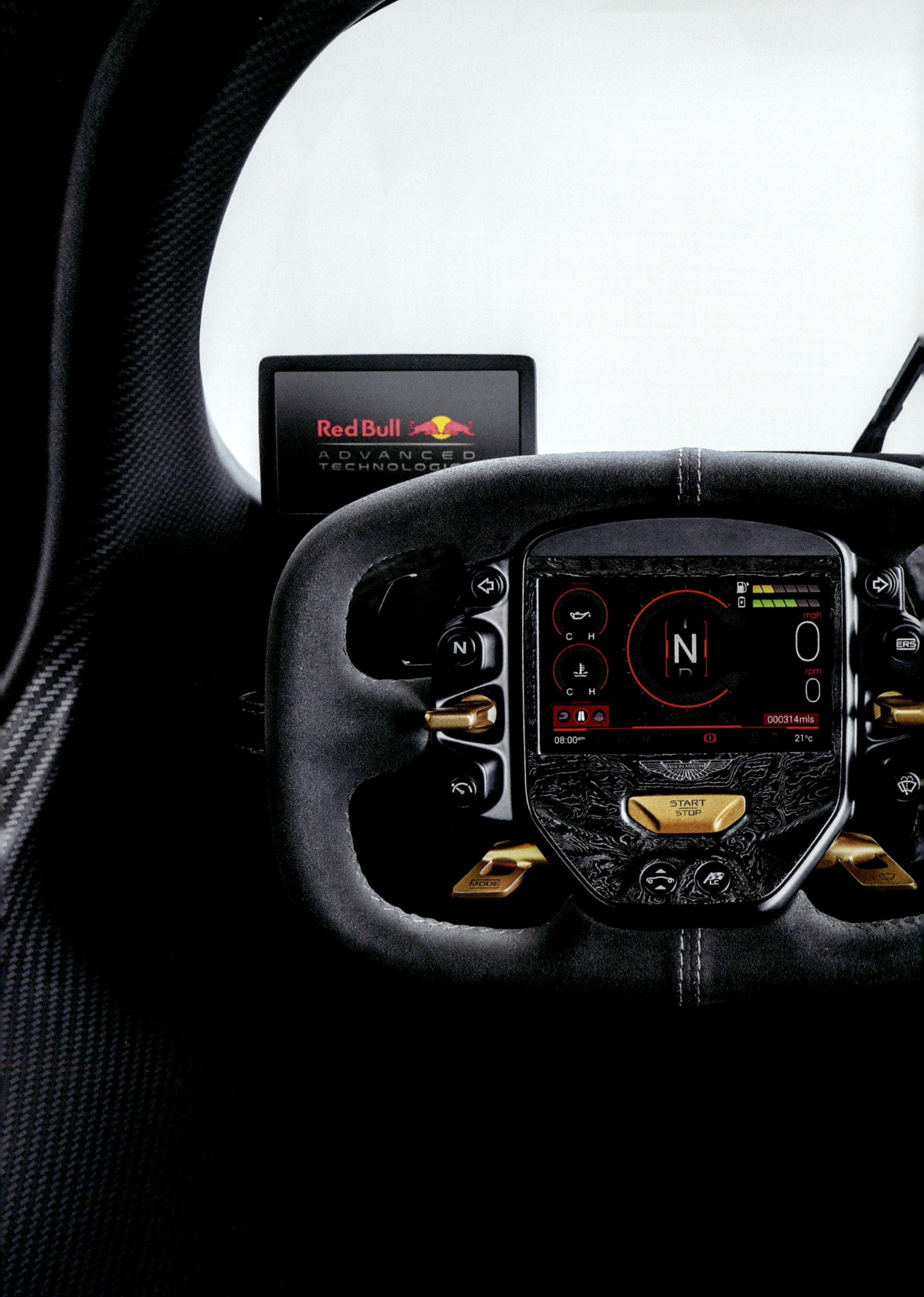

Red Bull
ADVANCED
N
ERS
mph
rpm
000314mls
08:00
21°c
START
STOP
MODE

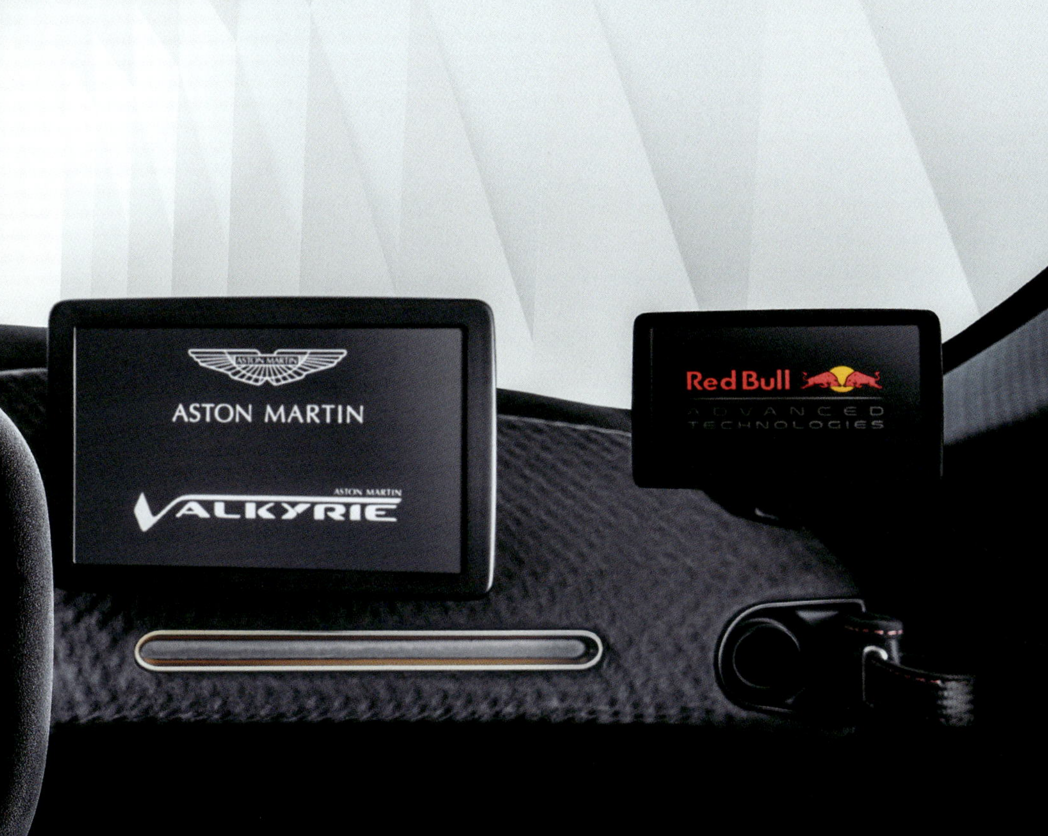
ASTON MARTIN
ASTON MARTIN
ASTON MARTIN
VALKYRIE
Red Bull
ADVANCED
TECHNOLOGIES

ASTON MARTIN VALKYRIE

Throughout the 2010s the styling of hypercars became increasingly extreme. A lot of this had to do with advances in computing power and ever more sophisticated CAD/CAM technology, which enabled manufacturers to better understand dynamic airflows and then sculpt cars into increasingly complex, higher-performing forms. But more than this, given the competitive nature of the hypercar market, manufacturers have come to the realization that to stand any chance of success in this high-risk business they need to be able to create offerings that not only have an ultra-wow factor in terms of performance, but that they must also have a strong sense of character, because that is what collectors ultimately connect with on an emotional level. It is also what first grabs attention at auto shows and turns heads in the street, so the outward appearance of a hypercar by definition needs to be pretty sensational. But another thing that has always been a defining characteristic of hypercars is their futuristic and highly technological aesthetic. The Aston Martin Valkyrie, which was first unveiled as a full-scale model at the marque's headquarters in Gaydon, Warwickshire in 2016, is a case in point. Although it might look to the uninitiated like some sci-fi concept, right from the beginning it was very much intended as a series-manufactured vehicle — though limited to a production run of 150 road-going examples (priced at $3.2 million each) alongside a further 25 track-only AMR Pro competition variants.

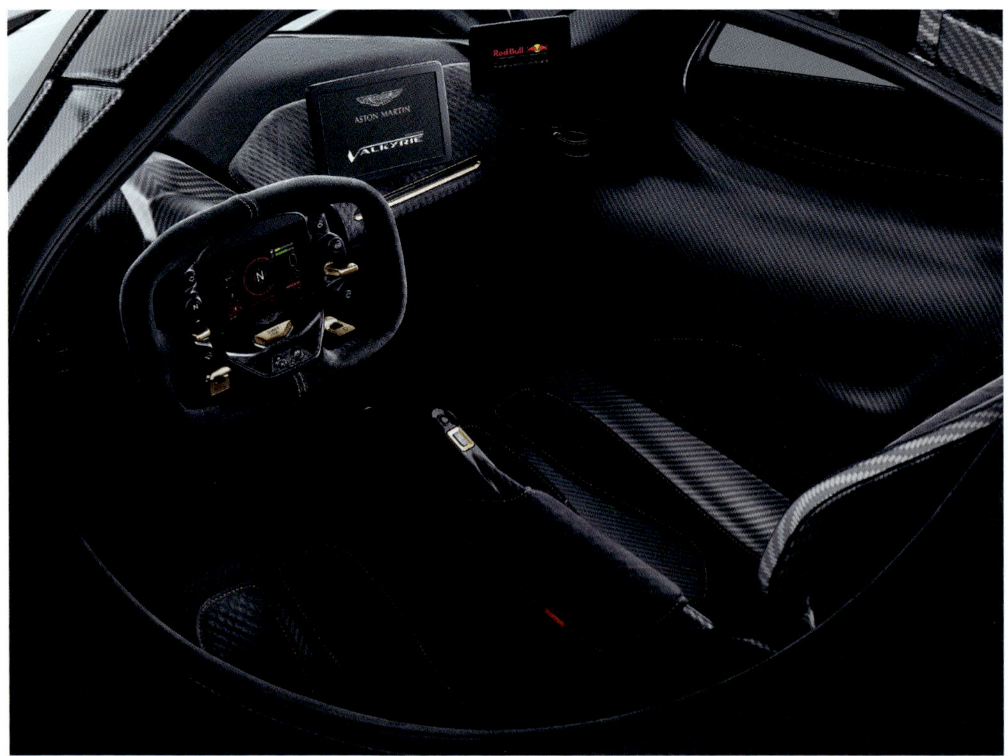

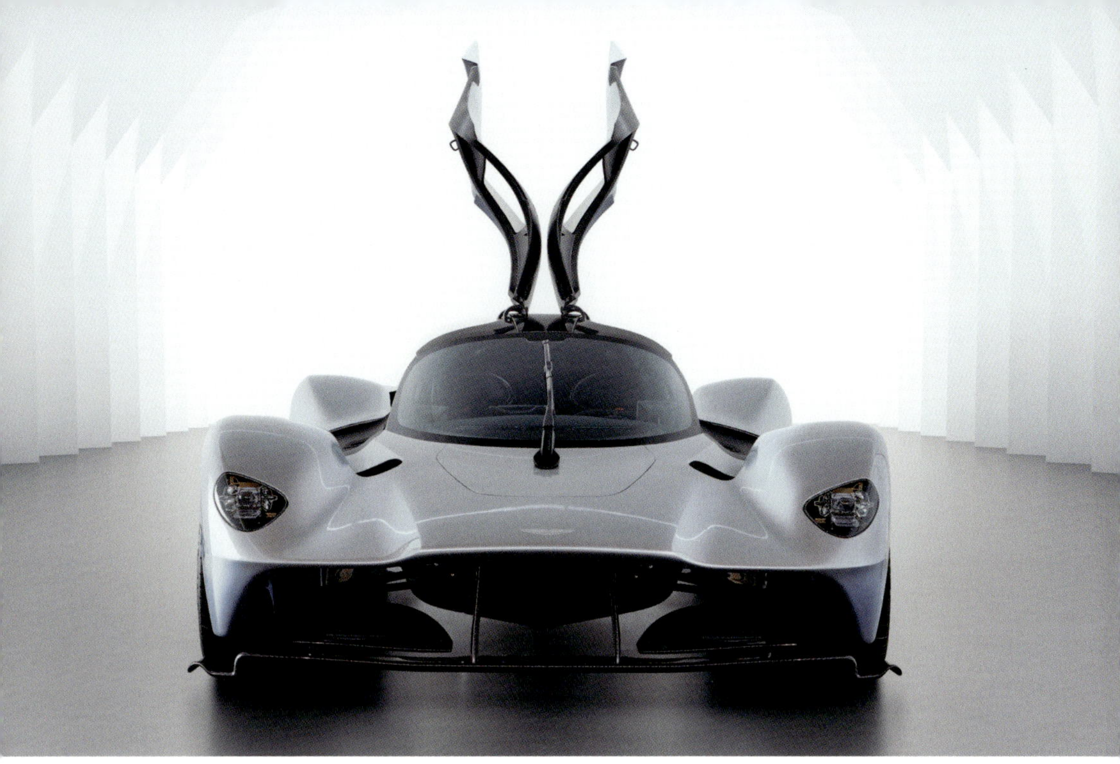

Previous: In order to minimize distractions and keep the driver focused on the road ahead all the Valkerie's switchgear is located on the steering wheel, while all the car's vital signs are shown on a single OLED display screen.

This remarkable vehicle is Aston Martin's most forward-looking hypercar to date and the result of a close collaboration between Aston Martin and Red Bull Racing, who both wanted to create a track-oriented hybrid that would also be suitable to drive on roads. Adrian Newey, one of the world's most talented designers of Formula 1 cars and Red Bull Racing's chief technical officer, assisted with the Valkyrie's design. In fact, such was the extent of his creative input the car's initial codename during development was Nebula — an acronym standing for Newey, Red Bull and Aston Martin, before it was changed to the more prosaic AM-RB 001. In 2017, Aston Martin revealed the full specifications of the car and also announced its production name: Valkyrie — in homage to Odin's spirit maidens of Norse mythology who ruthlessly determine the afterlife fate of slain warriors. This evocative appellation, which immediately conjures up "the power and honor of being chosen by the Gods," was adopted for two reasons: the first was it fitted with the marque's already established V naming tradition as previously used for the Volante, Virage, Vantage, Vanquish and Vulcan, while the second was that it perfectly captured the intentional otherworldly spirit of the car. Impressively, all 150 Valkyries were presold to customers in 2016, just on the basis of the earlier concept model. In order to dissuade any of these clients from attempting to sell on their build slots for quick profit — a practice known

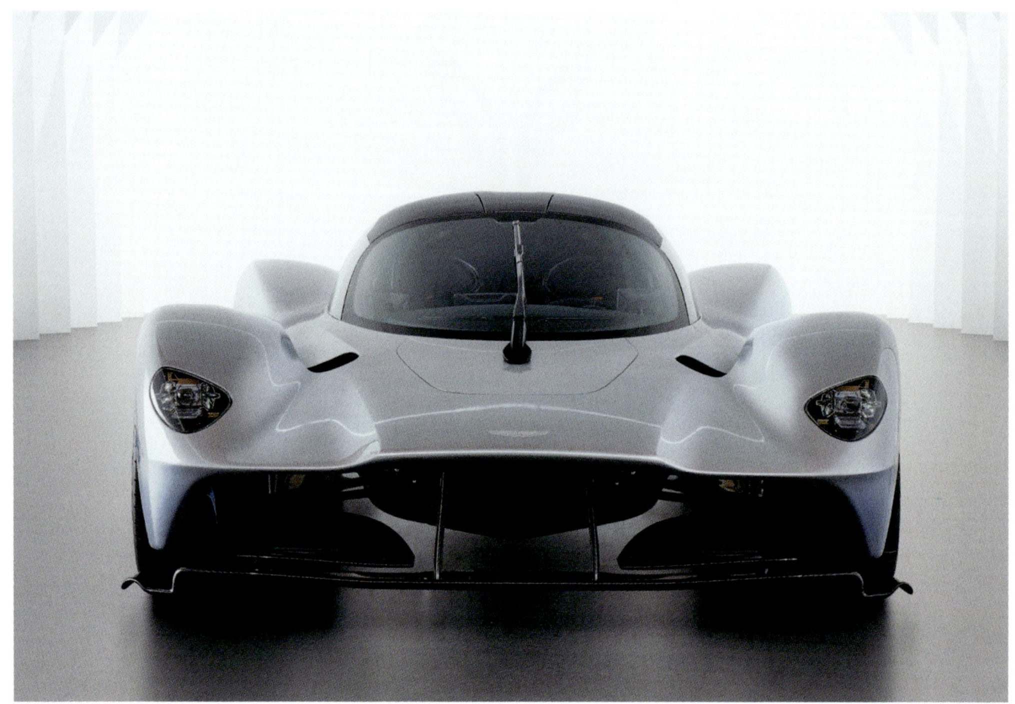

Above & opposite: The Aston Martin Valkyrie comes as close as possible to an F1 car without being restricted to the track. Its technology results directly from the company's involvement with Red Bull Racing Advanced Technologies and has all the hallmarks of Aston Martin's "crafted luxury." The car's striking aerodynamic exterior and open underfloor maximizes downforce and harnesses the atmosphere around Valkyrie. Its all carbon-fiber bodywork is formed into a radical body utterly honed for performance. This is Aston Martin's first ever hypercar.

as "flipping" — Aston Martin's CEO Andy Palmer warned on Twitter: "If they do and we identify who flipped, they lose the car. If they flip, then they never get another special" — meaning their name would not feature on the marque's privileged customer list for the next limited-run model. In late 2019, a Valkyrie was tantalizingly put through its paces at Silverstone, before production eventually commenced in 2020.

So, what makes the Valkyrie so special? Well, for a start, it challenges conventional auto-design wisdom with radical aerodynamics that unusually for a road car feature an open underfloor, which helps maximize downforce. Indeed, the design of its all-carbon-fiber body, though giving an oblique stylistic nod to Aston Martin's signature-shaped grille, was conjured up from effectively a blank sheet. As Miles Nurnberger, Aston Martin's creative director of exterior design, explains of its development, "Everything has been approached afresh. It truly is [based on] thinking from the ground, up." But all of this sophisticated skinning is only as good as what lurks beneath it, which in the case of the Valkyrie is pretty awesome, too. Its naturally aspirated 6.5-liter quad-cam V12 engine,

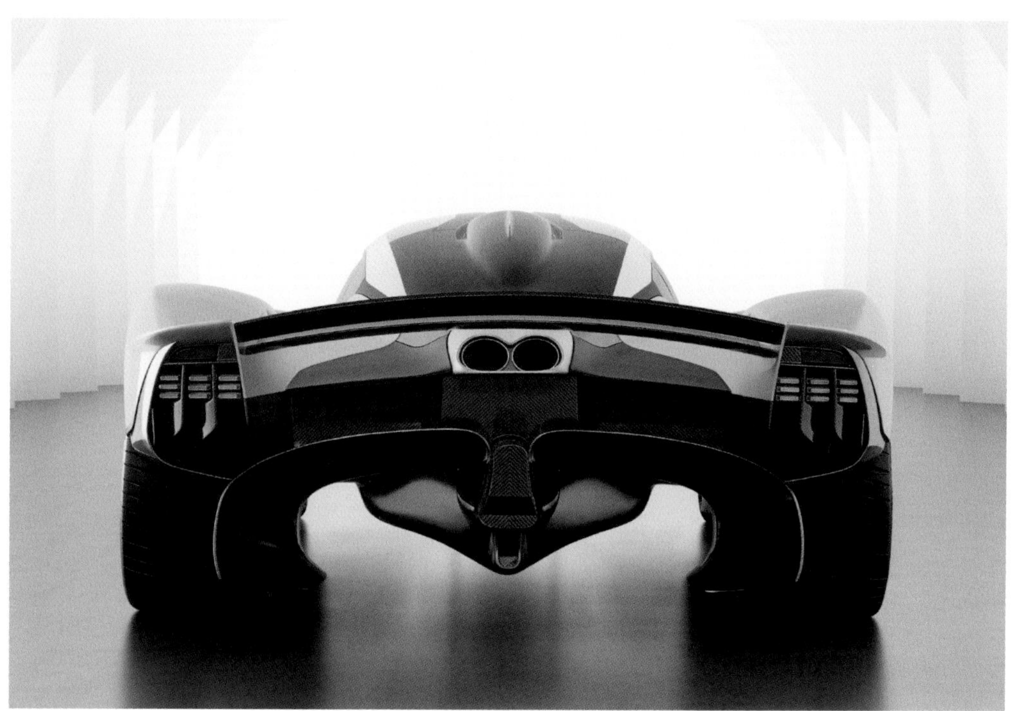

which was developed with the considerable expertise of engine specialists Cosworth, uses an advanced torque-enhanced hybrid system that during “take-off” employs an electric-motor-derived power boost. The power that this engine produces is not sapped by any superfluous weight, because the whole structure of the Valkyrie is made of lightweight carbon fiber, so not one single heavy steel component is used anywhere. Its state-of-the-art active suspension system also aids its handling, ensuring that it grips supremely well around corners whether on road or track. The upshot of all this design and engineering magic is outlandish speed, in excess of 250 mph (402 km/h). A veritable milestone for Aston Martin, the Valkryie is a dazzling vision of the automotive future that will no doubt influence the shape of things to come.

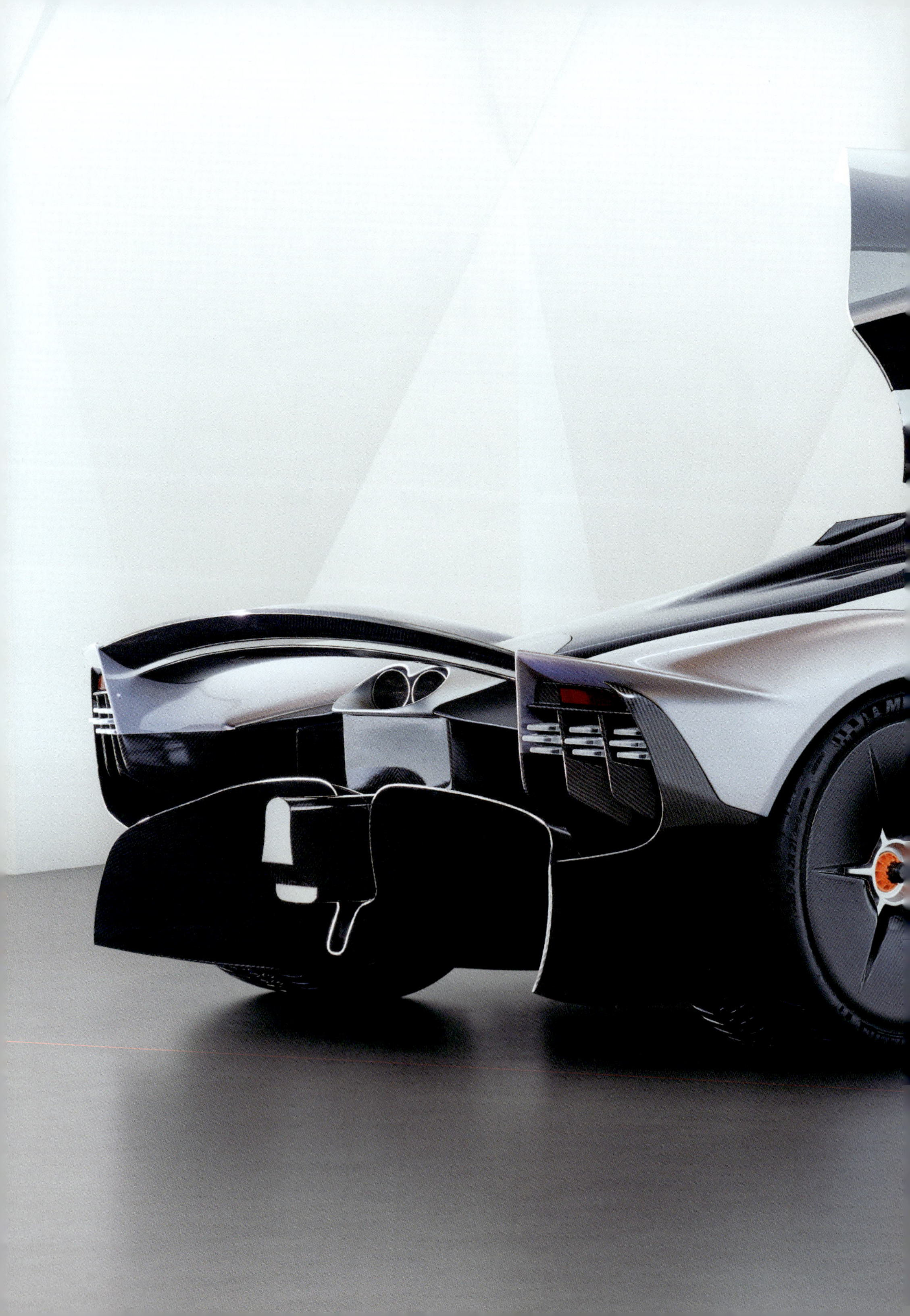

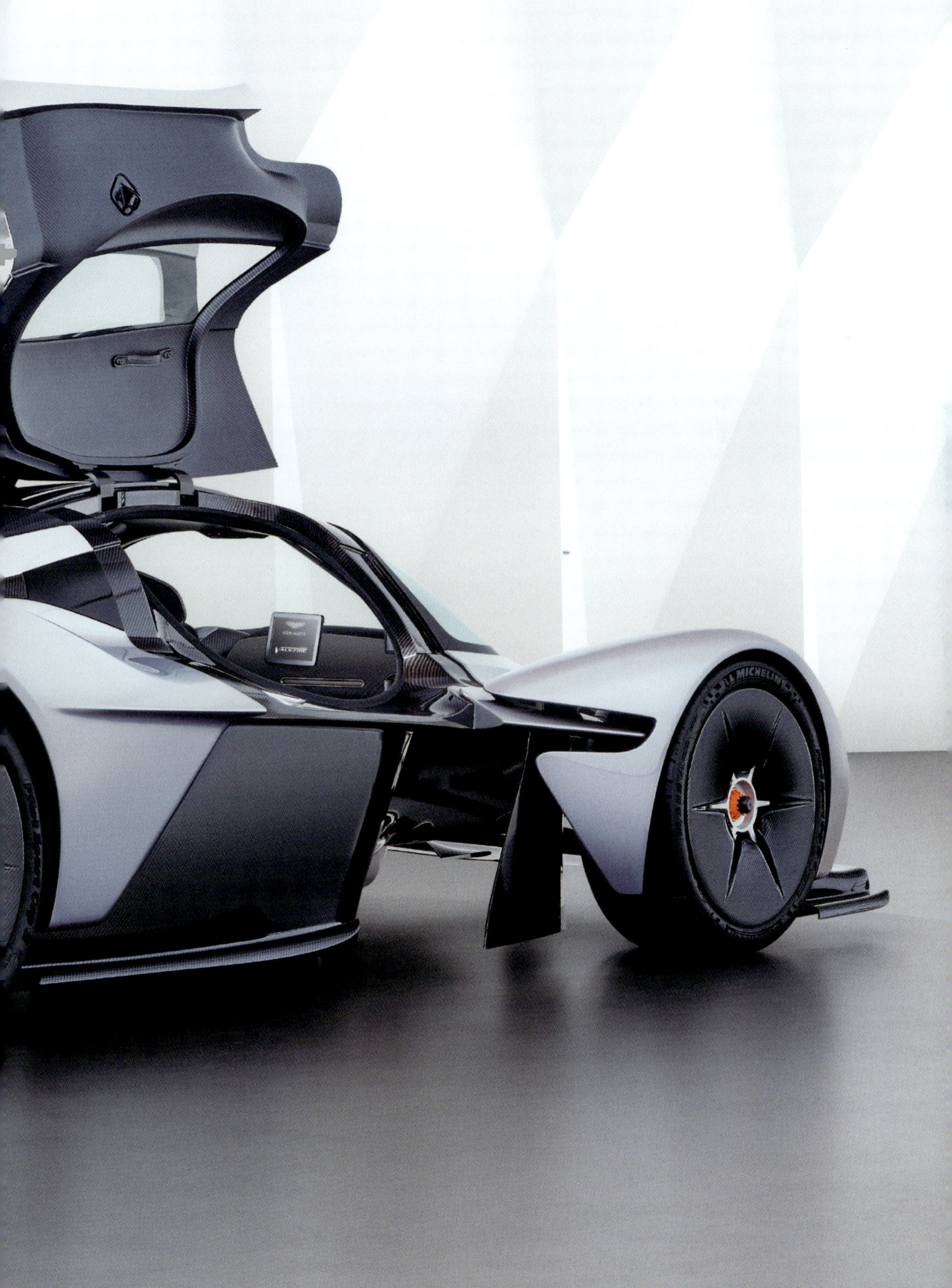
MICHELIN

2020

McLaren Speedtail

MANUFACTURED 2020–present | **ENGINE** 3,994 cc (244 cu. in.), twin-turbocharged DOHC per bank V8 & electric motor **HORSEPOWER** 1,036 peak combined (746 hp & 308 hp) **TOP SPEED** 403 km/h (250 mph) | **TRANSMISSION** 7-speed dual-clutch automatic | **NUMBER PRODUCED** 106

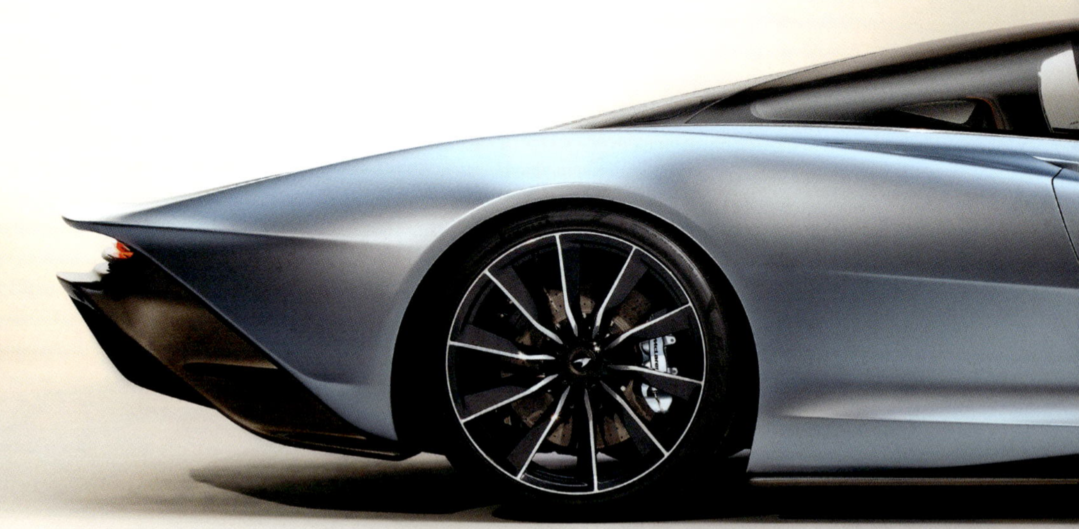

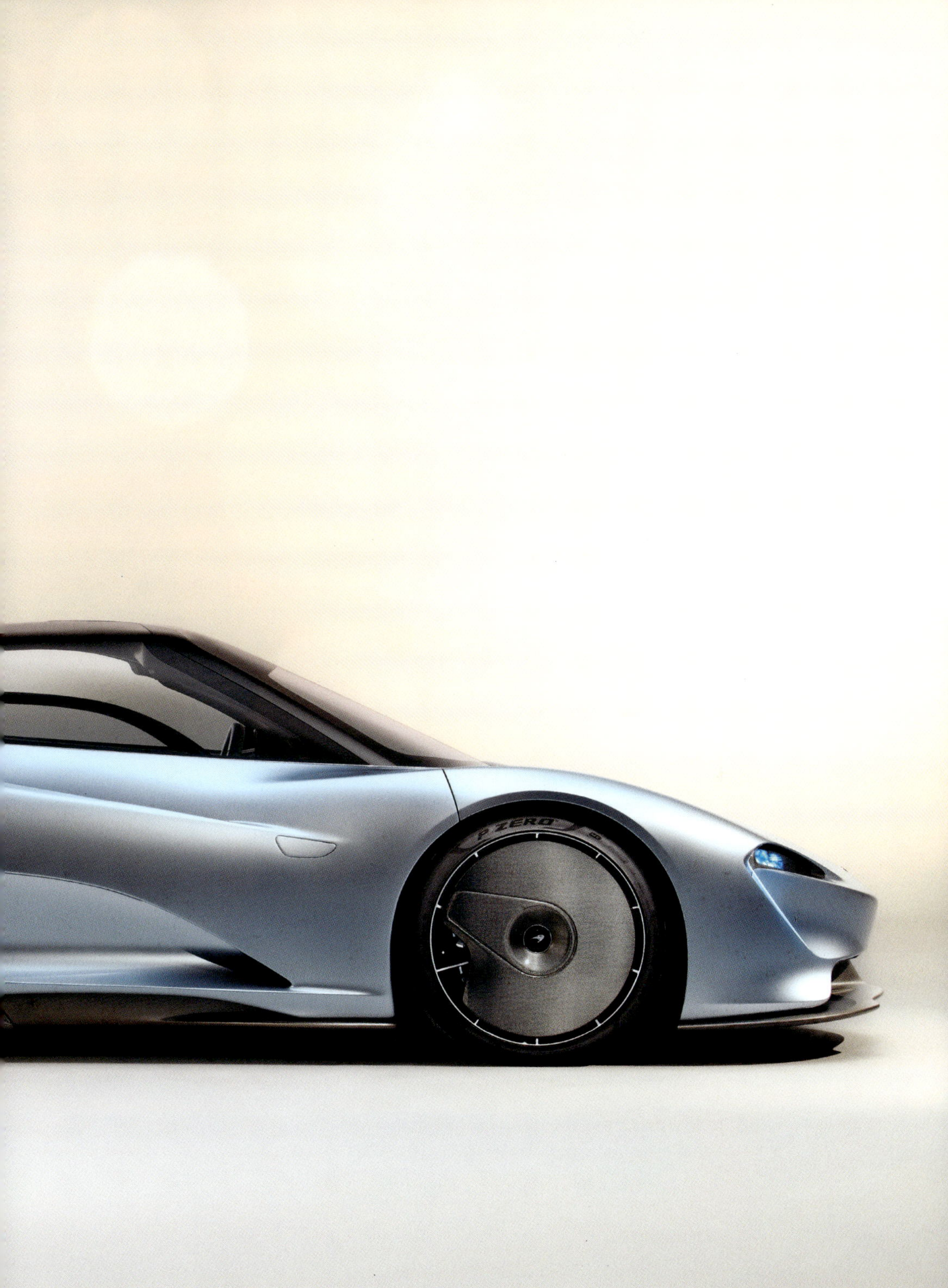
P ZERO

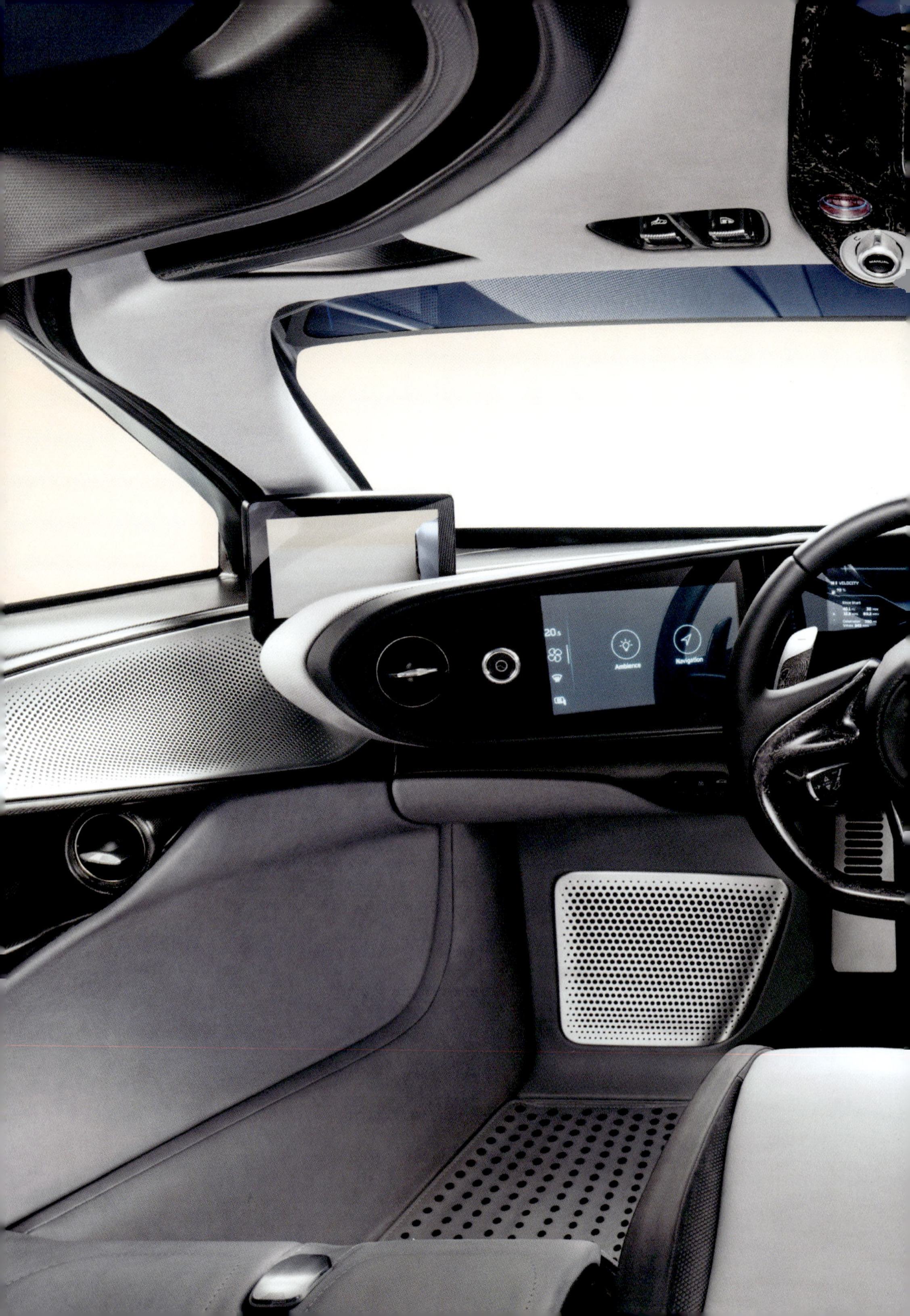
20 s
Ambience
Navigation
VELOCITY
Since Start

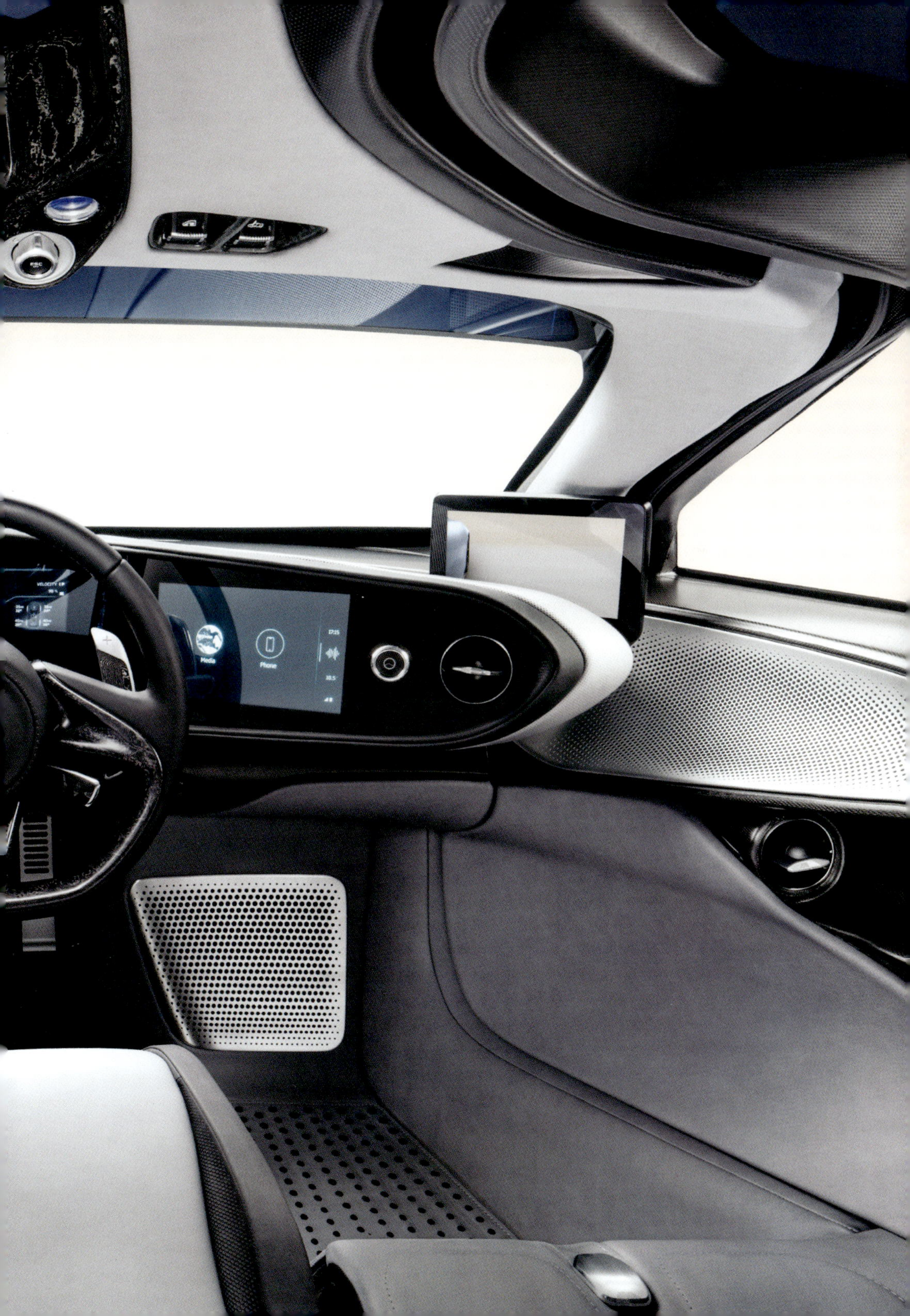
ESC
Media
Phone

Aerodynamics is the study of how forces act upon an object when it is propelled through air or water, and it is the data gleaned from such research that has long enabled car designers to hone their creations for maximum performance. Often when considering the aerodynamics of a car one immediately thinks of its front end, which is the first point of contact meeting the resistant air. Or maybe one thinks about its data-informed air-slipping side sections and strategically positioned airflow-enhancing vents. But the aerodynamics of a car's rear end are every bit as crucial for its high performance operation. This is the section where road-hugging downforce is enhanced, while at the same time the efficient streaming of air away from the vehicle is manipulated. So, like the muscular hindquarters of a racehorse, when a supercar's tail end looks "right" it is usually a good indicator that it will be a first-rate performer. The McLaren Speedtail is a prime example of this, and is named in homage to the extreme aerodynamic profiling of its rear section. As part of the car's radical streamlined form, this vital element enables the model to achieve a top speed of 250 mph (403 km/h). As McLaren explains, "The Speedtail's exterior is unlike anything else in the automotive world. Every element has been honed into the most aerodynamic shape possible. Air is channeled without interruption over, under and around the body — from the nose all the way to the innovative ailerons at the tail. While it's an undeniably jaw-dropping aesthetic, everything speaks of the Speedtail's extraordinary velocity. This is a car shaped for performance. With a design that draws on the way the natural world has adapted forms to create

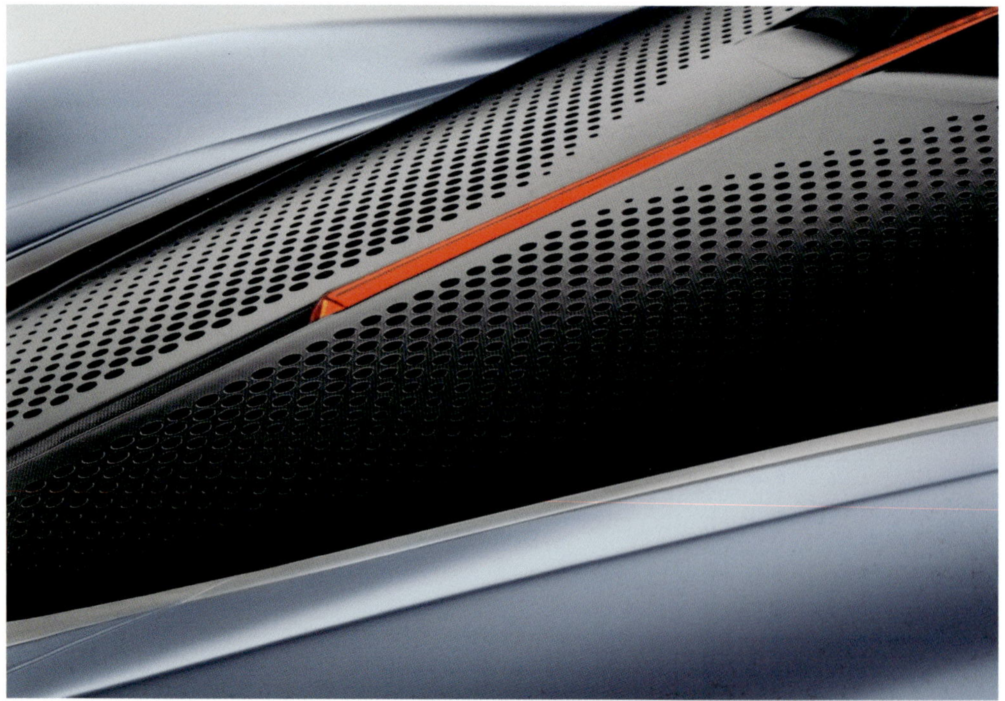

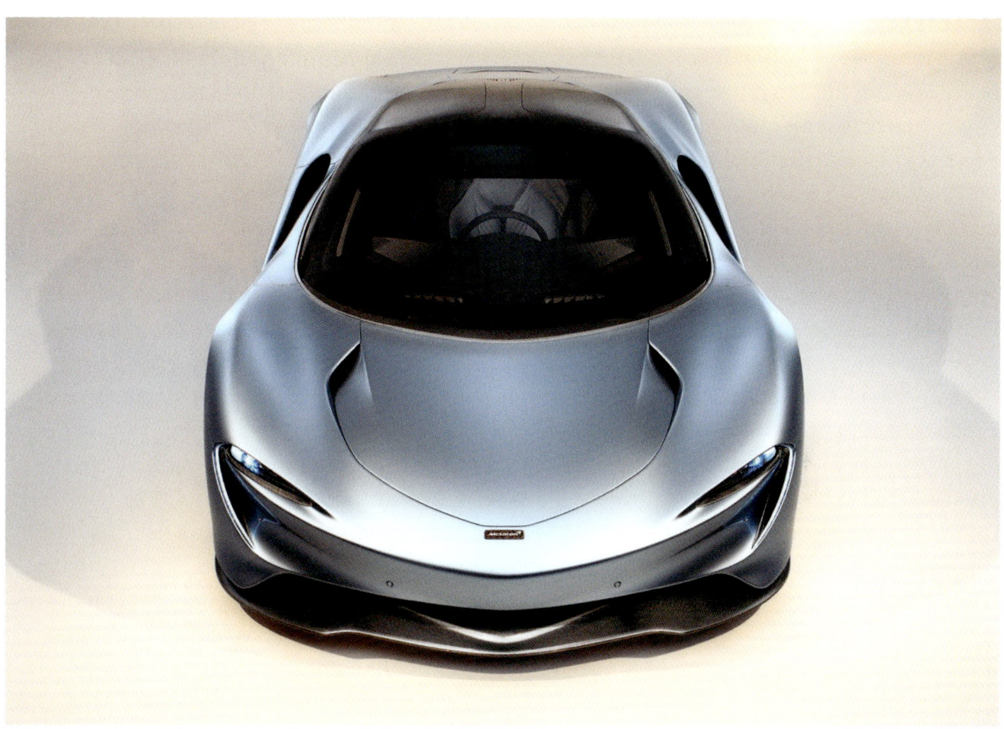

Previous: At the heart of the Speedtail's extraordinary and highly innovative interior is the driving seat. Its central position recalls McLaren's very first road car, the iconic F1, and offers the driver an unparalleled view of the road. This helps to create a unique sense of space and balance behind the wheel — a feeling that is amplified by the stunning use of glass and the seamless, clean dashboard design.

the ultimate in stealth and speed. This is automotive design innovation on a new level." As a consequence of this advanced organic essentialist approach to design, the Speedtail possesses not only a striking yet elegant aesthetic, but also a very distinct personality, which is expressed through its angled eye-like headlights and the configuration of its splitter, which forms a curious little smile and, of course, its elongated tail. This latter element's trailing edge innovatively integrates ailerons, which are controllable winglets, like those normally found on aircraft, and provide a next-level degree of aerodynamic control.

Like other cars in the McLaren line up, the Speedtail has been devised to be as "fat free" in its design as possible, and as such it adheres to the company's long-held mantra, "everything for a reason." Its undeniable beauty is the outcome of its state-of-the-art design expressing pure function. Yet its purposeful form only makes real sense when the Speedtail is viewed from above, for then its radical V-shape perfectly reveals the way in which air is channeled over its surfaces, thereby diminishing drag.

Created as a successor to the much-lauded F1 (see p. 418), the Speedtail is McLaren's first hybrid hyper-GT, yet it has been designed very much in the spirit of its illustrious forebearer. As the third member of McLaren's renowned "Ultimate Series," it has been specifically developed to be the most advanced auto design statement currently achievable. Like the F1, it also boasts an unusually configured three-seater cabin with a central driving position and has likewise been released as an ultra-exclusive edition, in this case just 106 units, all of which were quickly presold. In fact, interest far exceeded supply, even though this scintillating speedster's price tag was set at a cool $2.25 million. Following in the tracks of McLaren's F1 and Senna, the Speedtail's design introduces a number of innovative design firsts, most notably its lightweight carbon fiber front wheel covers which stay fixed in place over its 20-inch alloy wheels in order to smooth airflow over them and its pair of discreet HD cameras that glide out from its dihedral doors to replace conventional wing mirrors, thereby helping to minimize air turbulence.

Among today's current crop of hypercars, the Speedtail stands out for its pure streamlined elegance, which is derived from the single-minded vision of its creators to build the most aerodynamically refined car possible in the pursuit of sheer unbridled velocity. From the very first car in this book, the indomitable 1903 Mercedes-Simplex 40 hp created nearly 120 years ago, to this very latest one, the outstanding Speedtail, the passion for innovation has relentlessly driven the development of "ultimate" cars that are the unsurpassed auto-design expressions of their eras. These types of cars sit at the very apex of desirability when it comes to collecting because they are quite simply the very finest of all time. But more than this they also poignantly encapsulate the hopes, desires and dreams of those who have passionately dedicated their lives to their exacting realization.

Pages 504–505: Italian car designers Battista "Pinin" Farina (1893–1966, left) and his son Sergio (1926–2012), of Carrozzeria Pininfarina, September 28, 1956, discussing the Alfa Romeo 6C 3000 CM body type 2 "Superflow II" concept car that was displayed at the 1956 Paris Motor Show. The family surname was changed to Pininfarina in 1961.

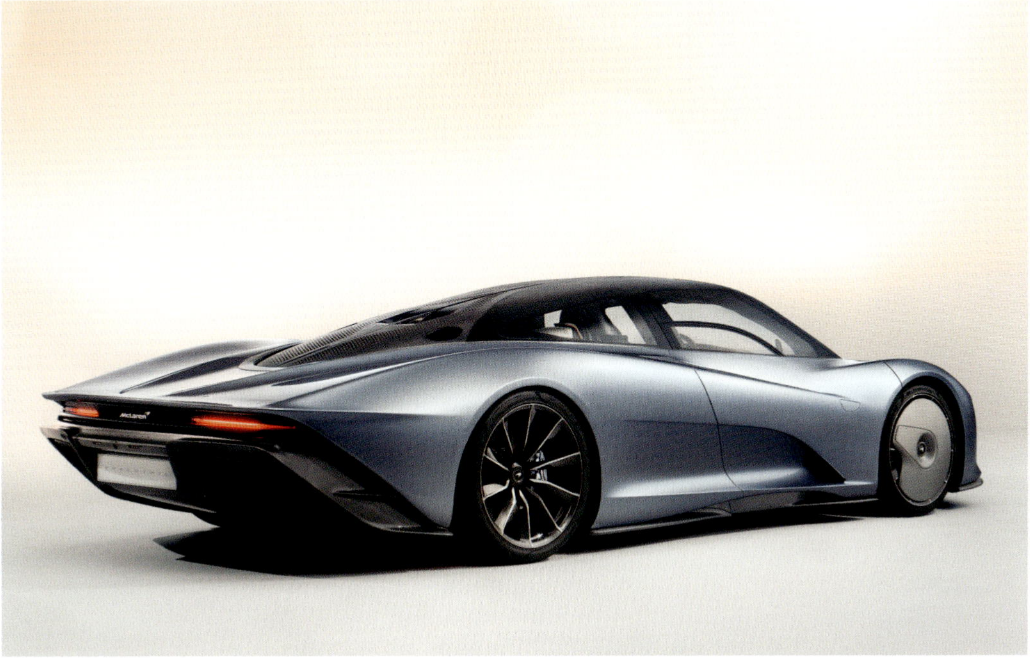

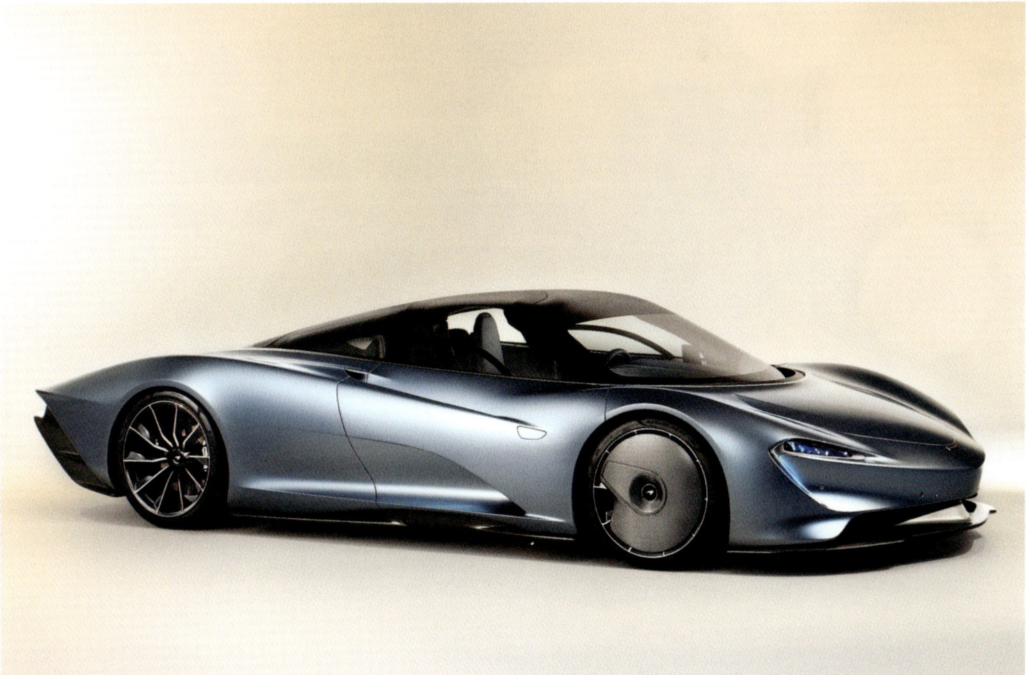

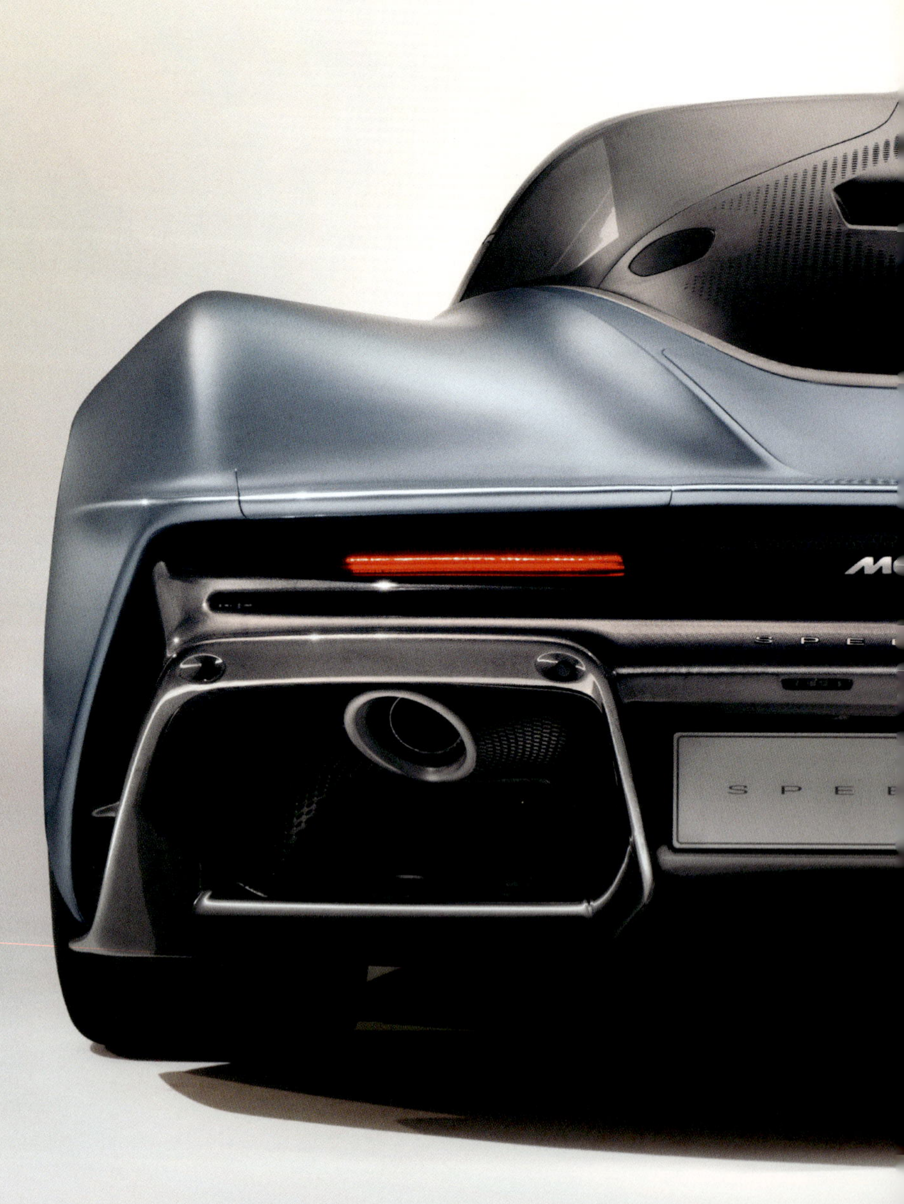

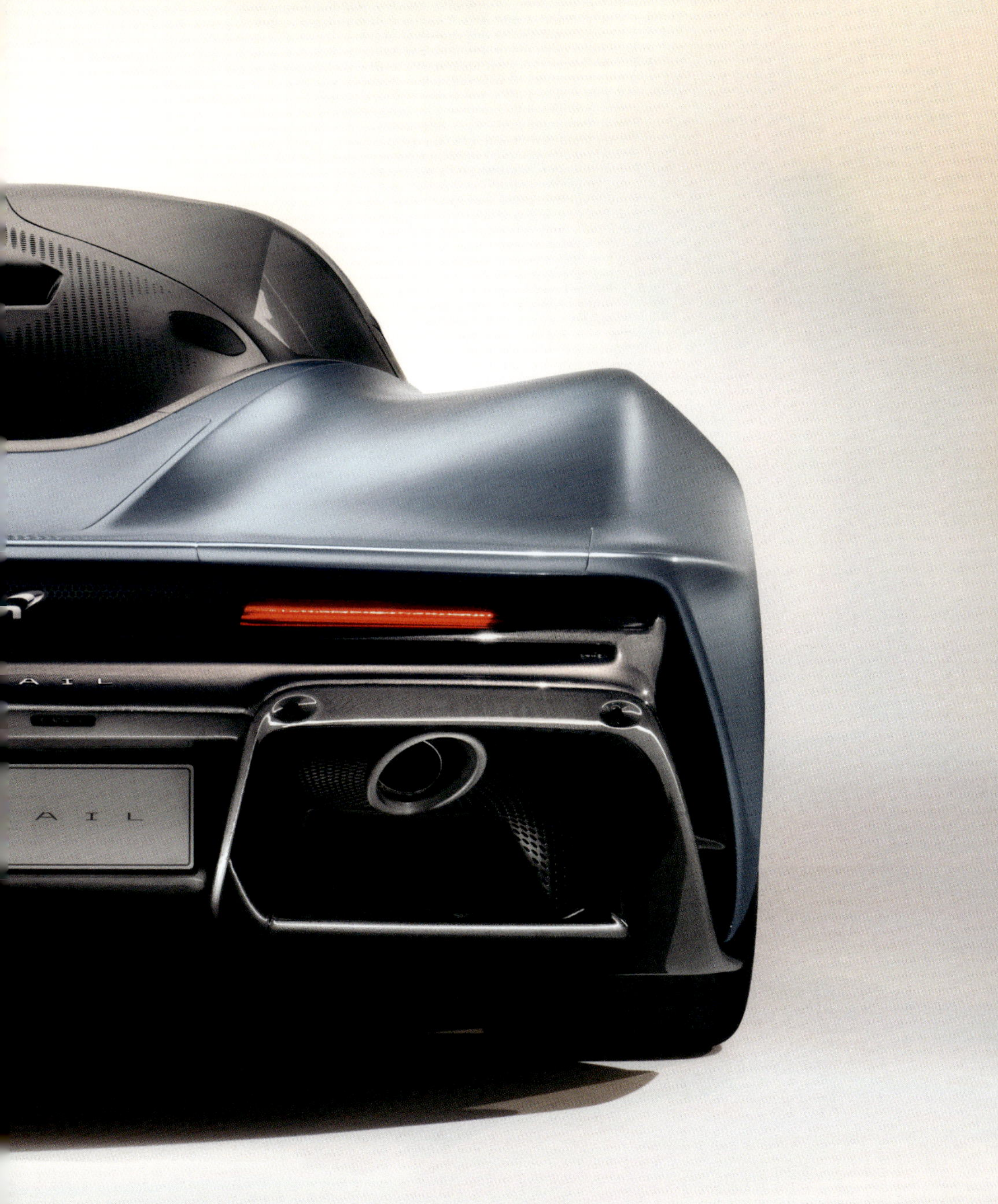

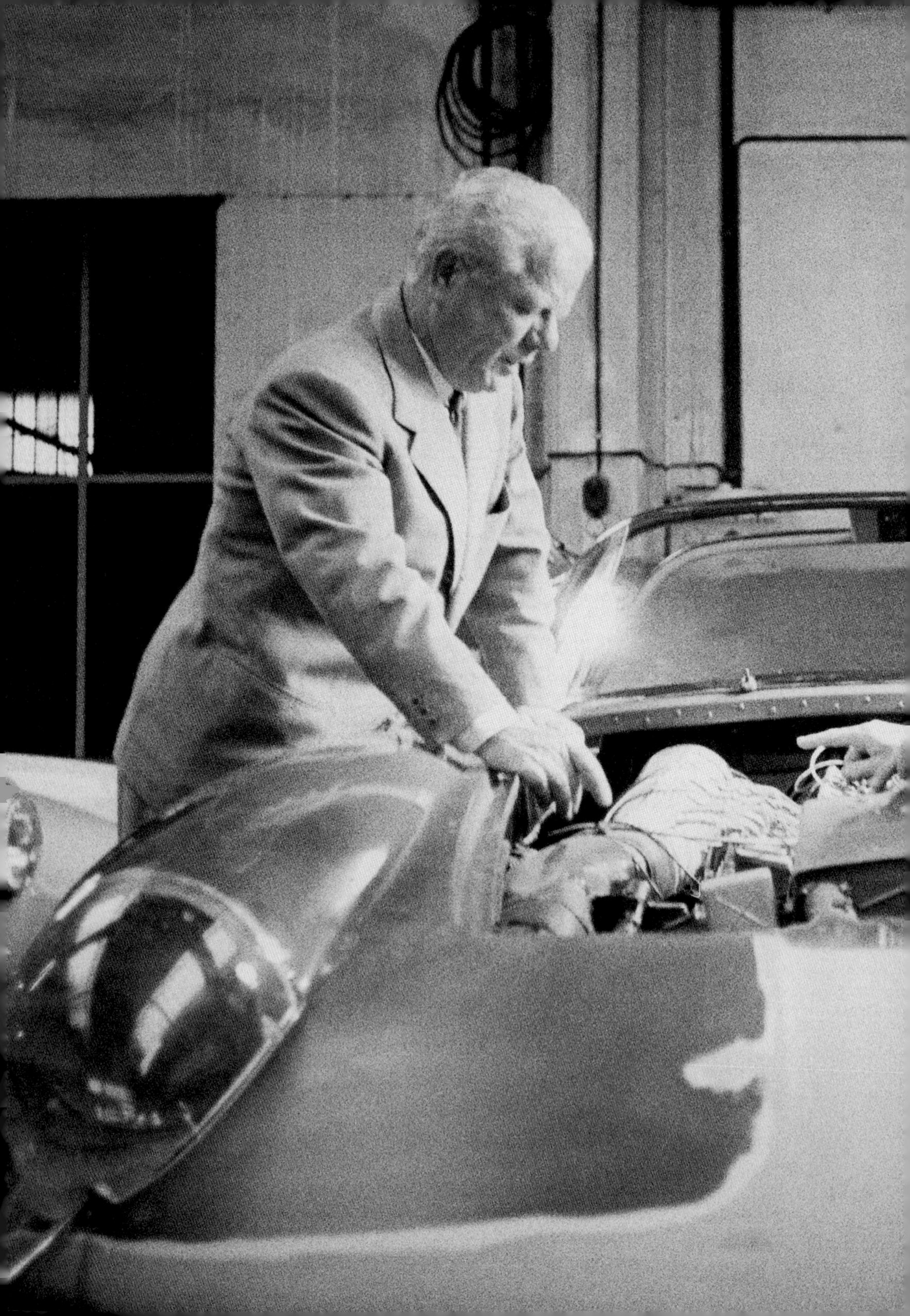

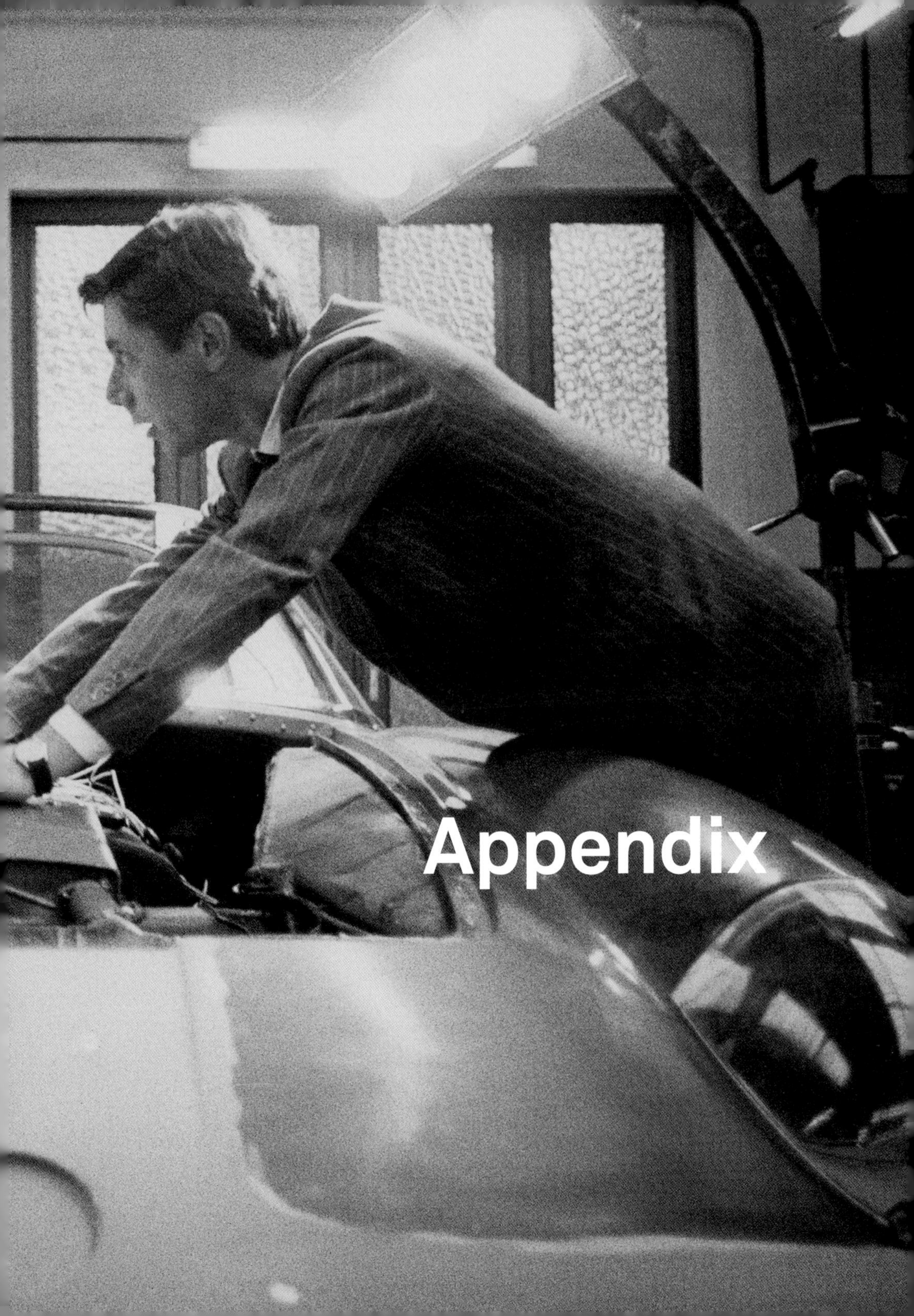

Appendix

Acknowledgments

By its very nature a book of this scale will always require a big team effort, so we would like to take this opportunity to thank all those involved in the project. First off, our heartfelt thanks must go to Benedikt Taschen and Marlene Taschen for committing to this wonderful book in the first place and for their subsequent insightful input. Immense gratitude must also go to our editors at TASCHEN, Simone Philippi and Pimploy Phongsirivech, for keeping the project on track and their logistical organization, and also Silvia Scamperle for her help with image sourcing. In addition, our thanks go to Andy Disl for his outstanding art direction. We are also grateful to Daniela Asmuth and Stefan Klatte for their exacting management of the book's production, Doug Adrianson and Aaron Bogart for their proofreading, Andrew Frankel for his help with fact-checking as well as for sharing his insights into the world of car collecting and Michael Furman for his help with imagery and invaluable wisdom. We would also like to express our enormous gratitude to Rob Myers for allowing us to use so many images from the RM Sotheby's archive. Likewise, we would like to acknowledge the crucial support that Ian Kelleher, Meghan McGrail, and Darin Schnabel of RM Sotheby's have provided over the course of this project. And lastly but by no means least, we would like to acknowledge the incredible assistance we have received while researching this book from various private collectors, salerooms, museums, specialist dealers, manufacturers, website owners, classic car clubs, photographers, and picture libraries who have very kindly allowed us to reproduce their beautiful imagery.

With special thanks to:
David Adams – Aston Martin Lagonda Limited
Robin Adams – RM Sotheby's
Giuseppe Allievi
Ing. Giovanni Bianchi Anderloni – Registro Internazionale Touring Superleggera
Nicole Daniell Auger – Bugatti Automobiles S.A.S.
Jennifer Augustin – Mercedes-Benz Museum GmbH
Rupert Banner – Bonhams
Walter Bäumer – InternationalMaseratiResearch.com
Ryan Bender – Gooding & Company
Sharron Bland – The International Club for Rolls-Royce and Bentley Enthusiasts
Heather Buchanan – Kahn Media
Kyle Burt – RM Sotheby's
Jonathan Butler – Alamy
Paul Chadderton – McLaren Automotive Ltd.
Paul Clarke
Simon Clay – simonclay.com
Emanuele Collo – Kidston SA
Fabrice Connen – dppi images
Hannah Corkish – Goodwood Motor Circuit
Rémi Dargegen – RM Sotheby's
Laetitia Desfontaines – Sotheby's
Robert Desimone – Barrett-Jackson
Natascia Di Maggio – Giorgio Nada Editore Srl
Thomas Drinkwater – Goodwood Motor Circuit
Per Einarsson – ultimostile.com
Patrick Ernzen – RM Sotheby's
Sebastian de Faber – Getty Images
Lynnie Farrant – Bonhams
Ian Ferguson – Vintage Sports-Car Club
Matthew Ferguson – Barrett-Jackson
Carmen Figini – Editoriale Domus / Quattroruote
Fotohalle Unger – RM Sotheby's
Andrew Frankel – A.L.F. Productions Limited
Laurent Friry
Marie-Louise Fritz – Bugatti Automobiles S.A.S.
Erik Fuller – RM Sotheby's
Christine Giovingo – Mecum Auctions
David Gooding – Gooding & Company
Diane Hall – Auburn Cord Duesenberg Automobile Museum

hamtramck-historical.com
Peter Harholdt – Photographs Peter Harholdt
Valerie Harrell – Dick Harrell Performance Center
Kandace Hawkinson – Pebble Beach Concours d'Elegance
Dennis Heck – Mercedes-Benz Classic
Gerhard Heidbrink – Mercedes-Benz Classic
Chelsey Hinsenkamp – Mecum Auctions
Martyn Hollingsworth – Jaguar Heritage Trust
Karissa Hosek – RM Sotheby's
Iris Hummel – Artcurial Motorcars
Dirk de Jager – RM Sotheby's
Juliet Jarvis – JJC / Automobili Lamborghini S.p.A.
Erwin Jelinek – Technical Museum Vienna
Loïc Kernen – loickernen.com
Simon and Georgina Khachadourian – Pullman Editions
Remco Kuiper – Automotive Literature Europe John Lamm
Matthieu Lamoure – Artcurial Motorcars
Dean Lanzante – Lanzante Motorsport
Christophe Lavielle – Librairie Motors Mania
André Le Roux – leroux.andre.free.fr
Pawel Litwinski – litwinski.com
Maurice Louche – editionsmauricelouche.com
Philipp Lücke – Philipp Lücke Automotive Photography
Brad Mace – Bentley Motors Limited
Julia Marozzi – Bentley Motors Limited
Christian Martin
Kate Matthews – Fiskens
Tobias Mauler – Porsche AG
Pieter Melissen – ultimatecarpage.com
Wouter Melissen – ultimatecarpage.com
Ryan Merrill – RM Sotheby's
Tony Merrygold – Jaguar Heritage Trust
Sam Murtaugh – Mecum Auctions
Jim Orr – The Henry Ford
Diane Parker – Historic Vehicle Association
Gemma Perrone – Centro Documentazione Alfa Romeo
Roberto Piccinini – Actualfoto
David Phillips – Michael Furman Studio
Eric Powell – Indianapolis Motor Speedway Museum
RacingSportsCars.com
Peter Raider – RM Sotheby's
Karam Ram – Jaguar Heritage Trust
Thomas Reinhold – McLaren Automotive Ltd
Chiara Reverberi – Ferrari S.p.A.
Chip Riegel – Chip Riegel Photography
Michael Roth – Indianapolis Motor Speedway
Sarah Jayne Rothwell – McLaren Automotive Ltd.
Yanouchka Sabbatini and JD Clerc – galerie123.com
Peter Sachs – The Klemantaski Collection
Mo Satarzadeh – RM Sotheby's
Zoe Schafer – LAT Images
Jack Schroeder – RM Sotheby's
Tim Scott – Fluid Images / RM Sotheby's
Tim Shipley – RM Sotheby's
Shooterz.biz – RM Sotheby's
Dennis Simon – centuryofspeed.com
Everett Anton "Tony" Singer – VintageAutoPosters.com
Peter Singhof – RM Sotheby's
Diana and Matt Spitzley – Spitzley / Zagari Archive
Chris Stephenson – The Revs Institute for Automotive Research
Cymon Taylor – Cymon Taylor Productions
TED7 – Ted7 Automotive Photography
Oli Tenent
Jörg Thilow – Porsche Museum
Time USA, LLC
Sophie Tobin McHugh – Aston Martin Lagonda Limited
Jens Torner – Porsche Museum
Guy van Grinsven – StudioPress Foto & Videoproducties BV
Debbie van Rijswijk – Louwman Museum
Franco Varani
Diana Varga – RM Sotheby's
Jacques Vaucher – arteauto.com
Francesca Vernia – Ferrari S.p.A.
Steve Wakefield – RM Sotheby's
Matthieu Waltmann – Bugatti Automobiles S.A.S.
Kevin Watters – Aston Martin Lagonda Limited
Tim Wheatley – Studio 397 B.V.
Laurie & Mike Yosha – Yosha Graphics
Michel Zumbrunn – Foto Zumbrunn

Credits

Robin Adams © courtesy of RM Sotheby's 430–437 (all)
Alamy / Heritage Image Partnership Ltd 38b
Alamy / Iconographic Archive 39
Alamy / Universal Images Group North America LLC 28
Aston Martin Lagonda 482–491 (all), 491
Automobili Lamborghini S.p.A / photo: Pietro Bianchi 454–455 (all)
Photos courtesy of Barrett-Jackson Auction Co, LLC 390–391, 396, 397, 392–393, 394, 399b
Bentley Motors Limited 20–21, 23, 24–25, 26, 27, 28
BMW Group Archive 61, 66, 68
Bridgeman Images 128
Bugatti Automobiles S.A.S. 56b
Centro Documentazione Alfa Romeo – Arese 43b, 77, 382–383 (all)
John Collins, courtesy Talacrest 2000 AD Limited 374–375 (all)
© Daimler AG, Mercedes-Benz Classic 11, 38t, 39
Patrick Ernzen © courtesy of RM Sotheby's 102–104 (all), 104, 108–109, 124–126, 127, 144–148 (all), 254–258 (all), 256, 262–263, 264–267 (all), 446–451 (all)
Ferrari S.p.A. 474, 475, 480–481
Ferrari S.p.A. / photo: G. Galliano 428–429
Fiell Archive 172b, 183t, 351t, 399t
Michael Furman 40–41, 42, 45t, 48–53 (all), 70–73 (all), 74, 92–94 (all), 96b, 99–100, 316–321 (all)
Michael Furman © courtesy of RM Sotheby's 8–15 (all), 18–19, 224–225 (all), 230–231, 346–348 (all), 349, 350
Getty Images / Bettmann 143b, 228b
Getty Images / Photo by John Dominis / The LIFE Picture Collection 193–194
Getty Images / Heritage Images 6–7
Getty Images / Keystone-France 408b
Getty Images / Klemantaski Collection 209t+b, 210–211, 240b, 373, 378t
Getty Images / Thomas D. McAvoy 162
Getty Images / Popperfoto 80–81
Getty Images / Jean Tesseyre 372t
Getty Images / Thurston Hopkins / Picture Post / Hulton Archive 504–505
Peter Harholdt 30–39 (all)
The Henry Ford 42 (both), 280 (all), 281b, 323, 324, 372b
Jaguar Heritage Trust 149tl+tr, 192t+b, 360–361 (all)
Kidston SA 2–3, 402–406 (all), 409b, 411–412
Klemantaski Collection 150b, 170, 172t, 182t, 206t, 221tr, 240t, 270–271, 272, 273tr
L'art et l'automobile 111t
Lanzante Limited / photo: Giles Rozier and Harry Rudd 465 (both), 467
Lanzante Limited / photo: Oli Tenent 462–463, 464, 468–469
LAT Photographic 29 (both), 111b, 150t, 182b, 183b, 220, 221tl, 247t, 261, 289b, 296b, 297, 314b, 315 (both), 335 (both), 340, 381b, 398
© Pawel Litwinski 412–417 (all)
© Archives Maurice Louche 238
Courtesy Lumsden and Fiskens 289t
Collection Flavien Marçais 88t
Christian Martin, courtesy Artcurial 196–295 (all)
McLaren Automotive Ltd 400–401, 424–425b, 494–501 (all)
Pieter Melissen / UltimateCarPage 22
Mullin Automotive Museum 222–223 (all), 275m+t
Novafoto-Sorlini Archive – Giorgio Nada Editore 161t, 164–165
Petersen Automotive Museum 188t, 193

Petersen Automotive Museum (photo: TED7)
4–5, 132–141 (all), 136, 184–192
Roberto Piccinini / Actualfoto 273tl+b
Porsche AG 141 (both), 142, 242–243
Porsche Cars History 163
Pullman Editions 379t
Quattroruote Archive 408t
RacingSportsCars.com / Alexis Callier Collection 161b
Peter Raider © courtesy of RM Sotheby's
58–60 (all), 62–65 (all), 67b
Revs Institute / Albert R. Bochroch Photograph Collection 101b
Revs Institute / Collier Collection
26, 101t
Revs Institute / European Motorsport in the 1950s and 1960s Photograph Collection
251t
Revs Institute / Eric della Faille Photograph Collection 381t
Revs Institute / Rodolfo Mailander Photograph Collection 90, 106b, 110t
Revs Institute / Duke Q. Manor Photograph Collection 351b
Revs Institute / George Phillips Photograph Collection
89, 100, 110b, 149b, 151b, 241t
Mo Satarzadeh © courtesy of RM Sotheby's
470–473 (all), 478t
Darin Schnabel © courtesy of RM Sotheby's
274–275, 276t+b, 298–299, 300t, 303–304, 326–330 (all), 331, 334
Tim Scott © courtesy of Fiskens
282–288 (all), 301
Tim Scott © courtesy of McLaren Automotive Ltd
418–421 (all), 427, 422–423 (all)
Tim Scott © courtesy of RM Sotheby's
82–84 (all), 86–87, 91 (both), 153–157 (all), 158, 159, 174–178 (all), 179, 180–181, 244–247 (all), 248, 249, 252–253, 290–292 (all), 293 , 295, 336–339 (all), 340, 341b, 342, 343, 344–345

Simeone Foundation Automotive Museum
44, 45, 56t, 57, 77, 76b, 97t, 151t, 221b
Peter Singhof © courtesy of RM Sotheby's
438–443 (all)
Spitzley Zagari Collection 409t
TASCHEN Archive 43t, 177t, 260, 278, 294
Cymon Taylor 166–168 (all), 171b, 171t
Time USA, LLC 101tl
Diana Varga © courtesy of RM Sotheby's
232–234 (all), 234, 236–237
VintageAutoPosters.com
229, 322, 329t
Steve Wakefield © courtesy of RM Sotheby's
1, 362–371 (all)
Wikimedia Commons 16t, 123t
Michel Zumbrunn 352–359 (all)
Emmanuel Zurini / DPPI 380

Selected Bibliography

Adatto, R. et al, *French Curves: Delahaye, Delage, Talbot-Lago: Mullin Automotive Museum*. Coachbuilt Press: Philadelphia, Pennsylvania, 2011

Adatto, R. & Furman, M., *Concours Retro-spective*. Coachbuilt Press: Philadelphia, Pennsylvania, 2015

Allievi, G., *Ferrari*. TASCHEN: Cologne, 2018

Ardizio, L., *Museo Storico Alfa Romeo: The Catalogue*. Giorgio Nada Editore: Vimodrone, Italy, 2015

Bayley, S., *Cars: Freedom, Style, Sex, Power, Motion, Colour, Everything*. Conran Octopus Ltd.: London, 2008

Bolsinger, M. & Becker, C., *Mercedes-Benz: Silver Arrows*. Delius Klasing Verlag: Bielefeld, 2002

Comer, C. & Shelby, C., *Shelby Cobra: Fifty Years*. Motorbooks: Beverly, Massachusetts, 2011

Engelen, G., *Milestones of Motorsports: Mercedes-Benz 300 SLR*. Hatje Cantz Verlag: Ostfildern, 2015

Fiell, C. & Fiell, P., Industrial Design A-Z. TASCHEN: Cologne, 2000

Fiell, C. & Fiell, P., Masterpieces of Italian Design. Goodman Fiell, London, 2013

Frankel. A., *Bentley: The Story*. Redwood Publishing, London, 2003

Friedman, D., *Shelby American Up Close and Behind the Scenes: The Venice Years 1962–1965*. Motorbooks: Beverly, Massachusetts, 2017

Heseltine, R. & Zumbrunn, M., *British Auto Legends: Classics of Style and Design*. Merrell Publishers Limited: London, 2012

Japp, C., Adatto, R. & Kruta, J., *The Art of Bugatti: Mullin Automotive Museum*. Coachbuilt Press: Philadelphia, Pennsylvania, 2010

Kimes, B.R. & Goodfellow, W.S., *Speed, Style, and Beauty: Cars From the Ralph Lauren Collection*. MFA Publications: Boston, Massachusetts 2005

Leffingwell, R., Ingram, C. & Furman, M., *Porsche Unexpected: Discoveries in Collecting*. Coach-built Press: Philadelphia, Pennsylvania 2014

Ludvigsen, K.E., *Porsche: Excellence Was Expected*. Bentley Publishers: Cambridge, Massachusetts, 2019

Nikas, J. & Furman, M., *The Face of Change: Portraits of Automotive Evolution*. Coachbuilt Press: Philadelphia, Pennsylvania, 2019

Nikas, J. & Furman, M., *Rule Britannia: When British Sports Cars Saved a Nation*. Coachbuilt Press: Philadelphia, Pennsylvania, 2017

Noakes, A., *Aston Martin DB: 70 Years*, White Lion Publishing: London, 2019

Simeone, F.A., M.D. (eds.), *The Stewardship of Historically Important Automobiles*. The Simeone Automotive Foundation / Coachbuilt Press: Philadelphia, Pennsylvania, 2012

Simeone, F.A., M.D. & Furman, M., *The Spirit of Competition*. The Simeone Foundation Automotive Museum / Coachbuilt Press: Philadelphia, Pennsylvania, 2009

Whyte, A., *Jaguar: Sports Racing & Works Competition Cars to 1953*. J. H. Haynes & Co. Ltd.: Sparkford, Somerset, 2002

Whyte, A., *Jaguar: Sports Racing & Works Competition Cars from 1954*. J. H. Haynes & Co. Ltd.: Sparkford, Somerset, 2002

Wollen, P. & Kerr, J. (eds.), *Autopia: Cars and Culture*. Reaktion Books: London, 2002

Zaugg, J., *Gentlemen, Start Your Engines! – The Bonhams Guide to Classic Sports & Race Cars*. Gestalten: Berlin, 2015

Authors' Note

For consistency's sake we have used metric followed by imperial measurements for top speeds and engine displacements within each entry's headline specification information, however, in the related body texts and captions we have decided to employ a more flexible system to reflect the nationality of the constructor. This means for cars made by British or American marques we use imperial measurements followed by their metric conversions, whereas for European-manufactured cars the protocol is reversed.

Page 1: 1966 Ford GT40 Mark II (chassis no. P/1016). This is the car that placed third in the epic 1-2-3 GT40 clean sweep at the 1966 24 Hours of Le Mans.

Pages 2–3: Lamborghini Miura P400 SVJ (chassis no. 4934). This example was the first of only four original factory-built examples of the performance-enhanced SVJ built during the Miura's initial production run.

Pages 4–5: 1957 Jaguar XK-SS (chassis no. XK-SS713). This is the most famous example of the car, which for many years was owned by Steve McQueen and now resides in the Petersen Automotive Museum in Los Angeles.

Pages 428–429: Flavio Manzoni, Senior Vice President of Design at Ferrari (wearing necktie), attaches great importance to model making. Here, he and his team are working on the clay model of the limited-production Ferrari Monza SP1 sports car. During the modeling process, scale and full-scale models are created by digitally controlled milling machines. Manzoni and team then work like artists on the model in order to connnect surfaces with each other, to be able to judge shapes and proportions better and to develop it step by step. This car was launched at the 2018 Paris Motor Show.

Page 512: Detail of the Aston Martin Valkyrie rear end showing its radical open underfloor, which maximizes downforce and harnesses the atmosphere aerodynamically around the car's body.

Imprint

EACH AND EVERY TASCHEN BOOK PLANTS A SEED!
Each year, we offset our annual carbon emissions with carbon credits at the Instituto Terra, a reforestation program in Minas Gerais, Brazil, founded by Lélia and Sebastião Salgado. To find out more about this ecological partnership, please check: www.taschen.com/institutoterra.
Inspiration: unlimited.
Carbon footprint: (almost) zero.

Want to see more? Visit taschen.com to view our current publications, browse our latest magazine, and subscribe to our newsletter.

Hohenzollernring 53, D–50672 Köln
www.taschen.com

Printed in Bosnia-Herzegovina
ISBN 978–3–8365–9166–9

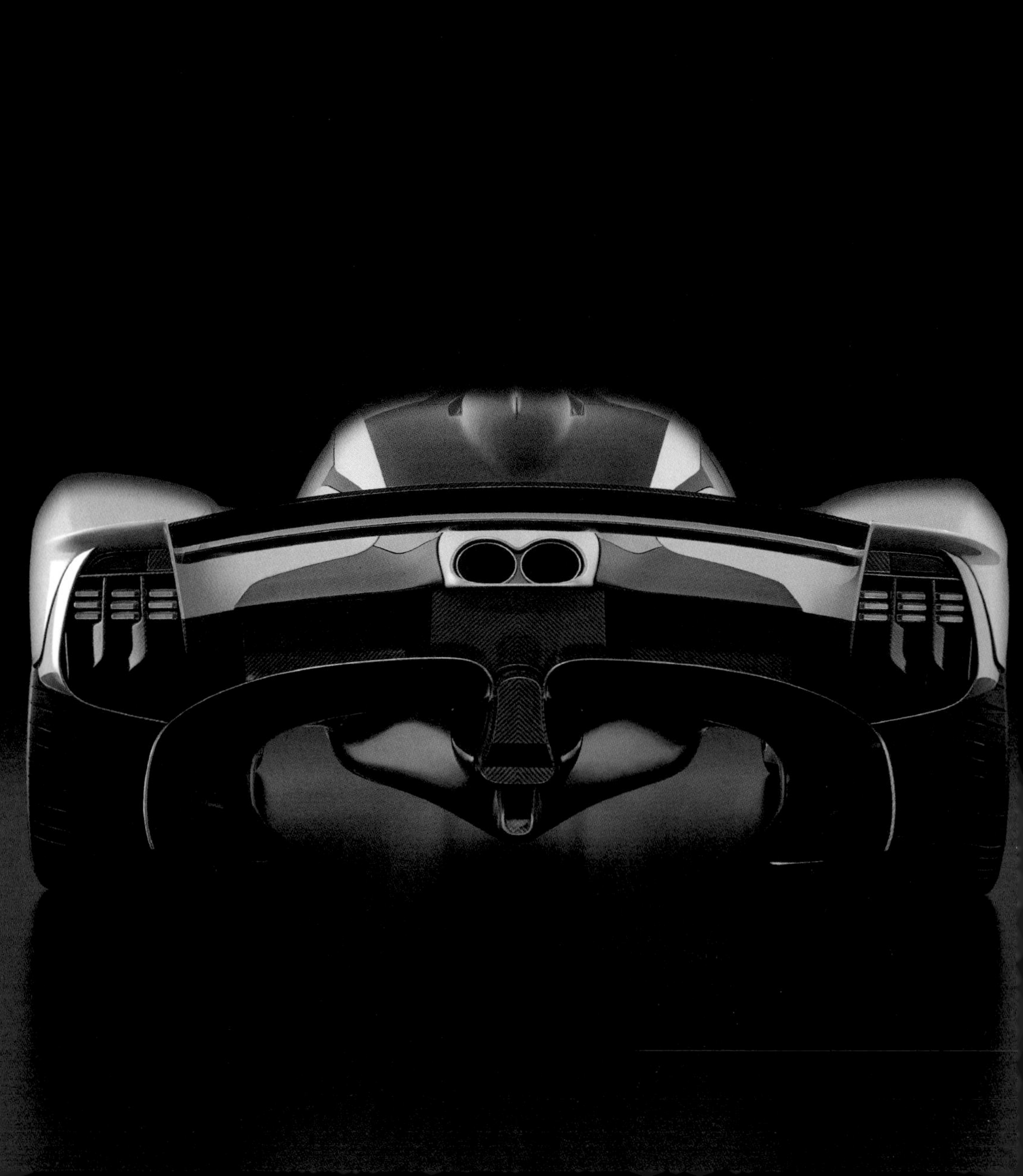